THE LIFE OF LENIN

Louis Fischer was born and educated in Philadelphia. In 1921 he was sent to Berlin by the *New York Post* and spent most of the next twenty-five years on roving assignments in Europe and Asia.
He was a leading authority on Russia, where he spent fourteen years, as well as on India and the Middle East. After 1959 he taught at Princeton, first at the Institute of Advanced Study, later on the faculty of the Woodrow Wilson School of Princeton University. Louis Fischer died in 1970.

A selection of books by Louis Fischer

The Life of Lenin
Russia, America, and the World
The Story of Indonesia
Russia Revisited
This is Our World
The Life and Death of Stalin
The Life of Mahatma Gandhi
The God that Failed (co-author)
Thirteen Who Fled (editor)
Gandhi and Stalin
The Great Challenge
Empire
A Week with Gandhi
Dawn of Victory
Men and Politics (an Autobiography)
Stalin and Hitler
The War in Spain
Soviet Journey
Machines and Men in Russia
Why Recognize Russia?
The Soviets in World Affairs (2 volumes)
Oil Imperialism

THE LIFE OF LENIN

Louis Fischer

**PHOENIX
PRESS**

5 UPPER SAINT MARTIN'S LANE
LONDON
WC2H 9EA

A PHOENIX PRESS PAPERBACK

First published in Great Britain
by Weidenfeld & Nicolson in 1964
This paperback edition published in 2001
by Phoenix Press,
a division of The Orion Publishing Group Ltd,
Orion House, 5 Upper St Martin's Lane,
London WC2H 9EA

A CIP catalogue record for this book
is available from the British Library.

Printed and bound in Great Britain by
Clays Ltd, St Ives plc

ISBN 1 84212 230 4

Grateful acknowledgment is made for permission to quote
throughout the text excerpts from *Brest-Litovsk, The Forgotten
Peace, March, 1918* by Sir John Wheeler-Bennett, published by St.
Martin's Press, Inc., and Macmillan & Co., Ltd., London.

Grateful acknowledgment is made to Sir Robert Bruce
Lockhart for permission to quote material from his book
British Agent, published by G. P. Putnam's Sons.

ON THE BEACH *of the island of Rhodes, between sessions of a conference on the problems of Asia and Africa, Robert M. Hutchins, former Chancellor of the University of Chicago, asked me what I intended to do next year. I said I had a strong wish to settle in a university town and write about Lenin. He mentioned the Institute for Advanced Study in Princeton, New Jersey. I hoped it could be arranged. Thanks to Dr. Hutchins, arrangements were made with George F. Kennan of the Institute faculty and Dr. J. Robert Oppenheimer, the Institute director. When, after my two happy years at the Institute, Mr. Kennan went on leave to serve as Ambassador to Yugoslavia, I transferred to Princeton University. In my third year under President Robert F. Goheen's academic roof, I finished this book.*

The Life of Lenin *is therefore dedicated to*

> Robert M. Hutchins
> George F. Kennan
> J. Robert Oppenheimer
> Robert F. Goheen

L.F.

CONTENTS

Illustrations

THE LIFE OF LENIN

I. TWO BROTHERS

LENIN was the founder of the Soviet state and the father of Soviet politics. Communist thinking and methods bear the imprint of his vivid, forceful personality. Born April 10, 1870, Lenin died on January 21, 1924, at the age of fifty-three, childless, but leaving many ideological heirs and millions of political offspring throughout the world.

There is a pretty baby picture of Lenin at the age of four, round-faced, with thick, curly blond hair, a faint smile, and deepset eyes. The Soviets have distributed it in millions of copies. Pavel Popovich took one with him as he entered his space ship in August, 1962, to orbit the earth forty-eight times. In April of the next year he presented the picture to the Central Museum of V. I. Lenin in Moscow. Before the communist revolution, an icon of the Virgin or of Christ or a saint hung between candles in a high corner of the living room of many Russian families. Communists welcome the substitution of a portrait of Lenin lit by an electric bulb. "Lenin Is Always With Us," reads a frequent headline in the Soviet press. The word "Lenin" or "Leninist" attached to a policy or theory lifts it beyond dispute. A quotation from Lenin wins an argument. The Kremlin encourages Lenin-worship. It projects a carefully shaped image of Lenin on the Soviet mind.

Lenin might have become a professor of economics, a successful lawyer, or a chess champion. Nothing in his ancestry, childhood, or adolescence offers a clue to his subsequent career as revolutionary and dictator. He was, however, a child of Russia—turbulent, violent—and the fruit of a tree with long roots in her varied soil.

The nationalist content of communism requires Lenin to be pictured as an ethnically pure Great Russian. The fact that he had non-Russian ancestors is therefore hidden away from all but the most curious. A 602-page official biography of Lenin written by P. P. Pospelov and eight other authors under the auspices of the Soviet Institute of Marxism-Leninism and published in 1960 in Moscow (*Vladimir Ilyich Lenin, Biografiya*) found space for only eight words about Lenin's ancestors: his paternal grandparents were "poor lower middle class people in Astrakhan"; his maternal grandfather was "a physician." The second, 1963, edition is equally uncommunicative.

The information lay at the authors' fingertips. Marietta Shaginyan, a well-known Soviet writer of Armenian origin, inspected crumbling local files and yellowed tax receipts and published an article in the November, 1937, issue of the Moscow magazine *Novy Mir* (*New World*), including facsimiles of some of the documents, which proves that Lenin's paternal grandfather was Nikolai Vasilievich Ulyanov, a poor tailor, probably a former serf, in the smelly fishing town of Astrakhan, where the Volga flows into the Caspian Sea. In his fifties, Nikolai Vasilievich, a Great Russian, married Anna Alexeyevna Smirnov, the illiterate daughter of a Kalmuck. In all the vast

1

Soviet literature on the great leader, these authenticated facts are nowhere reproduced. The Kalmucks are Buddhists with big, round, flat, yellow-brown faces and Mongol eyes. Lenin's high cheekbones and slanting eyes suggested this admixture of Asian blood.

Ilya Nikolaievich Ulyanov, the fourth and last son of the Russo-Kalmuck Astrakhan couple, came into the world when his father was 67 and his mother 43. Five years later the father died. Ilya's brother Vasili, 12 years his senior, a cart driver and merchant's assistant, never married; he took care of Ilya and paid for his education. Ilya became Lenin's father.

On his mother's side, Lenin had German blood. This piquant genealogical morsel strikes most Soviet publications dumb. The long, 19-page account of Lenin in the *Bolshaya Sovietskaya Entsiklopedia (Large Soviet Encyclopedia)* mentions Lenin's father; it does not mention Lenin's mother. Neither does a Soviet biography by Ex-Commissar of Education Platon M. Kerzhentsev published in New York in 1939 as the *Life of Lenin*. Another official biography by Emilian Yaroslavsky, a prominent Bolshevik and member of the Soviet Communist Party's Central Committee, published in Moscow in 1938, says merely that she was "the daughter of a physician." A separate brief entry in the *Large Soviet Encyclopedia* on Lenin's mother limits itself to the same meager statement—this in a country, whether tsarist or soviet, where every birth, baptism, school enrollment, and change of residence is registered and retained in the archives and where everybody at all times must have a passport indicating nationality. An English-language book entitled *Lenin's Mother*, by Ray Kovnator, published in Moscow in 1944 likewise ignores Lenin's German ancestry. It is also omitted from a 72-page volume by Maria, Lenin's youngest sister, about their father,[1] Ilya Ulyanov. But a book about the Ulyanov family edited and annotated by Lenin's oldest sister, Anna, asserts simply: Maria Alexandrovna Blank, the mother of Lenin, "was the daughter of a physician; her mother was a German."[2] Lenin's German grandmother died young, and his mother, Anna wrote, was raised austerely by a German aunt.[3]

These two mentions of Lenin's German maternal grandmother and Marietta Shaginyan's mention of his Kalmuck paternal grandmother are volubility itself compared with the silence that shrouds the ethnic origin of Dr. Alexander Dmitriyevich Blank, the father of Lenin's mother. Some maintain he was a Jew.

[1] M. Ulyanova, *Otets Vladimira Ilyicha Lenina, Ilya Nikolayevich Ulyanov (1831-1886) (The Father of Vladimir Ilyich Lenin, Ilya Nikolayevich Ulyanov)*. (Moscow-Leningrad, 1931).

[2] V. Alekseyev and A. Shver, *Semya Ulyanovykh v Simbirskye, 1869-1887 (The Ulyanov Family in Simbirsk, 1869-1887)*, edited and annotated by A. I. Ulyanova-Elizarova (Leningrad, 1925), under the imprint of the Lenin Institute of the Central Committee of the Russian Communist Party.

[3] A. I. Ulyanova-Elizarova, *Vospominaniya o Alexandre Ilyich Ulyanove (Recollections about Alexander Ilyich Ulyanov)* (Moscow, 1930), p. 33. Alexander Ilyich Ulyanov was Lenin's brother.

Asked in the 1922 census about his grandfather, Lenin, according to Marietta Shaginyan, answered, "I don't know." In a multi-racial country like Russia, racial origin is well known and usually avowed. But this and other information about Dr. Blank is elusive and vague. Maria, Lenin's sister, writes that in the beginning of the 1860's her father, Ilya N. Ulyanov, met "his future wife, Maria Alexandrovna Blank. Maria Alexandrovna was the daughter of a physician of petty bourgeois origin, a progressive person interested in ideas, strong and independent, foreign to any careerism and obsequiousness. Having retired, A. D. Blank bought a not-large estate in Kazan Guberniya [province]. . . ." An anthology on Lenin's youth which appeared in Moscow in 1958 quotes this passage and appends a footnote: "Maria Alexandrovna Blank [Lenin's mother] was born in 1835. Her mother died soon thereafter. Her father, Alexander Dimitrievich Blank graduated from the St. Petersburg Medical Academy, worked as a physician in the Smolensk, Perm, and Kazan provinces. After the death of his wife he retired."[4] There is no suggestion what it was he retired from, for he continued practicing medicine when he withdrew to his estate at Kokushkino. The name of his German wife, Lenin's maternal grandmother, is never given.

Nadezhda K. Krupskaya, Lenin's widow, added one detail about Dr. Blank in an article she contributed to *Bolshevik*, a communist party organ, in June, 1938: he was born in the Ukraine. Karl Radek, the most famous Soviet publicist and communist party leader, writing in the Moscow daily *Izvestia* of April 23, 1933, called Dr. Blank "a regimental surgeon" and added shrewdly, "In accessible sources it is possible to read little about Lenin's grandfather. Like all physicians of that period he probably inclined to a primitive materialism which, incidentally, was compatible with religion. At home Lenin's mother was educated in the religious spirit but not according to rules of Domostroi." Domostroi, a written Orthodox Church code of conduct dating back to the sixteenth century, described the submissive relationship incumbent upon all members of a family toward the feudal-religious master of the household. "Not according to Domostroi" means not Russian Orthodox. Lenin's maternal grandmother was a German Lutheran, and his mother was brought up as a Lutheran.

In his *Izvestia* article, published a few weeks after Hitler's accession to power, Radek, himself a Jew, declared that Lenin's "parents, the Ulyanovs, were more than mere physical participants in the forming of the Messiah who led the proletariat out of Egyptian bondage. Ilya Nikolaievich Ulyanov and Maria Alexandrovna Blank were persons who contributed considerably to the spiritual character of our teacher."

Those who knew the puckish Radek personally and read the products of his stinging, naughty pen would deduce that he meant to convey more than he said. Did he choose the Moses metaphor by chance? Was he hinting that in-

---

[4] *Molodiye Godi V. I. Lenina (The Early Years of Lenin)* (Moscow, 1958), p. 13.

accessible sources held a secret? The Kremlin has not taken the hint.

The riddle about Dr. Blank has inspired a hot polemic among émigré Russian experts. N. Valentinov, author of a book of reminiscences about Lenin published in New York in 1953, wrote in *Novy Zhournal* (New York, Vol. 61, 1960), "Where he was born, where he is from, I do not know, but I am certain, and I have already written this, that Blank was not a Jew." On the other hand, David N. Shub, whose *Lenin—a Biography* was published in New York in 1948, replying to Valentinov in a subsequent issue of *Novy Zhournal*, insisted that Blank is not a Russian but a Jewish name and that Alexander Blank, Lenin's maternal grandfather "was a converted Odessa Jew." In the same issue (Vol. 63), "Historian" takes a similar position. Anna M. Bourgina, however, rejected their view in a letter published in *Novoye Russkoye Slovo*, a New York Russian-language daily, of April 9, 1961. She cited several Russians named Blank who were definitely non-Jewish. Shub stood his ground in a reply to the Russian daily of April 23, 1961. N. Valentinov returned to the attack in the New York *Sotsialicheskii Vestnik (Socialist Courier)* of May, 1961, and refuted the statements of Shub and others identifying Alexander D. Blank as a baptized Jew and doctor's assistant of Odessa.

Only one conclusion is possible: reliable facts to prove that Dr. Blank was or was not a Jew have not been made public. The records were undoubtedly available in Russia's bulging archives, but the Bolsheviks saw fit to suppress them. This feeds the suspicion that there is something to conceal.

The Kremlin's secretiveness, when tens of thousands of pages about all other aspects of Lenin's life have been published in Russia, may be explained by the wish to create a nationalistic image of Lenin as a one hundred percent Great Russian without infusions of non-Russian blood. Dr. Blank, moreover, owned not a small farm but an estate and, until 1861, he owned many serfs. That flaw too does not belong in the popular picture of Russia's redeemer.

Shelve the hypothesis of a Jewish grandfather as unproven; even so, Lenin's ancestry spanned Eurasia from Central Asia to Central Europe. In this sense Lenin was what Russia is: a bridge between West and East, partaking of both yet struggling to be neither.

"Lenin" (pronounced Lenyin, accent on the first syllable) is a pen name. As author, editor, journalist, and leader, Lenin often wrote under the pseudonym of "N. Lenin." (He used several other pen names: V. Ilin, V. Frei, K. Tulin, Karpov, etc.) The "N" does not stand for anything. He was never Nikolai Lenin. He was born and as Soviet leader he signed: Vladimir Ilyich Ulyanov (Vladimir, the son of Ilya Ulyanov), often adding Lenin in parentheses.

The origin of the name Lenin is in doubt. It has been suggested that when he first signed it in December, 1901, he remembered a high school classmate named Lena. The official biography by Pospelov and others states, in its second edition (page 81), that when Lenin's relatives were asked they replied "he apparently chose it accidentally, but it is possible" it comes from the great Lena River in Siberia. It would have been more natural for him to use "Volgin" after the Volga River in whose valley he spent his childhood and youth. However, Georgi V. Plekhanov, the father of Russian socialism, had already adopted "Volgin"; Vladimir Ilyich Ulyanov therefore looked farther east and styled himself "Lenin"—of Lena.

Lenin's father Ilya lived all his life along the Volga, the water artery of Mother Russia. He entered the Astrakhan gymnasium (high school) in 1843, and was graduated with a silver medal in 1850. The same year he enrolled in the University of Kazan. In May, 1855, he was appointed physics and mathematics instructor in the upper grades of the Nobles Institute at Penza. When several members of the faculty were dismissed for holding progressive, therefore subversive, views, Ilya remained. An Institute report praised him for devotion to the study of science and the methods of teaching it. On November 23, 1861, he read a paper before an Institute audience "About Thunder and Lightning Rods." Eight months earlier, Tsar Alexander II had liberated Russia's serfs, but Ilya's title, which might have been an apt comment on the inadequacy and purpose of the reform, bore no political connotation.

Ilya married Maria Alexandrovna Blank in Penza in 1863, and moved to Nizhni Novgorod, site of the famous annual Volga fair. He taught there until 1869, when the tsarist authorities appointed him Inspector of Public Schools for the province of Simbirsk with headquarters in the city of Simbirsk. Here Lenin was born; here he spent the first third of his life.

Simbirsk, a sleepy river town, began as a fort. High above the Volga, Tsar Alexey in 1648 ordered a kremlin, or bastion, built of stout logs with tall wooden towers surrounded by a moat and fields. Simbirsk thus became the key stronghold in a defense line designed to protect the southeastern flank of the Muscovite state against encroachments by non-Russians from Asia. Cossacks and watchmen, numbering 15,000, held off a heavy attack in 1650. Raids by Tartars and Mongols continued till the end of that century.

By 1870, when Lenin was born, Russia's expansion into Siberia and Turkestan robbed Simbirsk of military importance. It grew, instead, into a shipping center for grain, fish, wool, and potash, and most of its 30,000 inhabitants were Mordvi, Chuvashi, and other Asians—the Volga boatmen who pulled the barges and worked the warehouses.

Simbirsk stands with one foot on the low Asiatic bank of the Volga and the second on the lofty European right bank; a railway bridge connected the two parts. The city center, on the right bank, lay between the great river and the lesser Sviaga. As a boy, Lenin often swam and fished in the meandering Sviaga.

The majority of Simbirsk homes were one-story cabins built of dark-gray boards. Some had attics. A few boasted two stories. Lenin was born in the wing of a house owned by a certain Pribilovsky. Later the family occupied the top floor of the same house, and after Ilya received his promotion, in 1874, from Inspector to Director, the Ulyanovs moved several times until, in 1878, they bought the wooden structure at 48 Moscow Street. There Lenin lived until he was seventeen.

Vladimir (the family affectionately called him "Volodya"), who became Lenin, was one of six children: Anna, born in 1864; Alexander (affectionately "Sasha"), born in 1866; Vladimir; Olga, born in 1871; Dmitri, born 1874; and Maria, born 1878. A brother named Nikolai, born in 1873, died several days after birth.

Vladimir closely resembled his father Ilya. Both had high-domed foreheads, reddish beards, bald heads, and short legs. Both could not pronounce the "r" after some consonants. Both possessed boundless energy and spent it without stint in stern, prodigious, impassioned labors. Both died early, Lenin almost fifty-four, the father just past fifty-four. No autopsy was performed on Ilya but the doctor said a brain hemorrhage brought on his death; sclerosis of the brain caused Lenin's.

When Ilya assumed his duties as Director in 1874, the entire province of Simbirsk had twenty schools in poor condition. He toiled indefatigably on the building of new schools, the repair of old ones, and the training of teachers. For assiduity and success over more than a decade he earned the title of Actual Councilor of State, the equivalent, says Marietta Shaginyan, of "a civilian general." This made him a high-ranking nobleman—fourth in a table of fourteen ranks—with hereditary status.[5] By 1886, the year of his death, Simbirsk province counted 20,000 pupils in 434 small primary schools, and hundreds in several excellent gymnasiums.

Ilya's work kept him away from home for weeks, occasionally months at a time, traveling by train, carriage, and sleigh to the remote reaches of his educational realm. Even when he remained in the city, he impressed his children as formidable and somewhat distant. The dominant member of the family at all times was his wife, Maria Alexandrovna, nee Blank, a remarkable woman. The few Soviet references to her agree that she was "distinguished by strong will and a determined character." Lenin's sister Anna, in her memoirs of her brother Sasha, writes that their mother, having grown up in a village, "did not know nervousness" in her early years. Dr. Blank, Anna adds in a statement that seems to hide as much as it says, "could not invite teachers to the home for his younger daughters as he had for the older ones in another situation. He did not approve of education in an institute." Lenin's mother's education, therefore, was left to her German aunt, who proscribed tea and coffee as stimulating and harmful but guided her studies

---

[5] *Bolshaya Sovietskaya Entsiklopedia (Large Soviet Encyclopedia)*, Second ed. (Vol. 41, p. 446), carries an article entitled "Table of Ranks," which states, "The law of Dec. 9, 1856, fixed a higher rank for the attainment of inherited nobility: the fourth—for civilian officials." According to the Table of Ranks on the next page, Actual Councilor of State was fourth.

well. Though Maria Alexandrovna never attended school she passed written examinations and qualified as a schoolteacher. She taught herself English and French and spoke a literary German and Russian. On her table stood a complete Shakespeare in English and Louis Adolphe Thiers's giant history of the French Revolution in French. Under her guidance, the children published a weekly handwritten magazine for the family entitled *The Sabbath*. She sewed their clothes on a Singer Sewing Machine. The Ulyanovs owned a piano which Mama Maria taught Volodya, the future Lenin, to play. He also sang to the accompaniment of his mother and his sister Olga. Dmitri, Lenin's younger brother, remembers Volodya's singing the lyrical songs of Heine and the aria of Valentin from Gounod's *Faust*.

Lenin's oldest sister, Anna, wrote in her memoirs that as a child Volodya was "lively, pert, and jolly, and loved loud games, and running around. He broke his toys oftener than he played with them." He smiled perpetually and liked to tease and play childish pranks. He learned to read at five, then was tutored by a teacher who came to the house and prepared him for the gymnasium which he entered at the early age of nine and a half years.

Volodya's closest playmate was his sister Olga, twenty months his junior. She learned reading with him and mastered it at the age of four. Olga, according to Anna, was "extraordinarily diligent. I remember, when Volodya was in one of his last gymnasium years, he listened to Olga doing her endless piano exercises in the neighboring room and said to me, 'There's somebody whose industry can be envied.' Having recognized this, Volodya began to develop his own diligence which surprised all of us in his later years."

Diligence was a family characteristic. Papa Ilya took over an underdeveloped school system and built it up into a new realm. Mama Maria ruled the home that was her world. Both had a strong sense of order and loved work. All their children absorbed these qualities.

With little effort, Volodya earned good marks in the gymnasium. In his last gymnasium class he averaged $4^{10}/_{11}$; the highest grade was 5. On days when marks were announced he would come into the house shouting, "Greek 5, Latin 5, Religion 5, Mathematics 5, and so forth and so on," and rush upstairs to his private room or into the adjoining room to watch Sasha's chemistry experiments and, occasionally, to assist.

Papa Ulyanov played croquet with his two older boys, Sasha and Volodya. He also taught them chess. He had whittled the set himself and later gave it to Volodya who lost it decades later. Soon enough the boys won against their father.

Dmitri Ulyanov devoted a whole section of his memoirs[6] to chess. Volodya,

[6] The memoirs of Lenin's family, physicians, political associates, chauffeur, cook, and many others have been collected and published in four encyclopedia-size volumes entitled *Vospominaniya o Vladimire Ilyiche Lenine (Reminiscences about Vladimir Ilyich Lenin)*, Vol. 1 (Moscow, 1956), 555 pages; Vol. 2 (Moscow, 1957), 734 pages; Vol. 3 (Moscow, 1960), 384 pages; Vol. 4 (Moscow, 1963), 643 pages. Dmitri Ulyanov on Lenin and chess, Vol. 1, pp. 62-66.

he wrote, began playing chess at nine with his father and Sasha. Later he played with Olga and Dmitri. "He was my teacher," Dmitri recollected, "and a very strict one, and that's why I preferred to play with father who let me take moves back." Volodya had a strict rule which he obeyed and enforced on others: "Under no circumstances take back a move. Once you've touched a piece you have to move it." He said if you are permitted to touch a figure and then another it spoils the game; much better to think out your move and be sure of what you are going to do.

The young Lenin played chess seriously, according to Dmitri. He gave weaker partners a piece ahead and if they proudly protested he would argue that it was no fun playing a game which did not challenge him to think hard and "extricate myself." Dmitri after a while began winning from Volodya, who was playing with only one castle. Dmitri then suggested that Volodya reduce his disadvantage by playing with one knight. Volodya replied, "Win three games in a row, then we'll change." Once they played "blind," but Volodya disliked it. Nor did he enjoy reading chess literature except to learn some classic openings and endings. "In any case," Dmitri wrote, "he never tried to make a systematic study of chess theory."

Lenin's sister Anna asserted in her memoirs that neither Sasha nor Volodya took any interest in political questions during their gymnasium years. Both parents were liberal conservatives. The mother did not go to church. Ilya did. Lenin once recalled how, when Alexander II was assassinated, in 1881, Ilya sadly buttoned on his official's uniform and went to the Simbirsk cathedral to mourn the autocrat whom he regarded as "the Tsar-Liberator." Occasionally, in those times of ferment, terrorist circulars pasted on telegraph poles demanded "Death to the Tsar"; now and then disgruntled peasants burned the homes or harvests of their landlords. It is doubtful whether these matters came to the attention of the Ulyanov children. No entry in the tsarist archives, eagerly combed by Soviet writers for evidence of subversion, indicates that the Ulyanovs ever merited police surveillance.

The outside world seldom intruded on the pleasant, placid family. Ilya sometimes entertained colleagues with whom he discussed school problems. Maria Alexandrovna rarely went visiting. She had enough to do at home. She may also have been conscious of the gulf between the self-educated woman of culture with a German Lutheran background and the petty bourgeois, status-seeking Russian merchant wives of provincial Simbirsk enclosed in its envelope of gossip-ridden atmosphere. The fetid social air was partly urban-generated; part blew in from the farmlands that stretched farther than any eye could see. It carried the odor of decadence. For, though the serfs on the estates had been freed by the Tsar, the proprietors still spoke of them as their "souls" and employed them by the hundreds at pittance pay. Some landlords collected magnificent libraries. But as a class they stagnated. Work was as abhorrent to them as change. By preference inert, they pursued pleasure to exhaustion.

There is a story of two Simbirsk landlords who used to meet regularly for hunting, card games, and vodka-drinking bouts. Each owned a large-caliber cannon. If one wished to invite the other he fired a cannon ball onto his estate. If the second accepted he fired back a shot. If he fired two shots he was inviting the first to come to his manor house. If each insisted on the other's visiting him, they continued the cannonade until their ammunition gave out, when they met halfway to decide what to do.

Sleepy Simbirsk had an illustrious son in Ivan Alexandrovich Goncharov (1812-1891) whose novel, *Oblomov*, was published in 1859. From then to now "Oblomov" has been the synonym for a bored, irresolute, phlegmatic Russian to whom time is a nuisance and struggle unknown. Goncharov, member of a rich merchant family, served in turn as secretary to the governor of Simbirsk province, to an admiral, and in the St. Petersburg Ministry of Finance: he obviously did not lean toward radicalism. But his *Oblomov* vivisected the spiritually sluggish, socially immobile, parasitic Volga landlord and held him up for national display. Oblomovism was regarded as the Russian's second nature. "Oblomovka"—the home of the Oblomovs—"is our fatherland," wrote a contemporary Russian critic. "Something of Oblomov is to be found in every one of us."

Lenin read the book and referred to it in speeches and articles. A phenomenon so characteristic of nineteenth-century Russia must have had some impact, however unconscious, on the two bright teen-age Ulyanov boys. They might have noticed it during summers spent at Kokushkino, the Volga estate of their maternal grandfather, Dr. Blank. It need not have turned them to revolution. Goncharov himself accepted a post as government censor the year after his classic novel appeared. His observations of social decay inspired him to no active protest.

A Russian's ration of Oblomovism depended on temperament and experience. Lenin had a passionate temperament. He had a shattering experience: the execution of his brother Sasha.

Papa Ilya Ulyanov died on January 12, 1886. Sasha did not attend the funeral; he was in St. Petersburg at the university. Could the passing of the stern father have lifted a subtle restraint from both boys? Replying to the 1922 census questionnaire, Lenin wrote: "Nonbeliever [in God] since the age of 16"—that is, shortly after his father's death. (This should have eliminated an oft-told tale that he tore off his cross when he heard a priest tell his father the boy should be beaten for being an atheist. But it still lives in Soviet mythology.) At approximately the same time Sasha rallied to the Narodnaya Volya, or People's Freedom (or Will) Party, whose members planted the bomb that killed Alexander II in a St. Petersburg street on March 1, 1881. The Tsar's emancipation of the serfs twenty years earlier had not moderated the terrorists' hatred of the absolute monarchy. Nor did his violent death appease them. No sooner had they killed him than they began planning an attempt on the life of his son, the big, blubber-bodied Alexander III. Sasha

Ulyanov, now heir to his father's title of nobility, volunteered for the deed.

At the bottom of the broad Nevsky Prospect, in the great square of Leningrad's central railway station, stands an equestrian statue erected before the revolution. The granite pedestal has the dimensions of a huge block from the famous pyramids near Cairo. The horse resembles a rhinoceros, heavy and long of body with short legs wide apart the better to support its ponderous master. Alexander III, father of the last Tsar, Nicholas II, who was executed with his family by the Soviet regime, sits astride the animal, a pancake Tartar cap on his round head. The neckless body, with chest bulging like a gorilla's, and fat, stumpy legs make the whole look like an unconscious caricature of tsarism. Its squatness, immobility, and dull weight mirror the inflexibility and brute stupidity of the autocracy which erected it. The Bolsheviks therefore preserved the monument and into its base, in large block letters, they cut the word SCARECROW, and under it this verse of Demyan Byedny, the Kremlin's bard laureate:

> My son and father were executed by the nation,
> But I, condemned to posthumous inglory,
> Stand here, a pig-iron scarecrow, for a country
> That has forever discarded the yoke of autocracy.

It was this penultimate crowned ruler of Russia that Alexander Ilyich Ulyanov, brother of Lenin, proposed to blow up with an amateur chemist's bomb. Before the conspiracy got very far he and his sister Anna, who was not involved, and several associates were arrested on March 1, 1887.

The moment Lenin's mother heard by letter that her children had been arrested, she left posthaste on horseback for Syzran—a distance of sixty miles, and she was fifty-two—and thence by rail to St. Petersburg, where she petitioned the Tsar for permission to see Sasha in the dread Schluesselburg prison. Alexander III agreed in writing. At the interview (March 30) Sasha knelt, embraced her knees, and wept. High officials had told her that if he recanted and asked the monarch for mercy his life would be spared. Sasha explained that he could not do it. He would have had to reveal the secrets of the conspiracy. "I am sorry for you, Mama, forgive me," he said, as she recounted the story later. "After that," she added, "I did not insist and no longer tried to persuade him. I knew it would be difficult for him."

The mother attended the trial. Of the fifteen defendants, five, among them Sasha, received the death sentence, two life imprisonment, and the others various terms of exile in Siberia and Sakhalin.

Following the trial the mother again saw Sasha and once more implored him to ask the Tsar for a milder sentence as several of his confederates had done. "I cannot do that after all I said at the trial," he replied. "That would be playing the hypocrite." He had said, "I want to die for my country."

As she was leaving he asked for a small volume of Heine's poems. She brought it to him on her last visit and kissed him good-by. He was executed on May 8, 1887. His mother accompanied him to the gallows and said, "Take courage. Take courage." He had just passed his twenty-first birthday.[7]

A Soviet legend, told in all official biographies, has it that when Lenin heard of his brother's arrest for an attempt on the Tsar's life he said, "No, we will go a different way. That is not the way to go."[8] This tale hangs on the thin thread of his sister Maria's memory, and she was then nine years old. She launched it at a meeting in February, 1924, just after Lenin's death.[9] To be sure, the poignancy of Sasha's hanging might have sharpened her memory, but to remember she would have had to understand what the words meant. They were intended to convey the impression that Lenin, already a Marxist, was opposed to the terror of the Narodnaya Volya and Narodniks (populists), and would go the way of working-class revolution, not of individual bomb throwing.

Irrespective of Maria's recollections, the story is not true. The truth reveals friction between Sasha and his brother Lenin and tensions beneath the placid surface of the Ulyanov family's life. The truth also has a significant bearing on the tortured course of the Russian revolutionary movement.

At an early age, according to Lenin's sister Anna, Volodya (Vladimir, that is) usually imitated Sasha, and when asked for his choice in any matter, he invariably replied, "Like Sasha." Actually, however, the two brothers were unlike in temperament, conduct, ethics, and appearance, so much so, in fact, that there is reason to think that Sasha, as well as Anna, even disliked Volodya.

Anna writes in her memoirs of her older brother that the family's children paired: she with Sasha, who was two years her junior; Volodya with Olga— a year apart; and Dmitri with Maria. An anthropologist, studying photographs, came upon another division—long heads: the mother, Anna, Sasha, and Dmitri; round heads: the father, Lenin, Olga, and Maria.

Anna notes how their father once characterized several of his children: he called Anna "sanguine"—"gay, loving life"; Volodya "choleric"; and Olga "melancholy." Anna calls Volodya "that frisky boy." In the winter of 1885-86, she writes, "I walked and talked a good deal with Volodya. This also happened the next summer." Volodya, she declares, "was then in a transi-

[7] Anna reports this in her memoirs of her brother Sasha and it was also told by Lenin's younger sister Maria in an article published in *Pravda* on Feb. 18, 1963. The article, according to an editorial note, was written by Maria early in 1937, several months before her death, for publication on the fiftieth anniversary of Sasha's hanging (May 8, 1937). The article, however, did not appear until twenty-six years later. Reason not stated. Perhaps Stalin objected to the glorification of a would-be assassin. Stalin was in perpetual fear of assassination; reports of assassinations abroad were either suppressed entirely or printed in two inconspicuous lines. That the conspirator was Lenin's brother only compounded Stalin's objection; he wished to deflect attention from Lenin to himself.

[8] See, for instance, *Vladimir Ilyich Lenin. Biografia*, by P. P. Pospelov and eight others. First ed. (1960), p. 9; second ed. (1963), p. 9.

[9] Some excerpts appeared in *Izvestia*, April 19, 1963.

tional period when boys become especially harsh and stubborn. In him, who was constantly pert and self-confident, this was particularly noticeable, the more so after the death of the father whose presence always acts as a restraint on boys."

In the autumn of 1886 Anna asked Sasha his opinion of Volodya. Sasha replied, "Undoubtedly a very gifted person, but we don't get along." This, she recalled, was said "decisively and definitely" and she even thought he might have said "we don't get along at all."

"Why?" she inquired of Sasha.

"Just so," he answered evasively, "leaving it to me," Anna writes, "to work it out for myself. I explained it to myself by the fact that Sasha disliked those features of Volodya's character which wound . . . his great mockery, impertinence, arrogance, chiefly when they were directed at mother to whom he would at times talk back in a way he never dared when father was alive. I remember the disapproving looks of Sasha when he heard such backtalk."

In the summer of 1887, after Sasha had been hanged, the mother told Anna "that once, when Volodya and Sasha were playing chess, she reminded Volodya of an order which he had not carried out. Volodya answered rudely and did not hasten to carry it out. Mother, apparently irritated, insisted. . . . Volodya again answered with some kind of impolite joke but did not move."

Whereupon Sasha calmly addressed Volodya: "You either go and do what Mama asks or I shall not play with you again."

Volodya immediately rose and did what his mother had ordered.

"It was these aspects of Volodya's character," Anna wrote in her 1930 memoirs of Sasha, and also "the things that then interested Volodya" which shaped her older brother's opinion of the young man who would be Lenin. Mockery and teasing, she says, were "absolutely foreign to the nature" of Sasha, whereas "mockery came natural to Volodya at all times and in his transitional period in particular." The time was the summer of 1886, Sasha's last summer on earth, "after the loss of father and when, apparently, Sasha's decision to become a revolutionary had ripened."

Although Volodya imitated Sasha from childhood, Anna declares, and respected him, "they were never close to one another." What widened the gulf in the last year of Sasha's life was politics. "That winter when I went on many walks with him, Volodya was in a hostile mood toward the gymnasium directorate, gymnasium studies, and to religion too, and did not object to abuse the teachers (in some of these tricks I too participated), in a word, he was, so to speak, in a period of throwing off authority." But they did not talk politics.

"In the summer of 1886," she writes, "I remember how Sasha and I were astonished that Volodya could reread Turgenev several times. He would lie on his cot and read and reread—and that in the very months when he occupied one room with Sasha who was diligently studying Marx and other political-economic literature . . . Volodya began reading Marx in Russian only in 1888-89 in Kazan. And so, at that time"—before Sasha's arrest and hanging —"Volodya had no definite political views."

Lenin (Volodya), therefore, could not have condemned terror and expressed a preference for "a different way" in the remark attributed to him by his sister Maria. In fact, it was Sasha who was the Marxist or near-Marxist. This is known in today's Russia. Thus a thin volume, published in Moscow in 1956,[10] states, "In 1885-1886, among his"—Sasha's—"books was also Marx's *Capital*. Alexander Ilyich"—Sasha—"stood at the crossroads between the Narodnaya Volya"—the People's Will Party of terrorists—"and the Marxists. He agreed with the draft program of the Marxist Plekhanov group 'The Liberation of Labor.' " The same thin volume reveals, for the first time in the Soviet Union, that shortly before his death Sasha translated a long article by Karl Marx from the German. The translation, which appeared as a 47-page pamphlet in Russian in Geneva in 1887, lies before me, yellow with age.[11]

Lenin understood the truth about his brother a few years later and shared it with a close associate, Isaac Christoforovich Lalayants, to whom he said that Sasha "considered himself a Marxist."[12] Nevertheless, the Lenin mythology in Russia remains unchanged: Lenin was the teen-age Marxist, the brother a non-Marxist terrorist.

To the extent that the judges permitted, Sasha made known his political views at the trial which ended with his death sentence. The information is from the court stenographic record.[13]

THE PRESIDENT OF THE COURT TO A. ULYANOV: "You were at the Petersburg University?"

ANSWER: "Yes, I was."

QUESTION: "Already in your fourth year?"

ANSWER: "Yes."

[10] B. Volin, *Lenin v Povolzhe, 1870-1893* (*Lenin in the Volga Region, 1870-1893*) (Moscow, 1956), pp. 33-34.

[11] Karl Marx, *Vvedenye k Kritike Filosofii Prava Gegelya* (*Introduction to the Critique of Hegel's Philosophy of Right*). With an introduction by P. L. Lavrov. Under the imprint of "The Socialist Library. Publication of the Narodnaya Volya Circle" (Geneva, 1887).

[12] I. Ch. Lalayants, *On My Meetings with V. I. Lenin in 1893-1900*. Moscow *Proketarskaya Revolutsiya* magazine, Issue No. 1 (1929). Quoted by *Novy Mir* magazine, Issue No. 4 (1963), p. 159.

[13] *Pervoye Marta 1887 goda. Dyelo P. Sheviryov, A. Ulyanov, P. Adreyyushkin, V. Generalov i drugiye* (*March 1, 1887. The Trial of P. Sheviryov, A. Ulyanov, P. Andreyyushkin, V. Generalov, and others*). With an Introduction by A. I. Elizarova [Lenin's sister Anna]. Text Prepared for Print by A. A. Shikov (Moscow, 1927). The material was from the Soviet Central Archives. The book was published in an edition of 2,000—Soviet editions always indicate the size of the printing—in place of the tens and even hundreds of thousands of copies in which most Soviet books, usually paperbacks, circulate. The 2,000 copies would have gone to libraries, which would make them available to specially trusted persons, and to a limited group of high officials.

QUESTION: "Despite your youth?"

ANSWER: "Yes, I was in my fourth year."

Replying to further questions, Sasha stated that his father had supported him until his death. At one time he gave lessons. Then the matter of the group's mimeographed proclamation arose.

QUESTION: "Who hectographed them?"

Sasha answered that he had.

QUESTION: "No other person participated?"

ANSWER: "No, one person helped."

QUESTION: "Then who?"

ANSWER: "I refuse to give the name."

During the trial Sasha, who had been separated from his comrades in prison, whispered to them that they should put all the blame on him. He was ready to die to exculpate the others. One of the conspirators, Orest Makarovich Govorukhin, son of a Don Cossack, fled abroad just before the attempt on the Tsar's life was made. When the court asked why he, Ulyanov, had not escaped, he replied, "I didn't want to escape. I wished to die for my country." In Western Europe, Govorukhin told the story of the plot.[14] He said, "Alexander Ilyich Ulyanov was the most remarkable personality among them. My acquaintance with him began in 1885 in Petersburg. He was then in the third year of the Natural Science Branch of the Physics-Mathematics Department. As a student he was industrious and gifted. . . . He wrote a competition essay for which he received a gold medal. Success encouraged him. He was already thinking of becoming a professor . . . with all his passion for science, nothing human was alien to him. . . . At that time, in his third year, he did not yet participate in revolutionary organizations." His attitude to Narodnaya Volya study circles was negative. He said, "They chat a lot and study very little." He always kept pictures of his father and mother before him in his room. When his father died, Anna reported, according to Govorukhin, Sasha felt so sad he contemplated suicide. "I never saw him carefree and joyful," Govorukhin continued, "he was ever deeply thoughtful and somber. He loved the theater, understood poetry, and especially loved music, but when he heard it he became even more somber and thoughtful." Finally, he joined a Narodnaya Volya circle in order, he said, to test the revolutionary ideas he heard against the reality of life. On February 19, 1886, he participated in a demonstration at the Volkov Cemetery in St. Petersburg in honor of the poets, Nekrasov, Dobrolyubov, and others, who had championed the liberation of the serfs.

[14] It was transcribed at the time and found its way into the files of Vladimir L. Burtsev (1862-1942), a Russian historian of the revolutionary movement, and remained there until published in full, with an introduction by the Menshevik writer Boris I. Nicolaevsky, in *Golos Minuvshova na Chuzhoi Stranye (The Voice of Bygone Days in a Foreign Land)* (Paris) Issue No. 4 (1928). Long excerpts were printed earlier in the Moscow *Proletarskaya Revolutsia. Istoricheskii Zhournal Istparta (Proletarian Revolution. Historical Journal of the History of the Party)*, Issue No. 7 (July, 1925), with an introduction by Anna Elizarova.

The police prohibited further demonstrations. It was decided to kill the Tsar. When a participant in an illegal demonstration was arrested and a paper with Sasha's name was found on him, Sasha feared deportation to Simbirsk, his home town. "Why, that's a terrible prospect," he exclaimed, "to live in the provinces, in Simbirsk for instance, where one can become quite dull. No books, no people."

The future of Russian capitalism, the future of the Russian village: could the commune, or mir, survive?—these questions occupied Sasha, according to Govorukhin. "With his concepts, he did not belong in the Narodnaya Volya, for he denied the possibility of seizing the government after an assassination, and denied the *active* significance of the village commune as a factor that would make Russia socialist. He was convinced that there were no substantive differences between the Narodnaya Volya and Plekhanov's social democrats" whom Lenin later joined. "Several members of the terrorist group were social democrats, there were no members of the Narodnaya Volya in it," but they kept the name because it conveyed a message. The message was: "systematic terror" to bring down the tsarist government or force it to make major concessions. Sasha believed not in individual terror but in multiple assassinations.

Page 289 of the stenographic record of the trial reads:

"DEFENDANT ULYANOV: As to my defense, I am in the same position as Generalov and Andreyyushkin. The factual aspect has been fully established and I do not deny it. Therefore, the right of defense consists only in the right to present the motives for the crime, that is, to tell of the thought process which convinced me of the necessity to commit this crime. I can trace to my early youth that vague feeling of dissatisfaction with the social system which, penetrating more and more into my consciousness, brought me to the convictions which inspired me in the present case. But only after studying the social and economic sciences did this conviction of the abnormality of the existing system become fully confirmed in me, and the vague dreams of freedom, equality, and brotherhood took shape for me in the strictly scientific forms of socialism. . . . There is only one correct path of development, that is the path of words and the press, scientific printed propaganda, because every change in the social system is a result of a change in the consciousness of society. This proposition is clearly stated in the program of the terrorist fraction of the 'Narodnaya Volya' party, and this is just the reverse of what Mr. Prosecutor said."

The prosecutor, Sasha Ulyanov contended, had falsely charged that the small band of terrorists had intended to foist their views on society. Sasha took a diametrically opposed view: "Given the government's attitude to intellectual life, not only socialist propaganda but even general-cultural propaganda is impossible; even the scientific examination of questions is seriously impeded. The government is so powerful, the intelligentsia so weak and so concentrated in a few cities, that the government can deprive it of the only possibility—the last vestiges of freedom of speech. . . . Having become convinced of the absolute subjective need of freedom of thought and expression, it was necessary to examine the objective possibility, that is, to examine whether there exist in Russian society the elements on which a struggle [for freedom] could depend. Russian society differs from Western Europe in two important aspects. It is inferior intellectually and we have no firmly united classes that might restrain the government. . . . For an intellectual person, the right to think freely and to share his thoughts with those who are inferior to him in development is not only an inalienable right, but even a necessity and duty."

Here the presiding judge interrupted and instructed Sasha "not to propound general theories which are more or less known to us" but to explain how this affected him.

"DEFENDANT ULYANOV: All this affected me personally, so from this point of view I cannot advance subjective motives."

The judge told him to be as brief as possible.

"DEFENDANT ULYANOV: All right. . . . Our intelligentsia is so weak, physically, and so unorganized, that at the present time it cannot enter upon an open struggle, and it is only through terror that it can defend its right to thought and to intellectual participation in the life of society. Terror is the form of struggle created by the nineteenth century, it is the only form of defense available to the minority which is only strong spiritually and in the conviction of its righteousness against the majority's feeling of its physical power. Russian society exists in such circumstances that it is only in these single combats with the government that it can defend its rights. . . . In the Russian nation you will always find ten persons who are so loyal to their ideas and who are so filled with the unhappiness of their country that it is no sacrifice for them to die on behalf of their cause. There is nothing that will frighten such people."

"PRESIDING JUDGE: You are speaking of what was, not of what will be."

"DEFENDANT ULYANOV: I cannot enter upon that. In order that my belief in the necessity of terror may be more fully demonstrated I must say whether it can or cannot bring any results. So this is such an indispensable part of my explanation that I ask permission to say a few words . . ."

"PRESIDING JUDGE: No. That's enough. . . . In other words, under the influence of these thoughts you recognized the possibility of participating in this evil deed?"

"DEFENDANT: Yes. Under their influence. I was convinced that terror could achieve aims, so this was not only a personal affair. I say all this not to justify my act morally or to prove its political efficacy. I wished to show that it is the unavoidable consequence of existing conditions, of the existing contradictions of life. It is known that we can develop our intellectual capacities but we do not have the possibility of putting them at the service of our country. Such an objective-scientific examination of the reasons, however strange they may appear to Mr. Prosecutor, will be more helpful, even for those who reject terror, than mere indignation. That is all I wanted to say."

Those were his last words.

He had not denied guilt. He had admitted it and justified it. He had written his own death sentence.

The death of a young person whose great talents are just beginning to unfold gives the living a lasting shock. Death in the hangman's noose by order of a hated autocrat adds fury to the shock. Alexander Ulyanov became a hero to Russians who had never seen or heard of him. He became a hero to Vladimir Ulyanov (Lenin) whose shock and fury were enhanced by the worst of all feelings: regret, regret not to have been close to the hero brother, not to have appreciated him, to have underestimated him. When, as a university student, Lenin was first arrested, a colleague in the cell asked him what he thought he would do after his release. "What is there for me to think?" Lenin replied. "My path has been blazed by my older brother."[15] Lenin's wife recalls that the evening she met her future husband they took a walk, and the courtship began with his telling her about the execution of Sasha. "The fate of his brother undoubtedly profoundly influenced Vladimir Ilyich," she writes.[16] Asked, upon his return to Russia in April, 1917, to write a sketch of himself, Lenin penned an eight-line "Unfinished Autobiography," first published in *Pravda* on April 16, 1927, and reprinted in the April, 1963, issue of *Novy Mir.* "My name is Vladimir Ilyich Ulyanov. I was born in Simbirsk April 10, 1870. In the spring of 1887, my older brother Alexander was sentenced to death by Alexander III for an attempt (March 1, 1887) on his life. . . ."

His mother's grief also affected Lenin. He could be cold and impersonal. But he loved his mother. Writing from exile in Siberia or from Western Europe, he often addressed her as "Meelaya Mama" (Darling Mother) and his letters, many of which have been published, were filled with tenderness and solicitude. She lived till July 25, 1916. The day after Lenin returned to Russia from abroad in April, 1917, to lead the revolution—the times were tense and events pressed—he went to the Volkov cemetery in Petrograd and prostrated himself on her grave.

II. ◰ LEADER IS BORN

ALEXANDER (SASHA) ULYANOV turned in despair to revolution though no brother of his was executed. Lenin too might have traveled the road to the

[15] Quoted in Moscow magazine *Novy Mir*, of April, 1963, from a book by B. Volin, *Student Vladimir Ulyanov (Vladimir Ulyanov as Student)* (Moscow, 1958).

[16] Nadezhda K. Krupskaya, *Memories of Lenin.* Translated by E. Verney (New York, 1930), Vol. I, p. 5.

Kremlin even if Sasha's neck had not been broken in the hangman's noose. Yet given the rising social ferment among Russia's intellectuals, given the fact that the autocracy reached into the Ulyanov home to extinguish its brightest light, and Lenin's course was set.

The tsarist authorities did not visit the sin of Sasha on his younger brother. The spring which brought death to Sasha brought Volodya a gold medal at the graduation exercise of the Simbirsk gymnasium. The next term he matriculated in the University of Kazan, his father's alma mater. The mother, probably hating the provincialism of Simbirsk as much as Sasha had, now moved with her children to Kazan, a larger city and more cosmopolitan. Two of her married sisters lived in Kazan: Anna Blank, now Madame Veretennikova, and Lybov Blank, first married to Ardashev, and after her second marriage Madame Ponomaryova. (These are samples, from a Soviet book published in 1956, of the kind of detailed data available in tsarist police archives. The address of every house where the Ulyanovs lived is also found in the files.)

Lenin's mother, Maria Alexandrovna, had money. When her husband died, the Kazan Regional invited her to accept the star decoration she was entitled to wear. She refused—perhaps it meant nothing to her; also she would have had to pay for it. But two days after her husband's passing Maria Alexandrovna applied for a pension and was soon awarded a large sum. She also received part of the income of the estate of her father, Dr. Blank. From these resources she met Volodya's tuition and other bills and supported the family. Later she sent money to Lenin in Siberia, and even after he had become a well-known revolutionary she transmitted gold roubles through the tsarist post office to him, at his request, in Western Europe.

The mother did not pay Volodya's tuition very long. On December 4, 1887, in his first semester at Kazan, he joined several hundred students who staged a mild demonstration against the university's inspector. He and some others were arrested and imprisoned for several days. On December 5 the university expelled him, and on the 7th, the police exiled him to his grandfather's estate at Kokushkino, province of Kazan—a not unpleasant punishment—to which Anna, Lenin's oldest sister, had been exiled after her arrest in St. Petersburg.

Vladimir Ilyich read voraciously, played chess, hunted, and skied. On May 9, 1888, one day after the first anniversary of his brother's execution, he applied for readmission to Kazan University but received a refusal. He thereupon requested permission to go abroad for study and a cure. This too was refused. In September, 1888, the entire Ulyanov family, Anna and Vladimir included, were allowed to live in the city of Kazan. Here he spent seven months in which, according to Soviet hagiography, he participated actively in Marxist circles. But in all that time he never met the leading spirit of those circles, Nikolai E. Fedoseyev, though Maxim Gorky, then a wandering Russian writer, encountered Fedoseyev at one of the open-house evening gatherings and was asked whether he could put the circles in touch with some workers.

On May 3, 1889, the Ulyanov family went to spend the summer in the village of Alakeyevka in Samara province. Maria Alexandrovna bought a house there. In October, 1889, the family moved to the city of Samara on the Volga. Thereafter, until August, 1893, almost four years, Lenin and his relatives spent summers in their new village home and the rest of the time in Samara. Lenin read law, began to raise a reddish beard and mustache and to grow bald.

During this Samara period Lenin twice visited St. Petersburg, in the autumn of 1890 and from September 7 to November 12, 1891—the dates were entered into his passport which is preserved in the Central Communist Party Archives in Moscow—to ascertain the conditions for taking the law examinations without attending a university and to read in the library of the Academy of Science. Nobody in the Ulyanov family worked, but its funds sufficed for travel and life in town and country.

On January 14, 1892, "Nobleman Vladimir Ulyanov," as the future Lenin then signed, applied to the Minister of Education in St. Petersburg for permission to take the law examinations.[1] He passed and obtained an official license to practice but only as an attorney's assistant and in a limited number of cases. He complained to the court. The court queried the police, which stated that it had no objection to lifting the restriction. Lenin was accordingly admitted to the bar as a full-fledged lawyer.[2]

In Samara Lenin took his first step toward Marxism. Soviet biographies would have it that he began reading Marx's basic work, *Capital*, when his older brother Sasha brought it home on summer vacation. But as his sister Anna testified, he read and reread Turgenev, which was natural enough for a teen-ager in a provincial town. They contend further that he became a full-fledged Marxist in Kazan. However, V. V. Adoratsky, who knew Lenin in Kazan and later became one of the editors of Lenin's collected works, affirms that in Kazan, "Narodnaya Volya members undoubtedly exercised a certain influence on Lenin." The Narodnaya Volya Party, variously translated as People's Will and People's Freedom Party for the Russian language, significantly enough, equates freedom with will, was, in the bleak provinces, still a terrorist organization.

Lenin himself, writing in 1902 in *Chto Delat?* (*What Is to Be Done?*) about his generation of revolutionaries, said, "Many of them began to think revolution as Narodnaya Volya followers. Almost all of them enthusiastically worshiped the heroes of terror. Repudiation of the enveloping feeling of this heroic tradition came only after a struggle and was accompanied by a break with persons who at all costs wished to remain true to the Narodnaya Volya and whom the young social democrats [Marxists] held in high esteem."

[1] *Molodiye Godi V. I. Lenina*, pp. 372 and 385.
[2] *Leninskii Sbornik* (*Lenin Collection*, also called *Lenin Miscellany*), Vol. II, edited by L. B. Kamenev (Leningrad, 1924), p. 444. Under the imprint of the Lenin Institute.

"This paragraph," Lenin's wife Krupskaya writes in her reminiscences, "is a piece of Lenin's biography."

In Samara, however, Lenin took to studying Marx's *Capital* with the industry that accounts for some of his greatness. There, again according to Adoratsky, "Lenin was already a Marxist though certain vestiges of Narodnaya Volya remained (a special attitude toward terror)." A special bond with his dead brother?

Indeed, the vestiges survived. In 1902 Stepan V. Balmashov, a nineteen-year-old Russian Social Revolutionary terrorist (the Social Revolutionaries, or SR's, were the heirs of the Narodnaya Volya), shot and killed tsarist Minister of Interior Dmitri S. Sipyagin. When Lenin, living in London, heard of this, he exclaimed, "A neat job."[3] To be sure, he later argued in writing that the life of a revolutionist was not worth that of a scoundrel like Sipyagin, but the spontaneous outburst of approval tells as much as the subsequent cogitation.

After nearly four years in Samara province, Lenin left on August 20, 1893, to live in St. Petersburg. En route he stopped at Nizhni Novgorod, and there, Adoratsky affirms, "he addressed meetings as a Marxist." A Lenin biographer says that at that time "the Marxists in Russia could literally be counted on one's fingers."

Vladimir Ilyich Ulyanov, nobleman and attorney, age twenty-three, arrived in St. Petersburg on August 31, 1893, to begin his life as an active revolutionary. He joined a shining galaxy of young Marxists which reflected the light of the star of the Russian socialist firmament, Georgi V. Plekhanov. It included Alexander N. Potresov, a year older than Lenin, son of an artillery officer; Vasili V. Starkov, an engineer of the same age; Gleb M. Krzhizhanovsky, twenty-one-year-old engineer; and, notably, Peter B. Struve, grandson of the famous German astronomer Friedrich Struve and son of the governor of the Russian province of Astrakhan. Born the same year as Lenin, Peter Struve had already been abroad twice and written an article for a German magazine on Russian agrarian catastrophes. He was a Westerner, a Marxist, and an opponent of the terror-minded, village-commune-oriented Narodnaya Volya. Lenin clashed with him.

A knotted skein of personal and political motives explains their clash. Struve was a liberal believer in legal Marxism. Lenin had not yet shed his "special attitude toward terror" and hence favored illegal activity. Lenin's manner exacerbated the antagonism. Vasili Starkov, a member of the St. Petersburg group, wrote a memoir in 1925 which conveys the flavor of the Lenin-Struve debate: "Vladimir Ilyich astonished us no less by his practical maturity than by his theoretical preparation and, I would say, by the sobriety of his thoughts. This latter quality of his mind was especially emphasized by his undeviating and uncompromising attitude toward principles amounting to, as we soon began to say, 'stone-hardness.' Very unyielding in formulating

[3] *Vospominaniya o Vladimire Ilyiche Lenine (Reminiscences about Vladimir Ilyich Lenin)*, Vol. 1, p. 215.

general principles, he showed himself relatively very flexible on questions of day-to-day tactics; in such matters he manifested no excessive rigor. I remember with what heat he defended against our attacks his view on terror as a method of political struggle . . . he expounded what, to us, was the heretical thought that in principle Social Democracy does not reject terror as a method of struggle. The main thing is ends, and every means of struggle, including terror, is good or bad depending on whether, in the given circumstances, it conduces to the attainment of those ends or, on the contrary, diverts from them. To us, brought up on the articles of Plekhanov which sharply criticized the program and tactics, based on terror, of the Narodnaya Volya . . . such views appeared heretical. I no longer remember how we achieved a truce, but Vladimir Ilyich, in any event, remained the same. Possessing the determination and perspicacity of a real leader, he could permit himself the luxury, to some extent, of being opportunistic in matters of the method of struggle, for he always knew how far one could go in such cases and at what moment questions of tactic began to affect purely programmatic issues which demand complete obstinacy . . . I believe Vladimir Ilyich remained the same until the last days of his life."

(Starkov's memoir, first printed in the Moscow magazine *Krasnaya Nov,* of November, 1925, was republished in the third volume of Lenin reminiscences [*Vospominaniya o Vladimire Ilyiche Lenine*][4] without the above passage.)

Lenin had made his first scratch on the history of the Russian revolutionary movement. He was assiduous, erudite, well-read, and a bruising debater. He was confidently bellicose. He attached overriding importance to political method.

Before leaving Samara, Lenin paid out of his own pocket, or his mother's, for the printing of 200-250 questionnaires with numerous queries to be answered by Volga villagers. He commissioned A. A. Preobrazhensky, an idealist who founded an agricultural commune in the Samara district, to collect the replies. They reached him in St. Petersburg. Lenin now became a writer so engrossed in economic and statistical researches that he neglected his work as assistant to M. F. Folkenshtein, a St. Petersburg attorney.

In the spring of 1894 Lenin wrote an article, furnished with tables of statistics, which ran to approximately 30,000 words; nobody wanted to print it—until 1927. A second, still longer, article on markets, produced in the autumn of 1893, circulated among St. Petersburg Marxists but was not printed; in fact it was mislaid and did not get published until 1937. Nothing deterred the 23-year-old. From 1893 until early in 1923, when hardened cerebral arteries stilled his tongue and stopped his pen, Lenin wrote an estimated 10 million words. They are all available in Russian in his collected works. They reveal in detail a man with iron will, self-enslaving self-discipline, scorn for opponents and obstacles, the cold determination of a zealot, the drive of a fanatic, and the ability to convince or browbeat weaker persons

[4] Vol. 3, pp. 18-20.

by his singleness of purpose, imposing intensity, impersonal approach, personal sacrifice, political astuteness, and complete conviction of the possession of the absolute truth. His life became the history of the Bolshevik movement. When difficulties depressed waverers, he plowed on to success and enthroned communism in Russia. What had theretofore been a lonely exile's polemics then became a great power's policies.

One of the St. Petersburg Marxists who read Lenin's lengthy script on markets was Nadezhda Konstantinovna Krupskaya, born a year before its author. Writing more than thirty years later she recalled the impression the article made on her: "One felt in the whole approach a lively Marxist who grasps situations concretely as they are, and as they develop. I wanted to get to know the newcomer more closely, to know his views more closely."

This tall, pale, grave schoolteacher, her hair pulled into a bun on the back of her head, first met Lenin at a Shrovetide party where Marxists ate bliny, or pancakes, and discussed the future of Russia. Someone suggested the need of literacy committees to educate the masses. "Vladimir Ilyich laughed," Nadezhda Krupskaya wrote in her memoirs, "and somehow the laughter sounded so wicked and dry—I never heard him laugh again in that way."

"Well," he said, "anybody who likes to save the fatherland with a literacy committee why, fine, we shall not interfere." She understood him; he preferred stronger methods.

Four years later these two Marxists were married.

There is good reason to believe—though such matters cannot be documented—that Lenin failed in an earlier attempt at marriage. He proposed to Appolinaria Yakubova, like Krupskaya a schoolteacher and a member of his Marxist group. Krupskaya wrote in her memoirs, "I had been particularly friendly with her as we had worked in the same Sunday Adult School beyond the Nevsky" in St. Petersburg. Appolinaria rejected Lenin's suit and married Professor K. M. Takhterev, the editor of *Rabochaya Misl (Workers' Thought)*, a Russian revolutionary magazine. In his disappointment, Lenin courted and won Krupskaya. Subsequently—it was 1900—Appolinaria in London and Lenin in Munich exchanged very long letters devoted exclusively to problems of ideology and socialist strategy which, on his part, nevertheless had personal overtones: he resented her "caustic remarks" and referred to "our old friendship." She apologized.[5] In 1902 Lenin and Krupskaya moved from Munich to London, where they first rented a most modest apartment near King's Cross Road. The landlady, however, protested that Krupskaya not only did not put up curtains, she wore no wedding ring. Appolinaria, speaking better English than Lenin or Krupskaya, told the landlady that the newcomers were legally married and that if she repeated her insinuations she would be sued for defamation. She desisted.[6]

[5] *Leninskii Sbornik (Lenin Collection)*, Vol. XIII, edited by V. V. Adoratsky, V. M. Molotov, and M. A. Savelev (Moscow-Leningrad, 1930), pp. 93-111.

[6] *Vospominaniya o Vladimire Ilyiche Lenine*, Vol. I, p. 215-216.

Lenin wanted Appolinaria to "remember." He later loved a woman. He was attentive to family and comrades. But these apart, he reveled in the hate which provided a vent for his inexhaustible reserves of bitterness and combativeness. His intolerance of even moderate opposition during the years of European exile compounded the absolutism of tsarism. Together, these antidemocratic proclivities split Russia's revolutionary movement with disastrous results for her history. A united movement might have saved that talented nation (which did not deserve the governments it got because it had no choice in the matter) from the horrors of red terror and red dictatorship. But the opposition to a government usually mirrors the general nature of that government, and Lenin's inner tensions, the nervousness his mother did not have, sharpened the reflection.

The main line of cleavage within the revolutionary forces was between the Social Democrats, or Marxists, and the Social Revolutionaries (SR's) who followed in the footsteps of the Narodnaya Volya. It was to emphasize what divided the Marxists from the SR's and to erase what might have united them that Kremlin scribes invented Lenin's rejection of his brother's terrorism, thus blotting out the Marxism of Sasha and the terrorist views of Lenin. This is where communist distortion of history began.

The Social Democrats and the SR Narodniks, or populists, did differ, however, on a major issue: the muzhik, or peasant.

In 1667 a Don Cossack named Stenka Razin raised the banner of revolt among the peasant serfs of the Volga region. Rallying them in their rags, this Russian Robin Hood captured Nizhni Novgorod, Tambov, Voronezh, and Simbirsk—a vast region—but was finally defeated, taken prisoner, brought to Moscow, and quartered on June 6, 1671. Like all Russian children, Lenin knew about Stenka Razin and probably sang "Vniz po Volge" ("Down Along the Volga") which recounts the partially legendary tale of that popular hero. On May 1, 1919, Lenin stood on the stone execution block in Moscow's Red Square where Razin had been done to death and dedicated a monument to him. "At this spot," Lenin said,[7] "he laid down his head in the struggle for freedom. Russian revolutionaries have made many sacrifices in the struggle against capitalism," for "no capitalist government can ever hold power except by violence and abuse."

In the spring of 1767, exactly a century after Razin's revolt began, Catherine the Great (1729-1796), by birth a German princess, eager to see Asia, boarded a boat at Tver and, accompanied in lesser craft by 2,000 highborn Russians and the entire St. Petersburg diplomatic corps, floated down the Volga to Simbirsk and thence returned overland to her capital. "Me voilà en Asie," she wrote to Voltaire from Kazan on May 29, 1767, "j'ai voulu voir cela par mes yeux." And in a letter to Count Nikita Ivanovich Panin dated Kazan, June 1, 1767, the Eastern despot with a French culture said in

[7] V. I. Lenin, *Sochineniya (Collected Works)*, Fourth ed., Vol. 29 (Moscow, 1952), p. 304.

Russian, "Here the people along the entire Volga are rich and quite well-fed, and although prices are high here, they eat bread, and nobody complains or suffers need. We are all healthy. . . . Catherine."[8]

The Tsarina's discovery of universal contentment among her Volga subjects was six years old when the bearded Emelyan Ivanovich Pugachev, aged thirty-one, a simple Cossack like Stenka Razin from the Don River basin, pretending to be Tsar Peter III, whom Catherine had dethroned, threw the torch of revolt into the regions inhabited by the Tartars, Bashkirs, Kalmucks, Kazaks, and Russian peasants on both sides of the Volga. Burning, looting, killing, living off the land, his ill-equipped, mobile bands occupied a tremendous slice of the empire—larger than Razin's conquests—from western Siberia, through the Urals, down to Tsaritsin (Stalingrad, Volgagrad), and up to Saratov, Samara, Simbirsk, and Kazan. Catherine's best generals, among them Alexander Suvorov, had to be dispatched against Pugachev. A Volga famine completed his undoing. Captured at Simbirsk, he was transported in a cage across the curious countryside and executed in an open Moscow square on January 10, 1775.

Pugachev's eruption was a major chapter in Russian history; Stenka Razin's a vivid one. Together they helped mold the views of Russian Marxists on the future of their country. The peasantry, they held, was capable of pillage, arson, and murder, but could not overthrow a government or seize power. Pugachev played as much on the muzhiks' loyalty to royalty—hence his claim to the throne—as on their dissatisfaction with poverty and serfdom. Lenin accordingly looked to another class: the workers.

In their 1848 *Communist Manifesto* Marx and Engels spoke of "the idiocy of rural life." Marxism has always been a city philosophy. It is worker-minded and factory-oriented. The landlord was a natural enemy and the peasant a potential one, for he dreamed of owning land, and if the dream came true he would be a petty capitalist clinging to small-scale, inefficient farming methods.

Many Russian intellectuals, however, viewed the village, filth and misery notwithstanding, as idyllic. The God-fearing, honest, suffering peasant, clad in picturesque homespun and bast or felt boots, and unspoiled by urban decadence or materialistic corruption, was not a capitalist. He labored to feed, clothe, and shelter his family, and traded only to the extent that he had to for these purposes. Village economy, to be sure, remained backward, indeed primitive, but also primitively socialistic. As early as the fifteenth century, the simple Russian tiller of the soil had evolved the obshchina or mir (commune) whose social goal was equality. Conditions varied with place and period, but at least some land and property, usually woods and pastures, were held in common. The commune decided on crop rotation. Acreage obtained after

[8] *Sbornik Russkago Istoricheskago Obshchestva (Collection of the Russian Historical Society)*, Vol. 9 (St. Petersburg, 1872), pp. 203-207.

the Tsar's emancipation of the serfs in 1861 was divided by the village assembly according to the size and working capacity of a family and redistrib-
uted at irregular intervals as changes in these circumstances required, care
being taken to provide each smallholder with a strip of good land and one of
poor and mediocre land. This periodic reshuffle and its resulting fragmentation persisted after the Soviet revolution, indeed until collectivization in 1929,
and though it handicapped production it testified to an egalitarian spirit
which the nineteenth-century Narodniks regarded as the essence of the socialistic Russia of their dreams.

Russian populism went through several phases from its first appearance in
the 1860's as the purely terroristic Narodnaya Volya to its last incarnation
as the Left and Right Social Revolutionaries who did not neglect peaceful
political action and rocked the Soviet regime even after it suppressed them
in 1918. The populist firmament sparkled with stars. In philosophy, though
not by affiliation, Count Leo Tolstoy was a populist. Western Europe's plutocracy offended him; its ideal of progress had no appeal. In 1884, at the age
of fifty-six, he abandoned the glittering aristocratic society of St. Petersburg
and Moscow where he had spent cluttered years and withdrew to his ances-
tral village. Exalting manual labor, he plowed, harrowed, and planted with
the muzhiks, walked barefoot, wore a peasant smock (which urban intellectuals affected, calling it a tolstovka), renounced his property, denounced the
state-directed Orthodox Church, devoted himself to village uplift, and
preached back-to-nature and nonviolence. Ernest J. Simmons, Tolstoy's biographer, quotes him as saying in 1881, "An economic revolution not only
may but must come"; and Tolstoy declared in 1886 that if the problem of
Russian poverty was not solved, "a workers' revolution of destruction and
murder" would occur. Tolstoy, the Christian anarchist-populist, feared the
people's violence.

Bakunin advocated it. Mikhail Bakunin (1814-1876), a landlord and
Guards officer turned anarchist-atheist, radiated radical ideas throughout Europe, and particularly into Spain, the Mediterranean Russia. His enemy was
the state, his politics the destruction of all government, his hero Stenka Razin, his goal a nation of self-sufficient peasant communes and small industrial
artels, or cooperatives, with a minimum of local administration.

Like Bakunin, Prince Peter Kropotkin (1842-1921), once a page in the
Tsar's court, adopted the credo of anarchism and nihilism and formulated
the doctrine of mutual aid: voluntary, grass-roots communism based on the
mir. Georgi V. Plekhanov (1857-1918), scion of the rich nobility, also began
as a Narodnik or populist. Later he joined the Marxist Russian Social Democratic Labor Party to become its leading theoretician and as such Lenin's
venerated mentor—until Lenin, brilliant but bellicose, first dethroned him,
then maligned him. These were some of the few (compared with the many
upper-class conformists) who, incensed by the cruel, wasteful, insensitive

tsarist regime, wanted another and joined the thin ranks of revolutionaries. Many questioned everything; the nihilists denied all; some would destroy everything.

The fury of the revolutionists matched the folly of the monarchy. Government by a handful encouraged a handful to consider taking their place by means of assassination or revolution. Church-propped tsarism bred atheism. The Tsar made the revolution. Because Russia was an underdeveloped country, her intelligentsia, as Sasha said at his trial, was weak, and her classes were not full-grown. The revolutionists therefore thought in terms of bombs or coup d'états, two not too different forms of violence.

No steel wall separated the populists from the Marxists. They borrowed from one another. But the Narodniks concentrated on the *narod*—the people —and the people were overwhelmingly peasants. Russian capitalism was still in swaddling clothes: the industrial working class in 1881 numbered approximately 1 million,[9] the peasantry 75 million. The Narodniks abhorred Western capitalism with its slums and exploitation and hoped their beloved Russia would skip capitalism, cross the capitalist bog on the mir bridge and, avoiding class war, pass directly from underdevelopment to agrarian socialism. The populists poured this social content into their mystic, messianic Slavophilism.

Marx himself admired the non-Marxist Narodnik terrorists "who carried their skins to the market" (his dry economic formula for the idealistic sacrifice of life) and compared them favorably with the Russian Marxists of the 1880's "who came to Geneva to make propaganda in Russia." He studied the Russian village commune from afar and did not altogether discourage its partisans. When Vera Zasulich, a prominent Russian Marxist and former terrorist, prodded Marx for his opinion on the commune, he replied in French on March 8, 1881 (he died in 1883): "The analysis presented in *Capital* does not, accordingly, offer arguments for or against the agricultural commune, but the special study I have made of the subject . . . has convinced me that the commune is the pivot of the social regeneration of Russia; however, if it is to be able to function as such the deleterious influences which assail it must be eliminated and then it must be guaranteed the normal conditions of spontaneous development."[10]

Friedrich Engels too saw a bright eastern gleam in the commune of Russia where, he believed in 1885, "a handful" of determined men could "make a revolution."[11] But the famine of 1891 and Russia's galloping industrial de-

---

[9] The first census in Russia, exclusive of the Grand Duchy of Finland, was taken in 1897 and showed a total of 128,924,289 inhabitants, of whom 16,785,212 lived in cities and towns. An official tsarist estimate for 1881 gave the number of factory workers in European Russia as 770,842, a figure which does not include miners. "Approximately one million" is derived by adding estimated miners, and factory workers in Asiatic Russia, to 770,842.

[10] Dietrich Geyer, *Lenin in der Russischen Sozialdemokratie. Die Arbeiterbewegung im Zarenreich als Organizationsproblem der revolutionaeren Intelligenz. 1890-1903* (Cologne-Graz, 1962), p. 8.

[11] *Ibid.* p. 10.

velopment altered his thinking; communes in hungry dustbowls no longer
seemed the seedbed of communism "but a dream of the past." Russia was
chugging down the world's mainstream of capitalist economic development.

Lenin avidly accepted Engels' new concept and expanded it with unpitying
repetitiveness in a hectographed pamphlet.[12] This assault on the Narodniks
and defense of the Marxists, first released in July, 1894, was a barrage of
poison-tipped darts aimed in particular at Nikolai K. Mikhailovsky (1842-
1904) and Nikolai F. Danielson (1844-1918) whom the 24-year-old Lenin
lampooned and quartered. He called the Narodnik leaders "subjective so-
ciologists" who dissected an individual's adversity without realizing that alone
the class struggle predetermined man's fate. It was a virtuoso performance
by a prodigy throbbing with youthful yearning to kill with sneering sarcasm.
The essay is wholly unsentimental and unclouded by doubt. The Marxist
mold of Lenin's mind was already set for all time. He scoffed at the Narodnik
notion of saving Russia by bridging the chasm between capitalism and socialism. The mir, he predicted, would break up under the impact of industrialization. The peasant would become either a smallholder or a city laborer.

Lenin welcomed the growth of Russian capitalism. With it would grow
the number of workers, the predestined "gravediggers" of capitalism. Russia,
he insisted, lived by no social laws made especially for her; the teachings of
Marx had universal application; Russian capitalism would share the fate of
Western capitalism; both must first expand, then succumb to the revolutionary proletariat united under the banner of international communism.

"United action, of the leading civilized countries at least," Marx and Engels wrote in the Communist Manifesto, "is one of the first conditions for
the emancipation of the proletariat." Such international action, they felt,
was possible because "The working men have no country. We cannot take
from them what they do not possess." Already, they declared, "National differences and antagonisms between peoples are vanishing more and more every
day." In fact "National onesidedness and narrowmindedness become more
and more impossible, and from the numerous national and local literatures
there arises a world literature."

The error of Marx and Engels in predicting the early demise of nationalism stemmed from the proposition, basic to all Marxist thinking, that political, cultural, and psychological developments keep in step with economic
changes. "The bourgeoisie," says the Manifesto, "has through its exploitation
of the world-market given a cosmopolitan character to production and consumption in every country. . . . The bourgeoisie, by the rapid improvement
of all instruments of production, by the immensely facilitated means of communication . . . compels all nations, on pain of extinction, to adopt the

---

[12] Lenin, Chto Takoye 'Druzya Naroda' i Kak Oni Voyuyut Protiv Sozial-Demok-
ratov (What are the 'Friends of the People' and How they Fight Against the Social
Democrats), in Lenin, Sochineniya (Collected Works), Second ed., Vol. I (Moscow-
Leningrad, 1927), pp. 55-221.

bourgeois mode of production." Since production and consumption had become international, or cosmopolitan, so, the *Manifesto* optimistically assumed, would literature, popular sentiment, and proletarian effort.

"Of all classes that stand face to face with the bourgeoisie today," the Marx-Engels *Manifesto* declared, "the proletariat alone is a really revolutionary class. The other classes decay and finally disappear in the face of modern industry; the proletariat is its special and essential product."

Peasants were too conservative to make a revolution, said Marx and Engels; "Nay, more," they added, "they are reactionary, for they try to roll back the wheels of history." This dictum branded the Narodniks as reactionary champions of the reactionary peasantry. The workers, on the contrary, were functional revolutionaries.

Studying conditions in their own time, Marx and Engels drew conclusions which worshipful disciples have sought to apply to all time. "The modern laborer," they wrote in the *Manifesto*, "instead of rising with the progress of industry, sinks deeper and deeper. . . . He becomes a pauper, and pauperism develops more rapidly than population and wealth. And here it becomes evident that the bourgeoisie is unfit any longer to be the ruling class in society."

This leads to class war. "The history of all hitherto existing society is the history of class struggles," the *Manifesto* affirms. When one class has outlived its usefulness to society it must yield to another. Since the class will resist it has to be crushed. "The Communists disdain to conceal their views and aims," the *Manifesto* avowed in its peroration. "They openly declare that their ends can be attained only by the forcible overthrow of all existing social conditions. Let the ruling class tremble at the communist revolution. The proletarians have nothing to lose but their chains. They have a world to win. Workers of all countries, unite."

This is the Marxist law. During his twenty-four years—1893 to 1917—as agitator, editor, and organizer, Lenin hewed as closely as necessary to the Marxist line: when life demanded change he deviated. He began, however, as an internationalist and Westerner firmly convinced that Russia, moving in the mainstream of world capitalism, was influenced by developments in Europe, Asia, and America and would, in turn, influence them. The populists rejected Europe. Lenin embraced it. They were Russocentric. He, at first, was not.

Narodniks and Marxists faced and fought one another across this gulf in the 1870's, 1880's and 1890's. But as Russian industry developed, the Narodniks discovered the working class. As Russia became more capitalistic they too saw the doom of the mir. Similarly, Lenin realized, late, that the Russian proletariat alone could not even launch, much less consolidate, his eagerly desired revolution. He accordingly courted the peasantry. Had the Narodniks and Marxists operated in a democracy, which erodes the sharp edges of ideology, they might have coalesced to combat the common tsarist enemy instead of devouring one another. Exile, moreover, is a hothouse where conflicts grow wild and hairsplitting dogmatists luxuriate. Most leading Russian revolutionaries of both schools spent years of banishment in Siberia and Europe. Siberia did not cool their controversial ardor nor did Europe teach them democracy. In England, Germany, France, and Switzerland they lived in Russia.

The dispute between Russian populists and Marxists looks like a fossil of history. It has a living counterpart, however, in India today. Life permits few analogies. Many differences of space, time, and character separate tsarist Russia from independent India. Yet in India too "Marxists" (champions of hasty heavy industrialization) vie with "Narodniks" or nonviolent, humanitarian Gandhian socialists. The Indian "Marxists," watching the economic patterns of the Soviet Russia, attach more importance to state industry than to private farming. The Indian populists, on the other hand, argue that India has a unique mission and must create her own way of life based on self-sufficient village "republics" engaged in cottage industries which will not pour their surplus labor into city slums and thus accelerate the pace of industrialization. Here there are noticeable similarities between nineteenth-century Russia and today's India. Nevertheless, the Narodniks-versus-Marxists struggle in India did not follow a Russian course. Under British rule, moderate "Marxists" and peaceful populists functioned within or near the Gandhi-Nehru-led Congress Party. Gandhi was a populist-socialist, Nehru a "Marxist" not unalterably committed to Marxism. Gandhi's personality united the camps. British democratic tradition softened their antagonism. India's Congress Party experienced none of the ugly factional wars, splits, recriminations, and government-spy infiltrations which contorted the Marxist movement in Russia and drove the Bolsheviks to extremism.

After India's national independence, the bond forged during the common crusade for freedom prevented ideological differences from fostering a mania of destruction. One concludes that the Russian Marxist war against the Narodniks was less an inevitable clash of conflicting philosophies than a reflection of the white-or-black politics of their autocratic country.

History, however, sometimes plays wicked tricks on politicians. History played a trick on the Kremlin. Russian populism survives in red dress. Russia, not Europe, ousted the capitalist class. Stalin's "socialism in one country" smacked of the nationalistic Narodnik program. Soviet Russia, her spokesmen contend, has skipped—and Red China was said to be leaping—from underdevelopment to socialism—a Narodnik idea. Russia, the Narodniks urged, must shun the decadent West; she had a unique role to play. Echoes of those ancient, un-Marxist ideas are heard hourly from the Kremlin battlements. Soviet propaganda is often geared to the deep imprint the Narodniks stamped on the Russian mind. Behind the mask of messianic communism can be seen the visage of messianic Russian nationalism which eclipses Marxist internationalism.

No nation can escape its past. It can only build on it. The Narodniks reflected Russia's past. Russia was not reached by the Renaissance. Russia was not touched by the sixteenth-century Reformation; her ties were with the Eastern Church of Byzantium. In the latter part of the seventeenth century and in the eighteenth, Peter the Great and Catherine the Great tried to open windows to European techniques and culture. But when Europe in the shape of Napoleon appeared on the Russian plains, Prince Kutuzov, aided by "General Winter," defeated it. In so doing Russia, like Spain, shut out the French bourgeois-capitalist revolution and erected a wall against Western Europe. The West was too progressive and too powerful to suit the upper layers of tsarist society.

Young Lenin, writing in 1895 about the death in London of Friedrich Engels, noted that both Marx and Engels knew Russian, read Russian books, "watched with sympathy the Russian revolutionary movement and maintained contacts with Russian revolutionaries. . . . Marx and Engels saw clearly that a political revolution in Russia would have enormous significance for the West European workers' movement. Autocratic Russia has ever been the bulwark of reaction in all of Europe. . . . Only a free Russia that is under no necessity to oppress the Poles, Finns, Germans, Armenians, and other small nationalities or constantly to incite France against Germany will relieve contemporary Europe of its military burdens, weaken the reactionary elements in Europe, and increase the strength of the European working class. This is why Engels, for the success of the workers' movement in the West, warmly desired the establishment of political freedom in Russia."[13]

On April 25, 1895, Lenin left St. Petersburg and went to Switzerland, Paris, and Berlin, met exiled Russian Marxists, and studied European conditions. From Salzburg, Paris, and Berlin he wrote very ordinary letters to his mother in Russia, describing the sights, telling her about "my tiresome stomach trouble," asking her to "send me another 100 roubles," and informing her that (in Berlin) he bathed in the Spree River every day. Back in St. Petersburg in September, he intensified his illegal political activities, writing leaflets for underground workers' circles, organizing strikes, teaching Marxism to factory hands, and getting acquainted with proletarian conditions. In these activities he was assisted by Nadezhda Krupskaya, his future wife, then employed as a clerk in the railway administration. Because of his brother's reputation, and because of his own activities, the tsarist police kept a close watch on Lenin. Propaganda among workers was not easy. In November, 1895, in an article entitled "What Are Our Ministers Thinking About?" Lenin urged the expediency of leaving the Tsar out of the argument, and speaking instead of the new laws that favor employers and of Cabinet ministers who are antiworking class. "We," his sister Anna quotes him as saying (*Novy Mir* magazine, June, 1963), "intend to speak of the ministers, not of the Tsar." The monarch was still "The Little Father" to workers and peas-

[13] Lenin, *Sochineniya*, 1895-1897 (*Collected Works*), Fourth ed., Vol. 2 (Moscow, 1950), p. 13.

ants. "Of course, if you start right away talking against the Tsar and the existing social system you only antagonize the workers," Lenin declared.

For several weeks Lenin eluded the police. "In general one sensed in him the good Narodnaya Volya training" of slipping out of the detectives' net, Krupskaya writes in her memoirs, cited in the same issue of *Novy Mir*. But in the night of December 8, 1895, he was finally caught. In prison, he commenced work on a major opus, *The Development of Russian Capitalism*,[14] published legally in St. Petersburg in 1899. He used the prison library and received books sent by members of his family whom he guided with long lists of the volumes he needed; this was permitted by law. They also supplied him with food parcels and money. Writing to his sister Anna on January 12, 1896, he said, "My health is satisfactory. I can have mineral water here; it is brought to me from a pharmacy the day I order it. I sleep about nine hours a day and dream about the various chapters of my future books." He slept so well, he explained in another letter, because he exercised every evening before going to bed, he did about "fifty prostrations" in quick succession, touching the floor each time "without bending the knees." The guard, peeping into his cell, must have been amazed, Lenin thought, that "this man had suddenly grown so pious though he had not once asked to visit the prison church." In the evening he also read "fiction for relaxation." He likewise managed to communicate regularly with cell neighbors, and they with theirs, by a secret code of knocks for letters of the alphabet. V. V. Starkov, a member of Lenin's St. Petersburg Marxist group, who was arrested with Lenin, writes in his memoirs that they even played chess by the knock code.

Once, as he passed through the prison corridor on the way to the courtyard for daily exercise, Lenin noticed that during that split moment he could see a spot on the pavement of the street below. He then wrote a letter requesting Krupskaya, who tells the story in her memoirs as quoted in *Novy Mir* of June, 1963, and Appolinaria to stand on that spot so he could see them. But Appolinaria, "for some reason," could not come and the scheme did not work.

The sojourn in jail was far from unpleasant. In fact, according to unpublished memoirs by his brother Dmitri, cited from unpublished archives in the June, 1963, issue of *Novy Mir*, Lenin expressed "a kind of regret that he was released too early. 'If I had been in prison longer I would have finished the book.'"

After a year in the St. Petersburg jail, Lenin received his sentence: banishment to Siberia. First, however, he received five days of liberty in St. Petersburg, during which he addressed a meeting of comrades, and four days in Moscow, where he stayed at his mother's. He then went in freedom, and at his own expense, into exile. The trip was adventure. He traveled for days by the slow Trans-Siberian Railway; he forded the cold Ob River on horseback, and the passage lasted an hour. "I have left my nerves in Moscow," he wrote his mother from Ob Station on March 2, 1897. "The reason for nerves was

[14] *Ibid.*, Vol. 3 (1951), pp. 3-359.

the uncertainty of the position and nothing else. But now that there is less uncertainty I feel well."[15] The certainty was three years in Siberia. From the Ob he moved on by train to Krasnoyarsk to wait there until the authorities gave him the name of his place of exile. He used the interval to advantage. "Yesterday," he wrote his sister Maria, "I went to the local and famous library belonging to Yudin who welcomed me and showed me his book treasures." Gennadii Vasilyevich Yudin was a prominent Krasnoyarsk businessman and bibliophile; in 1907 he sold 80,000 volumes of his collection to the Library of Congress in Washington, D.C., for 100,000 roubles (approximately $50,000). Lenin remained in Krasnoyarsk five weeks; he spent most of the time in the Yudin library, an hour's walk from his quarters ("I am very pleased with this walk and enjoy it, although it often makes me drowsy"), and in the town library, searching for data on the growth of Russian capitalism.

Finally, word came that he was to live in exile in the village of Shushenskoye on the right bank of the great Yenisey, near the town of Minusinsk. In correspondence he christened the village "Shu-shu-shu" and said it was "not a bad place." The river Shush flowed close by; there were woods not far away, and the foothills of the Sayan Mountains could be seen on the horizon to the south. The region moved Lenin to poetry: "In Susha, at the foot of Sayan . . ." But he never got beyond this first line, he informed his mother in a letter.

Lenin rented a room in a peasant's hut and enjoyed complete liberty of movement. He traveled miles from the village to hunt duck and snipe, swam in the Yenisey, communicated by letter with other subversive exiles, some of whom came to visit him. He went rather far afield to visit them. His mail was prodigious. "I received a pile of letters today from every corner of Russia and Siberia and therefore felt in a holiday mood all day," he told his mother on February 24, 1898. He also received letters from abroad as well as foreign periodicals and books. He corresponded with Marxist leaders in Russia and Europe. For the rest, he wrote articles which he hoped to publish in Russian magazines and worked on his book. His requests to the family were continuous: "I am sorry I did not bring a mackintosh cape," he wrote his mother, "for it is essential to have one here. Could you send me one in a small parcel?" To his sister Anna: "I should much like to obtain the classics of political economy and philosophy. . . . Send me your newspaper after you have read it." He thought of asking for a hunting dog but acquired a pup while on leave in the Minusinsk district "and I hope to have a sporting dog next year. To send one from Russia would be terribly expensive." In the winter of 1898 he wrote his mother, "You might send me some socks," and he wanted a ready-made suit, and, "If my straw hat is still in existence. . . . And then, there is one more thing—a pair of kid gloves, if they can be bought without

[15] This and other letters from prison and exile appear in *The Letters of Lenin*, translated by Elizabeth Hill and Doris Mudie (New York, 1937).

knowing my size (I doubt it). I have never worn them, neither in Petersburg nor Paris, but I want to try them in Shu-shu-shu—in the summer, against mosquitoes. You can put a net over your head, but the hands are always attacked. . . . I also want some paper, *ruled in squares*."

The paper, the gloves, the hat, the suit, and many books were to be brought to him by Nadezhda K. Krupskaya. She had been arrested on August 12, 1896, for organizing a strike, but was released, along with other women, when a female prisoner, Marya Vetrov, in the Peter and Paul Fortress jail in St. Petersburg set fire to herself. Soon thereafter, however, Krupskaya was exiled for three years to the northern Ufa province. She then asked to be transferred to Shushenskoye "for which purpose," she wrote in her memoirs, "I declared that I was his [Lenin's] 'fiancée.'" Apparently she was. Lenin expected her and when the government granted her request she went to Moscow, gathered up the presents for Lenin, and, traveling with her mother, Elizaveta Vasilievna, reached Krasnoyarsk on May 1, 1898, and Shushenkoye shortly thereafter. When she arrived at Lenin's log cabin he was away hunting. The peasant gave the two women the part of the hut not occupied by Lenin and set himself up in a lean-to in the barnyard. Neighbors came to look them over and welcome them. "Finally, Vladimir Ilyich returned from the chase. He was surprised to see a light in his room. The peasant owner said that Oskar Alexandrovich (a Petrograd worker in exile) had been in there drunk and thrown all the books about. Ilyich rushed to the entrance and I rushed out of the hut to meet him. We talked for a long time that night."

"As you know," Lenin wrote his mother on May 10, 1898, "N.K."—Nadezhda Konstantinovna Krupskaya—"has had a tragicomic condition made to her: If she does not marry *immediately*, she is to return to Ufa." But his own identification paper had not yet reached the district police superintendent. "Siberian methods!" Lenin fumed, "although it is already my second year in exile!!" Yet without that identification document "the district police superintendent does not know anything about me and cannot issue any certificate" enabling him to marry.

The Russo-Siberian red tape was at last cut and Miss Krupskaya married Mr. Ulyanov on July 10, 1898. Forthwith the newlyweds began translating Sidney and Beatrice Webb's, *The History of Trade Unionism* (1894). "I am afraid of making mistakes," he had written his sister Anna. "I ought to have (1) An English grammar, especially *syntax* and especially a section on the idioms of the language. . . . (2) A dictionary of *geographical* and proper names. The transcription and translation from English are very difficult and I am afraid of making mistakes." The translation was finished late in August and mailed to a publisher in St. Petersburg.

Krupskaya—this is the name by which she was popularly known in the Soviet Union—has left a detailed, woman's-eye description of life with Lenin in exile. For the eight roubles a month the government paid him he received, she wrote, "a clean room, board, washing and repair of laundry, and at that the sum charged was regarded as high. To be sure, dinner and supper were simple: one week they killed a sheep for Vladimir Ilyich and fed it to him day after day until he had eaten it; having eaten it they bought meat for him for a week, and the maid would chop the purchased meat in the barnyard trough where the cattle feed was prepared and cook cutlets for Vladimir Ilyich for a whole week." Dairy products "for Vladimir Ilyich and his dog," Zhenka, were plentiful. But the men in the Ziryanov family whose house they occupied often got drunk, and for other reasons too, they rented half a house and a vegetable garden for four roubles a month. "We began to lead a family life." At first Krupskaya would spill the soup and dumplings. "Later, I learned." She had to cook, transcribe the chapters of *The Development of Russian Capitalism*, and help translate German pamphlets into Russian. After work they took walks. "Vladimir Ilyich was a passionate hunter"; he acquired a pair of leather trousers and descended into swamps to shoot wild fowl. Lenin also put his legal knowledge to good use. He gave free advice to peasants and attracted settlers from near and far; this gave him an opportunity to study farming conditions in Siberia. "As a matter of fact," Krupskaya wrote, "Vladimir Ilyich, being an exile, had no right to practice law, but the Minusinsk district was liberal in those days. Actually, there was no supervision at all."

For relief Lenin studied a German grammar and read Turgenev in German translation; Anna sent these to him by request. In April, 1899, he received a gun from his mother. He had reassured her about his hunting: "Your worrying about my going out shooting is also unnecessary. There is nothing dangerous in it." He wanted from the family, "(1) A hardmuth pencil Number 6 . . . (2) A small box of sealing wax and some sort of seal for sealing letters . . . (3) A penwiper . . . (4) Small scissors . . . Now instead of a penwiper, I use the lapel of my jacket; I have decorated it beautifully; I borrow the landlord's scissors—sheepshears . . ." In winter he ice-skated. "I am reminded of the old days," he wrote his mother and Anna, "and I do not seem to have forgotten how to skate, although I had not done any for some ten years. Nadya"—Krupskaya—"also wants to learn, but I do not know if she will succeed."

The good life of the exile ended in February, 1900, when Lenin, refused permission to reside in St. Petersburg, went to live in Pskov, a city near the capital where he arrived on February 26. Krupskaya, whose term of banishment had not yet expired, returned to Ufa. She was ill. In March Lenin petitioned the Minister of Interior to allow her to live in Pskov. This was denied. On April 20, 1900, accordingly, he wrote "A Petition presented by the hereditary noble, Vladimir Ilyich Ulyanov, residing in the town of Pskov, in Archangel Street, in the house owned by Chernov," to "His Excellency the Director of the Department of Police" for permission "to reside for six weeks in the town of Ufa." This too was refused. But Lenin's mother interceded on his behalf, and she, he, and Anna were allowed to visit Krupskaya in Ufa for a month. Meanwhile he applied for a passport to travel abroad and received it two days after permission was granted. Tsarism was autocratic but not totalitarian. Lenin's biography: in jail, out of jail, in Siberia, out of Siberia and into foreign exile indicates that the tsarist secret police, though cruel enough, was less ruthless than its Soviet successor.

Instead of taking his passport and speeding to the west, Lenin left Pskov with Julius Martov, the future Menshevik leader, for St. Petersburg, where he had been denied the right to stay, carrying a suitcase full of subversive literature and a large sum of money. To elude the police the two conspirators left the long-distance train and changed to a local at Tsarskoe Selo where the Tsar lived. "Don't you know that at Tsarskoe Selo there's an agent behind every bush?" the police inspector said to Lenin after he and Martov had been followed into the big city and arrested the next morning. Lenin pleaded innocence and both were released. Lenin then traveled to Ufa. Krupskaya recalled that he remained "about a week." He shortened his visit to his wife to keep secret rendezvous with comrades in Samara, Syzran, and elsewhere. Finally he went abroad.

Lenin carried to Europe a reputation as author, journalist, and underground organizer. With these he obtained ready access to the colony of Russian revolutionary exiles whose zeal and brilliance concealed their numerical weakness. Talks he had in Germany and Switzerland with high-ranking Marxists, among them Georgi Plekhanov, who were his seniors in the movement, led to the publication of a Russian-language magazine abroad for smuggling into Russia—an old Russian tradition. The first issue of *Iskra* (*The Spark*), organ of "The Russian Social Democratic Labor Party," appeared on December 11, 1900. It contained an article by Lenin on "The China War."[16] The Boxer Rebellion had commenced in China. Lenin followed it angrily. "The greedy paws of European capitalists have reached out into China," he exclaimed, "and almost the first to do so was the Russian government which now swears to its 'unselfishness.' It 'unselfishly' took Port Arthur from China and began building a railroad through Manchuria under the protection of Russian troops . . . to call things by their correct names, one must say that the European governments (and first, perhaps, the Russian) have already commenced partitioning China. They commenced the partition not openly but secretly, like thieves. They have started to rob China as a corpse is robbed, and when this supposed corpse tried to resist—they threw themselves on him like wild beasts, setting fire to entire villages, drowning people in the Amur River, shooting and bayoneting unarmed inhabitants and their wives and children. And all these Christian acts are accompanied by outcries against the savage Chinese who dare to lift a hand against civilized Europeans."

The tsarist government has announced that its measures were temporary and undertaken "exclusively out of the necessity to repel the aggressive activi-

[16] Lenin, *Sochineniya* (*Collected Works*), Fourth ed., Vol. 4, pp. 347-352.

ties of the Chinese rebels"; they, Lenin continued to quote, "are in no sense evidence of selfish plans completely alien to the policy of the imperial government."

"Poor imperial government," Lenin mocked. "It is so unselfishly Christian and yet it is so unjustly insulted! It unselfishly seized Port Arthur several years ago and now it is unselfishly seizing Manchuria. It unselfishly floods the Chinese provinces bordering on Russia with swarms of its contractors, engineers, and officers whose conduct has aroused the indignation even of the Chinese, known for their obedience. The Chinese working on the construction of the railway are paid ten kopeks a day for living costs—isn't that unselfish on the part of Russia?"

Who benefits from this "mad policy" in China? "It is beneficial," Lenin replied, "to a handful of capitalist-aces who trade with China, a handful of manufacturers who produce goods for the Asiatic market, a handful of contractors now earning big money filling urgent military orders. . . . Such a policy is beneficial to a handful of nobles occupying high civil and military positions. . . .

"What good will the working class and all laboring people get from conquests in China?" Lenin demanded. Ruined families, he replied, and increased government indebtedness. ". . . colossal sums are being wasted by a government which uninterruptedly cuts the subsidies to starving peasants— bargaining over every kopek; which cannot find funds for public education; which, like a kulak [prosperous peasant] squeezes the life juice out of workers in state factories, out of petty employees in post offices, and others. . . . The tsarist government is threatened with bankruptcy yet it wastes money on conquests."

"The tsarist government," Lenin affirmed, "holds not only our people in slavery—it sends our people to pacify other peoples who rise up against their slavery (as it did in 1849 when Russian troops suppressed the revolution in Hungary)." The only salvation, Lenin concluded, lay in the "convocation of peoples' representatives who would put an end to the autocracy of the government and compel it to consider the interests of those who do not belong to the robber bands at court."

From Munich, where he had settled for a while, and where he made arrangement for the smuggling of *Iskra* into Russia (sometimes the tsarist border police confiscated a batch and arrested the messenger), Lenin wrote his mother on February 7, 1901. He had no coat. ". . . next winter, if I have to stay, I shall write for my padded coat. Without such a coat, you have either to wear vests or two suits, as I do. At first it was not very comfortable, but I am quite used to it now. . . .

"The carnival ended here the other day. It was the first time I had seen the last day of a carnival abroad—processions of people in fancy dress moving along the streets, playing the fool, and clouds of confetti (small bits of colored paper) thrown into your face, paper snakes, etc., etc. They know how to live in public, how to amuse themselves in the streets!

"I am quite well, probably because I run about a good deal and do not sit much. My life goes on as usual.

"Nadya's term of exile is coming to an end soon—in our style abroad March 24"—in the Western, Gregorian calendar—"and March 11 in yours" —in the Russian, Julian calendar. "I shall send a petition one of these days for a passport to be issued to her. . . .

"Do you go to the theater? What is this new play by Chekhov, 'The Three Sisters'?"

As promised, Lenin went from Munich to Vienna to Prague to apply at the Russian consulate for Krupskaya's passport. She left Ufa and repaired to Moscow with her mother to stay at the home of Maria Alexandrovna, Lenin's mother. Lenin's sister Maria was in prison for revolutionary activities. Anna had gone abroad. "I loved Maria Alexandrovna very much," Krupskaya noted in her subsequent memoirs. "She was so sensitive and attentive. Vladimir Ilyich inherited his mother's will power, and also inherited her sensitivity and attentiveness to people."

With her Russian passport, Krupskaya traveled to Prague and looked for her husband in the home of a Czech workingman where Lenin had lived. But Lenin had returned to Munich. She had his old Munich address. But he had moved. Finally she located his house, knocked at his door, and found him sitting at a table with his sister Anna and Julius Martov, a prominent Russian Marxist, one of the *Iskra* editors. She had failed to receive one of his letters giving the new address. He was "Herr Meyer."

In Munich, in London, in Paris, in Loguivy, the little resort on the northern coast of France where his mother and Anna spent part of a summer with him, in Geneva, Zurich, and Lausanne, Lenin drafted a program for the Russian Social Democratic Labor Party, wrangled with ideological dissenters inside the ranks and with political enemies outside, and commented on events involving Russia. He preferred to call the Tsar not Nicholas II or Nicholas Romanov but "Nicholas Obmanov" (the deceiver), "Nicholas the Bloody," "Nicholas the Hangman," and similar names. On February 15, 1902, *Iskra* published a Lenin article entitled "Signs of Bankruptcy."[17] "Yes," he averred, "the bankruptcy of the autocracy is beyond doubt." The terror waxed yet it failed to pacify the country; the peasants were being condemned to starvation—"hunger has become the normal condition of our villages." Then "how long will this bankrupt manage to live from day to day by patching the holes in his political and financial budget with skin from the living body of the national organism?" Russia was living fast. The end would come through the political mobilization of the masses, best of all by the revolutionary Social Democrats "who alone will be capable of inflicting the fatal blow on the autocracy."

There had been student strikes in the universities and strikes of workingmen in towns. Now Lenin turned to the peasants, whose importance in the struggle for freedom he was beginning to discover, and in a pamphlet printed

[17] *Ibid.*, Vol. 6, pp. 62-68.

in Geneva in 1903, addressed *To the Village Poor*,[18] he introduced his party to them: "The Russian Social Democrats seek first of all to win political freedom." The peasants had achieved only incomplete freedom from the abolition of serfdom. "Just as the peasants used to be the slaves of the land-lords they remain the slaves of the bureaucrats. Just as the peasants, under the law of serfdom, had no civil liberties, they still have no political liberty. Political liberty means the right of the people to manage their national political affairs. Political freedom means the right to elect its deputies to the national Duma [parliament]. All laws must be debated and enacted, all taxes and tributes must be levied only by this national Duma elected by the people. Political freedom means the right of the people themselves to elect all their officials to convene all kinds of meetings for the discussion of state affairs, to publish, without permission, any books or newspapers they choose.

"All other European nations achieved political freedom long ago. Only in Turkey and Russia the nations remain in political servitude to the government of the sultan and to the tsarist autocratic government. Tsarist autocracy means the unlimited power of the Tsar. . . . In all other European countries factory workers and landless farm workers can be elected to the State Duma and they have spoken freely before the entire nation about the impoverished life of the workers . . . no policeman dared to touch them with a finger. In Russia there is no elected administration. . . . That is why the workers march through the streets and write 'Down with the Autocracy' on their banners. That is why tens of millions of village poor must support this battle cry of the city workers and make it their own."

History is the chronicle of divorces between creed and deed.

In *Iskra* of July 15, 1903, Lenin quoted Marx: "The establishment of a democratic Poland is the primary requisite of the establishment of a democratic Germany."[19] Translating this into Russian politics, Lenin added, "The day is gone when a bourgeois revolution could create an independent Poland; today the resurrection of Poland is possible only through a social revolution in which the modern proletariat breaks its chains."[20]

A candidate's broken promises convert his judgments into an accusation.

During part of 1902 and of 1903 Lenin and Krupskaya lived in London. Since the police did not require identification, they used the name of Mr. and Mrs. Jacob Richter and had an apartment for several months at 30 Holford Square. They found the British labor leaders a reserved lot difficult to meet. Lenin spent most of his working time in the British Museum and much of his free time with Krupskaya riding atop buses to the suburbs which they preferred to the center of London. They especially enjoyed the trip to Primrose Hill where they were near the grave of Karl Marx and, Sundays, to Hyde Park Corner to hear the open-air orators. They scoffed at the Salvation Army

[18] *Ibid.*, pp. 327-392.
[19] *Ibid.*, p. 415.
[20] *Ibid.*, p. 417.

recruiters and preferred the atheist speakers. Sometimes they went to church, a socialist church, and were amused when the minister prayed to God to "remove us from the kingdom of capitalism to the kingdom of socialism."

During the summer of 1903 forty-three delegates of the party assembled first in Brussels and then, because of trouble with the Belgian police, in London—in a church—to hammer out a set of principles and to discuss organizational problems. On a number of issues the meeting divided between a faction led by Plekhanov and Lenin which won bolshe (more) votes and another led by Julius Martov which gained menshe (fewer); ever since then they have been known as Bolsheviks and Mensheviks. Their differences were a complicated skein of the accidental, personal, and political. One major issue separating them was Lenin's insistence on a tightly knit party of professional revolutionaries who gave not only their loyalty and sympathy, as the Mensheviks would have preferred, but all their time too to political work and who, therefore, were to function as soldiers and officers in an army under a single command.

Lenin did not avoid the Bolshevik-Menshevik rupture. He welcomed it, indeed invited it. He foreshadowed it in his thick *What Is to Be Done?* pamphlet, first published in 1902 and since then the bible of Bolshevik organizers.[21] The booklet was directed against "Economism," against the "Economists" who concentrated on improving factory conditions to the neglect of national political problems. But by implication it was directed equally against the Mensheviks and all other Russian political parties which deviated from the Leninist principles of organization. "Social Democrats," Lenin emphasized, "must not confine themselves entirely to the economic struggle; they must not even allow the organization of economic exposures to become the predominant part of their activity. . . . Revolutionary Social Democracy . . . subordinates the struggle for reforms to the revolutionary struggle for liberty and for socialism. . . . Why is it," Lenin asked, "that the Russian workers as yet display so little revolutionary activity in connection with the brutal way in which the police maltreat the people, in connection with the persecution of religious sects, with the flogging of the peasants . . .? It is because the 'economic struggle' does not 'stimulate' them to do this . . . if we, by any means whatever, degrade social-democratic politics to the level of spontaneous trade-union politics, we thereby play into the hands of bourgeois democracy." Lenin advocated not spontaneity but organization. He "had in mind an organization of revolutionists, as an essential factor in 'making' the political revolution . . . a Social Democrat must concern himself first and foremost with an organization of revolutionists capable of guiding

[21] *Collected Works of V. I. Lenin.* Vol. IV, *The Iskra Period,* 1900-1902, Book II (New York, 1929), *What Is to Be Done? Burning Questions of Our Movement.* pp. 89-258. *What Is to Be Done?* (*Chto Delat?* in Russian) is the title of a novel by N. G. Chernishevsky (1828-1889), whom Lenin read and quoted and who is regarded by the Bolsheviks as one of their ideological ancestors—though there was much of the Narodnik in him.

the *whole* proletarian struggle for emancipation. . . . Only an incorrigible utopian would want a *wide* organization of workers, with elections, reports, universal suffrage, etc. under autocracy." It would merely help the gendarmes "make the revolutionists most accessible to the police." The leaven and leaders of the organization, he declared, would be intellectuals. "*Such* 'pushing from the outside' can never be too excessive; on the contrary, so far there has been too little, all too little in our movement; we have bowed far too slavishly before the spontaneous 'economic struggle of the workers against the employers and the government.' We professional revolutionists must continue, and will continue, *this* kind of 'pushing' . . . no movement can be durable without a stable organization of leaders to maintain continuity . . . the organization must consist chiefly of persons engaged in revolution as a profession . . . in a country with a despotic organization, the more we *restrict* the membership of this organization" to professionals "the more difficult it will be to catch the organization." Here Lenin put his strategy of revolution in one sentence: Adapting Archimedes, he wrote, "Give us an organization of revolutionists and we shall overturn all of Russia."

Lenin was the original organization man. Men wedded to a purpose, he held, could alter circumstances, change mass consciousness, and make history. Lenin never sought numbers. He wanted a disciplined human battering ram. Organization took precedence over political program. Method was all-important, more important than policy. Indeed his policy was organization. In this respect and in his subordination of program to early armed action, Lenin, as Harvard Professor Michael Karpovich pointed out in the *Review of Reviews* for July, 1944, resembled Peter N. Tkachov (1844-1886), a maverick populist, resembled him but was not indebted to him. Yet both were sons of Russia, and if Tkachov had lived longer or later, he might, like Lenin, have placed his hopes not on the peasantry but on the proletariat. The proletariat, however, had to be led, Lenin said. The party must be its leader, and the party must serve its leaders. This attitude emerged from Lenin's whole philosophy of directed action.

It also reflected his psychological needs. When Lenin arrived in London in 1902 because the *Iskra* offices were moved there, he announced, according to Nikolai A. Alekseyev, the party representative in England, that though other *Iskra* editors would live as a commune, he was "absolutely incapable of living in a commune, he did not like to be with people all the time." Lenin was a tense person. Krupskaya wrote that "the bickering and squabbling that was such a marked feature of life in exile, greatly hampered his work."[22] Lenin's "nerves—wrought up by the philosophical disputes—were calmed" by lying in bed for hours and reading French grammars. Once when Maxim Gorky invited Lenin to the island of Capri to meet some Marxists harboring unorthodox philosophic notions, Lenin replied: "It would be useless and harmful for me to go; *I cannot and will not have anything to do* with people

---

[22] Nadezhda K. Krupskaya, *Memories of Lenin*, Vol. II, p. 28.

who have set out to propagate unity between scientific socialism and religion. There is no use arguing and it is absurd to upset oneself for nothing."[23] Krupskaya tells how disputes worked on her husband's nerves; he grew green and could not sleep. Often she took him away from the feuding émigrés to swim in the sea or climb mountains for relaxation.

For health and political effectiveness Lenin needed a small party united in obedience rather than a larger organization hiding divergent elements under a blanket of unity.

On this matter, the majority at the 1903 London Congress—after the Jewish Bund and others bolted—supported Lenin. With Plekhanov's help, he also put through a plank in favor of "the revolutionary dictatorship of the proletariat" which Marx had enunciated in the *Criticism of the Gotha Program* but which the more democratic Mensheviks opposed. Lenin likewise succeeding in eliminating Paul Axelrod, Alexander Potresov, and Vera Zasulich, all Mensheviks, from the editorial board of *Iskra*, leaving only himself, Plekhanov, and Julius Martov to run the magazine. But Plekhanov soon realized that Lenin expected him to tip the balance for him and against the Menshevik Martov. Leon Trotsky, a literary comet who suddenly flashed into Western skies from the Siberian tundras whither he had been exiled for revolutionary acts in his Ukrainian homeland, sided with Martov; he regarded Lenin as "a despot and terrorist."

Finally Plekhanov, refusing to be Lenin's rubber stamp, brought Axelrod, Potresov and Vera Zasulich back into the *Iskra* board, whereupon Lenin, to avoid mental torment and defeat on editorial policy, resigned.

Lenin's stormy spirit, however, could not remain suppressed for long. He needed a magazine. He had to have an outlet for his brimming ideas. Money came from secret sources; Maxim Gorky paid part of the cost. The rest may have come from several Russian capitalists like Pavel Morozov, a Moscow textile magnate and art collector, who often financed the enemies of their class. Soon Lenin, in Geneva, was editing *Vperyod (Forward)*; its first issue appeared on December 22, 1904, with an article by him on "The Autocracy and the Proletariat."[24] "The absolute monarchy," Lenin asserted, "is shaking." Vyacheslav K. von Pleve (also spelled Plehve) succumbed to a terrorist bomb on July 15, 1904. "V. K. von Pleve," writes Hugh Seton-Watson,[25] "believed above all in repression. He also believed that 'a small victorious war' would have a salutary effect on Russian opinion, and would divert the people's thoughts from revolution." The bomb he got was retribution for repression; the war he got, far from being small and victorious, assumed enormous proportions and in it Russian defeat followed defeat. "The greatest part of the Russian fleet," Lenin stated in his article, "has already been destroyed, the situation of Port Arthur is hopeless, the squadron [of Admiral Zinovii P.

[23] *Ibid.*, p. 23.
[24] Lenin, *Sochineniya (Collected Works)*, Fourth ed., Vol. 8, pp. 5-12.
[25] *The Decline of Imperial Russia* (New York, 1952), p. 138.

Rozhdestvensky] which is going [from the Baltic to the Pacific] to its rescue has not the slightest chance not only of succeeding but even of arriving there, the main army commanded by Kuropatkin has lost 200,000 men. . . . A military collapse is unavoidable; no less unavoidably, discontent, ferment, and resentment will grow ten times stronger."

Japan was "constitutional"; Russia "autocratic." In this difference, according to Lenin, lay the secret of victory and defeat. Russian liberals were protesting against the misconduct of the war and demanding a constitution limiting the prerogatives of the monarchy. They realized, as Lenin did, that Russia "must become a European country." The proletariat, he urged, should support these trends. Predicting still worse conditions, Lenin foresaw sudden, spontaneous outbursts of popular fury. "At that moment," he declared confidently, "the proletariat will rise and take its place at the head of the insurrection in order to win freedom for the entire nation, in order to give the working class the possibility of waging an open struggle for socialism on a wide front and enriched by all the experience of Europe."

Lenin hated tsarism. He hated the Narodnik SR's. He hated the Mensheviks a little less, but because they were still within the Russian Social Democratic Labor Party, together with the Bolsheviks, they were more of an obsession to him.

In Geneva, Lenin and Krupskaya and her mother occupied a tiny apartment. They nevertheless invited a young Russian Jewish revolutionary, Maria Essen, to stay with them. Early in the century she had been banished to remote Yakutia; in 1902 she fled, escaped from Russia, and made her way to Geneva where she met Lenin whom she knew from the copies of *Iskra* which had reached her and her comrades in the arctic wilds of Siberia. She had not been in Geneva long before Lenin urged her to return to St. Petersburg and help distribute *Iskra* there. She carried out this assignment from the end of 1902 till May, 1903, when she was arrested at a meeting. After a short spell in prison she worked in Kiev and again appeared in Geneva and became a house guest in the Ulyanovs' tight little home. Her published memoirs[26] reflect her intimate acquaintance with Lenin. "I would like to register one peculiarity of Vladimir Ilyich," she wrote. "He could scarcely bear going to museums and exhibitions. He loved the lively crowd, living speech, singing, and he liked to feel himself part of the mass of people.

"Lenin was indefatigable on outings. I remember one outing in particular. It was the spring of 1904. I was to return to Russia and we decided to go on a farewell 'spree'—to go together on an outing in the mountains. Vladimir Ilyich, Nadezhda Konstantinovna, and I went by boat to Montreux. We visited the somber castle of Chillon—the prison of Bonnivard so beautifully described by Byron. . . . We saw the pillar to which Bonnivard was chained and the inscription made by Byron.

[26] *Vospominaniya o Vladimire Ilyiche Lenine (Reminiscences about Vladimir Ilvich Lenin)*, Vol. I, pp. 244-261.

"We came out of the dark dungeon and were immediately blinded by the bright sunlight and the turbulent, exultant scenery. One wanted movement. We decided to climb a snowy peak. At first the ascent was easy and pleasant, but the farther we went the more difficult the road became. It was decided that Nadezhda Konstantinovna would wait for us in a hotel.

"To reach the top more quickly we left the road and pushed recklessly upward. With every step the climb grew more difficult. Vladimir Ilyich strode strong and secure, laughing at my effort not to fall behind. After a time I crawled on all fours, grasping the snow with my hands which melted in my hands but did not fall behind Vladimir Ilyich.

"Finally we got there. A limitless landscape, an indescribable play of colors. In front of us, as on one's palm, were all the zones, all the climates. Brightly the snow shines; somewhat lower, the plants of the north, and further down the succulent alpine meadow and the turbulent vegetation of the south. I attune myself to a high pitch and am ready to recite Shakespeare, Byron. I glance at Vladimir Ilyich: he sits, deep in thought, and suddenly exclaims: 'The Mensheviks really mess things up.' "

III. THE SPARK AND THE FIRE

LENIN'S MANNER was direct, his language simple. What he said could scarcely ever be misinterpreted; where he stood none could mistake. Nor did he allow others to equivocate; you were either for him or against him. Dissenting party comrades were furiously denounced; if they reverted to his orthodoxy he welcomed them back. He never mixed sentiment with politics. He had nerves but no feelings. Personal pride did not turn his head nor did humility bow it; he knew one truth—his own. He was cantankerous, intolerant, irritable. He pursued the goal of revolution with the optimistic persistence of a hunter. He considered violence a legitimate, indeed a preferred method, and advocated it coldly, openly. The end hallowed all means. Money and other forms of aid could not be tainted by their source; the cause purified them. Unambitious as an individual, abstemious to the point of ascetic self-denial (he gave up chess because it consumed too much time), he lived not for himself or his wife or friends or comrades but for an idea. He was a Marxist monk. Yet the idea had nothing in common with an ideal or vision or religion. No picture of a rosy heaven on earth moved him; for utopians who dreamed of a utopia without blemishes he had only scorn. He was a military politician. Like a good troop commander he planned to crush the opposing army, not merely to occupy its fortifications. Reconstruction schemes did not interest him until after victory. "On s'engage et puis on voit," he said, quoting Napoleon. Enter the battle, engage the enemy, acquire power, then see what can be done. He was a power man. The Russian word for power is vlast. The Russian word for government is vlast. Lenin aimed at destroying the power-holders and becoming the power-holder, the government. He hated the tsarist government with an icy hatred and gloated over its defeats.

January 1, 1905, brought Lenin joyous tidings. "Port Arthur has capitulated," he exclaimed gleefully. Russia's military might, "long considered the most dependable bulwark of European reaction," lay in the Manchurian dust and at the bottom of the Pacific Ocean. "Yes," Lenin wrote, "Europe's bourgeoisie has reason to be afraid. The proletariat has reason to rejoice. The catastrophe of our vilest enemy signifies not only the approach of Russian freedom. It also portends a new revolutionary upsurge of the European proletariat." He stressed the interdependence of revolution in Russia and revolution in Europe.

"Progressive, advanced Asia," Lenin added, "has struck a blow at retarded, reactionary Europe from which it cannot recover." He identified Japanese military prowess with progress. The Japanese military, he implied, had served the cause of liberty. "The capitulation of Port Arthur," Lenin declared, "is the prologue to the capitulation of Tsardom." Therefore, "the Russian nation has gained from the autocracy's defeat."[1]

The wretched performance of the Russian armed forces in the Far East hatched the 1905 revolution in which workers in Moscow and other cities fought on the barricades and, for the first time in history, organized short-lived soviets. The government gave a fillip to these efforts by a stupid mass massacre on "Bloody Sunday" (January 9, 1905) when thousands of St. Petersburg workers and their families, carrying holy icons and images of the Tsar and singing the national anthem and religious hymns, walked peacefully, led by Father Georgi Gapon, an Orthodox priest, into the square fronting on the Winter Palace royal residence only to be fired on by soldiers and Cossacks. The government, according to Lenin,[2] gave the casualties as 96 dead and 330 wounded. Newspaper reports put the dead and wounded at 4,600. Lenin regarded even these figures an underestimate.

Russia's cities were aroused. Lenin watched from afar and issued instructions. Revolutionary squads, he urged, should conduct independent military operations. As few as two or three persons might constitute a squad. "The squads," he wrote,[3] "must arm themselves, each man with what he can get (a rifle, revolver, bomb, knife, stick, a rag dipped in kerosene for setting fires, a rope or a rope ladder, a slab of guncotton, nails—against cavalry—and so forth and so on)." He appended detailed organizational suggestions for

---

[1] Lenin, Sochineniya (Collected Works), Fourth ed., Vol. 8, pp. 31-39.
[2] Ibid., p. 101.
[3] Ibid., Vol. 9, pp. 389-393.

squads and told them how to operate. They might climb to roofs or top stories and throw stones and boiling water on troops or attack small isolated units of soldiers or police in order to liberate prisoners or wounded rebels and to obtain weapons. "Of course," he cautioned, "any extreme is bad. Everything good and desirable, if carried to extreme, can become and indeed must, beyond a certain limit, become evil and harmful. Disorderly, unprepared petty terror can, if carried to extreme, only divide the strength and diminish it. That is true, and this should not be forgotten. But, on the other hand, one must under no condition forget this too, that the order for the uprising *has already been given*, the uprising has already *commenced*. To launch an attack, under favorable circumstances, is not only the right but the absolute duty of every revolutionary. The murder of spies, policemen, gendarmes, and blowing up of police stations, liberation of prisoners, seizure of government money and its use for the needs of insurrection—such operations are going on wherever the insurrection breaks out, and in Poland as well as in the Caucasus . . ."

Lenin hoped that the revolutionary squads would seek out members of the Black Hundreds (reactionary monarchists and pogromists), "beat them up, kill them, and blow up their staff headquarters." Sometimes one person would have to do this "at his own risk." This was the way to fight for freedom, he insisted. All other democrats were merely "quasi-democrats" and "liberal chatterboxes."

A case could be made for Lenin: he was answering the government's terror with revolutionary terror. Yet as an explanation of his politics this would be only a fraction of the truth and therefore near to an untruth. Lenin had neither an emotional commitment to terror nor a revulsion against terror. There is no evidence that Lenin was a follower of Tkachov, whom he mentions once—unfavorably—or that he was influenced by Sergey G. Nechayev (1847-1882), a conspiratorial Russian anarchist whose name never occurs in all Lenin's voluminous writings, speeches, and letters. Violence was in the Russian air and in the Russian tradition, but whereas violence to Tkachov and Nechayev was a principle and supreme political weapon, to Lenin it was a subordinate means. Lenin's first philosophical commitment was to revolution and to violence and terror in connection with revolution. A murdered tsar was succeeded by a new tsar and a murdered minister by another, sometimes a worse, minister. Assassinations alone could not topple the regime. Therefore a Nechayev-terrorist like Vera Zasulich, born in 1849, became a Marxist revolutionist in 1883. Time made a difference. Lenin came later than Tkachov and still later than Nechayev. The passing years wrought changes among the rulers and the underprivileged. Lenin saw the possibility of mass action by workers and disaffected soldiers. To him, killing by the squads was not isolated violence but a rehearsal for revolution and justified for that reason. In June, 1913, he likewise excused peasant violence: "The bitterness in the village is terrible. What is called hooliganism is, above all, the consequence of the incredible bitterness of the peasants and the *initial forms of their protest*." After the initial forms of protest would come, presumably, a revolutionary expression of peasant anger. Hence his approval. In these matters Lenin was a good Marxist-Engelsist. Engels wrote in 1889 that "any means that leads to the aim suits me as a revolutionary, whether it is the most violent or looks the most peaceful." Lenin too regarded violence dispassionately as a weapon to be used when necessary. Though he warned the squads against extremism, he rejected halfway measures in principle. A triumph, to be safe, required the adversary's destruction. He made this clear at a meeting in Geneva on March 18, 1908, to mark the twenty-fifth anniversary of the death of Karl Marx (who died May 14, 1883) and the thirty-seventh anniversary of the birth of the Paris Commune.

For seventy-two days, from March 18 to May 29, 1871, a commune, supported by workers and directed by some extremists and some moderates, ruled the city of Paris. Then Louis Adolphe Thiers, the French Premier, bombarded and crushed it, inflicting heavy casualties. "Two mistakes ruined the fruits of the brilliant victory" of the Commune, Lenin said to his Geneva audience. "The proletariat stopped midway"; instead of expropriating the expropriators, "it was carried away by dreams of the establishment of supreme justice . . .; the banks were not seized. . . . Second mistake—the excess magnanimity of the proletariat; it should have exterminated its enemies, but it attempted to use moral influence on them, it neglected the significance of purely military action in a civil war, and instead of crowning its victory in Paris with a decisive attack on Versailles, it procrastinated and gave the Versailles government time to gather its dark forces and prepare for the bloody week of May."

Moreover, the French proletariat "was blinded by patriotic illusions." The patriotism engendered by the great French revolution of the eighteenth century lived on in the socialists and even in such a true revolutionary as Louis Blanqui, and they listened to the "bourgeois lament: 'The Fatherland is in danger.' "

Nevertheless, Lenin continued,[4] the Paris Commune served to "dispel patriotic illusions and destroy the naïve faith in the nationalistic strivings of the bourgeoisie." The Russian workers learned a lesson from the Commune and from the acts of their own autocratic government. Hence, in the 1905 Russian revolution, they resorted to civil war. "There are moments," Lenin declared, "when the interests of the proletariat demand the merciless annihilation of the enemy in open armed battles." The Commune and the 1905 revolution were crushed. "But there will be new revolts in which the weaker side shall be the enemy of the proletariat and from which the socialist proletariat shall emerge fully victorious."

Revolution was Lenin's first and last love. "Revolutions are the locomotives of history," Lenin quoted Marx as saying. This seemed too technological. "Revolutions are the holiday of the oppressed and exploited," Lenin added

[4] *Ibid.*, Vol. 13, pp. 437-440.

in the next sentence. He thought, and thought constantly, of revolution not as a historian or a social scientist but as a lover, a lover of radical change and maximum upheaval. He hated the present.

Lenin and the Bolsheviks, however, were not the authors of the 1905 revolution. It was spontaneous rather than sponsored. Much unhappiness had accumulated in the chasms that characterized Russian society. A gulf separated the court from the country, the nobility from the spendthrift merchant class, the get-rich-quick industrialists from the long-working, low-living proletariat, the Great Russians from the hundred or more underprivileged national minorities, and the exploited peasantry from the landlords, the workers, and everybody else. Russia was not so much a land of class struggle as of class islands, a people chopped into segments that observed one another from afar in envy and incomprehension. Illiteracy and poor transportation deepened differences. Inequality exacerbated poverty. The few democratic institutions did not bridge the gulfs. Japan's victories, products of Russian backwardness and social divisions, filled liberals with anger and patriots with despair. Those who felt the need of change through constitutional reform were either infuriated or depressed by the Tsar's resistance to it. Other forces chose change through violent subversion.

The 1905 revolution may be said to have commenced in January when it took the form of street demonstrations, strikes, and protest meetings. Big things were happening in Russia and Lenin, in Geneva, wanted the news. When he was in power in the Kremlin years later he had to answer questionnaires submitted to all delegates at party congresses, and opposite the item marked "Profession?" Lenin put "Journalist." As a journalist, editing his newborn weekly, *Vperyod* (*Forward*), he eagerly desired to have the facts of the revolution. In a letter, dated February 15, 1905, to S. I. Gusev, secretary of the St. Petersburg Bolshevik Committee, Lenin said, "Do not forget that the strength of a revolutionary organization lies in the number of its links. . . . So far not one of the Petersburg people (shame on them!) has given us a single new link. . . . It is a scandal, it is murder, it is ruin. For God's sake, learn from the Mensheviks. In *Iskra*," edited by Mensheviks after the party split, "there is a wealth of correspondence" about Bloody Sunday. "You have read *Vperyod* to young people, haven't you? Then why haven't you linked us up with any of these young people?" He implored Gusev to "find for us *ten* new, young and loyal friends of *Vperyod* who know how to work, who know how to establish links and who will then manage to correspond without you. Remember this!" In the next letter, in March, 1905, Lenin pursued the same theme: "For God's sake, get hold of letters from the workers themselves. Why do they not write? It is a positive disgrace! . . . Another question: have you accepted the six selected workers for the [St. Petersburg Bolshevik] Committee? Answer without fail. We strongly advise you to accept workers on to the committee, at any rate half. Without this you will not strengthen yourself against the Mensheviks, who will send strong reinforcements from here."

The Bolsheviks and Mensheviks were planning rival congresses abroad. In the same letter, therefore, Lenin wrote: "I strongly advise an agitation among the three hundred organized [Bolshevik] workers in St. Petersburg that they should send *at their own expense* one or two delegates to the Congress with a consultative vote. That will probably flatter the workers and they will take up the matter enthusiastically. Do not forget that the Mensheviks will do their utmost to discredit the Congress to the workers by saying that there were no workers. This must be taken into account. . . . The St. Petersburg workers will surely be able to collect three hundred roubles"—$150—"for two worker delegates (or perhaps some Maecenas will present this amount for such a purpose)."[5]

These letters convey some idea of Lenin's intense partisanship and a clear idea of the scale of Bolshevik party activities during the early months of the 1905 revolution. The Mensheviks and Social Revolutionaries were stronger but not by much. The revolution was made by a power far greater than all of these combined: the tsarist system. Every revolution is bred by the enemies of revolution.

The 1905 revolution was born in Russia's sunken battleships and smashed battalions. Defeat in the Far Eastern war stunned the tsarist regime. Not knowing how to reassure the nation it did nothing or, confronted with harmless men, women, and children pleading on their knees in the snow for relief from sorrow, it gave them lead bullets. Awareness of the government's hesitations and folly communicated itself by social telepathy to the people. When the hand of the captain falters the crew takes liberties. Russia rebelled.

A diary of Russian events between October, 1904, and January, 1906, is remarkable for the frequency with which Warsaw, Lodz, Vilna, Riga, Tiflis, Kutais (Georgia), and Baku are mentioned. "Revolutionary demonstration in Warsaw," "anti-war demonstration in Warsaw," "general strike in Warsaw," "general strike in the Baku oilfields," "troops battle strikers in Baku," "martial law in Kutais province," "second general strike in Lodz," etc., etc. The endemic dissatisfaction of the workers, coupled with the hopes of self-determination and independence aroused by the Tsar's military weakness, created prolonged and serious troubles for the regime in Poland, the Baltic districts, and the multi-national Caucasus. Here and there peasants took advantage of the general disorder to pillage estates and seize land. Liberals pressed for constitutional reform. Students demonstrated. On January 20, 1905, the universities of Kiev, Warsaw, Kharkov, and Kazan were closed by the authorities. On February 4, a Social Revolutionary named I. P. Kalyaev assassinated the Grand Duke Sergey Alexandrovich, Governor General of Moscow. On March 15, Warsaw Director of Police Nolken was wounded by a bomb. The day Mukden fell to the Japanese, demonstrators sacked police headquarters in Chiaturi, Georgia. April 2, the province of Courland, Latvia, was placed under martial law. In April, too, a general railroad strike broke out in the Caucasus.

[5] *The Letters of Lenin*, translated by Elizabeth Hill and Doris Mudie, pp. 235-238.

Lenin chose April, 1905, to call a rump congress of the Russian Social Democratic Labor Party in London, limited to his followers among the Bolsheviks; at about the same time, the Mensheviks convened in Geneva. Lenin's open call for a complete split between these two factions ignored the demands in Russia for unity in the mounting political crisis.

On May 11, the governor of Baku was assassinated by an Armenian nationalist. The tsarist regime had resorted to a time-honored Russian expedient: when attacked, divert the attackers. In the Caucasus, the relaxation of law and order led to repeated massacres of Armenians by Moslems and of Moslems by Armenians. Government officials either abetted or connived at the barbarities. The record also shows innumerable pogroms of Jews in the Ukraine, Bessarabia, White Russia, and Poland. Tsarism was trying to cure social unrest with racial bleeding.

On June 14, the crew of the armored cruiser *Potemkin*, at Odessa, mutinied and seized the ship, an event immortalized by Eisenstein's great film. The worms in the meat were merely symbolic of the worms in the tsarist system. Lenin, sitting in Geneva, writing in his new weekly, *Proletarii (The Proletarian)*, for which he claimed the title of central organ of the entire party, correctly attached enormous significance to the defection of the *Potemkin* and its escape from Russian waters to Romania. He noted a foreigner's comment that this was a unique phenomenon: the revolution had come in possession of an armored cruiser and did not know what to do with it. There could be no revolution, Lenin implied, without revolutionary administration. He saw the need, therefore, of "a provisional revolutionary government." The life-and-death struggle was "only beginning." He put his hopes in the *Potemkin*. "And long live the revolutionary army," he closed, "long live the revolutionary government."[6]

Indeed the *Potemkin*, expecting further developments in Russia, steamed back to Feodosiya in the Crimea and asked for coal. The authorities offered bread instead. Meanwhile, loyal troops fired on the cruiser, which then returned to Constantzsa and submitted to internment with its crew of four hundred.

The flames of revolt rose higher. Cossacks, dragoons, and police were kept busy dispersing demonstrations with gunshot and knout. Every funeral of the victims occasioned more deaths.

Through the mediation of President Theodore Roosevelt, Japanese and Russian negotiators met at the United States Navy Yard in Portsmouth, New Hampshire, where, on August 23, 1905, the two belligerent nations signed a peace treaty.[7]

In the month of August, too, the Russian government announced its in-

---

[6] Lenin, *Sochineniya (Collected Works)*, Fourth ed., Vol. 8, pp. 533-537.
[7] The date in the Western calendar was Sept. 5. Until the Soviet government adopted the Western, Gregorian calendar, Russian dates were thirteen days earlier than Western dates.

tention to convene a Duma, or parliament, and on October 17 the Tsar proclaimed in a manifesto that Duma elections would take place. In the meantime, on September 13, the Petrograd Soviet of Workers' Deputies came into being—the first Russian soviet, or council. Before the year was out, city soviets had sprouted in Sevastopol, in Kiev, in Rostov, in Moscow, in Samara, in Kharkov, Vladikavkaz, and other cities.

The first chairman of the St. Petersburg Soviet was G. S. Khrustalyov-Nosar, an attorney and non-party man. When the government arrested him on November 26 and sent him to Siberia, Leon Trotsky was elected his successor. Trotsky, born Leon Bronstein on October 26, 1879, rebelled as a juvenile against his untutored farmer father, against his parents' Jewishness, and against their manual environment in the dull Ukrainian countryside. At seventeen, a brilliant adolescent, he came upon a questing, argumentative group of revolutionaries in the Ukrainian town of Nikolaev. Like all anti-tsarists, they split between populists (Narodniks) and Marxists. Leon sided with the former. A young woman, Alexandra Sokolovskaya, tried zealously to win him for Marxism. He remained obdurate. New Year's night, 1897, there was a party and Leon told friends he had become a Marxist, but when called upon to pronounce a toast he exclaimed, "A curse upon all Marxists, and upon all those who want to bring dryness and hardness in all the relations of life." He directed this remark to Sokolovskaya. Later he married her, embraced Marxism, went into Siberian exile with her, had two children with her, and at her self-sacrificing urging, escaped to Europe (in 1902) and never lived with her again.[8]

Enormously talented, contrary, and egoistic, Trotsky—this was his literary-revolutionary pseudonym—had commenced, in Siberia, to send reviews and articles to Russian revolutionary émigré publications in Europe, including Lenin's Iskra. Escaped from Siberia and Russia, Trotsky traveled, penniless, across Europe, across the English Channel, and knocked, early one morning, at the door of Lenin's humble London dwelling. Nothing is more characteristic of a young writer than to seek out his editor. Krupskaya opened the door and exclaimed, "Hello, the Pen has arrived." His talent had already won him that sobriquet. "They gave me tea in the kitchen, I believe," Trotsky said later of that visit. "In the meantime Lenin dressed."[9]

In Siberia, Trotsky had steeped himself in Western classics and Russian revolutionary literature and devoured the works of Russia's great nineteenth-century novelists and critics, giants who grew in fallow soil. He also read and dissected Nietzsche and Ibsen. On the train, fleeing from Siberia, "I read the Iliad," he subsequently recalled.[10] He was hungry for culture. In London,

---

[8] The story is told in vivid detail in Isaac Deutscher, The Prophet Armed, Trotsky: 1879-1921 (New York and London, 1954).

[9] Leon Trotsky, Lenin (Authorized Translation, New York, 1925), p. 7.

[10] Ibid., p. 12.

Lenin guided him through the streets and pointed out the sights. "I no longer know how he expressed himself," Trotsky wrote, "but the meaning was: that is 'their famous Westminster.' The 'their' meant, naturally, not the English but the enemy." When Lenin mentioned the British Museum or the high quality of the *Times* it was always "they"—"always as enemies," Trotsky reported.[11] Lenin probably sensed young Trotsky's avidity and feared he might swallow "their" civilization uncritically.

In the next three years, Trotsky's pen lifted him to eminence in the socialist movement. The 1905 revolution now gave free play to his tongue. He arrived in Russia in February and before long, thanks to a gift for fiery oratory and red-hot prose, he moved to the epicenter of the social turbulence. In October, 1905, at the age of twenty-six, with the revolution at maximum intensity, Trotsky became its leader.

Early in November, Lenin left Switzerland and, traveling through Stockholm and Helsingfors, arrived in St. Petersburg on November 7 or 8. He had been away from Russia for more than five years. He had left as a young agitator and organizer. He returned as the leader of the Bolsheviks. He remained in the background. On October 27, the first issue of a Bolshevik daily, *Novaya Zhizn (New Life)* had appeared in St. Petersburg. This fulfilled Lenin's great desire; in *Chto Delat? (What Is to Be Done?)* and elsewhere he had attached maximum importance to having a party organ that could raise its voice every morning. Lenin wrote articles for the newspaper, conferred with party committees, worked on Bolshevik agrarian policy, met party workers privately, and, on one occasion, November 13, addressed the St. Petersburg Soviet on the employers' lockout of workingmen who had sought, by stay-ins, to enforce an eight-hour day. The police were now on his trail; accordingly, he and Krupskaya went into hiding on December 6.

The 1905 revolution highlighted a significant contrast between Trotsky and Lenin. It did not reveal a black-and-white distinction; neither of them could properly be called one thing or the other. But Trotsky, at this period, was primarily a mass-appeal man, Lenin primarily an organization man. Trotsky needed a stage, Lenin an office. Trotsky wanted followers, Lenin wanted hard-working, obedient executives. Party ties meant little to Trotsky; he preferred the role of lone wolf outside the pack, neither subordinating himself to a group nor subordinating a group to himself except by the force of tongue and pen. Lenin, on the other hand, competed feverishly for his party's supremacy over other socialist parties. In fact, however, the Bolsheviks were very weak. Their organization could scarcely be called a skeleton. Its separate bones still needed to be joined and clothed with flesh and infused with blood. Lenin's role in Russia in 1905 was therefore not primary. His time had not come.

The revolution lacked coordination and power. The government, now at

[11] *Ibid.*, pp. 7-8.

peace with Japan, felt able to establish peace with its own people by the use of steel, lead, and leather. But before it was drowned in blood the movement of protest rose to a heroic climax in Moscow where, for five days, workers fought on the barricades against troops. Finally, the Tsar sent the Semyonov regiment by rail from Petersburg to Moscow. The rebels then succumbed to artillery shells.

This is not the way Lenin had imagined the revolution. Sometime in June or July, 1905, in Geneva, Lenin had a dream. It was a daydream about a revolutionary war, and being a military politician, he drew up the plan of attack. The imaginary circumstances were these: the Tsar had been overthrown in St. Petersburg but the tsarist government, though beaten, "was not annihilated, not torn out by the roots." A competing provisional, revolutionary government had been formed. It appealed to the people. It offered "complete freedom. The people themselves arrange their own lives. Complete republican freedoms, peasant committees for a *complete* transformation of agrarian conditions. . . . The Social Democrats are in the provisional government. . . .

"Moreover—a Constituent Assembly." In it the people "*may* prove to have a majority (workers and peasants). Consequently, [there will be] a revolutionary dictatorship of the proletariat and peasantry." This arouses "the frantic resistance of the dark forces." Meanwhile, the "peasantry has itself taken in its hands all agrarian arrangements, *all* land. *Then, nationalization* is carried through. . . .

"War. . . . Either the bourgeoisie overthrows the revolutionary dictatorship of the proletariat and peasantry, or this dictatorship ignites Europe and then . . ."[12]

Here he stopped. Russia "ignites Europe." The prospect beggared his imagination. It was his ultimate desire. The word "ignites," the idea of ignition, lies at the heart of Lenin's thinking about revolutionary strategy. *Iskra (The Spark)* was the name of the party magazine he first edited. Either a Russian spark would ignite the European revolution or revolution in Europe would throw a spark into the social tinder of autocratic Russia.

Anything less than revolution failed to arouse Lenin's ardor. When Nicholas II received representatives of local government zemstvos and of upper court circles in August, 1905, and promised to convene a Duma, Lenin contemptuously called the delegation "Revolutionaries in white gloves." He warned the workers the Tsar and the liberal bourgeoisie would sell them down the river of reaction. He urged his party to boycott the Duma and the Duma elections. He feared the effects of democratic reforms on the minuscule revolutionary organizations. Free elections to the Duma could only be

---

[12] Lenin put the fantasy on paper. It remained in his files until first published in 1926. Reproduced in Lenin, *Sochineniya (Collected Works)*, Second ed., Vol. VII (1931), pp. 330-332. Also in Fourth ed., Vol. 8, pp. 499-501.

guaranteed by "an armed nation which has organized itself as a revolutionary army, attracted to its side everything that is alive in the army of the Tsar, defeated the tsarist forces, and substituted itself for the tsarist autocracy."[13] He was for all or nothing. And when he saw the reality of Russia on his arrival in St. Petersburg in November, 1905, it was immediately clear to his perceptive brain that it would not be all. He consequently paid more attention to his tiny party faction than to the soviets.

Leaving St. Petersburg in December, 1905, Lenin went to Finland to a party conference, was back in Moscow in January, 1906, explaining why the Duma elections should be boycotted, attended a party conference in St. Petersburg in February, left for Finland again at the end of February, returned to Moscow in March for secret party meetings, conferred with "the leading nucleus of Bolsheviks"[14] in Petersburg in the middle of March, conducted the fourth congress of the Bolshevik party in Stockholm in April, ventured into Russia in May under the assumed name of Karpov, and shuttled between Russia and Finland during the rest of 1906 and most of 1907, with visits to London and Stuttgart for congresses. Leonid I. Roozer, a party comrade, recalls a meeting he attended in St. Petersburg in August, 1906, where he first saw Lenin and heard him address the twenty party members present. Roozer states, in his Soviet-published memoirs of Lenin, that "We, the party youth . . . were still, in considerable measure, under the influence of the revolutionary romanticism of the Narodnaya-Volya period."

In November, 1907, Lenin finally emigrated voluntarily from Russia, not to return until April, 1917, nine and a half years later. Early in January, 1908, after spending some time in Stockholm and Berlin, he settled in Geneva.

Writing to his mother from Stirsudden, Finland, on June 27, 1907, Lenin said, "I have returned feeling terribly tired . . . I am having a wonderful rest: bathing, walks, no people, nothing to do. No people and nothing to do is the best thing for me."[15] Mental fatigue was the natural consequence of party dissensions without clarity and his brief but saddening experience with the 1905 revolution. Tsarism still had an eleven-year lease on life during which it would continue the buoyant industrial growth that commenced before the beginning of the century and inaugurate the land reform of Prime Minister Peter A. Stolypin designed to create a class of capitalist farmers and weaken the patriarchal mir. Lenin apparently sensed this impending development. "And so, in this stage," he wrote at the end of 1905 or the beginning of 1906, in a statement first published in 1926, "the liberal bourgeoisie and the prosperous (plus part of the middle) peasantry will organize the counterrevolution." In response, "The Russian proletariat *plus* the European proletariat will organize the revolution. . . . The European workers will show us

[13] *Ibid.*, Fourth ed., Vol. 9, p. 173. Written on Aug. 16, 1905.
[14] *Ibid.*, Second ed., Vol. IX, editorial note, p. 602.
[15] *The Letters of Lenin*, p. 247.

'how it's done,' and then we together with them will make the socialist insurrection."[16] And on another occasion, "Let us not forget, too, that the complete victory of our revolution requires a union of the Russian proletariat with the socialist workers of all countries."

"Go ahead and shoot," Lenin exclaimed in the legal Bolshevik St. Petersburg *Echo* of July 7, 1906, when the shooting had ended. "Summon the Austrian and German regiments against the Russian peasants and workers. We are for a broadening of the struggle, we are for an international revolution." Russian reaction had reserve forces in European reaction, he declared. "But we too have a mighty international revolutionary reserve: the socialist proletariat of Europe, an organized party of three million in Germany, and strong parties in all European countries."[17]

This was the heart of Lenin's internationalism. One seldom finds any sense of brotherhood or love of peoples in Lenin's internationalism. That would have been subjective and sentimental. His internationalism was functional. It was political physics, action and reaction of one nation upon another with a view to igniting revolution. Alone the puny, feuding Russian revolutionary parties could not unseat tsarism. Russia's Marxism therefore needed foreign auxiliaries. This led Lenin to exaggerate Western revolutionary developments, in fact to create them where they did not exist. "That the socialist revolution is looming in Great Britain—this only blind people could fail to see," he wrote on October 16, 1908.[18] He also expected big events in the United States. He noted, on September 18, 1912, that the *Appeal to Reason*, a Haldemann-Julius weekly published in Girard, Kansas, had attained a circulation of 984,000, and would soon, its editors proclaimed, reach a sale of one million. "This figure—one million copies of a socialist journal which is shamelessly baited and persecuted by the American courts and which waxes strong under the fire of persecution—shows more clearly than long disquisitions," Lenin declared, "what kind of revolt is approaching in America."[19]

Lenin likewise expected aid from Asia. On November 20, 1911, he attended the Paris funeral of two French socialists, Paul and Laura Lafargue. Paul had been a member of the Paris Commune; Laura was the daughter of Karl Marx. At the age of seventy, M. Lafargue decided that his social usefulness was ended and entered into a pact with his wife; both committed suicide. Lenin, Krupskaya stated in her memoirs, approved. "If one cannot work for the party any longer," he said to her, "one must be able to look the truth in the face and die like the Lafargues." At their funeral, he deliv-

[16] Lenin, *Sochineniya (Collected Works)*, Fourth ed., Vol. 10, p. 74.

[17] *Ibid.*, Vol. 11, p. 88.

[18] *Ibid.*, Second ed., Vol. XII, edited by N. I. Bukharin, V. M. Molotov, and M. A. Savelev (Moscow-Leningrad, 1929), p. 349.

[19] *Ibid.*, Vol. XVI (1930), p. 148. (Note: For the period beginning about 1907 the second edition of Lenin's collected works, edited by distinguished Bolsheviks and published between 1929 and 1931, before considerable politically motivated changes had been made in the text and especially in the voluminous editorial notes, is more reliable than the later fourth edition.)

ered a completely impersonal speech. "To us, Russian Social Democrats," he declared, "who have suffered all the oppression of an absolutism saturated with Asiatic barbarism and who have had the good fortune to draw from the writings of Lafargue and his friends a direct acquaintance with the revolutionary experience and revolutionary thought of European workingmen, to us it is now particularly obvious how quickly we are nearing the triumph of that cause to whose defense Lafargue dedicated his entire life. The Russian revolution [of 1905] inaugurated the epoch of the democratic revolution in all of Asia, and [its] eight hundred million persons have now become participants in the democratic movement of the whole civilized world. And in Europe," Lenin concluded, "the signs multiply more and more that the epoch of the domination of so-called world bourgeois parliamentarianism is coming to a close and will yield to the epoch of revolutionary battles of the proletariat which, organized and trained in the spirit of the ideas of Marxism, will overthrow the rule of the bourgeoisie and establish the communist system."[20]

These prophecies notwithstanding, Lenin professed a repugnance for prophecy. He refused to project himself into the future. "If I say," he wrote on September 16, 1912: "the new Russia *should* be built *thus-and-so* from the point of view, say, of truth, justice, the equality of labor, and so forth, that will be subjectivity, which leads me into the area of chimeras. Actually, the class struggle and not my finest desires will determine the shape of the new Russia."[21] This abhorrence of subjectivity and of "finest desires" or higher aspirations turned Lenin and all Marxists against utopias. "Utopia," he declared, "is a Greek word: 'U' in Greek means 'no,' 'topos' means 'place.' Utopia—is a place that does not exist, a fantasy, an invention, a fairy tale. A utopia in politics is the kind of wish that cannot be fulfilled now or ever."[22] One such utopia, Lenin stated, was the Russian populists' dream to enshrine socialism through a land reform.

The contempt for utopias and dreamers tended to put eternal values and moral considerations to flight and make a fetish of "objective circumstances," of a realism that easily becomes the handmaiden of opportunism. Yet how objective was Lenin's prediction in 1911 that "so-called world bourgeois parliamentarianism is coming to a close," or his 1912 vision of the United States on the eve of a socialist revolution because a soon-to-be-forgotten weekly had a booming circulation?

After the 1905 turmoil, the tsarist regime recuperated from its military defeat and coldly repressed its subversives. No sparks were ignited in Russia or in Asia, America, or Europe. On the other hand, fires lit in the Balkans embraced the world in the flames of war. Out of them rose a new Russian revolution for which 1905 was but a rehearsal.

[20] *Ibid.*, Vol. XV (1929), pp. 264-265.
[21] *Ibid.*, Vol. XVI, p. 143.
[22] *Ibid.*, p. 163.

IV. THE ESSENTIAL LENIN

IN DECEMBER, 1903, Nikolai Volsky (literary pseudonym N. Valentinov) age twenty-nine, an adherent of the Bolshevik wing of the Russian Socialist Party, was arrested in Kiev, went on a hunger strike, was released on its eleventh day, and immediately, armed with a letter of introduction to Lenin from Gleb Krzhizhanovsky, a member of the party's Central Committee, fled from Russia, via the "underground railway," to Geneva. Arrived there he walked from the station to Lenin's home at 10 Rue du Foyer where Krupskaya opened the lining of Valentinov's coat to extract the letter and develop the part written in invisible ink. In the next months, the newcomer spent many hours in conversation and days in walks and picnics with the Ulyanov family. Decades later he produced a record of the experience.[1] He remembered Lenin as good at rowing, swimming, cycling, shooting, and exercising on the trapeze and on rings. He also admired Lenin's billiard game. Elizaveta Vasilievna, Lenin's mother-in-law, once remarked to the visitor that Lenin sewed on his own buttons and did it "better than Nadya." Lenin cultivated his body, according to Valentinov, for the sake of the revolution. A revolutionary never knew when his physical powers would be tested—in prison or in escaping from prison.

Krzhizhanovsky, Valentinov's sponsor, also wrote memoirs of Lenin. "We might begin," he said, "with the plain, modest outward appearance of Vladimir Ilyich. His small body, topped by the customary cap, could easily be lost, without attracting attention, in any factory district. A pleasant, dark-complexioned face of a somewhat Eastern cast—that is about all that can be said of his outward appearance. Dressed in a cloth coat, Vladimir Ilyich could just as easily remain unnoticed in any crowd of Volga peasants. . . . But one had only to peer into the eyes of Vladimir Ilyich, into those unusual, piercing, dark dark-brown eyes, full of inner power and energy, to begin to sense that you were face to face with a far from usual type. Most portraits of Vladimir Ilyich fail to convey that impression of special endowments which quickly replaced the first impression of a plain appearance."

Krzhizhanovsky met Lenin in St. Petersburg in 1893 when the young Ulyanov arrived from his home on the Volga. "Alone the fact," he wrote, "that he was the brother of Alexander Ilyich Ulyanov, one of the last famous Narodniks, executed in 1887, would have created most favorable conditions for his friendly reception in our [Marxist] midst." Thereafter, Krzhizhanovsky saw Lenin frequently in Siberian exile, in Paris, and as a very high Soviet official; he was for a time Chairman of the Gosplan, State Planning Commission. Lenin, he reported, had a powerful body. In exile, Krzhizhanovsky recalled, he once talked with Lenin about the way in which the good health of a person is reflected in clear, distinct emotions. Lenin agreed. "That's

[1] *Vstraychey s Leninim (Encounters with Lenin)* (New York, 1953).

quite right," he said. "If a healthy person wants to eat he really wants it; if he wants to sleep he won't start investigating whether or not he can sleep on a soft bed, and if he hates then he really hates."[2]

In Paris a well-known French sculptor told Krzhizhanovsky that "he found a tremendous resemblance between the outline of Lenin's forehead and the sculptures representing the great ancient philosopher, Socrates." Maxim Gorky noted the same resemblance.

Gorky had given money to Lenin-edited publications, was arrested for revolutionary activity in January, 1905, and joined the Russian Social Democratic Labor Party in the latter part of that year. On November 27, 1905, the Central Committee of the party met in Gorky's home in St. Petersburg; with Lenin present, preparations for an armed uprising were discussed.[3] Gorky told the committee about his impressions of the fighting mood in Moscow. Gorky and Lenin met again in January, 1906, in Helsingfors in a private apartment, and several times in April, 1907, in Berlin where they walked in the Tiergarten and went to theater. These encounters apparently escaped Gorky's mind when he wrote his recollections of Lenin after the latter's death. He put their initial encounter in London at the May, 1907, congress of the Russian Socialist Party. "So glad you've come," Lenin said as they shook hands in the church that gave hospitality to the congress. "I believe you're fond of a scrap? There's going to be a big scrap here."[4]

Before the "scrap" began, Lenin took Gorky to the Imperial Hotel at Russell Square and helped him register. He accompanied Gorky up to his room, uncovered the bed, and felt the sheets and found them damp.

Gorky saw Lenin with the eye of a novelist and heard him with the ear of a dramatist. "I did not expect Lenin to be like that," Gorky wrote. "Something was lacking in him. He rolled his 'r's' gutturally, and had a jaunty way of standing with his hands somehow poked up under his armpits. He was somehow too ordinary, did not give the impression of being a leader.

"Before me now stood a baldheaded, stocky, sturdy person . . . holding my hand in one of his, while with the other he wiped a forehead which might have belonged to Socrates, beaming affectionately at me with his strangely bright eyes.

"He began at once to speak about the defects of my book *Mother* . . ."

The congress opening found Gorky in a "festive mood," he was among his own people. But they immediately commenced "wrangling about 'the

[2] *Vospominaniya o Vladimire Ilyiche Lenine (Reminiscences about Vladimir Ilyich Lenin)*, Vol. 1, pp. 146-164.

[3] These and subsequent details about Gorky's relations with Lenin and the Bolsheviks are taken from *V. I. Lenin i A. M. Gorkii. Pisma, Vospominaniya, Dokumenti (V. I. Lenin and A. M. Gorky, Letters, Recollections, Documents)*, Second ed. (Moscow, 1961).

[4] *Vospominaniya o Vladimire Ilyiche Lenine (Reminiscences about Vladimir Ilyich Lenin)*, Vol. 1, pp. 365-392. The English translation has been borrowed from: Maxim Gorky, *Days with Lenin* (New York, 1932). I have slightly amended the translation where it departed from the Russian original.

order of the day.' The fury of these disputes at once chilled my enthusiasm, and not so much because I felt how sharply the Party was divided into reformers and revolutionaries—I had realized that in 1903—but because of the hostile attitude of the reformers to Lenin."

Georgi Plekhanov, the Nestor of the party, delivered the first address. Gorky said he spoke "like a preacher confident that his ideas are incontrovertible, every word and every pause of great value." The person who did "the most fidgeting on the Bolshevik benches" during Plekhanov's speech "was Lenin . . . he hunched himself up as though from cold, then he sprawled as though he felt hot. He poked his fingers into his armholes, rubbed his chin, shook his bright head, and whispered something to M. P. Tomsky. When Plekhanov declared that 'there are no revisionists in the party,' Lenin bent down, his bald spot grew red, his shoulders shook in silent laughter."

Julius Martov, the Menshevik, also took the floor. "This amazingly attractive man," Gorky wrote, "spoke with the ardor of youth and in particular, it seems, he deeply felt the tragic drama of the split, the pain of the dissension." ". . . we must put an end to the split," Martov implored. "The party is too weak to be divided." At the end of his speech, Martov began to shout against the militant Lenin group and against all work directed to the preparation of an armed uprising.

Now Lenin "hurries to the pulpit, and cries 'Comrades!' in his guttural manner. He seemed to me to speak badly, but after a minute I and everybody else were absorbed in his speech. It was the first time I had heard complicated political questions treated so simply. There was no striving after beautiful phrases, he presented every word clearly, and revealed his exact thought with great ease."

As the congress continued, Lenin became "bolder and more confident. With every day his speeches," Gorky reminisced, "sounded firmer and the Bolshevik element in the congress grew more uncompromising and inflexible."

The unity congress lasted twenty days. Its result was disastrous disunity. (Joseph Fels, a philanthropist, single taxer, and Philadelphia manufacturer of Fels Naphtha soap, lent the money that paid most of the expenses of the congress. It was repaid in 1923.)

The sources of dissension were numerous. On the eve of the congress Plekhanov accused Lenin of wanting to acquire "the conductor's baton"— the leadership of the party. This battle of the generals—Lenin, Martov, Plekhanov, Potresov, Axelrod, Zasulich—began far back and resulted in Lenin's exit from the editorship of *Iskra*. No human organization can shut out the crosscurrents of personal rivalry. Indeed, politics is often the mask worn by ambition. Lenin was not personally ambitious; he was stubborn. "Have a good look at that man," Rosa Luxemburg said to Clara Zetkin at the 1907 international congress in Stuttgart. "That's Lenin. Observe his obstinate, self-willed skull."[5] Clara Zetkin, a German communist leader, wrote this after Lenin's death. "Rosa," she added, "was distinguished by her accurate artist's eye."

When Lenin held an opinion it became an unbendable belief which he defended against the arguments of man and the evidence of events until a new view replaced it and then he defended that with equal certainty. Doubts occupied little space in Lenin's mental equipment. He banished them consciously, and avoided doubters. In 1905, he ardently advocated, and persuaded the Bolsheviks—but not the Mensheviks—to carry out a boycott of the first Duma. In 1920 he admitted his error.[6] He ardently advocated Bolshevik participation in the Duma in 1906. This change of front caused one of the hottest clashes at the 1907 London congress. For now the big issue was how the socialist parties were to behave within the Duma. Lenin rejected the Menshevik strategy of permitting occasional collaboration with nonsocialist, liberal bourgeois parties. He would not cooperate with the middle even against rightist reactionaries.

Cooperation requires give-and-take, and there was no give in Lenin's politics. He was a political isolationist who preferred plowing a lone furrow. Also, he had no liking for, and little comprehension of, democratic parliamentarianism. He regarded parliament as an institution to be used for revolutionary purposes, not to be worked for democratic purposes. This flowed from his assessment of revolutionary prospects. In 1907 he still thought the Russian revolution imminent. The suppression of the 1905-1906 revolt did not convince him. He anticipated a new insurrection and, since none would come for a decade, his logic wilted. On May 2, 1907, for instance, he began an article with this statement: "In a certain sense of the word, only nationwide revolution can be successful. This is true in the sense that for a victory of the revolution the united effort of the great majority of the population in the struggle for the demands of that revolution is indispensable." For emphasis he rephrased the proposition: "only a tremendous majority can vanquish the organized and ruling minority." He called this "a truism." But conditions change rapidly in a revolution. Before the revolution, and in the first phase of it, everybody—the workers, peasants, petty bourgeoisie, and liberal bourgeoisie—support "political freedom" and "national interests." However, when the capitalist-bourgeois elements realize, in the further course of the revolution, what "political freedom" means they waver and turn against the revolution. Then "Social Democracy *must* isolate itself from the petty bourgeois people." Either the hesitations of the petty bourgeoisie indicate how difficult it is to make a revolution but do not signify its end ("that is what we think"), and in that case "the social democrats, the proletariat,

[5] *Ibid.*, Vol. 2, pp. 451-476. German communist publications spell the name "Clara," not "Klara."

[6] Lenin, *Sochineniya*, Second ed., Vol. XXV (Moscow, 1920), pp. 171-250.

educate these people for the struggle . . . develop their class-consciousness, decisiveness, and determination," or this stage of the bourgeois revolution has ended, but "we think this view is incorrect." However, in certain "unfavorable" circumstances it might prove correct. "That would be nation-wide cowardice." The "social democratic proletariat *isolates* itself from it"—from the cowardice—"in the interests of the entire workers' movement." Thus he ended,[7] leaving many loose ends dangling in the mist.

He therefore returned to the subject at the fifth, 1907, congress of the party in London during the discussion of the socialist attitude toward the bourgeois parties in the Duma. His presentation was sweeping. "Our revolution," he said, "is undoubtedly bourgeois in its social-economic content. . . . Even the most complete victory of the current revolution, that is, the achievement of the most democratic republic and the confiscation of all landed estates by the peasants, would not in the least affect the foundations of bourgeois society. Private property of the means of production" and of land, as well as a market economy, "would remain." Capitalism's contradictions and frictions would even grow. "All this should be beyond dispute for every Marxist." But it does not follow that the bourgeoisie must lead the bourgeois revolution. "Only the proletariat is in a position to complete it, to accomplish its complete victory." Why? Because the specific of the Russian revolution was the land problem. "This struggle for land unavoidably drives the overwhelming mass of the peasants toward a democratic revolt, for only democracy, by making them dominant in the government, can give them land." Therefore, "Victory in the contemporary Russian revolution is possible only through a revolutionary-democratic dictatorship of the proletariat and the peasantry." This should be the goal of the socialist party, not a compact with bourgeois parties. "Our bourgeoisie is counter-revolutionary." Even the peasant aims were utopian. "In what, chiefly, does its"—the peasantry's —"utopia consist? Undoubtedly in the idea of leveling, in the conviction that the abolition of private ownership of land and the equal division of the land (or of its usufruct) are capable of destroying the sources of privation, poverty, unemployment, exploitation.

"From the point of view of *socialism* there is no dispute that this—is utopia, the utopia of the petty bourgeois. From the point of view of socialism this is a reactionary prejudice, for the proletarian revolution sees the ideal not in the equality of small owners but in large socialized production." Nevertheless, what the peasants wanted—private ownership of equal parcels of land —would stimulate Russian capitalism. "And this is advantageous not only to the peasantry, but also the proletariat."

Thus, the "revolutionary-democratic dictatorship of the proletariat and peasantry" would foster capitalism through a bourgeois revolution which the bourgeoisie and the peasantry opposed. The peasant, Lenin quoted Marx as saying, dreams of shutting himself off from society "on his own piece of

[7] *Ibid.*, Vol. XI, pp. 204-207.

land . . . on his own manure heap." And, "This private-property instinct repels the peasantry from the proletariat."

How, then, establish a proletarian-peasant dictatorship?

The outlook, to say the least, was grim. "Our revolution is experiencing hard times. We need all the will power, all the steadfastness and firmness of a united proletarian party to be able to resist the mood of skepticism, despondency, apathy, and abandonment of the struggle."[8]

Conclusion: "There can be no thought now of our supporting the liberals."[9]

Lenin had given an admirable description of his troubled mind. A successful revolution needs the support of the majority, and the majority—industry, business, and peasantry—were counterrevolutionary. Nevertheless, the revolution was not ended. Since the revolution continued, a revolutionary party must avoid relations with counterrevolutionary parties. It must pursue revolution, not play parliamentary politics. Lenin remained wedded to revolution and spurned the alternatives. The revolution, however, was in the doldrums, and so were Lenin and his small Bolshevik group. They remained becalmed until the First World War put wind in their sails. Then a minority won power.

Organizational problems aggravated Lenin's frustration. He had always attached inordinate importance to these, insisting that issues like centralized authority versus rank-and-file democracy, professional revolutionaries versus a loose body of sympathizers, were not technical; they reflected ideological fissures. In 1902, he had devoted a book, *What Is to Be Done?*, to these matters. In 1904, the same questions were treated in another book, *One Step Forward, Two Back. The Crisis in Our Party*,[10] of approximately 50,000 words minutely dissecting past debates with enviable industry and unquenchable belligerency. "Little mistakes in organizational questions," he insisted, led to big political differences. What he called organizational "tailism," or dawdling, "was the natural and inevitable result of a psychology of anarchistic individualism" elevated to a philosophy of life.

Here Lenin himself made a long leap from form to philosophy. He attacked intellectuals. Under the terms "intellectual" and "intelligentsia," he wrote, he included "all educated people, members of the free professions in general, practitioners of mental work (brain worker, the English say)"—he used the English word—"as distinguished from manual labor." "The factory," Lenin declared, "to some the worst kind of bugbear, is that highest form of capitalist cooperation which has united and disciplined the proletariat, taught it organization, put it at the head of all other strata of the toiling and exploited population." The factory was the proletariat's "school." "In the struggle for power the proletariat has no weapon except organiza-

[8] *Ibid.*, pp. 245-254.
[9] *Ibid.*, p. 257.
[10] *Ibid.*, Vol. VI, pp. 159-328.

tion." The intellectual, on the other hand, had a "deathly fear" of this "school." The petty bourgeois life of the intellectual molded his anarchistic consciousness. "This haughty anarchism is especially peculiar to the Russian nihilist. Party organization seems to him a horrible 'factory'; the subordination of a part of the whole, of the minority to the majority, appears to him as 'serfdom' (see Axelrod's feuilleton), the division of labor under the direction of the center evokes tragicomic screams from him against the transformation of human beings into 'little wheels and screws.' "

Lenin was an intellectual, a bourgeois intellectual and nobleman. But he was resolved not to be a man of lofty thoughts who did nothing. He scorned the all-negating nihilist. He derided the parlor revolutionary; nineteenth-century Russia had known thousands of them. He misquoted Chernishevsky as saying, "Whoever is afraid to soil his hands should not undertake political activity."[11] In other words, you cannot make an omelet without breaking heads. He would not merely think revolution or talk revolution, he would soil his hands and organize revolution—with the help of the workers. The Narodnik-populists made a cult of the peasant. Lenin made a cult of the worker. Because the typical Russian intellectual rather ostentatiously branded the mark of Oblomov on his own forehead, he tended to glorify the mass, the people, those close to the soil in one case, to the lathe in the other. Russian upper-class society was indolent and sophisticated. Lenin therefore put simplicity above sophistication; brawn above brain; organization above the individual. There was in this a measure of self-rejection, of self-suppression. Indeed, Lenin curbed his better nature. (He said so during the Soviet period.) Whether or not Plekhanov was right in accusing Lenin of wanting to seize "the conductor's baton" and direct the party, it seems true that Lenin had an inbuilt "conductor's baton" for himself. He consciously tried to direct himself; he organized himself.

On all questions now, on organization, the imminence of revolution, relations with bourgeois parties, parliamentary strategy, and ideology, the Bolsheviks and Mensheviks grew further apart. Lenin grew angrier. The number of persons he could tolerate grew smaller. It would have been better, in the circumstances, not to convene the 1907 London congress. Yet Lenin welcomed it. He preferred a labeled chasm to a papered-over gulf.

After the congress, Gorky invited Lenin to Capri. Lenin had no time; he was arranging for the publication of a new party magazine called *Proletarii* (*The Worker*), and asked Gorky to write for it. The correspondence continued. On February 7, 1908, Lenin boasted to Gorky in a letter, "The importance of intellectuals in our party is declining: from everywhere comes news that intellectuals are *running away* from the party." He called them "swine," and asserted happily, "The party is cleansing itself of this petty-bourgeois

<hr>

[11] *Ibid.*, Vol. X, p. 264. Chernishevsky had written, "Whoever is afraid to be covered with dust and soil his shoes should not go into politics." *Ibid.*, editorial note, p. 503.

filth. Workers are starting to do more. The role of professional revolutionists who are workers is expanding. All this is wonderful."[12] Apparently Gorky took umbrage, for on February 13 Lenin, replying to the novelist, wrote that there was some kind of "misunderstanding. Why, of course, I had no thought of 'driving out the intellectuals.' "[13]

In mid-March Lenin again put off his trip to Capri: "there is no money, no time, and I cannot leave the paper." Were these the sole reasons? "I will most certainly come to Capri," he told Gorky in a letter mailed from Geneva on March 24, 1908, "and I shall try to induce my wife to come, but I should like to come without getting involved in a philosophical fight."[14] The philosophers, notably Bogdanov, Bazarov, and Lunacharsky, were living with or near Gorky on Capri.

In "damned Geneva," as Lenin called it, he and Krupskaya were not enjoying themselves. ". . . we found it difficult to get accustomed to life in exile again," Krupskaya wrote. "Vladimir Ilyich spent his days in the library, but in the evening we did not know what to do with ourselves. We did not feel like sitting in the cold, cheerless room we had rented; we longed to be among people, and every evening we would go to the cinema or to the theater, although we rarely stayed till the end, but usually left in the middle of the performance and would go wandering somewhere, most often to the lake."[15]

In April, finally, Lenin went to Capri—alone. Just before leaving Geneva he informed Gorky that "I could come . . . but I repeat: only on the condition that I do not speak about philosophy or religion."[16] With Gorky, Lenin visited the Naples national museum, the environs of Naples, and the ruins of Pompeii, and drove up Mt. Vesuvius. They also went fishing together and talked. A photograph shows Gorky and Maria Feodorovna Andreyeva, his wife, watching Lenin and Bogdanov playing chess on Gorky's terrace in the midst of Capri's beauty. Lenin was wearing an enormous bowler; it had to fit over his Socratic brow and big skull. Lenin lost the game, "and when he lost," Gorky noted, he "grew angry and even despondent like a child." Apart from chess, Lenin and Bogdanov did not match wits. Once Lenin said, "Explain in two-three phrases what your 'position' gives to the working class and why Machism is more revolutionary than Marxism." Bogdanov began, but before he got far Lenin interrupted: "Drop it."

"Of course," Krupskaya asserted, basing her version on Lenin's report, "no conciliation with Bogdanov's philosophical views took place. Afterwards, Ilyich recalled how he had said to Bogdanov and Bazarov: we will simply have to separate for two or three years. . . . There was a big crowd at Gorky's place, much noise and bustle. Many played chess, others went boating. Ilyich said very little about the trip. He spoke mostly about the beauty of the scene

12 V. I. *Lenin i A. M. Gorkii*, p. 20.
13 *Ibid.*, p. 25.
14 *Ibid.*, pp. 34-36.
15 Nadezhda K. Krupskaya, *Memories of Lenin*, Vol. II, p. 14.
16 V. I. *Lenin i A. M. Gorkii*, p. 38.

and the quality of the local wine, but he was reticent about the discussion of the big questions that took place there. It was too painful a subject with him to talk about. Ilyich again became immersed in the study of philosophy."[17]

The Bolsheviks, still a fraction in the Russian Social Democratic Labor Party (the other fractions were the Mensheviks, the Latvian party, the Jewish Bund, the Trotskyist Center, etc.), now threatened to break into two fractions—on the rock of philosophy. The philosophy of Marx was being challenged by the philosophy of Mach. Bogdanov, Bazarov, Lunacharsky, and many more Bolsheviks were Machists. They also claimed to be Marxists. Lenin reviled them. But to defeat them he had to know more about Mach and about philosophy in general. He had read some of the philosophical writings of Marx, Engels, Feuerbach, Plekhanov, and Kant. In 1906 he had also read a book called *Empirio-Monism* by Alexander A. Bogdanov, the leading Russian Machist, and having read it he wrote Gorky saying, "I became unusually annoyed and angry"; Bogdanov, "was taking an exceedingly wrong non-Marxist line."[18] Lenin began writing a book in reply. In 1908 his anger with Bogdanov was intensified by political differences. "This was a very difficult period," Krupskaya affirmed. "In Russia the organization was falling apart. The police, with the aid of agents provocateurs, caught the most prominent party workers. . . . The masses withdrew into their shell as it were. They wanted to think over everything that had occurred [in the 1905-6 revolution]; everybody had become tired of general agitation. . . . This situation created a favorable environment for the growth of Otzovism."[19] The Otzovists, or Recallers, wanted to recall the socialist deputies and boycott the Duma, as Lenin had urged in 1905. Now he was for using the Duma. Bogdanov had joined the Recallers. This doubled Lenin's hostility to his philosophy. "It was obvious," Krupskaya wrote, "that the former solidarity of the Bolshevik fraction was gone, that a split was approaching and first of all a split with Bogdanov."[20]

With characteristic energy and burning zeal Lenin collected material for his book against the Machists. But some publications were not available in Geneva. "Moreover, the bickering and squabbling that was such a marked feature of life in exile, greatly hampered his work. He decided, therefore, to go to London and work in the British Museum and to finish his book there."[21]

John Strachey, British Labour member of Parliament and author, has recorded "the story told me by a friend of mine, Miles Malleson, the actor. Malleson used to go and read in the reading room of the British Museum in

[17] Krupskaya, *op. cit.*, p. 23. Krupskaya mistakenly puts the visit in May. She wrote the second volume of her memoirs in 1931.
[18] *Ibid.*, p. 19.
[19] *Ibid.*, p. 23.
[20] *Ibid.*, p. 18.
[21] *Ibid.*, p. 28.

the 1920's. He was a keen left-wing socialist, and he remembered that just as Marx had read there, so Lenin had read there. . . . There was an old curator in the Library who had been there for thirty years and Malleson was sure he must have been there during Lenin's days. Anxious to hear anything about this tremendous figure, he said to the curator, 'Do you remember Lenin coming and reading here?' The curator looked puzzled: 'Lenin—no—I don't seem to recall any gentleman by that name.' My friend," Strachey continued, "said, 'Oh, perhaps he was not using his party name of Lenin then, he was using his real name of Ulyanov. Do you remember a Mr. Ulyanov coming in?' The curator at once said, 'Of course, I remember Mr. Ulyanov; a very charming gentleman, short, and with a pointed beard. A very nicely-spoken gentleman. I remember him very well. Can you tell me, sir, what has become of him?' "[22]

Lenin's researches resulted in a book published in 1909, entitled *Materialism and Empirio-Criticism. Critical Notes on a Reactionary Philosophy*.[23] It is a defense of the Marx-Engels philosophy of historical materialism and an invective-ridden assault on the thinking of the Russian disciples of Mach.

Ernest Mach (1838-1916) was an Austrian physicist and philosopher who aimed to "economize thought" by erasing the dualism between what is psychological and what is physical and substituting the monist theory that the physical, a table, an apple, did not exist except in our senses, in our experience. The table would have no hardness, no color, the apple would have no taste, but for man's perceptions. In other words, Mach subordinated matter to the human mind. Marx-Engels materialism postulated the primacy of things, of matter, of environment, of the physical world. It was this physical world, the materialists declared, that shapes our consciousness. Mach stood materialism on its head, reversed it, contended that it was our consciousness that gave matter its qualities: tint, taste, size, shape, and so forth.

Lenin put his case clearly in *Materialism and Empirio-Criticism*: "Hence matter is primary, and mind, consciousness, sensation are products of a very high development. Such is the materialist theory of knowledge, which natural science instinctively holds." By "very high development" he meant the birth of man. Surely, the Marxists argued, matter existed before man. There were trees, rocks, seas, beasts, and so forth before a living person was there to perceive them. "Being" or environment or the presence of matter came first. Therefore, "Consciousness in general reflects being," Lenin wrote, echoing the Marx-Engels basic proposition of materialism. Man's sensations reflect the world around him. This point was important; from it followed the basic Marx-Engels proposition of historical materialism: "social consciousness *reflects* social being," as Lenin phrased it. Materialism relates to the relation-

[22] John Strachey, *The Great Awakening. Or: From Imperialism to Freedom. Encounter.* Pamphlet No. 5 (London, 1961), p. 7.

[23] New York, 1927, p. 311. Russian original in Lenin, *Sochineniya*, Second ed., Vol. XIII, pp. 11-292. The book was first published under one of Lenin's literary pseudonyms: V. Ilin.

ship between matter and man as an individual. Historical materialism relates to the relationship between society and man. The individual's relation to society, to his community, is not something evolved within, not self-generated, it reflects "social being," that is, social conditions. And social conditions vary. They are one thing for the capitalist, another for the worker and peasant. Thus, the whole argument centered around the class struggle and around revolution.

Bogdanov, however, insisted that "without consciousness there could have been no communion. Therefore, *social life in all its manifestations is a consciously psychic life. . . .*" It was not enough for man to have appeared on this earth. He had to want to associate, to form a community. Hence, society is a manifestation of "consciously psychic life." This was "empirio-monism" or "empirio-criticism," which undertook to integrate matter and mind and make them one, with mind in the controlling, primary position.

Lenin protested: "Materialism generally recognizes the objectively real being (matter) as existing independently of mind, sensation, experience, etc. Historical materialism recognizes social being as existing independently of the social consciousness of humanity." They are not one, he contended, they are independent, therefore plural. "You cannot eliminate even one basic assumption, one substantial part of this philosophy of Marxism, it is as if it were a solid block of steel," Lenin, the doctrinaire, stated, "without abandoning objective truth, without falling into the arms of bourgeois-reactionary falsehood." He called the Machist effort to unite matter and consciousness "conciliatory quackery." The Machists, he wrote, "are all wretchedly pulpy, a contemptible party of *middle-roaders* in philosophy, in every question confusing the materialist and idealist points of view." They claim to rise above materialism and idealism, "while *in fact* all these gentlemen *continuously* deviate toward idealism, and lead an incessant struggle against materialism." The expression "graduated flunkeys of theism," Lenin charged, "best befits Mach, Avenarius and their school."

The Mach philosophy drove materialist Marxists into a rage, for it threatened their socialism, their revolution. The Marxist wishes to alter material conditions, economic and social institutions, the state. The Machist maintained that all these physical things were in the eye of the beholder. Man is the thing, man not as bone, flesh, skin, and organs, but man as mind. The materialist called this idealism, the enemy and opposite of materialism. That way lay religion, surrender to the bourgeoisie, and betrayal of the revolution.

Potugin, a character in Turgenev's *Smoke*, written in 1866 (Lenin knew the novel well), says, "At that I called him an idealist, and then he was annoyed! He all but wept. I had to comfort him and promise that I would not betray him to his comrades. To earn the name of idealist—is that easy to bear?"

Idealism implied abandoning reality for illusion, for mysticism. In the lexicon of a certain type of nineteenth-century Russian intellectual it meant decadence. It made one a vague visionary, a superstitious obscurantist, a foe of progress and science.

To crush the idealistic Machists and their Russian brethren, Lenin did a colossal amount of work, and his book, which in fundamental ideas parallels Engels' *Anti-Duehring* without being as profound, shows it. He quoted extensively from Berkeley to prove that what the British bishop wrote in 1710 was plagiarized by Mach in 1872: "It is an absolute plagiarism from Berkeley." He studied Hume, Huxley, Hegel, Diderot, Fichte, and not only Mach and Mach's mentor Avenarius but dozens of minor commentaries on them, and not only Bogdanov, Bazarov, and Lunacharsky (subsequently Soviet Commissar of Education)[24] but dozens of lesser Russian Machists who would have been long forgotten if Lenin had not hoisted them into history with a pen dipped in gall. Lenin repeatedly gnawed at and worried every philosophic bone of contention between him and his political opponents. In retrospect it all looks like a tempest in a Russian émigré samovar. Lenin himself intimated that they quarreled over philosophy because the situation in Russia permitted them to do little practical work there. The whole Marx-Mach, Lenin-Bogdanov controversy reflected the pathological state of a small party led by a combative talent intolerant of opposition and frustrated because his organization, cut off from home base, was melting away from lack of accomplishment. The noise Lenin made in Paris or Geneva was in inverse ratio to the impact he made on Russia.

Lenin and Krupskaya had rented a small apartment in Geneva and began housekeeping. Lenin's sister Maria, who arrived from Russia, and Krupskaya's mother lived with them. Zinoviev and Kamenev settled in Geneva. Nevertheless, Krupskaya felt, "life in this small, quiet, petty-bourgeois town of Geneva seemed awfully dull. We longed to move to some big center. The Mensheviks and Social Revolutionaries had already moved to Paris. Ilyich hesitated. In Geneva, he said, the cost of living was not so high, and there were better facilities for studying. . . . Finally, Lyadov and Zhitomirsky arrived from Paris and began to persuade us to go there. They advanced arguments in support of this: 1. It would be possible to take part in the French movement; 2. Paris is a large city and there would be less spying; the latter argument convinced Ilyich."[25] David Zhitomirsky, a Bolshevik member, was a spy for the tsarist secret police.

"What the devil made us go to Paris?" Lenin protested after he had spent three and a half years in the great city, beginning in December, 1908. He hated it and so did Krupskaya. She has left some intimate notes on their life there. "Vladimir Ilyich took only very remote interest in the efforts we were

[24] V. Bazarov, co-translator of Marx into Russian, later served in the Soviet Gosplan, the federal Planning Commission. Alexander A. Bogdanov gave up politics soon after the Soviet regime was established and became the founder and director of the Moscow Institute of Blood Transfusion. He died from one of his experiments there.

[25] Krupskaya, *op. cit.*, p. 51.

making to fix up our new quarters. He had more important things to think about. We rented an apartment on the outskirts of the city . . . not far from the Parc Montsouris. . . . There was a room for my mother, one for Maria Ilyinishna [Lenin's sister] . . . and one for Vladimir Ilyich and myself and a living room. . . . The contempt with which the concierge looked upon our white deal tables, common chairs and stools was worth seeing. In our 'parlor' we had only a couple of chairs and a small table. It was not cozy by any means. . . . Life was full of turmoil and bustle in Paris. At that time Russian exiles were drawn to Paris from all parts. During this year Ilyich spent little time at home. Our people would sit in cafés until late in the night. . . . The conflict within the [Bolshevik] fraction was nerve-racking. I remember once Ilyich came home after a heated debate with the Otzovists [Recallers who favored a boycott of the Duma]. I could hardly recognize him, his face was so drawn and he could barely speak. We decided that we must take a week's holiday at Nice. . . . It was very difficult to study in Paris. The Bibliothèque Nationale was far from where we lived. Vladimir Ilyich would generally cycle there, but riding a bicycle in Paris was not what it was in the suburbs of Geneva. . . . Ilyich would get very tired from these rides. The library closed at lunch time. Then there was a lot of bother in getting books from the library. Ilyich railed against the library and against Paris. . . . In the end his bicycle was stolen. He used to leave it on the stairs at the house adjoining the Bibliothèque Nationale and paid the concierge ten centimes a day for this. When the bicycle was stolen the concierge declared he had not under- taken to watch the bicycle, but merely to allow Ilyich to put it up under the staircase. One had to be very careful riding a bicycle in Paris and in the suburbs. Once on his way to Juvissy, Ilyich collided with an automobile. He barely managed to jump clear but the bicycle was smashed." He had cycled to Juvissy to watch the flight of an airplane—it was 1910—and the car hit him. The owner was "a Viscount, the devil take him," he wrote his mother. Lenin sued. He won. In another letter home he reported that he had very much enjoyed his visit to the Grevin Museum of wax historical figures. But "Paris is in many ways a nasty hole," he told his sister Anna in a letter, and he could not adjust to it. He rarely played chess. Sometimes he and Krup- skaya walked in the Bois de Boulogne. Once they cycled out to the woods at Meudon; "delightful," he wrote his mother. In general, they were short of money. Krupskaya recalled that they ate horse meat; it was cheaper. Lenin tried to earn money by writing but often failed to find a publisher for his articles and books. In such situations he took a small salary from the party. Once his mother sent sturgeon and caviar from Saratov. He thanked her profusely. The present reminded him of the Volga, he said.

Lenin and the ladies of his household vacationed in the summer of 1909 in the village of Bonbon (Seine-et-Marne). "Ilyich did not work at Bonbon and we tried to refrain from discussing party affairs," Krupskaya wrote. The guests in the boardinghouse were little people, French petty bourgeois; "this mediocrity bored us. It was a good thing we were able to keep aloof from them. . . . On the whole, Ilyich had a good rest."

But soon again he was deep in the hot caldron of party quarrels. The Russian Social Democratic Labor Party was split into factions and the factions into fractions. For three weeks, from January 15 to February 5, 1910, the plenary session of the Central Committee of the party met in Paris with the avowed purpose of restoring unity. "The Long Plenum," Lenin called it in a letter to Gorky dated April 11, 1910. "Three weeks of suffering, every nerve is overstrained, a hundred thousand devils! To the serious and profound factors, unrecognized by many, have been added small, petty, has been added a mood of 'reconciliation in general' (without any clear idea, with whom, why, how), has been added hatred of the Bolshevik Center and its merciless ideological war, has been added, among the Mensheviks, squabbles and the desire to make scandals—and the result is a child with abscesses. Now here we are and suffering. Either—if all goes well—we lance the abscesses, drain the pus, and cure and raise the child. Or—if worse comes to worse—the child dies. Then we will live for a while without a child (that is, again set up a Bolshevik fraction) and then we will give birth to a healthier infant."[26]

What Lenin envisaged was the death of the party as a whole and the survival of the Bolshevik group, and, later, a new party. The prospects of curing the child, the party, through unity were dim indeed. Lenin abhorred compromise. He, in fact, deliberately widened the canyons. His letter to Gorky was somewhat disingenuous. Lenin wrote frequently to Gorky; he wanted his financial, literary, and organizational support. Gorky had a tremendous reputation among Russian common folk but he was a babe in the Russian socialist jungle full of saber-tooth publicists and orators. His love of the little man of factory and field brought him to Bolshevism yet, incapable of dogmatism, alien to the party schism that had goaded Lenin into the philosophical dispute, he leaned toward his friends, Bogdanov and Lunacharsky, whose culture and character he respected and whose effort to conciliate Marxism with religion, or at least with spiritual values, he could understand. (He had opposed the publication of Lenin's anti-Mach book.) Lenin did not wish to lose him. When Lenin wrote Gorky that if the child, the party, died, he would "again set up a Bolshevik fraction," he distorted. The Bolshevik fraction existed and its leader intended either to enslave the child or deliberately kill it. What mangled Lenin's nerves was the desire for conciliation and unity manifested at the Long Plenum by the majority consisting of the Mensheviks and some Bolsheviks. "Without any clear ideas, with whom, why, how," he exclaimed in his letter to Gorky. Just "reconciliation in general." Not with him, he implied. He could live for a while without the unruly, obstreperous child. "Then we will give birth to a healthier infant" whose subservience would give Lenin healthier nerves. Lenin now proceeded

[26] V. I. Lenin i A. M. Gorkii, pp. 49-52. The syntax of my translation follows Lenin's.

with plans for the artificial insemination of the youngster. It happened in Prague in January, 1912.

Lenin's mother was spending the summer of 1910 in Finland. He attended the Eighth Congress of the Second International in August in Copenhagen. He arranged to meet his mother in Stockholm. It was the last time he saw her. It was a sweet, tender ten-day reunion, a soft interlude in a life of hard struggle in which money played a major role. Lenin, as an organization man, never underestimated the power of money. It enabled him to publish newspapers and magazines, convene conferences, maintain party schools and offices, and move emissaries into and out of Russia.

Income from membership dues was minuscule. Wealthy fellow travelers helped with inadequate contributions. The Bolsheviks needed large sums to assert themselves against other fractions abroad and in Russia. They made a great financial coup by acquiring most of the Schmidt fortune.[27] Nikolai Pavlovich Schmidt, a nephew of Pavel Morozov, the Russian textile magnate and one of Bolshevism's big backers, was arrested in 1906 for the part his furniture factory played in the 1905 armed uprising in Moscow. The police tortured Schmidt and, according to Krupskaya, finally murdered him. Bertram D. Wolfe suggests that he died "either of torture or as a suicide" and later accepts the suicide version. Leonard Schapiro calls it suicide.[28] Krupskaya wrote that he left "his property to the Bolsheviks." Party or Bolsheviks? If the party was the heir, the Mensheviks would share the money with the Bolsheviks and other fractions, or, since the Mensheviks controlled the party at the time, the Bolsheviks would receive little or nothing.

Since Schmidt died officially intestate, his two sisters were his "legal heirs," and they actually acquired his fortune. The Bolsheviks now launched a daring adventure. A Bolshevik, acting under instructions, married the older sister with a view to thus obtaining the funds for his masters. His new affluence, however, apparently changed his social consciousness and he refused to be impoverished. Threats forced him to yield part of the wealth to the Bolshevik treasury. The younger sister, Elizaveta Pavlovna, was not yet of age. The Bolsheviks sent her a lover, Victor Taratuta, an officer of the Bolshevik group. He arranged a fictitious marriage between Elizaveta and another Bolshevik, Comrade Ignatiev. Krupskaya stated that "Elizaveta Pavlovna was actually the wife of another Bolshevik, Victor Taratuta."[29] Then the fictitious marriage, of which Krupskaya too wrote, was also bigamous. Most authorities call Taratuta "the lover." Whatever the ethics, the manipulation was effective, and the Bolsheviks, according to Schapiro,

[27] Bertram D. Wolfe, *Three Who Made a Revolution. A Biographical History* (New York, 1948), contains the most detailed account of the affairs, Chap. XXII.

[28] Leonard Schapiro, *The Communist Party of the Soviet Union* (New York, 1959), p. 107. Schapiro spells the name "Shmidt," Wolfe "Schmitt," Krupskaya "Schmidt." The pronunciation is the same in all cases; the name, being originally German, would be "Schmidt."

[29] Krupskaya, *op. cit.*, p. 25.

quoting a Soviet book by a top communist, received 280,000 roubles, about $140,000—an enormous sum for a puny organization. The operation could not have been conducted without Lenin. He directed even minor organizational activities.

For additional funds, the Bolshevik party, in 1907, staged an armed raid, in wild West fashion, on tsarist State Bank messengers escorted by mounted guards through the streets of Tiflis. Joseph Stalin managed the holdup from behind the scenes. The loot was fabulous, but much of it was in 500-rouble bank notes which were difficult to change because the serial numbers had been communicated to foreign banks. The best brains of the party, including Maxim Litvinov's (future Soviet Foreign Commissar), were mobilized for the task, and some of the notes were changed. Years later, "The 500-rouble notes which had not been changed were destroyed."[30]

These money acquisitions left the Bolsheviks in bad odor. The anti-Lenin majority at the Long Plenum in January, 1910, had voted for reconciliation and unity, concretely for disbanding fractions and factions. On this unrealistic condition, Lenin agreed at the sessions to turn over the moneys he had to three German socialist trustees: Karl Kautsky, Franz Mehring, and Clara Zetkin. But since the fractions remained intact in fact, Lenin kept the money. When the trustees, lost in the labyrinth of Russian émigré politics, proposed a peace conference to unite the embattled Russians, Rosa Luxemburg, a prominent left-wing German, originally Polish, socialist who had attended the 1907 Russian party congress in London, branded the peace conference a "fool idea" and added, "At this conference, naturally, only a handful of fighting cocks *living abroad* would rival in clamoring for the ear and soul of the German trustees, and to expect anything of *these* cocks is pure delusion. They are already so involved in quarrels and so embittered, that a general confab will merely give them an opportunity to unburden themselves of their old, oldest, and freshest insults."[31]

The unity "confab" never convened. Nevertheless, Lenin was subjected to heavy pressure from within the Russian party and by the international, especially German, socialist movement where it had become known that his funds were tainted. In June, 1911, accordingly, the trustees demanded that Lenin transfer the money to them. He gave up part of it.[32]

Lenin, now thoroughly disgusted with the Russian party's opposition to him, summoned a Bolshevik conference in Prague in January, 1912, attended by fourteen voting delegates (including two tsarist secret-police agents) chosen by him. After considerable debate—even in this minuscule,

[30] *Ibid.*, p. 51.

[31] Luise Kautsky (ed.), *Rosa Luxemburg Letters to Karl and Luise Kautsky from 1896 to 1918*, translated by Louis Lochner (New York, 1925), pp. 163-164. Quoted from *The Bolsheviks and the World War: The Origin of the Third International*, by Olga Hess Gankin and H. H. Fisher (Stanford University Press, Stanford, Calif., 1960), p. 25.

[32] Leonard Schapiro, *op. cit.*, pp. 121-122.

hand-picked "confab," differences of opinion arose—the conference proclaimed that it alone represented the Russian Social Democratic Labor Party and elected a new central committee to act for that party. The conference also asked the German trustees to return the money Lenin had transmitted to them. All other Russian socialists: the Mensheviks, the Latvians, the Jewish Bund, and the "non-faction" centrist unity faction led by Trotsky, who was editing the *Pravda (Truth)* newspaper in Vienna, with private funds from sympathizers, cried havoc and coup d'état. Deaf to their wailing, Lenin proceeded from Prague to Berlin to get his money back. He saw August Bebel, the foremost German Social Democratic leader, who gave him an unfriendly reception and "looked daggers" at him, Lenin told V. Adoratsky, then in Berlin, subsequently one of the editors of Lenin's collected works. Regarding Kautsky, Lenin spoke "very disrespectfully," Adoratsky wrote in his memoirs.[33] Lenin there conceived a hate for Kautsky. Before leaving Berlin, he decided to institute legal action against Kautsky and instructed Adoratsky to find an attorney for him. Whether the case ever came to court Adoratsky did not know. Much of the money remained with the trustees.

At this juncture Lenin made a major move. He left Paris and settled in Cracow, Austria-Hungary. "Almost Russia," he wrote his mother on July 4, 1912, announcing his arrival several days earlier. "And the Jews resemble the Russians, and the Russian border is nine versts"—six miles—"away. The women are barefoot and wear gaily colored dresses—just as in Russia." In the autumn he told his sister Anna that, "We are living better here than in Paris,—my nerves rest, more literary work,—fewer squabbles, it will be easier for us to meet,—if there is no war and I think there won't be." In November, 1912, he mentioned, in a letter to his sister Maria, also staying in Saratov, that there was much talk of war in which case, "it would be necessary to move to Vienna" (it apparently did not occur to him that Austria-Hungary might be at war with Russia and, far from going to Vienna, he would, as a Russian subject, be interned) or go to Stockholm.[34]

A photograph of Lenin[35] taken at the mountain resort of Zakopane in Galicia in 1913—he was forty-three—gives the impression of an elderly gentleman deserving the name "Starik" (Old Man) with which he sometimes signed letters to comrades. He had ten more years of life to achieve greatness.

From Cracow, and from other places abroad, Lenin corresponded regularly with his mother, his sister Anna and her husband Mark Elizarov, his sister Maria (Olga, his closest sister, a university student at St. Petersburg, had died of typhus and erysipelas on May 8, 1891. On October 5, 1893, on his

[33] *Vospominaniya o Vladimire Ilyiche Lenine (Reminiscences about Vladimir Ilyich Lenin)*, Vol. 1, pp. 271-272.

[34] All personal letters of this period are translated from Lenin, *Sochineniya*, Fourth ed., Vol. 37 (Moscow, 1957), *Letters to Relatives 1893-1922*, pp. 400 *et seq.*

[35] *Vospominaniya o Vladimire Ilyiche Lenine (Reminiscences about Vladimir Ilyich Lenin)*, Vol. 1, opposite p. 288.

first visit to the capital, Lenin wrote his mother about his visit to the Volkov Cemetery where Olga was buried. "Everything is in good order," he said. "The cross as well as the wreath."), and his brother Dmitri (Mitya). These letters were brief, banal, dutiful yet not without warmth but lacking any intimation of stature or literary distinction. One, of December 21, 1912, from Cracow to his mother in Saratov, conveys the flavor of many others: "Dear Mamochka! Today I received your letter and Anna's. Many thanks. Greetings to all of you for the holidays [Christmas]. I wish you the happiest holidays in good health and good mood. Today I received a post card from Maria [she had been arrested and exiled to Vologda in North Russia] with a view of the Vologda River. Judging by the postcard it's not such a bad little town. She writes that she's arranged her household pretty well. If Mitya is with you, a big greeting to him. To Mark likewise. I hope he's already well? Anna's handwriting is still bad. It's certainly a pity about her finger. We are all well. We intend to celebrate the Russian holidays more than the local ones. [The Russian Christmas came thirteen days after the local, Austrian Christmas.] A strong embrace, and I wish you all the best. Your V. Ul."[36]

In the next letter to his mother, with a postscript to Anna, he thanked her for the big package of sweets that arrived in February, 1913. "Now we'll celebrate 'New Year' once again. . . . We are having wonderful winter weather without snow. I bought ice-skates and am skating with great excitement. Reminds me of Simbirsk and Siberia. First time I've skated abroad. A strong hug for you, my dear, and I send a very big greeting to Anna. E. V. [his mother-in-law] and Nadya [Krupskaya] too [send greetings]. Your V. Ul."

He was well, and in good spirits, but Nadya was not. She revealed the facts of her illness in a letter to Lenin's mother on May 3, 1913, from Cracow, just before they left for Poronin, a village near Zakopane, where they would spend the summer. "I am an invalid and tire very quickly. I took electric treatments for a whole month, my neck has not become smaller, but my eyes have become normal and the palpitations of the heart have diminished. Here in the clinic for nervous diseases treatment is free and the doctors are very attentive. . . . I am eager to get to the village as soon as possible. Although we live on the edge of town and there are vegetable gardens opposite our house, and the other day a nightingale sang, it's still a city, the children yell, soldiers ride back and forth, carts . . ." Ten days later Lenin told his mother that Krupskaya had "Basedow's disease (which worries me a lot). . . . The village," he added, "is almost typically Russian. Straw roofs, poverty. Women and children are barefoot. . . . I hope the tranquillity and mountain air will improve Nadya's health. We lead a country life here—wake early and to bed almost with the chickens. Walk to the post office and railway station every day."

Krupskaya took electric treatments and iron, but her illness persisted.

[36] Lenin, op. cit., Fourth ed., Vol. 37, p. 406.

Lenin wrote his brother Dmitri, the physician, who, diagnosing at long distance, said no operation was necessary. But people kept telling Lenin that his wife might go blind, might have to lie in bed for a year or a year and a half without moving. Krupskaya, in transmitting these reports to Lenin's mother, insisted she was not that ill and would get well during the summer. To this letter, dated May 25, 1913, Lenin wrote a three-line postscript: "Dear Mamochka, A big hug to you and regards to all. Many thanks to Mitya for his letters. I am trying to persuade Nadya to go to Bern. She doesn't want to. But now she is slightly better. Your V. U."

Bern was the home of Professor Theodor Kocher, a Swiss surgeon who specialized in Basedow's disease operations. The disease is thyrotoxicosis or exophthalmic goiter or toxic goiter. It causes eye bulging, enlargement of the thyroid gland and neck, capricious appetite, extreme nervousness, palpitations of the heart, and energy drain. In June, therefore, Lenin, overcoming his wife's objections to surgery, went with her to Bern. The operation lasted "almost three hours without an anesthetic," Lenin wrote his mother on July 26. "While I was in the hospital," Krupskaya noted in her memoirs, Lenin lectured at Zurich, Geneva, Lausanne, and Bern on the problem of national minorities, a subject absorbing his attention. Then husband, and wife whose goiter complaint was never cured, returned to the mountain village of Poronin.

On June 16, 1875, five years after Lenin was born in Simbirsk on the banks of the Volga, a baby girl was born in Paris on the banks of the Seine. Her father, Theodor Stephan, a well-known French opera singer, and her mother Natalie, half-French and half-Scot, also an actress, named the child Inessa-Elizabeth. Theodor died young leaving his widow with three daughters and no finances. An aunt, who had been teaching music and French in Moscow, took Inessa and Inessa's grandmother to Russia where the girl was brought up. At seventeen she graduated as a schoolteacher and at eighteen she married Alexander Yevgenyevich Armand, son of a rich woolens manufacturer—employer of 1,200 workingmen in a factory at Pushkino, a village north of Moscow. The Armands were a Russified French family who had joined the Orthodox Church. The marriage certificate, dated October 3, 1893, giving the name of the church and the priest and Inessa's religion as Anglican and her young husband's as Orthodox, was preserved in the remarkable Russian archives and is now in the Marx-Lenin Institute in Moscow.

These and numerous other well-documented facts appear in a biography entitled *Comrade Inessa*, by Pavel Podlyashchuk,[37] who not only mined stacks of ancient papers throughout Russia but interviewed three of Inessa's surviving children, themselves grandparents when he talked with them. The book also contains photographs of Inessa. At twenty she was a great French

[37] Moscow, 1963, 165 pages.

beauty: fine oval face, curly hair, intellectual forehead, eyes far apart and wide open, finely arched eyebrows, a strong nose, sensuous mouth, and rounded chin that tells of passion and determination.

The Armands belonged to the top rung of Moscow's high capitalist society together with the Morozovs, Ryabushinskys, and Guchkovs. Inessa's husband Alexander engaged in charitable work and was a member of the Moscow Provincial Zemstvo Assembly, a form of grass-roots self-government promoted by the liberals. He founded a school for village children where Inessa taught.

In her youth Inessa was very religious and very rebellious. Reading *War and Peace* at the age of fifteen, her heart protested against Natasha's role as a female here to produce children. But five years after her marriage she was the mother of a son and two daughters. That year, 1898, on vacation in the Crimea, she read a book by Peter L. Lavrov, a leading ideologue of the Russian Narodniks. ". . . it is long since I have read a book that so corresponds to my own views," she wrote in a letter to the family. In 1901 she gave birth to another daughter and in 1903, in Switzerland, to a son. Near the shores of Lake Geneva she read Lenin's *The Development of Russian Capitalism*.

That Inessa was drawn to such writings echoed a storm within. In 1903 she left her husband, by agreement, and went to live with his younger brother Vladimir, taking the five children with her. Still restive, the 1905 revolution spoke to her soul. The police arrested her on February 7, 1905. Searching her quarters, officers found a Browning revolver with ammunition and "publications of the Social Revolutionary and Social Democratic parties." Released, nevertheless, on June 3, she became an active revolutionary propagandist among women. A photograph in the biography taken at Mezen in Archangel province in 1908, shows Inessa in a floor-length dress, hands folded in her lap, thick blond braids resting coquettishly on her bosom, and, forming an arc around and behind her five young men, in rakish poses, one with white collar and tie and black hat tipped at a flirtatious angle, another in a Napoleonic hand-in-jacket posture, and all looking like gay Lotharios rather than the revolutionary deportees they, and she, were. Vladimir, her lover, followed her into exile. Alexander, still the legal husband, took care of the children and supplied funds to her and Vladimir. But when Vladimir contracted tuberculosis and left for Switzerland, Inessa escaped from Russia and joined him there. He died two weeks after her arrival. In 1909 she was in Brussels and in 1910 she enrolled as a student in the Sorbonne University in Paris. That year Lenin met her. He was forty, she thirty-five. She was strong, bold, a rebel untamed, mature, and her sculptured face, seen in a large photograph in the biography, has a tinge of frustration, a touch of sadness, of resignation, but also of eagerness, of zeal, of wonderment. She was a very attractive woman. Lenin felt the attraction. She began to frequent the Lenin apartment in Paris. "I see her now," a contemporary wrote in 1921, "leaving the home of our Lenins. Her temperament was impressive. It seemed that her life was an inexhaustible well. She was a hot bonfire of revolution, and the red feather in her hat was like the tongue of its flame."

Inessa became a friend of the Lenin family. Krupskaya's memoirs mention her often: Inessa lectured at a Bolshevik party school near Paris on political economy; "Vladimir Ilyich wrote out the speech" he delivered at the funeral of the Lafargues "and Inessa translated it" into French; in 1912, "All our people in Paris at that time longed terribly to go to Russia; there were Inessa, Safarov, and others. We were moving" to Cracow—"a little nearer to Russia"; "Inessa . . . visited us in Zvezhintsa and stayed with us for two days. . . . She and Ilyich discussed the whole plan of work" she was to do in St. Petersburg; "While the conference was in progress"—in Poronin in September, 1913—"Inessa arrived. She was arrested in September, 1912, with a false passport. Conditions in prison were very hard and undermined her health; she showed symptoms of tuberculosis, but she had not lost any of her energy"; "All of us, the entire Cracow group, became very much attached to Inessa. She always seemed to be in good spirits and full of vigor. . . . It seemed cosier and livelier when Inessa was present . . . we were very glad to have Inessa . . . she seemed to radiate warmth and ardor. Ilyich, Inessa, and myself did a lot of walking. . . . Inessa loved music and made us attend Beethoven concerts. She herself was a good musician and played many of Beethoven's compositions very well indeed. Ilyich was particularly fond of the *Sonate Pathétique* and he always asked her to play it. . . . There was nothing in Cracow which could provide Inessa with an outlet for her abundant energies. She decided to make the rounds of our groups abroad and deliver a series of lectures and then to settle in Paris. . . . In January 1914 Malinovsky came to Cracow and he and Ilyich went to Paris." Lenin returned to Poronin about a month later.

The thirty-fifth volume of Lenin's collected works presents a selection of his letters and telegrams from 1912 to 1922;[38] it includes two he wrote to Inessa in 1913, four in 1914, two in 1915, six in 1916, and nine in the first three months of 1917 before he left Switzerland for Russia. None of these contains a declaration of love or an avowal of affection. But in the two 1913 letters and the first 1914 letter Lenin addressed Inessa as "thou"; in the second 1914 letter she is likewise "thou" but one "you" slips in. The third 1914 letter has no second person pronouns; "thou" is used throughout the fourth. In subsequent letters the "thou" disappears. She becomes "you." In all of Lenin's published correspondence, he never addressed anybody outside his immediate family with the intimate "thou." He was closely associated with many comrades, men and women, for many years; they

[38] Lenin, *op. cit.*, Fourth ed., Vol. 35 (Moscow, 1950). Lenin's letters to Inessa of Jan. 17, 1915, and January 24, 1915, from Bern were first published in the Moscow magazine *Bolshevik*, Issue No. 13, 1939; his letters to her of Nov. 20, 1916, Nov. 30, 1916, Jan. 19, 1917, two letters of Jan. 30, 1917, and one of Feb. 19, 1917, all from Zurich, were published in *Bolshevik*, Issue No. 1, 1949.

remained "you." Inessa was the single exception. Why he shifted from "thou" to "you" in her case is a matter for surmise. The "you" appeared after the commencement of the First World War. Greater caution? The Soviet editors of this 1950 volume, in which Lenin's letters to Inessa are published, most of them for the first time, chose to eliminate the salutation from some, the closing from others, and salutation, closing, and signature from several, although they were certainly present in the original. This is a remarkable procedure even for communist censors. It is therefore impossible to know what else was deleted at the beginning and end of the letters. In fact, none but the guardians of the Moscow archives could reveal whether any of Lenin's letters to Inessa were suppressed completely. Those now available reflect considerable attentiveness and, for Lenin, unusual playfulness, slight though it was. Normally he began all letters with "Dear Friend," in Russian. In one letter to Inessa he wrote "my dear friend," and in a second "Dear Friend" in English. His customary ending of a letter was the Russian for, "I firmly shake your hand, V.I." or "V.U." In one to Inessa he wrote, "I firmly, firmly, shake your hand, Your Lenin." In another he finished with the English, "Friendly shake hands, W.I." The body of his letters to Inessa was in Russian; they were, with one exception, very long, serious, and political. They would have flattered her by the tasks he assigned her, the importance of the ideas he shared with her, and the attention he paid to her work, her suggestions. While he was in Cracow and she in Paris in December, 1913, she was his representative there. Arguing against the Mensheviks and those Bolsheviks who, beginning about 1911, urged the liquidation of secret, subversive "underground" party work and the formation of a legal mass workers' party ("liquidators" he called them), Lenin exclaimed in a letter, "Comedians! They chase after words, not comprehending how devilishly complicated and cunning life is and how it creates *altogether new* forms. . . . Most people (99 percent of the bourgeoisie, 98 percent of the liquidators, about 60-70 percent of the Bolsheviks) do not know how *to think*, and merely *memorize* WORDS. They memorized the word: "Underground. . . . But how *its forms*"—the methods of underground work —"should be altered in the new situation, how for this purpose it is necessary to study and think anew, that we do not understand. . . . It interests me very much whether thou canst make our people understand this. Write in detail . . ."

Again from Cracow to Paris, Lenin instructed Inessa to take up the fight against "that lousy, foul nationalistic petty bourgeois who, under the flag of Marxism, preaches the *division* of workers according to nationality, a separate national organization for Ukrainian workers. Thou understandst why *I* cannot send such a draft" attack "in my name." He was a Great Russian and it would look like chauvinism for him to condemn a Ukrainian. He wanted Inessa to find a Ukrainian sponsor. "Rewrite my draft (I of course agree with *all* changes, but my direct protest against the division by nationalities must remain). . . . This must be done tactfully, quickly, against Yurkevich and *without his knowledge* for that rogue will foul things up."

In June, 1914, Inessa settled in Fiume with her children and from there she sent Lenin, in Poronin, a novel by V. Vinnichenko, a Ukrainian. He read it and wrote, "What rubbish and folly! Collect the largest possible number of 'horrors,' tie together 'vice' and 'syphilis' and romantic villainy and extortion of money by blackmail (with the sister of the fleeced victim becoming a girl friend) and the trial of a doctor. All this with hysteria, eccentricities, and with pretenses at his own theory about the organization of prostitutes." That was Lenin's characterization of the novel, but *Rech*, a Russian daily, had declared that the book was an imitation of Dostoyevsky and had good things in it. "In my opinion," Lenin commented, "imitation is certainly there, supremely bad imitation of the supremely bad Dostoyevsky. In isolation, of course, all the 'horrors' described by Vinnichenko do occur in life. But to bring them all together and *in this way*—means to paint evil black, frighten your own imagination and the reader's, to 'forget' yourself and him.

"It happened that I once spent a night with a sick comrade (white delirium)—and once I had to 'dissuade' a comrade from committing suicide (after an attempt) and some years later he did commit suicide. Both these reminiscences are à la Vinnichenko. But both these cases were tiny bits of the lives of the two comrades. And this pretentious, double-dyed fool Vinnichenko, in love with himself, made out of this a complete collection of horrors—a sort of 'twopence-worth of horrors.' Brrr. Filth, worthless, a pity to have lost time reading it." So the letter ends. It was not written by a man indifferent to his correspondent. He sometimes took such pain when writing to Gorky. (The suicide was Fedoseyev, an exile in Lenin's village in Siberia. "Better don't wish me comrades in Shushu who are intellectuals," Lenin wrote his sister Anna on January 24, 1898, apropos of·the incident.)

A Russian socialist "unity" conference was scheduled for Brussels in July, 1914, and Lenin, in Galicia, could not attend. "I am sure," he wrote her, "that thou art one of those persons who unfold, become firmer, grow stronger and bolder when they occupy a responsible position—and therefore I stubbornly *do not believe* the pessimists who say that thou—could hardly—Nonsense and nonsense! I don't believe it! Thou wilt manage very well."

On the line she was to take: "The essence is, in my opinion, to prove that we"—the Bolsheviks—"are the party. . . . In January, 1912, we excluded a group of liquidators from the party. Did they form a *better* party? No party. . . . Either accept our conditions or no rapprochement, not to speak of unity." That was the essential Lenin: coexistence on his conditions.

Later, Inessa sent Lenin the outline of a pamphlet she planned to write on women's rights. He criticized it in a letter dated Bern, January 17, 1915.

He advised her to discard her suggestion of "free love for women." That is "a bourgeois demand," not a proletarian one. "Free love" was a vague concept, he contended. Readers would understand it to mean "freedom from a serious approach to love," "freedom from child-bearing," and "freedom for adultery." That was what he called bourgeois "free love." His last sentence read, "The point is not what you *subjectively*" understand by free love. The point is "the *objective logic* of class relations in matters of love."

Lenin, in Bern, returned to the subject exactly a week later after Inessa had challenged his criticism. "Good," he wrote, "let's look at the question again." He had stated the three freedoms of bourgeois free love. The proletarian conditions would be: freedom from financial accounting in love, from economic worries, from religious prejudices, and so forth. She had written in her letter, "Even fleeting passion and sexual intercourse . . . are more poetic and cleaner" than "a kiss without love" of husband and wife. "I agree," he replied. "But you compare 'fleeting' (why fleeting?) 'passion' (why not love?)" with bad husband and wife relations. "A (fleeting) kiss without love is contrasted with a married kiss without love. Strange." He preferred "the contrast between vulgar and filthy petty-bourgeois-intelligentsia-peasant marriage without love and civil proletarian marriage with love (plus, IF YOU ABSOLUTELY INSIST, a statement that fleeting sex-passion may be filthy and may be clean)." His real preference, however, was for something else: "The truth is I am not inclined to engage in controversy. I would gladly throw away this letter and put the matter off till we have a talk." She was then living in Soerenberg, canton of Lucerne, a two-hour journey, approximately, from Bern. It is not known whether the talk took place. (From June to September, 1915, Lenin and Krupskaya resided in Soerenberg.)

Coming from Lenin, the conservative, the declaration that he would "gladly throw away this letter" and "have a talk," seems very meaningful, rather impulsive; free. In man-woman relations Lenin was a restrained, nineteenth-century Victorian. He put that stamp on Soviet Russia. Indeed, he was in most respects, and in most of his ideas, a son of the nineteenth century. Bolshevism made him a political radical, but political radicalism may cohabit with personal conservatism. Lenin spent his passions on politics, and there is no indication that much remained for love. Krupskaya, especially after she became ill, but before that as well, could hardly have aroused romantic feelings. He and she lived like two good comrades together. Then Inessa emerged, attractive, exciting, Russian yet French, sharing his politics, working for him, staying close by. That she was a light in his life is certain; Krupskaya's memories and his letters permit no doubt of it.

Lenin had few if any friends; he had many comrades. Politics often interfered with friendship. Writing to Gorky on January 10, 1913, about his disagreement with Bogdanov, Barzarov, and Lunacharsky on matters of philosophy, Lenin declared, "Have they understood that *Marxism* is more serious and deeper than they had thought, you cannot jeer at it, as Alexinsky did, or slight it as something dead, as the others did? *If* they have understood—a thousand greetings to them, and everything personal (inevitably introduced during a sharp struggle) vanishes in a minute. Well, and if they have not understood, nor learned, then make no demands: friendship is friendship and duty is duty. Against any attempt to revile Marxism or confuse the policy of the workers' party we will fight without sparing life." Now, late in 1916, Inessa Armand intimated that she inclined toward defense of one's country. To Lenin this was poison. He sought to save their relationship by convincing her. "Regarding defense of country," he wrote her in December, 1916. "It would be extremely unpleasant to me if we were to drift apart. Let us try again to come to terms." They did. She yielded to him.

The April, 1952, issue of *Preuves*, a political monthly, published an article entitled "Alexandra Kollontai," by Marcel Body. Kollontai was a prominent Russian Bolshevik; Lenin corresponded with her often before the revolution. He appointed her People's Commissar of State Charity in his first Cabinet. In 1923 she became Soviet Minister to Norway. Marcel Y. Body served as First Secretary of the legation and saw Madame Kollontai almost every day. The *Preuves* article is a memoir about Kollontai. She and Body often took walks in the outskirts of Oslo. Once they talked about Lenin's death at such an early age. "He could not survive Inessa Armand," Kollontai said. "The death of Inessa precipitated the illness which was fatal."

"Inessa?" Body exclaimed. He had never heard the name.

"Yes," Kollontai confirmed, "in 1921 when they brought her corpse from the Caucasus (where she died of typhus) and we marched in the funeral cortege, Lenin was unrecognizable. He walked with his eyes closed and every moment we thought he might fall to the ground."

Kollontai added that in Paris and elsewhere Krupskaya was "au courant." She knew that Lenin "was very attached to Inessa and many times she expressed the intention of going away. 'No, stay,'" Lenin said to his wife. Krupskaya would have stayed for the same reasons that many wives stay in such circumstances, and, too, because he was not only her husband, perhaps not chiefly her husband, he was her political leader, and she sacrificed herself to his needs even if they included Inessa. Staying meant serving the communist movement, her strongest passion. Wives often subordinate their personalities to the careers of lesser men. Finally, Lenin asked her to stay. If he had asked her to go she would have gone without a word or whimper in his presence: party discipline.

Angelica Balabanoff, then Secretary of the Third International (Comintern), also described Lenin at Inessa's funeral in her little book of reminiscences: "His entire appearance, not only his face, expressed such sadness that no one even dared to greet him with a nod of the head. It was clear that he wished to be alone with his tragedy. He seemed to have become smaller: his cap covered his face, his eyes seemed to have disappeared in the painfully restrained tears. And every time when our group was pushed by a movement of the crowd he let himself be pushed without any resistance, as though he were thankful for being brought nearer the corpse."

Inessa died on September 24, 1920, in Nalchik, a delightful mountain town in the North Caucasus region of the Kabardinians and Balkarians where she had gone for her health. She lies buried in the Red Square by the Kremlin wall near John Reed in a plot adjacent to the one containing the remains of Zhdanov, Frunze, Sverdlov, Djerzhinsky, and Stalin. Inessa was not that important, except apparently to Lenin. Her grave is now in the shadow of his mausoleum.

∽∿∽∿∽∿∽∿∽

Lenin wrote a letter to Maxim Gorky on March 24, 1908, from Geneva, and added a postscript: "I enclose some *important* information about spying at your place," in Capri. The tsarist secret police would naturally have wanted to know what the novelist's revolutionary friends were saying. Lenin, on guard himself, put Gorky on guard.

"In the spring of 1911 we at last succeeded in establishing our own Party school near Paris," Krupskaya wrote in her memoirs. The intention was to rival the Otzovists' or Recallers' school in Bologna, Italy, where Mensheviks like Plekhanov and Theodor Dan lectured, and the Machist philosophers' school in Capri. "Our own party" school proposed to enlist workers from Russia as pupils. One of those was Roman Malinovsky who arrived from Kiev, Krupskaya reported. "He had a beautiful voice." He was a metal worker active in his trade union. Lenin wished to court this new type of proletarian professional revolutionist.

Malinovsky rose rapidly from the meager Bolshevik ranks. Lenin selected him to be one of the twelve delegates to the 1912 Prague conference which usurped the leadership of the Russian Socialist Party and made unity forever impossible. At that conference Roman Malinovsky was chosen a member of the seven-man Bolshevik Central Committee. He now wielded considerable influence. In 1912, accordingly, the Bolsheviks succeeded in electing him as one of their six deputies to the Fourth Imperial Duma.

In December, 1912, Lenin called the Bolshevik Duma members to Cracow for a conference. "Malinovsky arrived first . . . Malinovsky gave one the impression of being a very intelligent and influential worker," Krupskaya's *Memories* state. "Malinovsky, Petrovsky, and Badayev," Lenin wrote Gorky on January 1, 1913, "send you their hearty greetings and best wishes. The Cracow base has proved useful." Malinovsky came to Cracow frequently and stayed in Lenin's house. In 1914, Lenin and Malinovsky traveled together from Cracow to Paris to Brussels for a congress of Lettish socialists. "In Paris Malinovsky delivered what in Ilyich's opinion was a very able report on the work of the [Bolshevik] Duma fraction," Krupskaya recalled.

On May 8, 1914, Malinovsky resigned his seat in the Duma and went to Germany, avoiding Cracow. It now transpired that throughout the entire period of his membership, first in the ranks and then in the top leadership, of the Bolshevik party, he had been an agent of the tsarist Okhrana and had kept the secret police informed on Lenin's and the group's activities and writings. Malinovsky was always on the side of extremism, of splits with the Mensheviks and liquidators. Lenin favored such policies; he therefore favored Malinovsky. The tsarist police also favored those policies. They weakened the subversive movement. Dozens of Bolsheviks, Mensheviks and others who opposed splits, who urged unity, were reported by Malinovsky and arrested.

Many persons had warned Lenin about Malinovsky, had told him Malinovsky was a spy. Among them was Nikolai Bukharin who came to Cracow. Lenin turned a deaf ear. Krupskaya affirmed that "Vladimir Ilyich thought it utterly impossible for Malinovsky to have been an agent provocateur. Only once did a doubt flash across his mind. I remember one day in Poronin, we were returning from the Zinovievs and talked about these rumors. Suddenly Ilyich stopped at a little bridge that we were crossing and said, 'It may be true!' and his face expressed anxiety." But Krupskaya reassured him: "What are you talking about, it's nonsense." At that, "Ilyich calmed down and began to abuse the Mensheviks, saying that they were unscrupulous as to the means they employed in the struggle against the Bolsheviks. He had no other doubts on this question."

Following the fall of the Tsar, the Provisional government, then the Soviet government, studied the Okhrana files, held hearings, and established, on the basis of rich, incontrovertible data, that Malinovsky had been a well-paid secret agent within the Bolshevik leadership. "But I never saw through that scoundrel Malinovsky. That was a very mysterious affair, Malinovsky," Lenin said to Gorky after he had become head of the Soviet government.[39]

It was mysterious indeed, for in 1918 Malinovsky, who had been living in Europe on an opulent separation payment given him by the Okhrana after rumors destroyed his usefulness to it, voluntarily returned to Soviet Russia and surrendered to the Bolshevik authorities. He was tried and shot.

Why did he return? The tsarist police archives had already been opened and he had been officially branded a spy.

Father Georgi Gapon, the Orthodox priest who organized the peaceful, religious demonstration of St. Petersburg workers who were shot down, with their wives and children, on January 9, 1905 (Bloody Sunday), did so on an assignment from the tsarist government. He had been asked to cooperate in organizing government trade unions to counteract true trade unions. The plan, fathered for the whole country by S. B. Zubatov, a high police official, was called "police socialism" by its opponents, and "Zubatovism." But Bloody Sunday shook Father Gapon; Lenin quoted him as saying, "We have no Tsar

[39] Maxim Gorky, *Days with Lenin* (New York, 1932), p. 58.

any more. Rivers of blood separate the Tsar from the people. Long Live Freedom."[40] Lenin credited the stories of Gapon's ties with the police but that, he added, did not exclude the possibility of Gapon's being "a sincere Christian socialist" whom Bloody Sunday converted to revolution.[41] Lenin took cognizance of the skeptics who questioned Gapon's bona fides, but ruled that "only facts, facts, and facts could decide, and the facts have decided this question in favor of Gapon."[42] A few weeks later Lenin wrote, "The proletariat has broken through the frame of police Zubatovism, and the entire mass membership of the legal workers organization, formed to fight the revolution, has, together with Gapon, taken the road of revolution."[43]

Shortly after Bloody Sunday, Father Gapon left Russia and announced his allegiance to the Russian Social Democratic Labor Party. He had several talks with Lenin in Geneva. "He made an impression on me of a wise and enterprising person undoubtedly devoted to the revolution although, unfortunately, without a sustained revolutionary philosophy," Lenin declared in a speech on April 23, 1905.[44] Gapon also talked with Plekhanov and exiled Social Revolutionaries and convened a conference in Geneva on April 2, 1905, of foreign representatives of eighteen Russian revolutionary parties with a view to forming a united front for an insurrection. Lenin attended. Subsequently, Gapon returned to Russia and was accused by anti-tsarists of resuming his earlier relations with the Russian police. The Social Revolutionary Party thereupon sentenced him to death as a traitor; the sentence by hanging was carried out in April, 1906, under the supervision of Pinhas Rutenberg, later a prominent Zionist in America and hydraulic engineer in Palestine.

Did Malinovsky think of Gapon when he returned of his own free will to Soviet Russia in 1918? Did he recall Lenin's favorable opinion of the police-priest turned revolutionary? When the rumors of Malinovsky's spy career were being investigated by Bolshevik headquarters, Malinovsky "in a state of suspense . . . idled around Poronin," Krupskaya recalled. Did Malinovsky confess to Lenin? He had committed rape, or some other crime, in young manhood and, with this as blackmail, the police recruited him for espionage. But the revolution, Malinovsky might have argued, converted him as it had Gapon; contact with Lenin and other Bolsheviks transformed him into an honest revolutionary. Lenin, so persuaded of the all-conquering force of revolution, might have given him a nod of comprehension. Lenin did not denounce him. Was Malinovsky throwing himself on the mercy of Lenin when he returned to Russia in 1918? During the First World War Malinovsky was interned in Germany as an enemy alien. Lenin and Krupskaya, fully aware of Malinovsky's withdrawal from the party and the Duma, sent him food and clothing, and revolutionary literature for distribution among fellow prisoners.

[40] Lenin, *op. cit.*, Second ed., Vol. VII, p. 80.
[41] *Ibid.*, pp. 84-85.
[42] *Ibid.*, p. 89.
[43] *Ibid.*, p. 106.
[44] *Ibid.*, p. 288.

Is this what impelled Malinovsky to expect friendly treatment from Soviet Chairman Lenin? At his Soviet trial Malinovsky, pleading that Lenin could not have been ignorant of his police assignment, asked to be confronted with Lenin. The Bolshevik leader did not appear.

ᴅᴇᴄᴏᴅᴏᴄᴏᴄᴏ

Spy-ridden, riven by dissension, the Bolshevik party was a broken reed. Lenin in Cracow repeatedly tried to correct the line of the St. Petersburg *Pravda*, the party's organ; as often as it zigged toward him it zagged away in the direction of legality and unity with other socialist groups. But the socialists remained divided.

It was in this disarray that the revolutionary forces confronted the First World War, the greatest cataclysm of Russian history.

The tsarist monarchy was decadent and the landlord class a brake on progress. Nevertheless, Russia had made notable advances. Industry, aided by foreign investments, was expanding with impressive speed. Prime Minister Stolypin's 1906 land reform, given a generation to take nationwide effect, would have created a stabilizing middle stratum of farmers more productive than the inadequately equipped peasants, more ambitious than the estate-owning Oblomovs. Actual and potential economic gains, plus the regime's rigorous repression in the years after the 1905 rebellion, worked havoc among the revolutionists. In an article dated December 12, 1914, Lenin alluded to the growth of Russian capitalism and admitted that "now" there was "little" revolutionary spirit, "but it exists."[45] *The Communist Party of the Soviet Union* by Leonard Schapiro, citing a Soviet book, gives the membership of the united Russian Social Democratic Labor Party in 1905 as 8,400. Disillusionment, defections, and persecution in subsequent years reduced it still further.

The war gave Lenin new hope. He desired his country's defeat. "For us *Russians*, from the point of view of the working class of *Russia*," he wrote on October 17, 1914, "there is not the slightest doubt, absolutely no doubt that the *least* evil would be now and immediately—the *defeat* of Tsarism in this war. For Tsarism is a hundred times worse than Kaiserism."[46]

A decade earlier Lenin had hoped that Russia would lose the war to "progressive" Japan. Now he preferred Germany to the Tsar. In both instances, he considered military disaster the necessary prelude to revolution. The revolutionaries themselves were incapable of overthrowing the monarchy, for, Lenin said, Russia is "the most backward country in which an immediate socialist revolution is impossible."[47] An outside instrument—the foreign foe—would first have to cripple the tsarist state. Here again was Lenin's theory of the spark. In this case not the European proletariat but a European autocrat would ignite the Russian revolution against autocracy.

[45] *Ibid.*, 1914-1915, Second ed., Vol. XVIII, p. 81.
[46] *Ibid.*, pp. 55-56.
[47] *Ibid.*, p. 170.

Except as a stimulus to revolution, Lenin was indifferent to the outcome of the war. He declared, "The war is being waged for the division of colonies and the robbery of foreign territory; thieves have fallen out—and to refer to the defeats at a given moment of one of the thieves in order to identify the interests of the thieves with the interests of the nation or the fatherland is an unconscionable bourgeois lie."[48]

Yet he refused to advocate peace. Marxism taught him, he said, "the impossibility of abolishing wars without abolishing social classes and establishing socialism." Of course, "History knows many wars which, despite all the horrors, brutality, calamity, and suffering inescapably connected with every war were progressive, that is, they benefitted the evolution of mankind."[49] The war that began in 1914 was no such war. Nevertheless, "At the moment," he wrote, "the slogan of peace is, in my opinion, wrong. It is the slogan of Philistines and clergymen. The proletarian slogan should be: civil war."

To promote civil war, Lenin urged fraternization with enemy troops at the front, new illegal revolutionary organizations, and revolutionary strikes. Civil war, he knew, required much preliminary propaganda for "in Russia—at least a majority of the well-to-do and middle peasantry and a very considerable portion of the poor peasants were evidently under the spell of bourgeois imperialism." Peasants constituted the bulk of the Tsar's armies. Agitation had to be directed against national patriotism or "chauvinism." As long as soldiers and citizens harbored nationalistic sentiments and believed in defense of the fatherland they would not precipitate a civil war. Lenin, accordingly, trained his polemical guns on nationalism. He identified the war with "the horrors of contemporary 'patriotic' barbarism."[50] Workingmen should shun it. Socialism's "basic truth" was in the *Communist Manifesto*: "The workers have no fatherland."[51]

Every day workers in the trenches were proving that they would fight and die for their country. Lenin repeated the texts. The socialists in the German parliament declared on August 4, 1914, "In the hour of danger we will not leave our fatherland unprotected," and voted overwhelmingly for credits to the Kaiser's war machine. French and Belgian socialists joined their governments to support the war. Lenin called this the "collapse" of the "opportunist" Second International. Nothing daunted, he insisted that "the working masses would overcome all obstructions and create a new International."[52] For "the greater the war sacrifices the clearer the working masses would see the betrayal of the workers' cause by the opportunists and the need of turning their arms against the governments and the bourgeoisie of every country."[53]

Lenin apparently realized that he had raised questions to which, first of all, Russians wanted answers. Did he have no feelings for his native land?

[48] *Ibid.*, p. 147.
[49] *Ibid.*, p. 193.
[50] *Ibid.*, p. 66.
[51] *Ibid.*, p. 65.
[52] *Ibid.*, p. 66.
[53] *Ibid.*, p. 66.

"Is the sense of national pride foreign to us class-conscious Great Russian proletarians?" Lenin asked rhetorically. "Of course not!" he replied. "We love our language and our motherland." True, Russia was "justly called 'a prison of nationalities.' " The Great Russians oppressed over a hundred national minorities within the tsarist frontiers. "We are full of a sense of national pride and for that reason we *particularly* hate *our* slave past (when landlord-noblemen led muzhiks into war to crush the freedom of Hungary, Poland, Persia, and China) and our slave present when the same landlords, allies of the capitalists, lead us into war in order to strangle Poland, the Ukraine . . ." He summoned Russians to throw off the yoke: "No one is to blame for having been born a slave. But a slave who not only is without a yearning for his own freedom but also justifies and exalts his enslavement (he, for instance, regards the strangulation of Poland, the Ukraine, etc. as 'defense of the fatherland' of the Great Russians), such a slave is a toady and cad who evokes a rightful feeling of indignation, contempt, and loathing."[54]

Lenin had given his answer: No patriotism for a slave state. He quoted Marx and Engels: "A nation cannot be free if it oppresses foreign nations." Russia was oppressing Poland, the Ukraine, etc.

In his own environment, Lenin found adherents for his policy of national defeat. Lenin's erudition, intensity, and fanaticism often mesmerized those around him. His austere mode of life, singleness of purpose, and crunching polemical power gave him authority. The merry twinkle in his slanting eyes, the simplicity of his manner, lent him a certain charm. Some were alienated by his intolerance of dissent, steam-roller tactics against opponents, and the pursuit of ends by any means—even holdups to refill the party exchequer. But those who agreed with him were conscious of a personal attraction. Distance, however, lent disenchantment, and in Siberia, for instance, some Bolsheviks joined exiled Mensheviks to form groups that believed in defending Russia. Here and there the defenders outnumbered the Leninist defeatists and advocated a reunification of the Bolshevik and Menshevik fractions into one organization.

In the ranks of his own diminutive fraction the issues of nationalism and national minorities excited heated polemics. It was the age of self-determination. Fact or fiction, many believed Austria-Hungary's attack on little Serbia had caused the war. The Kaiser's 1914 unprovoked invasion of Belgium aroused sympathy for that small nation. The Western alliance hoped to right this wrong. President Wilson would, in 1917 and 1918, enunciate the doctrine of self-determination for Poland and the ethnic minorities of the Austro-Hungarian Empire. It drastically unscrambled the map of Europe.

The same principle served Bolshevism as a weapon against the tsarist empire. *Socialism and War*, a pamphlet written by Lenin and Gregory Zinoviev and published in Geneva in 1915 in Russian and German, emphasized that

[54] *Ibid.*, pp. 80-81.

"nowhere in the world does the majority of the people suffer such oppression as in Russia: Great Russians constitute only 43 percent of the population, that is, less than half, and all the others are deprived of civil rights, like aliens. Of the 170 million inhabitants of Russia *nearly one hundred million* are oppressed and without rights." Moreover, "Tsarism is fighting the war for the conquest of Galicia and the final extinction of the freedom of Ukrainians, for the conquest of Armenia, of Constantinople, and so forth."[55] Therefore, anybody who wants to be "national," Lenin declared, must be a socialist, must recognize "the right of oppressed nations to liberation, to secession from the big powers that oppress them."[56]

Lenin, lover of absolutes, advocated "the right of self-determination for all nations and renunciation of all 'annexations,' that is, of all violations of that right . . . if one is to recognize the right of all nations then it is wrong to single out, for instance, Belgium alone, one must consider *all* oppressed nations in Europe (the Irish in England, the Italians in Nice, the Danes and others in Germany, 57 percent of the population of Russia, and so forth), and also those *outside of Europe*, that is, all colonies." The Belgian socialists who asked nothing more than the liberation of Belgium "are in effect defending the demands of the Belgian bourgeoisie which wishes to continue robbing the 15 million inhabitants of the Congo and to receive concessions and privileges in other countries."[57]

Nevertheless, Lenin found it possible to say, "We are in no sense undeviating supporters of small nations." Nor did he uphold the "petty-bourgeois idea of federalism." A protagonist of dictatorship, he asserted that "We are certainly, *all other conditions being equal*, for centralization." But things were not equal; the agent of centralization was the Tsar, and why, Lenin asked, should democrats and socialists help tsardom "throttle the Ukraine, etc."? However, "If history settles the matter in favor of Great Russian great power capitalism"—this underlines his doubts about an early Bolshevik victory—"then the socialist role of the Great Russian proletariat, as the chief motive force of the communist revolution bred by capitalism, will be all the greater." But before the proletariat could lead Russia it would have to be educated in "the spirit of the fullest national equality and brotherhood." The education would be "prolonged"; he knew his Russian masses. "Our model," Lenin declared, "will remain Marx who, having spent decades in England, became half-British and demanded freedom and national independence for Ireland in the interest of the socialist movement of the British workers."[58]

But if "the workers have no fatherland," why urge self-determination for small nations? Since socialism required, in Lenin's own words, "international unity after the destruction of today's national barriers," why set up new

[55] *Ibid.*, p. 198.
[56] *Ibid.*, p. 164.
[57] *Ibid.*, p. 227.
[58] *Ibid.*, pp. 82-83.

national barriers? In fact, having advocated, on November 1, 1914, a United States of Europe risen from a republican fire that devoured the German, Austro-Hungarian, and Russian monarchies,[59] he reconsidered the matter, or rather he allowed Karl Radek, subsequently a foreign affairs adviser of the Soviet regime, and Inessa Armand to dissuade him—a rare instance—and announced on August 23, 1915, that the slogan of the United States of Europe was "incorrect."[60] As politics, he said, the idea was "unassailable," but "from the point of view of the economic conditions of imperialism . . . a United States of Europe, under capitalism, is either impossible or reactionary." He now preferred "a United States of the world."[61]

What was the sense, then, in proposing the liberation of colonies or the self-determination of small nationalities? How could Lenin plead, in the same breath, for the widest internationalism and the narrowest nationalism? His own Bolshevik comrades, Nikolai Bukharin in particular, objected.

Bukharin, destined to become a prominent and popular Soviet leader, was only twenty-seven years old in 1915 when he fought Lenin on self-determination. Bukharin loved Lenin but was not blind. In October, 1916, on the eve of a journey to the United States where he stayed till May, 1917 (returning then, via Japan, to Russia), Bukharin wrote to Lenin: "I ask one thing of you: If you engage in polemics, etc., preserve a tone that will not force a split. It would be painful to me, painful beyond endurance, if joint work, even in the future, should become impossible. I have the greatest respect for you and look upon you as my revolutionary teacher and love you."

Lenin became more and more nervous as the war wore on. Personal poverty intensified his irritation. "As for myself," he wrote in a letter in the autumn of 1916, "I must say I need an income; otherwise it simply means perishing. Truly!! The fiendishly high cost of living—there is nothing to live on." Lenin's mother, who received a munificent annual pension of 1,200 gold roubles from the tsarist government and had sent part of it to her rebel son in Siberia and Europe, had been dead three months. Hence the dire financial difficulty. After urging his correspondent to "extract money forcibly" from a number of publishers, Lenin concluded gloomily: "If this is not arranged, then I shall not be able to hold out. Of this I am sure. This is very, very serious." (Thirteen months later he was head of the Soviet government.) In the same letter he lamented the loss of touch with the movement in Russia: "The sorest point now is the weakness of contact between us and the leading workers in Russia!! No correspondence whatever!! . . . It can't go on that way."[62]

Lenin's mental tensions and the fear of inviting his wrath made devoted

[59] *Ibid.*, p. 65.
[60] *Ibid.*, p. 233.
[61] *Ibid.*, pp. 230-233.
[62] *Ibid.*, Second ed., Vol. XIX, pp. 273-276. (The English translation is taken from Gankin and Fisher, *op. cit.*, pp. 250-251.) This letter, incidentally, is omitted from the fourth edition of Lenin's works published in the Soviet Union in 1952.

followers hesitate to differ with him. Nevertheless, a group of Bolsheviks living in Norway which included Bukharin and Yuri L. Pyatakov rejected Lenin's theses. "The slogan of 'self-determination' of nations," they declared in a manifesto, "is first of all *utopian* (it cannot be realized *within the limits* of capitalism) and *harmful* as a slogan which *disseminates illusions*. In this respect it does not differ at all from the slogans of courts of arbitration, disarmament, etc., which presuppose the possibility of so-called 'peaceful capitalism.' " The only self-determination they countenanced was in colonies where, because of underdevelopment, socialism and therefore a proletarian internationalist revolution were precluded. The manifesto closed with a piercing postscript: "By the way, all *extreme Lefts* have a well-thought-out theory *against* [the slogan of self-determination]. Are they all 'traitors'?"[63] They anticipated Lenin's name-calling.

Lenin's retort to Bukharin and comrades was waspish indeed: "They have *slipped into a swamp*"; "their 'ideas' *have nothing in common either with Marxism or revolutionary social democracy*"; "*every phrase is incorrect.*"

A. G. Shlyapnikov wrote to Lenin gently chiding him for his "unaccommodating disposition" and "tactlessness" toward the Bukharin group. Lenin remained personally intransigent. Substantively, however, he was moderate. He realized that so long as he and Bukharin sat on their high horses encased in the armor of theory and jousting, the elder with a literary lance dipped in poison, the junior with a brilliant verbal sword, they would get nowhere. Lenin accordingly got down to earth and took a stance usually regarded as "reformism." He contended that "Not only the right of nations to self-determination, but *all* the fundamental demands of political democracy are 'possible of achievement' under imperialism, only in an incomplete, in a mutilated form and as a rare exception." This was a concession wrapped in a contradiction: "all the demands" could be achieved "as a rare exception." "We must . . . demand the liberation of oppressed nations," Lenin said, "not in general, nebulous phrases, . . . not by 'postponing' the question until socialism is established . . ."

Lenin's aim remained "the inevitable merging of nations" under revolutionary socialism. But this goal could be reached "only by passing through the transition period of complete liberation of all the oppressed nations, that is, their freedom to secede." The transition period might be a capitalist period or "the transition period of the dictatorship of the oppressed class." Secession, whether from a capitalist state or a socialist state, carried certain definite implications. "Concretely," Lenin explained, "this political, democratic demand implies complete freedom to carry on agitation in favor of secession, and freedom to settle the question of secession by means of a referendum of the nation that desires to secede."

To protect his exposed theoretical flank Lenin gave the ideological screw another turn. He had just argued for secession. Now he opposed it. "This

[63] Gankin and Fisher, *op. cit.*, pp. 219 *et seq.*

demand" for self-determination, he wrote, "is by no means identical with the demand for secession, for partition, for the formation of small states. It is merely the logical expression of the struggle against national oppression in every form. The more closely the democratic system of state approximates to complete freedom of secession, the rarer and weaker will be the striving for secession in practice." Thus the leader of a "democratic" dictatorship need merely assert that his government recognized the unabridged right of secession to prove, to his satisfaction, that "in practice" nobody desired secession. Khrushchev used this gambit in New York in 1960 to argue that no national minority wished to secede from the Soviet Union.

Lenin saw all issues in the light of their possible contribution to the ultimate socialist revolution and meanwhile to the intensification of the class struggle. "The socialist revolution may begin in the very near future," he asserted in March, 1916.[64] Alternatively, "five, ten, or even more years may pass before the socialist revolution begins." The interval, long or short, had to be packed with acts that weakened capitalism, imperialism, and opportunistic socialism. Therefore Lenin's policy for tsarist Russia included the liberation of previously annexed territories: "Finland, Poland, Courland, the Ukraine, Khiva, Bokhara, Estonia, and other regions peopled by non-Great Russians."[65] "We," Lenin declared, "are by no means opposed to the fight for reforms."[66] Self-determination was one of the reforms within the gift of capitalist states.

Lenin was the practical politician even when he could not pay the rent for his room in a Swiss boardinghouse. As a practical politician, he diluted theory with expediency and hurtled with ease from internationalism to nationalism and back again. In theory he espoused large international states; in fact he hoped to break up existing large states the easier to destroy them.

Lenin's readiness to reckon with nationalism as an emotional reality and a potential revolutionary force riled not only Bukharin and other Russian Bolshevik leftists but also German socialist leftists, notably Rosa Luxemburg whose pamphlet, entitled *The Crisis in Social Democracy*, was published illegally in Germany in 1916 under the pseudonym "Junius." Lenin detected "faults and errors" in the publication, and, "for the sake of self-criticism," proceeded to criticize Junius and everybody else—except himself.

Junius' chief error was the contention that since this was the era of imperialism "there can be no more national wars." It followed, Lenin submitted, that every war, even if it started as a national war, "is *transformed* into an imperialist war." The fallacy of this argument is obvious. It was a half-truth. Its opposite also was true. "A national war," Lenin explained, "can be transformed into an imperialist war, and *vice versa*. For example,

---

[64] Lenin, *Collected Works*, Second ed., Vol. XIX (International Publishers, New York, 1942), p. 57.
[65] *Ibid.*, p. 84.
[66] *Ibid.*, p. 369.

the wars of the Great French Revolution started as national wars and were such. But after Napoleon had created the French Empire by subjugating a number of large, virile, long established national states of Europe, the French national wars became imperialist wars, which *in their turn* engendered wars for national liberation *against* Napoleon's imperialism."[67]

Lenin's dialectic approach, together with his illustrative example from the past, helps clarify more recent history—that of the regime he founded. The Second World War began a week after the signature of the Soviet-Nazi pact. This agreement sanctioned annexations by Germany and Russia. For Germany, and for Russia—though she was a nonbelligerent, the war was, therefore, an imperialist, expansionist war. Then Hitler invaded the Soviet Union in June, 1941, took back the peripheral lands Stalin had annexed, and struck at the heart of Russia. The war became, for the Soviets, a war of national survival. Later, the Red Army conquered foreign territories and the Kremlin annexed them or subjugated their peoples thereby transforming the national war into an imperialist war. This, in turn, engendered national revolts in East Germany, Poland, and Hungary against Soviet imperialism.

Lenin foresaw that at all times, even after the triumph of socialism, wars or uprisings for national liberation are possible. He consequently favored self-determination irrespective of the nature of the state, whether capitalist or not, and condemned those Dutch and Polish Social Democrats who "repudiate self-determination of nations even under socialism."[68]

Lenin thought self-determination and secession desirable under socialism, attainable under capitalism, and possible despite imperialism. To argue otherwise, he insisted, was "downright annexationism"[69] and hence imperialism. This accusation he flung repeatedly at leftist socialists in Poland and Holland who, enamored of the world socialist state of their dreams, would allow subject peoples to languish in "the prison of nationalities" until red redemption day.

Wedded to abstractions, the Polish socialists said, "Social-Democracy . . . under no circumstances supports the establishment of new frontier posts in Europe," because that would be tantamount to "the restoration of the barriers swept away by imperialism." Empires were creating big states. The socialists would take them over. Why, then, they argued, break up the empires in order to liberate dependent territories?

The Poles were chasing their dogmatic tails: they, like Lenin, opposed defense of the fatherland in an imperialist war; therefore, they could not defend the Polish fatherland with a view to Poland's liberation. To demand Polish independence would be to join the Polish nationalistic capitalists who wanted the same thing. An independent Poland, these internationalist socialists contended, would always be a battlefield between Russia and Ger-

[67] *Ibid.*, pp. 199-213.
[68] *Ibid.*, p. 207.
[69] *Ibid.*, p. 280.

many. Better, they said, to join the German and Russian proletariat in a struggle to overthrow all capitalists and create one big Russo-Polish-German socialist state. Yet the same Polish socialists who rejected Polish self-determination, urged self-determination for European countries and Asian and African colonies.

Lenin believed he knew how to avoid both pointed horns of this dilemma. "Undoubtedly," he admitted, "the situation is very confused." He consequently proposed two contradictory policies: one for the Russian and German socialists, who "must demand unconditional 'freedom of secession' for Poland"; another for the Polish socialists, who "must fight for the unity of proletarian struggles in small and big countries, without advancing, in the present epoch, the present period, the slogan of the independence of Poland."[70]

If the German and Russian workers, Lenin elaborated, were to participate in the annexation of Poland it would mean educating them and the peasantry "in the spirit of the most despicable servility," and make them nationalist supporters of their capitalist governments. If the Polish socialists urged independence for their country they would help their mortal class enemies: the bourgeoisie. This would weaken the class struggle, and for Lenin the class struggle was higher than principle. He wanted to keep it alive during the war even at the expense of the idea of self-determination and no annexations. But he left a significant reformist loophole: "This is not an argument against greater political freedom (and consequently against political independence) in periods between wars."

A Polish nationalist uprising by the proletariat and the bourgeoisie would have hastened the defeat of capitalist Russia which Lenin so devoutly wished. Yet he counseled against it. Did he recoil from encouraging national sentiments among the Polish workers? Political independence after the war could have the same effect. It actually did in 1920. Lenin failed to foresee or to see this.

Lenin wrote so much that he can be quoted two ways on several issues. Those who today defend the denial of self-determination to subject nationalities within communist empires can find theoretical support somewhere in Lenin's vast theoretical output. His posture with one foot on the left bank of internationalism and the world state, the other on the right bank of nationalism, self-determination, and secession, is a bridge under which many ships can sail. But the preponderance of Lenin's declarations was in favor of self-determination as an instrument against capitalist imperialism. And, being tough-minded, down-to-earth, and nonutopian, Lenin recognized the danger of socialist imperialism unless socialists remained loyal to their professions. "If," he asserted, "a Socialist party declares itself to be 'opposed to the

[70] *Ibid.*, p. 297. I have amended one word in the English translation: Lenin used the Russian "zaputannoye" which is rendered "complicated." ("Complicated" would be "slozhnoye"). "Confused" seems more correct. The confusion persisted in Lenin's mind and contributed to the Soviet disaster in the 1920 war with Poland when he adopted Radek's 1916 position and Radek took Lenin's 1916 position.

forcible retention of an oppressed nation within the boundaries of an annex-ing state,' the party thereby undertakes to abandon forcible retention when it comes to power."[71]

In this connection, Lenin quoted from a letter Friedrich Engels had writ-ten to Karl Kautsky on September 12, 1882. Engels offered advice to Euro-pean socialist governments. "One thing alone is certain," he affirmed: "the victorious proletariat can force no blessings of any kind upon any foreign nation without undermining its own victory by so doing." Lenin called this the "absolutely internationalist principle." He knew a socialist regime too could sin. In the autumn of 1916, for example, he declared that "the prole-tariat does not become holy or insured against mistakes or weaknesses only because it has carried out a revolution." What is more, a victorious socialist proletarian revolution might be motivated by "selfish interests." It might try "to ride on somebody else's back."[72] Lenin did not rule out the possibility of a socialist, Bolshevik, or communist government becoming imperialistic. He foresaw the pitfalls of a successful proletarian revolution in one country. "The difficulties of revolution are familiar to everybody," he said. "Having begun with brilliant success in one country, it may have to pass through painful periods; for final victory is possible only on a world scale and only as a result of the joint efforts of the workers of all countries."[73]

A revolution in one country is a national revolution and breeds national-ism. Big-power nationalism is the mother of imperialism. Lenin did not assume that a proletarian, socialist country would be automatically demo-cratic or automatically internationalist or automatically anti-imperialist.

V. CAPITALISM'S DEATH SENTENCE

FROM CRACOW, Lenin served as foreign correspondent for St. Petersburg newspapers. He was a good journalist, though not as good as Karl Marx in the New York *Tribune*. Lenin excelled as a pamphleteer. He once copied a saying from Napoleon's *Pensées*: "The cannon killed feudalism. Ink will kill modern society." Lenin made his contribution to the murder. He pre-

[71] *Ibid.*, p. 276.
[72] *Ibid.*, pp. 298-299.
[73] *Ibid.*, 1918-1919, Second ed., Vol. XXIII, p. 22.

ferred pamphlets built on a scaffolding of statistics; they fascinated him. But the libraries in and around Cracow were poor, and he was busy; many Bolsheviks came to see him there: Bukharin, Stalin, and so forth. Bukharin was jolly and a painter; Stalin a grim mountaineer who, with Lenin as mentor at his elbow, produced a brochure on the problem of nationalities.

Emissaries from St. Petersburg and other Russian cities constantly crossed the frontier illegally and legally into Austria-Hungary to visit Lenin in Cracow and bring him news of the movement and take back instructions to party headquarters in the tsarist capital. Among them was a rank-and-file young party member named Anna N. Nikoforova. Krupskaya met and welcomed her warmly. "Vladimir Ilyich and I have no children," she said. "So stay with us in place of a daughter." Anna stayed twenty days, from June 16 to July 5, 1914. It was a bustling household. Lenin labored long hours writing letters and articles. Krupskaya and her mother, when they had finished shopping, cooking, and cleaning, copied his manuscripts and correspondence by hand for transmission to St. Petersburg. Anna Nikoforova helped in this daily task. Some letters were copied in ordinary visible ink; in some, special messages were written between the lines in invisible chemical ink. When the mail was ready, Lenin put it on his back in a rucksack, mounted his bicycle and took it to the post office.[1] Supersecret instructions were carried orally or in a double-bottomed suitcase or in the lining of a garment by messengers like Anna. Krupskaya would have liked her to stay. But duty had precedence over "daughter."

On August 7, 1914, the Austrian police arrested Lenin on the charge of espionage; the First World War had commenced and he was a Russian on enemy territory. But through the intervention of Victor Adler, socialist deputy in the Austro-Hungarian parliament, and others, Lenin was released after twelve days in a county jail and traveled, via Vienna where he and Krupskaya stopped for a day, to neutral Switzerland. They settled in Bern. Krupskaya's reminiscences read: "We lived in Bern on Distelweg, a small, tidy, quiet street adjoining Bern forest which extended for several kilometers. Across the road lived Inessa."

In September and October, 1915, in Zimmerwald and in April, 1916, in Kienthal, the first two of a long chain of international peace conferences were held. Lenin attended both and defended the idea of converting the imperialist war into many civil wars. Nothing moved.

Lenin suspected that he would be marooned for the duration. This was the time, especially with fine Swiss libraries available, to write pamphlets. He had one ready early in January, 1916, and mailed it to Gorky in Petrograd on January 11. The accompanying letter was Lenin's first to Gorky in two years. Gorky had written Lenin in support of Bogdanov's Machist views. Lenin's brusque reply, in December, 1913, broke the tie between them. You say, Lenin wrote, quoting Gorky, that "God is the complex of ideas, evolved

[1] *Vospominaniya*, Vol. 4, pp. 164-172.

by tribes, nations, humanity, which awaken and organize the social senses with a view to binding the person to society and restraining zoological individualism." That theory, Lenin told Gorky, "is clearly connected with the theory or theories of Bogdanov and Lunacharsky. It is clearly untrue and clearly reactionary . . . All your definitions are thoroughly reactionary and bourgeois."

Gorky fell silent.

Lenin resumed the correspondence in January, 1916, when he sent Gorky his brochure entitled, *New Data on the Laws of the Development of Capitalism in Agriculture. Part One. Capitalism in Agriculture in the United States.*[2] Gorky did not publish it. It appeared in 1917 in Petrograd under the imprint of the party. In the same letter Lenin informed Gorky that "I am sitting down to work on a pamphlet about imperialism." He sat and worked from January to June, 1916, when he finished it.

Lenin was a stupendous collector of figures and quotations. For the pamphlet on American farming he copied whole pages of long columns of figures from the 1900 and 1910 U.S. Census reports and filled notebooks with excerpts in English from American books, magazines, newspapers, and government bulletins. The research for his book on imperialism was a gigantic undertaking. He covered 760 pages in twenty copybooks with statistics from many countries and long passages from books in English, French, and German. This material, in his meticulous handwriting and with his marginal remarks, has been preserved and printed.[3] Krupskaya helped, under her husband's direction, in copying long sections of J. A. Hobson's *Imperialism*.

Lenin's *Imperialism, the Highest Stage of Capitalism,*[4] is still a much-used major weapon in the missionary arsenal of the world communist movement. It reveals Leninist thought patterns and has shaped Soviet policy. The book was designed for legal publication in monarchist Russia. Just before it appeared, however, Lenin arrived in republican Petrograd, and though he found no time to revise the text he prefixed a comment, dated April 26, 1917, explaining that to obtain the tsarist censor's approval he had used some "damned Aesopian language." For instance, he said, he had cited Korea as an example of Japanese imperialism when he wanted to name Finland, Poland, the Baltic States, and Russia's Asiatic provinces as illustrations of tsarist imperialism. This foreword, and another prepared by Lenin on July 6, 1920, for the German and French editions, stressed, in similar words, the central thesis: that "imperialism is the eve of the socialist revolution." Lenin mustered all his considerable mental faculties and material to prove this proposition, and the result was a book which sentenced world capitalism to death. The First

[2] Lenin, *Sochineniya*, Fourth ed., Vol. 22, pp. 5-89.

[3] *Leninskii Sbornik*, Vol. XXII (Moscow, 1933), pp. 22-390; Vol. XXVII (Moscow, 1934), pp. 16-482; Vol. XXVIII (Moscow, 1936), pp. 19-405.

[4] All quotations are from Lenin, *Sochineniya*, Fourth ed., Vol. 22 (Moscow-Leningrad, 1948), pp. 175-290, or Lenin, *Collected Works*, Vol. XIX, 1916-1917 (New York, 1942), pp. 83-196.

World War, he maintained, was an imperialist war. He made "imperialist" synonymous with "annexationist, predatory, plunderous." He made imperialism synonymous with capitalism. Imperialism was doomed; therefore capitalism was doomed.

Lenin began his dissertation by heaping up a hill of statistics covered with a thicket of quotations to prove that the concentration of industrial production in ever-larger monopolies "is a general and fundamental law of the present state of capitalism's development." Cartels were "one of the bases of the whole of economic life." It followed that "capitalism has been transformed into imperialism."

Automatically, therefore, and irrespective of whether or not a capitalist country possessed colonies, it became imperialistic by reason of having entered the phase of monopoly capitalism. Lenin arrived at this judgment by several logical leaps: Parallel with the cartelization of industry, banks expanded and bought up cartels. Thereby "scattered capitalists are transformed into a single collective capitalist"—the giant bank. And "the old capitalism, the capitalism of free competition, and its indispensable regulator, the Stock Market, are passing away." So, "In spite of themselves, the capitalists are dragged, as it were, into a new social order, a transitional social order from complete free competition to complete socialization." But "the immense progress of humanity, which achieved this socialization, goes to benefit the speculators." These "speculators" are rewarded by a "prodigious increase of capital which overflows the brim, as it were, flows abroad, etc." Huge foreign investments imply imperialism.

The new era brought a new figure to the scene: the rentier, the stockowner and bondholder, who did not produce anything. He lived "by clipping coupons." He was divorced from creative enterprise. "Imperialism, or the domination of finance capital," Lenin wrote, "is that highest stage of capitalism in which this separation reaches vast proportions."

The rentier put his money at the disposal of the banks. The banks and trusts looked abroad for new fields to conquer. The "most typical feature" of the old capitalism was the export of goods. But "under modern capitalism, when monopolies prevail," Lenin submitted, "the export of *capital* has become the typical feature." This was due to the enormous "superabundance of capital" in all advanced countries.

Why was the overflow not used for development at home? "It goes without saying," Lenin argued, "that if capitalism could develop agriculture, which today lags behind industry everywhere, if it could raise the standard of living of the masses, who are everywhere still poverty-stricken and underfed in spite of the amazing advance in technical knowledge, there would be no superabundance of capital." But "As long as capitalism remains what it is, surplus capital will never be utilized for the purpose of raising the standard of living of the masses in a given country, for this would mean a decline in the profits of the capitalists; it will be used for the purpose of increasing those profits by exporting capital abroad to the backward countries" where "profits are usually high because capital is scarce, the price of land is relatively low, wages are low, raw materials are cheap."

Lenin was convinced that the situation could only change for the worse. "Where," he asked, "except in the imagination of the sentimental reformists, are there any trusts capable of interesting themselves in the condition of the masses instead of the conquest of colonies?" When John A. Hobson, in his *Imperialism,* a book Lenin valued highly, urged the need of greater consuming power for the people, Lenin expressed his skepticism in a parenthesis: ("under capitalism!") He rejected any suggestions of improvement either by raising farm productivity or by buying raw materials in the open market instead of obtaining them from colonial possessions. To increase agricultural output, he asserted, would lift the living standards of the masses and reduce profits. Capitalists had no interest in such a development. Buy raw materials in the open market? Shortage of supplies precluded that: "The more capitalism is developed, the more the need of raw materials is felt, . . . the more feverishly the hunt for raw materials proceeds throughout the whole world, the more desperate becomes the struggle for the acquisition of colonies." He quoted a gloomy prophecy from the multi-volume opus of Dr. Sigmund Schilder, published in Berlin in 1912: "In the more or less discernible future the growth of the urban industrial population is more likely to be hindered by the shortage of raw materials for industry than by the shortage of food."

"For example," Lenin added on his own behalf, "there is a growing shortage of timber—the price of which is steadily rising—of leather, and raw materials for the textile industry." Lenin also accepted as true a statement about "the exhaustion of the American oil wells." The age of scarcity had dawned. Hence imperialism.

Capital from Europe flowed to other continents. By 1914 Britain had exported capital totaling 75 to 100 billion French gold francs; France 60 billion; Germany 44. Lenin assumed, erroneously, that England sent the bulk of these funds to her vast colonial domains. France "invested mainly in Europe, particularly in Russia (at least 10 billion francs)." Germany divided her foreign financial activity "fairly evenly between America and Europe." Lenin accordingly referred to British "colonial imperialism" and to French "usury imperialism." By inference, German imperialism belonged to the latter category. Russia, though "economically most backward" and enmeshed in "a particularly close network of precapitalist relations"—presumably the village communes and Asian pastoral life, had also reached the stage of "modern capitalist imperialism." The other colonial powers were the United States, Japan, Holland, Belgium, and Portugal. Together they had "completed the seizure of the unoccupied territories of our planet." This did not mean that the partition of the world was final: "on the contrary, new partitions are possible and inevitable."

"Finance capital," Lenin affirmed, "is not only interested in the already known sources of raw materials; it is also interested in potential sources of raw materials." Therefore there ensued an "insensate struggle for the last available scraps of undivided territory, or for the repartition of that which has been already divided." The exhaustion of the American oil wells, for instance, had touched off a petroleum war for the "redivision" of global oil resources. Oil imperialism was a wheel within the wheel of colonial imperialism.

Once a territory has been seized, development begins: "The British capitalists are exerting every effort to develop cotton growing in *their* colony, Egypt." The "Russians are doing the same in *their* colony, Turkestan; and they are doing so because in this way they will be in a better position to defeat their foreign competitors, to monopolize the sources of raw materials and form a more economic and profitable textile trust in which *all* the processes of cotton production and manufacturing will be 'combined' and concentrated in the hands of a single owner." This is what Lenin called "socialization," though it was not the kind he preferred. He favored the same concentration in the hands of the state.

Great Britain went beyond annexing colonies and exploiting their riches. She made Argentina "so dependent financially on London," in the words of a German authority cited by Lenin, "that it ought to be described as almost a British commercial colony." Portugal, an imperial power herself, was actually, according to Lenin, "a British protectorate."

Karl Kautsky, the German socialist leader and thinker, expected the separate national imperialisms to unite in a "super-imperialism, a union of world imperialisms." In this phase, he predicted, "wars shall cease under capitalism," and there would be not rivalry but "joint exploitation of the world by internationally combined finance capital." Lenin denounced Kautsky's "ultra-imperialism" as "ultra-nonsense"—"grist to the mill of the apologists of imperialism." In Lenin's view, the uneven economic development of capitalist countries would intensify the competition between them. He looked for no international union of capitalist states or of national cartels. They would quarrel, compete, and tear one another limb from limb. They would not only wrangle over control of underdeveloped overseas regions, they would contend for supremacy and territory in Europe. He cited the "German appetite for Belgium" and the "French appetite for Lorraine." Germany wanted Belgium as "a base for operations against England," and "England needs Baghdad as a base for operations against Germany." Each imperialist nation was striving for hegemony. The quest of the trusts for colonial raw materials and food led to the political conquest of Asian and African territories to prevent their occupation by a rival country. He anticipated wars.

The flag, Lenin claimed, followed investments. The stockholders and bondholders, the rentiers or "coupon-clippers," "whose profession is idleness," availed themselves of the defense forces of their government. He quoted as proof Dr. Schulze-Gaevernitz, author of a book on British imperialism, whom Lenin himself called "the enthusiastic admirer of German imperialism." The learned German doctor wrote: "Great Britain grants loans to Egypt, Japan, China, and South America. Her navy here plays the part of bailiff in case of necessity. Great Britain's political power protects her from the indignation of her debtors." The same German author, summoned again as witness, declared that England "is gradually being transformed from an industrial state into a creditor state."

This sad fate had also overtaken Holland, "the model rentier state," and France, and Germany, and Switzerland, and Belgium. They loafed while colonial coolies slaved for them. Lenin called this the "parasitism, which is a feature of imperialism." Capitalism, he said, had entered its highest, parasitic phase. "The rentier state is a state of parasitic, decaying capitalism." It was the prelude to death, the overture to socialism.

"An increasing proportion of land in Great Britain," Lenin wrote, "is being taken out of cultivation and used for sport, for the diversion of the rich. . . . On horse racing alone Britain annually spends 14 million pounds sterling." Again he found a helpful German text by Gerhard Hildebrand: "Europe . . . will shift the burden of physical toil—first agricultural and mining, then the more arduous toil in industry—on to the colored races, and itself be content with the role of rentier."

Instead of rejoicing over the emergence of "moribund capitalism" Lenin discerned a cloud no bigger than a trade-union leader's hand. The enrichment of capitalists through monopoly "makes it economically possible for them to corrupt certain sections of the working class. . . . Imperialism has the tendency to create privileged sections among the workers, and to detach them from the main proletarian masses. . . . A section of the British proletariat becomes bourgeois. . . . Imperialist ideology also penetrates the working class," Lenin sighed. "There is no Chinese Wall between it and the other classes." Where, then, was the class struggle? and the proletarian overthrow of the capitalist class? and socialism?

He found balm, however, in what communists call "the objective forces of history." The German economists on whom Lenin leaned mentioned "interlocking": the interlocking of one industrial enterprise with others, the interlocking of industries with banks, and so forth. "But what does this word 'interlocking' express?" Lenin asked. It expresses "the changing social relations of production." Big enterprises "assume gigantic proportions"; they collect and compute masses of economic data, and then plan for tens of millions of people. Raw materials are transported "sometimes hundreds or thousands of miles . . . in a systematic and organized manner . . . a single center directs all the successive stages of work right up to the manufacture of numerous varieties of finished articles . . . these products are distributed according to a single plan among tens and hundreds of millions of consumers (as in the case of the distribution of oil in America and Germany by the American 'oil trust' . . .)." Is this not "the socialization of production"? And does it not follow that "private economic relations and private property relations constitute a shell which is no longer suitable for its contents, a shell which must inevitably decay"? The new "socialized" capitalism may, to be sure, "continue in a state of decay for a fairly long period (particularly if the cure of the opportunist [labor-socialist] abscess is protracted)." Nevertheless, the decaying "shell" of private capitalism "will inevitably be removed." Dr. Schulze-Gaevernitz, the German imperialist whose words were so often on Lenin's lips, had asserted that through an interlocking central body of management "we are on the way to . . . Marxism, different from what Marx imagined, but different only in form."

"A crushing 'refutation' of Marxism, indeed!" Lenin cried; it confirmed Marx. All that remained of parasitic, decaying capitalism was the form, the shell, and the shell too was in decay. If only "the labor aristocracy"—the "bourgeoisified workers . . . who are quite philistine in their mode of life, in the size of their earnings," could be won over for revolution!

But after two and a half years as master of Soviet Russia, Lenin's optimism wilted. For on July 6, 1920, in his introduction to the German and French printings of his *Imperialism* he denounced this well-paid "labor aristocracy" as "the real *agents* of the bourgeoisie in the labor movement, the labor lieutenants of the capitalist class, real channels of reformism and chauvinism." From the heights of power he saw, clearly, he believed, that in the worldwide "civil war between the proletariat and the bourgeoisie they inevitably, and in no small number, stand side by side with the bourgeoisie." Capitalism, therefore, had a longer lease on life than Lenin had suspected four years earlier. But the Lenin book remained a sacred text.

⸙⸙⸙⸙⸙⸙

Lenin did not conduct an inquiry in order to resolve a doubt. He wrote to demonstrate a firmly held article of faith: that capitalism was incorrigible and socialism "inevitable." The capitalist system would "never" improve the lot of the masses; that was not its business. Its business was to earn fatter profits in the colonies.

But "inevitable" and "never" belong to prophecy, not to social science. The thinker accumulates facts to distill a theory from them. A theory is an idea with longevity. A theory is a general law or principle, deduced from various phenomena, which serves as a guide to the understanding of other phenomena, past, present, and future. Lenin's theory of imperialism, however, was a wish—a wish that did not come true, the wish of a zealot, not the careful conclusion of a scientist.

Lenin adduced some facts to bolster his thesis about imperialism. But information is sterile unless married to imagination. To believe in the "exhaustion of the American oil fields" (in 1916!) and in the shortage of timber, leather, and cotton reveals a low opinion of man's ingenuity and of the earth's resources. Since Lenin wrote, unfathomable lakes of oil have been tapped in North and South America, Russia, the Middle East, Southeast Asia, and northern Africa. New fields are being discovered and developed. If petroleum reserves are ever exhausted, atomic energy, the sun, the sea's waves, the ocean tides, and undreamt-of sources will fill the void. Who can today take seriously the impending scarcity of fuel, much less of leather, timber, and cotton, or of their synthetic substitutes?

Lenin's tinted lenses distorted his vision of the world's material wealth. They also gave him a false picture of men, else how could he have accepted the strange notion that Holland was "the model rentier state" of coupon-clipping parasites "whose profession is idleness"? The industry of rich and poor in Holland is proverbial, as is that of the Swiss and the Germans. Though Lenin lived in Europe for years he failed to see the heart of the matter: that stamina, technical skill, and managerial talent were the root and trunk of the tree of prosperity. Holland and Switzerland, almost bereft of natural resources, had, with brain and brawn, made themselves opulent, and Dutch living standards were to rise still higher after 1949 when the Netherlands finally surrendered Indonesia which was 99 percent of her empire and a veritable treasure house of oil, rubber, tobacco, tin, and other metals.

Lenin's whole treatment of imperialism was crude, to say the least, compared, for instance, with that of J. A. Hobson. In his Russian preface to *Imperialism, the Highest Stage of Capitalism*, Lenin wrote, "I made use of the principal English work, *Imperialism*, J. A. Hobson's book,[5] with all the care that, in my opinion, that work deserves." Evidently, however, little of Hobson's capacity for refined analysis rubbed off on Lenin. If anything, Hobson, the non-Marxist socialist, was the delicate dialectician, Lenin the crude doctrinaire. From Hobson's dissection there emerged, without his indicating it, a clear vision of why and how the bourgeois nations should, and in fact did, rid themselves of the plague of imperialism, whereas Lenin's brochure posed a single, simplified possibility: capitalist decay and death or socialism. This made socialism "inevitable," but gave no ray of hope until the "inevitable" happened. History has proved Hobson a reformist realist, Lenin a dogmatic dreamer.

Hobson and Lenin did not diverge on the essence. Only they were poles apart on subtleties, and it was these subtleties that ultimately shaped the decisive anti-imperialist events of the 1940's, 1950's, and 1960's. Wrote Hobson: "It is not too much to say that the modern foreign policy of Great Britain has been primarily a struggle for profitable markets of investment. To a larger extent every year Great Britain has been becoming a nation living upon tribute from abroad, and the classes who enjoy this tribute have had an ever-increasing incentive to employ the public policy, the public purse, and the public force to extend the field of their private investments, and to safeguard and improve their existing investments."[6] Here the agreement with Lenin is total. "Aggressive Imperialism," said Hobson, ". . . is a source of

---

[5] *Imperialism. A Study*, first ed., 1902; second ed., 1905; third, entirely revised and reset edition, 1938 (London).

[6] *Ibid.*, pp. 53-54.

great gain to the investor who cannot find at home the profitable use he seeks for his capital, and insists that his Government should help him to find profitable and secure investments abroad."[7]

This is where Lenin's examination of imperialism began and ended. Hobson was more profound. First, he drew a distinction between colonialism and imperialism: "Colonialism, in its best sense, is a natural overflow of nationality" through emigration, and he gave Australasia and Canada as British examples. He might have added the thirteen North American colonies. He also mentioned Russia's expansion into Asia by forced colonization of Great Russians among the indigenous inhabitants. On the other hand, imperialism, in most instances, involves "a small minority wielding political or economic sway over a majority of alien and subject people." The cases of colonialism were few. Imperialism was more widespread; he termed it a "debasement" of Western nationalism.

Hobson preferred internationalism to nationalism. He quoted an English assertion that, "The eve of the French revolution found every wise man in Europe—Lessing, Kant, Goethe, Rousseau, Lavater, Condorcet, Priestley, Gibbon, Franklin—more of a citizen of the world than of any particular country. Goethe confessed that he did not know what patriotism was, and was glad to be without it. Cultured men of all countries were at home in polite society everywhere. Kant was immensely more interested in events of Paris than in the life of Prussia."[8]

Aggressive imperialism, Hobson noted, not only defeats "the movement towards internationalism by fostering animosities among competing empires: its attacks on the liberties and the existence of the weaker or lower races stimulates in them a corresponding excess of national self-consciousness."

In his introduction to the 1938 edition, Hobson alluded to "emotions that inspire aggressive national activities." He wrote: "The sort of patriotism that can be evoked in Italy, Germany, and Japan for such aggression does not really proceed from the economic necessities cited in its defense. It is rooted in some ineradicable pugnacity and predacity of the animal man." Whether or not one wholly accepts this point of view—and Hobson himself was in doubt, for he added, "this patriotism . . . is fed and directed in its activities by economic motives"—the English author was at least aware of the psychological ingredient in imperialism; Lenin ignored it.

Hobson also directed attention, in the early and last editions of his standard work, to "the itch for glory and adventure among military officers. . . . This has been a most prolific source of expansion in India." The defense services, Hobson affirmed, were "imperialist by conviction and by professional interest." Their influence on government policy was augmented by "sympathetic support on the part of the aristocracy and the wealthy classes, who seek in the services careers for their sons." Here he quoted James Mill, who had

---

[7] *Ibid.*, p. 55.
[8] *Ibid.*, p. 7.

called the British colonies "a vast system of outdoor relief for the upper classes." The number thus employed was small, "But it arouses that disproportionate interest which always attaches to marginal employment. To extend this margin is a powerful motive in imperialism."[9] Hobson did not regard "coupon-clipping" as the only economic consideration.

Nor did the non-Marxist Hobson believe that all capitalists had a common stake in imperialism. There can be clashing groups within the capitalist class. Hobson showed by statistical tables that the "manufacturing and trading classes make little out of their new markets, paying, if they knew it, much more in taxation than they get out of them in trade." Aggressive imperialism, he reiterated, was a "source of great gain to the investor who cannot find at home the profitable use he seeks for his capital," but it "costs the taxpayer so dear . . . is of little value to the manufacturer and trader," and "is fraught with such grave incalculable peril to the citizen."

In these words, penned early in the century, the British social scientist supplied the key to what happened in 1946 and after. Following the Second World War, Britain's available capital for investment in colonies shriveled. British manufacturers and traders expected better business from an independent India. Above all, "the grave incalculable peril to the citizen" if England, weakened by her war effort, had to sit on the lid of seething India was plain for all to see.

Furthermore, the very factor which, to Lenin, favored imperialism actually maimed it. For in 1945 the "labor aristocracy," "the opportunists," "the real agents of the bourgeoisie," "the labor lieutenants of the capitalist class," as Lenin termed them, became the British government under Prime Minister Clement R. Attlee. One of his first moves was to open negotiations which, within two years, gave India, Pakistan, Ceylon, and Burma their independence and started a trend that by 1960 had added Israel, Ghana, the Sudan, Malaya, Nigeria, and Sierra Leone to the long list of colonies liberated by the United Kingdom, Holland, France, Belgium, and the United States. (Japan lost her empire through military defeat.)

Lenin had envisaged an irresistible progression from old-style competitive capitalism to monopoly capitalism to imperialism and then, inescapably, to decadent, parasitic capitalism which the proletariat, if unhampered by opportunists, would easily crush in a revolt leading to socialist dictatorship. History played it differently. Democracy, in the shape of public opinion, political parties, trade unions, crusading groups, and individual reformers, plus national interests and capitalist self-interest, as well as science and new techniques of production, management, and distribution, has raised living standards so that in advanced capitalist countries the masses are no longer "poverty-stricken and underfed." Agricultural output has mounted to such an extent that developed capitalist countries not only feed themselves but help feed former colonies. Increased production on farms and factories and

[9] *Ibid.*, pp. 50-51.

the vast growth of the middle classes which give services—teachers, doctors, lawyers, writers, artists, entertainers, transport workers, food, drink and clothing distributors, government officials, journalists, radio and television personnel, publishing employees, advertising and public relations agents, etc.—have greatly expanded home markets. As a result capital, which formerly gravitated to colonies and to foreign countries, now can be more profitably and safely invested at home. That induces more expansion of production and more improvement in living standards, hence a richer market and still more investment at home.

Today, therefore, the situation which Lenin—and Hobson—described (and decried) has been reversed. The private capitalists of developed countries are investing their money in their own countries or in other developed countries and only a trickle goes to former colonies or present colonies. Once-dependent territories are receiving considerable sums, largely for political reasons, in government-to-government aid, but the capitalists are putting the bulk of their money—as they always did, even in the heyday of imperialism—in advanced nations with stable economies and stable political systems. Now the shoe is on the other foot: the former colonies are complaining that private capitalists are not investing enough. Thus Ambassador B. K. Nehru, India's Commissioner General for Economic Affairs, told the New York Economic Club on November 15, 1960, "the new inflow of private [American] capital into India during the last few years has been no more than $10 to $20 million per year, inclusive of retained profit. That sum is absurd."[10] One reason for capitalist shyness, Ambassador Nehru indicated, was "distrust." So many young regimes have nationalized foreign property and investments that new investments are discouraged. A weightier reason is the rising standard of living in modernized nations and the consequent expanded market for capital at home and in friendly foreign nations.

The concentration of capital on development at home stands Lenin's imperialism thesis on its head. So does the increasing number of colonies liberated by the parliamentary decision of metropolitan "motherlands."

The imperial powers, guilty of the exploitation and past neglect of their colonies, have prospered since they relinquished them. The loss of empire has netted the Western capitalist powers a material gain (though some groups suffered). It has also enriched the quality of freedom, for, as Marx and Lenin repeatedly stated, a nation cannot deprive another of liberty without limiting its own. Fulfillment of the clamant desire of the colonial peoples for freedom enhanced the freedom of their ex-rulers.

The eclipse of Western imperialism did not come from the negative process of decay and parisitism. It arose from three creative processes: the revolutionary upsurge in the colonies; the technological revolution; and the irresistible popular demand for an upward leveling of living standards in all Western countries.

[10] *Indiagram*, issued by the Information Service of India, Embassy of India, Washington, D.C., Nov. 15, 1960.

It would be unfair to blame Lenin for not foreseeing these developments. The future is ever elusive. One can only censure him for excluding the possibility of such developments. The inflexibility of his own ideology made him attribute a similar inflexibility to the social system he wished to destroy.

But the Western world proved adaptable and pliable. The British Labour government nationalized the Bank of England and several major industries and introduced free socialized medicine for all. Most of these innovations were retained by subsequent, severely capitalist Tory Cabinets. In the United States, regarded by communists as the citadel of unyielding capitalism, President Franklin D. Roosevelt inaugurated an era, not yet ended, characterized by the use of federal, state, and local government money to buoy, bolster, patch, refresh, or renew private businesses and whole industries, like farming. The federal government has also built giant water-power and irrigation works and subsidizes some of the biggest American private enterprises. The Austrian state, governed by a Catholic-socialist coalition, is the proprietor and manager of more than 50 percent of the industries and banks of the nation. In Israel, 60 percent of the nation's capitalism is owned by the socialist trade unions; private capitalists hold the remainder. India too, and many newly independent, underdeveloped lands have evolved a mixed economy in which private capitalism and state capitalism coexist in peaceful friction as if they were not the oil and water of the dogma-bound Marxists-Leninists. State capitalism, the Soviet synonym for socialism, bulks large in almost every capitalist country. Indeed, throughout Western Europe, private and state capitalism play pickaback for mutual benefit.

This synthesis of opposites is the essence of dialectics. Yet dialecticians par excellence like Lenin could not imagine it.

Lenin did discern an element of elasticity in capitalism when, during the First World War, he tried to persuade the Bolshevik left—the Bukharinites—that self-determination for national minorities was possible under capitalism. Such self-determination breaks up empires. This actually happened. For example, the strength of the Gandhi-Nehru–led movement was, in effect, recognized by Britain as a self-determination plebiscite, and London, reading the returns aright, granted India independence. Yet, though Lenin dimly perceived the possibility of such an evolution, he obstinately insisted that "imperialism is the eve of the socialist revolution," that dying, decadent capitalism would perish in a socialist upheaval. The survival of reformed capitalism and the rebirth of many former colonies as free nations within the United Nations prove him wrong.

Above all, Lenin mistook the role of the proletariat. In common with all nineteenth-century Marxists, he regarded the proletariat as the "gravedigger" of capitalism. The gravedigger is a poorly paid manual laborer, what the Russians call "a black worker." Black workers, however, have become blue-collar workers and have been joined, to an increasing extent, by white-collar workers. The emblem of the Third International, or Comintern, depicted a burly workingman lifting a huge hammer to smite the chains that encircled a globe. In private, Karl Radek used to say, "A chisel would be more effective." As skill replaced brawn, workers, in the West at least, no longer recognized themselves as the proletariat. Instead of descending to be the gravediggers of capitalism, the working class chose to be the plastic surgeon of capitalism—in England by liberating the colonies, and, there and elsewhere (in the United States through the influence of powerful trade unions and votes), by helping intelligent capitalists recast capitalism into the modern mold of the welfare state, mixed economy, and internationalism.

The sources of Lenin's errors were numerous: a temperamental predisposition to believe the enemy's illnesses incurable; a burning faith in world revolution and socialism and in the demise of capitalism as a preliminary thereof; an exaggeration of the prospects of international revolution; a tendency to see world conditions as a carbon copy of Russian conditions; a brittle, black-and-white, intensely partisan, fiercely vituperative approach to all questions; finally, perhaps most important, an underestimate of what the modern state could do by planning, enhancing the security to individuals, moderating antagonism between classes, and healing through reform.

❧❧❧❧❧

In 1940 two Soviet economists prepared a book,[11] packed with statistics on the growth of monopoly, to support Lenin's thesis of imperialism's, hence capitalism's, early demise. They cite Hitler in favor of colonialism. On February 11, 1933, he told the London *Sunday Express*, "Germany needs a great many things which she must obtain from colonies, and we need colonies just as much as any other power." In the Reichstag on March 23, 1933, Hitler declared, "We know that the geographical position of Germany, which is poor in raw materials, does not guarantee autarchy for our state."[12]

Quoting Hitler to prove Lenin seems a strange communist exercise. A quarter century of postwar West European liberation from colonies shows that Hitler represents the dead past of capitalist imperialism. At the height of his power he was already obsolete—because his ideas were. He believed in annexations. So do the Soviets; they annexed and expanded during and after World War II. But the West, despite monopoly, has turned its back on imperialism, therefore on war, and is slowly graduating from nationalism into internationalism, thus inaugurating a new, creative historical epoch. Lenin denied that this could happen. His followers, blind in their loyalty to his obsolete theories, cannot see it.

Nor can they see that far from being the highest (last) phase of capitalism, imperialism was actually its first phase; it belonged to the primitive, in-

---

[11] *New Data for V. I. Lenin's Imperialism the Highest State of Capitalism*, edited by E. Varga and L. Mendelsohn (New York, 1940).

[12] *Ibid.*, p. 175.

fantile phase of capitalism. Indeed, the first empire builders were the intrepid Spanish, Portuguese, and Dutch navigators who circled the unknown globe seeking gold, spices, silk, and Christian converts. The Dutch East India Company was ruling what is today Indonesia as early as 1613. Surely seventeenth-century Holland had not yet entered the era of modern capitalism. As late as the beginning of the nineteenth century, Great Britain was loath to annex the Dutch East Indies after conquering them during the Napoleonic Wars. Sir Thomas Stamford Raffles, the temporary British administrator, hoped to make Indonesia a second India. But the merchants of London and the balance-of-power politicians in Whitehall rebuffed him. The Indies did not seem to offer good trading profits, and England returned them to Holland.

Lenin would have been nearer the truth had he argued that the less developed the capitalism of a given country (Portugal, for instance) the more tenaciously it holds on to its colonies, and, secondly, that the surrender of colonies leads to prosperity and the prospect of internationalism and thus to modernized capitalism.

Imperialism is not a function or phase of capitalism. It antedated capitalism. It is a feature of any nation which is underdeveloped, yet strong militarily. and dominated by a caste wedded to the exercise of autocracy abroad and at home.

~~~~~~~~~~

Gorky admired Lenin's book on imperialism; in a letter he entitled it *Contemporary Capitalism*. "It has gone to the printer," he wrote on October 25, 1916, to M. N. Pokrovsky, the historian, "and we are sending the author his honorarium. I recently sent him five hundred roubles through his sister." That was apparently an advance payment.

The book did not appear until September, 1917. The long delay seems to have been due to the general disorganization of life and work in Russia during that fateful year.

VI. COMMUNISTS AND THE STATE

IN FEBRUARY, 1916, Lenin moved to Zurich because its libraries were better. There the first news of the fall of the Tsar reached him; he read it in the Swiss newspapers of March 14 and March 15, 1917 (new, Western calendar). The next day he wrote Inessa Armand: "I am beside myself with anger because I cannot travel to Scandinavia. I won't forgive myself for not risking going there in 1915."[1]

A day later, when the news was confirmed, he sent a letter to Alexandra M. Kollontai in Stockholm: "Well," he shrugged, "there it is. This 'first stage of the first revolution (born of the war)' will not be the last and not only the last Russian" revolution. He already had plans for another—his own, and for revolutions outside Russia. It was imperative that he reach Russia. "From the moment the news of the revolution came, Ilyich did not sleep, and at night all sorts of incredible plans were made," Krupskaya recalled. "We could travel by airplane. But such things could be thought of only in the semidelirium of the night." He thought of asking Swedish comrades to forge a Swedish passport for him; he would learn a few words of Swedish. Krupskaya ridiculed the idea: "You will fall asleep and see Mensheviks in your dream and you will start swearing, and shout, 'Scoundrels, scoundrels,' and give the whole conspiracy away."[2] She knew her husband.

Lenin did not desist. His imagination concocted more fantastic schemes. He wrote Y. S. Ganetsky, the Bolshevik party's representative in Stockholm (who tells the story in the assembled memoirs about Lenin, Vol. 1, p. 487), that "It is impossible to wait any longer. All hopes of a legal journey are vain." The note, slipped into a book which Lenin sent from Switzerland, continued, "Find a Swede who looks like me. But I know no Swedish. Therefore the Swede must be a deaf mute. In any event, I send you my photograph" for the false passport.

A laugh broke the soap bubble.

Lenin then schemed to travel through France and England. On March 19, 1917, he wrote Vyacheslav A. Karpinsky, the Bolshevik party chief in Geneva: "Obtain documents in your name for transit through England (and Holland) to Russia. I can wear a wig. A photograph will be taken *of me* already in a wig, and in the Bern [Russian] consulate I will present myself, already in a wig, with your papers. You will then have to leave Geneva secretly for at *least* several weeks (until a telegram comes from me in Scandinavia)." Karpinsky would hide in the mountains; Lenin promised to pay the expense.[3] One year older than Karpinsky, Lenin apparently hoped there was enough resemblance for the disguise to succeed.

This plan, too, evaporated; Lenin never mentioned it again though he remained in correspondence with Karpinsky. On March 24, for instance, he told Karpinsky, "We are against rapprochement with other parties." A day later Lenin amplified, in French: "Our tactic: complete distrust, no support of the new government, Kerensky is especially suspect, the arming of the proletariat is the only guarantee, immediate elections to the Petrograd Duma, aucun rapprochement autres partis." This last, Lenin emphasized, was the

[1] Lenin, *Sochineniya*, Fourth ed., Vol. 35 (Moscow, 1950), p. 237.
[2] Nadezhda K. Krupskaya, *Memories of Lenin*, Vol. II (New York), pp. 200-201.
[3] Lenin, *op. cit.*, Vol. 35, p. 242.

"conditio sine qua non."[4] The Bolsheviks, standing alone, would strive to overthrow Kerensky.

For a moment, however, Lenin despaired. "It seems," he wrote Inessa Armand late in March, "we will not get to Russia. England WILL NOT ADMIT US. Transit via Germany cannot be arranged."[5]

Suddenly the gloom lifted. "And so we are going through Germany Wednesday," he informed Karpinsky on April 2 or 3, 1917.[6]

Russia's participation in the First World War divided the military power of Germany (at one time she had more soldiers on the eastern than on the western front) and threatened her with defeat. The Kaiser attempted to sign a separate peace with the Tsar but was rebuffed. Alexander F. Kerensky told me in New York in 1963 that when the Russian monarchy fell its successor, the Provisional government, over which he did not yet preside, received overtures through unofficial Germans in Copenhagen with a view to a separate peace. Petrograd reacted by suggesting to the Allies the formulation and announcement of war aims that would stimulate peace sentiment in Germany. England and France demurred.

It was then that the Germans turned to Lenin. As early as September, 1914, an Estonian named Alexander Keskuela had spoken in general terms to Baron Gisbert von Romberg, the German Minister in Bern, about the unused resource of the Russian revolutionaries in Switzerland. Keskuela laid a memorandum, dated March 25, 1915, before Romberg outlining the immediate Leninist political program: the transformation of the imperialist war into a civil war. Romberg forwarded the document to German Chancellor Bethmann-Hollweg.

Shortly thereafter—in August, 1915—Count Ulrich von und zu Brockdorff-Rantzau, German Minister in Copenhagen, conveyed to the Foreign Office in Berlin information he had received from Parvus regarding revolutionary stirrings in Russia. A. L. Gelfand-Parvus was, in the 1890's, a Russian Marxist. Having emigrated to Germany in that decade, he became one of the antirevisionist leaders of the German Social Democratic Party. He maintained his connections with the Russian revolutionary movement; in 1902 he wrote a series of articles in *Iskra*, and when the 1905 Russian revolution broke out he went to St. Petersburg, became a member of the city soviet, and collaborated closely with its chairman, Trotsky, during the brief life of that body and in the evolution of the theory of permanent revolution which, for him, meant either that a revolution in Germany would spark a revolution in Russia or that a revolution in Russia would infect Germany. As a supporter of the Kaiser's war effort, he won the ear of German officialdom in favor of Lenin's trip through Germany to Petrograd. He may justly be called the father, with Brockdorff-Rantzau, of that famous and fateful

[4] *Ibid.*, pp. 245-247.
[5] *Ibid.*, p. 248.
[6] *Ibid.*, p. 254.

train ride. Someone characterized him as having "the body of an elephant and the head of a Socrates,"[7] the appropriate intermediary between the Kaiser and Lenin. He wanted, he wrote in 1919, to defeat tsarism and Western imperialism; a strong Social Democratic movement would alter German policy and conditions.[8] Ludendorff, the brain of the German military, agreed to freight Lenin and his comrades through Germany; revolutionary disturbances in Russia would enable him to transport troops from the eastern to the western front. Wilhelm II approved. Ludendorff admitted in October, 1937, that he had no idea in 1917 what Lenin stood for (and probably did not care) when he sanctioned the transit journey and provided the facilities. The Kaiser was at least equally ignorant.

For Lenin the case was simple: he yearned to work in Russia, and all other channels were closed. What Western or Russian enemies might say did not concern him. The Mensheviks, he knew, would not attack him; their own leader, Julius Martov, and his comrades took the same route somewhat later.

Quickly, Fritz Platten, a Swiss socialist, aided by Baron von Romberg, made the detailed arrangements for the trip. Lenin sizzled with joy. He settled the landlady's accounts and returned borrowed books to the library. Krupskaya packed. Time pressed and she had not finished.

"Go yourself," the wife urged Lenin. "I will leave tomorrow."

"No," he ordered, "we will go together."

Did Krupskaya plan to remain so that Lenin might have Inessa?

Anatoli Lunacharsky, future Soviet Commissar of Education, was among those who saw Lenin off at the Zurich railway station. He subsequently recorded his impressions: "In leaving, Lenin was composed and happy. When I looked at him, smiling on the platform of the departing train, I felt that he was filled with some such thought: 'Finally, finally, that has arrived for which I was born, for which I prepared, for which I prepared the entire party, without which our whole life would be merely preparatory and unfinished.' "[9]

The travelers from various parts of Switzerland assembled in Bern: Lenin and Krupskaya, Inessa Armand, Zinoviev and his wife, Gregory Sokolnikov, Karl Radek, who was no Russian, and others—altogether thirty-one adults and a curly-headed boy of four named Robert, son of a member of the Jewish Bund.

The car they entered at Bern was not sealed. Trotsky puts the words "sealed car" in quotation marks.[10] The Russians, in a special car for themselves, with a good cook, had only transit rights and no permission to alight. The conditions under which they traveled were stipulated in writing in Zurich by Lenin and accepted by Baron von Romberg:[11] there was to be no

[7] Werner Hahlweg, *Lenin's Rueckkehr Nach Russland 1917* (Leiden, 1957), p. 13.
[8] *Ibid.*, p. 14.
[9] *Vospominaniya*, Vol. 4 (Moscow, 1963), p. 213.
[10] Leon Trotsky, *My Life. An Attempt at an Autobiography* (New York, 1930), p. 298.
[11] *Leninskii Sbornik*, Vol. II, pp. 389-390.

inspection of passports or luggage at any time and no German voice in the choice of the car's passengers who, in effect, enjoyed diplomatic immunity and privileges. It was in this respect that the car was "sealed" or neutral. The Kaiser himself ordered that if the revolutionaries were barred from Sweden they be allowed to go through the German lines on the eastern front. He also approved of further transports of Russian émigrés via Germany.[12] At Halle, the train of the German Crown Prince was delayed almost two hours to let Lenin's pass. In Berlin, German Social Democrats boarded the train. Lenin refused to see them.

On April 7 Lenin telegraphed Y. S. Ganetsky in Stockholm, "Tomorrow twenty persons arriving." This apparently refers to the twenty Bolsheviks in the transport. Lenin asked Ganetsky to have the group met at Trelleborg, the Swedish port of arrival of the train ferry, and to summon two Bolsheviks, Leo Kamenev and Alexander G. Shlyapnikov, known as "Belenin," to Stockholm.[13]

Lenin had wired Ganetsky on April 1, 1917, "Reserve 2,000, better 3,000 [Swedish] crowns for our trip [from Stockholm to Petrograd]. Wednesday at least ten persons intend to depart. Telegraph. Ulyanov."[14]

Two thousand or three thousand crowns was a considerable sum. It has been charged that Ganetsky received German money for Lenin and the Bolshevik party.

Yaakov Stanislavovich Ganetsky was Jacob Fuerstenberg, born in Poland in 1879. Early in life he joined the socialist movement of Poland and Lithuania. The Fifth Congress of the Russian Social Democratic Labor Party, meeting in London in 1907, elected him to its Central Committee. He had energy, ideas, and business ability. In Stockholm, during the war, he engaged in the business of buying and selling contraceptives. The invoices were seen by Michael Futrell, who made a meticulous study of the evidence in the Ganetsky-Fuerstenberg case and presented it at seminars in St. Antony's College, Oxford, England.[15]

Mr. Futrell, employing great persistence and patience, and guided by documents, found and talked "for several nights" with Keskuela, the Estonian who first broached the idea of the trans-Germany journey to Romberg in Bern. He discovered that after first seeing Romberg in September, 1914, Keskuela had his one and only conversation with Lenin the same month or in October. Keskuela's motives, as is usual—especially in underground operators—were complicated. He was an Estonian patriot who hoped that a

---

[12] Werner Hahlweg, op. cit., p. 23. This book consists, in addition to the author's introduction, of the German text of the official German documents, from the German archives, relating to Lenin's journey through Germany to Sweden.

[13] Leninskii Sbornik, Vol. II, p. 394.

[14] Ibid., Vol. XIII, p. 265.

[15] Michael Futrell, Northern Underground. Episodes of Russian Revolutionary Transport and Communications through Scandinavia and Finland 1863-1917 (London, 1963).

Russia weakened by revolution would withdraw from his homeland and give it independence. He was also a Bolshevik active in the revolutionary movement in 1905-1907. Later he studied in German and Swiss universities. These experiences furnished him with excellent qualifications as a go-between. He too claimed the paternity of Lenin's "sealed car" journey. "It was I who launched Lenin," he maintained.[16] "From a document of 1919 in the German archives," writes Futrell, "it is known that Keskuela then reckoned the total sum received from the Germans at between 200,000 and 250,000 marks." This was then equal to $50,000 to $62,000. He comforted himself with the illusion that he had borrowed it, and, in fact, he repaid it with interest in September, 1923, when it was equal to less than $1. He had used the money to print Bolshevik literature in wartime Germany and elsewhere for distribution in pre-Bolshevik Russia.

With the nose of a political Sherlock Holmes and the assiduity of a serious scholar, Mr. Futrell also followed the trail of Ganetsky-Fuerstenberg.

Futrell does not give the text of a letter, dated "1917, later than November 29 (December 12)" New Style, that is, about five weeks after the Bolshevik seizure of power, which Lenin wrote the party's Central Committee in defense of Ganetsky. The Committee, in Lenin's absence, had decided not to appoint Ganetsky as the Bolshevik party's representative in Stockholm. "In other words, you annulled an earlier decision of the Central Committee." Lenin called the arguments against Ganetsky "bourgeois gossip." No condemnation without evidence, Lenin demanded. " 'But Ganetsky was engaged in trade with Parvus' says 'everybody,' " Lenin quoted. He replied, "Ganetsky earned a living as *an employee* in a commercial firm of which Parvus was a stockholder. This is what Ganetsky told me. This has not been denied." Lenin declared that "the excited comrades" could inquire of witnesses who had been in Copenhagen if they were serious. But he rejected "the anonymous accusers of Ganetsky." Their conduct was "the height of injustice."[17] Of course, Lenin won. Ganetsky retained his post in Stockholm and later served as vice-president of the Soviet State Bank and a member of the board of the Foreign Commissariat and of the Foreign Trade Commissariat. "In 1937 he became the victim of hostile slander"—the normal understated formula for execution by Stalin—"but was subsequently rehabilitated."[18]

Lenin's letter was more damaging than helpful to Ganetsky's prerevolutionary record; it reveals that a majority of the Bolshevik Central Committee were sufficiently impressed by the "bourgeois gossip" to recall Ganetsky from Stockholm. Lenin's "Ganetsky told me" would not be admitted in a court of law, nor is the absence of a denial (by whom?) conclusive.

Fuerstenberg-Ganetsky was arrested in Copenhagen on January 17, 1917, for exporting thermometers, hypodermic syringes, and other medical goods

[16] *Ibid.*, p. 18.
[17] *Leninskii Sbornik*, Vol. XXXVI (Moscow, 1959), pp. 18-20.
[18] *Vospominaniya*, Vol. 2, p. 713.

which were in short supply in Germany and Russia. Mr. Futrell of Oxford obtained permission to examine the court files of the case. Fuerstenberg was the chairman of the board of directors of the Danish Handels-og Eksport-komppagniet whose turnover amounted to tens of thousands of pounds sterling. Large shipments of contraceptives to Germany and Russia bulked large in his smuggling. He paid a fine and was deported to Stockholm, where he acted as Lenin's agent and perhaps continued to trade.

After he unraveled the tangled skein of evidence in the northern underground with unflagging diligence, Mr. Futrell reaches this conclusion: "Surveying Fuerstenberg's previous career, it is difficult to imagine that he would have devoted himself to money-making for any other principal purpose than aiding the revolutionary cause. . . . If he did finance the Russian (as distinct from Polish) Bolsheviks before the spring of 1917, it cannot have been on a large scale, as the general shortage of money for Bolshevik activity before April, 1917 (despite previous contributions from Keskuela), is beyond dispute. . . . Whether Lenin knew much or little about Fuerstenberg as a company director, he valued him as a Bolshevik, and it is not surprising that he fought for him in the central committee."

The fact that Lenin telegraphed Ganetsky in Stockholm on April 1, 1917, to "reserve" 2,000 or 3,000 Swedish crowns proves that he knew Ganetsky had money from some source. There is no proof that it was a German source. Parvus and Keskuela, however, probably financed Bolshevik activities with German funds.

During the eight or ten hours Lenin and his fellow travelers spent in Stockholm en route home, he was much in Ganetsky's company. The party then advanced from Sweden to Finland by train and sleighs. Thence by train to Petrograd. Krupskaya recalls that Lenin was agitated and fretful; he said he feared the Provisional government would arrest him.

Instead, at his arrival in the Finland Station at 11 P.M. on April 3 (April 16, Western style), the eve of his forty-seventh birthday, Lenin was conducted to the Tsar's waiting room where he received an official welcome from N. C. Chkheidze, president of the Petrograd Soviet, and M. T. Skobolev, Minister of Labor, both Mensheviks. Lenin "stood there," a skilled observer noted, "as though nothing taking place had the slightest connection with him—looking about him, examining the persons round him and even the ceiling of the imperial waiting-room, adjusting his bouquet (rather out of tune with his whole appearance) and then, turning away from" the official welcomers, addressed the "Dear Comrades, soldiers, sailors, and workers."[19] These were his constituency and he hoped to use them to overthrow the welcomers and capture the state for communism. Having captured it he intended to destroy it. So he said in one of his revered works, *The State and Revolution.*

[19] N. N. Sukhanov, *The Russian Revolution 1917. Eyewitness Account,* edited, abridged, and translated by Joel Carmichael, Vol. 1 (New York, 1962), p. 273.

Lenin started the book in Zurich. On March 4, 1917, writing from that city, he asked S. N. Ravich, a Geneva Bolshevik, to obtain and send him a copy of *La Commune de Paris et la Nation de l'Etat* par Michel Bakounine, Paris, 1899. "If you cannot buy or borrow it elsewhere," Lenin advised, "get it from the anarchists."

In the stormy weeks following his April arrival in Petrograd, Lenin put the manuscript aside. After the "July Days," when several Bolshevik leaders were arrested, he went "underground," first in Petrograd, then in Finland. From his hiding place he wrote Leo Kamenev on July 18, 1917 (new style), "Entre nous: if I am bumped off"—he thought he might be hunted down and killed—"I ask you to publish my notebook, *Marxism and the State* (it was left in Stockholm)"—on the way from Germany to Russia. "A blue cover, hard binding. In it are collected all quotations from Marx and Engels," and so forth. "There are many comments and remarks, formulations. I should think the work could be published in a week. I regard this as important not only because Plekhanov but Kautsky too has created confusion. Condition: all this absolutely entre nous."[20] He was not killed; he recovered the notebook from Stockholm, quickly completed the writing, and changed the title.

Published in Russia late in August, 1917, less than three months before the Bolshevik revolution, it remains communist scripture. The book documents Lenin's love of absolutes which he bequeathed to generations of political progeny. Its stark thesis reads: "While the state exists there is no freedom. Where there is freedom, there will be no state."[21]

In all countries the amount of freedom and fear moves up and down like the curve on a fever chart. It records the health of a society. Soviet citizens enjoyed more liberty in Lenin's time than in Stalin's and more under Khrushchev than under Stalin. To omit the factor of degree is to be dogmatic instead of dialectic. The quantity of freedom determines the quality of a state, whether it is more or less democratic, more or less dictatorial.

Every state limits the individual's freedom. It may also protect and thereby increase it. Lenin's total "no freedom" would justify the total unfreedom of totalitarianism.

Throughout *The State and Revolution*, Lenin maintains that the state will die and freedom dawn only when classes vanish. The state, in the words of Friedrich Engels quoted by Lenin, would someday lie "in the museum of antiquities, side by side with the spinning wheel and the bronze axe."

"According to Marx," Lenin wrote, "the state is an organ of class *domination*, an organ of class oppression of one class by another." Class conflict

[20] Lenin, *op. cit.*, Fourth ed., Vol. 36, p. 414.

[21] All quotations are from *The State and Revolution, Marxist Teaching about the Theory of the State and the Tasks of the Proletariat in the Revolution*, included in Lenin, *Toward the Seizure of Power. The Revolution of 1917: From the July Days to the October Revolution*, Book II (New York, 1932), pp. 149-347. The English translation, deficient in a few spots, has been checked against the original Russian in Lenin, *op. cit.*, Fourth ed., Vol. 25, pp. 353-462.

cannot be eradicated by the state: "the existence of the state proves that class antagonisms *are* irreconcilable," Lenin said. Therefore, Lenin proclaimed with customary vehemence, the proletariat must launch "a violent revolution" and "shatter, break up, blow up . . . the whole state machinery." In place of the old bourgeois state, he announced, the victorious proletariat would erect a new state different in essence and operation from all previous capitalist governments in Russia or outside.

Engels was not as clear or definite about the nature of the state as Lenin and as Lenin makes him appear to be. Engels, quoted by Lenin, did say that "at a certain stage of development" society became "entangled in an insoluble contradiction with itself" and "is cleft into insoluble antagonisms which it is powerless to dispel." This Lenin accepted as the whole of Marx. "According to Marx," was his comment on the Engels statement, "the state is an organ of class *domination*, an organ of *oppression* of one class by another." Engels, however, did not let the matter rest there. "But," he added, "in order that these antagonisms, classes with conflicting economic interests, may not consume themselves and society in sterile struggle, a power apparently standing above society becomes necessary, whose purpose is to moderate the conflict and keep it within the bounds of 'order'; and this power arising out of society, but placing itself above it, and increasingly separating itself from it, is the state."

Thus Engels saw, prophetically, at least the vague outlines of the modern state. He was skeptical; the state "apparently" stood above society. Yet it undertook "to moderate the conflict" and increasingly separated itself from society. No state-hater, whether Proudhon or Thomas Paine, or Marx or Engels, could accept an identity between state and society. "Society," Paine wrote in *Common Sense*, ". . . is a blessing," but government is "a necessary evil." The state, nevertheless, is inextricably enmeshed with society, and while "increasingly separating itself" from society cannot completely separate itself from it except under a totalitarian dictatorship. Elsewhere the conflict of interests is reflected in the state; it wavers between them yet also defends the national interest, the interest of society, and tries to conciliate clashing power units for the sake of the entire community. Lenin rejected this thought, implicit in Engels, as "the opinion of the petty-bourgeois politicians." To "moderate collisions," he declared in his book, meant to "deprive the oppressed classes of certain definite means and methods for overthrowing the oppressors." Indeed he contended that "if it [the state] is a force standing above society," a violent revolution and the destruction of the state apparatus are all the more necessary.

The State and Revolution, Lenin's most influential literary work, became communism's handbook of revolution. It deals with two problems: (1) how to make a revolution; (2) what kind of state to establish after the revolution.

Communists have understood the first task. But Lenin's prescription for postrevolutionary state-making, compared with the history of the Soviet state, shows that nowhere is Leninism weaker than in its ideas on the nature and function of government.

In the beginning there was violence. Lenin praised Engels' "panegyric on violent revolution." Friedrich Engels, Marx's German collaborator, had said that "violence . . . plays a . . . revolutionary role; . . . in the words of Marx, it is the midwife of every old society which is pregnant with the new." Victorious revolutions, according to Engels, gave society an "immense moral and spiritual impetus."

Lenin emphasized that "all revolutions which have taken place up to the present have helped to perfect the state machinery, whereas it must be shattered, broken to pieces. This conclusion is the chief and fundamental thesis of the Marxist theory of the state."

Lenin's two commandments were: first, strengthen parliamentary power in order to annihilate parliament; second, strengthen the government in order to annihilate it. The "proletarian state," Lenin asserted, "will begin to wither away immediately after its victory, because in a society without class antagonisms the state is unnecessary and impossible."

The first rule of revolution—the exaltation of parliament with a view to crushing it—was obeyed by the Bolsheviks in Russia in 1917-1918, and remains a fundamental tenet of communists. The use of parliament for anti-parliamentary purposes is established communist practice.

Communism in Russia and outside also obeyed one part of the second commandment: it strengthened the apparatus of government. But nowhere did the proletarian state wither away immediately after the victory. On the contrary, it struck deeper roots and pushed out new and powerful branches covered with dark foliage and laden with bitter fruit.

The failure of communist states to follow the Marxist-Leninist withering-away blueprint flows from Lenin's mistaken notion that a proletarian revolution would create "a society without class antagonisms." The prolonged Soviet civil war; the anti-Soviet uprisings of 1920 and 1921; the new lease granted the capitalist class by Lenin's New Economic Policy (NEP) of 1921; the stubborn, widespread resistance to agrarian collectivization after 1929, and a thousand other Soviet phenomena demonstrate that class antagonisms not only persist for decades under a proletarian state but are nurtured by it.

As late as January, 1963, *Kommunist*, the monthly political and theoretical organ of the Soviet Communist Party, stated, with habitual understatement, that "In Soviet society, certain vestiges of class distinction between workers and collectivized peasants have survived." From Lenin to Stalin to Malenkov to Khrushchev, moreover, incontrovertible evidence has accumulated of fierce and enduring rivalries between Soviet castes, or groups, or estates: the military officers, technocrats, national minorities, farm collective leaders seeking economic elbow room, party leaders bent on implementing political views or enhancing personal power—all of them communists yet all competing and attempting to bend the state to their purposes. Lenin left these human aspects of government out of account and ordained, simply, that the end of capitalism meant the end of antagonism and therefore the beginning of the end of the state.

Similarly, Lenin's *The State and Revolution* ignored the international class war. World revolution, the aim Lenin assigned to the Comintern, or Third International, implied a worldwide civil war. Lenin evinced passionate hostility for the bourgeoisie of all countries and recognized the implacable hostility of capitalism to the proletarian state. Yet he omitted this international factor from his most authoritative treatment of the state. In it, without regard to internal or frontier-straddling class war, and to the usual tensions between nations, he endlessly emphasized the inevitability of the withering-away process once the workers dethroned the class enemy and set up a national state.

The State and Revolution abounds in evidence that its targets were, first, Social Democratic reformers and, second, anarchists. It may be that Lenin did not see the towering obstacles to the state's disappearance because he was training his sights on his opponents. Polemical ferocity limited his theoretical clarity.

He lampooned "the petty-bourgeois democrats"—including the Russian Social Revolutionaries and Mensheviks and their "twin brothers, the social-chauvinists and opportunists of Western Europe"—who held "the wrong view that universal suffrage 'in the modern state' is really capable of expressing the will of the majority of the toilers and of assuring its realization." He criticized the German Social Democrats, notably Karl Kautsky, their ideological leader, for demanding a "people's free state." Lenin affirmed that "*no* state is either 'free' or 'a people's state.' Marx and Engels explained this repeatedly to their party comrades in the seventies." Furthermore, Lenin excoriated the "sham socialists" who believed in the "peaceful submission of the [bourgeois] minority to a [toiling] majority conscious of its aims." The exploiting class, he insisted, would have to be overthrown and thrown out by force. This can be done "only by the proletariat." For, whereas capitalism "atomized the peasantry and all the petty-bourgeois strata" it unites the working class. Therefore "only the proletariat—by virtue of its economic role in large scale production—is capable of leading *all* the toiling and exploited masses who . . . are incapable of carrying on their struggle for freedom independently."

Lenin likewise poured scorn on the "dreams" and "utopias" of anarchists who wanted to abolish the state. This attitude, he contended, merely postponed the proletarian revolution. The bourgeois state could not be abolished, nor could it wither away; it had to be *"shattered."*

Today, no communist leader would argue with anarchists about the abolition of the state or with anybody about the withering away of the state. Communist and noncommunist worlds are moving in the opposite direction: toward the expansion of state power. Yet it was Bakunin, the Russian anarchist-populist, who made the first translation into Russian of the *Communist*

Manifesto and not, surely, as a literary exercise, but because of a certain parallelism of goals if not of method. All revolutionaries regarded the state as the ally and agent of their oppressors. Engels, in *The Origins of the Family, Private Property, and the State,* had presented the fascinating thesis that the state (as well as the family) was a recent and transitory social institution. Anarchists subscribed to this view. The issue was: Anarchist abolition or Bolshevik withering? This abstract question, and the hot polemics that raged around it, agitated Lenin. They now lie in the museum of twentieth-century antiquities. The current struggle is between power states intent on greater power—a far cry from atrophy of the state which Lenin, writing in his most abstract mood only a few weeks before power became his, proposed for realization immediately after the proletariat's accession.

Marx, Lenin claimed, empirically altered and expanded his theories of the state after close study of the 1848 French revolution and especially of the Paris Commune of 1871. "The first decree of the Commune," Marx wrote in *The Civil War in France,* which is an analysis of the Commune's brief career, ". . . was the suppression of the standing army, and the substitution for it of the armed people." Furthermore, the Commune itself consisted of municipal councilors "chosen by universal suffrage" and "revocable at short terms." The majority of its members "were naturally workingmen, or acknowledged representatives of the working class." All Commune members and all persons in the public service received "workmen's wages." There were to be no "high dignitaries" with fat "representation allowances" for luxury living and entertainment. Judicial functionaries would lose their "sham independence." Magistrates and judges, like all other officials, "were to be elective, responsible, and revocable."

Thus, according to Lenin, "democracy . . . is transformed from capitalist democracy into proletarian democracy; from the state (that is, a special force for the suppression of a particular class) into something which is no longer really the state in the accepted sense of the word."

Lenin attached special importance to Marx's observation that the Paris Commune had abolished "all money privileges in the case of officials, the reduction of the remuneration of *all* servants of the state to 'workingmen's wages.' Here is shown," Lenin continued, "the *break* from a bourgeois democracy to a proletarian democracy. . . . And it is precisely on this most striking point, perhaps the most important as far as the problem of the state is concerned, that the teachings of Marx have been entirely forgotten."

Marx's teachings are indeed entirely forgotten. What would Lenin say now when high Soviet dignitaries, who are neither responsible nor revocable, live as kings lived in the heyday of monarchy and when an upper class of "public servants" earn from five to forty times "workingmen's wages"?

Lenin quoted Marx: "The [Paris] Commune made that cheap catchword of bourgeois revolutions, cheap government, a reality by destroying the two great sources of expenditure—the army and the bureaucracy." It did so immediately. Everybody, Lenin commented, "longs for 'cheap' government."

This can be realized "*only* by the proletariat," he declared. This has not been realized in Russia or any other communist-ruled country; the military and bureaucracy, on the contrary, obey the biblical injunction to be "fruitful, and multiply and fill the earth." The Soviet army and bureaucracy number millions, and they occupy a privileged social and economic position.

Lenin—was he really so naïve?—found that "Capitalist culture has *created* large-scale production, factories, railways, the postal service, telephones, etc., and *on this basis* the great majority of the functions of the old 'state power' have become so simplified and can be reduced to such simple operation of registration, filing, and checking that they will be quite within the reach of every literate person, and it will be possible to perform them for 'working-men's wages,' which circumstance can (and must) strip those functions of every shadow of any privilege, of any domineering." These were the "self-evident" democratic measures constituting the "bridge leading from capitalism to socialism."

All officials in communist countries are indeed subject to "instant" recall at any time by party bosses who are not elected by the people; Stalin "recalled" hundreds of thousands of officials from their beds to the execution dungeons. Recall continues to this day by Kremlin fiat.

Lenin's dream state sans privilege and sans domineering would be what Marx called "the people constituted in communes." The commune was not a "parliamentary body," but a working body: "executive and legislative at the same time." Lenin quoted and approved these definitions. "In parliaments," he wrote, "they merely chatter for the special purpose of fooling the 'common people' . . . we can and *must* think of democracy without parliamentarianism."

Parliament having been discarded, the baby state would undertake "gradually to reduce all officialdom to naught—this is *no* utopia." The new order would likewise abolish "wage slavery," and introduce "more and more simplified functions of control and accounting" to be performed by each citizen "in turn" so that these functions "then become a habit" and "finally die out as *special* functions of a special stratum of the population." No sitting bureaucrats, no standing army.

Lenin summarized his simple program as follows: "Overthrow the capitalists, crush the resistance of these exploiters with the iron hand of the armed workers, break the bureaucratic machine of the contemporary state—and we have a mechanism of the highest technical equipment, freed of 'the parasite,' which can be set in motion by the united workers themselves who hire the technicians, supervisors, bookkeepers, and pay them *all* and indeed *all* 'government' officials the wages of a worker."

The "whole people armed" was Lenin's answer to capitalist militarism of the standing-army type and his formula for workers' control. "Under socialism," Lenin reiterated, "*all* will take a turn in management, and will soon become accustomed to the idea of no management at all."

"Even the smallest country hamlet," Marx decreed, would have its autonomous commune. But Marx defended himself against the charge that communes might break up the unity of the nation. "Marx is a centralist," Lenin noted. Marx and Engels opposed federalism as a socialist goal. Centralism, however, Lenin wrote, would be voluntary, "a voluntary union of the communes of the nation, a voluntary fusion of the communes into a nation," not something "imposed and maintained solely by means of bureaucracy and militarism."

Before the revolution, Lenin did not hesitate to oppose compulsion. Writing in *Proletarskaya Pravda* of January 18, 1914, he chided Russian "liberals" and "reactionaries" for wishing to impose the study of the Russian language on schools attended by children of non-Russians. "We know better than you," he told the "liberals," "that the language of Turgenev, Tolstoy, Dobrolyubov, and Chernishevsky is great and mighty. . . . And we of course want every resident of Russia to have the possibility of studying the Russian language.

"We do not want only one thing: the element of *compulsion*. We do not want to drive people into paradise with a bludgeon."

In the post-Lenin years and especially in the post-Stalin years, when every wise word of Lenin was quoted and requoted, this passage somehow got overlooked. No bludgeon? No compulsion? Voluntary centralism? How many Soviet measures in the areas of economics, culture, and politics could have been introduced without bludgeons and worse? How many days would the "Russian Soviet Federated Socialist Republic," for that is its name, or the Soviet Union, which is also a federation of national republics, have survived as a centralized state if, as Lenin urged, centralism were "based on the 'complete destruction' of the centralized state apparatus—the army, the police, the bureaucracy"?

Said Lenin in *The State and Revolution:* "Engels, like Marx, insists on democratic centralism, on one indivisible republic. The federal republic he considers either an exception or a hindrance to development, or as a transitional form from a monarchy to a centralized republic, as a 'step forward' under certain special conditions. And among the special conditions, the national question arises." The unsolved nationalities problem is the reason why the Soviet Union, after many decades, remains to this day an un-Marxist, un-Leninist federation. Actually, it is Russia indivisible, a unitary state operated by a gigantic bureaucracy and centrally directed by a small communist party oligarchy ruling through compulsion.

The record of communist cruelty will scarcely stand comparison with Lenin's ringing affirmation in *The State and Revolution:* "We set ourselves the aim of destroying the state, that is, every organized and systematic violence, every use of violence against man in general." For a time, he continued, the minority would submit to the majority; "But striving for socialism, we are convinced that it will develop into communism; that, side by side with this, there will vanish all need for force, for the *subjection* of one man to another, and of one part of the population to another, since people will *grow accustomed* to observing the elementary conditions *without force* and *without subjection.*"

Then Lenin continued, "In order to emphasize this element of habit, Engels speaks of a *new generation*, 'reared under new and free social conditions,' which 'will be able to throw all this state rubbish on the scrap heap,' " including, Lenin adds, even the socialist state.

The Soviet Union has reared several new generations. They have not grown accustomed to nonviolence. They have, on the contrary, lived in a constant climate of force and pressure—within their country under Stalin's government-by-murder, inside and outside their country after Stalin. Might is right in many places and especially in the communist world. The Russian rulers have habituated themselves and their citizens to force in being and force in use. In practice, communism has traveled an uncomputed number of millions of light-years from *The State and Revolution*, which, nevertheless, retains its status as a holy script.

Nobody has recorded a Lenin laugh at himself for writing *The State and Revolution*. Perhaps he was too bitter to be amused.

After Lenin became master of the Soviet state, withering away did commence immediately, but what commenced to wither away was the idea of withering away. This manifested itself in big and little things. One such "minor" matter was revealed in 1960 in a Soviet magazine which published the reminiscences of P. Shumyakov, a Petrograd worker, about his encounters with Lenin in 1918.[22] Starvation stalked the great city. The daily food ration consisted of 100 to 125 grams of bread doled out irregularly and an occasional head of a herring or a morsel of stale dried fish. Active communists with extra political assignments lacked the physical energy to cope with them. The communists of the Viborg district of Petrograd accordingly discussed the question of establishing a closed restaurant where party members might take more nourishing meals. Some communists, writes Shumyakov, thought that active party workers should starve just like the workingmen; "but the majority took a different view"—that if the communists were physically exhausted the result would be "inevitable premature collapse with disastrous effects on the revolution," because without its organizers and leaders "the working class would fail as the motor of the revolution and the builder of a new society." This problem was brought to Lenin.

Lenin listened to the opponents of privilege and rejected their arguments. He said, "The heroics of personal self-sacrifice, which is their basic position, are, especially in present conditions, profoundly petty bourgeois; it originated with the SR's [Social Revolutionary populists]. The working class cannot march in the vanguard of the revolution without its activists, its organizers. The activists have to be cared for, and at the present time, within the limits

[22] *Istoricheskii Arkhiv (Historical Archive)*, September-October, 1960 (Moscow); article entitled "My Encounters with V. I. Lenin," by P. Shumyakov, pp. 140-147.

of existing possibilities, must be supported physically. A closed restaurant [Lenin declared] should be organized. The workers will understand the necessity of it." A few days later, Shumyakov recalls, the restaurant for the district (communist party) activists "was organized."

Shumyakov met Lenin again in Moscow in September, 1918. During the previous month a workers' squad in Petrograd had arrested two persons, " 'His Excellency,' the brother of 'His Excellency' Count Witte," a former tsarist prime minister, and, Shumyakov's memoir continues, "Voronin, the director-manager of 'The Voronin, Lyutch, and Chesser Stock Company.' " They were arrested and handed over to the Cheka for hoarding large quantities of canned goods, gold, bonds, and so forth. "Later we were informed that when the workers learned of the removal of the arrested men to the Cheka prison on Pea Street, they assembled and lynched them." Shumyakov reported this to Lenin. "Lenin," Shumyakov writes, "especially liked my story of the way we carried out the red terror in our district and in particular of the workers' violent reprisals against 'His Excellency Witte' and Manufacturer Voronin. In reply to my remark about our carelessness which resulted in the lynching, Vladimir Ilyich [Lenin] said, 'Well, there's no great harm in that, the workers knew whom they were punishing. In the course of a revolution such cases are undesirable but unavoidable.' "

Lenin's attitude to the closed restaurant for communists was sensible. His reaction to the lynching was practical; what's done is spilt milk even if it's blood. But privilege for communists and workers' license for red terror were the thin wedge of an ax that severed reality from the proclaimed ideal. Multiplied many times, applied to millions of communist and noncommunist servants of the state, the infringement of Lenin's rule that no official receive more than a workingman—today, the very notion would evoke horror and laughter in communist countries—has created a caste-conscious, status-seeking, luxury-lusting hierarchy who for decades have been sacrificing principle to power and justifying the most inhuman means by recourse to convenient, self-formulated ends that bear little resemblance to the goals born in the brains of Marx, Engels, and Lenin. In domestic policy and especially in international affairs the Soviet state accommodated itself to old Russia, to the sick psychology of Stalin, to necessity, and to opportunity. Lenin's *The State and Revolution* lies in the museum. The book is unique in all of Lenin's writings in that it is non-Marxist. For Lenin, the essence of Marxism was the class war. That, indeed, is the heart of Marx' and Lenin's teachings. But *The State and Revolution* shuts out the internal class war and the international class war. Adopting the utopian Nowhere (*Erewhon*) method he so reviled, Lenin described and prescribed a stateless society unrelated to reality then or in the foreseeable future or now in Russia and elsewhere. Despite its plethora of Marx-Engels terminology and quotations, the Lenin book is an aberrant intellectual enterprise, a fanciful exercise for so rock-hard a man, as un-Leninist as the mask he wore and the false name he bore in hiding while writing it.

Lenin admitted that the *"future* withering away" must "obviously be a rather lengthy process." But it would begin immediately after the overthrow of the bourgeoisie: "once the majority of the people *itself* suppresses its oppressors, a 'special force' for suppression is *no longer necessary*. In this sense the state *begins to wither away*."

Lenin was no sooner in government than the civil war and foreign intervention conduced to the aggrandizement of state power. Lenin also demonstrated, in deeds, from November, 1917, to his final illness that he believed in the greatest possible concentration of power in the single party that controlled the state. This was his prerevolutionary goal and his postrevolutionary practice. Party monocracy conformed with his principles and suited his willful personality. Autocracy also flowed from Russia's past.[23] Lenin slipped back into it by subjective inclination and the force of objective circumstances. The root of the evil may lie in the fact that a minority and not the majority of the people suppressed their oppressors. Therefore "the special force," the state, prevailed.

Twenty months after his party seized the Russian state, Lenin went to Moscow's Sverdlov University and delivered a lecture—July 11, 1919—"On the State."[24] Now the experienced statesman spoke. What had he learned? Lenin described the state, all states: "It has always been a definite kind of apparatus which differentiated itself from society and consisted of groups of persons who occupy themselves only, or almost only, or chiefly only with administration. People are divided between the administered and specialists who administer, who raise themselves above society and who are called the governors, the governors of the state. This apparatus, this group of people, which administers others, always takes over the apparatus of compulsion, physical force . . ."

Still later Lenin came full circle and, dialectically negating the negation, he discarded his theory of the withering away of the state. It happened, fittingly, at a meeting on March 6, 1920, of the Moscow Soviet celebrating the first birthday of the Comintern. He told the assembled communists that it was "impossible to put the question of the state in the old way; in place of the old, bookish formulation of this question a new, practical formulation has appeared as a result of the revolutionary movement. . . . So now the question of the state has been set on different rails. . . . To object to the necessity of a central government, of a dictatorship, of the unity of will has become impossible."[25]

The State and Revolution, mocked by the revolution, had been scrapped by its revolutionary author—a courageous act. Life killed a beautiful theory. Instead of the death of the state, the death of *The State and Revolution*.

[23] Jerome Blum, *Lord and Peasant in Russia from the Ninth to the Nineteenth Century* (Princeton, N. J., 1961), contains valuable data on the role of the tsarist government in agriculture, industry, and trade.

[24] Lenin, *op. cit.*, Second ed., Vol. XXIV, pp. 362-377.

[25] *Ibid.*, Second ed., Vol. XXV, pp. 71-77.

Lenin knew, from history, that the Russian state and the Russian people were two hostile, isolated, and uncooperative entities. The state to him was therefore an absolute, incurable evil. But when he achieved power, history overpowered him. Despite his efforts to win popular support, the party-state, like the monarchical state, became, by its very nature, an alien, unrepresentative force which accordingly had to extract obedience.

VII. PEACE IS A PROBLEM

WHAT MEN want shapes their destinies. It also reflects their dimensions. On the eve of the Bolshevik revolution, Lenin's aim was simple and great: to seize the Russian state. Atop the car in front of the Finland Station on his arrival in Petrograd in April, 1917, Lenin addressed the mass and finished with the slogan, "Long Live the Socialist Revolution."[1]

To this end he devoted his colossal energy. He proclaimed his desire. The First Congress of Soviets opened in Petrograd on June 3. The next day Lenin was given the floor for fifteen minutes. He made this historic avowal: "The Citizen Minister of Posts and Telegraphs has declared that there is no political party in Russia that would agree to take the entire power on itself. There is." It was the Bolshevik party. All parties, he said, were contending for power and "our party will not refuse it. It is ready at any moment to take over the government."[2]

This statement was a program. Lenin adhered to it throughout the stormy months that preceded and followed November 7, 1917; he aspired not merely to power but to monopoly power, not to communist membership in a coalition but to a communist state. Yet the Bolshevik party was puny.

Ten Days That Shook the World, published in New York in 1919, is a reporter's contribution to history. Its author, an American socialist, was there during the Provisional (Kerensky) regime when Russia was pregnant with Bolshevism. He was there, as a declared sympathizer, when the Bolshevik revolution was born, and he had eyes that saw and a pen that recorded vividly what he saw and what he heard from the mouths of soldiers, women, workers, and leaders in the center of the stage. Lenin read John Reed's book twice and wrote an introduction to it.

On July 16 and 17, 1917, Petrograd workers launched a revolt against the Kerensky government. Reed says, "The Bolsheviki, then a small political sect, put themselves at the head of the movement. As a result of the disas-

---

[1] Vladimir Ilyich Lenin. Biografia. Institute of Marxism-Leninism. Prepared by P. H. Pospelov and eight other editors (Moscow, 1960), p. 300.

[2] N. N. Sukhanov, The Russian Revolution 1917. Eyewitness Account, edited, abridged and translated by Joel Carmichael, Vol. II, p. 380.

trous failure of the rising, public opinion turned against them." Trotsky, Anatoli Lunacharsky, Alexandra Kollontai, and other leaders were arrested. Lenin went into hiding, wore a wig and facial makeup, and was supplied with a forged card of identity representing him as K. P. Ivanov, a workingman in an armaments plant at Sestroretsk, near Petrograd.

The "small political sect" became smaller still.

July, August, September, October, November 7: four months after the disastrous failure the "small political sect" was the Soviet government of Russia.

Two intertwined circumstances explain this sudden ascent to power. In September, 1917, General Lavr G. Kornilov, commander in chief of the army, marched on the capital with a view to setting up a military dictatorship. His attempt failed; the Petrograd garrison opposed him. Then the usual happened: danger from the extreme reactionaries was wind in the sails of the extreme revolutionaries. The Bolsheviks now said that they were the best, the only, safeguard against rule by tsarist generals. The red star began to rise.

This factor alone would not have brought victory to the small sect. Workers, peasants, and middle-class citizens who abhorred the rotten royal regime feared its restoration. They wanted a firm hand. Above all, masses of soldiers refused to fight. The army's discontent was the Bolsheviks' ladder to power.

The intimate connection between war and the Russian revolution is obvious. Tsarism drafted 14 million men and gave them no heavy field guns, no more than 4,100 machine guns, and limited quantities of light artillery with 1,000 shells for each piece. (The Germans had 3,000 shells for each.) Staff officers were not merely ignorant of modern military science, they held it in contempt. Generals at the front, nursing rivalries born in the Russo-Japanese War a decade earlier, did not cooperate on the battlefield. During the first five months of hostilities (August to December, 1914), the Russian army lost 300,000 men and 650 light cannon.[3] In 1915 the casualties were greater still, in fact staggering: 2 million soldiers killed and wounded, and 1,300,000 taken prisoner by the German and Austro-Hungarian forces. Raw recruits and green officers sucked up out of the vast Russian spaces plugged the gaping holes only to meet maiming and death on the same sickening scale: in 1916 the Russian army counted 2 million killed and wounded and 350,000 captured. When Russia left the war at the end of 1917, her military dead numbered 1,700,000.

Late in 1914 Sir George Buchanan, the British ambassador to Russia, noted "the pessimism that had already struck root in Petrograd."[4] Commenting on Russia's defeats in 1915, he said, "The only wonder was that the army remained intact."[5] It did not remain intact. "Long before the destruction of the Tsarist regime the army at the front had developed acute indications of

[3] John Shelton Curtiss, *The Russian Revolutions of 1917* (Princeton, N.J., 1957). Almost all the casualty figures below are taken from this study.

[4] The Right Hon. Sir George Buchanan, *My Mission to Russia and Other Diplomatic Memories*, Boston, 1923. Vol. I, p. 220.

[5] *Ibid.*, p. 236.

disintegration," wrote Alexander F. Kerensky in the *New York Times* of May 22, 1927. "By January, 1917, more than a million deserters were roaming about in the rear of the army."

The anger of the army spread throughout Russia. Men wrote home that they often went into an attack without even a rifle and only got one when a buddy was felled by an enemy bullet. As the war grew older and grislier, the blame for bad leadership was laid at the door of Nicholas II, the Tsar-Emperor, known to be kindly yet weak, and especially of the Empress Alexandra, the former Princess Alix of Hesse, Germany, who had fallen under the hypnotic spell of Gregory Rasputin ("the debauchee"), a profligate, illiterate Siberian peasant-priest said to possess the therapeutic powers which kept the Tsarevich, the Tsar's heir and only son, from dying of hemophilia.

In September, 1915, debacle having followed debacle, Nicholas assumed personal command at the front. "The result was," Sir George Buchanan wrote, "that the Empress, especially after Stuermer became President of the Council in February, 1916, virtually governed Russia." And by dominating the Empress, Rasputin virtually governed Russia—or so most diplomats, many politicians, and the people believed. The drunkard-monk made and unmade members of the Supreme Council or Cabinet and mesmerized ladies at court. The Empress's published letters to the Tsar[6] show she was the channel through which Rasputin, widely regarded as pro-German or favoring a separate peace with Germany, influenced Nicholas in matters of policy and strategy. Incensed, their patriotic feelings outraged, a prince, a grand duke, and a politician conspired to kill Rasputin and invited him to a dinner party on December 16, 1916. They filled him with poisoned wine and poisoned pastry. When he survived and tried to rush out of the palace they drew revolvers, shot him, and threw his body into the icy Neva River. But the corpse refused to sink. The Empress had it buried with pomp in the presence of her husband, three daughters, herself, and members of the government.

Mortal poisons coursed through the arteries of Russian society.

In one letter to the Tsar, dated August 8, 1916, the Empress, referring to Rasputin with the usual "our friend," had written, "Our friend hopes we won't climb the Carpathians and try to take them, as he repeats the losses will be too great again." Scoundrel though he was, the peasant at court knew the mind of his lowly countrymen: the losses were already too great.

Between white monarchy and red soviets, there was an eight-month republican interregnum of freedom. Lenin called the new Russia, "the freest, the most advanced country in the world."[7] But from ten thousand wounds this free yet unhappy country cried, Peace, peace, and there was no peace. The prolongation of the war was the prelude to Bolshevism.

---

[6] *Letters of the Tsaritsa to the Tsar, 1914-1916* (New York, 1924).

[7] Lenin, *The Revolution of 1917*, p. 98. This speech is omitted from the fourth edition of Lenin's works, published during the Stalin period. It is included in the fifth edition, published in 1962.

Hindsight, always helpful and often unfair, suggests that the infant Republic should have taken immediate steps to retire Russia from the war. The Provisional government ought to have been aware of the circumstances that attended its birth. Early in March, 1917, Petrograd, as well as other cities, witnessed a spate of strikes and bread riots. Troops dispersed street crowds in the capital with a volley of bullets. On the afternoon of Sunday, March 11, however, the Pavlovsky regiment refused to obey the order to shoot and was disarmed by the Preobrazhensky regiment. The next day the Preobrazhenskys themselves disobeyed the order to fire on the people and, instead, killed their officers. Instructed to disarm the Preobrazhenskys, the Volhynsky regiment imitated them.[8]

On Monday morning the mutiny spread. Mounted Cossacks fraternized with demonstrators. The 215,000 soldiers in and around Petrograd, a city of 2,300,000, and the 80,000 sailors in the Baltic fleet would not support the monarchy. A picked force sent by the Tsar from the front to quell the uprising quickly atomized and deserted on encountering rebel troops in the Petrograd suburbs. Late on March 12, 1917, the Tsar's government no longer existed. The Provisional government, a moderate revolutionary Cabinet, was set up with Prince Georgi E. Lvov as Chairman of the Council (Prime Minister), Paul N. Milyukov as Foreign Minister, and Alexander F. Kerensky as Minister of Justice. Two days later, the Governor General of Moscow wired to General Staff Headquarters, "In Moscow there is complete insurrection. Military units are passing to the side of the revolutionaries." The same thing happened throughout Russia. Forsaken by the army, Nicholas abdicated on March 15. The same day the Provisional government announced its own birth.

Trotsky has written, "There is no doubt that the fate of every revolution at a certain point is decided by a break in the disposition of the army."[9] The attitude of the soldiers dated the doom of tsardom.

When Lenin arrived in Petrograd from Switzerland at 11:10 P.M. on April 16, 1917, he walked out of the Finland station and mounted a waiting armored car to address a large crowd of supporters. On the same conveyance he then drove to Kshesinkaya palace, headquarters of the Bolshevik party. There had been no disorder; he did not use the vehicle for personal safety. The military car was a symbol of the key to political power.

Lenin forthwith took command of the Russian communist movement. His first task was to alter the Bolshevik party's course from tolerance of the Provisional government to hostility. Owing to the "capitalist nature of this government," he declared in his famous "April Theses,"[10] "the war on Russia's part remains a predatory imperialist war." He criticized the daily *Pravda*, edited by Stalin and Kamenev: "*Pravda* demands that the government re-

[8] Buchanan, *op. cit.*, Vol. II, pp. 60-61.
[9] Leon Trotsky, *The History of the Russian Revolution* (Ann Arbor, Mich., 1932), pp. 120-125.
[10] Lenin, *op. cit.*, pp. 95-103.

nounce annexations. To demand that a government of capitalists renounce annexations is balderdash." He wanted "not a parliamentary republic" but a "republic of soviets," and the "abolition of the police, the army, and the bureaucracy." His slogan read, "All power to the soviets." That meant, "Down with the Provisional government."

Many Bolsheviks believed at the time that Russia must first experience a bourgeois-democratic revolution under the Provisional government before she became ripe for a working-class revolution and dictatorship. But Lenin was in a hurry.

It required all of Lenin's stubbornness, stamina, self-assurance, and prestige to convince even the upper ranks of the party to swallow his accelerated program of revolt. This campaign of conversion absorbed his energy. As soon as he felt he was making progress he turned to the army. Six days after he reached Petrograd he spoke to the assembled Ismailov regiment and urged immediate peace and the transfer of all government power to the "soviets of workers' and soldiers' deputies." Five days later he addressed the soldiers of the Mikhailov armored division and two days after that he was the chief speaker at a meeting of the soldiers' section of the Petrograd Soviet.

Nor did Lenin neglect the general public. And no public was too small or insignificant. Shortly after his return from Switzerland he went to a neighborhood meeting on Officer Street (now Street of the Decembrists). He sat in the audience, a bourgeois audience dotted with clusters of workers and soldiers and with communists under instructions to make themselves heard. Eugenia R. Levitas, a pharmacist and party member, tells the story.[11] A speaker was denouncing the Bolsheviks. "You Messrs Bolsheviks," he exclaimed, "agitate here. But you do not go to the front to defend the interests of Russia, the interests of our fatherland!"

Applause.

Suddenly a heckler spoke up. "And what, in actual fact, must we fight for?" he said. "For the Dardanelles? Or for the fat profits of the Russian and foreign bourgeoisie who are waxing rich on the blood of our soldiers?"

All heads turned. It was Lenin. He had risen from his seat. With him stood Alexandra Kollontai and a group of Bolsheviks. Lenin strode to the platform, took off his coat and cap, and began to make a speech. Nobody interfered. Russia was free. He stressed the theme: "Who needs the Dardanelles—the workers or the bourgeoisie? Who owns land—the peasants who fructify it with their sweat and blood—or the landlords who squeeze the last juice out of the peasants? Who owns the mills and factories? Who owns the banks and all the wealth of the country—the workers or the Russian and foreign bourgeoisie?"

Soldiers and workers applauded, writes Miss Levitas.

By propaganda among soldiers and civilians Lenin was making a power transfusion from the Provisional government which he abominated to the soviets which he hoped to capture. Already the authority of the government was di-

<hr />

[11] *Vospominaniya*, Vol. 4, pp. 253-254.

minished by the authority of the Petrograd Soviet. Lenin called this "dual government." Dual government is no government, an overture to revolution.

When the Tsar fell, a period of confusion intervened in which the Petrograd Soviet, consisting of representatives of factory workers and the garrison, behaved like a second government in competition with the national government. Thus on March 14 the Petrograd Soviet issued its famous Order Number One drawn up on the initiative of a roomful of soldiers who happened by and an intellectual acting as their recording secretary. The document instructed all army units to elect committees of soldiers responsible to the Soviet; the committees would control weapons which shall "in no case be surrendered to the officer." Soldiers were citizens. Saluting off duty was abolished. Officers had to address soldiers with the egalitarian "you" instead of the humiliating "thou."[12]

"This is the death of the army," the monarchist V. V. Shulgin exclaimed when he read Order Number One.[13] It was not; it was only a sure sign that the patient needed a drastic cure. The best medicine would have been an end to massacre on the battlefield. Instead, and though the air crackled with effective propaganda against imperialism and annexation, Foreign Minister Milyukov on May 1, 1917, dispatched a note to the Allied governments, published in the Russian press, promising no "slackening on the part of Russia in the common struggle of the Allies" and fulfillment of "the obligations assumed toward our Allies."[14] This and previous Milyukov statements on war aims raised a popular storm which forced him to resign. Defending his stand on May 22, Milyukov said, "I fought, unfortunately in vain, against those who favored the new formula [no annexations and no indemnities, and the right of self-determination] . . . I did nothing which gave the Allies the right to say that Russia has renounced the Straits."[15] Milyukov asked the crumbling army to die for Constantinople, the Dardanelles, and Galicia. He admitted in his memoirs that he had tried to conceal this by "substituting circumscribing phrases"[16] for the truth.

Milyukov's attitude shocked the politically minded segments of the population, yet a Bolshevik book which appeared in 1957 conceded that in May "the soldiers, in the mass, had not yet grasped the class character of the policy of the Provisional government. . . . Unlike the soldiers, the predominant part of the workers had a deeper comprehension of Milyukov's note and supported the Bolshevik slogans."[17]

[12] Leon Trotsky, op. cit., p. 276.

[13] William Henry Chamberlin, The Russian Revolution 1917-1921 (New York, 1935), Vol. I, p. 86.

[14] Curtiss, op. cit., pp. 124-125.

[15] Ibid., p. 127.

[16] P. Milyukov, Rossiya na Perelom. Bolshevitskii Period Russkoi Revolutsii (Russia at the Turning Point. The Bolshevik Period of the Russian Revolution) (Paris, 1927), Vol. I, p. 63.

[17] Petrogradskiye Bolshevikii v Oktyabrskoi Revolyutsii (The Petrograd Bolsheviks in the October Revolution), compiled by the Leningrad Provincial Communist Party's Institute of the History of the Party (Leningrad, 1957), p. 96.

Though decomposition was proceeding apace it had not yet destroyed the army. Peace might still have restored health. The Provisional government nevertheless chose this juncture to launch a major offensive on the Galician front. It began early in July; General Alexei A. Brusilov was in command.

Conservative generals retained by the Republic had warned that the spirit of the troops and the state of their armaments made an offensive a precarious operation. Kerensky, now Prime Minister and War Minister in the reorganized Cabinet, knew the military mood. At the Riga front one day, after Kerensky had plied the soldiers with his silver oratory, a peasant infantryman spoke up: "You, Mr. Minister, tell us that we must fight for land and freedom. Of what good will land be to me if I am killed? All I shall get is three yards for a grave." The muzhiks back home were seizing estates and partitioning them. Peasant-soldiers wanted their share. They might be cheated out of it if they stayed in the trenches. An offensive could mean loss of farm, life, or limb.

What, in these circumstances, prompted the harried Provisional government to insist on active prosecution of the war?

Men were moved by mixed motives, often contradictory. Even Leo Kamenev, a prominent Bolshevik, later a first-rank Soviet leader, wrote in *Pravda* on March 28, 1917, "When army stands against army it would be the most stupid policy to propose that one of them should lay down its arms and disperse to its homes. This would be a policy not of peace, but of slavery, which a free people would reject with indignation. No, it shall remain staunchly at its post, answering bullet with bullet and shell with shell."[18] If it had the bullets and shells—and the will. Lenin's advent in Petrograd put an end to such patriotic pleas by Bolsheviks, but the sentiment survived. It also animated many noncommunist revolutionaries who feared that military disintegration would open the front to Germany and allow the Kaiser's legions to crush the revolution, perhaps to restore the Tsar. Foreign Minister Milyukov, reflecting a mystical nationalism, had said in a manifesto, "The Russian nation will not permit the Fatherland to withdraw from the great struggle humiliated and undermined in its life forces."[19] Kerensky, asked years later in New York why he had not taken Russia out of the war, replied simply, "We wished to remain loyal to our Allies." France and Britain were hard pressed; generations of their youth were drowning in blood and mud in Flanders and France. Suppose Germany won the war? What would be the future not only of the liberal revolution but of Russia as an independent power? Politicians directing a state from a seat in the crater of a volcano can hardly be expected to think clearly. The country was heaving under the Provisional government's feet; Petrograd was a city divided; the endless steppes and flatlands were in turmoil; the regime did not know how far its writ ran and what was its life span. None of this conduced to insight or

[18] Quoted by Chamberlin, *op. cit.*, Vol. I, p. 115.
[19] Milyukov, *op. cit.*, p. 64.

foresight. The mere routine of administration, the thousands of little acts that constitute governing, caused the best heads to spin dizzily.

While, moreover, day-to-day decisions, manipulations, intrigues, and plans are born in the head, man's basic predispositions—the seedbed where cerebral processes germinate and grow—originate in the emotions, the fruits of one's own or of previous generations' environment and experience. Passion, ambition, pride, envy, and vanity lead an existence which is independent of the mind but trigger it. Driven by one or several of all these forces, intelligent men may do foolish things. Not so intelligent men may do very foolish things. The successors to the Tsar felt insecure. They had formal power with less content than they needed. Weakness, the ridicule it evoked, and frustration maddened them. Lenin, who knew how to insert his sharp dagger when he found chinks in an opponent's armor, had no trouble piercing thin skin. He was offering himself and his party as an alternative to the ruling group. This infuriated the government and made his program abhorrent. He had traveled from Switzerland to Russia through Germany by arrangement with the German General Staff. He was accused at home of being a German agent. Documents were circulated to prove the charge. The nationalistic bourgeoisie now had an added reason to hate the anticapitalist Bolsheviks. For the ruling politicians to adopt a separate-peace policy would have meant to identify with Lenin, to be tarred with the same "German agent" brush. Lenin shouted, "Down with the Provisional government"; "Peace." Could Kerensky and his friends cry "Peace"? To say "Me too" to Lenin would have been to yield to him on the central issue of the day, the issue of life or death for millions. Then why not admit his party into the government, a step tantamount, everyone realized, to letting a man-eating tiger into the family living room?

The Provisional government was under continuing pressure from Great Britain, France, and the United States to remain at war, to increase its attacks on the enemy. Because socialists served inside the Provisional government and supported it, socialists were included in the Western missions to Petrograd, even in Elihu Root's mission dispatched by President Wilson. Few of these missionaries knew what was happening around them. R. H. Bruce Lockhart, the British consul general in Moscow in 1917, who spoke Russian, quotes with approval M. Grenard, the French consul general in the same city, to the effect that "The Allies were blinded in their desire to prolong the military collaboration of Russia at all costs. They entirely failed to see what was possible and what was not. Thus they were simply playing into Lenin's hands and estranging Kerensky from the people." In his 1957 book, *The Two Revolutions, An Eye Witness Study of Russia, 1917*, Lockhart compared the efficacy of the Anglo-French delegations to that of "a drop of water in the saltiest of seas." The American delegation added neither a drop of water nor a drop of common sense. All of them together sent Kerensky's brain whirling with the ambition to measure up to the expectations of the great governments that were making obeisances to him.

Another human factor shaped events. The toppling of the Tsar released a river of talk. The memoirists of the period, notably Sukhanov,[20] record mass meetings at the front; delegations moving from the front to the cities and from political parties to the front; dawn-to-midnight conferences in Petrograd, Moscow, and provincial towns where exhausted speakers harangued sleeping, snoring, shouting audiences; street-corner groups discussing current affairs; talk, talk, talk. It was natural that the government, headed by a great talker, would hope to distinguish itself by deeds. In the army the situation was chaos compounded. What better remedy for indiscipline than an attack on the enemy?

In his autobiographical book, *The Catastrophe*, published in 1927, Kerensky explained the need for the offensive. He wrote, "For no army can remain in indefinite idleness . . . the restoration of the fighting capacity of the Russian army and its assumption of the offensive was the immediate fundamental, imperative national task of Free Russia. For the sake of her future Russia had to perform this act of heroic sacrifice."

The sacrifice cost several hundred thousand men.

The July offensive in Galicia against the demoralized Austro-Hungarian forces gained initial successes. The Russians even took thousands of prisoners and a few towns. But when Germany sent reinforcements the spent Russians recoiled. The army of Kerensky was now in a state of disintegration; the lower the military value of the particles the greater their political velocity. For most soldiers politics was synonymous with peace, and peace with land.

Shortly after the Galician offensive collapsed, Kerensky summoned a secret conference at General Staff Headquarters. The minutes were preserved. General Anton I. Denikin, commander of the Russian western front, "cited cases where regiments which had promised to go into attack after hearing a speech by Kerensky or receiving a red banner, changed their minds and refused to attack when the hour of action came. 'The officers are in a terrible position,' declared Denikin, his voice shaking with emotion. 'They are insulted, beaten, murdered.' " General Klembovsky, commander of the northern front, described similar conditions in his area. "What can help?" he asked. "The death sentence? But can you really hang whole divisions? Courts-martial? But then half the army will be in Siberia. You don't frighten the soldier with imprisonment at hard labor. 'Hard labor? Well, what of it?' they say. 'I'll return in five years. At any rate I'll have a whole skin.' "[21]

General Kornilov's attempt in September, 1917, to use a sick army to cure a sick civilian government spread the contagion. Now Russia could play no effective role in the war. Now was the time to try to negotiate for peace.

[20] *The Russian Revolution 1917*, A Personal Record, by N. N. Sukhanov, edited, abridged and translated by Joel Carmichael from *Zapiski o Revolutsii (Notes on the Revolution)* (New York, 1955).

[21] Quoted by Chamberlin, *op. cit.*, Vol. I, pp. 231-233, from *Krasnaya Letopis (Red Chronicle)*, No. 6 (1923), pp. 9-64.

Measures intended to restore army discipline added to the anarchy. Suspicion and slander flowered. When the important city of Riga fell to the Germans without a struggle, the Left charged that the capitalists, preferring the Kaiser to communism, had abandoned it. Lenin went further. In a secret letter addressed to the Petrograd City conference of the communist party which met on October 7, 1917 (and first published in 1924), he wrote, "Does not the complete passivity of the British fleet as a whole and also of the British submarines at the time the Germans captured the Oesel Islands"—in the Baltic—"prove, taken together with the plan of the [Kerensky] government to move the capital from Petrograd to Moscow, that a *conspiracy has been agreed upon between Kerensky and the Anglo-French capitalists to surrender Petrograd to the Germans and in this manner to crush the Russian revolution?

"I believe that this is proved."

In invention, this statement could hardly be excelled. Lenin used it to spur the Petrograd party into overthrowing the Kerensky government immediately. Moreover, since his enemies had called him an agent of Ludendorff, he was returning the harmful compliment. Each side now called the other pro-German. The political morass was smothering the last traces of soldier morale. Whole units of the army and of the navy were obeying Bolshevik Party orders—not because they understood Marxism or communism; they hated the war.

The Provisional government no longer possessed the influence to wage war. Day by day, power oozed from its veins. At most it might declare peace. But even that apparently required more strength than it could muster. The picture can be pieced together from many sources; as good as any is Sir George Buchanan, the British ambassador, who kept a diary and copies of his dispatches.[22] The first entry is dated August 31, 1917: "I saw Kerensky this morning. . . . I told him that, though I was one of the few who had not abandoned all hope of Russia being able to pull herself together, I could not assume responsibility of sending favourable reports to my Government unless he could give me satisfactory assurances as regarded the maintenance of order in the rear as well as on the food and transport questions. . . . I told him that what preoccupies me most was the fact that the Socialist [noncommunist] members of the Government were afraid of making the army a really efficient fighting force lest it might one day be used against the revolution . . . I could not . . . conceal from him how painful it was to me to watch what was going on in Petrograd. While British soldiers were shedding their blood for Russia, Russian soldiers were loafing in the streets, fishing in the river and riding on the trains, and German agents were everywhere. He could not deny this, but said that measures would be taken promptly to remedy these abuses."

On September 3, Buchanan added some notes about the same interview with Kerensky: "He more than once spoke of the necessity of our doing our

[22] Buchanan, *op. cit.*, Vol. II, pp. 168 *et seq.*

utmost to shorten the duration of the war, as if he feared that Russia could not hold out indefinitely . . . if he wished the war shortened, he must help us by restoring the combative power of the Russian army. . . . He gave me positive assurances on all these points, but whether he will give effect to them I will not venture to predict. . . . I had, immediately after the Korniloff affair, discussed with my French, Italian and United States colleagues the question of making collective representations to the Russian government on the subject of both the military and internal situations. At a meeting which I had convoked for the purpose we had drafted the text of a note. . . . In that note . . . we emphasized the necessity of their reorganizing all Russia's military and economic forces." Reorganize all Russia's military and economic forces! Kerensky must have wept. The historian can only laugh.

Buchanan, accompanied by the French and Italian ambassadors, went to see Kerensky again on October 9. The Englishman paraphrased Kerensky as follows: "There must also be continuity of policy, and, in spite of all her difficulties, Russia was determined on carrying on the war to the end. He was leaving in the afternoon for the front in order to set the work of army reorganization in motion at once. He concluded by reminding us that Russia was still a great Power." A great power with a dying government and a dying army.

Buchanan conferred once more with Kerensky and with Foreign Minister Tereshchenko on October 25, thirteen days before Lenin and Trotsky ousted Kerensky and Tereshchenko. Kerensky said it was feared in certain quarters that the Allied governments "contemplated making peace at Russia's expense. I replied that we had already categorically denied this charge, and that he might rest assured that we would never abandon Russia if she did not first abandon herself."

Buchanan's diary entry for November 3 began, "Verkhovski, the Minister of War, has resigned. . . . At last night's meeting of the committee of the Provisional council he seems to have completely lost his head, declaring that Russia must make peace at once." Lost his head? He had found his senses. At last, someone in the government was talking sense. But it was too late.

Could Kerensky have taken Russia out of the war? When? And how?

Russia was not the only country suffering from war-fatigue and peacehunger. In a summary of the condition of the four Central Powers at the end of 1917, General Ludendorff wrote, "The Austro-Hungarian army was tired. . . . Its fighting power was small; it practically sufficed only against Italy . . . only the army kept the Dual Monarchy together." Of Bulgaria, another ally, he declared, "The nation and the army were tired of war. . . . Bulgaria would remain loyal as long as all went well with us." Turkey "was at end of her tether." In Germany, the brain and body of the Quadruple Alliance, Ludendorff asserted, "the spirit was better than in the countries of our

associates, but it had obviously sunk quite appreciably, and the general atmosphere had become worse."[23]

Winston Churchill took an equally dismal view of conditions in the
Western alliance. Describing the situation at the end of 1917 he wrote,
"This was undoubtedly a favourable opportunity for peace negotiations.
Russia down, Italy gasping, France exhausted, the British armies bled white,
the U-boats not yet defeated, and the United States 3,000 miles away constituted cumulatively a position where German statesmanship might well
have intervened decisively."[24]

In 1917, before the Bolsheviks took power, both belligerent camps in the
First World War were breaking under the burdens of war. They needed
peace. Yet they lacked the statesmanship, and mankind lacked an above-
the-battle agent or agency, to bring the two sides together before the climax
of slaughter on the western front in 1918.

Most wars in history could have been shortened before total victory
installed a bad peace. But the companions of war are a closed mind, disruption of human communication, and the will to win irrespective of consequences and costs. If the Western governments, including the American,
had had better information from Russia and realized that only peace could
rescue Kerensky; if Ludendorff, instead of introducing Lenin into Russia,
had possessed caution or vision enough to grasp the potential effect of his
act on Germany in coming decades—the war might have ended a year before
the armistice of November 11, 1918, and who knows if this might not have
prevented the rise of Hitler and the outbreak of the Second World War.

Churchill, never deficient in martial spirit, regarded the time ripe for
peace talks—if Ludendorff would only take the initiative. Conceivably, judging by Ludendorff's assessment of the German alliance's declining strength,
he might have welcomed peace overtures from the government of which
Churchill was a prominent member. In all belligerent countries voices were
calling for an end to mass destruction. Perhaps the most notable of these
was heard in England.

Lord Lansdowne, former Governor General of Canada, Viceroy of India,
Minister of War, Foreign Secretary, member of one of the oldest noble
families of Britain, was a man of great social eminence and political influence.
He had urged England to enter the war. In October, 1914, his second son was
killed in France. In October, 1916, while Lord Lansdowne was a member of
the Coalition government, Prime Minister Asquith asked the members of
the War Committee "to express their views as to the terms upon which peace
might be concluded."[25] Lansdowne, emphasizing the enormity of human

[23] Erich Ludendorff, *Meine Kriegserinnerungen, 1914-1918 (My War Memoirs)*
(Berlin, 1920), p. 433.
[24] Winston S. Churchill, *The World Crisis*, Vol. II, pp. 123-124.
[25] Lord Newton, *Lord Lansdowne, A Biography* (London, 1929), p. 449.

sacrifice, wrote on November 13, 1916, that "it is unfortunate that . . . it should be possible to represent us and our Allies as committed to a policy partly vindictive and partly selfish, and so irreconcilably committed . . . that we should regard as unfriendly any attempt, however sincere, to extricate us from the impasse." He was then leader of the Coalition party in the House of Lords and therefore presumably well-informed about the military impasse.

This secret memorandum produced no echo. He waited a year. On November 29, 1917, the London *Daily Telegraph* published Lord Lansdowne's famous letter.[26] "In my belief," it read in part, "if the War is to be brought to a close in time to avoid a world-wide catastrophe, it will be brought to a close because on both sides the people of the countries involved realize that it has already lasted too long." He then argued against insisting on Germany's unconditional surrender followed by a punitive peace. He was, of course, showered with abuse, but, as he subsequently revealed, "The Archbishop told me he was on my side . . . I am surprised—I wonder if I really am?—at the number of letters written to me by officers at the front to say they welcomed the letter."[27]

In all quarters there was a poignant yearning for an end to killing. A brave official peace bid by Britain or Germany or a group of neutral states or by President Woodrow Wilson just as America was beginning to throw its decisive military weight into the balance (and just as Russia was slipping toward Bolshevism) might have crystallized sentiment into action. But the bloodshed had produced mental anemia. Peace was a popular wish but not a popular policy.

A general cessation of hostilities would have benefited the Kerensky government and perhaps enabled Russia, "the freest, the most advanced country in the world," to continue her experiment in democracy. The alternatives were a separate Russian peace with Western acquiescence or without it.

It would have been wise yet almost superhuman for the Western Allies, uncertain of victory, teetering on the edge of an abyss, and counting their casualties in millions, to urge Russia to quit their ranks and thereby enable Germany to shift whole armies from the eastern to the western front. Yet in a few months, under Lenin and Trotsky, this was to happen despite Allied disapproval.

The question remains whether Kerensky could not have done what Lenin would do: sign a separate peace with the Kaiser. Why could Kerensky not do in 1917 what Lenin did in 1918 when Russia had grown still weaker? Is one forced to admit here that a man made history? Trotsky writes, "If neither Lenin nor I had been present in Petersburg, there would have been no October Revolution: the leadership of the Bolshevik Party would have prevented it from occurring—of this I have not the slightest doubt! If Lenin

---

[26] *Ibid.*, pp. 463 *et seq.*
[27] *Ibid.*, p. 472.

had not been in Petersburg, I doubt whether I could have managed to conquer the resistance of the Bolshevik leaders. . . ."[28]

VIII. THE END AND THE BEGINNING

"THE ARMY IS WITH US," Leon Trotsky, elected Bolshevik president of the Petrograd Soviet after his release from prison in September, said to John Reed on October 30, 1917. "The Provisional Government is absolutely powerless. The bourgeoisie is in control. . . . But it is force which the bourgeoisie lacks. The Army is with us."[1]

Trotsky's "the Army is with us" was part truth, part fiction. The army was not with the war-to-the-finish Provisional government. Many soldiers were "with us." But the majority of the army, of the population, and of the intelligentsia were not Bolshevik.

The decades since 1917 have produced ample evidence that citizens often side with communism not out of communist conviction or a knowledge of Marxism-Leninism but from opposition to existing conditions and the existing government. The millions of illiterate peasants in India, Indonesia, and other Asian countries, even the millions of literate workers in Italy and France, who cast their ballots for the communist party vote their unhappiness and fears, not their ideology. Some of these voters would be appalled if the communists came to power. Just so, numerous soldiers, workers, peasants, and intellectuals in Russia in 1917 supported Lenin and Trotsky to vent their wrath against the war and those who wished to continue it. But only a minority voted Bolshevik in the nationwide democratic elections to the Constituent Assembly.

This election, the one free, popular referendum in Russia's history, was held, ironically enough, on November 25, 26, and 27, 1917, under Soviet rule. The fact that the balloting occurred at all and that it resulted in a Bolshevik defeat was proof of a liberality which the Soviet system soon conquered. This made the vote all the more interesting as a unique pulse-taking or poll-taking at the very moment when Russia crossed the divide from democracy into dictatorship.

From the moment Lenin arrived in Petrograd in April, 1917, till Novem-

[28] *Trotsky's Diary in Exile 1935.* Translated from the Russian by Elena Zarudnaya (London, 1959), p. 54.
[1] John Reed, *Ten Days That Shook the World,* pp. 50-51.

ber, he and his party emphasized the necessity of convening the Assembly to draw up the Republic's constitution and decide who should rule. The elections aroused great public interest and mirrored national sentiment. The Bolsheviks tried hard to win. *Rabochii Put*, the Bolshevik daily that replaced the proscribed *Pravda*, said on October 21, "The proletarian revolutionary party—the only consistent and uncompromising party of revolution—the Bolsheviks must be elected to the Constituent Assembly in massed rows." On November 8, the day after the Bolshevik seizure of power, Lenin spoke publicly of the Constituent Assembly as the decision-making body in foreign policy.

According to communist figures,[2] the Social Revolutionaries won 410 of the 707 seats—a clear majority. The Bolsheviks won 175; Mensheviks 16; the Kadets (the Constitutional Democrats who got their name from the initials of the corresponding Russian words: *Ka* and *De*) 17; nationalities groups 86; miscellaneous organizations the small remnant.

Thus, 24.7 percent of the electorate, or roughly one quarter, cast their ballots for the Bolsheviks when the Bolsheviks were actually ruling Russia in November, 1917.[3]

This indicates that at the time Lenin and Trotsky formed the government of Russia they were not merely a party of 25,000 members, as is often suggested. They had achieved a considerable popularity—but not a majority. Compared with the 17,490,837 votes garnered by the Social Revolutionaries (SR's) the Bolsheviks received 9,562,358 out of a total count of almost 40 million. How explain the Bolsheviks' strength?

"The testimony is unanimous," writes Oliver Henry Radkey, "that soldiers swayed the mass at will and exerted a profound influence on the outcome of the elections." He cites several cantons in Tver province "where a single agitator dispelled the animosity to Bolshevism and won the populace over to his cause." Another canton of the same province, however, gave the SR's 12,000 votes and the Bolsheviks only 1,400 probably because, Radkey says, "in this locality returning soldiers from the front generally recommended the SR list."

In a letter dated October 10, 1917, and addressed to I. T. Smilga, a Finnish Bolshevik who commanded pro-Bolshevik armed forces around Helsingfors, Lenin wrote, "Of course, leave should be given sailors and soldiers. Men going on home leave to villages should be organized as a propagandist squad for systematic travel in all provinces and for village propaganda in general as well as for the Constituent Assembly." Lenin also approved of Smilga's proposal to split the SR's and join in a bloc with the Left SR's. "This alone,"

[2] Oliver Henry Radkey, *The Elections to the Russian Constituent Assembly of 1917* (Harvard University Press, Cambridge, Mass., 1950). These and all subsequent statistics and quotations, unless otherwise indicated, are from Mr. Radkey's authoritative work.

[3] In some regions the election took place later in the year or early in 1918. These results too are included in the tabulations.

Lenin remarked, "can give us solid power in Russia and a majority in the Constituent Assembly."

The SR's considered themselves socialists, utopian socialists, who hoped Russia could leap from underdeveloped capitalism into a heaven of village communes. Though Lenin had called their populist socialism "foul and stinking carrion," they enjoyed a tremendous following in the farming countryside. In the agricultural province of Kursk, for example, the SR's had a 7-to-1 election lead over the Bolsheviks. "Even so," says Radkey, "Lenin's party still occupies second place with more than 100,000 votes, relatively few of which could be proletarian." Who cast these votes? "The answer is that soldiers—either those from rear garrisons or those coming back from the front—everywhere conducted a fierce agitation on behalf of Bolshevism. . . . Thus was Bolshevism sustained in districts with little or no industry."

According to Radkey, who read the contemporary press in Petrograd, Moscow, and small towns, "The most effective and certainly the most ubiquitous propagandists of the Bolsheviks were the soldiers from the front and the sailors from the Baltic front." One soldier told the Saratov daily newspaper, "Nothing matters except to end this damned war and get home."

Bolshevik candidates' names were printed on List No. 7. Leninist agitators toured the steppes repeating one telling argument among women: "If you don't vote for Number 7, just wait till your mate gets home—he'll beat the hell out of you."

In a big country like Russia, distance—and bad roads and irregular trains—made politics. Thus in Viazma "cantons near the railway line went for the Bolsheviks and those further away for the SR's, simply because soldiers had worked the villages near the stations but had not penetrated into the interior." For a similar reason the Bolsheviks received 653,430 votes at the western front close by their headquarters in Petrograd against 180,582 for the SR's, but only 167,000 on the more remote Romanian front against 679,471 for the SR's. On the still more distant Caucasus front, the SR-Bolshevik ratio was 5 to 1.

The city of Petrograd, which cast 942,333 ballots, gave the Leninist ticket 424,027 votes; the SR's 152,230; the Mensheviks 29,167, and the Kadets 246,506. In Moscow, with 764,763 persons voting, the result was: Bolsheviks 366,148; SR's 62,260; Mensheviks 21,597; Kadets 263,859. Russia's two metropoles, accordingly, chalked up an impressive plurality for the Bolsheviks, but let the peasant-oriented SR's down. The middle- and upper-class Kadets, however, represented a considerable minority soon to be reduced by emigration, execution, etc., and cowed by terror.

Everywhere the percentage of participation was high. "The election on the whole," writes Radkey, "passed off normally: no one was killed and of the few who were beaten, some were on one side and some on the other."

Russia had elected her first representative parliament—the Constituent Assembly. Before it could convene the Soviet government arrested a number of Kadet and SR deputies. Then the Soviets outlawed the Kadet Party, thereby depriving all Kadet deputies of their mandates. Two Kadet deputies, F. F. Kokoshkin and A. I. Shingarev, a former minister of finance, were murdered in their hospital beds in the night of January 18, 1918 (New Style), by a group of soldiers and sailors.

The decimated Assembly met that day in the Tauride Palace in Petrograd. Before even the Speaker had been elected, Yaakov Sverdlov, a Bolshevik leader, asked the Assembly, in vain, to rubber-stamp the decisions already taken by the Lenin-Trotsky government. Later, by a vote of 244, against 153 for the famous Left Social Revolutionary Maria Spiridonova (the Left SR's were collaborating with the Bolsheviks), Victor M. Chernov was elected Speaker. His opening address floodlit the chasm. Amid howls and heckling from the Leninists and Left SR's, Chernov, a right SR, enunciated a political program which would have required the Bolsheviks to surrender the power they had just seized to a bloc which included their enemies—the Mensheviks and Right SR's—and submit to a parliament sure to outvote them and, ultimately, oust them from office. It was fatuous to expect zealous communist powermen to relinquish power so easily. Far into the night the debate raged, with Bolshevik Nikolai Bukharin and Menshevik Irakli Tsereteli scoring points in a brilliant oratorical draw. Finally, long after midnight, Speaker Chernov read a decree nationalizing land. Before the vote could be taken, a burly Kronstadt sailor named Zhelezniakov, armed with a pistol, approached the Speaker and said the Assembly must disperse because "the guard is tired."

Shouts from the hall: "We don't need a guard."

Chernov: "Whose instructions, from whom?"

The guard replied that Commissar Dibenko, a communist naval officer, had sent him to close the session. Chernov nevertheless read a second decree, which was likewise approved, urging the belligerent allies of Russia to fix, with her, the conditions of an immediate offer of democratic peace. Thereupon the Constituent Assembly adjourned at 4:40 A.M. (the guard had a right to be tired) after deciding to reconvene the same day, January 19 (New Style), at 5 P.M.[4] Armed Bolshevik patrols prevented further sessions.

Thus ended Russia's brief parliamentary experience.

What would have happened if the Bolsheviks had won a majority in the Constituent Assembly? They might have kept the parliament in being. Subsequently, leaders made attempts to justify the dispersal of the Assembly on theoretical grounds. The reason was much simpler: the Bolshevik minority faced a resolute but unarmed majority. The Bolsheviks therefore used arms to scatter their opponents.

---

[4] *Uchreditelnoe Sobraniye. Stenographicheskii Otchot. January 5-6, 1918, Pechataetsa po Rasporyazheniyu Predsedatelya Uchreditelnago Sobraniya (Constituent Assembly*, Stenographic Record, Jan. 5-6, 1918, Printed by order of the Speaker of the Constituent Assembly) (Petrograd, 1918), 100 pages.

The elections to the Constituent Assembly merely underlined a fact of which Lenin was well aware when he stepped on Russian soil in April, 1917: war-weary soldiers were a decisive element, perhaps the decisive element in the political situation. Kerensky fell for much the same reason and in much the same way as the Tsar fell: no fighting man—except at the Winter Palace and in Moscow where officer cadets battled against the red insurgents—would lift a finger for him. The ten days did ultimately shake the world, but they scarcely raised a ripple in Petrograd which was the eye of the storm.

Kerensky is the best witness of what happened on the fateful November 7, the day Bolshevism came to power: "My office [in the Winter Palace], midnight, November sixth . . . the Council of Cossack Troops, meeting all night, had proclaimed the *neutrality* of the Cossacks in the struggle of the Provisional Government against the Bolshevik uprising. . . . The government's commissar attached to the municipal administration, Rogovsky, appeared. . . . We learned from Rogovsky, among other things, that a considerable number of warships from the Baltic Fleet had entered the Neva in battle formation, that some of these ships had moved as far as the Nikolayevsky Bridge, and that this bridge had been, in turn, occupied by detachments of mutineers, who were already advancing further toward the [Winter] Palace bridge. Rogovsky drew our attention especially to the fact that the Bolsheviki were carrying out their plan without any trouble, meeting no resistance on the part of the government troops . . . the staff of the Petrograd military district was watching the developments with utter indifference. . . . The hours of the night dragged on painfully. From everywhere we expected reinforcements, but none appeared."[5]

Weary from loss of sleep, but with a courage born of conviction, confusion, and despair, Kerensky left the Winter Palace in a confiscated car followed by an automobile bearing the United States flag. He was going to the front to find troops who would return with him to Petrograd and oust the Bolsheviks. Outside the city, at Gatchina, he rallied a few soldiers and officers and attempted to make a last stand. In vain. The "force" melted away. Kerensky escaped.

In Petrograd itself, the government, as one French commentator wrote, "was overthrown before it could say 'ouch.' " Trotsky, who as chairman of the Military Revolutionary Committee was in personal charge of the insurrection, stated subsequently, "Demonstrations, street fights, barricades—everything comprised in the usual idea of insurrection—were almost entirely absent."[6]

From headquarters in the three-story Smolny Institute, formerly a school for daughters of the nobility, the Bolshevik Military Revolution Committee operated openly like the general staff of an army. "It was," Trotsky wrote

[5] Kerensky, *The Catastrophe*, pp. 326 *et seq.*
[6] Leon Trotsky, *The History of the Russian Revolution* (Ann Arbor, Mich.), p. 292.

in his history, "as though the Winter Palace and Smolny had changed places." On November 6, the eve of the revolution, the committee ordered: "All regimental, company and staff committees together with the commissars of the Soviet, all revolutionary organizations must be *in permanent session*. . . . Not a single soldier is to leave his unit without permission of its committee. . . . Dispatch immediately to the Smolny Institute two representatives of each unit."[7] At the same time garrisons in the environs of Petrograd were instructed to guard the roads and railroads and prevent Kerensky from marching on the city.

November 6. "At 17.00 hours," reads the official communist history of the day, "soldiers of the Keksholm regiment occupied the central telegraph office." That evening Kerensky sent instructions that the bridges connecting Petrograd with its suburbs be opened, "but the determined action of the revolutionary units of the Petrograd garrison and of sailors of the Baltic fleet disrupted those plans. . . . At 21.00 hours, sailors in Petrograd occupied the Petrograd Telegraphic Agency."[8]

At 22.45 hours, Lenin, who had been in hiding in Finland and in and near Petrograd since July, arrived at the Smolny disguised as a workingman and still wearing makeup. "In the square before the Smolny, armored cars rattled, a three-inch cannon stood ready, and wood had been piled up in case it became necessary to build barricades," Krupskaya wrote years later. "At the entrance were machine guns, field pieces . . ."[9] The Smolny and the thoroughfares leading to it were guarded by Lettish riflemen under the command of Jan Berzin who in 1936 was the chief Soviet military officer in Loyalist Spain.

November 6. "Midnight. Yaakov M. Sverdlov, member of the Military Revolutionary Committee, dispatched a telegram to P. E. Dibenko, chairman of the Central Baltic fleet, to send battleships with a landing party from Helsingfors to Petrograd. On November 7, at 1.25 hours, a unit of Red Guards from the Viborg district, soldiers of the Keksholm regiment, and revolutionary sailors under the command of M. D. Gorchayev, occupied the main postoffice." (The Red Guards, according to John Reed, were "armed factory workers . . . untrained and undisciplined, but full of Revolutionary zeal.")

At 2 A.M. on November 7, the first company of the sixth reserve sapper battalion captured the Nikolayevsky railway station. Simultaneously Red Guards took the Baltic railway station, the central electric power station, and other points. At 3 A.M., "on the summons of the Military Revolutionary Committee, the first echelon of Baltic sailors arrived from Helsingfors by the Finnish railway. At 3.30, the cruiser *Aurora* dropped anchor at the Niko-

[7] *Petrogradskiye Bolshevikii v Oktyabrskoi Revolyutsii (The Petrograd Bolsheviks in the October Revolution)*, compiled by the Leningrad Provincial Communist Party's Institute of the History of the Party (Leningrad, 1957), p. 375.

[8] *Ibid.*, p. 377.

[9] *Ibid.*, pp. 378-379.

layevsky Bridge. At about 6 in the morning, sailors . . . seized the State Bank." An hour later Red Guards together with soldiers fought their way into the central telephone exchange and cut off the telephones of the Winter Palace.[10]

All day of November 7 the military operations rolled on without cease or hindrance. At 10 in the morning, after a vast fleet had moved from the Kronstadt naval base into the Neva River and landed troops in the streets of the city, Lenin announced: "The Provisional government has been overthrown."

Joseph Stalin also described the events of November 6 and 7, 1917, in purely military terms.[11] Only one center of resistance remained, the Winter Palace, home of the last Tsar, last citadel of the democratic Republic. It was strongly defended and stubbornly held. First, pro-Bolshevik units surrounded it. Cruisers, gunboats, minelayers moved into range. At 21.45 hours the *Aurora* fired one blank shot from a six-inch cannon to signal the opening of the attack. The heavy artillery of the Peter-Paul fortress lobbed thirty to thirty-five shells in the direction of the palace without doing much damage. Therewith the assault began. It continued until 2:10 A.M. on November 8, when, five of the six armored cars having deserted to the Bolsheviks, the officer cadets, members of the women's "Death Battalion," and other defenders desisted. On hearing the news, "workingman K. P. Ivanov" immediately removed his wig and makeup and became Lenin.

The hunted, disguised conspirator was now head of a government. How did he react? Through the night, while runners brought messages about the fight for the Winter Palace, Lenin and Trotsky lay on the floor of a room in the Smolny, trying to snatch some sleep: "some one spread rugs on the floor and laid two cushions on them." Later in the morning, after the palace had been taken, Lenin, looking tired, smiled and said to Trotsky, "The transition from the state of illegality, being driven in every direction, to power— is too rough."

"It makes one dizzy," Lenin "at once added in German, and made the sign of the cross before his face. After this one more or less personal remark that I heard him make about the acquisition of power, he went about the tasks of the day."[12]

The sign of the cross. In a moment of great emotion, the subconscious brought back the child and Lenin acted like a religious Russian.

Thus ended Kerensky's rule. Thus Lenin's began. The cannons and rifles had spoken. Politics were born in barracks and battleships.

The Provisional government was the victim of the First World War; the Soviet government was the natural offspring of the same struggle. Russia

[10] *Ibid.*, p. 380.

[11] *Pravda*, Nov. 6, 1918, reproduced in English in *The October Revolution, A Collection of Articles and Speeches*, by Joseph Stalin, Marxist Library, Works of Marxism-Leninism, Vol. XXI (New York, International Publishers, 1934).

[12] Leon Trotsky, *Lenin* (New York, 1925), p. 102.

longed for peace. Soldiers and sailors threw their weight to communism because they wanted to go home. Small wonder, therefore, that when the Bolshevik state emerged from the womb of war its first squeak was "Peace."

IX. ℳAN MAKES HISTORY

WHILE LENIN was aspiring to the power he won on November 7, 1917, he rejected peace by negotiation. Instead, he regarded international revolution the Siamese twin of peace. In a "Resolution on War" drafted for a party conference in May, 1917, Lenin wrote, "This conference again and again protests the low-down slander spread by the capitalists against our party, namely, that we favor a separate peace with Germany." The idea was abhorrent to him: "We regard the German capitalists as the same kind of brigands as the Russian, British, French and other capitalists, and Kaiser Wilhelm the same kind of crowned brigand as Nicholas II and the monarchs of England, Italy, Romania, etc." Then Lenin formulated his prescription: "This war can come to an end *only* through the transfer of all political power in at least several belligerent countries to the hands of proletarians and semi-proletarians [the poor peasantry]." He explained how this would happen: the revolutionary class of Russia would destroy the economic domination of capitalists and "immediately and publicly" propose "to all nations a democratic peace based on the complete renunciation of annexations and indemnities. These measures and this open offer of peace would create complete confidence of the workers of all belligerent countries in one another and would inevitably lead to insurrections of the proletariat against those imperialist governments which opposed the proffered peace."[1]

Direct proletarian insurgent action, not parleying for a separate peace, was the way to end the war. Meanwhile Lenin advocated fraternization at the front between Russian and enemy soldiers. Plekhanov, once Lenin's Marxist mentor, demurred. "No, Mr. Ex-Socialist," Lenin replied on May 11, 1917, "the fraternization, which we favor on *all* fronts, leads not to a 'separate' peace between the capitalists of some countries but to a universal peace between the revolutionary workers of all countries *in spite of* the capitalists of all countries, *against* the capitalists, with a view to destroying their yoke."[2]

However, the charge that Bolsheviks wanted a separate peace would not die; it vexed Lenin. He welcomed the "virtual armistice" on the Russian front and asked what was bad about it. The objection that it might result in a separate peace "is clearly without substance," Lenin said. "For if the Russian government, the Russian workers and peasants *do not want* a sep-

[1] Lenin, *Sochineniya*, Second ed., Vol. XX, pp. 263-265.
[2] *Ibid.*, p. 313.

arate peace with the German capitalists (our party, as is well known, has more than once protested against such a peace . . .)—if nobody in Russia wants a separate peace with separate capitalists then how, whence, and by what miracle can such a peace come about? Who can impose it?"[3]

On May 27, 1917, Lenin delivered a lecture, first published in the Moscow *Pravda* of April 23, 1929, entitled "War and Revolution."[4] Here he took a look at the origins of war. "We Marxists," he asserted, "do not belong to the unconditional enemies of all wars. . . . There are wars and wars. It is necessary to understand what historic conditions produced a given war, what classes conduct it, in the name of what." For, he explained, quoting his favorite German military philosopher, Clausewitz, "War is the continuation of politics by other means." Whether a war is just or unjust depends on what class rules. If capitalists rule, the war is imperialistic.

Being imperialistic, the First World War was about old or new annexations. Lenin defined annexations: "Any people which has been united with another people not by the voluntary desire of its majority but by the decision of a Tsar or government is an annexed people, a captive people." He did not qualify "majority." He did not say a majority of workers and peasants. He said "majority." Majority will is not something officially estimated. It can be ascertained only by a free vote.

Lenin cited Courland (Latvia) and Poland as cases of forced annexation. He said, "Together those three crowned brigands [the rulers of Russia, Prussia, and Austria-Hungary] partitioned Courland and Poland. They partitioned them for a century, they tore the living flesh, and the Russian brigand tore away more because at that time he was stronger." Now Germany, grown stronger, was questioning that division. Joined to similar rivalries around the globe, Lenin declared, "This is what the war is about."

"Here," Lenin continued, "I pass to the last question. This is—the question how to end the war. . . . What nonsense, that we stand for ending the war by means of a separate peace. A war waged by the capitalists of all the richest powers, a war caused by decades of the history of economic development, cannot be ended by the renunciation of military activities on the part of one side—that is so foolish we are embarrassed to refute it. . . . A war conducted by the capitalists of all countries cannot be brought to a close without a workers' revolution against those capitalists. . . . The workers' revolution is growing in the entire world. . . . Of course, in other countries a revolution is more difficult [to achieve]. There they have no such half-wits as Nicholas and Rasputin. There the best men of their class are at the head of the administration." Yet the revolution is "inevitable." For the future is with the revolutionaries, and "the workers must conquer in all countries."

---

[3] *Ibid.*, p. 354.
[4] *Lenin o Mezhdunarodnoi Politike i Mezhdunarodnom Prave (Lenin on International Policy and International Law)*, Institute of International Relations (Moscow, 1958), pp. 283-302.

Nevertheless, Lenin did not propose a violent revolution. "We do not desire 'the seizure' of power," he affirmed, "for the entire experience of revolutions teaches that only that government is stable which is supported by a majority of the population. Therefore 'the seizure' of power will be adventurism, and our party would not go in for that." But "If the government were a government of the majority . . . if the Soviet of Workers' and Soldiers' Deputies took power and the Germans continued fighting the war—what would we do?" Lenin repeated the declaration he made in 1915 in Switzerland: "If the revolutionary class of Russia finds itself in power it must propose peace. And if the German capitalists or any other country, whichever it be, rejects our conditions, then it [the revolutionary class] will be all for the war. We are not proposing to end the war by one blow. We do not promise that. We are not preaching so impossible and impracticable a thing as ending the war by the will of one side."

Lenin expressed much the same thoughts, in condensed form, in *Pravda* of June 7, adding, "Japan will not give up [the Chinese province of] Shantung, nor England—Baghdad and her colonies in Africa without a revolution."[5]

In a *Pravda* article published thirteen days later under the title "Is There a Way to a Just Peace?" Lenin repeated his oft-repeated ideas but dotted some i's. The road to peace without annexations was "through a workers' revolution against the capitalists of all countries.

". . . Peace is possible. A just peace is a peace without annexations, without conquests. Let the German robber-capitalists and Wilhelm, their crowned robber, know that we will not come to an agreement with them, that we include among their conquests not only what they have stolen since the war began, but also Alsace and Lorraine, and the Danish and Polish lands of Prussia.

"We regard Poland, Finland, the Ukraine and other non-Great Russian lands as annexations of the Russian Tsars and capitalists.

"We regard all their colonies, Ireland, etc. as the annexations of the British, French, and other capitalists."

Instead of calling, in general terms, for a workers' revolution in "at least several" capitalist countries as the necessary prelude to a just peace, Lenin now named two: Germany and France, adding, "If the capitalists of England, Japan, America attempt to obstruct such a peace," there will be a worldwide revolution in which the workers "shall defeat the capitalists of *the entire world*."[8]

On September 8, a slightly novel note appeared in one of Lenin's newspaper articles. He found that "the Anglo-French imperialists are not ready to conduct peace negotiations *now*, whereas the German imperialists are." And the reason was that the Germans were thinking of a settlement with

[5] Lenin, *op. cit.*, Second ed., Vol. XX, p. 426.
[6] *Ibid.*, pp. 503-504.

the Western powers by means of "an exchange of annexations"[7]—they would barter territories and colonies.

Milyukov's paper charged that "The German government instructed Lenin to make propaganda for peace." Lenin retaliated by calling his accusers "knights of foul slander."

After Kornilov's uprising in September, 1917, the question arose whether the Bolsheviks would not, in view of the tense internal situation, join forces with the government and defend the country. Lenin, however, remained hostile to Kerensky. The Bolsheviks would continue their agitation against the Provisional government, "but it is necessary to consider the timing, we shall not now overthrow Kerensky." Moreover, the Bolsheviks would defend Russia *only after* the transfer of power to the proletariat, after the offer of peace, *after* the renunciation of the secret [international] treaties and of the ties with the banks, *only after*. Neither the capture of Riga nor *the capture of Petrograd* will make us defenders." Until the proletariat rules, "we are against war, we are *not* defenders."[8]

In the last week of September, Lenin wrote a thin pamphlet, published in October, entitled *The Threatening Catastrophe and How to Fight It*.[9] He painted the economic situation black; famine threatened. But the government did nothing. Lenin proposed, for immediate implementation by Kerensky: "(1) The unification of all banks into one bank and government control over its operations, or the nationalization of banks. (2) The nationalization of the syndicates, that is, of the big, monopolistic combines of capitalists (the sugar, petroleum, coal, metallurgical, etc. syndicates). (3) The abolition of commercial secrets. (4) The compulsory syndicalization (that is, the compulsory unification in combines) of manufacturers, merchants, and property owners in general. (5) The compulsory unification of the population in consumers' cooperative societies or the encouragement of such organizations and the control over them."

Lenin knew he was fooling nobody. His program, he said, would be called "not democratic but *already* socialist measures," and the press of the bourgeoisie, the SR's, and the Mensheviks would plead that "we are not yet ripe for socialism." But, he replied, Russian capitalism was monopoly capitalism. In wartime, monopoly capitalism tended to become state-monopoly capitalism. "This is indeed a step toward socialism," Lenin declared. For, "Socialism is nothing other than state-capitalist monopoly *directed to the welfare of the entire nation* and to that extent *ceasing* to be a capitalist monopoly."

How can socialism be a state-capitalist monopoly if, under socialism, the state is to wither away immediately? It cannot wither away if it operates or controls all of industry and commerce. Moreover, if, as Lenin assumed, the difference between capitalist monopoly and state-capitalist monopoly was

---

[7] *Ibid.*, Vol. XXI, pp. 102-105.
[8] *Ibid.*, pp. 116-119.
[9] *Ibid.*, pp. 159-192.

that the latter served the welfare of the entire nation whereas the former did not, then if state capitalism or socialism did not serve the welfare of the entire nation it might be indistinguishable from, and no better than, private capitalism. "Entire nation" in Lenin's mouth presumably meant all individuals in the nation, not one class, not one class more than, or to the exclusion of, another; not the nation as a state but the nation as human beings. Whether they have been served involves the whole record of the Soviet Union since 1917. In any case, Lenin's dictum stands: "Socialism is nothing other than state-capitalist monopoly." Socialism is state capitalism, and, even if state capitalism were to differ in purpose from private capitalism and be superior to it in achievement, in structure and essence it is capitalism.

Having laid down the law that socialism is another form of capitalism, Lenin expounded a view which reveals his innermost nature. "Here," he said, "there is no middle ground . . . it is *impossible* to go forward from *monopoly* . . . without going to socialism. Either to be in fact a revolutionary democrat—then you cannot fear steps toward socialism. Or to fear steps toward socialism . . . and then inescapably you go on to suppress, by *reactionary-bureaucratic* means, the 'revolutionary-democratic' strivings of the worker and peasant masses. There is no middle ground."

For Lenin there was never a middle ground. He was an either-or, black-or-red exaggerator. Is it not possible, however, to be red and black, to go forward to state capitalism ("socialism") and engage in reactionary-bureaucratic suppression of the people's democratic strivings? This might be one way of reading decades of Soviet history.

Now Lenin came to the point. The war, he explained, was transforming monopoly capitalism into state-monopoly capitalism "*thereby* bringing mankind inordinately closer to socialism. The imperialist war is the eve of the socialist revolution."

In the same last week of September, 1917, Lenin penned a secret declaration, not published until 1921, called *The Bolsheviks Must Take Power*.[10] "The majority of the nation is *for* us," he asserted unstatistically. "Why must the Bolsheviks take power *now?*" he asked. "Because the impending surrender of Petrograd [to the Germans] will make our chances a hundred times worse. . . . And it is impossible 'to wait' for the Constituent Assembly, for by the very same surrender of Petrograd Kerensky and Company *can always torpedo* it. Only our party, having taken power, can guarantee the convening of the Constituent Assembly. . . . A separate peace between the British and German imperialists should and could be prevented, but only by acting quickly."

At this juncture Lenin changed his tune on a vital matter. He proposed to the party an "*armed uprising* in Petrograd and Moscow (including Moscow province), the seizure of power, the overthrow of the government. It is necessary to recall and assess Marx's words about an uprising, 'An insurrection is an art' . . .

[10] *Ibid.*, pp. 193-194.

"To wait for a Bolshevik 'formal' majority is naïve: no single revolution waits for *that*."

Lenin was now ready to launch a violent revolution by the Bolshevik minority. On his insistence, preparations commenced.

๛๛๛๛๛๛๛

Lenin's statement that the Western nations were more revolution-resistant because they had no half-wit leaders like Nicholas II and Rasputin suggests that in his opinion the man counts. Lenin counted. Commenting on the Bolshevik victory in November, 1917, E. H. Carr says, "The triumph of the party seemed almost exclusively due to Lenin's consistent success in stamping his personal will upon it and in leading his often reluctant colleagues in his train."[11] John Reed quotes Lenin as stating on November 3: "November 6 will be too early. We must have an all-Russian basis for the rising; and on the 6th the delegates to the Congress [of Soviets] will not have arrived. . . . On the other hand, November 8th will be too late. By that time the Congress will be organized, and it is difficult for a large organized body of people to take swift, decisive action. We must act on the 7th, the day the Congress meets."[12]

The day before the Bolshevik uprising, Lenin, still in hiding, wrote impatiently, fretfully, to the Central Committee of his party, "It is clearer than clear that now, quite truly, any delay in the insurrection is like unto death. . . . It is necessary at all costs, this evening, tonight to arrest the members of the [Kerensky] government, to disarm (vanquish, if they resist) the officer cadets and others. We must not wait. We may lose everything."[13]

Leon Trotsky took the same view of Lenin's role. "If we had not seized power in October"—November, 1917 (New Style)—"we would not have seized it at all. Our strength before October lay in the uninterrupted influx of the masses, who believed that this party would do what the others had not done. If they had seen any vacillation at this moment on our part, any delay, any incongruity between word and deed, then in the course of two or three months they would have drifted away from us as they did formerly from the Social Revolutionaries and the Mensheviki. The bourgeoisie would have had a breathing spell and would have made use of it to conclude peace. . . . It was just this that made Lenin decide to act. From this sprang his uneasiness, his anxiety, his mistrust and his ceaseless hurry, that saved the revolution."[14]

Kamenev and Zinoviev were opposed to the revolution. Other top-ranking Bolsheviks considered it premature. If the Bolshevik leader had been Kamenev or Kamenevesque, the Bolshevik revolution might not have occurred. Timing is the essence of politics. Lenin knew how to tell time.

[11] Edward Hallett Carr, *The Bolshevik Revolution 1917-1923* (London, 1950), Vol. 1, p. 99.
[12] John Reed, *Ten Days That Shook the World*, p. 56.
[13] Lenin, *op. cit.*, Fourth ed., Vol. 26, p. 203.
[14] Leon Trotsky, *Lenin*, p. 87.

History creates the opportunity. The war created communism's opportunity. Lenin seized the ephemeral opportunity.

Lenin possessed no magic formula in Marxism. He said on September 11, 1917, "We do not pretend that Marx or Marxists know the road to socialism in all its concreteness. That is nonsense. We know the direction of the road, we know what class forces lead to it, but concretely, practically, this will be shown by *the experience of the millions* when they undertake to act."

Lenin groped as everyone does in politics, cutting theory to match reality. His greatness lay in the talent to recognize an opportunity and use it. He was thus a monumental opportunist. He first said he favored majority rule and supported the Constituent Assembly which would embody majority will. He accordingly said he opposed the violent seizure of power. Then he announced, but without proof, that the majority was behind him, seized power by military force, and disbanded the Constituent Assembly because its majority was against him.

Did Lenin dissemble when he promised not to overthrow the Kerensky government by an insurrection? Was he camouflaging the actual preparations for the coup d'état and protecting his party against suppression? Did he think advocacy of majority rule would attract to the Bolsheviks the popular majority who were for democracy?

From the fall of the Tsar to the fall of Kerensky Lenin vociferously repeated pledges not to conclude a separate peace. Was he trying to blunt attacks on himself as a "German agent" because they hurt his party?

On the other hand, Lenin undoubtedly believed in the "inevitable" world revolution and regarded the war as its incubator. But whether or not his faith in world revolution was sincere, the propaganda he waged for it could not have been free of calculation. The Russian people needed peace. He promised it to them in return for their support. Peace could be achieved in two ways: by a separate peace or a general peace that would end the war. To urge a separate peace was embarrassing and impractical. In revolutionary Russia, a general peace resulting from revolution in at least France and Germany looked like a logical proposition. And for Lenin it represented the best possible political platform: Make a Bolshevik revolution in Russia which will spark a European revolution which will bring peace.

X. A FATEFUL DAY

RISEN out of a war that depleted the nation, Bolshevism inherited weakness and compounded it. The entire Lenin era was one of national weakness. In fact Russia did not become a great power again until the Second World

War. Lenin could not have foreseen this in 1917, but from the first day in office he did sense his government's instability and sought to remedy it. The nine-line announcement, dated November 7, of the demise of the Kerensky regime, which he scribbled and edited on a scrap of paper, was an act of political courtship. To the soldiers he offered peace; to the peasants land; to the workers "control" over production. "Long live the revolution of soldiers, workers, and peasants."[1]

Lenin did not know whether his party would retain power. Two days after the coup d'état he telephoned the Helsingfors army and navy committee for reinforcements; Kerensky was trying to make a stand at Gatchina and "some of the Petrograd troops are tired." Lenin stipulated that he wanted men "loyal and ready to fight." Such soldiers were rare. He also urged that the detachments bring their own food. "Have you any reserves of rifles and bullets? Send as many as possible."[2]

Nor did Lenin ignore the political aspects of the quaking situation. He repeatedly assured his wavering followers and the country that he wished to avoid civil war. He favored "a coalition with the peasantry" and as proof he cited "the land law of our government, entirely copied from the SR platform," which "showed concretely the full and sincere readiness of the Bolsheviks to establish a coalition with the tremendous majority of the population of Russia."[3]

To admit that he had borrowed the SR land-reform program and that the SR's, the traditional foes of Bolshevism, represented the peasant majority could not have been pleasant for Lenin. Necessity motivated his sincerity. He still deferred to the Constituent Assembly, yet to be elected, as the highest authority.[4]

Lenin condemned those comrades who were critical of his peace offer because it was not an ultimatum to all belligerent powers to cease hostilities. Rigid postures, he argued, might hinder acceptance.[5]

The life of the young regime depended above all on Russia's exit from the world war. A variety of reasons—but one, the desire to stay in power, would be enough—explain the aim of the Bolsheviks to achieve a general cessation of hostility. Yet the "Decree on Peace," adopted by the Second Congress of Soviets at 11 P.M. on November 8, 1917,[6] before even the Cabinet, or Council of People's Commissars, had been formally appointed, was, like hundreds since issued by the Kremlin, so interlaced with propaganda as to arouse the skepticism of the recipients and give them the impression

---

[1] Lenin, *Sochineniya*, Second ed., Vol. XXII, p. 3.

[2] *Ibid.*, pp. 27-29.

[3] *Ibid.*, pp. 36-37.

[4] *Ibid.*, pp. 17-19.

[5] *Ibid.*, pp. 17-19.

[6] *Ibid.*, pp. 13-15. Also in *Dokumenty Vneshnei Politiki SSSR (Documents of the Foreign Policy of the USSR)*, Vol. I (Moscow, 1957). English text borrowed from George F. Kennan, *Soviet Foreign Policy, 1917-1941* (Princeton, 1960), pp. 116-119.

that its purpose was proletarian proselytism, not improved international relations. If, as Lenin had repeatedly charged, the capitalist powers were fighting to expand their empires, how could he expect the belligerent governments to "enter immediately into negotiations for a just, democratic peace" defined in the document as "peace without annexations (that is, without the seizure of foreign territories and without forced incorporation of foreign peoples) and without indemnities"?

This sentence introduced two paragraphs elaborating on the nature of imperialist conquests and another which said that "it would be the greatest of crimes against humanity to continue this war only to determine how the strong and rich countries should divide among themselves the weak peoples they have seized." Nevertheless, the Soviet government announced "its determination to sign at once a peace putting an end to this war on the terms indicated." With whom?

The Decree of Peace further stated that Petrograd was "proceeding immediately to the publication of the secret treaties ratified or concluded between February [March, New Style] and October 25, 1917 [November 7, New Style], by the government of the landlords and the capitalists." One wonders whether it occurred to Lenin, the new chairman of the Council of People's Commissars, or to Leon Trotsky, the first Soviet Commissar for Foreign Affairs, that none of the capitalist governments to whom this peace appeal was broadcast had ever received a paper couched in socialist terminology and whether they might not disregard it as being insolent. On the other hand, someone's pen here inserted the mollifying sentence that the Soviet government "by no means considers the above-mentioned terms to be in the nature of an ultimatum; it is prepared, that is, to examine any and every other terms of peace" providing they are "completely explicit—that every form of ambiguity and secrecy be absolutely excluded." Forthwith, however, the strident propagandistic tone reasserted itself and the decree proposed an armistice of no less than three months to allow time for the completion of "the peace talks in which there would participate representatives of all peoples and all nationality groups, without exception, who had been involved in the war or forced to take part in it." Did this mean that the British delegation would have to include Irishmen, Scots, Indians, Australians, Bedouins, and Sudanese? and the French delegation Moroccans, Senegalese, and Annamese? Moreover, the decree presumed to instruct the belligerent powers in the ways of democracy and constitutional practices, for it asked that the peace terms be ratified by "assemblies of accredited people's representatives of all countries."

Finally, the "Provisional Workers' and Peasants' Government," as the Soviet authority still modestly styled itself, in deference to the future Constituent Assembly, "also appeals in particular to the class-conscious workers of the three leading world peoples and greatest states participating in the war: England, France, and Germany. The workers of these countries have

rendered the greatest service to the cause of progress and socialism." It speci-
fied the services and in a peroration expressed the hope that the "workers
of these countries . . . will carry to a successful conclusion the work of peace
and with it the work of liberating the toiling and exploited masses of the
population from every form of slavery and exploitation."

Thus ended the historic document. One senses in it an ambivalence: a
desire for peace or at least for a brief truce, yet also defiance and denunciation
of the very political institutions and social forces to whom the plea was
addressed and on whom negotiations depended.

The secret of this dualism lies not in unclarity of thought but in uncertainty of fate. At birth, the Bolshevik regime made a low estimate of its life
expectancy. When the Soviet government was seventy-three days old, a day
older than the Paris Commune of 1871, Lenin, not given to transports of
joy, felt jubilant and told Arthur Ransome, *Manchester Guardian* correspondent in Russia, with whom the leader maintained friendly contacts, that now
he was happy; if the Soviet regime perished it would have outlasted the Commune and made an even bigger contribution to the coming world revolution.
There is other evidence in the form of conversational indiscretions by Lenin's
close coworkers that the Bolsheviks' attempt to remain in power was alloyed
with the wish to leave a good record if they did not. These conflicting motivation were reflected in the text of the Decree on Peace. They also affected the
course of the Brest-Litovsk conference. To be sure, the inevitability of world
revolution was a cardinal tenet and a deeply ingrained thought habit. But
in the context of late 1917-early 1918 this merely supports the thesis of the
Soviets' poor assessment of their longevity: Lenin and his friends saw little
possibility of their government's survival in the absence of a revolution abroad
which alone, they believed, could bring Russia peace and Bolshevism the
strength to survive. Lenin accordingly closed his presentation of the Decree
on Peace to the Soviet Congress with the stark prophecy that, "The workers'
movement will take the ascendancy and pave the path to peace and socialism."[7]

Sir George Buchanan, the British ambassador, wrote in the second volume
of his memoirs that he received notice of the formation of the Soviet government and the text of the Decree on Peace only on November 21. The
decree had been broadcast to the world but not submitted to foreign governments for thirteen days. Buchanan forwarded the message to London and
recommended that no reply be sent. Instead, he suggested a statement in
the House of Commons. On November 23, Lord Robert Cecil, Under
Secretary of State for Foreign Affairs, speaking on behalf of the British
Cabinet, declared, "The action taken by the extremists in Petrograd would
of course be a direct breach of the agreement of September 5, 1914"—the
Allied agreement not to parley for a separate peace—"and if adopted by the
Russian nation would put them practically outside the pale of the ordinary

[7] Lenin, *op. cit.*, Second ed., Vol. XXII, p. 16.

council of Europe. . . . There is no intention of recognizing such a government."[8]

These words forecast the pattern of relations between the great powers and the Soviets until Lenin's death and after.

Buchanan himself, inspired, he admits, by General Sir Alfred Knox who was present in Petrograd, reconsidered the matter and wired his Foreign Office on November 27, that "the only safe course left to us is to give Russia back her word and to tell her people that, realizing how worn out they are by the war and the disorganization inseparable from a great revolution, we leave it to them to decide whether they will purchase peace on Germany's terms or fight on with the Allies, who are determined not to lay down their arms till binding guarantees for the world's peace have been secured. . . . For us to hold to our pound of flesh and to insist on Russia fulfilling her obligations under the 1914 Agreement, is to play Germany's game."

If the ambassador had sent such a dispatch six months earlier and persuaded his superiors of its wisdom, and if the other Western ambassadors in Petrograd had done likewise and met with equal success, there might have been no Soviet government. There was nothing preordained by history or heaven in the development that occurred. But from the middle of 1917 until November, 1918, the anti-German Allies had one war aim: to win the war, and though Buchanan's proposal was discussed at the Inter-Allied conference which met in Paris on November 30, 1917, and received some approval from Prime Minister Lloyd George, Foreign Secretary Arthur J. Balfour, and President Wilson's special envoy Colonel Edward House, nothing came of it. The Western nations regarded the Russian people's compulsive interest in peace as a betrayal. Nor can one blame them; their sacrifices in life, limb, and treasure had been so enormous that anything less than victory seemed a mockery of the dead and maimed. Reason was on the shelf and emotions ruled politics. Surrounded by blood and the din of battle it is always difficult to think of the world a decade or even a year later. Given this attitude, the Western alliance naturally tried to keep Russia, even Bolshevik Russia, in the war. Her defection would be a subtraction.

The German approach was diametrically different. For Kaiser Wilhelm and his fighting confederates peace with Russia promised some gain, and any advantage, however small, appeared important in view of the heavy casualties, the length of the war, and its uncertain outcome. Since myopia is the common professional disease of politicians saddled with the urgent tasks of today, it was much easier for the Germans to see their way to talks with Russia that would accomplish her early exit from the war than for the Western governments to envisage decades of Russia's future history and plan to divert it. So, while the Western Allies fumed and yet sought to retain Russia in their camp, Germany agreed to parley.

[8] Judah L. Magnes, *Russia and Germany at Brest-Litovsk. A Documentary History of the Peace Negotiations* (New York, 1919), p. 14.

The greatest danger for the Soviets lay in the possibility that their readiness to negotiate with Germany would lead to a separate peace between the West and Germany at Russia's expense. Winston Churchill outlined such a barter-peace: "The immense conquests which Germany had made in Russia, and the hatred and scorn with which the Bolsheviks were regarded by the Allies, might well have made it possible for Germany to make important territorial concessions to France, and to offer Britain the complete restoration of Belgium. The desertion by Soviet Russia of the Allied cause, and the consequent elimination of Russian claims, created a similar easement in negotiations for both Austria and Turkey. Such were the elements of this great opportunity. It was the last.

"But Ludendorff cared for none of these things." Instead, says Churchill, Ludendorff decided on "a supreme offensive in the West" to win the war on the battlefield.[9] But an influential peace party existed in Berlin. Vienna yearned for a peace that would save the tottering empire. The Austro-Hungarian Foreign Minister, Count Czernin, threatened to sign a separate peace; his emperor countenanced secret Austrian peace conversations with France and England.[10]

Lenin and Trotsky of course could not have read Churchill's mind or Vienna's intentions. But rumors of a deal behind Russia's back at the cost of her body filled the air. *Rabochii Put (Workers' Path)*, the Bolshevik daily, carried a series of articles by Gregory Sokolnikov on October 2, October 4, and October 7, 1917, entitled, "On the Eve of Peace Negotiations," in which he referred to "rumors of a 'separate' peace between England and France and Germany at Russia's expense." He quoted a Kadet party newspaper's comment to the same effect. The Pope had called for peace; Baron Richard von Kuehlmann, the German Foreign Minister, Sokolnikov stated, had offered to liberate Belgium; Czernin had said he would renounce Austria's annexations and "rebuild Europe after the war on a new international foundation." To Sokolnikov this meant the "establishment of the stable, international domination by capitalist enslavers over the oppressed masses." The Pope, he affirmed, wanted similar reforms. The same reforms are "proposed by President Wilson and all the scoundrels of secret diplomacy in the Allied countries. Only one important 'reform' is not proposed by any of them: the annihilation of the monopoly power of the capitalists." Sokolnikov's conclusion was: ". . . the bargaining is on. Behind-the-scenes diplomacy is being conducted feverishly. . . . The imperialists are preparing a peace."

Clearly, a peace between the two warring blocs without Russia would have spelled the Soviet government's death. Sokolnikov feared it. Lenin feared it. Ludendorff and Hindenburg were no less opposed to a negotiated peace with

---

[9] Winston Churchill, *The World Crisis, 1916-1918*, Vol. II, pp. 123-124.
[10] Prince Sixte du Bourbon, *L'Offre de Paix Séparée de l'Autriche (December 5, 1916-Octobre 12, 1917) avec deux lettres autographes de l'Empereur Charles et une note autographe du Comte Czernin* (Paris, 1920). Also, August Demblin, *Czernin und die Sixtus-Affaire* (Munich, 1920).

the West; they hoped to win the war, retain the territory robbed from Russia and the West, and rule Europe. The West likewise was reluctant, in the fourth year of the war, to accept peace without victory over German militarism. While general peace, therefore, was an urgent, universal need, these factors combined to delay it—and to throw Bolshevism a life belt.

The Soviets and the Germans consequently found themselves alone—talking peace—in the dismal provincial town of Brest-Litovsk.

For the moment, and forgetting the blood spilled and to be spilled, Germany was "sitting pretty." The prospect of converting the eastern front's "virtual armistice" into an agreed settlement would permit still further withdrawals of troops, bolster flaccid morale, depress the people of the West, and perhaps, depending on the degree of Russia's internal collapse, permit additional annexations. The Kaiser's warlords were sanguine enough to dream of ending the war with a sanguinary triumph.

The Bolsheviks, on the other hand, felt uncomfortably isolated. Ludendorff had them at his mercy. If they proved recalcitrant, even his skeleton forces could take Petrograd, the Ukraine, and whatever else he wanted. Looking back to the days of Brest, Lenin said on December 6, 1920, "in the military sense we were a zero."[11] The Soviet government was in no condition to defend the country against Germany. As a precaution, in fact, Lenin, in March, 1918, moved his capital to Moscow; thenceforth the Kremlin, no longer the Smolny, became the synonym of the Soviets.

With all the cards—and arms—stacked against them the Bolsheviks apparently decided to act with the courage of their convictions and impotence. To be meek before the German Moloch would evoke criticism and despair at home, hostility in the West, and brutality from the spike-helmeted militarists. The Soviet delegation accordingly behaved with aggressive defiance. It played for time. It made demands. It shocked and irritated the mighty adversary. Unable to cope with Germany on the level of power, the Bolsheviks lured her representatives into a thought joust where, using ideas as weapons, they unhorsed them.

For the Soviets, the Brest-Litovsk conference was a joint exercise in unaccustomed diplomacy and customary propaganda.

As a preliminary to peace negotiations, Lenin, Commissar of Nationalities Joseph V. Stalin, and Officer Nikolai Krilenko on November 20 talked for two and a half hours by ticker-telegraph with General Nikolai N. Dukhonin, Russian Commander in Chief at Staff Headquarters in Mogilev, insisting that he conclude an immediate armistice on all fronts with the German, Austrian, and Turkish troops facing him. Dukhonin disputed the new government's authority, whereupon Krilenko was appointed his successor. When Krilenko, escorted by sailors, arrived at Mogilev, Dukhonin resisted. Soldiers and sailors backed the commissar and lynched the general. Krilenko then ordered "firing and fraternization to cease" and discipline restored. Blindfolded Russian

[11] Lenin, *op. cit.*, Second ed., Vol. XXV, p. 499.

plenipotentiaries entered the German lines on November 27, agreed to a cease-fire, and fixed December 2 as the beginning of the talks at Brest-Litovsk, the German east-front headquarters.

In the Russian front lines all was confusion and dissolution. The army, reduced to skin and bones by desertions in the last year of tsarism and the eight anarchic months of the democratic republic, had all but vanished as a fighting force. Why freeze in the trenches when a truce with Germany, Austria-Hungary, Turkey, and Bulgaria was imminent? The soldiers, most of them peasants, were going home to secure their ration of nationalized farmland. Workers wished to glimpse the new workers' regime and get out of lice-infested uniforms and the cold. For the Russian people the First World War had lost the last vestige of sense.

The inhabitants of the Bolshevik capital were suffering acute hunger in icy apartments. Conditions in Moscow and other cities were similar or worse. The White versus Red civil war had already cut off northern and central Russia from some food and fuel sources in the south.

Facing hostility from monarchists, Mensheviks, and Social Revolutionaries, the Bolshevik party was racked by internal schisms on the issue of war and peace, socialism or nonsocialism. The Soviets had little strength and many problems.

Petrograd was a tohu-vovohu capital full of ideological turmoil. The pre-Bolshevik officials of the foreign office refused to work for Trotsky, the new Commissar for Foreign Affairs. At the November 17 session of the All-Russian Central Executive Committee, a kind of parliament of soviets, the stenographers had declared a strike, in effect a political boycott (the communists called it sabotage). According to the credentials committee, the Bolshevik delegates numbered 300; Left Social Revolutionaries (SR's) 169; Right SR's 24; Mensheviks 68, etc., to a total of 670. The Bolsheviks were in the minority.

At this session, G. Zaks, speaking for the Left Social Revolutionary Party, raised a question which lay at the root of the subsequent Stalin-Trotsky controversy and is, in fact, relevant to much of Soviet history and foreign policy. It was, at that moment, relevant to the Brest-Litovsk conference. Zaks accused the Lenin-Trotsky government of "steering a course toward socialist revolution. But having blown up the bridge to the other shore, will we not remain isolated? So far we have received no real help from anywhere. Western Europe is shamefully silent. Socialism cannot be decreed."[12]

Could a Soviet government which excluded all non-Bolshevik parties ("blown up the bridge to the other shore"), and had received no aid from European revolutionaries, Zaks was asking, establish a socialist state by ukaze? He doubted the ability of the Bolsheviks to build socialism in one country.

Lenin replied in anger. His basic concept, the theory of the spark, on which Soviet strategy rested, was being questioned. "In the mouth of an interna-

[12] *Ibid.*, Vol. XXII, editorial note, p. 582.

tionalist," Lenin exclaimed, "the expression 'The West is shamefully silent' is inadmissible. Only a blind man cannot see the ferment that has seized the workers in Germany and in the West." To be sure, Europe's socialist leaders were acting like nationalistic patriots. "But the rank and file," Lenin insisted, "are ready, against the wishes of the leaders, to respond to our summons." He explained why he thought so: there had been a mutiny in the German fleet in July-August, 1917; the Spartacus group was intensifying its revolutionary activity in Germany where the popularity of Karl Liebknecht, "the indefatigable champion of the ideals of the proletariat," rose from day to day. Therefore "we believe in the revolution in the West."[13]

Lenin believed that the spark in Russia would ignite the tinder of socialist revolution in Europe; then the socialist revolution in the West would strengthen and save the new regime in Russia. But what, meanwhile, was to be the nature of this new regime? So far, the Soviet government consisted of Bolsheviks only. Not all trade unions and socialist parties supported it. Some Mensheviks clamored for a Soviet government without Lenin and Trotsky. The important railway workers' union, speaking through its executive committee VIKZHEL, demanded a government of all socialist parties: Bolsheviks, Mensheviks, and Social Revolutionaries. The Bolsheviks sent representatives to parley with VIKZHEL.[14] The non-Bolshevik socialists argued that the Soviet government was too narrowly based to cope with the incipient civil war and with mounting economic and political troubles. Lenin and Trotsky disagreed; at most they wanted a coalition with the Left Social Revolutionaries —an effort to split the solid anti-Lenin Social Revolutionary Party.

This issue caused a crisis in the Bolshevik party. On November 17, 1917, four members of the Bolshevik cabinet resigned. They were V. Nogin, Commissar for Trade and Industry; A. Rykov, Commissar for Internal Affairs (subsequently Prime Minister); V. Milyutin, Commissar for Agriculture; and T. Teodorovich, Commissar for Food. Five other prominent Bolshevik officials joined them in a manifesto which said, "We take the view that the formation of a socialist government of all soviet parties is an imperative necessity. . . . We assumed that apart from this there is only one way: the maintenance of a purely Bolshevik government by means of political terror." The exclusion of "mass proletarian organizations from the leadership of political life," the manifesto added, would conduce to "an irresponsible regime."[15] That day, Nogin, Rykov, Milyutin, Kamenev, and Zinoviev issued a similar statement condemning the insistence on a one-party government as "a policy of disaster for which they could not accept responsibility."[16] They were therefore resigning from the Central Committee of the Bolshevik party, a step Lenin de-

[13] Ibid., p. 47.
[14] The story of the VIKZHEL episode is told in detail in Raphael R. Abramovitch, The Soviet Revolution, 1917-1939, introduction by Sidney Hook (New York, 1962), Chap. 5.
[15] Lenin, op. cit., Vol. XXII, p. 511.
[16] Ibid., pp. 551-552.

nounced as "sabotage" of the revolution.[17] When several of these liberal Bolsheviks also protested the Soviet government's suppression of anti-Soviet newspapers, Lenin scoffed.

The controversy fizzled. The Bolshevik rebels returned. Lenin won. But today's victory may defeat tomorrow. In this controversy, the future horror of a one-party tyranny cast its shadows before. G. Zaks, who found Western Europe "disgracefully silent," and the dissident Bolsheviks, who noted the same phenomenon, had visions of a feeble Lenin-Trotsky regime resorting to terror in order to survive until European socialism, spurred by Russia, came to the rescue. They therefore preferred a strong coalition with fewer illusions about a crimson conflagration in the West. Lenin taxed the doubters with lack of faith. But he too doubted the viability of the Soviet regime unless Europe, rebuffing the charge of disgraceful silence, spoke the loud language of revolutionary action.

At Brest-Litovsk, accordingly, the Soviets conferred with the foreign diplomats and scanned the western horizon for red flames. Bolshevik eyes were in double focus.

XI. CHRISTMAS AND DECEMBER TWENTY-EIGHTH

IN 1919 Arthur Ransome of the *Manchester Guardian* had a talk with Lenin in the Moscow Kremlin. Lenin said, "Russia was indeed the only country in which the revolution could start." Ransome suggested that "one reason why it had been possible in Russia"—and impossible in England—"was that they had room to retreat."

"Yes," Lenin agreed, "the distances saved us. The Germans were frightened of them." In 1918, Lenin added, the Germans "could have eaten us and won peace, which the Allies would have gladly *given* them in gratitude for our destruction."[1] But the German military had studied the record of Napoleon's progress to and from Moscow. Beyond Moscow there was the broad Volga region, which Lenin knew because he was born there, and beyond the Volga lay the Urals and endless Siberia, which Lenin, Trotsky, Stalin, Kamenev, and almost all Bolsheviks knew because they had been banished there. Russia's distances comforted Lenin. If worst came to worst and Germany, disregarding a bad Brest-Litovsk treaty, attacked Bolshevism, the Soviet government, carrying its few files, could move away, exchange space for time,

---

[17] *Ibid.*, pp. 38-39.
[1] Arthur Ransome, *Russia in 1919* (New York, 1919), p. 119.

wait, and summon winter cold and scorched earth, instead of Western capitalists, to be their allies.

Peace had no terror; war had no virtue. These were the pillars of Lenin's policy toward Brest-Litovsk. There was an additional consideration: "And we are not yet through our troubles with the peasantry," Lenin told Ransome in 1919.[2] The Volga valley, Siberia, central Russia, and the Ukraine above all, were packed with potentially rebellious peasants. For Lenin this made successful peace negotiations imperative.

The revolution turned men's minds away from the outside world and inward to domestic problems: land distribution and power redistribution in village and town. Here the Soviet regime developed an inner contradiction: to win popular support it had to concentrate on difficulties at home; to survive it had to promote foreign revolution. Lenin believed that peace, no matter how expensive, would serve both these ends. Other communists disagreed. A separate peace with Germany, they argued, would be the death of world revolution and hence of the Soviet revolution. This issue shook the Brest-Litovsk conference and temporarily cracked the Bolshevik party, leaving Lenin in the minority.

Trouble started soon after the Soviet seizure of power when several Russian divisions at the front established contact with German troops opposite them and suggested local cease-fires. G. I. Chudnovsky, an eloquent communist, and commandant of the Winter Palace, chided Lenin for permitting such procedures. They would wreck the army. "What Lenin is doing now," *Izvestia* of November 25, 1917, quoted Chudnovsky as saying, "destroys the capacity of our soldiers to go into battle in case the German government refuses to enter peace negotiations and it becomes necessary for us to continue the war, bringing liberation to the German proletariat on the tips of our bayonets." Lenin denied the charge, but the exchange revealed the strategy of the revolutionary-war supporters. They would march toward Germany to help overthrow the Kaiser. Ludendorff, Hindenburg, and Hoffmann would presumably bow and bid them pass.

Lenin had equally naïve ideas about the dawn of peace. He reported on November 23, 1917, that Soviet radio messages urging peace were getting through to Europe and the Germans were not jamming them. "We," he continued, "can establish wireless contact with Paris, and when the peace treaty is drafted we will have the possibility of informing the French people that it can be signed and that it is up to the French people to conclude an armistice in two hours. We shall see what Clemenceau says then." The treaty would foment revolution. He realized, he added, that the struggle for peace would be difficult. "International imperialism will mobilize all its might against us, but no matter how great the strength of international imperialism, our chances are very favorable."[3] Perhaps he was whistling to keep the comrades

---

[2] *Ibid.*
[3] Lenin, *Sochineniya*, Second ed., Vol. XXII, pp. 74-75.

in the dark. Perhaps he was magnifying the probability of revolution. He always had.

Lenin proposed: revolutionary propaganda; a peace treaty with all the belligerents or, if that was impossible, with the four Central Powers only; then, revolution. His opponents proposed: a revolution but no treaty. Everybody favored propaganda. As a result, three operations proceeded simultaneously. The Soviets negotiated with the Central Powers at Brest-Litovsk, attempted to bring the Western entente into the negotiations, and made propaganda against the Central Powers and the Western alliance.

The communists feared a twosome with Germany. On November 28 the Soviet press announced that the German-led Quadruple Alliance had accepted the Russian invitation to conclude an armistice but added that the talks would be delayed until December 2 to allow time for an appeal to the Western powers to "identify themselves with our peace platform and enter into common negotiations with the enemy for the conclusion of an armistice on the fronts of all belligerent nations." Foreign Commissar Trotsky confirmed this in a note to the Allied missions in Petrograd. The British ambassador, Sir George Buchanan, wrote in his diary on November 27: "Trotsky has communicated to the Allied military attachés a note asserting that his government never desired a separate peace, but that it was determined to have peace. It will, the note concluded, be the fault of the Allied governments if Russia has after all to make a separate peace."[4]

The Allies returned no reply.

On December 2, half an hour late, the Soviet delegation arrived at Brest-Litovsk. It consisted of a worker, a peasant, and a sailor, as symbolic representatives of the new government's avowed constituency, and Adolf A. Yoffe, chairman, Leo M. Karakhan, secretary, Leo B. Kamenev, Gregory Y. Sokolnikov, Madame Anastasia A. Bitsenko, Captain S. D. Maslovsky-Mstislavsky, and other military experts.

"My cousin, Prince Ernst Hohenlohe," wrote Prince Max von Baden, "was placed at the dinner table next to Madame Bitsenko who had qualified by killing a minister. On December 5, 1905, she assassinated General and former War Minister Victor Victorovich Sakharov."[5]

"I shall never forget the first dinner with the Russians," General Max Hoffmann remarked. "I sat between Yoffe and Sokolnikov, the present Commissar of Finance. Opposite me sat the worker who was obviously embarrassed by the large quantity of silverware. He tried to catch this and that with the various utensils, but he used the fork exclusively for the purpose of cleaning his teeth. Directly opposite, next to Prince Hohenlohe sat Madame Bitsenko, and next to her the peasant [R. I. Stashkov], a thorough Russian

[4] Sir George Buchanan, *My Mission to Russia and Other Diplomatic Memoirs* (Boston, 1923), Vol. II, p. 225.

[5] Prinz Max von Baden, *Erinnerungen und Dokumente* (Berlin and Leipzig, 1927) p. 186.

phenomenon with long, gray locks and a tremendous, primeval-forest beard. On one occasion, the orderly could not refrain from a smile when, asked whether he wanted red wine or white, he inquired which was stronger, for it was the stronger brand that he would want."[6]

On the other hand, "Yoffe, Kamenev, Sokolnikov, above all the first, made an exceptionally intelligent impression. They spoke with enthusiasm of their task of leading the Russian proletariat to the peak of happiness and prosperity." They also, Hoffmann recalled, confided to him their plans for world revolution. This was open but it was scarcely diplomacy.

At the initial conference session on December 2, first Yoffe and then Kamenev delivered long speeches about Bolshevik peace principles, proposed negotiations with the Western Entente, and finally, according to a Soviet communiqué of December 5, "introduced a draft armistice agreement on all fronts the chief points of which were (1) prohibition of any transfer of troops from our front to the front of our allies," and (2) "The evacuation of the Moon Sound Islands by the Germans." From these dots in the Gulf of Riga Petrograd might be menaced.

The German delegation agreed not to evacuate, but to suspend hostilities on, the Moon Sound Islands and not to shift troops to France, Flanders and Italy unless orders to do so had been issued before December 5. Such orders had, in fact, been issued to many divisions, so this stipulation meant nothing. The Soviets wanted a six months' armistice; they accepted the German counteroffer of a ten-day truce (December 7 to 17) with fighting renewable on three days' notice. The Soviet delegation demanded and achieved a seven-day recess. Trotsky thereupon informed the British, French, American, Chinese, Italian, Japanese, Romanian, Belgian, and Serbian missions in Petrograd that "the negotiations . . . were suspended at the initiative of our delegation for one week in order to give an opportunity during this time to inform the peoples and the governments of the Allied countries." He called upon the Western nations to "express their readiness or their refusal to participate in the negotiations for an armistice and peace, and in case of refusal to state openly before all the world clearly, definitely, and correctly, in the name of what purpose the peoples of Europe must bleed during the fourth year of the war."

The missions did not reply.

Leo B. Kamenev had told the November 23 session of the All-Russian Central Executive Committee (VTSIK), a convocation of delegates from urban and provincial soviets, why the Bolsheviks attached so much importance to the nontransfer of troops from the eastern to the western front. It was "necessary," he explained, "so the French, British and Italian workers would not misunderstand us and think we were deserting them,"[7] by sanctioning German reinforcements to the fronts where those workers were engaged. The

---

[6] General Max Hoffman, *Der Krieg der Versaeumten Gelegenheiten* (Munich, 1923), p. 193.

[7] Lenin, *op. cit.*, Second ed., Vol. XXII, editorial note, p. 584.

official Soviet communiqué stated that troops were not to be shifted to the front of "our allies." Russia had allies: she was not altogether helpless, the Bolsheviks were intimating.

A further Soviet-Quadruple Alliance armistice was signed on December 15 to last until January 12 and indefinitely thereafter unless one side terminated it after a week's notice. This document likewise forbade the transfer of German troops to the western front. The Soviets did not want to antagonize their "allies," or anger the Western proletariats. Moreover, they wanted the German soldiers to remain in the east as targets of communist propaganda; the armistice permitted fraternization between German and Soviet servicemen "though there must not be present at any one time more than twenty-five unarmed persons from each side." Twenty-five were enough for Bolshevik antiwar propaganda purposes, and Ludendorff subsequently complained—and Churchill confirmed—that the propaganda demoralized some elements of the German army on the eastern front. It also hastened the withering-away process of the Russian army. The Russians convinced the foe and themselves that further fighting was fruitless. Military indiscipline enabled the Russians to walk home. The Germans stayed.

Next on the agenda, after the truce agreement, was a peace settlement. The peace conference opened at Brest-Litovsk on December 22 at 4:24 P.M. Five days later *Izvestia* complained that "refusal of the Allies to participate in peace discussions ties the Russian revolution hand and foot in its struggle for a general, democratic peace." But the West was hostile. A British Foreign Office official, spreading his wisdom before his superiors, wrote on November 12, 1917, five days before the Lenin-Trotsky seizure of power, "Bolshevism is essentially a Russian disease; it is Tolstoyism distorted and carried to extreme limits." (It was about as Tolstoyan as Genghis Khan's depredations and Stalin's blood purges.) "It is too soon to speculate on the immediate future of Russia," he continued; then, speculating, he declared that "it may be taken for granted that the Bolshevik government is already on its last legs."[8]

What war will do to warp minds, even in civilized Britain, may be judged by two editorial excerpts. The London *Morning Post* proclaimed on November 9, 1917, that the Bolshevik leaders were "Russian Jews of German extraction" paid by Germany. The usually dignified London *Times* of November 23, 1917, commenting on the Russo-German truce, declared, "It would be undignified for the Allies to expend words of reprobation on this step. . . . They know that the Maximalists [Bolsheviks] are a band of anarchists and fanatics who have seized power for the moment, owing to the paralysis of the national life. . . . They know that Lenin and several of his confederates are adventurers of German-Jewish blood and in German pay. . . . While the Bolsheviks are tolerated at the head of affairs, Allied help to Russia is out of the question." Passion had vanquished reason.

United States Ambassador Francis observed in a letter dated November 8,

[8] Quoted by Richard H. Ullman, *Intervention and the War. Anglo-Soviet Relations, 1917-1921* (Princeton, 1961), p. 3.

1917, "It is reported that the Petrograd Council of Workmen and Soldiers has named a Cabinet with Lenin as Premier, Trotsky as Minister of Foreign Affairs, and Madame or Mlle Kollontai as Minister of Education. Disgusting."[9] Later he wrote, "Of course, we would not, or I would not recognize any Ministry of which Lenin is Premier or Trotsky Minister of Foreign Affairs."

France took an equally antagonistic position. Paris instructed General Berthelot, French military attaché on the Romanian front, to inform the Russian authorities that "it would not recognize any government that proved itself capable of entering into an agreement with the enemy."[10] French Foreign Minister Stephen Pichon told the Chamber of Deputies on December 28, 1917, "Russia may treat for a separate peace or not. In either case the war will continue for us."

The British, American, and French attitudes were intelligible. Russia was deserting their ranks and parleying with their mortal foe. Hatred of socialism, communism, entered into the reckoning. Their attitude was intelligible but not intelligent. Russia was in a state of collapse, and the Bolshevik regime would have collapsed if it had not achieved peace. Elsewhere, however, hopes made peace unpopular. Now that the United States had declared war and associated itself with the Western Allies, they hoped to win. Now that Russia was prostrate, the German-manipulated Quadruple Alliance hoped to win.

Though the Western nations abstained from the Brest talks, they recognized the error of unmitigated intransigence. Diplomacy is the art of if. What if the Brest-Litovsk discussions broke down and the Soviets, in despair, needed Allied assistance to stem a German advance? What if the communist faction known to oppose a separate peace, abetted by Left Social Revolutionaries of similar view, gained the upper hand in Soviet circles? It is wise in international politics to keep in touch, to be available as an alternative, to be present for information or possible negotiation. But since exchanges between the Western embassies in Petrograd and the Soviet government might have been interpreted as signifying de facto recognition—which they wished to avoid—they employed unofficial go-betweens or officials of less than first rank to maintain contact with the Bolsheviks and offer to receive them back into the fighting fold.

The situation was tailored to order for Western intermediaries dismayed by their governments' inept handling of the Russian problem who saw here an outlet for their patriotism, idealism, ambition, and self-importance. Nothing is so flattering to a minor figure as a confidential and apparently important relationship with a chief of state. Lenin and Trotsky invited it. They gave much time to Captain Jacques Sadoul, a junior member of the French Military Mission to Russia; to R. H. Bruce Lockhart, a former British consul

[9] David R. Francis, *Russia from the American Embassy, April 1916-November 1918* (New York, 1921), p. 186.

[10] Petrograd, *Izvestia*, Nov. 27, 1917.

general in Moscow; and to Raymond Robins of the American Red Cross. The three reveled in their role. It contained essential elements of high adventure: secrecy, urgency, intimacy with topmost officials, and discussions that might determine the fate of nations. They thought they were writing history. In any event, they wrote themselves into history.

Arthur Ransome, a hearty Englishman with a walrus mustache who wrote children's books, volumes of literary criticism, and excellent reports for the *Manchester Guardian*, had ready access to Lenin, Trotsky, and other communist leaders. Lenin once asked him about Colonel Robins: "Had he really been as friendly to the Soviet government as he made out?"

"Yes," Ransome replied, "if only as a sportsman admiring its pluck and courage in difficulties," and Ransome quoted to Lenin what Robins had once said, "I can't go against a baby I have sat up with for six months. But if there were a Bolshevik movement in America I'd be out with my rifle to fight it every time."

"Now that," said Lenin, "is an honest man and more farseeing than most. I always liked that man."[11]

Robins saw Lenin often and Trotsky oftener. Sadoul and Lockhart also were in and out of Trotsky's tight little office. Lockhart, after seeing Prime Minister David Lloyd George, had been appointed "head of a special mission to establish unofficial relations with the Bolsheviks." The Bolsheviks ignored the fiction. Before proceeding to Russia, Lockhart had lunch with Maxim Litvinov, the Soviet representative in London, at a Lyons restaurant where Litvinov wrote a letter informing Trotsky that Lockhart was "going to Russia with an official mission."[12] On the eve of Lockhart's departure from England, Lord Milner, who visited Russia in 1917 and was a member of the War Cabinet and Secretary of State for War in 1918, told Lockhart his "main task must be to do as much harm to the Germans as possible, to put a spoke in the wheels of the separate peace negotiations."[13]

Lockhart arrived in Petrograd on January 31, 1918, and the next day saw Georgi Chicherin, acting chief of the Foreign Commissariat in Trotsky's absence at Brest-Litovsk. Lockhart gathered the impression from this and subsequent conversations that the Bolsheviks' "obvious policy was to play off the Germans against the Allies and the Allies against the Germans." Chicherin told the British agent that the negotiations at Brest "were going badly and that now was the great opportunity for England to make a friendly gesture toward Russia."[14] (At the Genoa Conference in 1922, Chicherin, promoted to Foreign Commissar, employed the same gambit in reverse; he informed the Germans that the negotiations with the British, which were going badly, were going well, and that if the Germans valued relations with Russia this was

[11] Arthur Ransome, *op. cit.*, p. 120.

[12] R. H. Bruce Lockhart, *British Agent*, with an introduction by Hugh Walpole (New York and London, 1933), pp. 201-202.

[13] *Ibid.*, p. 205.

[14] *Ibid.*, p. 219.

the time for them to sign the Rapallo Treaty, which they did.) The negotiations at Brest-Litovsk were indeed going badly for the Bolsheviks. But a friendly British gesture toward Russia might merely have hastened a separate peace on better terms for the Bolsheviks—and a separate peace was not what Lockhart, Robins, or Sadoul desired.

During the following months, Lockhart worked closely with Raymond Robins. "Robins, who was a philanthropist and a humanitarian rather than a politician," Lockhart wrote, "was a wonderful orator. His conversation, like Mr. Churchill's, was always a monologue, but it was never dull. With his black hair and aquiline features, he had a most striking appearance. He was an Indian chief with a Bible as his tomahawk. . . . Although a rich man himself, he was anti-capitalist. Yet, in spite of sympathies for the under-dog, he was a worshipper of great men. Hitherto, his two heroes had been [Theodore] Roosevelt and Cecil Rhodes. . . . Now Lenin was amused by the hero-worship, and of all foreigners Robins was the only man whom Lenin was always willing to see and who ever succeeded in imposing his own personality on the unemotional Bolshevik leader."[15] He had a personality to impose. Lenin was a zealot and Robins was a zealot. There are, apparently, warm zealots of the heart and cold zealots of the brain. Robins belonged to the former, Lenin to the latter, but the zealotry they had in common made them kin. Besides, Lenin must have been amused by an American, a gold digger in Alaska, a do-gooder in Chicago, and a passionately religious man, championing the cause of friendly relations with the anti-rich, antireligious Bolsheviks.

Robins had come to Russia during the Kerensky regime to work under Colonel William B. Thompson, chief of the American Red Cross. Thompson was a multimillionaire. He convened a small group of prominent Right Social Revolutionaries, including Catherine Breshko-Breshkovskaya, the "Babushka," or Grandmother, of the Russian revolution, Nikolai Tchaikovsky, and others interested in bolstering political and army morale and strengthening the anti-Bolshevik government. Aware that they needed money, Thompson drew on his personal account with J. P. Morgan and Company in New York and deposited a million dollars, "a cool one million dollars," as George F. Kennan put it,[16] in a Petrograd bank for the use of the group.[17] Robins was of the same swashbuckling, bighearted, expansive, unbureaucratic, undiplomatic type as Thompson. When Thompson left Russia at the end of November, 1917, to return to America, Robins succeeded him as first Red Cross officer. In 1915 Robins had been the leader of the National Christian Social Evangelistic campaign in the United States. In 1917 he was the evangelist fallen among Bolsheviks. His role required him to resist Russian retirement from the war. Impulsively, he added a conflicting task: fair play for the Soviet government.

[15] *Ibid.*, p. 220.
[16] George F. Kennan, *Russia Leaves the War* (Princeton, 1956), p. 57.
[17] William Hard, *Raymond Robins' Own Story* (New York, 1920), p. 37.

Sadoul was an attorney and member of the Chamber of Deputies and, early in the war, served as an aide to Albert Thomas, French Minister of Munitions and a socialist. Lockhart called Sadoul "the French Robins," but George Kennan noted that "Robins and Sadoul do not appear to have been drawn to each other or to have maintained any intimate sort of liaison. This may have been due in part to linguistic differences, but only in part. Each was an egoist, preoccupied with his own experiences. Each was inclined to attach to his own contacts with the Soviet authorities an overriding importance, not to be rivalled by any other."[18]

Robins and Lockhart, on the other hand, did collaborate. "I liked Robins," Lockhart declared. "For the next four months"—February to May, 1918—"we were to be in daily and almost hourly contact."[19] Both were romantics (*British Agent* drips with romance), and the situation mingled the excitement of an unexpected love affair with the thrill of exclusive admission to a private show of history in the making. Lockhart was only thirty years old.

The West had two strategies: an official one, emanating from London and Paris, and occasionally from Washington: to bring old Russia back into the war by supporting or encouraging anti-Bolshevik rebel governments, and an unofficial one: to persuade Lenin and Trotsky not to leave the war. While the governments and their embassies intrigued against the Bolsheviks, the three optimistic intermediaries were permitted, often inspired, by their embassies to prevent the Brest-Litovsk conference from ending in a peace treaty. Thus, brutally anti-Bolshevik United States Ambassador Francis, who never went near a Soviet office or official, wrote Robins commending his services as "a channel of unofficial communication with the Soviet government";[20] Lockhart and the British Foreign Office exchanged messages in code. Sadoul encountered greater difficulties and soon grew closer to the Soviets than to his French superiors.

The extent of Robin's failure may be measured by his greatest success. He was a father of Woodrow Wilson's Fourteen Points. The paternity of this statement of America's war aims is in dispute because it was apparently sired by so many who believed they planted the seed in the President's brain. Robins too claimed parenthood.

The text shows that when he wrote it Bolshevik Russia was uppermost in Wilson's mind. A number of Americans with experience in revolutionary Russia had placed suggestions on the President's desk pleading for a public enunciation of war purposes which, by indicating how much these coincided with the Bolsheviks' peace aims, would influence their behavior at Brest. On January 3, 1918, Colonel William B. Thompson left a memorandum for Wilson—who had refused to see him because, in the words of Thomas W. Lamont, a Morgan partner, "he did not want to talk to anyone who would

[18] Kennan, *op. cit.*, p. 383.
[19] Lockhart, *op. cit.*, p. 220.
[20] Hard, *op. cit.*, p. 72.

throw away a million dollars"—urging that "the President . . . speak to the Russian people . . . through a message to the American Congress" and "that America should now declare itself in agreement with certain of the basic Russian peace terms as quoted, such as no punitive indemnities, etc."[21]

Thompson suggested that the Soviets "if given any intelligent aid or support in the [Brest-Litovsk] negotiations" would reject a separate peace with Germany. Moreover, "it is possible, even now, to take entire charge of the Russian situation, bringing it around to our point of view absolutely."[22] This "absolutely" mirrors an absolute misunderstanding of Bolshevik mentality as well as Thompson's absolute optimism, a quality of the missionary he shared with Robins.

A similar appeal was made to President Wilson through Secretary of State Robert Lansing on December 29, 1917, by U.S. Ambassador Francis in Petrograd and may have been timed to reinforce Thompson's proposal. Francis begged the President "to reiterate in some public manner the noble expressions of your address in the United States Senate of January 22 last."[23] In that speech Wilson had asked, "Is this war a struggle for a just and secure peace or only for a new balance of power?" A balance of power has to be guaranteed. ". . . who can guarantee the stable equilibrium of the new arrangement? . . . There must be not only a balance of power, but a community of power; not organized rivalries, but an organized common peace." He advocated, too, "some definite concert of power which will make it virtually impossible that any such catastrophe should ever overwhelm us again." Here was the germ concept of the League of Nations. To facilitate his postwar peace-enforcing "concert of power," he had advocated "a peace without victory. . . . Only a peace between equals can last. . . . The right is as necessary for a lasting peace as is the just settlement of vexed questions of territory or of racial and national allegiance." As an example, he proposed "a united, independent and autonomous Poland."[24]

Francis referred Wilson to the January 22, 1917, speech in the belief that its views, especially those about an independent Poland (then under German occupation) and "the just settlement" of questions of territory and of "racial and national allegiance" or self-determination would find favor with the Bolsheviks. "The tired people of this country [Russia]," Francis added in a startling burst of comprehension, "will not fight for territory . . . for commercial advantage . . . for treaties made by governments they had overturned, but they possibly will struggle for a democratic peace." Even the weak word "possibly" was too strong.

Francis was using un-Franciscan language and, indeed, Kennan writes that

[21] Kennan, op. cit., p. 245.
[22] Ibid.
[23] Papers Relating to the Foreign Relations of the United States, 1918, Russia, Publication of the Department of State, in three volumes (Washington, 1931), Vol. I, p. 405.
[24] War Address of Woodrow Wilson, with an introduction by Arthur Roy Leonard (Boston, 1918), pp. 3-12.

"this message . . . reflects the influence Robins and [U.S. military attaché in Petrograd, Brigadier General William V.] Judson had brought to bear on him [Francis] over the Christmas season." Judson had been to see Trotsky with Robins.

The hand, or rather the tongue, of Robins may also be discerned in a telegram sent about the same time from Petrograd by Edgar Sisson, representative of the U.S. official Committee on Public Relations, to George Creel, the committee's Washington chief, who had frequent contacts with Wilson. Sisson wired, "If President will state anti-imperialist war aims and democratic peace requisites of America thousand words or less, short almost placard sentences, I can get it fed into Germany in great quantities in German translation, and can use Russian version potently in army and elsewhere."[25] Robins, who subsequently quarreled with Sisson for buying and giving world currency to forged documents that purported to portray the Bolshevik leaders as German agents, was, at the time of Sisson's telegram to Creel, on good terms with him.

It is clear, however, from Wilson's January 22, 1917, address to the U.S. Senate that the basic principles of the Fourteen Points were germinating in his mind long before he felt the prods of Thompson, Francis, Robins, Sisson, and others. The American voices from Bolshevik Russia could only have affected the timing and the target of the Fourteen Points speech; it was aimed directly at the Soviet government's policy in the Brest-Litovsk conference.

An appeal by Foreign Commissar Leon Trotsky "to the peoples and governments of Allied countries" dated December 30, 1917, probably precipitated Wilson's decision to give the world his Fourteen Points. Secretary of State Lansing was impressed "with the adroitness of the author" of the appeal. He called it "this insidious address." "I feel," his last sentence read, "that to make any sort of reply would be contrary to the dignity of the United States and offer opportunity for further insult and threats, although I do not mean that it may not be expedient at some time in the near future to state our peace terms in more detail than has yet been done."

Trotsky had begun his appeal by saying that the Brest parleys had been recessed for ten days to give the Allied nations "the last opportunity to participate in the future deliberations and thus insure themselves against all the consequences of a separate peace between Russia and the enemy countries." Two programs, he continued, had been presented at Brest: the Soviet program of "consistent socialist democracy" which would facilitate the self-determination of "every nationality, irrespective of its strength and the level of its development" and the unification of all countries for "economic and cultural collaboration." The second peace-aims program, submitted by Germany, Austria-Hungary, Turkey, and Bulgaria, on the other hand, was unsatisfactory. Now, "It is necessary to declare clearly and precisely what is the peace program of France, Italy, Great Britain, the United States. Do they demand, together with us, the granting of the right of self-determination to

[25] Quoted in Kennan, op. cit., p. 251.

the peoples of Alsace-Lorraine, Galicia, Poznan, Bohemia, the Yugoslav regions? If so, do they agree, for their part, to grant the right of self-determination to peoples of Ireland, Egypt, India, Madagascar, Indo-China and so forth just as the Russian revolution has granted this right to the peoples of Finland, the Ukraine, White Russia, etc.?

"For it is clear that to demand self-determination for peoples in the territories of enemy countries and deny self-determination to the peoples within one's own country and colonies would be the most undisguised, the most cynical kind of imperialism. . . . Hitherto the Allied governments have definitely shown no readiness, and by their class nature could show no readiness, to conclude a truly democratic peace. They are no less suspicious of and hostile to the principle of national self-determination than the governments of Germany and Austria-Hungary. On this question the class-conscious proletariat of the Allied countries harbor as few illusions as we do."

In the new session of the Brest-Litovsk negotiations, Trotsky continued, the Soviet government would not wait for the Allies. "If the latter continue to sabotage a universal peace the Russian delegation will nevertheless appear for the continuation of the talks. A separate peace, signed by Russia, would undoubtedly inflict a heavy blow on Allied countries, first of all on France and Italy. . . . But if the Allied governments, with the blind obstinacy characteristic of declining and dying classes, again reject participation in the negotiations then the working class will be faced with the iron necessity of tearing the government from the hands of those who cannot or will not give the peoples peace.

"In these days the fate of hundreds of thousands and millions of lives is being decided. If no armistice is concluded on the French and Italian fronts, new attacks as senseless, merciless and indecisive as all the preceding ones will swallow countless new victims on both sides. The automatic logic of these massacres unleashed by the ruling classes is leading to the complete annihilation of the flower of the European nations. But the peoples wish to live and have a right to it. They have the right and the obligation to push aside all who prevent them from living." Once again Trotsky appealed to the Allies to come to Brest-Litovsk and once again in a high peroration he promised help "to the working classes of every country that rebels against its national imperialists, its chauvinists, its militarists—under the banner of peace, the brotherhood of peoples, and the socialist transformation of society."[26]

Secretary Lansing was angered by Trotsky's provocative proclamation. He told President Wilson it constituted a "direct threat to the existing order

[26] *Dokumenty Vneshnei Politiki SSSR*, Ministerstvo Inostranikh Del SSSR (*Documents of the Foreign Policy of the USSR*, Foreign Ministry of the USSR) (Moscow, 1957), pp. 67-70. The document is dated Dec. 17, Old Style (Dec. 30, New Style), 1917, and signed "The People's Commissar of Foreign Affairs." It is reprinted, according to a footnote in the 1957 volume, from the *Izvestia* of Dec. 17, 1917 (Old Style), where the signature reads, "The People's Commissar of Foreign Affairs, L. Trotsky," The book omits Trotsky's name from the signature.

in all countries." The document, he complained, discussed rights of nationalities "without defining what a nationality is. . . . Is the Bolshevik idea of nationality based upon blood, habitation in a particular territory, language, or political affinity? . . . The suggestions of the Bolsheviks in regard to Ireland, India, and other countries . . . are in my opinion utterly untenable if it is desirable to preserve the present concept of sovereign states in international relations. . . . The document is an appeal to the proletariat of all countries, to the ignorant and mentally deficient, who by their numbers are urged to become masters. Here seems to me to lie a very real danger in view of the present social unrest throughout the world. . . . I think in considering this address it might properly be asked by what authority the Bolsheviks assume to speak for the Russian people. They seized the Government at Petrograd by force, they broke up opposition in the army by disorganizing it, they prevented the meeting of the Constituent Assembly chosen by the people because they could not control it, they have seized the property of the nation and confiscated private property."[27]

Lansing advised Woodrow Wilson "to state frankly the false premises on which it [Trotsky's appeal] is based." The President rejected Lansing's recommendation. Wilson was not angered, or, if he was, he chose to return a soft, indeed a flattering answer.

The two opening paragraphs of President Wilson's Fourteen Points speech on January 9, 1918,[28] dealt with the first major crisis at the Brest-Litovsk conference. On December 25—spirit of Christmas?—the representatives of the Quadruple Alliance had cheerfully accepted the Bolsheviks' favorite formula: "no annexations, no indemnities." On December 27 a Soviet military attaché at Brest asked General Max Hoffmann at dinner how much German-annexed Russian territory would be evacuated. "Not one millimeter," Hoffmann replied.[29]

At lunch on the 28th, Hoffmann reported in his memoirs, "I told Yoffe, who was sitting next to me, that I had the impression the Russian delegation understood the concept of peace without forcible annexations differently from the representatives of the Central Powers. The latter took the position that it was not a forcible annexation when parts of the former Russian Empire voluntarily and through the decision of authorized political bodies announced their separation from the Russian state and their union with Germany or some other country. . . .

"Yoffe looked as if he had been hit on the head. After lunch Yoffe, Kamenev, and Pokrovsky on the one hand, and the Foreign Secretary [Kuehlmann], Czernin and I on the other, conferred for several hours during which the Russians gave free expression to their disappointment and indignation.

[27] *Papers Relating to the Foreign Relations of the United States. The Lansing Papers 1914-1920*, in two volumes, Vol. II (Washington, 1940), pp. 346-349.

[28] Leonard, *op. cit.*, pp. 92-101. All subsequent extracts from the speech are quoted from this source, checked against others.

[29] M. N. Pokrovsky, *Vneshnaya Politika Rossii v 20. Veke (Russian Foreign Policy in the Twentieth Century)* (Moscow, 1926), p. 74.

Pokrovsky declared amid tears of anger that one could not speak of peace without annexations when eighteen provinces were being taken from Russia."[30]

Lenin made some notes on December 10, 1917, for a definition of "annexations." Not only wartime annexations but any area seized "since the second half of the nineteenth century" was to be regarded as annexed if its people had expressed their dissatisfaction "in literature, in decisions of parliaments, municipalities, meetings or similar institutions, in governmental or diplomatic acts inspired by the nationalist movements of those territories, in nationalistic disputes, clashes, uprisings, etc." At this point Lenin abandoned the task of definition and apparently passed the piece of paper to Joseph V. Stalin, Commissar of Nationalities and therefore, presumably, the expert on the fate of subject peoples. Stalin suffixed several interesting precisions on self-determination: "1. Every (stateless) nationality constituting a part of a given belligerent country is officially recognized as enjoying the right of free self-determination including the right of secession and the establishment of a separate state; 2. The right of self-determination is exercised through a referendum of the entire population of the self-determining region." Stalin further stipulated "the prior conditions guaranteeing the fulfillment of the right of a .nation to free self-determination." These included "the removal of troops from the confines of the self-determining nation" and the return of officials and others banished by the occupying forces.[31]

Neither General Hoffmann nor Kuelhmann nor Czernin benefited from this enunciation of Bolshevik doctrine, for it lay unpublished in the Soviet archives until 1929. In any case, it would have been ignored, as Stalin himself ignored it when he in turn became the conqueror after the 1939 Soviet pact with Hitler.

Indignant at German perfidy in accepting self-determination on Christmas Day and nullifying it through interpretation three days later, *Izvestia* called the Germans "wolves in sheep's clothing." The Soviet government daily organ, lacking adequate information, missed the point. The Brest-Litovsk policy of the Quadruple Alliance was made by wolves in wolves' clothing and sheep in sheep's clothing. The sheep wore sheep's clothing at the Santa Claus performance, then were forced by the wolves to change into wolves' clothing.

Austro-Hungarian Foreign Minister Czernin was one of the sheep. "Desperate cries for food from Vienna," he noted in his diary on January 16 while at Brest. The next day, "Bad news from Vienna and vicinity. Big strike movement . . . reduced flour ration."[32] He was under instructions from Emperor Karl to bring back a peace treaty, even a separate peace treaty with

---

[30] General Max Hoffmann, *op. cit.*, pp. 201-202.

[31] *Leninskii Sbornik.* Second ed., Vol. XI (Moscow-Leningrad, 1931), pp. 15-16. Also in Lenin, *Sochineniya.* Fourth ed., Vol. 26, pp. 313-314.

[32] Count Czernin, *Im Weltkriege* (Berlin, 1919), p. 323.

Soviet Russia, if Germany remained obdurate and too proud to negotiate a settlement. On January 2, 1918, British Foreign Secretary Arthur J. Balfour informed President Wilson that General Jan C. Smuts and Austrian Count Mensdorff-Pouilly-Dietrichstein had met secretly in Switzerland and held "friendly and unofficial" interviews about peace. Smuts' statement that British war aims did not include the destruction of Austria-Hungary, Balfour's report added, gave the Austrian representative "much satisfaction."[33] Austria-Hungary, doomed to destruction from within, would have spared Britain the trouble. At Brest, consequently, Czernin was mentally depressed, physically ill, and in a mood to swallow the Bolshevik "no annexations, no reparations" formula hoping, weakly, that it would apply to German annexations but not to his rickety imperial house of disparate ethnic cards. Evenings at Brest, the Central Powers civilians were required to change into dinner jackets. In his buttonhole, Czernin wore the decoration of the Order of the Golden Fleece.

Richard von Kuehlmann was another sheep. Kuehlmann, born at Pera, Constantinople, in 1873, rose to top rank in the German Foreign Office in the First World War and survived the Hitler period and the Second World War. He died in 1948, leaving the finished manuscript of his memoirs.[34] His father served as director of the Turkish railways; his mother was the daughter of a well-known German author. Kuehlmann possessed a brilliant mind stocked with social theory, law, and history. He enjoyed the protracted ideological duels with Trotsky at Brest and would have prolonged them for the sport. But, as Trotsky wrote a little later, General Hoffmann had no interest in these exercises and often "put his soldier's boots on the table around which the intricate legal arguments then revolved. On our side nobody doubted for a moment that the boots of General Hoffmann were the only concrete reality in the negotiations."[35]

After filling high diplomatic posts in London, Stockholm, and The Hague, Kuehlmann had been appointed ambassador to Turkey, where a summons reached him from Chancellor Georg Michaelis, who succeeded Bethmann-Hollweg in July, 1917, to come to Berlin and take charge of the Foreign Office on the Wilhelmstrasse. "I have already explained," he noted on his August 5, 1917, appointment, "that from the first day of the war I regarded the German outlook with little optimism. . . . In my view, the Central Powers' only chance of avoiding defeat was through a peace settlement before the end of the war. If the Central Powers finished this gigantic trial of strength with undiminished territory I considered this a success."[36]

Logically, therefore, Kuehlmann would have welcomed the Bolshevik appeal for a peace conference of all belligerents. Political developments in

[33] Ray Stannard Baker, *Woodrow Wilson, Life and Letters, War Leader, April 6, 1917-February 28, 1918* (New York, 1939), Vol. VII, p. 442.
[34] Richard von Kuehlmann, *Erinnerungen* (Heidelberg, 1948).
[35] Leon Trotsky, *Von Oktober bis nach Brest-Litovsk* (Pamphlet) (Chicago), p. 109.
[36] Kuehlmann, *op. cit.*, p. 471.

Germany heightened his receptivity. The German Reichstag, on July 19, 1917, had adopted a resolution urging a peace agreement without "compulsory acquisitions of territory and political, economical or financial violence." This was merely a sigh for peace quickly swept away by the winds of war. But peace was in the international air. Rumors of confidential, high-level peace talks circulated everywhere. When the United States went into the war on April 6, 1917, Germany's victory prospects fell and Kuehlmann's pessimism thickened. So did his sheep's cover. But at Brest-Litovsk the field marshals and generals in wolves' clothing disrobed him, stripped him of his pacifist clothing and Kris Kringle mask, and made him speak with the voice of Esau. He should have understood them. "I was basically opposed to any kind of concessions to France on the question of Alsace-Lorraine," he wrote of his attitude in 1917.[37] Hindenburg and Ludendorff took the same position on Poland and the Baltic region. He hoped to keep the conquests of an earlier war; they intended to keep the gains of this. He had, at a meeting of the Crown Council on September 11, 1917, won from Kaiser Wilhelm, against the opposition of Ludendorff and Hindenburg, the authority to sound out the British government on the possibility of peace if Germany liberated Belgium.[38] But at a Crown Council on December 18, 1917, at Kreuznach army headquarters, the Kaiser, yielding to the Ludendorff-Hindenburg team, did not approve Kuehlmann's policy of self-determination for German-occupied lands in Eastern Europe. The military had won, and the military meant Erich von Ludendorff, who, in addition to being quartermaster general of the German army, was the brain of Field Marshal Paul von Hindenburg, the "Wooden Titan." Together they often intimidated the Kaiser, if need be by threats of resignation. Their last card was a dictated peace at Brest-Litovsk and, as a corollary, victory in the West. Ludendorff believed in victory. Kuehlmann did not. Nor did Czernin. This separated the civilian sheep from the military wolves at Brest.

Kuehlmann confessed that "my position as chief German negotiator was extremely difficult."[39] He had to watch his step but he could not do so because he had to watch Ludendorff and Hindenburg, "the two demigods," as he called them, at headquarters in Kreuznach. They objected to the Soviet proposals for self-determination and the evacuation of occupied territories. "That the first point in Germany's agenda was the release of Russia from her alliance obligations to the Western powers, for this," Kuehlmann declared, "the demigods in G.H.Q. apparently had not the slightest comprehension."[40] Their angle of vision was not Kuehlmann's. Speaking of the Brest negotiations, Ludendorff asserted, "The really important matter was whether they were going to be conducted in such a manner that we could attack [in the West] and make certain of finishing the titanic struggle in

[37] Ibid., p. 473.
[38] Prinz Max von Baden, op. cit., pp. 142-143.
[39] Kuehlmann, op. cit., p. 523.
[40] Ibid., p. 535.

our favor . . . to save ourselves from the tragedy of being defeated. . . . On December 25, Count Czernin, in the name of the four allies, declared his agreement with the Russian proposals of peace without annexations by force and without indemnities. . . . The right of self-determination was applied in a manner that lacked clearness and did not accord with German interests. . . . Nothing was in accordance with the decisions arrived at [in a Crown Council at Kreuznach] under the presidency of His Majesty on December 18. Our future in the East was rendered doubtful . . . I spoke to General Hoffmann, regretting the way the negotiations were going. . . . We now learned that Count von Hertling [the new German Chancellor] had expressly approved Count Czernin's Christmas speech. . . . We made extensive concessions to the principle of self-determination. We dropped our contention that the people of the occupied countries, Courland and Lithuania, had already been permitted to avail themselves of this right, and allowed the inhabitants to be consulted again. All we demanded was that this should take place during our occupation. Trotsky maintained that we must first of all evacuate the country and that the people would exercise their right afterward. To evacuate the country was a military absurdity; we needed it for our existence and had no mind to deliver it up to unscrupulous Bolshevism."[41]

Events occurred so fast that by the time "the explosion of joy" over the Central Powers' Christmas declaration had brought "hundreds of thousands of workers and soldiers out into the streets of Petrograd to demonstrate for a democratic peace,"[42] the Soviet delegation was back from Brest with the sad news of the December 28 German volte-face.

A few months after Brest-Litovsk, Trotsky asked himself "why German diplomacy, two or three days before the unveiling of its wolfish appetite, had given expression to democratic formulas; what did German diplomacy expect to achieve thereby?" He concluded that the Czernin statement on Christmas Day was made on "Kuehlmann's own initiative." Trotsky thought "the secret of Kuehlmann's diplomatic step lies in the fact that he really supposed he could play a four-handed game with us. He apparently resorted to the following reasoning: Russia needs peace; the Bolsheviks came to power because they fought for peace; the Bolsheviks want to retain this power and they can do this only if they really reach a peace settlement. Of course, they have committed themselves to a concrete peace program, but what are diplomats for if we cannot make the people see black as white? We Germans will make things easier for the Bolsheviks by wrapping our robbery in democratic formulas. . . . In other words, Kuehlmann depended on a tacit understanding with us: We get back our nice formula unharmed and give them in return the opportunity to acquire, without protest, provinces and nations for Germany."[43] Karl Radek made the same assumption.[44]

[41] Erich von Ludendorff, *Ludendorff's Own Story, August 1917-November 1918* (New York, 1919), pp. 167-175.
[42] Karl Radek, *Vnesnaya Politika Sovietskoi Rossii* (Moscow, 1923), p. 15.
[43] Trotsky, *op. cit.*, pp. 107-108.
[44] Radek, *op. cit.*, p. 15.

This could, conceivably, have passed through Kuehlmann's mind. Perhaps he thought the Bolsheviks, in their adversity, would be compelled to sanction the quick reversal between Christmas and December 28. It is far more likely that the Kuehlmann-Czernin-Hertling sheep flock, which included many other German and Austro-Hungarian civilian politicians and, probably, Austro-Hungarian military as well, saw a successful, conciliatory Brest conference as a long step to a negotiated peace without victory in the West, but were overruled by the twin "demigods," one of wood, the other of steel, who regarded the negotiations as a big leap toward military triumph over the Western powers.

President Wilson understood this.

Addressing Congress on January 8, 1918 (the Fourteen Points address), Woodrow Wilson said, "The Russian representatives [at Brest-Litovsk] presented not only a perfectly definite statement of principles upon which they would be willing to conclude peace, but also an equally definite program of the concrete application of those principles. The representatives of the Central Powers, on their part, presented an outline of settlement which, if much less definite, seemed susceptible of liberal interpretation until their specific program of practical terms was added.

"That program proposed no concessions at all . . . the Central Empires were to keep every foot of territory their armed forces had occupied. . . . It is a reasonable conjecture that the general principles of settlement which they at first suggested originated with the more liberal statesmen of Germany and Austria, the men who had begun to feel the force of their own people's thought and purpose, while the concrete terms of actual settlement came from the military leaders. . . . The negotiations have been broken off. The Russian representatives were sincere and in earnest. They cannot entertain such proposals of conquest and domination.

"The whole incident is full of significance. It is also full of perplexity. With whom are the Russian representatives dealing? For whom are the representatives of the Central Empires speaking? Are they speaking for the majorities of their respective parliaments, or for minority parties, that military and imperialistic minority which has so far dominated their whole policy and controlled the affairs of Turkey and of the Balkan states, which have been obliged to become their associates in this war? The Russian representatives have insisted, very justly, very wisely, and in the true spirit of modern democracy, that the conferences they have been holding with the Teutonic and Turkish statesmen should be held within open, not closed, doors. . . . To whom have we been listening, then? To those who speak . . . the spirit and intention of the liberal leaders and parties of Germany, or to those who resist and defy that spirit and insist upon conquest and subjugation? Or are we listening, in fact, to both, unreconciled and in open and hopeless contradiction? These are serious and pregnant questions. Upon the answer to them depends the peace of the world."

The President then took cognizance of the Russian people's sincere will to peace. He said, "There is, moreover, a voice calling for these definitions of principle and of purpose which is, it seems to me, more thrilling and more compelling than any of the many troubled voices with which the troubled air of the world is filled. It is the voice of the Russian people. They are prostrate and all but helpless, it would seem, before the grim power of Germany. . . . Their power, apparently, is shattered, and yet their soul is not subservient. They will not yield either in principle or in action. Their conviction of what is right, of what it is humane and honorable for them to accept, has been stated with a frankness, a largeness of view, a generosity of spirit, and a universal human sympathy which must challenge the admiration of every friend of mankind, and they have refused to compound their ideals or desert others that they themselves may be safe."

These humane, honorable, frank, and large statements had been broadcast repeatedly by Lenin and by Trotsky on December 30. Wilson showered them with commendation. He also hoped they would not leave the war for their safety's sake. "They call on us," he continued, "to say what it is that we desire, in what, if in anything, our purpose and our spirit differ from theirs. . . . Whether their present leaders believe it or not"—he wanted Lenin and Trotsky to believe him—"it is our heartfelt desire and hope that some way may be opened whereby we may be privileged to assist the people of Russia to attain their utmost hope of liberty and ordered peace."

Mr. Wilson's purposes were to split Turkey and Bulgaria, the weakest links in the Quadruple Alliance chain, from Germany; to widen the split between the German military and civilians; and, above all, to break up the recessed Brest-Litovsk conference by aiming compliments at the Bolsheviks and offering to help them, in the spirit of Robins-Lockhart-Sadoul, if they stayed at war.

To further these objectives the President then proceeded to outline the peace, or war, aims of the United States:

1. "*Open covenants of peace, openly arrived at* . . .

2. "*Absolute freedom of navigation upon the seas* . . .

3. "*The removal* . . . *of all economic barriers and the establishment of an equality of trade conditions* . . .

4. "*. . . guarantees . . . that national armaments will be reduced* . . .

5. "*A free, open minded and absolutely impartial adjustment of all colonial claims* . . ."

Point Five might please the Bolsheviks.

Point Six was for their special consumption: "The evacuation of all Russian territory and such a settlement of all questions affecting Russia as will secure the best and freest cooperation of the other nations in obtaining for her an unhampered and unembarrassed opportunity for the independent determination of her own political development and national policy, and assure her of a sincere welcome into the society of nations under institutions of her own choosing; and more than a welcome, assistance also of every kind that she may need and may herself desire. The treatment accorded Russia by her sister nations in the months to come will be the acid test of their good will, of their comprehension of her needs as distinguished from their own interests, and of their intelligent and unselfish sympathy."

7. "*Belgium . . . must be evacuated and restored . . .*"

8. "*All French territory should be freed . . .*" and Alsace-Lorraine restored to her.

9. "*A readjustment of the frontiers of Italy . . . along . . . lines of nationality.*

10. "*The peoples of Austria-Hungary . . . should be accorded the freest opportunity of autonomous development.*

11. "*Rumania, Serbia, and Montenegro should be evacuated . . .*

12. "*The Turkish portions of the present Ottoman Empire should be assured a secure sovereignty, but the other nationalities which are now under Turkish rule should be assured . . . an absolutely unmolested opportunity of autonomous development and the Dardanelles should be permanently opened as a free passage to the ships of commerce of all nations under international guarantees.*

13. "*An independent Polish state should be erected . . .*

14. "*A general association of nations should be formed . . .*"

Half a million copies of the President's speech were printed by the Bolsheviks in German translation and sent into the German lines on the eastern front. Thousands of copies in Russian translation were placarded on the walls and hoardings in Petrograd and other cities. The Soviet radio disseminated it widely. "The American Y.M.C.A., availing itself of Bolshevik aid, distributed one million copies throughout the Russian lines, and another million, in German, within the German lines on the eastern front. Every [Soviet] newspaper carried it in full."[45]

"But despite this prodigal distribution," Wheeler-Bennett wrote, "the Fourteen Points were destined to have little or no effect upon the Brest-Litovsk negotiations." George F. Kennan concluded that, "All in all, it is difficult to conceive that the subsequent course of events at Brest-Litovsk would have been appreciably different had the Fourteen Point speech never been made."[46] These judgments are substantiated by history. The question is whether the speech did not do harm. Wilson's Sixth Point read, "The treatment accorded to Russia by her sister nations in the months to come will be the acid test of their good will, their comprehension of her needs as distinguished from their own interests, and of their intelligent and unselfish sympathy." Wilson and the United States did not pass the "acid test." In the months to come America engaged in military intervention

---

[45] John W. Wheeler-Bennett, *Brest-Litovsk, the Forgotten Peace, March 1918* (London, 1938), p. 147.

[46] Kennan, *op. cit.*, p. 264.

against the Soviet government. Then Russia was free to scoff and scorn. The acid test turned Wilson's sweet compliments into bitter disillusionment.

Sixteen days after President Wilson delivered his Fourteen Points address, Raymond Robins in Petrograd wired William Boyce Thompson in America: "Cannot too strongly urge importance of prompt recognition of Bolshevik authority and immediate establishment of modus vivendi making possible generous and sympathetic cooperation. Sisson approves this text and requests you show this cable to Creel."[47]

The Fourteen Points thrilled Robins. He could not have dreamt of a greater victory in his crusade to win American friendship for Soviet Russia. The telegram to Thompson shows that he expected the speech to bring concrete results in the shape, first, of U.S. recognition of the Bolshevik regime. This was not to be.

Robins, as well as Lockhart and Sadoul, failed. Their zeal, combined in Sadoul with ideology (he became a fervent Stalinist), in Robins with acceptance of the revolution as a reformation, and in Lockhart with understanding and a strong civil-servant sense of duty, availed nought because they aimed to bring Russia back into the world war. They offered the Bolsheviks survival through Western military aid. This was implicit, too, in President Wilson's address. Lenin realized, however, that this would be tied to a condition: the maintenance of a fighting front against the mighty Central Powers, tantamount, in his view, to belligerency and therefore to mortal peril for the revolution.

As Wilson stood before Congress to proclaim the Fourteen Points, Leon Trotsky was in a train going to Brest-Litovsk to resume negotiations with the Quadruple Alliance. The crisis precipitated by the December 28 disclosure of the German position against self-determination made it necessary for the Commissar of Foreign Affairs himself to see what remained to be done. The specter of Ludendorff and Hindenburg loomed large over the gutted citadel town. The words of Wilson were vague and unavailing. Trotsky believed, however, that his own words to the European working class were concrete and would be successful in extricating the Soviet government from the dilemma of impotence. Both men exaggerated the importance of eloquence and ideology. Lenin's attitude, which Wilson overlooked, was: Self-determination yes, but not at the cost of political survival. Trotsky had made so much of self-determination that the President thought the Bolsheviks would die fighting for it. Wilson erred.

President Wilson knew that his Fourteen Points had failed to achieve a practical result. He apparently realized that the nub of the problem was diplomatic recognition of the Soviet regime. One day, sitting in the White House, he swung around in his chair to his Hammond typewriter and banged out a letter to Secretary Lansing:

[47] C. K. Cumming and Walter W. Pettit (eds.), *Russian-American Relations: March, 1917-March 1920, Documents and Papers* (New York, 1920), pp. 76-77.

"January 20, 1918. Dear Mr. Secretary, Here is the ever-recurring question. How shall we deal with the Bolsheviki? This particular suggestion seems to have something in it worth considering, and I am writing to ask what your own view is. Faithfully Yours, [Signed in pencil] W.W."

The President attached the text of a cable, dated January 14, Copenhagen, from an American diplomat whose "suggestion . . . worth considering" was that one of the Western Allies establish diplomatic relations with the Soviet government with a view to "combating German intrigue in Russia." By tradition, by its newness on the scene, and "especially in the light of the President's recent message"—the Fourteen Points—the United States was "best suited among Germany's opponents to undertake the task."[48] America would speak to the Kremlin on behalf of the alliance.

This was one of those ideas that flow in a steady stream from officials and private citizens who seek to influence men in high office. It reached the President's desk, a success in itself, and excited his interest, but got lost in the labyrinth of government. Nothing came of it. The Allies were already discussing military intervention in Russia. Recognition was abhorrent to them.

The West offered nothing. Germany offered peace. Russia had to have peace. What kind of peace? This is what Trotsky sought to ascertain at Brest-Litovsk.

XII. ÕHE GENERALS AND THE COMMISSAR

WHEN LENIN and Trotsky were émigrés in Europe they exchanged insults in the normal style of the Russian revolutionary hothouse. Trotsky once called Lenin "unscrupulous"; Lenin once called Trotsky "an empty phrasemonger." In the moment of communist crisis, however, they buried their hostility and marched together toward November 7, 1917. On the establishment of the Soviet government, Trotsky was given the second most important task— second only to Lenin's over-all leadership: that of forging an early peace. In 1918, with internal war menacing the new regime, Trotsky took command of the Red Army. Lenin, irascible in prerevolutionary years when an adjective or a comma seemed worth a quarrel and the loss of a night's sleep, grew forgiving when he gained power. He could still fire broadsides at those who differed with him; he branded Zinoviev and Kamenev as "strikebreakers" for

---

[48] Both documents are from the files of the State Department in the National Archives. Photostats were generously placed at my disposal for publication by Professor Arthur S. Link, editor of *The Papers of Woodrow Wilson* at Princeton University.

their doubts about launching the revolution. But he elevated them to high places in the Soviet hierarchy. He was a stern ruler without being vindictive to party dissidents. In Western Europe he and Trotsky had split thin ideological hairs. Inside the Soviet government—despite disputes—they were senior and junior partners in the management of the revolution.

Soviet writers have distorted Trotsky's part in the revolution (and therefore the history of the revolution) by ignoring him or falsifying facts and suppressing documentation. Whole segments of the Soviet record were rewritten in order to vilify Trotsky and glorify Stalin. But massive authentic material remains for a portrait of the man and an estimate of his work.

Leon Trotsky had biological magnetism which excited those who came within the field, and excitement is the prerequisite of revolutionary action. He was a genius of the stinging word and sweeping argument. Trained in the aim-to-kill school of revolutionary polemics (object: to demolish rather than convince) he could whiplash enemies with his tongue and pen. When the Brest-Litovsk peace conference built a stage from which a Bolshevik could address the world the role fell to Trotsky because of his literary flair, quick mind, and intensity. He was thirty-eight.

Some said Trotsky had a Mephistophelian face. Actually he had the dark, pale face of a Russian Jewish intellectual: high brow, full lips, dense, curly hair, thick mustache, small pointed goatee, and weak, shortsighted eyes behind pince-nez. It was the fire within that gave him the visage of an angry fighter. He loved combat. Perhaps he invited it by his unharnessed individuality. The trodden path did not lure him. Challenged to choose one of two roads he chose a third. Before the revolution he accepted Lenin and opposed Lenin, supported and rejected Bolshevism, adopted Menshevism, and finally remained aloof from both and built his own little political home—until the prospect of decisive action in the Russia of 1917 drew him into the Bolshevik party. In 1905, the alternative was: absolute monarchy or bourgeois-democratic constitution; Trotsky, liking neither, coined the slogan, "No Tsar and a workers' government." During the Brest-Litovsk controversy, Lenin advocated peace and Bukharin war; Trotsky advocated "No war and no peace." To an either-or person like Stalin this kind of neither-nor man would have been irritating.

Trotsky was many-faceted. Steeped in politics, he loved literature. In the nineteen-twenties, many ranked him as Soviet Russia's foremost literary critic. Feet on the battlefield, hands on the steering wheel of the ship of state, he read new fiction and poetry and wrote beautiful prose. While making history he wrote history.

Trotsky was no less anticapitalist than Lenin, and no less class-conscious. But his judgments of people were more psychological than political. In London, in 1902, Trotsky took lodgings with Vera Ivanovna Zasulich and Julius Martov, both editors of *Iskra*. Vera Ivanovna, an older woman and a former terrorist, impressed Trotsky as "a curiously attractive person." She had a sharp eye. She once said to Lenin, "George [Plekhanov] is a greyhound. He shakes and shakes the adversary and lets him go, but you are a bulldog: you have a deadly bite."

"That pleased Lenin greatly," she told Trotsky.[1]

Once, Trotsky recalled, "I used the expression 'bourgeois-democratic revolutionaries.' 'But no,' Vera Ivanovna interrupted with a touch of annoyance or rather of vexation. 'Not bourgeois and not proletarian, but simply revolutionary.' "[2] Trotsky liked this approach, at least he did not reject it. But Lenin said to Trotsky, pejoratively, "In Vera Ivanovna much is based on ethics and feeling."[3]

Trotsky understood her. "She remained to the end the old radical intellectual on whom fate grafted Marxism," he wrote. "Zasulich's articles show that she had adopted to a remarkable degree the theoretical elements of Marxism. But the moral political foundations of the Russian radical of the seventies remained untouched in her until her death."[4]

There was in this analysis a touch of admiration, an appreciation of the old idealism which Lenin found objectionable. Though their names are linked in a historic adjective: the Lenin-Trotsky revolution, the two men were different. Lenin was as selfless as the human animal can be. Trotsky had a prima donna's sensitivity. It is doubtful whether Lenin could be hurt by hostility. Trotsky suffered. His ego was as great as his gifts. Indeed, while he deferred to Lenin he was also jealous of him. Instead of being pleased, in the later years of bitter banishment from the Soviet Union, with Stalin's admission that "All the work of the practical organization of the [Bolshevik] insurrection was conducted under the immediate leadership of the President of the Petrograd Soviet, Comrade Trotsky," he felt that Stalin's previous sentence: "The inspirer of the revolution from beginning to end was the Central Committee of the party headed by Comrade Lenin," was "designed to weaken the impression prevailing in the party that the leader of the insurrection had been Trotsky."[5] In defeat, credit for victories tastes doubly sweet, and no scorn is so fierce as that of a dictator denied.

Both Lenin and Trotsky were dictator types. They were therefore fated to part while aspiring to dictatorship and to join in the successful dictatorship when Trotsky had to choose between second fiddle or none, the more so since they agreed on essentials. A strict Marxist, Trotsky, like Lenin, believed in the intimate relationship between a viable Russian revolution and the European socialist revolution. They were internationalists of varying intensity.

Trotsky, writing during the First World War, declared, "The whole globe,

---

[1] Leon Trotsky, *Lenin* (Authorized Translation), p. 16.

[2] *Ibid.*, p. 19.

[3] *Ibid.*, p. 21.

[4] *Ibid.*, pp. 18-19.

[5] Leon Trotsky, *The History of the Russian Revolution*, Vol. III, *The Triumph of the Soviets*, translated from the Russian by Max Eastman (New York, 1932), Appendix 1, p. 373.

the land and the sea, the surface as well as the interior, has become one economic workshop, the different parts of which are inseparably connected with each other. This work was accomplished by capitalism." That led to imperialism. "What the politics of imperialism has demonstrated more than anything else is that the old national state . . . is now an intolerable hindrance to economic development. The present War is at bottom a revolt of the forces of production against the political form of nation and state. It means the collapse of the national state as an independent economic unity." Approximately forty years later, and ten years too late, the capitalist states of Europe, acting under the impact of aggressive Soviet imperialism, were to realize this truth and move toward international integration. "The nation," Trotsky affirmed, "must continue to exist as a cultural, ideologic and psychological fact, but its economic foundation has been pulled from under its feet. . . . The War proclaims the downfall of the national state. Yet at the same time it proclaims the downfall of the capitalist system of economy. . . . Capitalism has created the material conditions of a new Socialist economic system. . . . War is the method by which capitalism, at the climax of its development, seeks to solve its insoluble contradictions."[6] This is a vivid version of what Lenin would say in *Imperialism, the Highest Stage of Capitalism.*

The revolutionary antithesis to dying capitalist nationalism was, for Trotsky, "the United Europe of tomorrow."[7] But he focused on the "fight against tsarism." It was 1914. "What tsarism primarily seeks in Austria-Hungary and the Balkans is a market for its political methods of plunder, robbery and acts of violence." The Tsar exported tsarism. An army moves on its stomach and carries its master's mind with it. That, however, was only the ideological aspect. Tsarist Russia had been making buoyant economic progress. "The Russian bourgeoisie, all the way up to its radical intelligentsia," Trotsky wrote of pre-1914 Russia, "has been completely demoralized by the tremendous growth of industry in the last five years, and it has entered into a bloody league with the dynasty which had to secure to the impatient Russian capitalists their part of the world's booty by new land robberies."[8]

Dizzy with industrial success, Russia coveted Galicia and "strove to throw a noose around the neck of the Balkan peoples" leaving to the intellectuals "the task of concealing its robberies by sickening declamations about the defense of Belgium and France." Imperialism, born of economic power, found its ideological lackeys whom Trotsky called "liberals." There remained the Russian proletariat as "the sole champion of the war of liberation"—within Russia. "It makes the Russian Revolution definitely an integral part of the Social Revolution of the European proletariat." Conscious of Russian socialist

[6] Leon Trotsky, *The Bolshevik and World Peace*, introduction by Lincoln Steffens (New York, 1918), pp. 20 *et seq.*

[7] *Ibid.*, p. 29.

[8] *Ibid.*, p. 30.

weakness and a conscientious internationalist, Trotsky was offering Europe a revolutionary alliance.

During the war Trotsky lived as a refugee, harried and moving from Austria to France, to Spain, to the United States, seeking freedom for his pen. He could not have imagined himself the hero of peace negotiations at Brest-Litovsk. Yet he might have said there and in effect did say there what he wrote in 1914: "we have never looked for help from Hapsburg or Hohenzollern militarism, and we are not looking for it now . . . we should refuse to regard the Hohenzollerns not only as an objective but as a subjective ally. The fate of the Russian revolution is so inseparably bound up with the fate of European socialism, and we Russian socialists stand so firmly on the ground of internationalism, that we cannot, we must not for a moment, entertain the idea of purchasing the doubtful liberation of Russia by the certain destruction of the liberty of Belgium and France. . . . We are united by many ties to the German Social Democracy. We have gone through the German Socialist school."[9] For this reason, and for geopolitical reasons, Germany remained the centerpiece of Soviet foreign policy long after the 1917 Bolshevik revolution. But, unlike Lenin, Trotsky was furiously anti-German. Writing when it seemed the Kaiser would win the war, Trotsky referred to "the ancient race of Hindenburgs, Moltkes, and Klucks, hereditary specialists in mass-murder"; he argued that a German triumph against France "would mean the victory of the feudal-monarchial state over the democratic-republican state."[10] Lenin made no such distinction, harbored no such sentiments.

What of Russia? "Is it possible," Trotsky asked, "that the defeat of Tsarism might actually aid the cause of the revolution?" He answered with only a qualified affirmative. The Russo-Japanese War of 1904-1905 "gave a powerful impetus to the revolutionary events that followed. Consequently similar results may be expected from the German-Russian War." Yet he saw more deeply than most. He was not sure this development was desirable. The Russo-Japanese War "hastened the outbreak of the [1905] revolution; but for that very reason it also weakened it. For had the revolution developed as a result of the organic growth of inner forces, it would have come later, but would have been far stronger and more systematic."[11]

Between 1912 and 1914 "Russia's enormous industrial development once and for all pulled the country out of its state of counter-revolutionary depression." This was a slower but more conscious, an organic and more systematic, revolutionary development and Trotsky welcomed it. Now, "If we presuppose a catastrophal Russian defeat" in the First World War, he wrote, "the war *may* bring a quicker outbreak of the revolution, but at the cost of its inner weakness. And if the revolution should even gain the upper hand under such circumstances, then the bayonets of the Hohenzollern armies

[9] *Ibid.*, pp. 31-32.
[10] *Ibid.*, p. 108.
[11] *Ibid.*, pp. 85-86.

would be turned on the revolution. . . . That in such circumstances a Russian revolution, even if temporarily successful, would be an historic miscarriage, needs no further proof."[12]

Thus spake the prophet in 1914. His words offer a preview of the situation he confronted at Brest-Litovsk in 1918. Superficially, there was a big difference: within less than a year after the signing of the Brest peace, Germany suffered military defeat. That, however, does not affect Trotsky's assessment of the inherent frailty of a premature revolution. German arms caused the overthrow of tsarism. They were responsible for the overthrow of Kerensky too and therefore for the immaturity and debility of the Bolshevik revolution when it arrived prematurely on November 7, 1917. Had Trotsky been frank then or thereafter he might have called the revolution "an historic miscarriage." He knew the weakness of the revolution. This weakness confirmed his stubbornly held belief in the theory he had evolved years earlier while in European exile, the theory of Permanent Revolution which, in simple summary, meant: the retention of political power by the Russian revolutionary government and the development of state-owned industry without, however, attempting to revolutionize, socialize, the entire country, including agriculture, until revolutions in the West came to Russia's rescue and paved the way to the building of socialism on an international scale. Permanent revolution was Trotsky's answer to the premature revolution. Lenin too hoped for salvation from Europe. But he never thought that revolution could come too early.

An underdeveloped country inevitably has an underdeveloped ruling class —domestic or foreign—which may, in times of stress (world war and the aftermath or colonial unrest) be forced to surrender a territory too weak and too poor for expensive social transformations. Russia, being backward and weak, was ripe for violent revolution but unfit for socialism. That was Trotsky's long-range, pre-1917 estimate of Russia's prospects. More immediately, Soviet Russia was weak when Foreign Commissar Trotsky appeared at Brest-Litovsk in 1918 to baffle and defy the Kaiser's generals.

Lenin wrote endlessly, but he was not a literary man. Trotsky loved words. He knew their value in a revolution when they dispelled despair and kindled hopes. He knew their limitations when directed at "the ancient race of Hindenburg, Moltkes, and Klucks, hereditary specialists in mass-murder." He was too intelligent to waste energy in attempts to convert generals and field marshals. He concentrated, instead, on ending the imperialist war by starting civil wars in all belligerent countries. Lenin had formulated this idea before the Bolshevik revolution. That revolution showed how to finish the war in one country. Trotsky wanted peoples elsewhere to follow suit. This was his highest card, his finest illusion, as he neared Brest-Litovsk in January, 1918.

Several weeks earlier Trotsky had told the Petrograd Soviet that the Ger-

[12] *Ibid.*, pp. 78 *et seq.*

man and Austro-Hungarian governments had agreed to parley at Brest-Litovsk "under popular pressure." There was an element of truth in this statement, especially as applied to Austria-Hungary. But the natural wish of Berlin and Vienna to subtract Russia from the list of hostile belligerents would seem to be a much more satisfying explanation of the eager yes they returned to the Bolshevik truce proposal. With Russia definitely passive by signed agreement, German efforts would center on only one front where, as soon as winter yielded to thaw, her warlords intended to push to the English Channel and final victory. When the first Russian armistice offer was broadcast, Ludendorff telephoned General Max Hoffmann on the eastern front. "Well, but can one negotiate with those people?"

"Yes," Hoffmann replied, "one can negotiate. Your Excellency needs troops and these are the first you will get."[13]

That is why the Germans sat down with the Russians at Brest. But communists, even so sophisticated a communist as Trotsky, not to speak of a subsequent stupid variety, can never advance a reason for a reasonable act of a foreign government other than "public pressure." Trotsky believed that the oratorical honing of this democratic instrument was the best way of making Russia safe for dictatorship. This was not mere personal vanity. It was a broadly shared Bolshevik conviction.

The Bolsheviks wore blinkers which helped them move forward until they were mired up to the eyes in terror and lies. Trotsky also carried binoculars. With them he, like Lenin, swept the western horizon and saw what he wanted to see: the revolution of their salvation. It was the mother of policy. It fed Trotsky's courage. A journalist just a few months out of the talk-and-smoke-filled cafés of New York's East Side, he challenged German generals in a tone of superiority, for he felt that not only were right and the future his but he too was a general commanding the rising proletariat of a continent. The vision gave him strength.

Arrived in Brest, Trotsky "put the Soviet delegation into a monastery," as Hoffmann wrote: no meals with the Austro-Hungarian-German-Bulgarian-Turkish representatives; no personal conversations with them. One could not fraternize with imperial dignitaries at dinner tables and with common soldiers in freezing trenches. One could not sup genially with generals and call for their overthrow. The relations at Brest-Litovsk became cold and formal. The two sides talked across a gulf—as enemies. Militant communism faced organized militarism. The tempest of revolt thundered round the rock of reaction. Two worlds jousted in the battered town.

The time for negotiation had passed. In single combat between disarmed revolutionaries and Teutonic warlords, bargaining was precluded. The original Soviet scheme of a worldwide conference of belligerents had been still-born. In effect, therefore, the peace would be pro-German. The subtraction of a military zero does not seem capable of altering an equation. But suppose

[13] General Max Hoffmann, *Der Krieg der Versauemten Gelegenheiten*, p. 189.

the Kaiser availed himself of Russia's natural resources and mobilized her manpower? A Churchillian peace, an arrangement between the two belligerent camps at Russia's expense, raised equally ominous possibilities: Germany, already the world's strongest nation, could convalesce from the war, organize Russia, and fall upon the West again as in 1914. Wilson notwithstanding, therefore, the Western Allies were averse to peace without victory. Bolshevism made them more adamant. The German militarists, seeing Russia prostrate, became more arrogant. The prospect at Brest, accordingly, was a separate peace with advantages for Germany.

Alone in the Brest-Litovsk arena with the Kaiser colossus, the Bolsheviks felt ambivalent. They were hypnotized, as ever, by German efficiency and fighting prowess. Uninformed about America and America's military potential, underestimating Western stamina, the Soviet leaders believed the Quadruple Alliance would defeat the Anglo-French-American coalition, believed this not only during the Brest-Litovsk period in the first quarter of 1918 but also as late as September, 1918, two months before the German surrender. On August 27 the Kremlin signed a supplementary Brest-Litovsk agreement which provided, among other things, that Russia indemnify Germany with six billion marks in gold, goods, and bonds. In August and September the Soviets, still bedazzled by Germany, actually shipped to Berlin gold valued at 120 million gold roubles (approximately $60 million), an enormous sum for the struggling Lenin-Trotsky authority. Yet face to face with the awesome, armored German Goliath, the Bolshevik David expected that revolution, the one stone in his sling, would find the giant's exposed temple and slay him.

Approaching Brest in Trotsky's train, Karl Radek, a prominent publicist and member of the Soviet delegation, scattered anti-war, anticapitalist leaflets among the German soldiers guarding the tracks.[14] When the conference resumed, Trotsky demanded that it move to neutral Stockholm which had better radio, telegraphic, postal, and travel ties with the West than Brest. Trotsky wanted the conference to meet "under a bell-glass." "The elimination of secret diplomacy," he had said in his November 22, 1917, announcement of the publication of secret international treaties, "is the first condition of an honest popular and truly democratic foreign policy."[15] The Central Powers insisted on Brest.

The Germans, too, were conscious of the propaganda aspect. They knew the political world had tuned its ears and focused its eyes on Brest-Litovsk. "On December 28, 1917," Prince Max von Baden, the last Chancellor of

[14] Years later Radek described this scene to me with great glee.

[15] *Dokumenty Vneshnei Politiki SSSR.* Ministersvto Inostranikh Del SSSR. (*Documents of the Foreign Policy of the USSR.* Ministry of Foreign Affairs of the USSR) (Moscow, 1957), Vol. I, Nov. 7, 1917-Dec. 3, 1917, pp. 21-22. This statement by Trotsky is signed, "People's Commissar of Foreign Affairs." The name of Trotsky is kept secret though the usual practice in this series of volumes is to publish the names of the signatories.

Kaiser Germany, wrote later, "we committed the irreparable error: we created the impression in the whole world and the German masses that, in contrast to the Russian attitude, our acceptance of the principle of self-determination of peoples was insincere and concealed annexationist designs. We rejected the Russian demand for free and unconstrained plebiscites in the occupied territory on the ground that the Courlanders, Lithuanians, and Poles had already self-determined themselves. Never should we have regarded the arbitrarily created and expanded territorial councils as authorized parliaments."[16] The civilian sheep of the Central Powers wanted to make a better impression when the conference reconvened.

However, General Max Hoffmann soon tired of listening to endless irksome harangues from Leon Trotsky, the Jewish farmer's son. "There began," he wrote, "a speech-battle between Trotsky and Kuehlmann which lasted weeks and led to nothing. Only gradually did it become clear to the participants that Trotsky's chief purpose was the spread of Bolshevik doctrine, that he merely spoke through the window and attached no importance to practical work." Furthermore, "Trotsky's tone became more aggressive every day. One day I pointed out to State Secretary Kuehlmann and Count Czernin that in this way we could never reach our goal, that it was imperative to bring the negotiations back to a practical level."[17]

Trotsky tilted at Hoffmann and pierced his skin but drew silence instead of blood. In accordance with the truce agreement, the Russians were making propaganda among German troops and the Germans were doing the same, especially through a Russian-language daily, among Russian troops. Hoffmann complained that the Soviet publication sought to suborn German soldiers. "I refused to discuss the matter," Trotsky said in *My Life*, his autobiography published in 1930 after his expulsion from the Soviet Union, "and suggested that the General continue his own propaganda among the Russian troops—the conditions were the same, the only difference being the kind of propaganda. I also reminded him that the dissimilarity of our views on certain rather important questions had long been known, and had even been certified to by one of the German courts—the one that during the war had sentenced me in contumacy to prison. This indecorous reminder," Trotsky wrote, "created a great sensation. Many of the titled gentlemen almost gasped."

Kuehlmann, who was having his troubles with Hoffmann, apparently relished the general's embarrassment. Turning to Hoffmann, not, probably, without Schadenfreude, the Foreign Secretary asked, "Would you like to reply?"

"No, that's enough," the general snorted.

On the other hand, Kuehlmann reveled in the duel. He allowed Trotsky to draw him into lengthy debates on theory, history, and philosophy. The more rarefied their discussions the more Hoffmann fumed, but Kuehlmann,

---

[16] Prinz Max von Baden, *Erinnerungen und Dokumente*, p. 191.
[17] Hoffmann, *op. cit.*, p. 208.

at least as he remembered it decades later when he composed his memoirs, hoped to serve a cause. "Bolshevism," he wrote, "was for the world as a whole a new doctrine greeted by many with interest, by some perhaps not without sympathy. . . . The Bolsheviks had understood how to veil highly horrible reality in fine-sounding phrases; occasionally Bolshevism knew how to wrap itself in a democratic mantle of sorts. . . . One of my chief purposes consisted in tightening the thumbscrews on the Bolsheviks in this matter through the Brest-Litovsk discussions. I regarded it as one of my great debating triumphs when Trotsky had to admit to me in public session that Bolshevism was based not on any democratic principles but on armed might." Kuehlmann, the spokesman for German armed might, sadly complained in the next sentence that German propaganda organizations ignored his forensic successes, but, "Trotsky," as Kuehlmann recalled the scene in the 1940's, "twisted like an eel in an effort to avoid this admission. Finally, however, he was maneuvered into a corner so badly that he was forced into the unpleasant confession." Trotsky had confessed that "in a society based on classes, every government rests on force. The only difference was that General Hoffmann applied repression to protect big property owners, whereas we did in defense of the workers." Moreover, "we do not shoot peasants who demand land, but arrest landowners and officers who try to shoot the peasants." At the word "officers," Trotsky wrote in *My Life*, "Hoffmann's face grew purple."

Trotsky found some enjoyment in this "Marxian propaganda class for beginners," but Kuehlmann, reminiscing, recalled that Trotsky sent one of his confidential comrades to ask the German "to put an end to this terrible suffering." Kuehlmann was operating according to plan. "My plan," he declared, "was to tie Trotsky up in a purely academic discussion about the right of peoples to self-determination and about its practicable implementation."[18]

Fortunately, Trotsky's view of the same situation is available. To be sure, he paid Kuehlmann his due. He was, Trotsky asserted in *My Life*, "head and shoulders above Czernin, and probably above all the rest of the diplomats I met in the years after the war. He impressed me as a man of character, with a practical mind far above the average . . . and 'a considerable gift of casuistry.' " However, "Like a good chess player who for a long time has met only weaker players, and who has lost some of his skill, Kuehlmann, having met only his Austro-Hungarian, Turkish, Bulgarian and neutral diplomatic vassals during the war, was inclined," Trotsky remarked with characteristic conceit, "to underestimate his revolutionary opponents and play his game in a slovenly manner. He often astonished me, especially at the outset, by the primitiveness of his methods and by his lack of understanding of his opponent's psychology."

Kuehlmann played Trotsky's game. Trotsky wrote in 1923: "After the first

[18] Richard von Kuehlmann, *Erinnerungen* (Heidelberg, 1948), pp. 524-525.

break in the negotiations, Lenin suggested that I go to Brest-Litovsk. In itself the prospect of treating with Baron Kuehlmann and General Hoffmann was not attractive, but 'in order to delay the proceedings there must be some one to do the delaying,' as Lenin expressed it."[19]

Kuehlmann helped in the delaying and he realized it later, for a few pages farther along in his memoirs he asserted that "Trotsky had been sent to Brest to work a delay."[20]

Trotsky, accordingly, went to the peace conference with a dual goal: to delay the negotiations and speed the European revolution.

The Trotsky-Kuehlmann verbal wrestling match lasted—first round—ten days. Every detail of every Central Powers proposal was endlessly discussed till General Hoffmann yawned or roared. On January 18 Trotsky summarized what had emerged: Germany and Austria-Hungary, he asserted, "were cutting off from the dominions of the former Russian Empire 170,000 square kilometers of territory which includes the former Polish duchy, Lithuania, and considerable areas inhabited by Ukrainians and White Russians [Byelorussians]." The Quadruple Alliance, he added, refused to say when or even whether they would evacuate this huge domain. "Practically, it comes down to this: the governments of Germany and Austria-Hungary are taking over the fate of these peoples. We regard it as our political duty to confirm this fact openly. I propose a recess in the work of the delegations in order to give the government of the Russian Republic the possibility of making its final decision regarding the peace conditions presented to us."[21] No recess was declared, but Trotsky, accompanied by Leo B. Kamenev, left for Petrograd to report to his party comrades.

The Bolsheviks faced a host of enemies, from the conservatives to the Left Social Revolutionaries. All realized that a peace treaty would reinforce Lenin's power. Some opposed the peace for this reason, others out of patriotism. Among the Bolsheviks themselves, governing was a novelty, and the lust to rule had not yet flowered. Many put ideals above power. Internationalism, the keystone of Marxist teachings, held sway in most Bolshevik minds; it was buttressed by a conviction that the revolution could not endure unless it spread to other countries. They dedicated themselves to spreading it. A separate peace to save their own Russian regime seemed disgracefully selfish and would leave a black blot on the tombstone of the revolution when it inevitably succumbed in isolation. At the end of 1915 Lenin had written, "If the revolution were to bring it [the Bolshevik party] to power . . . we would propose peace to all belligerents on condition of the liberation of all colonies and all dependent, oppressed, and not fully independent peoples. Neither Germany,

[19] Leon Trotsky, *Lenin*, p. 103. Trotsky's introduction to this book is dated April 21, 1924, and internal evidence indicates that the chapters were written in 1923 or earlier.

[20] Kuehlmann, *op. cit.*, p. 544.

[21] *Bolshaya Sovietskaya Entsiklopedia* (Moscow, 1927), First ed., Vol. VII, columns 447-448.

nor England and France would, with their present governments, accept this condition. Then we would have to prepare for and wage a revolutionary war."[22] This is exactly what many Bolsheviks wished to do in 1918, only to encounter Lenin's fierce rejection.

Lenin was a genius at organizing and disorganizing. He had one formula for both processes: split. He split the original Russian Social Democratic Labor Party and molded his faction into the obedient Bolshevik order. He split Russian politics in 1917, dividing power between the Kerensky government and the soviets until the latter overthrew the former. He split foreign socialist parties which spurned the word of Moscow. Now, on the issue of the Brest-Litovsk peace, he was splitting his own party. The split resulted from the adherence of a part of the party to his principles, as he had enunciated them, for instance, in 1915, and his own subordination of those principles to practical considerations.

On January 10, 1918, the Moscow Regional Bureau of the Bolshevik party passed a resolution demanding "the termination of the peace negotiations with imperialist Germany." The same day the Petrograd committee of the party voted a resolution similar in content.[23] These were the two most important Bolshevik party units in Russia, and they probably reflected some sentiment in the provinces. By the time Trotsky and Kamenev, his brother-in-law, had returned to Petrograd from Brest-Litovsk, a sizable segment of the party was challenging Lenin's policy.

The revolution had not yet begun to devour its children, or even to intimidate them. Kerensky was gone, but the backwash of Russia's dead democratic revolution still carried freedom to its destroyers. A group of Bolsheviks accordingly took the liberty of organizing against Lenin and for a revolutionary war. It presented a formidable array of talent: Bukharin, E. Preobrazhensky, A. Bubnov, Madame Kollontai, Inessa Armand, Professor M. Pokrovsky, Karl Radek, A. Soltz, S. Kossior, E. Yaroslavsky, Y. Pyatakov, M. Uritsky, T. Sapronov, V. Kuibishev, Bela Kun, V. Smirnov, and many others who played and would continue to play key roles in Soviet affairs.[24] Soon they were to publish a newspaper, called *Kommunist*, in Petrograd and Moscow which was frankly anti-Lenin and anti-peace treaty. "We are on the eve of surrender," Radek wrote in the first issue of the Petrograd edition, "and that, chiefly, because the proletarian party, having won power, reckons first of all not with the interests of the working class but with the mood and pressures of the tired peasant masses." In the second issue of the Moscow edition of *Kommunist*, Radek declared that "in one country, and that in a backward country, it is impossible to introduce socialism."[25] Radek's two propositions in effect charged Lenin with betraying the revolution by not launching a revolutionary

[22] Lenin, *Sochineniya*, Second ed., Vol. XVIII, p. 313.
[23] *Ibid.*, Vol. XXII, editorial note, p. 599.
[24] *Bolshaya Sovietskaya Entsiklopedia*, First ed., Vol. VII, column 452.
[25] *Ibid.*, column 451.

war against European capitalism. Throwing the spark of revolution into Europe was not only Lenin's 1915 program; it was Trotsky's policy of Permanent Revolution. Yet now Lenin and Trotsky opposed revolutionary war, Lenin on the new pragmatism of survival for the sake of future achievements, Trotsky because Russia had no army to wage any war. Traveling between Petrograd and Brest, Trotsky saw that the Russian "trenches were almost empty." Therefore, "On the question of revolutionary war, there was not the slightest difference of opinion between Vladimir Ilyich and myself."[26]

To defeat, perhaps to convert, the Left Communist opposition, Lenin wrote out, in longhand, twenty-one "Theses on the Immediate Conclusion of a Separate and Annexationist Peace."[27] Alone the title indicated that he disliked the peace treaty but advocated its speedy acceptance. Lenin's theses spelled compromise. They pitted time against loyalty to principle and circumstances against adherence to past programs. He had written on September 11, 1917, "The transfer of political power to the proletariat—that is the crux of the matter. . . . Life will show what modifications will be necessary. This is the last thing to worry about. We are not doctrinaires. Our philosophy is not a dogma, but a guide to action."[28] This is the Leninist foundation of Soviet policy. On it he erected his twenty-one theses. Its first name is expediency. Its surname is the promise of success. It makes Soviet policy kin, in broad outlines, to the policies of all nations.

The leading Lenin thesis was a daring distortion. "The situation of the Russian revolution at the moment," it read, "is such that almost all workingmen and the great majority of the peasants undoubtedly are on the side of the Soviet government and the socialist revolution it has inaugurated. To that extent, the success of the socialist revolution in Russia is guaranteed." This, to put it mildly, was an exaggeration. Lenin, however, needed a bold show of confidence as a base for his logical pyramid. If the Soviet socialist revolution was secure and European revolution remote, why sacrifice life to a chance? To make this cardinal point, Lenin inserted another thesis—the sixth: "There is no doubt that the socialist revolution in Europe must and will come. All our hopes on the *final* victory of socialism rest on this certainty and this scientific prophecy." But when? "Since this can in no way be determined, all attempts to do so would, objectively, constitute a blind gamble." In other words, a bird in the hand is worth two possibly unfertilized eggs in the bush.

Lenin's remaining theses were debating darts aimed at his revolutionary-war opponents. He said, "the propertied classes" had already precipitated civil war. The Soviets would win it, but "an inevitable period of ruin and chaos" would follow. Moreover, the task of creating socialism in Russia promised to be "great and difficult" and must, "in view of the numerous petty-bourgeois fellow-travellers of the socialist proletariat" (the peasantry), and "in view of

[26] Trotsky, *Lenin*, p. 104.
[27] Lenin, *op. cit.*, Second ed., Vol. XXII, pp. 191-199.
[28] Lenin, *Toward the Seizure of Power. The Revolution of 1917: From the July Days to the October Revolution*, Book I (New York, 1932), p. 133.

the low cultural level" of the working class, "take a long time." Therefore the revolution needed a breathing spell of "not less than several months," he underestimated, to defeat the bourgeoisie first in its own country. Finally: the German military had won the battle of Brest-Litovsk and would annex Russia's borderlands and impose reparations on her. The question for Bolsheviks, therefore, was, "Accept this annexation peace now or launch a revolutionary war? There is, in fact, no in-between decision." If they fought, Lenin stated, "we would be fighting, objectively, for the liberation of Poland, Lithuania, and Courland."

Lenin read these theses on January 21 to a conference of delegates from Petrograd, Moscow, the Volga region, and the Urals who were to attend the Third Congress of Soviets. After pronouncing the words "Poland, Lithuania, and Courland," he added extemporaneously, revealingly, "But no Marxist who has not abandoned the basic ideas of Marxism and in general of socialism can deny that the interests of socialism stand higher than the interest of the right of nations to self-determination."[29] Then he sat down.

Trotsky now offered an in-between solution: break off the Brest negotiations; declare Russia out of the war; but do not sign the peace treaty.

Leading Left communists vehemently called for a revolutionary war.

The conference thereupon voted. Of the 63 delegates, 32, a majority, favored revolutionary war; 16 supported Trotsky; 15 supported Lenin.[30]

Three days later, on January 24, the Central Committee, highest executive authority in the communist party, debated the same problem. Sensing the mood of his comrades, Lenin had shifted ground. His motion now read, "We do everything to delay the signing of the peace." He no longer insisted on the "immediate conclusion of a separate and annexationist peace." Joseph Stalin, Gregory Zinoviev, and Gregory Sokolnikov sided with Lenin. "There is no revolutionary movement in the West," Stalin announced, "there are no facts, there is only a potentiality, and we cannot reckon with a potentiality."[31]

Trotsky moved, "We end the war; do not sign the peace; and demobilize the army." Bukharin and Uritsky stood with Trotsky. Uritsky accused Lenin of nationalism. "Comrade Lenin's mistake," he asserted, "is . . . that he looks at this matter from the point of view of Russia, and not from the international point of view."[32]

Lenin defended himself: the army was tired and military supplies were exhausted. If the Germans advanced they could take Reval (Tallinn) and Petrograd "with naked hands." By prolonging the war in these circumstances "we unusually strengthen German imperialism, and the peace will have to be concluded anyway, but then the peace will be worse because it will be concluded

[29] Lenin, *Sochineniya*, Second ed., Vol. XXII, p. 198.

[30] *Ibid.*, editorial note, p. 600.

[31] *Ibid.*, editorial note, p. 600, which quotes Stalin from *Protokoly Tsentralnovo Komiteta (Minutes of the Central Committee.)* In Stalin's *Sochineniya (Collected Works)*, Vol. 4, November, 1917-1920 (Moscow, 1947), p. 27, a servile or Georgian hand inserted an additional sentence: "Trotsky's position is no position at all."

[32] *Bolshaya Sovietskaya Entsiklopedia*, First ed., Vol. VII, column 451.

by someone other than ourselves. No doubt the peace which we are now being forced to conclude is an indecent peace, but if war commences our government will be swept away and the peace will be concluded by another government."

This was an argument for immediate peace. Yet his motion recommended delay.

Those who advocate revolutionary war, Lenin proceeded, believe it will foment a German revolution. "But Germany is only pregnant with revolution and with us a perfectly healthy baby has been born—the socialist republic which we might kill by starting a war." He did not agree with Stalin, Lenin said, about the dim prospects of revolution in the West, nor with Zinoviev who thought the signing of the peace would temporarily weaken the revolutionary movement in the West. "But the heart of the matter is that there the movement has not yet begun whereas we already have a newly-born, lustily-screaming infant, and if we, in this moment, do not say clearly that we agree to the peace we shall perish. For us it is important to hold on until the emergence of a general socialist revolution, and we can achieve that only by concluding peace." As for Trotsky's proposal: end the war, refuse to sign the peace, and demobilize the army, "that," Lenin averred, "is an international political demonstration."[33]

Following this spirited speech, balloting took place. Twelve voted for Lenin's motion to delay, 1 against; 2 for revolutionary war, 11 against, 1 abstention; 9 for Trotsky's motion, 7 against.[34]

Since these results have been subjected to much subsequent Soviet falsification they bear analysis. The Central Committee, elected at the Sixth Party Congress which met between July 26 and August 3, 1917, consisted of twenty-four members. Some of these may have been absent from the city at the time of voting. Or some abstentions may not have been recorded. It is interesting that whereas sixteen voted on Trotsky's formula only thirteen voted on Lenin's. The very long article on "The Russian Communist Party (Bolsheviks)" in the eleventh volume, published in 1930, of the first edition of the *Large Soviet Encyclopedia* (column 466) says, "At the session of the Central Committee . . . Trotsky's in-between resolution was passed." There was no complete conflict between Trotsky's motion and Lenin's. Trotsky would have voted for Lenin's because it proposed delay. The lone vote against delay was cast by Zinoviev, not Stalin.

The next day, the Central Committees of the Bolshevik and Left Social Revolutionary Parties met in joint session. "By a majority vote a resolution was adopted to present for the consideration of the Congress of Soviets the formula: 'Not to wage war, not to sign the peace.' "[35] This was Trotsky's formula.

[33] Lenin, *Sochineniya*, Vol. XXII, pp. 200-202.
[34] *Ibid.*, editorial note, p. 600.
[35] *Ibid.*, editorial note, p. 600.

The Third Congress of Soviets met in Petrograd from January 23 to 31, 1918. Its delegates included Mensheviks, Right Social Revolutionaries, United Internationalists, Left Social Revolutionaries, and Bolsheviks; 1,046 delegates in all. Lenin addressed them on January 24, and pointed out that the Soviet government had been in existence two months and fifteen days, "that is five days longer" than the Paris Commune. He dealt with the deteriorating domestic situation, but declared, in conclusion: ". . . in all countries the socialist revolution is ripening not by the day but by the hour." He finished with a flourish: "The Russian commenced—the German, the Frenchman, the Englishman will finish, and socialism will be victorious."[36]

Trotsky then reported on the issue of "War and Peace." After a discussion, the delegates voted a resolution approving the Soviet government's conduct of foreign affairs and granting it "the widest authority" in the matter of the peace treaty.[37]

With this, Trotsky left Petrograd for Brest-Litovsk late on the night of January 26, 1918. Judging by the votes of the several bodies, his instructions were unmistakably to protract the negotiations. No committee, congress, or conference had voted for signing the peace treaty. Trotsky's "No war, no peace" formula had won majority backing from the party's Central Committee whose decisions between party congresses are law. He was authorized, accordingly, to tell the Quadruple Alliance that Russia would not sign the treaty but was retiring from the war.

Trotsky left behind him a sad capital city. Food was so scarce in Petrograd, "speculation so monstrous," that Lenin ordered army squads of workers and soldiers to ferret out speculators. Anyone refusing to join a squad, Lenin urged, should have his ration card annulled. "So long as we do not apply terror to speculators—shooting on the spot," Lenin declared, "nothing will succeed." If the squads themselves started looting the speculators' hoards they were to be given the same Leninist medicine: "shooting on the spot."[38]

Conditions elsewhere were worse. Larger areas of Russia had come into the grip of civil war. The task of defeating the Whites would be herculean. Russia was still a military zero. En route to Brest, Trotsky again saw the abandoned Russian trenches. In January, the government officially demobilized all soldiers over thirty-five,[39] but men under that age had feet too, and their feet, as Lenin had said, voted against war. They walked home.

With these impressions and instructions Trotsky arrived in Brest.

During the Brest recess, Trotsky's Austro-Hungarian opposite number, Foreign Minister Count Czernin, had been to Vienna. There, addressing parliament on January 24, he said, "I demand not a square meter or penny from Russia." Hunger riots multiplied in the cracked realm of the Dual Monarchy.

[36] Ibid., pp. 205-218.
[37] Ibid., editorial note, p. 601.
[38] Ibid., p. 243.
[39] Dokumenty Vneshnei Politiki SSSR, Vol. I, pp. 103-104.

Emperor Karl had been in contact, behind Czernin's back, with the French government. Austria-Hungary, as sorely in need of peace as Soviet Russia, was threatening Germany with a separate peace with the Bolsheviks.

Baron von Kuehlmann could give Czernin understanding but nothing else, for he himself had earned the fierce disapproval of the German military. Early in January, Field Marshal von Hindenburg had complained in a long letter to the Kaiser against the dilatory tactics of Kuehlmann at Brest and also against General Hoffmann. Hindenburg wrote, "General Hoffmann is my subordinate and carries no responsibility in the Polish question." Nevertheless, "Your Majesty has, in the Polish question, given precedence to General Hoffmann's opinion over mine and over General Ludendorff's." He and Ludendorff, he went on, were convinced that their policies would strengthen the monarchy "whereas the contrary one could only lead down from the mountain up which Your illustrious forefathers have led Prussia and Germany." The Kaiser, Hindenburg asserted, could not expect "honest men who have loyally served Your Majesty and Germany to participate with their authority and reputation in dealings in which they cannot participate because of an inner conviction that they are harmful to the Crown and the Reich." Of course, it was for the Kaiser to decide. "My person and that of General Ludendorff need play no role where the nation's requirements are concerned."[40] This was a plain hint that they would resign—at a moment when, under their direction, the giant German "victory" offensive in the West was already in preparation—if the Kaiser preferred Hoffmann's views to their own.

The Kaiser sent Hindenburg an above-the-battle reply: The field marshal's letter again showed that he and the quartermaster general were "men whose complete loyalty and ability are indispensable to Me for the further prosecution of the war. My confidence in both of you cannot be destroyed by the circumstance that I and My political advisor, the Reich Chancellor, deviate in some point from your statement of the situation."

The Kaiser gave the Chancellor copies of this correspondence. The Chancellor gave copies to Kuehlmann. On January 12 Hertling met in Berlin with Ludendorff and Hindenburg. "There Ludendorff declared emphatically that he would ask for his dismissal if I [Kuehlmann] remained in office."[41]

Kuehlmann remained and Ludendorff did not resign. But the tensions weighed on the Brest-Litovsk conference. Ludendorff wrote in his memoirs: "On January 23"—a week before the resumption of the Brest parley—"at my request, the Field Marshal declared, during consultations at Berlin, that we must have the Eastern situation cleared up. Until it was it would be necessary to retain there good divisions that were fit for employment in the West. If the Russians delayed matters any further we ought to reopen hostilities. This would bring down the Bolshevik government, and any others that might suc-

[40] Kuehlmann, *op. cit.*, pp. 536-539; complete texts of this letter and the Kaiser's reply.
[41] *Ibid.*, p. 537.

ceed it would have to make peace." (Lenin said the same thing the next day.)

"What must the statesmen of the Entente," Ludendorff moaned, "think of our need of peace if we tamely submitted to this sort of treatment by Trotsky and his Bolshevist Government. . . . How necessary must peace be to Germany when she literally ran after such people and put up with open propaganda against her and her army." What would the world think "when we allowed ourselves to be treated thus by unarmed Russian anarchists"? In the resumed negotiations "everything was ordered in accordance with his [Trotsky's] ideas.

"However, the diplomats themselves now seemed to perceive that discussions with him led to no result. Secretary of State von Kuehlmann and Count Czernin proceeded to interrupt the negotiations and were back in Berlin on February 4. . . . In order to discuss the situation with Herr von Kuehlmann and Count Czernin I had gone to Berlin early in February. At our interviews on the 4th and 5th I received from the former a promise that he would break with Trotsky twenty-four hours after signing the peace with the Ukraine."[42]

The Ukraine was the crux.

Count Czernin's nerves "were completely shattered," Hoffmann wrote in his reminiscences of the Brest-Litovsk conference.[43] As the conference dragged on, the condition of Austria-Hungary and of Czernin's nerves deteriorated. "In order to prevent a famine, Berlin had to be asked for help. Berlin, to be sure, helped despite its own need, but this naturally prevented Count Czernin from making further threats to conclude a separate treaty with Trotsky or from trying to conclude one."[44]

But Germany, herself on short rations, mostly turnips, could not meet Austria-Hungary's requirements. Only the Ukraine, Russia's bread basket, could, and, said Hoffmann, if the Central Powers wanted Ukrainian grain "they would have to fetch it themselves."[45] However, the precondition of fetching it was a separate treaty with an "independent" Ukraine. This peace was Hoffmann's hidden trump against Trotsky.

Back in December, 1917, when the Soviets had summoned the nations of the world to come to Brest-Litovsk for peace deliberations, nobody accepted —except the Ukraine, and Lenin, who had times without number spoken of the Ukraine as a prisoner in tsarist Russia's "prison of peoples," could not object.

The Ukraine had, in fact, separated from Russia after the March, 1917, revolution and set up its own government under the presidency of V. K. Vinnichenko, age thirty-eight in 1918, a writer of fiction, a participant, at twenty-five, in the 1905 revolution against tsardom, and a member of the Ukrainian branch of the Social Democratic party. Subsequently, he organized a national-

[42] Erich von Ludendorff, *Ludendorff's Own Story. August 1914–November 1918*, pp. 178-179.
[43] Hoffmann, *op. cit.*, p. 197.
[44] *Ibid.*, p. 211.
[45] *Ibid.*, p. 217.

ist insurrection against the German occupation of the Ukraine, and later served the government of the Soviet Ukraine.[46]

This, by Bolshevik standards, is not a derogatory biography and when, therefore, representatives of Vinnichenko's government, which called itself the Central Rada or Central Soviet, reached Brest-Litovsk in December, the Petrograd delegation received it cordially. Trotsky wrote that, "On its first appearance in Brest-Litovsk the Kiev delegation described the Ukraine as a constituent part of the emerging Russian Republic."[47]

The Germans and Austro-Hungarians, however, opened separate talks with the Ukrainian delegates, hinted at diplomatic recognition, and encouraged Ukrainian secession. Here the Central Powers were the champions of self-determination—in the interest of bread and conquest.

Simultaneously, the Soviet delegation invited the Ukrainians to sign a treaty declaring Generals Kaledin and Kornilov counterrevolutionaries and agreeing "not to hinder [Moscow] in the struggle against them."[48] This meant the passage of Russian troops through the territory of the Central Rada en route to the North Caucasus and other areas held by the generals. The Ukrainians procrastinated and pressed their negotiations with the Germans.

The Bolsheviks did not regard their red Russia a "prison of peoples" and hence opposed Ukrainian separatism. Soviet forces attacked the Central Rada and overthrew it. When Trotsky returned to Brest late in January, he brought with him V. M. Shakry, Minister of War in the Ukrainian Soviet government, and I. G. Medvediev, President of the Ukraine. He claimed that they, not the Central Rada, represented power and people in the Ukraine. Brest-Litovsk had been declared Ukrainian ground. ". . . outside of Brest-Litovsk," Trotsky wrote, "the Rada had little territory."[49] Hoffmann reported that Trotsky told the conference "the power of the Central Rada had vanished and the only area over which its representatives had a right to dispose was their rooms in Brest-Litovsk." Hoffmann's comment read, "Unfortunately, according to my information about conditions in the Ukraine, there was reason to believe that Trotsky's statement was not unjustified."[50]

Nevertheless, the Quadruple Alliance signed a treaty with the nonexistent Ukrainian government on February 8, 1918. That government had no territory. Yet it made territorial demands. It demanded the Polish district of Cholm for the Ukraine. The Germans obliged. In return, the dispossessed Ukrainian "government" gave Germany the right to send troops into the Ukraine.

Soviet Russia faced a crisis. By taking Ukrainian grain Germany and Austria-Hungary would be denying it to starving Russians. German occupation

[46] Lenin, *Sochineniya*, Second ed., Vol. XXII, editorial note, p. 632.
[47] Leon Trotsky, *Von Oktober bis nach Brest-Litovsk* (Pamphlet), p. 110.
[48] *Ibid.*, p. 117.
[49] *Ibid.*, p. 118.
[50] Hoffmann, *op. cit.*, p. 213.

would also make it impossible for Lenin to dispatch troops through the Ukraine to cope with rebellious White generals in the North Caucasus. Moreover, occupation of foreign territory becomes an addiction and compulsively whets the appetite of the occupier for further conquest. Was Soviet Russia next?

The Quadruple Alliance's treaty with the ousted Ukrainians confronted Trotsky with a problem: was this the time to propound his No-war, No-peace formula? Did he know that on February 4 and 5, Ludendorff had extracted a promise from Baron von Kuehlmann "to break with Trotsky twenty-four hours after signing the peace with the Ukraine"? A break with Trotsky implied the end of the Brest conference (no peace) and a German invasion of Russia (war). There is no evidence that he did or did not know, yet he might have known from a planned German indiscretion, an accidental-on-purpose "leak," or he might have surmised, wisely, that Germany would not fail to take advantage of the Ukrainian treaty and face him with an ultimatum: sign or we invade you too.

But just as Kuehlmann had made a promise to Ludendorff so Trotsky had made a promise to Lenin. During the first Trotsky versus Kuehlmann round at Brest early in January, Trotsky had written to Lenin about his wish to stage a "pedagogical" demonstration by announcing that "we shall stop the war but without signing the peace." "It was my opinion," Trotsky declared in his book, Lenin,[51] "that, cost what it might, before signing the peace we must give the workmen of Europe a clear proof of the deadly enmity between us and governmental Germany." This indicates that the charge of "German agents" had penetrated and hurt. Trotsky was sensitive to the record, for the record makes an impression on men's minds and influences their future conduct. Trotsky intended, as he informed Lenin, to undertake his hazardous No-war, No-peace maneuver in order to wash away the "German agents" mud with which the Bolsheviks had been spattered. His gambit, he thought, would thereby facilitate the European revolution.

Lenin wrote back saying, "If you come here we will talk it over."[52]

Trotsky put his case to Lenin in the Petrograd Smolny in the second half of January. "That is all very attractive," Trotsky quoted Lenin as replying, "and could not be better if General Hoffmann were unable to march his troops against us. But there is little hope of that. He will send specially chosen regiments of Bavarian peasants, and what then?" Trotsky had said the German army would not march. "You have said yourself that the trenches are empty."

"Then we would be forced to sign the peace treaty," Trotsky argued, "and it would be clear to everyone that we had no other way out. By that alone we would strike a decisive blow at the legend that we are in league with the Hohenzollerns behind the scenes."

"Naturally," Lenin replied, "there is much to be said for that but, after all,

[51] P. 106.
[52] Ibid., p. 107.

it is too bold. For the moment, our revolution is more important than everything else."

Trotsky thereupon contended that the sentiment against signing the peace was strong in the party; the Left Communists had "played an active role" in the November, 1917, revolution and they counted many followers in the party. Signing the peace treaty would split the party.

"Better a split in the party than the danger of a military overthrow of the revolution," Lenin retorted. The split could be healed; the Left would return, but "if the Germans conquer us, not one of us returns."

"We will sign the peace under bayonets," Trotsky asserted. "Then the picture will be clear to the workmen of the entire world."

"But you will not support the solution of a revolutionary war?" Lenin demanded.

"Under no circumstances," Trotsky agreed.

"With this understanding," Lenin, according to Trotsky, agreed that "the experiment is not so dangerous. We risk the loss of Estonia and Latvia."

"Lenin's chief fear concerning my plan," Trotsky revealed, "was that in case of a renewal of the German attack we might not have time to sign the treaty; that is, that German militarism would leave us no time. 'This beast springs suddenly,' Vladimir Ilyich often remarked." There would be no opportunity to sign "under the bayonets."

Trotsky felt Lenin yielded to him and his intermediate formula because without it the majority in the party's high command would have opted for revolutionary war. Later, however, at the Seventh Congress of the Russian Communist Party (Bolsheviks) in March, 1918, Lenin disclosed that he and Trotsky had reached an agreement: "we hold out until the German ultimatum, after the ultimatum we capitulate."[53]

Now, on February 8, the Germans having signed the treaty with the Ukrainian government-in-exile-in-Brest-Litovsk, Trotsky decided to keep his promise to Lenin by making his "pedagogical demonstration" before the ultimatum. What Trotsky did not know was the story of a behind-the-scenes test of will between Kuehlmann, backed by Czernin, and the German military.

When the Ukrainian treaty was signed on February 8, Ludendorff wrote, "I now requested Herr von Kuehlmann to carry out his promise of the 5th and break with Trotsky, but he declined. On the same day a wireless message from the Russian government called upon the German army to refuse obedience to the Supreme War Lord," the Kaiser-Emperor. This raised the hackles of the generals. Here, accordingly, Hindenburg intervened. "At the request of the Field Marshal the Emperor now instructed Herr von Kuehlmann to present an ultimatum to Trotsky requiring acceptance of our former conditions" —German annexation of Poland, Lithuania, and Courland—"and further to demand the evacuation of the Baltic littoral"[54]—Latvia, Estonia, and the

[53] Lenin, *Sochineniya*, Vol. XXII, p. 333.
[54] Ludendorff, *op. cit.*, p. 18.

Moon Sound Islands, the staging ground for an easy German entry into Petrograd. The Kaiser's telegram ordered Kuehlmann to confront Trotsky with a twenty-four-hour ultimatum.

"But State Secretary von Kuehlmann," Hoffmann simplified, "had gained the impression just at this moment that it might be possible to reach a conclusion of the negotiations because Trotsky, under the pressure of the Ukrainian peace, had commenced, for the first time, to cope practically with the problem of peace. He had sent a question to the State Secretary inquiring whether it might be possible in some way to allow Riga and the near islands" —Moon, Oesel, and Dagoe—"to be retained in the Russian Empire." This Trotsky gambit may have been Kuehlmann's immediate excuse for delaying the promised ultimatum. The German also had in mind the prospect of peace negotiations with the West.

Kuehlmann accordingly did a courageous thing. Instead of complying with the Kaiser's wired instructions, he telegraphed the Kaiser to say, Hoffmann wrote, that "If His Majesty insisted on the presentation [of the ultimatum] the Reich government would have to look for another State Secretary. He would wait until 4:30 P.M., if until then no other order regarding the ultimatum demand had been received, he would pass from it to the agenda" of the conference. "Nothing arrived before 4:30, and Kuehlmann kept the ultimatum in his pocket."[55]

Trotsky may have sensed that there was an ultimatum in the air or in the offing. Faced with such an ultimatum he would have to accept, as he had promised Lenin, and abandon his favored historic formula. Accordingly, when State Secretary von Kuehlmann, who presided, opened the session of the Political Commission at 5:58 P.M. on February 10, 1918, Trotsky rose and said, "If ever this war was for defensive purposes it has long since ceased to be that for both sides. If Great Britain seizes African colonies, Baghdad, and Jerusalem this is still not a defensive war. If Germany occupies Serbia, Belgium, Poland, Lithuania, and Romania, and takes possession of the Moon Islands, this also is not a defensive war. This is a struggle for the division of the world. Today, this is clearer than ever.

"We no longer wish to participate in this purely imperialistic war. . . . We are equally unreconciled to the imperialism of both camps. . . .

"In anticipation of the time, we trust soon, when the oppressed toiler classes of all countries take power into their hands, like the toiling people of Russia, we are withdrawing our army and our nation from the war. Our soldier-peasant must return to his fields this spring to till peacefully the soil which the revolution transferred from the hands of the landlords to the hands of the peasants. Our soldier-workingman must return to his shop in order to produce not armaments but creative instruments and, together with the cultivator, build a new socialist economy.

[55] Hoffmann, op. cit., pp. 213-214. Interestingly enough, Baron von Kuehlmann's otherwise detailed memoirs, published in November, 1948, contain not even a reference to this authenticated episode which Ludendorff also alludes to: op. cit., p. 181.

"We are leaving the war. We announce this to all peoples and all governments. We are issuing a decree for the total demobilization of our armies facing the troops of Germany, Ausria-Hungary, Turkey, and Bulgaria. We
expect, and fervently believe, that other peoples will soon follow our example.
At the same time we declare that the terms offered us by the governments of
Germany and Austria-Hungary are fundamentally opposed to the interests of
all peoples. . . . We refuse to sanction the terms which German and Austro-
Hungarian imperialism write with the sword on the bodies of living nations.
We cannot affix the signature of the Russian revolution under terms which
carry oppression, misery, and unhappiness to millions of human beings.

"The German and Austro-Hungarian governments wish to hold the territory of peoples by right of military conquest. Let them do their deeds in the
open. We cannot hallow violence. We are leaving the war but are compelled
to refuse to sign the peace treaty."[56]

"The whole congress sat speechless after Trotsky delivered his statement,"
Hoffmann remembered.[57] "This, of course, completed the confusion in the
East," Ludendorff commented.[58]

Trotsky had a sense of the dramatic. Lenin was prosaic. Trotsky wished
to demonstrate freedom from a pro-German taint. Lenin had no taste for a
gesture that might hurt the Russian revolution. Trotsky remained loyal to
his agreement with Lenin: capitulation after a German ultimatum; no
ultimatum, no capitulation. For Trotsky this had international importance.
Lenin acquiesced to avoid a split in the party.

XIII. LENIN'S WILL POWER

WHEN TROTSKY sat down after delivering his No-war, No-peace speech, Baron
von Kuehlmann recovered quickly and defined the formal situation. He said,
"I conclude" that the Central Powers "are at the present moment at war
with Russia." Trotsky replied: military action now would not serve the de-

[56] *Mirnye Peregovory v Brest-Litovske. C 22/9 Dekabrya, 1917 po 3 Marta (Feb.
18) 1918.* Tom I, *Polni Tekst Stenogramm pod Redaktsiei i s primechaniami* A.A.
Yoffe (V. Krimskogo) c predisloviem L. Trotskogo. Izdatelstwo Narkomindela
(Moskva, 1920). (*Peace Negotiations in Brest-Litovsk, from December 22/9, 1917
till March 3 (February 18 Old Style) 1918,* Vol. I, Complete stenographic text edited
by and with commentaries of A. A. Yoffe—V. Krimsky—with an introduction by L.
Trotsky. Published by the Commissariat of Foreign Affairs (Moscow, 1920), pp.
205-208.

[57] Hoffmann, *op. cit.,* p. 214.

[58] Ludendorff, *op. cit.,* p. 181.

fense of the fatherland. Therefore, "I am deeply convinced that the German and Austro-Hungarian peoples will not allow it."[1] The session ended at 6:50 P.M. The Russians left the next day after brief desultory arguments with the enemy.

Reactions in the German-led alliance varied. Hoffmann reported, "Ambassador von Wiesner, one of Czernin's assistants, had, in a complete misunderstanding of the situation which was the rule with this diplomat, even telegraphed to Vienna that peace with Russia had been concluded." In German cities, flags to celebrate the peace were flown from buildings and homes for several hours until orders caused them to be furled. On the other hand, Hoffmann wired GHQ that "the armistice was automatically at an end." He was told, in reply, that the High Command shared his view. This implied a renewal of hostilities in the East.[2]

Kuehlmann nevertheless opposed a resumption of fighting. He put his view to a meeting of Central Powers representatives convened immediately after Trotsky's speech: The militarily impotent Soviets could be ignored. All German troops and supplies could be shifted with impunity to the western front in order to "inflict a decisive defeat on the Western powers." He favored this strategy the more because "I knew that Austria-Hungary . . . would strenuously resist a reopening of the war in the east. Bulgaria too was not expected to have much enthusiasm for a continuation of the war in the east. Turkey, which expected extensive conquests, would probably prefer a signed peace with significant annexation potentialities."[3] Thus at odds, the Germans entrained for Berlin.

"Demigods," Chancellor, and lesser notables now converged on the Homburg spa, vacation spot of the Kaiser. They deliberated all day February 13. The monarch came and went; he knew who would win. Kuehlmann, aware of the demigods' hostility, conscious of their desire to oust him from the Foreign Ministry, eager to stay partly to deny them the satisfaction of seeing him go, partly to implement his scheme of secret peace soundings in London, presented his case with studied mildness: the Soviet government's signature on a peace treaty "has little concrete value. The simplest thing to do is to adopt no official attitude toward Trotsky's statement" and shift all available forces west.

Such flabby negativism was no match for the iron determination of Ludendorff backed by Hindenburg. Mindful of Russian distances, he contemplated "no extensive operation." He wanted "a short but sharp blow." The Kaiser sanctioned the invasion.

The Bolshevik camp also had its iron will, Lenin's, but his opponents were more troublesome than Ludendorff's, and the story of the struggle is still surrounded with stench:

---

[1] *Mirnye Peregovory v Brest Litovske*, p. 210.
[2] Hoffmann, *Der Krieg der Versaeumten Gelegenheiten*, p. 215.
[3] Kuehlmann, *Erinnerinigen*, pp. 545-546.

"The enemies of the party and government, Traitor Trotsky and the group of 'left communists' hostile to the party, together with all counterrevolutionaries, beginning with the Mensheviks and Social Revolutionaries, ending with the White Guards, waged a fierce battle against Lenin and Stalin, against the signing of the peace. . . . In reality, Traitor Trotsky and the 'left communists' played the game of the German imperialists and of the counterrevolutionaries inside the country.

". . . On January 27 (February 9), 1918, with the help of Traitor Trotsky, Germany concluded a separate peace with the counterrevolutionary Central Rada. On the day of the signature of the treaty with the counterrevolutionary Central Rada, the German imperialists presented an ultimatum to the Soviet delegation: either a continuation of the war or an annexationist peace. January 28 (February 10), Traitor Trotsky broke off the peace negotiations though V. I. Lenin and J. V. Stalin, in the name of the Central Committee, had given the Soviet delegation instructions to sign the peace immediately. Traitor Trotsky, leader of the Soviet peace delegation, in violation of the direct orders of the Bolshevik party, announced to the Germans that the Soviet government refuses to sign the peace and simultaneously informed the German imperialists that the Soviet government continues to demobilize its army and will not wage war. In this way, the German imperialists received an excuse for armed intervention against the young, still not strong, Soviet Republic."[4]

Thus was history written in the heyday of Stalin's "cult of personality." The lies in this account are too numerous to enumerate. Some are obvious: Lenin and Stalin could not have instructed Trotsky, in the name of the Central Committee, to sign the peace immediately because the Central Committee had voted against immediate signature. The Germans had presented no ultimatum to the Soviet delegation; neither the official Russian stenographic record (*Mirnye Peregovory v Brest Litovske*) nor any contemporary report or record or chronicle mentions such an ultimatum. Kuehlmann had resisted the Kaiser's orders to deliver an ultimatum and did not, actually, deliver it. But Stalin's rewriters of history needed the invented ultimatum to create the impression that Trotsky had broken his promise to Lenin to sign the peace treaty if confronted with an ultimatum.

A book published in Moscow in 1963 (*Vneshnopoliticheskaya Dyeatelnost V. I. Lenina. Lenin's Activity in Foreign Affairs*) repeats the tale of Trotsky's disloyalty, but contradicts itself: On page 91 it quotes Lenin as saying to Trotsky, "we hold out until the German ultimatum, after the ultimatum we capitulate." Yet on page 111 it falsifies history by stating that at Brest Trotsky "refused, despite the decision of the Central Committee, to sign the peace treaty."

[4] *Bolshaya Sovietskaya Entsiklopedia* Second ed. (Moscow, 1951), Vol. 6, p. 86. The item *Brestskii Mir (The Brest Peace)* in the first (1927) edition of the same encyclopedia contains none of these accusations against Trotsky.

The reception given Trotsky when he returned from making his No-war, No-peace declaration conveys the flavor of full approval. On February 11 the Petrograd Soviet debated Trotsky's declaration and, with only one negative vote and twenty-three abstentions, overwhelmingly approved the resolution offered by Gregory Zinoviev, its chairman: "The Petrograd Soviet fully sanctions the declaration made by the Russian delegation at Brest on January 28 (February 10) 1918."

"Traitor Trotsky's" No-war, No-peace speech was printed in full in the January 30 (February 12) issue of the daily *Izvestia*, organ of the Soviet government. The next day, an editorial in the same paper entitled "Questions of War and Peace," began, "It has happened! Russia has left the imperialist war. It was out of the question for proletarian-peasant Russia to continue participating in a world war in which both belligerent groups . . . openly pursue predatory, rapacious aims. . . . But on the other hand, socialist Russia also cannot agree to the conditions the Austro-German imperialists intend to dictate to her."

Izvestia, clearly, took Trotsky's position.

On February 14, 1918, Trotsky reported to the All-Russian Central Executive Committee (VTSIK), the highest Soviet authority between Soviet congresses. After analyzing his action on February 10 at Brest, he exclaimed, "I think, comrades, we did the right thing." He added, "This does not mean to imply that a German advance into Russia is precluded. . . . But I believe I can calmly affirm that our position on this matter makes it much more difficult for German militarism to proceed against us. . . . We can only say this: if it is possible, in our completely exhausted and depressed country, to lift the spirits of the revolutionary forces, if the defense of our revolution and of its territory is at all possible, then it is only thanks to the situation just created. And that situation is a direct result of our exit from the war and our refusal to sign the peace treaty."[5]

After a discussion, President Sverdlov introduced a resolution which read, "Having heard and fully considered the report of the peace delegation, the Central Executive Committee fully approves the actions of its representatives at Brest-Litovsk."[6] The resolution was passed unanimously.

Trotsky was sitting in Lenin's office on February 18, engaged in a conversation with A. V. Karelin, a Left Social Revolutionary, Commissar for Property in the Soviet Cabinet and member of the Soviet delegation to Brest. The Left SR's had joined the Lenin government in December, 1917; one of their leaders was appointed Commissar of Justice, another Commissar of

[5] Leon Trotsky, *Von Oktober nach Brest-Litovsk*, pp. 111-121.

[6] Petrograd *Pravda*, Feb. 15 and 16, 1918. (Note: In January, 1918, Soviet Russia, by a Lenin-signed decree, adopted the Gregorian (Western) calendar. The decree went into effect on Feb. 1, 1918 (Old Style) which became Feb. 14, 1918 (New Style). Thereafter, only New Style dates were used. In this book, New Style dates have been used for events antedating this change. For instance, the Bolshevik uprising, which occurred on Oct. 25, 1917 (Old Style), is dated Nov. 7, 1917.)

Agriculture. In the early Brest-Litovsk phase, the Left SR's backed Lenin. They were a party with strong peasant support, and, Maria Spiridonova, their leader, said to Trotsky, "The peasant does not want war and will accept any peace whatever." Trotsky reported that when he returned to Petrograd after his first round in Brest, she said to him, "Sign the peace at once and annul the grain monopoly."[7] Gradually, however, the Left SR position changed. For a while they supported Trotsky's intermediate No-war, No-peace stand. Later, they moved still further from Lenin and reinforced the Left Communists' agitation for a revolutionary war. Lenin and Trotsky were discussing this problem with Karelin when a secretary entered and handed Lenin a telegram. Lenin read it, loked glum, and passed it to Trotsky. They quickly finished their conference with Karelin and remained alone. The telegram was from Soviet General Samoilo who had been left in Brest for contact.

The wire, dated February 16, announced "Today, at 19.30 hours, I received official notice from General Hoffmann that as of noon, February 18, the armistice with the Russian Republic is ended and the state of war renewed. February 17, morning, I depart, with the commission accredited to me, for Baranovichi and Minsk."[8]

As they sat there, therefore, Soviet Russia was at war with Kaiser Germany and had received two days' notice, instead of the seven agreed upon December 15, of the cancellation of the armistice. "They have deceived us and gained five days," Lenin said to Trotsky. "This beast lets nothing escape it. There is nothing for us to do but sign the old conditions if the Germans still agree to them."

Trotsky argued for a postponement until Hoffmann's troops actually attacked. The territorial sacrifices this entailed, he contended, "are necessary so that the German workman, on the one hand, and the French and English workman, on the other, may understand."

Lenin took sharp issue with him.[9]

Within minutes, the Central Committee of the Bolshevik party was convened. Lenin and Zinoviev spoke for signing the peace treaty without delay. Trotsky and Bukharin spoke against it. On a motion for the resumption of peace negotiations, Lenin voted in the affirmative and Trotsky in the negative. The motion was defeated: 6 for, 7 against. In the evening, the Committee met again. Trotsky reported the German capture of Dvinsk (Duenaburg). The Germans were advancing on a broad front. He now had the demonstration he wanted of German aggression. This altered his attitude. Lenin, Stalin, and Sverdlov demanded the resumption of peace negotiations. Uritsky, Lomov, and Bukharin were opposed. Trotsky would ask Germany for her peace terms. On a motion to sign the peace at once, seven members (Lenin, Smilga, Stalin, Sverdlov, Sokolnikov, Trotsky and Zinoviev) voted for; five

[7] Leon Trotsky, *Lenin*, pp. 110-111.
[8] *Mirnye Peregovory*, Vol. I, p. 263.
[9] Trotsky, *Lenin*, p. 112.

(Uritsky, Lomov, Bukharin, Yoffe, Krestinsky) against; Madame Stasova abstained. The Committee authorized Lenin and Trotsky to draft and send a reply to Hoffmann.[10]

Lenin drew a pencil and scribbled his text. Trotsky made several emendations. It protested the shortened, two-day notice of the annulment of the armistice and declared that the Soviet of People's Commissars [the Cabinet] felt "compelled, in the created situation," to sign "formally."[11]

The message was dispatched from the Tsarkoe Selo wireless station at 8:12 A.M. on February 19 over the signatures of Lenin and Trotsky. A day later, Hoffmann radioed that this could not be regarded as official "because of the absence of original signatures." He wanted them attested in writing and forwarded by courier to the High Command in Dvinsk.[12] This was done.

The Bolsheviks, however, were still at sixes and sevens and Lenin's control was far from firm. Mighty forces disputed his chosen course. For example, *Pravda* of February 20 declared in a first-page editorial entitled "Decision" that: "There can be no agreement, there is no possibility of an agreement between, on the one hand, the government of workers and peasants who have risen against Russian landlords and bourgeoisie, and, on the other hand, the government of German landlords and bourgeoisie."

Meanwhile, the Bolsheviks prepared to fight. "The socialist fatherland is in peril," *Pravda* of February 22 screamed in giant headlines, and called on workers and soldiers to defend Petrograd, "the red fortress of the world revolution."

There were the voluble Left Communist advocates of revolutionary war to cope with. Moreover, the Left SR's now assumed an intransigent, anti-treaty posture. In fact, at a meeting on February 21 of the Soviet of People's Commissars (Sovnarkom), the Left SR members voted against the acceptance of aid from the Western Entente. Joseph Noulens, French ambassador to Russia, had telegraphed Trotsky on February 21, "In your resistance to Germany you can count on the military and financial collaboration of France." The Left SR's cried havoc; they would not fight one imperialism with materials from another. The Cabinet meeting was accordingly adjourned. The next day Trotsky asked Jacques Sadoul to obtain an official note from Noulens repeating his offer. Noulens complied. When Trotsky reported this the same evening to the Central Committee of the Bolshevik party, Bukharin, Uritsky, and Lomov objected in principle to negotiations with imperialists on any subject; Sverdlov, Krestinsky, and Smilga were not opposed to the principle of a transaction but regarded it as practically unwise; Trotsky and Sokolnikov argued for acceptance of aid. Lenin could not attend the meeting but sent a mocking note: "Please register my vote in favor of taking potatoes and arms from the Anglo-French imperialist brigands." On Trotsky's motion for accept-

[10] Lenin, *Sochineniya*, Second ed., Vol. XXII, editorial note, p. 605.

[11] *Ibid.*, p. 260.

[12] *Leninskii Sbornik*, Vol. XI, p. 26.

ance of assistance, 6 voted yes, 5 no. Trotsky stipulated that "The Russian Social Democratic Labor Party"—that was still the name of the Bolshevik party—"retains its full independence in foreign affairs, gives the capitalist government no political guarantees." Bukharin thereupon resigned from the Central Committee. On February 22 the Sovnarkom too voted for acquiring foreign food and equipment.[13]

Irritated, as ever, by opposition, especially when it defended abstract principles at a moment of concrete, life-or-death crisis, Lenin lashed out at the dissenters. *Pravda* of February 21 published an article of 3,200 words and the next day an article of 1,000 words, both signed with a pseudonym, Karpov, but unmistakably Lenin's.[14] The first was entitled "Regarding the Revolutionary Phrase." "The revolutionary phrase," he said, "is a repetition of revolutionary slogans without considering objective circumstances." There followed a basic policy declaration: "Our press has always spoken of the necessity of preparing for a revolutionary war in the event of the victory of socialism in one country and the preservation of capitalism in neighboring countries. This is beyond dispute." Actually, however, they had been forced to demobilize the army and "not one voice had been raised against it." The reason was clear: it lay in "the social structure of a small-peasant, backward country reduced to extreme ruin after three years of war. The demobilization of the multi-million army and the creation of a Red Army on a volunteer basis —these are facts. . . . The old army had ceased to exist. The new army is only just being conceived." Some argued, he continued, that Germany could not attack. That, he replied, "is tantamount to a declaration that 'We know the German government will be overthrown *in the next weeks.*' In fact, they did not and could not know this, and therefore the declaration is a phrase. . . . Only if a separate peace is *completely* impossible will we have to fight, and *not because that will be the correct tactics but because there is no choice.* . . . We must fight the revolutionary phrase, we must fight it, absolutely fight it, lest some day they tell the bitter truth about us: 'The revolutionary phrase about a revolutionary war killed the revolution.' "

The second article Lenin called "Regarding the Itch." "An agonizing illness—the itch," read the first sentence. "And when the itch of the revolutionary phrase takes hold of human beings then alone the sight of it causes intolerable suffering." Why did he return to the subject of his article in *Pravda* the day before? Because "the same itch today jumped over to a new place (a very contagious disease this)." He was referring to the opposition that had developed earlier that day, February 22, to accepting military and other assistance from the Western Entente. He chose a revealing illustration to prove how wrong that stand was: the case of I. P. Kalyaev, a student and a terrorist SR, who, on orders from his party, assassinated Grand Duke

[13] Lenin, *op. cit.*, Second ed., Vol. XXII, editorial note, pp. 607-608.
[14] The articles are printed in full in Lenin, *op. cit.*, Second ed., Vol. XXII, pp. 261-269 and 272-274.

Sergei Alexandrovich, uncle of Tsar Nicholas, on February 4, 1905, and was hanged for it on May 10, 1905, in the Schluesselburg prison, where Lenin's brother had been executed for a similar attempt. "Now suppose Kalyaev," Lenin wrote, "in order to kill a tyrant, a monster, obtains a revolver from a terrible scoundrel, swindler, robber, promising to bring him bread, money, and vodka for the service. Can Kalyaev be condemned for his bargain with a robber in order to obtain a lethal weapon? Any normal person will say, No. Since Kalyaev could obtain a revolver nowhere else, and since Kalyaev's purpose was honest (the murder of a tyrant, and not murder for the sake of robbery) then Kalyaev should not be reprimanded for such an acquisition of a revolver, but praised.

". . . Well, and if the representative of an exploited, oppressed class which, after having overthrown the exploiters, published and annulled all secret and predatory treaties, is subjected to a bandit attack by the German imperialists, can it be condemned for 'a deal with the Anglo-French bandits' for taking arms and potatoes from them in return for money or timber, etc.? Can such a bargain be considered dishonest, disgraceful, dirty?

"No."

In the midst of battle, an ineradicable trauma (his brother's hanging) had dredged up the name of a successful assassin, Kalyaev, and brought it to the surface. Yet Lenin sensed the inadequacy of an individual's imaginary pact with the devil to serve a holy purpose and searched for a historic analogy. He found it, and wrote at the end of the article: "P.S. In their war of independence against England at the end of the eighteenth century the North Americans availed themselves of the aid of a rival, the same kind of colonial brigand as England: the Spanish and French governments. It is said that there are 'left Bolsheviks' who have sat down to write a 'Ph.D. thesis' on the 'dirty deal' of those Americans." In Lenin anger bred humor.

The Germans were moving closer to Petrograd. The capture of the capital would have lopped off one of the regime's proletarian legs and left it standing, infirmly, on the other, Moscow. Lenin's mind, pen, and tongue knew no rest. At 10:30 A.M., February 23, the Soviet government received the German reply to the Lenin-Trotsky radiogram of February 18, announcing Russia's readiness to sign a dictated peace. Correspondence with the Germans traveled at a slower pace than their troops. Ludendorff's "short but sharp blow" had not yet reached its targets. Hoffmann's long-awaited message of the 23rd outlined sterner terms than those contemplated at Brest-Litovsk: German "police" were to be stationed in Estonia and Latvia "until the establishment of stable governments"; the Soviet government would make peace with German-occupied Ukraine; Russian armed forces would evacuate the Ukraine and Finland; Russia would pay heavy indemnities; Turkey would annex Russian lands; the Bolsheviks were to conduct no propaganda in Germany or the territories she held.

The day these terms arrived in Petrograd, Lenin addressed three meetings

of key policy bodies: the Central Committee of the Bolshevik party, a joint
session of the Central Committees of the Bolshevik and Left SR Parties;
finally, a meeting of the All-Russian Central Executive Committee of the
Soviets (VTSIK), the nearest equivalent to a parliament, which still embraced Mensheviks, anarchists, and SR's as well as Bolsheviks.

At the Bolshevik party's Central Committee session, Lenin stated that if
the use of revolutionary phrases continued he would resign from the government and the Central Committee. He called this "an ultimatum. I present
it in this extreme case." Lenin, Zinoviev, Sverdlov, and Sokolnikov defended
the acceptance of the German terms immediately. (Germany had demanded
acceptance within seventy-two hours.) Bukharin, Uritsky, Djerzhinsky (a Pole),
and Lomov attacked the proposal. Trotsky said the party was divided, therefore he could not support a policy of revolutionary war. Stalin, surprisingly,
favored procrastinating, as Trotsky ("Traitor Trotsky") had at one stage.
Stalin declared, "It is possible not to sign but to commence peace negotiations." Lenin replied, "Stalin is wrong when he says it is possible not to
sign."[15] Stalin then voted with Lenin.

Lenin put three questions: "Shall we immediately accept the German
terms?" He, Stasova, Zinoviev, Sverdlov, Stalin, Sokolnikov, and Smilga
voted in the affirmative; Bubnov, Uritsky, Lomov, and Bukharin in the negative; Trotsky abstained together with Djerzhinsky, Krestinsky, and Yoffe.
Second question: "Shall we prepare for a revolutionary war?" in the absence
of an alternative. Unanimously adopted. Third: "Shall we consult the population of Petrograd and Moscow?" Yes, 11; no, 0; 4 abstentions.[16]

Lenin said to the joint Bolshevik-Left SR meeting, "Our Russian proletariat is not at all to blame because the German revolution is late. It will
come." We must sign, he added, and build railroads, organize the food supply, fashion a good army, "and by that time the German socialist revolution
will undoubtedly catch up."[17] No vote was taken.

Because of the protracted debate, the VTSIK did not actually assemble
until 3 A.M. on the 24th. Everybody was conscious of the ticking of history.
Time was running out. Lenin spoke first and repeated, with maximum intensity and emphasis, the arguments he had been using in the past few days.[18]
Julius Martov, the leader of the Mensheviks, and Right SR deputies opposed
the signing. A. J. Geh, leader of the "anarchists-communists," asserted that
his group was proclaiming "terror and partisan war on two fronts"—presumably against Germans and Russian Bolshevik-conservatives like Lenin; "it is
better to die than to live under German imperialism." B. D. Kamkov, a fiery
Left SR, an exponent of terror, derided the faint hearts that trembled before
Germany's terms.

[15] *Ibid.*, p. 277.
[16] *Ibid.*, editorial note, p. 608.
[17] *Ibid.*, p. 279.
[18] *Ibid.*, pp. 280-283.

President Sverdlov now called for a vote. The majority of those Bolsheviks who opposed signing walked out of the hall before the balloting. The tally showed: 116 for signing; 85 against; 26 abstained; 7 refused to vote.[19] This gave the Sovnarkom (Cabinet) authority to conclude peace.

On February 24 a Soviet diplomatic courier left Petrograd with the official announcement to the German government that Russia would sign the proffered treaty. Early the next morning a Soviet peace delegation took the train for Brest to sign the peace; it consisted of Sokolnikov, chairman; Adolf Yoffe; G. K. Petrovsky; Leo M. Karakhan; and Georgi V. Chicherin, deputy Commissar for Foreign Affairs. Sokolnikov and Yoffe had refused at first to go. Sokolnikov favored the signing but recoiled from doing it personally; Yoffe opposed the signing. Both bowed to a special order from the Central Committee.[20]

The delegation had not traveled far when they were stopped by a bridge that had been blown up. They reported this to Lenin by a telegram in which they requested him to inform German headquarters of their predicament. Lenin, suspecting that this was an excuse reflecting the delegates' reluctance to proceed, wired: "Don't fully understand your telegram. If you are wavering this is inadmissible. Send truce envoys [to inform the Germans] and try to reach the Germans as soon as possible."[21] Then he asked, and received, from the railway administration the numbers of the trains carrying the courier and the delegation and the exact time of their departure.

On foot and by a railway hand trolley, the delegates finally reached Pskov, 257 versts (a little over 160 miles) from Petrograd. The city was in darkness and disorganization, but before long Sokolnikov and his comrades discovered that the Germans had occupied it. And the Germans discovered them. After misadventures, misunderstandings, and explanations, they were given quarters for the night and facilities to proceed to Brest the next day. At Brest, the Soviet representatives demanded that the military advance stop, but on instructions from the High Command, Ambassador von Rosenberg, the German plenipotentiary, said this was impossible. He also informed the Russians that only three days had been allowed for negotiations preliminary to the signing of the treaty. The Bolshevik delegates decided to sign without discussion and without attempting to soften the terms. When the final treaty text was submitted to them on March 1, they realized that the terms were not only worse than those submitted by the Central Powers at Brest-Litovsk but worse than those received from Hoffmann on February 23. Nevertheless, the Russians agreed to sign at once in order to stop the invasion and to underline the fact that this was peace at the tip of a sword. Karakhan, secretary of the Soviet delegation, accordingly sent two telegrams to Lenin; one that they were signing, the second, asking for a train to take them home.

[19] Petrograd *Pravda*, Feb. 25, 1918.
[20] *Leninskii Sbornik*, Vol. XI, p. 29.
[21] *Ibid.*, p. 29.

However, the second telegram arrived first. Lenin forthwith drafted and dispatched an urgent order repeating Karakhan's telegram, interpreting it as "meaning in all probability the Germans have broken off the negotiations," and advising "all, all, all" throughout Russia to be "prepared for an immediate German advance on Petrograd and in general on all fronts."[22] Shortly thereafter Karakhan's first wire arrived.

Though the Russians were willing to sign the treaty on March 1, the Germans asserted that for technical reasons the copies of the treaty would not be ready for signing until March 3. Meanwhile the German army continued its advance unopposed. At the signing ceremony on March 3, Sokolnikov noted the worsened conditions, condemned the transfer to Turkey of the provinces of Kars and Ardahan and the city of Batum without consulting the inhabitants, and declared that the settlement had been violently imposed. In conclusion, Sokolnikov could not forbear to say, prophetically, "We do not doubt for a moment that this triumph of imperialism and militarism over the international proletariat will prove only temporary and transitory."

General Hoffmann shook himself and exclaimed, "Again the same ravings."[23]

The signing was completed at 5:30 P.M. on March 3.

༼ఞ·ఞ·ఞ·ఞ·ఞ·ఞ·ఞ༽

The Voronezh-Kursk front. August 1, 1919. Soviet Russia is deep in civil war. Leon Trotsky is Commissar of Defense, the leader of the armed forces of the country. Adolf Yoffe, editing the official stenographic report of the Brest-Litovsk peace conference, asks Trotsky to write an introduction. Trotsky agrees. He feels the need to present a clear image of himself to posterity. He wrote, "We went to Brest-Litovsk to conclude peace. Why? Because we could not fight." The Germans could have moved all their armies away from the eastern front without holding the Brest conference. But "they did not understand us." He reviewed the course of the negotiations and explained his reasons for the February 10, No-war, No-peace climax. The German offensive followed. "But in hindsight it is possible to say with complete certainty that the temporary rupture of the Brest-Litovsk talks and the advance of the German troops did not, in the final analysis, harm but, on the contrary, helped the European revolution. After the German conquest of Dvinsk, Reval, and Pskov, the English and French workers could not, naturally, believe that this was a matter of a behind-the-scenes collusion between Bolsheviks and Hohenzollerns. This for a long time made it difficult for the bandits of the Western Entente to attack us." He exaggerated the result of his gesture. But he could not have been wrong when he said in conclusion, "All's well that ends well."

Trotsky was a towering presence at the Brest conference. The hero, however, of Brest-Litovsk was Lenin. Lenin's policy toward the Brest-Litovsk

<hr />

[22] Ibid., pp. 31-32.
[23] G. Sokolnikov, Brestskii Mir (The Brest Peace) (Moscow, 1920), p. 31.

peace problem revealed his greatness. It lay in his ability to subordinate one side of his self and let another dominate. As a writer, propagandist, and thinker before the revolution Lenin was never inductive. He was deductive. He accepted truth as handed down by Marx and selected data and arguments to bolster that truth. He did not question old Marxist scripture, he merely commented, and the comments have become a new scripture. That was the aspect of Lenin that ruled him before he began to rule. It was due to the fact that a revolution denies experience, defies existing conditions. But to preserve the revolution, Lenin came down to hard earth.

As a statesman, Lenin observed, weighed, and reasoned, and arrived at decisions on the basis of reality. Power did not go to his head. It cleared it. Most other Bolsheviks attempted, at least in the early Soviet period, to achieve an integrity between their prerevolutionary and postrevolutionary selves. But for Lenin, power was too precious to be squandered on consistency. His responsibilities compelled a cold, objective assessment of circumstances, compelled a sober, practical unsentimentality stripped of illusions, slogans, cant, pride, attachment to theory, and attachment to past stands and statements. He paid lip service to what Stalin called "the potentiality" of European revolution but excluded it from his calculations. He judged the concrete situation. The situation in 1918 demanded peace at a high price. He saw this from the beginning and was ready to pay. He thereby saved the state he had created.

XIV. LENIN VERSUS THE LEFT

THE BREST-LITOVSK peace treaty[1] was humiliating to Russian nationalists and painful to Russian Bolsheviks. No laboratory tests had been devised to ascertain the percentage admixture of nationalism in Bolshevism. To some Lenin would have appeared in 1917 as the savior of the Russian nation from ruin and death in battle. As Chairman Nikita S. Khrushchev, referring to 1917, stated in his marathon address to the Central Committee plenary session on March 5, 1962, "It cannot be said that the workers and peasants of Russia

[1] Full Russian text, *Mirnii Dogovor mezhdu Rossiei c odnoi storoni i Germaniei, Avstro-Vengriei, Bolgariei i Turtsiei c drugoi (Peace Treaty between Russia on the one hand and Germany, Austria-Hungary, Bulgaria, and Turkey on the other)* (Moscow, 1918); also, in *Dokumenty Vneshnei Politiki SSRR (Documents on the Foreign Policy of the USSR)* Vol. I (Moscow, 1957), pp. 119-204. English translation in *Papers Relating to the Foreign Relations of the United States, 1918, Russia*, Vol. I, pp. 442-475.

knew the theory of scientific communism when they rose in revolt. Only a few advanced people—revolutionists, knew this theory profoundly. . . . They knew that the Bolsheviks stood for peace, opposed the imperialist war . . ."

But the sudden German invasion of Russia in February and March, 1918, the terms of the Brest treaty which deprived Russia of vast spaces inhabited by 55 million inhabitants, and the fear that, treaty notwithstanding, the Kaiser might take another big bite, were strong nationalistic arguments against Lenin's policy. Communist purists opposed it for other reasons. When, in pursuance of the party's Central Committee February 24 decision to ascertain the views of the population of Moscow and Petrograd, forty-two provinces (gubernii) were actually consulted, the returns must have shocked the pro-treaty Leninists. Six provincial cities opted for peace, twenty for war; eighty-eight county (ooyezdnie) towns and villages opted for peace, eighty-five for war.[2] Admittedly, this was no plebiscite. Those who replied to the query of the Soviet of People's Commissars (Sovnarkom) were soviets strewn throughout Russia. But in March, 1918, the soviets were representative and quite democratic, and the question, as stated in the long telegram, gave both sides with meticulous impartiality adding, in the penultimate, half-truth sentence: "The first point of view is defended by the Central Committee of the Bolsheviks and Lenin; the second point of view by the Central Committee of the Left SR's."

The results of the referendum indicate that Russia's fighting spirit was not dead; that the Left SR's carried much weight with the population and were necessary to the stability of the government; and that Lenin's views on the peace treaty had failed to convince many soviets.

Not only were the soviets democratic, the party was. The Moscow Regional Bureau of the Bolshevik party unanimously adopted a resolution on February 24, in which it "expresses its nonconfidence in the Central Committee because of its policy and its composition, and will, at the first opportunity, insist on new elections. Moreover, the Moscow Regional Bureau does not regard itself absolutely obliged to submit to the enactments of the Central Committee which may arise out of the implementation of the terms of the peace treaty with Austria-Germany."[3]

Nonconfidence in the Central Committee! Open defiance of its decisions! In the 1930's and thereafter such a thing became totally inconceivable, and if it had happened it would have ended with a bullet in the back of the head for the whole lot of them. But in an article in two parts in Pravda of February 28 and March 1, 1918, Lenin said of the Moscow resolution, "In all this there is not only nothing appalling, but also nothing strange. It is completely natural for comrades who differ sharply with the Central Committee on the issue of a separate peace to reprimand the Central Committee sharply and express their conviction on the inevitability of a split. All this is the legal right of members of the party, and this is fully understandable."

---

[2] Leninskii Sbornik, Vol. XI, pp. 59-61.
[3] Lenin, Sochineniya, Second ed., Vol. XXII, footnote, p. 297.

The Soviet regime stood up to the lower lip in swirling waters that threatened to rise to its eyes. Yet Lenin regarded disobedience in the top ranks of the party as normal and "understandable."

But what is strange and appalling, Lenin continued, was the explanatory note appended to the Moscow Bureau's resolution: "In the interest of the world revolution we consider it advisable to risk the possible destruction of the Soviet government which has now become a pure formality." This, Lenin declared, proved his point: for Russia to wage a revolutionary war against Germany meant to court death. The end of the Russian revolution would not help the German revolution, he argued; it would help the German reactionaries. The German workers, frightened by the fall of Russia's soviet regime, would recoil from establishing their own. "Perhaps," Lenin inquired, "the authors [of the resolution] suppose that the interests of the international revolution require its *instigation*, and such instigation would be only a war, not a peace which could create the impression on the masses of a sort of 'legalization' of imperialism? Such a 'theory' would represent a complete break with Marxism which has always rejected the 'instigation' of revolution that must develop in step with the ripening of acute class contradictions that breed revolution."

Lenin usually used hammer logic, scorn, biting epithets, but no eloquence. At the end of his second *Pravda* article, however, he waxed oratorical. "Why," he exclaimed, "cannot the grave military defeats suffered in the struggle with the colossi of contemporary imperialism toughen the national character of Russia too, tighten self-discipline, kill bragging and phrase-mongering, teach restraint, teach the masses the correct tactics of the Prussians who had been crushed by Napoleon: sign the shameful peace treaty when you have no army, gird your loins, and then lift yourself up again and again? Why must we succumb to despair at the first unprecedentedly grievous peace treaty when other nations have bravely borne more bitter disasters? . . . foreign conquests can only strengthen national sympathy for the Soviet government if . . . if it will not engage in adventures. The refusal to sign an indecent peace, if you have no army, is an adventure for which the people will justly blame the government guilty of this refusal. . . . We will not perish even from ten supremely burdensome peace treaties if we take a *serious* view of insurrection and war. We will not perish at the hands of the conqueror provided we do not allow ourselves to be destroyed by despair and phrases."

Lenin had worked himself up to a fever of fight. On March 1, the day the second part of his article appeared in *Pravda*, the same paper published an unsigned contribution from his pen urging the provinces to send flour to Petrograd, asking how many trained soldiers could be dispatched to the front immediately, how many Red Armymen were undergoing instruction. "All arms and shells must be accounted for; the production of new arms and shells must be resumed immediately. The railroads must be free of bag-carriers [individuals who went to villages to exchange city treasures for food] and hooligans." He called for "strict revolutionary discipline." Only if these requirements were met "will it be possible to speak seriously about war."

The capital was being moved to Moscow out of Germany's reach. The diplomatic corps had left Petrograd for Vologda and other remote parts. Trotsky would remain in the former capital to organize its defense. Lenin was preparing for the Seventh Congress of the Bolshevik party. Would it support him?

In February, 1918, Leo B. Kamenev, a Bolshevik of high party status, later Chairman of the Sovnarkom (Prime Minister) was sent, via England, to France. The purpose of his mission is in dispute and no Soviet material can be found to throw light on it except the statement of Georgi V. Chicherin, Commissar for Foreign Affairs, in 1919: "Comrade Kamenev, who was sent in February on an extraordinary mission to France, where he was not allowed to enter by the worst of our enemies—the Government of Clemenceau . . ."[4]

It seems extraordinary to accredit an extraordinary mission to a government as hostile to Soviet Russia as Clemenceau's was known to be, but the French embassy in Russia did furnish Kamenev's diplomatic passport with a diplomatic visa, and, given the class-angled vision of the Bolsheviks, it may be that Lenin and Trotsky expected Kamenev, once in France, to enlist proletarian sympathy, at least to indicate by his presence that the Bolsheviks were not bound hand and foot to Germany, and perhaps to obtain help even from Clemenceau for Russian resistance to a resumed German invasion if it occurred.

In the end of February and the early part of March, the Soviet leadership, including Lenin, manifested renewed interest in the three optimistic Western intermediaries: Robins, Lockhart, and Sadoul. The government did not know whether the German offensive would halt with the signing of the Brest peace treaty or whether the party congress and the subsequent Soviet congress would ratify it. Nonratification might invite a deeper military thrust. To resist it the Bolsheviks would want foreign assistance.

When U.S. Ambassador Francis left Petrograd for Vologda on February 27, Robins went with him, and Lenin gave Robins a handwritten letter to the Vologda Soviet asking it to be helpful to the ambassador and his staff. Francis arrived in Vologda on February 28, and on March 1 he wired the Secretary of State in Washington, "If Soviet government overthrown which highly probable Allies should cultivate new government to prevent its alliance with Germany."[5] Robins had different views. He was not the man to vegetate in a provincial town where marooned diplomats would be taking in one

[4] George Chicherin, *Two Years of Foreign Policy*, The Relations of the Russian Socialist Federal Republic with Foreign Nations, from November 7, 1917, to November 7, 1919 (Pamphlet) (New York, The Russian Soviet Government Bureau, 1920). Original Russian in Moscow *Izvestia*, Nov. 6 to Nov. 13, 1919.
[5] *Papers Relating to the Foreign Relations of the United States. 1918. Russia*, Vol. I, p. 389.

another's rumors. He returned to Petrograd on March 4 to be at Trotsky's elbow.

The next day he visited Trotsky in the Smolny. "Colonel Robins," Trotsky saluted him, "do you still want to beat the peace?" (The peace had been signed in Brest forty-eight hours earlier.)

"Mr. Commissioner," Robins said, "you know the answer to that question."

"Well, the time has come to be definite," Trotsky declared. "We have talked—and we have talked—about help from America. Can you produce it? Can you get a definite promise from your government? If you can, we can even now beat the peace. I will oppose ratification, at Moscow, and beat it."

Robins asked about Lenin's attitude toward American aid.

"Lenin agrees," Trotsky affirmed.

"Will he say so?" Robins wanted to know.

"He will," Trotsky assured.

"In writing?"

Trotsky bristled. "Do you want us to give you our lives?" he exclaimed. "The Germans are thirty miles from Petrograd. How soon will your people be within thirty miles?"

Robins nevertheless insisted on a written note.

"Be back at four," Trotsky said.

Robins was back at four with his Russian interpreter-secretary, Alex Gumberg, later a unique New Yorker. The three walked down the corridor to Lenin's office. The four then walked to the Cabinet room. Gumberg translated the document Trotsky had drafted.

Robins to Lenin, "Mr. President Commissioner!" (The title was Robins' own invention. It should have been Chairman Commissar.) "If the United States government answers this document affirmatively, will you oppose the ratification of the Peace of Brest-Litovsk at the All-Russian Congress of Soviets at Moscow?"

"Yes," Lenin replied.

"Very well," Robins said, and left hurriedly with Gumberg.[6]

Lenin's "Yes" was conditioned in the document by two sets of ifs: If the Congress of Soviets refused to ratify the Brest treaty, or if the Germans attacked despite the treaty, or if the Soviets renounced the treaty because of any German action—those were one set of ifs. Secondly: If the Soviet government could rely on receiving support of the United States, Britain and France; and, most important, more important than supplies: "Should Japan . . . attempt to seize Vladivostok and the Eastern Siberian Railway . . . in such case what steps would be taken by the other Allies, particularly and especially by the United States to prevent a Japanese landing in our Far East?" Finally, would Great Britain send help through Russia's northern

[6] William Hard, *Raymond Robins' Own Story* (New York and London, 1920), pp. 134-138.

ports—Archangel and Murmansk—and thereby "undermine the foundations of rumors of the hostile plans against Russia on the part of Great Britain in the nearest future"?[7]

It is clear what agitated Lenin and Trotsky. A German attack in the west, concerted with a hostile British landing in the north, and a Japanese invasion of Siberia would spell the Soviets' doom. Lenin had plans to retreat before a German incursion: first to Moscow, then to the Volga, then to the Urals, then east of the Urals to the Ural-Kuznetsky Basin.[8] The Lenin-Trotsky document given to Robins noted that Japanese action "would greatly impede the concentration of Soviet troops toward the east about the Urals." Lenin did not want the revolution to expire in an iron Germano-Japanese embrace. Japan was America's ally and rival. What would Wilson do?

The Lenin-Trotsky document was a dud; it never went off. George F. Kennan tells the story: "Robins, with the help of Consul Tredwell and Captain Prince (who had returned to Petrograd with Robins), tried that evening to wire Trotsky's message to Francis. Unfortunately, they were compelled to use the military code for its transmission; they had no other. But since Ruggles and Riggs, now on their way to Petrograd, had taken the military code books with them, the Embassy at Vologda had no means of decoding the message. When this fact became known to the Americans in Petrograd later that day, they were confronted with a pretty problem. . . .

"Tredwell, realizing the importance of the message, urged (in fact, practically ordered) Captain Prince of the Military Mission to despatch the message directly to the War Department in Washington, for transmission to the State Department 'adding that we were endeavoring to get it to the Ambassador as soon as possible.' Together with one of the officers of the Military Mission, Tredwell worked all night encoding the message, with a view to despatching it to Washington on the morning of the 6th. The message was evidently held, however, for clearance with Ruggles, who was arriving that night. Ruggles must have decided, for some reason, not to despatch it that night. His decision was probably connected with the fact that he himself expected to see Trotsky almost at once, and he no doubt wanted to send his own version of Trotsky's views; also with the fact that he (like the other Allied military attachés) was resentful of the free-wheeling negotiations of Robins and Lockhart. In any case, the records indicate that he did not actually despatch the message containing Trotsky's suggestions until nearly two weeks later. It did not reach Washington until March 22, by which time, of course, the Brest-Litovsk Treaty had long been ratified."[9]

Robins had no idea of these mishaps and thought Trotsky's message, and Lenin's concurrence, were known in Washington. While impatiently awaiting Wilson's reply he begged Lenin, in a personal interview, to be patient.

[7] *Ibid.*, pp. 138-139.
[8] Leon Trotzky, *Lenin*, pp. 116-117.
[9] *Russia Leaves the War* (Princeton, N.J., 1956), pp. 499-500.

But events took their course. The Seventh Congress of the Russian Communist Party (Bolsheviks)—the new party name adopted by the Seventh Congress—met in Petrograd from March 6 to 8, 1918. Unlike subsequent party congresses attended by thousands of delegates, this congress counted forty-six voting delegates—each representing 5,000 party members. It was a deliberative body which debated freely (twenty speakers took the floor), and voted freely—for ratification of the Brest peace treaty. *Pravda* of March 9, 1918, gave the vote as: 30 in favor, 12 against, and 4 abstentions. The editors of Lenin's *Collected Works* give it as: 28 for, 9 against, and 1 abstention.[10] Ovsyannikov counted 28 votes for and 12 against.[11] Latter-day, hollow-headed unanimity is much easier to record than the arithmetic of democracy.

The speech with which Lenin opened the congress was an unhurried tour of the horizon.[12] He talked at length, more like a teacher than a leader fighting for a majority. He spoke softly to his "young friends who call themselves left," and gently took them by the hand to show them the errors of their thinking. En route, he delicately, deferentially, demolished Trotsky's position too. Throughout, he remained master of himself and the situation, and calmly, repetitiously, laid down some laws of revolution and politics which are relevant, even today, to the acts of communists and anticommunists.

Bolshevik policy—land for the peasant, peace for all, and all power for the soviets—enabled "us to win so easily in Petrograd" in November, 1917, and to make "the following months of the Russian Revolution one uninterrupted triumphal procession."

Now the difficulties had commenced. "The more backward the country which happened, thanks to the zigzags of history, to begin the socialist revolution, the more difficult for it is the transition from old capitalist conditions to socialist conditions."

The "zigzags of history" were the First World War, the mother of Bolshevism. "Only thanks to the fact that our revolution occurred in the happy moment when the two giant groups of plunderers could neither destroy one another nor unite against us," did the Bolshevik revolution take over all of European Russia, spread to "Finland and begin to conquer the Caucasus and Romania."

Carried away by "this triumphal procession," some of the "intellectual supermen" in the front ranks of the party said, "We can handle international imperialism; there too we will see a triumphal procession." This was a miscalculation. ". . . in Europe it is immeasurably more difficult to start the

---

[10] Lenin, Vol. XXII, editorial note, p. 613.

[11] *Lenin i Brestskii Mir. Stati i rechi N. Lenina v 1918 godu o Brestskom mire—s vvodnoi statei i primechaniami N. Ovsyannikova (Lenin and the Brest Peace*—Articles and Speeches by N. Lenin on the Brest Peace—with an introductory article and commentaries by N. Ovsyannikov) (Moscow-Petrograd, 1923).

[12] Lenin, Vol. XXII, pp. 313-330.

revolution and here it was immeasurably easier to start, but it will be more difficult to continue it here than there." The dream, however, of the impending triumphal procession against European capitalism, Lenin declared, conduced to a false approach to the Brest-Litovsk negotiations: "A quiet domestic pet lay down next to a tiger and tried to convince him to conclude a peace without annexations and indemnities." You could only achieve this, Lenin scoffed, by attacking the tiger. Nevertheless, "the intelligentsia and some of the workers' organizations" wrapped their folly in phrases. They would not furl the flags of their triumphal procession; they would not accept humiliating peace terms. "Never," he paraphrased their utterances. "We are proud revolutionaries. We assert, above all, 'The German cannot take the offensive.'"

This notion was based on the assumption of the dawning German revolution. "Of course," Lenin agreed, ". . . there is no doubting the truth that if our revolution remained the only one, if no revolution erupted in other countries, our position would be hopeless. We took the whole situation into the hands of the Bolshevik party alone, we took it for ourselves, in the conviction that the revolution is ripening in all countries. . . . Our salvation from all these difficulties, I repeat, is in an all-European revolution." But this was "a completely abstract truth and, though guided by it, we must beware lest it, in time, become a mere phrase, for every abstract truth, if you apply it without any analysis whatsoever, is reduced to a phrase. If you say that behind every strike hides the hydra of revolution that is true and whoever does not understand that is no socialist. Yes, behind every strike hides the socialist revolution. But if you say that every given strike is a direct step toward a socialist revolution then you are uttering an empty phrase."

Lenin had preferred one-party rule and believed it could be maintained with the help of foreign revolutions. He chose to forget that the early triumphal processions of the Russian revolution were made possible by the quick spread of multi-party soviets, popular and democratic. He had sacrificed this inner strength to the dream of outside reinforcements, a dream induced by the endless chants of the abstract "truth" that the European revolution "is ripening." The refrain became an empty phrase. Lenin sang the refrain but refused to indulge in "instigation" of revolution until the fruit was ripe, not merely ripening. His Bukharinite opponents were prepared to sacrifice the Soviet state to the European revolt. This caused the split. Lenin did not fear it. There was a "guarantee," he said, "that we will not break our necks on this question," because the pre-1917 method of debating differences by means of mountains of literature and millions of words had yielded to "a new method of learning." It is "the testing of everything with facts, events, and the lessons of world history. You say that the German cannot attack. The corollary of your tactics was to declare that the state of war had been ended. But history taught you a lesson, it rejected this illusion. Yes, the German revolution is growing but not in the way we would desire, not with the speed that would please the Russian intellectuals, not with the tempo which our history introduced in November, 1917, when we could arrive in any city, proclaim the Soviet government, and nine-tenths of the workers would come over to us in a few days. The German revolution has the misfortune of not moving so fast. And who must take account of whom? We of it or it of us? We wanted it to take us into account, but history taught you a lesson. This lesson, because it is an absolute truth, is that without the German revolution we shall perish—perhaps not in Petrograd, not in Moscow, but in Vladivostok or still more remote places. . . . Nevertheless this does not by one iota shake our assurance that we must be able to bear up under the worst situation without bragging. . . . in Russia—in the country of Nicholas and Rasputin it was easy to start a revolution, it meant —lifting a feather. But to begin a revolution, without preparation, in a country where capitalism is developed and has created a democratic civilization and organized every last man—that is wrong, absurd. . . .

"Yes, we will see the international world revolution, but for the present it is a very good fairy tale, a very beautiful fairy tale—I fully understand that it is natural for children to love beautiful fairy tales. But I ask: is it natural for serious revolutionists to believe in fairy tales? . . .

"Everything I predicted has come to pass: in place of the Brest peace, we received a much more humiliating peace, the fault of those who did not take it in the first place." (A slap at Trotsky.) "Having been taught this lesson, we will get over our split, our crisis . . . because an immeasurably truer friend will come to our aid: the world revolution." Therefore: ratify the treaty. Lenin called it a "Tilsit Peace," the peace dictated by Napoleon to Prussia in 1807. "The Hoffmann of those days—Napoleon—caught the Germans at violating the peace, and Hoffmann will catch us doing the same thing. Only we shall try not to let him catch us so quickly."

The Brest treaty, signed on March 3, required the Soviet government to withdraw its troops from Finland, the Ukraine, and Romania. Bolshevik revolutions had occurred in those three countries. Lenin said, ". . . everybody will understand that, having signed the peace with the Germans, we do not stop our military aid: we send the Finns arms but not troops which have proven worthless." (Lenin's speech was first published in 1923, so he was revealing no secrets in 1918.) The German army suppressed all three revolutions.

Of the Congress Lenin asked that it ratify the treaty to get a respite, if only for a few days. Already, by signing when the German army was within arm's reach of Petrograd, they had saved the city, temporarily at least. Nobody knew for how long. "This animal jumps well. He demonstrated that. He will jump again. Of this there is not the shadow of a doubt. Therefore it is necessary to be ready, and not to brag, and to take even one day's breathing spell, for even one day can be used to evacuate Petrograd."

Lenin ended his long polemic with a brief, pessimistic paragraph: "Lose your illusions." We face "an epoch of the most trying defeats." It is necessary to be prepared for "persistent work in conditions of illegality, in conditions of undisguised German slavery. . . . If we can do that, then we, despite defeats, this can be said with absolute certainty, shall win."

The leftists were horrified at the defeatist concessions Lenin was prepared to make. They knew his attitude: on March 8, at the closing evening session of the party congress, he went so far as to say that he would "not renounce the use of bourgeois parliamentarianism" if they were thrown back. "To think that we will not be thrown back is a utopia." Should this happen, Lenin affirmed, should "hostile forces" in Russia drive them back and erect an old-style parliamentary state, they would exploit parliament and simultaneously strive to restore the new-type state, a soviet state. This bleak prospect confirmed the leftists in their anti-Leninist intransigence.

The opposition now opened up with heavy artillery: Bukharin, their leader, only twenty-nine years old; Radek, Uritsky, D. B. Ryazanov, Bubnov, and others. Lenin busily made notes and prepared his replies. "We of the left are always right," Bukharin said. "Past master, that Bukharin," Lenin jotted down. (Lenin was very fond of the witty, fiery, short, jovial, learned, and artistic Bukharin and affectionately called him "Bukashka"—little insect.) The breathing space would last "only a few days," Bukharin argued. "Will he try to make it longer?" Lenin wrote on a folded sheet of paper preserved in the archives.[13] The wavering of our party, Bukharin continued, is demoralizing the people, the party, and the army. "True," Lenin noted. "But who is wavering? The Central Committee, and in the Central Committee who? Why you, my 'left' friends." Like a good Marxist, Bukharin sought to attribute the division in the party to the class structure of Russia. The "compromisers," headed by Lenin, reflected the petty bourgeois "bag-carriers" and the tired peasants.

This was the gist of the leftist argument. They feared that Lenin's policy meant domestic peace with the peasantry and petty bourgeoisie. This would be tantamount to a cessation of the class war at home. They called for class war abroad: revolution.

As leader of the Soviet delegation at Brest, Trotsky had to speak. But he was distressed. Russia at that moment faced the first of many dilemmas of the premature revolution, a "miscarriage" brought on by the war which survived because of the war. The leftists were less interested in the Brest-Litovsk treaty than in the character of the revolution. If it was to be bourgeois-democratic, with nationalistic overtones, and not a proletarian dictatorship, they would despise it as a formality and prefer to offer it up on the altar of world revolution. Trotsky agreed with Bukharin, but he also agreed with Lenin, yet he disagreed with both. Torn this way and that, he made a bad speech. Trotsky had told the Petrograd Soviet in mid-February that if it became necessary to fight "we would have to lose ten soldiers for every

[13] *Leninskii Sbornik*, Vol. XI, pp. 62-64.

German."[14] He had added, however, "I consider a German offensive against us highly improbable, and if the likelihood of an offensive could be stated in percentages, then it would be 90% against an offensive and 10% for."[15] Now, he admitted his error to the Seventh Party Congress: "I was one of those who believed that Germany would not take the offensive. . . . Of course, we made a risky move" on February 10. The risk was, "Will the European proletariat support us or not? If not, we would be crushed. . . . Comrade Lenin believes that today, after Germany has occupied Reval and other cities, it is necessary to sign the peace today; the other wing, to which I belong, considers that today the only possibility for us, to the extent that it depends on our will, is to act as a revolutionizing force on the German proletariat." He objected, moreover, to peace with the German-puppet government of the Ukraine headed by Vinnichenko, but was aware that Lenin would go to that length too because the treaty compelled it. All these considerations put Trotsky at odds with Lenin. Nevertheless, he did not intend to resist the ratification of the treaty signed at Brest-Litovsk on March 3: "I will not propose that it not be ratified. I have great respect for the policy which was expressed in the signing of the peace treaty, in its ratification, and in this or that respite, even if it be of undetermined historic dimensions. Here it was shown, altogether correctly, in particular by Comrade Lenin, that war must be waged properly." To do so, Russia needed arms. "If America gives them to us we will accept them for our purposes without being apprehensive because they come from imperialists. We studied this matter with Comrade Lenin and concluded that America would give us military supplies because, naturally, that would serve her interests." The Bolsheviks would accept them to serve theirs. In the vote, Trotsky declared, he would abstain lest Lenin resign, as he had threatened. He could not contemplate such a split or contribute to it.[16]

(In fact, it was Trotsky who resigned. He had asserted on February 24 that he wished to withdraw as Commissar for Foreign Affairs, but Lenin persuaded him to stay, at least not to release the news of his retirement from the post. The information was made public on March 16, 1918, and the same decree announced Trotsky's appointment as "People's Commissar for Army and Navy Affairs.")[17]

∞∞∞∞∞∞∞

Anyone familiar with recent decades of Soviet history would assume that the affirmative decision of the Seventh Party Congress was Lenin's last hurdle in his race to ratify the peace treaty with Germany. But 1918 antedated the iron age, and the ice age, when the central Soviet government and

---

[14] L. Trotsky, *Sochineniya*, Vol. XVIII, p. 114.
[15] *Ibid.*, p. 115.
[16] *Ibid.*, pp. 137-140.
[17] *Ibid.*, editorial note, pp. 675-676.

the local soviets were rubber stamps for communist party fiats. The Sovnarkom (Cabinet) still included Left Social Revolutionaries, and the Fourth Extraordinary All-Russian Congress of Soviets, convened hastily on March 14, 1918, in Moscow's big, long, crystal-chandeliered Hall of the Nobles (now House of the Trade Unions) to vote on treaty ratification, consisted of 795 Bolsheviks, 284 Left SR's, 14 anarchists, 3 Ukrainian SR's, 24 Maximalists, 29 Center SR's, 11 Menshevik-Internationalists, 6 United Mensheviks, 21 no-adjective Mensheviks, and 17 nonparty delegates.[18] The Bolsheviks enjoyed a clear majority. The Left SR's, however, were now as adamantly anti-treaty as the Left Communists, and together, or separately, they could make more trouble than their numerical representation in the congress indicated. The Left SR's, in particular, had strong peasant support and strong terrorist proclivities. The Mensheviks and anarchists also were anti-treaty. At stake, accordingly, was the peace treaty and the fate of the soviets. If the parties opposed to the treaty seceded from the soviets, Lenin might gain what he bargained for and more: monopoly control of the soviets and, in consequence, mounting mass and class hostility. The Russian bourgeoisie, too, had not yet been crushed.

This Soviet congress and its aftermath were, in fact, a watershed in Soviet history.

The congress met against diplomatic background noises made by Lockhart, Robins, and Sadoul consulting with Lenin and Trotsky, with their home governments, with their friends hibernating in Vologda. The three optimistic intermediaries tirelessly appealed to harried foreign ministers and others to check Japanese intervention and try, with promises of arms and food, to win the Bolsheviks for war against Germany. The summit of their achievements and the end of their hopes was a telegram addressed by President Woodrow Wilson to the Soviet Congress: "May I take advantage of the meeting of the Congress of the Soviets to express the sincere sympathy which the people of the United States feel for the Russian people at this moment when the German power has been thrust in to interrupt and turn back the whole struggle for freedom and substitute the wishes of Germany for the purposes of the people of Russia. Although the Government of the United States is unhappily not now in a position to render the direct and effective aid it would wish to render, I beg to assure the people of Russia through the Congress that it will avail itself of every opportunity to secure for Russia once more complete sovereignty and independence in her own affairs and full restoration to her great role in the life of Europe and the modern world. The whole heart of the people of the United States is with the people of Russia in the attempt to free themselves forever from autocratic government and become the masters of their own life."[19]

Russians are enormously skillful at shelling sunflower seeds with their

---

[18] Lenin, op. cit., editorial note, p. 618.
[19] Papers Relating to the Foreign Relations of the United States. 1918. Russia, Vol. I, pp. 395-396.

teeth. The congress delegates quickly got to the kernel of Wilson's message: "the Government of the United States is unhappily not now in a position to render . . . aid." They could therefore indulge their true and insulting sentiments. President Sverdlov accordingly read the resolution, drafted by Lenin, in reply to Wilson: "The Russian Socialist Federative Republic of Soviets takes advantage of President Wilson's communication to express to all peoples perishing and suffering from the horrors of imperialist war its warm sympathy and firm belief that the happy time is not far distant when the laboring masses of all countries will throw off the yoke of capitalism and will establish a socialist state of society, which alone is capable of securing just and lasting peace as well as the culture and well-being of all laboring people."[20]

The applause which greeted the reading was taken by Sverdlov to indicate "that you all join in this resolution." Undisturbed now by diplomatic rustle off stage, the delegates settled down to the business before them.

The bigger the audience the broader the invitation to demagogy. Facing twelve hundred delegates instead of forty-six, Lenin repeated the arguments he had made to the party congress but added a touch of intelligentsia-denigration and a dash of bourgeoisie-baiting. Several times he sneered at the intellectuals who opposed him, though he was an intellectual himself— certainly not a peasant or worker, and seemed to suggest that whereas the villager and proletarian made judgments on the basis of common sense (it is better to run away when you are outnumbered; you cannot fight without arms), the intellectuals' values were impractical: they would face odds and annihilation to preserve the purity of their ideological concepts and because they thought their cause just. He reminded the intellectuals that it was the Russian capitalists who were inciting the Soviet regime to go to war against Germany; "That is required by the class interests of the bourgeoisie." Here was a shrewd sample of guilt-by-association wrapped in sly dialectics. The left had gone so far to the left that they found themselves on the right, in the company of the class enemy. He understood the Russian bourgeoisie; "it filled the columns of its counter-revolutionary newspapers."

"You have closed down all of them," a voice interrupted.[21]

"As yet, unfortunately, not all," Lenin replied. "I should like to see the proletariat that permits counter-revolutionaries, supporters of the bourgeoisie, and those who agree with it, to continue exploiting their monopoly of wealth to drug the people with bourgeois opium. There has never been such a proletariat."

In the Ukraine the bourgeoisie had made common cause with the Germans in order to topple the soviets. The Russian bourgeois aim was the same. This illumined the "depth of error of those who, like the party of Left Social Revolutionaries,"—not to mention the Left Communists—"allowed

[20] *Ibid.*, pp. 339-400.
[21] In the official stenographer's record of Lenin's speech, Lenin, *op. cit.*, pp. 388-402.

themselves to be captivated by a theory half desperation and half phrases, a usual thing in difficult moments in the history of all revolutions when, instead of eyeing reality soberly, . . . a serious, grave question is decided under the pressure of feelings, only from the point of view of feelings."

And again he held out the hope of salvation: ". . . we know, that somehow or other Liebknecht will be victorious, that is inevitable in the evolution of the workers' movement." Meanwhile, a breathing spell, etc.

The discussion which followed Lenin's address was not of a high order. Julius Martov, the leader of the Mensheviks, said Lenin wanted to sell them, in effect, a pig in a poke and no peasant at a county fair would buy it. There was a time, he continued, when "smart land officers forced peasants to sign such documents which delivered them into thirty years of peonage."

Kamkov, speaking for the Left SR's, asked how long a breathing spell the peace treaty would give them. His party could accept no responsibility for such a treaty. He called the Bolsheviks "salesmen of German imperialism."

Lenin gave notice that he would not reply to harsh words. But he did. He called the Mensheviks "stooges of the bourgeoisie." He furiously assailed the Left SR's. He denied they had a peasant following: "Among the peasantry they are the same soap bubble they proved to be among workers." On the one hand, the Left SR's "make eyes at us and on the other hand they appeal to the Kadets"—the bourgeois party, and say, "Reckon on us, you see, we are with you in spirit."

"That's a lie," delegates exclaimed.

The Fourth Extraordinary Congress of Workers, Soldiers, Peasants, and Cossacks—the official designation of the congress, decided to ratify the Brest-Litovsk peace treaty by a vote of 784 for and 261 against; 115 abstained, among them 64 Left Communists. Thereupon, the Left SR's resigned from the Sovnarkom. Lenin's speech had practically read them out of the government. He may never have wanted them in except for temporary, tactical reasons. He had not given them important Cabinet posts. He did not trust them.

The Left SR's proceeded to take drastic measures against the peace treaty and against the Soviet government.

XV. A MURDER IN MOSCOW

DURING the negotiations at Brest-Litovsk, Count Wilhelm Mirbach, who had served in the German embassy in Russia before the war, was in Petrograd to exchange civilian and military prisoners. He left Petrograd on February 18 and on February 23 reported to the Kaiser at army headquarters. After treaty ratification, Mirbach returned to Russia and on April 26, 1918, presented his credentials to President Sverdlov. Officially he was minister; some called him ambassador.

In Moscow, Mirbach did what tourists and other newcomers do; he walked through the streets, drove through the streets, and made notes. But his notes went to the German Kaiser, who made comments.

"In the hands of the Bolsheviks," Mirbach reported on April 30,[1] "Moscow, the sacred city, the embodiment of the power of the Tsars, the high place of the Orthodox Church, represents what is perhaps the most glaring destruction of taste and style that has resulted from the Russian revolution."

The Kaiser wrote in the margin, "This is not our concern; the world war is also lacking in style."

"Anyone who knew the capital in the days of its glory," Mirbach continued, "would hardly be able to recognize it now." He elaborated, and ventured into sociology: "There is seething activity in the streets, but they seem to be exclusively populated by the proletariat. Hardly any better-dressed people are to be seen—as if the whole of the previous governing class and the bourgeoisie had disappeared from the face of the earth. This may be partly connected with the fact that most of them are trying to conform externally . . . so as not to inflame the lust for loot and the unpredictable temper of the class which now rules the city. . . . Hardly anything can be bought in the shops except dusty remnants of past splendour, and these only at fantastic prices. The hallmarks of the whole picture are general unwillingness to work and aimless loafing."

The Kaiser: "The hallmark of the 'Social state of the Future.' "

"Russia," Mirbach added, "seems to be heading for an even worse catastrophe than that already produced by the revolution. Public safety leaves much to be desired." This last sentence could be his epitaph.

"The despair of the old governing classes," Mirbach confided, "is boundless, but they can no longer raise sufficient strength to put an end to the organized looting which is now prevalent."

The Kaiser remarked, "This will have to come from the outside."

"The cry for organized conditions," Mirbach said, "reaches down to the lowest strata of the people, and the feeling of their impotence makes them hope for salvation from Germany."

The modest Kaiser wrote, "Either England or America or *we* (indirectly through Russian generals)."

On May 16, 1918, Count Mirbach had "a fairly long discussion with Lenin about the overall situation," and summarized its contents for the German Chancellor. The Chancellor forwarded the document to the Kaiser,

[1] *Germany and the Revolution in Russia, 1915-1918*, Documents from the Archives of the German Foreign Ministry, edited by Z. A. B. Zeman (London, 1958), pp. 120-121.

who contributed his customary marginalia.[2] Lenin, in Mirbach's quaint phraseology, "trusts his lucky star with the utmost conviction and repeatedly expresses the most boundless optimism in an almost overpowering way." The Russian leader did admit, however, that "the number of his opponents has increased." The situation, he quoted Lenin as asserting, "demands intenser vigilance than it did a month ago." Indeed, Lenin told the German that "his opponents are no longer to be found exclusively among the parties on the right, but that they are now also being recruited in his own camp, where a kind of left wing has formed." These dissenters complained, the German reported, that the Brest treaty, "which he"—Lenin—"is still determined to defend with the utmost tenacity, was a mistake. More and more Russian territory was being occupied." Lenin wanted peace treaties with Finland and the Ukraine and requested German mediation toward that end.

"Not that Lenin spoke plaintively or querulously," Mirbach stressed in his last paragraph, "nor did he insinuate in any way that . . . he might be forced to turn back towards the other power. However, he was quite apparently concerned to describe the awkwardness of his position as graphically as possible."

The Kaiser: "He is finished."

The same day Mirbach telegraphed the German Foreign Ministry that the Western Entente was spending large sums of money bribing Russian regiments and warship crews and financing Right SR's. "I am still trying to counter efforts of the Entente and support the Bolsheviks," Mirbach stated. "However, I would be grateful for instructions as to whether overall situation justifies use of larger sums in our interests if necessary, and as to what trend to support in the event of Bolsheviks being incapable of holding out. If Bolsheviks fall . . . Entente has best prospects."[3]

This dispatch was received at the Wilhelmstrasse on May 18. Within a few hours Kuehlmann wired, "Please use larger sums, as it is greatly in our interests that Bolsheviks survive. . . . If further money required, please telegraph how much." Kuehlmann then ran through the possibilities if the Bolsheviks collapsed: the Left SR's "would fall with Bolsheviks," he assumed. The bourgeois Kadet party "are anti-German." Also, "We have no interest in supporting Monarchists' ideas, which would reunite Russia. On the contrary, we must try to prevent Russian consolidation as far as possible and, from this point of view, we must therefore support the parties furthest to the left."[4] This was the logic of the German monarchy's league with radicalism.

The Kaiser believed Lenin was finished, yet the Kaiser's Kuehlmann ordered the Kaiser's envoy in Moscow to give the Bolsheviks millions. The split personality of governments is never so evident as in wartime when unity is most necessary. In crises, moreover, diplomatic journalism sinks to low levels. Thus, Herr K. Riezler, counselor of the German Legation in

[2] *Ibid.*, pp. 126-127.
[3] *Ibid.*, p. 128.
[4] *Ibid.*, pp. 128-129.

Moscow, reported to the Wilhelmstrasse on June 4, 1918, that "The Bolsheviks are extremely nervous and can feel their end approaching, and all the rats are therefore beginning to leave the sinking ship. . . . Karakhan [Assistant Commissar for Foreign Affairs] has put the original of the treaty of Brest ready in his desk. He intends to take the document with him to America and to sell it, with the Emperor's signature on it, to the highest bidder."[5] (One wonders what Mr. Riezler paid for that piece of gutter gossip.)

Now General Ludendorff entered the act. The quartermaster general had enough to do. The great German offensive which was to carry Germany westward to victory, opened on March 21, 1918. An enormous artillery barrage and a colossal concentration of troops enabled the Germans to take considerable territory. But by the end of April the British, French, and American armies stemmed the advance. Ludendorff and Hindenburg studied their weaknesses ("certain divisions had obviously failed to show any inclination to attack"; soldiers at the front "showed poor discipline"; "The absence of our old peace-trained corps of officers"—killed in the war—"was most severely felt"),[6] regrouped their forces, brought up reserves, and launched another major attack on May 27. It succeeded but stopped for breath a few days later. The German military machine was commencing to falter. "The fighting took us forward into the trench system which we had abandoned in March, 1917," Ludendorff wrote.[7] This he booked as a triumph. He planned to renew the costly offensive on June 7 and postponed it because of insufficient artillery preparation. It began on June 9 but immediately met more Allied resistance and stronger counterattacks. Yet on June 9 Ludendorff had the peace of mind to pen a long memorandum for Kuehlmann on the Russian situation.[8]

Owing to manpower shortage, Ludendorff observed, "we have had to weaken our divisions there"—on the eastern front—"still further." What remained sufficed if no trouble erupted. ". . . because of the obscure policy of the weak Soviet government, we must look around for other allies in the East. In the North we have Finland, which has strengthened its military position as a result of our entry." He hoped to "find strong military support there."

Glancing southward he saw the Ukraine, "essential to our survival and to our supply of raw materials," but no Ukrainian army. Hence "we are justified in using our troops." Farther south, in Georgia, "we must organize a Georgian army. . . . An ethical point should be taken into consideration in this case; Georgia is a Christian state." Like Germany. "Georgia's recognition and protection will at the same time give Georgia security against the greedy Turks"—who were Germany's allies. On the other hand, "I should like to stress that Turkey must be taken into account and that we must, to a certain

[5] *Ibid.*, pp. 130-131.

[6] Erich von Ludendorff, *Ludendorff's Own Story, August 1914-November 1918*, Vol. II (New York and London, 1919), p. 245.

[7] *Ibid.*, p. 271.

[8] *Germany and the Revolution in Russia*, pp. 134-136.

extent, regard its wishes." However, "We should not forego running the Tiflis-Baku line under German control. There the Turks will have to give way to us. Also Baku should not be ceded to the Turks." Baku was the great oilfield, and the Tiflis-Baku railroad carried its oil to the refineries and tankers at Batum. German cities were dark, German airplanes flying fewer sorties because of petroleum deficiency. Therefore the infidel Turks would be kept out of Moslem Baku. Germany's Christian ethics floated on oil.

Finland and Georgia, Ludendorff knew, could not furnish much manpower; they were small countries. "We also have to enter into contact with the Caucasian Cossack tribes, which are trying to elude the grasp of the Soviet government."

So much for military matters. But war is high politics. Ludendorff accordingly presumed to instruct State Secretary Kuehlmann. In the political field, the general wrote, "I regard the dishonourable endeavours of the Soviet government with the gravest distrust. . . . We can expect nothing from this government although it lives by our mercy. It is a lasting danger to us which will diminish only when it recognizes us unconditionally as the supreme Power and becomes pliable through its fear of Germany and concern for its own existence. Therefore a strong and ruthless treatment of this government appears to me still to be indicated."

His ruthlessness implied deviousness: "Though we now negotiate officially only with the Soviet government, we should at the same time entertain relations with other movements in Russia. . . . We cannot rely on Kerensky's partisans, because they are dominated by the Entente. . . . We have to acquire contacts with the right-wing monarchist groups and influence them so that the monarchist movement would be influenced by our wishes."

In May, Kuehlmann told Mirbach to support the Russian communists; in June, Ludendorff told Kuehlmann to support the Russian monarchists. In 1917, Ludendorff introduced Lenin into Russia to overthrow Kerensky. In 1918, he hoped to strangle Lenin. Governing is not a science, it is an art, a complicated art, and Ludendorff was a mediocre artist.

Meanwhile, General Max Hoffmann chafed in the east. Problems besieged him. "Endless trouble with the Austrians in the Ukraine," read his diary entry for March 13, 1918. "They want to enter Odessa alone, and are behaving with their usual meanness when the knife is not at their throat."[9]

MARCH 14. "It almost looks as if not . . ." that is, as if the Russians will not ratify the Brest peace treaty. "In that case we must, of course, take Petersburg. . . . I am having the most frantic trouble with the Austrians in the Ukraine. It is a pity that the Italians do not attack"—attack the Austrians. The Italians were the enemy; Austria the ally. "One can deal with the Austrians only when they are in difficulties."

MARCH 21. "Much trouble with the Lithuanian government. . . . These people want to go back on their resolution of December by which, in return

---

[9] Major-General Max Hoffmann, *War Diaries and Other Papers*, Vol. I (London, 1929), p. 210. Subsequent entries from subsequent pages.

for their independence, they bound themselves to a close association with Germany." Independence? Self-determination à la Hoffmann.

MARCH 23. Two Germans visited Hoffmann, one a "German clergyman representing the German colonists [settlers] in South Russia and the Crimea. The cleryman talked a good deal about the right of self-determination, and, on this ground, suggested the union of the Tartars of the Crimea and the German colonists, thus combining the Crimea and the adjoining provinces into a German colony. I told him I had no objection." More self-determination à la Hoffmann.

APRIL 3. "There is further advance in the West, and they all seem confident. . . . Everything and everybody (even from the Staff) that could be spared has been shifted to the West. I often think that it is really a pity that Hindenburg and Ludendorff did not get me a Division. The command of a Division in the West at present would, anyway, be much more interesting and offer much better prospects than my dead post here."

APRIL 4. "We have now occupied the whole of the Crimea, and on the East we have nearly reached the boundary of the Ukraine. . . . Our operations in the Caucasus area were also conditioned by our needs in regard to war material. We had accordingly to get control of Baku and the Baku-Tiflis-Batum railway."

APRIL 26. "In the Ukraine the situation is coming to a head. The Government is making further difficulties, and I am afraid we shall have to look for another."

APRIL 30. "From the political point of view the chief event is that the Ukrainians have at last overthrown their Government." The "Ukrainians" were the Germans. "They have summoned a General to be Hetman of the Ukraine and Dictator. As this gentleman stands by the Brest-Litovsk Peace and other agreements regarding the delivery of corn, etc., this is very likely to our advantage." The gentleman was Hetman Skoropadsky, former tsarist general.

MAY 2. "The Don Cossacks have telegraphed to the German Emperor, asking him to help them against the Bolsheviks. . . . They are quite fond of us now."

MAY 6. "The efforts of G.H.Q."—Ludendorff—"and Eichhorn"—Field Marshal von Eichhorn, German commander in the Ukraine—"are, though they do not know it, driving the Ukraine back into the arms of Great Russia."

MAY 25. "I should have no objection to pushing farther and farther eastwards—I should like to get to India, except that the distances grow more immense, and our army does not."

JUNE 4. "I have an impression that in the West our advance has gradually come to a stand on the Rheims-Soisson line . . . if I were Ludendorff—"

JUNE 5. "There has been all manner of fighting in the Ukraine in the last few days."

JUNE 26. "Kuehlmann has made an ill-advised speech. I assume that he will probably disappear." He did; he resigned. He had sinned by discussing the improbability of military victory and the necessity of peace talks.

JULY 3. "According to our representatives in Russia, the days of the Bolsheviks are numbered." The days of "our" chief representative in Russia, Count Wilhelm von Mirbach, were numbered. He was murdered on July 6.

At three o'clock on the afternoon of July 6, 1918, two Russians, Y. Blumkin and N. Andreyev, appeared at the residence of Mirbach on Denezhny Pereulok (Lane). To the nine Lettish guards who were under personal instructions from Lenin to protect the ornate villa, once a merchant's home, Blumkin and Andreyev showed a pass signed by Felix Djerzhinsky, chief of the Cheka (All-Russian Extraordinary Commission for the Struggle against Counterrevolution). Blumkin and Andreyev were high Cheka officers. They had forged Djerzhinsky's signature. The Cheka stamp on the pass was put there by Alexandrovsky, Djerzhinsky's deputy, a Left SR. Blumkin and Andreyev were Left SR's. Herr Riezler, counselor of the German legation, received them, but they insisted on seeing Count Mirbach; they said the Cheka had arrested a German spy named R. Mirbach. Ushered into the minister's ground-floor office, Blumkin walked over to Mirbach, drew a small revolver, and fired point-blank. Thereupon Blumkin and Andreyev rushed to the open floor-to-ceiling window, but before jumping Blumkin tossed a hand grenade at the dying German. In leaping, Blumkin broke a leg. Both assassins escaped in a waiting auto, first to the Cheka building, then to the headquarters of the Popov Battalion. Popov too was an important Cheka official and a Left SR. He had several hundred men under his command.

The moment Djerzhinsky heard of the murder he drove with Karakhan to Denezhny Pereulok and then to the Popov headquarters, where he was joined by M. Y. Latsis, his first assistant, a Latvian, a former teacher. They demanded the surrender of the assassins. The Left SR's said they could search for them. Djerzhinsky and Latsis went from room to room breaking down doors, and when they failed to find their quarry, they threatened to arrest the Left SR's present. Instead, the Left SR's "temporarily detained" them in the cellar of the building.[10]

The death of the diplomat was the prearranged signal for a Left SR's insurrection designed to smash the Bolshevik government and precipitate war against Germany.

The peace treaty had been ratified, but few were satisfied, not even Lenin. Chicherin defined Kaiser policy after ratification as "gradual encroachment

[10] My account of the Mirbach murder and the Left SR revolt is pieced together from Lockhart's *British Agent*; Lenin, *Sochineniya*, Second ed., Vol. XXIII, pp. 554-555; and, chiefly, from *Krasnaya Kniga (Red Book)*, published by the Cheka in Moscow in 1919 and immediately withdrawn from circulation. In 1928 Vorobyov, the meticulous librarian of the Commissariat of Foreign Affairs in Moscow, permitted me to read it and make notes.

and infiltration" by the German army into "the depths of Russia." Early in April, Chicherin reported later, the German advance "reached the provinces of Great Russia." On April 26—the day Count Mirbach handed his credentials to President Sverdlov—German troops, Chicherin declared, "were moving further toward the north, advancing on Orel, Kursk, and Voronezh." From there they menaced Moscow. "The whole of May"—again according to Chicherin—"was an extremely unsettled time, owing to the gradual movements to the north and northeast, partly of German troops and partly of irregular bands supported by the former. But the main blows of the Germans at this time were directed toward the southeast . . . in the direction of the grain-producing Kuban." In the same period the Turkish army, "disregarding the treaties, were advancing in the Caucasus and were supporting there the fictitious counter-revolutionary governments." Most important "the boiling volcano of the Ukraine, surcharged with rebellion,"[11] continued to spew sparks into Moscow politics. Instead of Trotsky's No-war, No-peace, the Bolsheviks now had war and peace. Lenin's policy of peace for survival at any ideological price was being nullified by German political perfidy and military activity. The Left SR's, who had strong ties with the Ukraine, fumed. The communist party was in disarray.

The situation became even more desperate as a result of the rising tide of Allies intervention: by the Japanese, the Czechoslovaks, and others.

Narodnik and nihilist plotting against tsarism was an enraged protest against impotence. Facing overwhelming autocratic might, the individual terrorist with hidden bomb or Browning was power, an elusive, frightening power. He answered the tyranny of the state with the tyranny of terror. His strength lay in fearlessness. He bought the death of others with his own. The Left SR conspirators were gambling Samsons; they would topple the temple and entice the imperialists of both camps to fight in the ruins and perish. They would die, but so would the Philistines—and Lenin. Or, depending on the turn of the wheel, they would live and he would die.

The good politician is a good psychologist. Lenin knew the Russian: he can live for a long time on a diet of hope. To dispel the encroaching gloom that bred terror, Lenin spread optimism—not biological or evangelical optimism; that was alien to him. He found optimism in Marxism.

Lenin explained[12] that "the very deepest roots of the foreign as well as domestic policy of our state are formed by the economic interests, the economic conditions of the ruling classes of our state. These propositions, which are the foundation of the entire world outlook of Marxists . . . should not for a moment be forgotten lest we get lost in the jungle and labyrinth of diplomatic tricks—in the labyrinth sometimes even artificially created and contorted by men, classes, parties, and groups that love to or have to fish in

[11] George Chicherin, *Two Years of Soviet Policy*, pp. 6-15.
[12] Lenin, *op. cit.*, Second ed., Vol. XXIII, pp. 3-16. "Report on Foreign Policy" delivered May 14, 1918, to joint session of VTSIK and Moscow Soviet.

muddy waters." Lenin enumerated them: "the Kadets, the bourgeoisie, the landlords, and their leading yesmen—the Right SR's and Mensheviks." His silence about the Left SR's was earsplitting. He did not wish to alienate them: they could be dangerous enemies.

Russia "for the time being" remained "an oasis in the stormy sea of imperialist rapaciousness." Although it was natural for all imperialists to combine for the defense of capitalism into a union "which does not know a fatherland" and "which puts itself above the interests of the fatherland," they have not been able to do so. "Of course, this continues to be the basic economic tendency of the capitalist system" and in the end a union will emerge. But the world war had prevented its emergence. Therefore the waves of "imperialist reaction" that hurl themselves against "the little island of the socialist Soviet Republic" and that seem just on the verge of flooding it, actually break against one another.

Another capitalist contradiction was the enmity between the United States and Japan. "The crusade inaugurated against the Soviet Republic (the landing at Vladivostok and the support of Semyonov's bands) has been contained because it threatens to convert the hidden conflict between Japan and America into open war." This could change overnight "if the sacred interests of private property demand it," but for the present, these contradictions explain why Bolshevism is not submerged by imperialism. The Brest-Litovsk treaty was "the outer casing, the outer expression" of Russia's temporary ability to survive as a neutral. Nevertheless, "you know the value of treaties and of laws in the face of burning international conflicts—no more than a scrap of paper."

Lenin mentioned possibilities: Ameirca might come to terms with Japan about intervention in Russia; the Japanese bourgeoisie, now fighting Germany, might ally itself with Germany. The situation in the Far East, therefore, continued "rather unstable." But the existence of the Soviet regime stimulated workers in all countries to inhibit intervention.

Lenin was like a painter painting a dark cloud and then a silver lining, and then another black cloud and another bright lining. His picture was balanced between doom and salvation. Anything might happen, therefore the good might happen, and despair was unjustified.

In these fluid circumstances, Lenin said, the Soviet government needs to exercise "restraint and composure. I know there are, of course, wise fellows who think themselves very clever and even call themselves socialists and who insist that it was wrong to take power before revolution had erupted in all countries. . . . That is nonsense. The trials of a revolution are well-known. Having commenced with brilliant success in one country it will perhaps live through times of torment, for it is possible to succeed definitely only on a world scale and only by the joint efforts of the workingmen of all countries." Hence the necessity to "maneuver and retreat until reinforcements arrive."

After these "general propositions," Lenin said, he would pass to the concrete situation which "in the last days has created alarm and panic and enabled counter-revolutionaries to resume their subversive work against the Soviet government." Relations between Moscow and Finland, Turkey and the Ukraine, particularly the last, had grown dangerously tense. To obtain Ukranian grain and raw materials the Germans must "conquer every step" and overcome popular resistance to confiscations. Guerrilla war had commenced in the Ukraine against Germany; German troops were everywhere. No demarcation line existed between Soviet Russia and the Ukraine, or between Soviet Russia and German-held Georgia. Invasion might occur any day. Lenin was profoundly disturbed. There had been a small British landing in April in Murmansk and a Japanese landing the same month in Vladivostok. The extreme militarists had won control over German foreign policy. On May 5, the Bolshevik Central Committee adopted a resolution, drafted by Lenin,[13] to "Begin immediately the evacuation to the Urals of everything in general," to "Direct all forces to the defense of Ural-Kuznetsk region and territory against Japan as well as Germany," and to ask Mirbach to facilitate Russia's peace treaty negotiations with the Ukraine and Finland "although recognizing" that such a peace "portends new annexations."

This explains why Lenin spoke as he did on May 14. The question of war or peace, he declared in that speech, "hangs in the air." They had to mobilize their strength, slowly, because "objective circumstances offer no possibility of a summons to a universal, relentless repulse" (a world revolution). The Russian working class was weak. "Not our wish, but historic conditions, the heritage of the Tsarist regime, the flabbiness of the Russian bourgeoisie," that is what put the Russian proletariat ahead of other units of the international working class, "not because we wanted it, but because the situation required it. Nevertheless, we must remain at our posts until our ally, the international proletariat, arrives." Meanwhile, save "the oasis." Since November 7, 1917, Lenin declared, "we are defending the fatherland against the imperialists. We defend, we will win. We are for the state, we are defending not our great-power status: nothing remains of Russia except Great Russia"; the heart of Russia without the Ukraine, the Caucasus, the Baltic States, and so forth. Therefore the Bolsheviks are defending "not national interests; we declare that the interests of socialism, the interests of world socialism are higher than national interests, higher than the interests of the state. We are defenders of the socialist fatherland." Lenin was replying to charges that his motivation was Russian nationalism and the survival of the Soviet Russian state.

"My time is up," he said, "and I take the liberty of concluding with the reading of a radio telegram from Comrade Yoffe, the Soviet ambassador in Berlin." Yoffe had received assurances from the German High Command that "there would be no further advances" into Russian territory. The German government would cooperate in establishing peaceful relations between Moscow and Kiev and Moscow and Helsingfors. "The German government

[13] *Leninskii Sbornik,* Vol. XI, p. 76.

declares officially that . . . it wishes to live on peaceful terms with us, has no aggressive plans."

On this theatrical note of optimism, Lenin resumed his seat.

The speech and the climactic telegram precipitated a storm. Replying for the Left SR's, B. Kamkov demanded the denunciation of the Brest treaty and the launching of military attacks on German forces in the Ukraine. He was followed by E. Kogan-Bernstein, of the Right SR's, who called for the dismissal of "Lenin, the revolutionary without class consciousness," and the restoration of the Constituent Assembly. Julius Martov declared that his Menshevik party did not trust Lenin. Therefore he too asked that the Constituent Assembly be convoked. "Down with the dictatorship," he exclaimed as he finished. "Long Live the Republic."[14]

Lenin's policy was approved by a large majority.

The way of the propagandist is unabashed repetition. At the Moscow regional conference of the communist party on May 15, 1918, Lenin added nothing new in the debate on foreign policy, merely defending his tactic of maneuvering. However, in answer to the Left Communist attack on state capitalism—government ownership, operation, and control of industry, trade, etc., as distinguished from workers' conduct of factories under socialism— Lenin maintained that in the "painful transitional period from capitalism to socialism," large state-capitalist enterprises were the only means of putting industry on its feet. He praised the leather workers who had introduced workers' control in private shops.

The party conference voted 42 for Lenin, 9 for the Left.[15]

But on May 10, the district party conference in the important factory town of Ivanovo Voznesensk, having heard a report by Bukharin, had voted 12 against 9, with 4 abstentions, for the Left Communist policy of aggressive resistance to Germany.[16]

The Left Communists and the Left SR's could not reconcile themselves to Lenin's program of retreat, compromise, and ideological dilution. On June 14, 1918, Soviet Moscow nevertheless signed a peace treaty with the monarchist Ukrainian government; it created a bad taste in the mouths of many Bolsheviks and of non-Bolsheviks who were still members of the soviets. To Lenin, however, the treaty meant the possible elimination of one dangerous front.

Objective circumstances were far from favorable. Cut off from the bread baskets of the Ukraine and the Don-Cossack and Kuban-Cossack regions to the south, Great Russia was hungry. Lenin sent a letter to the workers of Petrograd acknowledging "the unusually grievous famine situation" in their city and also in Moscow, and many industrial centers and provinces. He referred, too, to "the debauch of speculation in grain and other food products."

[14] Lenin, *op. cit.*, Second ed., Vol. XXIII, editorial note, p. 536.
[15] *Ibid.*
[16] *Leninskii Sbornik*, Vol. XI, p. 89.

There was grain, but the rich, the kulaks (prosperous peasants), and speculators were hiding and hoarding it. "Who does not work, he shall not eat,"
Lenin quoted, and added, "How to do this?" He proposed, first, a government grain monopoly, that is, "an unconditional prohibition of all private
trade in grain and the obligatory delivery to the government of all surpluses at
a fixed price." Second, a strict accounting of all surpluses and the shipment
of such surpluses to deficit areas. Third, "correct and just" distribution of
bread among all citizens under the control of "the workers' proletarian state."

Lenin knew that opponents read his books and remembered. He accordingly answered their attacks before they made them: "It is necessary for only
a trice to consider these terms of victory over famine in order to grasp the
abyss of stupidity of the scornful anarchist twaddle which denies the necessity of state power . . . during the period of transition from capitalism to
communism and for the relief of the laborers from every form of oppression
and exploitation."[17] *The State and Revolution* lay in the museum.

Lenin urged workers organized in squads to enter the villages and bring out
the grain. The idea was condemned at a big Moscow conference. "Your
squads that go to collect grain," a speaker warned, "will get drunk and will
themselves be turned into home-brewers and robbers." Lenin admitted that
this "happened often"; the new socialist man was not made in a day. But
something had to be done. "We have no police, we will have no special
military caste, we have no apparatus other than the united class-conscious
workers."[18] The squads, consequently, were their sole arm against famine.
They were to comb the countryside for grain, split the village between poor
peasants and kulaks, organize the former into Committees of the Poor, get
information from them on hoards, bootleggers, and so forth.

The Left SR's roared with fury. Lenin was throwing the torch of class war,
civil war, into the village where the Right and Left Social Revolutionaries
found their chief popular support. The result would not be bread for the
cities but strife on the land and smaller crops.

In Petrograd, on June 20, a Right SR named Sergeyev fired six bullets into
the body of V. Volodarsky, a member of the communist party's Central
Committee and Petrograd's Commissar for Press, Propaganda, and Agitation.
Volodarsky died the same day.

This was an alarm signal. The Social Revolutionaries were seizing their
old weapon: terror. An explosion seemed imminent. The SR's were fiercely,
irrevocably opposed to Lenin's policy of peace with Germany and war with
the peasantry.

In this pent-up atmosphere, the Fifth All-Russian Congress of Worker,
Peasant, Soldier, and Red Army Deputies assembled in Moscow on July 4,
1918. There were 745 voting Bolshevik delegates, 352 Left SR's, 14 Maximalists, 4 anarchists, 4 Social Democratic Internationalists, 4 Poalei Zion,

[17] Lenin, *op. cit.*, pp. 26-31.
[18] *Ibid.*, p. 57.

1 Left Armenian, 1 Right SR, 10 non-party men. The Left SR's began the proceedings by charging the Bolsheviks with "artificially increasing the number of their representatives." This was an overture to fireworks.

In the debate on the agenda, Maria Spiridonova, Left SR leader, proposed that the Congress hear reports by delegates from the provinces on local conditions. "Our fraction," she exclaimed, "urges all those whose spines have been stung and whose necks have been cut" by the compulsory grain deliveries to vote for full information from the provinces. V. Karelin, of the Left SR's, demanded inclusion in the agenda of a motion against capital punishment, "that shameful phenomenon, heritage of Tsarism and the [Provisional government] coalition." Both suggestions were rejected.[19]

The Bolsheviks were right in denying the congress platform to reporters on countryside conditions. The non-Bolshevik newspapers were bulging with embarrassing information. The flatlands rocked with revolt. In April a party of sailors on a grain-requisitioning expedition was ambushed in the village of Tishanka, Bobrov district, by peasants organized under local soviet leadership; nineteen mounted men of the expedition were killed. In the same month four Red Guards on a similar mission were killed in the Shlykov district of Perm province. *Novaya Zhizn (New Life)*, Maxim Gorky's daily, gave details on May 18, 1918, of armed clashes in Penza province between peasant and punitive grain-procuring squads from big cities. The same paper, on June 6, reported this incident: about 300 unarmed peasants assembled at Jeshemlya station on the Northern Railway and stopped train #119 bound for Petrograd with grain. They begged for food but were shot down and bayonetted by the train guards. Scores of similar frays have been documented.[20] More fighting flared when incensed inhabitants insisted on fair soviet elections. The authorities had barred all but communist and Left SR candidates.[21]

The Fifth Soviet Congress seated in the Moscow Bolshoi Theater (Opera House), had, over Left SR protests, accepted the report of the credentials committee and drawn up the agenda. The next order of business was greetings from fraternal parties. A. Alexandrov, delegate of the Ukrainian Left SR's, who were engaged in daily armed skirmishes with German and Skoropadsky troops, mounted the rostrum and, turning to the box where Count Mirbach sat, demanded that the German diplomat be chased from Moscow. He also summoned the Soviet government to join the Ukrainian rebels' war with Germany. Trotsky, now Commissar for Military Affairs, asked to speak. He advocated "determined measures" against those who were congregating in Russo-Ukrainian border areas and agitating for war, the rupture of the Brest peace, and guerrilla attacks on Germans. The Left SR's shouted their

[19] *Ibid.*, editorial note, pp. 548-549.
[20] Raphael R. Abramovitch, *The Soviet Revolution. 1917-1939*, Introduction by Sidney Hook, p. 143 *et seq.*
[21] *Ibid.*, p. 146.

disapproval. Through the din Trotsky offered a resolution authorizing his War Commissariat to purge the army of "provocateurs and hirelings of imperialism," and establish "revolutionary order." He was answered by B. Kamkov, of the Left SR's, who called on the congress to send greetings to the military units which had broken army discipline and behaved like revolutionaries. The Left SR's thereupon left the meeting in a body and Trotsky's resolution was passed unanimously.

The next day, July 5, Maria Spiridonova spoke. Lenin, following her to the podium, characterized her speech as "extremely excited in places." He did not exaggerate. This young woman of twenty-nine was high-strung. In 1906, as a schoolgirl of seventeen, she waited with a gun in her muff on a railway-station platform, and when General Luzhensky, "pacifier" of a peasant revolt in Tambov guberniya, descended from his train, she, on party orders, fired and killed him. She then turned the revolver on herself, but Cossacks caught her, dragged her away, and raped her. She was condemned to death. The Tsar, in response to popular indignation, commuted the sentence to life imprisonment. After eleven years in Siberia, the March, 1917, revolution returned her to liberty and leadership of the Left SR's. This day, a little over a year out of foul confinement, she stood on the giant stage of the plush Moscow opera house and addressed the Fifth Congress in protest against the Bolshevik policy of goading the peasants into revolt by requisitions and sending punitive expeditions to pacify them. Clothed in simple, unadorned dress, her black hair pulled straight back, her pince-nez now on her nose, now at the tip of her gestures, she looked the typical, tense Russian rebel against tsarist autocracy.

"She is obviously nervous. Her delivery, too, is monotonous, but as she warms to her subject, she acquires a hysterical passion which is not unimpressive," wrote Bruce Lockhart, who was in one of the diplomatic boxes.

"Her attack is concentrated on the Poverty Committees." Committees of the Poor. "With pride she refers to the fact that her whole life has been dedicated to the welfare of the peasants. Keeping time to the rhythm of her sentences with an up-and-down swing of her right arm, she bitterly attacks Lenin. 'I accuse you,' she says, addressing Lenin, 'of betraying the peasants, of making use of them for your own ends and of not serving their interests.' She appeals to her followers: 'In Lenin's philosophy,' she shrieks, 'you are only dung—only manure.' Then, working herself up to a hysterical peroration, she turns on the Bolsheviks: 'Our other differences are only temporary, but on the peasant question we are prepared to give battle. When the peasants, the Bolshevik peasants, the Left Social-Revolutionary peasants, and the non-party peasants, are alike humiliated, oppressed and crushed—crushed as peasants—in my hand you will still find the same pistol, the same bomb, which once forced me to defend . . .' The end of the sentence is drowned in a wild torrent of applause. A Bolshevik delegate in the parterre hurls an indecent insult at the speaker. Pandemonium ensues. Brawny peasants stand up in their seats and shake their fists at the Bolsheviks. Trotsky pushes himself forward and tries to speak. He is howled down and his face blanches with impotent rage. In vain Sverdlov rings his bell and threatens to clear the theater. Nothing seems more certain than that he will have to carry out his threat. Then Lenin walks slowly to the front of the stage. On the way he pats Sverdlov on the shoulder and tells him to put his bell away. Holding the lapels of his coat, he faces his audience—smiling, supremely self-confident. He is met with jeers and cat-calls. He laughs good-humoredly. Then he holds up his hand, and with a last rumble the tumult dies."[22]

He could well be calm. The opera house was guarded by trusted armed communists. Inside, 745 Bolshevik delegates could outvote, outshout, and outfight less than 400 opponents. At a party caucus on the eve of the Fifth Congress, the Left Communists, denying rumors they would support the Left SR's, threw in their lot with Lenin. Above all, he felt certain of the strength of his arguments. He came to the point immediately. After a four-word reference to the tone of Miss Spiridonova's speech, he said the "chief factor" shaping Soviet policy, was the Brest treaty. His party had been wise in signing it; they had achieved a breathing spell with the result that "the peasant and the proletariat who do not exploit others, who do not profit from the people's hunger, are entirely and undoubtedly on our side, and, in any case, against those fools who would drag us into war, who are opposed to the Brest treaty."

"Uproar," reads the official stenographic record.[23]

"Nine-tenths are for us," Lenin persisted. While each of the imperialist camps was "stronger than we," "while Russia had not sufficiently recuperated to build a new kind of disciplined army . . ."

Shouts of "Kerensky" from the Left SR's. Lenin continued to attack the kulaks and those who shielded them. "Yes, comrades, whoever . . . shouts against the Brest noose does not see that the noose around the necks of the workers and peasants in Russia was put there by Kerensky, the landlords, the capitalists, and the kulaks."

A delegate yelled, "Mirbach." More "uproar."

"I am not at all surprised," Lenin commented, "that in the situation in which these people find themselves nothing remains but to reply with shouts, hysterics, curses, and wild attacks when there are no other arguments."

From the audience: "We have arguments." "Uproar," the record reads.

"Ninety-nine percent of the soldiers know what it cost in unbelievable suffering to end the war," Lenin continued. "They know that in order to wage war on a new socialist and economic base . . ."

"Mirbach will not permit that," roared a Left SR.

Lenin repeated his prescriptions: wait, prepare. The people would not fight the imperialists now, he declared. In passing, Lenin paid a compliment

[22] R. H. Bruce Lockhart, *British Agent*, with an Introduction by Hugh Walpole, (New York and London, 1933), pp. 295-296.

[23] Lenin, *op. cit.*, pp. 115-132.

to Trotsky for informing the world's workers from Brest that Russia wanted a democratic peace which the capitalists rejected. Having once criticized Trotsky, he now poured balm on Trotsky's wound. But he flayed the Left SR's: when the Bolsheviks asked them to join in the revolution before November 7, 1917, they refused. They took positions in the Cabinet only later, when the successful revolution was in office.

The Left SR's made so much noise at this point that he had to interrupt his speech. Yes, Lenin said when he was able to resume, "Truth pierces the eye." More interruptions. Lenin reminded them that the Bolshevik majority had not interfered with Maria Spiridonova's address. His political intuition told him something was in the making. He expressed a suspicion: "If these people prefer to bolt from the Congress the road is paved." But these people had other plans.

Again the old theme: "To talk now of the Brest noose means to throw the landlord's noose back on the peasant's neck." The Soviet government was of course making mistakes. Socialism had passed "from the area of dogma . . . to the area of practical work." The hands of the workers and peasants were "making socialism." They were inexperienced. "For Russia the time is gone, irrevocably gone, I am sure, when people debate socialist programs according to the books." Prerevolutionary speculations about postrevolutionary practice were obsolete, impractical. "We still do not know the socialism which can be put into the paragraphs" of a decree or constitution. Hence the need for discipline with patience. If, because of the Committees of the Poor, "our former comrades, the Left SR's, in all sincerity, which cannot be doubted, say, Our ways have parted, then we firmly reply, The worse for you, because that means you have abandoned socialism."

As to the death sentence: "I should like to see that people's court, that workers' or peasants' court, that wouldn't shoot Krasnov"—a tsarist general fighting the Bolsheviks in the south—"who is shooting workers and peasants. We are told that when the commission of Djerzhinsky"—the Cheka—"executes it is all right, but when a court, openly, before the eyes of the nation, declares, He is a counter-revolutionary and deserves to be shot, that is bad. People who have become so hypocritical are politically dead." ("Applause") "No, a revolutionary who doesn't want to be a hypocrite, cannot reject capital punishment. There has been no revolution, no epoch of civil war, in which there were no executions."

The Bolsheviks gave him a stormy ovation. The Left SR's sat on their hands.

The next day their hands murdered Mirbach.

Kamkov, the Left SR who succeeded Lenin at the rostrum, released a fury. He predicted that the Bolshevik Committees of the Poor and workers' requisitioning squads would be "tossed out of the villages by the scruff of the neck." The squads consisted, he said, "not of the best, class-conscious workingmen but of those who wish to rob the village." Under Lenin, "dictatorship of the proletariat has developed into the dictatorship of Mirbach." The Bolsheviks were "not an independent power but the lackeys of the German imperialists who have the audacity to show their faces in this theater."

The Left SR's rose and turned to the box where the German sat. "Down with Mirbach," they yelled. "Away with the German butchers. Away with the hangman's noose of Brest." Sverdlov had to adjourn the session until the following afternoon, Saturday.

Saturday afternoon, Blumkin killed Mirbach.

ოოოოოოოო

Immediately after the assassination, Left SR's, operating from their staff headquarters in the Morozov Palace on Triokhsvyatitelsky Pereulok, shelled the Kremlin, seized the Moscow Central Post Office and ordered two telegrams sent throughout the length and breadth of Russia: one, about the death by assassination of Mirbach; the second: "Stop all telegrams signed by Lenin, Trotsky, Sverdlov . . ." Left SR patrols captured a section of Moscow, blocked the streets, and arrested Bolshevik officials in government automobiles. Among those held was the President of the Moscow Soviet, Smidovich. According to Trotsky's statement to the Fifth Soviet Congress on July 10, the Left SR's disposed of artillery, hand grenades, and "from 800 to 2,000 soldiers." They had ordered their members in Petrograd and Vitebsk to come to Moscow. General M. A. Muraviov, defender of Petrograd against Kerensky and Krasnov, former Soviet commander in the Ukraine, now Soviet army commander on the Volga, undertook to march on Moscow to aid the Left SR's.

Trotsky was in charge of suppressing the revolt. He brought in two Latvian battalions from the outskirts of Moscow and laid siege to the Morozov Palace. The Central Post Office was retaken. By 2 A.M. on July 7 the revolt had been liquidated. An extra edition of *Pravda* on July 8 printed Lenin's assertion that Left SR's were fleeing the capital. This news reached General Muraviov on July 11 in Simbirsk. He committed suicide by shooting himself in the presence of the town soviet.

"I organized the Mirbach affair from the beginning to the end," Maria Spiridonova stated during her cross-examination in the Cheka on July 10. "We adopted a resolution on the necessity of assassinating Count Mirbach as part of a plan we had accepted of annulling the Brest treaty of peace."[24]

Her words rang true. This was the avowed program of the Left SR's. This was still the period of honesty. It produced a remarkable letter printed in *Pravda* of July 8, from Djerzhinsky to the Sovnarkom: "Since I am one of the chief witnesses in the case of the murder of the German ambassador, Count Mirbach, I do not consider it possible for me to remain in the All-Russian Cheka for the Struggle Against Counter-Revolution." He could not, he wrote, remain its chief or participate in its work. He could not, in other words, be prosecutor, judge, and witness. Such fine ethical considerations soon vanished under the blows of Soviet reality; before long Djerzhinsky resumed his labors above the death dungeons of Lubyanka Square.

[24] *Krasnaya Kniga*, p. 200.

Late in 1918 Lenin attempted a retrospective analysis of the Left SR
revolt on the occasion of the death of P. P. Proshyan, a Left SR who served
as Commissar of Post and Telegraph in the short-lived Bolshevik-Left SR
coalition cabinet. He had had a good opportunity, Lenin declared, to become
acquainted with Proshyan. Before the signing of the Brest-Litovsk peace
treaty, "it appeared that no really substantial differences remained between
us. Proshyan began to talk about the merging of our parties." Lenin was
skeptical (he believed in party purity) but welcomed Left SR collaboration
in the government. The treaty put an end to this. Yet "I must admit that I
never expected things to go so far as rebellion and the treason of Commander
in Chief Muraviov, a Left SR. But the case of Proshyan proved to me how
deeply *patriotism* had been implanted even in the most sincere and convinced socialists among the Left SR's." It was this "subjectivism of the populists that led to the fatal mistake in even the best of them who allowed
themselves to be blinded by the specter of the enormous power of German
imperialism."[25]

In 1918 patriotism and nationalism, born of the "subjectivism" Lenin so
disliked, were ideological crimes in Soviet Russia. It was patriotism, Lenin
charged, that aroused the Left SR's against the Brest-Litovsk treaty and
caused their break with the communists. But after the German revolution,
he declared in the last paragraph of the obituary, "a new rapprochement,
more stable than the earlier one, between Proshyan and communism, would
have been inescapable, but his premature death interfered."

These pithy words of Lenin are suggestive: International revolution would
dethrone patriotism; the absence of revolution enthroned it—and the "subjectivism of the populists" too. Revolution in industrial Germany would
cement the rapprochement between communists and Russian populists who
had shed their nationalism. The populists would become communists. In the
absence of a German or other revolution, communists might become patriots
and nationalists.

XVI. JOURNEY WITHOUT
A BAEDEKER

THE FIFTH All-Russian Congress of Soviets on July 9, 1918, excluded the
Left Social Revolutionaries from local, provincial, and national soviets.[1]
Since other parties had been barred earlier, this date marks the emergence

---

[25] *Pravda*, Dec. 20, 1918.

[1] *Bolshaya Sovietskaya Entsiklopedia*, Second ed., 1953, Vol. 24, pp. 403-404.
The exclusion did not take effect in all places immediately. In Baku, for instance,
the Left SR's remained in the city soviet, and several of their deputies supported the
communists in the latter part of July.

of the one-party system in Soviet Russia. The soviets became obedient instruments of the communist party.

In the same month of July, 1918, the Left SR leaders were "liquidated by the organs of the Soviet government."[2] Maria Spiridonova, Kamkov, and Karelin, the three top leaders, were among the exceptions. Kamkov escaped to Vitebsk, then to Kiev, and in both places fomented insurrections against the Germans. When the Bolsheviks occupied Kiev, they arrested him. He subsequently appeared in Berlin and edited the Left SR magazine *Znamya* (*Banner*).[3] Karelin too fled and joined the editorial staff of *Znamya* in Berlin.[4] Maria Spiridonova stayed in the Bolshoi Theater and calmly submitted to arrest by the Cheka. "In November, 1918, she was tried by the court of the Revolutionary Tribunal and sentenced to one year's imprisonment and amnestied several days later. After the amnesty she continued to prepare attacks on the Soviet government and was soon arrested again. At the present time [September, 1929] she has forsaken political activity."[5]

Blumkin, Mirbach's assassin, repented of his deed, according to Isaac Deutscher, citing *The Trotsky Archives* at Harvard University, "joined the Bolshevik party, won distinction in the civil war, and rejoined the Cheka. In the 1930's he was in sympathy with the Trotskyist opposition, but, on Trotsky's advice, continued to serve with the G.P.U. When Trotsky was an exile on Prinkipo Island, Blumkin secretly visited him there and returned to Moscow with a message from Trotsky to the opposition. Before he managed to deliver the message, however, he was arrested and shot."[6]

The Left SR revolt confirmed the collaboration between Lenin and Trotsky. Seconds after Lenin heard of the attack on Count Mirbach he telephoned Trotsky at the War Commissariat and asked him to come over. Trotsky arrived a few minutes later. Their conversation was interrupted by telephone calls giving further news. Mirbach was dead. They feared reprisals; Germany might invade. Lenin decided that he, President Sverdlov, and Foreign Commissar Chicherin visit the embassy to express their condolences.

"What ought we to say there?" Lenin wondered. "I have already talked to Radek about it. I wanted to say 'Mitleid' [sympathy] but we must say 'Beileid' [condolences]." Lenin laughed, then put on his coat and said to Sverdlov, "Let us go." "His face changed and became stone-gray. The drive to the Hohenzollern Embassy, to offer condolences over the death of Count Mirbach, was not an easy thing for Ilyich. As an inward experience it was probably one of the most difficult moments of his life."[7] But the political brain said, "Go."

[2] *Ibid.*

[3] Lenin, *Sochineniya*, Second ed., Vol. XXII, editorial note, p. 638, and Vol. XXIII, editorial note, p. 611.

[4] *Ibid.*, Vol. XXII, editorial note, p. 638.

[5] *Ibid.*, Vol. XXIII, editorial note, pp. 627-628.

[6] Isaac Deutscher, *The Prophet Armed. Trotsky: 1879-1921* (New York and London, 1954), footnote, p. 403.

[7] Trotsky, *Lenin*, pp. 156-157. In describing Lenin's emotions, Trotsky revealed his own.

All of 1918 was full of the most difficult moments in Lenin's life. Yet he never despaired. Arthur Ransome, British artist-journalist with a gentle sense of humor, said of Lenin, "He struck me as a happy man; every one of his wrinkles is a wrinkle of laughter and not of worry; the reason must be that he is the first great leader who discounts the value of personality." Lenin had wrinkles of laughter and wrinkles of premature sclerosis, and he did not worry because, though he faced a mountain of troubles, he did something about them. He was a doer. Instead of worrying he worked. He had an endless love of work and a mastery of small detail and mammoth undertakings. He shuttled from decisions on whether this military front or that should be reinforced to writing a recommendation for a needy comrade in search of an apartment in crowded Moscow. He possessed prodigious energy and spent it prodigally as if he knew he would not be there long. His vanity was minimal, a quality which no doubt created the impression that he discounted the value of personality. But he was too intelligent to discount the value of his own personality, and if he did, nobody else did, nor can history.

After Mirbach's murder the German menace subsided yet retained its fatal potential. Western intervention increased. Russian enemies of Bolshevism, abetted in many cases by foreign powers, attacked Soviet territory from every angle. If the Soviet victory in that civil war had to be put in one word it would be "Lenin"; if two words were allowed they would be "Lenin" and "Trotsky." What this means is that civilian politicians defeated tsarist Russia's best generals—Kaledin, Dutov, Krasnov, Yudenich, Wrangel, Denikin, and a host of others—and Admiral Kolchak.

Politics are a major ingredient in all civil wars. The quantity and quality of men and arms decide the issues of battles, but when battles are fought in suburbs and wheat fields rather than on a fixed front, and when citizens can therefore choose sides, the real battlefield is the mind of man, and that is where the tsarist generals lost the civil war and where Lenin won it. They stood for the past. He handed out promissory notes on the future.

But before Lenin could engage in high politics he had to begin very low and build the foundation of a new state in the smoking debris of the old. Every government is the successor to a government. The government which preceded the Soviet government vanished: soldiers, officers, officials. Lenin had to start, literally, with the doorman. On his second day in power he drafted instructions for the guard outside his office: Admit only members of the Cabinet if the attendant recognizes them; if not, demand to see their identification; all others must write their names and purpose of their visit "in two words" on a piece of paper. The attendant should bring this paper to the Chairman (Lenin) without whose permission no person is to be admitted into the office. "If nobody is in the office keep the door open in order to hear the ring of the telephone and ask one of the secretaries to answer. If somebody is in the room of the Chairman, always keep the door closed."[8]

Lenin would not have gone to the trouble of writing out these instructions

[8] *Leninskii Sbornik*, Vol. XXXV, p. 7.

if they had been unnecessary. He knew the human material available. His own nature also impelled him to deal with myriad details, and it was the good fortune of communism that he coped with them expertly, which often meant harshly. The civil servants of the Ministry of Finance went on strike when the Bolsheviks seized power. "If the strike continues in any section of the Ministry of Finance," Lenin decreed on November 12, 1917, "the chiefs of such sections will be arrested immediately."[9] On January 5, 1918, Lenin signed a proclamation conscripting men and women to clear the snow from Petrograd's streets and railway tracks. On January 16 he wrote a message to the staff of the Red Guard asking that thirty revolvers be issued to special watchmen inside the Tauride Palace where Cabinet and other meetings were held. At a Cabinet meeting in March, 1918, Lenin noticed persons present whose subjects were not then under consideration. He passed a note to the Cabinet secretary calling attention to this breach and adding, "They should be thrown out. But I record a strict reprimand against you and the other secretaries. You have been told a hundred times that persons should be invited *only* for the question that concerns them."[10]

If Lenin had had ten brains, twenty eyes, and forty hands he could have used them. Without leaving the capital, except to hunt or rest (there is no record of his having visited a front), he was everywhere. He commanded the army, managed the economy, and ran the state while constructing it from the cellar up. More than anything else, he had to win the civil war by winning popular support among workers, national minorities, and peasants. He did this with cold ruthlessness.

Examples:

In December, 1917, soon after the Bolshevik revolution, the Petrograd directorate of the mining, iron, and steel industry in the Urals was unable or unwilling to transfer money to the plants for workers' wages. The workers sent a delegate to Lenin. After fifteen minutes with the delegate, Lenin ordered Felix Djerzhinsky, chief of the Cheka, and A. G. Shlyiapnikov, Commissar of Labor, to "immediately *arrest* the management of the factories, threaten them with a (revolutionary) trial for creating a crisis in the Urals, and *confiscate* all Ural plants. Prepare a draft of the decree with all possible speed. Lenin."[11]

The Sovnarkom (Cabinet) decreed on January 1, 1918, that "capitalist-saboteurs" who threatened to create "unemployment and hunger" would be sent to the mines as slave laborers. Within days, Chief of Staff V. A. Antonov-Avseyenko in Kharkov, a large city in the Ukraine, received a complaint from workingmen that their Christmas bonus had not been paid. Antonov thereupon arrested fifteen of the biggest factory owners, locked them in second-class railway cars, and warned them that if the sum of one

[9] *Ibid.*, pp. 7-8.
[10] *Ibid.*, p. 15.
[11] Lenin, *op. cit.*, Fourth ed., Vol. 36, p. 419.

million roubles was not forthcoming in twenty-four hours the cars would be shunted to the coal mines. They paid and were released. Lenin telegraphed Antonov enthusiastic congratulations.[12] The factories were nationalized soon afterward.

Such episodes, instigated or encouraged by Lenin, were legion. His attitude was manifest in a note to all people's commissars (members of the federal Cabinet) dated August 29, 1918. He ordered: "(a) the improvement of the living conditions of the masses (raising wages for *workers*, people's teachers, and so forth) . . . (b) the participation of workers in management (the personal participation of outstanding workingmen and workers organizations, and so forth) . . . (c) the expropriation of landowners, capitalists, merchants, bankers, and so forth.

"The chief task is to demonstrate *concretely*, with facts, *exactly how* the Soviet government has taken definite steps *(the first)* toward socialism."[13]

The hand of a master was at work. For instance: The Moscow Soviet of Workers' and Soldiers' Deputies telegraphed Lenin asking him to confirm their dismissal of the Moscow governor and the appointment of a successor. Lenin wired back on November 19, 1917, "The Soviets have all power. Confirmation is not necessary. Your dismissal of one and appointment of another is law."[14]

Sincere or not, and in those early days it probably was, this action, one of many, displayed Lenin's talent as a teacher-executive, a propagandist-through-acts. It is easy to imagine the joy his telegram gave Moscow workers and soldiers: they were in charge, he was telling them; the soviet was real; they had power. This power evaporated. The soviets became a myth. But for the moment, what did the tsarist generals have to offer in exchange for Lenin's concrete championship of the workers against the employers? The generals were allies of the employers, had the same interests, associations, and social status.

Further to woo the workers Lenin enlisted them as volunteers of terror; he enabled them to wreak vengeance on those they hated. After the assassination of V. Volodarsky, a prominent Bolshevik, in Petrograd in June, 1918, Lenin was disappointed by the punitive measures. He wrote on June 28, 1918, to Zinoviev, communist boss of the city: "Only today we learned in the Central Committee that Petrograd *workers* wanted to answer the murder of Volodarsky with mass terror but that you (not you personally, the Petrograd Party Committee) restrained them.

"I resolutely protest.

"We compromise ourselves . . . *we put a brake* on the *perfectly* proper revolutionary initiative of the masses.

"That is im-poss-ible.

[12] *Ibid.*, p. 420.
[13] *Ibid.*, p. 294.
[14] *Ibid.*, p. 265.

"The terrorists"—the anti-Bolshevik terrorists—"may think we are weak sisters. This is tensest wartime. We must foster energetic action and demonstrations of mass terror against counter-revolutionaries, and especially in Petrograd whose example is decisive."[15]

The workers, however, were the element of the population easiest to woo and win. Russia's unenlightened employers normally paid the lowest possible wages and squeezed the biggest possible effort out of their work force; in this respect they had all the characteristics of the greedy rich in an under-developed country undergoing industrialization. The resulting anticapitalist sentiments of the mill and mine hands made them responsive, much of the time, to the pro-proletarian pronouncements of the Bolshevik party, particularly when, with the forceful elimination, by shrewd design, of the Mensheviks and other socialists, Lenin could now confront the workers with the stark alternative: the soviets and "dictatorship of the proletariat" or restoration of the old capitalism under absolutist tsarism.

There remained two large segments of Soviet Russia's population to court and conquer: the national minorities and the peasantry. During the First World War, Lenin stated that Great Russians constituted only 43 percent of Russia's inhabitants; 57 percent were members of ethnic or national minorities: Ukrainians, Byelorussians, Georgians, Armenians, Azerbaijani, Uzbeks, Tadjiks, Turkomans, Tartars, and many others—at least a hundred.

The civil war fronts were fluid, but generally speaking the Bolsheviks held the central Great Russian heart of the country whereas their foes operated, of necessity, in the peripheries inhabited by national minorities. The tsarist generals who dominated the anti-Bolshevik fighting camp were patriots of "undivided Russia," the same centralized Russia that had oppressed the national minorities before the revolution. In May, 1919, for instance, General N. N. Yudenich, commanding a mixed force of Russians and Estonians, approached Petrograd with a view to overthrowing the Soviets. But Yudenich was opposed to independence for Estonia. N. N. Ivanov, Minister of Public Works in Yudenich's Cabinet recorded a revealing conversation near Petrograd between himself and Yudenich. The general said, "There is no Estonia. It is a piece of Russian soil—a Russian province. The Estonian government is a gang of criminals who have seized power"—and set up a national authority in Reval—"and I will enter into no conversations with it."[16] When, therefore, a Bolshevik counteroffensive unrolled in August, 1919, the Estonians deserted and opened the front for the Reds to advance and repel Yudenich's nearly victorious thrust at Petrograd.

In the North Caucasus (southeast Russia), in the region of the Don and Kuban Cossacks, tsarist rebel generals felt solidly based because the Cossack atamans wielded special executive authority under the Tsar, and the large

---

[15] *Ibid.*, p. 275.
[16] N. N. Ivanov, *O Sobitiyakh Pod Petrogradom V 1919 godu (Events Outside Petrograd in 1919)* (Berlin, 1921), p. 16.

Cossack stanitsas, or settlements, rich in horses and livestock, enjoyed comparative prosperity. "Cossack," moreover, had become synonymous in Russian radical circles with mounted policemen of the monarchy, and the Cossacks, therefore, did not expect kindness from the revolution. In essence, the Cossacks were a conservative element and for the most part of Great Russian stock.

However, the moment the generals moved out of their natural habitat north and northwest toward Moscow, the atmosphere became less friendly.

It did not follow that the national minorities longed irresistibly for Bolshevik rule. Rather they hoped to take advantage of the chaos in central Russia and achieve independence.

Although Lenin championed "democratic centralism," which on his lips meant dictatorship from one center of authority, he took cognizance of Russia's fissiparous reality. A "Declarations to the Peoples of Russia," signed by Stalin and Lenin on November 15, 1917 (New Style), enunciated the principle of "emancipation" and announced "the equality and sovereignty of all the peoples of Russia," as well as "the right of the peoples of Russia to unhampered self-determination including secession and the establishment of independent states." Tsarist "oppression and arbitrary rule" would now "be replaced by a policy of a voluntary and honest union of the peoples of Russia."[17]

Nothing loath, taking the Bolsheviks at their written word and spurning the suggestion of union, Finland started the exodus in January, 1918; the Ukrainians, the largest national minority—some 37 million—followed suit almost immediately. Early in the same year Mensheviks created the independent Republic of Georgia—population approximately 3 million; and the Dashnaks, a nationalistic agrarian-socialist party, did likewise in Armenia. Others also seceded. Russia was falling apart at her ethnic seams.

The Fifth Congress of Soviets on July 10, 1918, approved a constitution, Bolshevism's first, which created the R.S.F.S.R. (Russian Soviet Federated Socialist Republic); in it, the territories of the numerous national minorities were to be autonomous. The minorities variously interpreted this as an invitation to return or a threat of "voluntary and honest union." In December, 1918, Latvia and Lithuania, released from German domination, set up Soviet republics which Moscow recognized as independent—"until the Congress of Soviets." Presumably the congress would induct them into the R.S.F.S.R.

The delicate national-minorities situation was exacerbated by international politics. Foreign powers fished in the seams. Germany supported Finland; Germany, then Britain, supported anti-Bolsheviks in Georgia and Azerbaijan; Russian Turkestan attracted British interest and after the exit of Germany and Austria-Hungary from the Ukraine, British and French eyes focused on that vital member of the former tsarist empire. Said Prime Minister David Lloyd George at the Guildhall on November 10, 1919: "You

[17] *Dokumenty Vneshnei Politiki SSSR*, Vol. 1, pp. 14-15.

must not imagine that I am reading from the present situation any sort of prediction that the Bolshevists are going to conquer the whole of Russia. I do not believe it. The free peasantry of the South have in their hearts a detestation of Bolshevism, and I do not believe that the Bolshevists will conquer that aversion."

The aversion existed. Lenin strained to dispel it. "For God's sake," he telegraphed on January 21, 1918, to Antonov-Avseyenko, military chief in Kharkov, "make *every* effort to *eliminate all and every* friction with the Central Executive Committee [TSIK] of Kharkov. This is *supremely important* from the point of view of the national interest. For God's sake, make peace with them and grant them *all* sovereign rights. I earnestly request you to dismiss the commissars you appointed. I very and very much hope that you will carry out this request and achieve *absolute* peace with the Kharkov TSIK. In this matter, *supreme* NATIONAL *tact* is required."[18] In other words, You, Antonov-Avseyenko, agent of Moscow, must not hurt the Ukrainians' nationalistic sensibilities by appointing commissars without consulting them.

On April 22, 1918, Lenin and Stalin telegraphed the Tashkent Congress of Turkestan Soviets: "You may be sure, comrades, that the Sovnarkom [Council of People's Commissars] will support the autonomy of your region on the basis of Soviet principles." The congress was asked to send a commission to Moscow to determine the relations "of your regional executive body to the Sovnarkom."[19]

Citizens of the national minorities, even highly placed communists among them, apparently found it difficult to believe in Lenin's nationalities' policy and in the longevity of their autonomy. Witness the July, 1921, letter sent to Lenin by S. G. Said-Galiyev, president of the TSIK of the Tartar Autonomous Soviet Socialist Republic, in effect the president of Tartaria. The president posed four questions and received four answers:

"1. Is the existence of the small autonomous republics of the RSFSR in general and of Tartaria in particular a necessity?"

Lenin replied, "Yes."

"2. If yes, for how long, or, to put it another way, until the fulfilment of what·tasks and the achievement of what purposes?"

Lenin replied, "For a long time."

"3. Is the view correct that 'the communists of the former ruling nation' —the Great Russians—'who are superior in all respects, should serve as teachers and nursemaids to the communists and laborers of the former oppressed nationalities whose name is attached to the given autonomous republics (or region or commune) and, as the latter grow, yield their places to them . . .'" [Omission in the Russian]

Lenin replied, "Not teachers and nursemaids but assistants," without

[18] Lenin, *op. cit.*, Fourth ed., Vol. 36, p. 433.
[19] *Ibid.*, p. 445.

indicating, however, whether he suspected that the Tartar president might have tongue in cheek.

"4. In all national republics, and in this case in Tartaria, among native communists (Tartars), there exist two quite distinct tendencies (groupings): one accepts the principle of class war and stimulates the further differentiation of the strata in the native population, and the other—has a touch of petty-bourgeois nationalism . . ."[Omission in the Russian]

Lenin replied: "I request exact, brief, clear references to the facts regarding 'the two tendencies.' "

Finally, President Said-Galiyev posed an unnumbered question to which Lenin returned no answer: "Is it correct that the first"—grouping—"should receive the full measure of support from the Russian Communist Party and its highest offices while the latter (to the extent that they are sincere and burn with a desire to serve the proletarian revolution and to the extent that their work is helpful) should merely be used and simultaneously educated in the spirit of pure internationalism but not preferred to the former"— grouping—"as happens of late, and not alone in Tartaria?"[20] This was a muted cry of pain, a gentle chiding: Moscow promoted petty-bourgeois nationalists among the ethnic populations—because they had more followers—and discouraged internationalistic communists. Rarely do the Soviet authorities permit such a deep peep into Lenin's strategy toward national minorities. War is war and civil war is worse, and Lenin took strength where he found it.

By and large the minorities' politicians accepted the fiction of autonomy and the important posts, however decorative, that came with it, in preference to the Tsar's irritating policy of Great Russian supremacy. Lenin attempted to lend the fiction as much reality as convenient, but this was often little indeed when armies, officers and communist officials obedient to Moscow were present and, of necessity in wartime, predominant on the territories of the national minorities. Lenin himself harbored no prejudices against the minorities, nor did his close collaborators, many of whom—Trotsky, Zinoviev, Kamenev, Rakovsky, Djerzhinsky, Sverdlov, Stalin, and so forth—belonged to racial minority groups. Lack of bias notwithstanding, however, some of these non-Great Russians (Stalin and Djerzhinsky, in particular) tried to out-Great Russian the Great Russians. Lenin once reprimanded Djerzhinsky for this zeal. Nevertheless, the Kremlin's and particularly Lenin's solicitude for the minorities was sensed on Russia's periphery although administrators on the spot were not as virtuous as remote policy-makers. The Kremlin could never be sure of the minorities' loyalty. It could be sure that they hated the White generals. This became a not inconsiderable asset. Indeed, independent Poland's fear of the "undivided Russia" mentality of the Whites probably played a decisive role in Bolshevism's victory over the generals—and, in 1920, over Poland.

[20] *Ibid.*, Said-Galiyev's letter, p. 661, editorial note. Lenin's reply, p. 499.

Every Soviet problem shriveled by comparison with the peasant problem. Of Russia's 159 million inhabitants in 1913, 18 percent lived in cities, 82 percent in villages.[21] Throughout the civil war lower middle-class and working-class unemployed (many factories had closed) tended to leave the hungry cities for food-producing farm areas. Moreover, most of the ethnic groups were overwhelmingly peasant; the Ukrainians probably 90 percent. Workers, even had they all been pro-Bolshevik, were a small minority.

In the civil war the countryside served a threefold function: it furnished most of the manpower to both sides; it supplied the armies and cities with food; it was the battlefield. The towns were the prizes; the rural areas were the fighting arenas. Victory in the internal war, therefore, would be the gift of the lowly muzhik.

Lenin had become increasingly aware of the crucial role of the peasantry in Russian politics. Before the revolution he wrote copiously about agrarian affairs. But, "I know Russia very little," he admitted to Gorky on Capri. "Simbirsk, Kazan, Petersburg, exile—and that's about all."[22] His experience of Russian village life was even more limited; as boy and teen-ager he spent summers at Kokushkino, a Volga estate of Dr. Blank, his maternal grandfather, which Lenin's mother and her sister Veretennikova, inherited. There he played with his cousins but never did any farm work. That would have been improper for the "child of landlords," as he later called himself. But he understood the political importance of the land question. When the revolution began, only peace took precedence in Lenin's mind over the peasants. After removing his wig and makeup on learning that the Winter Palace had been taken at 2 A.M. on November 8, 1917, Lenin appeared briefly before the Petrograd Soviet and went to the private apartment of V. Bonch-Bruevich, his secretary, for some sleep. There was no guard. Bonch fastened the front door with its chain, hook, and lock and loaded and cocked his revolvers. "It's our first night," he thought, "anything might happen." Lenin was given a small bedroom; Bonch lay down on a couch in another room. Lenin extinguished his light; Bonch too. Bonch was falling asleep when he heard Lenin get out of bed, switch on the electricity, and start writing. He wrote fast, scratched, and seemed to be rewriting. Early in the morning he tiptoed back to bed. He awoke several hours later and appeared in the living room fresh and smiling. "Happy first-day-of-the-revolution," he greeted the family. Breakfast over, Bonch and Lenin began walking to the Smolny Institute, headquarters of the infant Soviet state, but boarded a trolley car for the rest of the journey. "Seeing the exemplary order in the streets, Vladimir Ilyich beamed." In his pocket was the Decree on Land he had drafted in pencil during the night.[23] That evening (after the Decree on Peace had been

[21] SSSR v Tsifrakh v 1960 godu (The USSR in Figures for 1960) (Moscow, 1961), p. 65.
[22] Vospominaniya, Vol. 1, p. 381.
[23] Ibid., pp. 543-545.

adopted) he read it to the Soviet Congress which approved unanimously.

The decree "immediately abolishes landlord ownership of land without compensation." Estates, as well as uncultivated land, and land owned by churches and monasteries, with all their animals and equipment, were to be transferred to the county land committees of local soviets "until the Constituent Assembly" determined their disposition. "The land of common peasants and common Cossacks will not be confiscated." It was proposed further that when the Constituent Assembly met it would forever abolish private ownership of land and prohibit the sale, purchase, and renting of land. Peasants would enjoy the use and fruits of their nationalized plots, as would present owners of vegetable and fruit gardens in and near cities. The peasants would periodically redistribute the land in accordance with their ability to till it.

When Lenin finished reading, he said he had heard delegates shout that this was the policy of the Social Revolutionaries. "So be it," he exclaimed. ". . . Whether this is in the spirit of our [Bolshevik] program or of the Social Revolutionary program is not the essence. The essence is that the peasantry receive a firm guarantee that the landlord has vanished from the village, that the peasants themselves can decide all questions, can arrange their own lives."[24]

The peasants had already been arranging their own lives. Under the Provisional (Kerensky) government, peasants with clubs, stiffened by army deserters with rifles, drove out many landlords, sacked manor houses, and parceled out the estates. Lenin merely sanctioned a mood and a fait accompli. But land is not the only factor in land reform. The peasant, to be prosperous, also needs capital: tools, animals, money, as well as sons and skills. Despite the redistribution of land, therefore, some peasants were poor, others were relatively comfortable; some, the "middle peasants," in between. The Bolsheviks used this stratification to introduce virulent class struggles into the villages. The effect was a civil war within a civil war.

The complicated peasant situation was not as simple as it seemed. International politics added complexities. Ukrainian peasants, like many others, had seized landed estates. The treaty signed at the Brest-Litovsk conference by the Central Rada of the Ukraine with Germany and Austria-Hungary was followed by the return of landlords. The peasants blamed this on the Bolsheviks who had opposed the treaty but initiated the conference. The cold logic that the dead Rada would probably have entered into a pact with the Germanic powers in any case was too subtle. The peasant said: Bolshevism; Brest-Litovsk; land lost to landlords.

Angry with the Bolsheviks and the Rada, and subsequently with its heir, the government of Hetman Skoropadsky, peasants left home and formed marauding bands, often inspired by Left Social Revolutionaries and/or anarchists, who pillaged and killed. They did not hesitate to attack Red

[24] V. I. Lenin, *op. cit.*, Second ed., Vol. XXII, pp. 20-23.

Army detachments and, with gusto, ambush workers' squads who came from cities to fetch grain by force.

These squads needed allies within the village. They found them among the peasant poor, organized in Committees of the Poor, who, for varied reasons—envy, power drive, or intimidation by the urban invaders—joined in confiscating whatever food was available, usually in the barns, bins, and concealed pits of the better-off peasants (styled kulaks) and of the middle peasants. The civil-war-within-the-civil-war was thus envenomed. The aggrieved upper strata of the peasantry now favored the anti-Bolshevik White generals; at best they adopted an attitude of a-plague-on-both-your-houses. Or their allegiance changed with the color of the confiscators: when the Whites came to seize grain the muzhiks joined the Reds and when the Reds came for the same purpose they joined the Whites. Small wonder that in this civil-war-squared, which lasted from 1917 to 1921, villages, regions, and towns shuttled back and forth from one side to the other. No military map adequately reflected the chaos.

While Russia wallowed in this welter, Lenin and his aides had to forge a policy and push to victory. The task required almost superhuman faith and fortitude, reliance on the human frailties of the foe, and some luck. For this journey Marx was no Baedeker.

XVII. BUILDING A STATE

LENIN built his popular backing, and simultaneously he built the Soviet state, with rifle, trowel, whip, and pen. New Year's Day, 1918, he appointed Sergei Orjonekidze, a Georgian, "Extraordinary Commissar of the Ukraine." January 5, he wrote a letter to a soldiers' congress on the urgency of organizing a Red Army. January 14, he received the diplomatic corps. In the afternoon he presided over a session of the Cabinet and then delivered a speech at the departure of the first echelon of Red Army men for the front. Returning, his car was fired on but he remained unscathed. That week he prepared the political ground for the dissolution of the Constituent Assembly and wrote the ukase dissolving it. Meanwhile he was in touch with Trotsky in Brest by telephone. On January 26, he wired Orjonekidze that a bottleneck between Orel and Kursk blocked the movement of grain and coal, thus threatening Petrograd with famine and more closed factories. "We suspect sabotage of railwaymen at that spot," Lenin said. "We urgently request you to take the most merciless revolutionary measures. We ask you to dispatch a squad of dependable men. . . . Station several sailors or Red Guards on every locomotive. Remember that it is up to you to save Petrograd from starvation. Lenin."[1]

Four days later Lenin congratulated Staff Chief Antonov-Avseyenko in Kharkov on drawing Cossacks into soviet activities in the south. "As to the land problem in the Don region, I advise you to consider the text adopted the day before yesterday by the Congress of Soviets regarding the federation of Soviet Republics."[2] The Don Cossacks, Lenin was intimating, could enjoy autonomy and fashion their own land reform if they were pro-Soviet.

The last day of January, Lenin decreed the nationalization, without compensation, of the sea and river freight-carrying fleets of Russia.

During February, 1918, Lenin continued juggling all these balls and put others into the air. He cautioned N. I. Podvoysky, People's Commissar of War, to see to it that paper money sent by railway reach designated recipients. . . . If people's commissars were absent from Cabinet meetings their deputies could participate and vote provided they had been appointed by the Cabinet. . . . Telegram to Commander in Chief in Kiev, M. A. Muraviov, dated February 11, 1918: Unless Antonov has issued other instructions, move energetically on the Romanian front in agreement with Christian G. Rakovsky and his commission. This showed Lenin trying to avoid overlapping of orders and the resulting jealousies. Muraviov was to stop the Romanians from seizing Bessarabia. He failed. Soon, moreover, German and Austro-Hungarian troops entered the Ukraine, overthrew the Soviet government there, and drove out the Red Army. Antonov deployed his forces toward the southeast. February 23 telegram to Antonov from Lenin: "Capture Rostov-on-the-Don this very day no matter what."[3] After Trotsky's No-war, No-peace declaration at Brest-Litovsk, German units also pushed into western Russia. The chairman of the city soviet of Driss asked Lenin what to do. "Resist wherever possible," Lenin wired back. "Carry off everything valuable and food. Destroy all else. Leave the enemy nothing. Take apart the railway tracks—two versts out of every ten. Blow up the bridges."[4] Between sessions of the Cabinet, a committee of five would be in charge of current affairs; Lenin nominated Trotsky, Stalin, himself, Karelin, the Left SR, and Proshyan, likewise a Left SR.

In the same month, Lenin was fighting hard, against Left Communist and Left SR opposition, to achieve a peace treaty with the Germans at Brest-Litovsk. What with party conferences, Soviet conferences, private talks to convert opponents, articles in *Pravda,* and reading reports from Brest and sending instructions to Brest, this would have been a full-time job. Lenin searched N. Karayev's *History of Western Europe* and another book on

[1] *Leninskii Sbornik,* Vol. XXXV, p. 12.
[2] Lenin, *Sochineniya,* Fourth ed., Vol. 36, p. 431.
[3] *Ibid.,* p. 441.
[4] *Ibid.,* Vol. 35, p. 269.

Napoleon's wars with Germany for data supporting his contention that history did not end with the acceptance of peace at the tip of a conqueror's sword. Every conqueror has his day and death. He pressed these points home; on February 20, for instance, he addressed the Lettish fusiliers, then the backbone of the Soviet armed forces, who had openly declared their opposition to the peace treaty and their intention of waging guerrilla war against the Germans.[5] Their country, Latvia, would, they knew, be a victim of the treaty.

Antonov took Rostov. Lenin wired him on February 28: "Our warm greetings to all the selfless heroes of socialism, greetings to the revolutionary Cossacks." Mindful of the key role the Cossacks played in the White generals' strategy, Lenin again—he was the great repeater—instructed Antonov to let the Cossacks draft their land law and present it to the Sovnarkom for approval. "I have no objection to autonomy for the Don region."[6]

The Seventh Party Congress met on March 6, 7, and 8, 1918. Lenin spoke several times each day, wrote most of the resolutions. He set himself two goals: approval of the peace treaty and a new party program. Bolsheviks attach supreme importance to program. The party's program is the theoretical ground on which it stands and its plan for the future. The seizure of power in Russia changed the party's role. Lenin therefore proposed a new program and a new name. "Russian Social Democratic Labor Party" no longer suited him. The European socialists' pro-war record, he maintained, had besmirched social democracy. Moverover—echoes of *The State and Revolution*—since every state implied oppression there could be no democratic state and therefore no democracy. He accordingly suggested "The Russian Communist Party (Bolsheviks)." It was adopted by majority vote.

But when the Left Communists, with Bukharin in the van, demanded that the new program define communism or socialism, Lenin replied it was too early. "The materials for a characterization of socialism do not yet exist," he said. "The bricks with which socialism will be built have not yet been made. More than this we cannot say, and we must be as cautious and precise as possible." If they sketched a future beyond their reach the Western proletariat would suspect that "our program is only fantasy." A program, he contended, is a statement of "what we have begun to do and of the next steps that we want to take. We are in no position to describe socialism."[7]

Lenin therefore proposed only two additions to the old party program: first, a description of the imperialism manifested by all the First World War belligerents, and here he referred to his *Imperialism* book as offering the necessary ideas, and, secondly, the assertion, with proof, that the soviets were a new form of government, a new kind of state. On this issue, too, Bukharin challenged Lenin to describe socialism as a society without a state. Lenin refused: "We are now unconditionally for the state, but to say—give

[5] *Ibid.*, Second ed., Vol. XXII, p. 666.
[6] *Ibid.*, Fourth ed., Vol. 36, p. 442.
[7] *Ibid.*, Second ed., Vol. XXII, pp. 347-365.

a detailed definition of socialism in which there will be no state—here you can think up nothing except that then the principle of: from each according to his abilities, to each according to his needs, will be implemented. But this is still remote, and to say that is to say nothing, except to say that the ground under our feet is weak."

"To proclaim in advance the withering away of the state," Lenin warned, "would be to destroy the perspective of history." Yet he referred the delegates to his book, *The State and Revolution*, where he had proclaimed in advance that the state would begin to wither away immediately the proletariat seized power. It had seized power in Russia exactly four months before the congress convened. No withering away was in evidence. This discrepancy between prerevolutionary fantasy and postrevolutionary fact entangled Lenin in a jumble of contradictions. "The state is an apparatus for suppression," he told the congress. "It is necessary to suppress the exploiters, but they must not be suppressed by police, they must be suppressed by the masses." It was Lenin, however, not the masses, who ordered the Cheka to arrest the management of Ural industries and confiscate their properties. It was the Sovnarkom, under Lenin's guidance, that threatened capitalists with forced labor; the army and police, not the masses, put substance into the threat. Lenin likewise advocated an unreal nationwide system of "social bookkeeping, stock-taking, and investigation carried out by the population itself" in preparation for "further steps of socialism." This harked back to his tract on the state but had no relation to Soviet practice then (or since). Nevertheless, "the Soviet government is a new type of state, in the form of the dictatorship of the proletariat," and to Soviet "democracy we assign new tasks." In *The State and Revolution* he had written that no state could be democratic. This "democratic dictatorship" had passed "the law of the socialisation of the land," but "we will parcel out the land fairly in the interest, chiefly, of the small peasant economy." Capitalist farms on socialist soil. Apparently aware of these contradictions, Lenin said in conclusion, "Perhaps we are making mistakes, but we hope that the proletariat of the west will correct them. And we appeal to the European proletariat to aid us in our work."

From Tom Paine to Pierre Joseph Proudhon (1809-1865) to Mikhail Bakunin to Karl Marx, Friedrich Engels, and Lenin, hate of the state distinguished revolutionists. Liberal reformers, too, feared the state; they argued that that state governs best which governs least. For the more it governed the more it oppressed the weak and served the strong. Where this was especially true, in Russia and Spain, the anarchism of stateless equality and individual liberty found numerous followers. Marxism was born with this mark of anarchism. But Marx failed to notice that the evils of British capitalism flowed from a political system in which the government governed least. Had he lived he could have watched governments govern more—with benefit to the underprivileged. He and Lenin could not imagine a state as an instrument of society rather than of one class. To abolish the class state Lenin proposed to abolish classes. Instead, he stands unique in history as the deliberate architect of a one-class state. It became the oppressor of all classes. An extremist in a country of extremes—extremes of cold and heat, of wealth and poverty, of culture and illiteracy, of power and impotence—Lenin abominated the extremist state and created one.

The Seventh Party Congress of March, 1918, gave Lenin what he asked: approval of the Brest treaty, approval of a new program incorporating elements of his two most recent books, *Imperialism* and *The State and Revolution*. He continued the battle for the peace treaty and against bureaucratic "disorganization" and economic bankruptcy. On March 28, 1918, he dictated a draft of an article on the "Current Tasks of the Soviet Government" which stressed the pressing need of "practicality" and "efficiency." To this end, the recruitment of "bourgeois intellectuals" for government service was "indispensable." This implied no retreat from the principles of socialism, he declared. On the contrary, the bourgeois specialists would help the revolution.[8] Meanwhile, the financial situation had become catastrophic. A plan for solvency was presented. Lenin commented on April 18: ". . . even the best financial plan cannot now be fulfilled because we have no apparatus to carry it out." Provincial and local soviets were "not connected with one another" and were "cut off from the central government." They lacked the power to improve their own financial position and often succumbed to "separate groups, partly in conflict with the soviets, which do not obey the soviets and which, unfortunately, dispose of certain rifle strength."[9] Rival organizations levied taxes in the same locality. The state was in a state of dissolution, had withered. He complained.

Throughout March and April, 1918, Lenin concentrated on saving Russia from chaos. He made notes: "raise productivity"; "learn socialism from the big organizers of capitalism, from trusts"; "six hours of physical labor plus four hours running the state" (a sure road to more confusion); "Tailors system, Motion study," he wrote in English—a reference to the Frederick Winslow Taylor labor-saving method reviled by communists and others; "communal feeding"; "one-man management" of industrial plants; "draw with both hands from foreign countries"; "piecework pay according to results"; "don't steal, don't be a slacker . . ."; "the Soviet government plus Prussian railroad efficiency plus American technology and organizations of trusts plus American public school education, etc., etc. plus plus equals socialism."[10]

He wrote a note on April 23, to A. I. Rykov, then People's Commissar of Internal Affairs, to insist on the issuance of new currency for old. "Gukovsky"—Assistant Commissar of Finance—"is opposed, but I think the move must be made. Your opinion?"[11]

[8] *Ibid.*, pp. 412-425.
[9] *Ibid.*, pp. 428-429.
[10] *Leninskii Sbornik*, Vol. XXXVI, pp. 31-38.
[11] *Ibid.*, p. 39.

Lenin's note in April to A. D. Tsurupa, Commissar of Food, called attention to the "catastrophic food situation in Moscow province." The peasants too had to be fed, "otherwise they will eat all the seed and will not plow. What can be done? What have you done?"[12] On May 22, 1918, the Sovnarkom adopted Lenin's proposal to ship 10,000 poods (360,000 pounds) of grain from Tsaritsin to the Baku Soviet in exchange for oil. In May, too, Lenin wrote Commissar of Justice D. I. Kursky: "It is necessary *immediately*, with demonstrative speed, to introduce a bill providing that the punishment for bribery (usury, graft, pandering to bribery, and so forth) be not less than ten years imprisonment and, in addition, ten years of forced labor."[13]

These are but a handful of the bushelful of problems that weighed on Lenin in the first half of 1918. He also planned for the future (Moscow's and Petrograd's supply of electricity) and faced questions of principle and personnel. The Left Communists, for instance, favored workers' management of individual factories. At a May-June conference of the Councils of National Economy, V. V. Obolensky (also known as N. Osinsky) and V. M. Smirnov proposed decentralized control of industry. During a Cabinet meeting Lenin passed a note to Rykov saying that G. D. Weinberg of the All-Russian Council of National Economy had telephoned and told him of "foolish talk" by the Leftists about industrial management. "What happened?" Lenin asked. "What can we do?"

Rykov replied, "Smirnov and Obolensky literally invent 'wise foolishness.' At the plenary session they were defeated. In the commission on management a compromise was adopted: one-third of the management is to consist of workers of the factory, one-third of trade union representatives, and one-third of the technical staff." The central authorities could veto decisions of this troika.[14]

Lenin disapproved. He published his views on June 2, 1918: "Communism demands and assumes maximum centralization of the large enterprises of the entire country. . . . To deprive the All-Russian center of the right to subordinate directly to itself all plants of a given branch of industry in all corners of the country, which is what arises from the commission's proposal, would be regional anarcho-syndicalism, not communism."[15]

The Leftists, however, enjoyed considerable support. Immediately after the Bolshevik revolution decentralized syndicalism dominated industrial management. The workers and trade unions ran their enterprises, including railroad and river transportation. They were abolishing the state. To Lenin this was not communism. He gradually abolished worker and trade-union management; the federal government took over. Some called this "Militant Communism"; others "Military Communism." The Russian term can be translated "Military Communism" or "Wartime Communism."

[12] *Ibid.*, p. 41.
[13] Lenin, *op. cit.*, Fourth ed., Vol. 35, p. 271.
[14] *Leninskii Sbornik*, Vol. XXI, pp. 130-131.
[15] *Ibid.*, Vol. XXXVI, pp. 47-48.

Lenin seemed to be rushing off in fourteen directions. But there was method in his movements. He was consciously building a state in an administrative desert, building it with old capitalist rubble instead of new socialist bricks. He was preoccupied not only with urgent problems that demanded attention (army, peace treaty, food, management, and so forth) but also with matters that embellish a society. As early as November, 1917, he drafted a memorandum on the libraries in Petrograd. He wanted them reorganized on "principles applied long ago in the free countries of the west, particularly in Switzerland and the United States of America." He ordered the unpaid exchange of books between libraries in Russia and with foreign libraries. The reading room of the Petrograd Public Library, the former Imperial Library, "must be open, as in *private* libraries and in reading rooms for the *rich* in civilized countries, every day, including holidays and Sundays, from 8 a.m. to 11 p.m."[16] On May 25, 1918, he wrote a plan for the establishment of a Socialist Academy of the Social Sciences complete with a publishing department for Marxist books. At a Cabinet meeting on July 12, 1918, Lenin sent a note to Commissar of Education Anatoly Lunacharsky asking whether he had talked with Vinogradov, the secretary of the commission for the removal of tsarist busts and statues. Lunacharsky replied, Not yet. Back went the same piece of paper with another message from Lenin: "When are you going [to Petrograd]? The day and the hour?"

LUNACHARSKY: "Tomorrow at midnight."

LENIN: "Could you telephone Vinogradov and give him an appointment tomorrow?"

LUNACHARSKY: "Of course."

LENIN: "Have you his telephone number?"

Lunacharsky replied that he could get it. Then Lenin sent a note to his secretary at the Cabinet meeting: "Telephone Vinogradov in my name. Why hasn't he made an appointment with Lunacharsky? Lunacharsky is here [in Moscow]."

Lenin was anxious to have monarchist monuments removed and appropriate inscriptions (like "Religion is the opiate of the people") displayed on walls and buildings in Moscow and Petrograd. "I am astonished and outraged," he wrote Lunacharsky, that this had not yet been done. In August, 1918, he instructed the Education Commissariat to increase the enrollment of students in universities and to favor children of workers and poor peasants. In September, 1918, Lenin reprimanded Lunacharsky—a serious matter; reprimands were recorded in a communist's party card and clouded his reputation—for failing to display busts of Marx and propaganda texts in city streets: "I demand that the names of those responsible be sent to me so that they can be put on trial. Shame on the saboteurs and loafers." On November 19, 1918, Lenin decreed the establishment of state homes for orphans and other

[16] *Ibid.*, Vol. XXI. Lenin's early communications on cultural questions are published on pp. 204-215.

children. When a high official said at a Cabinet meeting that the Bolshoi and Mali theaters were unnecessary to a workers' state, they only wasted fuel and played old bourgeois operas like *Traviata, Carmen,* and *Eugene Onegin,* Lenin demurred and told the official that he "had a somewhat naïve idea of the role and significance of the theater." The theaters were saved.[17]

Lenin likewise took an interest in the new system of laws, courts, and prisons. He leaned toward severity. He condemned the judges who, on June 2, 1918, punished bribe-takers with six months' imprisonment instead of shooting. These judges should be expelled from the communist party: "their place is by the side of Kerensky and Martov, not next to revolutionary communists."[18] In a discussion of the functions of the Cheka he proposed that "false informers be executed." (Lying denunciations with a view to obtaining the victim's job or apartment or wife became a common social phenomenon in the Soviet Union.) On other occasions, however, Lenin intervened on behalf of persons wrongly accused, arrested, and sentenced. For instance: he telephoned a message to Djerzhinsky or his deputy, Peters, on November 2, 1918: "Is there a serious accusation against Professor [D. N.] Zernov [anatomist at the Moscow State University] whom you have arrested? Gorbunov and Krassin request his release." Similarly, Lenin's telegram, dated October 25, 1918, to the Tambov county executive committee: "You may not expel the sick woman Azanchevskaya from the room she rents from Mikhailov. Please have the Red Cross care for her. Wire your reply." Early in November, 1918, the Cheka arrested a dentist named K. S. Ginsburg for alleged contacts with the Kadet party. Two communists vouched for him. Lenin asked the Cheka for information. Later he wrote the Cheka: "I demanded this information on the evening of November 11. Since then 10½ hours have elapsed and I have had no reply. I repeat my demand." The Cheka had merely stated that the dentist could not be located although, Lenin insisted, he was in a Moscow jail. The Cheka quickly found Ginsburg and released him. Lenin later obtained the release from prison of a well-known Russian engineer and official of the Kerensky government named Palinsky. (He was executed in 1930 in connection with the Shakhti trial.)

Lenin also gave time and thought to social insurance, the Red Cross, the care and repair of public buildings, a national census, the creation of rest homes in the south for wounded soldiers, amendments to the constitution ("As socialist soviet governments are established in other countries, the R.S.F.S.R. enters with them into one Union of Federated Socialist Soviet Republics," etc.), the price of potatoes, the equipment of a bacteriological laboratory, silence at Cabinet meetings (note to his secretary Gorbunov: "No talking at sessions; only exchange of notes"), the translation of *The State and Revolution* into Finnish, the collection of books, pamphlets, newspapers,

---

[17] *Vospominaniya,* Vol. 1, pp. 171-172.

[18] *Ibid.,* p. 223. For Lenin's communications on questions of courts, the Cheka, and so forth, see *ibid.,* pp. 216-238.

and other matter for his office library, and regular mailings to him of clippings from foreign newspapers.

Lenin and the Bolsheviks were furnishing a permanent home. The Whites or anti-Bolsheviks behaved like temporary tenants. They recruited soldiers, confiscated grain, distributed ministerial portfolios, and printed paper money, but they were essentially an occupational force in transit, not a government. Their goal was Moscow. There they hoped to create a state. One could scarcely establish a national government in Taganrog or Irkutsk or Novocherkassk or Omsk or Archangel. A paramount factor in the Soviets' victory over innumerable enemies in the 1917-1921 civil war was their possession of Russia's capital city, in fact of both capital cities, Moscow and Petrograd. But this would have proved an inert advantage if Lenin had not used it assiduously to build the Soviet state. A revolution occurs when administration breaks down. The Soviet revolution won in November, 1917, because Lenin's "Dual Power" strategy, or the division of power between Kerensky and the soviets, disemboweled the government, just as years, indeed decades, of civil war and the consequent anarchy of administration lifted Mao Tsetung to the Chinese throne. Similarly, a functioning administration, a state, no matter how rickety, stiffens the army in the field and leads to victory in civil wars. An exception comes to mind: the 1936-1939 Spanish civil war. There the anarchists, the communists, and the touch of anarchism in every Spaniard weakened the government's administration and gave the palm to the stronger, foreign-supported army. Had Lenin adhered to his semianarchistic *The State and Revolution* his regime would have suffered the same fate. But in power he was not guided by books.

XVIII. CHICHERIN AND LENIN

THE combination of internal rebellion and foreign intervention against a feeble and new government threatened its life. Moreover, the fact that the Western Allies intervened while the German and Austro-Hungarians were still in Russia doubled Lenin's troubles. It also gave him an opportunity to experiment with his policy of divide and survive.

The motives of Allied policy toward Red Russia varied with each ally and from time to time. The official reasons given for military intervention were true in some cases and an excuse in others. When true reasons became invalid, intervention did not cease. Governments always find explanations for whatever they do.

At first, Western intervention in Soviet Russia was conceived as a win-the-war measure. In a long note addressed to the Imperial War Cabinet on June 22, 1918, Winston Churchill wrote, "There are two perfectly simple things to do . . . (1) Above all things reconstitute the fighting front in the East; (2) make a plan for an offensive battle in France in 1919."[1] This pessimism—victory no earlier than 1919, and the extra effort required to restore an anti-German battle line in Russia—embittered the West against the Bolsheviks for quitting the war. That they quit to save themselves was no balm to the millions of families who had given sons to Mars.

Another factor increased the bitterness. Lenin and Trotsky negotiated separately with Germany, the hated foe; maybe they were indeed German agents, some said. Bolshevik propaganda endeavored to soften the resent-ment; but words could not cool emotions generated by the long life-and-death struggle against the Kaiser coalition. A few in the West sympathized with Russian policy. To the vast majority, Bolshevism was betrayal.

The Bolsheviks did not reduce the encompassing antagonism. Their every act fed it. On December 3, 1917, Chairman Lenin and Commissar of Na-tionalities Joseph Stalin issued a Manifesto to All Toiling Moslems in Russia and the East which misinformed them that "the workers and soldiers of the West are already gathering under the banner of socialism, storming the fortresses of imperialism"; that India "has raised the banner of insurrection, organizing its Soviets of Deputies"; it urged the Arabs, Persians, Turks to do likewise. "We declare," the Manifesto read, "that the secret treaties of the deposed Tsar about the seizure of Constantinople . . . are now torn up and destroyed. The Soviet of People's Commissars is opposed to the conquest of foreign lands: Constantinople must remain in Moslem hands." The 1907 treaty with Britain regarding the partition of Persia was declared null. "Mos-lems of Russia! Moslems of the East! . . . we expect your sympathy and sup-port."[2] The British raj roared with rage. . . . On December 9, 1917, Foreign Commissar Trotsky discharged the Russian ambassadors in London, Tokyo, Washington, Rome, Peking, Madrid, Paris, Stockholm, The Hague, Bern, Brussels, Lisbon, Buenos Aires, Cairo, Bucharest, and Athens, and many other diplomatic and consular Russian representatives abroad.[3] Each became a nucleus of anti-Soviet intrigue. . . . On December 28, 1917, the Council of People's Commissars (Sovnarkom) ordered the confiscation of the assets of the Russo-Belgian Metallurgical Association.[4] . . . On January 19, 1918, the Soviet government disbanded the Constituent Assembly, freely elected under Bolshevik rule. . . . On February 10, 1918, the Soviets canceled all

---

[1] Winston Churchill, *The World Crisis, 1916-18* (London, 1927), Vol. 2, p. 191.
[2] *Dokumenty Vneshnei Politiki SSSR*, Vol. I, pp. 34-35
[3] *Ibid.*, pp. 43-44.
[4] *Ibid.*, p. 66.

foreign loans and promised not to pay interest on them.[5] This measure brought Moscow deep hostility from tens of thousands of Russian bond-holders abroad, especially in France. . . . On April 22, 1918, the Soviet government nationalized foreign trade, thus establishing a state monopoly of imports and exports, which, at the time, tended to cut off Soviet economy from world economy and to embarrass, if not paralyze, the activities of foreign companies dealing with Russia.[6] . . . On April 30, 1918, Lenin wrote a brief note to Raymond Robins, chief of the American Red Cross in Russia. Robins, in a warm letter to Lenin dated April 25, said he was about to leave Russia for the United States and thanked Lenin for facilitating the work of the American Red Cross. He expressed "the abiding hope" that the Soviet Republic would "develop into a permanent, Democratic Power, and that your ultimate aim to make Russia a fundamental economic democracy will be realized." Lenin's four-line English reply read, "Dear Mr. Robins, I thank You very much for Your letter. I am sure the new democracy that is a proletarian democracy is coming in all countries and will crush all obstacles and imperialist-capitalist system of the new and old world. With kindly regards and thanks, Yours truly Lenin."[7]

By limiting communism's scope to Russia, Robins, the sympathizer, had apparently stung Lenin and provoked a curt reprimand that reflected the Kremlin's bold design. Lenin, it seems, was unwilling to try to make friends outside the red camp. His attitude scarcely mitigated the world's mounting anger toward the Bolshevik state.

Would the Western Allies have intervened in Russia if the Soviets had not disclosed their dreams of world revolution and had not suppressed, confiscated, and nationalized? To simplify the if-question somewhat, Would the Allies have intervened if, say, Alexander Kerensky, the moderate democrat, had withdrawn his collapsing country from the war and signed a peace treaty with Germany without the assent of the West?

The answer is conjectural. The British, French, Italians, and Americans were not at once averse to helping the Bolsheviks organize a Red Army which might be called upon to fight Germany. In March, April, and May, 1918, War Commissar Trotsky asked Allied military personnel for aid in training Russia's new forces. The Kremlin had established the Red Army by decree in January, and created an officers' training corps in February. Some tsarist generals, colonels, and lesser ranks volunteered their services either out of Russian patriotism, anti-German sentiments, need of emolument, or love of warfare. But Trotsky wanted expert modern guidance and arms. The West

---

[5] *Ibid.*, p. 97.
[6] *Ibid.*, pp. 255-256.
[7] Robins' letter is from a photostat generously supplied by the State Historical Society, Madison, Wis. Lenin's letter is in the English original published in *Leninskii Sbornik*, Vol. XXXVI, Institute of Marxism-Leninism of the Central Committee of the Soviet Communist Party (Moscow, 1959), pp. 40-41.

seemed willing. On March 11, 1918, Colonel James A. Ruggles, chief of the United States Military Mission, had "a satisfactory interview with Trotsky," U.S. Ambassador Francis reported, "but no definite program [was] adopted." Captain E. F. Riggs, Assistant United States Military Attaché, "now [in] Moscow," Francis wired from Vologda to Secretary of State Robert Lansing on March 26, "reports Allies responding to appeal to assist army organization generously, having assigned thirty-eight [officers] therefor and Italians ordered ten from Italy. Have authorized military attaché to do likewise because it is unadvisable to refuse." Francis added that while the new Russian army was "nominally for defense, [its] real object is resistance to all existing governments and promotion of socialism throughout the whole world." Nevertheless, he said, the army "is only hope for saving European Russia from Germany." Finally the ambassador up north in Vologda on Soviet territory yet far from the Soviet world, revealed "my (real) and strictly confidential reason" for aiding the Soviet army: the "army so organized can by proper methods be taken from Bolshevik control and used against Germans, and even [from] its creators if prove that [they are] German allies. I anticipate not revealing last reason to Robins or Riggs."[8]

Deception of a foreign government and of one's own official may be fair in war but its fruit is sour. Nothing came of the talks to train the Soviet army. The Western Allies were frying other fish. Since no hurriedly assembled Red force could withstand a further German thrust into Russian territory, the Allies contemplated military intervention in Russia—in the north, at the Murmansk and Archangel ports, in the south, and in the Far East around Vladivostok (where there were no Germans).

Notably in London, but elsewhere too, the question arose, Was intervention possible with Bolshevik consent? Bruce Lockhart, British agent in Moscow, answered Yes, and so telegraphed to Foreign Secretary Arthur James Balfour.[9] The British War Cabinet, Prime Minister David Lloyd George presiding, met on April 22 and "decided that [General Jan Christian] Smuts should go to Kola [Murmansk] to see Trotsky."[10] Nothing on record shows whether Trotsky had been consulted or why Smuts never undertook the adventure.

Ambassador Francis wired Secretary Lansing on April 5 about his plan "to induce Soviet government to ask Allied assistance, so that when Allies enter Russia, will not meet with Soviet government's refusal, but Soviet government's welcome";[11] on May 2, he asked Raymond Robins, "Do you think

[8] *Papers Relating to the Foreign Relations of the United States. 1918. Russia*, Vol. I, pp. 487-488.
[9] Richard H. Ullman, *Anglo-Soviet Relations, 1917-1921. Intervention and the War* (Princeton, 1961), p. 137.
[10] Major General Sir C. E. Callwell, *Field-Marshal Sir Henry Wilson, His Life and Diaries* (London, 1927), Vol. II, p. 93.
[11] *Papers Relating to the Foreign Relations . . .*, Vol. III, p. 228.

the Soviet government would oppose Allied intervention if they knew it was inevitable?"[12] (A day earlier—May 1—Colonel Ruggles telegraphed the U.S. War Department from Vologda, ". . . we should negotiate with Bolsheviks *modus vivendi* by consent to immediate Allied intervention through Siberia and northern ports.")[13]

Irrespective of Robins' view or the Soviet government's assent, Ambassador Francis informed the Department of State on May 2 that "In my judgment [the] time for Allied intervention has arrived." He based his recommendation on Vologda-induced opinions: (1) "Mirbach is dominating Soviet government and is practically dictator in Moscow" and (2) Mirbach had told the Soviet government that Germany's advance into Russia would end "if Allies evacuated Murmansk and Archangel . . . I think such evacuation would be exceedingly unwise."[14] In other words, Allied intervention was a fact.

It started in March, 1918, upon the arrival of British and French naval forces. The Murmansk Soviet, acting without specific instructions from Moscow—no surprise in the prevailing Russian chaos—entered into an oral agreement with the Anglo-French command: the foreign military recognized the Murmansk Soviet's supreme power in the region, undertook to supply food and other commodities, promised not to interfere in internal affairs, and accepted an arrangement under which the supreme military authority of the area would be vested in a council of three (one Briton, one Frenchman, and one Russian) subordinated to the Murmansk Regional Soviet.[15]

Later that month, Lenin and Stalin in Moscow conducted a conversation by direct telegraph wire with Alekseyev (otherwise known as Yuryev), leader of the Murmansk Soviet. Stalin began with questions. Was the agreement with the Anglo-French written or oral? The Murmansker replied that it was an oral understanding recorded in the minutes of a meeting. Stalin: "What military forces are available to the Soviet of Deputies?" Alekseyev said, one hundred soldiers, a railway guard unit, and two hundred sailors. Stalin: "Another question: Are the British supplying food free or for value received?" On credit, Alekseyev replied. Stalin: "Answer another question: Neither the British nor the French ever give aid for nothing. Tell me, What obligations was the Soviet of Deputies required to accept in return for the military assistance from the British and French?" Alekseyev explained that Murmansk was the only British, French, and American point of access, during the war, to Russia. By assisting the region the foreigners were serving their own interests, not those of the region, "therefore no obligations are being or were demanded of us." Stalin: "Receive our reply. We believe that you have got yourself into some trouble, now you have to get out of the mess." As a first

---

[12] *Russian-American Relations (R. A. R.) March 1917-March 1920. Documents and Papers*, compiled and edited by C. K. Cumming and W. W. Petit (New York, 1920), p. 162.

[13] *Papers Relating to the Foreign Relations . . .*, Vol. I, p. 517.

[14] *Ibid.*, pp. 519-520.

[15] *Dokumenty Vneshnei Politiki SSSR*, Vol. I, p. 221.

step, Stalin urged the Murmansk Soviet to obtain from the British and French a written declaration denying the intention to remain as an occupying force.[16]

Alekseyev was proud of his bargain: the newcomers would feed his hungry population and keep robbers from the huge heaps of munitions and materials deposited in the area when the Western Allies were assisting Russia's war effort. There had been rumors, moreover, that the Finns and the Germans in Finland were poised to cut across the remote corner of north Russia to Murmansk and Archangel. Alekseyev and his people presumably preferred the British, French, and Americans, whom they knew as occasional prewar visiting seamen, to the Germans, whom they had fought on the eastern front.

Moscow, however, feared that the Anglo-French descent on Murmansk heralded the coming of a larger force which would march south to the heart of Red Russia with anti-Bolshevik intentions. On June 11 a first contingent of 150 American marines landed at Murmansk; reinforcements would follow. A British unit of 600 soldiers, commanded by Major General Sir C. Maynard, arrived at Murmansk on June 23.[17]

The north Russian situation was thus ripe for Soviet diplomatic action. Foreign Commissar Chicherin took it. In June, 1918, he sent Vosnisensky, one of his assistants and a Left Social Revolutionary—this was before the Left SR revolt in July—to interview Allied missions in Vologda. Vosnisensky saw Francis O. Lindley, the British chargé d'affaires, French Ambassador Joseph Noulens, and U.S. Ambassador David Francis, and gave them Chicherin's oral message: the Soviet government would not resist Allied military moves against the Germans in Finland but would fight if they advanced to Kandalaksha and Onega in the direction of Moscow. Chicherin told me of this demarche while I was writing my book on Soviet foreign policy.[18] He explained it further in an English-language, handwritten letter to me: "Entente troops were already landing in Murmansk. The Entente governments declared that it was only against the Germans in Finland, and Britishers were going to Finland, they formed the Finnish Rifles Corps. At that moment we catched"—his quaint English—"them by their word: you say you go only to Finland, then give us a pledge that you will not move to Kandalaksha and Onega against us."

The Vologda diplomats withheld the pledge.

Some weeks later Chicherin made a similar but opposite proposal to Ger-

[16] *Ibid.*, pp. 220-221. The transcript is entitled "From a conversation by V. I. Lenin and J. V. Stalin with Yuryev (Alekseyev), leader of the Murmansk Regional Soviet," and is signed "Lenin, Stalin," but Lenin's part in the conversation is not given. The transcript was taken from a collection of documents published in 1940, which may explain why Stalin but not Lenin is quoted.

[17] George F. Kennan, *Soviet-American Relations, 1917-1920. The Decision to Intervene* (Princeton, 1958), p. 373.

[18] *The Soviets in World Affairs*, two volumes (New York and London, 1930). Facsimile reproduction with new introduction by author (Princeton, 1951; Vintage paperback. 1960).

many. Eight days after Count Mirbach's murder, the Berlin government asked permission to send a battalion of uniformed soldiers to guard its legation in Moscow. The eight-day delay indicated vacillation on the Wilhelmstrasse. Moscow refused the request. It feared that the legation might become a Trojan horse which would, at some moment of high tension, disgorge its human contents to reinforce Russian counter-Bolsheviks. In the second half of July, a compromise face-saving formula for Kaiser and Kremlin was devised: the German legation staff would be expanded to 300 persons, "and additional forces were to come to Moscow in groups of thirty without arms and without German uniforms."[19]

Mirbach was succeeded by Karl T. Helfferich, wartime Deputy Chancellor. Admiral von Hintze, a former military attaché in St. Petersburg, had replaced Kuehlmann as State Secretary for Foreign Affairs. Though Hintze echoed the Ludendorff-Hindenburg dominant duumvirate, his Russian policy, as Chicherin viewed it in retrospect, was "conciliatory."[20] The German military were pulling in their horns; or the points of the horns had been broken off by the Western entente's growing power. Germany now pursued one aim in the East: to fetch grain from the Ukraine.

Moscow evidently did not understand this. Moved by desperation, ignorance, and cynicism, the Kremlin hoped to embroil Germany with the West on Russian soil and thus achieve immunity from both. Chicherin accordingly made a strange proposal to Karl Helfferich. He gave me the details. Helfferich refers to the matter in his book, *Der Weltkrieg*.[21]

Very few days after Helfferich reached Moscow, Chicherin went to see him with a two-forked plan for German military action on Russian soil. First, the Bolsheviks would open a corridor through which German troops already stationed in Finland would enter Russia and, avoiding Soviet cities (Petrograd, Petrozavodsk, and so forth), advance to meet the Anglo-French interventionist forces moving down from Murmansk and Archangel. Second, Germany, using her army in the Ukraine, Chicherin hinted, would attack the forces of anti-Bolshevik General Mikhail V. Alexeyev in the Don Cossack region.

Years later, Chicherin explained the scheme in the Soviet press: "When, in August [1918], the Entente in fact waged war against us, having occupied Archangel and advanced from there to the south and taken action in the east with the help of the Czechoslovaks and in the south by pushing the Volunteer Army of General Alexeyev forward, Vladimir Ilyich [Lenin] made an attempt to exploit the antagonism of the two belligerent imperialist coalitions in order to weaken the Entente offensive. After a long conference with Vladimir Ilyich, I personally visited the new German ambassador Helfferich

---

[19] *Ibid.*, Vol. I, p. 127.
[20] George Chicherin, *Two Years of Foreign Policy*, p. 16.
[21] Berlin, 1919.

to propose that we agree on common action against Alexeyev in the south and on the possibility of dispatching a German unit, with our consent, to attack the Entente forces near the White Sea. The further evolution of this plan was interrupted by Helfferich's sudden departure."[22]

The Lenin strategy of directing Western force against Germany and simultaneously channeling German hostility toward the West was used decades later by Stalin on a vaster scale. In both instances, Russia hoped to escape harm while others bled: "Exploit the antagonism of the two belligerent imperialist coalitions." For Lenin and Chicherin in 1918 it was a daring gambit. The fate of the Bolshevik revolution hung by a hair, by Lenin's wit.

The Allies spurned Chicherin's advice.

The Germans did nothing. In fact, Helfferich was called home on August 7 to participate in a Crown Council which, for the first time, discussed the possibility of Germany's defeat.

Chicherin worked with Lenin in magnificent rapport. Chicherin was naturally circumspect; the Soviet government's weakness made Lenin cautious. Both had brilliant intellects and could speak "shorthand" to one another. "In the first years of the existence of our Republic," Chicherin wrote in *Izvestia* of January 30, 1924, nine days after Lenin's death, "I talked with Lenin on the telephone several times a day, sometimes very long telephone conversations, in addition to private, personal conversations, and frequently discussed with him all the details of any more or less important current diplomatic matter." Chicherin's proposal to Helfferich and the Vosnisensky mission to Vologda were important.

Chicherin revered Lenin, despised Stalin, and disliked Trotsky. Chicherin was fastidious, aristocratic, highly educated. He naturally had nothing but contempt for Stalin, who lacked culture, finesse, and humanity. Trotsky could be brusque and arrogant. "One day," Chicherin recounted, "I was sitting in my office. It was the middle of 1918. The telephone rang; Trotsky. He always had an extremely disagreeable manner of talking over the 'phone. 'You have some vermin in Vologda,' Trotsky said, referring to the Allied diplomatic corps that had taken refuge there from Petrograd. 'Turn them out.'"

Chicherin explained that this would be embarrassing.

"Nichevo" (never mind), Trotsky replied, "turn them out."

"I went to see Lenin about the matter," Chicherin continued. "Lenin at that time needed Trotsky's support and urged me to reach an understanding with Trotsky. I then invited Karl Radek and Arthur Ransome [the British journalist] to go to Vologda and ask the envoys to move to Moscow. Instead they moved to Murmansk."

I write this from notes, which show the signs of age, made between August 24 and September 1, 1929, in Wiesbaden, Germany, where Chicherin was taking a cure. During much of the period from early 1927 to autumn, 1929,

[22] *Izvestia,* Jan. 30, 1924.

when I worked on my book about Soviet foreign policy, Chicherin received me every Sunday afternoon in the Commissariat of Foreign Affairs at the corner of Kuznetsky Must (Smith's Bridge). He had a phenomenal memory. As I entered his office he would say, "Good afternoon. Sit down please. Last Sunday I was telling you . . ." and picked up the story of Soviet foreign relations where he had left off the Sunday before although in the intervening six days he had talked with an endless queue of ambassadors and Soviet officials and probably attended the weekly Thursday session of the supreme Politburo to report, or a meeting of the party's Central Committee of which he had been a member since December, 1925.

A Soviet foreign minister, unless he is a Trotsky at the crest of his influence, does not make foreign policy. Soviet foreign policy during Chicherin's years was formulated by Lenin in consultation, discussion, and friction with the communist party's Central Committee or with the Politburo. After Lenin's death, policy was made by Stalin with or without the seven-man, later nine-man, Politburo. Chicherin carried out the policy determined by his political superiors. Nevertheless, there is, in any organization, considerable policy-making in the daily execution of policy. Moreover, policy decisions depend, to some extent, on reports about conditions, relations, negotiations. Chicherin delivered most of those reports. They were refracted by the prism of his mind. Cultivated European and anti-tsarist though he was, Chicherin had an anti-West European, notably anti-British, bias which resembled tsarist Russia's and sprang from Anglo-Russian rivalry in Central Asia and the Near East. British intervention in Soviet Russia strengthened the bias. Europe interested Chicherin because of its power, Asia because of its possibilities. British strength curtailed the possibilities.

Chicherin's quick brain, packed with history and information, his skill in drafting diplomatic notes, his persistence amounting to stubbornness, and his ascetic selflessness impressed Lenin and gave weight to his opinions.

Georgi Vasielevich Chicherin, Soviet Foreign Commissar from 1918 to 1930, was born in 1872 on an estate in the central Russian province of Tambov. His paternal ancestors, surnamed Ciceroni, came from Italy; Italians were frequently invited to Russia in the fifteenth and sixteenth centuries and later to build churches and palaces and to paint portraits at court. His mother's family were Narishkins; Natalya Narishkin, of Tartar descent, was Peter the Great's mother. Chicherin's sparse reddish goatee and downward-curving mustache and little squinting eyes conveyed a suggestion of Tartar origin. In Mongolian costume—he liked to wear exotic clothes—he looked like a khan.

Chicherin's father served as a minor official in the tsarist Foreign Ministry. In 1897 the son likewise entered the Ministry to work in the archives, a post that suited his personality, for he was maniacally meticulous. As commissar he would invade his typists' office to examine the addresses on outgoing envelopes and point out mistakes in his high-pitched squeaky voice. Knowledge of languages helped the young archivist. He would have earned promotion; he spoke German, French, Italian, and English fluently. (At times, however, his English was delightfully wrong, as when, replying to a request for an interview, he wrote me in 1930, "I am at present invisible.") But serving the Tsar held no attraction for Chicherin. In 1904 he, like hundreds of upper-class and middle-class Russian intellectuals vexed by tyranny piled on inefficiency, answered the call of social idealism and rebellion. He renounced possession of his estates, resigned from the foreign office, and emigrated to Berlin, then to Paris, where he collaborated as a Menshevik with the French Socialist Party. In the First World War he embraced Bolshevism, lived in London, and helped anti-war Labourites. This earned him a cell in Brixton jail, where, following the November 7, 1917, revolution, Labour leader Arthur Henderson, of the War Cabinet, visited him. Trotsky demanded Chicherin's release and announced that no British subject would be granted an exit visa from Russia until Chicherin was allowed to leave England. He left on January 3, 1918. In Petrograd, Chicherin became Deputy Foreign Commissar under Trotsky. On Trotsky's transfer to the War Commissariat, Chicherin succeeded him.

Chicherin realized that my history of Soviet foreign affairs was also the story of his lifework as foreign commissar, and he helped me endlessly during our Sunday-afternoon talks and on my visits to him in his sanatorium in Grunewald-Berlin. When my manuscript was finished and bound in black in two long, large volumes I felt I should ask him to read it. I also hoped he would impart more information. Hence my stay in Wiesbaden in 1929. I saw him every day for eight days. Each day he would read the manuscript for two or three hours and then receive me for two to three hours during which he would criticize, expound, comment on Soviet leaders, and reminisce. We met either in his apartment in Hotel Vierjahreszeiten or in the restaurant, where he ate an enormous meal, or in the bar, which was usually empty. I made notes and typed them out later. After my departure he wrote me twenty-five handwritten letters in English, some many pages long, some about the book, some personal.[23] In several he repeatedly called my attention to the same misspellings of proper names. In one dated August 28, 1930, after he had paged through the published two volumes which I sent him with an inscription of gratitude, he deplored my version of Vosnisensky's Vologda mission. I had written, "The Bolsheviks, harried as they were, could scarcely prevent an Entente landing in the north. Chicherin therefore made it clear to the ambassadors that while the Bolsheviks objected to intervention, they would resist landings only in case they were directed against the Communist government."

"What you have put down," Chicherin said in his letter, "is a complete misconception, it is totally untrue, and a mortal blow to my reputation. You have killed my reputation. I am in the greatest despair. I am near to suicide

[23] I have presented them to the Library of Yale University at New Haven, Conn.

owing to your blow. You represent me as having favoured entente landings, provided they would have declared their aim at the Germans. I would have been the greatest traitor and the greatest idiot if I had done so."

In a subsequent letter of September 3, 1930, Chicherin added, "The reader will not accuse Lenin of being such an idiot and a traitor but will accuse me." In the next sentence he indicated one reason for his concern: "The thing can make a noise already now abroad and in our ruling circles, so that an explanation can very soon become inevitable. This misfortune outweighs for me everything else."

There was no noise abroad or, so far as one heard, in Soviet ruling circles.

The letter continued: "In general my condition is much worse than a collapse. In the morning at 8½ or 9 A.M. I am a little fresher, I read the papers and speak to the secretaries, Korotkin or Nikolayev, then after 1½-2 hours (at 10½-11) begins the great Qualzustand"—suffering—"I am lying down immovably, boundless feebleness, not so much sleeping but principally halfdozing, partially hallucinating, subdelirante Zustaende"—subdelirious condition—"pain in everything; with the greatest difficulty I rise for dinner and supper and eat almost nothing. At about 9 or 10 or 11 p.m. the period of pause comes, some little renewed vitality for several hours, when I read papers, write letters, attend to the small practical matters of existence. During this period I looked into your book (very insufficiently) and am now writing this letter. During this period I also play Mozart, the best thing I have had and have in life, my ideal of beauty, the incarnation of cosmic universefeeling and of fiery real life, of human psychology and of immensity without shores, true nectar and ambrosia filling with complete satisfaction. In these hours I play and read and write and eat. But it is for a short time always. So it is not only delicate health, it is immensely worse—when and how comes the conclusion, is unknown. But I will not go down to posterity as having encouraged entente landings, which is complete untrue. Unfortunately the one paragraph in cause gives this wrong impression."

On September 26 Chicherin sent me a brief note asking that I correct the offending statement in the German translation of the book. "Please do the thing," he concluded. "It would be too bad to leave the world with this stain unwashed." Later he made the same request regarding the French translation. I changed the French edition,[24] but Hitler came to power before the German translation could be published.

Chicherin wrote me four further friendly letters about Soviet foreign policy and personal matters. In one of these he informed me that prior to the first British landing at Murmansk, "I had a most dramatic talk from the Kreml per direct wire with Yurief, the president of the Murmansk Soviet. I appealed to his Soviet feelings, spoke of the world-historical stake, entreated

[24] *Les Soviets dans les Affaires Mondiales* (NRF, Paris). When the Nazi armed forces entered Paris, they pulped some unsold copies of the book.

him to resist to the last to the invaders, better die than submit; he answered skeptically, mockingly, having no faith in the Soviet cause, putting forward the necessity of submitting to overwhelming force. This Yurief signed a local treaty in the name of Murmansk with the Britishers, giving legal base to the occupation of Murmansk. Later, when the Entente had evacuated the North, Yurief was shot."

A circumstance that might have contributed to Chicherin's distress over my treatment of the Allied landings was his summary dismissal as Foreign Commissar in August, 1930. He learned of it from the newspapers; Maxim M. Litvinov succeeded him. He wrote me of this event and added, "I send you my farewell greetings and hope to be in touch with you in future. My greatest joy remains to me: playing Mozart. He is for me the world in extract and the incarnation of the beauty of life. I am mostly in a very bad state, with some life coming back for a short time usually late in the evening."

For years Chicherin had occupied an apartment in the foreign office building. He rarely left it except to attend important sessions or a foreign journalists' tea in the Sugar King's Palace by the Moskva River. In the apartment he had a piano which he delighted to play. Despite his valuable experience in world politics, he authored only one book, a short volume on Mozart, which was read by some of my Soviet friends but withheld from publication. It was too sentimental and nonmaterialistic.

Chicherin was a genius. I have known two others: Sergey Eisenstein, the Soviet film producer, and André Malraux, the French novelist. Genius is more than intelligence and talent. Lenin, Trotsky, and Bukharin were as wise as, probably wiser than, Chicherin. The genius possesses an ineffable extra quality. He is, in many cases, an artist. Chicherin's music made him an artist, a frustrated artist. The genius may have physical frustrations or eccentricities which lend him an intensity of perception, imagination, and intuition denied most human beings. Genius inhabits poets and painters, but also generals and statesmen and perhaps mathematicians and physicists. They have mental gifts that elude measurement and cannot be traced to education or experience. They can conjure up inspired beauty or wisdom at random, draw it up out of a hidden well whose content is a puzzle even to themselves. Luminous names come to mind. Chicherin's is one.

Chicherin had no private life, no interest in women or men. Work, his piano, books—these were his sublimating passions. He usually worked through the night and, as often as possible, gave night appointments to foreign ambassadors. His only friend, whom he engaged in long nocturnal conversations, was the German ambassador, Count Brockdorff-Rantzau, fervently devoted to Germany's Eastern orientation.

If Chicherin had any other passion it was his illnesses. He treasured them like a hypochondriac and never went far from his physicians. As the 1920's grew older he grew in girth until he began to look like an inflated pear. He suffered from diabetes, poor eyesight, and nervous pains in his right leg. He died, a lonely forgotten man, in 1936. On his face, as he lay in an open coffin in the conference room of the Foreign Commissariat, and in his hands one could read the physical torment of his last years. Over his dead body, Ambassador Nikolai N. Krestinsky, soon to be sentenced to death in one of the Moscow trials, pronounced a funeral oration full of criticism.

Chicherin's colleagues appreciated his tremendous talents but few had smooth passage with him. He and his first deputy, Litvinov, feuded constantly, and it was common knowledge in the Foreign Commissariat that if Chicherin favored a proposal Litvinov would be sure to oppose it and if Litvinov advanced a scheme or idea Chicherin was certain to reject it. Apart from the fact that Chicherin looked to Asia and Germany whereas Litvinov wanted to build diplomatic bridges to Western Europe and the United States, the two gifted men did not mix chemically. Litvinov was full-blooded, dynamic, earthy, and disliked Chicherin's pernickety ways. He called him "an old maid." When I once told him that Chicherin had been talking to me about Soviet-German relations, he said, "His memory isn't as good as it was." Both had fine memories.

Lenin had his difficulties with Chicherin. Bukharin, Sokolnikov and Larin were going to Germany on June 4, 1918, for commercial negotiations. An exchange of notes between Chicherin and Lenin at a Cabinet meeting has been preserved and published:

CHICHERIN: "Could we have a conference with you *Sunday morning* to give instructions to Sokolnikov, Larin, and Bukharin who are leaving Tuesday?"

LENIN: "Wouldn't it be possible Saturday at five so as not *to spoil* the Sunday?"

CHICHERIN: "Five o'clock *is quite impossible* for me. That's the time I do my most important work."

LENIN: "At six? Six-thirty? Seven to eight?"

CHICHERIN: "I cannot get free until nine. You will have to meet without me. At five and until seven or eight Sokolnikov and Company have a meeting with the Germans" in Moscow.[25]

On May 24, 1918, Lenin received a letter from Ambassador Yoffe and Soviet Consul General (in Berlin) V. R. Menzhinsky, containing charges against Chicherin. He answered the same day: "Dear Comrades, Received your pessimistic and angry letter. Some of your accusations against Chicherin hit me. For instance, I insisted on transmitting our theses about concessions *through* the Germans in order to prove to them how earnestly we desire businesslike commercial relations. (The theses were formulated by common consent with the participation of Radek and other 'Leftist' fools.) . . . Your dissatisfaction with Chicherin is, in my opinion, exaggerated." He asked them to draft concrete proposals and send him copies of all telegrams and letters

[25] *Leninskii Sbornik*, Vol. XXI, pp. 246-247.

that went to Chicherin but to make them "brief, for I have no time to read." They apparently complained that Chicherin was nervous. "Don't you be nervous either," Lenin admonished.[26]

The meeting between Lenin and the delegates going to Germany took place as Chicherin had suggested and Lenin did consent to spoil his Sunday. "I am sitting at a session of the 'departing' (without Larin)," Lenin wrote to Yoffe. "I am listening to speeches against 'Yoffe's transferring the Commissariat of Foreign Affairs to Berlin.' The friction between you and Chicherin is sometimes used—more unconsciously than consciously—to intensify the friction. I am sure that you will be on guard and will not allow the friction to grow. I have followed your letters attentively and am firmly convinced that this friction is not important (there is chaos everywhere, inaccuracy everywhere). Patience and persistence, and the conflicts will be settled. Chicherin is an excellent executive; your policy is fully loyal, to implement the Brest Treaty; we have *already*, in my opinion, had successes, and from this it follows that the conflicts will be settled easily. If the German businessmen take economic benefits in the understanding that they can get nothing through war, we will burn *everything*, then your policy will achieve further successes. We can supply the Germans with raw materials. . . .

"Bukharin is loyal, but has gone to sickening extremes in his 'Left-foolishness.' Sokolnikov has gone astray again. Larin—is an unstable intellectual, a first-class bungler. . . . Prenez garde."[27]

"Chaos everywhere." A two-word summary of Soviet history until the middle of 1918. Writing of that period, Gregory Zinoviev, Politburo member, declared in 1923, before the Bolshevik Age of Idolatry, "It is only necessary to recall all those alarming days, all those difficult moments of crisis, to realize that had it not been for Comrade Lenin—who knows what would have happened to our revolution."[28]

XIX. LENIN WOUNDED

"WAS IT SUMMER, or had autumn commenced—I don't remember. But the night was dark, damp. There was a kind of hoarfrost, fog, haze. You could not distinguish the outlines of an object a few steps ahead. In the Kremlin it was quiet, but the silence was somehow alarming. The night before, a shot had suddenly been fired near the building of the Sovnarkom. Who fired and why no one knew.

[26] *Ibid.*, Vol. XXXVI, pp. 43-44.
[27] *Ibid.*, pp. 46-47.
[28] G. Zinoviev, V. I. Lenin. Kratkii Biographicheskii Ocherk (A Short Biographical Sketch) (Leningrad, 1924), p. 27. (The first sentence of the book reads, "Comrade Lenin is now 53 years old.")

"I was returning to the Kremlin at night from a meeting that had gone on very late. Conditions then were not very gay (it was the second half of 1918). The worse phase of our military defeats, desperate famine in the capital, feverish activity on the part of counter-revolutionary organizations. We returned literally wet from every meeting, worn out with fatigue—this was the exhausting battle we had to wage with traitors and informers. Their ally was hunger. And with the approach of winter there was also cold."

This is from an article in *Pravda* of January 22, 1927, by L. S. Sosnovsky, a member from 1917 to 1924 of the All-Russian Central Executive Committee (VTSIK), editor of *Bednota*, a peasant newspaper, and one of Russia's most prominent publicists in the 1920's. It was August, 1918, and some August nights, in Moscow, chill the bones. "In the Kremlin," Sosnovsky continued, "not a soul was to be seen. A few dozen more paces and I would be home. But on the pavement opposite a figure appeared out of the darkness. Lit up by a dim lantern or the light from a window?—but something prompted me:

"Isn't that Lenin?

"Alone? So late? And walking not in the direction of his apartment but toward the embankment? Is it he? Collar of the coat turned up, cap down over his forehead. It's undoubtedly he. Was it proper to abandon him alone in this disturbing quiet of a dark night? And what about the shot heard the evening before? I fingered the revolver in my pocket. I must go over to Lenin, not leave him alone. But perhaps he wants solitude. Is it right to bother him, draw him into conversation, disturb his lonely walk?

"No, it is terrible to go away. Suppose . . . My abandoning him could never be justified. I shall follow him . . . Lenin heard my steps and turned around. Now I had to address him so as not to alarm him.

" 'Hello, Vladimir Ilyich. . . . How come you are out so late and in such weather?'

" 'Hello . . . I couldn't sleep and have a headache. I decided to get some fresh air. And what about you?'

"I told him of the meeting from which I was returning.

"Vladimir Ilyich asked what factories I had visited in recent days and what was happening there. What was the mood of the workers? His ability to get from every person the facts he needed is well known.

"I told him about the very stormy meetings on the Prohorovka and in the Alexandrovsky railway shops, that we barely managed to get the floor, that we were literally pulled off the speaker's platform. The mood of the workers is bad. And there are good reasons why. Again, in the last few days, nothing has been distributed on the ration cards. It is terrible to look at the faces of the women workers. They bear the stamp of famine. And the SR's and Mensheviks shamelessly enflame the discontent, spread monstrous rumors, and fantastic accusations. It is extremely difficult to combat them. The people are hungry, suffering. Still, class consciousness wins out. But every day brings new wavering, new explosions of despair.

"Lenin scarcely interrupted me with questions; he listened, sadly shaking his head. He asked with special emphasis about the railwaymen and the metal workers: how are they?

"Then, interrupting my tale, he said over and over again, gloomily:

" 'Mm, yes . . . our worker has slackened, grown weak.' "

They stood there and talked on the narrow red-brick walk inside the Kremlin. "He has weakened, our worker has weakened," Lenin kept repeating. "Yes, our worker has grown slack."

The Soviet system was called "the dictatorship of the proletariat," the dictatorship of the working class, and now the working class, even in the capital city, had grown slack.

Lenin recognized the danger. He urged workers at a meeting in the Lefortovsky district of Moscow on July 19, 1918, to "Look the danger in the face. . . . We have enemies everywhere, but we also have new allies—the proletariat of the belligerent nations." And domestic allies too: "the great mass of poor peasants." He tried to explain the country's difficulties: "All the imperialistic animals of prey are throwing themselves on Russia and want to tear her to pieces because they know that every hour of the existence of socialist Russia prepares their destruction."

Again, in a speech to the Moscow provincial conference of factory committees on July 23, 1918, he sought to educate. In general, Lenin always courted but never cosseted his audience. He was a straight shooter. His method as a propagandist was repetition. He mixed unpleasant truth with world-revolutionary hope and salted the dish with an interesting idea or two that lifted his addresses high above the average. There were no flowers in them but also no weeds. Thus, on this occasion, he again emphasized that the Russian revolution was only "one unit of the international socialist army" and the success of the part depended on the success of the whole. "This fact is never forgotten by any of us." That Russia made the first socialist revolution was explained not by her economic development. "Quite the contrary: by the backwardness of Russia, by the inability of the so-called national bourgeoisie to cope with the proletarian battalions, its inability to conquer political power and through it to establish its own class dictatorship." Then a caution, since overlooked in Asia, Africa, and Latin America by his ideological children: "A revolution cannot be made to order, cannot be timed to this or that minute, but ripens in the process of historic development." This was sobriety. There followed the pink dream: "And the minute is near." It will arrive "inevitably."[1] Three days later, "The day of reckoning for the bourgeoisie of all lands is near. In Western Europe indignation grows stronger."[2]

In August, 1918, Lenin redoubled his efforts. As the weather worsened he tried to improve the political climate. On August 2 he delivered three speeches. That week news reached him of a peasant uprising in Penza

[1] *Pravda*, July 24, 1918.
[2] *Pravda*, July 28, 1918.

province in central Russia, west of the Volga and east of Tambov. He had sent Eugenia B. Bosh, People's Secretary of Internal Affairs in the Ukraine, to Penza for information about peasant discontent. She telegraphed her report: five rural districts had risen against the Soviet government. He wired instructions to the provincial executive committee, with a copy to Eugenia Bosh, "to carry out merciless mass terror against kulaks, priests, and White Guards; persons of doubtful standing should be locked up in concentration camps outside the city. Send an expedition" to the mutinous districts. "Telegraph about your actions." Three days later he wired again: "Altogether astonished by the absence of information on the progress and results of the suppression of the kulak uprising in the five districts. I do not wish to think that you have procrastinated or shown weakness in the suppression or in the exemplary confiscation of the property and especially of the grain belonging to the insurgent kulaks."[3]

Penza was not the only province experiencing peasant revolts.

At a meeting in Moscow on August 9 Lenin said, "The Russian revolution has thrown sparks into all the countries of the world; high-handed imperialism is nearing the brink of the chasm. Comrades, our situation is difficult" but we must "retain in our hands the banner of socialist revolution we have raised. The workers of all countries look to us with hope. You hear their voices: 'Hold out a little longer,' they say. 'We are surrounded by enemies, but we will come to your aid and, with forces united finally cast the imperialist wolves into the chasm.' "[4]

As August wore on, Lenin's mood grew grimmer. He begged workers and peasants in the provinces not to ally themselves with the Left Social Revolutionaries (who were obviously still a power among the peasantry) and not to neglect the middle peasant, the stratum that was better off than the poor but did not speculate and hoard like the kulaks. "Try to make concessions to the middle peasant, be more careful, be more just to him."[5] But no mercy for Left SR's! "You were wrong not to arrest them as is being done everywhere," he told a communist visitor from the hinterland. "All SR's must be expelled from all responsible jobs. Power in the provinces should now be taken into our hands completely."[6]

August 16—this was about the time of his nocturnal headache, insomnia, and talk with Sosnovsky—Lenin revealed his thoughts to the important Moscow Committee of the communist party: "One senses a great deficiency of strength. . . . At our meetings few new forces speak up."[7] He drove himself to the limit. In the midst of all his cares, he sent a long letter to the American workers. Michael M. Borodin, a participant in the 1905 Russian revolution who was to achieve fame in China, had come from Chicago to Moscow

[3] Lenin, *Sochineniya*, Fourth ed., Vol. 36, pp. 448-449.
[4] *Izvestia*, Aug. 11, 1918.
[5] Lenin, *op. cit.*, Second ed., Vol. XXIII, p. 173.
[6] *Ibid.*, editorial note, p. 560.
[7] *Ibid.*, p. 175.

and talked with Lenin. Under the inspiration of this encounter, Lenin wrote the letter, an indignant letter, and the Bolsheviks believed it was widely disseminated in the United States—thanks to John Reed. Lenin zealously defended the Brest-Litovsk treaty and flayed the imperialists who did not want peace. He protested the lies about Soviet Russia that circulated in the United States. "Oh, hypocrites," he cried, "oh, scoundrels, who libel the workers' government." He excoriated the double standard. "The British bourgeois forget their 1649, the French their 1793. Terror was legitimate and lawful when applied for self-benefit by the bourgeoisie against the feudals. Terror became monstrous and criminal when the workers and poor peasants dared to apply it to the bourgeoisie." Most of the letter was red-hot with anger. But toward the conclusion comes a cool paragraph: "We know, comrades-American-workers, that your help will probably not arrive soon, for revolution develops in different forms and at differing tempos (and it cannot be otherwise)." The phrase "different forms" is among Lenin's most neglected pronouncements. "We are betting on the inevitability of the international revolution but this does not at all mean that we, like simpletons, bet on the inevitability of revolution in a *known* short term. . . . Nevertheless, we firmly know that we are invincible, for humanity will not be crushed by imperialist slaughter but will master it. . . .

"We live as in a besieged fortress" but help from the outside will come. "In a word, we are invincible, for the world proletarian revolution is invincible."[8]

From these heights of faith he descended to Moscow factory meetings to face reality: the chaos of management under nationalization; hunger; the approach of winter.

The first requisite of the leader is physiological strength, biological power. Lenin's compact body had it. As the crisis deepened, as Western military intervention and domestic subversion spread, he tapped the reserves of his energy. On August 30, 1918, he addressed two meetings of workers. At the first he called attention to events in the Ukraine, the Volga region, Siberia, and the Caucasus; the soviets had been deposed by Russian counterrevolutionaries and foreign interventionists, and "Land has been restored to the nobility, factories and mills returned to their former owners, the eight-hour day annulled, workers' and peasants' organizations swept away"; the old tsarist police had reappeared. "Let every worker and peasant who still harbors doubts about the government look at the Volga, Siberia, the Ukraine, and then the answer, clear and definite, will come of itself."[9]

The same evening Lenin went to the industrial area across the Moskva River and talked to a large assembly of factory hands in the nationalized Mihelson plant. He found it necessary to debate with absentees: Kerensky,

[8] *Ibid.*, pp. 176-189. The letter, dated Aug. 20, 1918, was published in *Pravda* on Aug. 22, 1918.
[9] *Ibid.*, p. 200.

Milyukov, and others of the democratic Provisional coalition that overthrew tsarism. Wherever the kulaks and bourgeoisie rule, he added, "they give nothing to the toiling masses. Take America, the freest, the most civilized [country]. There they have a democratic republic. And what is the result? A handful of millionaires and billionaires insolently dominate, and the entire nation—is in slavery and bondage. . . . Wherever democrats rule real, unending robbery exists. We know the true nature of so-called democracy." The Soviets, to be sure, were having trouble with the peasantry, but he put his trust "in the factory-and-mill proletariat."[10]

Lenin finished his speech with the exclamation: "For us there is one alternative: Victory or Death." Before the applause had died he was advancing with short, quick steps toward the exit. Two Right Social Revolutionaries, Novikov and Fanny Kaplan, had heard the address. As Lenin came near them on the way out, Novikov extended his arm to push several workers aside so Fanny Kaplan could move closer to Lenin. Suddenly she whipped out a revolver and fired three shots. Two struck Lenin. He fell to the cobblestones.

Whether because of panic or because it was Russia, it did not occur to anybody to bring him to a hospital where doctors, nurses, X-ray apparatus, and supplies would be immediately available. He was taken by car to the house in the Kremlin in which he lived and allowed to walk up to his third-floor apartment. He collapsed into a chair in the vestibule. Four physicians were summoned. Later Dr. Vladimir N. Rozanov, a surgeon, was called for consultation.[11] The doctors found that one bullet had broken the left shoulder and injured the left arm; the second bullet "penetrated the apex of the left lung, penetrated the neck from left to right, and settled near the right sterno-clavicular joint." It had passed "immediately in front of the vertebra, between it and the gullet" without harming the large blood vessels of the neck. "If the bullet had deviated one millimeter in either direction, Vladimir Ilyich, of course, would already be dead." A serious hemorrhage into the left chest cavity had pressed the heart far to the right.

Dr. Rozanov felt for Lenin's pulse. It was weak; at times he lost it altogether. "Ah, it's nothing. They are disturbed for nothing," Lenin said. The doctor told him to keep quiet. Lenin whispered something again, and Dr. Rozanov again told him to be quiet. Lenin smiled faintly. During the examination which, Rozanov knew, was painful, Lenin made a wry face once or twice, but never moaned or groaned.

The five physicians withdrew to another room in the apartment for consultation. They had no doubt that the bullets should not be removed. The possibility of infection worried them. Lenin's physical strength gave them

---

[10] *Ibid.*, p. 201-202.

[11] The account that follows, including the details of the course of the bullets and of Lenin's condition and medical treatment, as well as the quotations, are from Dr. Rozanov's contribution to *Vospominaniya*, Vol. 2, pp. 325-346.

hope. His impatience troubled them. He talked and moved. When they returned to his bed, he said, "It's nothing, nichevo, good, it can happen to any revolutionist." They tried to impress upon him the need for silence and tranquillity. Later they put his arm in traction, partly because that was the proper treatment, partly to keep him still in bed.

Within forty-eight hours, Lenin's pulse was satisfactory. Gradually the blood in the lung from the hemorrhage was absorbed. Massage reduced the pain in the thumb and index finger of the left hand, the result of injury to a nerve. Lenin began to think of resuming work. The physicians insisted that he go to the government rest house at Gorky, not far from Moscow. Reluctantly he obeyed. At the end of September he came into the city for an examination. The medical authorities declared him in excellent condition. They taught him to massage his hand, and instructed him to guard his health and keep his apartment warm. Lenin laughed. "I ordered an electric stove brought," he said, "It was brought, but it turns out that this is against regulations. So what to do? It will have to remain—doctors' orders." They laughed. He tried to pay them. They refused.

Dr. Rozanov, who could distinctly feel the bullet in Lenin's neck with his fingers, asked whether the bullets gave him any feeling of discomfort. Lenin said, No, and added, "We'll remove them in 1920 when we will have finished with Wilson."

Maxim Gorky visited Lenin while he was recuperating in Gorky. "He had hardly regained the use of his hand and could scarcely move his neck. . . . When I expressed my indignation, he replied, as though dismissing something of which he was tired, 'A brawl. Nothing to be done. Every one acts according to his lights.'

"We met on very friendly terms, but of course there was evident regret in dear Ilyich's sharp and penetrating glance, for I was one who had gone astray"—on the question of Mach-vs.-Marx philosophy.

After several minutes, Lenin "said heatedly, 'He who is not with us is against us. People independent of the march of events—that is a fantasy. Even if we grant that such people did once exist, at present they do not and cannot exist. They are no good to any one. . . . You say I simplify life too much? That this simplification threatens culture with ruin, eh?'

"Then his ironic, characteristic, 'Hm, hm . . .'

"His keen glance sharpened," Gorky wrote in his recollections,[12] "and he continued in a lower tone: 'Well, and millions of peasants with rifles in their hands are not a threat to culture according to you, eh? You think the Constituent Assembly could have coped with that anarchy? . . . We have got to put before the Russian masses something they can grasp. The Soviets and Communism are simple.

" 'A union of the workers and intelligentsia, eh? Well, that isn't bad. Tell the intelligentsia. Let them come to us. According to you they are true

[12] Maxim Gorky, Days With Lenin, p. 39 et seq.

servants of justice. What is the matter then? Certainly, let them come to us. We are just the ones who have undertaken the colossal job of putting the people on their feet, of telling the whole world the truth about life—it is we who are pointing out to the people the straight path to a human life, the path which leads out of slavery, beggary, degradation.'

"He laughed and said without any trace of resentment, 'That is why I received a bullet from the intelligentsia.'

"When the temperature of the conversation was more or less normal, he said with vexation and sadness, 'Do you think I quarrel with the idea that the intelligentsia is necessary to us? But you see how hostile their attitude is, how badly they understood the need of the moment? And they don't see how powerless they are without us, how incapable of reaching the masses. They will be to blame if we break too many heads.' "

It apparently never occurred to Lenin that his attitude toward the intelligentsia (before and after the revolution) might have been partly responsible for theirs.

The day Lenin was shot, Moisay S. Uritsky, chief of the Cheka in Petrograd, died at the hand of a revolver-wielding Right SR student named Kanegisser.

This was the Bolshevik nadir.

That very evening President Sverdlov called for Red terror. He addressed the All-Russian Central Executive Committee (VTSIK) on September 2; the Committee thereupon adopted a resolution authorizing "a massive red terror against the bourgeoisie and its agents."[13]

Fanny (sometimes called Dora) Kaplan, aged thirty-five, was taken to a cell in the Cheka building on Lubyanka Square. Two days later the commandant of the Kremlin, Pavel Malkov, received an order to bring her to the Kremlin and put her under "a trustworthy guard." He drove to the Lubyanka, and took her by car to the Kremlin where he imprisoned her in a semibasement room under Sverdlov's apartment. On September 3, Varlam A. Avanesov, a high-ranking Bolshevik, summoned Malkov and showed him a Cheka decree: "Kaplan to be executed. The verdict to be carried out by Kremlin commandant Malkov."

Malkov told his story in 1958:

"The shooting of a person, particularly of a woman, is not an easy thing. That is a difficult, very difficult duty. But I was never called on to carry out a more just verdict. 'When?' I asked Avanesov. . . .

"Today, immediately," Avanesov replied.

"All kinds of fables and nonsense tales are in circulation: that Kaplan allegedly remained alive, that Lenin allegedly canceled the verdict at the last moment. There are even 'eyewitnesses' who 'met' Kaplan either in the Butirki prison, or in Solovkii, or in Vorkuta, and I don't know where else. These fairy tales were born of a petty bourgeois urge to represent Lenin as a

<hr>

[13] Lenin, *op. cit.*, Second ed., Vol. XXIII, editorial note, p. 563.

kindly fellow who graciously forgave enemies their evil deeds. No . . . No-body annulled Kaplan's death sentence. On September 3, 1918, the sentence was carried out, and I carried it out, I, a communist, a sailor of the Baltic Fleet, commandant of the Moscow Kremlin, Pavel Dmitrievich Malkov—with my own hands."[14]

The fact was officially announced on page five of Moscow *Izvestia* of September 4, 1918. Under a general two-column title, "White Terror," the first item read in full: "Execution of Roid-Kaplan. Yesterday, pursuant to the decision of the All-Russian Cheka, the Right SR woman, Fanny Roid (also known as Kaplan), who fired at Lenin, was executed."

"When I returned to Moscow from Stockholm," wrote Angelica Balaba-noff, a veteran Russian socialist and close friend of Lenin, he "was still recuperating at a house in the country." She sped to him by car. "Lenin was sitting on a balcony in the sun. At the sight of him and the thought of how close he had been to death, I was overcome with emotion and embraced him silently." He asked her many questions about the prospect of splitting foreign socialist parties and attracting dissidents to the international com-munist movement.

"Only when the time came for me to leave did we refer to what had hap-pened to him and indirectly to the Terror that followed. When we spoke of Dora Kaplan, the young woman who had shot him and who had been executed, Krupskaya [Lenin's wife] became very upset. I could see that she was deeply affected at the thought of revolutionaries condemned to death by a revolutionary power. Later, when we were alone, she wept bitterly when she spoke of this. Lenin himself did not care to enlarge upon the episode."[15] He said, "The Central Committee will decide" what is to happen to Dora Kaplan.[16] Dora Kaplan was already dead.

Tsarist tyranny bred individual terror. So, in the beginning, did Soviet terror. Then Lenin's massive state terror stopped individual terror.

ononononon

After Lenin had recuperated from his bullet wounds he obeyed doctors' orders to walk in the Kremlin grounds and, while doing so, stretch his left arm by scratching his back as high as possible. To quiet widespread appre-hension that he was dead the authorities decided to make a film of one of these strolls without telling him; if he had known he would have objected. V. D. Bonch-Bruevich, a close co-worker, made the arrangements and accom-

[14] *Moskva (Moscow Magazine)*, November, 1958. Issue No. 11, P. Malkov, "Zapiski Komendanta Kremlya" ("Memoirs of the Commandant of the Kremlin,") pp. 123-161.

[15] *My Life as a Rebel* (New York and London, 1938), pp. 187-188. The rebel remained a rebel and was active for decades in Europe as a leading anticommunist socialist.

[16] Angelica Balabanoff, *Lenin. Psychologische Beobachtungen und Betrachtungen* (Hannover, 1959), p. 47.

panied him but left his side on some excuse or other so that pictures of Lenin alone could be taken. After some time Lenin noticed men running wildly across paths and scurrying from building to building and he asked Bonch who they were. Bonch could no longer suppress the secret: they were photographers, he revealed. For a moment Lenin was angry, but when Bonch explained the purpose, and that the film would be exhibited to workers, Lenin acquiesced and cooperated.

XX. THE EMERGING PATTERN OF THE CIVIL WAR

WHEN FANNY KAPLAN made her attempt on Lenin's life, Trotsky was at the front near Kazan on the Volga. He rushed to Moscow. He was the heir apparent. True, he had joined the communist party only recently, in July, 1917, and on his record were years of opposition to Lenin and to Bolshevism. But the fire of revolution burned his sins to ash. Lenin had accepted him. To the country and to the party he stood next to Lenin, though several steps down, as a symbol of Sovietism.

Death hovered in Lenin's sick chamber. Had he died, powermen in the party apparatus might have resisted the succession of the stranger in their midst. Yet Trotsky was no longer a stranger. In the 1918 trough of Bolshevik fortunes, few would have dared to let the scepter pass to Stalin, still unknown, or to Sverdlov, a prosaic organization man, or to the youthful Bukharin, or still less to Kamenev or Zinoviev who, despite their long party membership, voted against launching the revolution on November 7. Trotsky had favored it and led it. This counted more than his Menshevik-non-Bolshevik past. Trotsky, dashing, daring, dynamic, was cast in a hero's mold. He was not one-piece marble, steel, or bronze. Rather his figure would have looked like an exhumed Greek statue restored with patches of clay. He was no Lenin, but there were no other Lenins; there was no one as electric as Trotsky.

Trotsky addressed the All-Russian Central Executive Committee in Moscow on September 2. He referred to "the front where Vladimir Ilyich's life struggles with death. Whatever defeats may be expected by us on this or that front—I am firmly convinced of our imminent victory—the defeat of no single part could be so difficult, so tragic, for the working class of Russia and the whole world, as would be the fatal issue of the fight at the front that runs through the breast of our leader."

In Lenin, Trotsky said, "Nature produced a masterpiece . . . a figure of blood and iron created for our epoch." Lenin embodied "the revolutionary thinking and the unbending energy of the working class." He was "the great man of our revolutionary epoch."

"I know and you know too, comrades," Trotsky cautioned, "that the fate of the working class does not depend on single personalities" but "that does not mean that personality in the history of our movement . . . is of minor importance." Karl Marx had been criticized for prophesying that "the revolution would be much nearer than was actually the case." Others answered with perfect right that as Marx stood on a high mountain the distance seemed shorter.

"Many have criticized Vladimir Ilyich, too, more than once—and I among them—because he did not notice many less conspicuous causes and accidental circumstances. I must say that this might have been a defect for a political leader in a time of 'normal' slow development; but this was the greatest merit of Comrade Lenin as leader of the new epoch. All that is incidental, external, or of secondary importance is omitted, and only the basic, irreconcilable antagonism of the class remains."

Why did Trotsky recall his differences with Lenin? They amounted to a charge, he was now saying, that Lenin had been inflexible, had overlooked the incidental and accidental factors of history, had looked at the world, like Marx, from a high mountain, and seen only the class struggle. Why remind his colleagues of past arguments? Because unmentioned they could be used against him by rivals. To recall them, he presumably hoped, was to dismiss them. And the next moment he recalled his collaboration with Lenin since the revolution: "Any one to whom it was granted, as it was to me in this period, to observe Vladimir Ilyich's work at close range could not fail to look with enthusiasm—I repeat the word enthusiasm—at this gift of the keen, penetrating mind that rejects all the external, the accidental, and superficial, in order to perceive the main roads and methods of action." The grubber in trivia is overcome by myriad minutiae. Lenin observed from the peak and saw the main road.

In addition to "a powerful mind, Vladimir Ilyich also was endowed with an inflexible will." The combination produced "the real revolutionary leader," bold, pitiless, hard, unyielding.

Then Trotsky talked about the civil war, the war with the Czechoslovaks and "the White Guards, the mercenaries of England and France." He was going back to the front in the assurance that Lenin "will soon be up again, to think and to work. In return we promise to fight with the enemy of the working class to the last drop of blood, to our last breath."[1]

Stalin did not come to Moscow when Lenin was wounded. During the first five months of 1918 he had busied himself with the drafting of a federal constitution and with affairs on the periphery of Russia, seat of the national

[1] Leon Trotsky, Lenin (Authorized Translation), pp. 196-205.

minorities. The volume of his collected works covering this period includes no important statement on policy or theory.[2] On May 29, the Sovnarkom appointed him special commissar for food supplies in southern Russia. He left Moscow on June 4 and arrived on June 6 in Tsaritsin, later known as Stalingrad and, more recently, Volgagrad. On July 7 he wired Lenin that "in Tsaritsin, Astrakhan, and Saratov," three big cities on the Volga, "the [state] grain monopoly [decreed by Moscow] and fixed prices [for bread] have been abolished by the [local] soviets." This was a measure of the administrative anarchy. "Bacchanalia and speculation," he added, "are rife." He acted very quickly, it would seem. "I have succeeded," he told Lenin, "in introducing rationing and fixed prices in Tsaritsin." Railway and river transportation were disorganized. Bataysk, a rail junction town near Rostov on the Don, had been captured by the Germans, he reported.[3]

The same day Stalin wrote Lenin a letter. "I am hastening to the front," it began. "I write only about concrete matters. (1) The railway line south of Tsaritsin has not yet been re-established. I am driving and scolding everybody, anybody who needs to be; I hope it will soon be restored. You may rest assured that we will not spare anyone, not myself, and not others, and we will certainly deliver the grain. If our military 'specialists' (shoemakers) were not asleep and idle the line would not have been cut, and if the line is restored it will be not thanks to the military but in spite of them." The military specialists were tsarist officers recruited, with Lenin's approval, by Trotsky. "(5) Things in Turkestan are bad. England is bossing the show through Afghanistan. Give somebody (or me) special powers (of a military character) in the region of southern Russia to take urgent steps before it is too late."[4]

On July 10 Stalin dispatched another letter to Lenin from Tsaritsin: "Comrade Lenin, A few words. If Trotsky will, thoughtlessly, hand out credentials right and left to Trifonov (in the Don region), to Antonov (Kuban region), to Koppe (Stavropol), to members of the French mission (who deserve to be arrested), and so forth, you may be sure that within a month everything in the North Caucasus will crash and this region will be lost to us definitely." To accomplish the task of obtaining grain, Stalin explained, "I need full military authority. I have already written about this but received no reply. Very good. In that case I myself will, without formalities, dismiss those commanders and commissars who are ruining the situation. This is what the common interest tells me to do, and, of course, the absence of a piece of paper from Trotsky will not stop me."[5]

These were the first brutal manifestations of the Stalin-Trotsky feud which shattered Soviet politics for decades and shook the world. Many years before

[2] Stalin, *Sochineniya*, Vol. 4 (Moscow, 1947).
[3] *Ibid.*, pp. 116-117.
[4] *Ibid.*, pp. 118-119. Parts of the letter were first published in *Pravda*, Dec. 21, 1929, Stalin's fiftieth birthday.
[5] *Ibid.*, pp. 120-121. First published in the 1947 volume.

the issues of agrarian collectivization, rapid industrialization, and the Chinese revolution that allegedly caused the historic duel could have arisen, Stalin was casting suspicion on Trotsky's loyalty and ability and demonstrating a consuming hunger for power and the defiant determination to seize it in competition with Trotsky. Lenin was able to bank the fire of Stalin's envy but never to extinguish it.

Stalin's rivalry with Trotsky runs like a black thread through the history of the Soviet civil war, adding to Lenin's towering burdens. When Fanny Kaplan's bullets laid the leader low, Soviet power was boxed in by the troops of both coalitions in the great European war and by anti-Bolshevik Russian armies. Germany had shorn Russia of Poland, the Baltic States, Finland, the Ukraine, the Crimea, as well as the Caucasus where the three republics of Azerbaijan, Georgia, and Armenia, having seceded from Soviet Russia, were in part occupied by Germans. In addition, Turkey seized the provinces of Kars and Ardahan and took possession of the Black Sea port of Batum. All in all, the German-led Quadruple Alliance held 400,000 square miles of Russian territory inhabited by 60 million persons. Germany thus constituted the western and southern sides of the box into which Bolshevism had been squeezed.

The nations of the Western Entente intervened in Russia after Germany did. Only the northern and eastern sides of the box were available to them. Tsarist officers who escaped from Soviet rule at the very beginning of the revolution ensconced themselves in a segment of the southeastern corner of the box, in the region of the Don and Kuban Cossacks, those famous horsemen whose mobility, before the day of tanks and, in a country like Russia with inadequate roads and railroads, was a major military asset. Great Britain began courting the generals immediately after November 7, 1917; on December 3, 1917, Prime Minister David "Lloyd George and the rest of the War Cabinet decided to guarantee to Kaledin all the financial support he needed, without regard to expense."[6]

General A. M. Kaledin had been elected ataman of the Don Cossack troops in June, 1917. Among his associates were General Lavr G. Kornilov, leader of the abortive coup d'état in Petrograd in 1917, General Mikhail V. Alexeyev, former tsarist chief of staff, and General of Infantry Anton I. Denikin. To the remote bidder, this seemed an impressive collection of Russian brass. But the Cossacks had been through too many world war battles to follow the generals so soon into a new war. They too needed a respite. A British officer sent to assess their value cabled, "Cossacks absolutely useless and disorganized."[7] Kaledin, defeated by Bolshevik troops in

[6] Richard H. Ullman, *Anglo-Soviet Relations, 1917-1921. Intervention and the War* (Princeton, 1961), p. 46. Mr. Ullman had access to the unpublished papers of Lord Milner, a member of the War Cabinet, and to other treasures of official documents. He quotes the text of telegrams sent to a British representative authorizing money payments to Kaledin "up to any figure necessary."

[7] *Ibid.*, p. 49.

February, 1918, resigned his atamanship and committed suicide. Kornilov was killed on April 13, 1918, in an assault on Yekaterinodar (now Krasnodar) in the Kuban region.[8] The British continued to cooperate with the Cossack commanders and later got better results for their money. But direct intervention by Allied troops was obviously a prerequisite to the establishment of an eastern front.

As a prelude, and in some respects a trigger, to the advent of foreign expeditionary forces, a remarkable spectacle was enacted by some forty to fifty thousand members of the Czechoslovak Legion who roamed for months over the vast spaces of Russia, fighting, and destroying soviets, as they went. Their famous Anabasis commenced in and around Kiev and took them thousands of miles east by slow trains to Vladivostok, then back to Siberia, and back and forth across Siberia and into European Russia as far as the Volga.

During the early years of the First World War, many Czech and Slovak officers and privates in the Austro-Hungarian army willingly surrendered to the Russians; they had no heart for fighting in the ranks of their oppressors. Soon the idea occurred to them to form, together with Czech and Slovak civilians resident in Russia, a corps that would serve the Western Allies. The Tsar rejected the proposal: it would have angered Austria-Hungary and thus closed the door to a separate peace with the Viennese Kaiser; it might have given a fillip to separatism among the ever-restive ethnic minorities in Russia. The Czechs and Slovaks, to be sure, were brother Slavs, but they were republican antimonarchists and most of them were Roman Catholic. These factors weighed more than Pan-Slavism, a synthetic spirit that could be turned on and off as politics required. The prisoners remained prisoners.

The republican Provisional government which overthrew the Tsar adopted a different policy. Nudged by Thomas G. Masaryk, future President of Czechoslovakia then in Russia, and by General Maurice Janin, chief of the French military mission in Petrograd, it ordered the release of the prisoners and their training and equipment for war. The French mission took over the training. In May, 1917, Masaryk wrote, "I came to an agreement with the French Military Mission to send thirty thousand prisoners to France. . . . We were promised . . . that transports would be sent via Archangel as soon as possible."[9] French liaison officers were attached to all the units of the corps. Russian officers joined them. When Masaryk visited General Nikolai N. Dukhonin, Russia's Chief of Staff, on October 9, 1917, it was "explicitly agreed with Dukhonin that our army would be used only against the foreign enemy." The Kornilov uprising had already taken place, another uprising

---

[8] *Razlozheniye Armii v 1917 Godu (The Disintegration of the Army in 1917)*. Prepared for publication by N. E. Kakurin from documents in the tsarist archives, with an introduction by Y. A. Yakovlev (Moscow-Leningrad, 1925). An appendix contains biographical data on tsarist military personnel.

[9] This early history of the Legion follows T. G. Masaryk, *Die Welt Revolution. Erinnerungen und Betrachtungen. 1914-1918* (Berlin, 1925); and Eduard Beneš, *Der Aufstand der Nationen* (Berlin, 1928).

might take place, and Masaryk did not want his men embroiled in Russian domestic affairs. The Czechoslovak Legion was to fight in France under the eyes of the world. This would be Czechoslovakia's visa to independence.

Came the Bolshevik revolution, the Bolshevik peace negotiations with Germany, and the German army's entry into the Ukraine in the spring of 1918. The Czechoslovaks had to get out of the Ukraine. An idea was conceived and adopted to move the corps "from Kiev to France by way of Siberia—a fantastic plan," Masaryk admitted. The corps became part of the French army. "We were financially dependent on France and the Allies."[10]

France, weak from loss of blood, welcomed the prospect of Czechoslovak reinforcements on the western front. Every platoon counted. But, according to Dr. Masaryk, "England would have preferred to see us in Russia, or actually, in Siberia." Masaryk, who knew Russia well, declared, "I had thought of the war against the Bolsheviks and against Russia. I would have attached myself and our corps to an army which would have been strong enough for a struggle against the Bolsheviks and the Germans, and which would have defended democracy." His next sentence read, "There was only one possibility for the fight against the Bolsheviks—the mobilization of the Japanese."

This approximated the British position adumbrated "around the beginning of April," 1918, by British military planners in a document submitted to the Allied Permanent Military Representatives. It "envisaged the advance of an Allied expeditionary force from Vladivostok to the area of the Urals, and possibly the Volga. The Japanese were to form the 'mobile base or nucleus' of this force; but they were to enjoy . . . 'the eventual assistance *of Czech and other elements which can be organized on the spot.*'"[11]

The British scheme seems to have gained support from the French, and after a discussion between high-ranking representatives of both nations in Versailles on April 27, a second document was drafted on the disposition of the Czechoslovaks. It provided that all Czech troops that had not passed Omsk on their way to Vladivostok were to be routed to Murmansk and Archangel where, while awaiting transport for France, "they could be profitably employed in defending Archangel and Murmansk and in guarding and protecting the Murman railway." The Czechoslovaks who had moved eastward beyond Omsk were to cooperate with the Allies in Siberia.[12]

George F. Kennan comments: "The wording of this note, together with the fact that as much as six weeks later no serious move had yet been made by either government to provide shipping either to Vladivostok or at the northern ports, makes it very difficult to believe that the idea of dividing the Corps was anything other, in the minds of its authors, than a disingenuous one, designed to give perfunctory recognition to the principle of the eventual

[10] Masaryk, *op. cit.*, p. 198.

[11] George F. Kennan, *The Decision to Intervene* (Princeton, N.J., 1958), p. 145. Kennan cites the document from the National Archives in Washington, D.C. Kennan's italics.

[12] *Ibid.*, pp. 146-147. Cited from National Archives in Washington, D.C.

removal of the Czech units to France but actually to assure their availability for service in Russia in the event of Allied intervention."

The intention to keep the Legion in Russia was the essence, the rest was consequence. For the British and French it would have been preposterous to transport the Czechoslovaks from Vladivostok across the Pacific, through North America, and across the Atlantic to the western front when they themselves planned to send their own troops to Russia. It made just as little sense to bring the Legion to Murmansk and Archangel, and ship it from there to France and then ship British and French forces to Murmansk and Archangel. This was the logic of the retention of the Czechoslovak corps in Russia. The incidents, the minor and major irritants, were secondary. Sometimes subordinate issues make history. In this case, surface troubles wrapped history in mist.

The Soviets had stated their purpose, on March 26, to disarm the Czechoslovaks but allow them to keep a few weapons for guarding trains and depots. When Thomas Masaryk heard of this in Tokyo he told U.S. Ambassador Roland S. Morris, "This report is very favorable: the army is en route to France and needs no weapons because it will be re-equipped there."[13] Eduard Beneš likewise expressed his approval. He added, however, that on April 13, 1918, "at the military conference, the view of a part of the commanders of the first division was adopted against surrendering the arms at the next station to the Bolsheviks—in accordance with the agreement with the Soviets."[14] Two Czech officials in Moscow, Dr. Maxa and Chermak, telegraphed the corps commanders urging fulfillment of the agreement. The commanders, closer to reality and their British and French sponsors, paid no heed.

An incident occurred at Chelyabinsk in west-central Siberia on May 14. Two trains were standing on the tracks, one full of Czechoslovak troops, the other packed with Hungarian prisoners of war. No love was lost between these minorities of the mottled Austro-Hungarian Empire. As chance would have it, a Hungarian hurled a piece of iron into the Czechoslovak train and fatally injured one of the soldiers. Promptly, the Czechoslovaks lynched the Hungarian. After that the Legion refused to give up its arms in accordance with its decision of a month earlier.

Arthur J. Balfour, British Secretary of State for Foreign Affairs, heard of this incident "only months later."[15] The same is true of Lord Robert Cecil, Balfour's undersecretary. Yet on May 18, four days after the incident, Cecil wrote to French Premier Clemenceau that he saw "one possible plan" of "creating a diversion in the East." The plan was to use the Czechoslovaks as a trigger. Cecil was convinced that "they could be used to start operations in

---

[13] *Die Welt Revolution*, p. 216.
[14] *The Soviets in World Affairs*, Vol. I, pp. 110-111.
[15] Ullman, *op. cit.*, p. 168.

Siberia." In the event he had "little doubt that the Japanese would move and the Americans would find it difficult to hold back."[16]

Diplomat proposes and life often disposes otherwise. The Cecil scheme, however, worked out exactly as he and his government contemplated.

The first large-scale descent of Western troops on Soviet Russian soil occurred in the far north. By July 1, 1918, 4,000 British, French, American, Canadian, Italian, and Serbian soldiers had landed at Murmansk on the Arctic Ocean. By mid-July they had occupied Kandalaksha, about one hundred miles south of Murmansk, and the intervening territory as well as Kem, on the White Sea. On August 2, Archangel being free of winter ice, a landing was made there. Ten thousand Western soldiers were now present in the Russian north—but no Czechoslovaks; they had a task in Siberia and the Volga region. On September 4, 4,500 Americans disembarked at Archangel. As the Western forces moved inland under tremendous terrain and climatic hardships, Bolshevism melted away.

This was the northern side of the box the Western Allies were building in Russia. They needed an eastern side. Throughout 1918 British, French, Italian, and Japanese officials repeatedly pressed the United States government to sanction intervention in Siberia and, if possible, participate in it. Woodrow Wilson remained adamantly opposed. Then Wilson's hand was forced. The Czechoslovaks quarreled with the Vladivostok Bolsheviks during June, and on the 29th of the month they drove out the soviet and took over the city. Forthwith, the British and Japanese landed troops from their warships in the harbor. Secretary of State Lansing communicated the news to the President by telephone on July 3. The same afternoon Lord Reading, British ambassador in Washington, submitted to Wilson yet another appeal from the Allied Supreme War Council urging intervention in Siberia. The next day, during the July 4 holiday celebrations, Lansing drafted a paper for the President in which he declared that the Czech capture of Vladivostok and their military victories in Siberia "materially changed the situation by introducing a sentimental element into the question of our duty," and recommending that American troops be sent to Siberia.[17] The "sentimental element" was Wilson's attachment to the idea of a postwar independent Czechoslovakia outlined to him in person by the urbane Masaryk. Within forty-eight hours Wilson and the key men in his administration approved a memorandum which provided that 7,000 American and 7,000 Japanese troops were to go ashore at Vladivostok and filter into the interior. The first large Japanese units entered the city on August 3. Early in November, not 7,000 but 70,000 Japanese armed men were in Siberia. The United States kept the agreement. A British battalion augmented the foreign forces.

Between the German coalition and the Western alliance the Bolsheviks

[16] *Ibid.*, pp. 169-170.
[17] Kennan, *op. cit.*, p. 395.

were thus constricted into an irregular rectangle which included Petrograd and Moscow and points south and east and an arched tail that hung down from it along the lower reaches of the Volga to Astrakhan where the river flows into the Caspian Sea.

There was nothing regular in the fighting fronts of the Soviet civil war that began in 1917 and ended in 1921. Certainly in the early phases there was nothing that could be described as a continuous front line. A war map of the opposing forces would have looked more like a weather chart with patches marked "high" and "low," and "low" patches within the "high" patches and vice versa. Whites and Left and Right Social Revolutionaries operated inside the Bolshevik zone, and when the Czechoslovaks or the British or Germans or Turks or Japanese or Americans marched into an area and ousted the soviets, the communists and the pro-communists did not disappear. They continued to conduct guerrilla warfare and work in the underground against the ostensible masters. The patches on the chart were blown hither and yon by the winds of war. Towns, villages, whole provinces changed hands interminably. Some Ukrainian cities and rural regions were conquered and reconquered as many as seventeen times, and each conqueror printed his own currency which peasants, factory workers, and merchants had to accept only to find that it had become worthless when a new conqueror arrived and introduced his paper bills which, in turn, lost their entire value with the advent of the next rulers. While traveling through the Ukraine and other parts in 1922 and 1923, Soviet citizens would, after the most superficial acquaintance, take me into their confidence and untie the knots of kerchiefs containing wads of Petlura money and Skoropadsky money and Kerensky money and inquire naïvely yet poignantly whether they could get anything for this dirty trash which represented so much toil.

It was inevitable, indeed necessary, that the foreign armies seek domestic allies. For they knew, Russia being the size of North America, that 200,000 or 300,000 troops from outside could neither conquer nor rule her. The Germans, with superior forces in the Ukraine, could not protect their own highest officials, much less take the peasantry's crops. The anti-German coalition partners faced the problem of overthrowing the Lenin-Trotsky regime and of enthroning a viable substitute that would not be fatally handicapped by foreign sponsorship. Nobody thought out this problem; everybody functioned on a day-to-day basis, from hand to mouth, from foreign purse to Russian palm. The Japanese bought Gregory Semenov, ataman of the Ussuri Cossacks, who was a brigand and led his men in depredations against all and sundry. The Czechoslovaks, the best army in the Russia of mid-1918, and a decisive power if concentrated, were strung out along thousands of miles of the Trans-Siberian Railway equipped with ancient fragile rolling stock which stood in repair shops more than it rode the tracks. They sought respectable Russian associates; they gave aid to liberal, sometimes socialist, but sometimes reactionary foes of Bolshevism and assisted them in setting up anti-

Soviet soviets. The Allied diplomatic missions in Vologda, Murmansk, Archangel, and elsewhere poured out roubles as though they were river water. Bruce Lockhart, the British agent in Moscow, wrote "of the French, who, as I knew from their own admission, were supplying funds to Savinkoff. Their promises, too, were extravagant. The Whites were led to believe that Allied military support would be forthcoming in decisive strength. . . . Encouraged by these hopes, the anti-Bolshevik forces began to increase their activities. On June 21st, Volodarsky, the Bolshevik Commissar for Press Affairs in St. Petersburg, was assassinated."[18]

Intervention, assassinations, and insurrections were interlinked directly through conspiracy or indirectly through political climate. On July 1 the British and French landed in Murmansk. On July 6 Mirbach was killed and the Left SR's rose in revolt in Moscow. The same day Right SR's, led by Boris Savinkov, staged an insurrection in Yaroslavl where the Volga intersects the north-south railway line from Archangel to Vologda to Moscow. Three days later similar revolts erupted in Ribinsk, near Yaroslavl, and in Arzamas and Murom, railway and river junction towns on the east-west line between Moscow and Kazan. On August 1 an Allied landing took place in Archangel. On August 6 the Czechoslovaks captured Kazan. On August 30 Uritsky was assassinated and Lenin wounded. If either the longitudinal or latitudinal approach to Moscow, or both, had been cleared by the confluence of foreign intervention and Russian plot, Bolshevism might have foundered. But the foreign expeditionary forces were smaller than the anti-Bolsheviks had expected; Savinkov's insurrection in Yaroslavl lasted fifteen days but its initial impetus was spent before those in the other towns had commenced; and Trotsky with an army stood athwart the path between Moscow and the Czechs at Kazan.

Boris Savinkov was tried in Moscow the evening of August 21, 1924. How and why he re-entered Russia after having fled abroad when his role in the civil war ended is not known; the GPU probably lured him in, as it did others. The trial, however, was not a faked frame-up like the Moscow trials of the 1930's. In a courtroom, which accommodated about one hundred and fifty persons, one saw Felix Djerzhinsky, the gaunt chief of the Cheka, Chicherin, the handsome Karakhan, Radek, Leo Kamenev, then Assistant Prime Minister, and other Soviet celebrities who surely would not have come to hear the defendant recite a script the GPU had written and rehearsed with him.

Savinkov, then about fifty years old, was a known terrorist, prominent revolutionist, and novelist. The right side of his face looked as though a hand had pushed it upward out of symmetry with the left, and in the left cheek there was a deep gash from cheekbone to jowl. His eyes gave the impression of being focused on something he had seen before—death.

Replying to a question by Chief Justice Ulrich of the Soviet Supreme

[18] R. H. Bruce Lockhart, *British Agent*, p. 289.

Court, Savinkov testified, "I have already named [French] Consul Grenard, the military attaché [French General] Lavergne, and the French Ambassador Noulens. They told me your government will be deposed . . . it was necessary, they said, to carry out armed attacks . . . occupy the upper Volga . . . the upper Volga will serve as a base for the advance on Moscow."

The Chief Justice asked about subsidies. Savinkov declared: "They gave the money to me . . . I received two hundred thousand roubles through a Czech by the name of Klecanda. All in all, I received two million Kerensky roubles from the French."

ULRICH: "That was in May, 1918?"

SAVINKOV: "Yes, in May-June, 1918. Later when we determined on the risings, the French gave us two million in one payment specially earmarked for the risings."[19] This confirmed Lockhart's statement that the French "were supplying funds to Savinkoff."

Lockhart himself paid out money to anti-Bolsheviks. He had, at first, sought to establish friendly relations between the British government and the Soviet government. When he saw intervention impending he believed Kremlin approval could be won. But British intervention with hostile intent faced him with a dilemma. "Almost before I had realised it," he wrote in his memoirs, "I had identified myself with a movement which, whatever its original object, was to be directed, not against Germany, but against the de facto government of Russia."

He tried "to explain the motives which had driven me into this illogical situation. . . . Why then had I given my adherence to a policy which seemed to hold out little promise of success and which was to expose me to widespread accusations of inconsistency? . . . I ought to have resigned and come home. Today, I should have been enjoying the reputation of a prophet who had predicted the various phases of the Bolshevik revolution with remarkable accuracy. . . . The motives for my conduct were two. Subconsciously, although I did not put the question at the time, I was unwilling to leave Russia because of Moura." Moura was a Russian woman of the aristocracy, aged twenty-six, whom Lockhart loved. "The other motive—and it was the all compelling one, of which I was fully conscious—was that I lacked the moral courage to resign and to take a stand which would have exposed me to the odium of the vast majority of my countrymen."

Accordingly, "I increased my contacts with the anti-Bolshevik forces." Nevertheless, he still gave the Kremlin the benefit of some doubt. When he heard, on July 17, that the day before Tsar Nicholas and the Tsarina and their family had been executed in a cellar in Yekaterinburg (now Sverdlovsk), he felt "that, alarmed at the approach of the Czech troops, who had now turned in their tracks and were at open war with the Bolsheviks, the local Soviet had taken the law into its own hands." The actual order for the execution was signed by Chairman Beloborodov, of the Central Executive Com-

[19] Fischer, op. cit., Vol. I, pp. 118-119.

mittee of the Ural region, but he would hardly have acted without consulting Moscow. Leon Trotsky states in *Trotsky's Diary in Exile 1935* that he had favored a widely publicized trial of the Tsar. But on returning to Moscow from the front on one occasion, President Sverdlov informed him that the Tsar, the Tsarina, and their children had already been shot. "We decided it here," Sverdlov told Trotsky. "Ilyich believed that we shouldn't leave the Whites a live banner to rally around, especially under present difficult circumstances." Trotsky in exile defended Lenin's extermination of the entire family. "The execution of the Tsar's family," he wrote, "was needed not only in order to frighten, horrify, and dishearten the enemy, but also to shake up our own ranks. . . . In the intellectual circles of the Party there probably were misgivings and shakings of heads. But the masses of workers and soldiers had not a minute's doubt. They would not have understood and would not have accepted any other decision. *This* Lenin sensed well." Bruce Lockhart, however, records a contrasting public attitude. "I am bound to admit," he states, "that the population of Moscow received the news with amazing indifference. Their apathy towards everything except their own fate was complete." When individuals behave as though their fate resides within the four walls of a home, tyrants are safe.

Lockhart also noted that in response to British intervention in north Russia, "The broad masses of the Russian people remained completely apathetic. . . . To have intervened at all was a mistake. To have intervened with hopelessly inadequate forces was an example of paralytic half-measures, which in the circumstances amounted to crime. Apologists for this policy maintain that it served a useful purpose in preventing Russia from falling into the hands of Germany and in detaching German troops from the Western front. By June, 1918, there was no danger of Russia being overrun by Germany."

Nevertheless, Lockhart commenced "to supply financial aid to pro-Ally organizations." The French, he wrote, had been doing all the financing. "Now that we had reached an open rupture with the Bolsheviks I contributed my share." When he was arrested and confined in the Cheka's Lubyanka prison he had on his person the notebook which contained "in cryptic form an account of the moneys I had spent." He asked the innocent guard to take him to the toilet where, under the eyes of the Russian, he flushed the compromising pages down the drain.[20]

The Allies spent huge sums of money to oust the Bolsheviks and introduced thousands of troops into Russia. In mid-1918 the Soviet regime was at its weakest. Why did these efforts fail? Popular apathy, resulting from the disillusioning world war and reinforced by fear of terror and the presence of hunger (hungry people do not usually rebel; Russians were not yet hungry in 1917), was a major factor. The bickerings among the anti-Bolsheviks were equally defeating. Lockhart received a letter from the monarchist General

[20] Lockhart, *op. cit.*, pp. 284 *et seq.*

Alexeyev in south Russia stating that he would "sooner cooperate with Lenin and Trotsky than with Savinkoff or Kerensky."[21] There were scores of such splits. Nor were the anti-Red forces ever concentrated for a mortal blow at the communist system. Forty to fifty thousand Czechoslovaks could have taken Moscow, though its retention was another matter. But those 40,000 to 50,000 troops were strung out thousands of miles along the Trans-Siberian in order to keep open their lines of communication with Vladivostok. The foreign expeditionary forces in north Russia likewise failed to come within striking distance of Moscow or Petrograd. Distance favored the Bolsheviks, division hampered the anti-Bolsheviks.

Despite intervention, conspiracy, successful assassinations, therefore, and with Lenin wounded and the Bolsheviks frightened by the event, no collapse occurred.

The Soviets nevertheless needed a victory to bolster their morale. It arrived on September 10, 1918; Kazan was taken from the Czechoslovaks. "Samara Next," read the big-print headlines of September 11. The next day the Moscow papers reported that Simbirsk, Lenin's native city, had been captured from the Czechs. The Czechoslovak Legion was stretched too thin. It drew back into Siberia. The Soviets were encouraged.

At the Kazan front Trotsky received a telegram: "I greet with rapture the brilliant triumph of the Red Army. May it serve as a guarantee that the alliance of the workers and the revolutionary peasants will completely smash the bourgeoisie, entirely break the resistance of the exploiters, and secure the victory of world-wide socialism. Long live the socialist world revolution. Lenin."[22]

The telegram, sent so soon after the attempt on Lenin's life, meant that he was getting well. It heartened his followers.

[21] *Ibid.*, p. 288.
[22] *Pravda*, Sept. 12, 1918. This telegram is reproduced in the Fourth edition of Lenin's *Collected Works*, Vol. 28 (1950), p. 74, without mention of Trotsky's name.

XXI. WOODROW WILSON AND RUSSIA

FOR DECADES, no honest and adequate history of the Soviet civil war was on sale in the Soviet Union or otherwise available to Soviet readers. Books, articles, plays, and novels were taboo unless they depicted Joseph Stalin as the author of victory and Trotsky the conniving traitor who conspired to crush the revolution he had led. After the Twenty-second Congress of the Soviet Communist Party in October, 1961, which voted to remove the mummy of Stalin from the Red Square mausoleum, official notice was taken of the distortions which the Kremlin had sponsored for years. "In the interpretation of the history of the November, 1917, revolution, of the civil war, and of the building of socialism, serious mistakes were permitted," wrote Mikhail A. Suslov, a member of the party's supreme Presidium (formerly the Politburo), and one of the chief permissive culprits. "In the works on the history of the civil war, for instance," Suslov's article in the February, 1962, *Kommunist* continued, "one front, contrary to fact, was assigned primary importance, the significance of another reduced, depending on whether Stalin was present at this or that moment; almost all victories in the civil war were regarded, first of all, as results of Stalin's activities . . .

"It is necessary to speak of this because this incorrect interpretation of the facts was included in the *Short Course*,[1] and it penetrated into literature and school textbooks. And the biography of Stalin stated positively that the direct organizer and inspiration of the most important victories of the Red Army was Stalin, that he originated most of the important strategic plans. The role of Lenin and of the party in the leadership of the defense of the country was minimized."[2]

I. Smirnov, another contributor to the same issue of *Kommunist*, declared, "And since an objective analysis of historic facts was not always demanded of researchers, there developed among some"—read, all—"historians of Soviet society and historians of the party a nihilistic relationship to sources and a skeptical relationship to the study of archives. . . . During the period of the [Stalin] cult of personality many completely innocent persons were subjected to unjustified repression." ("Repression" is a euphemism for execution and life imprisonment and banishment.) "Among them were most prominent and talented leaders of the party and the Soviet government; the names of these persons were unceremoniously deleted from history books." The biggest name deleted was Leon Trotsky's. When included it was to revile him.

[1] *History of the Communist Party of the Soviet Union (Bolsheviks). Short Course.* Edited by a Commission of the Central Committee of the C.P.S.U. (B.) (New York, 1939). According to statements made by N. S. Khrushchev in his secret speech at the Twentieth Party Congress on Feb. 25, 1956, and by other speakers, Stalin edited and in part wrote the *Short Course.*

[2] *Kommunist*, February, 1962, pp. 20-21. (This is the monthly "theoretical and political journal of the Central Committee of the Soviet Communist Party.")

The same "nihilistic" disregard of truth dominated the history of foreign intervention in Soviet Russia. The past became a football of current Soviet foreign policy, so that one could distill from the distorted story of intervention in 1918-1920 the Kremlin's thoughts in 1938 or 1959. Thus, Stalin's *Short Course*, a compulsory study manual for communists and more millions of noncommunists, published in the Soviet Union in 1938, stated, "The British and French troops landed in the north, occupied Archangel and Murmansk . . ." No mention of the American troops who participated in that operation. "The Japanese troops landed in Vladivostok, seized the Maritime Province, dispersed the Soviets . . ."[3] No mention of the Americans who also intervened. In 1938 Stalin was courting the United States.

The *Short Course*, which rewrote history, was superseded in 1959 by a new history of the party[4] which rewrote the rewritten history and added innumerable bald lies. In this book the Soviet reader, who might still have a copy of the *Short Course* on his shelf, was told that "the American, British, and French imperialists landed troops in Murmansk in the spring of 1918."[5] Further, "In the Far East and Siberia, the American monopolies and the United States government itself supplied arms and munitions to the Russian counterrevolutionaries on a vast scale. The United States was not only the arsenal of arms for the Russian counterrevolution";—the English-language edition reads, "not only supplied arms to the Russian counterrevolution"— "American troops participated together with the Japanese interventionists in military operations against the partisans, persecuted and executed civilians. The interventionists plundered national property. They exported timber, furs, gold, and raw materials worth tremendous sums without paying compensation."[6] The exaggeration of America's role in Siberia as "the arsenal" of the counterrevolution and executioner and plunderer reflected heightened Soviet rivalry with America in 1959 and 1960. This treatment is called "socialist realism," a literary method which permits the present to alter the past and presents future plans as accomplished fact.

Falsification pervades official Soviet histories of the Soviet civil war. A collection of documents published in Moscow in 1960 is furnished with an introduction, signed by "The Institute of Marxism-Leninism of the Central Committee of the Soviet Communist Party," which asserts, "The documents in this volume undeniably demonstrate the leading role which the imperialists of the United States of America played in the organization of the war against the Soviet Republic."[7]

---

[3] P. 227. American intervention is recalled casually.

[4] *Istoriya Kommunisticheskoi Partii Sovietskovo Soyuza (The History of the Soviet Communist Party)* (Moscow, 1959; English translation, Moscow, 1960).

[5] Russian edition, p. 276; English translation, p. 298.

[6] Russian edition, p. 279; English translation, p. 301.

[7] *Iz Istorii Grazhdanskoi Voini v SSSR (From the History of the Civil War in the USSR).* A Collection of Documents in Three Volumes, Vol. One, May, 1918-April, 1919, p. vi.

After this introduction there follow 699 documents, many dealing with purely domestic aspects of the civil war, others with foreign intervention. The first document quotes a speech by Lenin in Moscow on July 29, 1918, in which he referred to the "participation of the Anglo-French imperialists" in the Czechoslovak uprising, "the imperial and financial manipulators of England and France," "the landing by the British of more than ten thousand troops" in Murmansk, and again and again of "Anglo-French imperialism"; not one word, however, about the United States or America or American imperialism.[8] But an editorial note on this address refers to "the Trans-Caspian counterrevolutionary revolt inspired by the Anglo-American imperialists,"[9] without citing any evidence of American participation because there is none.

The lengths to which Soviet scholars-in-uniform will go in misrepresenting their own history is shown by Document Number 12 in the same volume. It gives the text of the "Statement of the Soviet Government Regarding the Japanese Landing in Vladivostok," issued in Moscow on April 5, 1918. Midway in the document, three dots indicate an omission. From another Soviet book of documents published in 1957,[10] one sees that the omission is a paragraph in which this sentence occurs: "The American government was apparently opposed to the Japanese invasion."[11] Since the sentence contradicted the anti-American thesis of the Institute of Marxism-Leninism it was left out.

Document Number 29 of the Institute's collection is a telegram dated June 26, 1918, from Lenin to Yuryev of the Murmansk Soviet saying that "Soviet policy was equally hostile to the British and the Germans," and adding, "We will fight the British if they continue their policy of plunder."[12]

There is no question that the Americans did intervene militarily in north Russia as well as the Far East. But far from playing "the leading role" in the anti-Soviet intervention, the United States dragged its feet, procrastinated, resisted mighty, concerted pressures from almost all Allied governments, and finally agreed, with unfeigned reluctance, to join in an action in which it did not believe.

The Russian question tormented President Wilson for many months, indeed for almost a year, before he sanctioned American intervention. It is difficult to know exactly why he agreed to it, but there are clues. Early in 1918 Samuel Gompers, president of the American Federation of Labor, urged Wilson to send a message to the Constituent Assembly in Moscow. Wilson replied on January 21, 1918: "I liked your suggestion about a message to the Russian Constituent Assembly, but apparently the reckless Bolsheviki have already broken it up because they did not control it. It is

[8] *Ibid.*, pp. 3-8.
[9] *Ibid.*, p. 775.
[10] *Dokumenty Vneshnei Politiki SSSR*, Ministry of Foreign Affairs of the USSR, Vol. 1 (Moscow, 1957).
[11] *Ibid.*, p. 225.
[12] *Iz Istorii Grazhdanskoi Voini v SSSR*, p. 29.

distressing to see things so repeatedly go to pieces there."[13] On July 8, 1918, Wilson wrote Colonel House, "I have been sweating blood over the question of what is right and feasible (*possible*) to do in Russia. It goes to pieces like quicksilver under my touch."[14]

Woodrow Wilson was said to have a one-track mind. It seems he also had a "one-piece" mind. He tried to fit the Russian jigsaw puzzle together into a neat pattern, but it repeatedly went to pieces. He had lived all his life in a democracy and had studied the processes of democratic government which, with all their variations, gyrations, and minor explosions, remain within a broad, predictable groove. He accordingly addressed the Bolsheviks in his Fourteen Points speech as though they were a new species of liberal democrats. He had no other terms of reference. When the Bolsheviks dispersed the Constituent Assembly he thought the act "reckless." In fact, it would have been rash for Lenin to do anything else.

Wilson was wise enough, after these experiences, to realize that he did not understand the Bolsheviks. He sweated blood over the problem of what to do, but a solution eluded him. That being the case, his orderly mind said, Do nothing; you cannot have a policy toward an incomprehensible situation. In 1918, and indeed in 1919, Wilson's preferred policy toward Russia would have been no policy, especially in view of his preoccupation with the hundreds of titanic tasks facing a warring nation unaccustomed to waging war. He was a one-front man. He wished to concentrate on the western front where Germany could win or lose.

Those who have read the record, however, are aware of the powerful pulls exerted on Wilson by the military and political giants of America's allies. Foch, Clemenceau, Lloyd George, Balfour, and scores more made known to him their conviction that intervention in Russia, with American participation, was indispensable to victory. He was a stubborn person, but he wanted victory, and he was a reasonable person. It would have been unreasonable to pit his opinion, consciously based on an incapacity to penetrate the problem, against the opinions of men of experience closer to it who doggedly demanded action.

Nor could Wilson ignore the law of coalition and alliance. A partner cannot forever frustrate the wishes of all other partners on a matter they consider vital without undermining the partnership. Wilson knew intervention in Russia was wrong. But in the end his allies wore him out.

Soviet scholars-in-uniform, who write of politics purely in terms of class and imperialism and productive forces, who write of politics as a science yet do not hesitate to falsify fact and document, have of course dismissed President Wilson's psychology as irrelevant. But then they are demonstrably bad historians or un-historians.

[13] Ray Stannard Baker, *Woodrow Wilson. Life and Letters. War Leader, April 6, 1917-February 28, 1918* (New York, 1939), Vol. VII, p. 486.
[14] Xerox copy of original seen in the Woodrow Wilson archives at Princeton University.

Even as Wilson agreed to intervention he deliberately tied one hand behind America's back and held action down to a minimum. What is more, he tried to square his conscience by denouncing intervention at the moment of intervention. Cynics may discern in this an element of hypocrisy and they are perhaps right. It was also a reflection of Wilson's tortured soul. The statement announcing American intervention in Russia was signed by Acting Secretary of State Frank L. Polk. It nevertheless reads like undiluted Wilsonism.[15] U.S. Supreme Court Justice Louis D. Brandeis, who knew Wilson well, wrote to Edwin A. Alderman, president of the University of Virginia, on May 11, 1924, "Mr. Wilson . . . should be judged by what he was and did prior to August 4, 1918, the date of the paper justifying the attack on Russia. This was the first of his acts which was unlike him; and I am sure the beginning of the sad end."

The paper violated Wilson's personality and therefore helped undermine it. It declared, "In the judgment of the Government of the United States, a judgment arrived at after repeated and searching considerations of the whole situation, military intervention in Russia would be more likely to add to the present sad confusion there than to cure it, and would injure Russia rather than help her out of her distress.

"Such military intervention as has been most frequently proposed, even supposing it to be efficacious in its immediate object of delivering an attack on Germany from the east, would in its judgment be more likely to turn out to be merely a method of making use of Russia than to be a method of serving her. Her people, if they profited by it at all, could not profit from it in time to deliver them from their present desperate difficulties, and their substance would meantime be used to maintain foreign armies, not to reconstitute their own or to feed their own men, women, and children. We are bending all our energies now to the purpose, the resolute and confident purpose, of winning on the western front, and it would in the judgment of the Government of the United States be most unwise to divide or dissipate our forces."

Thus far, the statement would justify Wilson's delays in sanctioning intervention. It answered his foreign critics and spoke to his conscience. It continued: "As the Government of the United States sees the present circumstances, therefore, military action is admissible in Russia now only to render such protection and help as is possible to the Czecho-Slovaks against the armed Austrian and German prisoners who are attacking them"—a popular fiction tale at the time—"and to steady any efforts at self-government or self-defense in which the Russians themselves may be willing to accept assistance.

[15] Published on Aug. 4, 1918, it had in fact been typed by Woodrow Wilson the day before on his Hammond typewriter. Professor Arthur S. Link, director of the Woodrow Wilson Papers at Princeton University, allowed me to make a Xerox copy which shows President Wilson's inked corrections. Wilson had originally written it as an aide memoire on July 17, 1918, and circulated it to members of his Cabinet for comments.

"With such objects in view the Government of the United States is now cooperating with the Governments of France and Great Britain in the neighborhood of Murmansk and Archangel. The United States and Japan are the only powers which are just now in a position to act in Siberia in sufficient force to accomplish even such modest objects as those that have been outlined. The Government of the United States has, therefore, proposed to the Government of Japan that each of the two governments send a force of a few thousand men to Vladivostok, with the purpose of cooperating as a single force in the occupation of Vladivostok"—a vain expectation—"and in safeguarding, as far as it may, the country to the rear of the westward-moving Czecho-Slovaks; and the Japanese Government has consented." The Japanese government had long been clamoring for it.

The United States and Japan agreed to send 7,000 troops each to Vladivostok and Siberia.

It did not take long; it was August 26, in fact, when John K. Caldwell, U.S. consul in Vladivostok, cabled to the Secretary of State in Washington: "Following from Stevens: About 18,000 Japanese troops disembarked Vladivostok already. Six thousand additional troops moved by way of Changchung to Manchouli front. Japanese dominating everything possible. . . . Situation is critical."[16]

One is driven to the old-fashioned thought that even a statesman should not do what he knows is wrong.

XXII. LENIN AND THE GERMAN REVOLUTION

THE WORLD SITUATION was undergoing drastic change. Germany's plight was increasing. A mighty French counterattack at Soissons on July 18, 1918, took the German army by surprise and forced a retreat. Field Marshal Hermann von Eichhorn, German commander in chief in the Ukraine, and his adjutant, Captain von Dressler, were assassinated by B. Danskio, a Left Social Revolutionary, in Kiev on August 1. Gathering grain with bayonets in the Ukraine, never successful, suffered a further setback. Germany and Austro-Hungary would be hungrier.

Under cover of a dense morning fog on August 8, British, Australian, Canadian, and French divisions smashed into the German line in France and broke it. "The situation was uncommonly serious," Ludendorff wrote.

[16] *Papers Relating to the Foreign Relations of the United States, 1918. Russia,* Vol. II, pp. 328-329.

"August 8 put the decline of [Germany's] fighting power beyond doubt. . . . The war must be ended." Five days later Ludendorff told Hindenburg, the Chancellor, and Secretary of State Admiral von Hintze "that it was no longer possible by an offensive to force the enemy to sue for peace. Defense alone could hardly achieve this object, and so the termination of the war would have to be brought about by diplomacy."

The next day the same sad gentlemen conferred with Kaiser Wilhelm II. Hintze, tears in his eyes, summarized Ludendorff's views. "The Emperor was very calm. He agreed with State Secretary von Hintze, and instructed him to open peace negotiations if possible, through the medium of the Queen of the Netherlands."[1]

The German army stood defeated. Germany had succumbed on the field of battle. Ludendorff had said so. Yet Ludendorff and a little corporal—Adolf Hitler—knowing the romantic Germans' love of myths, cultivated and won widespread acceptance for the fable that Germany lost the First World War as a result of the Dolchstoss, the "stab-in-the-back" administered by communists, socialists, pacifists, and Jews on the home front. (This big lie was a ladder that helped Hitler climb to power in 1933.)

With monarchist Germany sliding into the grave, it made no sense for Ambassador Helfferich to return to Moscow from the Crown Council's considerations of imminent German collapse. The German embassy moved to Petrograd, nearer to German soldiery in the Baltic States. Later it moved to the Russian city of Pskov, occupied by General Hoffmann's troops. There it lost its diplomatic functions—presumably Helfferich's intention. He and Major Schubert, his military attaché, harbored a red-hot hate for Bolshevism and hoped it would go away if they did.

General Max Hoffmann idled in the war's forgotten eastern backwater, sizzling with envy of Ludendorff, yearning for an energy outlet. "I think it absolutely essential that we should attack soon" in Russia, he confided to his diary on August 26, 1918. "If the Entente sets up a Tsar without our cooperation we shall be eliminated from Eastern Europe for the next half-century."[2] Apparently he would have cooperated with the Allies to set up a Tsar.

Hoffmann, drunk with dreams of action and conquest, could not see the truth. Light came from the West and sobered him; the Armistice signed on November 11, 1918, ended the First World War with Germany's total submission.

Hoffmann blamed the debacle on other German generals. "We should have won the war in the West in August, 1914, in a gallop" if the first offensive into Belgium had been conducted according to the Schlieffen Plan. Instead the right wing was weakened to strengthen the left. Whose fault?

---

[1] Erich von Ludendorff, *Ludendorff's Own Story. August 1914-November 1918*; pp. 328-335.
[2] Major-General Max Hoffmann, *War Diaries and Other Papers*, Vol. One (London, 1929), p. 232.

Supreme GHQ. Nor should the Germans have been stopped on the Marne. Fault of Moltke. Then, rather than dig in for years of trench warfare in the West, a quick and massive frontal attack was in order. The "Second GHQ" missed the opportunity. After that, the war could be won only in the East. But the warlords muffed the chance to smash Russia and, by surrendering Belgium, achieve a *status quo ante* peace in 1917.

Unexpectedly, despite these blunders, the Bolshevik revolution offered Germany a second opportunity to win the war "by establishing order in Russia and signing an alliance of friendship with a new Russian government," and wait in the West. This strategy would have brought no victory but also no collapse. Ludendorff, however, "wanted to win. Yet he did not employ all his forces, nor did he employ them wisely." Having failed to break through, Ludendorff might have remained on the defensive in the West and sued for peace while Germany was still strong. He preferred to engage the exhausted remnants of the army; he thereby delivered the disarmed country to the "hate of Britain, the fanatic vengeance of the French, and the mentally unbalanced Wilson."[3]

Thus Hoffmann's autopsy of the war. Ludendorff introduced Lenin into Russia but failed to reap the harvest. In Hoffmann's logic, the Brest peace was a mistake. Germany should have ousted the Soviets and made Russia a servant satellite. Hoffmann blamed this blunder on Ludendorff's uncontrollable urge to defeat the West in military combat and achieve hegemony over Europe.

At a deeper level, Germany's defeat in the First and Second World Wars may be ascribed to her inability to determine whether she was an Eastern or a Western power, whether her chief rival was Russia or the Anglo-French. She consequently grappled with both and succumbed. Historic parallels usually diverge. Yet there is a family resemblance between the Brest-Litovsk peace treaty of 1918, which enabled Ludendorff to plan the blow that would crush the West, and the Soviet-Nazi pact of August 23, 1939, which encouraged Hitler to turn from Poland to attack the West.

The November, 1918, armistice lowered the curtain. Kaiser Wilhelm II abdicated and went into exile in Holland, never to return (though he lived to see Hitler's army invade the Netherlands). Germany became a republic. This was revolution. The Bolsheviks expected more.

We are "with you head and heart," Clara Zetkin, a leader of the Spartacus League, which incubated the German Communist Party, had said in a letter. "This," Lenin replied on July 26, 1918, "gives us confidence that the best elements in the west European working class will yet come to our aid—notwithstanding all the difficulties."[4]

---

[3] General Max Hoffmann, *Krieg der Versaeumten Gelegenheiten*, pp. 231-232.

[4] V. I. Lenin. *Ueber Deutschland und Die Deutsche Arbeiterbewegung. Aus Schriften, Reden, Briefen*. Besorgt vom Institut fuer Marxismus-Leninismus beim ZK der SED (East Berlin, 1958), p. 443.

Two days before the attempt on his life, Lenin addressed the All-Russian Educational Congress. "Comrades," he began, "we are living through one of the most critical, important, and interesting moments of history—the moment of the approaching world socialist revolution. . . . All signs indicate that Austria and Italy are on the eve of revolution. . . . In more stable and stronger nations like Germany, England, and France, conditions are somewhat different and less noticeable, but the same process is coming to a head. The collapse of the capitalist system and of the capitalist war is inevitable. The German imperialists have not been able to suppress the socialist revolution."[5]

Lenin did not ignore Soviet problems. Only eighteen days after he was wounded he sent a message to a conference of proletarian educational organizations complaining that not enough workingmen were promoted to "the running of the country." Next day his brief article in *Pravda* implored Soviet newspapers to print "less politics," "more economics," and fewer superfluous words. "In place of two hundred or four hundred lines, why not," he demanded, "discuss in twenty or forty lines such simple, well-known, clear phenomena, already largely understood by the masses, as the foul treachery of the Mensheviks, those lackeys of the bourgeoisie, [and] the Anglo-Japanese crusade for the restoration of the sacred rights of capitalism? More economics," he nevertheless insisted, not economics in general, but the economics of daily work: "Where is the blacklist of lagging factories which, since nationalization, have become models of chaos, collapse, filth, hooliganism, idleness, where is it?"[6]

But Germany was uppermost in Lenin's mind. A novel note sounded in his greeting to an assembly of worker and trade-union representatives on October 3. Theretofore, he had used the declared imminence of world revolution to dispel gloom; now he used it to stir enthusiasm for work. Russians would be saved by the world revolution, he said, if they deserved it: ". . . the Russian proletariat is not only watching events. . . . It has posed the question of harnessing all its strength *in order to help the German workers. . . .* The Russian proletariat will now understand that tremendous sacrifices are soon to be asked of it in the interest of internationalism. . . . Let us begin to prepare immediately. Let us show that the Russian workingman can work much more energetically. . . . Above all, let us increase tenfold our efforts to collect reserves of grain." Let citizens join the army: "We have decided to build an army of one million by spring, but we need an army of three million. We can have it. And we shall have it."[7] World revolution, until then a dream symphony, was becoming a marching song.

To influence German events, Lenin planned a major work—a pamphlet attacking the evolutionary unhurried attitude of Karl Kautsky, theoretician

[5] Lenin, *Sochineniya*, Second ed., Vol. XXIII, p. 197.
[6] *Ibid.*, pp. 211-214.
[7] *Ibid.*, pp. 218-224.

of German social democracy. But a brochure would take time to write, and Lenin was impatient to bring the Berlin brew to a boil. He accordingly prepared a preliminary article, entitled "The Proletarian Revolution and the Renegade Kautsky," which *Pravda* printed on October 11, 1918. "Europe has *no* revolutionary party," he moaned. "There are parties of traitors like Scheidemann, Renaudel, Henderson, the Webbs and Co., or souls of lackeys like Kautsky. There is no revolutionary party." To be sure, "a revolutionary movement can overcome this lack, but it remains a great misfortune and a great danger. Therefore it is necessary in every way to expose traitors like Kautsky." Lenin then appealed to the German workers to make a revolution "without considering the national sacrifice (only in this does internationalism consist). . . . The interests of the international workers' revolution are more important than the safety, security, and tranquillity of this or that national state, especially one's own." He evidently feared German working-class patriotism. He apparently was thinking of the safety and security of the new Soviet state.

Socialism derived from spontaneous conception in a number of nations. But the cradle of the modern socialist movement was Germany and its parents were Marx and Engels, two prolific Germans who spent their most creative years in England imbibing British statistics and emitting universal theories. The direct line of Marxist succession ran from Marx to Engels to Kautsky. Karl Kautsky (1854-1938) codified Marxist social laws, systematized Marxist thought, and taught socialism to the German Social Democratic Party (SPD) which August Bebel, Wilhelm Liebknecht, and Ferdinand Lasalle had organized in 1863. Its origins were pacifist and internationalist; Bebel, a workingman with a flare for oratory, opposed credits in 1870 for the Franco-Prussian War and supported the Paris Commune.

Kautsky found a foe in Eduard Bernstein (1850-1932), whose book on evolutionary socialism laid down these propositions: the class struggle was waning; the middle class, balance and bridge between employers and workers, was growing; capitalism was not on the verge of collapse; therefore, social and economic reforms were obtainable. Kautsky and Bebel, rejecting Bernstein, preferred revolution to reform. In Siberian exile, Lenin and Krupskaya translated, in two hectic weeks, a pamphlet by Kautsky attacking Bernstein. In April, 1911, and again in October, 1911, Lenin, in letters to Maxim Gorky, praised Kautsky's politics. In 1912 Kautsky signed the Basel Manifesto which summoned socialists to bury bourgeois rule if war came.

Bebel's death in 1913 spared him the mental anguish and political contortions to which the First World War subjected the SPD. Marx had excoriated absolutist tsarism; he regarded British imperial power as a necessary counterpoise to it. Bebel had frowned on Germany's naval rivalry with England. The SPD had advocated the general strike as a weapon to prevent war. Yet in 1914 the SPD members of the Reichstag, with few exceptions, voted in favor of military credits. Emotion overruled reason. Patriotism banished pacifism. Nationalism eclipsed internationalism.

Kautsky, however, as well as Bernstein, remained anti-war and, with Hugo Haase and others, joined the small Independent Socialist Party.

Presumably, then, Kautsky would have welcomed the seizure of power by the anti-war, revolutionary Bolsheviks. This was the attitude of Karl Lieb-knecht who inherited the repugnance his father, Wilhelm, had manifested for monarchist Russia. Instead, Kautsky saw in the dictatorship of the pro-letariat a new form of Russian absolutism.

It is easy to understand Lenin's wrath. After eleven months of rule, he already knew that Soviet Russia was not equipped, and the outside world not inclined, to facilitate his task of building a strong state in short order. But now the homeland of Marx was about to give birth to revolution. Surely it would be a Marxist revolution, a younger yet better-endowed brother of the Soviet revolution. Anyone who obstructed this development invited the Kremlin's fury. Kautsky did. In 1918 he published in Vienna a sixty-three-page pamphlet entitled *The Proletarian Revolution*, "almost one third" of which, Lenin charged, "is devoted by this windbag to twaddle that must be very agreeable to the bourgeoisie, for it amounts to beautifying bourgeois de-mocracy and obscuring the question of the proletarian revolution." Lenin admitted that Kautsky "knows Marx almost by heart"—no small feat—yet he wrote eighty-one pages to demonstrate that Kautsky did not understand Marx.[8]

The gravamen of Lenin's contention was that, though no state is demo-cratic, the Soviet state is more democratic than any bourgeois state. Kautsky denied this. The Lenin-Kautsky polemic, therefore, was the progenitor of the worldwide debate that has since raged on the nature and advantages or disadvantages of the Soviet system. Lenin gave the gist of Kautsky's views and then elaborated his own, highly seasoned with pepper, on the sins of capitalist freedom and the virtues of soviets. In subsequent decades, his followers' contribution to the controversy has been repetition.

"Literally," Kautsky argued, "the word 'dictatorship' means the abrogation of democracy. But, of course, taken literally this word also means the un-divided rule of one individual who is not bound by any laws." Lenin, unable to foresee Stalin's twenty-three years of personal despotism, said this "is obviously untrue." Kautsky likewise declared that to Marx "the dictatorship of the proletariat" was not a form of government "but a state of things that must necessarily supervene whenever and wherever the proletariat has con-quered political power." To prove this he recalled Marx's opinion that "in

---

[8] *Ibid.*, pp. 331-412. Also Lenin, *Izbrannie Proizvedeniya (Selected Works)*, In Six Volumes, Vol. IV, 1918-1920, pp. 86-160. English, *The Proletarian Revolution and Kautsky the Renegade* (Pamphlet) (London. March, 1920). I have amended this translation wherever comparison with the original required it. Lenin wrote the bro-chure in October-November, 1918. In March, 1920, he began work on an introduction to the London pamphlet in which he intended to analyze and condemn the policies of J. Ramsay MacDonald and his Independent Labour Party ("independent in words, but in fact fully dependent on bourgeois prejudices"), but after writing about a page and a half—reproduced in *Leninskii Sbornik*, Vol. XXXVI, pp. 100-101—he quit for lack of time. Lenin equated MacDonald with Kautsky.

England and America the transition can take place peacefully, and therefore, in a democratic way." Marx, according to Kautsky, believed in dictatorship as a temporary necessity but not as a permanent good, a necessity to the seizure of power, not a desirable system of government. And if, as in the two Anglo-Saxon nations, the transition to socialism could be accomplished democratically, dictatorship was unnecessary.

Lenin sought to kill Kautsky with argument and epithet. Kautsky's "monstrous distortion of Marxism . . . is simply a flunkey-like subserviency to the opportunists, that is, in the last resort, to the bourgeoisie." Kautsky "forgot" the class struggle. "It is impossible to enumerate all the absurdities uttered by Kautsky, for every phrase in his mouth represents a bottomless pit of apostasy." Lenin's use of the word "apostasy" is revealing; Kautsky had abandoned a religion, a dogma. Its core was class war. "Did the dictatorship by slaveowners in ancient societies mean the abrogation of democracy for the slaveowners?" Lenin asked. "Everbody knows it did not." Dictatorship denies democracy to the class "against which the dictatorship is wielded," he asserted, but "not necessarily" against the class that wields it.

Kautsky found the very idea of a class dictatorship untenable. A class, he held, cannot govern. Only "organizations" or "parties" can govern.

"You are talking nonsense, sheer nonsense, Mr. Muddle-Head," Lenin commented.

The proletariat never governed the Soviet Union. The party governed, and a dictator or an oligarchy dominated the party.

Perhaps Lenin's vitriol made him "forget." In his pamphlet *Two Tactics of Social Democracy in the Democratic Revolution*, published in Geneva in 1905, he noted that, "From the vulgar bourgeois viewpoint, the concept of dictatorship and the concept of democracy are mutually exclusive." Clarity dawns when this statement is compared with his 1917 notes on Marx's *The Critique of the Gotha Programme* which he made in preparation for writing *The State and Revolution*. One note reads, "In fact, democracy excludes freedom." Therefore dictatorship and democracy are alike, not mutually exclusive. Lenin explains that he is talking of both bourgeois democracy and proletarian democracy: "The dialectic (process) of development is: from absolutism to bourgeois democracy; from bourgeois democracy to proletarian; from proletarian to none at all." None-at-all-democracy would see freedom.

Lenin pointed out in the same 1905 pamphlet that the dictatorship of a class differed from a personal dictatorship; a democratic dictatorship also differed from a socialist dictatorship. The difference, apparently, consisted in the temporary nature of a proletarian or socialist dictatorship. Here Lenin leaned on Marx, who wrote in the *Neue Rheinische Zeitung* of September 14, 1848, "After a revolution, every provisional government requires a dictatorship, in fact an energetic dictatorship." To which Lenin commented, "What does Marx tell us in these words? That a temporary revolutionary government must function as a dictatorship."

This confirmed Kautsky. According to Marx, Kautsky had written, the dictatorship of the proletariat is "not a form of government" but a temporary condition after the conquest of power. However, much hinges on the interpretation of "provisional" and "temporary." Does it mean three months or three years or thirty or forty years or half a century? In a sense, of course, everything is temporary.

(Lenin indicated the duration of "temporary" in an article published in the November, 1919, issue of *The Communist International*. "Socialism," he said there, "is the abolition of classes. The dictatorship of the proletariat has done everything it could for this abolition. But it is impossible to abolish classes immediately. And classes *have remained* and will remain during the entire period of the dictatorship of the proletariat. The dictatorship will be unnecessary when classes disappear. They will not disappear without the dictatorship of the proletariat.")

Dictatorship involved the use of maximum force. That precluded freedom. In the 1905 pamphlet Lenin wrote, "Great questions in the life of nations are decided only by force." This tenet he never forsook. He lived by it. He emphasized it in 1918 in attempting to demolish "the renegade" Kautsky who, he declared, "is mortally afraid of the *revolutionary violence* of the oppressed class," because he had become "a liberal who mouths banal phrases about 'pure democracy.' . . . When Kautsky has 'interpreted' the concept of 'the revolutionary dictatorship of the proletariat' so that revolutionary violence by the oppressed class against the oppressors disappears, the world record of the liberal distortion of Marx has been beaten; the renegade Bernstein has been proved to be a puppy compared with the renegade Kautsky." Violence, Lenin predicted, would flare during the transition to socialism in America and England, for "the need of such violence against the bourgeoisie is caused especially . . . by the fact that there exist an army and bureaucracy. But in the seventies when Marx was making his observations, these institutions did not exist in England or America (though now they *do* exist)." This was a revision of Marx and a revision of fact; Britain and the United States in the 1870's possessed bureaucracies and access to armies. Lenin, however, believed in the universal application of social laws, tolerated no exceptions, and cut particulars to suit his generalizations. This mental attitude lay at the root of his conviction that since Russia had made a revolution the world would make one.

The Germans, however, Lenin feared, might not make a proletarian revolution; they might remain within the framework of capitalism. He therefore inveighed against capitalist freedoms. "Kautsky shamelessly disguises bourgeois democracy," he wrote, "ignoring for instance, what the most democratic and republican bourgeois of America or Switzerland do against striking workingmen. Oh, the wise and learned Kautsky hushes up these things! He does not understand, this learned politician, that such silence is infamy. . . . Oh, scholarship. Oh, this refined flunkeyism before the bourgeoisie. Oh, this civilized manner of belly-crawling before the capitalists and licking their boots. If I were a Krupp or Scheidemann or Clemenceau or Renaudel I would pay Mr. Kautsky millions. . . .

"The learned Mr. Kautsky has 'forgotten'—no doubt accidentally forgotten—a 'detail,' to wit, that the ruling party in a bourgeois democracy grants the protection of minorities only to another *bourgeois* party, whereas in every *serious, basic, fundamental* question, martial law and pogroms take the place of 'the protection of minorities.' " Next came a Lenin law which he underlined: "The more developed a democracy the closer it is to a pogrom or civil war whenever a basic political divergence imperils the bourgeoisie. The learned Mr. Kautsky might have observed this 'law' of bourgeois democracy in the Dreyfus affair in republican France, in the lynching of Negroes and of internationalists in the democratic republic of America, in the example of Ireland and Ulster in democratic England, in the persecution of the Bolsheviks and the organization of pogroms against them in April, 1917, in the Russian democratic republic. . . .

"Take the bourgeois parliament. Is it to be supposed that the learned Kautsky has never heard that *the more developed* a democracy is *the more* the stock exchange and bankers subject bourgeois parliaments to their control?"

By contrast, Lenin submitted, "Proletarian democracy, of which the Soviet regime constitutes one of the forms, has given the world a hitherto unknown development and expansion of democracy for the gigantic majority of the population, for the exploited and the laborers." Soviet diplomacy is democratic and "carried out openly." Everywhere else "the masses are deceived—in democratic France, Switzerland, America, and England this is done in an incomparably broader and refined manner than in other countries. Participation in bourgeois parliaments (which *never decide* serious questions in bourgeois democracy; the bourse and banks decide them) is fenced off from the toiling masses by thousands of barriers, and the workers know and feel full well, they see and realize, that the bourgeois parliament is an institution *foreign* to them, an *instrument* of bourgeois oppression of the proletariat."

But "The Soviet government is a million times more democratic than the most democratic bourgeois republic. . . . Instinctively, reading the fragments of truth in the bourgeois press, the workers of the entire world sympathize with the Soviet republic just because they see in it a *proletarian* democracy, *democracy for the poor*, and not a democracy of the rich as is the case in every bourgeois democracy, even in the best. . . . In Russia, on the other hand, the bureaucracy has been smashed . . . , the old judges have been driven out, the bourgeois parliament has been dispersed, and instead the workers and peasants have received a form of representation *far more accessible* to the workers and peasants in particular. . . .

"Kautsky does not understand this truth, so comprehensible and obvious to all workers, for he has 'forgotten,' 'lost the knack' of putting the question, 'Democracy for what class?' . . . He argues like Shylock, 'A pound of flesh,' nothing else.[9] Equality for all citizens—otherwise there is no democracy."

Having denounced Kautsky, now as "a most learned armchair fool," now as writing with the "innocent air of a ten-year-old girl," Lenin attacked Kautsky's analysis of the suppression of the Russian Constituent Assembly. The elections to the Assembly, Lenin argued, were held too early, before the Bolsheviks reached maximum popularity. He gave the statistics: in the elections to the All-Russian Congress of Soviets, the Bolsheviks polled 13 percent of the votes on June 16, 1917; 50 percent on November 10, 1917; 61 percent on January 23, 1918; 64 percent on March 20, 1918; and 66 percent on July 17, 1918.[10]

These are remarkable figures. For, according to Lenin, the Mensheviks and Right SR's were excluded from the soviets on June 14, 1918.[11] The Left SR's were excluded early in July, 1918. A rise of only 2 percent between March and July, 1918, therefore suggests a popularity bottleneck. The use of the state apparatus to suppress rivals and prod the electorate should have made the soviets "monolithic" much earlier.

Lenin was saying that he disbanded the Constituent Assembly because the Bolsheviks lost the election; they would have done better later. This amounts to the proposition that the anticipation of different circumstances alters cases.

Lenin welcomed the "abuse" showered on Soviet Russia because that "will accelerate and deepen the split between the revolutionary workers of Europe and the Scheidemanns, and Kautskys, the Renaudels and Longuets, the Hendersons and Ramsay MacDonalds and all the old leaders and the old traitors of socialism. The masses of the oppressed classes, the class-concious and honest leaders of revolutionary proletarians will be *with* us . . . . More than any party in any country, Bolshevism has helped in a practical manner to further proletarian revolution in Europe and America. . . . Not only the all-European but the world proletarian revolution is ripening under the eyes of all, and it was aided, accelerated, and supported by the victory of the proletariat in Russia."

Lenin finished his anti-Kautsky pamphlet on November 9, 1918, and proposed to write a conclusion the next day. During the night news reached him of the revolution in Berlin, where power had passed to the soviets. In the morning Lenin penned the last sentence of the pamphlet: "The conclusion which I had intended to write on Kautsky's pamphlet and on the proletarian revolution has been rendered superfluous."

Life, however, wrote its own conclusion, which disappointed Lenin. At first,

[9] This reference to Shylock is omitted from the English pamphlet published at the time by the "British Socialist Party," the forerunner of the British Communist Party.
[10] London pamphlet, p. 57.
[11] *Ibid.*, p. 63.

all went well. Karl Liebknecht was released from prison on October 23. Three days later Ludendorff resigned his command. For a moment it looked as if Liebknecht might be his successor. On November 3 naval ratings mutinied at Kiel, and on November 9 Liebknecht proclaimed the German soviet republic from the balcony of the royal palace. With chaos threatening and soviets springing up in many cities, Chancellor Prince Max von Baden handed over his post to Fritz Ebert, an SPD member of the Imperial Cabinet. Philipp Scheidemann, the other SPD member of the Cabinet, learning of Liebknecht's act, proclaimed the democratic republic. Ebert served as Imperial Chancellor for just one day—November 9. Late that night General Wilhelm Groener telephoned from the German High Command offering Ebert armed assistance. Ebert accepted. "This telephone alliance," as Gerald Freund called it,[12] saved the republic and doomed the revolution.

The next day Ebert appealed to the Berlin Soviet of Workers and Soldiers and won its approval of his government. Subsequently, he was elected chairman of the Council of People's Commissars. This name on the political show window was a translation from the Russian, a concession to the passing revolutionary gale. The stock on the shelves inside, however, was moderate socialism; the majority in the Council consisted of nonrevolutionary SPD members.

The German soviets intended to put an end to the war. The end of the war put an end to them, the fight went out of them; on December 19, 1918, the Congress of Soldiers' and Workers' Soviets fixed January 19, 1919, for the elections to a Constituent Assembly. Four days later, revolutionary soldiers and sailors and armed Spartacus civilians invaded the Chancellery and captured Ebert. The next day, soldiers of the regular army, obeying Hindenburg and government orders, released him. Seeing the specter of counterrevolution, the Independent Socialists in the Cabinet resigned. Fierce street fighting broke out in Berlin. In some districts the revolutionists triumphed. But on January 16 troops commanded by SPD leader Gustav Noske entered Berlin and, mounting machine guns and cannon at strategic crossroads, retook the capital. That same evening political gangsters, probably first-generation Nazis, murdered Karl Liebknecht and Rosa Luxemburg and threw their bodies into an urban canal. Therewith the flames of revolution flickered, then died. The National Assembly met in Goethe's Weimar on February 6, 1919, and elected Ebert President and Scheidemann Chancellor of a coalition government supported by the SPD, the Catholic Center Party, and the Democratic Party. Therewith the Weimar Republic began its meandering—now healthy, creative and gay, now sorrowful—course.

The German communist revolution failed because the workers and intellectuals did not believe in it, the farmers did not need it, and the army, middle class, and temperate politicians opposed it. Lenin should have known

---

[12] *Unholy Alliance*. Russian-German Relations from the Treaty of Brest-Litovsk to the Treaty of Berlin. With an introduction by J. W. Wheeler-Bennett (London and New York, 1957), p. 33.

that the fate of the German revolution would not be determined by the "apostasy" of Kautsky or the "treachery" of Social Democrats. Communism teaches that great events obey "the iron logic of history" and "objective historical necessity." By these criteria alone the German revolution was bound to differ from the Russian. Bolshevism seized power because the world war ripped the fabric of Russian society to shreds and ruined the Russian army. But the German army, after losing 1,834,524 men in battle, counted, on November 11, 1918, 3,403,000 soldiers in 183 divisions. Mutinies and flurries notwithstanding, this force stood by the new republic in its early infancy. German society, moreover, was intact despite the multiple dislocations of war. It required the fourteen postwar years of madness and muddle in Germany, the West, and Moscow to spawn Hitler's totalitarianism.

To these objective factors might be added some subjective ones: the SPD, thanks to the corrosive effect of wartime compromises, was no longer the party Bebel knew. At war's end its leaders faced the irresistible temptation of power in association with the bourgeoisie. Finally, eleven months of Bolshevik dictatorship in Russia killed what taste the SPD, and Kautsky, had for revolution. Bolshevism needed a communist Germany and helped make it impossible.

Lenin had done everything to make it possible—by words hurled at Kautsky and by covert deeds. On October 22, Lenin appeared in public for the first time since the attempt on his life. Speaking for some forty minutes at a joint meeting of the All-Russian Central Executive Committee, the Moscow party committee, and factory and trade-union committees, he noted numerous signs of revolution throughout Europe. He quoted from an Italian bourgeois newspaper's report on the tour of Samuel Gompers, the American trade-union leader, through Italy. "The Italian workers," it said, "behave as though they would allow only Lenin and Trotsky to travel through Italy." In Germany, Lenin added, the formation of soviets, and the leftist line of the Independent Socialist Party, were sure symptoms of the dawn of revolution.

Apparently restored in strength and invigorated by the prospects of revolution abroad, Lenin addressed two meetings on November 6, three on November 7, and two on November 8. At one meeting he said, "Germany, as you know, has expelled our ambassador from Berlin, citing the revolutionary propaganda of our mission in Germany. As though the German government had not previously known that our embassy carries revolutionary infection! But if Germany's government previously kept quiet about this it was because she was strong. Then she did not fear us. But now, after military defeat, we have commenced to terrify her."

Lenin knew the truth; it was not so much infection as planned subversion. The Soviet ambassador, Adolf A. Yoffe, bought arms for the German revolutionaries and financed their propaganda. Years later I heard the facts from him. In 1927, in Moscow, a mutual friend, George Andreichin, a Soviet communist of Bulgarian ancestry, said Yoffe would like to see me. I had never met Yoffe, but he heard of my work on a book about Soviet foreign policy and apparently wished to speak to an outsider for the record. Only subsequently did I understand why; several weeks after our talk, Yoffe committed suicide—November 17, 1927—in protest against Stalin's increasingly high-handed political acts. He felt powerless to delay the dawn of the new repressive era except by indicating, with his death, that he refused to live under it. He told me Stalin's policies filled him with anguish. And without any transition, but as though to suggest that he was a militant communist and could not, therefore, abide Stalin, he rose slowly from his sick bed and drew from his files the 1919 report on his activities in the Berlin Soviet Embassy. The embassy, he asserted, "was the staff headquarters of the German revolution. I bought secret information from German officials and passed it on to radical leaders"—most of them top functionaries of the Independent Socialist Party—"for use in their public speeches and in articles against the Kaiser government. I bought arms for the revolutionists and paid 100,000 marks for them. Tons of antimonarchist and anti-war literature were printed and distributed at my embassy's expense. We wanted to pull down the monarchy and stop the war. Your President Woodrow Wilson pursued the same aim by other means. Almost every day after dark, Independent Socialists slipped into the embassy to consult me." Yoffe was the experienced conspirator and they wanted his advice, money, and guidance. "In the end," he said ruefully, "we accomplished little of permanent value. We were too weak to launch a successful revolution." He meditated for a moment and then added, "But we probably shortened the war by a month and saved lives."

Subsequently I found confirmation in print in an article written by Yoffe for a Soviet magazine.[13] "More than ten Independent Socialist Party newspapers," he declared there, "were directed and supported by the Soviet embassy in the German capital. It is necessary to emphasize most categorically that in the preparation of the German revolution, the Soviet embassy always worked in close contact with German socialists."

Lenin had attached great importance to the presence of Yoffe in Berlin. We have this on the authority of Karl Radek. When the German Independent Socialists begged the Soviet government not to pay the next installment of its reparations to Germany under the Brest-Litovsk treaty, Lenin said, "It is worth paying so that Yoffe can remain in Berlin." Radek added, "and we sent the gold." At that time—the autumn of 1918—Lenin instructed Radek to proceed to Germany to guide the revolution. Eight years later Radek published his memoirs of the adventure.[14]

Though Kark Radek accompanied the Soviet delegation to the Brest-Litovsk conference, he never held office in the Soviet government, he was merely a publicist, the best in Russia and perhaps, in his prime, in the world.

---

[13] Vestnik Zhizn, No. 5 (Moscow, 1919).
[14] Karl Radek, Noyabr. Stranichka iz Vospominanii (November. A Little Page of Reminiscences), Krasnaya Nov (Moscow, November, 1926), pp. 139-175.

He was a witty imp and an ugly Puck. He had dense, curly, disheveled black hair which looked as if he never combed it with anything but a towel; laughing, nearsighted eyes behind very thick glasses; prominent wet lips; sideburns that met under his chin; no mustache, and sickly sallow skin. But the sharpness of his tongue, the brilliance of his humor, and the catholicity of his information soon led one to overlook that face. His rooms, first in the Kremlin, then in the soot-colored tenement for high brass on the Moscow River embankment, were cluttered with breast-high piles of newspapers from many parts of the world; he read them and numerous periodicals with lightning speed, and as he turned the pages he commented to his visitor, joked, and swore. In the early 1920's, before my Russian was adequate, we spoke German; he was a Polish Jew educated in Germany. Later we shifted to Russian. Sometimes when I telephoned, his wife would answer and arrange for my visit to her husband. Sometimes he answered the phone. I would say, "Comrade Radek." He would reply, "Comrade Radek is not here." Whereupon I gave my name and he would usually give me an appointment. One found him, bleary-eyed and unkempt and apparently unwashed, prone on his bed, partially hidden by the capitalist press. He was a compulsive conversationalist. At the beginning of a visit he would struggle visibly between reading and talking and when, soon enough, the latter won, he could not be stopped. If I had just returned from America or Germany or England or Spain, he would put a question, for instance, "Well, how is Roosevelt's New Deal getting along?" and before I could formulate the first sentence and open my mouth he would reply to his own query. This was a satisfactory procedure. I knew what I knew, I wanted to know what he thought. He started as a revolutionary enthusiast, he ended as a cynic believing in nobody and nothing.

Once, in his apartment in the inner sanctum of the Kremlin, he served tea—China tea sent him from China by the "Christian" General Feng Yu-hsiang with a message, "from the little brother of the revolution to the Big Brother of the Revolution"—Radek acquired expert knowledge of China and became rector of Moscow's Sun Yat-sen University. His phone rang. During the telephone conversation, a click was heard, and Radek said to the person at the other end of the line, "Some spy has plugged himself in. The devil take him," and continued imprecating the Stalin administration. Inevitably, he was awarded a term of exile in Siberia. Later he, like other Trotskyists, recanted and returned to Moscow where, in his last years, he played the loudest trombone in the cacophony of Stalin's personality cult. Stalin nevertheless put him in the dock in the second of the famous Moscow frame-up trials (January, 1937) and had him sentenced to prison. Fantastic tales circulated about Radek's ultimate fate: he was choked to death by cell inmates for turning informer against former comrades; he was released during the Second World War to conduct communist propaganda in Poland; he had been restored to favor and again advised Stalin; etc., etc. All reflected the public concept of various aspects of his irrepressible personality. A Soviet book published in 1961 says he died in 1939, presumably while serving his sentence.

Radek was the author of many political anecdotes, the illegal currency of totalitarianism. Two samples:

(1) Stalin summoned leading communists and invited suggestions on an easy, quick, and cheap way of making the people happy. Radek whispered something to his neighbor who put his hands to his mouth to stifle a laugh. "What is it, Radek?" Stalin asked.

"No, no, no, it's just a joke. You won't like it."

"Tell it to me, I promise no harm will come to you," Stalin assured.

"An easy, quick, and very cheap way of making the people happy would be to hang you on the Red Square."

(2) Rabinovich told Levine that he had accepted a new job. They were building a tower at the western frontier of the Soviet Union and he would stand on top of it and shout when he saw the world revolution coming.

"But why do you want a job all the way out there?" Levine protested. "Does it pay well?"

"No," Rabinovich replied, "but it's permanent."

In 1918, however, Soviet reality had not yet robbed Radek of faith. The ripening·of the German crisis stirred his revolutionary zeal; he was the number one "German" among the Russians. As Lenin's counselor on German affairs he enjoyed tremendous prestige. In the first paragraph of his reminiscences of the German revolution he reported that Yoffe, in Berlin, summoned him to the direct telegraph wire in Moscow and told him of the German government's decision to ask President Wilson for an armistice. "I, of course, immediately transmitted the news to the government," Radek wrote. He called it "a message of liberation," for until then the "noose around the neck of Soviet Russia was being drawn tighter every day" by the combined if disparate efforts of the Germans, the Western Allies, and the Russian Whites. Bukharin, in Berlin on a "commercial mission" (he was a philosopher of communism and knew nothing about business), informed Moscow of the rising tide of revolution. When Karl Liebknecht was liberated on October 23, 1918, "we felt," Radek recorded, "that the German revolution now had a leader." Presently, what Radek called "a revolution" broke out in Austria. "Lenin and Sverdlov instructed me to write an appeal. 'But where can we have it printed? There are no [German] compositors.'

" 'We'll find them,' Bela Kun replied. 'Just provide bread and sausage.' Kun found them among the Hungarian prisoners of war."

The next morning news of an Austrian revolution brought marching columns to the square fronting the Moscow Soviet. Wave on wave they came; the square was jam-packed. "Suddenly," Radek wrote, "there was a cry which grew like a whirlwind. Into the crowd an automobile moved slowly. We guessed that Lenin could not contain himself in the Kremlin and, for the first time since he was wounded, he drove out. Bela Kun and I ran to meet him. His face showed extreme excitement. . . . Until late in the evening columns of workingmen and workingwomen and soldiers were on the march. The world revolution had commenced. The masses heard its iron steps. Our isolation was ended."

This Austrian "revolution" was the November 12, 1918, proclamation of a republic to replace the monarchy. In the crowd massed before the Viennese parliament building a handful of communists shouted party slogans and some communist soldiers fired a few shots. The democratic surge submerged them.

Several days later, the Radek memoirs continued, "the German embassy telephoned to say that Berlin was calling." He went there with Chicherin. First they spoke by direct telegraph ("Hughes" they named it) with Oskar Kohn, an Independent Socialist member of the Reichstag, and then with Georg Haase, a representative of the government of people's soviets. The latter thanked the Russians for their offer of grain, but, "Knowing that there is famine in Russia we request that the bread you wish to contribute to the German revolution be given to the starving in Russia. . . . The American President Wilson has guaranteed Germany the bread and fats necessary to feed our population for the winter."

Radek commented: "The leader of the German revolution, Haase, receives bread and lard from the leader of the American plutocracy, Wilson. He does not need help from the Russian revolution." To Radek this was "a Judas Iscariot betrayal."

A few days passed and a telegram arrived from Berlin inviting a Soviet delegation to the German Congress of Soviets. The Kremlin selected Radek, Yoffe, Bukharin, Ignatov, and Christian G. Rakovsky, chairman of the Soviet government of the Ukraine. "We met with Lenin and Sverdlov to discuss our line of conduct at the congress. After the conversation, Lenin asked me to stay. . . . 'A grave phase is commencing. Germany has been crushed. The Entente's road into Russia is open,' Lenin said." He saw the Allied armies invading the Ukraine from bases in Hungary, Romania, and the Dardanelles. Radek thought the troops, eager for peace, would not fight.

"They will dispatch colored troops," Lenin insisted. "How will you make propaganda among them?"

"We will agitate among them with cartoons," Radek replied. "Besides, colored troops would not stand our climate. If revolution does not come soon in Entente countries and they are able to send troops to the land of revolution their troops will become disaffected here."

"We shall see," Lenin remarked.

Lenin then discussed the mission to Germany. "Remember," Lenin emphasized, "that you will be in action in the enemy's rear. Intervention is inescapable, and much depends on the situation in Germany."

Radek talked back: "The German revolution is much too great a development to be regarded as a diversion in the rear of the enemy." Lenin was the national leader thinking in terms of Russia's safety.

Radek, Ignatov, and Bukharin proceeded westward to the German front line. There had been skirmishes with the Red Army. The Germans refused to pass the Soviet delegation. Radek got in touch with Sverdlov, Sverdlov consulted Lenin, and Radek was given permission to make his way illegally to Germany so he could appear at the Soviet Congress as representative of the Soviet Communist Party.

Imagination, ingenuity, courage, and energy carried Radek through a dozen traps and trials, and finally, "dirty, filthy," he reached Berlin. His first act was to buy a copy of the *Rote Fahne*, the communist daily newspaper. He went to its office and there found Fanny Ezerskaya, Rosa Luxemburg, Karl Liebknecht, Paul Levy, and other top communists. "What is the situation in the Berlin Soviet?" Radek asked, after the surprise of his sudden appearance had subsided.

"We have no organized forces there," was the reply.

"But what organized forces do we have in Berlin?"

"We are only just gathering our forces," they told him. "When the revolution began we had in Berlin no more than fifty persons."

That evening they met in a workers' eatery. The question of the Soviet terror precipitated an argument. "Rosa was hurt that Djerzhinsky was head of the Cheka: 'Terror has not crushed us,' she said. 'How can you put your trust in terror?'"

Radek replied, "Our trust is in the world revolution. We have to gain several years' time. Then how can you deny the significance of terror? . . ." Liebknecht agreed with Radek. Rosa was not mollified. "Maybe you are right," she said. "But how can Joseph"—Djerzhinsky[15]—"be so cruel?" Never an orthodox communist, she differed with Lenin on many basic issues.

Radek was a keen observer; he quickly sized up the German situation. Cab drivers in a saloon told him, "Wilson is a decent fellow." "He forced that scoundrel, the Kaiser, to flee." "He is now supplying Germany with bread." "He will give us a good peace."

This was the voice of the people, Liebknecht declared: "Anybody who tried to speak against the Entente in defense of the revolution would be devoured by the crowd." The First Congress of the communist party, which heard Radek's greetings from Russia, depressed him: "I did not feel that the party really existed."

To have contemplated a German proletarian revolution in those circumstances was the acme of irresponsibility in Berlin as in Moscow. Lenin grossly miscalculated German conditions. His predictions were fantasies. He encouraged his German comrades to make a putsch, to seize power by a coup d'état. There could be no question of a mass-supported, popular uprising. It is bad political generalship to believe that a platoon one favors can defeat an army one abominates. The Kremlin foolishly assumed that Russian requirements converted its wishes into foreign realities. Hopes alone do not make history.

After the murder of Rosa Luxemburg and Karl Liebknecht, Radek, walk-

[15] His given name was Felix; friends called him Joseph.

ing the streets, saw a poster offering a reward for information about his whereabouts. He took quarters in the apartment of the widow of an army physician where he dictated revolutionary appeals and a pamphlet. On February 13, police agents broke open the door, shouted "Hands up," and transported him to Moabit Prison in Berlin. He was put in chains.

The cross-examination in camera was long and painful, and Radek never knew whether or not he would be lynched by angry soldiers who guarded the jail. Finally, the investigation came to an end, but he was not released. Moscow had apparently seized some German hostages for him and negotiations were proceeding about their exchange. Meanwhile, he could receive visitors. Radek's prison cell now became a political salon. "One of my first guests," he wrote in his memoirs, "was Talaat Pasha, former Grand Vizier and head of the Young Turk government, and his war minister, the hero of the defense of Tripoli, Enver Pasha." Radek urged them to go to Russia. Enver did.[16] (Talaat was assassinated in Berlin on March 15, 1921, by an Armenian.)

"Without any preliminary negotiations," Radek continued, "Rathenau came." Walther Rathenau, the president of the German General Electric Company, future foreign minister of the German Republic, author and thinker, impressed Radek at their first interview with his "great abstract wisdom, the absence of intuition, and pathological self-love. Crossing his legs, he asked permission to present his views on the world situation. He spoke for over an hour listening to the sound of his own voice." No compulsive talker likes another. Rathenau said: "Soviet Russia will not be conquered. . . . The question is whether you can build a new society. The entire world stands at the crossroads. There is no return to the old capitalist system. A breakdown of social relationships is taking place, but the working masses themselves can only destroy, constructive work requires brains; the working class can only create a new society under the leadership of an aristocracy of the spirit. That will not be a society of equality, for equality is impossible. . . . Marx propounded only the theory of destruction. In my books you will find the theory of constructive socialism."

Radek smiled.

"In Germany the victory of the revolution will be impossible for many years," Rathenau continued. "The German worker is a philistine. Several years from now I will probably come to Russia as a technician and you, the powers that be in the Soviet government, will receive me in silk clothing."

"Why silk?" Radek asked.

"Because after many years of the asceticism of the illegal revolutionary you, having won, will want to enjoy life."

Maximilian Harden called on the prisoner; he was the radical Radek of bourgeois Germany. "Socially," Radek proclaimed, Harden "was a mixture of Carlyle and Nietzsche." Harden's power as a publicist lay in his opposition

---

[16] For an account of Enver's adventure in Russia see, Louis Fischer, *The Soviets in World Affairs*, Vol. I, pp. 382-390.

to the government of Kaiser Germany. Radek's pen failed him when he sold it to Stalin.

Baron Georg F. W. F. von Reibnitz came to the cell in Moabit. He had been on Ludendorff's staff. "Reibnitz," Radek stated, "was the first representative of the breed which received the name of 'national Bolshevik,' with whom I had dealt." When the German government dropped its charges against Radek, and since he could not return to Russia because of the hostages and transit difficulties, he moved into Reibnitz's apartment where he remained eight weeks. There he met Colonel Walter Bauer, Ludendorff's right-hand man. Bauer gave Radek to understand that "we are invincible and that we were the allies of Germany in her struggles against the Entente." There he also received a visit from Admiral Paul von Hintze, the Kaiser's Foreign Secretary, likewise a Ludendorff man. "He stood for a deal with Soviet Russia," Radek asserted in his 1926 recollections.

Radek entered jail a world-revolutionary. His visitors ignored this aspect, looked behind it, and recognized in him the spokesman of a national power, a potential partner. Right met left, the right that would destroy the democratic Weimar Republic met the left which hated bourgeois democracy, and if they did not see eye to eye they lent one another their ears (and later their votes and hands). Radek came to Germany to make a revolution. He stayed to make Soviet foreign policy. The 1922 Rapallo Treaty and the bonds between the Soviet government and the German army first took form in a prison cell and in the guest room of Ludendorff's aide.

Radek left Germany convinced that "a revolution, even one limited to Europe, would be a very prolonged process." He carried to Moscow this thought and "the works of Einstein, then unknown in Russia."

Trotsky, in exile from the Soviet Union, called the history of the German workers' movement after 1914 "the most tragic chapter in modern history." This was a subjective judgment. It was his tragedy and it was Lenin's. For Lenin, the failure of the German revolution broke a tryst with destiny. In the transformation of Radek's mission there was implicit the transformation of the Soviet system. Bolshevism was thrown back on itself to fight its own battles and to merge gradually with Mother Russia.

XXIII. LENIN AND MAXIM GORKY

WHEN THE CAPITAL MOVED from Petrograd, Lenin took a suite in Moscow's National Hotel at the corner of Mokhovaya (now Karl Marx Prospect) and Tversakaya (now Gorky). Later he and Krupskaya acquired an apartment of five small rooms in the Kremlin with a total floor space of twenty-six square yards. A visitor, who came to see Krupskaya and stayed for tea with her and Lenin and Lenin's sister Maria, recalled that the household had only two teaspoons which passed from hand to hand. Black bread and butter were served with the tea. It was the hungry year of 1919.

A group of peasants visited Lenin in his office and commented on how cold it was. "There's no wood, we have to economize," he explained. They sent him a load of kindling.

Lenin hated waste. He insisted that officials use the telephone to save paper. He told journalists to be brief; *Pravda*, the party daily, was appearing as one sheet printed on brown wrapping paper. He disliked wasting time too. Sessions of the Central Committee of the party were called for 10 A.M. He opened them at 10:15 sharp. Speakers were given two minutes; Lenin watched his watch. Elena D. Stasova, secretary of the Central Committee, reports that Lenin also objected to wasting government property. When A. D. Tsurupa, a prominent Bolshevik, neglected his health, Lenin wrote him saying that since communists were government property they had no right to harm themselves. Krupskaya and Maria Ilynichna, Lenin's sister, told Stasova that Lenin was sleeping badly. Stasova put through a resolution of the Central Committee by telephone ordering Lenin to take a vacation, and informed him of the fact by phone.

"When must I go?" he inquired angrily.

She told him. He went. He hunted, fished, and collected mushrooms in the woods around Moscow.[1]

In the first summer after the revolution, Lenin occasionally spent Sundays or weekends at Tarasovka, a village vacation spot near Moscow. He tried to be alone, but failed because he did not have his own dacha or summer bungalow —usually a rickety log cabin with open terrace. Several families occupied the dacha as tenants, and he had their company at meal and tea times. Besides, writes his sister Maria, there were no screens and Lenin suffered from the buzzing and the stings of mosquitoes. Once he could not sleep all night and fled to Moscow at dawn. His cook, A. M. Sisoyeva, remembered that when he saw a fly on a loaf of bread he told her that bread must be covered. During the second summer (1919) Lenin rested from time to time at the government's dacha in the village of Gorky, where he went mushroom hunting and brought back a basketful to the cook.

Later Lenin and Krupskaya had a maid named Olympiada Nikoforovna Zhuravlova, formerly employed in an iron foundry in the Urals. Lenin, according to Krupskaya, found that Olympiada "possessed a strong proletarian instinct" and he liked to have dinner, supper, and tea in the kitchen so he could talk with her.[2]

Krupskaya's health had been bad since her operation in Bern. Early in 1919

---

[1] *Vospominaniya*, Vol. 1, pp. 315-323.
[2] *Ibid.*, Vol. 2, p. 399.

it deteriorated. V. D. Bonch-Bruevich, Lenin's chief executive secretary, suggested that she needed a long vacation away from Moscow. "Long vacation!" Lenin exclaimed. "She won't hear of it. Try to persuade her."

"You're the only one who can persuade her," Bonch replied. He had an idea: since Krupskaya was active in the field of education, organizing schools, recruiting teachers, preparing proletarian textbooks, she might be willing to stay in one of the schools in the woods at Sokolniki, a suburb of Moscow, where she could work and observe. Lenin liked the proposal and asked Bonch to go there and ascertain whether accommodations were available. "Don't tell anybody why you came. Note the road well . . . I'll try to prepare Nadya"— Krupskaya.

Bonch found that she would be comfortable. "Nadya is inclined to go. I'll tell you definitely tomorrow morning," Lenin said and returned to "his unceasing, tense, extremely nerve-racking work constantly interrupted by telephone signals: the flashing of lamps, the buzzing of 'bees' on the switchboard in the neighboring room announced calls from Petrograd, Nizhni Novgorod, Kursk, and other places. Equably, calmly, without raising his voice, Vladimir Ilyich issued hundreds of instructions, received reports, transcribed the most important of them, drafted telegrams, radiograms, telephonograms, sent notes and letters by couriers on motorcycles—all this simply, and outwardly quiet, as though it was not work. From time to time he would walk quickly to the map and mark the positions at the fronts in accordance with the latest information."[3]

The next morning, as Bonch entered Lenin's office with the first batch of papers, Lenin said, "Nadya agrees . . . She's packing. . . . Taking a pile of work with her, but she can scarcely talk, scarcely breathe. . . . Will she get well? . . . We'll go toward evening, only don't tell anybody, tell absolutely nobody."

All went well; Nadya settled in the Sokolniki school; Lenin drove out now and then to see her. Once Lenin invited Bonch to come along; the children were having a Christmas-tree party (early January, 1919). They bought a few sweets and presents; Moscow shops had little to offer in those days. It was a gay affair. Lenin joined a ring of children as they danced around the Christmas tree and sang. The song was about the tree itself. Then they played koshka-mishka or cat-and-mouse: a ring is formed, and one child within the ring—the cat—must try to get out to catch a second child—the mouse—outside the ring. The segment of the ring closes where the cat attempts to break through; the cat tries another segment and that too must close quickly. Lenin, holding hands with two pupils, took charge of the ring's strategy of blocking the cat's assault on the mouse.

The fresh air and relaxation helped Krupskaya, and she remained in the Sokolniki woods. On January 19, 1919, a Sunday, Lenin went out again in a car driven by his thirty-year-old chauffeur, Stepan Kasimirovich Gil, who tells

[3] *Ibid.*, pp. 441-444, as told by Bonch.

the story.[4] The streets were high with snow; no one to clean them. The car was moving along softly and nearing Kalanchevskaya Square when they heard a shout, "Stop." Gil stepped on the gas. Several blocks farther along, several men in the middle of the road with revolvers in their hands cried, "Halt. Stop the car." Gil, seeing this was not a patrol, drove straight at them. "Stop, or we shoot," one of the men yelled. Gil wanted to speed past but Lenin told him to stop.

"Get out. Step lively," the men ordered.

Lenin opened the door and said, "What's the matter?"

"Get out. Don't talk," came the reply.

One of the armed men jerked Lenin toward him. Lenin showed his pass, with photograph and name, and said, "What's the matter, comrades? Who are you?" Maria Ilynichna and a man companion also came out of the automobile. One of the armed men searched Lenin's pockets and took his wallet and a small Browning. Maria, her temper aroused, exclaimed, "What right have you to search him? Why, he's Comrade Lenin! Show your papers!"

"We don't need papers," somebody replied. "We can do anything."

Gil, who had remained seated at the wheel with his revolver cocked, did not dare use it. In an exchange of shots, Lenin might be killed. The holdup group now asked Gil to leave the car. When he obeyed, they all got in and drove off. "Pretty clever," Lenin said. "We, though armed, surrendered the machine. What a disgrace!"

Gil explained his fears of provoking a battle. "Yes, Comrade Gil," Lenin agreed, "you're right. Force would not have worked here. Apparently we are alive because we didn't resist."

Nearby stood the building of the Sokolniki Soviet. They walked over to phone the Kremlin for a car. But the watchman would not let them in; he asked Lenin for his pass.

"I'm Lenin," Lenin said, "but I have no pass. I've just been robbed."

The guard looked skeptical. Gil showed his identification, which served for all of them. Inside they found nobody. In a small room they awakened a sleeping telephone operator who rang the Kremlin. A car came.

Lenin ordered a search for the stolen automobile. The roads out of the city were blocked by snow, he reasoned, and in Moscow a big car could not be hidden. The Cheka and the criminal police spread a net and discovered Lenin's abandoned machine that same night. Near it lay a dead policeman and a dead soldier. The robbers escaped. But many criminals were caught during the search.

In the spring of 1919 a group of Cossacks from the Don were delegated to Moscow to interview Mikhail I. Kalinin, appointed President of Soviet Russia (President of the VTSIK) in March on the death of Sverdlov. Kalinin, himself of peasant origin, said Lenin was interested in the mood of peasants and Cossacks and had invited them for the next day at 3 P.M. In the waiting

[4] *Ibid.*, pp. 435-438.

room, Lydia Fotieva, Lenin's secretary, warned them against staying too long: "Vladimir Ilyich has not slept several nights." Promptly at three they entered Lenin's office. They were awed by the idea of seeing him but not by him; his questions quickly brought them down to earth: Had they provided seed for the families of peasant soldiers at the front? Were the Cossacks enlisting in the Red Army? What view did the Cossacks take on farm cooperatives and communes? (Their reply is not known but can be surmised.) The audience was repeatedly interrupted by telephone calls from the fronts, from factories, from all parts of the country. Each time, Lenin came back to them with a smile. They had traveled to Moscow, like thousands of others who arrived every day, to make requests of various commissariats for arms, transport, and preferences. "Go and knock," he advised them. "If no one opens, phone me." He had a sensitive ear.

Pravda of February 15, 1919, published Lenin's answer to a letter, printed in *Izvestia* (the government organ) on February 2, from a peasant named Gulov, fighting in the Red Army. Gulov, Lenin wrote, asked about the government's attitude toward the middle peasants, those who were neither grain-selling, prosperous kulaks nor uncomfortably poor, and "tells about reported rumors alleging that Lenin and Trotsky are on bad terms, that there are allegedly big differences between them, especially regarding the middle peasant."

Trotsky had already issued his denial in *Izvestia* of February 7, branding the rumors as lies spread by landlords and capitalists and their agents. "I, for my part," Lenin now affirmed, "fully confirm Comrade Trotsky's declaration. There are no differences between us, and in the matter of the middle peasants there are no differences not only between us and Trotsky but in general in the communist party to which both of us belong. In his letter, Comrade Trotsky explained fully and clearly why the communist party, and this workers and peasants government, elected by the soviets and belonging to that party, does not regard the middle peasants as their enemies. I sign my name with both hands under what Comrade Trotsky has said." But knowing the mind of the peasant, rich, middle, and poor, Lenin added, "Free trading in grain means freedom for the rich to get rich and freedom for the poor to die. . . . The capitalist government and 'freedom to trade' will not return. Socialism shall win."

(Lenin's article appears in the thirty-sixth volume of the fourth edition of his collected works, published in Moscow in Russian in 1957. The authorities did not feel free to suppress it. But they added an editorial note: "L. D. Trotsky—the bitterest enemy of Leninism . . . After the victory of the November socialist revolution, Trotsky, for a while, formally agreed with the policy of the party on the peasant question.")

But Lenin doubted the peasantry's loyalty, and on April 30, 1919, he asked Zinoviev to assemble some "three hundred to six hundred Petrograd workers, highly recommended by the party and the trade unions, and distribute them in ones and twos" to administer villages in all parts of Russia. "Without such groups of absolutely dependable and experienced Petrograd workers we will achieve no big improvement in the village."[5]

Petrograd, "Paris of the North," city of light, lived in an envelope of gloom, cold, and hunger. The cult of the worker and peasant made a political puppet show of the lowly and lowered standards of behavior. Maxim Gorky, a resident of the former capital, growled. "In 1919," he wrote, "there was a congress in Petrograd of 'the village poor.' From the villages in the north came several thousand peasants, some hundreds of whom were housed in the Winter Palace of the Romanovs. When the congress was over, and these people had gone away, it was found that not only the bathtubs of the palace but also a great number of priceless Sèvres, Saxon, and oriental vases had been befouled by them for lavatory use. And this was not done out of necessity—the toilets of the palace were functioning and the water system was working. No, this vandalism was an expression of the desire to sully and debase things of beauty."[6]

As a public figure, Maxim Gorky was at that moment probably better known and more loved than Lenin. The intellectuals, and many workers and peasants, whether or not they had read his stories, knew him. Unlike Lenin who had stepped out from nobility to serve a cause, Maxim Gorky was a man of the people who served the people in his own way. Lenin treated Gorky with special deference and usually received him at home. When he was to come to the Sovnarkom office, Lenin would arrive early and say to a secretary, "Have you remembered to tell the booth at the Kremlin gate not to delay Gorky there?" Half an hour later, Lenin would phone his secretary to ask whether a car had been sent to fetch Gorky. Lenin never kept Gorky waiting; he received him out of turn. A Gorky visit, a secretary recalls, always meant work for Lenin's staff.[7] Gorky brought a fileful of requests about persons, most of them intellectuals, artists, and writers, who had been arrested, or subjected to class discrimination, or denied creative expression. The official sun shining on workers and peasants left the intellectuals in the shade and made Gorky unhappy. Gorky "is coming here tomorrow, and I would very much like to pull him out of Petrograd where he has become overstrung and depressed," Lenin wrote on July 7, 1919, to Krupskaya who was on the *Krasnaya Zvezda (Red Star)*, a Volga propaganda boat with speakers aboard which stopped at cities and lesser centers to preach. Lenin hoped to persuade Gorky to join the ship; that would have been a big political coup. (Lenin added: "Mitya"—his brother Dmitri—"has left for Kiev. The Whites, apparently, have recaptured the Crimea. Our life is just the same: we vacation Sundays at 'our' dacha. Trotsky's health is better, he's left for the south, I hope he pulls through. I expect improvement from the replacement of

[5] Lenin, *Sochineniya*, Fourth ed., Vol. 36, p. 466.
[6] *Vospominaniya*, Vol. 1, p. 380, and *Days With Lenin*, p. 35.
[7] *Vospominaniya*, Vol. 2, pp. 420-422.

Commander in Chief Vatsetis by [General S. S.] Kamenev (of the eastern front). . . . I embrace you firmly, please write and telegraph oftener. Your V. Ulyanov. N.B. Obey the doctor: eat and sleep more, then by winter your working capacity will be *fully* restored.")[8]

The next day Lenin wrote Krupskaya again: "I saw Gorky today, tried to convince him to go on your boat . . . but he refused unconditionally."[9] "Unconditionally" implied that Gorky did not give his health or work as the reason. He did not wish to join the Volga showboat and identify with the Soviet regime. He was not anti-Soviet; but he had a strong commitment to freedom and the persecution of intellectuals tormented him. Petrograd felt this persecution more than other places. It was the window to Europe, a European city; Moscow was the door to Russia, an overgrown urban village. The window was clouded over with political hoarfrost. The weather vane pointed east to Asia. Western hostility was partly to blame for the bad weather. But blame is no balm. Intellectuals resented the cold wind blowing out of the Moscow Kremlin. Gorky resented it. Made of pure Russian clay, he had nevertheless tasted of the West and needed it.

He returned to Petrograd. Lenin did not give up. He wrote Gorky again on July 19, 1919, coaxing him to come to the government rest house at Gorky, twenty miles south of Moscow: "I often go for two days to the village where I can put up very comfortably for a short or longer period. Come, really! Wire, *when*; we will get you a compartment [on the train]. . . . A little change of air, you truly need it. I expect your reply. Your Lenin."[10]

Gorky declined and gave vent to his bitterness. Lenin replied on July 31, 1919, in a 1,000-word letter, probably the longest he wrote during the civil war—a chilling letter of controlled anger.[11] "Dear Alexey Maximich," it began. "The more I read and reread your letter, the more I think of the connection between its conclusions and the information in it (and what you told me in our talks), the greater becomes my conviction that this letter and your conclusions and all your impressions are diseased."

Petrograd, Lenin continued, has suffered much: hunger, danger of military attack, and so forth. "Your nerves clearly cannot stand that," Lenin wrote. "This is not surprising. But you remain obstinate when you are told to change your residence, for to allow your nerves to be frayed until they are sick is altogether unreasonable. . . .

". . . You begin by mentioning dysentery and cholera; and immediately there follows a kind of diseased animosity: 'brotherhood, equality.' Unintentionally you make it appear as though communism is to blame—for privations, poverty, and the diseases of a besieged city!!

[8] Lenin, *op. cit.*, Vol. 37, p. 454.
[9] *Ibid.*, p. 455.
[10] *Ibid.*, Vol. 35, p. 346.
[11] *Ibid.*, pp. 347-350. "Maxim Gorky" is a literary pseudonym. His name was Alexey Maximovich Peshkov. "Gorky" means "bitter."

"Further there are some kinds of hostile attacks on 'fenced-in' literature (what kind? why connected with Kalinin?). And the conclusion, it seems, is that 'the negligible remnant of intelligent workingmen' say that 'they have been betrayed' 'into the hands of the muzhik.' "

Gorky's letter, Lenin declared, had referred to "vestiges of the aristocracy." "Their mood," Lenin said, "influences you unhealthily. You say you see persons 'of the most varied strata.' It's one thing to see, another thing to feel this contact every day in everything." Gorky's profession, Lenin hinted, required him "to receive" scores of "embittered bourgeois intellectuals." These "remnants," Gorky had written, "have something like warm sympathy for the Soviet regime," but "the majority of the workers" are thieves, bandwagon "communists," and so forth. "And you," Lenin commented, "go so far as to reach 'the conclusion' that a revolution cannot be made with the help of thieves, cannot be made without intellectuals.

"This is an altogether diseased mentality," Lenin charged. Much was being done, Lenin affirmed, to draw intellectuals into the service of the state. But "in Petrograd this cannot be 'seen,' for Petrograd is a city with an unusually large number of bourgeois persons who have lost their places in society (and their heads) and 'intellectuals,' but throughout Russia this is an undisputed fact. In Petrograd or from Petrograd one can understand this only if you have exceptional *political* knowledge together with especially great political experience. This you do not have. And you occupy yourself not with politics, and not with observing *the work* of political construction, but with a peculiar profession which surrounds you with angry bourgeois intellectuals who have understood nothing, forgotten nothing, learned nothing. . . .

"If you are *to observe* you must observe at the bottom where it is possible *to see* the work of the building of a new life, in a workers' quarter in the province [whose boredom Gorky knew too well], or in a village—there it is not necessary to grasp a totality of complex data, there it is possible only to observe. . . .

"You have put yourself in a position in which you cannot directly observe the life of the workers and peasants, that is, nine-tenths of the population of Russia." (On other occasions, Lenin had hailed Petrograd as the model proletarian city; and Gorky, Russia's most sensitive artist-observer, had observed peasants in congress in the Winter Palace.) "You stubbornly reject advice to leave" the city. "Naturally you have made yourself ill. You write that life has become not only difficult but 'quite disgusting.' No wonder. . . ." Gorky had steeped himself in the misery of the intellectuals but in Petrograd "*you cannot* observe and study what is new in the army, in the village, in the factory. . . . This country is committed to a feverish struggle against the world bourgeoisie. . . . Life has become loathsome, there is 'a deepening divergence' with communism. Wherein lies this divergence I cannot understand. You give no proof of any divergence in policy or ideas."

Lenin finished by again urging Gorky to "make a radical change in your environment, in your contacts, in your work, otherwise you may make your life altogether loathsome.

"I firmly shake your hand. Yours, Lenin."

Some of the "vestiges of aristocracy" for whom Gorky interceded were aristocrats of the spirit or of the pen or brush. One was the Grand Duke Nikolai Mikhailovich, a cousin of the last Tsar and a historian who wished to retire to Finland to write. After Gorky put the Grand Duke's case to Lenin, Lenin gave him a letter to the Petrograd authorities asking them to accede to Gorky's request. On returning to Petrograd, Gorky learned that the Grand Duke had been executed. Gorky talked about this episode to Boris I. Nicolaevsky, a prominent Menshevik writer, in Berlin in 1922 and 1923 and aired the suspicion that Lenin himself or a person in Lenin's entourage had ordered the Grand Duke's execution at the very time Lenin gave Gorky the letter. The suspicion of duplicity is supported by a telegram reproduced in *Leninskii Sbornik* (Vol. XXI, p. 279), in which Lenin advised Zinoviev in Petrograd to delay the Grand Duke's departure for Finland.

Nothing, nevertheless, destroyed the Lenin-Gorky relationship. Gorky was a one-man civil liberties union; Lenin was his final court of appeals. Gorky saved the lives of many writers, artists, and intellectuals. Lenin needed Gorky, famous throughout Russia as a writer about the masses, for the masses, with the masses. Had he not identified himself with the communist party? To alienate him would have broken a Soviet prop. Lenin and Gorky continued to meet in Moscow, Gorky bringing his dossier of injustices, Lenin attempting to "correct" Gorky's views.

Gorky's memoirs about Lenin, written after the leader's death, are a hymn of praise.[12] But he gently stood his ground, an unregenerate defender of freedom. "I often used to speak with Lenin about the cruelty of revolutionary tactics and life.

" 'What do you want?' he would ask in astonishment and anger. 'Is humaneness possible in such a struggle of unprecedented ferocity? Where is there any place for softheartedness or magnanimity? Europe is blockading us, we have been denied the expected aid of the European proletariat, from every side counterrevolution is creeping up on us like a bear, and we— what should we do? Shouldn't we, haven't we a right to fight back, to resist? Well, excuse me, we are not fools. We know: what we want cannot be done by anyone except us. Do you think that I would be sitting here if I were convinced of the contrary?

" 'What is your criterion for measuring the number of necessary and superfluous blows in a fight?' he once asked me after a heated discussion. I could only answer this simple question lyrically. I think that there is no other answer.

"I often overwhelmed him with various requests, and at times I felt that

[12] *Vospominaniya*, Vol. 1, pp. 365-392; also, *Days With Lenin*.

my interventions on behalf of people made Lenin pity me. He would ask, 'Doesn't it seem to you that you are occupying yourself with inconsequential matters, trifles?'

"But I continued to do what I thought was necessary, and was not put off by the cross, angry looks of a person who knew who the enemies of the proletariat were. He would shake his head vigorously and say, 'You are compromising yourself in the eyes of the comrades and the workers.'

"But I pointed out that comrades and workers 'in a state of passion and irritation' frequently adopted a too frivolous and a 'simple' attitude toward liberty and toward the lives of valuable people, and that, in my view, this not only compromised the honest, difficult affairs of the revolution by excessive and at times senseless cruelty, but was objectively harmful to the revolution, for it repelled many people with great qualities from participating in it.

" 'Hm, hm,' Lenin muttered skeptically, and pointed out to me many instances when intellectuals betrayed the workers' cause. 'Between you and me,' he said, 'many betray and desert not only out of cowardice but out of selfishness, out of fear of being embarrassed, afraid that their favorite theory might suffer in a clash with reality. But we are not afraid of that. Theories and hypotheses are not something 'holy' to us, they are tools.' "

". . . do you really pity people?" Gorky asked on another occasion.

"I am sorry for the clever ones," Lenin replied. "We haven't enough clever people. We are for the most part a talented people, but mentally lazy." (Mental laziness often results from political tyranny. Thinking is not encouraged when its expression is penalized.)

One evening Lenin and Gorky and others gathered in the apartment of Yekaterina Pavlovna Peshkova, Gorky's former wife, to listen to Isaiah Dobrovein play Beethoven. He played the Appassionata. "I know of nothing greater than the Appassionata," Lenin commented. "I would like to listen to it every day. It is marvelous superhuman music. I always think with pride —perhaps it is naïve of me—what marvelous things human beings can do."

"Then," Gorky's report continues, "screwing up his eyes and smiling, he added, rather sadly, 'But I can't listen to music too often, it works on my nerves, makes me want to say kind, stupid things and pat the heads of people who, living in this vile hell, can create such beauty. But now one must not pat anybody's head—they might bite off your hand, and you have to beat them on the head, beat them without mercy, although we are ideally opposed to the use of force against anyone. Hm, hm, this is an infernally difficult job.' "

Lenin's personality had many chambers, and there is no master key to all. But his comment at that evening musicale unlocks many of them. The most infernal difficulty of the job was to repress the humaneness in him and cultivate the capacity to crack skulls. He put on an iron glove to cover the velvet hand. He saw to it that his personality, with whatever softness was left in it, never got in the way of duty. He disciplined himself before he disciplined others. He curbed himself so he could curb others. He had sold his soul to the idol, Revolution, and obeyed its cruel dictates. No Elysian sonata must remind him of the finer things of life. Music worked on his nerves because he had to work to shut out its message. He was at war in the service of her majesty, Victory, and he opened his ear only to bugles. He neither smoked nor drank. Fighting was his food. Work was his drug. But he slept poorly. Gorky called Lenin "the helmsman of so vast and ponderous a ship as our leaden, peasant Russia." It pulled him down.

XXIV. ᏫHE LONG ARM

ONE MORNING Lenin left his bedroom and placed a note where his wife and Maria could see it: "Please wake me no later than 10 in the morning. It is now 4:15, I can't sleep; I'm quite well. Otherwise I lose tomorrow."

Despite his insomnia, Lenin did not wish to "lose tomorrow" because all Soviet threads ended in his hand. He operated as a one-man political-military staff against foreign intervention and civil war.

When the First World War came to an end, and with it the need of a second front in the east, Russians expected a respite. Not Lenin. He said to Chicherin, "Now Das Weltkapital will advance against us."[1] He used the German term for world capitalism.

Some capitalist politicians were inspired by hatred of communism, some by hostility to Russia—Russia as a nation. Soivet weakness tempted other countries to tamper with the world balance of power. Given nationalism and the rivalry it spawns, few governments could resist the rare opportunity to bite into a great land mass and rip off a piece or establish a sphere of influence. The United States, an amateur in the professional balance-of-power game, avoided entanglements in Europe yet aimed to curb Japan's growing strength in the Pacific. President Wilson, opposed in principle to the game, played it by opposing it: he would listen to no scheme to overthrow the Soviet regime or dismember Russia, for a weak Russia could not counterbalance Japan in the Far East.

"I attended a dinner that King George V. gave to the President at Buckingham Palace, one or two days after Christmas, 1918," wrote David R. Francis, U.S. ambassador to Russia. The dinner over, "King George, who was escorting Mrs. Wilson out of the reception room, when he met me, said: 'Mr. Ambassador, what do you think we ought to do about Russia?'

[1] Repeated to me by Chicherin. Lenin said, "Na nas idyot Das Weltkapital."

"I replied I thought the Allies should overturn the Bolshevik Government.

"The King rejoined by telling me he thought so, too, but President Wilson differed from us."[2]

Francis, who had just left Soviet Russia, sought an audience with Wilson. The President delayed. When they finally met, Francis presented a plan: ". . . that the Allied missions return to Petrograd to occupy their domiciles accompanied by 100,000 Allied troops and abundant food supplies." The Soviet government would be overturned.

"The President," Francis reported, "said he would give the plan consideration."[3]

This is a Chief Executive's polite way of saying No. He never considered it.

Japan disguised nothing. For her rivalry with America, and to further her designs on China, she wanted to annex Russia's Far Eastern Maritime Provinces and the island of Sakhalin and possess their raw materials. Tokyo's Russian puppets in Siberia—Ataman Semenov and Ataman Kalmikov—refused to collaborate with Admiral Kolchak or any Russian who favored an "undivided Russia."

The British and French also aimed to divide Russia. Lord Milner, member of the British War Cabinet, and Premier Georges Clemenceau signed a convention in Paris on December 23, 1917, "On the Subject of Activity in Southern Russia." France was to operate in the northern areas of the Black Sea, England in the southeastern areas of the Black Sea against the Turks. "With this reservation, the zones of influence assigned to each government shall be as follows: The English zone: the Cossack territories, the territory of the Caucasus, Armenia, Georgia, Kurdistan. The French zone: Bessarabia, the Ukraine, the Crimea. The expenses shall be pooled and regulated by a centralizing inter-Allied organ."[4]

Though this was a wartime agreement, it could hardly have been intended as a plan for wartime operations; neither Britain nor France was in a position to move into southern Russia in 1917 or 1918 and fight the German army of occupation. Nor could Allied fleets have passed through the Dardanelles into the Black Sea until they had won the war. The convention only makes sense as a scheme for a postwar balance-of-power partition of southern Russia. In fact, after victory England and France each entered the zone delineated for it in the agreement. But, lacking sufficient troops for their original purpose, they shifted to supporting White champions of an undivided Russia.

The manpower problem shaped postwar Allied policy toward Russia.

[2] David R. Francis, *Russia From the American Embassy* (New York, 1921), p. 307.
[3] *Ibid.*, p. 311.
[4] Full text first published in Louis Fischer, *The Soviets in World Affairs*, Appendix, Vol. II, p. 836. The document, in the French original, was handed to me in 1929 by the Librarian of the British Foreign Office. Winston S. Churchill, *The Aftermath* (New York, 1929), pp. 167-168, described the convention without quoting its text. It is mentioned by Crosby in Paris telegram 2955, Dec. 27, 1917 (*Foreign Relations 1918, Russia*, Vol. II, pp. 597-598), and by George F. Kennan, *Russia Leaves the War*, pp. 179-180 note.

January 12, 1919, the first day the statesmen assembled in Paris to concoct a peace for Germany, they discussed a military crusade against Russia. Wilson objected. Communism, he said, was indeed "a social and political danger" but there was "a great doubt in his mind whether Bolshevism can be checked by arms."[5] He preferred to negotiate with it. Prime Minister David Lloyd George echoed him: "the Bolsheviki movement is as dangerous to civilisation as German militarism." If, however, they undertook to kill Bolshevism by the sword, "the armies would mutiny. . . . The mere idea of crushing Bolshevism by a military force is pure madness. Even admitting that this is done, who is there to occupy Russia?"

He had been told, reads the official summary of Lloyd George's remarks, "that there were three men, Denikin, Kolchak and [British General] Knox. In considering the chances of these people to overthrow the Bolsheviki, he pointed out that he had received information that the Czecho-Slovaks now refused to fight; that the Russian army was not to be trusted. . . . If the Allies counted on any of these men, he believed they were building on quicksand. . . . If a military enterprise were started against the Bolsheviki that would make England Bolshevist, and there would be a Soviet in London."[6]

At a session of the Peace Conference on January 21, 1919, Lloyd George asked his colleagues what contribution their countries could make toward a volunteer army of 150,000 to combat communism. "President Wilson and M. Clemenceau each said none." Italian Premier V. E. Orlando was equally negative.

"We are sitting on top of a mine which may go off at any moment," Field Marshal Sir Henry Wilson noted in his diary on January 17. "Ireland tonight has telegraphed for some more tanks and machine guns and is evidently anxious about the state of the country." Five days later he told the British Cabinet that "we dare not give an unpopular order to the troops, and discipline was a thing of the past. [General] Douglas Haig said that by February 15, we would have no army in France."[7]

Marshal Foch informed Sir Henry Wilson on February 3, that "his men won't stand it much longer, and will demobilize themselves as the Belgians are doing."[8] Lloyd George in Paris received news on February 2 of riots in Glasgow and strikes in London and Liverpool. French labor too was restive. The French government opposed the presence of Bolshevik representatives at the peace conference: "they would convert France and England to Bol-

[5] Ray Stannard Baker, Woodrow Wilson and World Settlement, Written from his Unpublished and Personal Material (London, 1923), Vol. I, p. 166.

[6] Minute of the Conversation in Foreign Minister S. Pichon's office in the Quai d'Orsay on Jan. 16, 1919, reproduced in the Hearings of the Committee on Foreign Relations of the U.S. Senate, in Senate Document 106, p. 1235.

[7] Major-General Sir C. E. Callwell, Field-Marshal Sir Henry Wilson, His Life and Diaries, Vol. II, p. 164.

[8] Ibid., p. 168.

shevism."[9] Led by Bela Kun, communists established a Soviet government in Hungary on March 21. Bavaria went communist on April 5. An expensive French encounter with the Red Army at Kherson in the Ukraine and a mutiny in the French fleet at Odessa on April 27 brought an order from Paris for the evacuation of all French forces from south Russia.

It was no time for the weary soldiers of anemic nations to wage war again in remote Russia. Only Japan did that. The European powers and the United States sent officers, technicians, and arms. The armies that landed in north Russia during the war were soon ordered home.

Except for the Japanese, foreign troops, though present in thousands, played a minor role in the Russian civil war after November, 1918. It was Russian versus Russian. The anti-Bolsheviks had the advantage of heavy arms shipments from the Allies and the disadvantage of disunity. Their fate depended on joint effort. If they could keep the Bolsheviks in a box and attack all sides of it simultaneously, triumph was assured. They agreed, accordingly, to unite behind Kolchak. But Yudenich, far off on the Baltic Sea, could not communicate with Kolchak in Siberia or with Denikin in the North Caucasus. Indeed, Denikin had trouble maintaining contact with Kolchak. Paris was accordingly chosen as White coordinating center in Russia's civil war.

The Supreme Council, consisting of Premier Clemenceau, President Wilson, Prime Minister Lloyd George, Prime Minister Orlando, and Japanese chief representative Saionji, on May 26, 1919, addressed a note to Kolchak,[10] which began: "It has always been the cardinal axiom of the Allied and Associated Powers"—the United States was the Associated Power—"to avoid interference in the internal affairs of Russia." But "they are prepared . . . to continue their assistance." The note then stated that the powers would aid and recognize Kolchak if he and his friends convoked the Constituent Assembly "as soon as they reach Moscow," and call free elections, forbear from re-establishing the monarchy, recognize the independence of Finland, Poland, Estonia, Latvia, Lithuania, and the Caspian and Caucasus Republics, and pay Russia's foreign obligations.

Colonel John Ward, British troop commander at Omsk, Kolchak's Siberian capital, told me that the admiral's royalist supporters and "undivided Russia" advisers opposed acceptance of these conditions. Ward suggested a soft answer. On June 4, accordingly, Kolchak replied that he would convene the Constituent Assembly and, being a democrat, could not prejudge its decisions about the form of government or the alienation of Russian territory. He did agree to Polish independence.

Mr. S. D. Sazonov, tsarist foreign minister from 1910 to 1916, was Kolchak's foreign minister, with seat in Paris. He attempted to coordinate the activities of the Whites in Russia and to relate them to the wishes of the

[9] Senate Document 106.
[10] British Blue Book, *The Evacuation of North Russia, 1919.*, Cmd. 818.

Allied and Associated powers. In May, 1919, he spent ten days in London which, according to a telegram dated June 1 and decoded and typed out on stationery of the Omsk Foreign Ministry on June 5,[11] pleased him. He had an audience with the King, twice conferred with members of Parliament "of various parties," and felt that England would help. In a long letter to Kolchak's prime minister, Peter V. Vologodsky, carried by messenger from Paris on June 17, Sazonov added details. Lord Curzon gave him a friendly reception. Winston S. Churchill and Sir Samuel Hoare expressed sympathy for Kolchak. To the argument that Britain, France, and the United States were in no position to ship soldiers to Russia, "I invariably replied that we are not asking aid in manpower but seek support in arms and munitions and insist that the powers withhold direct and indirect assistance to the separatism of various groups and nationalities."[12]

Admiral Alexander V. Kolchak (1873-1920) was commander of the Russian Black Sea fleet in 1916. Prime Minister Kerensky sent him to England in August, 1917. Thence he proceeded by British cruiser to Canada and, somewhat later, by special railway car, to New York and Washington where he interviewed President Wilson and high-ranking naval officers. From America he reached Japan and offered his services, through British Ambassador Sir W. Conyngham Greene, to the British army. It assigned him to duty in Mesopotamia. En route to that dry front a telegram intercepted him at Singapore "ordering him" to retrace his steps to Peking. There the British released him for service in Siberia. He soon became War Minister in the Omsk anti-Bolshevik government which included Social Revolutionaries and enjoyed British, French, and Czechoslovak support. On November 17, 1918, he carried out a midnight coup d'état, arrested Vladimir M. Zenzinov, Nikolai D. Avksentyev and other SR ministers, purged the socialists from the government, and declared himself "Supreme Ruler of Russia." The French and Czechoslovaks, suspecting a hidden British hand in this monarchist-militarist overthrow, turned against Kolchak and may have been responsible, together with the Bolsheviks, for the admiral's doom. The British government favored a military regime in Siberia.[13] Whether its representatives on the spot actually inspired the Kolchak coup is unproved and immaterial. In the encircling chaos, the expedient of a strong-man authority exercised a natural attraction on foreigners remote from the scene. But in the socialist climate of Russia, the expulsion of socialists from the anti-Bolshevik government was water on Lenin's mill. Kolchak promised to convene a Constituent Assembly and arrested Right Social Revolutionary Victor Chernov, chairman

[11] From the secret archives of Kolchak's Foreign Ministry seized by the Red Army in Omsk and Irkutsk and deposited in the Moscow Commissariat of Foreign Affairs where, in 1928, I was allowed to see them, make notes, and photostat some.

[12] *Posledniye Dni Kolchakovshchini (The Last Days of Kolchak's Rule)*, A Collection of Documents, Soviet Central Archives (Moscow, 1926), pp. 95-100.

[13] Richard H. Ullman, *Anglo-Soviet Relations, 1917-1921. Intervention and the War*, p. 273.

of the one-day Constituent Assembly in January, 1918. That loaded the guns of Soviet satirists.

General Denikin in the North Caucasus, General Yudenich in Estonia, and General Miller in the Archangel region, accepted Kolchak as their chief. Denikin went so far in his subordination as to ask the admiral for an increase in pay. In green ink, Kolchak wrote approvingly across the request, "Necessary grant same salary as Chief of Staff of Commander-in-Chief."[14] Britain was supplying much of the money and most of the arms to these anti-Soviet forces. Two thousand British commissioned and noncommissioned officers were assigned to Denikin alone. The duties of this mission, Secretary of State for War Winston S. Churchill told the House of Commons on December 16, 1919, "are confined to advice and supervision in the distribution and use of British materials." The next day, in the same place, he said, "Every effort has been made by the mission to reorganize the railways, and with the same object technical materials to the value of 500,000 pounds sterling and commodities and clothing to a similar value are being sent out by the War Office." Much earlier, on May 21, 1919, the *Manchester Guardian* had reported the "very valuable assistance" being given to Denikin. "Great Britain is supplying complete equipment with arms and guns for 250,000 men."

The influence that accrues to the purposeful giver enabled Britain to act as a liaison agency in coordinating the disparate blows rained on Soviet Russia by her several opponents. It was a nerve-racking enterprise hindered by personal rivalries, regional jealousies, distance, and politics. Denikin, for instance, had to consider the urge for autonomy among the Cossacks, the spine of his army. The presence of foreigners and foreign arms made it difficult for the White generals to pose as national redeemers. The Bolsheviks wore no such albatross. They appeared as Russia's defenders, a surprising yet profitable role. The generals stood for landlords, Great Russian supremacy over national minorities, limited civil liberties, and nineteenth-century capitalism. But the fall of the Tsar had given the people a taste for a new life. The generals started the civil war because they were convinced, rightly, that their way of life would die if the Bolsheviks stayed. But they were warriors of a lost cause. The Kerensky regime killed the ancient order and its chances of restoration. After Kerensky, the choice was new Red or old White, and the people preferred the unknown. Bolshevik weakness brought chaos which enhanced freedom. The masses therefore identified freedom with the Soviets. No peasant could foresee that his acquisition of a farm without payment in 1917 or 1918 would be nullified through collectivization in 1929. All this was communism's enormous asset.

Arms presented a minor problem. Four big cannons, for instance, were standing in the yard of the Putilov factory in Petrograd, completed during the world war but never used. Russian industry could manufacture sufficient artillery. The famous small-arms plant at Tula remained in Bolshevik hands

[14] Photostat opposite p. 205, Fischer, *Soviets in World Affairs*, Vol. I.

and Lenin watched over it as it hatched munitions. G. N. Kaminsky, later Commissar of Health and executed by Stalin, was in charge and had authority from Lenin to call him directly if difficulties arose. In April, 1918, Kaminsky informed Lenin that the Tula armory workers were not getting their wages and bread rations. Lenin took immediate steps.[15] Moreover, the Soviets followed the usual procedure in internal wars: they enriched their armies with weapons captured from the enemy. In the 1920's, before the Bolsheviks manufactured their own tanks, the annual May Day and November 7 parades on the Red Square included British tanks taken from Denikin. Nonferrous metals and other raw materials were stockpiled by the tsarist and Kerensky governments and left for Bolshevik use in the civil war and in peacetime.

Russia, moreover, had ample manpower, much of it trained in the simple arts of firing a rifle and using a bayonet. The civil war was fought with rifle and bayonet, saber and sword, a few cannons, crude machine guns mounted on horse-drawn buggies, and a rare tank, armored train, and gunboat. Once, when Denikin's horsemen, the famous Mamontov raiders, cut deep into Soviet territory and struck Bolshevik forces in the rear, Lenin suggested using low-flying airplanes against cavalry. He had read about this being done abroad, he wrote vaguely; could not some "X.Y.Z." military expert answer "quickly" whether it was feasible for them.[16] Apparently the reply was negative. In the same month—September, 1919—Trotsky, in the field, issued a ringing call, "Proletarians to Horse," which brought Budenny's rough-riding cavalry army into effective action on a wide arc.

With technology subordinate, morale counted most. General Denikin, retired to Lake Balaton, Hungary, in 1923, had unhappy memories of the civil war: "Russian life in that period (Summer, 1918)"—he took the same gray view of the later period—"reveals a striking anomaly of Russian mentality due to the underdeveloped political and national consciousness of the Russian people. Tens of governments and tens of armies sprang up on the vast spaces of the country wearing all the colors of the political spectrum, from Red to Southern. All of them mobilized men on the territory they occupied. The people submitted to everything—with the greatest reluctance, offering passive but very seldom active resistance, yet submitted and fought, sometimes exhibiting the highest valor, sometimes disgraceful cowardice; they abandoned 'the defeated' and deserted to 'the victors' and with ease exchanged the red cockade for the tricolor triangle and back as though these were merely decorations on a uniform. All exertions of the Red, White, and Black leaders to attach national significance to the struggle failed. All the five years of Russia's time of troubles witnessed a deep internal process of the disintegration and formation of social strata, of explosions of popular anger, of false appearances of national excitement, but there was no armed national struggle."

[15] *Leninskii Sbornik*, Vol. XXXVI, p. 72.
[16] Lenin, *Sochineniya*, Fourth ed., Vol. 36, p. 472.

To these dismal reflections, normal in a defeated leader, Denikin appended a thought on the Red Army. He found that it resembled the old Russian army because organization and training were in the hands of tsarist generals employed by the Bolsheviks. Trotsky and the other communist commanders were merely "supervisors." The generals "contributed knowledge," the communists "added will power." With the same knowledge by similar men in the Red camp and the White, will power made the difference between victory and rout. Most tsarist officers served communism loyally. Denikin wrote, "From those who occupied important posts in the Bolshevik camp and who shared my ideas we certainly received not the slightest concrete help which would have compensated for their sacrifice. . . . During the two and a half years of war in South Russia, I know of only one instance of deliberate sabotage of a major Bolshevik operation which seriously threatened my armies."[17] The Bolsheviks held the wives and children of tsarist officers as hostages; sometimes wavering old-army commanders were shot as examples to others.

Lenin sanctioned and defended the use of tsarist military. "Some of our comrades"—Stalin and the Bukharinites—"are indignant," Lenin said in Petrograd on March 12, 1919, "because tsarist servants and old officers stand at the head of the Red Army. . . . The question of experts must be seen in its wider aspects. We use them in all branches where we, naturally lacking the experience and scientific preparation of the old bourgeois specialists, cannot manage with our own personnel. We are not utopians who think that the building of a socialist Russia can be carried out by some sort of new men; we make use of material left us by the old capitalist world." The old specialists were under surveillance and "we compel them to perform the work we need. This is the only way to build. If you cannot build a building with the material left to us by the bourgeois world then you are not communists but phrase-mongers."[18]

Lenin and Trotsky hired tsarist experience and attached it to their spirit. Only a minority of the Red Army were imbued with spirit. But in a situation of balanced apathy, a few tip the scales. The few were communist party members and fellow travelers. Some joined it for safety or to be little dictators under the big dictators. But the danger exceeded the safety, for when the enemy breached the line, communists were hurled in to hold or die. No soldier could say the communists merely used him as cannon fodder; they were the cannon's first meal. Every battlefield has seen the contagion of fear. If an officer falters, the unit may run. Courage too is contagious. When communists stood, or advanced under fire, those behind were sometimes too human to retreat.

The communist party was the Soviet spearhead in the civil war. Lenin toughened, tempered, and honed it. In *Pravda* of September 21, 1919, he

[17] General A. I. Denikin, *Ocherki Russkoi Smuti (Essays on Russia's Time of Troubles)* (Berlin, 1924), Vol. 3, pp. 143-145. Lenin owned a copy of the first volume of Denikin's memoirs on which he wrote this comment: "The author approaches the class war like a blind puppy."

[18] Lenin, *op. cit.*, Second ed., Vol. XXIV, pp. 35-36.

expressed his approval of a proposal by Zinoviev to purge the party, "follow-ing the Petrograd example," of "hangers-on" and then increase its member-ship by attracting the "best elements of the mass of workers and peasants." Communists were taught to talk politics in the army during noncombat hours. But their chief contribution, a major one, was exemplary heroism in combat. A party member whose valor failed faced a firing squad.

The element of politics was further emphasized by Lenin's appointment of civilian lieutenants at various fronts. Trotsky was at one front, Leo Kame-nev, Stalin, Orjonekidze, Sokolnikov, and others elsewhere. Each front had its own Revolutionary War Council (Revvoiensoviet) in which communists predominated. Lenin, advised by these lieutenants and councils and by the Politburo and tsarist experts, functioned as supreme strategy coordinator, gadfly, dynamo, and scold. In August, 1918, for instance, he telegraphed the Astrakhan provincial executive committee, copy to provincial party organi-zation: "Is it really true that in Astrakhan they are already talking about evacuation? If this is true, merciless measures must be taken against cow-ards; immediately assign dependable and tough persons to the organization of the defense of Astrakhan."[19]

Telegram dated October 20, 1918, to Commander in Chief Vatsetis at Arzamas: "Greatly surprised and disturbed by delay in the capture of Izhevsk and Votkinsk," two towns in Vyatka province taken by hostile elements in August, 1918. "Please adopt the most energetic speed-up measures. Tele-graph exactly what you have undertaken. Sovnarkom Chairman Lenin. VTSIK President Sverdlov."[20] The towns were recaptured in the second week of November.

Lenin to Vatsetis, December 23, 1918: "The Council of Defense inquires: 1) Is it true that two weeks ago in battles in the area of Balashov, our units surrendered 25 to 30 cannon to the enemy during two or three days fighting, and if true what have you done to punish the guilty and prevent similar occurrences? 2) Is it true that two weeks ago you issued an order for the capture of Orenburg"—in the Urals—"and if true why is the order not being carried out? 3) What has been done to stabilize the situation of our units at Perm which have asked Moscow for urgent help?"[21]

Lenin to Trotsky on location near Kursk, January 2 or 3, 1919: According to report from the Caucasus front, "the Krasnovites"—forces of General Krasnov—"have occupied Raigorod on the banks of the Volga south of Sa-penta thus threatening, first, our military shipments from Vladimirovka to Tsaritsin, second, the safety of the Astrakhan-Saratov line. Please act. Accord-ing to the same report, the British fleet, comprising four ships, has shelled Staro-Terechnaya, south of Astrakhan, set fire to two of our barges, and steamed back unscathed into the [Caspian] sea taking with them our hospital

[19] *Ibid.*, Fourth ed., Vol. 35, p. 293.
[20] *Ibid.*, p. 307.
[21] *Ibid.*, p. 312.

ship, *Alesker* with medical personnel. Where is our fleet and what is it doing? Lenin."[22] (An editorial note states that this telegram was written by Stalin and signed by Lenin. Trotsky, deep inland at Kursk, would scarcely have been in a position to know what was happening far off in the Caspian Sea or to do anything about it. Stalin and Zinoviev had been trying to turn Lenin against Trotsky and apparently succeeded at least for a time.)

The founding congress of the Communist International (Comintern) or Third International was welcomed by Lenin on March 2 in Moscow. On March 4 he addressed the delegates, most of whom—with the exception of the Russians—represented weak or nonexistent foreign parties, and gave them a summary of the arguments he had presented some months earlier in his *The Proletarian Revolution and Kautsky the Renegade* pamphlet. The congress was dull.

But Lenin was sanguine, or naïve, or purely propagandistic: he told the Soviet in Petrograd on March 12, 1919, that, "Soviets are becoming increasingly popular in the West and there is a struggle for them not only in Europe but also in America. Everywhere soviets are being formed which sooner or later will take power into their hands. At present, an interesting moment is being experienced by America where soviets are being established." Lenin had more verifiable news for the Eighth Congress of the Russian Communist Party (Bolsheviks) which heard him announce an exciting event: the Red revolution in Hungary. "We are certain," he declared in his closing speech on March 23, "that this will be our last difficult half-year. We are especially confirmed in this conviction by the news which was announced to the congress the other day, the news of the victory of the proletarian revolution in Hungary. If hitherto, Soviet power was achieved only among the peoples constituting the former Russian empire, if hitherto, short-sighted people who cannot easily part with routine, old habits of thought (although they belong to the socialist camp), could think that alone the peculiarities of Russia were the cause of this unexpected turn toward proletarian Soviet democracy, that in the peculiarities of this democracy were perhaps reflected, as in a distorting mirror, the ancient peculiarities of Tsarist Russia, if such an opinion could still exist, it has now been destroyed at its roots. . . . The difficulties facing the Hungarian revolution, comrades, are tremendous. Compared to Russia it is a small country which can be smothered much more easily by the imperialists. But no matter what the difficulties to be encountered by Hungary, we have here, in addition to a victory of Soviet power, *a moral victory for us* . . . the dying beast of international imperialism . . . will perish and socialism will conquer the world."[23]

Hungary and Russia were of course different. But in bourgeois Hungary, as in tsarist Russia, the capitalist class was weak. This, plus the vestiges of feudal economy and the strength of feudal mentality, made both highly

[22] *Ibid.*, p. 314.
[23] *Ibid.*, Second ed., Vol. XXIV, pp. 176-179.

vulnerable to communism. In the second decade of the twentieth century, Lenin had advocated more capitalism for Russia (and for China), because he felt, with Marx, that only the country that had a full measure of capitalism was ripe for communism. This was the thesis of his *Imperialism* book: monopoly capitalism built the short bridge to socialism. But the seizure of power in Russia and the failure of the 1918 German revolution showed the reverse to be true. The weaker the capitalism and the stronger the feudalism the better the chances of revolution. In such a situation an added political factor is usually necessary to convert susceptibility into reality. In Russia it was the fall of the Tsar, in Hungary the fall of the Austro-Hungarian Empire; both introduced enough anarchy to undermine the state and smooth the rebels' road to power. Hungary's small size and greater exposure to foreign pressure made the fortunes of the two revolutions diverge, but Lenin hoped to make them converge.

At 5 P.M. on March 22, Radio Budapest called him. Twenty minutes later, in the Moscow radio station, he said, "Lenin at the microphone. I want to speak to Comrade Bela Kun." Budapest replied that Kun was at a meeting. Ernst Por, substituting, declared, "The Hungarian Soviet Republic offers the Russian Soviet government an armed alliance against all the enemies of proletariat. Please inform us immediately about the military situation."[24]

Lenin understood; Hungary needed military assistance to survive. But he was no gambler. He wanted assurances before he acted. He therefore sent a radio dispatch to Bela Kun on March 23: "Please inform what concrete guarantees you have that the new Hungarian government is actually communist and not only socialist, that is, social-traitors.

"Do the communists have a majority in the government? When will the congress of soviets meet?"

To forestall the conclusion that he was demanding a Hungarian carbon copy of the Russian soviet system, Lenin added, "It is altogether certain that, in view of the unique situation of the Hungarian revolution, the simple imitation of our Russian tactic would be a mistake. I must warn you against such a mistake, but I should like to know what, in your opinion, are the real guarantees."[25] Lenin's doubts were due to the participation of several supine Social Democrats in the Bela Kun cabinet. His hesitation, however, soon vanished; communist Hungary opened up a rosy vista. The European continent seethed. Armies were mutiny-minded. Germany was still a red hope. Lenin in a speech quoted the *Frankfurter Zeitung* of March 23: ". . . the spark might fly at any second from Budapest to Vienna and perhaps even to Prague and further." If Moscow, he said, could save Hungary, Europe might save Russia. Hungary's salvation, as seen from the Kremlin, lay in reaching across Romania, which separated the Soviet Ukraine from Red Hungary. On March 26, Soviet Commander in Chief Vatsetis wired Antonov-Avseyenko, in

---

[24] *Ibid.*, editorial note, p. 768.
[25] *Ibid.*, p. 183. The German original, in Lenin's handwriting, is printed in *ibid.*, opposite p. 180.

The Ulyanov family. *Left to right,* Olga,
Lenin's mother holding Maria, Alexander (Sasha), Dmitri,
Lenin's father, Anna, Vladimir (Lenin).

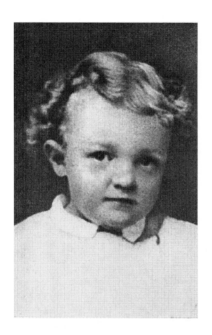

Top left, Lenin aged four. *Top right*, Lenin's brother
Alexander (Sasha) shortly before his execution. *Lower left*,
Lenin aged twenty-one. *Lower right*, Lenin aged twenty-seven.

Lenin in bowler playing chess at Capri, 1908,
with Gorky and his wife in the background.

Inessa Armand with other exiles in northern Russia, 1908.

Inessa at the age of twenty.

Inessa in her mid-thirties
when she met Lenin.

Tsar Nicholas II
and his cousin George V
of England.
The Bettmann Archive

Nicholas II shoveling snow
during his internment at
Tsarskoe Selo early in 1918.
The Bettmann Archive

Lenin in 1917.

Lenin in disguise as K. P. Ivanov,
a factory worker, in late 1917.

General Erich von Ludendorff.
The Bettmann Archive

Alexander F. Kerensky.
The Bettmann Archive

Lenin's group in Stockholm, April 1917, enroute to Petrograd;
Lenin in center with umbrella. *Malmström, Stockholm*

Trotsky, Lenin, Kamenev. *United Press International Photo*

Lenin in hiding in 1917.

Lenin in his office, 1918.

Krupskaya addressing soldiers during the civil war.

Lenin in Gorky village, 1922.
Between Anna, Lenin's sister, and Krupskaya
is Lenin's nephew, Victor.

Lenin and Maxim Gorky,
1920.

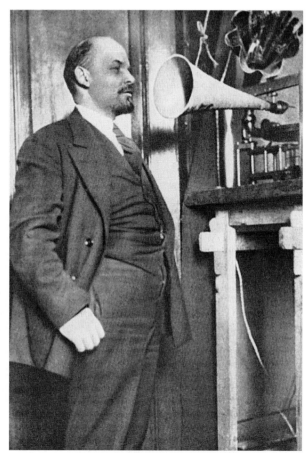

Lenin recording a speech
in Moscow, 1919.

Karl Radek. *United Press International Photo*

Chicherin in Mongolian costume.

Leon Trotsky
Bettmann Archive

Stalin, Lenin, Kalinin in 1919. *Sovfoto*

The Central Executive Committee and foreign press, October 1922. Indicated from left to right are Kamenev, Lenin, Zinoviev, Kalinin and Louis Fischer.

On preceding page, Lenin addressing workers in a Moscow square, May 1919, *Sovfoto*

Zinoviev and Kamenev (executed in 1936).
United Press International Photo

Bukharin and Lenin's sister Maria in *Pravda* office. (Bukharin was
executed in 1938.) *United Press International Photo*

Lenin in park at Gorky.

charge of operations around Kiev, to establish "direct intimate contact with the Soviet armies of Hungary."[26] Several weeks passed in preparations and preliminary skirmishes. On May 13 Lenin telegraphed Bela Kun, "yesterday Ukrainian troops, after defeating the Romanians, crossed the Dniester River."[27] The Soviet army was en route to Hungary. Furthermore, Ataman Gregoriev, an independent peasant-partisan leader, who had been fighting by the side of the Bolsheviks in the Odessa-Kherson region, was ordered to invade Bessarabia, a Russian province annexed in January, 1918, by Romania.

Just at this juncture, Gregoriev turned against the Bolsheviks, probably because of conscription of peasants and the confiscation of village grain. Moscow had to divert forces against him. An even greater blow to the dream of red hands across Romania was the advance of Kolchak in March from Siberia through the Urals toward the Volga. In April he loomed larger. The Western press reported him heading for Moscow. Simultaneously, Denikin began moving up from the south into the Donets coal basin of the Ukraine. In May, Yudenich rallied his Russian and Estonian troops against Petrograd. The offensive to rescue Hungary turned back. On June 18, Lenin sent a coded message, through Foreign Commissar Chicherin, to Bela Kun advising him to negotiate an armistice with the Western Entente.[28] The Bela Kun communist government of Hungary succumbed on August 1, 1919.

Soviet Russia had to look to her own defense. The spring of 1919 brought maximum dangers. Foreign ventures to fan sparks into revolutionary fires were abandoned. Lenin showered his lieutenants in the field with hot telegrams. To Gregory Sokolnikov at the southern front on April 20: "I am intensely disturbed by the slackening of the operations against the Donets Basin and Rostov. Speed-up is necessary, but of course only with adequate strength. . . . It is the greatest scandal that the suppression of the Cossack uprising has been delayed. Answer in detail."[29] The Cossacks joined Denikin.

To the commander of the southern front on April 22: "Sokolnikov wires me that Denikin in the Donets Basin has used the pause to excellent advantage, gathered strength, and collected much fresher forces than ours. The peril is immense. . . . From Podvoysky's reports I see that in the Ukraine, even not counting Odessa, there is a great deal of war material, it should not be saved up, but used immediately for the formation of Donets workers' units and new units for the capture of Taganrog and Rostov. Have all officers in the Ukraine been mobilized? No matter what happens you must quickly and significantly increase the forces against Denikin. Telegraph in greater detail and compel your code clerks to code more accurately so that everything can be understood."[30]

[26] Quoted from the archives of the Soviet War Commissariat. See Fischer, *The Soviets in World Affairs*, Vol. I, p. 194.

[27] Lenin, *op. cit.*, Fourth ed., Vol. 36, p. 468.

[28] *Ibid.*, Vol. 36, p. 471. This telegram was first published in 1954 in a Budapest communist book.

[29] *Ibid.*, Vol. 35, p. 315.

[30] *Ibid.*, p. 316.

Lenin to the Soviet government of the Ukraine on April 24, 1919: "No matter what happens, no matter with what exertions, and with the greatest possible speed, help us finish off the Cossacks and capture Rostov even at the expense of a temporary weakening in western Ukraine, because otherwise ruin threatens."[31]

The same day, however, he ordered the Revvoiensoviet of the western front to retake the city of Vilna. Twenty-four hours later he wired Antonov in Kiev, copies to Rakovsky, Podvoysky, and Leo Kamenev, to throw Ukrainian troops into the fray and capture Taganrog "immediately and no matter what. Telegraph. Lenin."

Late in April, the Second Ukrainian Army took several French tanks from the forces of Denikin and presented one to Lenin. This was a gesture. Lenin needed no tank in the Kremlin. The tank remained at the front. It was an old custom to give a token trophy to the monarch. Lenin seized the opportunity for propaganda: "This gift is dear to all of us, dear to the workers and peasants of Russia as proof of the heroism of our Ukrainian brothers, dear also because it demonstrates the complete collapse of the once apparently so powerful Entente."[32] The telegram was a three-barreled shot. It pleaded for Russian-Ukrainian friendship; unless the Ukraine fought Denikin he might defeat the Russians. It identified Denikin with the foreign enemy. And it raised hope of victory; the enemy was slipping. At the same time Lenin instructed *Pravda* to show that the SR's, who played a role in the Ukraine, favored the kulaks and secession from the Russian union and thereby helped Denikin, Kolchak, and the bourgeoisie.[33] Guilt by alleged association.

Communists were being dispatched to the fronts. M. M. Kostelovskaya received an order to proceed to the eastern anti-Kolchak front as head of the political section of the Second Army. She inquired of Lenin how she was to understand this. He replied, "To be understood just for what it is: a decision of the Central Committee of the party. *This is wartime.* Everybody does *what is most difficult.*"[34]

No one was a free agent. "No caprices," Lenin wrote A. E. Badayev, Food Commissar of Petrograd. "You're not a young lady. . . . Do your work, *we accept no resignations.* Hereafter, carry out *all* instructions from Moscow and don't talk indecent nonsense about 'intrigues.' Greetings. Lenin."[35]

Lenin's telegram torrent had the effect of bringing his long political arm and feverish sense of haste right into front-line councils and remote offices. He could punish, promote, praise, dismiss, transfer, and reprimand. The law of dictatorship requires its chief to manifest his omnipresence. If he cannot do it in person he does it with a stinging verbal prod which carries intimations of his resources and power. On May 6 Lenin scolded the Revvoiensoviet of

[31] *Ibid.*, Fourth ed., Vol. 35, p. 318.
[32] *Ibid.*, p. 322.
[33] *Ibid.*, p. 321.
[34] *Leninskii Sbornik*, Vol. XXXVI, p. 75.
[35] *Ibid.*, p. 75.

the southern front for procrastination in suppressing Gregoriev's insurrection. "Shall I send you still more Chekist forces? Wire in greater detail."[36]

In Mid-May Yudenich approached Petrograd, cradle of the revolution. Lenin tolerated no independent action by the Petrograd authorities, even though Zinoviev himself was in charge there. He telegraphed Zinoviev for full information: Why were several factories in and near Petrograd evacuated? Who ordered the ships scuttled? How many workers had been mobilized, how many remain in the plants? Were all being used for defense purposes?[37]

Urgent telegram to the southern front, May 19: "The attack on Petrograd increases tenfold the danger and the supreme necessity of suppressing the" —Gregoriev—"revolt immediately at all costs . . . are the Voronezh and Tambov communists who were sent to you actually arriving? Do you need further reinforcements and exactly what kind? . . . Delay is extremely dangerous. Sovnarkom Chairman Lenin."[38]

In the west and south, peril and gloom. Suddenly, the dawn of victory lit up the eastern sky. Kolchak's thrust toward Moscow was blunted. His armies splintered. For Lenin this seemed too good to be true. He wanted reassurance. On May 12, 1919, he telegraphed the Revvoiensoviet of the Fifth Army: "Do you guarantee that the reports attributed to you regarding the demoralization of the Kolchakists and their mass desertion to you are not exaggerated? If you vouch for them, what steps have been taken, first, to hasten the advance and consolidate the victories, second, to send the Kolchak deserters, who have experienced his bestialities and are capable of raising the spirit of our army, into all units of both the eastern and southern fronts?"[39] It was true. Kolchak was retreating. Just as the Supreme Allied Council in Paris recognized him as "Supreme Ruler" of Russia and inquired what he would do when he reached Moscow, he commenced to collapse.

On the other hand, Denikin was moving forward fast through the Ukraine. He occupied Kharkov on June 25. The Reds abandoned Tsaritsin on July 1. Yudenich was breathing into Petrograd. Lenin's expectation that the first semester of 1919 "will be our last difficult half-year" had been dashed. Krupskaya wrote, "The second half of 1919 was more difficult than the first."[40]

XXV. PEACE IS A WEAPON

THE REVOLUTION, though out of swaddling, seemed doomed to die under enemy blows. "Especially difficult," Krupskaya wrote in 1938, "were Septem-

[36] Lenin, *op. cit.*, Fourth ed., Vol. 35, p. 324.
[37] *Ibid.*, p. 326.
[38] *Ibid.*, p. 327.
[39] *Ibid.*, p. 325.
[40] *Vospominaniya*, Vol. 2, p. 392.

ber, October, and the beginning of November . . . the Whites decided to conquer the centers of Soviet power—Moscow and Petrograd. From the south Denikin began to advance, captured many of the most important places in the Ukraine, from the West Yudenich moved ahead, he came quite close to Petrograd itself. The White victories inspired the hidden foe. At the end of November, a counterrevolutionary organization, connected with Yudenich and subsidized by the Entente, was discovered." Had this occurred after Franco encircled Madrid in 1936, the organization would have been called a "Fifth Column," the inside civilian arm of the besieging army outside, and if there was no Allied subsidy someone blundered. That happened often.

As wife, Krupskaya knew what few others learned. "All the while Denikin and Yudenich were winning," she wrote, "Vladimir Ilyich received a great number of anonymous letters containing curses, threats, and caricatures. The intelligentsia still wavered. . . . Anarchists, supported by SR's, exploded a bomb on September 25 in the headquarters of the Moscow Committee of the party on Leontevsky Lane which cost the lives of many of our comrades."

Individuals had to be molded into an army. Officials had to be welded into a government. Hunger ruled city and land. "And though Ilyich never for a minute weakened in his faith in victory," Krupskaya continued, "he worked from morn till night, and out of great anxiety he could not sleep. He would awake in the middle of the night, get out of bed, and begin to check by telephone: had this or the other of his orders been carried out? think up some kind of additional telegram to send. During the day, he was rarely at home, sat in his office most of the time: receiving callers. In those busy months I saw him less than usual, we almost never took walks. I hesitated to go to his office since I had no business there: I was afraid to interfere with his work."[1]

To dine in the Kremlin restaurant for high officials would have exposed Lenin to small talk, serious talk, and requests. Krupskaya therefore went to the restaurant for the family dinner. She was often seen treading cautiously on icy Kremlin pavements with a big chunk of black bread under her arm and carrying in front of her a full pot of soup by its two ears. But though her trip to the restaurant was timed for Lenin's return home she rarely found him there. Maria would phone his office. He promised to come right away. After ten or fifteen minutes, Gora, Anna's adopted son, telephoned the office. "Vladimir Ilyich," the boy would plead, "well when will you come? The soup is getting cold and we are sitting at the table, hungry, and waiting." Many days Gora—he was thirteen in 1919—finally ran over to Lenin's office, took the pen from his hand, and dragged him home. "Now, let's have your cold soup," Lenin would say.

"Now sit and wait till we heat it on the stove" was Maria's reply.

Never did Lenin participate in the seven-course, sixteen-toast dinners that became de rigueur in the days of Stalin and Khrushchev. He rarely went to theater or concerts. In the autumn of 1919 he attended a song-and-dance

[1] *Vospominaniya*, Vol. 2, p. 392.

performance in the Bolshoi Theater by Shalyapin, Nyezhdanova, Sobinov, Geltser, and other stars. He sat alone in an orchestra seat wearing his overcoat; the building was unheated. As the final curtain descended and the lights brightened the public discovered him and somebody shouted, "Long Live the Leader of the World Revolution, Vladimir Ilyich Lenin." He fled by a side door.[2]

Commissar of Education Anatoly Lunacharsky, primary patron of the arts, could recall "several" Lenin visits to the theater and "I think exclusively" to Stanislavsky's Moscow Art Theater. Lunacharsky often staged concerts in his own apartment where Shalyapin, Koussevitzky, and a Stradivarius quartet appeared. He always asked Lenin and Lenin always asked to be excused: "Busy." Once Lenin said, "Of course, it's very pleasant to listen to music, but imagine, it affects my mood. Somehow, I cannot bear it."

Lenin's personal librarian recalls that he asked her for newspapers, magazines, foreign pamphlets, dictionaries, books on India, on history, philosophy, and theory, but never a novel.[3] "I have no time" was his answer to many a suggestion and invitation. Life consisted of war and politics, which to Lenin were one. Moments of relaxation were far between. "At the end of 1919," Krupskaya wrote, "we had frequent visits from Inessa Armand with whom Ilyich liked to talk about the prospects of the movement. Inessa had an older daughter who had already been at the front and who was almost killed in the bomb explosion on September 25 on Leontevsky Lane. I remember how Inessa once came with her youngest daughter, Varya, then quite a young girl who later became a devoted member of the party" and Lenin enjoyed talking with her, as he did with their maid, Olympiada, about the bright communist future. In the presence of the woman he loved and of her daughter he allowed himself to wake-dream about better times.

Did Lenin have flashes of sadness? Did he, in the long nocturnal hours of insomnia, have feelings of loneliness? There are no data for an answer, there is only the supposition that being human implies moments of weakness. On the other hand, in personal emotions as distinguished from political passions, Lenin was a man in a minor key. His 1918 congratulatory telegram to Trotsky on the Red Army's first big victory, at Kazan, startled the recipient by its "I greet with rapture" first sentence, and Trotsky commented on "the intensely elated (for Lenin) tone" of the message.[4] Lenin was not given to elation. He rarely rose to the upper register of emotion or fell to the lower register. Sentiments that might overwhelm him were shut out. Doubts that might depress him were banished. Others, Foreign Commissar Chicherin, for instance, did doubt. In a letter to Lenin on October 12, 1919, apropos Kautsky's new book, *Terrorism and Communism*, Chicherin said, "To the

[2] *Ibid.*, p. 419.
[3] *Ibid.*, pp. 583-588.
[4] Leon Trotsky, *The Stalin School of Falsification*, Introduction and footnotes by Max Schachtman, translated by John C. Wright (New York, 1937), p. 40.

extent that I have time to read our literature, it seems that here we do not adequately treat the role of state capitalism under proletarian political power. . . . We do not yet have communism but state capitalism."

Lenin replied, "Ours is the first stage of the transition to communism struggling against *peasant* and capitalist efforts to defend (or restore) commodity production."

Describing the Soviet system, Chicherin noted "the unequal pay even to the extent of piece work, and forms of compulsion which sometimes recall the old [tsarist] regime and the centralization even of management which restricts factory self-management."

Lenin wrote in the margin: "This is not the specter of capitalism. This comes from the enemy's struggle and from the level of culture, not from capitalism. Unfortunately we have almost no centralization."

Chicherin heavily underlined his last thought: "We have a Red Army of state capitalism with an apparatus of powerful compulsion but not an army of communism."

Lenin demurred. He wrote, "This is altogether untrue."[5]

It was not that Chicherin had a better understanding of Soviet politics than Lenin. Nor was Lenin writing circumspectly for publication. Chicherin's letter and Lenin's marginalia did not see the light of day until years later. But Lenin, the prophet of state withering, refused to admit even to himself that he was the father of state capitalism instead of some form of communism. Hear no music. Speak no heresies. See no retreats. Lenin was racing to the finishing line: victory in the civil war, and blinkers were part of his harness.

However, in deeds, as distinguished from creeds, Lenin faced unpleasant truths squarely. A report he delivered in person to the Moscow Soviet on April 3, 1919, was typical. The situation "is extraordinarily difficult . . . Rostov . . . is semiencircled." Hindenburg, despite the end of the war, was helping the Allies' military effort in Latvia. A water main in Petrograd had been blown up by enemies. The railroad near Samara on the Volga had been rendered useless by the removal of rails; grain destined for Soviet cities was thereby ruined. Passenger traffic on all lines had been stopped to help move freight; this expedient produced good results. In the Ukraine the peasants were so frightened by the pro-landlord German regime that even after the departure of the Germans the peasants "do not dare seize landed estates." There and elsewhere, he affirmed, SR's and Mensheviks sabotaged the Soviet government's military and economic efforts. "Of late, the Soviet government has commenced to close their newspapers and arrest them. Some comrade-workers, observing this, say, 'That means those Bolsheviks—and I am one of them—were wrong when they involved us in certain concessions to petty-bourgeois democracy [by allowing opposition newspapers to appear]. Why did we make concessions if we must now close down the newspapers and arrest them? Is there any consistency in that?'

[5] *Leninskii Sbornik*, Vol. XXXV, p. 78.

"My answer is as follows: In a country like Russia where petty-bourgeois elements do all the farming, in such a country we cannot long survive without the support of the petty-bourgeois stratum. This stratum is now moving toward its goal not in a straight line but in zigzags. If I am pursuing an adversary who moves not in a straight line but in zigzags, I also must, in order to overtake that adversary, move in zigzags."

The Kremlin treasures this Leninist tactic in domestic and foreign affairs.

The village worried Lenin. Village communists, he continued, went to extremes and did not distinguish between the kulak, who used hired labor, and the middle peasant, who lived by his own labor. "No socialist in the world has ever proposed taking private property from the smallholder. The smallholder will continue to exist for many years."

Those extremist village communists thought that war communism was militant communism and accordingly molested the middle peasant. But Lenin, who wrote on Chicherin's letter that the Soviet system was a stage of communism, preferred the middle peasant's bread to communistic suppression of private property. He was a practical, plastic politician. His hope of success, he said, lay in "the confidence and class-conscious attitude of the workers" of Russia and in the "only possible conclusion: that our cause is near to victory in the entire world."[6]

The peasants were too numerous to crush, and since they zigzagged between acceptance and rejection of the Bolsheviks, Lenin zigzagged with them and connived at private capitalism so that what he called communism might endure. He remitted some peasant taxes. But he hated the Mensheviks and they were few. There had been a strike in the munitions city of Tula. He blamed the Mensheviks for instigating it. "Somebody," he said at a trade-union meeting, "asked me, 'Is that proved?' I reply that if I were an attorney, or a shyster lawyer, or a member of parliament, I would be under an obligation to prove it. I am neither the one nor the second nor the third, and I won't even try to do this and I see no point in it." Perhaps, he conceded, some Mensheviks, including Martov, and his paper, *Vsegda Vperyod* (*Ever Forward*), were against the Tula strike. "But in a political struggle, when the Whites are strangling us, is it possible to differentiate? Have we any time for such things? . . . Maybe in two years, when we shall have defeated Kolchak, we will study the matter. But not now. Now it is necessary to fight."[7]

More than the Tula strike was involved. The Mensheviks were urging the government to "Stop the Civil War." This referred not to the fight with the Whites but to the Soviet policy of using armed workers to foment strife in villages between the Committees of the Poor and the not-so-poor peasants. Often the government sent food to feed the committee adherents and then urged them to plunder the others. By thus splitting the peasantry, Lenin hoped to win supporters and undermine the SR's whose political roots in the countryside he had not been able to pull up. SR's and Mensheviks now

[6] Lenin, *Sochineniya*, Second ed., Vol. XXIV, pp. 207-220.
[7] *Ibid.*, p. 239.

formed a united front for survival. Despite their expulsion from the soviets, these two parties often dominated local politics. If Lenin ceased waging civil war within the population of Bolshevik-held territory, the SR-Menshevik coalition might submerge the meager Bolshevik forces. Lenin accordingly fed the fires of the civil war within the anti-White civil war, and, in particular, vented his wrath on the Mensheviks. He suppressed Martov's newspaper.

Lenin's hatred of world capitalism was equally boundless. He saw himself in a death embrace with it. But it was strong whereas the Mensheviks were weak. Therefore he offered profitable business deals to American and European capitalists. He also zigzagged in parallel zigzags to the outside enemy's zigzags. As at Brest-Litovsk, so now, he sought the pause that gave Russia a saving respite.

Early in 1919 the victorious Western powers made a zigzag toward peace. They knew they could not send a large army to overthrow the Bolsheviks. The chief delegates at the Versailles Peace Conference accordingly asked President Wilson on January 21, 1919, to draft a proposal for an all-Russian (Red and White) peace parley conditioned on an armistice in the civil war. Mr. Wilson had his plan ready the next day: the Russian factions, including the Soviets, were to assemble on Prinkipo Island near Instanbul on February 15. It was adopted. Great Britain appointed Sir Robert Borden as its delegate. Wilson appointed William Allen White, the Emporia, Kansas, editor.

The Soviets, whom Wilson designated as participants in the Prinkipo conference, were never invited. But on January 23, the Moscow radio station monitored a news item about the scheduled meeting, and five days later Chicherin wirelessed to Wilson that Moscow had not received an invitation. After waiting in vain till February 4, the Soviet government accepted the invitation that had not been sent. Its long radio message declared the Kremlin's readiness "to recognize its financial obligations to its creditors in Entente countries, . . . to guarantee the payment of interest on its loans with a definite quantity of raw materials, . . . to grant citizens of Entente countries mining, lumbering, and other concessions, . . . to include in the general agreement with the Entente powers a pledge of noninterference in their internal affairs."[8]

President Wilson told a private meeting of the Democratic National Committee on February 28, 1919, what Lloyd George's reaction to the Kremlin's radiogram had been: "I never saw a man more angered than Mr. Lloyd George who said, 'We cannot let that insult go by. We are not after their money or their concessions or their territory. That is not the point. We are their friends who want to help them and must tell them so.'" But Mr. Wilson added, "We did not tell them so because to some people we had to deal with the payment of foreign debts was a more interesting and important matter."[9]

[8] Fischer, The Soviets in World Affairs, Vol. I, pp. 167-168.
[9] Joseph P. Tumulty, Woodrow Wilson as I Know Him (London, 1922), p. 374.

On the same occasion Wilson called the Bolsheviks "the most consummate sneaks in the world." He too thought the Bolshevik reply "studiously insulting." He understood the Soviets to be saying: "We are dealing with perjured governments whose only interest is in striking a bargain, and if that is the price of European recognition and cooperation, we are ready to pay it."

Lenin and Chicherin discerned in the proposed Prinkipo conference an Entente zigzag and made a complementary zigzag. Lenin took a hard, cynical view of capitalists: Their god was Mammon; toss a dollar into their midst and they will scramble indecorously for it; they could be bribed by the prospect of profit; if the Kremlin succeeded in luring them into doing business with Russia they would change or at least moderate their governments' anti-Bolshevik policies. But Lenin failed to see that the unalloyed moneyman would be an uncompromising anticommunist. It was the politicians who agreed to parley. As Lloyd George put it, "By opposing Bolshevism with arms, they were in reality serving the cause of Bolshevism. The Allies were making it possible for the Bolsheviks to argue that the Imperialistic and Capitalistic Governments were endeavouring to exploit the country and give the land back to the landlords and so bring about a reaction. If it could be shown that this was not true, and that the Allies were prepared to deal with the rulers of Russia, much of the moral force of this argument would disappear. . . . If . . . the Allies would swallow their pride and natural revulsion which they felt for the Bolshevists and see the representatives of all organized groups in one place, he thought it would bring about a marked reaction against Bolshevism."[10]

This did not exactly bear out Wilson's statement that "We are their friends who want to help them." Premier Clemenceau was even less friendly. But, he said, "Bolshevism was spreading. . . . If Bolshevism, after spreading in Germany, were to traverse Austria and Hungary and so reach Italy, Europe would be faced with a very great danger. Therefore, something had to be done against Bolshevism. . . . He admitted his remarks did not offer a solution. The great misfortune was that the Allies were in need of a speedy solution . . . had he been acting by himself, he would temporize and erect barriers to prevent Bolshevism from spreading. But he was not alone, and in the presence of his colleagues he felt compelled to make some concession, as it was essential that there should not be even the appearance of disagreement amongst them. The concession came easier after having heard President Wilson's suggestions" for a conference of all Russian factions.

Arthur James Balfour, British Foreign Secretary, "said that he understood that all these people were to be asked on an equality. On these terms he thought the Bolshevists would refuse, and by their refusal they would put themselves in a very bad position.

"M. Sonnino"—Italy's Foreign Minister—". . . did not agree that the

---

[10] Official secret minute read to the U.S. Senate Committee on Foreign Relations by Mr. William C. Bullitt on Sept. 12, 1919, and reproduced in William C. Bullitt, *The Bullitt Mission to Russia* (New York, 1919), pp. 18-31.

Bolshevists would not come. He thought they would be the first to come, because they would be eager to put themselves on an equality with the others." Therefore he favored a conference without the Bolsheviks. Italy's Prime Minister Orlando, however, supported the scheme of a conference with the Bolsheviks, yet also approved Clemenceau's policy of a "cordon sanitaire," and only refrained from pressing for a solution by force of arms because "The occupation of Russia meant the employment of large numbers of troops for an indefinite period of time."

Baron Makino "wished to support the proposal" but he "thought they should under no circumstances countenance Bolshevist ideas." The Japanese army had succeeded in this purpose. "The conditions in Siberia East of the Baikal had greatly improved."

Motion adopted.

"M. Clemenceau suggested that the manifesto to the Russian parties should be based solely on humanitarian grounds."

So conceived, the conference was bound to abort. William Christian Bullitt, then a member of the U.S. Peace Commission in Paris, later first United States ambassador to the Soviet Union, testified before the Senate Foreign Relations Committee on September 12, 1919, that "The French—and particularly the French foreign office, even more than M. Clemenceau—and you can observe it from that minute were opposed to the idea," of the Prinkipo conference—"and we found that the French foreign office had communicated with the Ukrainian Government and various other antisoviet governments that if they were to refuse the proposal, they would support them and continue to support them, and not allow the Allies, if they could prevent it, or the allied Governments, to make peace with the Russian Soviet Government."[11]

The French foreign office, charged with issuing the invitations, issued none to Moscow. When Moscow invited itself and offered sordid monetary profits, Wilson and Lloyd George were offended. The Prinkipo conference never met.

Lenin could not penetrate the capitalist world's mind because it was not of one mind. Its words did not conform with its deeds or its deeds with its intentions. Indeed, how could Lenin know the capitalist mind when some statesmen did not know their own minds?

Frustrated by French sabotage of the Prinkipo conference, Wilson and Lloyd George, though ostensibly angered and insulted, resolved to try again. But on February 19, Clemenceau was fired at and wounded, and with this hero's halo around his head no Prinkipo-like proposal could survive his objection. Accordingly, Bullitt was sent to Moscow by Colonel Edward M. House, Wilson's confidential adviser on foreign affairs, and Secretary of State Robert Lansing with the knowledge of Lloyd George's staff but without the knowledge of the French who were deliberately kept uninformed.

[11] *Ibid.*, p. 32.

Early in February Wilson discovered from a memorandum which "he had from unimpeachable sources" that the French government press was instructed "to emphasize chaotic conditions in Russia."[12] Chaos in Russia implied possible Bolshevik collapse; so why negotiate? On February 15, moreover, Wilson sailed for America to mend home fences and Lloyd George went to London to deal with labor disputes. Colonel House substituted for the President, Winston S. Churchill for the Prime Minister. "The first thing that Winston Churchill did"—on February 19—"was to demand instant action against Russia, and he practically supported Foch's Napoleonic scheme, which was now resurrected with new determination, for applying military force against Soviet Russia."[13] Lloyd George reprimanded Churchill.

Three days later Bullitt left Paris for Moscow. The divisions among the Allies, and within the British government, and between some civilians and most of the military, who exaggerated the efficacy of force, boded ill for his mission.

The Bolsheviks, however, did not know the inside story. They expected big results from their talks with Bullitt. Chicherin in Moscow wrote to Christian G. Rakovsky, chairman of the Soviet government of the Ukraine, "The decision is very important. If we did not reach an understanding, the policy of blockade will be pressed with vigor. They"—the Allies—"will send tanks, etc. to Denikin, Kolchak, Petlura, Paderewski, etc." Four days later, on March 17, Chicherin sent a second note to Rakovsky: "He"—Bullitt—"does not believe big concessions can be achieved in Paris."[14]

For Bullitt, too, it was important to reach an understanding. He came from a rich, upper-class, Rittenhouse Square, Philadelphia family. Sitting in his ambassadorial villa in Moscow in the 1930's, he said to me, "F.D.R., John Reed, and I belong to the same social class." He had married Louise Bryant, the widow of John Reed. Class was no greater gulf for Bullitt than it was for Reed or Lenin. Man can rise above class if not above himself. Every envoy hopes to end his assignment with a triumph. In addition, peace with Russia had become indispensable to a peaceful world, perhaps, as it seemed for a moment, to capitalist survival. Bullitt realized this. In his seven days in Moscow—March 8 to 14, 1919—he talked at length with Lenin, Chicherin, Litvinov, and others. They sent him back to Paris with a peace offer and economic offers which he regarded as reasonable and acceptable. But on his return to Paris he was rebuffed. He had traveled from Moscow to Petrograd, and through Finland to France. In the French capital he saw Colonel House immediately. "Colonel House went to the telephone and called up the President right away and told him that I was in, and that he thought this was a matter of the utmost importance, and that it would seem to be an

[12] Ray Stannard Baker, *Woodrow Wilson, Life and Letters*, Vol. I, p. 297.
[13] *Ibid.*
[14] In 1928 I visited Rakovsky in Saratov, where he lived as a Trotskyite exile, and he searched in his huge travel trunk and found these letters written by hand by Chicherin and allowed me to copy them.

opportunity to make peace in a section of the world where there was no peace; in fact, where there were 23 wars. The President said he would see me the next evening down at Col. House's office, as I remember it," Bullitt told the U.S. Senate Foreign Relations Committee. "The next evening, however, the President had a headache and he did not come. The following afternoon, Col. House said to me that he had seen the President and the President had said he had a one-track mind and was occupied with Germany at present, and he could not think of Russia, and that he had left the Russian matter to him, Col. House." Bullitt continued to see House "every day, indeed two or three times a day, on the subject" of the Soviet peace proposals. "Colonel House," Bullitt testified, "reported to me that he thought in the first place that the President favored the peace proposal; in the second place, that the President could not turn his mind to it, because he was too occupied with Germany, and finally—well, really, I have no idea what was in the President's mind."

Bullitt talked with Secretary of State Lansing, General Tasker H. Bliss, and other members of the U.S. delegation to the Peace Conference and to the entire American commission, minus President Wilson. "We had a long discussion," he declared, "at the end of which it was the sense of the commissioners' meeting that it was highly desirable to bring about peace on the basis" of Lenin's proposals.

"The next morning," Bullitt recounted, "I had breakfast with Mr. Lloyd George at his apartment. Gen. [Jan Christian] Smuts, Sir Maurice Hankey [Secretary of the British Cabinet] and Mr. Philip Kerr [Lloyd George's secretary, later Lord Lothian] were also present, and we discussed the matter at considerable length. I brought Mr. Lloyd George the official text of the [Soviet] proposal." He had read it earlier. (Bullitt had telegraphed it by State Department code from Helsingfors.) He handed it to Smuts with the statement, "General, this is of the utmost importance and interest, and you ought to read it right away." Smuts did so immediately and agreed that it was of "the utmost importance."

Then Lloyd George revealed his mind: "Mr. Lloyd George, however, said that he did not know what he could do with British public opinion. He had a copy of the *Daily Mail* in his hand, and said, 'As long as the British press is doing this kind of thing how can you expect me to be sensible about Russia?'" Lloyd George thought aloud of sending a prominent Englishman whose views might influence the British electorate. He mentioned Lord Lansdowne and Robert Cecil and Smuts and the Marquis of Salisbury but wondered whether they could go. Finally he urged Bullitt to publish the report of his mission to Moscow and the Soviet peace plan. Wilson vetoed that.

Thwarted by Wilson, depressed by Lloyd George, Bullitt felt betrayed. To disappointment was now added indignation: "About a week after I had handed to Mr. Lloyd George the official proposal, with my own hands, in the presence of three other persons, he made a speech before the British Parliament, and gave the British people to understand that he knew nothing whatever about any such proposition. It was the most egregious case of misleading the public, perhaps the boldest that I have ever known in my life." Bullitt sent a clipping of the Prime Minister's speech with a letter to Wilson. The President did not reply.[15] Bullitt resigned from the State Department.

Bullitt, an elegant charmer with a white-and-gold smile and ready repartee, liked Lenin when he met him in 1919. "Face to face Lenin is a most striking man—straightforward and direct, but also genial and with a large humor and serenity."[16] Bullitt was twenty-nine years old.

Lenin explained his attitude to the Bullitt mission in particular and to peace proposals in general when he addressed the Seventh All-Russian Congress of Soviets on December 5, 1919. He said, "We must repeat our peace proposal in the most business-like and tranquil manner. We must do this because we have already made such a proposal many times. And every time we made it we gained in the eyes of every educated person, even an enemy, and the blush of shame appeared on the face of that educated person. That is what happened when Bullitt came here, when he was received by Comrade Chicherin and talked with me and when we, in the course of several hours, concluded a preliminary treaty of peace. . . . And when we signed the treaty, the French and British ministers made this kind of a movement." Here Lenin kicked. "Bullitt," he continued, "was left with a worthless piece of paper and they said to him, 'Who could have expected that you were so naïve and so foolish as to trust in the democracy of England and France?' . . . The result is that they have put themselves on display before the entire world either as rogues or youngsters—they can choose!" By disavowing Bullitt, by rejecting other Soviet peace offers, Lenin declared, the Soviets won sympathizers even among the foreign bourgeoisie who remembered that "they too at one time fought against their own tsars and kings."[17]

Lenin saw the propaganda and public relations advantage of reiterated peace offers. Those Bullitt received were indeed far-reaching. They took the form of a proposal to be made to the Soviet government by the Allied and Associated governments. All hostilities in the former Russian Empire and Finland would cease and not be resumed until a peace conference convened in a neutral country a week after the truce began. "All existing de facto governments which have been set up on the territory of the former Russian Empire and Finland to remain in full control of the territories which they occupy at the moment when the armistice becomes effective." These governments and foreign governments were "to agree not to attempt to upset by force the existing de facto governments." Officials of Soviet Russia and of the Allied and Associated powers and anti-Soviet governments in Russia would be permitted free and unhindered right to enter the territories of one another, and Soviet Russia would obtain transit rights through the territories of non-Soviet

[15] *Op. cit.*, pp. 65-99.
[16] *Ibid.*, p. 64.
[17] Lenin, *op. cit.*, Second ed., Vol. XXIV, pp. 602-603.

Russian governments. An amnesty, the lifting of the Allied blockade of Soviet Russia, and the recognition by Moscow and the other Russian governments of old Russia's financial obligations were also provided for.[18]

Bullitt's report submitted to the American Peace Commission in Paris and to Lloyd George also contained a dark description of Soviet life: "Russia today is in a condition of acute economic distress. . . . Only one-fourth of the locomotives which ran on Russian lines before the war are now available for use." Moscow was receiving "only 25 carloads of food a day, instead of the 100 which are essential . . . Petrograd only 15 carloads, instead of the essential 50 . . . every man, woman, and child in Moscow and Petrograd is suffering from slow starvation. . . . Typhoid, typhus, and smallpox are epidemic in both Petrograd and Moscow.

"Industry, except the production of munitions of war, is largely at a standstill."[19]

The economic situation threatened to cripple the Soviet government. The Red Army was green. In contact with the enemy, it still ran away oftener than it fought. Trotsky had commenced to mold it into a fighting force by means of executions for indiscipline, the use of communist political commissars to stiffen morale, and the use of tsarist officers for training and leadership. But Lenin needed time. He had faith in time. He believed that the pro-landlord interests of the anti-Boishevik governments would undermine their strength; Russia's peasants were in an insurrectionist mood. He believed that once the workers tasted the White regimes they would prefer soviets. Lenin was no pacifist. Peace to him was not an end. It was a means to an end: the consolidation, and if possible the extension, of Soviet power.

The West rejected peace with the Soviet government for a different reason. "The principal reason was entirely different," Mr. Bullitt told the U.S. Senate committee. "The fact was that at this moment, when this proposal was under consideration, Kolchak made a 100-mile advance. There was a revolt of peasants in a district of Russia which entirely cut off supplies from the Bolshevik army operating against Kolchak. Kolchak made a 100-mile advance, and immediately the entire Paris press was roaring and screaming on the subject, announcing that Kolchak would be in Moscow within two weeks; and therefore everyone in Paris, including, I regret to say, members of the American commission, began to grow very lukewarm about peace in Russia."[20]

Kolchak did not reach Moscow in two weeks. Moscow's long arm reached out to Siberia and killed him. But Lenin could not be sure. He wanted a respite.

Lenin, however, was not a one-weapon statesman. In the first week of March, 1919, he launched the Third International (Comintern) to spread revolution abroad. In the second week he saw Bullitt and prepared the peace offer to the Entente. In the third week, the Eighth Congress of the Russian

[18] Bullitt, op. cit., pp. 39-43.
[19] Ibid., pp. 49-50.
[20] Ibid., p. 90.

Communist Party (Bolsheviks), answering SR and Menshevik charges of Bolshevik Bonapartism and militarism, adopted a 3,000-word resolution "On the Military Question," which described "the old social democratic program" of a popular militia as having had "an undoubtedly educational significance" (along with the demand for equal, universal suffrage) in the period of imperialism. Now, however, "when the class war is being transformed into a civil war, thus tearing the veil from bourgeois rights and bourgeois-democratic institutions, the slogan of 'people's militia' "—or what Lenin, late in 1917, in *The State and Revolution*, called the "whole people armed"—"has lost all sense." At first, the resolution continued, "we created an army on the basis of volunteering." But now the Red Army was not a militia, but "permanent" and "regular." There would be no further elections of officers. Commanders of the tsarist army who "either adopted the Soviet point of view out of conviction or saw themselves compelled, by the force of circumstances, to serve it conscientiously," would be employed in the Red Army together with political commissars backed by cells of communists in the ranks. This army would not only defend "the socialist community"—"fatherland" was still taboo— "but it would permit the giving of decisive aid to the proletariat" of imperialist states "in their struggle against imperialism."[21]

The failure of peace-diplomacy and the recession of European revolution left Soviet Russia with one instrument to combat her domestic and foreign enemies: political-military force. There would be no breathing space and no proletarian aid from abroad. The new state had a new army, the key to its fate.

XXVI. ONE TOUCH OF IDEALISM

A RUSSIAN ARMY unit moved on its empty stomach until it pillaged a village. Divisions traveled hundreds of miles on foot. Heavy equipment was hauled in

[21] Lenin, *op. cit.*, Second ed., Vol. XXIV, pp. 709-717.

peasant sleighs and carts which had to be pulled out of the mud of rutted roads or pushed over roadless steppes. Limping locomotives drawing soldier-filled cattle cars across the frozen countryside stopped regularly to allow the men to cut down trees along the right of way for heating the boilers. No statistics were kept; but frost, hunger, and disease probably killed more persons than bullets and shells. Only toil-hardened muzhiks, workers inured to poverty, and convinced communists and anticommunists could stand the strain. Perhaps only Russia—and China—could survive such an ordeal. A small country like Italy or England or a twentieth-century country like the United States would have died of plague and famine from three and a half years of paralyzed production, distribution, transportation, and communications. Russia's backwardness led to Bolshevik victory.

The Russian civil war consisted of great sweeping movements. Trenches and sieges were rare. Success therefore required the manipulating of forces by a central authority. Here the Soviet government enjoyed a distinct advantage over its enemies. Denikin in the south tried to form a junction with Kolchak in the east but failed to take Tsaritsin, which would have been the link. Miller and Tchaikovsky in the Archangel region also reached out to Kolchak; their arms proved too short. The Bolsheviks, however, shifted troops incessantly from one arc to the other of their 5,280-mile front; Lenin supervised the gears, hinges, and swivels. He himself was a stationary human generator producing stinging energy and kinetic power for the entire military enterprise.

Early in 1919, as Trotsky explained to the plenary session of the Moscow Soviet on April 1, 1919, Denikin, supplied with arms and advisers by England and France, moved toward Moscow. The army facing Kolchak was then stripped to check Denikin.[1] Kolchak consequently made the 100-mile advance which so misled the peacemakers in Paris in March-May, 1919. In May, 1919, danger threatened the Bolsheviks on the eastern as well as the southern front. Lenin bristled. On May 21 he wired the southern-front command that, according to information from Beloborodov, his eye-and-ear deputy in the area, "orders took three days to reach units and armored cars are without fuel. I am tightening things here, you do the same. The Tambov army committee telegraphs that it has sent you 669 communists . . . I am surprised that with these, and with 2,000 officer cadets, and a division, you procrastinate in adopting decisive measures against the insurrection" of Ataman Gregoriev "which must be suppressed immediately. Wire more details. Chairman Sovnarkom Lenin."[2]

Five days later he urged the Sovnarkom of the Ukraine "not to relieve a single soldier fighting Gregoriev, to decree and carry out the complete disarmament of the population," which apparently sympathized with the ata-

---

[1] Trotsky, *Sochineniya*, Vol. XVII. *Sovietskaya Respublika i Kapitalisticheskii Mir* (*The Soviet Republic and the Capitalist World*), Part II: *Grazhdanskaya Voina* (*The Civil War*), pp. 99 *et seq*.

[2] Lenin, *Sochineniya*, Fourth ed., Vol. 35, p. 328.

man, "to execute mercilessly on the spot for every hidden rifle. The essence of the moment is: a speedy victory [against Denikin] in the Donets Basin, the gathering of all rifles in the villages, and the creation of a stable army . . . mobilize every workingman. Read this telegram to all prominent Bolsheviks. Lenin."[3]

In that May month Kolchak's army, moving westward, devastated the land like locusts. As he advanced toward the Volga, therefore, villages and then whole counties rebelled in his rear in the Urals and Siberia. His young officers, more than he himself, were monarchistic and landlord-minded. They dispossessed the peasants, reinstated the estate owners. "You will be received with church bells," Boris I. Nicolaevsky said in Moscow after passing through nominally Kolchak territory.

Blocked by the Red Army, harassed by recalcitrant villagers who cut off his food supply and sniped at his soldiers, Kolchak halted and changed focus from Moscow and Paris to Siberia. Lenin counseled hot pursuit: "Unless we conquer the Urals this winter, I regard the death of the revolution inescapable. Strain every nerve. . . . Look attentively for reinforcements. Mobilize the entire population in front areas. Check on political work. Wire me results every day in code," he demanded of the Revvoiensoviet of the eastern front on May 29. "Read this telegram to all prominent communists and to the workingmen from Petrograd. . . . Pay the closest attention to the mobilization of the Orenburg Cossacks. You will be held responsible to see that units do not begin to become demoralized and that depression does not set in,"[4] presumably because of the prospect of continued fighting.

Presently, the anti-Kolchak front had to be deprived once more to save Petrograd and strengthen the southern front. Lenin telegraphed the Revvoiensoviet of the eastern front on June 9: "Grave deterioration near Petrograd and breakthrough in south compels us again and again to take troops from your front. There is no alternative . . . break with routine. Mobilize everybody in front regions from the ages of 18 to 45, and assign them tasks like the capture of the nearest big factories such as Motovilikhi, Minyara, promising to release them if they succeed. Assigning two or three persons to each rifle, summoning them to chase Kolchak out of the Urals, mobilize 75% of party and trade union members. There is no other way, you must begin to work in a revolutionary manner . . . Lenin."[5]

The transfer of regiments and armies from one front to the other depended on the significance attached by the Bolshevik leaders to this or that strategic objective; here differences of opinion occurred. In the beginning of 1919, for instance, Trotsky favored a plan "to entrench ourselves in the Urals and throw the maximum of our forces to the south in order to liquidate the threat [from Denikin] against Moscow." Others, including Smilga, Lashevich, I. N.

[3] *Ibid.*, p. 329.
[4] *Ibid.*, p. 330.
[5] *Ibid.*, p. 332.

Smirnov, and K. I. Gruenstein, advocated a fight to the finish with Kolchak in Siberia. Trotsky was outvoted in the Politburo. The pursuit of Kolchak gathered momentum.

Lenin felt fully confident. On September 3, 1919, addressing a Moscow meeting of noncommunist workers and soldiers, he recalled that as soon as the capitalists achieved power in Siberia they expelled the Mensheviks and SR's from the Omsk government and did not summon a Constituent Assembly but established "a dictatorship of landlords and officers." This proved to the proletariat, he said, that "there can be no reconciliation between labor and capital." Some workers had believed in the coalition of the bourgeoisie but "tens of thousands of Siberian workers and peasants shot and flogged to death paid for their trustfulness." Now they had turned against Kolchak. The same development, he predicted, would take place in the Ukraine to the detriment of Denikin.[6]

Denikin, nevertheless, kept moving forward. He captured Kursk, 330 miles from Moscow, on September 20, 1919. Simultaneously, General Yudenich, repulsed earlier in the year, renewed his offensive against Petrograd.

Again, the question of priority. Pursue Kolchak? Block Denikin? Defend Petrograd?

The communists were recruiting Petrograd party members and workers and sending them south to stop Denikin. Lenin now gave precedence to the southern front. He urged the proletariat of other cities to follow Petrograd's example. "The Denikinists," he declared on October 3, 1919, "reckon on sowing panic in our ranks and on forcing us to think only of defensive operations, and only in one direction. . . . The foreign radio screams to the entire world about the open road to Moscow. That is how the capitalists want to frighten us.

"But they shall not succeed in frightening us . . . Denikin will be broken as Kolchak has been broken." Nevertheless, he did not underestimate the peril. "A serious danger has been created by the fall of Kursk. Never has the enemy been so near Moscow."[7]

On October 14 Denikin took Orel, 245 miles from Moscow.

Apparently, Lenin panicked; he proposed surrendering Petrograd. It was the cradle of the revolution. With Moscow it was the twin pillar of the revolution. Yet Lenin thought of abandoning it. In such matters he was totally unsentimental. Russia is big. Survival is worth a city. Lenin feared, at this juncture, that Soviet Russia might not survive. "The military power of the Entente *can* crush (but still in fact has not crushed) us," he wrote in a greeting dated October 10, 1919, to Italian, French, and German communists.[8] Six days later, from the balcony of the Moscow Soviet, Lenin addressed worker-communists who had arrived from Yaroslav and Vladimir

[6] *Pravda*, Sept. 11, 1919.
[7] *Ibid.*, Oct. 4, 1919.
[8] Lenin, *op. cit.*, Fourth ed., Vol. 30, pp. 34-44.

provinces en route to the front. He told them frankly of the "terrible danger" represented by Denikin and Yudenich. "The situation is extraordinarily difficult." But there was hope outside. "We know that in the entire world, in all countries without exception, the revolutionary movement grows, more slowly than we should wish, but grows steadily. And we also know that the victory of the working class in the whole world is guaranteed." He painted a rosy future whenever the present was black. "The imperialists," he said, "may destroy one or two more republics, but they cannot save world imperialism, for it is doomed, it shall be swept away by approaching socialism."[9]

It was this pessimism that impelled Lenin to suggest the abandonment of Petrograd. "During the advance of Yudenich on Petrograd," Trotsky wrote, "Lenin at one time thought it was not worthwhile trying to defend the city and that we ought to move the line of defense nearer Moscow. I objected. Comrade Zinoviev supported me and I think also Comrade Stalin."[10]

Trotsky was in Petrograd prepared to hold the city. Lenin wired him there: "Last night transmitted in code . . . the decision of the Council of Defense. As you see, your plan was adopted." Lenin, the chairman of the council, had been outvoted—and he acquiesced. Nevertheless, his vision of disaster persisted and he authorized Trotsky to act as events demanded. "An attempt to outflank and cut off Petrograd," Lenin's telegram continued, "will, of course, bring corresponding changes which you will carry out on the spot. Assign someone in each department of the local executive committee to collect Soviet papers and documents in preparation for an evacuation."[11]

"Fifth columns" in Moscow and Petrograd aggravated the danger. Lenin blamed "this 'intelligentsia' folk" for skillfully "sowing panic."[12] The Cheka fished with a fine net and caught sharks, flounderers, and minnows. The sins of conspirators were often visited on the innocent. Maxim Gorky and his wife Maria Feodorovna complained to Lenin. "Measures for release," he replied, "have been taken. (It is impossible not to arrest the *entire* Kadet and near-Kadet crowd as a precaution against plots. They are capable, all of them, of helping the plotters. It is criminal not to arrest them. It is better that tens or hundreds of intellectuals sit"—go to jail—"for a day or a week than that 10,000 be killed. Yes, yes, it's better.)" Meanwhile, a "Committee for the Defense of Moscow" proclaimed the fourth week of October "Defense Week." For further defense—against typhus—Lenin, in the same week, ordered the urgent construction of baths, with delousing rooms, at Moscow's railway stations.

After the fall of Orel, Tula, approximately halfway between Orel and Moscow, was Denikin's next target. Lenin wrote to the Tula Revolutionary

[9] *Ibid.*, pp. 48-49.
[10] Trotsky, *The Stalin School of Falsification*, Introduction and Explanatory Notes by Max Schachtman, translated by John G. Wright (New York, 1937), p. 44.
[11] *Ibid.*, pp. 44-45.
[12] Lenin, *op. cit.*, Fourth ed., Vol. 30, p. 52.

Committee (Revkom) on October 20, urging its leaders to end conflicts among themselves and close civilian administrative offices wherever possible. "In Tula," he declared, *"the masses* are by no means with us." Therefore intensive propaganda should be conducted in the army, in the reserves, and among men and women workers. "If you lack sufficient personnel, write, we will help from Moscow. . . . Are you building blockhouses? . . . Do you have the materials? the workers? Are Red Army soldiers training?"[13]

On October 24 Lenin met the graduating class of Sverdlov University in the capital. The occasion, he said, was not only a celebration. Half the class had volunteered "in order to render new, extraordinary, and substantial aid to the troops battling at the front." Lenin regretted this necessity. The students had been trained to take the place of factory workers who, having borne the burden of administering the country, were "extremely exhausted." But "no choice remained."

Lenin then surveyed the civil war situation. In the north, in the Murmansk-Archangel region, "the British were compelled to withdraw their forces. . . . That front, once especially dangerous because the enemy, possessing sea access, enjoyed the most favorable conditions," was now manned by "an insignificant number of Russian White Guards of nearly no importance."

On the Siberian front, where Kolchak, aided by the Western powers, and by Poles and Czechoslovaks, had scored many successes "because the local workers and peasants were late in mobilizing . . . we now feel most firmly established." Bolshevik troops had arrived at the Irtish River, on which Omsk, Kolchak's capital, was situated.

On the western front, facing Poland, quiet reigned. "There remain two fronts—Petrograd and southern." A quick improvement had intervened at Petrograd. "You know from the reports of Zinoviev and Trotsky that losses have been replaced, that former vacillations have vanished, that our troops are advancing and advancing successfully against the most desperate resistance. Comrade Trotsky has informed me by telephone from Petrograd that in Dyetskoye Selo"—the former Tsarskoye Selo—"which was recently captured by us, White Guards and bourgeois people who stayed behind fired from individual homes and resisted more stubbornly than in previous battles. The enemy senses that this is the turning point of the war and that Denikin is in a situation where he must be helped by diverting our forces directed against him. But we can say definitely that they have not succeeded in this. . . . Not one unit on the Petrograd front was drawn from the south, and the victory which we have begun to achieve and which we shall carry to a final triumph will be attained without the slightest weakening of the southern front where the outcome of the war with the landlords and imperialists will be decided." He promised that outcome "in the near future."[14]

[13] *Ibid.*, Vol. 35, pp. 360-361.
[14] *Pravda*, Oct. 26 and 28, 1919.

His prediction was based on an accomplished fact: the Red Army had re-captured Orel on October 20 and driven Denikin back. Lenin also knew about Makhno's activities.

It seems probable that Denikin, like Kolchak, suffered defeat almost as much because of what happened behind him as by the resistance of the Red Army at the front. Denikin's rear was chewed up by Makhno, an anarchist guerrilla leader.

Nestor Ivanovich Makhno fought against the Bolsheviks at one time and against Denikin at another. The Whites courted him and so did the Reds. In 1918 he had a long talk with Lenin in the Kremlin.[15] He was a unique revolutionary figure.

Put your hand on the lower half of a frontispiece photograph of Makhno in his autobiography, leaving only the head exposed, and you have the like-ness of a woman with a high, rounded, dense shock of black hair thickly packed on the neck and hugging the temples and ears; beautiful, deep, oval eyes and perfectly formed eyebrows; a small nose; and broad, sensuous lips. But he wears military harness and a uniform, and in his belt is a saber. On his hips, not shown in the picture, are probably two revolvers. This is how he looked at the age of thirty-four or thirty-five, in 1918 or 1919, the zenith of his strange career.

A stormy Ukrainian petrel, Makhno served years of hard labor in a Moscow prison and in Siberia, and returned, in the autumn of 1917, to his passionately loved village of Gulyai-Polye near Yekaterinoslav (now Dnieper-petrovsk) and Alexandrovsk (now Zaporozhe). The peasants had seized land. When civil war raised the specter of landlordism restored, the people of Gulyai-Polye organized for "the defense of the revolution" and obtained arms from the Bolshevik-Left SR soviets in neighboring towns.

Makhno called himself a "communist-anarchist." Gulyai-Polye under his direction became an independent commune where small workshops were managed by their employees and peasants cooperated voluntarily in their daily tasks. Moscow was remote, Bolshevism incomprehensible. Politics van-ished. Gulyai-Polye was a diminutive republic with Nestor Makhno as "Father." If the residents had an ideology it consisted of Ukrainian sep-aratism mingled with anti-Semitism and dislike of Great Russians.

Isolation on this populist-anarchist island was short-lived. In March-April, 1918, after Germany signed the separate treaty in Brest-Litovsk with the fictitious Central Rada, German and Austro-Hungarian troops occupied most of the Ukraine, including Gulyai-Polye. Makhno, away from home in search of more arms from the Bolsheviks, did not attempt to return; he proceeded southeast to Taganrog where he convened a conference of communist-anarch-

[15] Nestor Makhno, *Pod Udarami Kontr-Revolutsii. Pod Redaktsei, s Predisloviem i Primechanyami T. Volina (Under the Blows of the Counter-Revolution*, edited, and with Introduction and Notes, by Comrade Volin) (Paris, 1936), Book Two, pp. 126-135.

ists, many of them escaped from Gulyai-Polye, who, after blaming the Jews for the German entry into their village, resolved to retake it at harvesttime in late summer. Makhno meanwhile would tour Russia to survey the revolution.

Makhno, uneducated, seems to have been a highly emotional if not neurotic person. In his memoirs he tells how he learned at a railway station of the fall of his native Gulyai-Polye. He was shaken. He entered a waiting Red Army train. The soldiers, he writes, later reported to him what happened. They said that "I wept and fell asleep in the railway car on the knees of a Red Army soldier. But I don't remember that. I thought I was not asleep and only felt a kind of alarm. I felt badly, but I was able to walk and talk. I recall that I could not understand where I was." Makhno possessed a hysterical quality which engendered heedless courage and gave him a magnetic attraction. He loved action. He loved freedom. He hated the state.

Touring churned-up Russia, he went from Taganrog to Rostov to the Tsaritsin area to Saratov. Everywhere he met anarchists fleeing from "the persecution directed against us by the then befouled Lenin and Trotsky and the Bolshevik-Left SR Chekists." The anarchists either hid, which aroused Makhno's ire, or joined with Red Fleet deserter-sailors to form armed bands that wreaked vengeance on Chekists. On one occasion, Chekists transporting a bound terrorist commander met three anarchists on a road outside Saratov and decided to seize them too. But the three hurled hand grenades, liberated the commander, and escaped with him. When this became known in Saratov, the anarchists, "numbering 15 to 20," Makhno writes, rushed to a river boat and sailed for Astrakhan. Though Makhno's destination was Moscow, in the opposite direction, he went along. Later he returned by Volga boat to Saratov and, having obtained a railway ticket from the city Revolutionary Committee which respected his status as chairman of the "defense of the revolution committee" of Gulyai-Polye, he entrained for Moscow.

Makhno here commenced to call the Bolshevik regime "the paper revolution"; it had spawned a bureaucracy. He noted the speculation; trains full of Russians bringing flour from the villages. In Moscow he met Kozlovsky, a fellow inmate of his tsarist prison, now a precinct police commissar. "The revolution demands this," the commissar apologized. Makhno scoffed and considered him "a hangman of the revolution."

On April 13, 1918, the Cheka had descended on the anarchist groups of Moscow with a view to suppressing them. Many anarchists were arrested, others went underground. Makhno sought them out, tried to convince them that the traditional anarchist hostility to organization was the cause of their weakness; they needed to become a party. Prince Peter A. Kropotkin, the Nestor of Russian anarchism, who had seen the inside of tsarist and French jails, was living in Moscow, his native city, at the time, having returned to Russia from England in the middle of 1917. Makhno interviewed him. Kropotkin was seventy-six, disappointed in the revolution, disillusioned with Lenin. Makhno questioned the sinking giant. "To all the questions I put to him I received satisfactory replies" is Makhno's laconic summary of the exchange. When he told Kropotkin of his proposed return to the Ukraine to conduct revolutionary activity among the peasants, the author of *Memoirs of a Revolutionist* withheld advice and stressed the risks. In parting, the old man said to the young fighter, "Selflessness, strength of spirit and of will on the path toward the projected goal, conquers everything."

These words spoke to Makhno's heart; he possessed unlimited strength of will. "I approached the gates of the Kremlin," he declares in his memoirs, "with the definite intention of seeing Lenin no matter what happens, and, if possible, Sverdlov too, and to talk with them." Terror notwithstanding, the revolution had not entered its iron age, and the bureaucratic state, which Makhno abhorred, was, fortunately for him, inefficient. He did get to Sverdlov's secretary who, fascinated by Makhno's report on the mood of the Ukraine's peasantry, brought him to the President of Soviet Russia. Sverdlov too found Makhno's information valuable and telephoned Lenin. When he put down the receiver, the President said, "Comrade, tomorrow at one o'clock come straight to me and we will go over to Comrade Lenin."

There is no mention in the great library of literature by and about Lenin of the leader's talk with Makhno in June, 1918. Many peasants, singly and in delegations, came to see him; it was his way of taking the pulse. Perhaps no record was kept. Perhaps the censors have suppressed it. Makhno provides the account, and there is no reason to question his veracity.[16]

Lenin welcomed Makhno "in a fatherly manner," shook the visitor's hand, and put his left hand lightly on Makhno's shoulder and directed him into an armchair. He asked Sverdlov to sit down and then sat down himself. Lenin inquired three times how Ukrainian villagers understood the slogan, "All power to the soviets." Each time Makhno said this meant self-government and economic self-management on local and county levels.

Did Makhno approve?

"Yes."

Then the peasantry, Lenin suggested, is "infected with anarchism"?

"And is that bad?" Makhno asked.

"I do not wish to say that," Lenin replied. "On the contrary, it would be comforting, for it would hasten the victory of communism over capitalism and capitalist power."

Lenin might well have made this statement. Peasants yearning to be politically and economically independent would oust their landlords and abandon the conservative parties. But Lenin added that anarchists were unable to organize the proletariat and poor peasantry and could not, therefore, defend the achievements of the revolution against counterrevolutionaries, whereas the firmly knit proletariat could. Here he cited the Red Guard

[16] *Ibid.*, pp. 126-135.

squads of Petrograd workers whose "revolutionary heroism" he admired.

"You, Comrade Lenin," Makhno objected, "having information at second or third hand, exaggerate this" revolutionary heroism. At times it was "pale and negligible." The squads attacked only along the railway lines and sometimes held railway stations, but five or ten miles away, out in the countryside, the villagers never heard of them.

"I remember," Makhno wrote in his mid-1930 memoirs published in Russian in Paris, "how disturbed" Lenin was at this statement. Makhno recalled Lenin's "great emotional alarm only possible in a person animated by the struggle against a social system he hates and thirsting for victory over it."

Then what, Lenin inquired, "are the revolutionary propagandists doing in the villages"?

Nothing, Makhno answered.

Lenin folded his hands, leaned forward, and was lost in thought. Turning to Sverdlov, he said, "In reorganizing the Red Guards by merging them into the Red Army we are taking the right road to the final victory of the proletariat over the bourgeoisie." Lenin always rejected guerrilla fighting. He preferred tightly organized, firmly disciplined military formations under central control.

"What do you propose to do in Moscow?" Lenin asked Makhno.

He was preparing, he replied, to return to the Ukraine in July.

"Illegally?"

"Yes."

"Anarchists," Lenin remarked to Sverdlov, "always accept selfless sacrifice, but as shortsighted fanatics they miss seeing the present by focusing on the remote future. . . . I regard you, Comrade, as a realist. . . . If only one-third of the anarchist-communists of Russia were like you we communists would be ready, on certain conditions, to work together with them in favor of a free organization of producers."

For that brief moment Lenin reverted to the anarchism present in the original idealistic concept of communism: the free, voluntary organization of producers without a state. But just as anarchists neglected the present for the future, so Lenin, and Leninists since him, ignored the future for the present. They reaped a harvest of lies, death, and power-madness. There is always an urgent present to block the advent of the ideal future.

That single flash of Lenin's idealism moved Makhno: "I felt I was beginning to venerate Lenin whom I so recently held responsible for the destruction of the Moscow anarchist organization."

"Yes, yes," Lenin declared, rising from his chair. "The anarchists are always strong on thoughts about the future; in the present, by reason only of their empty fantasies, they are pitiful, with no ground under their feet, and actually have no connection with that future."

"I am a semiliterate peasant," Makhno, looking at Sverdlov, rejoined, "and

I cannot debate the confusing ideas about anarchism just uttered by Comrade Lenin." But in the Ukraine the anarchists had demonstrated that they could deal with reality by going into battle against the Germans, against the troops of Hetman Skoropadsky, and against all counterrevolutionaries. He was returning to the wars.

"Do you want my help?" Lenin asked.

"Very much."

Lenin ordered Sverdlov to make the necessary arrangements. Makhno was supplied with a false passport in the name of Ivan Yaakovlevich Shepel, a teacher and officer, and an officer's uniform. In the next two years, Makhno's immersion in day-to-day realities must have astounded, and at times appalled, Lenin. Out of the Ukrainian earth, out of the peasants' ire, Makhno stamped an army. By May, 1919, with Denikin slicing north to Moscow, that army was a factor that disturbed the Kremlin. "Temporarily, as long as Rostov has not been taken," Lenin wired Leo Kamenev in Kiev on May 7, 1919, "it is necessary to deal diplomatically with Makhno's troops, send Antonov [Antonov-Avseyenko] there and make Antonov responsible for Makhno's army. Telegraph a detailed report. Lenin."[17]

In that month the Central Committee of the Russian Communist Party, alarmed by the White advance and Ataman Gregoriev's revolt, ordered the mobilization of 20,000 workers in the Ukraine, including Donets miners. The Kharkov Coal Trust asked Lenin to exempt the miners; he refused but made an exception for diggers at the coal face. The Bolsheviks needed every man, and were losing men. The Red Army seized peasant horses for its new cavalry. The peasants protested, joined Makhno, joined Gregoriev. "The development of Makhnoism was fostered by the wholesale imposition of communes and state farms without taking account of realistic possibilities and of the peasantry's land requirements."[18] Makhno's swelling forces fought under the black anarchist flag, received arms from the Reds, and harassed Denikin, but attracted Ukrainians disgruntled with Russian Bolshevism and its local agents. Trotsky, irritated, denounced Makhno on June 2, in *Na Puti* (*On the Road*), the newspaper printed on the armored train which served him as headquarters. Nevertheless, Makhno prospered. In July Gregoriev came to see him, proposed an alliance against the Bolsheviks and Petlura, a Ukrainian nationalist guerrilla leader. Makhno regarded both Gregoriev and Petlura as foul birds of a feather, equally counterrevolutionary. Gregoriev was murdered in Makhno's camp. Makhno telegraphed the news to Lenin. Makhno wished to demonstrate that he was the revolutionist supporting the revolution which Lenin, he held, had betrayed.

The Red Army was in retreat before Denikin. Retreating units entered Makhno's army. By August, 1919, Makhno commanded four infantry brigades, one cavalry brigade, an artillery detachment, and a machine-gun regi-

[17] Lenin, *op. cit.*, Fourth ed., Vol. 36, p. 467.
[18] *Bolshaya Sovietskaya Entsiklopedia*, First ed., Vol. 38, column 500.

ment with 500 machine guns—15,000 men in all, and reinforcements coming in daily. "There is good evidence that the Whites soon came to regard Makhno's new army as their toughest immediate opponent."[19] On September 26 Denikin surrounded Makhno. Fighting for twenty-four hours under their black flags and "Liberty or Death" and "Land for the Peasants, Factories for the Workers" banners, Makhno's men withstood the onslaught, took the offensive, and inflicted a severe defeat on the Whites. Makhno now rampaged across the Ukraine, tapping Denikin's blood, taking his cities (Krivoi Rog, Nikopol, Alexandrovsk, Melitopol, and Mariupol), and seizing his supplies. On October 20 Makhno entered Yekaterinoslav just as the Red Army entered Orel. The two successes were related. Denikin might not have been held at Orel on his dash to Moscow if Makhno had not hollowed out his rear. By the end of 1919 White Denikin, victim of red and black, died militarily, escaped to Europe, wrote his reminiscences of defeat in five large tomes.

As the Bolshevik army marched south, flooding the Ukraine, Makhno withdrew before it. It pursued him, overtook him, he fought; his force was destroyed. He fled to Romania, then Poland, then Paris, where he died in 1935 of tuberculosis of the lungs. "Our military command has failed shamefully in allowing Makhno to get away (despite our great superiority in strength and the strict orders to catch him)," Lenin wrote to Comrade E. M. Sklyansky, Trotsky's first assistant. Lenin blotted Sklyansky's party record with another "warning."[20]

XXVII. ŎWO SOULS IN ONE BREAST

IN THE AUTUMN of 1919, Peter Orkhimenko, author and translator of poetry, escaped from his Ukrainian home town of Kamenka when the Whites captured it, and, after troubles galore, arrived in Moscow "as poor," in his own words, "as Job." To earn money, he translated some English verses of Joseph Edwards Carpenter and brought them to Pravda, where Maria Ilynichna, Lenin's sister, worked as secretary of the editorial board. The poems were printed on November 7, 1919. Several days later Orkhimenko, in the Pravda office for the honorarium, told Maria about his straitened condition. Maria

[19] David Footman, Civil War in Russia (London, 1961), p. 272. This book contains a detailed account of the Makhno adventures.
[20] Lenin, op. cit., Fourth ed., Vol. 35, p. 404.

told her brother. Lenin wrote a letter to Abel Yenukidze, secretary of the VTSIK, Leo Kamenev, and Central Committee secretary E. D. Stasova: "I beg you to help the bearer, Comrade Peter Orkhimenko, with clothing, a room, and food. If there are difficulties of any kind in rendering the aid please 'phone me. V. Ulyanov (Lenin)."[1]

This was not Lenin's only act of kindness to a comrade. Moreover, on the testimony of many, he loved children—and cats. He had had a brown cat in Geneva. During her visit to Lenin at Gorky shortly following the August 30, 1918, attempt on his life, Angelica Balabanoff saw two cats in the household. Lincoln Eyre, an American journalist who went to Lenin's Kremlin apartment, noted that the dictator was "fond" of his several cats.[2]

Lenin's private tenderness and political ruthlessness were unrelated phenomena. "Lenin loved Martov," says Boris I. Nicolaevsky, prominent Menshevik publicist. But Lenin hated, harassed, and suppressed the Menshevik party led by Martov. This was not schizophrenia. Lenin resembled a soldier who would not conceivably murder in civilian life but kills on the battlefield. In the chasm between personal morality and public immorality lie most of the world's evils.

Angelica Balabanoff, friend of Mussolini when he was a socialist, friend of Lenin, a socialist of long experience with Western socialist parties, was Soviet Russia's unofficial representative in Stockholm. She had been instructed to foster European Left Socialist sympathies for communism. "Every Saturday ships came to Stockholm from Petrograd; they brought me cases full of newspapers and very much money." She hesitated to spend the money when Soviet citizens were hungry and Soviet industry and agriculture languished. She aired her misgivings in a message to Lenin. He replied, "Dear Comrade, Thanks, thanks, thanks," each "thanks" thrice underlined, "you have served our movement extremely well. But I beg you not to economize. Spend the money by the millions, yes, by the tens of millions." Back in Moscow, just after Lenin had been wounded, she went to his villa at Gorky and carried with her some Swedish cheese. Refreshments and tea were served. Lenin apologized for the "privileges" he enjoyed: "The sugar was brought to me from the Ukraine; the bread from Central Russia; the meat was ordered by my physician and I don't know where it comes from." She offered him the cheese. "Give it to Moscow's children," he urged.[3]

In March, 1918, N. P. Gorbunov, secretary of the Sovnarkom, in collusion with Bonch-Bruevich, raised Lenin's monthly salary from 500 to 800 roubles. Lenin demanded an explanation. None was given. In an official note, dated May 23, Lenin said the increase was "clearly illegal" and contravened government decrees. He administered "a stern reprimand" to Gorbunov, who

---

[1] Lenin, *Sochineniya*, Fourth ed., Vol. 36, p. 475.
[2] New York *World*, Feb. 21, 1920.
[3] Angelica Balabanoff, *Lenin*, Hannover, West Germany, 1959, pp. 47-48.

recalls that several days earlier Lenin had instructed him to raise the salary of Assistant Finance Commissar Gukovsky to 2,000 roubles and salaries in commissariats generally.[4]

Lenin abhorred luxury, and he had a personal commitment to austerity and equality that harks back to original socialist principles. Others, he knew, were made of softer stuff.

. Angelica quit her Stockholm post. Lenin appointed her Commissar of Foreign Affairs of the Soviet Ukraine—as though the Ukraine were an independent country. In Kiev, reality struck Angelica. "Harmless people were being arrested and, often, executed . . . when an area was evacuated a considerable portion of the population was shot [by the Cheka] lest they be useful in any way to the enemy."

Angelica's distress mounted when she learned of the activities of a "scoundrel," posing as foreign ambassador to the Ukraine. He speculated in money, sold passports to citizens eager to go abroad, and reported his clients to the Cheka. Incensed, Angelica rushed to Moscow and interviewed Felix Djerzhinsky, Cheka chief. The "scoundrel," he told her, was a Cheka employee. She appealed to Lenin. "Comrade Balabanoff," Lenin said, "when will you begin to understand life? Decoy spies? If I could I would put decoy spies in Kornilov's army."[5]

For Lenin the end hallowed this means too.

For Angelica it killed the end.

Angelica, an individual, free inside, though she was still inside Russia, could afford the luxury of criticizing the corrupt practices of government. Lenin, a state lashed to his back, bent under its weight. All states lie and spy. There are, however, degrees of unscrupulousness. A dictatorship, thanks to its harnessed press, hobbled public opinion, and unlimited police power, is likely to excel in unprincipled acts—especially in wartime, and it is always wartime in a dictatorship.

Judging by the number of times Lenin defended his dissolution of the Constituent Assembly in January, 1918, judging by the number of times he tried to explain or explain away his book, *The State and Revolution,* Lenin must have been uncomfortable about both. He lectured the students of Moscow's Sverdlov University *About the State* on July 11, 1919, in the midst of the civil war.[6] During the first two minutes he told them three times that the question of the state was "a difficult one," "one of the most complicated and difficult questions," and it was further "confused by bourgeois scholars and writers." A minute later, again, "I have already spoken of the fact that scarcely any other question has been so deliberately and inadvertently confused by the representatives of bourgeois science, philosophy, jurisprudence, political economists, and publicists as the question of the state. Very often

[4] Vospominaniya, Vol. 2, p. 59.
[5] Balabanoff, op. cit., p. 68.
[6] Lenin, op. cit., Second ed., Vol. XXIV, pp. 362-377.

this question is still merged with religious questions" not only by religious persons but by those "who regard themselves as free of religious prejudices." They teach that the state "is something divine, something superhuman."

The question of the state "is now the focus of all political discussions and all current political disputes." The issue is: "Does the state in a capitalist country, in a democratic republic—especially in one like Switzerland or America—in the freest democratic republics, does the state represent the national will, the combined nationwide decision, the national will, etc.,—or is the state an apparatus through which its capitalists can maintain their power over the workers and peasants? This is the basic issue around which all the political arguments of the world move. What do they say about Bolshevism? The bourgeois press abuses the Bolsheviks. You will not find a single newspaper which does not repeat the popular charge against the Bolsheviks that they are the destroyers of the people's rule. . . . There is at the present time not a single very wealthy newspaper in the wealthiest countries . . . which does not repeat . . . that America, England, and Switzerland are progressive countries based on the people's will whereas the Bolshevik republic is a government of bandits, that it knows no freedom and that the Bolsheviks are the destroyers of the idea of democracy and even went so far as to disband the Constituent Assembly. These terrible accusations against the Bolsheviks are repeated throughout the world. These accusations bring us to the question: What is a state?"

Here Lenin referred the students to Engels, who, in Lenin's words, taught that "any state in which private ownership of land and the means of production exists, where capital rules, no matter how democratic it might be, is a capitalist state, it is a machine in the hands of the capitalists to subjugate the working class and the poor peasantry. And universal suffrage, a Constituent Assembly, a parliament—all this is form, a sort of promissory note, which does not in the least alter things in essence."

"No matter what forms cover the republic," Lenin continued, "though it be the most democratic republic, if it is bourgeois, if it retains private ownership of land, factories, and mills, and if private capital holds the entire society in hired slavery . . . that state is an apparatus for the oppression of some by others. And this apparatus we will take into the hands of the class which must overthrow the power of capitalism. We reject all old prejudices that the state means universal equality,—that is deceit: as long as there is exploitation there cannot be equality. The landowner cannot be the equal of the worker, nor the hungry man the equal of the well-fed. The apparatus which was called the state and before which people stand motionless with superstitious respect and belief in the old fairy tales that this is a national government—this apparatus the proletariat discards and says: that is a bourgeois lie. We have taken this apparatus away from the capitalists, taken it for ourselves. With this apparatus or with a club we shall smash all exploitation, and when no possibility of exploitation remains on the earth, when there are no more owners of land, owners of factories, when it will no longer be true that some eat their fill while others starve—only then, when no such possibility remains, will we scrap this apparatus. Then there will be no state, there will be no exploitation. This is the view of our communist party."

In the utopian *The State and Revolution* Lenin had promised that the state would begin to wither away immediately the Bolsheviks seized the Russian state. Now he postponed that consummation until the Greek Calends, until "no possibility of exploitation remains on earth."

In conclusion, Lenin told the Sverdlov students that "I hope to return to this question in subsequent lectures—again and again." Did he wish to hurl another brick at the thin-glass utopia of *The State and Revolution*? He actually returned to the university on August 29, 1919, but, according to the editors of his *Collected Works*, no record of the second lecture exists.[7] This might have been by oversight or by design. What more was there to say after he had scrapped one of his major theoretical books when it still stood high in the curriculum of compulsory studies?

Two souls coexisted in Lenin's breast, that of the theorist-propagandist and that of the statesman, and the twain apparently never met, for, if they had, peaceful coexistence would have become impossible. His actions were untrammeled by abstractions. His abstractions lived in an unreal world apart from his actions.

Were his tireless prophecies on the early advent of the world revolution one of his abstractions, like his insistence in 1917 on the imminence of the death of the state? He repeated the refrain on July 20, 1919, in response to questions of the United Press. "Capitalism," he asserted, "is ripe and overripe. It has outlived itself. . . . The collapse of capitalism is unavoidable. . . . *The Soviet Republic* has arrived to take its place." He proclaimed that "the triumph of the International Soviet Republic is assured."

Lenin did not believe in peaceful coexistence in the real world. He posed the eternal question, the question that implied struggle: "Kto kovo." Who whom? Who would destroy whom? His answer was: Communism would destroy capitalism. He omitted the date.

Meanwhile, and in conclusion, he offered the United Press some humor: Soviet Russia would run a race with America or any other country. "A little illustration," Lenin wrote, of capitalism's suppression of freedom: "the American bourgeoisie misleads the people, boasting of freedom, equality, and democracy in its country. But neither this nor any other bourgeoisie, no government in the world, can accept, it is afraid to accept, competition with our government on the basis of real freedom, equality, and democracy: suppose a treaty grants our government and any other government a free exchange of views . . . pamphlets in the name of the government in any language and containing the text of laws of the given country, the text of its

[7] *Ibid.*, editorial note, p. 787.

constitution, and an explanation of the superiority of the given country. Not a single bourgeois country in the world would dare to enter into such a peaceful, civilized, free, equal and democratic agreement with us. Why? Because all, except the Soviet governments, exist by reason of their oppression and deception of the masses."[8]

This was before the age of the iron curtain, the Berlin wall, Soviet jamming, and other communist devices which hamper free exchanges. Some democracies add their own devices.

In *The State and Revolution* Lenin declared that freedom and the state were irreconcilable. Now that he had abandoned the idea of state withering, he also buried the idea of the incompatibility of liberty and the state. The Soviet state, he said, was democratic. In fact, in a written interview with Isaac Don Levine of the Chicago *Daily News* on October 5, 1919, Lenin went further. Replying to a question, he affirmed in English in his own handwriting, "Yes, the Soviet government is the most democratic government of all governments in the world. We are willing to prove it."[9]

How could he have proved it?

XXVIII. COLD VICTORY

IN THE AUTUMN of 1919 Admiral Kolchak's army counted 103,000 men; "the strength of the Bolshevik forces was approximately the same." The figure and the estimate are General Denikin's.[1] They are accepted with a grain of salt and a dash of skepticism because desertions and inactivity on wide segments of the so-called front would have reduced the number of troops engaged in combat.

The northern theater of operations, centering on Murmansk and Archangel, Denikin wrote, had always been of "secondary importance" owing to "the wild nature" of the arctic wastes and the consequent communications and transport difficulties.

Yudenich, in September, 1919, when he approached Petrograd, had an army of 17,000; the Red Army opposing him was 27,000 strong "and could bring up considerable reinforcements."[2]

Denikin himself commanded 93,000 warriors in October, 1919. The Bolsheviks confronted him with 130,000. At one time, however, he had 98,000 soldiers under him, the Reds 140,000 to 160,000. These were on duty in a

---

[8] *Ibid.*, pp. 402-405.
[9] Photostat helpfully given me by Isaac Don Levine.
[1] General A. I. Denikin, *Ocherki Russkoi Smuti*, Vol. 5 (Berlin), p. 216. (The end of the manuscript is dated Brussels, 1926.)
[2] *Ibid.*, p. 224.

vast area from Orel in central Russia to the Caucasus more than a thousand miles away.[3] On the Soviet side, moreover, the number of men in contact with the enemy would have constituted less than half of those in training, in reserve, and in transit. Harsh climate, shortage of armaments, and roadlessness and crippled railroads further diminished the intensity of battlefield activity.

By November, 1919, Yudenich vanished. Denikin describes the circumstances that led to the end of the threat to Petrograd which had so alarmed Lenin. Yudenich recognized Kolchak as his "Supreme Ruler." Kolchak communicated directly and only with Yudenich, not with the government of which Yudenich was the Defense Minister. The government resented the slight and resented Yudenich. Yudenich had one army. General Rodzianko commanded it. Yudenich was Rodzianko's "Commander in Chief of the Front" but with no function not exercised by Rodzianko. Hot friction developed between the two commanders. A third military man in the Yudenich camp, "Father" Bulak-Balakhovich (who preferred killing Jews and robbing peasants to fighting the Bolsheviks), joined N. N. Ivanov, a minister in the Yudenich government, and plotted Yudenich's overthrow. The Estonians abetted the intrigue. Rodzianko arrested Bulak-Balakhovich. Bulak fled to the Estonians. The Estonians withstood British and Yudenich pressures to support the military campaign against Petrograd. If Yudenich won, if Kolchak won, there would be no Estonia. On the other hand, Soviet Foreign Commissar Georgi Chicherin, on August 18, 1919, offered Estonia negotiations with a view to peace and independence.

Despite these unfavorable omens, Yudenich hurled his little army at Petrograd on September 15. He advanced. The Estonians obstructed. In the midst of the operation, Yudenich dismissed Rodzianko. Denikin hints that each commander coveted the glory of entry into Petrograd. The Reds defended the city. On November 1, Yudenich retreated. Estonia concluded a truce with Moscow in December. Yudenich vanished.

Denikin was next. He writes that not only his reserves but also a part of his active army was "diverted to 'the internal front' for the pacification of revolts by Makhno and other 'atamans' which flooded" vast areas of the Ukraine. Makhno, with, Denikin estimates, 10,000 to 40,000 men, roamed the White rear capturing supplies, cutting communications, and defeating large contingents that otherwise would have faced the Red Army. When the Bolshevik forces re-formed for a counteroffensive, Denikin had no reserves. In a nine-day swaying battle between Budenny's Red rough riders and General Shkuro's White cavalry, the Whites were pushed across to the right bank of the Don where Budenny pursued and hacked them into useless fragments. Meanwhile, the main Soviet army, outnumbering Denikin two to one, drove him out of Orel.

Denikin now encountered destructive difficulties with the national minorities of the North Caucasus and of the Caucasus to the south. "Soviet gold,"

[3] *Ibid.*, pp. 230-232.

he thought, "carried full weight." There were weightier reasons. "The British did not help." Peasants rebelled wherever Denikin trod. A report to Denikin described the retreat: "robbery and speculation"; "chaotic evacuation complicated by rushing waves of refugees"; "the army, as a fighting force, does not exist."

"Great and varied were the sins of the Volunteer Army"—Denikin's army —he admits, "but of course no greater than" those of other White armies "and of that—the Caucasian—commanded by Baron Wrangel." Personal feuds plagued the White forces. In an angry farewell confrontation between Wrangel and Denikin at Taganrog, Wrangel declared, "The Volunteer Army has discredited itself by thefts and violence. All is lost here. . . . A different flag is necessary. . . . But not a monarchist flag."[4] Exit Denikin. Wrangel took command of the remnants.

Admiral Kolchak also went the way of all Whites. Pushed by the Red Army, impeded by peasant and workingman revolts, he abandoned his March-to-May, 1919, gains in the Volga Basin and withdrew into the Urals, then into Siberia. Here not only Russians but Czechoslovaks harassed the "Supreme Ruler." The Czechoslovaks still held the Trans-Siberian Railway and decided who could use it. Some of them made a financial profit out of this advantage. As he fled eastward, even Kolchak needed the Czechoslovaks' permission to board a train. They kept the trains running, if not on time, at least running—which was a political and technical miracle in a region where murders, burnings of villages, sacking of factories, theft of fuel, confiscation of food supplies, and armed attempts by leaders to hold sleeping cars for comfort and early escape had ceased to be news. The Czechoslovaks' first concern by October, 1919, was to get out of this cold caldron, reach Vladivostok, and thence their European homes. They consequently gave priority to the transportation of their own troops and accumulated belongings. Kolchak's personnel took second place.

Finally, Kolchak received a special car which carried him from Omsk, his former capital, more than a thousand miles eastward to Irkutsk. From there he sent a "most urgent" telegram, dated "The Train of the Supreme Ruler, November 25, 1919," instructing his Foreign Minister Sazonov in Paris to ask the Czechoslovak government in Prague to recall its representatives in Siberia and "substitute others who can at least behave decently."[5] He also complained to Generals Knox and Janin, the British and French military chiefs in Siberia.

The admiral was pitiful. He told the Prime Minister of his government, "I am breathing new life into Russia . . . and will stop at nothing in pacifying the Czechs, our prisoners of war."[6] Kolchak was breathing his last. Early in January, 1920, a multi-party workers' group seized Irkutsk. On January 4

---

[4] *Ibid.*, p. 260.
[5] *Posledniye Dni Kolchakovshchini,* Centrarkhiv (Moscow-Leningrad, 1925), pp. 113-114.
[6] *Ibid.*, p. 140.

Kolchak resigned as Supreme Ruler and appointed Denikin, already defeated, his successor in Europe and Ataman Semenov, the Japanese puppet, his heir in eastern Siberia.

Now the Czechoslovaks feared for their own fate. They did not wish to become prisoners of the Reds. They accordingly made a deal with the new workers' authority in Irkutsk: the workers would permit trains carrying Czechoslovaks to pass unhindered toward Vladivostok; the Czechs would allow the workers to capture Kolchak's car. Some say the Czechs had obtained French General Janin's approval of the bargain. Peter Fleming, in *The Fate of Admiral Kolchak* (New York, 1963), states that "General Janin and [Czechoslovak] General Syrovy were responsible" for Kolchak's arrest and surrender to the workers' council.

The workers' authority in Irkutsk sentenced Kolchak to death. One report has it that Lenin wanted Kolchak brought to Moscow. The Irkutsk Revolutionary Military Soviet declared, however, that Kolchak supporters were preparing to seize the city and liberate the admiral. This was probably an excuse.

Early on February 7 the Bolshevik executioner went to Kolchak's cell. The admiral heard the death sentence and asked whether he might smoke his pipe. Permission was granted. The executioner took from Kolchak a handkerchief with a knot holding a poison pill. Kolchak said, "I beg you to inform my wife, who lives in Paris, that I bless my son."

"I will do so if I don't forget," the executioner replied.

Shortly after 4 A.M., a semicircle of Red Army men fired twice at the admiral. His corpse was pushed under the ice of the Angara River.[7]

More favored by fate, General Denikin traveled in a British ship to Constantinople.

The Russian civil war (1917-1921) was a protracted, expensive, disastrous enterprise. It ruined the nation's economy and piled endless new sufferings on a people already sorely tried by three and a half years of world war for which they were ill-prepared and in which they were poorly led by a rotten monarchy and bureaucracy. The war of Whites against Reds exposed many millions to deadly epidemics. It depleted Russia's blood, brains, and treasure. Hordes of orphaned waifs (besprizorniye) and uprooted adults roamed city and countryside and robbed and killed for sustenance and devilment. The nation had lived so long in the embrace of death that violence became more normal than tranquillity. One life more or less made little difference. This attitude made a difference of tens of thousands of lives.

The civil war left a legacy of lawlessness and physical exhaustion. It therefore accentuated two conflicting yet complementary qualities of the Russian psyche: the penchant to anarchy and the habit of subservience. Bolshevism had to curb the one and reinforce the other. Lenin drew attention to a third aspect of the national mentality: "our common weakness, perhaps connected with the Slav character,—we are not sufficiently stable and steadfast in the

[7] S. P. Melgunov, *Tragediya Admirala Kolchaka (The Tragedy of Admiral Kolchak)*, Part Three, Vol. Two (Belgrade, 1931), pp. 172-175.

pursuit of the goals we set ourselves."[8] This too explains the seesaw nature of the civil war. People swung from Red to White and back with the greatest of ease in accordance with self-interest and circumstances. Only a minority heard the voice of principle.

"The chief difficulties are already behind us," Lenin told the Seventh All-Russian Congress of Soviets on December 5, 1919. But twice before, he warned, once in the east, again in the south, they had allowed the enemy to escape and fight another day. "There is not a shadow of a doubt," that the Western powers, "in a bandits' alliance of international and Russian capitalism," will again intervene and attempt to restore a government "of landlords and capitalists." But Bolshevism had allies; "we regard ourselves and can only regard ourselves as one of the squads of the international army of the proletariat, in fact a squad which occupied a forward position not at all thanks to its development or preparation but thanks to peculiar circumstances in Russia . . . therefore, the victory of the socialist revolution could only be considered as final when it became the victory of the proletariat in at least several advanced nations." Here the idea of world revolution was used to dampen careless optimism and, optimistically, to foster stamina; the battle was not yet over, and would not be over until Germany or/and France and/or England went communist. Lenin did not yet know that communism could win power only where the "peculiar conditions in Russia"—economic and political backwardness and the dislocation of world war or civil war— were reproduced.

Meanwhile, even their partial victory was due to support from the Western workers who had prevented the bourgeois governments from bringing their full forces to bear against Russian Bolshevism: "we have won over from England, France, and America their workers and peasants."

Meanwhile, likewise, they needed the dictatorship. "We did not paint sweet pictures for our peasant, that he could abandon the capitalist system without the iron discipline and a firm government of the working class. . . . We said it frankly: dictatorship is a harsh, heavy and even bloody word, but we said that the dictatorship of the workers would bring him"—the peasant—"the overthrow of the yoke of the exploiters, and we have been proved right." Thus Lenin spoke to the Soviet Congress on December 5; and the next day he added, "Terror and the Cheka are an absolutely necessary thing. . . . Our Cheka is organized very well. . . . We are told that the soviets seldom meet and are not re-elected with sufficient frequency." Moreover, it had been charged that the Central Executive Committee of the Soviets (VTSIK) was not convened. "Comrade Trotsky answered that beautifully by saying the VTSIK was at the front."

The Cheka worked well; the democratic soviets worked intermittently. Comrade Trotsky lived long enough to discover that soviets not convened in wartime can be ignored in peacetime.

Lenin seemed to realize at this point that his defense of terror and dicta-

[8] Lenin, *Sochineniya*, Second ed., Vol. XXIV, p. 628.

torship was bald but not educational. He had stated his policy, not the politics that justified it. To affirm endlessly, as he did in his Sverdlov University lecture and at other times, that capitalism provided neither freedom nor democracy nor equality carried little conviction to a country turned in on itself by enveloping hardships. Lenin accordingly looked back at the Constituent Assembly which met in Petrograd for one day in January, 1918. Almost two eventful years had passed since then, yet the subject interested him, perhaps troubled him. In 1918 the Social Revolutionaries (SR's) published a collection of articles in Moscow, including an essay analyzing the elections to the Constituent Assembly. Lenin now wrote a 6,000-word analysis of this analysis.[9] For some reason, he considered only the November, 1917, poll, though elections in a number of areas were held in December and January. But this did not affect his conclusions.

First, Lenin noticed that the SR author had made a mistake in adding: the total number of votes cast in November was not 36,257,960 but 36,262,-560. The discrepancy was infinitesimal. Lenin, however, politely called attention to it.

Citing the figures of N. V. Sviatitsky, the SR writer, Lenin stated that the Russian SR's had received 16,500,000 votes. The Bolsheviks garnered 9,023,963 votes—here he quoted the exact statistic—or 25 percent. The Kadets and other "parties of the landlords and bourgeoisie" received 4,620,-000 votes, or 13 percent. The Mensheviks and their allies received 4 percent.

Lenin also credited the SR's with the votes of Ukrainian and Moslem parties of similar political coloration, thus raising the SR total to 20,900,000, or 58 percent. This grouping gave the SR's a formidable appearance, but it served Lenin's purpose. He stated that, "the Bolsheviks were, at the time of the Constituent Assembly elections, the party of the proletariat, the SR's —the party of the peasantry." But the Ukrainian and Moslem SR's were by no means all peasants. Many were workers and intellectuals. Lenin, however, had to explain why in the Ukraine the SR's won 77 percent of the votes, the Bolsheviks only 10 percent. Since he could not admit that workers would not vote Bolshevik, he called all the Ukrainian SR's peasants and blocked them with the predominantly peasant SR's in central and western Russia and in the Urals and Siberia. He now felt warranted in scoffing at those who asserted that the Bolsheviks constituted a minority of the proletariat. "We hear such statements from Mensheviks (their count was 668,000 plus 700,000 to 800,000 in the Caucasus compared with 9 million for the Bolsheviks) as well as from the social traitors of the Second International."

Having thus, by statistical manipulation, scored his first point—that though the Bolsheviks were a minority in the population they were a majority of the working class—Lenin could ask, "How was such a miracle

---

[9] *Ibid.*, pp. 631-649. Also, *Ibid.*, Fourth ed., Vol. 30, pp. 230-251. Lenin's article was first published in the November-December, 1919, issue of *Kommunisticheskii Internatsional*.

possible: the victory of the Bolsheviks, with one-quarter of the votes, over the petty-bourgeois democrats in alliance (coalition) with the bourgeoisie who in combination had three-quarters of the votes?"

Lenin's reply was a brisk summary of the first two years of Soviet history. "In both capitals, Petrograd and Moscow," he said, the communists received more votes than the SR's and Kadets together. Reformist democrats to the contrary notwithstanding, "the economic and political fact" is that the city and village are unequal. This was so under capitalism and "in particular during the transition from capitalism to communism. The city cannot be the equal of the village. The village cannot be the equal of the city in the historic conditions of the present epoch."

Lenin no longer used the threadbare Bolshevik argument that the Constituent Assembly had been dispersed because circumstances changed between the time of the nominations and the elections. He wished to establish a far more important proposition: that a majority among the workers gave the communists greater rights than a majority among the entire population. "The city inescapably *leads* the village," he wrote. "The village inevitably *follows the city*. The only question is *which class* of the 'city' classes can lead the village." His answer, naturally, was: the working class. "Further, the Bolsheviks . . . had on their side . . . 'the fighting fist' in the capital cities. To have the decisive superiority of forces at the decisive place at the decisive moment—this 'law' of military success is also the law of political success, especially in that furious, seething war of classes which is called a revolution."

Moreover, Lenin showed that in the army "the Bolsheviks received *slightly fewer* votes than the SR's. The army, in other words, was by October-November, 1917, *half Bolshevik*. Without this we could not have won. But, with almost half the votes in the army as a whole, we had a preponderant superiority on the fronts *near the capitals*."

The political general was, in fact, writing his dispatch, for the record, on the military-political victory of November 7-8, 1917. Here, too, the numerical majority mattered less to Lenin than bigger battalions in a few key spots. Those bigger battalions, however, aided the revolution by their apathy, their neutrality. Only a tiny fraction of the pro-Bolshevik soldiers and sailors sufficed to topple the Kerensky regime.

Though this explained the success of the November 7-8 coup, Lenin set himself a larger task: to explain why the Bolsheviks had retained power. He wrote, "*State power in the hands of one class, the proletariat, can and must become a weapon for drawing the nonproletarian toiling masses to the side of the proletariat, a weapon for winning those masses away from the bourgeois and petty bourgeois parties.*"

The "petty-bourgeois parties" were, in Lenin's mind, the Mensheviks, and, chiefly, the SR's. Several hours after the Bolsheviks seized the state, Lenin said, they used the state to attract the peasants away from the SR's by adopting the SR agrarian program, "word for word."

The SR's, Lenin declared, were indignant. "They screamed that, 'The Bolsheviks have stolen our program,' but people only laughed at the SR's for this: that party is good which had to be beaten and driven out of the government in order to carry out everything in its program that is revolutionary and useful to the toilers!"

Lenin was revealing his big cynical design: he used the SR agrarian program and brought the Left SR's into the Bolshevik government with the intention of driving them out of the government as soon as he considered it strong enough as a result of the stratagem. Lenin was always, before the revolution and after, intolerant of coalitions. A coalition, or rule by two or three, is incompatible with a dictatorship, or rule by one.

How Lenin's design worked in the provinces may be seen from a typical example: Tula. "For the speedy victory of the Soviet government in the counties of the province, the formation of a bloc between the Bolsheviks and the Left SR's had serious significance. On December 23, 1917, the Tula Left SR's announced their recognition of the Soviet government and submission to its decrees." This followed the entry of the Left SR's into the central Soviet government in Moscow. "Knowing the instability of the Left SR's," the account continues,[10] "the Bolshevik party entered into a temporary bloc with them because a considerable section of the peasantry still followed them. This bloc weakened the strength of the opponents of the Soviet government, struck a blow at the anti-Soviet parties, the Mensheviks and Right SR's, and helped rally the working masses of the village around the Soviet government and the communist party." The coalition was a temporary device to destroy the partner in the coalition.

But Lenin did not see himself as a historian when he wrote his December, 1919, analysis of the November, 1917, Constituent Assembly election. He related that election to the civil war. "See what regions proved to be least Bolshevik," he wrote. In the East Ural and Siberian provinces the Bolsheviks received 12 percent of the votes. In the Ukraine, 10 percent. In the Great Russian Volga-Black Earth region, 16 percent. "And these were the provinces where the governments of Kolchak and Denikin retained power for months and months." In those parts the peasants wavered. When the Bolsheviks gave them land, demobilized the army, and ended the war they sided with the Bolsheviks. The Brest-Litovsk peace treaty "offended . . . their deepest petty-bourgeois feelings, their patriotism. The dictatorship of the proletariat was especially disliked by the peasantry where the grain surpluses were largest and when the Bolsheviks showed that they would insist on the delivery of those surpluses to the state at fixed prices." Then the peasants of the Urals, Siberia, and the Ukraine turned to Kolchak and Denikin. Later still, the peasants realized the hollowness of the democracy of the Whites and rebelled against them.

[10] *Uprochnenie Sovietskoi Vlasti v Tulskoi Gubernii (The Stabilization of the Soviet Government in Tula Province), A Collection of Documents and Materials for 1918* (Tula, 1961), pp. 4-5.

Given the unreliability of the peasants, Lenin concluded that the proletariat, working near the centers of capitalist industrial and political power, "expresses the real interests of the overwhelming majority of the toilers under capitalism," and could, "even when it constitutes a minority of the population," overthrow the bourgeoisie and then attract the support of "semi-proletarians and petty-bourgeois" peasants who do not yet understand "the purposes" and "the inevitability" of the dictatorship of the proletariat.

Lenin had now explained why parliamentary elections did not interest him: minorities under communist leadership were entitled to employ their strength against majorities; a minority government would find the means of managing and neutralizing the majority. Lenin's honesty shines by comparison with the intellectual gyrations of his apologists who have endeavored over the decades to demonstrate the "democracy" of the dictatorship.

But dictatorship in itself neither feeds nor warms. "You know," Lenin told a meeting on December 19, 1919, "how very much our working class hungers and freezes." There might be comfort in company: "And we know," he continued, "that not only has backward Russia . . . been ravaged, but also the most advanced and richest countries, the countries of the victors, France and America for instance, have reached a state of complete ruin." Bolshevik leaders habitually seek solace in comparisons; this time, America had caught up with Russia in ruination. The refrain was the same; his last sentence read: "Notwithstanding all hardships and sacrifices, we ourselves will arrive at, and bring the workers of all countries to, complete victory over capitalism."

"Applause," the record reports.

Photographs of Lenin in this cold, hungry winter of 1919-20 show him at work in the Kremlin—carrying logs. The communist party of Moscow and other cities had been organizing "Communist Subbotniks" or sabbaths on which leaders, laborers, officials, and intellectuals did socially useful manual work. Lenin, in June, 1919, wrote a pamphlet enthusiastically approving the innovation, became a participant himself, and on December 20, 1919, made a speech about this welcome institution. Their ruling party had changed its name to "communist," he said. The reason, as he had once put it, was a wish to doff the shirt soiled by the pro-war Social Democrats of Europe and wear a white one. But the name was without content. "From the expropriation of the landlords and capitalists we have merely received the possibility of building the most primitive forms of socialism, but in this there is still nothing communistic." Soviet economy contained only the "very weak embryo of socialism" side by side with the "overwhelming domination of old economic forms," to wit, private farming and "the wildest, unrestrained speculation." Even the beginnings of what he called socialism were threatened by the louse. Shortage of soap, limited bathing facilities, and dirty living quarters provoked a population explosion of lice; the result—widespread typhus. Soldiers and civilians beguiled their leisure hours with the popular sport of louse-hunting. "Either the louse will defeat socialism," Lenin had said on December 5, 1919, "or socialism will conquer the louse."

With peasants, speculator rats, and billions of lice biting into the vitals of socialism, at last one communist phenomenon emerged; it was, Lenin asserted, the communist sabbaths, "that is, unpaid, large-scale work for the common good by individuals without rate fixing by any government, by any state." This was "communism in action." It helped the state and it helped to flush out impure elements and impure influences which had found a home in the communist party during the period of "disintegrating capitalism."[11]

Since Lenin, only the millions of slave laborers in Soviet concentration camps have performed unpaid, large-scale work. For them every day for years was a "communist sabbath."

As 1919 came to an end Lenin was able to say in a letter to "the workers and peasants of the Ukraine" that they had won a victory. Denikin, their invader, had been defeated. They could therefore ponder their political future: "Should the Ukraine be a separate and independent Ukrainian Soviet Socialist Republic bound in a union (federation) with the Russian Soviet Socialist Federated Republic, or should the Ukraine merge with Russia in one soviet republic?" The Ukraine could be independent "and in that case exactly what federational tie should be established between that republic and Russia?"

We, Lenin added, "are opposed to nationalist enmity, nationalist discord, national isolationism. We are internationalists. . . . We are striving for a close union and complete merger of all the workers and peasants of all nations of the world in one universal Soviet Republic."[12] He left the Ukrainians little choice. They joined in a federation with Russia.

XXIX. ŎALES OF A HUNTER

THE Hall of Trade Unions, formerly the Hall of Nobles, in Moscow is packed with tense spectators. In the center of the stage sits the Supreme Military Tribunal. To its right, in a guarded box, are a group of prisoners; to its left— Nikolai V. Krilenko, chief Soviet prosecutor, in green hunter's costume. He stalks his prey, bares his teeth, screws up his face in grimaces of hate. He demands the death sentence for all defendants. He was the outstanding actor in the first Moscow show trials in the late 1920's and early 1930's. In 1937 he himself succumbed to the Stalin terror. Arrested and imprisoned, he died in 1940.

Krilenko was a passionate prosecutor, a passionate chess player, a passionate mountaineer, and a passionate hunter. He took Lenin hunting. Hunting

[11] Lenin, *Sochineniya*, Second ed., Vol. XXIV, pp. 650-654.
[12] *Ibid.*, pp. 654-660.

was a favorite pastime of the nobility in the tsarist period. Lenin resorted to it for relaxation. "The best thing about this is that here for two days there hasn't been a single telephone call," Lenin remarked to Krilenko as they plodded through the woods and swamps of Smolensk chasing white part-ridge and black grouse, "not a single message, not a single question."[1]

Nevertheless, says Krilenko, Lenin could not wash away city thoughts. He himself would initiate political conversations. "Of course," Krilenko added, Lenin "was not a total stranger to the excitement of sport, to the so-called 'passion of the hunt,' but it played a negligible role in him." He wanted a rest for his weary brain. His health was worse.

Once Lenin and Krilenko went fox hunting. The Russian method in this aristocratic sport consists in forcing the fox into a very large circle marked by red flags from which there is only one exit and, by handclapping and yells, to impel the fox to that exit where the hunter waits. The fox came straight at Lenin, who did not notice him because the animal's bright red fur was cov-ered with snow fallen from the spruce trees. When Lenin became aware of the fox's presence he was transfixed and "stared . . . and stared . . . and did not shoot." The fox looked at Lenin as he slowly raised his gun, then lifting his tail, made off like lightning.

"Why didn't you shoot?" Krilenko exclaimed.

"He was so beautiful and pretty," Lenin apologized. "I'm not a hunter but a shoemaker."

For a summer hunt Krilenko and Lenin had to travel twenty-five miles by peasant carts. Lenin, in blue blouse with a leather strap around his waist and his famous gray cap, sat, somewhat bent, beside the driver of the first cart; Krilenko and a companion were in the second.

"Who is that in front? Isn't it Lenin?" the driver asked Krilenko.

"No, no," Krilenko retorted.

"Well, if you say no it's not," the peasant said, but Krilenko felt he was skeptical. "The fact itself," Krilenko wrote in his 1928 memoirs, "that the leader of the world revolution, Lenin in person, Chairman of the Sovnarkom, the terror of the world bourgeoisie, the 'dictator' as the world bourgeois press pictured him, was being jolted up and down in a simple peasant cart appar-ently did not seem at all strange or incomprehensible to the driver."

On that hunt Lenin and Krilenko spent two nights in a peasant's hayloft. Lenin allowed nobody to serve him and did not complain though he was clearly fatigued. Early one morning Krilenko woke Lenin as agreed. Lenin said he had not slept and was racked by a severe headache. But he would not hear of postponing or canceling the trip into the swamp.

Lenin tried desperately. He imitated the call of birds, and sat patiently in a field shack waiting for game. But his bag was always meager. His biggest wish, to kill a wolf, Krilenko reports, was never fulfilled. In failure, Krilenko wrote, even the most cultured hunters swear; Lenin never.

[1] *Vospominaniya*, Vol. 2, pp. 425-429.

Jan Ernestovich Rudzutak also hunted with Lenin. Rudzutak, son of a
Latvian farm laborer, himself a shepherd and farm laborer, rose, thanks to his
energy, organizational ability, revolutionary zeal, and communist orthodoxy,
to the highest ranks of the Russian Communist Party (Bolsheviks) including
membership from 1926 to 1932 in the supreme Politburo. "Rudzutak was a
crystal clear and to the end a sincere communist," wrote *Pravda* of August
15, 1962, the seventy-fifth anniversary of his birth. "In 1938, in the period
of the cult of personality"—euphemism for Stalin terror—"he became a victim of unwarranted repression"—read: he was executed. "At the Twenty-
second Congress of the Soviet Communist Party [October, 1961], Comrade
N. S. Khrushchev mentioned the dear name of J. E. Rudzutak too as one of
those loyal Leninist and prominent leaders of the party and government who
were killed though innocent."

Lenin knew Rudzutak in 1920 as secretary of the Soviet trade-union organization. They made appointments Saturday evenings in the winter of that
year to hunt on Sundays. At 4 A.M. Lenin would wake him with a telephone
call. Lenin, in felt boots, a black horse-leather jacket, hunter's accouterments,
a package of sandwiches, a tin box filled with small pieces of sugar and tea,
stood at Rudzutak's door by the time he was ready. Once, after a freezing day
of unsuccessful hunting, their auto-sleigh broke down some forty miles from
Moscow. It was already dark. They decided to walk the mile and a half to the
next railroad station. Loaded with ammunition they dug their way through
the snowdrifts. En route they stopped at a village soviet to telephone the
Kremlin. Some persons standing around the office thought they recognized
Lenin but to make sure, Rudzutak wrote in his reminiscences,[2] they asked for
the visitors' identity papers. Rudzutak presented his and vouched for his companion. As they were leaving, a member of the soviet put the direct question,
"Aren't you Lenin?"

"Yes, yes," Lenin replied.

The member thereupon drove the hunters to the railroad station. The Moscow railroad authorities, on the telephone, offered to send immediately a locomotive and passenger car. Lenin refused; a freight train was due in forty
minutes and he would take his place in that, if permitted.

Lenin and Rudzutak were accommodated in the caboose. The train personnel told them that "of the twenty or more freight cars in the train, about
ten had been left behind at various stops on the road because of hot boxes or
for other reasons." At the first station, railroad workers entered the caboose,
shook Lenin's hand, and drew him into conversation. They objected to the
armed squads that were confiscating grain in the villages. (Most railwaymen
were part-time peasants.)

One Sunday Lenin shot a rabbit. He rushed over to see his prey. Meanwhile another rabbit appeared but got away. Rudzutak censured Lenin:
"Why, you, you chase after the dead and let the living escape."

[2] *Ibid.*, pp. 430-431.

"I won't do it again," Lenin promised.

Whenever they looked in on a peasant's hut, Rudzutak recalled, Lenin inquired about the details of daily life and needs of the people. "He could learn as well as teach."

Now and then Stephan Gil, his chauffeur, drove Lenin out into the countryside to places he did not know; Lenin liked to talk with peasants and feel their political pulse; it recorded their economic heartbeats. Once, in the village of Bogdanikha, Gil stopped the car. A crowd gathered immediately. Any man traveling by automobile would be regarded as an important official. The peasants began putting questions to Lenin and making complaints. Above the din a booming voice was heard. It came from an old, gray-haired muzhik. "Listen, folks," he shouted. "Here you have before you the top Bolshevik, Lenin. Let's tell him about our hard lot. Who, better than he, can help us?"[3]

Everybody talked at once. Lenin said, "This is not good, comrades. If you all talk I won't understand anything. Choose one person who can tell me everything in orderly fashion. And you listen, and if he omits something or makes a mistake—straighten him out."

They chose the gray head.

"He recounted to Lenin the scandalous goings-on in the village." It appeared that the village soviet had taken from the poor peasants all their grain and seed. "People were left without a pound of flour or a single potato."

Lenin asked for a detailed written statement, with names. "There are enemies at work here," he told the crowd. "They are striving to create peasant discontent. We shall investigate."

Three hours later, after visiting neighboring villages, Lenin was back and received the written statement. He forwarded it, with comments, to the Cheka. Subsequent events demonstrated to Lenin, unless he knew it at the time, that the "enemy" was the law; if the members of the soviet had not delivered the village quota of grain, even though that meant depriving even the poorest, the Cheka would have been barking at their heels. They would have been "the enemy."

Gora, the adopted son of Lenin's sister Anna, often accompanied Lenin on a hunt with Dr. Dmitri Ulyanov, chauffeur Gil, and a secret service man. For hours, he writes,[4] they would wander in the woods looking for wild fowl and rabbits. When Lenin missed, Dmitri lost his temper and scolded his brother with a vehemence that "frightened him after he had cooled off." Lenin listened contritely. Lenin, Gora says, was not a particularly good shot or a passionate huntsman, but he enjoyed the change of scene. He liked to get away from it all. In fact, he had to get away from it all. His ill-health was becoming a source of worry to himself and his comrades, including Krupskaya.

---

[3] *Ibid.*, pp. 432-435.
[4] *Ibid.*, p. 137.

XXX. RUSSIAN VERSUS POLE: THE GRAND DESIGN

AT THE BIRTH of 1920, after 784 days of Bolshevik revolution, everything in Soviet Russia and everybody, including Lenin, was worn out and run down. "How old are you?" Mikha Tskhakaya, a Georgian Bolshevik, asked Lenin in Geneva in October, 1916.

"I'm an old man, an old man," Lenin replied, "I am already forty-six."

Now, in 1920, he was fifty and much older. He had four years to live, and serious illness reduced them to less than three working years, years of brain-busting economic problems, murderous famine, war, disputes, and disappointments.

In January, 1920, Lenin wrote his fourth outline (the other three were prepared between October, 1919, and December, 1919) of a pamphlet on the dictatorship of the proletariat.[1] He was too busy or too tired to begin writing the text. Perhaps, however, there was another restraint. Perhaps he recalled his comments on the death of Friedrich Engels in 1895. Marx and Engels, he had declared, "became socialists after being democrats, and the democratic feeling of *hatred* for arbitrary political rule was extraordinarily strong in them."[2] Lenin never doubted the need for dictatorship. But it was becoming increasingly difficult to clothe the iron idol of Soviet dictatorship in the flowing robes of liberty. By 1919 and 1920 Lenin could not have been unaware of the illegal assaults on the soviets and all other forms of proletarian democracy. His 1920 outline on dictatorship included a note reading: "The successes of democracy: congresses, meetings, the press, religion, women, the oppression of nationalities." These were intended themes for his pamphlet. He knew the congresses and meetings were manipulated. The press was manacled. Religion was ridiculed. Women were free to work as hard as men. The nationalities, to be sure, had won a new freedom. But in a June 22, 1920, Politburo decree, written by Lenin, Moscow's agents in Turkestan were ordered to transfer power "gradually but undeviatingly" to the local soviets "under the control of reliable communists." Those communists were either Russians or took their instructions from Moscow. In general, the decree concluded, the goal was "the overthrow of feudalism, not communism."[3] The nationalities had a long row to hoe to democracy.

As 1920 dawned, Lenin expected peace. The Whites had been defeated. "Attempts are being made to incite Poland against us, but these efforts will fail, and the time is not remote when we will conclude peace with everybody, though they say they refuse to recognize us."[4] In every article and speech

[1] Lenin, *Sochineniya*, Second ed., Vol. XXV, pp. 5-12.
[2] *Ibid.*, Vol. I, p. 415.
[3] *Leninskii Sbornik*, Vol. XXXVI, p. 106.
[4] *Pravda*, Feb. 13, 1920.

384

Lenin boasted of the Soviet peace agreement with little Estonia: "We have cut a window through to Europe." The capitalists of all countries, he claimed, had obstructed this assumption of relations, "but we defeated them." After that first victory more would follow, "opening for us the possibility of the exchange of goods with Europe and America."[5] The Soviet people were hungry for hope.

Lenin now concentrated on the task of raising his country from the dead. He spoke often of the need to transfer "from the front of blood to the bloodless front" of labor, the front of bread. "In one place," he said, "a peasant has bread, but his neighbor is hungry, yet he prefers to sell the bread to the hungry man for a thousand roubles rather than lend it to the workers' government."

"Quite right," a heckler exclaimed.

It was not right, Lenin retorted. "We say, 'Each for all, and somehow we will get along without God.' " He asked the peasants to lend their grain to the government "because for the time being we have nothing to give in exchange, and colored pieces of paper are not money."[6]

This was the crux of the Soviet economic situation in 1920. This was the heart problem of war communism.

Lenin had kept his eye on economic questions even in the thick of war. In 1919 he encouraged the formation of consumers' cooperatives with predominantly working-class membership. Producers' cooperatives and communes appeared in villages. Producers' cooperatives sprang up in cities too. In one instance a producers' cooperative was organized in Petrograd by the owners of a printing plant so as to elude nationalization. Lenin ordered the Cheka to liquidate the cooperative and transfer the plant to the Petrograd Soviet.[7] In September, 1919, Lenin urged the chairman of the Petrograd Soviet to excavate shale deposits near the city for their fuel oil content ("The bourgeoisie should be mobilized for this, let them live in mud huts"), and inquired whether sugar could be made from sawdust. He likewise wrote Gleb Krzizhanovsky about the use of the immense peat bogs outside Petrograd as raw material for the generation of electricity. He broached the idea of an "electrified" Russia ("in ten—twenty?—years") operating as a grid and receiving current here from shale, there from peat, here from waterfalls, there from petroleum. "Let's talk about this on the telephone," he concluded the second letter to Krzizhanovsky.[8] Lenin also wrote enthusiastically to a man who proposed a newspaper "without paper": radio.

Lenin was always alive to the value of propaganda media for communist theories. But he would not allow theory to interfere with practice. Communist theorists were insisting that communism required a directorate of

[5] Lenin, *op. cit.*, Second ed., Vol. XXV, p. 24.
[6] *Ibid.*, p. 15.
[7] *Leninskii Sbornik*, Vol. XXXVI, pp. 102-103.
[8] Lenin, *op. cit.*, Fourth ed., Vol. 35, pp. 371-372.

three or five or seven to manage a factory. Lenin, however, believed in one-man management. Again and again in 1920 he vetoed the proposal of multiple managers and verbally chastised its proponents. Even seven workers in a collegium, he told the central trade-union organization on March 15, 1920, would not be tantamount to the broad participation of workers in the conduct of an enterprise. "Stop whining and be grownups," he implored his audience. What industry needed was bourgeois specialists, not proletarian collegiums.

Lenin was expert at mixing a dash of hard truth with a dose of lurid propaganda. Addressing the All-Russian Congress of Toiling Cossacks ("toiling" took the curse off "Cossacks") on March 1, 1920, he boasted that all the great powers—England, France, America, Japan—in fact Winston Churchill's "fourteen countries," with their "millions" of soldiers and their fabulous resources—were defeated by ruined Russia because "we had allies" in the enemy camp: the soldiers who refused to fight Bolshevism. "And we have never concealed the fact that our revolution is only the beginning, that it will arrive at a successful conclusion only when we inflame the entire world with such a revolution, and we fully understood that the capitalists were the enraged enemies of the Soviet government." The struggle was not ended. The struggle against Soviet Russia was a rehearsal "with fire and sword" for the last decisive battle. The imperialists were preparing. Already "three-quarters of Finland has been bought up by the American billionaires. Only the Russian Socialist Republic has raised the banner of true freedom, and throughout the world sympathy is moving in its favor." Thanks to such pressures, Germany and the Allies had lifted the blockade of Russia in January, 1920. In all countries, "in Paris, London, etc., . . . in all cities, the bourgeois intellectuals are demonstrating under the slogan, 'Hands Off Soviet Russia.' . . . That is why they lifted the blockade. They could not restrain Estonia, and we signed a peace with her and can trade with the entire world. We have opened a window to the civilized world. We enjoy the sympathy of the majority of labor, and the bourgeoisie is worried about how it can initiate trade with Russia more speedily."

All was not well in the capitalist world, Lenin told the Cossacks. "Japan and America are on the eve of war, and there is no possibility at all of preventing such a war in which more tens of millions will die and twenty million will be mutilated." France and England also were at swords' points over colonies. "True," Lenin conceded, "they might still incite Poland against us." But he reassured the Poles. He knew their hatred of the old Russia which thrice helped slice them into three parts. "Therefore we understand the hate which fills the soul of a Pole, and we say to them that never shall our army . . . cross the frontier where they now stand." But if Poland, stoked by France, made war on Russia, "We say, 'Just try. You will be taught a lesson you shall never forget.' " This was music in the ears of the Pole-hating Cossacks.

The Bolsheviks, Lenin continued, had not wished Russians to die for the Tsar's crown and Constantinople. But "the Russia which has liberated herself, which has suffered through two years of her Soviet revolution, that Russia we shall defend until the last drop of blood."

However, all must begin to concentrate on the "bloodless front" where grain grew and the forges roared. The Russian peasant, "for the first time in thousands of years," was working for himself. On the other hand, "when the Soviet government takes grain from the peasants at fixed prices, it compensates them only with paper." The value of the paper was far less than the value of the bread, but the government had nothing else to give. The peasant must deliver grain to the state on trust until industry was restored. "Would even only one sated peasant refuse to give bread to a hungry worker if he knows that that worker, when fed, will repay in goods?"[9]

Lenin would soon have his answer. The peasants would say it not with flour but with bullets.

On March 25 Lenin warned the Moscow Soviet—workers, for the most part—that France was instigating Poland against them. Great sacrifices would be required of factory hands, for they faced further hunger. "We must remember that we are carrying out a socialist revolution in a country whose majority are peasants"—the key to the Soviet situation then and for decades thereafter. The peasants were "perverted by capitalism" and believed "in the antique freedom of trade which they regarded as their holy right," an attitude, he stressed in a political sideswipe, which the SR's and the Mensheviks defend. But it was the duty of the soviets to get rid of speculators "and conquer the old traditions of capitalism." For the reconstruction of industry they needed bourgeois technicians, and to supervise the technicians they needed a watchdog "Workers and Peasants Inspection" commission.[10]

Lenin's thoughts had been turning more and more to economics, but not yet to a new economic policy. He still expected to extract the peasant's grain by promises and pleadings or by force. His thoughts also turned to foreign affairs; he formulated a guiding principle: Foreign Commissar Georgi Chicherin was to draft a Soviet declaration of peace. "In that text," Lenin instructed, "there must be a proposal of direct peace and peaceful negotiations, without any mention of conditions (draft an alternative text which will confirm all previous proposals, but in such a means as not to commit us)."[11]

Lenin now created a fiction, the Far Eastern Republic in eastern Siberia, with capital at Chita, to act as a "buffer," Lenin called it, between Japan and Soviet Russia. On December 15, 1919, Lenin had telegraphed the Omsk Revvoiensoviet to capture the Kuznets Coal Basin but not to pursue Kolchak's spent troops farther; forces were needed elsewhere.[12] Some leading Bolsheviks objected to the "buffer state." They apparently feared it as a divisive example to multi-ethnic Russia. "The opponents of 'the buffer state' should be fiercely scolded," Lenin wired Trotsky on December 19, 1920.[13] Lenin was concerned

[9] *Ibid.*, Second ed., Vol. XXV, pp. 46-62.
[10] *Ibid.*, pp. 65-70.
[11] *Leninskii Sbornik*, Vol. XXXVI, p. 83.
[12] *Ibid.*, p. 85.
[13] *Ibid.*, p. 97.

with the remnants of Denikin's armies commanded by Baron Wrangel and with the possibility of a Polish attack. He saw no wisdom in grappling with a superior Japanese army. The "buffer state" was appropriately camouflaged for anyone who chose to respect the thin disguise.

Further to strengthen the Soviet regime's military power, men of the large conscript labor army—another feature of war communism in its later phase —were transferred to the Red Army. Stalin protested and wired Lenin requesting permission to come to Moscow and argue his case. Lenin refused. Stalin, he wrote on the back of the telegram, "is looking for an excuse to make trouble. The commander in chief was perfectly right." First defeat the Denikin remnants, then permit peacetime routine. A telegram, drafted by Lenin, was sent by the Politburo telling Stalin he could not be summoned to Moscow because of the importance of the Caucasus front.[14] At the same time, however, whole divisions of the fighting forces were shifted to the conscript labor army for work on the railroads which had sunk into paralytic confusion. In addition, the communist party mobilized thousands of its members for the same task.

The towering nonmilitary problem remained: the capitalist "perversions" of the peasant who asked a real return for his produce. The Sovnarkom had decided by majority vote on January 3, 1920, that where fodder could not be obtained at arbitrary government-fixed confiscatory prices, state procurers might pay market prices. Lenin had cast his ballot against this measure but was outvoted. In the same month A. D. Tsurupa, People's Commissar of Food, complained that the Sovnarkom resolution disrupted his procurement operations; now all peasants wanted to sell at market prices. When Lenin was shown Tsurupa's letter he wrote that it would be "unpleasant" to change the Sovnarkom decision so soon. He suggested waiting "a month or so and then re-examining the matter."[15] Meanwhile agents in the field, under orders to obtain fodder and other grains or else, paid what the market required. One of them confessed this to Lenin, who merely smiled. The government had to have fodder for army animals and for the horses that hauled timber from the forests. Horses were the first effective anticommunists.

Leon Trotsky, War Commissar, spent the winter of 1919-20 trying to salvage the transportation system. In its crippled state it threatened to kill the national economy. "The railway transport position is catastrophic. Bread transport to Moscow has ceased," Lenin wrote. He recommended merciless measures: "*Decrease* the individual bread ration for those workers who do not transport workers, *increase* it for transport workers. Let thousands perish, but the country must be saved."[16] Trotsky temporarily took charge of the railroads. He studied general conditions; his conclusion was that war communism must go and make way for arrangements which fostered economic

[14] *Ibid.*, p. 97-98.
[15] *Ibid.*, p. 89.
[16] *The Letters of Lenin*, translated and edited by Elizabeth Hill and Doris Mudie, p. 457. Russian original in Lenin, *Sochineniya*, Second ed., Vol. XXIX, p. 390.

self-interest and personal incentive. In February, 1920, he laid his knowledge and ideas before the Central Committee of the party in Moscow. He condemned the existing system of grain requisitions which penalized better producers by taking more from them. He condemned the equal distribution of industrial goods (what little there was) irrespective of the quantities of farm produce seized. He proposed, instead, that consumer commodities be offered not to villages as units but to peasant individuals in accordance with the surpluses they delivered to the state. He would thus create legal barter. He spoke of restoring the free market where peasants could trade. He suggested a tax to replace confiscations.

The Central Committee voted 11 to 4 against Trotsky's proposals.[17] Lenin had attacked them vehemently.

Presently, economic issues and foreign trade and diplomatic hopes were pushed brusquely to the periphery of the Kremlin's attention, and everybody focused on one event: the Poles invaded Soviet territory on April 26, 1920. The Bolsheviks were at war again, this time with a foreign state abetted by France and, indirectly, by Britain. The Polish army moved with speed. It captured Kiev, the Ukraine's major city, on May 8.

Polish leaders had long dreamed dreams of a greater Poland embracing the Ukraine as far as Odessa and all of Lithuania. Bolshevism, some Poles believed, was their historic opportunity. Yet, while Kolchak fancied himself in the Kremlin, while Yudenich was beating on the gates of Petrograd, and while Denikin wondered about the weather in Moscow, Poland held her fire. Instead of smiting Russia in her worst hour, the Poles waited until all the Whites, except weak Wrangel in the far-off sunny Caucasus and Crimea, had been felled by Red arms. Then they struck. The reason for their procrastination was the fear of helping the Whites to victory and thereby raising the specter of a monarchist or nationalist Russia, restored in strength and reasserting the Tsar's former authority over the province of Poland. With the tsarist generals in the dust, that fear vanished, and the Poles could indulge their ancient expansionist designs at the expense of Red Russia bled white by the Whites.

Count Alexander Skrzinski, Polish Foreign Minister in 1922-1923 and from 1924 to 1926, explained Polish political thinking. "Undoubtedly," he wrote, "Denikin would have received with great gratitude the help of the Poles, but only on the understanding, scarcely concealed, that such help was forthcoming from Poles as faithful subjects of Russia."[18]

Lenin, shrewdly suspecting Polish apprehensions of a White victory, sent secret emissaries in 1919 to Marshal Pilsudski, master of Poland, to negotiate. An unofficial truce was arranged.[19] On April 19, 1919, however, Poland occupied Vilna; on August 8, Minsk. These were straws in an ill wind. On

[17] Leon Trotsky, *My Life. An Attempt at an Autobiography* (New York, 1930), p. 464.
[18] Count Alexander Skrzinski, *Poland and Peace* (London, 1923), p. 39.
[19] Details in Fischer, *The Soviets in World Affairs* (Vintage Books, New York, 1961), pp. 166-169.

January 28, 1920, Lenin, Trotsky, and Chicherin warned the Poles not to launch "an unwarranted, senseless, and criminal war against Soviet Russia," and clearly defined the Russo-Polish and Ukrainian-Polish frontiers which the Red Army would not violate.

Poland needed peace as badly as Russia. Herbert Hoover's American Relief Administration (ARA) distributed $50 million in food to Poles during February-August, 1919. It continued, indeed augmented, its relief measures in 1920 while Poland continued her war preparations. In January, 1920, 34,000 cases of typhus were registered in Poland. In June, 1920, the ARA was feeding 1,315,000 Polish children. "There she was six months ago," said Mr. Herbert Asquith in the British House of Commons on August 10, 1920, "a population stricken with disease and famine, and it is no exaggeration to say on the verge of national bankruptcy, and it was under these circumstances that she started this campaign . . . it was a purely aggressive adventure. It was a wanton enterprise."

Aggression is never a rational enterprise.

Poland's prostrate condition did not discourage Pilsudski. It encouraged Lenin.

Anticipating a Polish offensive, the Soviet government opened negotiations with Lithuania on March 31, 1920, which resulted in a peace treaty on July 12, and with Latvia, which resulted in a peace treaty on August 11. The Kremlin was neutralizing Poland's potential partners. Finland signed August 14, 1920. On the other hand, French efforts to recruit Hungary and Romania for the war against Russia proved fruitless.[20]

Before even Poland attacked Soviet Russia, Lenin saw the expected invasion in terms of a European revolution—and Europe was then the world. "The victory of the communist revolution in all countries is inevitable," he affirmed at a March 6, 1920, meeting of the Moscow Soviet celebrating the first anniversary of the founding of the Third International, or Comintern.[21] In the beginning, he recalled, they had hoped that the end of the world war would spark the world revolution, for at that moment the workers were armed. He still did not know, he confessed, what had interfered with the fruition of their hopes; Moscow's information was fragmentary and unsatisfactory. Nevertheless, Lenin was in no doubt that the Second International of moderate socialism "is dead, and that the masses of workingmen in Germany, England, and France are joining the communists . . . even among the backward strata of workers in such countries as England a change has intervened, and it is possible to say that the old forms of socialism are dead forever. Europe is moving toward revolution not as we moved, but in essence Europe is going through the same process."

Lenin never did figure out why Europe had not followed Russia's lead to revolution. "Opportunism is the chief enemy," he wrote in July, 1920,[22] in

[20] *Ibid.*, pp. 182-183.
[21] Lenin, *op. cit.*, Second ed., Vol. XXV, pp. 71-77.
[22] *Leninskii Sbornik*, Vol. XXXVI, p. 113.

the midst of the Polish war. Yet he failed to dissect "opportunism" or "reformism." He merely quoted Ramsay MacDonald as saying, "We know that all this will pass, it will straighten itself out." Lenin's immediately following comment reads, "The roots of opportunism: bribery of the upper stratum of workers," and he mentioned the sum. But Lenin should have been the first to recognize that "opportunism" or "reformism" was not a subjective phenomenon. "Bribery" meant higher wages paid by a richer, stronger capitalist class eager for a home market and greater social tranquillity. It meant, moreover, working-class hopes that democratic methods—the franchise, increased purchasing power, and strikes—would extract bigger benefits than violent revolution. But such was Lenin's total commitment to revolution that he could discern no virtue in any alternative. In February, 1920,[23] he ridiculed Otto Bauer, the Austrian socialist leader, for asserting that "expropriation of the expropriators" destroyed the productive capacity of a country and therefore ruined the masses. Better, Bauer said, to carry out expropriation "in an orderly, regulated fashion," by means of taxes. This, to Lenin, was a most revolting form of counterrevolution. Yet a comparison today between the economic status and political power of the Austrian workingman and the Soviet workingman would lead one to wonder who was right: Lenin with his violence or Bauer with his "revolution by taxation." Lenin was a prisoner of Russia's history. Russia had never known gradualism from below. She had had only reforms from above or revolutions from below. This, indeed, might have been the real explanation of Lenin's undeviating attachment to revolution and to a tight communist party of professional engineers of revolution. The strange fact is that Lenin, an educated man, ignored the effect of national history on the course of revolution. By intellectual legerdemain, he wiped out the seventy-two years of Western economic development since Marx and Engels had published *The Communist Manifesto*, and ordained that revolution everywhere was the sole road to salvation. Marx misled Lenin. Lenin's was the either-orism of an extremist behind opaque national windows. He did not realize that the more economically developed a country the less it has to gain and the more it has to lose from revolution.

But now Lenin would test his theories with a bayonet. He would push over the European opportunists with the Russian soldier's rifle butt. The Poles had penetrated far into the Ukraine. The Red Army repulsed them quickly, and in June, 1920, it stood on the old Polish frontier. Soviet Moscow was stirred as never before. One blow of the red fist could crumble the rotten walls of European capitalism.

On March 15, 1920, a part of the German military staged the Kapp putsch in Berlin. It was put down quickly with the help of a general strike. The German communists redoubled their activity. Lenin informed the Ninth Congress of the Russian Communist Party on March 29 that everything in Germany was proceeding well according to a pattern they knew; the abortive Kornilov military uprising in Petrograd in September, 1917, had led to the

[23] Lenin, *op. cit.*, Vol. XXV, p. 37.

Bolshevik revolution of November 7, 1917. The putsch by Dr. Wolfgang Kapp would yield similar fruit. He felt "certain that the day is not far off when we shall march hand in hand with a German Soviet government."[24] Necessity was the mother of his hopes. Neglect of national differences was the mother of his illusions. One of the basic principles of Marxism, frequently reiterated by Lenin, is "the uneven development" of capitalist countries. This dissimilarity naturally affects the prospects of an anticapitalist revolution. Lenin overlooked it. Poland too was ready for revolution, Lenin felt. ". . . the revolutionary movement there is growing," he told the party congress on March 29.

When, accordingly, the Red Army drove the Polish army out of the Ukraine, Lenin favored hot pursuit into Poland and through Poland toward Germany. Other Bolshevik leaders were opposed.

Stalin was opposed. In an interview in the Kharkov *Kommunist* of June 24, 1920,[25] he elaborated on the military difficulties that faced them. "We are at war not only with the Poles," he declared, "but with the entire Entente which has mobilized all the dark forces of Germany, Austria, Hungary, and Romania, and which is supplying the Poles with all manner of comforts." Therefore, he argued, "I regard as out of place this bragging and harmful self-satisfaction which some comrades have manifested: some of them are not satisfied with the successes at the front but shout about 'a march on Warsaw,' others, not satisfied with the defense of our Republic from enemy attack, proudly assert they will only be reconciled with 'a Red Soviet Warsaw.'" He told them that this did not correspond with the policy of the Soviet government. But when Stalin learned that it did correspond with the views and intentions of Lenin, he changed his mind and sided with the master.

Trotsky was opposed. The army and the country were exhausted. Julian Markhlevsky, Lenin's chief secret negotiator of the 1919 truce with Poland, a Pole and a communist, gave the chances of a Polish revolution a low rating. Karl Radek, born on Polish territory, a foreign affairs expert, held an equally pessimistic opinion. Djerzhinsky, the Cheka chief, a Pole by birth, likewise frowned on a Russian march into Poland. Yet when Trotsky proposed an immediate end of the war against the Poles, "I was supported, as far as I can remember now, only by Rykov. All the rest were won over by Lenin during my absence . . . it was decided to continue the offensive."[26]

Why did Lenin order the Soviet invasion of Poland when Trotsky and Radek would have vetoed it? All three were equally committed to world revolution; none scrupled about the use of violence. Lenin knew the straitened condition of Russia as well as Trotsky. Radek realized from his 1918 stay in Berlin that neither Germany (nor Poland) was ripe for revolution. Trotsky had an aversion, probably reinforced by his Soviet expe-

[24] *Ibid.*, Vol. XXV, pp. 94-115.
[25] Stalin, *Sochineniya*, Vol. 4, pp. 332-333.
[26] Trotsky, *op. cit.*, p. 457.

rience, against premature revolutions. He would logically speak out against an attempt to harness the crippled Soviet child to a Polish or German fetus. He opposed a revolutionary drive into Poland for the same reason that Lenin opposed a revolutionary war against Germany during the Brest-Litovsk crisis: Germany and Poland were merely pregnant with revolution—and even that was not a diagnosed fact.

Lenin, however, rejected Radek's information and Trotsky's doubts. He was ruled, as always, by needs, not by knowledge. Revolution is a gamble in impossibilities. Lenin wanted an extension of the Russian revolution to revive its spirit and give it a transfusion of advanced Western technology and power. Trotsky and Radek found the use of the army for this purpose uncongenial. Perhaps one difference between Lenin and them was the difference between the topmost leader and everybody else. The head of a state is more than the first among equals, more than the superior among unequals. His responsibility is unique and adds a unique quality to his psychology; the fate of the entire national enterprise rests on him. A person below the highest rung can indulge his skepticism. The man at the summit of power cannot afford the luxury of "maybe." Lenin must have felt in his bones and brains that the red torrent of the Russian revolution had become a pale trickle; Bolshevism was incapable of lifting a hundred million peasants out of the "perversions" of capitalism. Only a foreign anticapitalist weight could right the balance against Russian petty bourgeois capitalism. Trotsky and Radek, to be sure, made the same gray estimate of the prospects of socialism in a backward, peasant nation. The key to their varying approaches to revolution-by-invasion must probably be sought deep in the subconscious. A Russian war against Poland would be a popular war. General Brusilov, of world war fame, volunteered for duty on the Bolshevik General Staff and issued a call to tsarist officers to fight for the fatherland. Russian nationalism flared. Trotsky hated it. Lenin had tapped a new pocket of power. All Bolsheviks believed in force. Lenin believed in it more than most. He believed in the export of revolution on the tips of bayonets.

Lenin brooked no opposition in this matter. He had the army and would use it. He would teach Poland a lesson by setting her aflame; the fire might spread to Hamburg, Berlin, Munich—or farther. He had read Henri Barbusse's *Le Feu* and drawn political conclusions from it. The First World War, hated by millions of soldiers, had, he was convinced, disemboweled the capitalist system. Pierce its empty body and it would fall, deflated, into the gaping grave. He loosed the Red Army on Poland. The Red cannon roared revolution. The European proletariat would hear and act, thereby saving the Russian revolution from the economic attrition that threatened it. Moscow's choice lay between foreign revolution and capitulation to Russian capitalism. Lenin pinned his faith on revolution. Trotsky's faith burned lower; he did not expect the solution of urgent domestic problems to come from the outside at that moment and in that manner. He had already opted for a new economic policy. Stalin's faith did not burn at all. As early as August 19, 1917, he wrote in a newspaper editorial, "Once upon a time it was said in Russia that the light of socialism came from the West." But things had changed. In 1917 "the West exported to Russia not so much socialism and liberation as slavery and counterrevolution."[27] The subsequent years increased his antagonism to the West.

Lenin's will won. At Brest-Litovsk his role was restraint. In Poland it was release.

An army about 150,000 strong, led by General Mikhail Tukhachevsky, "a young Napoleon," aged twenty-seven, delivered the main thrust westward from the historic plains of Smolensk. Between July 4 and July 20, it advanced twelve miles a day, an enormous distance in the foot-and-cart era.

Lenin had his reward. For the first time, it seems, since November, 1917, a mood of exhilaration gripped the Soviet people. "Give us Warsaw" was scribbled on fences and walls. Communist youths and Russian and Ukrainian nationalists clamored for "war to the victorious end."

Tukhachevsky's sweeping progress stunned the Poles. "On the [Polish] military," Marshal Pilsudski wrote, "this march produced the effect of a kind of monstrous kaleidoscope." It seemed, he added, "like something irresistible . . . the government trembled."[28] Outside Warsaw, waiting for the trembling to induce death, were Felix Djerzhinsky, Felix Kon, and Julian Markhlevsky, all well acquainted with Polish conditions. They lived in a Roman Catholic priest's home. From a hill nearby they could see Warsaw which they intended to tint red. Lenin had constituted them "The Polish Provisional Revolutionary Government."

A second Soviet army, commanded by General A. I. Yegorov and supported by mounted Cossack roughriders, their mustachioed General Simeon Budenny leading, had slashed southwest into Polish eastern Galicia. The political commissar with this army was Joseph Stalin.

Poland reeled under the double onslaught. In Moscow, Russians and assembled foreign communists rejoiced and daily tallied the kilometers gained.

One non-event chilled the jubilation and puzzled Lenin: the expected Polish revolution was conspicuously absent. The peasants of the fields and the workers of the towns (except in eastern Byalostok) received the Russian and Ukrainian intruders with sullen quiet. No spirit of international brotherhood moved them. If the Soviet armies inspired any sentiment it was not revolution but its antidote: Polish nationalism. Radek had predicted it.

In an analysis of his Polish campaign which Tukhachevsky delivered before the Military Academy in Moscow on February 7 and 10, 1923, he

[27] Stalin, op. cit., Vol. 3, pp. 234-235.
[28] Joseph Pilsudski, L'Année 1920. Édition Complète avec le Text de l'Ouvrage de M. Toukhatchevski 'La March Au-Dela La Vistule' Et les Notes Critique du Bureau Historique Militaire de Varsovie. Traduit du Polonais (Paris, 1920), pp. 112-114.

expressed complete agreement with Lenin on the prospects of European revolution in 1920. "What was the condition of the proletariat in Western Europe? Was it prepared for revolution? Could it, enlivened by the socialist avalanche which descended from the east and which brought it freedom, have given help? . . . Could Europe have reinforced the socialist movement by the explosion of a revolution in the West? The facts reply in the affirmative. . . . There can be no doubt that if we had been victorious on the Vistula the revolutionary fires would have reached the entire continent. . . . The export of revolution was possible. Capitalist Europe was shaken to its foundations, and without our strategic errors, without our defeat on the battlefield, perhaps the Polish war would have become the ring linking the November, 1917, revolution with revolution in Western Europe."[29]

Tukhachevsky then drew this "essential conclusion" from "our 1920 campaign: the defeat was due not to politics but to strategy."[30] The great strategic error, he held, was committed by the Soviet army in the southwest, commanded by Yegorov and Budenny under the orders of Stalin, already ambitious to make history. While Tukhachevsky took Warsaw he would take Lvov (Lemberg) and approach Austria or Germany. But Tukhachevsky had traveled too fast and too far, and when he stood at the Vistula in early August eager to subdue that last barrier to Warsaw the Poles made a stand. Tukhachevsky telegraphed repeatedly to general headquarters asking urgently for reinforcements. Headquarters summoned Yegorov and Budenny to abandon their own objectives and succor Tukhachevsky. They did not hear. Trotsky blames Stalin by name.[31] Tukhachevsky merely mentioned the number of the army.

Tukhachevsky turned and returned to Russia. Yegorov and Budenny also withdrew to the homeland. Lenin's greatest attempt to kindle revolution in Europe had ended in cold failure.

Tukhachevsky said, in his 1923 retrospect, that the Polish bourgeoisie and intellectuals had rallied behind their shaken government and, by preventing the workers from rising, lent it a new stability. As a soldier, however, he demoted the social factor and stressed strategy as primary. Lenin, the author of the defeat, looked deep into the political heart of the matter and blamed himself. Trotsky declares that "Lenin, of course, understood better than anyone else the significance of his 'Warsaw' mistake, and returned to it more than once in thought and word."[32] Trotsky does not cite Lenin's words. Clara Zetkin did. A prominent German communist, she met with Lenin, not for the first time, in 1920 and he spoke to her frankly about the collapse of his policy of revolution by bayonet and saber. She noted his statements and published them in Russia and elsewhere after his death.

[29] *Ibid.*, pp. 230-232.
[30] *Ibid.*, p. 254.
[31] Trotsky, *op. cit.*, p. 458.
[32] *Ibid.*, p. 459.

Lenin had gone to see her because she was ill. "Like so many who at that time came to Moscow from the West," Comrade Zetkin wrote in her memoirs,[33] "I had to pay tribute to the change in my manner of life, and had to take to my bed. Lenin visited me. Anxiously, like the best of mothers, he inquired whether I was receiving proper care and nourishment, good medical attention, etc., and if I wanted anything. Behind him I saw Comrade Krupskaya's kind face. Lenin doubted me when I said that everything was going well. He was particularly excited about the fact that I was living on the fourth floor of a Soviet house, which, it is true, has a lift theoretically, but one which does not, in practice, function. 'Just like the desire and the will of the Kautskians for revolution,' he remarked sarcastically. Soon the little vessel of conversation drifted into political channels."

They talked about Poland. She told him how "The early frost of the Red Army's retreat from Poland had blighted the growth of the revolutionary flower fostered in our thoughts when the Soviet troops, by a bold and rapid advance, had reached Warsaw." She told him of the excitement among German communists when the Soviet soldiers "in impossibly old scraps of uniform and civilian clothes, in bast shoes or torn boots, spurred their small, brisk horses right up to the German frontier," and how the German bourgeoisie and petty bourgeoisie "with their reformist followers from the working class," observed these events "half pleased," because Poland, the "hereditary enemy," was being beaten, and "half afraid," because of the approach of the Red Army.

Lenin listened, then "sat silently for a few minutes," sunk in reflection. "Yes," he said at last, "so it has happened in Poland, as perhaps it had to happen. You know, of course, all the circumstances which were at work; that our recklessly brave, confident vanguard had no reserves of troops or munitions, and never once got even enough dry bread to eat. They had to requisition bread and other essentials from the Polish peasants and middle classes. And in the Red Army the Poles saw enemies, not brothers and liberators. They felt, thought and acted not in a social, revolutionary way, but as nationalists, as imperialists. The revolution in Poland on which we counted did not take place. The workers and peasants, deceived by the adherents of Pilsudsky and Daszynsky, defended their class enemy, let our brave Red soldiers starve, ambushed them and beat them to death."

Lenin proceeded to praise Budenny as "the most brilliant cavalry leader of the world." However, "all the excellencies of Budyonny [an unorthodox but sensible phonetic spelling] and of other revolutionary army leaders could not make up for our deficiencies in military and technical affairs, still less for our political miscalculations—the hope of a revolution in Poland. Radek predicted how it would turn out. He warned us. I was very angry with him, and accused him of 'defeatism.' But he was right in his main contention. He knows affairs

[33] Klara Zetkin, Reminiscences of Lenin (London, 1929), pp. 18-23.

outside Russia, and particularly in the West, better than we do, and he is talented. He is very useful to us. We were reconciled a short while ago by a long political conversation over the telephone in the middle of the night, or rather towards morning."

It was a fantasy to expect that the armies of Tukhachevsky and Budenny with a combined strength, at the end of the Russian offensive, of less than a hundred thousand, in military and civilian tatters and bark shoes, short of munitions and reserves, and depending for food on confiscations from hostile peasants, could have vanquished and then held down twelve million angry adult enemies. In Poland they would have been the exposed target of resolute armed resistance. In Germany they would have been a laughingstock. Significantly, Lenin referred to Budenny, never mentioning Tukhachevsky, the hero of the Polish campaign, and that clearly, because the cavalry was, Moscow believed, carrying revolution to Germany by Cossack saber. A small fraction of Germany's army could have tossed Budenny back. In fact, Pilsudski withdrew all his forces opposing the Budenny-Yegorov troops and threw them against Tukhachevsky in front of Warsaw.

Tukhachevsky had a magnificent brain, vast organizational talent, noble carriage, and great charm (despite a goiter). He could charm a lady or an army, and he was a hero to Soviet youth. (None of these assets contributed to longevity in the Stalinist 1930's.) In his 1923 post-mortem of the 1920 Polish adventure he tried to ascertain why he had failed. The military man looked for military mistakes, and he found them in others and ignored his own; he had moved too far to the north and west in the direction of the Polish Corridor and Danzig instead of attacking Warsaw head on in mid-August. As to the Polish revolution, it was an article of faith; workers who are expected to make a revolution make one unless blocked by their bourgeois masters and opportunist labor leaders. He never examined this untouchable "truth." Though the facts gainsay it for half a century, it remains dogma, the demagogue's beloved peroration.

Lenin, however, was a politician and he looked for the political error. He named it: "our political miscalculation—the hope of a revolution in Poland." A war waged to fulfill a hope, a hope born of doctrine out of ignorance. The Polish "workers and peasants," Lenin said to Zetkin, "deceived by Pilsudsky and Daszynsky, defended their class enemy." The First World War should have taught Lenin that workers and peasants would defend their country against an invader, class notwithstanding. But The Communist Manifesto announced in 1848 that "the working men have no country." Therefore they sinned in defending their country in 1920. How they were "deceived" nobody ever explained. Had Lenin forgotten so soon the fierce Polish nationalism and ferocious Polish anti-Russianism resulting from three partitions of Poland with Russian help? (There would be yet another with Soviet help.) He of course knew the facts; he expressed them at a meeting on October 2, 1920, when he explained the Russian defeat at Warsaw by "the patriotic upsurge" in the city which stiffened the Polish troops.[34]

The excuse that Lenin regarded revolution in Poland and then Germany as indispensable to the preservation of the Russian revolution is untenable. A revolution in Poland would merely have broadened the area of misery. A revolution in Germany (most unlikely eventuality) would have brought French and British military intervention and involved Soviet Russia in large-scale warfare.

The Soviet invasion of Poland is best booked as the "miscalculation" Lenin himself called it, a mistake—and a monumental one. Few statesmen die without such blots on their records. Lenin's is interesting because it stemmed from his schematic concept of world events, from the unreliability of doctrine as a guide to politics, from slavery to a dogma. He blundered because he considered his ideology immune to blunder. He overestimated the lure of revolution. He also misjudged the entire situation. Russia was too weak to conquer by force and lacked an idea that could conquer despite insufficient force.

The warfare in Poland had enabled Baron Wrangel, commanding Denikin's remnants, to come out of the Crimea into the North Caucasus and the Ukraine. The communist party Politburo therefore divided the front in two: the Polish and the anti-Wrangel segments. Lenin wired this decision to Stalin. From the Ukraine, Stalin replied, "Received your note regarding the partition of the fronts, the Politburo should not occupy itself with trifles. I can work at the front at most for two more weeks. I need a rest, find a substitute. . . . As to the mood of the Central Committee in favor of peace with Poland, it is impossible not to notice that our diplomacy sometimes succeeds very well in destroying the results of our military victories."

Lenin countered, "I don't quite understand why you are dissatisfied with the division of the fronts. Give your reasons. . . . Our diplomacy is under the direction of the Central Committee and will never destroy our victories unless the Wrangel danger creates vacillation inside the Central Committee. From the Kuban and Don regions we are receiving alarming, indeed desperate telegrams about the growth of the insurrectionary movement. They insist on speeding up the liquidation of Wrangel. Lenin."[35]

Lenin's polite language barely concealed his irritation. This exchange of telegrams, moreover, revealed Moscow's mixed mood and forked policy in early August, 1920. Stalin opposed peace with Poland. So did many leading Bolsheviks in the capital. All concerned, including Lenin, were apparently so euphoric over Soviet military victories in Poland that they believed they had won the war and could dictate a humiliating peace. If Poland balked at the terms, Moscow contemplated a winter campaign when frozen Polish marshes and solidified minor rivers might not impede progress. On the other hand, as

[34] Lenin, *op. cit.*, Second ed., Vol. XXV, p. 399.
[35] *Leninskii Sbornik*, Vol. XXXVI, pp. 115-116.

Lenin's shrewd telegram to Stalin indicated, anti-Soviet revolts in the Kuban and Don regions might induce him and his associates in the Central Committee to "vacillate," to abandon the gamble of revolution in Poland, and parley for a peace of safety.

In fact, while Tukhachevsky was still marching toward Warsaw, Leo Kamenev and Leonid Krassin, in London to achieve a trade agreement with the British government, assumed the black cloth of diplomats and commenced to negotiate for peace, with England as intermediary. It was to these talks that Stalin had objected in his message to Lenin. (The communist party's Politburo consisted of Kamenev, party secretary Krestinsky, Lenin, Stalin, and Trotsky; Bukharin, Kalinin, and Zinoviev were "candidates" or alternate members.)

The foremost power in world diplomacy, Great Britain sought to play a role in the Russo-Polish peace. She had attempted to inject herself into the war. Lord Curzon, the British Foreign Secretary and, as a former Viceroy of India, an indomitable foe of Russia black or Russia red, warned the Soviets, in a note dated July 12, not to cross the Curzon Line drawn by the Allied Supreme Council on December 8, 1919; it separated Poland and Russia and ran from Grodno to Byalostok to Brest-Litovsk, then south along the Bug River. Tukhachevsky crossed it. There was agitation in England to go to the aid of Poland. There was agitation in Labour circles in favor of Russia; under Ernest Bevin's guidance, the dockers refused to load munitions for the Poles. (Czechoslovak transport workers obstructed the transit of war matériel from France to Poland.)

Leo Kamenev communicated Moscow's peace terms for Poland to Lloyd George. Kamenev, however, deliberately suppressed one of the terms: that a civilian militia of 200,000 workingmen be established in Poland. The British government telegraphed the Polish government to accept. The Poles fought on. The French fumed.

The Soviet peace terms in their entirety were the kind a victorious country dictates to a defeated enemy. Lenin revealed them in a public declaration adopted by the VTSIK (All Russian Central Executive Committee —highest organ of the Soviet government) on September 25. The strength of Poland's army was to be reduced (to 60,000); her war industries were to be "demobilized"; arms not needed for the army and militia would go to Russia; and the Volkovisk-Graivo railway ceded to Russia. Moreover, a plebiscite was to take place in East Galicia (largely inhabited by Ruthenians, who are related to Ukrainians) conducted "on the Soviet principle, that is, voting by toilers."[36] Portrait of Poland as a satellite.

Late in September, when the VTSIK declaration was published, the military situation in Poland had changed to Soviet Russia's disadvantage, and the Wrangel menace persisted. Lenin faced a clear alternative: fight a winter war in Poland or bow to reality. He scrapped the peace terms presented to

[36] *Ibid.*, pp. 123-136.

the Poles in August. He granted Poland a new frontier with Russia well to the east of the Curzon Line, more favorable, that is, than the boundary fixed by the Allied Supreme Council in December, 1919, and conceded East Galicia to Poland, merely urging a plebiscite there, not on the Soviet principle but "on the usual bourgeois-democratic principle."

The VTSIK declaration stated, further, that by these new proposals Soviet Russia had done everything possible and necessary to secure peace. Rejection, Lenin wrote, "would mean, we are convinced, that Poland had, probably under the pressure of the imperialists of France and of other Entente countries, decided on a winter campaign." Therefore the Soviet government demanded acceptance of the VTSIK proposals within ten days. Delay beyond ten days "predetermined the question of the winter campaign."

Poland accepted on October 5—the tenth day. The final peace treaty was signed in Riga on March 18, 1921.

The day before the drafting of the VTSIK declaration—September 22— Lenin addressed the All-Russian Conference of the communist party. The situation was difficult "but it in no sense represented a naked loss for us," he asserted. ". . . Poland cannot vanquish us whereas we were not and are not far from victory." The Soviet army still held considerable Polish territory. Then, too, the Russian march on Warsaw had shaken Europe, especially England, where Labour's intervention against British support of Poland had actually created "dual power," after the manner of Russia under Kerensky: "The British Mensheviks, according to the testimony of competent persons, already regard themselves as a government and are preparing to take the place of the bourgeoisie in the near future. This will be a further step in the general process of the British proletarian revolution." Events in England had had a tremendous effect on the world labor movement and especially in France. They will soon know, Lenin added, whether they would be forced into a winter campaign in Poland, but if that was their fate, "we will win, no doubt about it, and notwithstanding exhaustion and fatigue."[37]

The VTSIK declaration showed the hand of Lenin, the serious statesman. The party conference heard the voice of the propagandist who, relying on "competent persons," frivolously assumed that the British "Mensheviks" were "clearing the road of the British working masses to the Bolshevik revolution." Lenin saw the world through distorting Russian spectacles. The wish was father to the mistake; Russia's experience incubated his false prophecies.

Lenin's insistence on the invasion of Poland fitted into a grand design. The conception was indeed grandiose. "If Poland had become a soviet country," he said in a speech on October 2, 1920,[38] "if the Warsaw workers had received from Soviet Russia the help they awaited and welcomed, the Versailles Peace would have been destroyed, and the entire international system,

[37] Lenin, op. cit., Second ed., Vol. XXV, pp. 377-380.
[38] Ibid., pp. 398-408.

achieved by victories over Germany, would have collapsed. France would then not have had a buffer separating Germany from Soviet Russia. . . . The situation was that, given several more days of victorious progress by the Red Army, not only would Warsaw have been taken (that would not have been so important) but the Versailles Peace would have been ruined."[39] This, he said, would have indicated to Germans that the Bolsheviks were their allies, "that in its struggle for survival, the Soviet Republic was the only force in the world that was combating imperialism—and imperialism now means the alliance of France, England, and America." In any case, France was "on the way to bankruptcy," and even the old leaders of the British workers "who formerly opposed the dictatorship of the working class have now come over to our side." The advance of the Red Army would threaten the whole edifice of capitalism.

Lenin had been warned not only by Radek and Trotsky but also by Paul Levi, a German communist leader. Angelica Balabanoff invited Lenin and Levi to her Moscow quarters. Hardly was Lenin seated than he posed the question that obsessed him. "How soon after the entry of the victorious Russian troops in Warsaw will revolution break out in Germany?" Lenin asked.

"Three months," Levi replied, "or three weeks, or perhaps not at all."[40] Lenin shook his head, stood up, and left. He would allow nothing to deflect him from giving the roulette wheel of history a mighty spin.

Lenin's grandiose brain-building crashed by the waters of the Vistula. Lenin did not hide the fact. "The disillusionment is too great," he told a conference of Moscow communist party officials on October 9—four days after Poland accepted his amended peace terms. "Six weeks have already passed from the moment we commenced to retreat, and we have still not stopped retreating." From the heights of hope he fell to the depths of depression. Yet he sought and found bright patches: More food had been taken by the government from the peasants than in the previous year. (Obviously, for the government, now that Kolchak and Denikin were gone, controlled far more territory.) "Inside Poland there is a great crisis: economically Poland is far more destroyed than we." By signing the peace "we gain time and will use it to strengthen our army." Furthermore, "On the front against Wrangel the balance of forces favors us. . . . In the Far East, the situation is such that Japan will have to leave because a winter campaign is an impossibility for her. This strengthens us. At the present time, an American billionaire (Washington B. Vanderlip) is in Moscow conducting negotiations with us for a concession on Kamchatka. By granting this concession, we aggravate the relations between Japan and America."

As against these favorable factors, Lenin noted that conditions in Turke-

[39] *Ibid.*, p. 402.
[40] Angelica Balabanoff, *Lenin*, p. 89.

stan and the Caucasus were "more complicated." The Turks were advancing into Armenia and wanted to seize Batum on the Black Sea and Baku, the oil city on the Caspian Sea. Secondly, the Kremlin could not, in defeat, exploit the differences between England and France. Thirdly, "I cannot say, in detail, how well armed our army is. Recently, there was an insufficiency of bullets, but now the difficulties are fewer." He did not trust the Poles or the French: "Undoubtedly, the Poles will also use the armistice to reinforce themselves . . . we must do the same."

In a concluding paragraph of three sentences Lenin swept away the illusion that the advent of Bolshevism had inaugurated a new era of open diplomacy. "As long as there is war," he said, "there must be secret diplomacy as one of the weapons of war. We cannot reject it. The evaluation of such diplomacy depends on the general evaluation of war."[41]

Leo Kamenev was conducting secret diplomacy with the British government. Lenin telegraphed him in code: "That we have aroused the workers— that is no small gain."[42] This was his small consolation for the big defeat in Poland.

Remained Baron General Peter von Wrangel. He commanded 75,000 well-equipped, foreign-equipped troops. The Bolsheviks confronted him with 150,000 men. In October, after the Russo-Polish armistice, the Red Army attacked Wrangel in the Ukraine. The Bolshevik commanders were sanguine. Lenin read their reports and wired, "I fear [your] excessive optimism. Remember, it is necessary, at all costs, to enter the Crimea immediately behind the enemy. Prepare more thoroughly, verify whether all fording possibilities for the capture of the Crimea have been studied."[43] Eight days later, October 24, 1920, Lenin again warned the local commanders that Wrangel "is clearly withdrawing his units." Hence the optimism. Lenin suspected that Wrangel was "already trying to hide in the Crimea." He urged an intercepting cavalry attack.[44] Lenin's suspicions were justified; Wrangel drew back from the Ukraine into the Crimean bottle and pulled the tight cork in with him by fortifying Perekop, the thin isthmus, in places less than several hundred yards wide, connecting the Ukraine to the Crimea. The Red Army, finding no fords, assaulted Perekop frontally. The Whites had dug row on row of trenches. Wave after wave of attackers advanced into the narrow neck only to be mowed down. More waves came on, using the piles of corpses as cover. It was the bloodiest battle of the Soviet civil war—the last White gasp. By November 12 Wrangel and his surviving followers took to their ships, Allied and Russian ships, and sailed for Constantinople and permanent exile.

The Japanese were still in the Russian Far East but remained passive. At last the Bolsheviks enjoyed peace in the encircling gloom of myriad problems.

[41] *Leninskii Sbornik*, Vol. XXXVI, pp. 129-132.
[42] *Ibid.*, p. 119.
[43] Lenin, *op. cit.*, Fourth ed., Vol. 35, p. 392.
[44] *Ibid.*, p. 395.

XXXI. LENIN LAUGHS

THE RED VICTORY over Kolchak, Denikin, Yudenich, and lesser Whites indicated to the world that the Soviet government was not an ephemeral phenomenon. The Russo-Polish war aroused sympathy and antipathy in the West but also curiosity, and serious interest, for here was something new under the sun, and it cast a long shadow. The great enigma, the little big man in the Kremlin, became a prime target of foreign journalists, labor leaders, writers, social scientists, friends and foes. What shape did the crimson "anti-Christ" take? Whence his power? What was his future? Every visitor to Russia wanted to be able to say on returning, "I saw Lenin." Those who did not make the trip, usually from fear, occasionally from loathing, tried to communicate with him from afar.

Lenin failed to enrich the world's treasury of jokes. In the Everest of Leniniana only one Lenin joke is recorded: "What is the worst punishment for bigamy?" he asked. He answered: "Having two mothers-in-law."[1] He told this to his mother-in-law.

He had his own kind of humor. For instance: A journalist on the staff of the London *Daily News* telegraphed Lenin in September, 1920, that the published reports of the French and German socialist delegations on their stay in Soviet Russia "had done more harm to your cause than all the anti-Bolshevik propaganda of recent years." In particular, the report of the delegates of the German Independent Socialist Party, who had gone to Moscow to study the wisdom of joining the Comintern, stated that "workers who refused to work in Russia were shot," that "75 percent of the population of Russia were peasants, and that they were neither socialists nor communists," that "rightist militarism" ruled in Russia, that "deserters were executed and workers were not permitted to strike." In the cities too, neither socialism nor communism existed, and "instead of the dictatorship of the proletariat there existed only a dictatorship over the proletariat."[2]

Lenin chose to reply. He was not surprised, he said, that Social Democrats and Kautskians, who sided with the bourgeoisie and shot revolutionary workers, did not like what they saw in Soviet Russia. "If you assume that the reports of the French, German, and British workers' delegations did more harm to Bolshevism than all anti-Bolshevist propaganda," Lenin continued, "let us conclude a treaty: you in the name of the anti-Bolshevik bourgeoisie of all countries, I—in the name of the Soviet Republic of Russia. In accordance with this agreement, let delegations of workers and small-holding peasants (that is, working peasants, those who, by their labor, create profits for capitalists) be sent to Russia, and let each delegation live in Russia two months. If the reports of these delegations are beneficial to the cause of

[1] *Vospominaniya*, Vol. 3, p. 39.
[2] Lenin, *Sochineniya*, Second ed., Vol. XXV, editorial note, pp. 634-635.

anti-Bolshevik propaganda, the international bourgeoisie will cover the cost of their journeys. However, considering that this bourgeoisie in all countries of the world is very weak and poor, and that we in Russia are rich and strong, I agree to obtain a discount from the Soviet government so that it will pay three-fourths and only one-fourth will burden the millionaires of all countries."[3]

Lenin must have laughed.

H. G. Wells had heard of Lenin's laugh, but Lenin did not laugh much in his meeting with the novelist. Wells arrived in Petrograd at the end of September, 1920, and disliked what he saw and heard. He was also amused. "Directly I got to Petersburg," he wrote, "I asked to see a school, and on the second day of my visit I was taken to one that impressed me very unfavorably. It was extremely well equipped, much better than an ordinary English grammar school, and the children were bright and intelligent; but our visit fell in the recess. I could witness no teaching, and the behavior of the youngsters I saw indicated a low standard of discipline. I formed an opinion that I was probably being shown a picked school specially prepared for me, and that this was all that Petersburg had to offer. The special guide who was with us then began to question these children upon the subject of English literature and the writers they liked most. One name dominated all others. My own. Such comparatively trivial figures as Milton, Dickens, Shakespeare ran about intermittently between the feet of that literary colossus. Being questioned further, these children produced the titles of perhaps a dozen of my books. . . . I left that school smiling with difficulty and thoroughly cross with my guides.

"Three days later I suddenly scrapped my morning's engagements and insisted upon being taken at once to another school—any school close at hand. I was convinced that I had been deceived about the former school, and that now I should see a very bad school indeed. Instead I saw a much better one than the first I had seen. The equipment and building were better, the discipline of the children was better, and I saw some excellent teaching in progress. . . . All this was much more satisfactory. Finally by a few questions we tested the extraordinary vogue of H. G. Wells among the young people of Russia. None of these children had ever heard of him. The school library contained none of his books. This did much to convince me that I was seeing a quite normal school."[4]

[3] *Ibid.*, pp. 375-376.
[4] H. G. Wells, *Russia in the Shadows* (London, 1921). Wells's book was published in Russian translation in Moscow in 1959, in its entirety, with all its denigrating and offensive remarks and descriptions: "It will be best if I write about Marx without any hypocritical deference. I have always regarded him as a Bore of the extremist sort"; after attending a session of the Petrograd Soviet: "It was in fact a mass meeting incapable of any real legislative activities; capable at the utmost of endorsing or not endorsing the Government in control of the platform"; "Nothing will be left of Russia but a country of peasants; the towns will be practically deserted and in ruins, the railways will be rusting in disuse. With the railways will go the last vestiges of any gen-

In Petrograd Wells met Maxim Gorky, who telephoned Moscow and arranged for Lenin to receive the Englishman. Accompanied by Feodor A. Rothstein, later Soviet ambassador to Persia, and "an American comrade with a large camera," Wells passed through various gates and cordons and offices. "We got to Lenin at last and found him, a little figure at a great desk in a well-lit room that looked out upon palatial spaces. I thought his desk was rather in a litter. I sat down on a chair at a corner of the desk, and the little man—his feet scarcely touch the ground as he sits on the edge of his chair—twisted round to talk to me, putting his arms round and over a pile of papers. He spoke excellent English. . . . Meanwhile the American got to work with his camera, and unobtrusively but persistently exposed plates. . . .

"I had come expecting to struggle with a doctrinaire Marxist. I found nothing of the sort. I had been told that Lenin lectured people; he certainly did not do so on this occasion. Much has been made of his laugh in the descriptions, a laugh which is said to be pleasing at first and afterwards to become cynical. This laugh was not in evidence. . . . Lenin has a pleasant, quick-changing brownish face, with a lively smile and a habit (due perhaps to some defect in focussing) of screwing up one eye as he pauses in his talk; he is not very like the photographs you see of him because he is one of those people whose change of expression is more important than their features; he gesticulated a little with his hands over the heaped papers as he talked, and he talked quickly, very keen on his subject, without any posing or pretences or reservations, as a good type of scientific man will talk.

"Our talk was threaded throughout and held together by two—what shall I call them?—*motifs*. One was from me to him: 'What do you think you are making of Russia? What is the state you are trying to create?' The other was from him to me: 'Why does not the social revolution begin in England? Why do you not work for the social revolution? Why are you not destroying Capitalism and establishing the Communist State?' These *motifs* interwove, reacted on each other, illuminated each other. The second brought back the first: 'But what are you making of the social revolution? Are you making a success of it?' And from that we got back to two again with: 'To make it a success the Western world must join in. Why doesn't it?' "

---

eral government. The peasants are absolutely illiterate and collectively stupid, capable of resisting interference but incapable of comprehensive foresight and organization. They will become a sort of human swamp in a state of division, petty civil war, and political squalor, with a famine whenever the harvests are bad; and they will be breeding epidemics for the rest of Europe. They will lapse towards Asia." When the English edition of Wells's book reached Lenin in 1921, he read it carefully, marked many passages with "NB," and underlined—and double-underlined—others: for instance, "In Russia I must confess my passive objection to Marx has changed to a very active hostility"; and so forth. These Lenin markings are shown in the Russian edition: Gerbert Wells, *Rossiya vo Mgle* (Moscow, 1959). The purpose of publishing the Russian translation, as indicated in an introduction by Gleb Krzizhanovsky, was to prove Wells wrong in predicting the ruin of Russia.

The Lenin-Wells duet commenced "with a discussion of the future of the great towns under Communism." Mounting his cosmic imagination, Wells saw "the dying out of the towns of Russia." He predicted that "most of the towns would dissolve away."

Lenin "agreed quite cheerfully. 'The towns will get very much smaller,' Lenin admitted. 'They will be different. Yes, quite different.'"

And what about industry? Wells inquired. It "has to be reconstructed—as fundamentally?"

"Did I realize what was already in hand with Russia? The electrification of Russia?" Wells reported Lenin as replying.

Wells, who could soar on the wings of fantasy into the earth's far future, refused to fly with Lenin; his book called him "the dreamer in the Kremlin." Lenin, he said, after denouncing utopians "like a good orthodox Marxist . . . has succumbed at last to a Utopia, the Utopia of the electricians. . . . Can one imagine a more courageous project in a vast flat land of forests and illiterate peasants, with no water power, with no technical skill available, and with trade and industry at the last gasp? . . . I cannot see anything of the sort happening in this dark crystal of Russia, but this little man at the Kremlin can. . . . While I talked with him he almost persuaded me to share his vision."

Lenin also predicted the replacement of peasant farming by "large-scale agriculture. The Government is already running big estates with workers instead of peasants . . . come back and see what we have done in Russia in ten years' time."

Wells said he "realized that Communism could after all, in spite of Marx, be enormously creative. After the tiresome class-war fanatics I had been encountering among the Communists, men of formulae as sterile as flints, after numerous experiences of the trained and empty conceit of the common Marxist devotee, this amazing little man, with his frank admission of the immensity and complication of the project of Communism and his simple concentration upon its realization, was very refreshing. He at least has a vision of a world changed over and planned and built afresh."

Wells argued, however, that capitalism could be "civilized" through reforms "into a Collectivist world system." Lenin laughed briefly. To him capitalism "is a scramble, and it will inevitably make wars." Wars, Wells objected, "sprang from nationalist imperialism and not from a Capitalist organization of society."

"But what do you think of this new Republican Imperialism that comes to us from America?" Lenin suddenly asked.

"Here," Wells wrote, "Mr. Rothstein intervened in Russian with an objection that Lenin swept aside." Disregarding Rothstein's "plea for diplomatic reserve," Lenin dotted the i's of the new U.S. imperialism and, with relish, outlined the project that the American, Mr. Washington B. Vanderlip, a temporary tenant, like Wells, of the government guest house in the "Sugar

King's Palace" on the Moskva River, had held up to dazzle the Soviets: America would give economic assistance to Russia and recognize the Soviet state. "There was to be," Wells reported, "a defensive alliance against Japanese aggression in Siberia. There was to be an American Naval station on the [Russian] coast of Asia, and leases for long terms of sixty or fifty years of the natural resources of Khamskhatka [Kamchatka] and possibly of other large regions of Russian Asia." "Did Wells think that this made for peace?" Lenin wondered, or would it be "the beginning of a new world scramble"? And how, Lenin teased with a laugh, would British imperialists like it?

"Our multifarious argumentation ended indecisively, we parted warmly . . ." and Wells and Rothstein left the Kremlin together, the latter still grumbling over Lenin's "indiscretion" about fishing for America's favor with economic bait and naval bases.

Another Englishman had interviewed Lenin several months before Wells and saw deeper into the leader and the Soviet system. He was Bertrand Russell. Philosophy apparently served him better in 1920 than fiction-writing served Wells. "Soon after my arrival in Moscow," Russell wrote,[5] "I had an hour's conversation with Lenin in English, which he speaks fairly well. An interpreter was present, but his services were scarcely required. Lenin's room is very bare; it contains a big desk, some maps on the walls, two book-cases, and one comfortable chair for visitors in addition to two or three hard chairs. It is obvious that he has no love of luxury or even comfort. He is very friendly, and apparently simple, entirely without a trace of *hauteur*. If one met him without knowing who he was, one would not guess that he is possessed of great power or even that he is in any way very eminent. I have never met a personage so destitute of self-importance. He looks at his visitors very closely, and screws up one eye [his left eye had defective vision], which seems to increase alarmingly the penetrating power of the other. He laughs a great deal; at first his laugh seems merely friendly and jolly, but gradually I came to feel it rather grim. He is dictatorial, calm, incapable of fear, extraordinarily devoid of self-seeking, an embodied theory. The materialist conception of history, one feels, is his life-blood. He resembles a professor in his desire to have the theory understood and in his fury with those who misunderstand or disagree, as also in his love of expounding. I got the impression that he despises a great many people and is an intellectual aristocrat."

Bertrand Russell was in Russia from May 11 to June 16, 1920. His observations led him to see three possibilities: "The first is the ultimate defeat of Bolshevism by the forces of capitalism. The second is the victory of the Bolsheviks accompanied by a complete loss of their ideals and a regime of Napoleonic imperialism. The third is a prolonged world-war, in which civilization will go under and all its manifestations (including Communism) will be forgotten."

[5] Bertrand Russell, *Bolshevism: Practice and Theory* (New York, 1920, 192 pages; London, 1920, 131 pages).

Russell derided Bolshevism as "an impatient philosophy. . . . The ultimate source of the whole train of evils lies in the Bolshevik outlook on life: in its dogmatism of hatred and its belief that human nature can be completely transformed by force." He regarded Bolshevism as a "tragic delusion destined to bring upon the world centuries of darkness and futile violence." Part of the Soviet lack of liberty "has been inherited from the tsarist regime." But, "A great part of the despotism which characterizes the Bolsheviks belongs to the essence of their social philosophy."

Russell had intended, with a friend, to study "whether the Soviet system is really superior to Parliamentarism" as a form of representative government. "We were not able to make any such study, because the Soviet system is moribund. . . . The Moscow Soviet meets rarely. . . . The Presidium [of the Soviet] meets daily." It "consists only of orthodox Communists."

Russell also criticized the operations of Soviet economics. But as a philosopher he devoted much thought, and in his book much space, to the theory of Bolshevism. "Marxian Communism," he stated, lacked "the changing fluidity and skeptical practicality of modern science . . . , to Marx . . . , self-enrichment seemed the natural aim of man's political actions. But modern psychology has dived much deeper into the ocean of insanity upon which the little barque of human reason insecurely floats." Russell mentioned factors other than economics that shaped man's views and acts: climate and sex. These are materialistic yet Marxist materialists disregard them. He also included nationalism as a Marxist-neglected element in human affairs. Marxism made "Marxists rigid and Procrustean in their treatment of the life of instinct." But "there comes a point at which men feel that amusement and ease are worth more than all other goods put together." Another Russellian prediction deserves a high grade: "It is sheer nonsense to pretend that the rulers of a great empire such as Soviet Russia, when they have become accustomed to power, retain the proletarian psychology, and feel that their class interest is the same as that of the ordinary workingman." Finally, Russell defined a communist "as a man who entertains a number of elaborate and dogmatic beliefs—such as philosophic materialism, for example—which may be true, but are not, to a scientific temper, capable of being known to be true with any certainty."

The untruth shall make you unfree.

Alas, Russell discussed none of these basic matters with Lenin. He put superficial questions which he, and many others, might have answered in advance for Lenin. First question: Could the revolution in England be non-violent? Lenin "waved aside the suggestion as fantastic. I got little impression of knowledge or psychological imagination as regards Great Britain." Second question: Was it possible to establish communism firmly and fully in a country containing such a large majority of peasants? Lenin "admitted that it was difficult, and laughed over the exchange the peasant is compelled to make, of food for paper; the worthlessness of Russian paper struck him as comic." But conditions would improve. Electrification would help. What they really needed, Lenin confided, was "revolutions in other countries. Peace between Bolshevik Russia and capitalist countries, he said, must always be insecure." Reverting to the peasant problem, Lenin "described the division between rich and poor peasants, and the Government propaganda among the latter against the former, leading to acts of violence which he seemed to find amusing. He spoke as though the dictatorship over the peasant would have to continue for a long time, because of the peasant's desire for free trade."

In summarizing the impression Lenin left, Russell wrote, "I think if I had met him without knowing who he was, I should not have guessed that he was a great man; he struck me as too opinionated and narrowly orthodox. His strength comes, I imagine, from his honesty, courage, and unwavering faith—religious faith in the Marxian gospel. . . . He has as little love of liberty as the Christians who suffered under Diocletian. . . . Perhaps love of liberty is incompatible with whole-hearted belief in a panacea for all human ills. If so, I cannot but rejoice in the skeptical temper of the Western world. I went to Russia a Communist; but contact with those who have no doubts has intensified a thousandfold my own doubts, not as to Communism in itself, but as to the wisdom of holding a creed so firmly that for its sake men are willing to inflict widespread misery." The price "mankind must pay to achieve Communism by Bolshevik methods is too terrible" and "even after paying the price, I do not believe the result would be what the Bolsheviks profess to desire."

Emma Goldman and Alexander (Sasha) Berkman also came to praise and stayed to curse. Deported from the United States in December, 1919, these two famous anarchists reached Russia in January, 1920. They had lauded the Soviet government at public meetings in America. Arrived in Petrograd, Miss Goldman was aglow with ecstasy. "Soviet Russia! Sacred Ground, Magic People! You have come to symbolize humanity's hope, you alone are destined to redeem mankind. I have come to serve you." Thus, in her autobiography,[6] she described her sentiments as she descended on Soviet soil. The two anarchists soon discovered "the gagging of free speech at the session of the Petro-Soviet that we attended . . . better and more plentiful food was served Party members at the Smolny dining room . . . many similar injustices. . . . Thirty-four different grades of rations—under alleged Communism!" They nevertheless shielded their faith against the assaults of fact: "But Sasha and I held on to our firm belief that the Bolsheviki were our brothers in a common fight." Hope for humanity shut their hearts to inhumanity. Hope dissolved the black clouds, leaving only silver linings. They knew about "taking hostages for political refugees, not exempting even old parents and children of tender age." They knew about the "nightly . . . street

[6] Emma Goldman, *Living My Life* (New York, 1931), Vol. Two, pp. 504-993.

and house raids by the Cheka." Yet "I would not see with my inner eye the truth so evident to my outer sight," Emma Goldman wrote. There have been many like her.

Angelica Balabanoff arranged an appointment for the two anarchists with Lenin. After waiting an hour, the door to Lenin's office opened. They stepped in. "Two slanting eyes were fixed upon us with piercing penetration." Miss Goldman describes the room and adds, "The background seemed most fitting for one reputed for his rigid habits of life and matter-of-factness." The surroundings were of "severe simplicity." She also noted his "emotional economy" and his "quick perception. . . . No less amazing was his glee over anything he considered funny in himself or his visitors. Especially if he could put one at a disadvantage, the great Lenin would shake with laughter so as to compel one to laugh with him." Lenin began by aiming a quiverful of arrows at them from "his flint-like brain": What were the chances of revolution in the U.S.A. in the near future? Why hadn't they remained in America to abet it, even from prison? Now that they were in Russia how would they contribute here? "Sasha was the first to get his breath. He began in English, but Lenin at once stopped him with a mirthful laugh. 'Do you think I understand English? Not a word. Nor any other foreign language. I am no good at them, though I have lived abroad many years. Funny, isn't it?' And off he went in peals of laughter."

He spoke fluent English with Wells and Russell. The laughter might have indicated he knew they knew he was lying.

Berkman addressed Lenin in Russian. Why were anarchists kept in Soviet prisons? "Anarchists?" Lenin interrupted, "nonsense! Who told you such yarns . . . ? We do have bandits in prison, and Makhnovtsy [followers of Nestor Makhno], but no *ideiny* anarchists [anarchists guided by principles]."

Emma Goldman suggested that "capitalist America also divides the anarchists into two categories, philosophic and criminal." Did he not, then, believe in free speech?

"Free speech," Lenin replied, "is a bourgeois prejudice, a soothing plaster for social ills. In the Workers' Republic economic well-being talks louder than speech." The dictatorship of the proletariat "faces very grave difficulties, the greatest of them the opposition of the peasants. They need nails, salt, textiles, tractors, electrification. When we can give them these, they will be with us. . . . In the present state of Russia all prattle of freedom is merely food for the reaction trying to down Russia. Only bandits are guilty of that, and they must be kept under lock and key." This sentence offered them a peep into the Soviet future. Blithely ignoring their known love of liberty and horror of organization and the state, Lenin urged Goldman and Berkman to work with the Comintern in support of Soviet purposes abroad. They could not agree. For a year after talking with Lenin their anti-Bolshevik bitterness rose in the cup, but it did not overflow until Kronstadt poured into it—until the Kremlin used concentrated military power to suppress a peasant-anarchist-pro-freedom revolt of the sailors on the Soviet naval base in 1921. "Kronstadt" later became a synonym for the last straw that makes a communist or Soviet sympathizer get off the Red camel's back, the last zag that throws riders off the locomotive of communist revolution.

Angelica Balabanoff, who brought Goldman and Berkman to Lenin's attention, had her "Kronstadt" before they did. She knew Lenin well, visited his home; he consulted her. She knew the European socialist movement, especially the Italian. Once, in 1920, he summoned her to his office; what was her opinion about the situation in Italy? She thought Italy manifested considerable enthusiasm for revolution. "But, Comrade Balabanoff," Lenin interrupted, "don't you know that a revolutionary development in Italy now would be a disaster, a tragedy? Italy has neither grain nor coal, and no raw materials at all. . . . Do not compare the Russian nation with other nations. No other people could have suffered so much. . . . We have no use for a second Hungary." No premature revolution in a small country.

But this conversation gave proof to Angelica of the "hypocrisy of Bolshevik policy and of Lenin personally." For even while he pointed out to her the dangers involved in an Italian revolution, Giacinto M. Serrati, the leader of the Italian revolutionary socialists, who was saying the same thing, found himself expelled from Moscow's favor and denounced as a traitor. The Kremlin replaced him with Bombacci, characterized by Lenin, in a remark to Angelica, as "an idiotic illiterate" and by another top Bolshevik as "a long-bearded idiot." Later, wrote Angelica, the Bolsheviks abandoned him; he thereupon joined the fascists and was hanged with Mussolini from the same gallows.[7]

Angelica found herself surrounded by cynicism, insincerity, and dishonesty. To this was added the state-inflicted poverty of the people. "I myself saw and experienced," she writes, "how one went to the country and from one peasant hut to the other to exchange a needle for an egg"—the result of world war and civil war but also of Lenin's love of class war.

She accordingly told the Central Committee of the party that she wished to leave Russia. A long delay intervened. Endlessly she begged Lenin to hasten her departure. At last, he said "with irritation, 'Well, yes, if you prefer Italy to Russia we shall immediately accede to your request.'"

Instead, however, the Central Committee ordered her to a sanatorium in southern Russia and, when, pleading good health, she refused, it offered her a heavy-duty post in the south. Ultimately, the Soviet authorities allowed her to leave. Despite decades of anticommunist socialist activity in the West, she retained her respect for Lenin. "Both Lenin and Trotsky," she wrote, "were motivated by a single desire: to serve the cause of the people; to this aim they devoted their entire life. But even at close range did it in different ways." Lenin was totally impersonal. He "tried to persuade, de-

[7] Angelica Balabanoff, *Lenin*, pp. 97-98.

manded obedience," but all in an impersonal way. He made everybody feel
his equal. "This involved no strain, it was his nature, his true self. To his
opponents he was an intolerant, stubborn, cruel and unjust foe, but he always treated them as enemies of *Bolshevism*, not as *his personal* opponents.
Often one hears that Lenin was 'modest.' In my opinion, this was not true.
Modesty presumes a judgment, a comparison between oneself and another.
To Lenin this was immaterial. It was characteristic of him that he wished
to learn from others, especially after he came to power. . . . Trotsky thought
and acted quite differently. He served the revolutionary ideal with the same
self-denial as Lenin; but every act, every one of his thoughts had to carry
the stamp of his personality: 'Trotsky said this, Trotsky wrote this.' " His
temperament and "biting irony" multiplied his enemies. "Even when he
wanted to be friendly, he wrapped himself in a layer of ice." Lenin cared for
neither applause nor disapproval. He was the "village schoolmaster"; when
the lesson was over, the speech delivered, he walked out with hurried steps;
"he was the avowed foe of every kind of exhibitionism." On the other hand,
Trotsky loved the plaudits and acclaim of the multitude.

Lenin was all function. Trotsky was function and form.

"Lenin," Angelica wrote in her thin little memoir of Lenin in the 1950's,
"could keep apart his opinion of a person as a person from his opinion of that
same person as an instrument in the service of Bolshevism. He did not like
Trotsky." He disliked Trotsky's vanity. But he worked with Trotsky in the
closest harmony after the revolution—disputes notwithstanding.

Trotsky was punctual, punctilious, puritanical, meticulous. "Think of it,"
he once said to Angelica, "my father wants to visit me, but he has no shoes
and I can't get any for him. How can I ask shoes for my father when there
are so many people here who have none?" Lenin might have made an exception for his parent.

Trotsky dressed simply, usually in unadorned Red Army uniform, but was
elegantly groomed. Lenin's "dress was nondescript," Lincoln·Eyre reported
to the New York *World* of February 21, 1920, "—a slightly soiled soft white
collar (even soiled white collars are a rarity in Russia), a black tie and a dark
brown business suit, the trousers stuffed into knee-high boots of thick felt
[valenki], the warmest kind of foot covering."

Lenin received Eyre in his Kremlin office and then allowed himself to
be induced to take the American journalist and Victor O. Kubes, a photographer, to his private apartment—rarely opened to bourgeois foreigners—
where he submitted to questions and the orders of the motion-picture cam-
eraman. "And you represent the New York *World*," Lenin greeted Mr. Eyre,
"the organ of your government, is it not?"

"Apparently," Lincoln Eyre wrote in his newspaper of February 21, 1920,
"Lenin was in the best of spirits. His rather grim sense of humor was to the
fore. He laughed frequently, usually at the ironic quips in which he so de-
lights. There was about him that mental alertness, that intellectual electricity,
which is perhaps the most salient characteristic."

While Lenin obeyed the photographer's directions "with smiling docility," Eyre studied the statesman: "With his bald pate, squinty eyes, broad nose, thickish lips, unkempt reddish gray beard, Lenin is decidedly homely, not to say ugly. But his homeliness is that of the bulldog, having about it nothing unwholesome and repulsive. His wide and slightly bulging forehead, revealing the thinker, moreover, redeems his face from the heavy, almost brutish quality it might otherwise reflect." Lenin spoke "rather slow but very pure English . . . he tackled each topic brought up with the unhesitating promptitude of one who knows his own mind thoroughly."

Lenin also took orders from an English sculptress, Clare Consuelo Sheridan, a cousin of Winston Churchill, who came to Moscow with warm recommendations from Leo Kamenev and won Michael Borodin's aid in reaching Lenin's office. She was a handsome aristocrat for whose beauty several exalted communists developed an acute appreciation. Lenin remained immune to her feminine pulchritude, but, she wrote, "He has a genial manner and a kindly smile which puts one instantly at ease." During the first, four-hour sitting on October 7, 1920, "he never smoked, and never even drank a cup of tea." He worked at his desk. When he had a telephone call, "his face lost the dullness of repose and became animated and interesting. He gesticulated to the telephone as though it understood." In the second and final sitting the next day, she prevailed on him to leave his papers and pose on a revolving stand she brought to his office. She had little conversation with Lenin. In reply to her question why his secretaries were women, he said curtly the men were at war. She asked whether he had read H. G. Wells. He had started *Joan and Peter* but did not read it to the end. "He liked the description in the beginning of the English intellectual bourgeois life." Was Cousin Churchill Russia's most hated Englishman? Lenin "shrugged his shoulders and added something about Churchill being the man with all the force of the capitalists behind him." A comrade appeared for audience. "Lenin laughed and frowned, and looked thoughtful, sad, and humorous all in turn. His eyebrows twitched, sometimes they went right up, and then again they puckered together maliciously."

On the revolving stand Lenin told her "he never had sat so high." She kneeled before him to study his face from another angle. Laughingly she asked, "Are you accustomed to this attitude in women?" A secretary entered to impede the answer. "They talked rapid Russian together, and laughed a good deal."

". . . he looked upon me resentfully as a bourgeoise," she wrote later. Perhaps she thought so because he did not react to the heavy charm barrage she hurled at him; it had brought lesser giants to her knees.

"Give me a message to take back to Winston.

"He answered, 'I have already sent him a message through the [British Labour] Delegation, and he answered it not directly but through a bitter newspaper article in which he said I was a most horrible creature . . .' "

Back in England, she wrote a book in which she described her Soviet experiences and read heads (Lenin's, Trotsky's, Djerzhinsky's, Zinoviev's) as a palmist reads hands.[8] Lenin disliked the book.[9]

In Petrograd months after the revolution, Lenin and his wife took occasional strolls by the banks of the Neva without a guard and without being recognized.[10] This elderly couple could have passed unnoticed in the streets of Moscow in 1920. But by that time he had become a world figure, a world mystery, to some a bogey, to some a hope. In Soviet Russia he was loved and hated, admired and scorned. None could be indifferent to him, because he had power, because he stood for an avowed political and social program which his party and government translated into actions that affected every human being in Russia and many outside. He knew what he wanted. He was all of one piece, a great, rough-hewn, unpolished chunk of granite much more impressive than any sculptor's bust. He chose politics as his life and gave it all his life. There could have been no conflicts within, no regrets, rather much joy. That history, unexpectedly, granted him the chance to do what he, as a young man, set out to do must have afforded him endless satisfaction. He laughed at foreigners and took pleasure in confounding them; they were unbelievers. He had been borne to the summit on the wings of faith in himself and his purpose. This was happiness in an unhappy country. The summit is cold. He lived there in isolation in a bare hut while all below was turmoil, toil, trouble, death, and despair. He consequently delayed too long to introduce the changes forced on him in 1921. He refused to descend. This can be strength and it can become a weakness.

XXXII. EAGER UNDERTAKER

LENIN'S RELIGION was violent revolution. It was his god and he is its saint. Yet many communists regarded him as a rightist, and he repeatedly attacked the leftists.

The Ninth Congress of the Russian Communist Party, which met in Moscow from March 29 to April 5, 1920, proposed to celebrate, prematurely, Lenin's fiftieth birthday. He protested, and when the laudatory speeches commenced he got up and walked out, and telephoned every few minutes from his Kremlin office inquiring when the oratory would cease so he could return to the session.[1] He spurned all manifestations of "the cult of personality."

[8] *Mayfair to Moscow. Clare Sheridan's Diary* (New York, 1921).
[9] *Vospominaniya*, Vol. 2, p. 232.
[10] *Ibid.*, Vol. 3, p. 157. Told by Krupskaya.
[1] *Vospominaniya*, Vol. 2, pp. 36-37.

Four days after his fiftieth birthday, Lenin completed the writing of a 30,000-word pamphlet entitled *The Infantile Disease of "Leftism" in Communism*.[2] It might have been entitled "How to make a Communist Revolution in a Democracy." It is studded with shining examples of Lenin's tactical thoughts and fallacious thinking. It reflects his assessment of revolutionary prospects, and helps, among other things, to explain the Polish misadventure and more recent Soviet foreign policies.

The Soviet invasion of Poland was a leftist deviation, a revolutionary war (not devoid of rightist nationalist undertones), the kind Bukharin, Radek, and others advocated and Lenin opposed during the Brest-Litovsk negotiations. Yet Radek, the leftist, opposed the Polish invasion which Lenin advocated. Before the Polish war, Lenin was a rightist. After the invasion, he sometimes spoke like a rightist and sometimes like a leftist but usually acted like a rightist, and when he did he provoked leftist opposition at home. Others too shifted ground; Bukharin was first an extreme leftist, then an extreme rightist. If leftism fails, can rightism be far behind? And vice versa. Politics is round, like the revolving globe. Go west—and you reach east; go east, you come to the west. The choice of political direction is not made in a vacuum, it is an accommodation to circumstances; this was Lenin's message in the *Infantile Disease* brochure. It is a handbook on how to succeed through accommodation. "Right" and "left" are vague, often misleading, terms.

The Lenin pamphlet began by stating that "the Russian pattern" of revolution "reveals to *all* countries something very important about their inescapable and early future." This became a refrain. He believed it. It also established his authority to lecture, and occasionally to hector, foreign communists who failed to follow the Soviet road to the acquisition of power. In the pursuit of this goal he placed obedience higher than ethics.

Foreign communist readers recognized the mind of Lenin in a passage in the pamphlet admonishing them not to quit the trade unions. To do so would be a gift to reactionary trade-union leaders. Communists must, on the contrary, infiltrate the unions. They would, to be sure, encounter every kind of obstacle. "It is necessary to know how to resist all this," Lenin wrote, "to submit to all and any sacrifice, even—in case of need—to use any subterfuge, shrewdness, illegal method, deceit, the concealment of truth, anything to penetrate into the trade unions, remain in them, and at all costs conduct communist activity." He cited an example from life in tsarist Russia.

Lenin, however, was not immoral. Nor was he moral. He was amoral, he had no interest in what was virtuous or wicked, only in what served his purpose or threatened to defeat it. He formulated the simple alternative: "Who-whom?" Who downs whom?—and the choice of weapons is free, the choice of holds is unrestricted.

In an address on October 2, 1920, to a congress of the Russian Communist Union of Youth (now called "the Leninist Komsomol"), Lenin defined mor-

[2] Lenin, *Sochineniya*, Second ed., Vol. XXV, pp. 171-249.

ality:[3] Youth should be educated in "communist morality." Is there such a thing? "Of course, yes." But it is not bourgeois morality which originates with God. "We don't believe in God and we well know that the priesthood, the landlords, and the bourgeoisie spoke in the name of God with a view to accomplishing their exploiting purposes. . . . We reject all morality derived from extra-human, extra-class concepts. We say that is deception . . . we say that our morality is completely subordinate to the interests of the class struggle of the proletariat . . . we have not yet had time to abolish classes; the division between workers and peasants still remains." If a peasant has surplus grain not required by his family and cattle while others starve and he says, "the more they starve the dearer I can sell my grain," that is exploitation. "We say: morality is that which serves the destruction of the old exploiting society and the unification of all working people around the proletariat engaged in creating a new communist society . . . we say, for a communist all of morality consists of this tight solidarity discipline and of the class-conscious mass struggle against exploitation. We do not believe in eternal morality." The only form of immorality he mentioned was economic exploitation, the equivalent, in Soviet Russia at that time, of private trade.

For the effective prosecution of the class struggle against exploitation, Lenin, in his *The Infantile Disease of "Leftism" in Communism*, handed down a key commandment: Be Inside; Bore From Within. To prove its wisdom he reviewed the history of Russian Bolshevism and the qualities that explain the movement's triumph: "one of the basic conditions for the victory over the bourgeoisie is unconditional centralization and the strictest discipline of the proletariat." Russia had it. Thanks to tsarism, moreover, Russian revolutionists emigrated to the West and acquired "as no other country in the world," a wealth of international contacts and revolutionary theories; the best was "Marxism, the only correct revolutionary theory." Russian experience demonstrates that there is a time for victories and a time for setbacks. "Revolutionary parties," Lenin preached, "must continue their studies. They studied how to advance. Now they should understand that this science has to be supplemented by the science of how better to retreat." During a revolutionary trough, revolutionaries "must certainly learn to work legally in the most reactionary parliaments, in the most reactionary trade unions, cooperatives, insurance and similar organizations." That would constitute retreat. It was something the Western "leftists" balked at doing. They preferred to boycott parliaments and trade unions, and they excoriated moderate communists ready to compromise. Lenin lashed back. He urged British communists to join the Labour Party. Sylvia Pankhurst, suffragette and leftist communist, said in a personal conversation with Lenin in Moscow that if the communists joined, "those gentlemen will expel us." He replied, "That would not be *at all* bad."[4] One does not begin with radicalism, Lenin wrote

[3] *Ibid.*, pp. 384-397.
[4] *Ibid.*, p. 363.

in his pamphlet. He recalled—what many had forgotten—that before the Bolshevik revolution he did not propose "All power to the soviets" until a change had occurred "in the mood of the soviets" favorable to his party. He also repeated an earlier statement: after the fall of Nicholas II, "Russia became a bourgeois democratic republic, freer—and during a war—than any country in the world." Such a republic, with a Constituent Assembly added, was better than one without an assembly, and a soviet republic was still better. Without these fine distinctions, without thorough and prolonged preparation for them, "we could not have won in November, 1917," or retained power.

Lenin then listed the compromises the Bolsheviks made from the birth of the party in 1903 until 1917, how it adapted itself to other parties, cooperated with them, borrowed from them, coexisted with them. The list is long but lacks conviction; the first Lenin law had always been: "no rapprochement with other parties," no collaboration even with fractions of his own party that failed to accept his program and obey him. Lenin was a dictator long before November, 1917. If he could not lick his opponents he left them and established his own weekly paper or his own party. He did not bore from within, he battered from without. He nevertheless branded as "leftist infantilism" the ideas of those communists in Germany, Holland, and England who took their cue not from what he said in 1920 but from what he did before 1917. He accused the Western leftists of "denying partyness and party discipline"—a sin he regularly committed except when he imposed the discipline.

It was "comic childish nonsense" to talk, as the European leftist communists did, of "the dictatorship of leaders *or* the dictatorship of the masses." Lenin contended that the two were identical, the dictatorship was implemented through mass organizations: soviets and trade unions. "The German 'leftists' complained of the 'bad' leaders of their parties," Lenin wrote, "and succumb to despair, going so far as the ridiculous 'denial' of 'leaders.'" The masses, they proposed, should dictate. But part of the training of good leaders came from participation in parliaments, and "criticism . . . should be directed not against parliamentarianism or parliamentary activity but rather against those leaders who cannot—and still more against those who *will not* —use parliamentary elections and the floor of parliament in a revolutionary, communist manner." "Revolutionary manner" was translated by Lenin on August 2, 1920, in a talk to the Second Congress of the Communist International. If you can break up parliaments "by an armed uprising in all countries—that is very good," he said. But "we are also compelled to conduct the struggle for the destruction of parliament within parliament." This had happened in Russia. "We know very well," Lenin recalled, "that our dispersal of the Constituent Assembly on January 5, 1918, was not hampered but facilitated by the circumstance that within the counterrevolutionary Constituent Assembly there was a consistent Bolshevik, as well as an inconsistent Left Social Revolutionary, soviet opposition." (Actually, armed Bol-

shevik guards dispersed the Assembly without regard to its membership.)
It was wrong, therefore, to boycott bourgeois parliaments.

The German leftists, Lenin charged, made another mistake in refusing to
recognize the Versailles Peace Treaty imposed on Germany by the Allies. "It
is necessary to understand," he wrote, "that the tactic is radically wrong
which repudiates the obligation of a Soviet Germany (if a Soviet Germany
should soon arise) to recognize the Versailles Treaty for a time and submit
to it. . . . To tie one's hands in advance, to say openly to the enemy, who
is better armed than we, that we will fight him, and when we will fight him,
is folly, not revolutionary." Lenin assumed that the Allies would allow the
German Communist Party to govern Germany if it promised to cooperate
with the treaty's perpetrators. He underestimated the imperialists.

Now the Kremlin pamphleteer turned to England, where "both conditions for a successful proletarian revolution are clearly ripening." The conditions were: "a majority of the workers (or, in any case, a majority of the
class-conscious, thinking, politically active workers) have fully understood
the necessity of a revolution and are ready to die for it," and, second, a crisis
within the ruling classes. To win Britain for communism, Lenin advised,
"we must, first, help Henderson or Snowden [the Labour Party leaders] defeat Lloyd George and Churchill (still more correctly: compel the former
to defeat the latter, for the former fear their own victory!); second, help the
majority of the working class to be convinced, through its own experience,
that we are right, that is, that the Hendersons and Snowdens are wholly
unsuitable, that they are petty bourgeois and treacherous, and that their
bankruptcy is inevitable." To this end, the British communists must offer
the Labour Party an alliance. If Labour accepted, the communists could
bore from within; if it refused, the communists could expose the Hendersons and Snowdens.

This was pure fantasy. Drawing no distinction between developed countries and nineteenth-century, underdeveloped Russia, forgetting that the Soviet government was the child of the First World War and that the war had
ended, unmindful of the resources of capitalism and the conservatism and
strength of Labour and, in Germany, of the Social Democrats, Lenin looked
upon the Western nations as so many Russians destined to repeat Russia's
revolutionary experience in which the red tail wagged and then swallowed
the big black dog.

Lenin's final chapter gave a summary of his wrong conclusions. "In less
than two years" soviets conquered Russia and were recognized as "the gravedigger, the heir, and the successor of parliamentarianism and bourgeois democracy in general" throughout the world. The next statement worked havoc
with working-class movements in many countries during the decades that
followed: "The history of the workers movement now shows that in all countries . . . communists would," on the road to victory, "live through a struggle (which has already commenced) above all and chiefly against *its own*

Menshevism . . . , that is, against opportunism and social chauvinism." This formula split and weakened the labor forces almost everywhere and, in Germany, gave a strong helping hand to nazism on its ascent to power and pestilence. The communists, in addition to fighting the "Mensheviks" or democratic socialists, would also have to combat what Lenin called " 'Leftist' Communism." Lenin thus placed himself in the middle, a vital center, determined, like blind Samson, to push against the pillars to the right and left of him. He underestimated not only the world capitalists but also the world labor movement. He blundered further in believing that, while the working class of each country must evolve in its own way, it would move "far more speedily" toward victory over the bourgeoisie than had Russian Bolshevism: "In their thinking the advance guard of the proletariat has already been won over" for communism. "That is the chief thing." Now the advance Red Guard would proceed to win over the main body of labor.

Lenin loved statistics which, though often used, unconsciously or maliciously, to mislead are precise in themselves. Yet he made hasty diagnoses and large generalizations from small, stray facts a year out of date. His was a fine brain squeezed into a doctrinal strait jacket of a priori judgments, a fine brain where dogma, once admitted, bored from within and made holes in his analyses—especially of foreign situations. He swore by the beard of the prophet—Marx. Marx and wishes were the fathers of his thoughts. An enslaving fatalism possessed his mind; "Everybody will agree," Lenin wrote in the conclusion of the brochure, "that the conduct of that army will be unwise or even criminal which does not prepare to master all varieties of warfare, all the means and methods the enemy has or can have. But this applies even more to politics than to military affairs. . . . By mastering all means of struggle we can surely win, for we represent the interests of the truly progressive, truly revolutionary class." He decided who represented whom. He decided who would defeat whom. The Marxist scriptures had predetermined it. Lenin saw himself clad in the armor of science and tilting with an unbreakable lance against the fragile walls of the citadels of capitalism. Actually it was all messianic delusion. Lenin once said that "the real essence, the real soul of Marxism is: the concrete analysis of a concrete situation." It was missing in his treatment of the European situation in April, 1920.

At bottom Lenin's misapprehensions of the outside world were due to the fact that, though not conventionally nationalistic, he was Russo-centric. He spent years in Switzerland, but his writings and oral statements contain no evidence of an understanding or appreciation of that country of communes. He knew its democracy and British democracy, yet he abhorred their parliamentary system, the capstone of their edifice of freedom, and regarded it as a sham to be swept away and replaced by soviets. Since Russia was capitalistic and autocratic, all forms of capitalist government stank in his Slavic nostrils. He would have substituted a "democratic" dictatorship on his Muscovite model. He urged his foreign comrades to adapt their national political patterns by adopting the Russian pattern. Proletarians of the world unite! You have only your national individuality to lose. You have Russia to gain. Small wonder the West did not lend him its ears. He came to bury it. No one loves his own impatient undertaker.

To accelerate the burial of the bourgeoisie, Lenin proposed not only to attack the victim through the front door—Europe—but also through the back door—Europe's colonies. He scoffed at bourgeois equality; it could not be attained except by the elimination of class divisions in the developed and "little-developed" countries. Alone the cooperation of the "working masses of all nations and countries for the combined struggle to overthrow the landlords and bourgeoisie can guarantee victory over capitalism without which the annihilation of national oppression and inequality is impossible." The petty bourgeois nationalists who proclaimed their internationalism but retained their "nationalist egoism" were doomed to failure in the colonies. On the other hand, "proletarian internationalism demands, first, the subordination of the proletarian struggle in one country to the interests of that struggle on a world scale; second, it requires the ability of a nation which is achieving victory over the bourgeoisie to make the greatest national sacrifice for the sake of the overthrow of international capitalism."

Communist parties in underdeveloped lands, Lenin wrote,[5] must help the independence movements combat the influence of the priesthood "and other reactionary and medieval elements," and undermine "Pan-Islamism and similar tendencies seeking to combine the independence movement against European and American imperialism with a reinforcement of the position of the khans, landlords, mullahs, and so forth." But, he cautioned, the communist parties must never merge with the independence movements; they should assist yet remain separate. For in addition to promoting the independence of colonies, the communist parties had a special role: to expose the deceit of the imperialist powers who grant independence to countries and at the same time keep them "completely dependent economically, financially, and militarily. . . . In the present international situation, there is no salvation for dependent and weak nations except in a union of soviet republics" embracing all continents.[6]

In April, 1920, the anti-leftist *Infantile Disease* pamphlet. In June, 1920, this extreme leftist program of sovietism in the backward colonies. In practice, however, Lenin frowned on attempts to establish soviet republics even in countries contiguous to Soviet Russia, in Persia, for instance—in 1921. Lenin wanted no more trouble.[7] Red Army troops had invaded Persia in 1920 in pursuit of White units. Lenin favored their withdrawal in accordance with the February, 1921, Soviet-Persian Treaty. By that time, however, the Bol-

[5] *Ibid.*, p. 289.
[6] *Ibid.*, pp. 285-290. "Preliminary Draft of Theses on National and Colonial Questions for the Second Congress of the Communist International." Written on June 5, 1920, first published on June 14, 1920, in the *Communist International* magazine.
[7] Leninskii Sbornik, Vol. XXXVI, p. 144.

sheviks had driven the Menshevik government out of Georgia by military force. Sergo Orjonekidze, the Bolshevik viceroy in Tiflis, and Stalin, his Moscow mentor, thwarting Lenin's wishes, reinforced the Russian soldiers in the north Persian province of Ghilan. Feodor Rothstein, Muscovite ambassador in Tehran, protested to Lenin. Rothstein submitted that Persia, a poor, retarded country, with no working class, was unprepared for a proletarian revolution. To export one would complicate Russian relations with the Shah and with the British who might then reoccupy southern Persia. "It seems to me you are right," Lenin wrote to Rothstein in reply.[8]

His view thus stiffened by Lenin, Rothstein urged Riza Khan, virtual ruler of Persia and subsequently the Shah, to march into Ghilan and suppress the tribal leaders, notably Kuchik Khan, a puppet supported by Stalin. Kuchik was defeated and fled into the mountains, where he froze to death. Riza had Kuchik's head brought to Tehran for display. "Among the prisoners taken by Riza were Russian peasants from the [central Russian] province of Tula," Chicherin told me. "Those were the soldiers of Stalin's Ghilan Soviet Republic," Chicherin sneered.

Stalin was furious. He blamed Rothstein for the collapse of his effort to sovietize—and thereby annex—northern Persia. He raised the matter in the Politburo. Chicherin described the proceedings to me. Stalin pressed his complaint.

"Good," said Lenin, with a gleam in his eye and dictated to the stenographer: "A strict reprimand to Comrade Rothstein for killing Kuchik Khan."

"No," a Politburo member objected, "it was Riza who killed Kuchik Khan."

"Good," Lenin agreed, "a strict reprimand to Riza Khan for killing Kuchik Khan."

"But we cannot reprimand Riza," Stalin interjected, "he is not a Soviet citizen."

Whereupon Lenin burst into a laugh and the subject was dropped. Adopting a rightist, antirevolutionary position, Lenin had used ridicule to flatten Stalin, historically a rightist who, in this Iranian escapade, followed a leftist-revolutionary, indistinguishable from a nationalist-imperialist, course.

Thus, Lenin preached rightist moderation in Europe and planned leftist extremism for Asia and Africa, and in his capacity as statesman responsible for the fate of his country behaved with rightist circumspection. Lenin was a remarkable combination of inflexible dogma and flexible procedures, of granite and boa constrictor.

---

[8] While I was writing The Soviets in World Affairs, Ambassador Rothstein read to me from his diary into which he had entered the text of his letter and Lenin's. He exacted a promise from me not to publish this until after his death.

XXXIII. THE "NEW" DIPLOMACY

FOR THREE YEARS the Soviet state had teetered on the brink of destruction. Yet it survived. Certain survival amid encircling troubles induced sober stocktaking. Lenin faced harsh facts and told truths that hurt. He viewed the world in a new perspective. "Three years ago," he reminisced on November 6, 1920, ". . . as we sat in the Smolny . . . if someone had told us that night that things would be as they are today, that we would win this victory of ours, nobody, not even the most inveterate optimist, would have believed it. We knew then that our victory would be a victory only when our cause succeeded in the entire world, because we launched our action exclusively in the expectation of a world revolution."[1]

In another address on November 20, 1920, Lenin put the essence of the communist outlook from that day to this: "It has transpired that neither one side nor the other, neither the Soviet Russian Republic nor the whole remaining capitalist world has won a victory or succumbed to defeat, and at the same time it has transpired that, although our predictions have not been fulfilled simply, quickly, and directly, they have been fulfilled to the extent that they have given us the main thing, and the main thing was to secure the possibility of the existence of the proletarian government and the Soviet Republic even in the event of the delay of the socialist revolution in the entire world."[2]

Of necessity, Lenin shifted his primary emphasis from external revolution to domestic entrenchment, for, being practical, he moved away when he encountered an immovable object. But hope remained, and Comintern activity remained: "We always knew and will not forget," he had said on November 6, 1920, "that our cause is an international cause, and so long as a revolution does not take place in all countries—including the wealthiest and most civilized—our victory is only half a victory, or perhaps less."

What had enabled the Soviet state to survive? "Three such mighty powers as England, France, and America could not unite against us," Lenin declared on November 6, "and were defeated in the war which they began against us with united forces." He exaggerated. Those powers used only a minuscule fraction of their might against the Soviets. And if they could not unite how did they fight with "united forces"? But Lenin wanted to make a point: the great nations had failed in their anti-Soviet endeavors because "they are semi-corpses . . . because . . . the bourgeois class is rotten." Therefore Russia was safe and the world revolution a possibility. Herewith Lenin set a permanent

---

[1] Lenin, *Sochineniya*, Second ed., Vol. XXV, p. 473.
[2] *Ibid.*, pp. 483-484.

Kremlin fashion: inflated failures in other countries were offered as balm for the deep wounds of his own countrymen and mirages of world revolution as the circus when bread and other commodities fell short of demand. Lenin, however, added a touch of realism: it would have been "insanity" to promise that "Russia with her own strength could make over the entire world." It was more pressing now to remake Russia. "Communism is the Soviet government plus the electrification of the whole country," he declared in his November 20 address, "for without electrification industry cannot be improved." He expanded on the detailed program. He realized, nevertheless, that this was only one aspect of the enormous task before his government. "The economic foundations for a real socialist society are still absent." Moreover, the country had witnessed "a rebirth of bureaucracy."

The mass of the workers and peasants, Lenin knew, lacked the literacy and culture necessary to lift the economy and eliminate the bureaucracy which had eaten into the party and state hierarchies. The energies and the lives of the most devoted citizens had been taken by the civil war; persons of little courage and less imagination and big love of red tape now manned the apparatus of government. Compared to the tens of millions of petty bourgeois in village and town, "we are few," Lenin complained. Enthusiasm was at a low ebb. The desire for a safe berth in an office, where pedantry predominated over devotion, soared high. Those fitted by education and training to perform the myriad acts of governing were not distinguished by sympathy for Bolshevism, whereas few communists and procommunists were as yet equipped for administrative work. The idea that any cook, any laborer, could govern had withered in three years' time.

Bureaucracy was the infantile disease of a government which controlled, managed, and directed everything—economics, politics, education. As statism grew older, the disease became permanent. Lenin saw this when he neared the end of his life.

Meanwhile, he had to forge a new foreign policy and domestic policy. Foreign policy is the twin of domestic politics in all countries, including communist countries. Thus Lenin opened his speech on December 6, 1920[3] to a meeting of the secretaries of the communist party units of Moscow with these words: "Comrades, I saw [from reports of the earlier proceedings of the meeting] with satisfaction, although I must admit, with surprise too, that the question of concessions [to foreigners] has aroused great interest. From all sides, and chiefly from the lower ranks [of the communist party] cries are heard. They ask: 'How can this be: we drove out our own exploiters and call in alien exploiters?' "

Another question was implicit in this one: If the Soviets admitted foreign capitalists into Russia on concessions, would they next legalize domestic capitalism? The civil war had ended with the defeat of Baron Wrangel. Now Soviet citizens wondered, and communists worried, about the fate of military

[3] *Ibid.*, pp. 498-513.

communism. Some regarded it as militant communism and hoped it would stay. They favored many of its features: in the villages, seat of the petty bourgeois, capitalist majority, the upper and middle peasants were being leveled downward by requisitioning and confiscatory taxes; a number of state farms—"agricultural factories"—had been established; villages had been forcibly collectivized here and there, and "communes" were not unknown; private trade was proscribed; foreign trade was a state monopoly; the government directed all manufacturing, mining, lumbering, transportation, etc.; communists voluntarily imposed a low ceiling on their personal incomes; the state was the sole patron of the arts, literature, theater, the cinema. Capitalism exorcized; the state supreme. This looked like socialism. Yet Lenin, in a decree dated November 23, 1920, offered large-scale concessions to foreign firms. What did this portend?

In his defense, Lenin outlined a new Soviet foreign policy. It amounted to a balance-of-power policy. "So long as we have not conquered the whole world," he said, "so long as we remain economically and militarily weaker than the capitalist world, we must follow this rule: it is necessary to be able to use the contradictions and contrasts between the imperialists." The Bolsheviks had done this at the time of the Brest-Litovsk negotiations, Lenin recalled. But every year "the western powers are recuperating from the [first world] war." To be sure, the Comintern now had nuclei in all the world. Nevertheless, "the speed, the tempo of revolutionary development is much slower in the capitalist world than here. It was apparent that when the nations got peace, a slackening of the revolutionary movement would inevitably follow. Therefore, without guessing about the future, we cannot at present depend on an acceleration of the tempo. Our task is to decide what to do now. People live in states, and each state lives in a system of states which exist in a system of a certain political balance in relation to one another."

Lenin thus proclaimed that, whether it is called capitalist or communist, a nation-state is a nation-state and lives by the rules of nation-states; it must, unless it wishes to upset the balance of power by war or exported revolution, submit to the principle of balance. The idea that a socialist country cannot be imperialistic seems plausible, and a socialist state with a socialist foreign policy would probably prove it true. But when a country, no matter what it calls itself, adopts the nineteenth-century balance-of-power foreign policy which Lenin outlined, it may well succumb to all the ills a nineteenth-century capitalist nation is heir to.

Lenin next noted that capitalists owned and controlled most of the planet's raw materials, and "it is necessary to take this into account, to make use of it." We cannot wage war against the Entente, he continued. We have to exploit the differences between the powers "which are explained by deep economic causes." But this must not be done in the petty manner of "the miniature politician and cheap diplomat." The Soviets would play for big stakes. The "basic contradictions in the contemporary capitalist world" could be exploited. "The first, the nearest to us, is the relation between Japan and America. A war between them is being prepared . . . it is inescapable, that is indubitable." But "can we remain indifferent in such a situation and merely say, as communists, 'We will make propaganda for communism in those countries?' That is correct, yet it is not all. The practical task of communist policy is the task of making use of that enmity, inciting one against the other." Lenin reasoned that Japan had "fifty million inhabitants"; the United States with "one hundred and ten million" was far wealthier than Japan. "Japan has seized China with four hundred million inhabitants and the richest coal deposits in the world." It would be "ridiculous," he declared, "to think that a stronger capitalism will not take from a weaker capitalism everything the latter has robbed." This created a "new situation. Japan and America want to wage war for supremacy in the world, for the right to grab," because America "has no colonies at all." Moreover, "America is inescapably opposed to colonies, and if she tries to touch [this problem] more deeply she will help us tenfold. The colonies are boiling with indignation and when you touch them, whether you like it or not, whether you are rich or not rich—and the richer the better, then you will help us, and the Vanderlips will come flying." Therefore Japan, eager to acquire colonies, would inevitably come into conflict with the U.S.A., Lenin believed. In this war, "we communists must use one country against the other. Are we not committing a crime against communism? No, for we are doing this as a socialist state conducting communist propaganda and compelled to use every hour given it by circumstances to grow strong with maximum speed. We have commenced to grow strong, but we are growing strong very slowly. America and other capitalist countries are growing in economic and military might with diabolical speed. No matter how we muster our strength, we shall grow incomparably slower. We must use the situation that has been created. That is the entire essence of the Kamchatka concession." The concession would help make an imminent war more imminent.

A man "named Vanderlip," Lenin stated, "has been here. He is, if we are to believe him, a distant relative of a well-known billionaire. Unfortunately," Lenin explained, "our counterespionage in the Cheka, which is working magnificently, has not yet embraced the United States of America,[4] and hence we still have not established the exact relationship of those Vanderlips. Some even say there is no relationship. I will not undertake to judge: my knowledge is limited to the reading of a book by Vanderlip." An editorial note gives the title of the book as *What Happened to Europe*.

Lenin confused two men. The book, published in New York in 1919, was written by Frank A. Vanderlip, president of the National City Bank of New York from 1909 to 1919 (he also wrote *From Farm Boy to Financier* in 1935), "who was not engaged in any mining venture in connection with a distant relative whom he barely knew."[5] The distant relative, Washington

[4] This address was first published in 1924, after Lenin's death.
[5] From a 1963 letter to me from Frank A. Vanderlip's widow. She also sent the excerpt from the Vanderlip Genealogy.

Baker Vanderlip, Jr., Lenin's visitor, the lobbyist for the Kamchatka concession, also wrote a book, *In Search of a Siberian Klondike*. He had explored Nigeria, the Philippines, and Central Alaska, and "When the rich sands of gold were found on the Yukon River and later in the Beach Sands of Cape Nome," reads the Vanderlip Genealogy, ". . . [Washington B.] Vanderlip was engaged by a Russian firm to make an extended prospecting tour through the territory north of the Okhotsk Sea and along the shores of the Bering Sea. His experiences in these regions during the summers of 1898 and 1899 have been described very interestingly" in his volume on the "Siberian Klondike." Twenty-one years after he walked the shores of the Bering Sea he walked into Lenin's Kremlin office to prospect again.

"So now this Vanderlip," Lenin proceeded, "brought with him a letter to the Sovnarkom." Lenin described it as "very interesting because it says with extraordinary frankness, cynicism, and crudeness, 'We are very strong in 1920; in 1923 our fleet will be still stronger. Japan, however, interferes with our strength, and we shall have to fight her, but it is impossible to wage war without kerosene and without oil. If you sell us Kamchatka, I give you a guarantee that the enthusiasm of the American people will be so great that we will grant you diplomatic recognition. The Presidential elections next March will be won by our [Republican] party. But if you do not rent Kamchatka to us I declare there will be no such enthusiasm.' This is the almost verbatim content of the letttter."

Who wrote this letter to the Sovnarkom? Lenin did not say. "Sell Kamchatka" or "rent Kamchatka"? Lenin's paraphrase mentioned both. In Lenin's version, it was a foolish letter. Yet "When this letter was received," Lenin revealed, "we said to ourselves, 'We must grab this with both hands. . . . If we give America Kamchatka which belongs to us juridically but actually has been occupied by Japan, we gain.' There you have my political considerations and, on these grounds, we immediately decided to conclude an agreement with America." They bargained with Vanderlip, Lenin said, "because no merchant will respect us if we do not bargain. But when we reached the point of signing, we declared, 'Everybody knows who we are, but who are you?' "

This, one would think, should have been the first question, before they seized the offer with both hands. "It transpired," added Lenin, "that Vanderlip could give no guarantee, then we said that we would yield, for this was only a draft, and you yourself said that it would come into force only when your party succeeds, and it has not succeeded, and therefore we will wait."

The whole affair was amateurish.

Lenin went on to ask, "Who is Vanderlip? . . . he wanted to meet me . . . Vanderlip came, we talked about all these matters, and then, when he began to say that he had been in Siberia, that he knows Siberia, that he came of a working-class family like all American billionaires, etc., that he appreciates only what is practical, that he appreciates only what he has seen, then I replied, 'Now you, being practical people, look about, see what the Soviet system is, and introduce it in your country.' He glanced at me, surprised at the turn of the conversation, and said to me in Russian (the whole conversation had been conducted in English): 'Maybe.' I asked in astonishment how he knew Russian. 'What do you mean?' [Vanderlip replied] 'I covered most of the Siberian provinces on horseback for twenty-five years.' When we parted, he said, 'I will have to report in America that Mr. Lenin . . . has no horns. . . .' We had a polite farewell. I expressed the hope that, on the basis of friendly relations between the two countries, not only would the concession agreement be concluded, but that mutual economic aid would develop normally." Subsequently, telegrams from abroad reported that "Vanderlip compared Lenin with Washington and Lincoln," Lenin said. "Vanderlip asked me for a portrait with an inscription. I refused, because when you give a portrait you write, 'To Comrade So-and-so,' and it was impossible to write, 'To Comrade Vanderlip.' And nevertheless such telegrams [praising Lenin] arrived: this makes it clear that this story played a certain role in imperialistic policy." Why is not so clear.

Thus ends the tale of the concession that never was. No concession. No diplomatic recognition until 1933. No Japanese-American war until 1941, and then it was not the war Lenin foresaw.

In addition to the "contradiction" between the United States and Japan, Lenin, in the same address, dealt with a second "contradiction which we must make use of, the contradiction between America and the rest of the capitalist world." America was hated everywhere, he reported, and in America a rising chorus demanded an agreement with Russia. "America," he asserted, "cannot make peace with the rest of Europe—that is a fact demonstrated by history." The question of a concession would be viewed in the Kremlin in the light of that "fact." America would make peace with Russia. Negotiations for a trade agreement with Great Britain were proceeding in London (the treaty was signed on March 16, 1921). Lenin wrote a note to Chicherin on November 19, 1920, saying that according to his information "America will immediately join (the trade agreement of Russia with England)."[6] Brittle logic required the United States, eager to trade, rebuffed by Europe, worried about Japan, to link her fortunes with Russia.

"And the third contradiction is between the Entente and Germany," Lenin continued. Germany could not live under the conditions imposed by the Versailles Peace Treaty; "and Germany must seek an ally against world imperialism . . ."—an intimation that the ally might be Soviet Russia.

These were three reasons, Lenin summarized, why it "is necessary to favor concessions with all our soul—or omit soul—with all our calculations." World economy could be restored only by using Russia's raw materials. "And now Russia presents herself before the entire world and declares: 'We under-

[6] *Leninskii Sbornik*, Vol. XXXVI, p. 143.

take to restore the international economy—here is our plan.' This is the right thing economically." The Bolsheviks would say to the capitalists of the planet, "You are no good . . . isn't it time, gentlemen, for you to reach an understanding with us?" The world capitalists, unable to manage their economy without the communists, would reply, "Why, indeed, it is time, let us sign a trade agreement." Here, again, was a manifestation of Lenin's Russo-centrism and of distorted economic determinism.

At best, Lenin's score for prophecy was one out of three; Germany did negotiate the Rapallo Treaty with Soviet Russia in 1922. His disquisitions about America and Japan and about America and Europe and the dawning economic collaboration between the U.S.A. and Russia amounted to whistling in the doldrums.

In the peroration, Lenin left reality far behind him. He proposed a pooling of all the world's raw materials for the restoration of the global economy—an excellent idea but, in his mouth, poison to those who would have had to assent. He added, "We represent 70 percent of the population of the world"—the populations of all the colonial and semicolonial (China, Persia) regions. He could make such a claim because he believed in representation without authorization. "For us it is important," he said, "that there be no famine anywhere. You capitalists cannot eliminate it, but we can." Before many moons, he invited capitalist America to enter Russia and feed millions of famine victims in the Volga Valley and the Ukraine.

Lenin still believed, against mounting objective evidence, that the proletarians of the outside world would solve Russia's pressing problems by overthrowing capitalism, and that, at the same time, proletarian Russia would solve the pressing problems of the capitalist world. Only one of these things could happen. Neither did.

XXXIV. CAVIAR AND HORSES AND THE DEATH OF A BELOVED

LOOKING AT HIS HANDIWORK, Lenin might have seen a super-Laocoön, a great giant writhing in endless coils of red tape while sons and daughters and a whole nation looked on helplessly. Occasionally, the giant resembled Lenin himself. Now and then Lenin cut the paper fetters from a finger or hand or arm or leg of the giant and gave him limited movement. Lenin abhorred bureaucracy and did not behave like a bureaucrat, yet he created a bureaucratic state, and much of his energy was spent protesting its perversions, escaping from its toils, and getting things done quickly by personal intervention.

Petitions to the all-highest for small favors and big decisions are in the old Russian tradition. When Tsar or supreme commissar, by a stroke of the pen or a spoken "Yes," settled a matter which might have been left to a third assistant secretary, he demonstrated his kindness, accessibility, and indispensability. (He also invited more appeals.) The normal functioning of an autocracy tends to absolve the autocrat, in the eyes of the people, from responsibility for the system's sins. The good is remembered, the evil is blamed on lesser men.

An actress, N. Nikulina, of Moscow's Mali Theater, wrote to Lenin on September 3, 1920: "Only a desperate situation compels me to disturb you with a humble request. I am seventy-four years old, and of these, to the extent of my strength and ability, I gave fifty-one to the service of my beloved Moscow. . . . Knowing how closely-packed the people live, I gladly helped and surrendered several rooms in my little house. All that remained to me were two cold passageways, which I needed and which do not afford comfortable living. Now I am threatened with the loss of these. I beg you, help me . . . a few words written at your order will be a sufficient guarantee for me."

Lenin made a marginal notation: "Investigate and telephone: leave her in peace."[1]

This was a humane act. But it would have been far more humane if the Soviet government had passed legislation or imposed regulations to prevent the myriad injustices that became endemic under communist rule.

Maxim Gorky addressed a letter to Lenin on March 5, 1920, from Petro-

[1] *Leninskii Sbornik*, Vol. XXXV, p. 149.

429

grad in which he asked that the higher-calorie ration for 1,800 scholars in the city be retained. "I also beg you to telephone Felix Djerzhinsky and tell him to release the chemist Sapozhnikov from prison quickly." Sapozhnikov, Gorky explained, had been working on valuable discoveries of materials for the prevention of disease. "And also: it is necessary to give Manukhin the possibility of doing research on an anti-typhus serum, and here one can do nothing. . . . I telegraphed [Commissar of Health] Semashko—he doesn't answer. Pardon me for plaguing you, but this is extremely important, you will understand that yourself!"

Lenin replied on March 19. The scholars would continue to receive their rations. "Sapozhnikov was released on March 9." Manukhin is to send a detailed proposal to Semashko.[2]

But what of the many hundreds of Sapozhnikovs without access to the Gorky of the golden touch and direct pipeline to Lenin? How many cries of despair reached Lenin depended, of necessity, on his secretaries, who naturally sought to protect him from harassment. The Soviet system, however, possessed no built-in protection against arbitrary officials. The dictatorship, operating through a proliferating bureaucracy, could not, without destroying its grip on the nation, permit recourse to courts or local legislatures or a free press or free assemblies where individuals might seek redress of their grievances. The citizen could only acquiesce in fear or complain in person, usually after queuing for hours with fellow sufferers, in the hope of reaching the heart of a bureaucrat too frightened or too overworked or too disinterested to take remedial action. A tiny percentage of the aggrieved, hoping their reputations would open a breach in the secretarial barrier surrounding Lenin or some other member of the Politburo or of the Central Committee of the communist party or of the federal Cabinet, could appeal to those who might take effective action. (But even Gorky failed to extract a reply from Semashko.) A dictatorship is a state without law and therefore without order in the sense of orderliness. The dictator's wish or whim is law and he or he and his close colleagues are the state. Since there is no law there are no normative rules of procedure, no comforting security for inferior officials who, accordingly, do nothing they can avoid doing because anything they do involves a risk. "Passing the buck" then becomes a habit, and responsibility and decision-making shift upward toward the top while those below sink into the slough of routine. When the little bureaucrat leaves home in the morning he leaves his soul and human milk behind. In the office he abandons initiative, abdicates his will and becomes an automatic instrument, sometimes an instrument of the dictatorship's cruelty, but his sense of guilt is minimal, for he says to himself, "I merely pushed the document from my desk to that desk." The dictators do everything; they have to.

On June 14, 1920, Lenin decreed: Having learned from three comrades that a "perfectly healthy spruce tree" had been cut down on June 14, 1920, in the park of the government sanatorium in the village of Gorky by order of

[2] *Ibid.*, pp. 110-112.

Comrade Vever, the sanatorium director, Vever was to be imprisoned for a month. Provided Vever had not been punished previously, he could be released conditionally after one week with a warning that if he committed a similar act again he would be imprisoned for three weeks and dismissed from his job and the workingmen and office employees involved would likewise be penalized.[3]

Vever got no hearing. Lenin served as prosecutor, jury, and judge: all self-appointed. Sentence was handed down on the day of the crime.

Lenin's note of June 29, 1920, to the secretariat of the party's Central Committee: "Compel the State Publishing House to publish quickly (with abridgements) the book of [John Maynard] *Keynes:* 'Economic Consequences of the Peace.' "[4]

Nothing was too small for Lenin's attention. In the midst of the Russian war with Poland he hunted for film so that a motion picture of the trial of Kolchak's ministers could be released without delay. The photo-cinema section of the Commissariat of Education had informed him by letter that speculators had sold out the last available prerevolutionary film at exorbitant prices and that, despite his telegraphic instructions to buy film abroad, none was available. On this letter he wrote a message to Commissar of Foreign Trade Krassin: "Please *press firmly* and gratify the request *quickly.*" The same day, July 8, 1920, he ascertained that the Commissariat of Health owned some film. He directed that it be delivered to the producers of the Kolchak picture.[5] Hard is the lot of a dictator in an economy of scarcity. Oil, coal, and even wood were in short supply. Lenin suggested a competition, with money prizes, for the invention of large wooden thermos containers. Eventually constructed of plywood "and shavings," they were found to be light, inexpensive, and capable of keeping food warm "up to twenty hours."[6] On May 15, 1920, Lenin sent one carload of meat and one of fats from Moscow to Orekhovo-Zuyevo, a textile town in Moscow province, and, to the same place, one carload of wheat from Nizhni Novgorod as "a gift to the children." He added, "For the time being, there is no salt." These shipments constituted the April-May ration of the factory city; "From May 25, improvement."[7] In July, six carloads of caviar were brought to him from Azerbaijan which produces the grayest and best. "For the CHILDREN," Lenin ordered.[8] No champagne went with it. On September 9, 1920, Lenin wrote to an official in Tambov, central Russia, that Krupskaya requested help for two acquaintances, an old woman named Anna Azanchevskaya and her daughter; "feed them well. . . . How are things in Tambov Province? Famine? . . ."[9] A steady flow of telegrams reached Lenin from far and near beg-

[3] *Ibid.,* p. 132.
[4] *Ibid.,* p. 134.
[5] *Ibid.,* pp. 136-137.
[6] *Ibid.,* p. 135.
[7] *Ibid.,* p. 125.
[8] *Ibid.,* p. 141.
[9] *Ibid.,* p. 150.

ging for bread and fuel. Railroad bottlenecks and transport inefficiency aggravated the results of bad crops and peasant refusal to sell for worthless roubles. He did what he could, telephoning and telegraphing to districts with surplus, urging shipments to relieve starvation. Suddenly the direct line from his office to Kharkov ceased to function. He told the Commissariat of Posts and Telegraphs to repair the break "immediately." The Russian army on the Polish front had taken over the buildings of the Smolensk University. The Sovnarkom passed a resolution ordering evacuation. Army headquarters paid no heed. Lenin wired on November 2, 1920, saying he was putting the question of this disobedience and punishment therefor on the agenda of the Sovnarkom's next session.

As essential supplies vanished, the number of bureaucrats multiplied. How many office workers were on the government payroll? Lenin asked his statisticians for round figures within four weeks and exact data "in how many weeks?"

The Moscow Soviet published a report at the end of 1920 on the year's activities: its executive committee had discussed one political question, eight economic questions, forty-six questions of organization, one health question, and eleven miscellaneous matters. "Monstrosity," was Lenin's marginal notation; "it should have been just the reverse"—and he drew a chart showing how he would have preferred it: a very short column representing organization issues, an equally short column for political issues, and a very tall column representing the time devoted to economic questions. Lenin's indignation was justified, but he was wrong in remonstrating, for officials discuss—and think—as a prelude to action, and when action and the decision to act are the monopoly of superiors, officials talk about themselves: what committee or person pushes what paper where. Lenin's Kremlin had sucked all power out of the soviets. The 1917 slogan of "All power to the Soviets" was converted by practice into all power to the communist party.

Organizational matters always obsessed Lenin. To Comrade Botin, builder of the Nizhni Novgorod radio station, one of Russia's first, Lenin wrote on June 4, 1920, chiding him for "distrust of the 'specialist.'" The specialist was a famous inventor. Second, Botin did too much of "the black" preparatory work which might have been done by others, by mechanics, electricians, etc.[10] Botin promised to reform.

The telephone connection with Chaika [Sea Gull] Sanatorium had been cut because, according to Lenin's information, one pole near a certain village whose name he was not sure of, "sounds something like Ivankovo," had been destroyed. He asked the telephone network to make the repairs and report to him.[11]

Anna, Lenin's older sister, was working in the Commissariat of Education. She had been given an assistant whom she did not know and with whom she could not cooperate smoothly. There were frictions and petty misunderstand-

---

[10] Lenin, *Sochineniya*, Fourth ed., Vol. 36, pp. 484 and 657.
[11] *Leninskii Sbornik*, Vol. XXXV, p. 167.

ings. Anna told her brother. At a Cabinet meeting in the autumn of 1920 he wrote her a note about the matter. The principle of administration, he said, should be, "I am in charge . . . I am responsible. Person X, who is not responsible and not in charge, interferes with me. That is a squabble. That is chaos . . . I demand his removal."[12]

In November, 1920, Lenin, worried by predictions of widespread harvest failures, proposed the manufacture of electric plows for deep plowing. His fertile but fatigued brain worked overtime. A note to Chicherin: Could he, or, if he is too busy, someone else, examine his *The Infantile Disease of "Leftism" in Communism* or the chapter on England and look "for mistakes or tactless statements"? Suggested corrections might be written out in pencil on separate pieces of paper, he modestly urged. A note to Semashko: Comrade Dmitry Eroshenkov was free from work for several weeks; could the Health Commissariat employ him? He had invented a disinfection chamber. A note to the Foreign Commissariat dated June 9, 1920: a man named Weisbein, at Rue Victor Considérant 5 in Paris, had a suitcase of his party and personal papers. Could it be brought to Moscow?[13] John Reed wanted to see Lenin for five minutes "today," August 17, 1920, on "a very important matter." Lenin: "If he insists and only for five minutes, let him come now."[14] A note to Bukharin suggesting that *Two Pages from Roman History, Plebs and Labor Leaders, The Warning to the Gracchi*, by the American socialist Daniel De Leon, be published in Russian translation with an introduction and notes by Louis C. Fraina (Lewis Corey). "I will also write several words." The translation never appeared. A note to M. N. Pokrovsky congratulating him on his new Russian history. It should be translated into European languages, Lenin said, and be used as a textbook in Soviet Russia. (Stalin later proscribed it.) But, Lenin remarked, a chronological index ought to be included.

Insurrection in Tambov province. On October 15, 1920, Lenin commanded the army to liquidate it "immediately and completely." On the 19th he commanded the Cheka to do likewise. "Our forces, especially cavalry, are weak" there, he told Djerzhinsky.[15] Workers and office employees throughout the country were being granted bonuses to foster efficiency. Did this not open wide the gate to "wholesale abuse"? Lenin wondered.[16]

During the early months of 1920, Lenin's beloved Inessa Armand was ill. He himself was ill. He wrote her early in February: "Please write me what is the matter. The times are bad: typhus, influenza, Spanish flu, cholera. I am just out of bed and do not yet go out. . . . What is your temperature? *Don't you need anything* for a cure? I beg you very much to write me frankly. Get well. Your Lenin."[17] Again to Inessa on February 16-17: "To leave the house" with fever "is plain insanity. I urgently beg you not to leave the house

---

[12] *Vospominaniya*, Vol. 2, pp. 293-294.
[13] *Leninskii Sbornik*, Vol. XXXV, pp. 131-132.
[14] *Ibid.*, p. 143.
[15] *Ibid.*, p. 158.
[16] *Ibid.*, p. 107.
[17] *Ibid.*, p. 108.

and tell your daughters *from* me that I beg them to watch and *not to let you out* (1) until the complete restoration of normal temperature, and (2) until the doctor permits it."[18] In August of the same year Lenin arranged for Inessa to be accommodated in a sanitorium in the North Caucasus where she died in September. Meanwhile, he had delivered a volumeful of speeches, formulated a new foreign policy, and governed a collapsing country during the war against Poland and the shifting fortunes of the war with Wrangel. The Kremlin robbed where it could. During the Red Army's temporary retreats in the face of the Baron's forces, Stalin drafted an order to the military on the Crimean and Caucasian fronts "making it mandatory for our divisions, in withdrawing, *to take* from the population all food surpluses and *all horses.*" Lenin signed it and added, "without offending the workingmen."[19] With all his headsplitting preoccupations and multiple backbreaking tasks he answered "Yes" when his office librarian asked whether he wanted some books published in Tiflis and "Please" when she offered him a bound volume of the Paris *L'Europe Nouvelle.*[20] On September 1, 1920, he modestly begged the Ryumantsev Library (now the great Lenin Library in Moscow) to lend him two Greek dictionaries: Greek-German, Greek-French, Greek-Russian, or Greek-English; and a history of Greek philosophy; and the best philosophical dictionaries, whether German, French, Russian, or English—the newest. What other modern ruler of a country in convulsion called for such reading matter? Lenin knew reference books could not be taken out of the library, but he asked if he could have some of these volumes "for one evening, say a night, after the library has been closed. I would return them by the morning."[21] He was tense, overwrought, and worked through most of the night. Small wonder that as 1920 neared its black end Lenin, on December 28, wrote, "today I feel quite ill from insomnia."[22] But come death, war, sickness, famine, and bureau rats gnawing at the guts of government, the state must go on and the helmsman must go on too.

XXXV. STALIN, LENIN, AND TROTSKY

ON THE VERY first day of the Bolshevik revolution, Leo Kamenev proposed the abolition of the death sentence. Trotsky argued for retention. The motion passed. Lenin was still in hiding. When he arrived at the Smolny and heard

[18] *Ibid.*, p. 109.
[19] *Ibid.*, p. 144.
[20] *Ibid.*, p. 180.
[21] *The Letters of Lenin*, Edited by Elizabeth Hill and Doris Mudie, p. 461. Russian original in Lenin, *Sochineniya*, Fourth ed., Vol. 35, p. 388.
[22] *Leninskii Sbornik*, Vol. XXXV, p. 172.

what had happened, he exclaimed, "Nonsense! How can you safeguard a revolution without executions?" The Soviet government accordingly decided not to make an announcement. "Somebody said, 'It is better simply to apply the death sentence, then it will be clear that there is no alternative.' In the end, that is where the matter rested."[1]

No taint of liberalism attached to Trotsky or Lenin in office. Trotsky, to boot, seems to have been conscious, always, of his Menshevik and anti-Bolshevik past which he felt he had to live down not by suppressing his views even when he disagreed with Lenin but by adopting policies characteristically Bolshevik in severity. This never did violence to his personality, rather the contrary.

With all their differences in family background and experience, Lenin and Trotsky were well matched as leaders of Soviet Russia. They championed uninhibited centralized power. They frowned on pro-Soviet guerrilla groupings—a kind of battlefield syndicalism—and insisted on absorbing them into the Red Army. They employed tsarist officers in the armed forces and bourgeois specialists in the national economy.

On substance, in these and similar matters, Lenin and Trotsky did not diverge. Both were stern executives who fostered maximum concentration of authority in the one person charged with a task. Both considered democracy in administration self-defeating. "Theirs not to make reply, theirs not to reason why" would have reflected the Lenin-Trotsky attitude toward soldiers and alike toward civilians in the mass. In the army, Trotsky was a merciless disciplinarian; Lenin approved. Once Trotsky had a regimental commander and a political commissar shot for moving their troops without instructions. The act stimulated subdued murmurs of criticism against him which his highly placed enemies, notably Stalin and Zinoviev, fanned into a small political fire. He raised the question at a Politburo session and justified the draconic deed. "Absolutely," Lenin interjected and, while the proceedings stopped, for he was presiding, he took a sheet of his Chairman of the Government stationery and wrote on the lower half: "Comrades: Knowing the strict character of Comrade Trotsky's orders, I am so convinced, so absolutely convinced, of the correctness, expediency, and necessity for the success of the cause of the order given by Comrade Trotsky, that I unreservedly endorse this order. V. Ulyanov (Lenin)."

Lenin handed the paper to Trotsky in the presence of the Politburo and said, "I will give you as many forms like this as you want."[2]

Trotsky liked to have Lenin's sanction. Lenin completed him. He was Lenin's perfect complement. Neither intellectual ever wavered in making full use of the great power the revolution gave him.

When Kolchak, Denikin, and Yudenich had been defeated and Trotsky transferred his considerable talents to the labor front, he conscripted, or mili-

[1] Trotsky, article in *Pravda*, April 23, 1924.
[2] Trotsky, *My Life*, p. 469. The date on the document is "July, 1919."

tarized, the railway workers. A controversy flared. The issue: government (that is, communist party) control over workers or workers' participation in management? Trotsky favored complete control over workers. He had organized the Red Army, imposed strict discipline on it, yet instilled it with fighting spirit, and forced the rank and file as well as communist commissars to accept orders from military experts whatever their politics. This made him the chief architect of victory in the civil war. It brought him prestige, respect, and popularity if not love or power in the party, which was the source of power. Trotsky now proposed to impose the discipline of battlefield and barracks on factory, railroad, coal mine, and oil field. To those who argued that the workers needed protection by trade unions against exploitation he replied that workers need no protection from a workers' state.

Early in 1920 Trotsky had wanted to abolish war communism, to legalize private trade, and relieve the peasantry of requisitions—measures which would have granted freedom to capitalist peasants. Several weeks after this program was voted down, he wanted to conscript the working class. Years later, in his autobiography-in-exile, he offered an explanation for the reversal: "When the change to the market system was rejected, I demanded that the 'war' methods be applied properly and with system, so that real economic improvements could be obtained. In the system of war communism in which all the resources are, at least in principle, nationalized and distributed by government order, I saw no independent role for trade unions."[3]

Stalin took the Trotsky view on workers' conscription. He ordered the 42nd Division on the southwestern front which had fought Denikin to "put aside its arms so as to join the battle against economic ruin and to supply the country with coal." The division was to enter the Ukrainian Labor Army on March 7, 1920.[4] Ten days later, addressing the Ukrainian Communist Party Conference, Stalin praised the work of the larger, Trotsky-sponsored, All-Russian Labor Army: "The repair of locomotives and railway cars is progressing; the mining of fuel is developing and advancing." In another speech to the same gathering on March 19, he said, "One comrade here declared that the workers are not afraid of militarization because the best workers are disgusted with the absence of order. That is absolutely true." In 1918, he recalled, partisan or guerrilla units were instructed to enroll in the regular Red Army. "A similar thing must be done now in crumbling industry."[5]

Stalin's estimate of the popularity of conscription was confirmed by Arthur Ransome of the *Manchester Guardian* on a trip to Yaroslavl in north-central Russia. Ransome journeyed from Moscow in March, 1920, with Karl Radek and Yuri Larin, a former Menshevik, to a provincial party conference, Radek to defend the party's position on labor armies and trade unions, Larin to oppose it. "Workman after workman came to the platform and gave his

[3] *Ibid.*, p. 464.
[4] Stalin, *Sochineniya*, Vol. 4, p. 292.
[5] *Ibid.*, pp. 294-304.

view," Ransome wrote.[6] ". . . The Red Army served as a text for many, who said that the method which had produced that army and its victories over the Whites had been proved successful and should be used to produce a Red Army of Labor and similar victories on the bloodless front against economic disaster. Nobody seemed to question the main idea of compulsory labor. . . . The one thing on which the speakers were in complete agreement was the absolute need of an effort in industry equal to, if not greater than, the effort made in the army."

The next day Radek appeared at a meeting of railwaymen in Yaroslavl. "He led off," Ransome said, "by a direct and furious onslaught on the railway workers in general, demanding work, work and more work, telling them that as the Red Army had been the vanguard of the revolution hitherto, and have starved and fought and given their lives to save those at home from Denikin and Kolchak, so now it is the turn of the railway workers. . . . He addressed himself to the women, telling them in very bad Russian that unless their men worked superhumanly they would see their babies die of starvation next winter. I saw women nudge their husbands as they listened. . . . And the amazing thing is that they seemed pleased. They listened with extreme attention, wanted to turn out some one who had a sneezing fit at the end of the hall, and nearly raised the roof off with cheering when Radek had done."

Many factories were closed. More than half the country's locomotives were either limping badly or out of use. The difference between a living national economy and a dead one was so obvious to even the untutored eye that most workingmen recognized hard work and discipline as being in their self-interest. Centuries of submission to tsarism, moreover, made obedience to the state a habit. And this, Larin told them, was their state. "The November, 1917, revolution," he said in the daily *Ekonomicheskaya Zhizn* of March 20, 1920, "transformed the united proletariat from hired slaves of capitalism into the boss of industry in the person of the proletarian government." Here Lenin, reading the article, wrote in the margin, "Now that's right."

"The hireling-class has become the owner-class," Larin continued.

"Stupid," Lenin commented.[7]

Lenin saw a delicate yet decisive discrepancy in Larin's thinking. The boss of industry, Lenin agreed, was the united proletariat incarnated in the government. The workers had vested their title of ownership in the state. The workers, consequently, were no longer the owners and it was "stupid" to say they were. Lenin did not believe they were although Soviet propaganda repeated endlessly, It's your mill, your mine, your railroad, give it your all. Some took this seriously and wished to manage their property.

The state owned, therefore it managed; management, Lenin held, was the

[6] *The Crisis in Russia* (New York, 1921), pp. 68 *et seq.*
[7] *Leninskii Sbornik*, Vol. XXV, p. 113.

job of managers appointed by and serving the party. The communist party in 1920 had 600,000 members.

The Russian trade unions in 1920 counted three million members. There were those in the trade unions and in the upper ranks of the party who felt that the unions, the organized working class, should play a primary role in directing the nonagricultural sector of the national economy. The issue provoked a debate which shook Soviet politics in 1920 and 1921, and left a scar on Soviet history. The opposition objected to Lenin's idea of one-man management of factories and as a substitute offered management implemented by a collegium or board consisting of technical specialists and of workingmen delegated by the unions. Lenin objected.

The official trade-union position was outlined in the March, 1920, theses of Mikhail Tomsky, chairman of the All-Russian Central Council of Trade Unions and member of the communist party's Central Committee, later of the Politburo. He proposed the "basic principle" of "collegial management of industry" to be applied, except rarely where one-man management is permissible, from top to bottom: in the All-Russian Council of National Economy, the supreme government organ, as well as in single industrial plants. The trade unions, however, were to avoid duplication and "harmful" friction between themselves and the supreme government organ. In the interest of rehabilitating the economy, finally, the unions "must in every way support the work of labor armies and the successful introduction of labor conscription."[8]

This was a straddle. Tomsky countenanced one-man management. He had little difficulty, in 1921, in joining Lenin.

A more intemperate stand was taken by the Workers' Opposition, led by A. G. Shlyapnikov, ex-Commissar of Labor and former Commissar of Trade and Industry, and by Yuri Lutovinov and S. Medvedyev, of the Metal Workers Union, abetted, as the one intellectual among workingmen, by the beautiful Alexandra Kollontai, feminist of aristocratic bearing and sizzling rebel temperament. She preached free love, to Lenin's disgust, and lived it. At the moment she was living with Shlyapnikov. She put the Workers' Opposition case in a pamphlet.[9] She wrote, "Who, after all, shall be called upon to create new forms of economy; shall it be the technicians, businessmen who by their psychology are bound up with the past, and soviet officials with communists scattered among them, *or the working class collectives which are represented by the trade unions?*" She urged the communist party to "lend its ear to the healthy class call of the broad working masses. Through the creative powers of the rising class in the form of industrial unions we shall go toward the reconstruction and development of the creative forces of the country; toward

[8] Lenin, *Sochineniya*, Second ed., Vol. XXV, Appendix No. 1, pp. 543-544.
[9] Alexandra Kollontai, *The Workers' Opposition* (Chicago, 1921); cited by Robert Vincent Daniels, *The Conscience of the Revolution. Communist Opposition in Soviet Russia* (Cambridge, Mass., 1960), pp. 128-129.

purification of the party itself from elements foreign to it; toward correction of the activity of the party by means of going back to democracy, freedom of opinion, and criticism inside the party."

Clearly, Kollontai and her friends were concerned with more than trade unions. Conditions within the party, the motor of the Soviet state, disturbed them. They wanted the trade unions to perform an independent function and therefore to acquire at least limited power. They wanted this for the sake of the workers and trade unions, but also of the party which, if it did everything, might grow bureaucratically sclerotic and politically autocratic.

The Workers' Opposition found reinforcement in the Democratic Centralists guided by V. N. Maximovsky, an anti-Brest-Litovsk-peace man in 1918, Assistant Commissar of Education, subsequently a professor; T. V. Sapronov, a house painter, in 1925-1927 a spokesman of the Right opposition and therefore excluded from the communist party; and N. Osinsky (Valerian V. Osinsky-Obolensky of the princely Obolensky family), an economist, also an antagonist of the Brest treaty, later Soviet ambassador to Sweden and alternate member of the party's Central Committee.

Osinsky, Sapronov, and Maximovsky presented their theses to the Ninth Congress of the Russian Communist Party in March, 1920. They began with an academically objective preamble: Neither collegial workers' management nor one-man management "is the only and unconditional basis" of industrial organization. Neither possesses "absolute technical superiority." But a collegium of workers has social and political value. "A collegium is the highest-level school of government leadership." (Lenin had been calling the trade unions "the school of communism.") Nothing other than a collegium teaches people "to decide private questions from the point of view of the interests of the whole community." Besides, a collegium, consisting of workers and specialists, would "draw former bourgeois specialists into the channel of comradely reciprocal action, saturating them with the proletarian spirit," and at the same time control them until they had outlived old capitalist psychology and habits. The collegial system would, they continued, prevent the "bureaucratic deadening of the government apparatus."

Rykov also sensed danger. Alexey Rykov, confirmed "right-winger," President of the Supreme Council of National Economy (VSNH) in 1920, subsequently Soviet Chairman or Prime Minister, declared, "There is a possibility of so constructing a state that in it there will be a ruling caste consisting chiefly of administrative engineers, technicians, etc.; that is, we should get a state economy based on a small group of a ruling caste whose privilege in this case would be managing the workers and peasants."[10] Seeing the future darkly was not the monopoly of "leftist" oppositionists.

To prevent bureaucratic abuses, the Soviet government, in March, 1919, created the Workers and Peasants Inspection, in Russian: "RKI" or

[10] Arthur Ransome, *op. cit.*, p. 104.

"Rabkrin." Stalin, already Commissar of Nationalities, was named Commissar of Rabkrin. The new commissariat secured the services of many zealous communists bent on banishing favoritism, formal, letter-and-punctuation official attitudes toward human beings, and the flight from action and responsibility which characterized civil servants. But the biggest fact in Rabkrin was Stalin. His position required him to eradicate unfairness, corruption, nepotism, apathy, and red tape in the state and party machines. He collected, sifted, and evaluated evidence about all important officials. He decided a man's fate. He could end a man's career. The watchdog Rabkrin had a murderous bite. On Stalin's leash, it spread dread and sycophancy. It enhanced his power which he used to recruit henchmen.

Stalin possessed the prime prerequisite for the Rabkrin job: brutal ruthlessness. It is this that might have induced Lenin to appoint him. Nobody knows why Lenin picked Stalin. Perhaps personal power for personal power's sake was so alien to Lenin that he did not see it in Stalin. Perhaps others recoiled from the purging and snooping involved. Perhaps it was too early for Lenin to recognize the real Stalin. Lenin knew Stalin's capacity to superintend bank robberies that replenished the party treasury and to conduct the roughest kind of political warfare against Mensheviks. When Stalin, bearing this reputation, arrived in Cracow in February, 1913, Lenin, according to Krupskaya's second volume of memoirs, "wrote to Gorky about Stalin as follows: 'We have a wonderful Georgian here.' " After the revolution, Stalin's letters to Lenin were unusually rude and crude. Lenin might have regarded this as being in the nature of an undereducated Georgian hillman untouched by European culture and accustomed to the fierce feuding of wild mountaineers. Until Lenin died (and for several subsequent years) Stalin behaved like a retiring comrade who sought neither popularity nor publicity, indeed sacrificed them on the altar of harsh duty. This apparent self-effacement masked the megalomania which ultimately assumed psychotic magnitude and cost the lives of millions. But those enjoying the benefits of hindsight must be cautious in apportioning blame for lack of foresight. It is unfair to judge the past as the future. Lenin could hardly have anticipated Stalin's massacres of life and talent in the 1930's, 1940's, and 1950's.

With hindsight the world knows that Stalin hoped to erase the "Lenin-Trotsky" adjective which history prefixed to the Bolshevik revolution and substitute "Lenin-Stalin." For some years, in the communist world, he did. Stalin rejected his drunkard-shoemaker father who beat him. As a student in the Orthodox theological seminary in Tiflis he rejected God the Father and became an atheist. A psychoanalyist might say that in Lenin Stalin sought the father he had never had. The father-hero. "I had hoped to see the mountain eagle of our party," Stalin wrote of his first, prerevolutionary sight of Lenin, "the great man, great physically as well as politically. I had fancied Lenin as a giant, stately and imposing." A political analyst might say that Stalin exhibited to Lenin a canine faithfulness calculated to win acceptance, approval, and promotion. But Trotsky barred Stalin's way to the side of Lenin by being there. Also by his scarcely disguised scorn of Stalin. In the autobiography Trotsky said Stalin "always repelled me." Trotsky, the intellectual man of the world, held Stalin in contempt for his vulgarity, lack of culture, and provincialism.

The haughty Trotsky and the envious Stalin were fated to come to blows. The trouble began early. "I insist categorically on the removal of Stalin," Trotsky wired Lenin on October 8, 1918, from the fighting front. Stalin was at Tsaritsin, later Stalingrad, later Volgagrad. Lenin transferred Stalin to the Ukraine. "The Tsaritsin methods," Trotsky remonstrated to Lenin by wire on January 10, 1919, "which led to the complete disintegration of the Tsaritsin army cannot be permitted in the Ukraine." Lenin urged Trotsky to reach an understanding with Stalin. That proved impossible. In June, 1919, Stalin asked the Central Committee of the party to dismiss Trotsky from the command of the Red Army. The committee gave Trotsky a vote of confidence.

Trotsky complained to Lenin in 1919 that Stalin had been drinking wine from the Tsar's cellars in the Kremlin. Lenin summoned Stalin to his office for the triangle confrontation. "If the rumor reached the front that there is drinking in the Kremlin," Trotsky argued, "it will make a bad impression." The sale of alcoholic beverages was illegal at that time in Russia.

"How can we Caucasians get along without wine?" Stalin protested.

"You see," Lenin interjected lightly, "the Georgians cannot do without wine."

That ended the discussion. "I capitulated without a struggle," Trotsky wrote in a *Life* article dated October 2, 1939.

Lenin witnessed the rivalry between Stalin and Trotsky. He saw their mutual hatred. Yet he could use both. To harass the bureaucracy the chief of Rabkrin needed an abrasive, aggressive personality. No one was more abrasive than Stalin. Democracy might have curbed bureaucracy, democracy in the form of free trade unions or of participation in management through the trade unions. But any democracy clashed with Lenin's sacred principle of party autocracy, the party without competitors.

Lenin tried to block debate on the trade unions. "Fortunately," he wrote in a February, 1920, letter to locals of the Russian Communist Party on the eve of the Ninth Party Congress, "the time for purely theoretical considerations is gone. . . . It is necessary to go forward, it is necessary to be able to understand that we are now faced with *practical* tasks."[11] And when, nevertheless, Tomsky and the several opposition groups published their theses, Lenin complained at the Ninth Congress in March, 1920, that "the discussions about the socialist society contain not an iota of practicality, nothing businesslike." The theses were "basically wrong."[12]

Theory and big ideas about the structure of society, Lenin affirmed, be-

---

[11] Lenin, *op. cit.*, Second ed., Vol. XXV, pp. 42-45.
[12] *Ibid.*, p. 111.

longed to the prerevolutionary period. He went further. He told the Congress of Soviets on December 22, 1920, that he hoped to see the "very happy epoch when fewer and fewer politicians would talk less frequently and at less length and more engineers and agronomists would address" Soviet Congresses.[13] (He said this toward the end of an eighty-minute discourse.)

But Lenin could not dictate to the party, and despite his reiterated desires, the debate on the role of trade unionism, which was really a debate on the role of the working class in a socialist society, continued with animation. In December, 1920, at the plenary session of the party's Central Committee, Lenin was defeated and a resolution backed by Trotsky and Bukharin won a majority.

Lenin reacted more in pain than in anger. Distress or anger or both must have been there, but he held himself in check. He attacked Trotsky frankly yet gently and balm went with each blow. Not that he spared Trotsky; he feared a split in the party. For Trotsky had a formidable following. The debate on the trade unions, Lenin began at the national congress of mineworkers on January 23, 1921,[14] was taking on "an unhealthy character," it "too soon assumed the form of a fractional struggle." He had forebodings of a fractional fight between himself and Trotsky. Lenin considered the trade-union issue "the widest, unlimited question" affecting every aspect of Soviet life, "and I accuse Comrade Trotsky" of approaching it too hastily and presenting his successful resolution to the Central Committee without sufficient preparation. This "has happened to each one of us and will happen again, because all our work is conducted in the greatest haste. The mistake is not a big one, each one of us has acted in a hurry." All the more reason for care in a dispute which may cause the party to break into factions. "Because here even a person who is not very fiery, something I cannot say of my opponent"—Trotsky—"may easily fall into error." Trotsky had accused Mikhail Tomsky and Solomon A. Lozovsky, trade-union officials, of "exclusiveness," of "hostility" to new blood, of bureaucracy. They kept workingmen out of the trade-union leadership. Is it right, Lenin asked, for "a person of such great authority, such a major leader" to attack party members in this manner? With such "thoughtlessness"? It was a "fundamental error. This is no way of behaving." Lenin objected to Trotsky's words and the tone. "Although I said earlier," Lenin declared, "that I might perhaps 'act as a buffer' " —between contending sides—"and not participate in the discussion, for it is harmful to tangle with Trotsky, harmful for us, harmful for the party, harmful for the Republic," but after Trotsky's attack he felt compelled to speak.

Lenin quoted Trotsky as having said in November, 1920, that there ought to be a "shake-up" in the trade unions. "Trotsky made a mistake in saying

---

[13] *Ibid.*, Third ed., Vol. XXVI, pp. 24-48. (The third edition is identical with the second but appeared later.)

[14] *Ibid.*, pp. 97-108.

so. Here it is clear, politically, that such an approach produces a split and hurts the dictatorship of the proletariat." For this reason Lenin had advised against the public debate; he preferred deliberations in a commission. "But comrades said, 'No, how is that possible? It would violate democracy.' Comrade Bukharin went so far as to talk about 'the sacred slogan of workers democracy.' Those were exactly his words. I read this and—I almost made the sign of the cross."

The audience laughed. Lenin was mocking Bukharin's devotion to workers democracy. His opponents, Lenin continued, were condemning bureaucracy. But "The battle against bureaucracy requires decades. This is a most difficult battle and anybody who tells to us that we will free ourselves at once from bureaucracy if we adopt an anti-bureaucracy platform is simply being a charlatan." Of course there was bureaucracy, Lenin admitted. "Some government departments have thirty thousand employees in Moscow alone. That is not a pound of raisins. To cure such a thing is like breaking through this wall," he said, pointing. Bureaucracy would be fought. "We shall not give up compulsion. Not a single sensible workingman will go so far as to say that it is possible now to do without compulsion or that it is possible now to disband the trade unions or to put all industry in their hands. It was Comrade Shlyapnikov who could blurt out such a thing." Industry run by workers was syndicalism; Lenin rejected it. "Marxists fought syndicalism everywhere in the world." When we electrify the country, Lenin said, in twenty years— and that would be very quick, "Let us talk then about giving rights to the trade unions, but to talk about it earlier is to deceive the workers. . . . Does every workingman know how to run the government? Practical people know that this is a fairy tale. . . . We haven't even liquidated illiteracy. We know how workers who are connected with the peasantry lend themselves to nonproletarian slogans. Who among the workers have been governing? Several thousand in all of Russia and that is all." Gone with the revolution was Lenin's naïve notion that governing consisted of simple operations—registering, filing, and checking—which any literate person could perform.[15] Russia had many tens of thousands of literate workingmen. Gone was Lenin's prerevolutionary dictim that "every cook" should be taught to share in government administration.[16]

To say that the trade unions themselves and not the party should govern the country, Lenin continued, "will sound very democratic, this is how to catch votes, but not for long. It will destroy the dictatorship of the proletariat."

In a last paragraph Lenin stressed his most important thought: "To govern it is necessary to have an army of tough revolutionary-communists, it is and

---

[15] In *The State and Revolution*.

[16] N. Bukharin and E. Preobrazhensky, *The ABC of Communism, A Popular Explanation of the Program of the Communist Party of Russia*, translated by Eden and Cedar Paul (London, 1922), p. 171.

it is called the party." This was the rock on which Lenin had stood through-out his career. The Party Above All. The party was the agent of revolution, the vehicle of power, the machine of dictatorship. The "syndicalist nonsense" of the workers, not the party, managing industry, Lenin concluded, "ought to be thrown into the wastepaper basket."

Workers could and did become bureaucrats. Workers as workers, through their trade unions or individually, remained an insignificant factor in manage-ment and government. A booming bureaucracy, driven by the party, governed.

Lenin's political flesh was torn by the horns of a dilemma: he tolerated nothing that diminished the party's power or fractured its unity. Yet undimin-ished power, with the government, as the party's agent, monopolizing admin-istration in all fields—economic, political, social, cultural, educational—led to bureaucracy, bad bureaucracy because of illiteracy and the doubtful loyalty and slothful ways of the literate.

Lenin's speech on the trade-union controversy makes it clear that the unity of the party was threatened by Trotsky's differences with him. To the world and to the Soviet people, Lenin and Trotsky together symbolized Bolshevism; they were the leadership.

Friction between Lenin and Trotsky warmed Stalin's heart.

Slowly, at first almost imperceptibly, then more rapidly, Trotsky shifted his ground until he stood closer to the Workers' Opposition than to Lenin, yet remote from both. Like most communists who alter their policies, he attributed the change to changed conditions. But Stalin, whispering behind the scenes, could call it regression to an anti-Leninist past and charge that Trotsky was unstable, unreliable. Stalin also attacked in public. His article in *Pravda* of January 19, 1921, said, "Our differences" concern "*the methods of strengthening labor discipline in the working class.* . . . Two methods exist: the method of *compulsion* (the military method) and the method of persuasion (the trade-union method). . . . One group of party officials headed by Trotsky, flushed with the success of the military method in the army, as-sumes that it is possible and necessary to transplant these methods among workers, into the trade unions. . . . Trotsky's mistake is in his underestimat-ing the difference between the army and the working class."

Stalin, Lenin, and Trotsky had favored and had implemented the party's decision to organize labor armies. Trotsky no longer supported labor con-scription; he was now for management by nationalized trade unions. Stalin did not care to notice. Apostle of compulsion, he extolled "persuasion."

Lenin created a salubrious climate for Stalin's anti-Trotskyism. "The party is ill. The party is quivering with fever," Lenin wrote in a thin pamphlet on January 19, 1921. "We must have the courage to look the bitter truth straight in the face." He entitled the brochure *The Crisis in the Party*.[17] In it he accused Trotsky of "fractionalism." In Lenin's lexicon, this was most grave, more grave, he said, than Trotsky's mistaken ideas about trade unions.

[17] Lenin, *Sochineniya*. Third ed., Vol. XXVI, pp. 87-94.

It is one thing, and permissible, to make proposals. It is another, and intolerable, to rally forces behind them in opposition to the will of the party majority. This, Lenin maintained, is what Trotsky had done.

Instead of keeping the trade-union debate inside the party, Lenin affirmed, Trotsky had, in a pamphlet dated December 25, 1920, on *The Role and Functions of the Trade Unions*, carried the problem to a wider public. Lined up against Lenin and Zinoviev, Lenin said, were Trotsky and Bukharin, and the workers were asked to choose.

Here, Lenin harked back to a December 30, 1920, meeting where he had declared that, "Our government is, in fact, not a workers government but a workers-peasants government."

"What kind?" Bukharin had heckled.

"I was wrong and Bukharin was right," Lenin admitted in the *Crisis* pamphlet. "I should have said, 'A workers government is an abstraction. We in fact have a workers government with, first, this peculiarity, that the peasants, not the workers, constitute a majority of the national population, and, second, it is a workers government with a bureaucratic distortion.'"

Having given Bukharin his due in recognizing that workers needed protection against the rural majority and the bureaucrats, Lenin assailed Bukharin's proposal that the trade unions be represented in all government trusts and combines. "That is a complete departure from communism to the position of syndicalism. That, in essence, is a repetition of Shlyapnikov's slogan, 'Trade-unionize the state,' in other words, hand over the All-Russian Supreme Council of National Economy—VSNH—in bits to particular trade unions.

"Communism says, The communist party, vanguard of the proletariat, leads the non-party mass of workers, educating, preparing, teaching, training that mass ('the school' of communism), first the workers, then the peasants, so that it can achieve and has achieved the concentration in its hands of the management of the entire national economy.

"Syndicalism entrusts to the mass of non-party workers, divided into factories, the management of the branches of industry ('trusts and combines'), thereby destroying the necessity of the party."

Lenin was apparently sanctioning syndicalism but at a remote date when the working class had been prepared.

Now Lenin attempted to still the storm. "Bukharin's mistakes are a hundred times worse than all of Trotsky's mistakes taken together. How could Bukharin have gone so far as this rupture with communism? We know all the softness of Comrade Bukharin, it is one of his qualities for which he is so loved and for which he cannot but be loved. We know that he was once called 'soft wax.'" Demagogues and unprincipled persons made their impressions on the wax. "But of course it would not occur to anybody *to explain* what happened as unprincipled demagogy, to attribute everything to it." Lenin invited all ideological wanderers to repent, "recognize their mistake, correct it, and turn over this page of the history of the Russian Communist

Party." Bukharin, in particular, must return to the right path, for "Whereas we have to some extent absorbed what was healthy in the 'democratic' 'Workers Opposition,' Bukharin has had to take hold of the *unhealthy*."

Lenin was trying to please everybody. Even Sapronov and Osinsky "are, in my opinion, valuable party men." Hitherto the party platform had been: defense against the extremes of bureaucracy. Now they had added to the platform a struggle "against those *unhealthy* elements of the opposition which have gone so far as to reject all 'militarized economy,' to reject not only 'the method of appointment' "—of managers—"which has predominated until now, but of any 'appointing,' that is, in the final analysis, the rejection of the role of leadership of *the party* in relation to the mass of non-party people." Party appointees must man key points, Lenin insisted.

The final appeal in the last paragraph: "The capitalists of the Entente will undoubtedly try to use the illness of our party for another invasion and the Social Revolutionaries for staging conspiracies and uprisings. This does not frighten us, for we shall all unite as one, without fear of recognizing the illness but conscious of the fact that it demands of all greater discipline, greater tenacity, greater firmness at every post."

Lenin's oil failed to calm the tempest, it fed the fires. His peace efforts encouraged the dissidents. All was now confusion inside and outside the communist party.

For the attention of the Tenth Party Congress (Moscow, March 8-16, 1921), the Lenin group, the Trotsky-Bukharin opposition, the Workers' Opposition, the "Buffer Fraction," the Democratic Centralists, and the "Ignatovites" (allies of the Workers' Opposition) submitted resolutions, some many pages long, about Soviet trade-unionism. The Trotsky-Bukharin proposal[18] bore the signatures, impressively, of seven of the twenty members of the Russian Communist Party's Central Committee: Trotsky, Bukharin, A. A. Andreyev, Felix Djerzhinsky, chief of the Cheka, N. Krestinsky, E. A. Preobrazhensky, Christian G. Rakovsky, and L. P. Serebryakov. (Krestinsky, Preobrazhensky, and Serebryakov comprised the party Secretariat.) In addition, five members, notably Pyatakov and Felix Kon, of the Central Committee of the Ukrainian Communist Party subscribed, as well as two members of the presidium of the All-Russian Trade Union Council, twenty-one first-rank trade-union leaders, and eighteen prominent Moscow communists, among them: Larin, Gregory Sokolnikov, Y. Yakovleva, G. Krumin, and V. Likhachov. Trotsky had done just what Lenin hated, he had rallied a mighty minority against the majority leadership of the party. This was "fractionalism."

The Trotsky-Bukharin proposal elaborated a radical readjustment of Soviet society. The trade-union leaders, it charged, were cut off from the directors of the national economy. From time to time they agreed on something or collided, but they functioned apart; Lenin wished to preserve the separation.

[18] *Ibid.*, Appendix 2, pp. 551-562.

"The platform of the 'Workers' Opposition' is based on the altogether proper and correct urge to concentrate the management of industry in the hands of the trade unions," but it would institute elections of workers' representatives to participate in the management of each factory and of the highest economic offices of the Republic, and this, "irrespective of the intentions of the authors of the idea, would lead to the mutual isolation of factories and plants, to the destruction of the centralized economic apparatus and the loss of the party's dominant influence over the trade unions and also over the economy." Instead, the Trotsky-Bukharin group advocated "The gradual concentration of the management of industry in the hands of the trade unions," thus transforming "the trade unions into organs of the workers state, that is, the gradual fusing of the trade union and Soviet organizations." (Or what Bukharin called "the state-ification," "the governmentalizing" of the trade unions.) "The Commissariat of Labor is abolished with the transfer of its basic functions to the trade unions." And, "immediately," "one-third to one-half" of the top personnel of the All-Russian Central Council of Trade Unions and of the government's All-Russian Council of National Economy must "be identical."

The proposal made a second point: "In this way, conditions would be created under which the party units, while completely retaining the general direction of affairs in their hands, would not have to meddle in the work of individual unions."

Moreover, "All specialists without exception must pass through the filter of the trade unions."

This to Lenin spelled heresy, and if carried out, usurpation. His filter for all appointments was the party. The party must "meddle" in the work of every cog. Management of industry by unions largely noncommunist in membership would, in the Leninist conception, chip away and ultimately dismantle the paramountcy of the party. Trotsky should have known that Lenin would fight this tooth and claw and resign rather than accept it. The Trotskyist merging of the unions with the government might kill them or enable them to wag the bureaucracy. It meant centralization, as against the fragmentation of authority proposed by the Workers' Opposition, but not Lenin's kind of centralization. The centralized "trade-union state" would have interposed itself between the party and the proletariat. Lenin spurned the notion. He countenanced only direct dictatorship by hard-core communists under maximum discipline. The trade unions were too big and diffuse to be trusted with anything more important than taking their members to school. Trotsky was doomed to defeat. His platform antagonized the party-supremacists without satisfying the worker-democrats who wanted independent trade unions that subtracted power from the party-state.

Nevertheless, the debate lived on. Civil war's end and peasant unrest stamped the end of 1920 and the first two or three months of 1921 as a turning point. Many proletarians were consciously or subconsciously aware of the sharply contrasting alternatives: power for workers under socialism or bureaucratic dictatorship. Peace granted the freedom to talk and quarrel. Men sensed that this was the historic hour of decision about the shape and fate of the Soviet state and they wished to put a hand on the future. "Everybody whom I asked about it began at once to address me as if I were a public meeting," wrote Ransome, who was making inquiries about the tide of the trade-union battle. He finally isolated three elements: (1) "all but a few lunatics have abandoned the ideas of 1917, which resulted in the workmen of a factory deposing any technical expert or manager whose orders were in the least irksome to them. Those ideas and the unfairness they caused, the stoppages of work, the managers sewn up in sacks, ducked in ponds and trundled in wheelbarrows, have taken their places as curiosities of history." (2) ". . . industrial conscription . . . , at least inside the Communist party, seemed generally taken for granted." (3) Workers' control was still in dispute, with the majority against it and favoring one-man-manager control under the yoke of the party.[19]

Workers' control was a remembrance of things past: socialist aspirations, whereas industrial conscription recognized the hard facts of the current economic chaos. Labor armies under military discipline and worker-managed factories under self-discipline were mutually exclusive policies. Faced with the choice between practical necessity and alluring ideology, Lenin chose the practical.

Toward the autumn of 1920, however, a noise outside the debating halls, the noise of shooting and shouting, began jamming the talk on trade unions. The din came from the peasants, unrepresented in the party or the unions. They clamored for capitalism.

How could Lenin yield to capitalism in the villages and simultaneously to socialism in the factories? How could he liberate the peasant to trade and subject the worker, the apple of the revolution's eye, to military discipline? In the end, therefore, both workers' control and conscription went with the village wind. The peasantry without votes vetoed the trade-union programs of the opposition and of Lenin. Conscription of workers was impossible when the peasants were rebellious and unnecessary because the workers were docile. "Putting it brutally, so as to offend Trade Unionists and Communists alike," Ransome summarized, the trade unions became "a gigantic megaphone through which the Communist party makes known its fears, its hopes, and its decisions to the great mass of the industrial workers."[20]

A megaphone is a large but inanimate instrument.

It was the Tenth Party Congress in March, 1921, that performed the last rites on all pro-trade-union opposition and on the trade unions as a free institution. Therewith the working class submitted to communist party rule. Domination of the party now loomed as Stalin's objective. He labored silently

[19] *The Crisis in Russia*, pp. 102-103.
[20] *Ibid.*, p. 107.

behind the scenes. Krestinsky, Preobrazhensky, and Serebryakov, who had signed Trotsky's trade-union proposal, were not re-elected by the Congress to the Central Committee. They therefore also lost their key organization posts in the party Secretariat where Vyacheslav M. Molotov, Emilyan Yaroslavsky and V. M. Mikhailov, all Stalin men, replaced them. Mikhail Frunze, a critic of Trotsky's military views, Klementi Voroshilov, Stalin's right-hand commander at Tsaritsin, Sergo Orjonekidze, Stalin's appointee to the leadership of the Caucasus, and several other creatures of Stalin entered the Central Committee. The Central Committee again elected the same small Politburo of five: Kamenev, Lenin, Stalin, Trotsky, with Zinoviev, added for supporting Stalin, in place of Krestinsky, out for supporting Trotsky. Molotov became an alternate member, or "candidate," of the Politburo.

These were tremendous shifts in the power balance in favor of Stalin and against Trotsky. Stalin's climb to the peak of the Soviet pyramid had commenced—during Lenin's supremacy and with Lenin's acquiescence. Sentiment never intruded on Lenin in politics. He felt far closer to Trotsky as a person than to Stalin. He had much more in common with Trotsky than with Stalin as a person and a great deal in common with Trotsky politically. But in the trade-union controversy, Trotsky broke discipline and, Lenin believed, almost broke the party, whereas Stalin, for purposes which Lenin failed to discern, stood by the master in the cause of party unity. And party discipline, "partyness," took precedence in Lenin's mind over individuals, the working class, and doctrine.

XXXVI. ᴔHE EVENING BEFORE CAPITALISM

IN LENIN'S OFFICE a sign, placed there after he had been wounded by Fanny Kaplan in 1918, read, "No Smoking." The office might have displayed another sign with the wise words of a Kostroma peasant who attended the Eighth All-Russian Congress of Soviets in Moscow in December, 1920. Lenin assembled the noncommunist peasant delegates on December 22 for an off-the-record conference where he encouraged them to speak their minds. While they did so he scribbled excerpts from their statements; later he circulated his notes to the members of the party's Central Committee and to Cabinet commissars.[1] A Byelorussian tiller said, "Give us salt, iron, and everything so that we can *sow* our land. That's all I will say." A Tver cultivator declared the peasants got nothing out of the collective farms. Another from central Russia

[1] *Leninskii Sbornik*, Vol. XXXV, pp. 190-193.

complained that "the slothful and the industrious peasants are subjected to equal confiscations, which is unjust." The next speaker told Lenin, "Bread, iron, and coal—that's what we need. And equipment." Criticizing by indirection, a delegate urged that "the poorest should learn from the industrious. The industrious ought to be encouraged." The man from the Donets Basin exclaimed, "We ask thirty-five thousand [poods] of seed. But people only carry briefcases and did nothing."

Good journalist that Lenin was (in one questionnaire he wrote "journalist" as his profession), he sketched an incident when the delegate from the northern province of Cherepovets said: "Some are called lazy, but the fact is they have no plows or harrows. There ought to be a law that the poor peasant should be helped. Compulsion is absolutely necessary."

"Enough, enough," the angered audience shouted. The peasant resumed his seat. Lenin wrote "NB"—mark this well. Even peasants picked to attend a Soviet Congress disliked the Lenin-made class war.

Then spake the villager from Kostroma on the Volga: "The peasant needs incentive. I cut timber under the lash. But you cannot farm under the lash."

"No Smoking." "No Farming Under the Lash."

Commissar's lash replaced Tsar's knout.

The collectivistic-minded Bolsheviks treated the village as a collective and confiscated its surpluses, sometimes its seed and food, thus depriving the peasants of the material and spirit needed to work with nature. In *Between Man and Man*, Martin Buber distinguishes a collective from a community: "Collectivity is not a binding but a bundling together . . . community is being *with* one another. . . . Collectivity is based on organized atrophy of personal existence, community on its increase and affirmation in life lived toward one another." Community-binding would create rival nuclei of power which communists abhor. Collectives atomized the peasantry. Soviet policy bundled the peasants together in an atrophied, atomized existence. When this happened, under or after Lenin, the peasants staged a prolonged strike. They were striking in 1920 and the first months of 1921.

One desire the peasant delegates did not disclose to Lenin, the desire to keep and sell their surpluses at a profit on the free market. For Lenin had asserted on November 26, 1920, "We regard the freedom to trade as a crime."[2] A capitalist crime. But the peasants did demand the equivalent of private trade: the end of requisitions. A Petrograd peasant at the conference with Lenin: "Requisitions. In our place there was such *compulsion* that revolvers"—of collector police—"were put to temples. The folks were indignant." The Perm peasant: "To lift up agriculture it is necessary to liberate us from under the lash. The lash is requisition of food." But for requisitioning the villagers might have had food to eat, seed to sow, and something to sell.

The Bolshevik revolution is often regarded as the advent of communism or socialism. Actually, it was primarily nationalistic, it served the national in-

[2] Lenin, *Sochineniya*, Second ed., Vol. XXV, p. 513.

terest by withdrawing Russia from the war, and it was also capitalistic, it helped the peasants to hold or get land. But power and military necessity whetted the Bolsheviks' appetite for collectivism, and they vetoed the peasantry's wish for capitalistic economic freedom. The villagers considered this a breach of promise; the Kremlin let them have land but took its fruits. As the civil war veterans returned to their huts and plows, they cried, "What were we fighting for?" (Za chto borolis?)

Peasant discontent was the brother of worker discontent. In fact, the workingman, denied socialism, favored village capitalism. ". . . in Petrograd, the heaviest category of workers, the transport workers, were receiving only 700 to 1,000 calories of food a day. The Petrograd workers attempted to organize food collecting expeditions in the neighboring countryside, in defiance of the prohibition of free trading. The government's action in suppressing these expeditions raised discontent to fever heat." Cold sharpened the discontent. "The situation was aggravated in February [1921] by a fuel crisis which led to the closing of many factories." Strikes broke out. "That this question of food collection was uppermost in the minds of the demonstrators and strikers is evident from the fact that all the resolutions passed at the numerous strikers' meetings demanded the right to trade freely with the villages and the abolition of the punitive detachments which existed to suppress such trading as was carried on illegally. . . . The strikes and demonstrations . . . were assuming the character of a general strike." The Petrograd Committee of the Communist Party, Zinoviev-bossed, "quickly and effectively suppressed" the strikes "by the combined method of force and concessions. On February 24 the Petrograd Guberniya [Provincial] Communist Committee declared a state of emergency, mobilized the whole party for dealing with the situation, and among other measures of wholesale repression, arrested all the members of the menshevik and social revolutionary organizations still at liberty." At the same time "food-finding expeditions by the workers were sanctioned, and a large quantity of food was hastily rushed to Petrograd."[3]

In most countries policy lags behind necessity, for governments are heavy animals too tied down by what is to speed into what should be. Delays are longer in dictatorships where little except the brains of the dictators can spare the people the high cost of a harmful and obsolete dogma-imposed policy. The Kremlin realized the need for bigger crops. But when, early in 1920, Trotsky suggested a new economic policy tantamount to the enfranchisement of village capitalism, the Central Committee, committed to communist doctrine, said No. The leadership therefore thrashed around for an entire year seeking substitute incentives to stimulate production. Toward the end of 1920 this search grew mad. The nation's stomach was near-empty and its century-tested patience had begun to crack.

[3] All quotations in this paragraph are from Leonard Schapiro, *The Origin of Communist Autocracy. Political Opposition in the Soviet State. First Phase. 1917-1922* (London, 1955), pp. 296-298.

Lenin estimated that "nine-tenths and more probably 99 percent" of Russia's agricultural area was cultivated by private householders.[4] "I know," he told the communist caucus at the Eighth Congress of Soviets on December 24, 1920, "that the collective farms are so disorganized, in such a lamentable condition, that they deserve the name of almshouses. . . . The condition of most state farms is below average. We must lean on the individual peasant householder, that's what he is and he will not change in the near future, and there is no use dreaming about any transition to socialism and collectivization."[5]

Hence the urgency of doing something about the private peasant. But what? Socialism was out, capitalism not officially in. This narrowed the margin for maneuver. "From general discussions," Lenin said on December 24, "we must pass to the question of how to take the first practical, indispensable step this spring and under no circumstances later, and only such a formulation of the question will be businesslike . . . for us it is necessary to begin first of all with what is absolutely indispensable, namely, with the saving of the seed. . . . It is being eaten. It should be saved. How in that case are we to act most practically? It should be taken to the general warehouse, and the peasant should be given the security and the certainty that the seed will not become the victim of red tape and unjust distribution but that our aim is to place under the state's protection the quantity of seed necessary for a complete sowing."

This is all that Lenin suggested. With the nation's agriculture crumbling around his ears, with rumblings of revolt drawing near, this is all he could fit on the thin line between not-collectivism and not-capitalism.

Three days later the communist delegates to the Soviet Congress caucused again and Lenin addressed them once more on the peasant problem. It was a short speech, like the previous caucus speech, it too dealt with a single aspect of the problem, and it was not published until 1959.[6] Lenin discussed prizes for peasants.

The communist fraction at the Soviet Congress had adopted an amendment to the resolution which the party was submitting to the Congress; the amendment would have eliminated prizes to individual peasants and given them only to collectives or to villages as a whole. The Central Committee of the party found this amendment unwise and commissioned Lenin to speak against it. He said:

[4] *Leninskii Sbornik*, Vol. XXXVI, p. 151.

[5] Lenin, *op. cit.*, Third ed., Vol. XXVI, pp. 53-57. The speech was secret and did not appear until Lenin's *Collected Works* were published years after his death. The Soviet Congress comprised 2,537 delegates of whom 1,728 were voting delegates and 809 nonvoting. Of the voting delegates, 1,614 (93%) were communists, 114 non-party, and one Bundist. Of the nonvoters, 722 were communists, 65 non-party, 6 Bundists, 8 Mensheviks—among them, Fyodor I. Dan, a leader, 3 Poale Zion, 3 SR's, and 2 anarchists. Because of the presence of non-party people and other-party delegates, the communists caucused separately.

[6] *Leninskii Sbornik*, Vol. XXXVI, pp. 149-153.

The Central Committee appreciated the fraction's fears that prizes might be given to kulaks. But that was no reason for rejecting all prizes and awards. When the Central Committee debated the matter, "I, at least, took this position: here it is necessary to weigh the pros and cons, and ask the local people." He thought it wrong to abandon the idea of prizes for individual cultivators, but if the local authorities considered it practical, then prizes for village communities should be given priority without, however, excluding prizes for private peasants. Of course, he continued, the kulaks were the best farmers and there were many of them, and if they were not careful, most of the prizes would go to kulaks. Moreover, if the prizes took the form of agricultural equipment we would be guilty, "and not even indirectly, of being participants in the development of kulakism" and enhancing the kulak's influence in his village. Nevertheless, Russia had twenty million individual peasant households and it was "basically incorrect" not to stimulate their productivity. "To be sure, it would be desirable to improve the [agricultural] economy through collectivism, by entire districts. . . . If you, working in the localities," can do this, "fine. But are you sure you can succeed, that this isn't a fantasy which, in practice, will result in tremendous errors?" Therefore, awards and rewards go first to whole villages, and in the second place to individuals, care being exercised that if the individual uses any kulak methods: makes money by lending money or "speculation," or hires labor, he is disqualified.

Then this question: Machines and equipment to raise production or things to beautify the home and ease daily living? "We say, 'Give the individual cultivators only consumer goods and household articles and, of course, medals'" like the Order of the Banner of Red Labor.

The amendment was withdrawn.

Save the seed and confer prizes. That was Lenin's policy.

Saving the seed by collecting it from the peasants and storing it in state granaries for later distribution among the same peasants would expose some to hunger and impress all with the government's lack of trust in them, thus multiplying their distrust in the government. No amount of official propaganda could convince the peasant that a government guilty for years of confiscating his crops would return the seed. The scheme never worked.

The policy toward prizes, a drop in the sea of Bolshevism's problems with the peasantry, reflected communist inhibitions, the cause of innumerable Soviet headaches. A strong body of party opinion opposed any prizes for individual peasants, and it required Lenin's prestige to overcome the objection. The peasant, absent partner in the "Workers' and Peasants' Dictatorship," remained the bogey of Marxists, especially when industry and enterprise earned him the pejorative title of kulak, the Russian word for "fist." The kulaks grew better crops, had surpluses, sold them ("speculated") illegally in the market, became moneylenders to the poor and slothful, accepted payment in the form of labor, and in these and subtle ways acquired power in the village and used it to no pro-Soviet purpose. Therefore the government had to hamper the progress of the good producers and thereby reduce the national harvest in a hungry country. But even the poor and middle peasants, though eligible for prizes, could receive them only in the form of consumers' commodities, not of a plow or harrow, for added equipment would help increase output and tempt them, indeed compel them, to "speculate"; what else could they do with surpluses? That made them kulaks. If, moreover, a peasant's cow calved and his horse foaled he too became a kulak and invited discrimination and got no prize.

The Kremlin was killing the spirit that raised the golden grain and filled the Soviet stomach.

Almost always Lenin proved invincible in debate. This testified to his superior intellect but also to the mesmeric effect of supreme power which awed even Bertrand Russell and H. G. Wells, not to speak of Soviet citizens. Moreover, Lenin concentrated on one practical issue, in the trade-union debate on party unity, in the peasant discussion on the immediate problem of conserving the seed, and he made these seem paramount. But focus on the practical may lower the horizon and blur perspective. Party unity equals oligarchy and ultimately cult of personality. The eating of next season's seed was a symptom, not a first cause. It is the lash that caused the trouble. Lash and prize are an unmatched team which cannot pull a plow. The peasant preferred one well-fed horse.

Lenin's emphasis on the practical at the expense of the ideological was good Marxism. For Marxism aims to change material conditions or objective circumstances. Changed objective circumstances change consciousness and therefore change ideology; they might in fact transform it into its opposite. The activity of Marxists could thus spell the death of Marxism. In its extreme manifestation, stress on the practical may exclude the political, especially under a dictatorship where politics, which is a struggle for power, tends to vanish because the dictator's power monopoly precludes a struggle against him. This was not yet the case in Lenin's day, but he paved the way to it for his heirs. On December 20, 1920, for instance, on his initiative, the Central Committee of the communist party directed *Pravda* and *Izvestia* "to transform themselves more into *production* than political publications and to teach the same to *all* newspapers of the Russian Soviet Federated Socialist Republic." The end product several decades later was dullness. Professors, under party orders, taught philosophy as a tool to raise factory output. The pursuit of steel, shoes, and underwear loomed larger than ideology. Propaganda bathos, exemplified by *Pravda* editorials, and peremptory commands drove thought underground.

Because he had the power to make decisions, Lenin could not devote himself only to peasant problems and trade-union questions. Other matters, some large, most small, divided his attention. On the last day of 1920, answering a request from Azerbaijan in the Caucasus for more textiles—the expected quid pro quo was oil for the north—he instructed Rykov and Stalin to meet with Nariman Narimanov, Chairman of the Azerbaijan Republic, for preliminary talks.[7]

About the same time, a minor party official named Zaligin in a small provincial center informed Lenin by telegram from prison why he had been arrested: A local communist chairman had married the daughter of a capitalist hostage, and to make the sin worse, the wedding took place in a church; he, Zaligin, thereupon proposed to the communist unit that the chairman be expelled from the party. A majority voted for expulsion. The minority appealed against the decision to the provincial party committee whose representative, on arriving in the town, annulled the vote and clapped Zaligin in jail for making the proposal in the first place. Lenin ordered Zaligin's immediate release and a thorough investigation.[8]

Lenin loved dictionaries. Late in 1920 he instructed his secretary to import for him: a French-German, a German-French, two English-German, one Italian-German, and one German-Russian, all published in Germany. They were his barbiturates. He read them during sleepless nights to calm his nerves. Then he slept late. A member of the Cabinet wished to see him one morning. Lenin replied, "I can't before 11:30, I'll try to see him between 11:30 and noon *if* I don't oversleep."[9]

The Swedish Red Cross requested permission for Ivan P. Pavlov (1849-1936), a physiologist, and Nobel Prize winner in 1904, to work in Sweden. Lenin asked his secretary on January 6, 1921, to draft a reply that would say Pavlov had not asked to leave ("Is it true he does not wish to go abroad?"). Moreover, Pavlov must be granted "some privileges." Lenin added, "Since my letter" to the Swedes may be published, "it is very desirable" to include in it a statement about these privileges.[10] Apparently, Pavlov was unhappy and the Swedish Red Cross invitation might have been designed to help him, for "in January, 1921, Lenin signed a special decree" providing for the publication of Pavlov's scientific papers, better conditions for him and his family, and improved working facilities.[11]

Pavlov was angry and skeptical when Fedor N. Petrov, representing the Education Commissariat, visited him in Petrograd after the decree had been published. "Well, how can Russian science develop?" Pavlov exclaimed. "The dogs are dying, no food for them; the experimental rooms are collapsing; I can't conduct any experiments; what is to come of this?"

Petrov said Lenin had ordered Professor Pavlov's wishes to be gratified: "How much money do you need?"

"Can you provide the money? Gold is necessary for the purchase of equipment abroad."

[7] *Ibid.*, p. 159.
[8] *Ibid.*, p. 160.
[9] *Ibid.*, Vol. XXXV, p. 201.
[10] *Ibid.*, pp. 205-206.
[11] *Bolshaya Sovietskaya Entsiklopedia*, First ed., Vol. 43, column 745.

Petrov asked how much gold. Pavlov sat down and drew up a modest budget amounting to one thousand gold roubles (approximately $500). The Soviet government gave him the sum.

On January 10, 1921, Dr. Dmitri I. Ulyanov, Lenin's brother, director of the Department of Sanatoriums in the Crimea, wired Commissar of Health Semashko in Moscow, copy to Lenin, that the peninsular authorities were obstructing his work by putting their particular interests above those of the federal Republic. Lenin asked Semashko for a copy of his reply. Semashko telegraphed the Crimean provincial communist headquarters on January 13: sick workers from Petrograd and Moscow would begin to arrive in the Crimea on January 20; they must be provided with automobile transportation from the rail terminus to the seacoast, with rooms, food, heating; should the chief Crimean health officer "not understand these basic national obligations to the workers of the Republic, I beg you to appoint somebody in his place." Lenin then wired his brother that he had seen his telegram to Semashko and Semashko's instructions to the Crimea; "Let me know if an improvement is noticeable. Lenin."[12] Coldly businesslike; nothing personal.

The Council of Labor and Defense, an inner Cabinet, studied the coal-mining situation on January 24, 1921. Lenin summarized in a brief memo: "Rubbish and dirt are being mined, not coal. There is no sorting. They give rubbish to the railroads and keep the good for themselves. Coal sold in bags to individual private buyers . . ."[13]

Prince Peter Kropotkin, a former page in the Tsar's court, Russian anarchist, and noted geographer, lay dying. Semashko asked authorization for a special train to take a concilium of physicians to Kropotkin's bedside in a country place not far from Moscow. The Commissariat of Transportation said it needed Lenin's permission. Lenin on February 5: "Permit train to Kropotkin."[14] The old rebel died on February 8, and was buried in Moscow city. He had returned to Russia in June, 1917, and stayed on although the unfolding of Bolshevism and the persecution of anarchists broke his great spirit.

Distracted though he was by many other matters, Lenin's January, 1921, speeches and writings on trade unions would have filled a good-sized book; it was the burning issue. But on February 4 he addressed the Moscow Expanded Conference of Metal Workers and found its interest riveted not on unions but on food. For two entire days, February 2 and 3, the 850 delegates from factories in the city and province of Moscow had discussed the report of the Commissariat of Food delivered by Andrey Yanuaryevich Vishinsky, long a Menshevik, now a Bolshevik of 1920 vintage (subsequently prosecutor in the Moscow show trials and still later Foreign Minister). The delegates treated him roughly. "Speakers sharply condemned the food policy, criticized

[12] *Ibid.*, pp. 206-207.
[13] *Ibid.*, p. 210.
[14] *Ibid.*, p. 213.

the officials of the People's Commissariat of Food, and demanded the cancellation of all privileged rations, including those of the Sovnarkom [Cabinet], and equalization in the distribution of food supplies. Having heard the closing remarks of A. Y. Vishinsky, the workers, declaring that the report of the representative of the People's Commissariat of Food failed to satisfy them, demanded a report by V. I. Lenin. Mensheviks and SR's present at the conference exploited the mood of the delegates and developed at the conference an intensified anti-Soviet agitation as demonstrated by the notes passed up to the Presidium during the report of A. Y. Vishinsky and the speech of L. B. Kamenev. In these notes such demands were made as the convocation of the Constituent Assembly, the organization of an All-Russian peasant union, etcetera. As a result of the heated discussion the conference adopted a resolution on the food question demanding the abolition of all privileged food rations, an end to the practice of distributing among workers the products of their own plant, the improvement of meals in factory cafeterias, etcetera . . . the delegates to the conference protested against the decree establishing committees to supervise sowings, and some of them defended the SR-advanced idea of creating peasant trade unions."[15]

Facing the embittered, embattled metal workers on February 4, Lenin must have known that just as the Tsar and Kerensky made the Bolshevik revolution by sins of commission and omission (Kerensky has said the Tsar's regime "committed suicide"), so he, Lenin, could be held responsible for the ugly temper of the delegates and their receptivity to Menshevik and SR suggestions. The conference's shrill whistle was the sound of steam escaping through a vent from a subterranean accumulation of heated resentment that would soon explode. How did Lenin cope with it? The sulking peasantry, eager for capitalism, had found an ally in the workingman, backbone of the dictatorship whose stated aim was socialism. Not only did the worker need the peasant's crop, most workers were part peasant, they were only a generation or two removed from the village, and many still had land in the village either personally or through their families. Lenin would have been better served by a more class-conscious proletariat unsympathetic to the capitalist-class-conscious peasantry.

"From the words of comrades who have spoken," Lenin began his speech, "I learned that you are v˖ry much interested in the sowing campaign. Very many think that there is a kind of cunning in the Soviet government's policy toward the peasants. Our policy in this area is such that we always frankly explain it before the eyes of the whole mass. The root question for the Soviet government is that after our victory we still do not have victories in other countries. If you read our constitution attentively you will see that we promise no nonsense of wheels but speak of the necessity of a dictatorship, for the entire bourgeois world is against us. . . . The capitalists' military power is stronger than ours, but they failed, and we say, The worse is behind us,

[15] Lenin, *op. cit.*, Third ed., Vol. XXVI, editorial note, p. 640.

but the enemy will still try. There is not one European who has visited our country who says that they would have managed without ragged people and 'queues' or that England, after six years of war, did not suffer from similar conditions."

Always the comfort of company in misery; even Europeans could not have done it better; the fault is not ours—there has been no world revolution; they must be on guard against the foreign foe; things had improved nevertheless. Old propaganda refrains.

Then he moved closer to the heart: "We are told that the peasants do not enjoy the same conditions as workers, that you are being cunning here, but we openly avow this cunning. . . . The peasants are another class; socialism will come when there are no classes, when all means of production are in the hands of labor. We still have classes, their annihilation will require long, long years and whoever promises to do it quickly is a charlatan. The peasant lives separately, and he sits, as an owner, apart, and he has the grain: with it he can enslave all." These words were designed to dissociate workers from peasants.

This impression is reinforced by what followed: "We do not promise equality, there is none in our country. There can be none so long as one person has bread in abundance and the other has none. . . . We have a dictatorship of the proletariat, the word frightens the peasants, but this is the only means of uniting the peasants and compelling them to proceed under the leadership of the workers. . . .

"What policy do the capitalists pursue in America? They distribute land free of charge and the peasants follow them and they tranquilize them with words about equality. Either you succumb to such deceit or you understand it and unite with the workers and expel the capitalists.

"There you have our policy and you can find it in our constitution. . . . We promised no one equality: if you wish to be with the workers—come with us, come over to the socialists, if you don't wish—go to the Whites. . . . We promised no rivers of milk. . . .

"They tell us: re-examine the sowing campaign. I say: nobody has suffered as much as the worker. During this period, the peasant received land and was able to harvest his grain. This winter the peasants are in a desperate situation and their dissatisfaction is understandable.

". . . What is the chief purpose of the sowing campaign?—to sow all the land, otherwise we perish—inescapably. Do you know how much grain we have taken from them this year? About three hundred million [poods], but without that what would the workers have done? Even so they lived in hunger. . . . We cannot promise to relieve the peasants of their privations all at once, for that the factories would have to raise their output a hundredfold. If the workers had not been supported even with this scant ration we should have had to close down every industry. . . . But you help us carry out the sowing campaign so that all fields are sown, then we can master the difficulties."[16] In a last sentence, he asked advice on how to improve procedures.

Lenin had already heard the advice and would hear more of it from hodok lips. The hodok, or walking messenger, was in an old muzhik tradition. In tsarist times, when a village or group of peasants felt aggrieved, a hodok would go forth to lay the case before an official, the highest accessible. Often bearded and long-haired, dressed, usually in a tulup, a tight-waisted, knee-length, smelly sheepskin coat with the fleece nearer the body for greater warmth, a sheepskin cap, and plaited bark or leather or felt boots, the hodok trudged hundreds of miles over snow and ice, with a credential or petition in a purse tied around his neck and hanging down inside his homespun blouse, until he came to a provincial capital, and if the grievance did not find an open ear or friendly response, he moved on, spending nights on the floors or atop the Dutch ovens of wayside inns or of kabaks (vodka shops) or the huts of hospitable peasants, and finally, in St. Petersburg, he camped at the gate or on the doorstep of a bureaucrat or minister who either sent him packing or gave him a loaf of black bread and a rouble and promised to investigate but normally did nothing. Many hundreds of these hodoks crisscrossed the plains of Russia in the early Soviet years; one saw them in the streets of Moscow. President Sverdlov, then President Kalinin, had regular reception days for hodoks and sometimes arranged by telephone for Lenin to see a few. They brought the village with its high skies, tasty folk language, heavy odor, and hard life into his aseptic Kremlin office. Lenin was a good listener. "In January and February, 1921, Lenin received peasants from the provinces of Tver, Tambov, and Vladimir and from Siberia and other areas—and almost all told him of their firm conviction that requisitions must be abolished if the material incentive of the peasants in improving their farms is to be stimulated. Talking with hodoks, Lenin drew conclusions about local conditions and the mood of the peasants."[17]

Lenin did not need the hodoks to open his eyes. Since October, 1920, a peasant uprising had been gaining recruits and raging with increasing vehemence in Tambov province in central Russia.[18] On October 21, 1920, Lenin sent a note to the Commissariat of Food saying peasants from Stavropol in the North Caucasus complained that the cooperative stores had wheel grease, matches, and other commodities, but would not distribute them. "Herring have decayed, yet were not given out. The discontent is terrible. The provincial food commissar explains that when you finish [delivering] confiscated grain we will give things out. Confiscations amounting to twenty-

---

[16] *Ibid.*, pp. 147-149.

[17] P. N. Pospelov and eight others. *Vladimir Ilyich Lenin. Biografia* (Moscow, 1960), pp. 485-486.

[18] *Leninskii Sbornik*, Vol. XXXV, p. 158.

seven million poods are excessive and they are taking *seed*. It is alleged there will definitely be *reduced sowing*."[19] Lenin kept urging the manufacture of several deep-plowing electric plows—the Commissariat of Agriculture promised fifty in November, 1920, if the Supreme Council of National Economy made them in a hurry—but the peasants, in their millions, would have produced far more with their wooden plows if relieved of requisitions and persecutions (no herring or grease until you bring in grain marked for requisition), and further discrimination against good farmers. The brake on Soviet agriculture was not technology but politics.

The Sovnarkom, on November 30, 1920, approved a resolution drafted by Lenin instructing a commission to ascertain, within a week, whether local money taxes could be abolished and to study "the necessity of preparing, simultaneously with the abolition of money taxes, the substitution of a tax in kind for requisitions."[20] Requisitions, limited only by the whim of the collector and his readiness to threaten the peasants with the accompanying Chekists' revolvers, were made after the harvest; they therefore induced the tillers to sow less. A tax in kind would presumably be fixed in advance of planting and stimulate larger sowings.

It is not known whether or what the commission reported after a week. More than two months passed; more hodoks besieged Lenin. The stormy metal workers too must have made an impression on him. Sitting at a Politburo session on February 8, he wrote out a "preliminary rough draft" of theses on the peasant question and read them to his four colleagues, Kamenev, Stalin, Trotsky, and Zinoviev: "(1) Grant the wish of the non-party peasantry for the substitution of a grain tax in place of requisitions (in the sense of the removal of surpluses); (2) Reduce the size of this tax below last year's requisitions; (3) Approve the principle of coordinating the size of the tax with the diligence of the cultivator in the sense of reducing the percentage of tax in accordance with the increase in the diligence of the cultivator; (4) Extend the freedom of the cultivator to use his surplus after taxes in the local economic turnover on condition that he pays his tax quickly and in full."[21]

Point Four was a comforting communist circumlocution for: legalize private trade, or legalize what Lenin had branded a "crime." But who would weigh diligence and how? The procedure promised free rein to vengeful communists and arbitrary bureaucrats. What if diligence made a man a kulak? Nobody ever determined the legal economic height of a kulak. An official measured it without rules.

Lenin's rough draft lay on his desk for a month before being submitted, in more elaborate form, to the Tenth Communist Party Congress in March,

[19] *Ibid.*, p. 159.
[20] *Ibid.*, pp. 176-179.
[21] Lenin, *op. cit.*, Fourth ed., Vol. 32, p. 111.

1921. Meanwhile, with the planting season approaching in the southern regions, the peasants waited for a lifesaving Kremlin ukaze.

On February 6, Lenin requested two books received from Germany: Professor G. F. Nikolai's *Sechs Tatsachen als Grundlage zur Beurteilung der heutigen Machtpolitik* (*Six Circumstances as a Basis for Judging Today's Power Politics*), and F. Jung's *Reise in Russland* (*A Visit to Russia*).[22] Three days later he ordered two London publications, H. N. Brailsford, *The War of Steel and Gold*, and Z. Kahan-Coates, *The Life and Work of Friedrich Engels*, as well as three German volumes, Karl Marx, *Die Klassenkaempfe in Frankreich* (*The Class Struggles in France*), Marx and Engels, *Reichsgruendung und Kommune* (*Reich Establishment and the Commune*), and Franz Mehring, *Freiligrath und Marx in ihrem Briefwechsel* (*Freiligrath and Marx in Their Correspondence*).[23] Yet February, 1921, was probably the busiest month in his life. His chief preoccupations, listed by a staff member, were: organizing shipments of food from the provinces to Moscow and Petrograd to prevent starvation, the nationwide fuel crisis, creating a state planning commission, convening the electrotechnical congress in Moscow, coordinating the work of the various economic commissariats, offering concessions to foreigners, remedying the shortage of industrial raw materials, and reorganizing the Commissariat of Education.

Lenin's Directives of the Central Committee to the Communist Officials of the Commissariat of Education[24] noted that the party had lowered the admission age to polytechnical schools from seventeen to fifteen "solely as a temporary practical necessity due to the poverty and ruin of the country under the burden of wars imposed on us by the Entente." Nevertheless, professional education must be combined with "general polytechnical knowledge" even for fifteen-year-olds. "The basic shortcoming of the Education Commissariat is its deficiency in businesslike approach and practicality," its failure to find bourgeois teachers with decades of experience ("Of course . . . noncommunist specialists must work under the supervision of communists" and general subjects "particularly philosophy, the social sciences and communist training must be formulated by communists"), and its unsatisfactory distribution of printed matter with the result that "newspapers and books are gobbled up by a thin stratum of Soviet employees and very few reach the workers and peasants. This entire operation must undergo a radical reorganization."

In a *Pravda* article,[25] Lenin commented on his own Directives. He ridiculed the debate on "Polytechnical or Monotechnical Education" in which

[22] *Leninskii Sbornik*, Vol. XXXVI, p. 189.

[23] *Ibid.*, Vol. XXXV, p. 214. Ferdinand Freiligrath (1810-1876) was a German revolutionary poet and friend of Marx in the 1850's, who later disagreed with Marx and broke with him while living in London.

[24] Lenin, *op. cit.*, Third ed., Vol. XXVI, pp. 156-159.

[25] *Ibid.*, pp. 160-167.

some communists agitated for purely professional or technical training without courses in the social sciences, ideology, and philosophy. "General disquisitions and vain attempts to 'underpin' such reduction [of standards] are pure nonsense. Enough of this game of general disquisitions and so-called theorizing." Experienced teachers "undoubtedly exist. We suffer from the inability to find them." He called for *"less* 'management' and more practical work, that is, fewer general discussions, more facts and proven facts to showing what, under what conditions, and to what extent we are advancing or standing still or going backward."

Lenin's own impressions justified the conclusion, he said, that, "at the present moment . . . only the first forward step is being taken in the transition from capitalism to communism."

Actually, however, Soviet Russia was on the eve of changes that would take her two steps backward toward capitalism. That happened in March, 1921, and this made February Lenin's busy month. In the twenty-three working days of the month, again according to his staff member, he presided over forty Cabinet, Politburo, Central Committee, Council of Labor and Defense, and other sessions; received sixty-eight persons, including several hodoks; delivered four public addresses, meticulously prepared; wrote two articles, one on the Education Commissariat, the second on planning; regularly read several dailies; paged through "every new book which appeared in Russia or was sent from abroad." In addition to the major problems debated at the forty sessions, Lenin was "buried under a heap" of lesser business "which he tried, and taught others, 'to carry to a close' without fail."[26]

For his numerous tasks Lenin needed that scarcest commodity—time. Because their country was backward and had few clocks and watches, or because the land is vast and the peasants slept for months and the aristocracy played for years, Russians had little sense of time. Instead of making a virtue of punctuality, they made a habit of lateness, especially in coming to meetings. They also liked to talk long. I once heard Zinoviev, who had a thin, high-pitched voice, deliver a four-hour speech. But Lenin was a time-miser. He arrived before the moment fixed for the opening of a session and presided with a watch, which had a second hand, on the table in front of him. Three to five minutes were allowed for reports by himself or other members of the Sovnarkom or Council of Labor and Defense (STO) and he held up his watch when the time had elapsed. To torture colleagues still further, smoking, on his doctors' orders, was prohibited in his presence although most Russians, particularly at tense moments, are rarely without the hollow paper stem of a Russian cigarette between their teeth. But since the alternative was smoking or exploding they would congregate in an anteroom (where they could also listen to the proceedings) until he "grumbled and recalled them to their seats." A. A. Andreyev, a member of the party's Central Com-

[26] *Leninskii Sbornik*, Vol. I, edited by L. B. Kamenev, pp. 196-197.

mittee and in 1920 and 1921 of STO, who records these memories,[27] adds that "In presiding at sessions, Lenin never expected his opinion to be regarded as the last word. If the slightest shade of difference in opinions or proposals emerged, voting was the rule at all sessions of the Central Committee and STO. . . . I never saw him gloomy or even severe at meetings. But he literally grew furious when he heard of the failure to carry out a decision or of an unconscientious attitude to work or of an infringement of party or state discipline. In such cases he gave the official a fierce dressing down and demanded that the strictest punishment be meted out." If a speaker talked generalities, Lenin would interrupt him demanding "precision and truly businesslike proposals. At the same time, Lenin could, like nobody else, listen even when his mind has been made up on a question; slightly screwing up one eye and looking cunning, he would merely smile." But "Without the Central Committee, without discussion in the Central Committee he never decided any important question. Lenin strictly adhered to the idea of collective leadership in the Central Committee as in the Sovnarkom."[28]

Most committee meetings were held in a chamber adjoining Lenin's private office. There he also received some visitors. This made it easier for him to terminate the interview by saying he had to return to his desk for a telephone call or some other reason. In conserving time and energy he had an effective coadjutor in Lydia A. Fotieva, age thirty-eight in 1919, a party member since the age of twenty-three, imprisoned for anti-tsarist subversion, active among Bolshevik émigrés abroad, and Lenin's personal secretary as well as private secretary of the Sovnarkom and STO during almost all his career as a statesman. Her memoirs, the expected mixture of demonstrable or plausible fact and breathless adulation, shed light on his character, idiosyncrasies, and work methods.[29] If people smoked in the office he said to her it would be better to remove the No Smoking sign than to have its injunction infringed. When an official disobeyed instructions "Lenin ordered the guilty one arrested on the spot for two or three days, and added, 'To be arrested on non-work days and released for work days, so the work does not suffer.'" He was strict with himself too and accepted no privileges. In 1918-1919, a sheepskin mat lay under his desk to keep his feet from freezing. Somebody replaced it with a polar-bear skin. Lenin protested and called it a

[27] *Vospominaniya*, Vol. 2, pp. 7-42.

[28] Soviet treatment of the past always reflects conditions in the present. The book containing Andreyev's memoirs appeared in 1957 when Stalin was under attack for "the cult of personality." This passage from Andreyev is followed by, "It is necessary to say that neither at sessions, meetings, congresses, nor in the press did Lenin ever permit the slightest praise or glorification of his personality or his services and he opposed the cult of personality so alien to Marxism." That did not preclude the posthumous glorification of Lenin, largely sincere, partly a stick to beat Stalin, who deserved it well.

[29] *Vospominaniya*, Vol. 2, pp. 204-222.

luxury and "an altogether unnecessary reform in our ruined country." He fought bribery as "the damned legacy of tsarism" to be punished with "no less than ten years in prison and, after that, ten years of forced labor." His orders, Miss Fotieva writes, were unfinished business until proof of compliance was laid before him. She notes his punctiliousness about small things: Although his office staff had telephoned down to the guard booth at the Kremlin gate to admit his caller, the person was held up below and again upstairs; why? He frequently sent urgent messages and letters to colleagues in Moscow by bicycle courier, and admonished a secretary not to dispatch the packet without first ascertaining whether the recipient was at home, in his office, at a meeting, or elsewhere; "Seal the letter in an envelope and if necessary sew it and seal it with wax. And Lenin asked slyly, 'Do you know how to do that?' Then he added, 'Be sure to write, "To Be Opened By Nobody Else," and warn the messenger that the addressee must sign a receipt.'"
The receipt had to be shown to Lenin. Once one of his letters was delayed and he sent an angry note to the executive secretary of the Sovnarkom saying, "Yesterday I discovered that an urgent document I gave Fotieva was forwarded 'ordinary,' that is, in an idiotic way, and was several hours late, and had I not intervened again it would have been delayed for days." If it happened again "I shall resort to severe punishment and dismissals." "Lenin was polite and friendly to all, and very simple in his relationships. He never forgot to express thanks for a service, even the most insignificant, for instance when he asked for a newspaper." His staff had to inform him within twenty-four hours of the receipt of written complaints and within forty-eight hours of oral complaints. Miss Fotieva was under instructions to record in the minutes of the Sovnarkom and STO the names of late-coming members and extent of their lateness. ". . . people who came to see Lenin in a depressed mood, having lost faith in themselves, left him inspired."

Heaps of reports were submitted to Lenin in writing. "Usually," Miss Fotieva remarks, "Lenin began reading documents at the end, that is, where the practical proposals began, leaving out 'the literature,' as he called it. If the practical proposals were businesslike, Lenin read the entire paper. Lenin read with unusual speed." He had a highly evolved sense of responsibility. "A leader," Fotieva quotes him as saying, "is responsible not only for what he himself does but also for the deeds of those whom he leads." Hence his scrupulous scrutiny of what colleagues and subordinates wrote, suggested, and did. He likewise took into consideration the response of others to his acts. "Nadezhda Konstantinova [Krupskaya]," Miss Fotieva writes, "said that even in purely personal matters Lenin would ask himself, 'What will the workers say to this?'" Every leader is on parade and must think of his constituency but Lenin may also have been trying to justify his inhibitions which reduced purely personal matters to a minimum. Except during illnesses, most of his life was spent in the office or in the neighboring conference room where, throughout 1918 and 1919, the Sovnarkom met every day, excluding Sunday, from 8:30 P.M. to 1 or 2 A.M., according to Fotieva who attended. Later it convened somewhat less frequently.

Lenin's office hours were long and intense. The office, on the third floor of a Kremlin building, was simply furnished in consonance with the style of its occupant. Every piece of furniture—left by the Tsars—was functional except an old clock which fell behind one minute, and sometimes fifteen, every twenty-four hours. Constant repairs did not help, yet Lenin would not allow it to be removed. "Another clock will be no different," he declared. In the end he permitted a substitution.

Lenin, Fotieva writes, allowed no draperies in his office; the blinds were never lowered; "it was as though he felt cramped and stifled in a room cut off from the outside world by lowered blinds." The temperature had to be kept under fourteen degrees "[Reaumur; 63.5 degrees Fahrenheit]." "If the temperature was raised as much as one degree he could not bear it."

He had three telephones on his small desk (he rejected a large, better one), and used them frequently. On the left side of the desk there usually lay folders full of papers. Comrade Fotieva says she tried for several years to arrange the papers systematically and Lenin acquiesced, then frustrated her efforts. The folders were marked "Urgent," "Not Urgent," "Important," "Less Important," "Seen," "Not Seen," and each paper was furnished with a label about its contents. From these folders Lenin "raked up" the papers he needed and when he left the office he put them in the center of his desk with a large pair of scissors on them. "This meant, 'Don't Dare to Touch.'" Or he filled a separate folder with papers from all the other folders and took them to his Kremlin apartment for homework. "This folder lived a living life, Vladimir Ilyich worked on it. But in the end this folder was packed to bursting because he inserted all new papers, which for any reason attracted his attention, into this folder, and for some time, nobody except him touched them. Having received permission from Lenin, I sorted them into the several folders.

"The desk drawers were always locked except for the top left drawer in which he deposited papers with his instructions. Several times a day we took them out for immediate action.

"Once after a delegation from Bokhara had left at an hour when Vladimir Ilyich usually went home for dinner, the door between his office and the conference was locked on the inside. Assuming that it had been locked by a Cheka employee who guarded another door and disturbed because Lenin's instructions [on the papers in the top left drawer] could not be carried out, we banged desperately on the door. After several minutes, it was opened by a smiling Vladimir Ilyich. He was dressed in a Bokharan national costume which the Bokharans had presented to him and he had taken it into his head to try it on." (Alas, no photograph.)

Lenin disliked soft, padded chairs. He sat at his desk on a plain wooden chair with a wicker seat and back. On the desk was a small electric lamp with a green glass shade. Alone in the office, he did not turn on the chandelier, and he never left the office without switching off the light. Every day he tore a page from the wall calendar. Near a door leading to the corridor stood a small table laden with maps and atlases. He enjoyed studying maps. He had pasted on the Dutch oven in the office a little map of the territory where Russia meets Turkey. Miss Fotieva, thinking he did not need it, wanted to remove it. He objected, saying he was accustomed to having it there. "In general, Vladimir Ilyich liked customary, unchanging surroundings. It was as though in this quiet of the room and of things that were always the same and always in the same places he found rest from the rich varied events of life." The explanation sounds plausible. He was also finicky and conservative.

Several bookcases and bookshelves and a revolving bookcase were heavily laden with old friends and new arrivals. Miss Fotieva puts their total at two thousand. These included thin Russian paperbacks and fat dictionaries and reference volumes. He told his secretaries to guard against books being appropriated by visitors. In some valuable volumes he wrote, "Lenin's copy." Foreign and Soviet newspapers also abounded in the office.

There was no photograph of Lenin in his office, in the conference room, or in any Sovnarkom or other office which he might visit; he would not tolerate them. A portrait of Karl Marx stood on a shelf above his office sofa. Lenin did not want to pose for photographs and relented only under the combined power of the photographer's prolonged persistence and his staff's supplications; after all, the country needed to see him, and he never traveled except twice to Petrograd and to a few Moscow villages. Nor did he relish sitting for painters or sculptors. He did submit to Nathan I. Altman who made a bust and to Clare Consuelo Sheridan.

Office was Lenin's sanctuary. He shared it with no secretary or assistant. In that office and in the connecting conference chamber he and select comrades labored throughout February, 1921, while Russia burned with resentment and rebellion. They faced a complicated task: to decide whether and how to reverse gears and back the cumbersome machinery of state into capitalism without losing control of the power apparatus. They naturally procrastinated and applied ineffective palliatives.

On February 1, 1921, the Sovnarkom decided to import 300,000 tons of coal, Lenin told the Tenth Party Congress, and pay in gold. It would have been better, he said, to import mining equipment, but the coal crisis was too "acute."

On February 9 the Soviet government's Central Executive Committee (VTSIK) decreed that all local soviets must be convoked immediately and all power restored to them. This merely proved they were dead, and Russians knew Bolsheviks did not believe in resurrection. Something very grave was happening in the villages, something political which alarmed Lenin even more than meager plantings. Alexis de Tocqueville had written in *The Old*

Regime and the French Revolution (1856), "It is only government by a single man that in the long run irons out diversities and makes each member of a nation indifferent to his neighbor's lot." This was the effect of Stalin's quarter century of despotism, but in Lenin's time, with politics still alive, men were indifferent to their neighbor's growling stomach, not, however, to the Kremlin's encroaching arm. The peasants were fighting back. Kulaks, that is, muzhiks with surplus bread, not only sold it under their aprons at illegal markets, they were lending sacks of grain to poor and middle peasants and thus acquiring good reputations and great influence. It was now: Kulaks versus the Kremlin. Lenin faced the muzhik, angry and hungry, and wrath made all peasants kin. Lenin knew that the divide-and-rule-the-village policy had boomeranged. "In the early months of 1921 . . . in diverse districts of the country," reads the official 1960 Lenin biography, "kulak uprisings erupted; in a number of places"—the usual vague communist understatement for communist troubles—"the kulaks succeeded in involving middle peasants, dissatisfied with requisitions, in anti-Soviet actions."[30]

Strikes in Moscow, Petrograd, and elsewhere. Peasants revolts in Tambov province, in Tobolsk province in western Siberia, and in eight provinces of the Ukraine where "twenty-eight partisan detachments, some of them a thousand or more strong, were operating" against communist punitive expeditions.[31] Lenin understood the problem and he knew there was only one solution: abandonment of requisitions and legalizing private trade. He had been pondering this solution since November. The Politburo on February 16, 1921, authorized *Pravda* to discuss "The Substitution of Requisitioning by a Tax." On the following day, and on February 26, two authors, P. Sorokin and M. Rogov, used statistics to show the advantages of a tax system. The party Central Committee, on February 24, approved the introduction of a tax in kind to replace requisitions, but Lenin objected to a suggestion that this important news be published immediately. "We will decide at the [communist party] Congress when to publish," he urged. "In my opinion, publication should take place before the [sowing] campaign, that is, right after the party Congress."[32]

Lenin changed his mind. In a speech on February 28, to the plenary session of the Moscow Soviet, he attributed "our terrible crisis" to a mistake: they had overestimated their grain reserves, the same kind of mistake they had made in the Polish war by overestimating their offensive power. But the workers were no worse off than the workers of Vienna who were dying from capitalism. In the first half of 1920, he said, the Soviet government had not put aside enough food "to have something in the second half for a black day." He added, "Revolution, in certain circumstances, means a miracle.

[30] Pospelov and others, *op. cit.*, p. 485.
[31] Leonard Schapiro, *op. cit.*, pp. 218-219. Detailed account of the Tambov uprising in William Henry Chamberlin, *The Russian Revolution 1917-1921*, pp. 436-441.
[32] Lenin, *op. cit.*, Third ed., Vol. XXVI, editorial note, p. 652.

If we had been told in 1917 that we would, for three years, survive a war with the entire world and that as a result of that war, two million Russian landlords, capitalists, and their children would find themselves abroad and we would prove to be the victors none of us would have believed it. A miracle occurred. . . . Just because a miracle occurred here it robbed us of the faculty to calculate in advance. That's why all of us are very, very imperfect."

Thus far, Lenin refused to confess to a false policy and admitted only a miscalculation. Nevertheless, the date of the opening of the Tenth Party Congress, he announced, had been moved forward; it would meet next week. "But there is no reason for us to succumb to panic. . . . From the point of view of a healthy person, we will not have enough bread and the supply cannot immediately be increased . . . but if we calculate correctly so as to give to those in greatest need and take more from him who has larger surpluses than from him who, in the last three years, has given his last piece of bread" they could create a reserve. "Have the peasants of Siberia and the Ukraine understood this calculation? Not yet." The peasants of those regions and of the North Caucasus "usually have hundreds of poods of surplus and they are accustomed to think that for such surplus they should immediately be given consumers goods which we can get from nowhere when factories are idle."

Coming from other lips Lenin would have characterized the speech to this point as "literature." He had not mentioned either cause or policy effect. Now he reported receiving news from the Deputy Commander in Chief of the Soviet armed forces, who was in Siberia. "He wires that communications have been re-established and four trains of grain are on the way to Moscow. At one time there had been disturbances and kulak uprisings." Uprisings serious enough to cut the rail connection with European Russia. "These insurrections," Lenin declared, "signify that a segment of the peasant population refuses to be reconciled either to requisitions or taxes. Somebody here spoke of taxes. This makes a lot of sense. . . . When the non-party peasant says to us, 'Let us consider together what the small peasant needs; he needs assurance: I will give you so much, then I shall farm.' We say, Yes, that's a deal." He promised that the matter would be put before the party Congress in a week, and "we shall examine it and make a decision that will satisfy the non-party peasant, also satisfy the broad masses." Lenin was anticipating the Tenth Party Congress, in theory the supreme political authority of the country. Knowing the laws of leadership, he felt sure that the Congress would obey him when necessity commanded.

Lenin knew the peasants were not in revolt against "requisitions and taxes," they were rebelling against requisitions; they preferred taxes, taxes fixed in advance, "then I shall farm." Meanwhile, he added, an enemy had shot and killed a communist in Moscow, and there had been arrests in Petrograd where—he quoted Zinoviev's report—the Mensheviks had "pasted up proclamations calling for strikes." But, Lenin concluded, "we have survived greater difficulties."[33]

Revolts, strikes, arrests, and economic catastrophe had forced Lenin to adopt the New Economic Policy (NEP). The peasants would plant, reap, and sell at will. The workers, their trade unions nationalized à la Trotsky and Bukharin but robbed of power à la Lenin, would labor under the lash of the party and the heel of the bureaucracy. This was the NEP.

XXXVII. ᲢHE STEEL THAT BENDS

SUDDENLY, a red flame flashed across the Russian sky—the Kronstadt revolt. This revolt differed from the insurrections in Tambov, Siberia, and the Ukraine; the rebels of Kronstadt were revolutionists, not capitalist peasants.

The revolt may be said to have begun on February 28, 1921 with a conference of sailors on board the battleship *Petropavlovsk*. The same day the crew of the *Sevastopol* met to support the decisions of its sister ship. Units of the Kronstadt garrison voted to join the movement. What they decided became known on March 1, at a huge mass meeting in Yakornaya Ploshchad (Anchor Square) in the heart of Kronstadt. The assembly was addressed by Soviet Russia's President Kalinin and Commissar of the Baltic Fleet N. N. Kuzmin. These pro-Kremlin speakers failed, however, to dissuade the sailors, whom Trotsky had called "the pride and glory of the Russian revolution," and their soldier colleagues from adopting, in Kalinin's presence, a resolution clearly opposed to Leninist principles and Soviet practice. It demanded, for all of Russia, the re-election of soviets "by secret ballot" after "free preliminary agitation"; "freedom of speech and press for workers, peasants, anarchists, and left socialist parties"; freedom of assembly; free trade unions and peasant unions; liberation of radical political prisoners; abolition of search parties which boarded trains to seize food bought from peasants; equal rations for all except for workers in harmful occupations; complete freedom for the peasant to cultivate his land as he sees fit and to keep as much cattle as he can tend without hired labor; freedom for in-

[33] *Ibid.*, pp. 176-186.

dividual artisans to ply their craft without hindrance.[1]

The resolution, adopted unanimously, was signed by the meeting's chairman Petrichenko and secretary Perepelkin. Stepan Maximovich Petrichenko, leader of the revolt, was a twenty-year-old petty officer on the *Sevastopol*, born in a peasant family in the Ukraine, the stronghold of anarchists and the Left Social Revolutionary Party. Lenin told the Tenth Party Congress on March 8 that those in Kronstadt who aspired to take power from the Bolsheviks represented "an indefinite conglomerate or union of ill-assorted elements apparently even slightly to the right of the Bolsheviks or perhaps even 'left' of the Bolsheviks."[2] He added, however, that "at the same time, White generals played a big role" in the Kronstadt revolt. "You all know this. This is fully proved." This was a plausible inference. All the Kronstadt armed forces, naval and land, joined in the insurrection, therefore the tsarist generals attached to those forces joined. The second edition of the *Large Soviet Encyclopedia* states that the rebels had 10,000 troops, 68 machine guns, and 135 cannons mounted on ships and forts.

The Soviet government did not parley with the Kronstadt rebels. When delegates from insurgent Tambov saw Lenin on February 14, he agreed to remit the province's requisitions.[3] But to parley with Kronstadt about freedom that would limit the dictatorship's freedom was something the communist party could not contemplate. Instead, the Politburo ordered an immediate military assault on the island under the direct command of Trotsky, General Sergey S. Kamenev, a former tsarist officer who began his service in the Tsar's army in 1900, and General Tukhachevsky, a former tsarist officer.

The Kronstadt naval base is situated on Kotlin Island, in the Gulf of Finland, sixteen miles due west of Petrograd. Oranienbaum, a town on the mainland to the south of Kronstadt, is less than ten miles from the base. The mutineers took no offensive action against Petrograd or against Oranienbaum where they might have captured large supplies of food for use in case of siege.

Trotsky arrived in Petrograd the night of March 4, and the following morning issued an ultimatum, signed by himself and General Kamenev: "The Workers and Peasants Government has decreed that Kronstadt and the rebellious ships must immediately submit to the authority of the Soviet Republic. . . . Only those who surrender unconditionally may count on the mercy of the Soviet Republic."[4]

The first shots were artillery shells lobbed into the island from mainland

---

[1] Full text in Raphael R. Abramovitch. *The Soviet Revolution 1917-1939*, pp. 197-198; in Chamberlin's *The Russian Revolution 1917-1921*, Vol. 2, pp. 495-496; and in Alexander Berkman, *The Bolshevik Myth* (New York, 1925), pp. 297-298.

[2] Lenin, *Sochineniya*, Third ed., Vol. XXVI, p. 214.

[3] *Bolshaya Sovietskaya Entsiklopedia*, Second ed., Vol. 2, p. 528.

[4] Alexander Berkman, *The Kronstadt Rebellion* (Pamphlet, 42 pp.) (Berlin, 1922), pp. 31-32.

positions at Sestroretsk and Lissy Noss on March 7 at 6:45 P.M. The next day the Kronstadt *Izvestia* said, "The first shot has been fired. . . . Standing up to his knees in the blood of the workers, Marshal Trotsky was the first to open fire against revolutionary Kronstadt which has risen against the autocracy of the communists to establish the true power of the soviets."[5]

This reflects what the rebels thought of themselves and of the Bolshevik regime.

Now, March 8, the Tenth Communist Party Congress convened in Moscow attended by 990 delegates representing 732,521 card-carrying members. Attacks by Trotsky's forces on March 8, March 10, and March 12 were beaten back by the rebels. At the March 12 evening session of the Congress, "approximately three hundred Congress delegates were mobilized and sent off the same evening to the Kronstadt front."[6]

That more than 30 percent of the leading communists of the nation— a much higher percentage if over-age and militarily untrained communists like Lenin are excluded—had to be rushed into the Kronstadt battle indicates the low morale of those facing the rebels. Some Bolshevik units had deserted to the islanders although Trotsky's forces consisted in the main of communist cadets at officers' training schools. Yet they needed stiffening by Congress delegates.

Another assault commenced on March 16. The rebel battleships were frozen fast in the ice. The entire gulf between the mainland and Kronstadt was solid ice, one foot thick in places. Fresh snow covered the ice. The Kremlin communists wrapped themselves, and the horses that pulled their guns and munitions, in white sheets for camouflage and stormed the forts and ships under raking fire. Where shells broke the ice hundreds were drowned. A few forts fell to the attackers in the morning of the 17th, and by March 18, after cruel hand-to-hand combat, Kronstadt succumbed. Then a quiet massacre began. Stepan Maximovich Petrichenko with several thousand comrades escaped across the ice to Finland. A number of his followers, interviewed by the Associated Press in the refugee camp in Terijoki, Finland, said "his greatest fault was his reluctance to kill communist agitators when he was President at Kronstadt."[7] The same AP dispatch reported a Finnish demand that the Soviet government remove from the ice around Kronstadt the great number of corpses which would be swept to Finland's shores when the thaw came.

D. Fedotoff White, who was in Petrograd several days before the Kronstadt revolt, has assembled considerable evidence on its causes, and comes to the conclusion that "the bluejackets were an independent lot, difficult to manage, and were far from constant in their support of the Soviet government in the period between 1917 and 1921. That they were imbued with

---

[5] *Ibid.*, pp. 34-35.
[6] Lenin, *op. cit.*, Third ed., Vol. XXVI, editorial note, p. 649.
[7] *New York Times*, March 30, 1921.

a strong revolutionary spirit did not necessarily mean that they were willing to lie on the Procrustean bed of the communist dictatorship." During the rebellion, he adds, 497 members of the communist party at Kronstadt "(about one-quarter of the total membership) had voluntarily resigned their membership, 211 were excluded from the party after the crushing of the rebellion." One reason for the defections was offered by the ex-communists in the Rif Fort: "During these entire three years many egoists and careerists have joined our party; as a result of this, bureaucracy developed."[8]

Stepan Petrichenko, the rebel leader, presented another reason to his Associated Press interviewer at Terijoki: "For years, happenings at home while we were at the front or at sea were concealed by the Bolshevist censorship." When the civil war ended and they went on home leave, "our parents asked why we fought for the oppressors. That set us thinking." Most of the parents of the sailors were Ukrainian peasants touched by Makhno anarchism and Left Social Revolutionary populism. Ukrainians have a history of defiance and dissidence.

All presumed causes of the Kronstadt revolt should be set in a frame of spontaneity. If the uprising had been carefully planned it would have coincided with the Petrograd strikes and demonstrations in the second and third weeks of February. Any deliberate strategy would have required the mutineers to wait until the ice melted so their assailants could not advance across it.

Civil war's end brought relaxation. The nation was tired. The party was depressed. The soviets were dead. The population was hungry and cold. The next harvest would be poor. No further explanations are needed for the actions of hotheaded twenty-year-olds whose hopes had been chilled by reality.

The Kronstadt revolt is usually credited with being the father of the NEP. This ignores a missing link. Just as the trade-union discussion is almost invariably reduced to Trotsky's labor conscription versus Lenin's "school of communism," thus omitting Trotsky's abandonment of militarization in favor of trade unions as government agents in managing industry, so Lenin's February 28 speech to the Moscow Soviet, in which he promised the essentials of the NEP, has been eclipsed by the dramatic sequence of Kronstadt revolt and Tenth Party Congress decisions inaugurating the NEP. Soviet Russia would have gone NEP without Kronstadt. The revolt merely swept away a negligible communist minority's doubts. The Soviet system had become a communist system without soviets. The Kronstadt rebels wanted a democratic soviet system open to all proletarian-peasant socialist groups but not dominated by one—a hopeless undertaking in view of Lenin's genius to compromise on major issues and retain the essence—power. The NEP was an economic Brest-Litovsk: surrender to survive.

Characteristically, Lenin's first words in opening the Tenth Congress on

[8] D. Fedotoff White, *The Growth of the Red Army* (Princeton, 1944), pp. 127-157.

March 8 urged party unity. Discussions and quarrels within the party in the presence of domestic and foreign enemies were "a truly astonishing luxury." Now there must be "not the slightest trace of fractionalism."[9]

This statement could have been nothing more than an argument against disputes within the party. Yet it seems correct to assume that Lenin at this juncture feared the Soviet government might be overthrown. ". . . in view of the economic situation," he told the party Congress on March 8, "the Soviet government is unstable." Then he spoke of food and famine. It was Siberia and the North Caucasus that produced the best harvests, but those were the very regions where the Soviet regime was weakest and transportation most impeded, therefore the government had to collect grain from the poor-crop districts "and this has made the farm crisis extraordinarily acute." In Europe the revolution "is ripening" and the economic crisis "is growing worse," yet "if we assumed from this that help in the form of a proletarian revolution would come from there we would simply be crazy people." The Russian proletariat constituted not merely a minority of the population, it was "a small minority." A continuation of the methods of wartime communism, he added, "would certainly mean the collapse of the Soviet government and of the dictatorship of the proletariat." Not only was the peasantry discontented, "In the recent period, undoubted ferment and dissatisfaction have been found among non-party workingmen."

At the March 13 session of the Congress, Bukharin, a staunch critic of Lenin's trade-union policy, nevertheless reported for the Central Committee on questions of party organization, and the resolution he offered on behalf of Lenin, the committee, and the majority, received 369 of the 694 votes in the Congress, against 23 for the Workers' Opposition, and 9 for the Democratic Centralists. The rest of the delegates were at the Kronstadt front. But Trotsky, having arranged for the final assault on the mutinous fortress, was back at the Congress on March 14 and resumed his dispute with Lenin over the trade unions; Bukharin on this issue supported Trotsky.

Lenin replied: "Comrades, today Comrade Trotsky argued with me very politely and chided me and called me excessively cautious. I must thank him for the compliment and express regret that I cannot return it. On the contrary, I have to speak of my incautious friend . . ." Trotsky maintained in a *Pravda* article of January 29, 1921, that discussion of the role of the trade unions in the management of industry must continue and that those who wish to suppress it are creating differences in the party. This was not true, Lenin declared: "Comrade Trotsky, before an audience of responsible party workers in the Bolshoi Theater, criticized me for blocking the discussion. I accept this as a compliment. I did block the discussion in the form it took, because such a speech at the approach of a difficult spring was harmful. Only blind people could not see that.

   [9] Lenin's pronouncements at the Congress in Lenin, *op. cit.*, Third ed., Vol. XXVI, pp. 199-283.

"Comrade Trotsky is smiling now . . . and is surprised that I criticize him for not raising the matter in the commission. But this is very important, Comrade Trotsky, very important, for failure to take this up in the trade-union commission [of the party] is a breach of discipline of the Central Committee. And when Trotsky does the public speaking the result is not a quarrel but a quaking in the party and bitterness." Lenin would have preferred to sweep the trouble under the commission. The airing of the trade-union controversy disturbed Lenin almost as much as its substance. He presumably believed that life would take care of the substance; the trade unions, he felt, could not manage industries, and in the end bureaucrats obeying party orders would do the job. What really troubled him was the freedom of public debate, the venom it injected into the party's veins; the doubts it left in the minds of communists and noncommunists; the energy he had to expend in beating down the opposition. Most distressing, Trotsky and his considerable following might remain in opposition. That is why the controversy still rankled after the direction of industry by trade unions had become a dead issue; a crack in the party when the peasants were discontented, the workers in ferment, and the economic horizon black might indeed doom the Soviet government.

To meet the crisis Lenin had two proposals: oil, timber, mining, and manufacturing concessions to foreign companies and abolition of requisitioning.

The readiness of the Soviet government to grant concessions to foreigners aroused hostility. Would not concessions, a communist had asked Lenin at a party caucus on December 21, 1920, during the Eighth Congress of Soviets, be tantamount to a recognition of the longevity of capitalist states and an admission that communist views on the imminence of world revolution were wrong? "The point is not that we recognize longevity," Lenin replied, "but that gigantic forces are pushing them into the abyss. Our existence and the hastening of our escape from a critical situation and from hunger is a gigantic force and a revolutionary factor much greater, from the viewpoint of world economy, than the few pennies they will earn from us." Besides, the Soviets would gain in machinery, etc.

"If American unemployment is accelerating revolution, don't we, by granting concessions, enable America to get through the crisis, that is, we retard the revolution?" another party member asked.

Lenin thought little of the objection. Someone sent up a similar question. Lenin: "If capitalists could prevent crises at home, capitalism would be eternal. They are, however, blind pawns in the general mechanism—the world war showed that. The crisis of capitalism grows month by month, disintegration in the whole world proceeds further and further and only in Russia has an upward trend commenced toward a stable and serious improvement."

Lenin brushed aside suspicions that foreign capitalists might suborn their

Soviet workers with higher wages and better conditions. One communist stated that hostility to concessions "reveals not at all a healthy mood but rather a patriotic feeling in the powerful petty bourgeois stratum of the village and in the urban middle class." Lenin dismissed this interpretation. He welcomes the "revolutionary patriotism" that had brought them victory despite hunger.[10]

Lenin's efforts notwithstanding, the prospect of admitting foreign capitalists to operate in Soviet Russia continued to arouse antagonism, and not only among rank-and-file communists or the petty bourgeoisie. On January 16, 1921, Maxim Litvinov wired Lenin from Reval, Estonia, regarding the receipt, from the Royal Dutch-Shell Company, of a request for monopoly export rights of petroleum and kerosene and for a concession to mine oil in Soviet regions not yet producing oil. Lenin replied, "I *favor experimental* negotiations, supremely cautious."[11] A few days later Lenin said that "the question is so important, the *exact* text of *instructions* should be drafted."[12] On January 24 the Supreme Council of National Economy said negotiations with the Royal Dutch were desirable. The Sovnarkom sanctioned negotiations for oil concessions in Baku and Grozny on February 1, 1921.[13] Nevertheless, and despite the near collapse of Russia's nationalized industries, despite near famine, despite revolts, despite Lenin's insistence on concessions, the opposition to them persisted. At a February meeting of the Central Committee, Rykov, chairman of the Supreme Council of National Economy, passed a note to Lenin: "We are in a position to teach Europe. . . . We can do everything ourselves." Then Stalin passed a note to Lenin: They, the capitalists, "will pump water. . . . The conditions have not been clarified. . . . The proposal is frivolous, not thought out . . . they will pump water, not oil. . . . The workers cannot be convinced." Tomsky took a diametrically different view. He passed a note to Lenin saying, "The workers will succumb." They will say, "It's better next door. . . . Today, miracles of heroism, tomorrow, Beat the Jews."[14] In other words, workers now heroic supporters of the soviets might soon turn reactionary. And Tomsky was the trade-union leader.

Usually, however, Lenin had the last word and the largest vote. He told the party Congress that, "by granting concessions for one quarter of Grozny and one quarter of Baku"—then the only two important oil fields—"we can use this grant—if it materializes—in order to overtake the advanced technique of advanced capitalism on the remaining three-quarters." The Congress agreed, and on March 19 Lenin telegraphed Leonid Krassin, who was in London seeking to conclude a commercial treaty with the British govern-

---

[10] *Kommunist* magazine, April, 1963, first published this Lenin quiz. The Institute of Marxism-Leninism supplied an introduction to the text which said, "V. I. Lenin accepted concessions as permissible in principle as one of the forms of state capitalism."

[11] *Leninskii Sbornik*, Vol. XXXVI, p. 165.

[12] *Ibid.*, p. 167.

[13] *Ibid.*, Vol. XX, p. 146.

[14] *Ibid.*, p. 147.

ment, "The party Congress has approved the policy on concessions in Grozny and Baku which I defended. Accelerate negotiations for them as well as for all other concessions. Inform me more frequently. Lenin."[15] He was in a hurry and he was sanguine. In fact, he hoped to make the maximum use of concessions to foreign firms. "Look at this," Lenin wrote on a note and passed a letter to Trotsky at a meeting on March 28, "(interesting) and return to me. I shall be talking to Kharkov this very day." The letter, according to an editorial note, was probably a letter from Pyatakov in Kharkov protesting the idea of opening the Donets coal basin in the Ukraine to foreign concessionaires. "Isn't it amusing about concessions?" Lenin added. "Baku and Donets-Basin 'patriotism.' But to give one quarter of the Donets Basin (+ Krivoi Rog)"—iron deposits—"to concessionaires is most desirable. Your opinion?"

"There is no reason to exclude the Donets Basin from concessions," Trotsky wrote on the back of Lenin's note and returned it to him.[16]

Vanderlip was still in Moscow seeking the key to Kamchatka. The day after the Congress closed Lenin drafted a letter to him in English which read, exactly, as follows:

> Moscow, March 17, 1921.
> Mr. Washington B. Vanderlip.

Dear Sir:

I thank you for your kind letter of 14th cr., & am very glad to hear of President Hardings favourable views as to our trade with America. You know what value we attach to our future American business relations. We fully recognize the part played in this respect by your syndicate & also the great importance of your personal efforts. Your new proposals are highly interesting & I have asked the Supreme Council of National Economy to report to me at short intervals about the progress of the negotiations. You can be sure that we will treat every reasonable suggestion with the greatest attention & care. It is on production & trade that our efforts are principally concentrated & your help is to us of the greatest value.

If you have to complain of some officials please send your complaint to the respective Peoples Commissary who will investigate the matter & report if necessary. I have already ordered special investigation concerning the person you mention in your letter.

The Congress of the Communist Party has taken so much of my time & forces that I am very tired & ill. Will you kindly excuse me if I am unable to have an interview with you just now. I will beg Comrade Chicherin to speak with you shortly.

> *Wishing you much success I remain*
> *Yours truly Wl. Oulianoff (Lenin)*[17]

[15] *Ibid.*, Vol. XXV, p. 217.
[16] *Ibid.*, Vol. XX, p. 151.
[17] *Ibid.*, p. 189. "Oulianoff" is the French spelling. Chicherin once wrote me, "I spell Tchitcherin, the Britishers spell Chicherin."

". . . very tired and ill" was not an excuse. Lenin had talked on his feet to the entire assembly for many hours, and there must have been, as in all such conventions, exhausting behind-the-scenes arguments, personal interviews, lobbying, and committee sessions. More than concessions, more than Kronstadt, more even than requisitions, it was the disappearing tail of the trade-union controversy that cost him most tons of energy, for it involved the value he held dearest: party unity. His first words and his last to the Congress were devoted to that subject. Citing the innumerable sensations published abroad about the Soviet situation ("Moscow Rising Reported"; "Petrograd Fighting, Red Batteries Silenced"; "Sinowjew Verhaftet"; "Petrograd et Moscou Seraient aux Mains des Insurgents Qui Ont Formé un Gouvernement Provisoire"; "Trotsky Arrests Lenin"; "Lenin Arrests Trotsky"), Lenin said they showed "to what extent we are surrounded by enemies," and this limited the permissible measure of differences within the party. Of course, "You cannot expect of people who have just engaged in a struggle to understand this measure immediately. But when we look at our party as the hearth of the world revolution and at the campaign which the syndicate of states of the entire world is now waging against us, we must not be in doubt. Let them conduct their campaign . . . we know that, having closed ranks at this Congress, we shall emerge from our differences absolutely united and with a party, more tempered, which will go on to greater and greater decisive international victories." Gavel.

The major task of the Tenth Party Congress was to introduce a new period of Soviet history: the NEP. It did this by substituting a produce tax in place of compulsory requisitions. That left the peasant, or some peasants, with a surplus to sell in private trade.

Here was a Lenin paradox: he gave economics precedence over politics, but economics were primarily politics to him. Thus his address to the party Congress on the tax in kind began: "Comrades, the question of replacing requisitions with a tax is first of all and above all a political question, for the essence of this question is the relationship of the working class to the peasantry." This relationship, good or bad, would "determine the fate of our revolution." However, "the interests of the two classes diverge, the smallholder does not want what the worker wants." Again, as before, Lenin stressed what divided the classes and the nation. "We know," he continued, "that only an agreement with the peasantry can save the socialist revolution in Russia as long as there is no revolution in other countries." But "We know that, to put it mildly—without recording the word mildly in the minutes— this agreement between the working class and the peasantry is not durable, and frankly speaking, it is considerably worse." Many communists had believed, Lenin said, that the economic roots of the smallholding peasantry could be transformed—that private farming could become socialist farming. They were visionaries. "And that was not especially bad. How could a revolution have been launched in a country like ours without visionaries?" Attempts at forming collectives and communes, however, "had played a negative role. . . . Peasant neighbors laugh or display malice." The government had to satisfy some peasant demands. "First, there is need of a certain freedom of turnover, freedom for the small private cultivator, and second, we have to procure goods and commodities." Now he interpreted "freedom of turnover" more precisely than ever before: "Freedom of turnover—that is, freedom of trade, and freedom of trade means back to capitalism.

"The question is asked, how can that be, can a communist party recognize freedom of trade and go over to it? Aren't these irreconcilable contradictions?" He gave no answer. Future laws and regulations would shape the reform in practice. The Congress "must decide this question in principle and inform the peasantry about it because the sowing season is at hand. The small producer had to have a stimulus . . . a vast agrarian country with poor transportation, endless expanses, different climates, different farming conditions, and so forth, inescapably assumes a certain freedom of trade on a local scale between local agriculture and local industry. In this respect we sinned very much by going too far: we went too far on the road of nationalizing trade and industry by shutting off local turnover. Was that a mistake? Undoubtedly." The kulak, to be sure, would benefit from the new measures. But the peasant was becoming a middle peasant, he was growing more. "In general the situation is this: we must satisfy the middle peasantry economically and accept freedom of turnover, otherwise it is impossible, economically impossible, for the proletariat to retain power in Russia while the international revolution is retarded."

The Congress and the party supported Lenin on the tax, on the NEP, and on concessions because war communism was obsolete and socialism impracticable. The only expedient was retreat. Here Lenin showed his mastery. In November, 1917, he knew when to advance and seize. In March, 1921, he knew how to retreat and relinquish. He realized that retreat without discipline ended in rout and ruin. The Congress saw his wisdom and therefore supported his plea for party unity (which meant submission to his leadership).

Lenin was the steel that bends.

XXXVIII. ЦENIN ON MARX

WHAT was the Soviet system now?

A government decree, approved by the Sovnarkom on April 5, 1921, permitted factories, "as an experiment," to pay part of their workingmen's wages in the goods produced by those workingmen so that they could exchange them for food.[1] Lenin explained four days later that, "Textile workers,

[1] *Leninskii Sbornik*, Vol. XXXVI, p. 216.

for instance, will, on condition that the government's needs are covered, receive some of the textiles as pay and exchange them on their own for bread."[2] This meant that workers as well as peasants would engage in private trade.

Lenin was usually indifferent to definitions, but when challenged he tried to comply. Bukharin, whom Lenin had called "a magnificent educated Marxist-economist," asked him during the inauguration of the NEP in March-April, 1921, about the nature of the new social system. The proletarian government, Lenin replied, owned the factories and railroads and had a monopoly of foreign trade. This made it the sole seller and transporter of manufactured goods. It sold the commodities to workers and employees for money and to peasants for grain. The state would try to organize the entire population in cooperative stores. "Why is this *impossible?*" Lenin protested. "And this is *capitalism* plus socialism."[3]

The sale of commodities by workers to peasants and by peasants to workers and by both to employees was certainly private capitalism. Where, however, did Lenin see socialism? He wrote a 29-page pamphlet in March-April, 1921, entitled *On the Tax in Kind*,[4] in which he discussed "the significance of the new policy and its conditions." It opened with a 10-page quotation from his 1918 brochure on the problems that then faced the Soviet government. "State capitalism," he had written, "would be a step *forward* compared with present conditions in our Soviet Republic." The name "Socialist Soviet Republic" means "the determination of the Soviet government to achieve the transition to socialism and not at all that the existing economic order is socialistic." Having taken a step backward from 1918 and legalized private capitalism in March–April, 1921, Lenin could scarcely call the new economic order socialistic.

Words like "socialism," "communism," "capitalism," and "colonialism" are empty bottles into which one person pours poison and another wine; they are not scientific terms, nor are they unchanging terms. They change in time and space. To some, socialism implies internationalism, freedom, equality, and release from poverty and exploitation, to others nationalism, inequality, dictatorship, low wages, no trade unions. For some, socialism signifies a condition, to Lenin it announced an intention. In many countries, socialism begins with nationalization of foreign capital—Instant Socialism. In others, socialism is a synonym for total state capitalism: the state holds all capital and controls the entire economy and therefore the entire population. Hitler was a nazi—a national socialist. In one country, socialists have abandoned Marxism, oppose nationalization, and support a welfare-state, high-wage capitalism. Elsewhere, they were always non-Marxist socialists, favor limited nationalization, nationalism, and highly evolved social welfare. The

---

[2] Lenin, *Sochineniya*, Second ed., Vol. XXVI, p. 307.
[3] *Ibid.*, Fourth ed., Vol. 36, p. 497.
[4] *Ibid.*, Vol. XXVI, pp. 321-352. (One page is an illustration of Lenin's handwritten manuscript, the reverse side is blank.)

president of one country calls himself a Marxist, is a mystic Moslem, behaves like a sultan, believes in democracy, and courts domestic communists, Moscow and Peking. The president of another admits having flirted with the ideas of Marx, Engels, Lenin, Hitler, Gandhi, Hannibal, and Cromwell. An African prime minister says he saw a white man beating his father, and that opened his mind to socialism.

Socialism is a shirt of many colors.

". . . our task," Lenin had written in 1918, "is to learn state capitalism from the Germans, imitate it with all our strength, not to spare dictatorial methods in order to accelerate the imitation of westernism by barbarous Russia, not to refrain from barbarous means in the struggle against barbarism."

Conscious cultivation of barbarism in a barbarous country breeds bigger barbarism. In order to introduce into Russia Kaiser Germany's state capitalism which was not Marxism? Before and after November, 1917, Lenin wrote in 1918, he had regarded state capitalism as "a step and steps to socialism." Now, coming to 1921, he stated that he was wrong in 1918 in assessing the time factor: "The periods have proved to be longer than we then assumed." The steps from state capitalism to socialism were obstructed by the petty bourgeois peasantry. " 'War Communism' was imposed by war and ruin." It had to be replaced by "a certain (if only local) freedom of trade" and, hence, "the resurrection of the petty bourgeoisie and capitalism." Meanwhile, state industries languished, he said.

"Is it possible," Lenin asked, "to combine, unite, the Soviet state and the dictatorship of the proletariat with state capitalism? Of course it is possible," he answered. "As long as the proletariat firmly holds power in its hands, firmly holds transport and big industry in its hands," private trade was "not terrifying to the proletarian state."

Angelica Balabanoff hated the NEP and told Trotsky so. He said, "If one wants the ends one must also want the means."[5] She spoke in the same vein to Lenin, evoking the specter of inequality. He said, "You know well that it was a necessity. Otherwise Russia could not have held out."

But "the workers will lose their faith in the future, in socialism."

"Of course," Lenin replied in a tone that was "at once sad and sarcastic." "If you can suggest a different way . . ."[6]

Lenin bent his socialism to necessity. Marx taught Lenin that all history, except, Engels added, the history of primitive peoples, recorded the course of class wars. The NEP, however, flowed not from a war between classes but from combined proletarian and peasant class pressures on the Soviet government. War and the premature revolution in an underdeveloped country created a sharp antagonism between the Kremlin and the toiling masses and forced Lenin to yield to their primary needs. His Marxism was malleable. For him, politics (which he would have reduced to economics) came first, ideol-

[5] Angelica Balabanoff, Lenin, p. 125.
[6] Ibid., pp. 146-147.

ogy—when convenient. This accounts for Lenin's successes; a more brittle approach would have killed the communist regime.

It is idle to speculate on what Marx would have thought about the Russian revolution. He might have said revolution devours its fathers. It is just as idle but more interesting to speculate on the fate of Marx if there had been no Lenin, no Soviet revolution in Russia. Early in the twentieth century, Western socialists who had accepted the master's teachings were revising him beyond recognition. Marx was already being Bernsteinized out of existence. Socialists gradually accommodated themselves to capitalism as capitalism accommodated itself to modern requirements. International war sublimated class war. Later the capitalist system, finally fulfilling the Marx-Engels prophecy in *The Communist Manifesto,* moved toward internationalism and threatened to usurp it from communists and some socialists becalmed in nationalism. If Russia, caught in this Western current, had been swept into modernized, feudal-free capitalism under a constitutional monarchy or liberal republic and thereby avoided Lenin's communist-party regime, Marx might have been remembered as the false prophet of the demise of world capitalism instead of as the spiritual father of the father of a country where his name became a meaningless adjective. Or he would have had to wait until a party in a large underdeveloped country—China?—came to power officially proclaiming itself Marxist. One wonders, however, whether China's political development might not have been altered by Russia's, and, too, whether a revolution in China need have carried the banner of Marx. India became independent and launched an industrial revolution without him. Other Asian and African and Latin-American peoples might have acclaimed Marx as little as they did Hegel, Bakunin, Proudhon, Mill, Jefferson, Sombart, Mazzini, Henry George, Max Weber, or Keynes. The Latins had their own Bolívar. Mexico made her revolution with indigenous forces and ideas. Perhaps Lenin rescued Marx from the veil of time that obscures many seminal social thinkers of the past.

Lenin rescued Marx, then stood him on his head by demonstrating that communists could triumph only in a country where the peasantry was predominant, poor, and atomized, the working class weak, industry underdeveloped, the church a corrupt instrument of government, democracy anemic, and the state a broken reed, where, therefore, the seizure of the state by an aggressive, determined political phalanx proved to be an easy yet decisive operation with grim repressive consequences.

One of the earliest articles of the young Lenin, which appears in the first volume of his collected works, was written on the death of Friedrich Engels in London on August 5, 1895. "Marx and Engels," Lenin states, "both knew Russian and read Russian books, took a lively interest in Russia, followed the Russian revolutionary movement with sympathy, and were in communication with Russian revolutionaries. [For a time, they supported the anti-Marxist populists.] Both were *democrats* and hence became socialists, and the democratic feeling of hatred for arbitrary political rule was extremely strong in them."

When Lenin said "democratic" he meant two different things: the arbitrary dictatorship that would replace the hated arbitrary tsarist dictatorship and the bourgeois-democratic revolution to be launched by the antibourgeois proletariat. The latter seems a paradox, but it contains a large element of plausibility. The bourgeoisie of his underdeveloped country, Lenin reasoned, was too ridden with autocracy and feudalism to save itself by revolution. Therefore, the forward-looking proletariat, in its own and the national interest, would make a democratic bourgeois revolution for the bourgeoisie, and then, having thus thinned the ranks of its enemies and augmented its rights and power, it would dig the grave of the bourgeoisie and march on to socialist dictatorship.

Lenin wrote another article, published in March, 1913, over the initials "V.I.," entitled "Three Sources and Three Constituent Parts of Marxism."[7] In it he affirmed that "an impartial social science is impossible in a society founded on class struggle. In one way or another every governmental and liberal science defends wage slavery, and Marxism has declared ruthless war against this slavery. To expect impartial science in a wage-slave society is rather stupidly naïve."

This is not wholly untrue. Does it follow that Marx, who wrote in a wage-slave society, did not produce an impartial social science? Or was Marx an exception, and might there not be others? (The Soviet Union is a low-wage-paying society.)

"The teaching of Marx . . ." Lenin continued, "is complete and symmetrical, offering an integrated view of the world."

It would thus be a philosophy containing all the answers, and indeed Lenin wrote, "The philosophy of Marx is that finished philosophic materialism which has given humanity in general, and the working class in particular, the greatest of all instruments of understanding."

The three sources of Marxism referred to in the title of the article were "the German philosophy, English political economy, French socialism." Marxism was their "legitimate inheritor."

The three constituent parts of Marxism were materialism, economic theory, and the class struggle.

"The philosophy of Marxism," Lenin stated, "is materialism." But Marx, he added, did not merely borrow eighteenth-century materialism. "He enriched materialism with the acquisitions of the German classic philosophy, especially the system of Hegel which led in its turn to the philosophy of Feuerbach. The chief of these acquisitions is the dialectic—that is, the understanding of evolution in its fullest, deepest and most universal aspect."

Marx did more, Lenin claimed: "While deepening and developing philosophical materialism, Marx carried it through to the end, extending its mode

---

[7] Lenin, op. cit., Second ed., Vol. XVI, pp. 349-353. English translation borrowed from Capital. The Communist Manifesto, and Other Writings by Karl Marx. Edited and with an introduction by Max Eastman With an Essay on Marxism by V. I. Lenin (xxi-xxvi) (New York, 1932). The essay was first published in the St. Petersburg legal magazine Prosveshcheniye (Enlightenment), Issue No. 3, 1913.

of understanding nature to the understanding of human society." Philosophical materialism, according to Lenin, explained nature; historic materialism explained society.

Historical materialism showed "how out of one setup of social life, another higher one develops in consequence of the growth of the productive forces—capitalism, for example, out of feudalism.

"Just exactly as man's knowledge reflects a nature existing independently of him . . ."—this is the Marxist argument against Machism—"so also the social understanding of man (that is, his various views and teachings, philosophic, religious, political, etc.) reflects the economic structure of society. Political institutions are a superstructure resting on an economic foundation."

But philosophy, religion, and politics—the superstructure—may outlive the economic system. Supernatural, pagan, and mystic elements in several religions defy not only economic evolution but scientific progress as well.

Since economics was the determining factor in mankind's beliefs, thought, and social organization, "Marx," Lenin wrote, "gave most of his attention to the economic structure." Here Marx's major contribution was "the doctrine of surplus value . . . the keystone of the economic theory of Marx." Lenin explained it in these terms: "The wage-worker sells his labor power to the owner of land, factories and the instruments of labor. One part of the working day he spends in order to meet the cost of supporting himself and his family (wages), but another part of the day he spends working for nothing, creating surplus value for the capitalist." Surplus value was "the source of profits, the source of the wealth of the class of capitalists."

This, presumably, applies whether the owner of the land and factories is one person, one firm, or one state, and the important question for workers and farmers is what part of the day they spend working for nothing; under capitalism they have struggled, with success, to reduce its duration. But Marx envisaged a violent class struggle which, in Lenin's words, would result in "the victory of labor over capital."

The abolition of private capitalism and of surplus value would make sense if the state too were abolished. But where the state is the sole employer and sole capitalist it can take greater advantage of the workers than a private employer in an advanced country. The Soviet state is a highly expensive and most inefficient machine. It reduces the wages of the worker and the income of the peasant by financing billion-rouble schemes (like the use of the virgin lands in Kazakstan for cereal production), by imperialism, by an expansionist foreign policy in distant continents, and by vast armament expenditures connected with that policy. The money comes from the surplus value created by the working class and the peasantry.

A year after he wrote his article on Marxism Lenin wrote a brief biography of Marx. Apparently, the editors of the *Granat Biographical Encyclopedia*, published in Russia, had seen the article and invited him to contribute the item on Karl Marx for their new seventh edition. He began the writing in and near Cracow in July, 1914, and finished it in Switzerland on November 17,

1914, but in an introduction to a separate printing of the piece in May, 1918, he said, "it was written (as far as I remember) in 1913," obviously confusing it with the article, a minor human error. A facsimile of the first manuscript page of the biography (in the second edition of Lenin's collected works) written in his quick yet careful hand, in ink, begins: "*Karl Marx* was born ..." The facsimile of the same page in the fourth edition shows that Lenin drew a hooked line over Karl and under Marx making it read: "*Marx Karl* was born ..." The biography,[8] couched in encyclopedia style, devotes four and a quarter pages to a framework of facts about Marx's life and twenty-eight pages to Marx's teachings. Marx, says Lenin, was born on May 5, 1818, in Trier, Germany. His lawyer father was a Jew converted to Protestantism. "The family was prosperous, cultured, but not revolutionary." Marx read law at the university in Bonn, then in Berlin, yet gave more time to history and philosophy. He wrote his thesis on the philosophy of Epicurus. Marx "was then still a Hegelian idealist." He was still, in other words, "the young Marx," the humanist of whom Lenin disapproved. But "the young Marx" was indeed very young, and, "In Berlin," as Lenin noted, "he joined the circle of 'left Hegelians' ... who tried to draw atheistic and revolutionary conclusions from Hegel's philosophy."

Marx hoped to become a professor but "the reactionary policy of the government" prevented his obtaining a university post. Instead he was appointed chief editor of the *Neue Rheinische Zeitung* in Cologne at the age of twenty-four. The newspaper took "a radical bourgeois" line in opposition to the government which applied the censor's blue pencil so drastically that Marx resigned after three months. Three months later the authorities shut the paper down. "Journalism showed Marx that he was inadequately acquainted with political economy, and he commenced to study it assiduously." [At the age of thirty, Marx, assisted by Engels, brought down one tablet of the law from the socialist Sinai: *The Communist Manifesto*.]

In effect, using his 1913 article as an outline, Lenin began the exposition of Marx's teachings with a statement about philosophical materialism. Here he quoted Marx: "To Hegel, the life-process of the human brain, *i.e.* the process of thinking, which, under the name of 'the idea,' he even transforms into an independent subject, is the demiurgos of the real world, and the external world is only the external, phenomenal form of 'the idea.' With me, on the contrary, the idea is nothing else than the material world reflected by the human mind, and transformed into forms of thought."[9]

---

[8] *Karl Marx. Kratkii Biograficheskii Ocherk s Izlozheniem Marxizma (Karl Marx. Brief Biographical Essay with an Exposition of Marxism)*, in Lenin, *Sochineniya*, Second ed., Vol. XVIII, pp. 5-43; Fourth ed., Vol. 21, pp. 30-62.

[9] *Karl Marx. Capital. A Critique of Political Economy*, Vol. 1, *The Process of Capitalist Production*. Translated from the Third German Edition, by Samuel Moore and Edward Aveling and Edited by Frederick Engels (Chicago, 1915). Author's Preface to Second Edition, pp. 16-26. (The date of this preface is London, Jan. 24, 1873.)

Marxists give precedence to nature, to the objective world. The mind is its mirror—without autonomy. Opposed, said Engels, are the idealists—a better term would be idea-ists; that way leads to religion, theology, metaphysics in the sense of "drunken speculation" as opposed to "sober philosophy."

Now Lenin erected a bridge from philosophical materialism to revolution. Evolution had been generally accepted. "This idea, however, in the formulation which Marx and Engels, building on Hegel, gave it, is far more many-sided, far richer in content, than the current idea of evolution." They said evolution "proceeds in a spiral, not in a straight line, higher, by lurches, catastrophes, revolutions; 'interruptions of gradualness'; the transformation of quantity into quality . . ."

Marx, Lenin added, applied this same principle to history and the social sciences. "If materialism in general explains consciousness in terms of objective circumstances, and not in reverse order, then in application to the social life of mankind materialism demanded the explanation of social consciousness in terms of social objective circumstances," social conditions.

Man's role in society is fixed by his relationship to production, Marx said, and this relationship, Lenin quoted, "is definite, necessary, and independent of the wishes" of the persons concerned.

It follows that every individual has a niche, willy-nilly, in a class which molds his attitudes, views, and social philosophy. Classes have contradictory interests. "And the modern era," Lenin insisted, "the era of the complete triumph of the bourgeoisie, of representative institutions, broad (but not universal) suffrage, a cheap mass press, etc., the era of powerful and ever growing trade unions and unions of employers, etc., has revealed the class war (although very often in a one-sided, 'peaceful,' 'constitutional' form) as the motive power of events." The middle classes, Marx maintained, the petty merchants, artisans, and peasants, struggle against the bourgeoisie to save themselves from perishing, they are reactionary, and if they are revolutionary it is because, Marx asserted defensively, "they defend not their present but their future interests: inasmuch as they abandon their own point of view in order to accept the point of view of the proletariat."

Marx should not be blamed for failing to foresee the contrary process that has occurred in the twentieth century: the vast expansion of the middle class, the class of service which, in all Western countries, outnumbers the farmers and is beginning to equal or exceed the size of the working class. The working class in the West, moreover, is acquiring property—homes, cars, stocks and bonds, complicated kitchen equipment, entertainment paraphernalia (television sets)—and, true to Marx, is therefore acquiring the social consciousness (psychology) of a middle, capitalist, class. Marx lived too early to suspect this. Lenin, had he looked, might have discerned the first shoots of this great social revolution in Europe. But his one good eye was so sharply focused on another kind, the bloody, barricade kind of revolution which the rulers of

Russia were fostering, that he, as blind as they, did not see the modern miracle of technology, social mobility (in some places less than others), and rising living standards.

". . . every historical period," Marx, in his introduction to the second edition of *Capital*, quoted a Russian reviewer as saying, "has laws of its own." Marx called this "the dialectical method." But the great dialecticians, Marx and Lenin, judged future periods by their own, and Lenin, to boot, judged the world by his own country.

There follows a chapter on Marx's economic laws which lead to the conclusion that capitalist production methods undermine the sources of wealth: in agriculture it exhausts the soil, in industry the workingman. "From the preceding," Lenin begins his next section on socialism, "it is clear that Marx deduces the inevitability of the transformation of capitalist society into a socialist society entirely and exclusively from the economic laws of the movement of contemporary society."

To extrapolate the future from the present is a risky business. The present itself is often baffling. Lenin, being anti-utopian, refused to draw even the vaguest description of the future socialist society; it depended on too many unknown factors. Yet he, and Marx, offered long-range and short-range prophecies on the future of capitalism. A long list of failures has not stopped their disciples from imitating them. The several fathers of "scientific socialism" manifested an irresistible proclivity for prognostication. Thus Friedrich Engels, quoted by Lenin,[10] wrote on April 6, 1887, "I do not think that present conditions can continue for even a year. And when a revolution breaks out in Russia then Hurrah!" Engels went further. In a letter dated April 23, 1887, he thought he saw in the crystal ball that Bismarck was persecuting German socialists because "it seems" he "wants to prepare everything for the event that, when revolution erupts in Russia, which is a question of several months, Germany might immediately follow her example."

"The months," Lenin sighed, "proved very and very long. . . . Yes, Marx and Engels were greatly mistaken and frequently mistaken in determining the proximity of the revolution, in their hopes for the victory of the revolution. . . . But *such* mistakes by the giants of revolutionary thought . . . are a thousand times nobler, more grandiose, and *historically more valuable, more justified*" than the skepticism of counterrevolutionaries. Then Lenin ventured his own prediction—it was April 19, 1907: "The Russian working class shall win freedom for itself and by its revolutionary acts, full of mistakes, give Europe a push—and let vulgar men plume themselves on the faultlessness of their revolutionary inaction."

For the sake of revolution, Lenin pointed out in the same article, socialists accept strange bedfellows. He cited another letter of Engels, dated January 27, 1887: "Where would we have been today if in the period between 1864 and 1873 we had always wished to go hand in hand only with those who

[10] Lenin, *Sochineniya*. Second ed., Vol. XI, pp. 165-179.

openly avowed themselves partisans of our program?" It was better, Engels said elsewhere, for "a workers party to begin organizing on the basis of a not altogether pure program." Revolutionists, Lenin stressed, must avoid "parliamentary idiocy," a favorite phrase of Marx, and philistinism. Loyalty to program and consideration of one's constituency—the party—would have been "parliamentary idiocy" in a crisis like that Russia faced in 1921. Lenin was too great a tactician, too impatient with ideological strait jackets, to worry whether the NEP was compatible with long-nursed theories. It was necessary.

In the same spirit of practicality, a capitalist system might introduce socialist features. Or perhaps capitalism and socialism are not what they used to be and not what their champions think. Only primitives have sharp shapes and stark tints. More sophisticated productions mix colors and mingle forms. No social phenomenon is altogether one thing or its opposite. It is the percentages in the mix that determine the quality and quantity of freedom. The hybrid NEP, far more capitalistic than socialistic, was a salutary interlude bringing more groceries and liberties than the war communism that preceded it or the Stalinism that succeeded it. War communism was a failure wrapped in a war that was a success. The NEP was an ounce of socialist intention wrapped in a pound of capitalist cure. It raised living standards, saved the Soviet state, made Lenin the capitalist peasants' hero, and, by making money flow freely, threw a life raft to theaters, writers, and musicians. In the NEP period, Russia as a nation and Russian individuals accumulated the capital which, collected in cruelty, enabled Stalin in 1928 to move toward the modernization of Russia.

XXXIX. LENIN ON ART AND LITERATURE

IN 1918, Soviet Russia had no dial telephones. The next year a closed circuit dial system—called the "Kremlin commutator"—was introduced to enable less than two hundred top leaders to keep in touch with one another and with Lenin without resorting to human operators. Inessa Armand, a minor party official, had a dial phone installed in her apartment on Neglinaya Street near the brick wall, since razed, of the "Chinese City" adjoining the Kremlin.

That year the Komsomol (League of Communist Youth) held a conference in Moscow's Hall of Columns. It wanted to hear Lenin and sent a dele-

gation to invite him. The delegation consisted of three young men and
Inessa Armand, the daughter of Inessa Armand, Lenin's friend. Lenin called
the daughter "Inessa Little."

But when the delegation announced at the Kremlin gate that they wished
to see Lenin the guard barred them and remained impervious to the usual
arguments. Inessa Little then said to her comrades, "Come," and led them
to her apartment. All four entered her mother's room where the dial phone
stood. Inessa Little dialed Lenin's office number. A secretary answered. Inessa
Little, deepening her voice, said she wished to speak with Lenin. "Who is
speaking?" the secretary inquired.

"Inessa Armand."

She was put through immediately.

Resuming her natural voice, which resembled her mother's, she said,
"Vladimir Ilyich, a delegation of our youth conference instructed me and
my comrades to ask you . . ."

"Who is speaking?" Lenin inquired.

"Inessa Little."

"Little but shrewd," Lenin exclaimed. "What a trick." He chatted with
her for a few moments in good humor but rejected the invitation. He was
too busy.[1]

After the mother's death, according to Inessa Little's memoirs,[2] she, her
sister Varvara (Varya), and her brother were under Lenin's guardianship.
They frequently visited the Lenin apartment in the Kremlin. One evening,
February 25, 1921—the NEP was about to be launched—Inessa Little sat
chatting with Krupskaya when Lenin came home. "While talking he walked
quickly, as usual, up and down the room. That evening, I remember, he was
lively and gay, and inquired how I lived and worked." Then he asked about
Varya who lodged in the dormitory of the Higher Art-Technical Studio
(Vkhutemas).

"Let's go, Nadya," said Lenin to his wife, "and visit Varya and see how
the young people live."

It was 11 P.M., but Krupskaya, somewhat reluctantly, agreed. They took
Inessa Little along. A guard accompanied them. The dormitory was on Myas-
nitskaya (now Kirov) Street opposite the corner post office. Lenin and Krupskaya were greeted enthusiastically; students poured into a central hall. He
returned their greetings and went to inspect the bedrooms. There was practically no furniture in the dormitories; beds were boards on trestles. Painted
slogans, drawings, and newspapers covered the walls. Lenin pointed to the
drawing of a locomotive with what he called "dynamic" lines. The artist's
imagination amused him. Lenin read a placard with the words of a line
from Vladimir V. Mayakovsky, the revolutionary poet:

We toss reinforced concrete into the sky.

---

[1] Moscow *Literaturnaya Gazetta*, April 20, 1963.
[2] *Vospominaniya*, Vol. 3, pp. 327-330.

"Lenin, smiling, commented, 'But why into the sky? We need reinforced concrete on earth.'"

They discussed Mayakovsky's verse. "Vladimir Ilyich liked the excitement with which the young people spoke about their beloved poet and about the revolutionary spirit of his verse. However, on the question of poetry too a hot argument broke out because it developed that among the youth there were many advocates of futurism in this branch of art as well. In the end, tired of arguing, Lenin declared jokingly that he would make a special study of futurism in painting and poetry, would read the literature on the subject, and would then come again and definitely defeat them in the discussion."

He asked whether they read the Russian classics. "It transpired that they knew them quite badly and many roundly rejected them as 'old-regime legacy.'" Lenin reproached them. "He told them how he himself loved Pushkin and appreciated Nekrasov." "Why," Lenin said, "a whole generation of revolutionaries learned from Nekrasov."

The exalted visitor also inquired into their physical needs. Did they have enough to eat? Yes, they reassured him, "at most we have four days in the month without bread." The remark, says Inessa Little, "amused Lenin."

It was late. "We did not accompany Vladimir Ilyich and Nadezhda Konstantinova so that they might leave unnoticed. The times, remember, were troubled."

Subsequently, Krupskaya told Inessa Little that Lenin had talked with Education Commissar Lunacharsky about his visit to the artists' dormitory. "Lenin said to him reprovingly, 'Our youth is good, very good, but what are you teaching them!'"

Lenin is not on record as ever having visited the Louvre or the National Gallery in London or any art museum or exhibition of painting in Paris, London, Switzerland, Munich, Berlin, or, for that matter, in Moscow or St. Petersburg. He attended few concerts. He did know, however, that he disliked futurist painting and Mayakovsky's futurist poetry. Lenin was not a modern. He made a new regime but he was made by the old regime with its wondrous genius that flowered into literature, music, science, and its debasing absolutism and riches-and-poverty extremes, seedbed of Marxist revolution. Both Russia's strains, the noble and the ignoble, chained Lenin to her past and turned his back to the future.

Lenin loved clarity. "I have the courage," he said to Clara Zetkin, "to display myself as a 'barbarian.' I cannot regard the works of impressionism, futurism, cubism, and other 'isms' as the highest revelations of the artistic genius. I do not understand them. I get no joy from them."[3] His heirs are loyal to the master. He knew how much the Tsars and their censors had harmed literature and art; the authorities proscribed Tolstoy's Kreutzer Sonata, for instance, and it was published only after Countess Tolstoy interviewed Alexander III and persuaded him to lift the ban. Many of the

[3] Clara Zetkin, Leben und Lehren einer Revolutionaerin (East Berlin, 1949), pp. 52-54.

world's greatest nineteenth-century novels appeared in print crippled by the Tsar's censor, and some works, notably Tolstoy's, were published abroad because the autocracy feared dissent. "Think of the pressure exerted on the development of painting, sculpture, and architecture [he omitted literature] by the mores and moods of the Tsar's court," Lenin said to Clara Zetkin. "In a private-property society the artist produces commodities for the market, he must have customers. Our revolution has lifted the weight of this very prosaic condition from the artists. It has made the Soviet state their protector who gives them commissions. Every artist, and everybody who considers himself one, takes it as his right to create freely according to his ideal, whether it is good or not. There you have the ferment, the experimenting, the chaotic."

Lenin nevertheless added, "But of course we are communists. We must not drop our hands into our laps and allow the chaos to ferment as it chooses. We must try consciously to guide this development too and mold and determine its results."

The Soviet government has guided the development of art and literature by a crudely capitalistic method: the state pays the piper and calls the genre.

Lenin enunciated the principle that should guide the guidance: "Art belongs to the people," he told Comrade Zetkin, ". . . it must be understood and loved by them." If he could not understand modern art, how would they? "Should we give sweet, sophisticated biscuits to a minority when the masses of workers and peasants lack black bread? I mean this, obviously, not only in the literal sense but also figuratively. Let us always concentrate on the workers and peasants. We must learn for their sake to manage and to calculate. Also in the realm of art and culture."

Reduce art and literature to the lowest common denominator of comprehensibility and may the minority perish in the desert.

Russia, Lenin explained, is a tremendous and poor country, and "While in Moscow perhaps ten thousand today and again ten thousand tomorrow drug themselves with brilliant theater performances, the millions call for the art of spelling, of writing their names, of learning arithmetic, of learning that the earth is a sphere and not a flat surface."

"Comrade Lenin," Clara Zetkin interposed, "do not complain so bitterly about illiteracy. To a certain extent it probably made it easier to make the revolution."

"That is correct," Lenin agreed, "but only within certain limits, or rather: for a definite period of our struggle. . . . Illiteracy is scarcely compatible, not at all compatible, with the tasks of economic construction."

Lenin's task in 1917 was indeed facilitated by economic backwardness and also by "darkness"—the absence of enlightenment in the laboring strata of town and land. Lenin, moreover, distrusted intellectuals and disliked futuristic poets and painters because they experiment, they strike off in different directions as talent and temperament, but not the communist party, command. They doubt. They think. They rebel against orthodoxy. Sovietism, however, is a new orthodoxy. Lenin was a revolutionary, not a rebel. He wanted changed institutions and a changed economy, he did not envisage man changing himself. That required freedom.

Although Lenin thus sowed the dragon's teeth which later sprouted in the Soviet cultural wasteland, his own bark was worse than his bite or that of his less-cultured successors. Art and literature, fortunately, were Lenin's neglected stepchildren. "Throughout his life," Culture Commissar Lunacharsky wrote in 1924, "Lenin had very little time to occupy himself at all intently with art, and, since dilettantism was always alien and hateful to him, he did not like to express himself on art. Nevertheless, his taste was very definite. He liked the Russian classics, liked realism in literature, in painting, etc."[4] Once, Lunacharsky relates, he and Lenin and Kamenev went to see an exhibit of models for a statue to replace the monument of Alexander III near the Cathedral of Christ the Savior in Moscow. When Lenin was asked his opinion, he said, "I understand nothing here. Ask Lunacharsky." But when Lunacharsky himself said he saw nothing worthwhile in the assembled art, "Lenin was very glad and said to me, 'And I thought you would put up some kind of futuristic scarecrow.'" On another occasion Lenin, together with Lunacharsky, examined a model of a proposed statue of Karl Marx to be erected in Moscow. Lenin studied it from all sides and approved but urged Lunacharsky to tell the artist to make Marx's hair resemble the original, otherwise there would be little likeness.

Lunacharsky says Lenin cut the budget for the Bolshoi ballet, calling it a "piece of pure landlord culture" and of the Bolshoi opera whose "pompous court style" he regarded as "specifically landlord." On the other hand, Lenin repeatedly stressed the enormous importance of the cinema as an instrument of a propaganda and political education for the millions.

Trotsky was an artist, therefore he had fewer chances to survive in the man-eating jungle of Soviet politics. To him art meant life. Lenin's interest in art was political. He could control his own instinctive reaction against nonconformism and radicalism in literature and art. But he thought the "leftists" of both domains might infect politics. In 1918, new-wave artists and writers, interpreting the revolution as a charter to deviate, organized the Proletkult, or Proletarian Culture, a body of writers, painters, and sculptors, notably the Symbolist poet and prose author Andrey Bely; the novelist, short-story writer, and dramatist Yevgeny Zamyatin, an irrepressible heretic; Nikolai Gumilyov, a gifted "Acme-ist" poet; and Valeri Bryusov whom Trotsky called a "rationalist" and "ecletic." The Proletkult opened study circles and studios for workers in factories, for youths in universities, for sailors and soldiers. All its sponsors did not reject the revolution or accept it. They merely used it as an opportunity to spread their ideas and models of a new culture. Lenin feared, according to Lunacharsky's memoirs, that it would detract workers from work

---

[4] *Vospominaniya*, Vol. 2, pp. 322-326.

and education. He feared even more a serious diversion from his concepts of Marxism. In August, 1920, he asked Professor M. N. Pokrovsky, Deputy Commissar of Education, to explain the juridical position of the Proletkult; who appointed its officers; where it got its money. Pokrovsky replied on August 24 that it was "an autonomous organization" subsidized by his commissariat. As soon as he could spare the time, Lenin drafted a resolution, dated October 8, 1920,[5] declaring the Proletkult must not advance "special ideas, but Marxism." Soviet Russia needed "not *the invention* of a new proletarian culture but *the development* of the best forms, traditions, and results of *existing* culture from the viewpoint of the philosophy of Marxism and the living conditions and struggle of the proletariat in the period of its dictatorship."

When the Politburo took up the question three days later, however, Bukharin and Lenin clashed on the issue of the Proletkult.[6] Bukharin was to speak at the Proletkult congress that month. Lenin sent a note to Bukharin minimizing their differences and seeking agreement on larger questions. "Proletarian culture equals communism," Lenin wrote. No communism yet, no proletarian culture, Lenin implied. The party, and not an autonomous organization, Lenin added, carries out policy. He had objected to an independent role in industry for trade unions. He objected equally to an independent cultural organization outside the party, and considered the quest for autonomy an effort to elude party control, the more so since the Proletkult's moving ideological spirit was A. A. Bogdanov, the Machist, with whom he had crossed doctrinal swords before the revolution. Hardly an accident, Lenin would have thought; the Symbolists and Futurists were not realists, materialists, or Marxists. "*In actual fact*," Lenin had written in his controversy with Machists in March, 1910, "all the phrases about 'proletarian culture' conceal a struggle *against* Marxism." Now Lunacharsky, one of Bogdanov's fellow Machists, was Education Commissar, the Proletkult had been thrust into his care, and he had remained an aesthete, a mild, art-loving modern. This heightened Lenin's aversion to the Proletkult. Further, he generalized in his note to Bukharin, "The proletarian class equals the Russian Communist Party which equals the Soviet state. Don't we agree on all this?"[7] Here is Leninism in one sentence.

Lenin also "instructed me," Lunacharsky recalls in his memoirs, "to go there"—to the Congress—"and definitely indicate that the Proletkult must submit to the leadership of the Commissariat and regard itself as its organization, etc. In a word, Vladimir Ilyich wanted us to draw the Proletkult to the state; at the same time he took steps to draw it to the party." Lunacharsky pleads that his speech to the Congress was temperate, but when Lenin heard

[5] *Leninskii Sbornik*, Vol. XXXV, p. 148.

[6] V. I. *Lenin o Literature i Iskusstvye* (V. I. *Lenin on Literature and Art*). A Miscellany (Moscow, 1960), editorial note, p. 747.

[7] *Leninskii Sbornik*, Vol. XXXVI, p. 132.

of it, "He summoned me and gave me a dressing down. Later, the Proletkult was reorganized in accordance with the instructions of Vladimir Ilyich."

In truth, however, Lunacharsky and Bukharin continued to resist Lenin
and assist the Proletkult. As late as September 27, 1922, *Pravda*, edited by
Bukharin, published an extra-long article by V. Pletnyov on proletarian culture. Lenin marked it: "KEEP" in two places and underlined the word four
times. He also made numerous marginal remarks. But instead of keeping it
he sent it to Bukharin saying, "I am sending you today's *Pravda*. Now why
print foolishness? . . . I marked two examples of folly and put down a series
of question marks. The author [Pletnyov] should study not 'proletarian' science, he should simply study. Is it possible that the editors of *Pravda* did not
explain his mistakes to the author? Why this is *the falsification* of historical
materialism! Playing with historical materialism! Your Lenin."[8]

Where Pletnyov wrote, "The creation of a new proletarian class culture is
the basic goal of the Proletkult," Lenin wrote in the margin, in pencil, "Ha-
ha!" Where Pletnyov explained that only the proletariat could establish a new
culture and not the few bourgeois individuals who joined it, Lenin remarked,
"And but the peasants?" Pletnyov declared in ringing tones that "The feeling
of class solidarity, the feeling of 'We,' is inculcated by the circumstances that
'we' will build the locomotive, the ocean liner, the airplane (without collective efforts this task is insoluble) as well as by the circumstance that in the
struggle against the bourgeoisie every worker is bound in unity by the social
inequality between his class and other classes and by the clear-cut consciousness that the locomotive of revolution can be built only by the forces of 'we,'
by the forces of class unity. These conditions determine the class consciousness of the proletariat which is alien to the peasant, the bourgeois, the intellectual: doctor, lawyer, engineer, raised on the principles of capitalist
competition where 'I' is the foundation and divide et impera the principle
of rule."

In this passage, Lenin underlined the word "peasant" twice and "bourgeois" and "intellectual" once, and penciled in the margin, with sober skepticism, "And what is the percentage of locomotives in disrepair?" This took
the poetry out of Pletnyov's "locomotive of revolution." How could Russia's
railways get moving without bourgeois intellectuals to repair broken-down
locomotives? Could workers alone do the job? The peasants are religious,
Pletnyov proceeded, they depend on nature, but the worker knows that production depends on his efforts in the mine and factory. "And on Saturday he
gets his pay. Here"—unlike in the farmer's field—"everything is mathemat-
ically exact." Lenin underlined the last sentence and sought to destroy it
with, "And the religion of the workers and peasants?" Not only the peasant
was religious.

Passing to culture, Pletnyov pontificated that "The task of creating a proletarian culture can be solved only with the forces of the proletariat itself and

[8] Lenin, *Sochineniya*, Fourth ed., Vol. 35, p. 475.

by scientists, artists, engineers, etc., who rise from its own ranks." Lenin wrote "Superfiction." Pletnyov declared, "Well, and are there many among us who can teach electrification?" "That's the point," Lenin debated. "This is against V. Pletnyov,"[9] who had said the proletariat would build locomotives, ocean liners, and airplanes.

Not only had Pletnyov written patent nonsense, he was hoist with his own petard. First he argued, using Marxist-Leninist methods of analysis, that since class, job, and economic status (or objective conditions) determine consciousness: ideas, sentiments, religion, philosophy, and art (or culture), it followed that if the petty-bourgeois peasantry and bourgeois technicians build locomotives, airplanes, and factories and produce goods and sell them they will share in the creation of Soviet culture and it would not be proletarian culture. Lenin strengthened this contention by pointing out how much the country's economy leaned on peasants and bourgeois specialists; moreover, many workers were as religious, and, he might also have said, as culturally backward, as peasants. Therefore, Pletnyov, speaking for the Proletkult, had demonstrated that in NEP Russia proletarian culture could not be born. But then, with complete inconsistency, he also argued that "the creation of a new proletarian class culture was the basic goal of the Proletkult." Lenin rightly laughed at this. For how could any organization, even one as mighty as the communist party, much less a small autonomous unit like the Proletkult, create a proletarian culture in a predominantly nonproletarian nation? One could no more do that than create a proletarian culture in capitalist America (or a Christian culture in Hindu India). The Proletkult mistake was a Machist mistake stemming from the false assumption that consciousness took precedence over class and economics. This flew in the face of every tenet of historical materialism which gives priority to economic institutions as the foundation of the political, and, of course, cultural superstructures. Small wonder Lenin fumed when he found Pletnyov "playing" with and falsifying historical materialism.

The Proletkult, by proving that a proletarian culture could not exist in NEP Russia, proved that the Proletkult should not exist in NEP Russia. The Kremlin abolished it in 1923.

As early as 1905 Lenin had decided that writers must hitch their wagon not to the proletariat but to the star of the party. He proclaimed the "partyness" of literature and art the first commandment of socialist culture. "Down with non-party writers!" Lenin cried in an article in Gorky's St. Petersburg legal daily *Novaya Zhizn (New Life)* of November 26, 1905. "Down with literary supermen! . . . Literature must be made a component part of organized, planned, unified social-democratic party work." He knew this was "alien and strange for the bourgeoisie and bourgeois democracy." He nevertheless insisted that "literature must definitely and without fail become a part of social-democratic party work inseparably connected with its other parts.

[9] V. I. Lenin o Literature i Iskusstvye, pp. 567-579.

Newspapers must become organs of various party organizations. Writers must join party organizations without fail.

"Calm yourselves, gentlemen," Lenin continued, addressing the bourgeoisie. "First, we are speaking of party literature and of its submission to party control. Everybody is free to write and speak whatever he pleases, without the slightest limitation. But every free organization (the party included) is also free to expel those members who use the name of the party to propagate anti-party views. Freedom of speech and of publications must be complete. But then the freedom of organizations must be complete."[10] Lenin also felt that "Non-partyness is a bourgeois idea. Partyness is a socialist idea." And, too, "materialism includes partyness within itself."

Exactly twelve years later the party ruled the Soviet state. In effect, this has meant the insistence on partyness in Soviet art and literature—Kremlin insistence that in their creative work artists and writers serve the party and through it—and only through it—the state, the revolution, and communism.

For Lenin, art was a handmaiden, not a goddess. In Capri, Gorky reports, Lenin, confronting A. A. Bogdanov, said, "If you write a novel on the subject of how the sharks of capitalism robbed the workers of the earth and wasted the oil, iron, timber and coal—that would be a useful book, Signor Machist."[11]

Years later, in the Kremlin, Lenin "frequently and with strong emphasis referred to the value of Demyan Byedny's work for propaganda but added, 'It's somewhat crude. He follows the reader whereas he ought to be a little ahead.' "[12] Demyan Byedny, a racy rhymester, wrote lilting verse on current themes. His "partyness" was exemplary.

On the other hand, Gorky testifies, Lenin "mistrusted Mayakovsky, and was rather irritated by him." Mayakovsky was an individualist, a literary "superman," in Lenin's terms. Mayakovsky "shouts," Gorky quoted Lenin as saying, he "invents some sort of distorted words, and doesn't even get anywhere in my opinion—and besides is incomprehensible. It is all disconnected, difficult to read. He is talented? Very talented even? H'm, h'm. We shall see. But doesn't it seem to you that people are writing a lot of poetry now? There are whole pages of it in the newspapers and volumes of it appear every day." Demyan Byedny was completely comprehensible and superficial: "people are writing a lot of poetry now" has been the anguished cry of other Soviet leaders. Rebel poets find followers.

At a Kremlin concert for Red Army soldiers, Lenin, sitting in one of the front rows, "was rather taken aback and bewildered," Krupskaya records in her memoirs, as an actress named Gzovskaya, reciting a Mayakovsky verse:

> Our god—the advance,
> Our heart—the drum,

[10] Lenin, *op. cit.*, Second ed., Vol. VIII, pp. 386-390.
[11] Maxim Gorky, *Days with Lenin*, p. 20.
[12] *Ibid.*, p. 59.

advanced straight on Lenin. "When Gzovskaya was followed by some actor who read Chekhov's *The Evil Doer,* he heaved a sigh of relief." Revolutionary poetry shocked the quiet-loving revolutionary.

Lenin reacted fiercely against Mayakovsky's poem 150,000,000. "Aren't you ashamed," he wrote to Lunacharsky on May 6, 1921, "to have voted [in the Education Commissariat's collegium] for the publication of Mayakovsky's 150,000,000 in an edition of 5,000?

"Nonsense, foolish, double-dyed folly, and pretentiousness.

"In my opinion, we should publish only one out of ten of such works and *not more than* 1,500 copies for libraries and cranks.

"And Lunacharsky should be flogged for his futurism. Lenin."

Lunacharsky replied weakly that he did not like the poem but that the poet Bryusov had praised it, and when the author himself recited it he won great success among workers.

Not satisfied, Lenin turned to Lunacharsky's deputy, Professor Pokrovsky, an orthodox Marxist historian, and begged him to join in the fight against futurism. He again protested the big printing of 150,000,000. (The figure was for the then population of Russia.) "Can't this be stopped?" Lenin pleaded. "It should be stopped. Let us agree to print those futurists only twice a year and in *not more than* 1,500 copies." Lenin also complained that Lunacharsky had favored the futurists over "an artist-'realist' " like Kiselev. "Cannot dependable anti-futurists be found?" Lenin concluded. (*Pravda* of December 16, 1962, used the last sentence of Lenin's letter as ammunition in Chairman Khrushchev's campaign against abstract painters and rebel poets like Yevtushenko.)

Lenin's reaction, though stormy, was mild compared with the physical extermination and barbarous persecution of artists and writers in subsequent Soviet decades. By employing the weapon of political pressure, Lenin did, however, smooth the path to those harsher methods.

Almost all of Lenin's literary criteria were at least partly political. He liked Pushkin's poetry for its classic quality. But Pushkin was ever in conflict with the tsarist authorities and sympathized with Russia's early nineteenth-century revolutionists. Lenin also relished the poems of Nekrasov whose "troubled, uneven verse," writes Avrahm Yarmolinsky, "dwelt upon the miseries of the oppressed masses and voiced the peccavi of the gentry, aware of their debt to the people, as well as the aspirations of the democratic intelligentsia." On the other hand, Lenin did not enjoy Afanasy Fet, the poet, because, Krupskaya says in her memoirs, "Fet was an out-and-out feudalist and not worth while even dipping into."

Jan A. Berzin, a Latvian communist, Soviet diplomat and, in 1919-1920, secretary of the Executive Committee of the Comintern, writes in Volume 3 of the assembled memoirs about Lenin, that when they lived in the same house in a Finnish summer resort in 1906, Lenin "once came into my room and saw on my table the latest verses of [Konstantin D.] Balmont and [Alexander A.] Blok. 'What, you too fascinated by this balderdash! Why this is decadence. What do you find in it?' "

Berzin, taken aback, began to object and showed him some of the poems. "Hm," Lenin murmured, "doesn't sound bad, smoothly written, but still this doesn't make much sense."

In Siberian exile, Krupskaya records, Lenin usually spent his evenings reading Hegel, Kant, and the French naturalists (he also read Schopenhauer) "or, when very tired, Pushkin, Lermontov, and Nekrasov." After being banished to the Caucasus for subversive ideas, Lermontov had written:

> Land of masters, land of slaves, farewell,
> Unwashed Russia, it's good-by I say:
> You in your blue uniforms, and you
> Who were fashioned only to obey.

Also in Siberia, Lenin read Goethe's *Faust* in German (later in Paris he read it in Russian) and a little volume of Heine's poems, perhaps the same that his mother brought to her older son Sasha on the eve of his hanging. A report found in the archives of the Okhrana (the tsarist secret police) when they were opened in 1917, stated that on Lenin's first trip abroad he carried *Faust* and a book of Nekrasov's verse; all the other books dealt with economics. In Paris, says Krupskaya, Lenin "eagerly scanned Victor Hugo's poems Châtiments, devoted to the 1848 revolution. . . . These poems contain a good deal of naïve bombast, but one nevertheless feels in them the breeze of the Revolution." Lenin's poetic favorites ran the gamut from classic genius to vaudeville rhyme. Krupskaya affirms that her husband "was very fond of going to various cafés and suburban theaters [in Paris] to listen to the revolutionary singers who sang in working-class districts." Such cultural slumming gave Lenin some contact with the proletariat from which he was otherwise far removed. (". . . it's only a pity," Krupskaya wrote Lenin's mother from Paris in December, 1909, "that we see little of real French life.")

Krupskaya comments, too, on Lenin's taste in fiction: "Vladimir Ilyich, when choosing a novel, had a special liking for books in which social ideas were clearly reflected in the literary work."

Lenin's Kremlin librarian noted that he once asked her for a novel by George Eliot; one wonders why and which. George Eliot (Marian Evans, 1819-1880) translated *Das Wesen des Christentums (The Essence of Christianity)* by Feuerbach, a precursor of Marx. That might have been Lenin's bond with her. The novel, according to the informed guess of Ruth Adams, an English literature professor, was *Felix Holt, the Radical*. Lenin recommended to others Henri Barbusse's novel *Le Feu* about the murder, mud, and lice of World War I trench life, presumably after having perused it. In 1908 he attended a lecture on Shakespeare delivered by a Mr. Mobbs at the University of Geneva. In Paris, in 1912, Krupskaya and Lenin saw a performance of Sophocles' *Electra*. In Siberia, Lenin received from his mother some Emile

Zola novels in German, and he pasted Zola's picture into an album he kept of favorite writers. Later he read Zola's *La Joie de Vivre* in French and used a description in it of the birth of a child as a homily on revolution: "The birth of man is connected with an act which transforms the woman into a tortured, tormented, bleeding, half-dead piece of flesh mad with pain. But would anybody recognize as a person an 'individual' who saw *only* this in love, only the results which transform a woman into a mother?" Did anyone, Lenin asked, renounce love and childbirth only for this reason? So with revolutions. Some cowards retreated before the prospect.

For a person of his vast education, with his knowledge of European languages, including Italian, Lenin's contact with non-Russian literature was meager. He read for purpose, not for pleasure or culture. He filled many notebook pages with quotations from Clausewitz on military-political affairs. But de Tocqueville, Montesquieu, and Burke, as well as Jefferson, Madison, and Jay, were of no use to him, and there is no indication that he read them. Nor could art help the proletariat seize power. Nikolai L. Meshcheryakov, an old Bolshevik, long an acquaintance of Lenin, and deputy chief editor of the *Large Soviet Encyclopedia*, writes in his memoirs that early in the twentieth century he traveled in Belgium with Plekhanov who, on their arrival in Liège, asked him about a certain famous painting. "Lenin," Meshcheryakov adds, "was not interested in such matters. He was completely swallowed up in the workers movement."[13] It is difficult to imagine Lenin insisting, as Trotsky did in the introduction, dated July 29, 1924, to his book *Literature and Revolution*,[14] that "the development of art is the highest test of the vitality and significance of each epoch." Trotsky also stated, "It is very true that one cannot always go by the principles of Marxism in deciding whether to reject or accept a work of art." But Lenin would have agreed with his second-in-command that "Culture feeds on the sap of economics."

Not unexpectedly, Lenin found the theater too theatrical. Lunacharsky testifies that Lenin rarely went to the theater and then only to Stanislavsky's classical-realistic Moscow Art Theater which the leader esteemed highly. In Europe, Krupskaya writes, "We seldom went to the theater. We might pay an occasional visit, but the inane nature of the play, the artificiality of the acting, always jarred on Ilyich's nerves. Generally, we left the theater after the first act. . . . But once we did sit to the end. I think that was at the end of 1915, in Bern, when they were showing L. Tolstoy's play, *The Living Corpse* . . . Ilyich followed the play with intensity and excitement." After the revolution, "We went a few times to the Moscow Art Theater. Once we saw *The Flood*, a play by a Swede named Henning Berger, about the behavior of human beings during a Mississippi River disaster. Ilyich liked it immensely. We wanted to go to the theater the next day. They were playing Maxim Gorky's *The Lower Depths* . . . it irritated" Lenin. After that, Krup-

[13] *Vospominaniya*, Vol. 1, p. 221.
[14] New York, 1925. Translated by Rose Strunsky.

skaya relates, "he gave up going to the theater for a long time. I believe we went another time to see Chekhov's *Uncle Vanya*. He liked it. And finally, the last time we went to the theater was in 1922, to see Dickens' *Cricket on the Hearth*. Ilyich was already bored after the first act. Dickens' middle-class sentimentality began to get on his nerves . . . and [he] walked out in the middle of the [next] act."

Gorky once wrote that Feodor M. Dostoyevsky "always portrays man as 'helpless in the chaos of dark forces.' " This is probably the reason Lenin's overwrought nerves were irritated by Gorky's *The Lower Depths* and by Dostoyevsky who, to boot, is regarded by communists as religious, reactionary, nihilistic, and mystic. They applaud, however, his rejection of the decadent West.

In Lenin's millions of words in the twenty-seven fat volumes of the second, Blue, edition of his *Collected Works*, plus the thirty-six volumes of the *Leninskii Sbornik*, which contains letters, telegrams, notebooks, notes, messages, and scraps, sixty-three volumes in all, and in the additional material, found subsequently and published in the fourth and fifth editions of his works, there occur only five brief, incidental mentions of Dostoyevsky, four unfavorable.

By contrast, Lenin was fond of Anton Chekhov (1860-1904). When he finished reading Chekhov's short story, *Ward Number 6*, in Samara, in the 1890's, he told Anna, his oldest sister, "I felt really terrified, I couldn't stay in my room, I got up and walked out. I had the feeling that I myself was locked up in Ward Number 6." Lenin delighted in other Chekhov stories and remembered the characters. He also enjoyed Chekhov's plays. Once Gorky took Lenin to an evening of theater in the Moscow Hall of Trade Unions. Vasili I. Kachalov, a beloved actor of the Moscow Art Theater, writes that in a room backstage Gorky turned to him and said, "I've just been arguing here with Vladimir Ilyich about the new theater public. . . . What does it need? I say it needs only the heroic style. But Vladimir Ilyich asserts that it needs lyrics, Chekhov, worldly truth. At that moment the intermission ended and Vladimir Ilyich and Gorky returned to the auditorium."[15]

From Siberia in 1898, Lenin asked his mother to send him a twelve-volume set of Turgenev in Russian. He enjoyed Turgenev's limpid classic style. After receiving it he wanted Anna to send him Turgenev in German so he could study German by comparing the two versions. He read Turgenev many times, Krupskaya remembers, although he called the novelist a "liberal"—no compliment in Lenin's mouth—and remarked on his loyalty to the Tsar. Writing in 1907 about "the tragedy of the Russian radical"—"radical" too was no word of praise—Lenin referred to Turgenev's charming, moving story, *Asya*. The Russian radical, he said, sighed decades long for meetings, for freedom, but when he came to meetings—during the 1905 revolution—and found "that the mood was to the left of his own, he grew sad and sighed: 'It's hard

---

[15] V. I. *Lenin o Literature i Iskusstvye*, p. 688.

to judge,' 'no more than ten per cent'" are for revolution, "'you should be more cautious, gentlemen.'" And Lenin compared that type of radical with the "ardent hero" in *Asya* who, when he finally came face to face with his beloved, ran away from her.[16]

Lenin read Count Leo Tolstoy's *Anna Karenina* several times. He knew *War and Peace*, of course, as well as most of the major works of Tolstoy. "Once I came to him"—to Lenin in the Kremlin—"and saw *War and Peace* lying on the table," Maxim Gorky writes. "Yes. Tolstoy," Lenin said. "I wanted to read over the scene about the hunt, then I remembered that I had to write to a comrade. Absolutely no time for reading. Only last night I managed to read your book on Tolstoy." Then Lenin talked to Gorky about Tolstoy: "What a Colossus, eh? What a marvellously developed brain! Here's an artist for you, old chap. And do you know something still more amazing? You couldn't find a genuine muzhik in literature until this Count came on the scene."[17]

Lenin mentioned Russia's great novelists and poets in incidental remarks or to drive home a political nail; Tolstoy was the only genius-giant about whom he wrote at length, for Tolstoy was more than a writer, he was by all odds the largest personal phenomenon in Russian life in the second half of the nineteenth century and until his death in 1910. As such he played a remarkable role in the descent of the Russian monarchy. Lenin therefore found him a proper subject for comment.

On August 28, 1908, all of Russia and many followers and readers outside celebrated the novelist-patriarch's eightieth birthday. Lenin made this the occasion for an article entitled, "Leo Tolstoy as the Mirror of the Russian Revolution" in which he subjected the Count to Marxist analysis.[18]

As a really great artist, Lenin stated in the first paragraph, Tolstoy had to "reflect in his works at least some of the important aspects of the revolution." The legal Russian press, "overflowing with articles, letters, and notices regarding the eightieth jubilee of Tolstoy, is least of all interested in an analysis of his works from the point of view of the nature of the Russian revolution and its motive forces. All of this press is full to nausea of hypocrisy, twofold hypocrisy, official and liberal. The first is the vulgar hypocrisy of bribed scribblers who were told yesterday to badger L. Tolstoy and today—to discover his patriotism and try to be decent while Europe watched." The second type Lenin found even more revolting, for though the liberals glorify Tolstoy as "the great God-seeker" they do "not believe in the Tolstoyan God, neither do they sympathize with his criticism of the existing social order." Lenin then proceeded to discuss the "crying contradictions in the works, views, and teachings of the Tolstoy school:

[16] *Ibid.*, p. 235.
[17] *Days with Lenin*, pp. 50-51.
[18] Lenin, *op. cit.*, Second ed., Vol. XII, pp. 331-335.

"On the one hand an artist of genius, contributing not only incomparable pictures of Russian life, but literary productions of the first rank that belong to world literature. On the other hand, a landowner, wearing the martyr's crown in the name of Christ. On the one hand, an extraordinarily powerful, direct and sincere protest against social lies and hypocrisy; on the other, a Tolstoyan, that is, worn-out, historical sniveler called the Russian intellectual, who, publicly beating his breast, cries, 'I am bad, I am vile, I am striving after moral self-perfection; I no longer eat meat and now live on rice cutlets.' On the one hand, relentless criticism of capitalist exploitation, the exposure of governmental violence and of the comedy of justice and governmental administration, revelations of all the depths of contradictions between the growth of wealth and the achievements of civilization, and the growth of poverty, the brutalization of the working masses. On the other hand, weak-minded preaching of 'nonresistance to evil' by force. On the one hand, the soberest realism, the tearing away of all masks of whatever kind. On the other hand, advocacy of one of the most corrupt things existing in the world, that is, religion—an attempt to replace the official state clergy with priests by moral conviction, that is, cultivating a clericalism of the most refined and hence most loathsome kind."[19]

Few live according to all their high-minded principles. Tolstoy tried. Lenin, calling for a Russian revolution from safe Europe and accepting gold roubles sent by his mother out of her tsarist pension and her income from his grandfather's—Dr. Blank's—estate, might have been nailed to a board of contradictions too. Tolstoy's gift to Russia's future was his soberly realistic "tearing away of all masks," and, having looked at himself in the brutal mirror, his effort to achieve a Christlike life. Lenin did Tolstoy an injustice by saying the artist wanted a new "clericalism," he in fact opposed all organized religion and all organizations—he was therefore poles apart from organization-man Lenin. Tolstoy was an anti-church, anti-state, anti-violence anarchist for whom Lenin could have had only "loathsome" incomprehension.

The contradictions in Tolstoy's ideas, Lenin continued, "were no accident" —the beloved phrase of every variety of determinists—"but a reflection of the contradictory conditions surrounding Russian life in the last third of the nineteenth century." It reflected the peasantry's "protest against the advancing capitalism, the ruin, the mass loss of land, to which the patriarchal Russian village was to give birth. Tolstoy is comic as a prophet discovering new recipes for the salvation of mankind. . . . Tolstoy is great as the mouthpiece for those ideas and moods which took shape among the millions of the Russian peasantry at the time of the bourgeois revolution in Russia." The peasants, after the abolition of serfdom in 1861, were bitter, and eager to wipe out landlordism, the "official police-church," the "landlord government," and to create "a society of free and equal small peasants." Tolstoy,

[19] This entire paragraph is borrowed from Ernest J. Simmons, *Leo Tolstoy*, Vol. II, *The Years of Maturity 1880-1910* (New York, Vintage Books, 1960), pp. 366-367.

Lenin insisted, reflected this yearning more truly than he did the desire for "an abstract 'Christian anarchism.'" The peasantry, nevertheless, did not know how to fulfill its yearning. "A segment of the peasantry wept and prayed, reasoned and dreamt, wrote petitions and sent 'interceders'—altogether in the spirit of Leo Nikolayevich Tolstoy!" Tolstoy reflected "a ripened drive for improvement, the wish to get rid of the past—an unripe dreaminess, lack of political training, and revolutionary flabbiness." But under the hammer blows of the reactionary government, under the influence of socialist agitation, "not only the socialist proletariat but also the democratic masses of the peasantry will inevitably push into the foreground more and more hardened fighters less and less capable of succumbing to our historic sin of Tolstoyism."

When Tolstoy died in 1910, Lenin wrote a similar article. "The liberals," he declared, "give first prominence to Tolstoy as 'a great conscience.' Is that not an empty phrase . . . ? Is that not a detour around the *concrete* questions of democracy and socialism which Tolstoy *raised?*"

But a month later, on December 31, 1910, Lenin joyfully noted that "the death of Leo Tolstoy has, for the first time after a long interval, inspired *street demonstrations* with predominantly student participation but also, to some extent, of workers." Many factories downed tools on the day of the funeral; this represented "a beginning, if only modest, of demonstration strikes."

"That they have commenced to beat students," Lenin wrote Gorky on January 3, 1911, "is comforting, but Tolstoy cannot be forgiven for his 'passivism' or anarchism or populism or religion."[20] Lenin could not forgive Tolstoy for not being Lenin. Relentless, Lenin returned to the battle against Tolstoy in an article dated February 4, 1911: "Like the populists, he does not wish to see, he closes his eyes, he turns away from the thought, that that which is 'packing up' in Russia is nothing but the bourgeois social system." Lenin did not wish to see that for Tolstoy the important thing was not the bourgeois system or the proletarian system but their content, their treatment of the human being. Unlike Lenin, political forms did not matter to him. Unlike Lenin, social content did. A bourgeois system might be worse than a nonbourgeois system, a proletarian system might be better—if it improved man. To the materialist Lenin such considerations were immaterial in both senses: ". . . in our day, the attempt to idealize the teachings of Tolstoy, the justification or softening of his 'nonresistance,' his appeal to the 'Spirit,' his appeals to 'moral self-improvement,' his doctrine of 'conscience,' and universal 'love,' his preaching of asceticism and quietism, etc., will bring the most immediate and deepest harm."[21]

Here was the juxtaposition of nineteenth-century Russia's two greatest sons, Tolstoy and Lenin, two irreconcilables.

[20] Lenin, *op. cit.*, Second ed., Vol. XV, p. 58.
[21] *Ibid.*, pp. 100-103.

The Russian writers whose writings most influenced Lenin were not novelists, playwrights, or poets but publicists, essayists, and literary critics, notably Vissarion G. Belinsky (1811-1848), Alexander I. Herzen (1812-1870), Nikolai G. Chernishevsky (1828-1889), Nikolai A. Dobrolyubov (1836-1861), and, to a lesser extent, Dmitri I. Pisarev (1840-1868), and the critic and satirical novelist Mikhail Y. Saltikov-Shchedrin (1826-1889). Lenin was by all odds closest to Chernishevsky who, like Belinsky and Dobrolyubov, believed that literature should serve a social purpose; they reviled art-for-art's-sake in a Russia where everybody but a few million people was undernourished, uneducated, and underprivileged. This attitude lodged in Lenin's intellectual bloodstream long before the revolution and stayed there.

None of these literary critics was a Marxist. They were in revolt against tsarist backwardness, cruelties, and inanities. Alexander Herzen, an illegitimate son, was exiled to eastern Russia as a youth of twenty-two for participating in a radical discussion group. Later he inherited a fortune of $250,000 from his father and fled with it in 1847 to London where, from 1855 to 1862, he edited and wrote most of the famous fortnightly *Kolokol (The Bell)*, thousands of copies of which were smuggled into Russia and placed by unseen subversive hands on the tables of Alexander II, grand dukes, princes, ministers, generals, and admirals.[22] But whom the gods wish to destroy they first make illiterate. The men who misdirected the destinies of "Holy" Russia knew the Cyrillic alphabet, they could read, but they read without understanding. They could not even understand signs, the signs of the times. Leaders of underdeveloped countries usually slumber along with their people, little realizing that in the long night the people dream of vengeance—a dry fuel that ignites in a hot crisis—in a war particularly. (Lenin himself warned the monarchy on May 8, 1912: "The first impact of the storm came in 1905. The next begins to grow before our eyes.")

Lenin said, "Herzen belonged to the generation of revolutionaries of the first half of the nineteenth century who came from noble and landlord stock." Herzen, quoted by Lenin, had written that the Russian nobility raised up social trash, yet also "the men of December 14 [upper-class officers and civilians who in 1825 rebelled against absolutism], a phalanx of heroes reared, like Romulus and Remus, on the milk of the wild wolf. . . . Those were some kind of epic heroes struck from pure steel from head to foot, warrior-champions who consciously courted sure death in order to stir the younger generation to a new life and to cleanse the children born in the midst of executions and servility.

"Among those children," Lenin commented, "was Herzen."

When revolution swept Europe in 1848, Herzen, Lenin affirmed, was "a democrat, a revolutionary, a socialist." But after the failures of the revolutions Herzen's skepticism and pessimism took possession and his "bourgeois illu-

[22] *Encyclopedia of Russia and the Soviet Union*, Editor, Michael T. Florinsky (New York, 1961), pp. 213-214.

sions about socialism" collapsed. Actually, Herzen, until shortly before his death, stood with Bakunin, the anarchist-populist. He believed in the village commune though he saw that "The Russian peasant . . . is isolated in his little commune. The distance between villages in this great wide land robs him of contact with his own people."[23]

In the same article, Lenin praised Herzen for condemning Alexander II's punitive campaigns in Poland. Herzen's hostility to aggressive Russian nationalism lost him many readers and the sympathies of friends, among them Turgenev, but, Lenin said, "Herzen saved the honor of Russian democracy." And in the next sentence, Lenin wrote, "When news arrived that a Russian serf killed his landlord for dishonoring his niece, Herzen added in *Kolokol*, 'And he did very well.' " Lenin lauded these manifestations of Herzen's "strong characteristics."

Lenin saw Herzen as the first of three phases of the continuing Russian revolution. "First—the noblemen and landlords, the Decembrists and Herzen. The ambience of these revolutionists was small. Very far from the people. But their cause was not lost. The Decembrists awakened Herzen. Herzen expanded revolutionary agitation. It was taken up, broadened, reinforced, tempered by the middle-class revolutionary intellectuals beginning with Chernishevsky and ending with the heroes of the 'Narodnaya Volya' [Lenin's brother was one of them]. Herzen called them 'the young navigators of the coming storm.' But this was not yet the storm itself. The storm—is the movement of the masses themselves."[24] The proletariat.

Herzen died the year Lenin was born, Chernishevsky when Lenin was nineteen. Chernishevsky has a greater claim than Herzen to the paternity of Lenin's aesthetics and politics. Herzen was by far the finer stylist. But that mattered little to Lenin. Chernishevsky was the better materialist; he preached socialism—socialism without Marx, nonetheless socialism. Tsarist prison, which always came to the aid of the revolution, granted Chernishevsky the time to write a mediocre novel: *Cho Delat?* (*What to Do?* or, *What Is to Be Done?*). Lenin gave the same name to his well-known pamphlet—1902—on organization problems. ". . . to Bazarov's science, self-improvement, and nihilism"—Bazarov was the hero of Turgenev's *Fathers and Sons*—". . . the more political hero of Nikolai Chernishevsky's *What Is to Be Done?* added a hazy vision of socialist utopia and of revolutionary action."[25] Lenin overlooked the utopia because he welcomed the action. "Chernishevsky," Lenin wrote in March, 1911, "was a socialist-utopian who dreamt of the transition to socialism through the old, semi-feudal peasant commune. . . . But Chernishevsky was not only a socialist-utopian. He was also a revolutionary democrat, he was able to influence all the political events of his epoch

[23] A. I. Herzen, *Dvizheniye Obshchestyennoi Misli v Rossii* (*Changes in Social Thought in Russia*) (Moscow, 1907), p. 181.
[24] Lenin, *op. cit.*, Second ed., Vol. XV, pp. 464-469.
[25] George Fischer, *Russian Liberalism* (Cambridge, Mass., 1958), p. 50.

in a revolutionary spirit, advancing . . . the idea of the mass struggle for the overthrow of all old governments." This spoke to Lenin's heart—and also Chernishevsky's reference, in another novel, to Russia as "pitiful nation, nation of slaves, from top to bottom—all slaves";[26] and the fact that "the spirit of the class struggle flows through all his"—Chernishevsky's—"works."[27] Moreover, Lenin declared in March, 1909, Chernishevsky criticized Kant for his "metaphysical theory of the subjective nature of our knowledge." This, according to Lenin, put Chernishevsky with Engels in the anti-Mach camp— a golden compliment. When, therefore, Georgi Plekhanov, in a book entitled N. G. *Chernishevsky*, chided Chernishevsky for being too idealistic and displaying only "the rudiments of materialism," Lenin in 1910-1911, remarked, "Because of the *theoretical* difference between the idealistic and materialistic view of history Plekhanov *overlooks* the practical-political and *class* difference between a liberal and a democrat." The democrat, in Lenin's terminology, was Chernishevsky, and Lenin, as usual, ranked theory far below the practical politics of the class struggle. He forgave Chernishevsky his philosophical backsliding so long as he was for revolution. Krupskaya reports that Lenin's picture album contained two photographs of Chernishevsky. She also writes of Chernishevsky's influence on Lenin and actually suggests that he helped Lenin become a Marxist.[28] N. Valentinov (Volsky) reports a conversation he had in a Geneva café in January, 1904, with Lenin in the presence of two other comrades. Replying to a remark by Valentinov, Lenin exclaimed, "Do you realize what you are saying? How could the strange and absurd thought ever occur to you to attach the label of primitive and untalented to the works of Chernishevsky, the greatest and most talented spokesman of socialism before Marx! Under his influence hundreds of persons became revolutionists. . . . He, for instance, fascinated my brother, he also fascinated me."[29]

Presumably, Chernishevsky would have looked askance at the Proletkult just as Lenin did—for that organization was Machist-inspired and Machist in outlook: subjective, individualistic, idealistic, and actuated by the expectation that its "supermen" and ordinary mortals could, by acts of will, concoct a national culture proletarian in character despite the nonproletarian nature of the majority and the noncultured condition of the proletariat. Nevertheless, the Proletkult lived on until 1923 when grave illness would soon remove Lenin from the scene. For though Lenin was implacable toward political enemies of the state he was permissive, not punitive, toward cultural deviants. He wished not to murder them or still their pens and brushes, but to curb them and circumscribe their influence by restrictions on the use of paper, clubrooms, and amenities. His own culture inescapably affected his attitude

[26] Lenin, *op. cit.*, Second ed., Vol. XVIII, p. 81.
[27] *Ibid.*, Vol. XVII, p. 342.
[28] *Memories of Lenin*, Vol. I, p. 198.
[29] *Vstrachey s Leninim*, pp. 102-103. This passage, though written by an anti-Bolshevik Menshevik, is quoted in V. I. *Lenin o Literature i Iskusstvye*, p. 649.

toward culture. Bred in a home of books by a father devoted to schools and a mother to literature, his outlook had to differ from that of a shepherd-peasant-worker and low-brow hillman. He did, however, believe in censorship and control. Thus on September 13, 1921, he asked the Politburo—which complied—to prohibit the sale of "pornography and books with religious content." He had inserted another item in the resolution: "Permit the free sale of foreign books (novels)," but deleted it. Nevertheless, and though art-for-party's-sake stood high in his credo, he did not want the revolution to drain away the country's cultural lifeblood. There was as yet no iron curtain, the doors were not shut, and scores of Russia's best writers and musicians and fine painters like Vassily Kandinsky and Marc Chagall (as well as scientists) went west either because they could not bear the empty stomachs and stoves or because they could not take the revolution's restrictions. Gorky, Trotsky, and Lunacharsky were constantly nudging Lenin's elbow and reminding him, in effect, that Bolshevism must not add cultural anemia to economic poverty.

"Art," Trotsky wrote in his introduction to *Literature and Revolution*, "needs comfort, even abundance. Furnaces have to be hotter, wheels have to move faster, looms have to turn more quickly, schools have to work better." But there was no comfort, and furnaces were cold during the three and a half years of civil war communism. "I burned my furniture, my sculptor's stand, bookshelves and books, books beyond count or computation," a Petrograd author moaned in 1920. "If I had owned wooden arms or legs I should have burned them and found myself limbless in the spring. . . . Everyone gathered in the kitchen; in the abandoned rooms stalactites grew. . . . The Arctic Circle had become a reality and its line passed through the region of the Nevsky Avenue."[30]

Lenin abhorred futurism, but Trotsky, who said it was not "a revolutionary art," felt it "contributes to a greater degree more directly and actively than all other tendencies in forming the new art." Trotsky regretted that "The years of revolution became the years of almost utter poetic silence." He wrote in *Literature and Revolution*, "But what is one to say about the psychoanalytic theory of Freud? Can it be reconciled with materialism, as, for instance, Karl Radek thinks (and I also), or is it hostile to it?" Trotsky was a dissenter in power and not without influence on Soviet policy toward the arts. (His book on literature mentions Marx, Engels, Aristotle, but never Lenin. Did he find that Lenin had said nothing significant on the subject?)

Maxim Gorky too held unconventional views on art and especially on how the revolution should treat artists and the intelligentsia generally. Lenin treated Gorky with touching deference but did not always yield to his civil rights entreaties. Lunacharsky, present at one interview between Lenin and

[30] Victor Shklovsky, *St. Petersburg in 1920*, translated and quoted by Gleb Struve in *Soviet Russian Literature 1917-1950* (Norman, Okla., 1951), p. 28.

Gorky, recalls its substance: Gorky complained of searches and arrests among Petrograd intellectuals, "Among the very people who at one time were of service to all of us, to your comrades, and even to you personally, Vladimir Ilyich, and hid us in their apartments, etc."

Lenin smiled and said, "Yes, fine, good people, but that is just why their apartments must be searched. That is just the reason why now and then, reluctantly, they have to be arrested. You see, they are fine and good, their sympathy is always with the oppressed, they are always against persecution. And what do they now see before them? The persecutors—that is our Cheka, the oppressed—they are the Kadets"—Constitutional Democrats, a bourgeois party—"and the SR's who escape from it. Apparently, duty, as they see it, requires them to become their allies against us. And we must catch active counterrevolutionaries and make them harmless. The rest is clear. And Vladimir Ilyich laughed a completely amiable laugh."[31] Lenin gave Gorky a lesson in dialectics and distortion and laughed.

In 1921 Gorky once brought Lenin a number of books published in Berlin and suggested that they also be published in Russia. Lenin paged through them. He approved the publication of a book on locomotives. Then he looked at a volume of old Indian tales. "In my opinion," Lenin said, "this is premature."

"Those are very good stories," Gorky retorted.

"Spend money on this?" Lenin said.

"It is very inexpensive," Gorky argued.

"Yes," Lenin answered, "but for this we pay in gold. And there will be famine this year."

Alexander K. Voronsky, the first editor of the Moscow monthly *Krasnaya Nov*, who was present and reported the encounter, remarked, "It seemed to me then that two truths clashed: one would say, 'Man does not live by bread alone.' The other replied, 'And what if there is no bread?' "[32]

Within several weeks, Gorky appealed to America to feed millions of starving Russians.

XL. THE PARTY

FAMINE is a phenomenon of underdeveloped countries. Soviet Russia in 1921 was an underdeveloped country in which the collapse of industry, the paralysis of transport, the havoc of war, and the peasant's reluctance to reap his crop for the government collector aggravated the effect of the 1921

[31] V. I. *Lenin o Literature i Iskusstvye*, pp. 670-671.
[32] *Ibid.*, pp. 685-686.

drought in the Volga and the Ukraine. Maxim Gorky appealed for aid to "All Honest People." "Give bread and medicine," he pleaded. A conference of European government representatives, meeting in Paris and Brussels, declared itself ready to weigh the question of relief if the Soviets acknowledged their debts. Herbert Hoover, on behalf of the American Relief Administration (ARA), promised aid forthwith.

In the summer of 1921 at least twenty-five million persons in the Volga valley alone were without food. The ARA commenced operations in September, 1921, and continued them until July, 1923. It saved millions of lives in the Volga and the Ukraine.

Now there was no politics except economics. When, after the NEP was introduced, Michael Farbman, a Russian-speaking Englishman, correspondent of the London *Observer*, asked Karl Radek, "Is there a danger of the [communist] party degenerating or being transformed?" Radek replied, "Certainly, we are being transformed daily. In Switzerland, as revolutionary exiles, we never paid any attention to rainfall, being preoccupied by Marxian discussions. And now we are more concerned with rainfall and drought than with the philosophy of Mach and Avenarius. Osinsky, the present Commissar of Agriculture, was then translating Verlaine, and was totally indifferent to ploughing and sowing. Now he is obsessed by agriculture, and fights only with locusts and other pests. Kissilov used to be absorbed in plans for annoying the bourgeoisie; now all his thoughts are given to the proper organization of the Moscow tramways. . . . In former days we thought a bourgeois only worth wiping out; now we wonder if he will make a good factory director."[1]

It was the Age of Practicality, the Age of Lenin. Disaster had dethroned doctrine and made a virtue of economic success no matter what the cost in Marxist ideology. The Bolshevik revolution was a leap from war into civil war. Soviet Russia then took a leap into the kingdom of necessity. Now collapse threatened the revolution unless it could supply necessities to sustain the population in life and labor. The crisis evoked Lenin's gigantic effort to revive Russia's economy.

"The gross output of agriculture in 1920 was only about *one-half* the prewar output," according to the Stalin-edited history of the Soviet Communist Party. "The output of large-scale industry in 1920 was a little over *one-seventh* of pre-war. . . . The total output of pig-iron in 1921 was only 116,300 tons, or about 3 percent of the pre-war output. There was a shortage of fuel. Transport was disrupted. Stocks of metal and textiles were nearly exhausted. There was an acute shortage of such prime necessities as bread, fats, meat, footwear, clothing, matches, salt, kerosene, and soap."[2]

---

[1] Michael S. Farbman, *Bolshevism in Retreat* (London, 1923), p. 303.

[2] *History of the Communist Party of the Soviet Union (Bolsheviks). Short Course*, edited by a Commission of the Central Committee of the C.P.S.U. (B.), (New York, 1939), p. 248.

Socialism—the modern name for state capitalism—appeals to an under-developed country. Civil war and foreign intervention made Russia more underdeveloped in 1921 than in 1917. The Marxists accordingly decided that the country needed an additional period of private capitalism to prepare it for socialism. Capitalist underdevelopment enabled the communists to conquer. Capitalist development would now enable them to survive. In the unspecified future, total state capitalism would take over from private capitalism.

Some communists were more ambitious. Lenin rebuked them. He wrote on February 19, 1921, to Gleb Krzhizhanovsky, chairman from 1921 to 1930 of the Gosplan (State Planning Commission): "Milyutin is writing non-sense about planning. . . . We are poor. Hungry, ruined poor. A whole integrated, real plan is for us now 'a bureaucratic utopia.' Don't go after it. Immediately, without losing a day or an hour choose WHAT IS MOST IMPORTANT bit by bit, a minimum of industrial plants, and RESTORE THEM."[3] In the same temper, Lenin said in *Pravda* of February 21, 1921, "The essence of the matter is that we are unable to understand situations and we substitute intellectual and bureaucratic scheming for living work. . . . We must learn to administer Russia . . . Less intellectual and bureaucratic conceit . . ."[4]

Lenin was practical to the point of ragpicking. He wrote to Krzhizhanovsky in April, 1921, that the Planning Commission was not to occupy itself with long-range plans but with "Fuel today. For 1921. Now, for spring. The collection of scrap, waste, unused materials. Use them *for* barter for bread."[5] And on May 30, 1921, he insisted that sacks for grain be speeded to the Ukraine together with consumer goods. He demanded daily written reports on the extent of fulfillment.[6]

From now until he was incapacitated Lenin occasionally ascended to misty mountain heights for an ideological spree; most of the time a ton of bread was worth more to him than a heavy tome on Marx. In the Chuvash Republic on the Volga, he learned, 1,260,000 pounds of meat could not be brought to the railway depot owing to the absence of motor transport. He urged the local authorities to act "in battle formation. . . . Telegraph immediately on measures taken."[7]

So sensitive was Lenin to the mood of the masses, so aware of the weakness of the regime, that he wrote Vyacheslav Molotov in mid-April, 1921, "Unless memory deceives me, the newspapers published a Central Committee letter or circular about the May First holiday with instructions to *expose the lie of religion* or something of that nature.

"This should not be allowed. It is untactful. Just at Eastertime *something else* should be recommended: not to expose the lie, but *definitely to avoid*

[3] Lenin, *Sochineniya*, Fourth ed., Vol. 35, p. 405.
[4] *Ibid.*, Vol. 32, pp. 114-122.
[5] *Ibid.*, Vol. 35, p. 409.
[6] *Leninskii Sbornik*, Vol. XXVI, p. 251.
[7] *Ibid.*, Vol. XXXV, p. 226.

any offense to religion. A supplementary letter or circular should be issued. If the Secretariat [of the Central Committee] does not agree, then [the question should be raised] in the Politburo." A circular in Lenin's sense appeared on April 21.[8]

(Until he became very ill, Lenin never dictated. He wrote his notes, speech outlines, instructions, and telegrams by hand. In the middle of a message to his private secretary, Lydia A. Fotieva, on June 6, 1921, he wrote, "My ink, as you see, is rotten. Please send me a small bottle of good fountain pen ink.")[9]

The concession to Washington B. Vanderlip remained on Lenin's mind. In April, 1921, he dispatched a memorandum to Foreign Commissar Georgi V. Chicherin: "Has it been explained to Vanderlip that we could grant the Americans a concession to *tremendous* oilfields (Baku, Grozny, Emba, Ukhta) and that America would thereby beat England? Telephone as soon as you have read this."[10]

Opposition to concessions continued strong among communists and workers. Lenin summarized their arguments and, in rebuttal, said: "Is it possible now to formulate our task as: we can do it ourselves, or is this leftist infantilism, or foolish doctrinairism?" To grant concessions to one-fourth of the Soviet oil fields, he added, would be "ideal for training," and would permit the communists to overtake capitalist technique on two-fourths; "three-fourths would be an inaccessible ideal. . . . Then in thirty years (the concessions period is of medium duration) world victory is guaranteed, and in fifteen years we shall probably buy out" the concessionaire. He was attempting to drug the opposition with prophecy.

Lenin's motivation for concessions is interesting: "In view of the gigantic danger of the collapse of the Soviet government as a result of economic ruin and backwardness . . . our task can be put only in this way: *overtake* with the aid of an alliance with foreign capitalism."[11] He shrank from nothing.

Lenin seems to have been desperate. He wrote to Krzhizhanovsky on April 13, 1921, "We must assume that in 1921-22 we shall have the same or an even greater crop failure and fuel famine." To alleviate pockets of the worst distress they would have to reduce their small gold hoard by buying food, fuel, and industrial equipment abroad. Each purchase, he told Krzhizhanovsky, must be justified in detail.[12] Lenin supervised these gold expenditures with a miser's parsimony.

Lenin's black thoughts on the next year's harvest sprang from his knowledge of Russian history: one bad crop tended to induce another, because when he is hungry the peasant eats the seed for the coming planting.

[8] *Ibid.*, p. 233.
[9] *Ibid.*, p. 259.
[10] *Ibid.*, Vol. XXXVI, p. 215.
[11] *Ibid.*, pp. 194-197.
[12] Lenin, *op. cit.*, Fourth ed., Vol. 35, p. 415.

Moreover, Lenin could not be sure that news of the end of requisitions had reached and convinced the village. The muzhik was a hardheaded skeptic who would wonder whether the communists had indeed changed their red spots. Lenin therefore went to the gramophone-inscribing-studio in Moscow and solemnly, and in full obedience to the flustered technicians, made three records: one on the new system of tax in kind replacing requisitions, the second on concessions, the third on cooperatives.[13] (He had inscribed eight records in 1919. All eleven original plates found a safe repository in the Education Commissariat.) Since Russian radio broadcasting was an infant, records which could be played by itinerant propagandists were the best means of bringing the master's voice to the muzhik's ear.

The record on the tax in kind, especially addressed to the village, contains only 218 words. Lenin emphasized the strictly official character of the tax; it had been decreed by the Central Executive Committee—VTSIK—and seconded by the Sovnarkom, or Cabinet, in Moscow. "Why was it necessary to replace requisitions with the tax in kind? Because requisitions proved excessively heavy"—the Russian words are simple—"and inconvenient for the peasants. . . . Besides, animal deaths from dearth of fodder handicapped the transport of timber from the forests, handicapped the work of factories which make products to be exchanged for peasant grain. . . . The tax in kind amounts to half of requisitions. . . . The size of the tax will be known to each peasant in advance, that is, already in the spring. This will mean less abuse in tax collections. As a result, the peasant will be more interested in expanding his sowings, improving his farm, and trying to increase his harvests. . . . The peasant will now work on his farm with greater security and greater diligence, and that is the main thing."

The record on concessions explained in simple terms the nature of a concession and assured the workers and peasants that the foreign "capitalist-lease-holder" would bring only advantage, no peril: Concessions "Yes, will mean to develop capitalism, but this is not dangerous, for the government remains in the hands of the workers and peasants, and the property of land-lords and capitalists will not be restored." Lenin apparently thought the peasant might fear the return of his estate owner.

Co-op stores, Lenin said, would help in the distribution of commodities. Government officials, he added, must not limit these activities, must, on the contrary, foster them. Producers' co-ops were probably more attractive. They would enable smallholders and craftsmen, Lenin explained, to prepare dairy products, vegetables, and articles made from wood, iron, and leather and thereby "improve their living conditions"—in effect, by selling them on the free market.

Together, the three Lenin records were the primitive equivalent of a "fireside chat."

The famine was heavy in the land. The ARA opened kitchens for children

[13] The texts of these in *ibid.*, Third ed., Vol. XXVI, pp. 335-357.

in Moscow and Petrograd, and started feeding the starving as far east as Oren-burg in the Urals. Numerous authenticated cases of cannibalism occurred. A fourth of Russia's population—thirty-five million—now suffered from contin-uous acute hunger. Several million orphaned waifs (*besprizorniye*) roamed roads, railway tracks, and city streets, living on alms and crime.

As the Kremlin's problems multiplied its support dwindled. A document compiled by the party's Central Committee in the first week of May, 1921, and placed before Lenin for his corrections and comments, referred to "our at times sickly party cells" (units) and to the "wall that has grown up between communists and non-party workingmen."[14]

The wall broke the bond between the proletariat, consisting largely of non-party workingmen, and the communists—the bond which, in theory, justified the existence of the Soviet state. Bricks of worker discontent made the wall a dark reality.

The Central Committee's letter was a re-editing of a letter Lenin had drafted several days earlier which began: "The experience of non-party con-ferences has fully demonstrated that they have become an arena for Menshe-vik and SR agitation." The Central Committee letter kept this text but toned it down by burying it in the middle of its version and saying the Mensheviks and SR's "won no significant successes when they appeared openly. . . . There-fore they disguise themselves with increasing frequency as non-party people." Lenin did not object to the changes. In his draft,[15] he had urged "supreme caution in arranging non-party conferences, never allowing them to convene without the most meticulous preliminary preparation in each individual fac-tory. The provincial party committees"—who received the Central Commit-tee's letter by telegram in code—"must answer to the party for guaranteeing the success of each non-party conference."

Often this involved the arrest of actual or alleged Mensheviks and SR's in advance of the conferences.

These conferences were held to justify the party's policies to noncommu-nist, non-party workingmen and arouse their enthusiasm. Usually a repre-sentative of the Central Committee addressed them. One such representative or "instructor"—G. K. Korolov of Ivanovo Voznesensk—is known to have objected to the assignment and complained to Lenin, who replied on May 31, 1921: "The decision of the Central Committee regarding high-ranking itinerant party officials is a decision of the plenary session of the Central Committee. It is therefore beyond argument. (I personally fully agree with it.) . . . Central Committee's machine must be strengthened and *brought into closer touch with local groups.*" Korolov had apparently said he was weak on theory. Lenin commented, "You don't have to be a theoretician. It is enough to be *a party member.*"[16]

[14] *Leninskii Sbornik*, Vol. XXXVI, pp. 226-228.
[15] *Ibid.*, Vol. XX, pp. 329-330.
[16] *Ibid.*, p. 331.

The party and the proletariat were in a slough of despondency. In the draft of a speech to be delivered on May 18, 1921, at the communist fraction of the All-Russian Congress of Trade Unions—no text of the speech itself nor even a press summary is extant—Lenin noted one item he intended to discuss: "The extreme nervousness, excitability, dissatisfaction of the workers." Also their "profoundest indignation at such phenomena as 'cigarette lighters,' stealing, et cetera."[17]

That the primary leader of a country should mention "cigarette lighters" suggests their importance: matches being either unavailable or of such bad quality that they were useless, workers in factories spent their time making crude cigarette lighters for their own households and for sale; their factories lacked the raw materials and sometimes the fuel and power for more productive pursuits. On May 22, accordingly, Lenin laid before the Politburo a resolution, immediately adopted, requiring the trade unions to "achieve, with unusual speed, a reduction in the number of industrial plants and of workers by concentrating the latter in the least number of the best and largest plants."[18] Six days earlier Lenin had written Chairman Krzhizhanovsky of the State Planning Commission (Gosplan) on the need to give special attention to factories producing consumer goods easily exchangeable for the peasants' grain; to cut the personnel and budget of the navy "almost to annihilation"; reduce the size of the army to 1,600,000 by September 1, 1921, and then to half of that; and eliminate 25 percent or 50 percent of government employees.

These measures roused the trade unions to ferocious opposition. The communist fraction of the trade-union congress, reflecting workingmen resentments, adopted a resolution offered by D. B. Ryazonov which Lenin called "an anti-party resolution." Not only did Tomsky, the top trade-union leader, fail to combat Ryazonov's motion, "he did not even bring to the attention of the fraction the draft resolution written by the Central Committee's commission." The Committee, in plenary session, consequently ordered both Tomsky and Ryazonov ousted from trade-union activity. Only after Lenin addressed the communist fraction of the trade-union congress did it reject Ryazonov's resolution and pass "by a large majority" that submitted by the party.[19]

Something was rotten in Russia.

Banditry flowered in the soil of poverty and political confusion. In the Central Russian province of Voronezh, for instance, remnants of Antonov's anti-Bolshevik partisans were "carrying out murders of party and Soviet officials" as late as May, 1921.[20] Lenin ordered reprisals.

If Lenin's spirit flagged for even a moment he gave not the slightest sign

[17] *Ibid.*, Vol. XXVI, p. 237.
[18] *Ibid.*, pp. 240-241.
[19] *Ibid.*, p. 237, text and note.
[20] *Ibid.*, p. 253.

of it. On the contrary, he rebuked comrades for succumbing to depression. M. G. Sokolov, a third-rank Foreign Commissariat official, scheduled to deliver a speech on May 18, 1921, in the line of party duty, made an outline and sent it to Lenin for comment. Lenin replied immediately in a long letter —two pages in print.[21] Sokolov felt quite free to criticize Lenin on fundamentals: he disliked Lenin's pamphlet on the tax in kind. On the one hand, he said, you "implant *state capitalism*" by inviting foreign capitalists, presumably also former Russian capitalists, to lease land and forests, on the other hand, you talk about "expropriating the landlords."

Lenin replied: the landlords and capitalists remain expropriated; their leases would be short-term.

Sokolov argued further that "*spontaneous activity* on the part of the masses is *possible* only if we *wipe off the face of the earth* the abscess which is called bureaucratic central boards and centers" in industry.

Lenin replied that though he had not visited the provinces "I know this bureaucracy and all the harm it does. Your mistake is to think that it can be destroyed at once like an 'abscess.' . . . It is possible to expel the Tsar, drive out the landlords, banish the capitalists. We have done this. But it is impossible 'to expel' bureaucracy in a peasant country. . . . It is possible only *to reduce* it by slow, steady work. . . . Surgery in *this* case is absurd . . . only a slow cure—everything else is either quackery or naïveté. You are indeed naïve. Pardon my frankness. But you yourself write about your youth." Lenin then told Sokolov that his attitude "resembles despair. And for us to despair is either comic or shameful. . . . And don't let your spirit fall. If you deliver your speech (and I have absolutely no objection), please read my letter to you too. I shake your hand and beg you not to yield to 'the spirit of dejection.' Lenin."

Agriculture Commissar Osinsky, who had been traveling in the country, returned to Moscow with the impression that peasants regarded the tax in kind as a temporary measure and did not take it seriously. Twice bitten, the muzhik was thrice shy. What was worse, a leading communist official in a county asked a member of the party Central Committee in Moscow to tell him "in secret" whether "requisitioning will be restored in the autumn."[22] He would not have been the only "wise" one to think that the NEP was a short-term ruse. Lenin accordingly called a special conference to confirm the lasting nature of the new policy.

Each year during Lenin's crisis rule, a party congress met to make policy; it had supreme authority in Soviet Russia. (In Stalin's much more stable time, the Fourteenth Party Congress convened in 1925, the Fifteenth in 1927, the Sixteenth in 1930, the Seventeenth in 1934, the Eighteenth in March, 1939,

[21] Lenin, *op. cit.*, Third ed., Vol. XXVI, pp. 362-363.
[22] B. M. Shekhvatov, *Lenin i Sovietskoye Gosudarstvo. 1921-1922 (Lenin and the Soviet State. 1921-1922)* (Moscow, 1960), note, pp. 66-67.

and the Nineteenth in 1952.) Between congresses, under Lenin, a party conference assembled to assess the situation and pass ad hoc resolutions. The Tenth Congress had concluded its sessions on March 16, 1921. Yet Osinsky's report of peasant skepticism, and the possibility therefore of muzhik sabotage of the next harvest, caused Lenin to summon the special conference on May 26, 1921. He spoke three times.[23] He told the peasants the tax in kind would not be abolished. He told the workers they too could trade. He said, "Inasmuch as the peasantry constitutes a component part of capitalist society, so does the working class constitute a component part of that society. Therefore, if the peasants engage in private trade then we"—the workers—"must trade." The Mensheviks and SR's influenced the workers. "They are the more dangerous at a moment when the working class is compelled to live through a period of interrupted production"—circumlocution for unemployment. Result: "a state of unbalance, uncertainty, despondency, unbelief seizes certain layers of workers." A conference convoked to discuss the peasant became a bid for workers' support.

Imbalance in the Soviet proletariat; stability, however, in the international situation—the only ray of hope Lenin saw. For the rest: work hard, agitate, and trust in the future.

Why did not the nation rise in revolt against the communists?

Lenin had little talent for friendship—he used people too much. Millions worship him. Hundreds of thousands adored him in his lifetime. They admired his steel will, iron courage, razor-sharp brain, adamantine determination. Many loved him. He loved one woman—Inessa Armand. But his only friend—probably—was Julius Martov, the Menshevik leader, who worked with Lenin on *Iskra* magazine. Lenin respected his ability, honesty, and revolutionary sincerity. Outside of his family, and Inessa, Lenin addressed nobody with the intimate "thou." He did with Martov. While in London in 1902, Lenin and Martov "drank Bruderschaft." This is a German custom adopted by Russians: two men stand side by side, link arms, kiss, then drink wine, and thereafter they are "brothers" and address each other as "thou." The third volume (page 399) of the *Leninskii Sbornik* contains a letter, dated Zurich, April 17, 1902, in which Martov uses the second person singular in writing to Lenin. He would not have done this unless Lenin had shown the same intimacy toward him. Subsequently, however, the "brothers" broke off relations. Politics had brought them together; politics separated them. In 1920, after the Russo-Polish war, German socialists asked Lenin to allow Martov to leave Russia. The Soviet political and economic situations were so threatening that Lenin might have feared the Cheka, sometimes a law unto itself and sometimes a state within a state, would arrest Martov and make a martyr of him. He accordingly facilitated Martov's departure abroad. Raphael R. Abramovitch, a collaborator of Martov, followed several months later. On

[23] Lenin, *op. cit.*, Third ed., Vol. XXVI, pp. 385-411.

February 23, 1921, in the week of the pre-Kronstadt strikes in Petrograd, Boris I. Nicolaevsky and other Mensheviks were lodged in Moscow's Lubyanka prison.

The Menshevik party was beheaded.

After the Right SR revolts in north Russia in 1918 and the Left SR insurrection in Moscow in July, 1918, the Social Revolutionary leaders either fled west or were incarcerated or placed under strict surveillance. Their organization collapsed.

Earlier, the Russian bourgeois parties had been dissolved. In 1921 their leaders were dead or outside Russia.

A successful revolution must have effective leadership.

A nation that has suffered heavy losses of lives and limbs in one long civil war and sees war ruins all around it does not revolt and thus initiate a second civil war immediately thereafter. Nor does a nation revolt when it is starving. Hungry, dispirited people are not the material of a revolution. Despair does not make a revolution. Hope does. Hope and despair could, but not despair alone. Russia had hoped, it now despaired of quick results through revolution.

Revolution breaks out where administration breaks down. Administration had broken down in Russia in 1917, not in 1921. The Soviet government, with its long Cheka arm and omnipresent communist party eyes, ears, and brain, stood before the cowed, confused, undernourished, atomized nation as a colossus which Lenin, not without design, constantly reminded them had defeated numerous domestic and foreign enemies. Inured by tsarism to submission, Russia submitted to Lenin.

The key to Lenin's communism is the party. If one wishes to prejudge the judgment of history one might say that Lenin's greatest innovation was the removal of the heart and soul from politics and their replacement with a party organization. This was the new "Marxism": the party, the state, the nation, and the leader merged into one identity to which the people owed allegiance. This is what constitutes totalitarianism. The party is above the state and the government and morality, but not above personality. The person, however, operates through the party, and if he loses control of the party his personality shrinks. If he has complete control of the party and hence, after Lenin, of the country, his personality becomes a cult. In Soviet history, domination of the communist party has been the biggest political prize.

Before 1917 Lenin conceived of the communist party as a band of professional revolutionists. The Bolshevik revolution transformed it into an order of monks in armor. They fought with arms to win battles, with propaganda to win minds, with plan, energy, and technique to win victories on the economic front. The reward for valor was a more perilous post. The reward for hard work was harder work. The communist code banned fleshpots. The ascetic Lenin set the standard of puritanism.

But power is a lure for the strong who yearn to exercise it and the weak who are transfixed by it. Moreover, power is twin to privilege—especially in have-not countries where the use of an automobile or of a better apartment or, as in revolutionary Russia, access to a better official restaurant, was not only a status symbol but the difference between privation and comfort. The Soviet Communist Party, accordingly, attracted selfless idealists and self-seekers.

In March, 1920, at the time of the Ninth Party Congress, the party gave its membership as 611,978; at the time of the Tenth Party Congress in March, 1921: "almost three-quarters of a million."[24] Nobody knew for certain the motives of those who joined. But the party assumed that some were band-wagon-jumpers. On the other hand, believers in communism-around-the-corner felt disillusioned by the NEP turn to capitalism and left the party which, in consequence, was threatened with an excess of opportunists.

Lenin ordered a purge.

The purge took the form of re-registration. Every member of the party had to apply for membership again by registering. This afforded an opportunity to expel undesirables by refusing to register them. Lenin drafted the terms of re-registration which the Politburo adopted, with some changes, on June 21, 1921.[25] In each party cell, "a group of old members (not less than five to seven years in the party) and all of them workers" would conduct the re-registration.

According to figures quoted by Leonard Schapiro, in 1921 only 8 percent of the party membership had joined before March, 1917, and only 41 percent of the total membership were workers. Not all of the 8 percent would have qualified for the "five to seven years" category. Thus, the burden of passing on the new membership fell on approximately 3 percent of the total, some of whom, to boot, might have been deficient in discriminating intelligence and political experience. Here, perhaps, the bureaucrats of the party machine amended Lenin's draft. He assumed that being a worker was a sufficient guarantee of discipline and loyalty. His draft therefore also asked that the formalities connected with re-registration be reduced to a minimum in the case of "real workers really working in their factory" and of "peasants engaged on their own plot of land." He knew that many who had been workers and who still appeared in the party records as workers were actually officeholders reveling in their recently acquired bureaucratic power and prerogatives.

Lenin's draft provided for the exclusion from the party of members even "slightly doubtful, unreliable, who have not proved their stability" as communists. They could return after "supplementary investigation and tests." Likewise to be excluded were members of other parties who had joined the communist party after October, 1917; officials of the tsarist and Provisional (Kerensky) governments; as well as members occupying posts "connected with any privileges." Soviet government officials were to be subjected to espe-

[24] Leonard Schapiro, The Communist Party of the Soviet Union, p. 231, where official figures are cited.
[25] Leninskii Sbornik, Vol. XXXVI, p. 263.

cially severe investigations and cross-examinations by workers. Each communist applying for re-registration required recommendations from other members in good standing "several of whom must definitely be workers belonging to the party for five or seven years." During re-registration, admission to the party was to be closed for six months.

Despite Lenin's favoritism to workers, their ratio in the party membership fell from 57 percent in 1918 to 41 percent in 1921, while that of white-collar workers and intelligentsia rose to 31 percent.[26] Subsequent efforts to correct this anti-proletarian imbalance failed because of the natural desire of workers and peasants to improve their status after joining the party, the more so since they were considered worthy of greater trust and therefore promoted into the waxing bureaucracy. In time, the party, which began as an austere order, became a privileged caste. Not the least of its privileges was the luxury of power. Communists requited privilege with assiduous service, thus strengthening the dictatorship even as its ideology was being corroded by the NEP and its moral fiber by terror. The self-perpetuation of the party and of the dictatorship became a primary end.

The party would remain the effective instrument of government. But Lenin was worried about its Marxist purity. He had cause for concern: Isaac Christoforovich Lalayants, exiled to Samara for underground subversive activities, met Lenin there in 1893. Lenin's family—mother, Anna and her husband Mark Elizarov, Lenin, Maria, and Dmitri—occupied an apartment in the home of a merchant named Ritikov; Lenin introduced Lalayants to all of them and to the revolutionaries in the town.

A quick affinity developed between Lenin and Lalayants and between them and Aleksey Popov who shared their views. The "troika" met to discuss politics either at Lenin's or Popov's house or over beer glasses on a Volga River pier. In later years they met now and then. Lalayants was one of the founders of the Russian Social Democratic Labor Party to which Lenin belonged, worked on the magazine *Iskra*, spent years in Siberian and European exile: the biography of a Russian revolutionist.[27]

On September 5, 1921, Lenin received a letter about Lalayants. He replied the same day: "I am very grateful for the news of Lalayants. I am extremely sorry that he is not in the ranks of the Russian Communist Party. If possible I would ask you to write more fully why he stands outside the party, when he left it, how he lived in Siberia under Kolchak, etc." Lenin was also interested in finding work for Lalayants, "perhaps in Moscow."[28] Lalayants came to see Lenin in the Kremlin on January 12, 1922. He accepted a post in the Commissariat of Education but refused to join the party although Lenin then regarded him as "undoubtedly a devoted revolutionary."[29]

[26] Leonard Schapiro, quoting Soviet figures.
[27] *Vospominaniya*, Vol. 1, *Memoirs of Lalayants*, pp. 100-112.
[28] *Leninskii Sbornik*, Vol. XXXV, p. 277.
[29] *Ibid.*, p. 278.

Lenin clearly felt disturbed by the knowledge that a veteran revolutionary, once a member of the party, rejected membership in the party after it had staged the eagerly desired revolution. Lalayants was not alone. The Soviet state attracted careerists by its opportunities and often repelled believers by its opportunism.

XLI. THE STATESMAN'S SALT

IN THE SMOLNY in mid-November, 1917, Gregory I. Petrovsky was sitting in the waiting room of the Sovnarkom (Cabinet) when, by chance, Lenin entered. "Just in time," Lenin exclaimed as he smacked Petrovsky on the back. "Now we are going to appoint you Commissar for Internal Affairs." That is how Petrovsky became a member of the Soviet government. He had been a Bolshevik deputy of the tsarist Duma.

Nikolai P. Gorbunov, age twenty-five, distributed literature and arms among Petrograd workers before the communist revolution. After November, 1917, he worked in the Smolny giving information to visitors. One day he was summoned by V. D. Bonch-Bruevich, Lenin's secretary. "I came to him and he, without any explanation, dragged me upstairs to the third floor into the small corner room where, in the first days, Vladimir Ilyich worked. . . . I see Vladimir Ilyich who greets me and to my astonishment, says, 'You will be the secretary of the Sovnarkom.' I received no instructions from him at that time. I had not the slightest idea about my job or in general about secretarial duties. Somewhere I confiscated a typewriter on which, for quite a long time, I had to bang out documents with two fingers; no typist could be found." The office furniture consisted of one desk. Lenin called him into the first Cabinet meeting to take the minutes though he knew no shorthand and his spelling was not perfect.[1]

This haphazard method of recruitment survived the Soviet government's infancy. The central apparatus of the communist state suffered for many years from a shortage of qualified civil servants whose loyalties were assumed. Loyalty, never taken for granted, was at such a premium, and class status so highly esteemed, that talent took third place.

Provincial, county, and local governments were pasted together with even less attention to ability. Yet they exercised important functions, and especially during the civil war they operated with considerable autonomy owing

[1] *Vospominaniya*, Vol. 3, pp. 160-166.

to disruption of telephone, telegraph, and railway communication (Russia, notoriously, had few roads and few automobiles or trucks), and because of territorial self-interest. Distances and huge empty spaces and the variegated racial composition of the nation militated against Russian national cohesion and in favor of regional independence. Economic scarcity intensified separatism. Cities and provinces were forced to shift for themselves in obtaining food and other commodities. This was true even in Moscow. In mid-1921 Moscow workingmen with favored ration cards received only a quarter of a pound of bread per day, and bread for centuries has constituted the major part of the Russian's diet. With the advent of the NEP, the Moscow Soviet (municipality) decided that it could no longer depend on the federal Commissariat of Food to supply its population's flour needs and sent expeditions as far afield as the Urals and the Kirghiz Republic in Central Asia to buy grain. Cities, counties, and regions commenced competing with one another and raising prices—a boon for the much-harassed peasantry.

When this problem was laid before Lenin he nevertheless approved of Moscow's initiative. Turning to the unhappy federal Food Commissariat's representative at the discussion, he said, "Enough room remains for us to collect grain. Russia is vast."[2]

To check fissiparous tendencies and excessive regional rivalry, however, there was always "the flaming sword" of the vigilant-punitive Cheka. It supplied the mortar and, if need be, the lead. Felix Djerzhinsky, head of the Cheka, was now in charge of transportation as well as of executions. He supervised each action of the Soviet government and watched for spies and conspiracies in every branch of the state, including the army. The NEP did not diminish his tasks; it added a new dimension: the curbing of Russian capitalists or Nepmen who appeared the moment the rock of war communism was rolled away. Not all of these were of the pint-sized, fly-by-night species. In August, 1921, for instance, the Soviet government agreed to rent small and medium coal mines in the Donets Basin to private entrepreneurs. "These measures helped raise coal output and moderated the coal famine to some extent." Certain communist officials, however, objected to this capitalist infiltration and brought their complaint to Lenin in the Kremlin. He made light of it. "We must," he declared, "expose the panic-makers who try to convince people that the achievements of the November, 1917, revolution are perishing."[3]

Lenin created the Cheka on December 20, 1917, to cope with panic-making counterrevolution, banditry, sabotage, and chaos. One of its first tasks was to stop the "wine pogroms"[4]: the cellar of the Winter Palace and of the villas of the rich and noble were being looted by soldiers, sailors, and workers. Drunkenness led to crime; crime reaching the proportions of administrative breakdown, encouraged the enemies of the Soviets. Lenin chose Djerzhinsky

[2] *Ibid.*, Vol. 4, pp. 264-266.
[3] *Ibid.*, pp. 403-404.
[4] *Ibid.*, pp. 130 and 296.

as Cheka chairman for a good reason: he was a thin austere man, as austere as Lenin, a monk's monk. The Cheka, guardian of the new state, had to be above temptation, above corruption, above corrosive privilege. In time it succumbed to the absolute corruption of power over life and death. Kremlin materialists decided that privileges were the best antidote to the lure of privilege. Thenceforth the secret police enjoyed the best their country could offer in office buildings, housing, food, uniforms, wives, and travel facilities in Russia and Europe.

But although Lenin was a political animal, a powerman, and placed a high evaluation on political instrumentalities like the Cheka and the communist party, he was an economic determinist too, his politics were economically determined, and he knew that in the short run, short because of Russian poverty, the Bolshevik regime could not live on terror and poor administration alone. The people wanted bread, clothing, medicine, minimum comforts, entertainment, education.

Resources, however, were limited. Unemployment was general; the NEP increased it. Nationalized factories, now forced to give a strict accounting of expenditures and income, discharged their superfluous and least efficient workers; many were teen-agers and young men and women. The League of Communist Youth (Komsomol) intervened on their behalf. On July 1, 1921, the Council of Labor and Defense (STO) put the matter on its agenda. Lenin presided. Komsomol spokesmen were invited to attend. In the waiting room, the assistant executive secretary of STO warned that the rules allowed them a maximum of five minutes for their statements, but Lenin, knowing the nervousness of youth before exalted superiors, did not restrict their time. They pleaded for retraining schools and a minimum employment of under-age workers. (In heavy industry it was fixed, in May, 1922, at 7 percent.) Lenin stressed the importance of feeding teen-agers undergoing retraining; he suggested that they receive no less than half the ration given to school children.[5]

The STO met on Wednesdays and Fridays at 6 P.M. Sessions lasted until 10 and sometimes till midnight. The Sovnarkom met on Tuesdays from 6 to .10 P.M. in regular session, and sometimes again during the week for an extraordinary session. Lenin opened the meetings punctually no matter how few members were present. On his instructions, each case of lateness and its extent were noted in the minutes. Cabinet members arriving late received an admonitory shake of the head from Lenin or an oral rebuke. For a second instance of lateness, members were fined a day's salary, and for a third a reprimand in the official press.[6] As a result, lateness and absences fell to zero when Lenin presided—and that was always until he became ill.

Not alone the highest officials participated in Sovnarkom or STO sessions; others came to report, to discuss, and receive orders. The waiting room was

---

[5] *Ibid.*, pp. 463-466.
[6] E. B. Genkina, *Lenin Predsedatel Sovnarkoma i STO (Lenin—Chairman of the Sovnarkom and STO)* (Moscow, 1960), pp. 31-33.

usually filled with people playing chess, reading newspapers, or chatting in the acrid tobacco smoke. Lenin put a stop to this practice; persons who were not members of the supreme bodies but had business with them were to stay in their offices or at home until summoned by telephone or messenger. He had a highly developed (and somewhat un-Russian) sense of order and efficiency. He hated waste.

Lunacharsky recalled that even after he fell ill and still presided at sessions, Lenin laughed as happily and infectiously as before "especially when he caught somebody in a curious contradiction." Old and new revolutionaries laughed with Lenin "over the jokes of the Chairman himself who was very fond of making a pun."[7] (No puns ever quoted.)

During 1921 and 1922 the Sovnarkom held 124 sessions, STO 201. In these two years the Sovnarkom took up 1,221 questions, STO 4,422. For the period between November 1, 1920, and November 1, 1921—figures for other periods are unavailable—23.8 percent of the matters on STO's agenda concerned supplies: food, raw materials, and fuel; 19.6 percent concerned industry, transport, and construction; 12.3 percent labor; 7.5 percent organization. The Sovnarkom, or Cabinet, likewise dealt with organization questions: 20.5 percent of the total on its agenda; 13.7 percent with finance; 10.5 percent with food, raw materials, and fuel.[8] There was considerable overlapping in the work of the two bodies.

Before the revolution the Bolsheviks had no view of Russia's economic future except the further development of private capitalism under which the working class would burgeon. This view survived the revolution. The Kremlin's chief purpose during the NEP period consisted in stimulating industrialization through state capitalism and private capitalism and in permitting private farming and private retail trade to expand as long as they did not become a political hazard to the regime.

This was the frame within which Lenin worked in 1921, 1922, and until March, 1923, when a stroke ended his career though not his life. The peasants were his major concern. They had power: they might refuse to plant above their family needs or to sell to the government; they might impede administration by swelling the tide of banditry, at the time a widespread phenomenon due to poverty and politics. On the other hand, the proletariat, bereft of trade unions, suffering from unemployment and undernourishment, less given to guerrilla warfare than the villager, and more receptive than he to Bolshevik slogans (more interpenetrated by communists) could be depended on to remain resigned or cooperative.

Russian life was primitive. Except in the vast drought areas, the peasant had bread and cucumbers for his family; he could brew vodka from rye, wheat, or potatoes, make tea from herbs; his wife and daughter perhaps made a few homespun articles of clothing. But he needed nails, salt, and matches. He needed much more, but he could not live without salt, and cooking and

[7] *Ibid.*, pp. 37-38.
[8] *Ibid.*, pp. 25 and 27.

smoking without matches, especially in summer when the oven was quenched, created problems. Lenin watched salt production. Russia's output before the war, he noted in a brief memo on April 25, 1921, was 122 million poods. In 1918, work at the chief salt sources ceased. In 1919, 40 million poods were distributed from prewar reserves, in 1920 only 25 million poods. The production program for 1921 was 62 million.[9]

Salt was indispensable to the people and useful to the government. Lenin advised the Ukrainian authorities on August 6, 1921, to sell salt "exclusively" for grain and "under no condition for paper money." He wanted none of the state's useless currency. Secondly, sell salt only to those counties, villages, and householders "that have paid not less than one quarter or one half of their taxes." Thirdly, use the army to collect the tax in kind "so that the military units receive additional allowances at the expense of the local peasants until they pay their tax."[10] Compelling and crude.

In addition to wielding the gavel at frequent Sovnarkom and STO sessions, Lenin presided at the weekly meetings of the five-man Politburo elected by the new Central Committee of the communist party after each party congress. The Politburo was, in fact, the governing body of Russia. So severe was the food situation that on July 9, 1921, the Politburo ordered the transfer of a maximum number of communists to "the food front" even if this meant the closing of branches of the government or entire federal commissariats.

To the same Politburo meeting Lenin submitted an interesting suggestion. Half a million "(and even perhaps as many as a million?)" young men should be conscripted by the army in the famine regions. This would relieve starving families of one mouth to feed. "And secondly, station these half million in the Ukraine so that they can help in food-collecting, being deeply interested in it especially after clearly realizing and feeling the injustice of the gluttony of the rich peasants in the Ukraine."[11]

The Tsar disbanded a disobedient Duma based on limited suffrage. Lenin disbanded the Constituent Assembly elected by universal suffrage. Stolypin and the Bolsheviks tried to force the peasantry into government-desired molds. Traditional Russian compulsion, sharpened into economic instruments, served Lenin too. Money was one of his weapons. In August, 1921, he wrote Professor M. M. Pokrovsky of the Education Commissariat, "Comrade Lunacharsky has returned. At last! Harness him, for Christ's sake, to work with all his energy for technical training, for the integrated labor school, etc. Don't allow any money to go to theaters!" And to Lunacharsky on the 26th of the same month, Lenin wrote, "I can't see you at all, I'm ill. I advise you to bury all theaters. The Commissar of Education should occupy himself not with theaters but with the spread of literacy."[12]

At the meetings of the Politburo and Central Committee the members

[9] *Leninskii Sbornik*, Vol. XXXV, p. 237.
[10] *Ibid.*, p. 270.
[11] *Ibid.*, Vol. XXXVI, pp. 275-276.
[12] *Ibid.*, Vol. XXXV, p. 275.

voted and the majority decided. But Lenin often reversed the majority. Thus, in 1921, a majority of the Politburo rejected Professor Yuri V. Lomonosov, who had worked for the Tsar and (in America) for Kerensky, as chairman of a Soviet commission to buy locomotives abroad. "But Vladimir Ilyich," writes Sophia B. Brichkina, his secretary at the session, "succeeded in persuading them that Y. V. Lomonosov should head the commission."[13]

Lenin was a dictator, but not the kind of dictator Stalin later became. He employed maximum violence with minimum mercy against people he considered his political enemies: those who disputed the monopoly of the communist party and its edicts. Inside the Bolshevik power apparatus, however, he wore out and argued down his communist opponents, at worst he demoted or dismissed them, sometimes excluded them from the party, and on rare occasions banished them, but did not send them to the executioner's dungeon. He dictated by force of will, persistence, vitality, superior knowledge, executive talent, polemical vigor, practical sense, and persuasion. Power itself is a powerful argument, and used by a shrewd politician like Lenin with his prestige and success (he saved the Soviet revolution) it sufficed to overwhelm antagonists in the party. His nimble intelligence impressed, as his indomitable determination discouraged, opponents. They knew he could not be defeated. He would not yield ground after he had made a decision; he never hesitated to make a decision. He was strong, and his political armor had no personal inferiority chinks. Its metal was reinforced by renunciation; nobody could accuse him of wanting anything for himself. No other Bolshevik leader (Trotsky, Rykov, Djerzhinsky, Stalin, Kamenev, Bukharin, or Zinoviev) possessed a fraction of Lenin's self-confidence, the fruit of fanaticism. But he tempered fanaticism with sobriety. He confessed to mistakes because his position was impregnable. He welcomed criticism and thereby disarmed it. Unitary leadership, immune to popular veto, was his supreme law. Russia had known the system for centuries. He perfected it. Lenin sat in the Kremlin because of tsarist and Kerensky laxity. He countenanced none of it.

XLII. ᴆHE THIRD INTERNATIONAL

IT IS FUTILE to argue with the past. Yet one cannot escape a feeling that, given different leadership, the Bolsheviks could have formed a united front before and after the revolution with the Mensheviks and Social Revolutionaries and thereby achieved greater popularity and reduced the need for post-1917 official terror.

[13] *Vospominaniya*, Vol. 4, pp. 468-480.

The same Leninist preference for a communist party monopoly was imposed on the global communist movement with equally harmful results— not only for communists. This emerged at the Third World Congress of the Communist International (Comintern) which sat at Moscow from June 22 to July 12, 1921. "The Italian Question" bulked large in the discussions; Lenin spoke to it on June 28.

Fascism, spurred by a depressed economy and disappointment with Italy's benefits from the World War I peace, was on the march. Black Shirts and communists and socialists had clashed in the peninsula's cities. Common sense dictated the unity of all anti-fascist forces. Moscow ruled otherwise.

Moscow ruled the Comintern. The First Comintern Congress of March-April 1919, was an almost entirely Russian affair; few representatives elected by foreign communist parties attended. The Second Congress met in Petrograd and Moscow from July 19 to August 6, 1920; owing to the Allied blockade and military intervention, many delegates from newly formed communist parties and old semicommunist socialist parties could not reach Soviet Russia. In any case, Moscow, the mother and Mecca of the communist world, would have dominated—and did dominate—the proceedings. Moscow was Lenin. He wrote the nineteen theses,[1] later the famous Twenty-one Conditions, under which a party could attain membership in the Comintern.

The theses and everything else the Russians proposed were "adopted unanimously" except that Serrati, leader of a real party, the radically inclined Italian Socialist Party, abstained on certain matters claiming that what Lenin offered "did not completely correspond to the needs of a revolution in the West."[2] The Italians, moreover, privately suggested a twenty-second condition: that Masons be excluded from communist parties. Lenin and Trotsky spurned the idea. Some Italians thought the Kremlin leaders were secret Masons. Others believed more soberly that they did not understand the significance of this issue in the West.

Lenin's Twenty-one Conditions required parties applying for Comintern membership to expel "revisionists," "opportunists," "lackeys of the bourgeoisie," and similar vague, unscientific categories, and become a band of professionals stripped for the impending world revolution. Lenin felt, and said, that the effects of the First World War, which incubated the Soviet revolution, were still the decisive ingredient of Europe's social-political life. Russo-centric, and absorbed, as he was, in fighting the West (indeed, at the time of the Second Comintern congress, the Russian army had invaded Poland) Lenin saw visions of a red Europe just when it began to turn black.

Although the vision should have vanished when the Third Congress convened in June, 1921, the controversy with the Italians, and to an extent with the Germans, continued to swirl. Between the Second and Third Congresses, the Comintern had registered two triumphs: in September, 1920, a Congress

[1] Lenin, *Sochineniya*, Second ed., Vol. XXV, pp. 321-325.
[2] *Ibid.*, editorial notation, p. 622.

of the Peoples of the East met in Baku which Chicherin once called "a finger pointing to Asia." Zinoviev, Karl Radek, and Bela Kun presided over the proceedings, apparently on the assumption that Christians had less in common with the largely Moslem gathering of 1,891 delegates from thirty-seven nationalities. Before the revolution, Lenin once took pencil in hand and calculated that the imperialists with one-quarter of a billion inhabitants ruled colonies with a population of two and a half billion. This was Moscow's message. "The infantry of the East will reinforce the cavalry of the West." On the evening of September 1, Zinoviev, having harangued his colorful audience for several hours, reached a dramatic climax: "The Communist International turns today to the people of the East and says to them, 'Brothers, we summon you to a Holy War, first of all against British imperialism.' "

Every man in the hall jumped to his feet. They drew studded daggers from their twisted belt sashes, Damascan swords from their scabbards, revolvers from their holsters, and lifting them on high, shouted, "Jehad, Jehad. We swear, we swear." (A permanent organization was set up and future assemblies of a similar nature were planned, but the first was the last.)[3]

Zinoviev's second victory of the year was his unexpected, unprecedented appearance at Halle, where he addressed the Independent Socialist Party of Germany for four hours and succeeded in splitting off a considerable segment to reinforce the infant German Communist Party.

"Split" was the slogan of the Third Comintern Congress. The Congress heard a startling complaint from the Germans: "Not for a second do we disregard the difficult situation in which the Russian Soviet Government finds itself as a result of the delay in the progress of the world revolution. At the same time we foresee the danger that out of these difficulties there might emerge a real or imaginary contradiction between the interests of revolutionary world proletariat and the temporary interests of Soviet Russia."[4] Decades passed (until the Sino-Soviet dispute) before any communist again dared to suggest, even in the gentle understatement of the Germans, that the Kremlin might be tying world communism to the chariot of Russian nationalism. At the First Comintern Congress, in 1919, the Russian Bolshevik Party was represented by Lenin, Trotsky, Bukharin, and by Foreign Commissar Georgi Chicherin.[5] One remembers a "friendly cartoon" in *Pravda* by Deni showing Chicherin's embarrassment at an electrically charged Zinoviev speech calling for world revolution. It belonged to the period when the Soviet government, creature of the Russian Communist Party, endeavored to dissociate itself in diplomatic notes from the Comintern, likewise a creature of the Russian Communist Party. At birth, however, the umbilical cord, in the person of

[3] Louis Fischer, *The Soviets in World Affairs*, Vintage Books (New York, 1960), pp. 205-206.

[4] Lenin, *op. cit.*, Third ed., Vol. XXVI, editorial note, p. 673.

[5] Leon Trotsky, *The First Five Years of the Communist International* (New York, 1945), Vol. One, p. 18.

Chicherin, was in full view, and all his polemical skill failed to conceal it in subsequent years. For government mother and Comintern child wore an undeniable resemblance, and it was only natural for the weak, harassed parent to avail itself of the services, however paltry, of her offspring. The new non-Soviet communist parties needed the money, the facilities, and above all the prestige of the first communist state, and they paid for these in the coin of serfdom and everything that came in its train: loss of identity, death of revolutionary spirit, and aid to the advent of fascism in Italy and Germany. Moscow was a matriarchate which practiced infanticide.

Especially the Italians bridled at wearing the red badge of cowardice Moscow wanted to pin on them. "What is the meaning of the cock-and-bull stories of Serrati and his Socialist Party that the Russians only desire that they be imitated?" Lenin exclaimed in his June 28 speech. "We demand quite the opposite." Lenin knew that the Italian socialists, though inclined toward communism, balked at subjugation to Moscow. During the party conference in Reggio Emilia in the fall of 1920, the delegate from the Comintern was greeted with sarcastic cries of, "Long Live the Pope," and while he spoke some delegates unloosed "a pigeon in the halls to caricature Zinoviev's ambassador as a message carrier without a will of his own."[6]

No sooner, however, had Lenin paid lip service to the principle of independence than he asked the Italians to imitate the Russians. "Comrade Lazzari [a colleague of Serrati's] has said," Lenin declared, " 'We are in a preparatory period.' " Preparatory to a revolution and the establishment of the dictatorship of the proletariat over Italy. "That is the utter truth," Lenin agreed. "You are in a preparatory period. The first stage of that period is the break with the Mensheviks like that which we carried out in 1903 with our Mensheviks." The Italians were divided among socialists, centrists, and communists. "We in Russia," Lenin asserted on July 1, "already have considerable political experience in the struggle against centrists. As early as fifteen years ago, we fought our opportunists, and centrists, as well as the Mensheviks, and won not only against the Mensheviks, but against the semianarchists."

In February, 1917, Lenin said, the Bolsheviks "were a minority compared with the Mensheviks." But "we are organized and disciplined Marxists. . . . The leftist phrases of the Italians have bored us Russians to nausea. We are organization men. . . . A quite small party is sufficient to attract the masses. In certain moments there is no need for large organizations." And, sensing unspoken criticism, Lenin added, "Perhaps we are being accused of preferring to keep such gentlemen"—Mensheviks, SRs, and Anarchists—"in jail. But without that a dictatorship is impossible."

In these speeches to the Third Congress Lenin had condemned the Italian socialists for occupying some factories. That to him was anarchism. In the same addresses he taught them from Russian experience how to prepare for a

[6] Ypsilon, *Patterns for World Revolution* (Chicago-New York, 1947), p. 54.

communist revolution and a proletarian dictatorship. In nothing did he allude to the danger of Mussolini's progress to power. Mussolini, the former socialist, former editor of the socialist daily *Avanti*, was training his Black Shirts for the seizure of authority in Rome. Successive Italian governments were weak. Instead of telling the Italian socialists and communists to unite for resistance to fascism they were to split and adhere to the Comintern. Lenin said, "I and all of us and the Russian delegation must insist that not one letter of the twenty-one theses be altered." Turati, an old comrade of Serrati, was branded an "opportunist" by Lenin. He had to be expelled before the Italians earned admission to Mecca-Moscow.

The theses were not altered. The party split. The Lenin-pure Italian communists joined the Comintern. Mussolini "marched" on Rome in a sleeping-car compartment and seized the state without a struggle. Thousands of Italian communists and socialists went to jail and exile.

At the root of this folly—repeated almost exactly during Hitler's ascent—lay the apparently ineradicable communist need to prophesy the defeat of the enemy, and, hence, to underestimate his potential for survival and growth. Soviet Russia, moreover, inherited from tsarist Russia a sense of inferiority which the communists converted into the myth of invincibility. Chancellor Count Golovkin, conferring the title of emperor upon Tsar Peter the Great on October 22, 1721, said, "By thy untiring labours and by thy sole leadership" —cult of personality—"we have stepped forth from the darkness of insignificance and ignorance on to the road of glory and have joined in equality with the civilized States of Europe."[7] Russians have always been ashamed and proud of their country, so ashamed as to conceal it behind "Potemkin Villages" of propaganda exaggeration, so ashamed as to feel they must aspire to equality with the civilized states of the West, yet so proud as to think it was unique and could lead the West. In the Comintern the Kremlin believed it had an instrument for leadership of the West, an instrument, to boot, which would undermine the capitalist enemy. The Bolshevik revolution failed to spark the world revolution. Italy might. In reflective moments, Lenin knew Italy had neither food nor fuel to withstand the trials of revolution. But the acceptance of foreign parties of revolution as their sole goal was, first, a confirmation of Bolshevik wisdom and, also, a means of linking them to the Comintern, to the Kremlin, to Russia's fate, and of blocking the reforms required by an evolving capitalism. The more the prospect of revolution receded the more raucous grew the voices of prophecy and the closer non-Soviet communists were forced to serve Soviet foreign policy.

Lenin wrote a letter to the Comintern Chairman Gregory Zinoviev, on June 11, 1921, saying "I unconditionally insist" that Otto V. Kuusinnen, a Finn who later became a Soviet citizen, "and only he (that is, not Bela Kun)" deliver the report to the forthcoming Congress. Because "he knows and

---

[7] Ian Grey, *Peter the Great. Emperor of all Russia* (Philadelphia and New York, 1960). Quotation preceding Chap. One.

THINKS," and Lenin then added in German: *"Was sehr selten ist unter den Revolutionaeren"* (a very rare thing among revolutionaries).[8] With this attitude he could not have expected much of the Comintern or much opposition to his absolute control. It was a creaking fifth wheel to the Russian cart.

Bela Kun had earned Lenin's disrespect for failing to stay in power in Hungary; the revolution's collapse there was laid to Kun's collaboration with social democrats. A Moscow sin. Nevertheless, Bela Kun served as the Kremlin's agent in Germany at the time of the March, 1921, abortive communist uprising. Doomed to die before it started, this frail thrust for power raised hopes in Moscow which withered overnight. Among the German communist leaders who had advised against it was Paul Levi. Irate, he planned to resign from the leadership and expose the criminal adventure in a pamphlet. Lenin wrote him and Clara Zetkin a letter in German on April 16, 1921,[9] in response to theirs. Either honestly or disingenuously, Lenin washed his hands of the affair: "As far as the recent strikes and insurrectionary movement in Germany are concerned, I have read absolutely nothing. That a representative of the Comintern Executive"—Bela Kun—"advocated stupid tactics, excessively leftist, immediate action 'in order to help the Russians,' I readily believe: this representative is often too leftist." But "Why not wait? The Congress meets here on June 1. Why not a private talk here *before* the Congress? Without public controversy, without resignations, without pamphlets about differences. We have so few tested leaders."

Levi, refusing to be mollified, resigned, and attacked.

Thus, the Comintern rattled along during Lenin's lifetime and, until its demise in 1943, ever loyal to the motto, "In order to help the Russians," and in so doing usually helping reactionaries, not Russia.

XLIII. SOVIET FOREIGN POLICY

LENIN rejected sociology because it studied individual cases, not class causes, and argued, in an article written at the age of twenty-five, that Russian populists (Narodniks) related sociology to "the proposition, theoretically without content, that personality makes history." Yet when communist party members fell ill under the strain of unexpected turns in Soviet policy, he recommended "an attentive-individualized relationship, at times even a kind of cure, for representatives of the so-called opposition who have undergone a

---

[8] *Leninskii Sbornik*, Vol. XXXVI, p. 259-260.
[9] *Ibid.*, pp. 220-223.

psychological crisis in connection with their Soviet [government] or party careers. It is necessary to try to tranquilize them, explain matters to them in a comradely manner and find work for them . . . which suits their psychological peculiarities." Lenin's recommendation for psychotherapy was accepted by the Politburo on October 26, 1920.[1] Politics permitting, he endeavored to husband the regime's human resources. In the midst of extinguishing careers he took steps to save some.

As the manager of a giant enterprise Lenin knew he could not be rigid, he had to maneuver, to be one thing now and another later. For the spread of revolution he ordered the Red Army's advance into Poland in the summer of 1920. But he ordered restraint in the reconquest of parts of the former tsarist empire. Thus the Politburo, on November 27, 1920, approved Lenin's written proposal "To adopt toward Georgia, Armenia, Turkey, and Persia the most conciliatory policy, that is, a policy directed above all to the avoidance of war." Georgia was then governed by the hated Mensheviks who leaned on the hated British. Armenian nationalists had set up an anticommunist government in Erivan. Yet Lenin advised against attacking either: "Not to make our task an invasion of Georgia, or Armenia, or Persia," he repeated for emphasis, because he knew that Georgian and Armenian communists in Moscow were advocating just that. In addition, he urged special caution in Moslem Azerbaijan. (The Red Army captured Baku, Azerbaijan's capital, on April 27, 1920.) He decreed reinforced communist control over Azerbaijan and the Caspian Sea and, specifically, the employment of "a maximum number of Moslem-communists."[2]

In September, passion: the summons to a Holy War in Central Asia; in November, caution: instructions to eschew military action in the same area. Nothing obliges statesmen to be consistent.

Conditions nevertheless conduced to limited Bolshevik successes in east and west. British intervention in Soviet Russia was variously motivated, depending on the man who shaped policy. Churchill wanted to overthrow the Soviets. Foreign Secretary Lord Curzon, student of Persia, former Viceroy of India, continued the traditional policy of keeping "the Russian bear" far from the Khyber Pass by maintaining British influence in Central Asia. The Soviet revolution enabled England to expand this influence into Azerbaijan and Georgia, later into Georgia alone.

But England was eager to heal her war wounds. Pressures were brought to bear on Curzon to withdraw British troops from Georgia and the Georgian port of Batum on the Black Sea. With strikes at home, confusion at the Paris Peace Conference, and turmoil in India, Ireland, and Egypt, Prime Minister Lloyd George desired the reduction of Britain's global commitments. In 1919 Sir Henry Wilson, Chief of the Imperial Staff, agreed to withdraw from Siberia and north Russia but "I would strengthen our position on the line

---

[1] *Leninskii Sbornik*, Vol. XXXVI, pp. 137-138.
[2] *Ibid.*, p. 144.

Batoum-Baku-Krasnovodsk-Merv."[3] This was a Curzon line. Time, however, wrought further linear shrinkage. Lloyd George persuaded Italy to replace England in Georgia. Rome seemed sympathetic. But the move aroused antagonism and contributed to the fall of the Orlando Cabinet. "When I assumed the direction of the government in June, 1919," writes Francesco Nitti, "an Italian military expedition was under orders for Georgia. The English troops, who were in small number, were withdrawing. Italy had, with the consent of the Allies and partly of her own desire, prepared a big military expedition. . . . Georgia is a country of extraordinary natural resources"—an extraordinary exaggeration—"and it was thought that she would be able to furnish Italy with a great number of raw materials which she lacked." Nitti vetoed Italy's involvement.[4]

The British Cabinet discussed the issue on September 2, 1919. "Curzon favored our leaving a brigade there. So did Milner; but Bonar Law, [Sir Edward] Montagu, Austen [Chamberlain] and I"—Sir Henry Wilson— "opposed this."[5]

The British garrison left Batum on July 7, 1920; the city reverted to the Georgian Menshevik Republic.

Deprived of foreign military support, Georgia would have been an easy target for a Russian assault if the Red Army were not otherwise engaged—in Poland; in the Crimea against Wrangel. Its hand was free early in 1921. War Commissar Trotsky pressed for action. So did Stalin and Sergo Orjonekidze whose Georgian blood intensified their Bolshevik aggressiveness. The Red Army invaded, and in February, 1921, communists took over Menshevik Georgia.

Events in little Georgia mirrored a larger situation: the era of violent Western intervention in Soviet affairs was at an end. In London, Leonid B. Krassin negotiated with the British government on commerce, debts, and credits. In Riga, Adolf A. Yoffe labored to conclude a permanent peace treaty with Poland.

Yoffe felt unhappy. The Kremlin had been using him as "a trouble-shooter," shifting him from one difficult post to another. His nerves wore thin. He aired his complaints in a letter to Lenin. Lenin, suggesting therapy, replied on March 17, 1921.[6] "First, you are mistaken in reiterating (repeatedly) that 'I am the Central Committee' " of the communist party. "It is possible to write this only in a condition of great nervous irritation and overstrain." Lenin cited instances when he was outvoted by the old Central Committee to which Yoffe belonged. "Then why be so nervous as to write AN ABSOLUTELY IMPOSSIBLE, ABSOLUTELY IMPOSSIBLE phrase that I am the Central Committee. That is overstrain.

[3] Major-General Sir C. E. Callwell, *Field-Marshal Sir Henry Wilson*, Vol. II, p. 188.
[4] Francesco S. Nitti, *Peaceless Europe* (London, 1922), p. 147.
[5] Callwell, *op. cit.*, Vol. II, p. 219.
[6] *Leninskii Sbornik*, Vol. XXXVI, pp. 208-209.

"Secondly, I have not a trace of dissatisfaction with you or distrust in you. Nor have the members of the Central Committee, as far as I know, and talked with them, and saw their attitude toward you.

"Then how is the matter to be explained? By the fact that *fate has tossed you about*. . . . You are one of our first and best diplomats." Good officials have to be transferred from one key post to another. "If you think of this coldbloodedly you will see that this is the truth.

"You were not elected to the VTSIK?" (Central Executive Committee of the government.) "Just ask Trotsky how many times the opinion and decision of the Central Committee" of the party "wavered in principle on this question. Many times! 'Democracy' *compelled* the selection of a maximum number of new members. . . .

"My *personal* view, in complete frankness: (1) You are in serious need of rest. . . . Consider whether it would not be better abroad, in a sanitorium. In Russia it would not be good. . . .

"Rest. Then come to Moscow. We'll talk. . . . Your Lenin."

Many chief executives have encountered similar problems. Communists are not immune.

The absorption of Georgia and the relaxation of outside pressures on Soviet Russia that it reflected gave Moscow greater maneuverability in foreign affairs. In mid-1921 Lenin, surveying the world scene, saw "a certain equilibrium . . . between bourgeois society, the international bourgeoisie as a whole, on the one hand, and Soviet Russia—on the other." The armed struggle between them had ceased. But this was "a relative equilibrium, a most unstable equilibrium." The breathing spell might suddenly end. The Red Army had to be strengthened; "there is no other way. Now in relation to our practical policy" —he was addressing the Third Comintern Congress on July 5—"the fact that some equilibrium exists in the international situation has a certain significance, but only in the sense that we must recognize that the revolutionary movement, to be sure, has progressed, but that the development of the international revolution during this year has not advanced in a straight line as much as we had expected." When the Bolsheviks made the revolution in 1917, "We thought: either the international revolution comes to our aid, and then our victory is fully secured, or we will do our modest revolutionary work in the consciousness that, in the event of defeat, we will nevertheless have served the cause of revolution and that our revolution would help other revolutions. . . . Even before the revolution and also after it we thought: either immediately, or at worst very soon, revolution will come in other, more developed capitalist countries, or, if this is not so, we must perish." Within three minutes he repeated this idea three times, almost entirely in the same words.

Lenin then advised his foreign-communist audience to observe the million and a half or two million Russian bourgeois persons who had fled abroad. The Russian people within Russia had suffered at the hands of the bourgeoisie, "nevertheless, if we cold-bloodedly evaluate the organization and the political clarity of the views of the Russian counterrevolutionary emigration living abroad we will be convinced that the class consciousness of the bourgeoisie far exceeds the class consciousness of the exploited and oppressed."

Lenin was in a pessimistic mood.

At this point he splashed more black paint on the picture: "But in addition to the class of exploiters, there exists in all countries—perhaps with the exception of England—a class of small producers and of small farmers. The chief problem facing the revolution is the struggle against these two groups." The exploiters can simply be expropriated and driven out, "which is what we have done." But in most capitalist countries the small producers and small farmers constitute "approximately 30 to 45 percent of the population. If we add to them the petty bourgeois element of the working class we get even more than 50 percent. They cannot be expropriated or driven out."

Was Lenin revising his concept of revolution? Did he intend to imply that as the weight of the middle class, including middle-class workers, rises the prospects of revolution grow dimmer? In the next sentence Lenin suggests just such a conclusion: "Theoretically, all Marxists solved this problem well and easily; but theory and practice—are two different things, and to solve this problem practically or theoretically is not at all the same. We definitely know that we made big mistakes." But Soviet experience would be "beneficial for the coming proletarian revolutions and they can better prepare themselves technically for the solution of this problem." He gave no indication how.

Lenin then dilated on Soviet economic difficulties and policy changes and alluded to foreign socialist criticism of the Russian dictatorship. He asked: "According to what principle should we have acted? According to the principle of justice or of majority? No. We must behave practically. We must distribute [privations] in such a manner as to preserve the proletarian government. That is our only principle."

This brought Lenin to the question of concessions to foreign capitalists: "We recognize quite openly that in a system of state capitalism, concessions mean a tribute to capitalism. But we gain time," time to extend the use of electricity. The Russian peasant in German prisoner-of-war camps had learned "what constitutes the real basis of life, of cultured life. Twelve thousand kilowatts are a modest beginning." The development of heavy industry was the only road to peasant plenty. The Russian peasantry had been reached by Soviet propaganda. This demonstrates that "the broad masses—and in more advanced countries too—can learn more from their own practical experience than from books." At the time of the Kronstadt revolt, "Ferment among the peasants was very strong, discontent also dominated among workers. They were tired and exhausted. There is a limit to human strength. They starved three years, but it is impossible to starve four or five years." The Mensheviks and Social Revolutionaries tried to make political capital out of the situation. Their slogan was "Soviets Without Bolsheviks." The government would "continue its merciless struggle against these elements. Dictatorship is a condition of intensified war. We are in just such a situation. . . . And we say, 'In war we act as in war: We promise neither freedom nor democracy of any kind.' . . . This," he concluded—his farewell sentence to the Third Comintern Congress—"is what I wanted to tell the comrades about our tactics, the tactics of the Russian Communist Party."[7]

It is probably legitimate to suspect that his own fatigue and oncoming illness as well as the delay in the approach of the world revolution combined to sharpen Lenin's perception of reality and the desire to teach the Comintern delegates a lesson in the supremacy of practicality over theory. He also hoped to induce in them an appreciation of Russia's problems and of her consequent deviation from the course that dogmatic revolutionists might expect of a revolution. In the future they would be called upon, he knew, to defend many distasteful Soviet acts in domestic and foreign affairs; he was saying, in effect, Comrades of the Comintern, governing is a cruel task, and no doctrinal scripture helps.

The original concept of the Third International was a Moscow powerhouse supplying a European or perhaps a world grid that would spark revolutions. But soon the Bolsheviks became aware of Russian uniqueness; the red specter seen hovering over hemispheres had dissolved. Rituals and liturgy connected with the first purpose remained. Zeal, however, sought new outlets—chiefly in building power organizations. The Soviet government thought it had useful agents. More often than not the foreign communist parties were an awkward liability to the Soviets who were everywhere accused of conducting subversive activities. Similarly, the Kremlin was an impediment to the foreign communist parties; the tie to a remote nation whose acts, bad or good, they glorified, branded them as passive tools and political fools. But they needed Moscow for morale and money, and Moscow needed them to keep alive the deceptive dream of world revolution, sometimes too as an aid in espionage. The Comintern gave the Soviet government a sense of a messianic mission that hallowed sordid deeds. Mutual embarrassment notwithstanding, therefore, divorce between the Russian state and the Third International was unthinkable. They could not prosper together, neither could they live apart. (Later, empire replaced the Comintern.)

Lenin did not address the Comintern Congress after July 5, but on July 11 he delivered a significant speech in German to a conclave of members of the German, Polish, Czechoslovak, Hungarian, and Italian delegations to the Congress. He prepared himself well for this occasion. He wrote out a twelve-point outline and a four-point conclusion, and then a seven-point digest of the outline. The outline, digest, and speech were kept secret until 1959.

The March, 1921, attempt at a communist revolution in Germany had been a farcical fiasco with tragic results, and Paul Levi's pamphlet, *Unser Weg. Wider den Putschismus* (*Our Way. Against Putschism*), attacking

[7] Lenin, *Sochineniya*, Second ed., Vol. XXVI, pp. 450-465.

that dismal adventure had struck home in the Kremlin. Lenin wished to avoid repetitions of premature revolutions without, however, discouraging Europe's communists altogether.

He was encouraged, he said, by three recent events: the strike of Berlin's municipal employees, the strike of the textile workers of Lille, and the third "and most important fact": In Rome, a demonstration of 50,000 working-men against fascism, "communists, socialists, and also republicans," including 5,000 war veterans in uniform. "This shows that there is more fuel in Europe than we had thought. . . . Europe is pregnant with revolution."

But "it is impossible to work out the calendar of revolution in advance. We in Russia can hold out not only five years but longer." (Hence, he inti-mated, they need not hurry.) "Don't be afraid to say that *all of us* returned from Moscow (after the Third Congress of the Communist International) more cautious, wiser, more judicious, 'more rightist.' *Strategically, this is correct.* The more to the right now, the nearer the target tomorrow: il faut reculer, pour mieux sauter. It may be 'tomorrow' but it may be in two or three years. Don't get nervous. . . . Our only strategy now is to become stronger, and therefore wiser, more judicious, 'more opportunistic,' and we must say this to the masses. But after we have won over the masses thanks to our judiciousness, we can then apply the tactics of the offense."

In sum: "Don't be nervous, don't be afraid to 'be late.' . . . It is possible to 'put a brake' on 'actions' at any given moment, BUT we must be IMPLA-CABLE in *revolutionary* propaganda."[8]

What ideas did Lenin's speech plant in the confused minds of the dele-gates? At least they knew that the command was a definite "reculer" now and a vague "sauter" for the indefinite future. Meanwhile, the "opportunism" Lenin counseled would enable the Comintern in the coming years to coun-tersign every zigzag of Soviet foreign policy.

Addressing the Comintern delegates in July, 1921, Lenin could not have had in mind an event which occurred in January, 1923, but he must have envisaged the possibility. Adolf A. Yoffe, Soviet "troubleshooter" in Ger-many, later in Riga, was "troubleshooting" in China in 1922. In January, 1923, he met Chinese President Dr. Sun Yat-sen in Shanghai and there, on January 26, they issued a joint statement. Dr. Sun declared that the Soviet system could not be introduced into China "because the conditions do not exist here for the successful establishment of Communism or Socialism. Mr. Yoffe absolutely agrees with this view."[9] Yoffe acted with the Kremlin's, presumably with Lenin's, approval.

[8] *Leninskii Sbornik*, Vol. XXXVI, pp. 278-284.

[9] Translated from the fortnightly bulletin of the Soviet political representative in Peking, dated Feb. 1-15, 1923, which I saw in the archives of the Commissariat of Foreign Affairs in Moscow. The document, however, does not appear in *Dokumenty Vneshnei Politiki SSSR (Documents on the Foreign Policy of the USSR), Vol. 6, November 20, 1922-December 21, 1923* (Moscow, 1962). Published by the Ministry of Foreign Affairs of the USSR. The joint declaration is quoted in my *The Soviets in World Affairs*, Vol. II, pp. 540-541, and in the Vintage Books edition (New York, 1960), p. 397.

The Sun-Yoffe declaration (Moscow felt ashamed of it in subsequent years) was true; a communist revolution in China would have been premature. But truth is not the major preoccupation of international politics. Moscow made the truthful avowal in order to facilitate normal government-to-government relations with China. The revolutionary birthright was sold for a mess of diplomacy. The pursuit of foreign revolution, even in under-developed China, had become a minor Moscow theme. Thereafter the Kremlin supported Dr. Sun and Chiang Kai-shek with a view, chiefly, to impeding Japanese penetration and substituting Russian for Western influence. And where it was possible, without inviting punishment from a strong country, to implant Soviet power, Lenin did that too: late in 1921, Red Army units entered isolated, defenseless, anti-Chinese Outer Mongolia; a treaty was signed with Mongolian puppets, and the land of the Mongols was severed from the bloated body of China. Nor did Moscow relinquish to China the Chinese Eastern Railway which the Tsar's government had built across Manchuria. This policy of imperialism combined with revolutionary restraint probably sowed the seeds of subsequent frictions between Red China and Red Russia.

The motives of the Soviet government, like the motives of most governments, were mixed. As the author of a famous book on imperialism Lenin appeared to all the world in the golden armor of anti-imperialism. Yet though anti-imperialism and self-determination are opposite sides of the same coin, the Kremlin managed to so interpret self-determination on the territory of the tsarist empire as to make it tantamount to no self-determination and, in the case of Menshevik Georgia, for example, to the annexation of a state that had seceded from Russia. Early Soviet anti-imperialism, therefore, was partly ideological and largely a realistic necessity: a weak country cannot be imperialistic in the face of objections from a great power. Lenin made a virtue of this frailty. He dramatically renounced the imperialist gains and aims of tsarism. At the same time he showed a sharp interest in former tsarist territories.

"The first three months of its existence," wrote Foreign Commissar Chicherin, "was the period of revolutionary political offensive, when the Soviet government freely sent forth its revolutionary slogans to the toiling masses of the whole world. . . . But the first period of exhilarating victories was soon over."[10] Came the Brest-Litovsk peace conference, the German offensive into Soviet Russia, and in November, 1918, Germany's defeat in the First World War. Action followed immediately on Estonia, Latvia, and Lithuania. The moment the Kaiser's government fell, these three former tsarist provinces were declared under Soviet rule. The Soviet government of Estonia announced its birth in a manifesto dated November 29, 1918 (no place): "The

[10] George Chicherin, *Two Years of Foreign Policy*, Soviet Russia Pamphlets, No. 3 (New York, The Russian Soviet Government Bureau, 1920), pp. 3-4. Also Moscow *Izvestia*, Nov. 6 to 13, 1919.

international proletarian revolution has arrived."[11] On December 17, 1918 (no place), the Soviet government of Latvia "In the name of the World Revolution," proclaimed its existence.[12] The Lithuanian government had done likewise the day before (no place).[13] It is likely that each of these governments administered nothing more than a room or two lent it in Moscow by the Kremlin. On December 24, 1918, the Soviet government of Russia declared its "readiness to render all indispensable aid and support" to these governments,[14] and a "Congress of the Soviets of Lithuania," meeting at an undisclosed location between February 17 and 21, 1919, decided to unite with Byelorussia, already a part of the Russian federation, and to negotiate with Soviet Latvia, Estonia, and the Ukraine to enter into a federation with Russia.[15] But Russia's arm was too short, circumstances were not propitious, non-Soviet governments soon prevailed in the three Baltic countries, and Moscow recognized their independence and dealt with them as independent states until, by the terms of the Soviet-Nazi Pacts of August-September, 1939, they were reabsorbed into the Russian reich.

It would require an exercise in expert hairsplitting to determine whether the attempted sovietization of the three small Baltic countries in 1918-1919 stemmed from Russian nationalism or world-revolutionary impulses. The fact that Stalin annexed these states when Moscow possessed the power to do so might be taken as proof that the earlier motive too was imperialistic. But it is not conclusive. The chaos that reigned after Germany's 1918 defeat presented the Russian government with an attractive opportunity which its members probably never stopped to analyze. Lenin in those heady days might well have thought that the revolutionary lunge into Europe had commenced. Objectively, both labels—attempt at revolutionary expansion and at reoccupation of tsarist territory—fit Lenin's moves in the Baltic region in 1918 and 1919.

In Central Asia, however, the region of historic rivalry between British lion and Russian bear, Soviet policy marched under signs marked "Withdraw" and "Renounce." All acts were avowedly anti-imperialist and couched in revolutionary phraseology, with Britain still the target. Chicherin, Lenin's executive officer and, at times, mentor in foreign affairs, especially Asian affairs, was very Russian and very anti-British. In private conversations he repeatedly prophesied the end of the British Empire. The Dominions—Canada, Australia, New Zealand, and South Africa—he used to say in the 1920's, will soon desert England and leave her a shriveled, second-rate power. He hoped Russia might make a contribution to this end by undermining the British raj in the realms lying between India and Soviet territories in Central Asia and the Caucasus, chiefly Afghanistan and Persia.

[11] *Dokumenty Vneshei Politiki SSSR*, Vol. I, pp. 587-588.
[12] *Ibid.*, pp. 616-618.
[13] *Ibid.*, pp. 612-616.
[14] *Ibid.*, pp. 627-628.
[15] *Ibid.*, Vol. II, pp. 76-77.

The King of Afghanistan, Emir Habibullah, was assassinated "by an un-known miscreant" in February, 1919. On February 21 the Emir's third son, Amanullah Khan, succeeded to the throne. He had sympathized during the war with the Young Afghan movement which was anti-British and pro-Ger-man, and his father, Habibullah, sentenced him to death. The prince evaded the execution and waited.

On April 7, 1919, King Amanullah addressed a message to "His Majesty, the President of the Great Russian State" (Kalinin, the ex-peasant), inform-ing him of his coronation, calling him "my great and kind friend" who, together with his "comrades," had, as "the friends of mankind," taken upon themselves "the honorable and noble task of caring for the peace and wel-fare of men and have proclaimed the principle of the freedom and equality of the countries and peoples of the entire world." The Afghan government offered to establish relations with the Soviets.

Kalinin and Lenin replied on May 27, congratulating the new monarch, and adding, "May the aspiration of the Afghan people to follow the Russian example be the best guarantee of the strength and independence of the Afghan state. . . . The establishment of permanent diplomatic relations between the two great peoples opens a broad possibility of mutual aid against any encroachment by rapacious foreigners"—read England—"on the free-dom and property of others."[16]

Lenin received the new Afghan ambassador at 7 P.M., October 14, 1919. Striding to greet him, Lenin exclaimed, "I am very happy to see in the red capital of the Workers-Peasants Government the representative of the friendly Afghan people who suffer and are struggling against the imperialist yoke."

"I extend a friendly hand to you," the ambassador rejoined, "and hope that you will aid the entire East in liberating itself from the oppression of European imperialism."[17]

The Afghans' flowery Oriental language and the Soviets' slogans of anti-imperialism rang true to the old tones of Anglo-Russian rivalry. Afghanistan and the Soviets had the same interest in expelling England from Central Asia.

On August 18, 1907—old calendar—the Tsar's government, still suffering from the hangover of defeat by Japan, had signed an Anglo-Russian conven-tion which left Afghanistan outside the Russian sphere of influence and at least in principle, therefore, inside the British sphere. Both contracting par-ties had agreed not to interfere in Tibet. But they divided Persia. They rec-ognized the north as a Russian sphere of influence, the south as a British sphere, and the zone between as nobody's sphere.

Commissar of Foreign Affairs Trotsky informed the Persian government on January 14, 1918, that Soviet Russia considered the 1907 convention "once and forever annulled." All privileges enjoyed by the tsarist govern-

[16] *Ibid.*, pp. 174-175.
[17] *Ibid.*, pp. 261-262.

ment and by tsarist agents and Russians still operating in Persia were declared void. Tehran acknowledged the Soviet act in a formal note; British troops stood on Persian soil.[18]

Soviet withdrawal created a power vacuum. The result was, in the words of Lord Curzon's authorized biographer, "a Persia picketed on all sides by British forces."[19] From Persia, British troops fanned out into the Caucasus and Russian Turkestan. But the defeat of White General Denikin on land and on the Caspian Sea brought the Soviet Russians to the Persian port of Enzeli (now Pahlevi). The British retired. Subsequently, Red Army units, under orders from Georgian communists, notably Stalin, entrenched themselves in northern Persia and established the "Soviet Republic of Ghilan" which Lenin and Chicherin ultimately succeeded in dismantling. Persia, with no proletariat, they contended, was not ready for a communist revolution. The "revolution" Stalin had exported Lenin reimported.

War Minister Riza Khan Pahlevi, later self-appointed Shah and founder of the new Pahlevi dynasty, staged a coup d'état on February 21, 1921, and formed his own Cabinet which immediately abrogated the Anglo-Persian agreement of August, 1919, and on February 26 signed the Soviet-Persian Treaty. In it, the Soviet government renounced all conventions and agreements concluded by the former government of Russia with third powers "to the detriment of Persia." But Article VI stipulated that if third powers sent military forces into Persia with a view to imperil the territory of Soviet Russia and "if the Persian government, after a warning from the Russian Soviet government, proves unable to repel this danger, the Russian Soviet government shall have the right to introduce its army into the territory of Persia in order to, in the interests of self-defense, take the necessary military measures."[20] This meant: if a British army re-enters Persia a Soviet army would too.

Riza was neither a revolutionary nor a reformer. He was a ruler type, and he realized that to rule he must rid Persia of the two powers that had dominated her. Amanullah fancied himself a Peter the Great of Central Asia. He dreamed of modernizing Afghanistan, removing the veil from women, curbing the might of the obscurantist Moslem mullahs. But he was a weakling ahead of his time, and the forces of stagnation ousted him and sent him into well-paid exile in Italy. Kemal Pasha Ataturk, by contrast, was a ruler and a revolutionary reformer, a strong person, a dictator with enormous energy, a professional soldier, and a political doctor. In 1853 Nicholas I called Turkey "the sick man of Europe." The imperial ambitions reflected in the Tsar's dictum did not diminish its truth. Turkey had commenced to lose its virility and therefore its possessions even before the First World War.

---

[18] Ibid., Vol. I, pp. 90-93.
[19] The Earl of Ronaldshay, The Life of Lord Curzon (London, 1928), Vol. III, p. 212.
[20] Dokumenty Vneshei Politiki SSSR, Vol. III, pp. 536-544.

Defeat in that war, during which Kemal Pasha won victories—against the British—reduced Turkey to her hard Anatolian core, and there, in the fresh air and amid the soil, sand, and rock of the wind-swept plateau, Kemal began the cure. He shifted the capital from Asiatic Constantinople (Istanbul) on the European side of the Bosporus to the new European city of Ankara on the Asiatic side. He expelled the Sultan, abolished the Caliphate, and made Turkey a secular state. The veil, harem, and purdah were prohibited. A modified Latin alphabet replaced the cursive Arabic script, so conducive to illiteracy. Kemal decreed that the muezzin calling the faithful to their mosques be in Turkish, not Arabic. He proscribed the fez and prescribed Western hats. The most popular photograph of Ataturk, engraved on the national currency too, shows him in white tie and tails, the furthest remove from the traditional caricature of Turkey as a man in tasseled Oriental fez, baggy trousers, and moccasins with curled-up tocs.

Kemal combined Paris and Anatolia, gentleman and Tamerlane. His sex-drink-card orgies, during which he vanished for days, were succeeded by prolonged outbursts of creative turbulence and a prophet's reforming zeal. Volcanic and intemperate, Kemal rode his horse into the heart of a nation close enough to the primitive to admire his rough, masculine stamina. He broke heads and precedents with equal abandon. Cast in a hero's mold, he gave his people a sense of living an epic. A poor, small, and backward country, Turkey nevertheless felt rejuvenated.

Kemal preferred his own revolutionary nationalism to Lenin's, his own one-party totalitarianism to the Kremlin's. He banned communist activity and persecuted suspected communists. But Kemal's anticommunism did not hamper Soviet Russia's military, economic, and political cooperation with Turkey. Both countries were interested in pushing back the influence of the Western powers.

In the two hundred and forty years between 1677 and 1917, Russia and Turkey had fought thirteen wars. This gave rise to the fiction of an ineradicable hostility. There is no such thing. Nations are too practical to be guided by history. As long as Russia and Turkey harbored territorial designs on each other they feuded and hated. When both lost their empires and, enfeebled, their imperial appetites, they became friends.

Kemal addressed a letter to the Soviet government on April 26, 1920, announcing Turkey's readiness to "participate in the struggle against foreign imperialism which threatens both countries" and suggesting a military and political alliance.[21] Chicherin replied coldly, and proposed normal diplomatic relations. Kemal persisted. In a note to Chicherin dated November 29, 1920, he referred to "our close union" and to the "proletarian masses of the world" through whose efforts, aided by the "oppressed peoples of Asia and Africa," "the rule of the bourgeoisie" and of "international capital" "would end."

[21] Fischer, *op. cit.*, p. 286.

Clearly, Kemal needed Moscow. Moscow was preoccupied with the remnants of Wrangel, with Georgia, with economic problems. Yet Kemal pressed. On November 16, 1920, Turkish Foreign Minister Bekir Semi was in Moscow appealing for military aid. Greece, abetted by England, had invaded Anatolia.

"It need no longer be a secret," Karakhan said to me while I was writing *The Soviets in World Affairs*, "that we helped Kemal with much cannon, money, arms, and military advice." Leo Karakhan, Assistant Commissar of Foreign Affairs, a handsome, astute Armenian, apparently enjoyed revealing classified information; he also told me of Soviet military assistance to Chiang Kai-shek and gave me for copying a dossier of correspondence between Chiang and Sun Yat-sen, on the one hand, and Chicherin, on the other. He had an independent spirit, manifest in his private affairs, and disclosing secrets seems to have fed his sense of individual independence, an asset for which he paid with his life; he was executed on December 19, 1937, for refusing to confess to uncommitted crimes.

Before Simeon I. Aralov, a former army officer, left Moscow to serve as first Soviet ambassador to Kemalist Turkey, Chicherin took him to see Lenin.

"So, old chap," Lenin greeted him, "you finished fighting and you've become a diplomat. Good. You beat your sword into a plowshare. A necessary, good thing. Sit down, please. . . .

"Of course," Lenin began, "Mustapha Kemal Pasha is no socialist, but, it seems, he's a good organizer, a talented military man, he's carrying out a bourgeois-national revolution, a man of progressive inclinations, a wise statesman. He has understood the significance of our socialist revolution and takes a favorable view of Soviet Russia. He is conducting a war of liberation against aggressors. . . . It is said that the people believe in him. We should help him, that is, we should help the Turkish people. That is your job. Respect the Turkish government and people. Don't be proud. Don't interfere in their affairs. England has incited the Greeks against them. . . . You face· a serious task. . . . Although we are poor we can help Turkey materially. And we should. . . . The Turkish people will feel that they are not alone.

"Tsarist Russia fought Turkey for centuries," the soliloquy continued, "and this, naturally, put a big stamp on the memory of the people. . . . You know, distrust vanishes slowly. This therefore is a big, patient, cautious, attentive job; it will be necessary to convince wisely, to explain, not with words but with deeds, the difference between the old Tsarist Russia and Soviet Russia. That is our task, and you, as ambassador, are under an obligation to carry out the Soviet policy of noninterference in their affairs, to be the champion of real friendship between our peoples. Turkey is a peasant, petty-bourgeois country. She has little industry and what little exists is in the hands of European capitalists. There are few workers. You must keep this in mind." In other words, no proletarian revolution.

Moscow would help Kemalist Turkey, Lenin told Aralov. "What kind of help, we will let you know; most likely we will help with arms, if necessary we will give other help too.

"Learn the language, be in touch with simple people, with public personalities, don't surround yourself with fences and fortress walls as the ambassadors of the autocratic Tsar did. . . . Are you going with your children? That's excellent. The children will learn Turkish, and it is necessary for you to study it too. That is very important."[22]

Therewith Lenin sent the envoy on his way to Ankara.

Russia did help Turkey. (France also helped.) But before Soviet assistance was given, an incident almost ruined Soviet-Turkish relations. In February, 1921, just as Russian troops were taking over Georgia, Kemal moved troops toward the Georgian city of Batum, and on March 11, 1921, his men occupied the city. Batum was then the terminus of Russia's only oil pipeline; it carried kerosene from Baku to the Black Sea port and thence north into Russia or south for export. This economic factor apart, Russia would have incurred additional Georgian nationalist hatred by allowing the Turks to annex an important Georgian city. Red Army units approached to give battle. For five days the Turkish and Soviet commanders parleyed. Finally, Kemal yielded Batum, and Moscow accepted Turkish rule over the provinces of Kars and Ardahan.

Lenin knew the intimate relationship between Soviet foreign policies and domestic policy. The need to placate Georgia, and top Georgians like Stalin who disliked Kemalist Turkey, had to be considered. Soviet Armenia and Azerbaijan were brought into the treaty negotiations between Moscow and Ankara. If this did not decrease their dependence on the Kremlin it might at least give the impression abroad, particularly among Asians, that the Tsar's former inland colonies had acquired a new dignity. On March 31, 1921, Lenin agreed in writing with a note Chicherin sent him on the necessity of curbing tactless antireligious propaganda in the large Moslem-inhabited areas of Russia. He kept himself informed on the strivings for secession among nationalists in the Ukraine, the Caucasus, and Turkestan; discontent in these regions could cause disturbances and require repression. The facts would become known abroad and damage Soviet Russia's reputation among dependent peoples. Turkestan is one example.

When Tomsky, the trade-union chief, failed to support Lenin's trade-union policy, Lenin exiled him to an important post in Turkestan. There Tomsky collided politically with G. I. Safarov, a member of the Turkestan Bureau of the Central Committee of the Russian Communist Party. The dispute centered on the application of the NEP in Turkestan. Tomsky favored its application. Safarov argued that Turkestan should be an exception—a region

---

[22] S. I. Aralov, *Vospominaniya Sovietskovo Diplomata* (*Memoirs of a Soviet Diplomat*) (Moscow, 1960), pp. 34-37. Aralov is one of the very few Soviet officials—Ivan Maisky is another—who have published memoirs in Russia.

without NEP and with the old war communism which had been discarded elsewhere in Soviet Russia.

Tomsky wrote Lenin, who replied on August 7, 1921. "Of course, you are right that 'nine million sheep' are *indispensable* to us (Moscow). Take them no matter what. And send them *immediately* to us in STO. . . .

"In an attempt to iron out the differences between you and Comrade Safarov, we are sending Comrade Yoffe." Yoffe the foreign-policy and do-mestic-policy "troubleshooter."

In the next paragraph Lenin expounded his plan: "I think that both ten-dencies can and should be combined. 1) Bread and meat for Moscow first of all. 2) A series of concessions (to this end) and prizes for 'merchants.' 3) Most certainly *the New Economic Policy*. . . . 4) Definitely, Moslem *Committees of the Poor* and 5) Attentive, cautious relationship to *the Mos-lem poor* and a number of concessions.

"You can and must combine and *reinforce* the wise, cautious line which safeguards the interests of our 'world policy' in the *entire* East."[23]

The quotation marks around "world policy" were Lenin's. He seemed to be mocking his own grandiloquence. But his next letter dissolved the quotes.

Yoffe, on arriving in Turkestan, soon penetrated to the nub of the diffi-culty. He informed the Politburo in Moscow on September 9 that the strife between Tomsky and Safarov was "enflaming the hostility between the Rus-sian and native populations and between various nationalities."

Safarov had been depriving the so-called kulaks of their wealth in cattle and farm equipment and distributing it among the poor peasants—the same class-war practice that proved so disastrous in the central regions of Russia. Moslem victims of Safarov's folly blamed the Great Russian officials, their traditional enemies since tsarist days. Tomsky, on the other hand, insisted that these violent pre-NEP methods be dropped. But if, as is likely, some of the kulaks and merchants who stood to benefit from the NEP were Rus-sians, and if the Moslem poor suffered at their hands, they would resent Tomsky's introduction of the NEP. Safarov's methods bred anti-Russian sentiment. So did Tomsky's. Moreover, Yoffe made it clear that the Kremlin had to choose: Safarov or Tomsky. Lenin's wish to have his cake: "*most cer-tainly the New Economic Policy*," and eat it: "Definitely, Moslem *Commit-tees of the Poor*" was impracticable.

The situation caused confusion and dissension in remote Moscow. Lenin admitted in a letter to Yoffe dated September 13, 1921, that, "There exist some differences of opinion on this question in the Central Committee" of the party. "It is most important to have more precise information. I person-ally *very much* suspect 'the Tomsky Line' . . . of Great Russian chauvinism and, more correctly, *a leaning* in that direction.

"For our entire Weltpolitik"—world policy—"it is devilishly important

[23] *Leninskii Sbornik*, Vol. XXXVI, pp. 305-306.

to win the trust of the natives; win it three and four times; *to prove* that we are not imperialists, that we *shall not* tolerate a tendency in that direction.

"This is a world issue, without exaggeration a world issue.

"We must be extremely strict in this matter.

"This will have its effect on India, on the East, we must not joke about this, here we must exercise a thousand-fold caution. With communist greetings, Lenin."[24]

In the end, Safarov, not Tomsky whom Lenin suspected of Great Russian chauvinism, was removed from Turkestan, given a post as consultant on Eastern affairs for the Comintern and investigated. When he complained, Lenin wrote to him, "Comrade Safarov, Don't get nervous, it's intolerable and shameful. You're not a fourteen-year-old girl." Lenin told Safarov that he considered the case against him absurd. Nevertheless, the Central Committee was sending Gregory Sokolnikov, a first-rank Bolshevik, to Turkestan to study the knotted situation.[25]

To win over the natives of Turkestan, to prove that Bolsheviks were not imperialists, was for Lenin a world issue. Success in Turkestan would matter in India and throughout the Orient. Lenin saw globally. Turkestan and the Caucasus could be bridges or barriers. Curzon and Churchill did not know Lenin's views on the significance of Turkestan. But they regarded him as a red reincarnation of a Romanov, a commissar in the place of a tsar, a tsar with no crown on his head but a dangerous idea in it. Now the bear had velocity, they thought. It is doubtful whether Lenin, despite all his illusions about the imminence of world revolution, shared their estimate of Russia's new potential for expansion. By 1921 his down-to-earth practicality must have told him that an idea is best carried at the tip of a swift sword or in a big moneybag.

Moreover, there were for Lenin two Englands, the one he should have liked to humble in Asia, the second, the world banker, merchant, and manufacturer, he had been courting in London. There were therefore (at least) two Lenins, or two souls lying peacefully together in one breast, loyal to his only principle: the preservation of the Soviet system. To this end, Russia had to trade with capitalism, and capitalism's citadel then was England which also had to trade to survive and prosper. But some in Britain put empire above commerce. To them the Lenin peril in Asia and red propaganda in the home islands loomed larger than business profits. Other forces took a less alarmist view of the communist menace, in fact believed they could reduce it by normal trade relations. Large British companies hoped to resume operation of their considerable properties in Russia; they applied for concessions. The Kremlin held out hopes. Still others, however, though equally avid to buy and sell, wanted to make trade contingent on the payment of tsarist Russia's debts. Either in response to pressure from these creditors or to avoid

[24] *Ibid.*, pp. 320-321.
[25] *Ibid.*, pp. 381-382.

extra strain on the wartime Entente that was shredding rapidly, Prime Minister David Lloyd George queried Paris on its attitude to an Anglo-Russian trade treaty. Foreign Minister Aristide Briand replied on November 25, 1920,[26] in an ingenious note. The French government, it stated, "has no objection to the resumption of commercial relations between individuals." But since Soviet individuals were prohibited, by the state foreign trade monopoly, from trading abroad, Briand was saying that he did object to trade with Soviet Russia. He furthermore made trade conditional on the settlement of Russia's prewar and wartime debts. But suspecting the Bolshevik will and ability to pay old debts, the French proposed the establishment of "a special organization charged to direct the execution of the engagements incurred. . . . Indemnification must therefore be sought by methods which foster the exploitation of the resources of the country." Briand dreamed of making Soviet Russia an economic colony of the West.

The Bolsheviks did not have to reject this scheme. The British did. Lord Hardinge of Penshurst, speaking for Foreign Secretary Lord Curzon of Kedleston said on June 24, 1921, "His Majesty's Government are unable to agree . . . that the resumption of trade with Russia and the recognition of Russian debts should not be dealt with independently."

The United Kingdom and Soviet Russia had signed a trade agreement on March 16, 1921. Both parties regarded it as a preliminary to a peace treaty and the resumption of diplomatic relations. This broke the ice, broke the effective big-power blockade against business transactions with the Bolsheviks. Now, indeed, "a certain equilibrium," in Lenin's words, had been established between his Russia and the outside world.

XLIV. ☐ DREAM DIES

A CERTAIN EQUILIBRIUM had been achieved inside Soviet Russia too. But famine and poverty disturbed it. So did a residual radicalism. Thus, Lenin wrote to Leo Kamenev, member of the Politburo and chairman of the Moscow Soviet, on April 14, 1921, "They say that the workers will, in three or four months, demand the abolition of the freedom to trade, that, it is said, they don't want the bureaucrats to eat bread rolls." Here was an embryonic class struggle manifesting itself in jealousy: government employees or bureaucrats were benefiting more from the NEP than workers. What did Lenin propose to do? "Should not measures be taken in advance?" his letter to

[26] Correspondence between His Majesty's Government and the French Government respecting the Anglo-Russian Trade Agreement. British White Paper. Russia, No. 2 (1921). Cmd. 1456 (London, 1921).

Kamenev continued. "1) Get to work immediately and with all energy on rest homes. Increase their number by summer and autumn. Then we will buy 'bread rolls' from time to time for the 'vacationers' in turn. 2) Consider special *queues* for purchases for children or 'prize' presents. But the first is more important. Drop me a line on your opinion and about what's happening. Salut! Lenin."[1]

Lenin cannot have placed a high value on the proletariat's class consciousness if he thought it could be appeased with a stay in a rest house, usually a capitalist's confiscated villa, and the occasional distribution of tasty white buns or by rewarding workers with children's toys.

At the Tenth Congress of the Russian Communist Party in March-April, 1922, that stormy petrel, D. Ryazanov, offered a motion prohibiting all party newspapers from printing advertisements. Anastas I. Mikoyan amended this to apply only to *Pravda*. Lenin's sister Maria and other *Pravda* editors present refrained from opposing the Mikoyan amendment. Lenin had not attended that session. At a subsequent one, he passed a note to Kamenev: "They say, the Congress voted against advertisements in *Pravda*. Can't this be corrected, it's an obvious mistake."

"You can't," Kamenev replied. "They voted twice. This"—the advertising —"makes them sick. It will be necessary to find other means of support: book ads, fees for announcements of meetings, for Central Committee information, etc. L.K."[2]

Lenin seemed more commercial than the party.

The greatest threat to Soviet Russia's stability, far greater than the vanishing radicalism, was Lenin's health.

I. A. Semyonov, a Red Army veteran and party member employed in the Don region in the food supply department, came to Moscow with the explicit purpose of informing Lenin about the highhandedness of the authorities, theft by officials, and the inefficiency of the administration in the Don which, he wrote in a letter to Lenin, had caused "various uprisings of workers and working peasants." Semyonov added that he would "wait three days" for Lenin's reply. "If there is none I shall commit suicide."

Distressed, Lenin gave the letter to his secretary, Lydia Fotieva, and instructed her in writing, on July 13, 1921, "*Quickly* find the author, receive him, calm him, say I'm ill, but I will act on this matter." He also asked her to make several carbon copies of Semyonov's complaint, one for Molotov, and, "In forwarding the letter to Molotov add in my name: I propose to send to the Don a Control Commission consisting of one member of the VTSIK and ten (or twenty) students of Sverdlov University (they are to take the author with them) and *to shoot on the spot* those proved guilty of stealing."[3]

[1] *Leninskii Sbornik*, Vol. XX, p. 277.
[2] *Ibid.*, Vol. XIII, pp. 29-30.
[3] *Ibid.*, Vol. XX, p. 333.

Lenin felt ill. Any loud noise shocked him, and the bells of his telephone were therefore replaced with small electric lights which flashed when calls came in. On July 8, 1921, he requested the Orgburo—Organization Bureau of the party—or the Secretariat of the Central Committee, of which Molotov was a key official (after telephoning the four other members of the Politburo for their assent), to grant him a month's vacation with the right to come to Moscow from nearby Gorky two or three times a week to attend meetings of the Sovnarkom and STO. The next day, the Politburo acceded to his request on condition that he attend meetings only of the Politburo "but not of the Sovnarkom or STO except in special cases—if the Secretariat of the Central Committee so decides."[4]

But he remained in Moscow during July for the Comintern Congress and other meetings and was as active as ever and dealing with key problems as well as with many peripheral questions: On July 13, for instance, he asked Borodin, who had lived in Chicago, to send him all available material on the Farmer-Labor Party of South Dakota; he had received and read it by July 26, and urged Borodin to write it up in an article for the *Communist International* magazine.[5] About the same time he asked for copies of the Czechoslovak communist newspaper *Rude Pravo* and of the Czechoslovak German-language daily *Vorwaertz* which contained reports on the Czechoslovak Communist Party Congress in May. On July 22, he urged the appropriate authorities to accelerate the importation of coal-mining machinery. The next day, in a letter, he dealt with horse breeding. That same day he turned his attention to irregularities in the Petrograd rationing system and proposed the arrest "for one Sunday" of the three guilty officials in charge and a warning: "next time for a month and dismissal." A day later one of his communications concerned the detailed operations of the fishing industry, and still another day later he asked Chicherin to have somebody prepare a pamphlet exposing the activities of the Georgian Mensheviks. So it went. His fertile brain knew no rest. He was so constituted. He apparently believed that without his prods and verbal bombs and lashings things would not move.

Tense, fearful of administrative drift, he tried, against doctors' orders and the Politburo's decision, to keep his hand on the Kremlin machine. From Gorky during his vacation the reminders, orders, memoranda, complaints, and barbs flooded his own office and those of others in Moscow. But he saw fewer people. On August 2, 1921, for example, he wrote V. V. Adoratsky, a close and valued comrade, "I'm on vacation. Ill. Cannot receive you." And he relented to the extent of doing some light reading. Boris I. Nicolaevsky, then in a common cell at the Lubyanka prison with Menshevik comrades, had received from Mrs. Lydia Dan, wife of the Menshevik leader, a French book of adventure, *Les Exploits de Rocambole*, by a second-rate author, Ponson du Terrail (1829-1871), whose popularity created the word

[4] *Ibid.*, Vol. XXXVI, p. 272.
[5] *Ibid.*, pp. 287 and 295.

"rocambolesque": the epitome of adventure. The Mensheviks devoured the volume, in fact had to share it with the SR's, Gots, Timofeyev, etc., in the neighboring chamber who "telegraphed" their eagerness by a code of alphabetical knocks on the wall that separated them. So the book passed from hand to hand, from Menshevik to SR and back, until Mrs. Dan suddenly reappeared and said she had to return the book at once, the library had asked for it: Lenin was ill, and he requested it. Anti-Bolsheviks idle in jail and the prime Bolshevik resting in Gorky had the same formula for forgetting— vacuous adventure stories. The Mensheviks decided Lenin had had his first stroke. This is not confirmed.

It ran against Lenin's nature and nerves to be idle. On vacation he wrote an article entitled "New Times, Old Errors in a New Form," which *Pravda* published on August 28, 1921. It dealt with instability, with "the petty-bourgeois vacillation" of the peasantry which "penetrated in varying degrees" into the proletariat. This vacillation, he found, was "unavoidable as long as the deepest roots of capitalism have not been removed."

The NEP, he reported, encouraged Moscow's enemies. The fellow travelers of the Mensheviks said, "The Bolsheviks have turned back to capitalism, here they will meet their death. The revolution has, despite everything, proved to be a bourgeois revolution. . . . Long live democracy! Long live reformism!"

It is true, Lenin explained, that the Bolshevik revolution began by being bourgeois. But "in the ten weeks or so" between November 7, 1917, and the dissolution of the Constituent Assembly on January 19, 1918, "we did more for the real and complete annihilation of the vestiges of feudalism in Russia than the Mensheviks and SR's did in the eight months [March-November, 1917] of *their* stay in power."

That first phase of the Bolshevik revolution was bourgeois. A bourgeois revolution destroys its predecessor, feudalism, according to Marx and Lenin. At the same time, however, Lenin noted, the Bolsheviks commenced "the socialist, proletarian revolution" by "striking a blow felt around the world at the fetishes of petty-bourgeois democracy: the Constituent Assembly and bourgeois 'freedoms' like freedom of the press for the rich." Also, "We created a Soviet type of state" and "we expanded, as never before, the forces of the working class and the use of the state's power by *them*."

Now they had entered a new phase: "The Entente has been forced (for how long?) to end intervention and the blockade." But there was a new enemy: "The enemy is the petty-bourgeois primordial force which surrounds us like air and penetrates heavily into the ranks of the proletariat. And the proletariat is declassed, that is, knocked off its class tracks. Factories and mills are idle—the proletariat is weakened, fragmented, and enfeebled."

All this encourages the "lovers of 'left' phrases." He had heard enough of them. "We do not minimize the danger. We look it straight in the face . . . the danger is great . . . cries of panic do not affect us. . . . The Mensheviks shout that the tax in kind, the freedom to trade, the legalization of concessions, and state capitalism constitute the collapse of communism." But the Soviet regime was developing "new forces" within the proletariat. "The best representatives of the proletariat are now ruling Russia. They had created the army and led it, created local government, etc., managed industry, and so forth. If there is bureaucratic distortion in management we do not conceal it, we expose it and fight it." New recruits from the proletariat to man the government apparatus would come in slowly. The working class had suffered grievously during the civil war. They had to expect "a *slackening* of the growth of the *new* forces within the working class." Therefore, Lenin urged, "More initiative and self-help in the localities. . . . Get to work, slower and more careful work, more sustained and more persistent work."[6] Thus he closed. He could not have been happy about the Soviet situation. He looked the danger straight in the eye. That did not reduce its size.

Exactly a month passed without a public statement or published article by Lenin—an unprecedented phenomenon. Then on September 20 a very brief statement from his pen appeared on the party purge. Former Mensheviks who had managed to slip into the communist ranks were to be expelled. Also, "The party must be purged of pickpockets, of bureaucratized officials, of dishonest, soft communists."[7]

Presently, Lenin grappled tentatively with Stalin. The issue: bureaucracy.

Bureaucracy plays a special role in a communist country. Every government rests on a bureaucracy, on the men and women who write and answer letters, draft and file documents, gather information, give orders, collect taxes, hire and fire others, and so forth. But the Soviet bureaucracy is a bureaucracy wrapped in an autocracy without democracy. The Soviet system has, by intention, no independent legislature. Executive and legislature are one and the judiciary is subject to it. This three-in-one body, moreover, is the sole employer of all gainfully employed, the sole operator of all industry, the master of agriculture, the arbiter of education and culture, the one banker, the one trader, the one foreign-policy-maker. In these circumstances, the bureaucracy which runs the executive rocks the country. It is, to be sure, the creature and agent of the dictator or of the dictatorial oligarchy, and bureaucrats can be dismissed or punished without notice or redress. But until the moment when the ax falls they exercise a frightful power against which there is little recourse except in rare cases—a handful out of a million —when *Pravda* or some other newspaper "makes a scandal" and exposes a wayward official.

Lenin became the father of this monster by the act of establishing the communist dictatorship and the Soviet state. He and many of his colleagues soon recognized the danger inherent in their handiwork and cried havoc. Nevertheless, the Frankenstein grew with the proliferation of the functions

[6] Lenin, *Sochineniya*, Second ed., Vol. XXVII, pp. 5-11.
[7] *Ibid.*, pp. 12-13.

of the government and the party. Lenin then tried to put the beast in harness: that was the Workers-Peasants Inspection (Rabkrin), and he placed the reins in Stalin's hands.

On September 27, 1921, Lenin wrote a long letter to Stalin on an aspect of Rabkrin's work. It was first published in 1929 in the *Leninskii Sbornik*, Vol. VIII, and again the next year, with Stalin's reply to Lenin.[8] In a typical approach, Lenin went from the general to the specific. "The function of the Workers-Peasants Inspection," he began, "is not only and not even so much 'to catch' and 'to prove guilt' . . . as *to be able to correct*. Competent and timely correcting—that is the chief function of Rabkrin."

Had Lenin penetrated to the black mind of Stalin and discovered a detective who "catches" and a prosecutor who "proves guilt"? Or is the question prompted by what the world learned subsequently about Stalin's character? But Lenin did say that Stalin concentrated on the punitive to the neglect of the corrective.

In order to correct it is necessary to study and inspect, Lenin taught. Many government enterprises had much in common, bookkeeping, for instance. Rabkrin should have a number of experienced persons who could "in the least time (send a person for half an hour or an hour to the given establishment) investigate whether bookkeeping has been set up, whether it has been set up properly, what are the shortcomings of the set-up, how they can be corrected, and so forth."

Lenin's diatribe against Stalin's Rabkrin was provoked by a preliminary report that came to his desk on the mounting fuel crisis in the autumn of 1921; it "convinces me that *the basic principle* of work has not been fixed in the Rabkrin as it should be. In this draft report there is *no study* of the situation, *nor an approach to its improvement*." The government enterprises Rabkrin had investigated, Lenin conceded, were working badly. "Bookkeeping was bad." An official in charge did his job badly. "But to find the guilty chief is only a very small fraction of the work. Has Rabkrin performed its task and duty? *Has it correctly understood its task?* This is the main question. And the answer to this question has to be in the negative."

The author of the preliminary report, Lenin pointed out, wrote that "The responsible officials are overburdened to exhaustion with work and at the same time the technical apparatus of subsidiary organizations . . . *is full of idle employees*. I am sure that this is a valuable and absolutely true observation and that it applies *not* only to the Fuel Trust but *to* all or 99 percent of all enterprises and departments."

How to change this? "I don't even faintly know. Rabkrin should know." For failure to suggest cures, Lenin blamed not only the author of the draft report: "It is clear to me that this applies not only to the author."

Stalin understood; Lenin meant him. He replied the same day. But he chose not to defend himself, he defended the author of the preliminary re-

[8] *Ibid.*, pp. 14-20, and editorial note, p. 501, for Stalin's letter.

port, thus shifting the blame from himself. "Your accusations against the author of the 'preliminary' report," his first sentence read, "*are possibly* premature, because *the real* report has not yet been presented to you." The preliminary "reportlet" was designed, among other things, to "facilitate *the preliminary* examination for you, or, according to the current expression, to 'interest' you in the question. Incidentally, I am prepared to admit a priori that our shabby inspection will still be thrashing around on the easy old path of 'catching,' *still* so long as we do not reinforce it with communists and provide its leading personnel with material rewards. . . . A pair of engineers conducting an investigation of fuel offices earn less together than a messenger in Sverdlovsk. The other day I had to give them several hundred thousand roubles each." The author of the preliminary report, Stalin noted, was a communist named Loninov, and in a P.S. he added, "Loninov said the day before yesterday that he would append to his report a plan of concrete steps for the improvement of the apparatus of the fuel enterprises." Stalin directed Lenin's thought to Loninov.

The fourth anniversary of the Bolshevik revolution on November 7, 1921, would be an occasion for rejoicing and self-congratulation. Lenin prepared the holiday climate in an article finished on October 14 and published in *Pravda* of October 18—twenty days before the event. It probably provided a cue to a thousand celebration orations throughout the country. As usual, he wrote it in his quick-flowing handwriting with few corrections. "The direct and immediate task of the revolution in Russia," he said, "was a bourgeois-democratic task: to destroy the vestiges of medievalism, eliminate them completely, cleanse Russia of that barbarism, of that disgrace, of that great brake on the entire culture and progress of our country. And we have a right to be proud that we carried out this cleansing more decisively, with more speed, courage and success, more widely and deeply from the point of view of its effect on the mass of the nation, on its bulk, than the great French Revolution more than one hundred and twenty-five years ago."

He itemized: they had uprooted the remnants of bondage: the monarchy; the estates: the nobility and gentry; the private ownership of land; religion; the inferiority of women; the oppression of nationalities.

"The cowards, the windbags, the self-loving narcissuses and little Hamlets waved their cardboard swords—and did not even annihilate the monarchy!" Lenin exclaimed in an attack on the Provisional (Kerensky) government. But "We threw out the monarchist filth as nobody else ever." (The reference is probably to the execution of the Tsar's family, for the Provisional government had overthrown the monarchy.)

"Take religion or the denial of rights to women or the oppression of unequal non-Russian nationalities. These are all questions of the bourgeois-democratic revolution. The vulgar men of petty-bourgeois democracy chattered about this for eight months; *not one* of the most advanced countries of the world has *completely* solved *these* questions in a *bourgeois-democratic* sense." We did. "We really have combated and are combating religion. We have given *all* non-Russian nationalities *their own* republics or autonomous regions." Women had been liberated.

These reforms, as he called them, were incidental "by-products" of "main and real *proletarian*-revolutionary socialist work. We always said that reforms are the by-products of the revolutionary class struggle. . . . The bourgeois-democratic transformation—we said and demonstrated in deeds—is the by-product of the proletarian, that is, the socialist revolution. . . . The first merges into the second. . . . The second consolidates the first. Struggle and only struggle determines the extent to which the second succeeds in out-growing the first."

Here Lenin's mind was at its clearest. The Bolsheviks had to make a non-socialist revolution first in order then to be able to make their socialist revo-lution. No leaps. A feudal society could not by one bound become socialist or communist.

But he had called the first revolution "bourgeois-democratic," and he knew that socialists, liberals, and others the world over looked in vain for democ-racy in the new Russia. He replied: "Let the hounds and hogs of the dying bourgeoisie and of the petty-bourgeois democracy intertwined with it cover us with heaps of curses, oaths, and ridicule for the failures and mistakes in our building of *our* Soviet system." There had been many mistakes. How could it have been otherwise in creating a new social system? "But we have a right to be proud that it fell to our happy lot *to begin* the construction of the Soviet state, to *begin* therewith a new epoch in universal history, the epoch of the domination of *a new* class oppressed in all capitalist countries and moving everywhere to a new life, to victory over the bourgeoisie, to the dictatorship of the proletariat, to the deliverance of mankind from the yoke of capital, from imperialist wars."

This was Lenin's eloquence at its best. No trace of illness.

Millions upon millions throughout the world were learning that they could not escape from *"the hell"* of the imperialist world and imperialist peace *"except through a Bolshevik struggle and a Bolshevik revolution. . . .*

"We started this process. Exactly when, in what period, the workers of which nation will carry it to its conclusion is immaterial. The essential thing is that the ice has been broken, the road has been opened, the way has been shown. . . . *The first Bolshevik revolution* has torn *the first hundred million people* on earth out of the imperialist war and the imperialist world. The second will snatch all mankind from such wars and from such a world."

It would have been unlike Lenin, however, to allow the golden victory bells to drown out the call of duty and the echo of his disappointments. "The difficulties are boundless," he wrote on the last page of his article. "But we have learned . . . an art that is indispensable to revolution—pliability, the ability to alter our tactics quickly and abruptly . . . choosing a new road to our goal if the former road has proved to be inexpedient or impossible for the time being."

This was his error: "Lifted up on a wave of enthusiasm," he said, "we expected . . . or perhaps it would be more correct to assert that we assumed without sufficient thought that we could, by direct command of the proletarian government, set up government production and government distribution according to communism in a petty-bourgeois country. Life exposed our mistake. A series of transitional steps were needed: state capitalism and socialism to prepare the transition to communism over a period of years. Not on enthusiasm directly, but with the aid of enthusiasm born of the great revolution, on personal interest, by personal incentive, on the basis of business accounting." Hence the New Economic Policy. "The proletarian government had to become a cautious, zealous, able 'boss,' a good *wholesale merchant* . . . there is no other transition to communism now, in present conditions, next door to the capitalist (the still capitalist) West. A wholesale merchant is apparently an economic type as far removed from communism as heaven is from earth. But this is one of those contradictions which, in living life, leads from a small-holding peasant economy through state capitalism to socialism. Personal initiative raises production." Nevertheless, "At all costs, no matter how difficult the torments of the transition period, the poverty, the starvation, and the ruin, our spirits shall not quail and we will carry our cause to a successful conclusion." End of article.[9]

To sum up: Lenin maintained that the first Bolshevik revolution, the bourgeois-democratic revolution had triumphed (although some of his paper claims: the elimination of religion, the liberation of women, and the equality of nationalities underestimated the drag of tradition). In discussing the second revolution, the socialist or communist revolution, Lenin revealed an un-Leninist utopianism: the expectation that communism could be established immediately in backward Russia, and by government fiat. One would have thought that communism could result only from the joint, voluntary effort of millions of individuals who had matured spiritually, culturally, and educationally in a highly developed economy—not by Kremlin command. Before the revolution Lenin repeatedly declared that Russia must become fully capitalistic before she became socialist. Why, then, had he assumed that socialism was possible on ruins, underdevelopment, and ignorance? But by October, 1921, he knew that the country would indeed need decades of private capitalism and state capitalism to lift it out of backwardness.

In his first speech in months, an address to political educators on October 17, 1921, Lenin enumerated three enemies: "communist swagger" or idle boasting that uses big words to disguise "slovenliness, loafing, Oblomovism, and backwardness"; second, illiteracy; third, "bribery." This long talk was one of the very rare occasions on which Lenin explained how, "approximately," he had thought communism would come to Russia: "We decided that through requisitions the peasants would give us the necessary quantity of bread and we would allot it to factory and mills—and the result would be communist production and distribution. Unfortunately, this is a fact. I say

---

[9] *Ibid.*, pp. 24-30.

unfortunately, because considerable experience has convinced us of the error of this notion."

Lenin thus admitted that military communism, which helped complete the ruin of Russia and intensify the famine, was not merely a war measure but also a deliberate attempt to make Russia communist, a fantastic, futile, fatal adventure, product of the great illusion: a state marked for withering, but actually in a state of dissolution, would create a one-two-three push-button communism; unmodernized, illiterate peasant Russia would avoid the capitalist phase of development and leap into socialist paradise. This was the old, somewhat modified, Narodnik-populist dream of unique Russia destined to lead the world up from hell. It dwelt deep in the heart of Lenin's practicality.

But now they had capitalism and that raised the big question: "Kto Kovo," Who whom? Who would defeat whom? "The enemy within is anarchic capitalism and anarchic private trade . . . the war is not ended." And therefore, "We must not expect a direct transition to communism. We must build on the personal initiative of the peasant." In this peacetime war the Bolsheviks had to be ruthless. Of course they had introduced the death penalty. "Sentimentality is no less criminal than self-seeking in war." In addition, he hoped the communist party would expel "one to two hundred thousand communists who have attached themselves to the party and who not only cannot fight red tape and bribery but interfere with the struggle against them." Russia needed a much higher culture. To achieve it would be a slow process. The government had to learn the art of business, learn it from capitalists, concessionaires, and renters of land in the Soviet country. In theory, Lenin was opposed to the renting of land. "There must be no renting," he said in a letter to Commissar of Justice D. I. Kursky dated October 25, 1921. "But the renting of state farms"—sovhozi—"or of 'uncultivated land?' . . . This is really a transfer of management."[10] By this legal legerdemain Lenin legalized renting and gave it a sweeter-smelling name; food was more important to him than socialist principles. The famine eclipsed everything. Everybody tried to help. Lenin's sister Anna, her adopted son remembers, donated the old Ulyanov family silver to the relief fund for the starving.[11]

Capitalism on rented land could feed and save.

Lenin had faith in the second—the socialist—revolution yet to come. This was his right. But his claims for the first—the bourgeois-democratic—completed revolution rested on paper, on decrees, not on life. He himself would soon discern that the national minorities had attained less than they wished, less than he wished. The peasants would learn from Stalin that they had no land, no freedom to till as they wished, no escape except into the abhorred collectives. The liberation of women had a shimmer of reality: they could vote for the one candidate in elections, they could be elected, they could, in

[10] *Ibid.*, p. 53. This letter is omitted from the fourth edition of Lenin's *Collected Works (Sochineniya)*, Vol. 33, August, 1921-March, 1923 (Moscow, 1950).

[11] *Vospominaniya*, Vol. 2, p. 137.

Moslem areas, discard the veil and go to school. But a statement in the Moscow *Kommunist* of November, 1963, casts some light on the fate of Soviet women. The author writes on page 82, that the average length of life of a Russian woman, which was two years less than that of the average man sixty-five years ago, is now eight years less. He attributes this disastrous reduction of the Soviet woman's life span to the multiplicity of abortions and to "the traumas of living conditions and working conditions." Most adult Soviet women are wives, mothers, and wage earners. The revolution brought them formal freedom and excessive burdens.

Before the first, capitalist-democratic revolution was half-successful, Lenin launched the second, anticapitalist, antidemocratic revolution. He thereby ruined both. This was his historic mistake.

XLV. ☉HE USES OF GOLD

CIRCUMSTANCES, some of his own doing, forced Lenin to court capitalists. He did it with zest for the good of Bolshevism and because he had sponsored the concessions policy and induced reluctant communists to accept it. But the remaining rich in Russia could be counted by a first-grade child, and foreign firms prepared to operate in the Bolshevik state were few in number. Capitalists, Lenin to the contrary notwithstanding, find a developed nation more attractive to work in than an underdeveloped one with a limited supply of everything they need: qualified workingmen, experienced technicians and engineers, sufficient electric power, efficient transportation facilities, and industries to supply their many requirements in machinery, materials, spare parts, and repairs. Moreover, most capitalists did not understand the Kremlin's politics or hated it and were therefore cold to invitations to come in and cooperate with the communist regime. Of those prepared to do business with Bolshevism, the vast majority preferred to buy from and sell to the Soviets outside rather than invest inside.

The important exceptions were foreign companies whose properties, usually mines, had been confiscated after November 7, 1917. They hoped for restitution and the resumption of operations in approximately the same conditions to which they had become accustomed in tsarist Russia. Probably the largest of these was the Russo-Asiatic Corporation of Great Britain dominated by Leslie Urquhart. Leonid Krassin in London had been negotiating with Urquhart before and after the signature of the Anglo-Soviet commercial agreement. In June, 1921, Lenin wrote Krassin that "We agree to grant a concession to all our enterprises" in Siberia. "Regarding the duration" of the concession "—bargain. We will give a certain amount of Soviet money. Regarding the percentage" of the products mined which the Soviets would receive "—bargain." Krassin had suggested 25 percent. Lenin agreed. "We agree regarding immunity"[1]—immunity of foreign personnel from arrest and harassment.

[1] *Leninskii Sbornik*, Vol. XXXVI, pp. 261-262.

From his vacation spot at Gorky on August 22, 1921, Lenin telephoned State Planning Commission Chairman Krzhizhanovsky: since Urquhart was seeking a concession to work "almost all the copper mines of Russia," he should "guarantee us a percentage" of the output to be delivered soon after production. Moreover, Urquhart was to make it possible for the Soviet government to receive from him "the necessary equipment to develop our own mines." Lenin also wanted to know from Krzhizhanovsky how the proposed concession would foster Russia's electrification.[2]

Meanwhile, the authorities in the Kirghiz Soviet Republic, where the copper mines were located, received orders from Moscow to proceed with mining, and in September the Russian director of the mines was summoned to Lenin's office. On his return, he wired Lenin that during his absence the chief engineer had closed down the mines and dismissed the workers. "Among the workers," he stated, "propaganda is being conducted in the sense that the Soviet government cannot restore the mines and only the Englishman Urquhart can do it. Confirmed facts that the Englishman Urquhart sent letters, money, and clothing" to the engineers who "are awaiting the arrival of the Englishman Urquhart with great joy."[3] This revealed local communist opposition to the concession. Lenin and his associates nevertheless favored it.

Royal Dutch-Shell had held considerable properties in the Baku oil fields, and the resumption of official trade relations between London and the Soviet government encouraged the company's president, Sir Henri Deterding, to hope for a concession. Lord Curzon intervened on behalf of the oil trust. The following letter went from the Foreign Office to Krassin, the Soviet negotiator in London:

> *Foreign Office.*
> *October 19, 1921.*
>
> *Monsieur Krassin,*
> *Sir,*
>
> *The Marquis Curzon of Kedleston is informed by Colonel J. W. Boyle that the Royal Dutch-Shell group are anxious to obtain a concession from the Soviet Government for the production of oil from their properties in South Russia and the Caucasus.*
>
> *I am directed to inform you that it is with the full approval and support of His Majesty's Government that Colonel Boyle has addressed himself to you on this subject. His Majesty's Government trust that these negotiations may result in early and satisfactory settlement.*
>
> *I am,*
> *Sir,*
> *You most obedient servant,*
> *(Signed) Esmond Ovey*[4]

[2] *Ibid.*, pp. 311-312.
[3] *Ibid.*, Vol. XXIII, p. 67.
[4] Soviet Ambassador Ivan Maisky drew this letter from the files of his embassy in London and allowed me to copy it.

Lenin favored the granting of this concession too.

Lenin was especially eager to bring American industrial enterprise into Soviet Russia. In part, this stemmed from his concept of world politics. He regarded the United States as the hostile rival of England and Japan, Russia's two traditional enemies. Germany had been Russia's enemy in the First World War, but that was not the Bolsheviks' war. On the other hand, Germany's finances were depleted. France had played a leading role on the White side in the Soviet civil war, and the antagonism continued thereafter. Moreover, and above all, a large number of small French investors had bought tsarist Russian gold bonds which the Kremlin refused to honor, and the communists saw this as a high hurdle to friendly economic relations. Nor did they think of France as the most technically advanced nation. They paid this compliment to America. Technological, financial, and political considerations, accordingly, induced the Soviet leadership, and Lenin and Trotsky in particular, to hope that the United States would participate heavily in Russia's reconstruction. Relations between tsarist Russia and the U.S.A. had always been a diplomatic backwater: official contacts, of course, and occasional patches of friction or friendship, but the record of the past was so bare as to encourage the Soviets to hope for a bright future. In 1918, therefore, when the Soviet government nationalized all foreign properties, Lenin himself, acting on a suggestion from Colonel Raymond Robins, exempted American industrial properties. The holdings of the Singer Sewing Machine Company, International Harvester, and Westinghouse Brake Company, for instance, were not subjected to confiscation. To be sure, the U.S.A. intervened with troops in the civil war, but the Soviets played this pianissimo, indeed sometimes omitted it from histories, and only after the Second World War, when Russia rose to the rank of the world's second power and America, in effect, became the military replacement of Japan and Germany, and, to an extent, of Great Britain, did Moscow assume an anti-American stance.

Two nineteenth-century patterns blended in Lenin's mentality: balance-of-power politics and the primacy of economics in politics. Herbert C. Hoover, however, put politics above economics. The Secretary of Commerce in the new President Harding administration, responding to Soviet courtship of America and reacting to the NEP, said on March 21, 1921, "The question of trade with Russia is far more a political question than an economic one so long as Russia is under the control of the Bolsheviki. Under their economic system, no matter how much they moderate it in name, there can be no real production in Russia, and therefore Russia will have no considerable quantities to export, and, consequently, no great ability to obtain imports. . . . That requires the abandonment of their present economic system."

Moscow chose to overlook Hoover's rebuff. Deputy Foreign Commissar Maxim M. Litvinov appealed to the U.S. government to establish normal commercial and diplomatic relations. Secretary of State Charles Evans Hughes replied in the Hoover spirit. Lenin was not deterred. On May 24,

1921, the Far Eastern (Chita) Republic, a Siberian subsidiary of Moscow, signed an agreement with the Sinclair Exploration Company for the exploitation of the oil resources of northern Sakhalin and, as a political supplement, a right to build two ports on the island's east coast facing Japan. Northern Sakhalin was then occupied by the Japanese. The implication was plain: if Harry F. Sinclair's friends in Harding's Cabinet moved Japan out he could have the oil. Meanwhile, the offer to Washington Baker Vanderlip of a large mining concession in Kamchatka—with a base opposite Japan for the U.S. Navy thrown into the deal—still stood.

Lenin hunted whales and simultaneously fished for trout. Urquhart, Sinclair, Vanderlip—these would be major hauls if they materialized. But he apparently wanted to have an American concessionaire to display at home and abroad; the scale did not much matter. Lenin accordingly invited to his Kremlin office a young American physician, Armand Hammer, who had come to Russia to exchange grain for furs and other commodities. While he supervised the food distribution in the Urals, local authorities drew his attention to asbestos deposits which were no longer being worked. Their wish quickly scaled the hierarchical ladder and reached the summit: Lenin.

On Lenin's desk lay a copy of the *Scientific American* magazine. "Look here," Lenin said to Hammer as he rapidly turned the pages, "this is what your people have done. This is what Progress means: building, inventions, machines, development of mechanical aids to human hands. Russia today is like your country was in the pioneering stage. We need the knowledge and spirit that have made America what she is today."

Lenin spoke fluent and correct English.

He was grateful, Lenin said, for Hammer's food and medical aid. But "What we really need is American capital and technical aid to get our wheels turning once more. Is it not so?" Would Hammer be interested?

Dr. Hammer said his "own affairs" were "insignificant."

"Not at all," Lenin contradicted. "That is not the point. Someone must break the ice." And he offered the asbestos concession. When Hammer intimated that the preliminaries might take months during which he would have to idle around in Moscow, Lenin exclaimed, "Bureaucracy, this is one of our curses." He would appoint a committee of two: one from the Cheka, the other from Rabkrin. "You may be assured that they will act promptly. It shall be done at once."

As soon as a tentative agreement was reached, Lenin wanted Dr. Hammer to inform him of the fact. "Business men are not philanthropists, and unless they are sure of making money they would be fools to invest their capital in Russia." On Hammer's suggestion that he might encounter labor troubles, Lenin assured him there would be none.[5] The concessions contract was

---

[5] Dr. Hammer has told the complete story of his Russian experiences in Armand Hammer, *The Quest for the Romanoff Treasure*, Foreword by Walter Duranty (New York, 1936), pp. 241.

signed in Moscow on October 28, 1921, by, among others, Maxim Litvinov of the Foreign Commissariat. Concessions were foreign policy. Several days thereafter, on the eve of Dr. Hammer's departure for the United States, Lenin wrote him a letter of good wishes and saying, in English, "The beginning is extremely important. I hope it will be the beginning of extreme importance." Some time later, Lenin wrote Zinoviev, ". . . it is extremely important for us that his [Hammer's] first concession would be a full success." He wrote this in English and added a translation in Russian.

Hammer made a hole in the ice but did not break it. Other small concessions to German, Scandinavian, British, and American companies likewise bored holes in the glacier that covered Russia's relations with the outside world. But the big thaw that would crack the ice and hurl huge blocks into the air waited upon some big event, a change of climate or at least a change of seasons. The Urquhart concession or a major oil concession might have improved the Soviets' international position. Instead, the negotiations with Urquhart struck a reef in October, 1921, and were broken off. Further deteriorations in Soviet foreign affairs impelled Commissar Georgi Chicherin to suggest several radical measures to Lenin in a letter dated October 15, 1921. Chicherin urged, first, that Lenin and Trotsky resign from the Executive Committee of the Third International (Comintern), and, further, that the Soviet government issue a statement, signed by Lenin, Trotsky, and Chicherin, recognizing tsarist Russia's debts. Lenin replied the next day. "My and Trotsky's withdrawal from the Executive Committee of the Comintern is out of the question," he stated. Krassin would deal with the question of debts. The difficulty with Urquhart was temporary and the rupture came over the percentage of output to go to the Soviet government; Urquhart offered 5 percent, the Russians asked 10. On the general Kremlin position, Lenin took a firm stand. "The British and French wish to rob us. We will not permit that. We will pay no attention to their 'dissatisfaction' with this." He listed improvements: one concession had been signed; trade with Germany was growing; trade with Italy was beginning and Italy had offered a loan. Only relations with England and France had taken a turn for the worse and "in my opinion, *no* retreats or measures are necessary." The agreement with Hoover's ARA for relief to famine sufferers "is a real advantage," he concluded.

Despite the sharp tone of Lenin's letter, Chicherin raised the issue again in a letter dated October 17. The Foreign Commissar re-emphasized the need of a public declaration, signed by Lenin, Trotsky, and himself, recognizing the tsarist debt. Lenin circulated Chicherin's letter among the members of the Politburo with a note of his own in opposition to Chicherin's proposals: "Such steps merely evoke an impression of our weakness."[6]

Chicherin, however, was capable of a quiet yet immovable stubbornness. Even two pointed written rebuffs from Lenin did not shake his conviction

[6] *Leninskii Sbornik*, Vol. XXXVI, pp. 338-339.

that the Soviet government should, to better its standing with England and France, issue a conciliatory statement on the debt problem. He accordingly drafted the statement and laid it on Lenin's desk and on the tables of other Politburo members. After studying this extremely long and eloquent document, Lenin made only three minor corrections, and with those corrections the Chicherin note was forwarded on October 27, 1921, to the governments of Great Britain, France, Italy, Japan, and the United States.[7] Chicherin asserted that the Soviet government had from birth sought economic relations with the other nations and was always ready to permit foreign capitalists to earn profits while helping Soviet Russia exploit her natural resources. The Russian government "is deeply persuaded that no nation is obliged to pay the cost of the chains it has worn for ages." Nevertheless, it "is ready to give way on this important question" (here Lenin amended the sentence to read: "is ready to make a number of substantial concessions on this important question") and would pay the Tsar's pre-1914 debts "on favorable conditions which provided it with the practical possibility of meeting these obligations." This meant loans and credits.

Chicherin then proposed the early convocation of an international meeting to deliberate with the Soviet government on these matters: the germ idea of the Genoa Conference of April, 1922.

In domestic affairs too, Lenin told the Moscow Provincial Party Conference on October 29, 1921, the retreat was not yet complete. "But defeat is not as dangerous as the fear to recognize one's defeat, the fear to draw all the conclusions from it." They had already benefited from some retreats. The small mines which the government had rented to private producers in the Donets coal basin "are working well, providing the government, in the form of rent, with thirty percent of their coal output." But the retreat in the spring of 1921—the NEP—was insufficient. The Kremlin had then believed in barter, in exchanging factory goods for peasant produce. Instead, "what has emerged is ordinary buy-sell trade. Make an effort to accommodate yourselves to it, otherwise the elemental force of buy-sell and of the circulation of currency will overwhelm you. That is why we are in the position of people who must still retreat in order, finally to advance in the future. . . . We now find ourselves in a position where we must move backward a little further, not only to state capitalism, but also to government regulation of trade and currency."

Some might ask, "Then what remains here of communism?" Such a mood existed in many places. Comrades were saying, "Well, all is lost." For these he had no soft words of comfort. They had to face the truth. "We must accept the terms of cash capitalism." They had to recognize money. This was dangerous. But had any revolution been free of peril? "The disappearance of danger would mean the end of the war and the scrapping of the dictatorship of the proletariat, but of this, of course, nobody among us now dreams."

[7] *Ibid.*, Vol. XXXV, pp. 284-288.

In the end, however, they would conquer, for the forces that favored them were growing in all countries.[8]

Average citizens owned millions, and some petty merchants owned billions, of Soviet paper roubles whose real value dropped daily. They yearned for gold, the basis of tsarist currency. Lenin's logical mind told him that since Russia's economy rested on cash capitalism he had to deal with the problem of gold, and he accordingly wrote an article entitled "On the Significance of Gold Now and After the Complete Victory of Socialism," which *Pravda* published on November 6 and 7, 1921.[9]

The first paragraph struck a note of sobriety: "The best way to celebrate the anniversary of the great revolution is to concentrate attention on its un-solved tasks." This was especially true when the revolution faced new situations.

"What is new in the present moment is the necessity for our revolution to resort to 'reformist,' gradualist, cautiously roundabout methods of action in basic matters of economics."

"Reformist" and "gradualist" had been nasty communist epithets hurled at Western liberals and nonrevolutionary socialists. In ears trained to Bol-shevik noises, these words sounded like irritating discords. Here Lenin asked interesting questions which, he probably knew, were exercising the minds of many communists: "If, having tried revolutionary methods, you admit their failure and adopt reformist methods, does that not prove that you are declar-ing the revolution to have been altogether a mistake? Doesn't this show that it was wrong to begin at all with revolution, and that we should have begun with reform and limited ourselves to reforms?"

This is what the Mensheviks are saying, Lenin commented. But, "For a true revolutionist the great danger, perhaps even the only danger, is exag-gerated revolutionism, the forgetting of distinctions and of the conditions for the appropriate and successful application of revolutionary methods. . . .

"What," he exclaimed, "warrants the conclusion that 'the great, victorious, world' revolution can and must apply only revolutionary methods?"

Nothing, he replied.

These seem to be surprising statements. They actually flow from Lenin's ruling principle that the end justifies all means, even means like capitalism, reformism, and gradualism. In a sense, however, this use of means that are diametrically opposed to the end raises the question, Why pay the initial high price of revolution? Lenin's answer was that their bourgeois-democratic revolution had been a success in Russia (abolition of landlordism, liberation of women and nationalities, freedom from religion), and that in the world "The epoch of bourgeois-democratic parliamentarianism has come to an end. A new chapter of universal history has opened: the epoch of proletarian dictatorship."

[8] Lenin, *Sochineniya*, Second ed., Vol. XXVII, pp. 57-78.
[9] *Ibid.*, pp. 79-85.

Meanwhile, Russia confronted strange phenomena: "Communism and trade?!" But, he added, "if one thinks *economically*, they are not further apart than communism is from small-holding, peasant patriarchal farming."

And that is very far indeed.

Lenin had only one answer to the unanswerable questions he raised: world revolution. It was also his answer on the role of gold which he had not yet mentioned in the article. "When we conquer on a world scale," he now announced, "we will build lavatories of gold on the streets of several of the biggest cities of the world." That would be "the most 'just' and obviously-edifying use of gold" for those who have not forgotten that tens of millions were killed and thirty million crippled in the 1914-1918 war for the sake of gold and that "in 1925 approximately or in 1928 or thereabouts, they are certainly preparing to kill twenty million people and cripple sixty million in a war either between Japan and America or between England and America or something of that sort."

Speeches and articles reflected the evolution of Lenin's thinking, but they were only a small part of his activity. A thousand requests assailed him daily. A hundred tasks awaited him at every committee meeting. He never learned to do less than the possible. "I'm tired and ill. I'm going away," he wrote to a comrade on December 6, 1921. The Central Committee of the party had voted to give him another vacation at the state farm at Gorky and issued instructions that no documents, reports, or letters were to be sent to him there. Physicians believed complete rest would avert a serious illness.

From Gorky, nevertheless, he telephoned a message to his secretary for Stalin about a communist who had been excluded from the party without sufficient grounds; wrote a letter to Kamenev regarding the selection of a new commissar of agriculture; telephoned a second message for Stalin on Rabkrin's study of animal husbandry; telephoned a letter protesting the exclusion from the party of Nadezhda S. Alleluyeva, daughter of an old Bolshevik family where Lenin had lived in hiding part of the time between July and November, 1917 (she was restored to membership); and telephoned another letter on behalf of another woman excluded from the party (she too was reinstated).

On vacation, his mind never stopped working. But he did escape from telephone calls and visitors, and he enjoyed walking in the woods with Krupskaya picking mushrooms and berries and, now and then, playing with his nephew, the son of his brother Dmitri, and with the children of the kitchen staff and maids.

XLVI. ɎHE FUTURE WAS PRESENT

ON DECEMBER 17, 1921, Lenin, back from vacation, began preparing his report to the Ninth All-Russian Congress of Soviets, the highest government authority (subject, however, to the orders of the communist party). He prepared by showering colleagues with questions: To Chicherin "or if he cannot do it, to Litvinov," and to Radek, about the internal political situations in Romania and Poland, about "the alliance of the four powers, England, the United States, France and Japan, concluded at the Washington Conference" in November, 1921; "Is it all right to tell of the proposal to invite Russia and Germany" to the (Genoa) conference in April, 1922? He also asked Chicherin and others for figures on foreign trade; how many locomotives had been purchased abroad, etc.? A question to Osinsky about seed given to peasants. Questions to Smilga about coal, oil, peat, and timber production. To Chairman of the Supreme Council of National Economy Bogdanov about steel production, the Hammer concession in the Urals, the textile industry—"not more than half a page on each item . . . the briefest index figures which could be used in my report to illustrate the great difficulty of the situation and the slight signs of improvement." He likewise requested data on the progress in electrification, in education. And a note to Trotsky: "Could you include the economic work of the army in your theses and report" to the Congress?[1] He then wrote a long, detailed outline of his projected address.

Lenin's address to the Congress was the government's report to the nation on the year's developments since the last Soviet Congress. He spoke—December 23, 1921—in the midst of frost and famine, a terrible time of interminable troubles enough to break the stoutest heart. He undertook, therefore, to inspire hope. He had warned others against "communist boasting," but now he indulged in it himself. Addressing an audience and a country cut off from uncensored information, he felt free to feed Russia's ancient inferiority-superiority complex by distortion: "Materially in the economic and military sense we are endlessly weak, but morally—not taking this from the point of view of abstract morality but understanding it as the relationship of the real forces of all classes in all countries—we are stronger than any other country." The capitalist nations had refused the Soviet government diplomatic recognition, yet they traded with it. A thousand locomotives had been ordered abroad. "We have already received the first thirteen Swedish, and thirty-seven German" locomotives. "This is the smallest beginning, still it is a beginning . . . we are overpaying, nevertheless they are helping our economy. They brand us as criminals yet they help us. . . . We see, as I have

---

[1] *Leninskii Sbornik*, Vol. XXIII, pp. 277-280.

already told you, that our estimate of conditions has, by and large, proved to be more correct than theirs. And not because they have no people who can understand things correctly—on the contrary, they have more than we—but because you cannot understand things correctly when you are on the path to destruction." Imports and exports had risen. The figures were "negligible, meager, ridiculously small," but this beginning showed that there were stronger forces at work in the world than the threats they had heard for years to cease being what they were or be destroyed. "Is such a thing conceivable at all, however, as the existence of a socialist republic in a capitalist encirclement? This appeared to be inconceivable militarily as well as politically. But that this is possible politically as well as militarily has been demonstrated as a fact." And now economic coexistence was a fact.

At home, the government aimed above all to link the working class with the peasantry. "This tie is trade." This was the essence of the NEP. ". . . we are carrying out this policy seriously and for a long time, but, as has already been remarked, not forever. It was necessitated by our poverty and ruin and the enormous weakening of our heavy industry." In this area too they had registered some success. But progress would be slow "for we must achieve success in the midst of economic war and in a situation not of help from our neighbors but of enmity. But our road is the true one, because it is the road at which the other countries shall inevitably arrive." Meanwhile, he had good news for them: "I should inform you that the last few days have brought us very considerable success in the struggle against hunger. You have probably read in the press that in America twenty million dollars have been allocated for the relief of the starving in Russia."

Sowing in the famine areas had increased over previous years. Fuel production too had risen. But they had not learned to trade. The private merchant, the private industrialist, "can do business at one hundred percent profit, say in finding raw material for industry, in a way no communist or trade-union man can. And right here is the significance of the NEP. Learn." Communists were better at writing resolutions than working. "Pardon me, please. What do you call the proletariat? It is the class that works in heavy industry. And where is that heavy industry? What kind of a proletariat is it? Where is your industry? Why is it standing idle? Because there are no raw materials? And have you been able to collect them? No. You will write resolutions about collecting them and end up in a mess."

All in all, however, the NEP had started them on the right road. And this aim of linking the workers with the peasants "is not only a Russian aim but a world aim . . . it will confront all socialists. Capitalism is perishing. . . . A new society, based on the union of workers and peasants, is inescapable. Earlier or later, twenty years earlier or twenty years later, it will come, and for it, for that society, we are helping to work out the forms of the union of workers and peasants."[2]

[2] Lenin, *Sochineniya*, Second ed., Vol. XXVII, pp. 113-141.

Starving, underdeveloped Russia was leading the way to world communism by permitting private trade between peasants and private profiteering merchants. In the black night of famine and retreat to capitalism Lenin discerned the remote star of world revolution. Inner necessity was the mother of this illusion.

To make the New Economic Policy credible the peasant had to have security against secret-police swoops on his crop; the Nepman wanted safety from arrest and confiscation of earnings and wares. Lenin accordingly told the Congress of Soviets that the Cheka, renamed, would be shorn of some of its powers unless counterrevolution raised its head again. But a thorn by any other name . . . The GPU (State Political Directorate) came forth from the Cheka on February 6, 1922. On March 1, Lenin wrote J. X. Peters, second-in-command of the GPU, "The State Political Directorate can and must fight bribery, etc., and such, and punish by shooting according to court sentence. The GPU must come to an agreement with the Commissariat of Justice and through the Politburo give the necessary instructions to the Justice Commissariat and all government offices." The Commissariat managed the courts, and the Politburo nudged by the GPU gave instructions to the Commissariat. Justice remained political—as under the Cheka.

The NEP also created new problems for the trade unions, Lenin wrote in a long statement which the party's Central Committee published as its own on January 12, 1922. Given the effort of every government factory to raise productivity and achieve "a non-deficit and profitability," there was bound to be increased friction between workers and directors. The communist party, the Soviet government, and the trade unions "must openly recognize the existence of an economic struggle." The trade unions should endeavor to regulate disputes, and if these disputes led to "open conflicts in the form of strikes in government enterprises" the trade unions should strive for just settlements. However, "Any direct interference by trade unions in the management of enterprises . . . must be recognized as unconditionally harmful and intolerable."[3]

The Soviet newspapers of February 3, 1922, announced that the International Union of Metal Workers, meeting in Hannover, Germany, had adopted a resolution in favor of calling a general strike if war threatened. "I propose the following," Lenin wrote the Politburo: "To place a number of articles in Pravda and Izvestia recalling the fate of the [1912] Basel Manifesto with a thorough explanation of all the infantile folly or all the social-treason being repeated by the metal workers," and, second, that the next Comintern Executive meeting pass a resolution to show that "only a previously prepared and experienced revolutionary party, with a good underground apparatus, can successfully conduct the struggle against war, that, moreover, the means of conducting the struggle is not a strike against war

[3] Ibid., pp. 147-156.

but the formation of revolutionary cells in the fighting forces and their preparation for carrying out a revolution."[4]

Lenin telephoned the statement to his secretary for the members of the Politburo and others. He was again ill in Gorky. He telephoned A. D. Tsurupa, Deputy Chairman of the Sovnarkom (Lenin was Chairman), on January 21, "I cannot return before three and perhaps four weeks."[5] In fact, the Politburo voted on February 2 to "extend" Lenin's vacation "until the Eleventh Congress of the [Communist] Party" at the end of March.[6]

Lenin was allergic to vacations. They offended his overpowering sense of duty. And they must have puzzled him. During his January-February-March, 1922, stay in Gorky he felt ill, slept badly, suffered stomach upsets. But his brain functioned as vigorously as ever. A year later, in March, 1923, that brain would be scarcely alive and his body would be partially paralyzed, and in January, 1924, brain and body would die. Yet during the year that preceded the mental collapse which ended Lenin's career, his intellectual grasp remained supreme and he dominated Soviet Russia as never before. His prestige grew and so did his command of persons and situations. Nobody could have suspected in those twelve months from March, 1922, to March, 1923, that they were seeing the flaming tail of a comet and not the rising sun. He might have lived in full vigor for ten or fifteen years more and thereby changed all of Soviet history and much world history.

In fact, Lenin's last year was his greatest. It was probably also his saddest, for it is impossible to suppose, judging by what he said, that he failed to realize where he had failed.

In this highest and last phase of his life Lenin faced two central problems: foreign policy and bureaucracy. Foreign policy involved the question of Russia's existence in a hostile international environment. Bureaucracy was synonymous with the management of the state or the functioning of the dictatorship. All Soviet citizens were its objects, all farming and art, all industry and education, all travel and news dissemination, all publishing and construction, all politics—everything except the very personal aspects of private life.

Throughout 1922 Lenin applied his tongue and pen and political arm to Soviet foreign affairs. Early in the year he had occasion to reprimand Chicherin, his Foreign Commissar, with whom his relations were usually smooth. Chicherin, seeking to throw a bridge to America and knowing American criticism of Soviet atheism, wrote two letters to Lenin, on January 20 and 22, suggesting that priests and clergymen be given the right to vote and to be represented in the soviets. Lenin bristled. On January 23, in a letter to the Politburo, quoted in the Pospelov *Biografia* (Second ed., p. 585), he said, "I have now received two letters from Chicherin. . . . He raised the

---

[4] *Ibid.*, p. 166. This statement is omitted from the fourth edition of Lenin's *Collected Works*, Vol. 33, August, 1921-March, 1923 (Moscow, 1950). It embarrassed Stalin's Kremlin.

[5] *Leninskii Sbornik*, Vol. XXXVI, p. 403.

[6] Lenin, *op. cit.*, Fourth ed., Vol. 33, p. 493.

question whether it is not desirable, in return for adequate compensation, to agree to a small amendment of our Constitution, namely the representation of parasitic elements in the Soviets. To do this to please the Americans. This Chicherin proposal shows, in my opinion, . . . that he should be sent immediately to a sanatorium, any connivance in this sense . . . would, in my opinion, represent a dangerous threat to all negotiations."

During January and February Lenin drafted a detailed plan for a long article to be entitled "Notes of a Publicist." The outline, found among his papers after he died, dealt chiefly with domestic problems but included such items as "Levi and Serrati," the two dissidents who had withdrawn from the Comintern: "Ireland"; " 'The United Front' of the West European proletariat and the British elections"; "Two global fronts and 'the Middle,' 'the Half-Bolsheviks,' compare the *Hindu*-Tolstoyan." The two fronts, presumably, were the capitalist front and the envisioned proletarian front, and in between stood "Half-Bolsheviks" like the Hindu-Tolstoyan, Lenin's only reference to Gandhi whom he did not understand, for the Mahatma was indeed a Hindu and Tolstoyan but the antithesis of Bolshevism. The outline also read: "Include in title: On the Genoa Conference."[7]

Lenin commenced writing the proposed article, did a few pages, but never finished it. He treated several of the questions, however, in speeches, letters, and telephone messages. On February 1, for instance, he dictated a long letter on the telephone from Gorky to Bukharin and Zinoviev about the united proletarian front. A conference of the Second, Third, and the Second-and-a-half International was scheduled to meet in Berlin in April. Lenin wanted the Comintern delegates there to "declare officially that we regard the Second and the Second-and-a-half International as nothing else than inconsistent and wavering participants in a block with the counterrevolutionary world bourgeoisie and that we are going to the conference on the united front with a view to achieving the greatest possible unity in direct action upon the masses in the interest of exposing the political errors of the entire position of the Second and of the Second-and-a-Half International," just as they, he believed, intended to expose the "incorrectness of our position." The very next day, Lenin telephoned another message to Bukharin saying he was "astonished and shocked" at not having had a reply to his first message. "I request an answer."[8]

PART ONE ✎ THE GENOA CONFERENCE

Of all foreign policy issues, the Genoa Conference bulked the largest. This was the first international conference to which the great powers invited

[7] *Ibid.*, Second ed., Vol. XXVII, editorial note, pp. 525-526; also *Leninskii Sbornik*, Vol. XXXVI, pp. 414-418.
[8] *Leninskii Sbornik*, Vol. XXXVI, pp. 418-420.

the Soviet government, and they invited it because they proposed, in view of the NEP, to achieve economic coexistence with Soviet Russia by participating on a large scale in her reconstruction and thus remolding her politically and economically. Lenin insisted on the most thorough preparation by each member of the Soviet delegation to the conference. He himself expected to lead the delegation. "We declared from the very beginning that *we greet Genoa and will go there; . . .* we are going there as merchants," he told a session of the communist fraction of the All-Russian Congress of Metal Workers on March 6. (Formally, he was on vacation in Gorky; that, however, could not prevent him from addressing a meeting in Moscow.) "We know," he continued, that the purpose of the Genoa Conference and its diplomatic preliminaries is trade. "*The bourgeois countries must trade with Russia;* they know that without some form of mutual economic relations their collapse will go further than it has gone hitherto." These words reflected a deep communist conviction: the capitalist nations needed Russia for their economic salvation. They would be forced to trade with her and to give her loans, otherwise, Bolsheviks argued, where would they invest their overflowing supply of capital? The Soviet representatives, Lenin cautioned, would have to learn how to conduct trade negotiations. "Here it is necessary to make our brains more flexible and throw off all our communist or, more correctly, our Russian Oblomovism and much else too. . . . There was a type in Russian life—Oblomov. He always lay in bed and made plans. Since then much time has passed, Russia has made three revolutions, and still the Oblomovs remain, because Oblomov was not only a landlord but also a peasant, and not only a peasant but also an intellectual, and not only an intellectual but also a worker and a communist. . . . We must trade with the capitalist nations so long as they exist as such." But if those nations imagine that they will think up something new and confront the Russians with new conditions at Genoa "then allow us to say to them (I hope I will be able to say this personally to Lloyd George in Genoa)—you, gentlemen, are not surprising anyone. You are traders and you bargain well . . . I said that I expect to speak personally with Lloyd George about these matters in Genoa and to say to him that there is no point *in frightening us with trifles,* because only those who frighten lose prestige. I hope that this possibility will not be denied me by my health which for some months has prevented me from participating directly in political affairs and does not allow me to fill the Soviet posts assigned to me. I have reason to expect that in a few weeks I can return to my direct participation in the work."

Lenin did not go to Genoa and did not speak personally to Prime Minister David Lloyd George. His health deteriorated sharply in the conference month of April and in May. There was fear, too, of his being assassinated abroad, and hundreds of Soviet citizens telegraphed the Kremlin—in those days such actions were probably spontaneous—urging that he stay home. But his chief reason for absenting himself from Genoa was health. "I am ill and stupid," he wrote in a letter dated March 3, 1922.[9] He was ill but not stupid, and his saying he was stupid was his way of making others look stupid, for in the same sentence he asked Commissar of Foreign Trade Krassin, to whom he addressed the letter, or a deputy to "explain to me in popular language and in not more than ten lines" the difference between abolishing the Soviet monopoly of foreign trade, which Lenin held to be a keystone of the communist regime, and allowing foreign businessmen to enter Soviet Russia to buy and sell. "Concretely? Popularly? What is the difference?" Lenin demanded. He saw no difference. There was no difference. The monopoly of foreign trade constituted the Kremlin's defense against alleged schemes the Western powers had for Genoa to re-enter the Russian market with their exports, purchase raw materials from any dealer, and thereby undermine Moscow plans for industrialization. The foreign trade monopoly, instituted long before Genoa, was the equivalent of 100 percent protectionism. No outsider would compete with a Soviet enterprise.

Commissar of Foreign Trade Krassin and Commissar of Finances Gregory Sokolnikov were at odds on the future of the trade monopoly. Lenin discussed the question with Kamenev, Stalin, and Zinoviev, and on March 3, the same day, he sent a letter to Kamenev saying, "I have thought rather long about our conversation. . . . My conclusion—Krassin is undoubtedly right. We cannot now retreat any further from the monopoly of foreign trade. Otherwise, foreigners will buy up and export everything of value." Sokolnikov was making "a gigantic mistake which will surely ruin us unless the Central Committee corrects his policy in time and makes sure of the actual execution of the corrected policy. His mistake is abstractness, being carried away by something schematic (which was always the sin of Sokolnikov, a talented journalist and fascinated politician)"—fascinated by abstract ideas. "It is a tremendous error," Lenin further told Kamenev, "to think that the NEP has put an end to terror. We shall still return to the terror and to economic terror. Foreigners are already bribing officials and 'they are exporting the remnants of Russia.' . . . The monopoly is a polite warning: My dear man, a moment will come when I shall hang you."[10]

These comments were, in effect, Lenin's instructions to Chicherin, leader and acting chairman of the Soviet delegation to the Genoa Conference. Lenin apparently had a premonition that he would not go as chairman of the delegation to Genoa for on February 25 he telephoned a note to Stalin and Kamenev: he rejected Chicherin's proposal "and I insist on my earlier formula." Chicherin had asked the Politburo to appoint a troika to lead the Soviet delegation at Genoa. Instead Lenin wanted Chicherin to exercise all the powers of the chairman, and only in case of Chicherin's departure or illness would the chairman's powers pass in turn to one of two troikas, first, Litvinov, Krassin, and Christian G. Rakovsky, second, Litvinov, Yoffe, and

[9] *Ibid.*, pp. 442-443.
[10] *Ibid.*, pp. 443-446.

V. V. Vorovsky. The Politburo voted for Lenin's arrangement.[11]

Eager to make the Soviet delegation immune to error, Lenin read Western newspapers and books and forwarded them to delegation members. On March 6, for example, he sent Chicherin and Litvinov, L. Haden Guest's *The Struggle for Power in Europe, 1917-1921, An Outline Economic and Political Survey of the Central States and Russia*, published in London in 1921. "If you haven't seen this," read Lenin's accompanying note, "look into it or instruct somebody to read it and tell you. The author, apparently, is a dangerous scoundrel, a rascally labor lieutenant of the capitalist class."[12] The last six words Lenin wrote in English.

Lenin's greatest worry was that the powers at Genoa would regard the NEP as their opportunity to help re-establish capitalism in Russia. Hence the emphasis in his March 6 speech to the metal workers: "We can assert with complete firmness that the retreat which we began we can already check and are checking. Enough." And again, a few minutes later, "Enough, we shall make no more concessions!" Moreover, "If the capitalist gentlemen think that they can delay further and the later it is the greater the concessions, then I repeat, we must say to them, 'Enough, tomorrow you will get nothing.'" Repetition never troubled Lenin. He expressed this same thought three more times. Also that they were going to Genoa as merchants: "We, as merchants, establish connections and we know what you owe us and what we owe you and what must be your normal and even your abnormal profit."[13]

He had left the door open. The speech was published in *Pravda* on March 8, for the outside world to read. But Soviet communists also read it, and some rejoiced at the thought that NEP retreats were ended. Indeed, Commissar of Justice Kursky took it to heart and, according to information given Lenin by an adjutant, refused to draft a declaration of civil rights, including individual property rights, on the grounds, as Kursky phrased it, that "the retreat has been rescinded." Angrily, Lenin wrote Kursky, "I must warn you that such a motivation is ridiculous and that the procrastination you have employed and are employing is intolerable." Lenin ordered Kursky to have the declaration ready and in Deputy Chairman Tsurupa's hands within forty-eight hours.[14]

Meanwhile Chicherin prepared with characteristic meticulous assiduity for the Genoa Conference. By March 10 he had formulated a statement of principles. He immediately delivered it to Lenin, who responded four days later.[15]

Chicherin begged Lenin to read the statement and "give your instructions. We must present 'the broadest pacifist program.' But we have none. There are only separate fragmentary mentions in the original directives of the

---

[11] *Ibid.*, p. 434.
[12] *Ibid.*, p. 447.
[13] Lenin, *op. cit.*, Second ed., Vol. XXVII, pp. 168-179.
[14] *Leninskii Sbornik*, Vol. XXXVI, pp. 462-463.
[15] *Ibid.*, pp. 451-455.

Central Committee. I am here for the first time essaying this task." Lenin's reply began, "Comrade Chicherin! I read your letter of March 10. It seems to me that you yourself have made an excellent presentation of the pacifist program."

Neither Chicherin nor Lenin was a pacifist. On January 24, 1918, Lenin had sent a two-sentence note to Chicherin: "The bearer is a pacifist who wants to talk about peace. If you can find a free minute perhaps you will meet his request."[16] The communist leaders were contemptuous of persons who wanted "to talk about peace." Lenin, however, did exempt religious conscientious objectors from military service. In December, 1918, Vladimir G. Chertkov, Count Leo Tolstoy's collaborator and translator, came to see Lenin in the Kremlin to plead the cause of the objectors. The result of the interview was a Sovnarkom decree of January 4, 1919, releasing religious conscientious objectors and nonreligious ethical objectors like Chertkov from military service providing they agreed to serve "chiefly in hospitals for contagious diseases or do other corresponding work chosen by the conscript."[17] In tsarist Russia objectors on religious and political grounds were excused from military service. It was an administrative convenience: forcibly conscripted objectors often practiced civil disobedience and caused indiscipline. Under the Lenin decree "several hundred persons" were exempted from military service. When Stalin came to power, exemptions stopped.

The communists wanted peace because they needed it, but given their conception of capitalists and imperialists as incurable warmakers, Chicherin and Lenin could only have regarded their "pacifist program" as propaganda, and indeed Lenin's letter to Chicherin implies as much: "The whole art consists in stating it"—the "pacifist program"—"and our merchants' proposals clearly and loudly *before* the dispersal (if 'they' bring things to an early dispersal). You and our delegation possess this ability. As I see it you already have approximately thirteen points." Lenin had marked the proposals in Chicherin's letter with Arabic numerals 1 to 13 and underlined some phrases one, two, three, or four times and here and there made marginal remarks: "Correct!" "True!" "*That's it.*" The thirteen points, Lenin said, were "excellent." "We will intrigue everybody by saying, 'We have a very broad and complete program.' If they don't allow you to read it, we will *publish it* with a protest.

"At all times 'a tiny' reservation: We, as communists, have *our* communist program (The Third International), *but* we regard it as our duty as merchants *to support* (even on a one in ten thousand chance) *the pacifists* in the

---

[16] *Ibid.*, Vol. XXXI, p. 240. The *Sbornik* editor states that the name of the bearer is unknown. Apparently, neither Lenin nor Chicherin received him.

[17] This information was communicated by Vladimir V. Chertkov, the son of Tolstoy's friend, from Moscow in July, 1963, to Olga Biryukova, the daughter of Paul I. Biryukov, another prominent Tolstoyan, in Geneva. Olga Biryukova generously shared the information with me.

OTHER, that is, the bourgeois camp (including in it the Second and Second-and-a-half International).

"This will be venomous as well as 'friendly' and will contribute to the demoralization of the enemy. With such tactics we shall gain *even* if Genoa fails. *We will not make* a deal that is not profitable to us. With communist greetings, Your Lenin."

Lenin was right in suspecting that "they" might break up the Genoa Conference soon after it opened. His suspicion is, in fact, the clue to the Soviet behavior at Genoa and also to the Rapallo Treaty which the Soviets signed with Germany near Genoa. The conference was indeed doomed before it started.

The idea of Genoa sprang from the imaginative mind of Prime Minister Lloyd George whose Liberal-Conservative Coalition government threatened to dissolve in a sea of personal rivalries and political crosscurrents. He could not have known that in the autumn of 1922 the Conservatives would abandon him, his Cabinet would fall, and he, age fifty-nine, resourceful, forceful, influential, would lose the election and live on until 1945, yet never return to office. He could not have foreseen this, but he was a politician and he sensed that, beset by troubles in India, troubles with trade unions, troubles in his own party, and the "loss" of Ireland, he needed a dramatic victory in international affairs to extend his stay at Number Ten Downing Street. The most immediate world problems were Germany and Soviet Russia. He hoped to solve both at Genoa where, as he put it, "big men meet big men." For this reason, "Citizen Lenin" was invited by name.

Success required the active aid of France; also of the United States. The Harding-Hoover-Hughes administration adopted a quarantine policy toward Russia. Except for famine relief, it wanted no contacts with Bolshevism. The U.S.A., accordingly, abstained from the Genoa Conference.

Aristide Briand, the French Premier and Foreign Minister, desired a fruitful issue of the Genoa Conference to reinforce his shaky position. Briand, with Lloyd George, in January, 1922, had settled the preliminaries of Genoa off the record between tees, drives, and putts on the golf course at Cannes. It is known, however, that Briand asked a British guarantee against German aggression in lieu of the Anglo-American guarantee which failed when President Wilson was denied Senate consent for the peace treaty. Lloyd George offered a guarantee against unprovoked attack but not the permanent General Staff consultations on which Raymond Poincaré had set his heart. Poincaré, moreover, resented negotiating with Germans about reparations. He was incubating his own scheme for reparations collections: the occupation of the German Ruhr (which occurred in January, 1923). Nor did Poincaré see eye to eye with Lloyd George on Russia. Briand, accordingly, received a hasty summons from the French President to interrupt his golf-and-diplomacy game at Cannes and return to Paris where he reluctantly yielded the premiership to Poincaré. Jean Louis Barthou became foreign minister and France's chief delegate at Genoa. This, as well as the knife at Lloyd George's political throat in London, boded ill for the conference. Lenin therefore counseled Chicherin to expound his "pacifist program" at the first opportunity.

This program declared: ". . . the existing international political and economic forms serve as a fig leaf for the predatory imperialists and, in particular, as a weapon against us. The League of Nations is simply an instrument of the Entente which has already employed it against us. You yourself," he wrote Lenin, "have pointed out that arbitration between bourgeois and soviet governments is impossible, nevertheless, arbitration is an indispensable part of the pacifist arsenal. . . . We must introduce something new into the customary international forms in order to interfere with the transformation of these forms into an instrument of imperialism. . . . As a result of the world war [not, be it noted, of the Bolshevik revolution] the independence movements of all oppressed and colonial peoples have been strengthened. The world powers are beginning to crack at the seams. Our program must bring all oppressed colonial peoples into the international scheme. The right of all peoples to secession or home rule should be recognized. . . . The novelty of our international scheme must consist in the participation, on an equal footing with European peoples, of all Negro and other colonial peoples in conferences and commissions and the right to block interference in their domestic affairs. A second novelty should be the obligatory participation of workers organizations" in international conferences. His third proposal was foreign aid by the strong to weak nations. "Simultaneously, we shall urge a general reduction of armaments . . . the abolition of submarines, chemical gases, rockets, flame throwers, and aerial warfare. . . . We shall propose to the capitalists of the advanced nations the construction of a superhighway from London to Moscow and Vladivostok (Peking) and explain that this will open the untold wealth of Siberia to general exploitation . . . we shall propose the planned redistribution of gold now lying unused in the vaults of American banks" as well as the planned redistribution of food, raw materials, and manufactured commodities.

"P.S.," Lenin added in his approving letter to Chicherin. "Why should we not 'be venomous' (and 'friendly') and propose in addition . . . the cancellation of all war debts and . . . *the revision* . . . of the Versailles and *all* war treaties? We will cover them with shame and spittle 'in a friendly way.' . . ." Finally, the Soviet government would, as an exception pay smallholders of Russian bonds if they were workers or peasants.

Lenin clearly felt Russia had nothing to gain at Genoa and therefore nothing to lose by enunciating Chicherin's "pacifist program." With this in mind, the heavy artillery of the Soviet delegation—Chicherin, Litvinov, Krassin, Yoffe, Rakovsky, Rudzutak, Preobrazhensky, Sapronov, and Vorovsky—arrived in Berlin in March, 1922, en route to the Italian seacoast.

The communist diplomats, notably Chicherin, who had a sharp aversion to the League of Nations and to the two great Western powers (England and France), dived immediately into intense negotiations with a view to a German alliance in all but name. The two pariahs, the losers in the war and the Muscovite revolutionaries, would link forces against the moneybag conquerors. The Eastern, pro-Russian school of politicians, traditionally strong in Germany under the monarchy, was reinforced by defeat at the hands of the West. Chicherin moved in his element.

Soon the text of what became the Rapallo Treaty—it shaped Soviet-German political, military, and economic relations until Hitler's advent—reached the drafting stage, and Chicherin urged signing. Foreign Minister Walther Rathenau, a Westerner, a philosopher, author, and liberal and former director of the German General Electric Company, held back. He still hoped for a settlement of Germany's painful reparations problem at Genoa. He put his faith in the "International Consortium" projected by France for the rehabilitation of Russia. When America refused to join, this became the "Europa Consortium." The British had other ideas. Leslie Urquhart, suing for a concession to his expropriated mining properties in Siberia, was a member of his country's delegation to the Genoa Conference. The Royal-Dutch Shell group had high expectations of obtaining an oil concession in the Caucasus. The British preferred not to mingle their economic efforts and export-import expansion with those of other countries. Nevertheless, Rathenau believed the idea of the consortium might prevail. So did the heads of several large German banks. Above all, Germany was eager to reappear on the international stage, and Rathenau rightly feared that signing a treaty with the Soviets on the eve of the conference would lead to German exclusion from its sessions.

The Germans and the Russians accordingly entrained for Genoa with the provisional Rapallo Treaty in their briefcases.

Chicherin mounted the world platform on October 10—the first Bolshevik to do so—and delivered his "pacifist program." He spoke flawless French, then translated himself into English.[18] The tone was more subdued than in the original Lenin had seen. Chicherin welcomed Italian Prime Minister Facta's statement that here there were no victors or conquered and Lloyd George's declaration that all at the conference were equal. Therefore coexistence was possible: Though the Soviet government stood on the principles of communism, the Soviet delegation recognized that "in the present historic epoch" the parallel existence of the old and the newly born social systems enabled them to cooperate for purposes of economic rehabilitation. The Soviet delegation did not come to Genoa to make propaganda for its the-

---

[18] Complete text in *International Economic Conference of Genoa. Provisional Verbatim Record. First Plenary Session* (Official conference document in Italian, French, and English) (Genoa, 1922). Russian text in *Dokumenty Vneshnei Politiki SSSR.* Vol. 5 (Moscow, 1961), pp. 191-195.

oretical views but to establish business relations with the governments and businessmen of all countries on a mutual basis of equality and complete and unconditional recognition. Russia was the largest country in Europe and was prepared to open her gates for transit to the Far East and for the exploitation of her vast soil, timber, coal and ore resources, especially in Siberia. But the economic restoration of Russia and, with it, the elimination of the economic chaos of Europe, would take a wrong road if it made intolerable demands related to Russia's hated past. (He was referring to the payment of tsarist debts.) The Soviet government had adopted new legislation, corresponding to the New Economic Policy, which provided the legal guarantees necessary to economic collaboration with capitalist states.

However, all efforts to restore world economy would fail as long as the threat of war hung over the planet. Therefore the Russian delegation would, in the course of the conference, propose a general reduction of armaments and support all proposals to lighten the burden of militarism: limitation in the size of armies, the abolition of poison gases and air warfare, and the prohibition of the use of weapons of destruction against civilian populations. (No mention of submarines.)

In addition, the Soviet government hoped future conferences would include representatives of all peoples. Chicherin then urged the convocation of a World Congress convened on the basis of the equality of all peoples whose right to dispose of their own fate would be universally recognized. Workers' organizations should participate officially in such congresses. These congresses would create technical commissions to aid underdeveloped countries. One desirable form of assistance was the redistribution of the world's gold resources in the proportions that existed before the war by means of long-term loans without causing any actual harm to the nations now in possession of great gold hoards. This redistribution of gold should be accompanied by the systematic redistribution of manufactured products, fuel, etc.

French Foreign Minister Barthou took the floor to reply. Of course, he conceded, every delegation has the right to raise any question, but they were meeting under the terms of the Cannes conference, and its resolutions envisaged no such universal congress as Chicherin had adumbrated, nor did they mention disarmament. These questions were therefore excluded and he was declaring simply but very firmly that any program on disarmament offered by the Russian delegation would meet with not only protest but precise, categorical, final, and decisive rejection.

Chicherin jumped to his feet. The agenda of the Genoa Conference already contained questions unmentioned at Cannes. There was as yet no definite agenda for the Genoa Conference but, "since we have come here for purposes of reconciliation," his delegation would abide by the will of the conference. On disarmament, he merely wished to say that since Briand had affirmed at the Washington conference on arms limitation that France could not disarm because Russia was armed, "we assumed that if Russia agreed to disarmament, the reason indicated by M. Briand would be eliminated."

The Franco-Soviet duel threatened to end the conference at birth. Lloyd George poured wit on the troubled waters. Chicherin had not laid down any conditions, he interpreted, but rather made some general remarks which, useful in themselves, might nevertheless be somewhat dangerous. He hoped Chicherin would not insist on his universal, ethereal, noble, but very questionable congress. They would all enter the kingdom where there are neither wars nor conferences before Chicherin's world assembly could meet. As to disarmament, he favored it in general.

This satisfied Barthou, who wanted no congress or disarmament, and Chicherin, who had expected neither. But, in effect, Genoa's first session showed that the conference, as a conference, would be barren of results. Lloyd George accordingly invited the Russians to negotiate privately and secretly in his Villa d'Albertis by the blue sea.

These talks dealt with Western claims on Russia and Soviet claims on the West for damage inflicted during the civil war; also with Western demands for payment and Muscovite demands for credits and loans to enable Russia to pay. The direct outcome was zero. The indirect result was the Rapallo Treaty.

While France, Belgium, and Italy participated with Britain in the Villa d'Albertis discussions, the Germans were excluded. For days they felt spurned. Repeated attempts to establish personal contact with Lloyd George failed. They gathered the impression that the West was reaching a commercial and financial agreement with Russia at their expense.

The Germans had no knowledge of the impasse in Lloyd George's villa. When Russian and German delegates met by appointment in a Genoa café, the Soviet representatives said all was going well. Rumor even had it that the Allies and the Soviets were on the verge of a settlement.

It was Saturday evening, and the atmosphere in the Hotel Eden, the German headquarters, was anything but paradisian. The Germans went early to bed. At one in the morning—Easter Sunday—a telephone call from Yoffe awakened Baron Ago von Maltzan, the Easterner among the Germans; he invited the German delegation to come to the Hotel St. Margherite, the Russian residence, to sign the Rapallo Treaty drafted in March in Berlin. What about the Villa d'Albertis talks? Maltzan inquired. Those were going fine, Yoffe replied; a recess had been called over Easter Sunday and Easter Monday.

Maltzan immediately woke the Germans and they gathered in their pajamas to deliberate. After some hesitation, they decided to sign and they did so at 6:30 P.M. Easter Sunday, April 16, 1922.[19]

[19] More on the Genoa Conference and Rapallo Treaty in Fischer, *The Soviets in World Affairs.*

Two days later Lenin telephoned a message from Gorky to Stalin, Kamenev, and Trotsky inquiring whether the treaty should be published immediately or when it became clear that the Genoa Conference was breaking on the rocks of discord. The Politburo voted to publish forthwith.[20]

The Soviet diplomats at Rapallo had tricked the Germans into signing. Yet they would have achieved the same effect without dissembling, for the Russians as well as the Germans got nothing out of Genoa; this and their isolation except from each other would have brought them together in any case.

Now Lenin thought Lloyd George was tricking them. Two days after the Rapallo Treaty was published in the Soviet press—April 19, 1922—he sent a note by telephone, again to Stalin, Kamenev, and Trotsky, recommending that a telegram be dispatched to Chicherin and journalist Sosnovsky in Genoa, copy to *Pravda* and *Izvestia* "as instructions to our press," saying: "All the news from Genoa indicates that we are succumbing to a deception. Lloyd George, who is making noises against France, is thereby disguising his chief aim—to force us to pay debts in general and the debts of former owners in particular. It is time to begin systematically exposing this customary maneuver of British diplomacy, expose it in our own and in the foreign communist press. Lenin."

Simultaneously Lenin sent a telephonogram to Stalin with the suggested text of a telegram to Chicherin "if the members of the Politburo do not object." It read: "Comrade Chicherin. I never doubted that Lloyd George is acting under the pressure of British sharks and that England will not abandon France, but I think that this must not alter our policy one iota and that we must not fear the dissolution of the conference. We must under no condition agree to recognize private debts. I think I know the real situation. Lenin."[21]

The real situation was that France and Britain were drifting apart. Lenin not only did not fear the dissolution of the conference, he hinted that Moscow, with Rapallo secured, might provoke the dissolution. The Kremlin had had a telegram from Rudzutak of the Soviet delegation in Genoa in criticism of an action by Chicherin. Reacting to Rudzutak's wire, Lenin dispatched a letter to Stalin "for the Politburo": Chicherin was making a mistake. Without achieving anything practical, "he might deprive us," in case of a rupture, "of the only explanation which is fully advantageous, important in principle, and gives us a sure gain in the future, namely a rupture on account of our refusal to restore the private property of foreign capitalists." Lenin therefore asked the Politburo to send a telegram to Chicherin "for all the members of the delegation" and "in my name," supporting Rudzutak's view: "We regard as a very dangerous error every step and every phrase which might rob us of the only beneficial excuse for a rupture . . . the excuse that we disagree

[20] *Leninskii Sbornik*, Vol. XXXVI, p. 473.
[21] *Ibid.*, p. 474.

unconditionally with the restoration of the private property of foreign capitalists." Lenin promised that this would lead to "our complete diplomatic
and commercial victory in the very nearest future. I repeat again that we
gave you the absolutely exact text of our maximum concessions from which
we shall not retreat one iota. As soon as it is fully clear that an agreement
is impossible on the basis of these concessions, we authorize you to break off
[the negotiations] while retaining for propaganda and future diplomatic advances these two trumps: 1) The importance in principle of the Russo-German treaty, 2) Our difference of opinion on the restoration of the property of
capitalists."[22]

The next day—April 25—the Politburo sanctioned Lenin's text of the
telegram to the delegation in Genoa.

Hopelessly deadlocked on this primary issue, neither Chicherin nor the
other chief delegates provoked a rupture. The conference dragged on into
May and did not die until it sired another conference, held in The Hague
in June and July, which also led to nothing. Russia never paid her old debts.

Ill and away from the Kremlin in Gorky, Lenin received all important
information, and all important decisions on foreign affairs issued from him.
He never sinned against formalities; he never had to. He consulted the Politburo, and it did his bidding.

Lenin still dominated Soviet politics.

PART TWO   ✍   THE BOG OF BUREAUCRACY

Soviet Russia in 1922 had a population of approximately 145 million
thinly spread over an area as large as North America; only 18 percent lived
in towns, the remainder in scattered villages. To rule such a country with a
few railroads, few roads, less than a dozen short highways, sparse telephone
lines, and an infant radio broadcasting system would have been a colossal
task even if unfettered local government had been highly developed. To
rule it from within the red-brick, crenelated walls of the Moscow Kremlin
defied the possible. Lenin's writ ran only where enough communists and
GPU-men could impose it, and this certainly did not embrace all the territory
and inhabitants of his realm. Occasional visits by tax-collecting agents was
as much as millions of muzhiks ever saw of the Soviet regime in those days.
Newspapers rarely reached the peasants and they were not interested or could
not read. In these circumstances, efficient government would have required
a large corps of supermen capable of resisting gravity in the bottomless bog
of red tape. Actually, the Soviet supermen could be counted on the fingers
of one hand. Perhaps there were four—Lenin, Trotsky, Kamenev, and Djerzhinsky—encumbered with many thousands of pygmies and more lackadaisical
Oblomov pen-pushers and paper-passers. These ruled unhappy Russia.

"*We are being sucked into* a foul bureaucratic swamp," Lenin wrote Dep-

[22] *Ibid.*, pp. 475-476.

uty Chairman Tsurupa on January 24, 1922. "Wise saboteurs deliberately drag us down into the paper bog. The majority of the people's commissars" —members of the federal Cabinet—"and other dignitaries unconsciously 'put their heads into the noose.' . . . The center of gravity of your work should be just this transformation of our abominable bureaucratic work, the struggle against bureaucracy and red tape, the check on the execution of instructions." Lenin likewise complained of "the disgraceful plethora of commissions. . . . You must . . . free yourself from the bustle and hurly-burly which *is killing all of us* and give yourself the possibility of thinking quietly about the work *as a whole.* . . . Please consider all this and write me. With a communist greeting. Lenin."

"More on the question of a new style of work," Lenin began a second letter to Tsurupa dated February 20. The activities of the Sovnarkom and STO should be improved so that "the people's commissars do not dare to bring up every detail, and instead decide it themselves and *be responsible* for it themselves." It was necessary "to study people and look among them for *capable* officials. That is now the essence; without that, all orders and decisions are dirty bits of paper. Give me an answer."

Tsurupa replied immediately, but the reply apparently displeased Lenin, who wrote him on February 21: "The chief thing, in my opinion, is to move the center of gravity from the writing of decrees and decisions (in that our folly reaches idiocy) to *the choice of personnel* and the checking of fulfillment" of orders. "That is the essence. . . . *You and Rykov* must devote nine-tenths of your time to this (it is ridiculous to expect from the Rabkrin and from the executive secretariats more than the fulfillment of *simple* tasks). With us everything has sunk into the disgusting bureaucratic bog of 'departments.' . . . Departments are excrement. Decrees are excrement. The search for personnel, the check on fulfillment—that is everything."[23]

These letters to Tsurupa were criticisms of Rabkrin. Stalin was People's Commissar of Rabkrin, the watchdog of bureaucracy. Its performance had convinced Lenin that it could do no more than execute "simple" tasks, not the gigantic task of eliminating the corruption, inefficiency, and other evils of the sagging government machinery. Lenin was apparently grooming Tsurupa to succeed Stalin as head of Rabkrin.

Many phenomena in the bureaucracy perturbed Lenin. On December 1, 1921, V. V. Oldenborger, chief engineer of Moscow water supply and member of the Moscow Soviet, committed suicide. *Pravda* did not report this event until January 3, 1922, and then, Lenin complained to the Politburo, "with complete inadequacy." He urged a thorough investigation, which found that Oldenborger had been driven to his death by persecution in which communists had a hand. He had been an engineer of the Moscow waterworks

---

[23] Lenin, *op. cit.*, Second ed., Vol. XXVII, pp. 156-165. The fourth edition of Lenin's *Collected Works*, Vol. 35, omits the last of these letters (dated Feb. 21, 1922) because it contains a criticism of Stalin's Rabkrin.

since 1894. In the same communication, Lenin mentioned the murder of engineers and technical specialists.[24]

Lenin saw this as a double-barreled threat: the communists were untrained and inefficient and were intolerant of trained and efficient noncommunists inherited from the past. He bore down heavily on communists. "The target of the next party purge will be the communists *who imagine* that they are executives," he told the communist metal workers on March 6, 1922. In the same speech he criticized communists who were good enough party members and had been to jail before the revolution and possessed other virtues and had therefore been placed at the head of a state trust though they lacked any business sense. "Our worst domestic enemy," he proclaimed, "is the communist who occupies a responsible position (and also not responsible position). . . . He has not learned to fight red tape, he cannot fight it, he shelters it. We must get rid of this enemy." In past party purges "hundreds of thousands, approximately, had been thrown out, and that was excellent," but other "self-seekers," "bandwagon-riders," and "thieves" remained. He would urge the impending party congress, he said, to expel them.

The idea that communists abused party membership to the detriment of noncommunists and of effective administration seems to have obsessed Lenin. He dwelt on it even in a lengthy salute to a new philosophical monthly, *Under the Banner of Marxism.* "Comrade Trotsky," the article began, "has already said everything important about the tasks" of the magazine in its first and second issues, "and said it very well." He, Lenin, wished to stress an announcement by the publication that it sought to unite all materialists, whether Marxists or not. This he welcomed. "One of the biggest and most dangerous mistakes of communists (and, in general, of revolutionists who have successfully begun a great revolution) is to suppose that it is possible to complete the revolution with the hands of revolutionaries alone. . . . There can be no thought of any successful communist development without a union with noncommunists in the most varied fields of activity."

The new journal, Lenin added, "must be an organ of militant atheism. We have government departments or, at least, government offices which conduct such work. But the work is very sluggish, extremely unsatisfactory, and apparently suffers under the burden of the general conditions of our authentically Russian (even though Soviet) bureaucracy."[25]

The legacy of the past lay heavy on the present.

"I have a deathly fear of reorganization," Lenin wrote Finance Commissar Sokolnikov. "We are always reorganizing and do nothing practical. Remember my words: if there is an evil enemy in the Finance Commissariat it is the fascination with reorganization and the weakness of practical work." Sokolnikov had suggested the reorganization of the budget, gold, and currency

---

[24] *Ibid.,* p. 155, and editorial material on pp. 517 and 584, as well as in *Leninskii Sbornik,* Vol. XXXVI, pp. 395-396.

[25] Lenin, *op. cit.,* Second ed., Vol. XXVII, pp. 180-190.

department of his commissariat. "Guard, protect [treasure] and combat theft under the general supervision and pressure of Trotsky. . . . That suffices. And that is very much." The center of attention should be on trade, first internal trade, then foreign trade and, "on the basis of trade, the restoration of the rouble."[26] Minor business transactions involved millions of inflated, almost worthless, paper roubles.

Now Lenin discovered "slackness" in the Presidium—the permanent commission—of the VTSIK, the intermittent Central Executive Committee. "This is not surprising," Lenin remarked, "for all its members are up to their eyes in twenty activities, as is customary in our 'Oblomov' republic." He also mentioned "the usual chaos."[27]

On the eve of the Eleventh Communist Party Congress, the Central Committee mailed a searching personal questionnaire to all members of the party —more than half a million. When Lenin received his in February, 1922, he wrote Molotov of the Central Committee's secretariat: "Either a fool is in charge of your statistics, or somewhere in these 'sections' . . . fools and pedants occupy important posts, and you, apparently, are too busy to keep an eye on them. 1) It is necessary to throw out the chief of the Statistical Section. 2) It is necessary to shake it up to its roots. . . . Otherwise we ('combating bureaucracy') nurture the most disgraceful and stupidest bureaucracy under our very noses." Lenin wanted the results of the questionnaire collated within a month. "Then dismiss nine-tenths of the Statistical Section . . . and begin building it anew. You must free yourself of trifles. . . . Write me, or telephone and we'll talk about this more thoroughly."[28]

Relentlessly Lenin tilted at the bureaucrats, for bureaucracy was the state and the state was all. He told State Planning Commission (Gosplan) Chairman Krzhizhanovsky that, "Comrade Trotsky writes in one of his letters to the Central Committee about the bankruptcy of our planning organization. This is true to the extent, for instance, that the administrative side of the Gosplan's work is undoubtedly in disorder. The *personal* responsibility of each member of the Planning Commission for *certain* important functions has not been fixed." Without "general supervision" over the fulfillment of the plan "everything is equal to zero." Lenin then suggested a scheme for assigning tasks to each member of the Gosplan.[29]

Lenin viewed the problem of bureaucracy in terms of persons, their efficiency, their lack of culture, the inadequacy of supervision by Molotov, by the Gosplan, by the Rabkrin, the adequacy of Trotsky's supervision, but never in terms of system. Russia's bureaucracy was complicated by the existence of two bureaucracies: the government bureaucracy and the party bureaucracy. The party bureaucracy is manned by communists, the government

---

[26] *Leninskii Sbornik*, Vol. XXXVI, pp. 403-405.
[27] *Ibid.*, pp. 424-425.
[28] *Ibid.*, pp. 425-426.
[29] *Ibid.*, pp. 432-433.

bureaucracy by as many communists as can be found. But the government apparatus moves only when it is plugged into the party powerhouse. It stands limp like a robot until an impulse—a decision—from the party gives it life. In a dispute between a communist powerman with no knowledge and an expert with no power, the latter lost unless the matter came to the attention of Lenin or another high-ranking unconventional party officer. Within the party bureaucracy, however, fear of mistakes and uncommensurate punishment drove decision-making ever upward until it became the monopoly of the Central Committee or of the Politburo and these, knowing the trembling below, seized the initiative with such frequency that everybody else lost the knack and taste for it and gladly saw it float away.

Reproached, a party bureaucrat might reply, "It's not my fault. See the higher-ups." A government bureaucrat, perhaps with some secret satisfaction, might tell the petitioner, "I had nothing to do with it. Apply to the party committee." This widespread washing of hands, disconcerting to the already helpless citizen, was Russia's darkest political phenomenon as the Eleventh Party Congress began to arrive in Moscow for its opening on March 27. The discussion of bureaucracy eclipsed economic planning. Shortages: the shortage of reliable information about raw material reserves, skilled labor, technical and managerial personnel, all of which were in limited supply, would have given a broadly conceived plan the contours of a castle in the sky. Lenin knew this. In *Pravda* of February 22, 1921, he stated his persisting view that, "There is not and cannot be any unified economic plan other than that already made by the Goelro"—State Commission for the Electrification of Russia—which provided for the construction within a decade or more of a network of hydroelectric and thermal power plants as the basis of future industrialization. What with a killing famine, a dying rouble, and paralysis of industry, Lenin's realistic brain dismissed further planning as a fantasy and concentrated on the two or three small electric-generating plants abuilding. For the rest, at the party Congress and elsewhere, he attacked the snake of bureaucracy that had coiled itself in endless rings around his organization—the new Soviet party-state.

Before the Eleventh Congress met, the Central Committee gathered in plenary session. Lenin asked to be excused for reasons of health. His strength, he said, would not permit him to attend the plenum as well as the Congress. But he dictated a minutely itemized outline of his major address to the Congress and submitted it to the plenum, which approved.[30]

The party congress is the highest political authority in Russia—unless some person or oligarchy usurps its authority. Lenin neither usurped nor imposed his authority. He was authority. One can have authority because one has power, but that is really power, not authority, or at most authority arising out of power. Pure authority is the influence and credence accumulated by an individual or institution as a result of faith, love, achievement, or deport-

[30] Lenin, *op. cit.*, Second ed., Vol. XXVII, pp. 207-208.

ment. Lenin had such authority, and power too, a mighty combination. He believed in maximum power for the state. His instructions to Justice Commissar Kursky in formulating the civil code were: "Not to follow the Commissariat of Foreign Affairs blindly. *Not to play up to Europe* . . . not to miss the smallest opportunity *to expand* the interference of the state in 'civil' relationships."[31] But Lenin ruled not by power alone. In his years of leadership he harvested authority too, and, in many hearts, affection. Power, authority, and affection were at zenith when he addressed the Eleventh Congress of the Russian Communist Party (Bolsheviks) which sat from March 27 to April 2, 1922. It was the last party congress he attended.

The Congress consisted of 522 voting delegates representing the 532,000 members of the communist party, and 165 nonvoting delegates. In the second half of 1921, 169,748 members or 24.8 percent of the total membership, had been expelled for ideological backsliding, corruption, indifference, disillusionment, drunkenness, and similar sins.[32]

The party congress was not yet the large mass meeting of Stalin and Khrushchev's days—with thousands of delegates—and debate and discussion were therefore possible. Under Lenin's chairmanship, a presidium was elected comprising, in the order mentioned by the nominating committee: Lenin, Trotsky, Zinoviev, Kamenev, Stalin, Molotov, Tomsky, and twelve lesser figures. A. Yenukidze, Anastas I. Mikoyan, and Sergey M. Kirov were elected secretaries. After further formalities and a brief argument about the agenda, Lenin called on himself to deliver the report of the Central Committee. He had opened the proceedings with a two-minute statement. The past year was the first in which they could devote themselves in peace to "the basic tasks of socialist construction." Famine and war's ruin still plagued them, but if the party remained united they had nothing to fear. "In the entire world, the communist movement is growing, not as quickly as those of us had expected who measured it by the tempo of wartime and of war's end, nevertheless it at least grows solidly, firmly, broadly, and deeply." Communist parties existed in almost all countries of the world—he apparently overlooked one or two continents—"And if we, in collaboration" with them, "can soberly evaluate our situation without fear of recognizing our mistakes we shall come out of these difficulties as victors."

Now Lenin drew his watch from his vestpocket, looked at it, wrapped the chain around a finger, and began his long report. He devoted a few remarks to the Genoa Conference, which had not yet commenced. He did not vouch for its success, but, "Through Genoa, if our partners there are sufficiently comprehending and not too stubborn, without Genoa if they take it into their heads to be stubborn, we shall attain our goal." For the "most urgent, prac-

[31] *Leninskii Sbornik*, Vol. XXXV, pp. 334-335.
[32] These figures and all quotations from Congress proceedings in *Odinnatsatii Syezd RKP (B), March-April, 1922. Stenograficheskii Otchot* (Eleventh Congress of the RKP (B), March-April, 1922. Stenographic Report) (Moscow, 1961). Lenin's speeches also in Lenin, *Sochineniya*, Second ed., Vol. XXVII, pp. 219-272.

tical" interests of the capitalist nations "require the development, stabilization, and expansion of trade with Russia. . . . I do not promise when it
will happen, I do promise that it will happen."

He then surveyed Russia inside. "The chief question, of course, is the
New Economic Policy." It served as a test of the union between city and
countryside. Does this union now exist? "Not yet." They might have to
remake the policy "and even remake everything many times from the start
. . . we do not prejudge, we approach our greatest task in the world with
sober eyes." The NEP meant that "We are building our economy with the
peasantry. We must remake it repeatedly and arrange it so that there will be
a link between our socialist work in heavy industry and farming." The communists must show that they can help the peasant. "Either we demonstrate
this or he will send us to the devil. That is absolutely inevitable." The peasant is saying, "Well, if you haven't the ability, we'll wait, maybe you'll learn."
But, Lenin warned, "This credit is not unlimited." Someday the peasant
"will ask cash." Progress would be slow, "endlessly slower than we dreamt."

The second facet of the NEP was the competition between state and private enterprise. The prerevolutionary capitalist, Lenin admitted, had supplied the population. "He did it badly, he did it by extortion, he insulted
us, he robbed us. That every worker and peasant knows who does not think
about communism because he does not know what sort of thing it is. 'Nevertheless, the capitalists did supply the people, and can you do it? You can't.'
Now those were the opinions heard last spring. . . . We don't know how
to manage. That is what this year has shown." Lenin said he would have
liked to prove this by examining the record of several state trusts. "Unfortunately, for a variety of reasons, largely because of illness," he had failed
to do this. But he knew, from observation, "that we do not know how to
manage. Either we show in the next year that we can or the Soviet government cannot survive. And the greatest danger is that not everybody realizes
this." They had "to pass an examination in competition with the ordinary
salesman, the ordinary capitalist, the merchant, who goes to the peasant and
does not argue about communism, just imagine, he does not argue about
communism,—but he does argue that if it is necessary to get something, to
trade properly, to build, then I will build expensively but maybe the communists will build more expensively, if not ten times more expensively. Now this
kind of propaganda is the essence of the matter, that is the root of economics. . . . The communist, the revolutionary, who made the greatest revolution
in the world on which if not forty pyramids then forty European countries
look down in the hope of getting rid of capitalism, he must learn from the
ordinary salesman."

His next point, Lenin said, concerned state capitalism. "Pity that Comrade
Bukharin is absent from the Congress,"—he was abroad—"I should have
liked to have a little argument with him, but I had better postpone it to the
next Congress. On the question of state capitalism, it seems to me that our

press in general and our party in general makes the mistake of lapsing into intellectualism, into liberalism, and we philosophize on the interpretation of state capitalism, and page through old books. And there you will find references to something altogether different, to the state capitalism which exists under capitalism, but there is not a single book about state capitalism under communism. It did not occur even to Marx to write one word on this question, and he died leaving not one precise quotation and no incontrovertible instructions." In this unenviable situation, with no guidance from the deceased master, "We must now therefore extricate ourselves by our own effort." Lenin felt lost but free, free to say that state capitalism under communism was different from state capitalism under capitalism. In Russia, "the state is we, the proletariat, we, the vanguard of the working class." Elsewhere, the state was the capitalist class. But he immediately contradicted himself. "Now, however, we have lived through a year, the state is in our hands, but has it this year behaved in the NEP according to our ideas? No. . . . How did it behave? The machine tears itself out of our hands: as though there is a man who drives it, but the machine does not go in the direction it is driven but where somebody, somebody illegal, somebody unlawful, God knows where he came from, either a speculator or a private capitalist or both—but the machine moves not at all as, least of all as, the one who sits at the wheel imagines."

The state was in the driver's seat but did not drive. The real driver was the private capitalist. State capitalism is capitalism—even without private businessmen and certainly, in Lenin's time, when capitalists drove the machine by economic radar. Lenin discovered no "incontrovertible" instructions in Marx on state capitalism under communism. Marx did, however, analyze the nature of capitalism, and he found that wages, money, a market economy, are the characteristics of capitalism. Names like "socialism," "communism," are politically elusive; economically they are irrelevant. The worker in a Soviet factory and the worker in a capitalist factory works for wages and buys according to his earnings, and in advanced Western capitalist countries he buys more because the cost of the Soviet state and bureaucracy exceeds the cost of the bourgeois state and capitalist profit; chiefly because the production-conscious Soviet economy, being underdeveloped, devotes a larger percentage of the gross national product to investment than do most consumer-conscious developed capitalist countries. Someday the Soviet imbalance between investment and consumption will change, it has changed to an extent. Still, it is the market that decides, and a market economy is a capitalist economy whether the state manages all or manages little. Lenin, however, asserted without analysis or proof that the nature of the state alters the nature of state capitalism.

"Now," Lenin said, "I pass to the question of the cessation of the retreat. . . . We must now say in the name of the party: Enough! The aim of the retreat has been achieved. . . . Retreat is a difficult affair, especially for those revolutionaries who are accustomed to advance, . . . especially when they are surrounded by the revolutionaries of other countries who dream only of beginning their advance. Seeing that we retreat, some of them even broke out into tears in a childish, intolerable manner, as happened at the last session of the expanded Executive Committee of the Comintern. . . . The most dangerous thing in a retreat is panic. . . . When such a retreat takes place in a real army and when a proper retreat is turned into a rout, cannon are set up and the command is, 'Shoot.' And quite rightly." In this connection, Lenin mentioned the Workers Opposition. He advised them and others to "Stop being clever and deliberating about the NEP. Let the poets write verse, that's why they are poets." (Some poets had bemoaned the reintroduction of capitalism.) "But economists should not deliberate about the NEP," they should form more mixed companies, partnerships between the state and Russian private capitalists or foreign capitalists. Eighteen of these, Lenin announced, had already been established. Too much discussion, too many committees. "Of hundreds of committees in our party not five can show practical results." Here he told the story of French imported canned goods:

"The Moscow Consumers Association had to buy canned goods. For this purpose, a French citizen appeared on the scene. I don't know whether he did this in the interests of foreign policy and with the knowledge of the leaders of the Entente or following the approval of Poincaré and other enemies of the Soviet government (I think our historians will investigate this after the Genoa Conference), but it is a fact that the French bourgeoisie participated not only theoretically but also practically, for a representative of the French bourgeoisie arrived in Moscow and sold canned goods. Moscow is starving, next summer it will starve still more, meat has not been brought in and, judging by all the known qualities of our Commissariat of Railways, will probably not be shipped in. They"—the French bourgeoisie—"sell canned meat (if they haven't gone rotten, of course—that a future investigation will reveal) for Soviet roubles. What could be more simple?" (He did not explain why the Frenchman wanted 160 billion Soviet roubles, the price of the canned meat. Perhaps it was to buy Soviet raw materials.)

Despite the hunger and the right price in roubles, Commissar of Foreign Trade Leonid Krassin did not presume to make the purchase but consulted Leo Kamenev, a member of the Politburo who placed the matter before the entire Politburo. "Naturally," Lenin mocked, "how could Russian citizens decide such a question without the Politburo of the Central Committee of the Russian Communist Party! Imagine, how could 4,700 responsible"—high-ranking—"officials make a decision about the purchase of food abroad without the Politburo? This is of course a supernatural idea. . . . When I first heard of this, I sent a written proposal to the Central Committee: in my opinion, everybody employed in Moscow government offices, except members of the VTSIK who, as you know, enjoy immunity, everybody except members of the VTSIK, should be sent to the worst Moscow prison for six hours, and the officials of the Commissariat of Foreign Trade for thirty-six hours. . . . This was simply the usual Russian intellectualist inability to do anything practical. . . . It was a typical affair. And not at all limited to the capital city of Moscow. . . . Any salesman who had gone through the school of a large capitalist enterprise could have transacted such a deal, but 99 percent of the responsible communists are incapable of doing it."

Lenin next cited an event in the Donets Coal Basin in the Ukraine. Friction developed between the mine management there and the central coal board in Moscow. The Central Committee of the party in the Kremlin decided not to dismiss the Donets management and, if disputes occurred, to collect all the facts for investigation by Moscow. "The Ukraine is an independent republic, but in party matters it sometimes, how shall I put it most politely, makes a detour." The Ukrainian Communist Party met in congress, "Apparently, there was an intrigue and a whole mess, and if the Party History Department studies the matter it will not get to the bottom of it even in ten years. But in fact, and despite the unanimous instructions of the Central Committee, that group" of managers in the Donets Basin "was replaced with another group."

In the case of the canned goods, Lenin censured officials for lacking initiative. In the coal case, he deplored Ukrainian initiative.

But, Lenin confessed, there is no way out of this dilemma, "for we have one government party which governs" and nobody can prevent a member of the party from complaining to the Politburo or bringing minor transactions to its attention.

Actually, the party's Politburo gradually yet deliberately ignored or overrode the government Cabinet (Sovnarkom) during Lenin's illness; more and more problems were passed to the Politburo thereby facilitating the ultimate monopoly of power by one member of the Politburo—Joseph Stalin.

To cope with the steady drain of authority away from the government, Lenin suggested to the Congress that all questions be laid first before the Sovnarkom where his deputies, Rykov and Tsurupa, would shoulder an enlarged share of his responsibilities and attempt to inject efficiency into the people's commissariats of the government. In the next breath, however, he unconsciously revealed why this would not work: "We have eighteen people's commissariats of which no fewer than fifteen are worthless." The eighteen people's commissars and Lenin and his two deputies constituted the Sovnarkom. If fifteen of them directed worthless commissariats, the Politburo would not leave decisions to them. But perhaps the Politburo's dominance helped make them worthless. Lenin avoided this dilemma. He did say, in conclusion, "We must admit and must not fear to admit that 99 percent of all communists have been placed in positions for which they are not fit and they cannot conduct their affairs and must now learn. If this is recog-

nized, and since we have sufficient possibility of doing so, and, judging by
the general international situation, there will be enough time to learn, this
must be done at all costs."

"Stormy applause," reads the stenographic record.

Meeting adjourned.

Any person saturated with impressions gathered from reading the proceedings of party congresses in the reigns of Stalin and Khrushchev, whose
reports received the unanimous hallelujahs due miraculous revelations, must
marvel at the volume of blunt criticism directed at Lenin's report to the
Eleventh Congress. Each speaker in the discussion was limited to fifteen
minutes. Skripnik rose first. N. A. Skripnik, member of the party since 1897,
became a high official of the Ukrainian Soviet government and party. He
was executed on Stalin's orders in 1933 and subsequently rehabilitated as
innocent. "Unfortunately," he told the Congress, Lenin said nothing in his
report about the relations of the more advanced capitalist countries to backward nations. "And it was necessary to speak of this . . . for the party remains the representative of the liberation of all toiling masses on the entire
globe, it is the spark thrown into the powder cellar of the enslaved East,
of all colonial peoples. But, in conducting this policy outside Soviet territory, we can accomplish our task only if we pursue the same policy inside
Soviet territory." Lenin's casual remark that "The Ukraine is an independent republic, but . . ." shocked Skripnik. He feared the old slogan of "Russia,
one and undivided."

From his seat, Solomon Lozovsky, trade-union leader and later Deputy
Foreign Minister, shouted, "The Russian Communist Party, one and undivided."

"Thanks for the elucidation," Skripnik replied. "But in relation to the
Ukraine and the other Soviet republics . . . there is a tendency to abolish the
statehood of the workers and peasants. . . . The question of the liquidation
of the worker-peasant statehood of the Ukraine" was posed in Russia and
outside by non-Bolshevik émigrés. He asked clarity on this issue from the
Central Committee in the Kremlin. In effect, Skripnik saw a looming conflict
between Russian centralism, garbed as federalism, and the desire of the national minorities for greater autonomy in their own affairs, including the
affairs of the Donets mines whose coal, however, was indispensable to the
all-Russian economy.

"It seems Lenin devoted too little space in his report to an evaluation
of the international situation," said the next speaker, V. A. Antonov-Avseyenko, who stormed the Winter Palace on November 7, 1917, and commanded the Ukrainian front in the civil war; an old party member. He
questioned Lenin's view that the capitalist countries were under a necessity
to trade with Russia. "This perspective has been sketched too optimistically."
For a long time "until the development of the world revolution, which undoubtedly will take place, we shall live in a besieged fortress and must under

no condition entertain any serious hopes of substantial aid from foreign capital." This proved to be a much more realistic conception than Lenin's prognosis of the capitalist world seeking economic salvation in Russia.

Antonov-Avseyenko also touched on the peasant problem: "In the village, kulak dominance is growing; the kulaks are beginning to buy land from poor peasants." He quoted Engels, who had written, in his treatise on the German peasant wars, that a leader who came to power before his class possessed sufficient material possibilities of enforcing his rule would have to carry out the ideas of another class hostile to his own. This was Trotsky's idea of the premature revolution. (Antonov later became a Trotskyite, but still later entered the Soviet foreign service and worked in Spain during that country's civil war. Finally, in 1939, he met the fate of most of the Soviet officials who had been in Spain: execution on Stalin's orders.) His last word to the Congress was: We must tighten our belts, strain our muscles, and depend "on our own strength and resources without expecting the slightest real results from the link with capitalism."

The delegates expected fun and fireworks when David B. Ryazanov mounted the rostrum. Though he directed the Marx-Engels Institute in Moscow and was therefore an authority on the socialist fathers, he had become the oppositionist par excellence and differed with Lenin respectfully yet drastically. He felt embarrassed, he affirmed, to criticize the Central Committee for it was a quite extraordinary organization. "They say the British Parliament can do everything except transform a man into a woman. Our Central Committee is much more powerful: it has already transformed more than one very revolutionary man into an old woman, the number of such women is multiplying unbelievably. . . . Comrade Lenin drew one conclusion: the Communist Party is absolutely unsuited for the whole new condition in which it has to work." What accounts for this lack? he demanded. The Central Committee, he replied, undermines democracy within the communist party. "So long as the party and its members do not participate in the collective deliberations on all the measures which are carried out in its name, so long as these measures fall like snow on the heads of members of the party, there will be created what Comrade Lenin called a mood of panic. . . . Comrade Lenin said today that we are putting a period to this retreat. I have heard about this period but I do not know where they have put it. . . . We have stopped retreating—where have we stopped? . . . This must be said and it has not been said." Ryazanov chided Lenin for denigrating the working class. If the proletariat was weighed down with unreliable elements, "on whom will we lean?" He hoped all workers in big factories would join the communist party.

This brought applause.

Ryazanov also felt unhappy about Lenin's attitude toward foreign affairs. Lenin had said to the Congress that the Soviet press paid too much attention to the Genoa Conference. On the contrary, Ryazanov contended, "We must behave like Lloyd George, like Poincaré." They create a public opinion, he believed, which prevents them from making too many concessions to other countries. There should have been a lively agitation in all Russian factories toward the same end.

While the debate rolled on, Lenin, sitting either on the stage or on the wooden steps leading to it, made notes. The discussion continued all day March 27 and was resumed on March 28. Some speakers were surprisingly outspoken. D. Manuilsky of the Ukraine, who subsequently became the symbol of orthodoxy in the Comintern and at other posts, said, "Comrade Lenin is not adequately informed." (This in reference to the Donets coal mines.) S. P. Medvedyev of the Workers Opposition stated that some excellent communists were resigning from the party because they did not wish to be "voting puppets." Lenin, he added, was concerned with the peasantry, tried to win over the peasantry, but was neglecting the working class. V. Kossior of the trade unions said he knew from experience that the Politburo insisted on dealing with minor matters, such as who should be appointed assistant chief of a section of the All-Russian Central Union of Trade Unions. It did not have to decide about buying French canned meat. It dragged this and many similar matters into its agenda.

Then Trotsky spoke in defense of Lenin. Some of the party's mistakes and some of the people's hardships were due to the fact that the Russian revolution was the first socialist revolution. "If we had appeared in the arena of social revolution not as the first country, but as the second, if the proletariat in Germany or, say, France, were now in power, if imperialist blows had not threatened us, what would have been our economic policy? . . . We would have confiscated only those enterprises which we could have organized in the given condition of our organizational resources and strength." They would have allowed middle-sized plants to remain in the hands of private capital. But, "we were surrounded by enemies. Who were the capitalists and directors in every factory, in every plant? They were units of the world counterrevolution."

Trotsky recalled how delegations came to him early in the revolution from factories in the Urals. "My heart ached: 'What should we do? We can certainly seize them'—the factories—'but what do we do then?' Talking with the delegations, however, it became clear that military measures were absolutely necessary." Otherwise the directors and their capitalist connections and finance would have been used to undermine the Bolshevik regime. "From the abstract-economic point of view our policy was mistaken." But politically they had had no choice.

For Trotsky, war communism was not an attempt to introduce socialism, it was a military necessity, wrong but imposed. This is the truth. Subsequently, some tried to justify its horrors and high cost by claiming the virtue of socialism for it. But the moment the civil war ended, Trotsky proposed ending war communism. Lenin and others rebuffed him at that time. Vanity —or was it insecurity?—impelled him now to recall his rejected wisdom: "When did the mistake begin? There were differences of opinion, no sense in reverting to them. When could the tax in kind" and with it the NEP "have been introduced—six months earlier or a year earlier?" We lost a year, Trotsky was saying, because the party did not follow me.

In the discussion, Shlyapnikov had suggested that the NEP was a maneuver. Yes, Trotsky agreed, "Retreat is a maneuver. Does it alter our program? It does not. Does it change methods? Yes, it introduces great changes."

Shlyapnikov had taken his case against Lenin to the Comintern. He had a perfect right to do that, Trotsky stated. But by this step, he said to Shlyapnikov, you draw a line between "We" and "They." You go into opposition, and the enemy press abroad cites you and your comrades with gusto. "In the intermission, just before I rose to speak," Trotsky said, "a comrade whom I have known at various fronts for a long time as one of our best officers came up to me and told me that his mother and sister had died of hunger in the Volga region. Such cases are not infrequent! . . . I asked him, 'How come, comrade, couldn't you have found ways of helping them?' But he answered, 'I didn't know.' There is the fact. A deeply tragic fact, of course. And here you have our inefficiency, our inability, our damned postoffice." But, he added, if you put yourself in the position of "We" and "They," that would mean "exploiting the disastrous condition of the country as a banner which could become the banner of a Kronstadt, only of a Kronstadt!" For this demagogy the audience rewarded him with applause.

Trotsky's fifteen minutes were up, and Tomsky, the presiding officer, inquired whether he might be given more time. "Please, please," the delegates cried. Tomsky accorded him a second quarter of an hour.

The basis for further work in peacetime was "specialization," Trotsky declared. It consists "in the study of details and minor matters of a definite profession. . . . That is the foundation of everything. . . . Clearly, the party . . . cannot decide all questions. Every economic question is complicated. But people often think that if this complicated question is put before the provincial party committee or the Orgburo or the Politburo it immediately becomes simple. It is thought that the very manager who cannot cope with his economic work when he is chief of the provincial economic council becomes heaven's anointed if he is appointed secretary of the provincial party committee." As a result of such an approach, the provincial party committee is converted into "an undifferentiated, one-sided, unspecialized apparatus, an always-hurried, always-breathless Soviet"—government—"apparatus. And here is the worst aspect of bureaucracy, that is, a relationship to a situation without knowing the substance of the situation, and the formal approach to situations then inevitably penetrates into the party apparatus." At the same time, "it depersonalizes Soviet agencies. No government official at any post feels that he is responsible. . . . The more stubborn, the tougher official knows that the provincial party committee will immediately reconsider and he is discouraged."

This was a brilliant, penetrating analysis not only of the existing situation but of something well-nigh ineradicable in a country where the one political party deals with all, even small, economic and other matters. "The ruling party," Trotsky urged, "should not be a party which directly manages every detail."

Lenin took the same view, but he and Trotsky and their comrades had created a party-state and they were consequently powerless to prevent the party from sticking its fingers into every transaction whether it concerned canned meat or coal or baby carriages. After the Congress, the party's involvement in economic affairs grew even more complete.

Trotsky also agreed with Lenin about the necessity for making concessions to the peasantry. "The overwhelming percentage of our Red Army soldiers are ordinary peasants in civilian life, and they say, 'Give us a free market.'" But "if the entire European or world bourgeoisie again attacks us we shall again possibly introduce war communism, as we are accustomed to call it, and it will be more merciless than in the time of recent civil war.

"That, however, would be the result of a total rupture of our present economic policy which is based on the expectation of a prolonged period of peaceful coexistence, peaceful commercial collaboration with bourgeois countries."

That was the Soviet line after the NEP.

With this the debate came to a close, and now it was Lenin's turn for rebuttal. Looking at his notes like a nearsighted man with one good eye, he dealt with his opponents' objections. "First of all on the question of state capitalism. 'State capitalism is capitalism,' Preobrazhensky said." Preobrazhensky, co-author with Bukharin of *The ABC of Communism*, had made this statement in the debate. "I affirm," Lenin replied, "that this is scholasticism." No book had been written on the subject. "Nobody could have foreseen that the proletariat would acquire power in one of the least developed countries." The NEP had been accepted by the party and the country with almost no protest. "The capitalism which we admitted had to be admitted. . . . The literary arguments which have been made so far about state capitalism belong, at best, in a history text book . . . our state capitalism now is unlike that about which the Germans wrote. It is the capitalism which we allowed to enter. Is that true or not? Everybody knows it is true. . . . And here it has been said truly that we had to consider the peasantry as a mass and grant it the freedom to trade. Every thinking worker understands that this is necessary for the dictatorship of the proletariat. . . . If the peasant needs the freedom to trade in present conditions and within definite limits we have to give it to him, but that does not mean that we will permit him to trade in raw brandy. For that we shall punish. It does not mean that we permit trade in political literature which calls itself Menshevik or Social Revolutionary and which is entirely supported with the money of the capitalists of the entire world. . . . Of course, we permit capitalism. . . . Without it the peasant cannot live and labor."

It was at last clear to the delegates that when Lenin spoke of state capitalism he meant private trade. The muzhik's wife goes to the railway station with a dozen eggs and finds eager customers. A Moscow Nepman buys a pig in a village and sells it to a private butcher in town. All are capitalists operating with state sanction. Preobrazhensky called this capitalism. Lenin called it state capitalism; capitalism permitted by the state. Perhaps he applied the term "state capitalism" to private capitalism in order thereby to disqualify it as a description of the Soviet economic system which he could then call "socialism."

But suppose the state sells eggs or bread or nails or candles? Suppose the state manufactures felt boots and markets them? Is that state capitalism? It looks like capitalism, it uses the procedures of private capitalism. Nobody at the Congress mentioned this kind of economic activity. The subject for discussion was the peasant's petty trade. Lenin regarded it as state capitalism. He called it "the capitalism which we allowed to enter"—that was obviously private capitalism. The practical Lenin, under the pressure of life, allowed private capitalism to return. But Lenin the ideologist and propagandist did not wish to give his opponents, and the world, the satisfaction of admitting this in debate. He thus sowed confusion which persists until today.

Much earlier, however, in an address on April 29, 1918, Lenin had expressed himself with greater clarity. Then he spoke of "state-capitalist enterprises" run by bourgeois specialists under Soviet government control. Such state capitalism, he declared, "would be a forward step." And "state capitalism would be our salvation . . . state capitalism under Kerensky democracy would be a step toward socialism, and under the Soviet government it would be three-quarters of socialism." Again in a May, 1918, pamphlet, Lenin enumerated private capitalism, state capitalism, and socialism as separate forms, and he differentiated between them. "It is not state capitalism which combats socialism here," he said at that time, "but the petty bourgeoisie plus private capitalists who together fight state capitalism and socialism simultaneously."

How, then, could the private-capitalistic NEP be state capitalism? Only government-managed, nationalized industry is state capitalism and there was very little of that in Russia in 1922; most factories were idle.

The fact is that the productive use of capital is capitalism, and its two major forms are private and, as under the Soviets, state. (In most so-called "capitalist" countries, both forms coexist.)

In his report to the Congress, Lenin had said that when a retreat becomes a rout, cannons are set up and orders given to shoot. In the debate, Workers' Opposition leader Shlyapnikov complained that the cannons would be aimed at the opposition. Lenin laughed: "Poor Shlyapnikov! Lenin intended to mount cannon against him. We are talking about measures of coercion by the party and not at all about cannon. We spoke of cannon for those in Russia who now call themselves Mensheviks and SR's and who arrive at the conclusion that you, they say, are talking about a retreat to capitalism, and we are saying the same thing: We agree with you! We hear this regularly, and abroad there is tremendous propaganda that the Bolsheviks want to keep the Mensheviks and SR's in prison yet they themselves introduce capitalism."

The Russian peasant cannot live without private trade, "But we affirm that he can live without SR and Menshevik propaganda. To anyone who affirms the contrary we say, We prefer to perish to the last man but we shall not yield our place to you. And all our courts must understand this. When we cross over from the Cheka to state-political courts we should declare at this Congress that we do not recognize courts as being above class. Our courts must be elected and proletarian, and the courts must know what we permit. The members of the court must know definitely what is the meaning of state capitalism."

The trouble with Preobrazhensky, Lenin continued, is that "He is a theoretician . . . a propagandist who is concerned with various means directed to the end of making propaganda. Everybody knows and appreciates this strong side of him, but when he discusses political and administrative matters the outcome is rather strange." Preobrazhensky had proposed a new party authority, an Economic Bureau to function side by side with the Politburo, which made political decisions, and the Orgburo—Organization Bureau of the party—which dealt with organizational questions. "Create an Economburo?!" Lenin exclaimed. "Why, everybody has just said and everybody agreed, and we were unanimous (and that is very important, for actions depend on this unity) that the party apparatus must be separated from the Soviet government apparatus."

Unanimity is unanimity and history is history, and history records that despite unanimity at the Eleventh Party Congress in March-April, 1922, the party apparatus was not separated from the Soviet government apparatus; on the contrary, the party ultimately swallowed the government. The Leninist division of functions became a fiction.

Lenin saw the problem. "It will be extremely difficult to do this"—to separate party from government. "We have no people! Here Preobrazhensky lightheartedly charged that Stalin heads two commissariats. And who of us has not sinned? Who has not taken several posts simultaneously? Yes and how could it be otherwise? . . . I think that Preobrazhensky himself could not name a candidate other than Comrade Stalin" as Commissar of Nationalities. "The same holds for the Commissariat of Workers and Peasants Inspection"—Rabkrin. "That is a giant undertaking. But in order to be able to inspect it must have at its head a person with authority, otherwise we will wallow and sink in petty intrigues." That person, Lenin believed, was Stalin.

Lenin would learn within a few weeks that Stalin saw a bigger future for himself.

Returning to Preobrazhensky's proposal to establish an Economburo, Lenin said this appeared to be "a good scheme: on the one hand, the Politburo, then the Economburo and the Orgburo. But this is smooth only on paper, in life it is laughable! I cannot at all understand how a person who has any feeling for living politics, after five years of the existence of the Soviet state, could introduce and insist on such a proposal. . . . Any political question can be organizational and vice versa. . . . You cannot mechanically separate the political from the organizational." Furthermore, "Politics is concentrated economics."

Therefore the Politburo centralized all political, economic, and organizational responsibility within itself and handed down ukases and decrees to obedient government bureaucrats. Truly, as Lenin had said before, the communists and he as their leader fought bureaucracy and nurtured it under their very noses. Lenin advocated the separation of party and state but in fact placed all power in the hands of the party's Politburo, and one day Stalin would make robots of his Politburo colleagues.

Kossior of the trade unions had pointed out during the debate on Lenin's report that the Politburo meddled in minor matters and even appointed third-rank officials. "But the Central Committee," Lenin replied, "cannot direct policy if the right to assign people is denied it. Even though we have made mistakes, shifting some people here and there, I still permit myself to think that the Politburo of the Central Committee has in its time committed a minimum of mistakes."

Lenin's dilemma was clearly visible. The power to appoint is indeed the key to omnipotence. He gave it to the Politburo. It named the big bureaucrats and small bureaucrats in government offices and even in trade-union positions. What was left of the separation of party and state? What of the war against bureaucracy?

Lenin finished his rebuttal with an appeal for unity. With unity they had won "victory over all the armies of the world." They needed unity to win the battle against bureaucracy.

Lenin did not address the Congress again until he closed it with a five-minute speech on April 2. "Comrades, we have arrived at the end of the work of our Congress. The first striking distinction between this Congress and the preceding one is the great cohesion, the greater unanimity, the greater organizational unity. Only a small fraction of one part of the opposition in the last Congress has placed itself outside the ranks of the party." (This referred to a segment of the Workers' Opposition that had been expelled.) . . . The proletarian revolutions which are ripening in all advanced countries of the world cannot succeed in performing their task without combining the ability of fighting selflessly and advancing with the ability to retreat in revolutionary order. . . . Now we have decided to recognize that the retreat is ended."

The workers must move ahead in step with the peasants. "This task can, in the present international situation and with the existing productive forces of Russia, be accomplished very slowly, cautiously, in a businesslike manner, testing every step a thousand times in practice. If some in our party will oppose this supremely slow, supremely cautious movement, they will be lonely ones." What lies ahead is study; the youth must be educated, everybody must study. Trotsky had told the Red Army that the coming year is "The Year of Study." That held for everybody. "I declare the Eleventh Congress of the Russian Communist Party closed."

The delegates departed.

Stalin commenced to work. He had not spoken at the Congress, not once taken the floor. But on its last day the Congress elected a new Central Committee of twenty-seven which met on April 3 and elected its Politburo, enlarged from five to seven: Kamenev, Lenin, Rykov, Stalin, Tomsky, Trotsky, and Zinoviev, and Bukharin, Kalinin, and Molotov as alternate members. At the same session the Central Committee, in Lenin's presence, also elected its secretariat: Stalin, V. V. Kuibishev, and Molotov, with Stalin as General Secretary. There had been another candidate for General Secretary: Ivan Nikitich Smirnov, a friend of Trotsky. Lenin threw his support to Stalin. (Smirnov was executed on Stalin's order in 1936.)

The General Secretaryship of the party was a new office. Lenin regarded it as a temporary expedient during his illness. Until 1919 there had been no party secretary. The Eighth Congress in March, 1919, elected as secretary Nikolai N. Krestinsky, a modest, mild person with negligible influence and a supporter of Trotsky. The Ninth Congress elected a secretariat of three: Krestinsky, Preobrazhensky, and Serebryakov, all friendly to Trotsky. But the Tenth Congress swept them out and elected three Stalinmen: Molotov, Mikhailov, and Yaroslavsky. Now, in April, 1922, Stalin, a member of the Politburo, a foremost leader, agreed to become General Secretary, and on April 25 he retired from his two posts in the Soviet government as Commissar of Nationalities and Commissar of the Rabkrin. The party, he knew, was the powerhouse of Russia. Lenin dominated it while his health was good, and the secretary therefore played a subordinate role. But Stalin calculated shrewdly that, with Lenin ill, the office of General Secretary could make him master of the party and the dictator of Russia if Lenin died. This is what happened, and the story is history. Stalin reached the communist summit, occupied it to the exclusion of others for two and a half decades, and murdered millions.

XLVII. STALIN VERSUS LENIN

PROFESSOR FELIX KLEMPERER, a distinguished German physician, was flown from Berlin to Moscow to examine Lenin during the Eleventh Party Congress in March-April, 1922. Dr. Otfried R. Foerster, a neurologist of Breslau, Germany, came on the same mission. Lenin's condition conceivably or probably influenced Stalin's final decision to quit his two posts in the Soviet government and take the office of General Secretary of the party.

Professor Klemperer returned to Berlin on April 3, and on the 5th he gave an interview which was published in the *New York Times* of April 6. A summary was cabled to Moscow and passed to Lenin. "Please," he wrote on April 7, "get me that copy of the *Times* on loan when it arrives."[1]

Dr. Klemperer declared in the interview, in which he did not tell all, that "Lenin is a man of strong physical constitution and great working energy who for a long while has worked intensively fourteen to sixteen hours daily. Recently, his capacity for work diminished, and he and his friends resolved to ascertain just what was the matter with him." Hence the invitation to the two German specialists.

"We arrived about simultaneously and were well received. We obtained our first information from the People's Commissar of Public Health, Dr. Semashko, who gave us two of his assistants, Dr. Rozanov and Dr. Maretzka, a woman, as permanent associates. We examined Lenin and found only a moderate neurasthenia, the result of overwork. Of more serious complaints, such as an affection of the nervous system or internal organs, there were none. Apart from a few general prescriptions regarding exercise and diet, no medical advice was necessary. We recommended that Lenin should take care of himself for a while and go on a vacation."

The vacation was the subject of a conversation on April 6 between Lenin and Sergo Orjonekidze, the top communist in the Caucasus and a close friend of Stalin. Orjonekidze suggested a stay in the Caucasus. Lenin wrote Orjonekidze the next day. "My nerves still hurt and my headaches continue." To be cured he needed a long vacation. He had been thinking of the Caucasus (then three days by train from Moscow). "I must frankly confess that my distrust of the 'outlying districts' is exceptionally great; from this distrust (and from sick nerves) I expect some kind of 'joke' instead of a cure." Even just outside Moscow promised arrangements were not made and he had to return to the city until "the joke was cleared away." But you cannot "go back to Moscow" from a far place like Tiflis or Novorossisk. "I must admit I fear a long journey: it might end in fatigue, nonsense, commotion, and squabble instead of a nerve cure."[2]

[1] *Leninskii Sbornik*, Vol. XXXV, p. 345.
[2] *Ibid.*, pp. 344-345.

Orjonekidze replied reassuringly the same day or the next. Simultaneously, Kamo appeared on the scene and asked Lenin to take him along to the Caucasus. Kamo, an Armenian whose real name was Semyon A. Ter-Petrossian, had been a boyhood buddy of Stalin in his home town of Gori, Georgia. Stalin used Kamo to rob banks for the benefit of the Bolshevik party's exchequer before the revolution. It was Kamo, with Stalin acting as director behind the stage, who on June 25, 1907, carried out the renowned holdup of two State Bank messengers in Tiflis and got away with 341,000 gold roubles, a huge sum.[3]

Kamo could have heard of Lenin's projected trip to the Caucasus only from Stalin or Orjonekidze. Lenin, suspecting nothing, wrote Orjonekidze on April 8 or 9 saying he had no objection to the company of Kamo but must know "the altitude above sea level of the house indicated, because Nadezhda Konstantinovna"—his wife Krupskaya—"had a bad heart and could not stand high altitudes."[4]

Stalin's idea of moving Lenin to the Caucasus where he would have been cut off from the Kremlin, except for occasional telegrams and courier pouches, was still alive on April 17 when Lenin again inquired of Orjonekidze by letter about altitudes—Abastuman and Borzhom were being considered—and about accommodations, heating, etc.[5]

Health Commissar Semashko telephoned Dr. Rozanov on the evening of April 20 and asked him to come see Lenin the next day. Professor Dr. Moritz Borchardt was arriving from Berlin for consultation because it had been decided to remove the bullets lodged in Lenin's body in 1918 by Fanny Kaplan.[6] "I was very surprised at this and inquired why." Semashko told Dr. Rozanov that Professor Klemperer had diagnosed Lenin's headaches as due to lead poisoning from the bullets. Dr. Rozanov raised his Russian eyebrows. "As a surgeon who had treated thousands of wounded this idea struck me as quite strange." Semashko agreed.

In the morning Rozanov picked up Professor Borchardt at his hotel and together they drove to the Kremlin. In Lenin's office, and at his suggestion, they dispensed with the woman interpreter and walked through to the Lenin apartment. There Lenin told them about his headaches and Klemperer's diagnosis. When Lenin said that Klemperer advised removing the bullets, Borchardt first looked astonished. "Unmoeglich" (impossible) escaped from his lips, but then he moderated his dissent in order not to disavow a colleague. On the other hand, Rozanov declared firmly that the bullets could not cause the headaches because the body had formed a tight fibrous sac around them through which nothing could penetrate. The bullet in the neck, under the right sterno clavicular joint, could be felt without

[3] Lenin, *Sochineniya*, Second ed., Vol. XII, p. 566.
[4] *Leninskii Sbornik*, Vol. XXXVI, pp. 468-469.
[5] *Ibid.*, Vol. XXXV, p. 345.
[6] From here the account follows Dr. Rozanov's memoirs in *Vospominaniya*, Vol. 2, pp. 340 *et seq.*

difficulty "and I did not object to its removal." But he vigorously protested against removing the other bullet from its deep bed in the left shoulder where it could not be reached without an extensive and painful dissection. Neither bullet, Dr. Rozanov believed, inconvenienced Lenin, and an operation was unnecessary.

"Oh, well," Lenin said, "let's get rid of the one so people won't pester me and worry."

It was agreed that the operation be performed at noon on April 23 in what is now called the Botkin Hospital where Dr. Rozanov worked. Rozanov invited Borchardt to come at eleven to inspect the operating theater. The German, however, asked permission to come at 10:30. Dr. Rozanov assumed he wanted a more extensive tour of the institution.

Instead, Professor Borchardt, "to my and my assistants' great astonishment," arrived carrying a heavy suitcase full of all kinds of appliances. In Rozanov's view, only a few instruments were necessary. "I reassured him and told him we had everything, everything had been prepared, and the novocaine solution" for the local anesthetic "and the gloves were ready," so there was plenty of time to see the hospital. But Professor Borchardt planned to spend the hour and a half preparing for the operation. Borchardt then invited Rozanov to perform the operation with his assistance, but Rozanov suggested that he would assist while Borchardt operated.

Lenin appeared promptly at twelve with Commissar Semashko and a bodyguard. "So," Semashko inquired, "who will operate?"

"The German, of course," Rozanov replied, "else why did he come here?" Semashko agreed.

The operation was successful. Lenin apparently was not nervous and knit his brow only when the extraction took place. Dr. Rozanov had anticipated that Lenin would leave the hospital in thirty minutes, but Professor Borchardt insisted that he remain twenty-four hours. This raised the unexpected question: Where to put Lenin? "All wards were crowded," writes Dr. Rozanov, "but with whom? I knew the illness of everyone but had absolutely no idea what might be in the minds of my patients." For security reasons, therefore, it was decided to vacate a section of the women's division. Lenin objected to staying in the hospital but complied when told he had to be under observation.

The wound healed quickly after several changes of bandages. At the last treatment, Rozanov asked Lenin how he felt. "In general, not so bad, but I have a headache at times, don't sleep well, and my mood is bad."

Rozanov counseled a vacation.

"You, Comrade Rozanov, need a vacation yourself. You too don't look well. Go abroad, I will arrange it for you," Lenin countered, suggesting a trip to Germany. The physician preferred the seashore at Riga, and he also recommended a stay in the Crimea for the nurse. Lenin wrote to Semashko asking him to provide the necessary funds and passports, and when this achieved nothing he wrote to Stalin. The Secretariat of the Central Committee granted Lenin's request, and Dr. Rozanov and his son traveled to Riga.[7] The nurse too went on vacation with her adopted child.

Lenin left for Gorky.

In Gorky he met two defeats. The Genoa Conference, he wrote Stalin, was somewhat of a real "step toward a truce" between the capitalist world and Russia; therefore the size of the Red Army should be reduced by one quarter. This Lenin proposal, dictated over the telephone at 2:30 P.M., May 20, 1922, was rejected by the VTSIK four days later.[8]

Observing the VTSIK session from Gorky (it sat from May 12 to May 26), Lenin decided that this, Soviet Russia's nearest imitation of a parliament, needed surgery. In a letter dated May 23 "To Comrade Stalin for the Politburo," Lenin proposed that 60 percent of the members of the VTSIK be "workers and peasants who hold no Soviet government jobs," and that "no fewer than 67 percent of the members of the VTSIK be communists." The Politburo debated the matter on May 26 and passed the subject to a commission.[9] Not that Stalin or the Politburo was shocked by Lenin's wish to determine who would occupy the benches of parliament. That had already been done. But how could the bureaucrats in the national legislature be cut to only 40 percent?

At ten in the morning on May 26, Dr. Rozanov heard the agitated voice of Lenin's sister Maria over the telephone: her brother was not well; pains in the stomach, and vomiting. An automobile quickly fetched Rozanov and took him to the Kremlin where he found Commissar Semashko, Dr. L. G. Levin, a prominent Moscow general practitioner, Lenin's physician brother Dmitri, and several others. They repaired to Gorky in two cars.

A doctor already in attendance reported that the vomiting had stopped but not the headaches. However, there were indications of paresis, or partial paralysis, of the right leg and right arm and a speech disturbance. And so on that day, writes Dr. Rozanov, "Death for the first time clearly wagged its finger."

Physicians and family tried to comfort Lenin. "No," he contradicted, "this is the first bell."[10]

All tests for syphilis were negative. Nevertheless, an expedition of medical personnel was sent to Astrakhan, home of Lenin's paternal grandparents, to do researches. "They found so much dirt that it is better not to speak of it." Alexey I. Rykov, Deputy Chairman under Lenin and, after Lenin's death, Chairman or Prime Minister, made this statement to Boris I. Nicolaevsky in 1922 or 1923 when both occupied the same room as house guests of Maxim

[7] *Leninskii Sbornik*, Vol. XXXVI, pp. 490-491.
[8] *Ibid.*, p. 488.
[9] *Ibid.*, p. 492.
[10] *Vospominaniya*, Vol. 1, p. 401. Told by Semashko.

Gorky in the little town of Sarow, near Berlin. Nicolaevsky's younger brother was married to Rykov's sister; they had frequent talks abroad though they were political "enemies," Rykov a Bolshevik, Nicolaevsky a Menshevik. (Rykov was fearless in this respect. He attended the cremation in Berlin in 1923 of Menshevik leader Martov.)

Lenin's will and body fought back. He exercised as well as he could, rested, walked though with difficulty, and obeyed the doctors' orders. Early in June, Professor Klemperer received a second summons to Russia. On returning to Berlin at the end of June, he told newspapermen that "The evening before I left Moscow I walked in the garden with Lenin and he felt relatively well. He is not capable of concerning himself with brain work very long. He cannot read very long either, and if he reads a book, magazine or newspaper he gets a headache." He added that Lenin's present illness had no connection "with his former wounds," rather with "the last thirty years of life" in which he worked "sixteen hours daily or more." He denied that Lenin was suffering from "progressive paralysis."

Several weeks after his first May 26 stroke, Lenin began to practice writing. "Lydia Alexandrovna," he wrote Miss Fotieva, his secretary, on July 12, "You can congratulate me on my recovery. The proof: this handwriting which *begins* to be human. Start preparing books for me (and send me the list) 1, scientific, 2, novels, 3, political (send the last after the others, because they are not yet allowed). Greetings. Lenin."[11]

The next day Stalin visited Lenin. The visitor quoted Lenin as saying, "I am not permitted to read newspapers. I am not permitted to speak about politics. I carefully make a detour around every piece of paper on the table lest it turn out to be newspaper and then I would be guilty of a breach of discipline."

Stalin laughed showing his short blackened teeth. "I laugh," he reported in *Pravda,* "and praise to high heaven the discipline of Comrade Lenin. At the same time we ridicule the doctors who fail to understand that professional politicians, received in audience, must talk about politics."

Lenin, Stalin wrote in the same issue of *Pravda*—September 24, 1922— was avid for news and hungry for work. He asked about the Genoa and Hague Conferences, about inflation, and about industry. "He became very animated on hearing that the crop outlook was good. He asks questions and makes mental notes," Stalin wrote, "but is in no hurry to express an opinion, complaining that he has fallen behind the news." Lenin was also interested in the trial of the SR's.

That trial took place in Moscow between June 8 and August 7, 1922. In the defendants' box were thirty-four SR's, including eleven members of their party's Central Committee, notably Gots and Timofeyev. At the Berlin meeting in April of the three Internationals: the Second, Third, and Second-and-

[11] *Leninskii Sbornik,* Vol. XXXV, p. 351.

a-half, the Kremlin representatives, Radek and Bukharin, under Western socialist pressure and in an attempt to achieve the united front which would facilitate communist infiltration of European labor movements, had agreed to exempt the accused SR's from capital punishment. On hearing this, Lenin dictated an article published in *Pravda* on April 11, 1922, entitled "We Paid Too Dearly." He said, "Our representatives were wrong, in my opinion, in agreeing to the following two conditions: the first condition, that the Soviet government will not apply capital punishment in the case of the forty-seven SR's [the number was reduced before the trial]; second condition, that the Soviet government would permit representatives of all three Internationals to be present at the trial."

Emile Vandervelde of Belgium, Theodor Liebknecht, and Kurt Rosenfeld served as attorneys for the defendants at this, Moscow's first show trial. Twelve of the SR's were sentenced to death, among them: Abram R. Gots, Yevgeni M. Timofeyev, Lev J. Gershtein, and Mikhail J. Gendelman-Grabovsky. Others received lengthy prison terms; several were acquitted. The court stated, however, that the death sentences would be carried out only if the SR's persisted in their armed struggle in Russia against the Soviets.[12] (Some survivors were shot in 1938.)

Perhaps Stalin and Lenin formulated the verdict as they sat on a bench at Gorky in July.

A diadem of doctors, each a star, Russian and German, gave their warmth and light to the leader. He responded well. *Pravda* of July 29 announced that Lenin was no longer a patient, he was merely on vacation. Leo Kamenev told the semiannual All-Russian Conference of the Russian Communist Party on August 4 that Vladimir Ilyich showed rapid improvement. He would soon return to work. "I saw him only yesterday," Kamenev said. (On September 16, Kamenev became Deputy Chairman of the Sovnarkom and STO—Lenin's third deputy.)

Every day telegrams of good wishes deluged Lenin. A factory in Voronezh, a Red Army unit, a provincial party committee—from all corners of Russia cheering messages which, between the lines, reflected worry, clogged the little postoffice in the village of Gorky. *Pravda* printed some of them inconspicuously. (*Pravda*, incidentally, was covering a page or more of its four, six, or eight pages with advertisements, some on page one, and they were very conspicuous: large ugly letters, crude drawings, and thick borders.)

The September 24, 1922, issue of *Pravda* included a free pictorial supplement on white paper in contrast with the daily gray—a unique publishing venture in a country where all publishing is politics. The tabloid-size supplement was devoted entirely to Lenin, and every square inch of it yelled: We want him back! Bukharin, the most sensitive among the Bolsheviks, who wore his heart on his sleeve and a smile on his face, expressed the feeling in simple words: we are issuing this supplement to show that Lenin is well. "He will

[12] Lenin, *op. cit.*, Second ed., Vol. XXVII, pp. 537-538.

be with us for a long time, for a long time," Bukharin hoped. But let's not burden him too much, he pleaded lovingly. "Lenin again takes his stance at the rudder of the machine of state. He, and with him the whole country, is recovering."

Kamenev's contribution to the supplement reflected no mean journalistic talent. He said it the unusual way. "What interests Lenin?" he asked. He answered: U. S. Senator [William E.] Borah and the recently published letters of Korolenko to Lunacharsky; the collection of taxes; the internal situation in Poland and the work of the ARA; the activities of [Soviet government] trusts and the position of Hoover in the coming American elections; V. Shulgin's book and the foreign trade turnover; the impending trade-union congress and Russia's planted acreage; his sister Maria's photography and the bad work of the Educational Commissariat; "and much, much more."

"What does Lenin condemn?" "Very much and first of all, with special emphasis, our bureaucratic apparatus."

"What does Lenin praise?" The American comrades who brought twenty tractors to Perm and the Perm peasants who quickly repaired the bad Russian roads so the tractors could get there.

"What does Lenin talk about least?" "His recent illness."

"How did I learn all this?" "During an hour's walk around the house in which Lenin lives."

Stalin compared his visit to Lenin on July 13, when they, he stated, laughed at the physicians and Lenin offered no opinions, with his September 15 visit. "This time," Stalin wrote in the special supplement, "Lenin was surrounded by a pile of books and newspapers (they have permitted him to read and to speak about politics as much as he wishes). There are no traces of fatigue and overwork. . . . His inner calm and confidence have returned in full. Our old Lenin, shrewdly eyeing his visitor, screwing up his eyes . . ." Here Stalin abruptly broke off the description and enumerated the many aspects of Soviet foreign policy and domestic conditions they had reviewed. He quoted Lenin as saying, "The situation is difficult but the worst days are behind us. The harvest makes matters definitely easier. The improvement of industry and finances should come after the harvest." They must now fight bureaucracy. As to the foreign situation, Lenin added, the powers, all of them, England, France, Germany, America, were greedy and would fall out. "We need not hurry."[13]

The feature of the supplement, however, was the pictures and they were calculated for large audiences, including those who could not read communist words and the skeptics who did not believe them. The cover displayed a single photograph: Lenin in a semimilitary jacket and flat cap, Krupskaya in a white dress. His beardless face and head seemed to have shrunk; he made an attempt to smile. She looked grief-laden. She had been through a difficult period, never leaving his side for many weeks. Inside there was a photograph

[13] Stalin's article in J. Stalin, *Sochineniya*, Vol. 5, pp. 134-136.

of Lenin seated, alone, in overcoat and cap and high laced shoes. Thick veins stood out on his gnarled hands; Stalin and Lenin; Kamenev and Lenin; Lenin smiling and walking hand in hand with little Vitya, his thin-boned, five-year-old nephew; again Lenin walking, hands in his trouser pockets. And Lenin reclining deep in a collapsible chair, with Krupskaya nearby on a bench in a different dress, not in a different mood. Another photograph, not used in the supplement, showed Lenin without a beard, Krupskaya without a smile, Lenin's sister Anna, Vitya, and the joyful young daughter of the cook. Anna gave birth to no children. Maria, her sister, never married. Lenin and Krupskaya had no children. Vitya (Victor), who became an engineer, was the son of Lenin's younger brother Dmitri and the only offspring of the entire Ulyanov family of Simbirsk.

The pictorial supplement did more than depict Lenin alive and well. It heralded his return to work. In fact, he was already back in the driver's seat.

Government offices in Moscow began sending him reports. One of the first came from Rabkrin, the Cerberus of the Soviet bureaucracy. In May, 1922, after Stalin left it for the General Secretaryship of the party, Trotsky had proposed the abolition of Rabkrin. Its staff numbered 12,000, and Trotsky regarded them as constituting a barren limb of the bureaucracy. Lenin declared, "Trotsky is quite wrong. With our hopeless 'departmentalization' even among the best communists, the low quality of government employees, and the intriguing between departments (worse than anything in the Rabkrin)" to which Trotsky had alluded "we cannot get along without Rabkrin now." But its work had to be improved, its staff of 12,000 cut to 2,000, and their salaries tripled.[14] (Most of the employees were communists.)

In August, when Lenin received the Rabkrin report, the staff was down to 8,000. Lenin, replying to A. I. Svidersky, temporarily in charge, urged a further reduction to 2,000. Tsurupa, whom Lenin had designated to replace Stalin as Commissar of Rabkrin, was still in Germany. "Those famous Germans treated *only* his heart" though in fact he had had a nervous breakdown. Svidersky himself was ill. "I believe," Lenin wrote him, "you must first get a complete cure, have a new set of teeth put in and learn to eat with them, and then, with all your strength, go after Rabkrin," and, helped by two or three members of the board, "*begin* a radical transformation immediately."[15]

One need not decide whether Lenin's interest in Svidersky's dentures was personal kindness or political concern. Svidersky, veteran Bolshevik, had lived in a house with Lenin in a Finnish summer resort in 1906. Undoubtedly a bond existed between them. But in a politician, especially in a passionate one-track politician like Lenin, it is difficult to analyze the ingredients of an official act. In reprimanding a comrade who neglected his health, Lenin frequently used the expression, "You should be prosecuted for careless use of state treasure—yourself." On May 18, 1922, Lenin wrote Stalin recommending a vacation and cure for I. I. Skvortsov-Stepanov: "He is a sickly person.

[14] Lenin, *op. cit.*, Second ed., Vol. XXVII, p. 389.
[15] *Leninskii Sbornik*, Vol. XXV, p. 354.

But very valuable as an intellectual worker. He should get the vacation he asks; I strongly support that. After his cure and rest he will be most valuable both as *a professor*, and Nota Bene, as a publicist."[16] Similarly, Lenin mingled the personal and political in a note to Abel S. Yenukidze, the secretary of the VTSIK, on January 9, 1922: "Please help Sergey Frolov, a peasant representing the village of Alakeyevka in Samara province, to buy and procure grain and also to supply the village with seed for the spring sowing. Since I was personally known in that village"—Lenin lived there occasionally between 1891 and 1893—"I regard it as politically useful that the peasants not leave Moscow without some assured assistance."[17] After Inessa Armand died, Lenin, childless, loved no one, not even himself, and being extremely impersonal by nature and political by dedication, he looked at everything, including his own health and life, from the viewpoint of the cause and the state.

The NEP was bearing fruit in the shape of buy-and-sell-anything Nepmen, a fresh crop of little capitalists thriving in the red soil of communism. The Finance Commissariat wanted to reach into their pockets. Deputy Finance Commissar M. K. Vladimirov put the problem to Lenin in a letter. "In regard to the catching of 'Nepmen' I advise cautious thinking," Lenin wrote. He wondered whether the government should introduce a turnover tax or a compulsory loan "or which first."[18] In other words, both.

Among the books Lenin received was one by a Soviet author on the Frederick Winslow Taylor system of labor efficiency. Lenin began a review but did not finish and it remained among his unpublished papers until 1928.[19] He thought the volume, though repetitive, might be used as a textbook in trade schools and middle-grade schools. "To learn to work," he said, "is now the chief and truly national task of the Soviet Republic." The elimination of illiteracy, of course; "but by no means should we limit ourselves to that, and at all costs adopt everything really valuable in European and American science."

"I see from the newspapers," Lenin wrote to his deputies who presided over the Cabinet in his absence, "that the situation in the Donets Coal Basin and Baku is desperate. What do you think? Shouldn't we take *some millions* from our gold reserve? Won't it be worse to be too late, and leave them without help? You might order a *short* memorandum (not more than 5 to 10 lines) so I can *clearly* understand the situation. Lenin."[20] A week earlier, September 17, 1922, he had asked Deputy Finance Commissar M. K. Vladimirov "how much gold we have left and how much of it is free of obligations?"[21]

The Kremlin had sent Lenin the draft agreement for a mammoth con-

[16] *Ibid.*, Vol. XXXVI, p. 487.

[17] *Ibid.*, Vol. XXXV, p. 312.

[18] *Ibid.*, Vol. XXXVI, p. 494.

[19] *Ibid.*, Vol. VIII; reprinted in Lenin, *Sochineniya*, Second ed., Vol. XXVII, p. 302.

[20] *Leninskii Sbornik*, Vol. XXXV, p. 354.

[21] *Ibid.*, p. 496.

cession in Siberia to Leslie Urquhart, the British mining magnate. Lenin still hoped his concessions policy would make a major contribution to Soviet Russia's reconstruction. The last letter he wrote before his "first bell" rang on May 26 was directed to Stalin and marked "URGENT" and "Secret"; it dealt with the concession granted the American, Armand Hammer. Lenin called it "a little path to the American 'business' world"; and, "we must make every use of this path." But when he studied the draft agreement with Urquhart, which might have become a broad highway to the British business world, he told Stalin in a letter dated September 12, "Having read Krassin's agreement with Urquhart I oppose its confirmation. While promising us income in two or three years, Urquhart takes money from us immediately. That is absolutely intolerable. . . . I propose that we reject this concession. It is slavery and robbery." This time Lenin's word did not suffice. The Politburo argued the matter at its sessions of September 14, 21, and 28, the Central Committee on October 5, and only there did Lenin's objections prevail. The Sovnarkom officially rejected the concession on October 6, 1922.[22] At bottom, Lenin's hostility arose from his belief that the foreigner expected to invest too little foreign currency but to take Russian currency from the Kremlin for current expenses. Such expenditures would aggravate inflation. In a letter on another question, Lenin spoke of an official receiving a monthly "salary of two hundred million—pennies."

Urquhart never returned to his Siberian properties.

The failure of the Genoa and Hague Conferences and the banging of the door in Urquhart's face gave Lenin a clear view of the Soviet future. Gone was the illusion, in him if not in other communists, that the capitalist world would be forced to save itself by saving communist Russia's economy. The situation, he asserted in a message to the Congress of Trade Unions on September 18, "is particularly difficult" because the government lacked the means necessary to restore heavy industry, "the most important basis of socialism." In capitalist countries, big industries obtained capital through loans. "They do not want to give us a loan until we restore the property of the capitalists and landlords, and that we cannot do and will not do. There remains the hard and long way: to save slowly and increase taxes. . . . As long as we remain alone, the task of restoring our national economy lies on our shoulders with extraordinary weight." The strength of all workers and peasants must be harnessed to this task, "we must perfect, and cut the costs of, our government machinery which is still very bad." But if any worker or peasant grows despondent at the slow pace and high price of economic revival "let him recall the recent past with its rule by capitalists and landlords. Such memories will bring back the inspiration to work."[23]

Lenin himself felt the inspiration to work. In September he issued commands to the secretariat of the Council for Labor and Defense—STO: "I will

[22] *Ibid.*, Vol. XXXVI, p. 495.
[23] Lenin, *op. cit.*, Second ed., Vol. XXVII, pp. 303-304.

be back October 1 or 2. Tuesday, October 3, I shall preside. Meeting from 5 to 9. With one recess of a quarter of an hour.

"Warn the smokers. *No smoking.* STRICTLY. In the interval, tea and smoking (in the next room)." He wished to see his deputies before the session. "You must arrange all this *well.*"[24]

Even in a hungry land man does not live by bread alone. People want food and when they want it they talk about it almost to the exclusion of everything else. They also want money and jobs. Yet in the famished, fatigued Russia of 1921 and 1922 another subject agitated many minds and the minds sent unseen waves through the thick brick Kremlin walls to the eardrums of the communist leaders, and to Lenin in the village of Gorky. The subject was nationalism. The Bolsheviks talked world revolution and internationalism. The talk served many purposes even when it did not serve the announced purpose. But their big problem was nationalism. In fact, the test of Bolshevik internationalism consisted in giving reality to internationalism within the boundaries of Russia. For Russia was her own international composed of Ukrainian, ethnically Byelorussians, Uzbeks, Tadjiks, Turkomans, Azerbaijanis, Armenians, Georgians, Jews, Tartars, Buryats, Mongols, Kabardini, and scores of other national minorities who, in sum, now and then equaled, depending on territorial losses and conquests, the number of Russians (ethnically Great Russians). The minorities who suffered oppression under the Tsar had expected a new life from the communists. Some indeed expected independence; this is how they read the prerevolutionary debates and the post-revolutionary decrees of the Bolsheviks. The last thing they expected was a heavy Muscovite hand, however helpful, pushing them around. The monarchy had bred vibrant nationalist sentiments among the Ukrainians, Balts, Finns, Georgians, Armenians, and others. Like all colonial peoples they preferred self-rule to better rule by outsiders. But they found after the Soviet revolution that the presence of the Red Army, the secret police, and Moscow-sent commissars exploded the dream of independence. Lenin's first political principle was centralized control vested in a nationwide, highly disciplined communist party whose members obeyed Kremlin commands. This made a mockery of self-determination and the pledge of the right to secession, especially since Lenin held pessimistic views of the future of small nations, forebodings which his heirs took pains to justify. Lenin's focus on the class struggle, moreover, led him to underestimate the force of nationalism.

How much of their personality could the national minorities assert under these Soviet-Russian circumstances? By 1922 a satisfying answer to this question was the best the non-Russian peoples envisaged. In practice, this meant: What is federalism? Is it the false façade of centralism? This issue came to a head in September, 1922, as Lenin, vigorous once more, prepared to quit Gorky and come to Moscow.

A cleavage developed between Stalin and Lenin. Perhaps the controversy

[24] *Leninskii Sbornik,* Vol. XXXV, p. 353.

acquired acerbity from Lenin's sense that Stalin was reaching for too much power.

The problem arose when Moscow decided to reorganize the Soviet state. Originally, the Russian Soviet Federated Socialist Republic (R.S.F.S.R.), established on the first day of the Bolshevik revolution, embraced all the national minorities whose regional governments were titled autonomous republics or, in the case of smaller units, autonomous territories. This made them parts of the Russian federation, of Russia as of old. It was recognized subsequently that this arrangement did little for their national pride or for communist boasts of a new era in the life of ethnic minorities. Moscow therefore tried, by various devices, to give them the illusion of sovereignty. On February 22, 1922, for instance, the Ukraine, Armenia, Azerbaijan, Byelorussia, Bokhara, Georgia, the Far Eastern Republic, and Khiva, all member states of the Russian Federation, went through the motions of signing an agreement with it authorizing it to represent them at the Genoa Conference and to negotiate treaties on their behalf.[25]

Later that year a further step was taken in the same direction: the Kremlin proceeded to launch the Union of Soviet Socialist Republics (U.S.S.R.) which the Ukraine, Byelorussia, the Caucasus Federation (Azerbaijan, Georgia, and Armenia), and other peripheral regions would join "voluntarily" as constituent and "independent" republics or states.

After Stalin's mummy was removed from the mausoleum in Moscow's Red Square, the Soviet authorities admitted that for decades, while his "cult of personality" flourished, the story of the establishment of the U.S.S.R. was distorted and wrapped in lies to make it appear as his handiwork when in fact, they contend, Lenin fathered it. The unraveling of the mystery began in 1959 with the publication of theretofore withheld Lenin letters; since then the attacks on Stalin's misrepresentation of his role have grown in number and vituperation.

One article charges that "Already in the period of the civil war, Stalin regarded the independent Soviet republics as indistinguishable from autonomous republics," and he wished to place all of them under the direct jurisdiction of the Cabinet (Sovnarkom) in Moscow and of the VTSIK (Central Executive Committee) in Moscow.[26] It is not customary in Soviet circles nowadays to give Stalin the benefit of any doubts, especially where Lenin is involved, yet he may have been right in regarding "the independent" Soviet republics as merely autonomous in some local matters and actually ruled by the central Soviet government through the Kremlin-dominated communist party. His mistake, stemming from a tendency to disregard the feelings of individuals and of millions, was to put autonomy instead of independence

[25] *Voprosi Istorii KPSS (Questions of the History of the Soviet Communist Party)*, Vol. 6 (Moscow, 1962). Article by M. S. Akhmedov, "Lenin and the Creation of the U.S.S.R.," p. 25.

[26] *Ibid.* Article by D. A. Chugayev—pp. 173-181—entitled "The Formation of the U.S.S.R.: An Historical Survey."

into his proposals for the constitution of the new U.S.S.R. Lenin, more subtle, more conscious of the efficacy of yielding on appearances without yielding on substance (especially since the victims of this political legerdemain were helpless), saw no sense in Stalin's "autonomy-ization," to give it its clumsy Russian name.

On substance, that is, on the supremacy of Moscow, Lenin and Stalin agreed. Yet they quarreled.

Lenin, still in Gorky, mobilized his supporters against Stalin. "Comrade Kamenev," he wrote on September 26, 1922. "You have probably received from Stalin the resolution of his [constitution drafting] commission on the entry of the independent republics into the R.S.F.S.R. [Russian Soviet Federation of Socialist Republics]. If you haven't received it, please get it from the secretary and read it immediately. I discussed it yesterday with Sokolnikov, today with Stalin. Tomorrow I am seeing [P. U.] Mdivani [a Georgian communist suspected of "independence-ism"]. In my opinion this is supremely important. . . . Stalin has already made one concession. In Article I, say, instead of 'Entry' into the R.S.F.S.R.—'Formal union together with the R.S.F.S.R. in a Union of the Soviet republics of Europe and Asia.' The spirit of this concession is, I hope, understood. We recognize ourselves"—we the R.S.F.S.R.—"as having equal rights with the Ukrainian Soviet Socialist Republic, and others, and together and as equals enter with them into the new union, the new federation, 'The Union of Soviet Republics of Europe and Asia.' " There would be a federal VTSIK embracing all the republics. "It is important for us," Lenin added, "not to give ammunition to the 'independencers,' not to destroy their *independence*, but to create a *new floor*, a federation of *equal* republics. . . . Stalin has agreed to postpone the presentation of his resolution to the Politburo of the Central Committee until my arrival. I am arriving Monday, October 2. I want to have a meeting with you and with Rykov"—his two deputy chairmen; the third, Tsurupa, was still ill—"for two hours in the morning, say from noon till two, and, if necessary, in the evening, say from 5 to 7 or 6 to 8."[27]

Before leaving Gorky, Lenin also had talks there with Orjonekidze and three other Georgians, and with A. F. Myasnikov, the chairman of the Sovnarkom of Armenia. He was lobbying against Stalin.

To Lenin's letter to Kamenev of September 26, Stalin replied the next day, sending copies of the reply to Lenin and all members of the Politburo. The second edition of Lenin's *Biografia* by Pospelov and others describes Stalin's letter (p. 611) as written in "an intolerably coarse tone toward Lenin. Although Stalin agreed with the proposal of Lenin regarding the creation of the U.S.S.R., it is clear from the text of his letter"—unpublished—"that his consent was formal. He objected to the establishment of a Union Central Executive Committee" TSIK or "parliament"—"in addition to the VTSIK of the R.S.F.S.R., and proposed that it"—the VTSIK of the R.S.F.S.R.—

[27] *Leninskii Sbornik*, Vol. XXXVI, pp. 496-498.

"be transformed into a federal TSIK. Lacking an understanding of the international essence of the idea of establishing the U.S.S.R., Stalin considered Lenin's position as 'nationalistic liberalism.' "

There was, apparently, not much loyalty among top Bolsheviks, for after seeing Lenin in Gorky, Kamenev wrote Stalin, according to the account in the Pospelov *Biografia*, based on secret archives, that "Lenin has prepared to to go to war in defense of independence." To which Stalin replied, "Against Lenin, in my opinion, firmness is necessary." Lenin and Stalin were declaring war on one another.

October 6, when the party Central Committee discussed the new constitution of the U.S.S.R., Lenin, though back in Moscow, could not attend because he had a swollen cheek. That day, however, he sent a note to the Politburo: "I declare war to the death on Great-Russian chauvinism. I shall eat it with all my healthy teeth as soon as I get rid of this damned tooth. We must *absolutely* insist that in the Union TSIK, *the presidency* shall go in turn to a Russian, an Ukrainian, a Georgian, and so forth. *Absolutely!* Your Lenin."

On this message, Stalin wrote, "Correct. J. Stalin."[28]

Since Stalin thought Lenin correct what divided them?

Had Stalin capitulated to Lenin again?

How could Stalin, the Georgian, be a Great Russian chauvinist?

Was Lenin serious in his defense of independence for national minorities?

No part of tsarist or Kerensky Russia achieved independence from communist rule without fighting against Soviet armed force, and Georgia, Armenia, and Azerbaijan, briefly and uncertainly independent, were subdued by the Red Army and reincorporated into Russia.

What, then, was Lenin's concept of independence? And how did it differ from Stalin's concept of autonomy?

Communists reply that the several national republics: the Ukraine, Byelorussia, Tadjikistan, Uzbekistan, and others, acceded to Soviet Russia and the Soviet Union voluntarily. If one objects that the people were not asked, that there was never a plebiscite on the matter, the communists contend that under a proletarian dictatorship the will of the workers decides, and if one argues that the workers were a small minority in all of Russia and especially in the underdeveloped regions of the national minorities and that even the workers were not asked for their opinions, the answer is: the communist party embodies the will of the workers and it favored "independence" within the Soviet federation. Thus, the article by D. A. Chugayev in *Vosprosi Istorii KPSS* states that "the principle of a workers' government is one of the fundamental principles of the construction of a socialist multi-national state." A workers' government is entitled to interpret independence as dependence. And this position is not without cogency, for an independent Ukraine or an independent Azerbaijan would not be a Soviet country ruled by a proletarian

---

[28] Lenin, *op. cit.*, Fourth ed., Vol. 33, p. 335.

dictatorship. Since, in the official view, only anti-Soviet elements would wish to secede from the U.S.S.R., Moscow, by its own rules, is justified in denying them the right to national independence through secession.

Lenin therefore agreed to clothe the national minorities in the robes of independence while exercising "democratic centralism" from Moscow. Being a Great Russian by culture and part of his ancestry, he realized that the Great Russian half of Russia might, even under communism, oppress the non-Russians and thereby sow fissiparous tares. Stalin, on the other hand, feared even the name and the trappings of independence. He, being a Georgian, knew the strength of separatistic nationalism not only among the three million Georgians but also, and in particular, among the forty million Ukrainians, as well as in other ethnic populations. The shingle and the dress of independence might encourage some to look for its substance. Many who in fact sought a mere suspicion of the substance were murdered by Stalin during his quarter century of autocracy which reached into every remote corner of the vast Russian realm. The Georgian despot believed in Russia one and indivisible. Therefore he yielded quickly to Lenin in September, 1922, and abandoned his proposed autonomy within the R.S.F.S.R. for "independence" inside a federal union. But he continued to resist Lenin on the essence: how power was to be divided between Moscow and the capitals of the constituent republics of the union.

On this and on other issues a rift opened between Lenin and Stalin in December, 1922, when Lenin's health again deteriorated.

XLVIII. WHEN I SAW LENIN

I FIRST arrived in Russia in the latter half of September, 1922, knowing not a word of Russian, no Russians and no foreigners, and next to nothing about Russia. I came because in the aftermath of the First World War and of the bad Versailles peace, Western Europe, where I had lived for nine months, seemed to be suffering from anemia and lack of direction; in Russia, by contrast, there was, according to reports from critics and supporters, a sense of purpose.

To make the acquaintance of a city I walk. I walked for hours every day through the cobble-stoned streets of Moscow. A boy in a brown homespun jacket squats on the sidewalk with a three-pound bag of sunflower seeds between his legs. Men customers take their purchases into coat pockets, women into sacks. By the boy's clothing and bast shoes I judge him to be a peasant. Presently a woman appears dressed in similar brown homespun, her head and neck bound in a babushka, a pair of dented old milk cans slung over her shoulders, and motions to the youngster. They trudge off together to the railway station. Their day of capitalism is done.

On a sloping street called Kuznetsky Must several women stand at the State Bank corner; each holds up in her two hands a white cotton bra, more in a pack on her back. Farther down, a red-faced woman offers five pair of gloves in one hand and six scarves in another. Elsewhere, a wrinkled veteran has suspended a board by strings from his shoulders and attached it by a rope around his waist; on it lie several boxes of matches and several packets of cigarettes.

The central thoroughfares of Moscow were lined with such venders. The lure of doing what for five years was proscribed by law and the desire to acquire millions of paper roubles and rapid gain attracted hordes into the petty commerce of curb and street.

Men who have obviously seen better days stand at corners selling old coverless books from perambulators and pushcarts. Homemade shoes are sold at sidewalks and the maker nails on rubber heels while the customer leans against a wall and supports himself on one foot.

Toward the end of September, it was beginning to get cold, yet more business was apparently being transacted in the open air than in shops. Every day, however, stores were opening. As I passed them on my regular round each morning, I noticed how they gradually unfolded. First, the boards that had shielded a plate-glass window since the Bolshevik battle for Moscow in November, 1917, were removed, and behind it the private owner displayed, amid ancient cobwebs, a box of the finest foreign face powder, two bottles of Parisian perfume, silk gloves, and delicate porcelain figures, a combination. apparently, of old stock and personal household possessions that might suggest excessive opulence. The next week the second window of the same store came out of its wooden cocoon; this was the hat and cap division, clearly the result of homework by the Nepman's wife.

Thus capitalism, by stages, reared its head in Soviet Russia.

I lived comfortably and ate well in the Savoy, the only hostelry that housed bourgeois foreigners. Evenings I went to the opera or ballet or theater, or studied Russian, or played poker with journalistic colleagues. The foreign correspondents were a competitive yet tight, friendly fraternity. One afternoon I was sitting in the living room of Jim Howe, the Associated Press man, when Michael Farbman, a lanky, apple-cheeked, curly-haired, Russian-speaking Englishman, came in glowing and worried. He had just had an interview with Lenin, "a scoop," the first given to any journalist in months, but would it get to the London *Sunday Observer* in time? It did. He took the interview on October 27, 1922, a Friday, and the *Observer* published it the next Sunday.[1]

"Had I not known of his illness," Farbman wrote, "I should not have sus-

---

[1] The interview was printed in *Pravda* on Nov. 10, 1922, and appears in Lenin, *Sochineniya*, Second ed., Vol. XXVII, pp. 311-316.

pected it." Lenin "appeared full of life and health." He sat down opposite Farbman, "pulled his chair very close up, and began talking with a look of deep earnestness," but he smiled, and indeed laughed "a great deal, and chiefly at two things: in the first place, at English wisdom in inventing the two-shift party system, so that one shift can rest while the other is working hard."

"As you know," he said, "we in Russia have only one party, and have to wear ourselves out without a relieving shift."

Lenin laughed again when he spoke of the Conservative-Liberal coalition trying to frighten the country with the revolutionary danger of electing the Labour Party to office. "Can anyone still believe that of [Arthur] Henderson and his party?" Lenin asked and guffawed.

None of this appears in the Russian versions. *Pravda* and Lenin's *Collected Works* printed only Farbman's written questions and the written replies. Edouard Herriot, the leader of the French Radical Socialist Party, neither radical nor socialist, had been in Moscow negotiating with the Soviet government. Did this represent a turning point in Soviet foreign policy? Farbman inquired. No, Lenin said, "Every approach to France is very desirable for us," but, "We consider friendliness to both England and France possible, and that is our aim." In fact, "we even believe that peaceful and friendly relations of these countries with Russia constitute one guarantee (I would almost say the strongest guarantee) that peace and friendship between these countries will be upheld."

Russia in the role of peace bridge between England and France.

With the end of the Greco-Turkish War, in which Britain supported Greece (and Russia supported Turkey), Lenin affirmed in answer to another question, the settlement of "differences between us and England" should be facilitated. In the peace conference that always follows a war, France had proposed that Russia participate only in the second part when the question of the Turkish Straits would be under discussion. Did Russia wish to be a full member of the conference for prestige reasons? Farbman wondered.

"I hope our international policy during the past five years has proved," Lenin replied, "that we care very little about prestige. . . . No nation is so indifferent to prestige and more ready to meet the claims of prestige with hearty laughter than Russia. I believe that modern diplomacy is speedily approaching a time when it will treat questions of prestige in the same way we do." But Russia rejected a limited role at the impending conference on Turkey and the Straits. "We believe that such a limitation would lead to some very practical and immediate economic friction which might hit France and England in the nearest future."

Thereupon, Lenin enunciated Soviet Russia's policy toward the Turkish Straits (Dardanelles): "Our program includes the closing of the Straits to all armed ships in peace as well as in war," and "full freedom for commercial shipping."

(When Russia is weak she wants the Straits closed to all warships; when she is strong she wants them open.)

Would the Soviet government agree, Farbman now asked, to control of the Straits by the League of Nations "if," the Russian texts add, "the League membership included Russia, Turkey, Germany, and the United States," or "would you advocate a special commission for this purpose?"

"It goes without saying," Lenin affirmed, "that we are opposed to the League of Nations and not only because of the characteristics of our economic and political system but from the point of view of international peace. The League of Nations has on it the birthmark of its war origin; it is to such an extent enmeshed in the Versailles Treaty, so much permeated with unfair discrimination as between nations, that I believe our negative estimate of the League of Nations needs no further comment."

Here Farbman turned to an issue that agitated British business: the Urquhart concession. Was Russia's refusal to ratify it "a victory for the left Communist wing"?

On October 5 Lenin, who was no "left Communist," and Pyatakov had spoken against the Urquhart concession at a meeting of the party's Central Committee. The next day Lenin, writing to Pyatakov and reminding him of this fact, said the Central Committee had delayed final action for want of more information. The essential question which needs to be studied, Lenin told Pyatakov, was whether the concession would give Urquhart a monopoly of the nonferrous metals mined in Siberia. Moreover, how many roubles would the Soviet government be required to pay Urquhart for current expenses; how much would he invest in pounds? From Lenin's letter it is clear that the Central Committee was interested only in the economic aspects of the concession, and if there were any hidden political considerations they arose only in Siberia where the regional authorities feared the presence of an efficient foreign enterprise paying higher wages and thus creating disaffection among workers in state enterprises. Farbman did not know this; Lenin's letter was not published until 1959 in Volume XXXVI of the *Leninskii Sbornik*. And Lenin had no intention of even hinting at Soviet motives in rejecting the concession. Instead, with statesman's tongue in cheek, he told the Englishman that because of past illness "I am not informed on all details," but he knew "left Communism" had nothing to do with the Kremlin's attitude. "Here are the real facts": and he made a long propaganda statement on Russia's exclusion from the impending conference on the Greco-Turkish War and the Straits. This "raised such indignation in Russia" that it "consolidated not only the Right and Left of the Communists, but also the great mass of the Russian people." Now there would be a public discussion on the concession in the press, Lenin said.

That was the concession's burial.

Farbman's last question mentioned recent arrests of Nepmen. Did that signify "a return of nationalization and confiscation"? No, Lenin assured him, "those arrested are not tradespeople but speculators who tried to sell platinum and gold for smuggling purposes." The VTSIK, now in session, "is working out laws to consolidate the new economic policy and render im- possible any departures from it."

On October 31, four days after the Farbman interview, I learned that Lenin would speak that morning to the VTSIK—the communist "parlia- ment"—his first public appearance since April. The guard at the Kremlin gate honored my foreign correspondent's credential—I was writing for the New York *Evening Post*—and directed me up the red-brick walk to the Tsar's palace.

It was easy to imagine ladies, in tiaras, pearls, ermine, and Paris gowns, on the arms of bemedaled generals, grand dukes in uniform, and aspiring indus- trialists in black, sweeping up the fifty-eight broad marble steps that lead from the vestibule to the throne-room floor. At the top of the stairs, covering an entire wall, hangs a painting by Ilya Y. Repin, still alive in 1922, showing Alexander III, the penultimate Tsar, intended target of Sasha Ulyanov's amateur bomb, receiving a delegation of peasants. Within the gold frame of the picture is the Tsar's reply to his humble supplicants: "Thanks for your greetings. Go home and tell your brothers that he who speaks to them of the division of the land, so that each peasant may have his own plot and dwell- ing, is trying to mislead them. Nothing of the kind can come to pass." Such words gave this palace to the Bolsheviks.

A long corridor guarded by high marble pillars and crystal vases taller than a man leads to the throne room. This is a huge chamber lit by hundreds of tiny electric bulbs in ten mammoth crystal chandeliers. On the walls the double-headed eagle, the gilded crowns, and other emblems of the imperial family have remained intact. But in place of the throne is a dais and on it a long table, covered with red cloth, at which sit the Soviet leaders. Lenin and Stalin are absent.

Nikolai V. Krilenko is delivering a report on Soviet justice. The delegates, a few in leather commissar jackets, some in the crude army uniforms they wore throughout the civil war, their heavy boots resting on the exquisite par- quet floors, sit on little gilded ballroom chairs that have been moved around into bunches with gaps between. I take a seat among them. Informality reigns.

Presently Lenin, unaccompanied, walked in through one of the side doors used by delegates and foreign and Russian journalists and sat down on one of the gilded chairs. For a few moments nobody paid any attention. Then heads began to turn, delegates nearby murmured "Lenin," and there was a ripple of applause. The presiding officer waved Lenin to the dais.

The little man—I judged him to be five feet two or three—with a bald head, parched yellow-brown skin, and a small sparse reddish beard, walked, but walked so fast it seemed he was running on tiptoe, to the stage. More applause but no great ovation, no shouts of "Long Live . . ." Nor did he applaud. The leader applauding his applauders dates from the period of the "cult of personality" when, at the mention of Stalin's name, everybody stood, clapped, and shouted and was afraid to cease demonstrating lest he be suspected of hostility to the "Boss." These performances, repeated several times at every meeting, sometimes lasted ten to fifteen minutes before the chairman dared to call a halt. When Stalin was present he began to applaud and when he stopped everybody stopped.

For a while Lenin on stage listened to Krilenko's report. Then Krilenko yielded to Lenin. He rose, called attention to the watch in the palm of his hand, and said the physicians had permitted him to talk no more than twenty minutes. I understood no word, or perhaps five or ten words, but I read the text later and have reread it recently. What is remarkable is its quality—in no way inferior to that of his speech in the heyday of his intellectual power. Yet in December "the second bell" would ring and in March, 1923, the same illness rang the third, and then his mighty brain well-nigh died; he no longer wrote or delivered speeches or participated in public affairs.

Lenin began with two news items: The Red Army had taken Vladivostok and driven the last remnants of armed Whites out of Soviet territory. He praised "the glorious" Red Army. But other factors had contributed. They were the international situation and "our diplomacy." In the near future, Soviet diplomacy would face another task at the Lausanne Conference on the Near Eastern (Turkish) question. "I believe that there too . . . we shall be able to defend the interests of all federal republics together with the R.S.F.S.R."—an obeisance to the "independent" national republics.

Now, he turned to domestic affairs where "we have achieved considerable successes." For instance, the labor code and its provision of the eight-hour day at a time when capitalist countries were suffering from unemployment and employer crusades against workers. "Compared with them we are less cultured, our productive forces are less developed, and our ability to work is worse than anywhere." But because we recognize our faults and fight them "we shall succeed in overtaking other countries with a speed of which they never dreamed."

He congratulated the VTSIK on adopting a criminal code and a land tenure code. If they had to be changed it could be done quickly. "In this respect, as all of you well know, the speed of our legislative processes are, unfortunately, unequaled in other countries. We shall see whether the near future will not force them to try to overtake Soviet Russia in this respect too."

But the battle against bureaucracy did not move with the same speed. In August, 1918, a census of city, provincial, and federal employees in Moscow showed a total of 231,000. Reductions were ordered. In October, 1922, a second census was taken. They expected a lower figure. "It proved to be—243,000." The government apparatus throughout the country was twice as large as before and "often it works not for us but against us. There is no fear of saying this even from the podium of the highest legislative body of our republic." He hoped for improvement but "Years and years must pass before our government machinery can be improved." Much depended, he said in closing, on the cultural level of the nation.[2]

When Lenin finished a recess was called and everybody grouped for a photograph. Some delegates sprawled on the floor. In the center row, from left to right, sat Kamenev, Lenin, Zinoviev, President Kalinin, and I with F. A. Mackenzie, a big-jawed Canadian employed by the Chicago *Daily News*, George Seldes, the very anti-Soviet correspondent of the very anti-Soviet Chicago *Tribune*, and Savel Zimand, a free-lance New York writer on economics. Elsewhere stood Jim Howe of the AP. We had simply wanted to be in the picture, and no one questioned us. After the posing and "just one more" had ended, we surrounded Lenin, and Mackenzie congratulated him on his recovery. "I do not understand English," Lenin said in English, and, with a laugh, he turned and escaped from foreign encirclement.

During the entire month of October, Lenin had been presiding at meetings of the Politburo, Central Committee, Cabinet (Sovnarkom) and Council of Labor and Defense (STO). As was his wont, he listened with both ears but passed notes to participants on subjects not under discussion. This simultaneous concern with several matters, the physicians had said, caused excessive fatigue, and it was accordingly agreed that the officials give their replies to the secretaries who would hand them to Lenin after the sessions. Lenin noticed at one session that he was getting no replies. "It seems you are intriguing against me," he wrote in a note to Lydia Fotieva, his private secretary. "Where are the answers to my notes?"[3]

Ever since his return from convalescence in rural Gorky on October 2, his old habits of driving several teams and prodding others had reasserted themselves. This was the result of his nervousness but also the cause of more nervousness and yet he might have been no less nervous if he had been sensible about his health, for then he would have worried about possible disaster. There can be no doubt that without his executive ability and dynamic energy the Soviet system would have succumbed in its early youth. Lenin not only made the revolution on November 7, 1917, his administrative talent kept it alive in the troubled years that followed. After him, Stalin needed drive, big intrigues, and a smoking revolver. Lenin did it with notes:

SEPTEMBER 25, 1922, TO THE COMMISSARIAT OF JUSTICE: "What is happening in your office about issuing the code or laws of the Soviet government? Is the codification law sleeping or preparing something for its fifth-year jubilee? It must be awakened; and write me two words. Lenin."[4]

OCTOBER 10. Letter to the assistant chief of fuel division of the Supreme Economic Council (VSNH): the American tractors, brought to Perm by the American Harold Ware, had worked well in the state farm to which they were

[2] Lenin, *op. cit.*, Second ed., Vol. XXVII, pp. 315-321.
[3] *Leninskii Sbornik*, Vol. XXXV, p. 356.
[4] *Ibid.*, Vol. XXXV, p. 352.

sent, but, according to information, they would have accomplished still more had it not been for the absence of the necessary quantities of gas and lubricating oil. In place of gasoline they had kerosene. This had to be corrected.[5]

EARLY OCTOBER: How large was the gold reserve; information needed before October 10.[6]

OCTOBER 16. How much foreign currency in the Soviet exchequer?[7]

OCTOBER 16. Request to the Commissariat of Foreign Trade for a monthly statement on exports and imports and income.[8]

OCTOBER 17. Memorandum to the Sovnarkom and STO: "I support the petition for the construction of paper pulp factory in Karelia and for the mining of mica. If there are no special obstacles, please speed up the matter."[9]

OCTOBER 21. Lenin received a request from the Dynamo Factory for the first signature in the autograph book it was inaugurating on November 7. "Remind me in *November*," he wrote his secretary.[10]

OCTOBER 24. Order to his secretaries: No private conversations at sessions of the Sovnarkom and STO.[11]

LATE OCTOBER. To Stalin: the territory of the suggested Urquhart concession should be reduced. "The important thing is the need to reduce the sums received by Urquhart so that our income is not put off until 1934 (?). Lenin."[12]

OCTOBER 26. To Krzhizhanovsky and Pyatakov about the purchase of peat-digging machine abroad.[13]

OCTOBER 27. Letter to the Commissariat of Education on the reduction of the state's subsidies to some theaters and to the Proletkult.[14]

OCTOBER 28. To Molotov: Had the half million gold roubles been released to Armenia for the purchase abroad of tractors and work animals? "What about other aid measures for the Armenians? The matter should be speeded up and checked."[15]

LATE OCTOBER. Note on the preparation of a world atlas. It was to show "the shameless domination by the four imperial powers (We will translate it into all languages, make it a textbook; add supplements every two years) . . ."[16]

LATE OCTOBER OR EARLY NOVEMBER. Memorandum on the stabilization of the rouble.[17]

[5] *Ibid.*, Vol. XXXVI, p. 501.
[6] *Ibid.*, p. 502.
[7] *Ibid.*
[8] *Ibid.*, Vol. XXXV, p. 354.
[9] *Ibid.*
[10] *Ibid.*
[11] *Ibid.*
[12] *Ibid.*, Vol. XXXVI, p. 505.
[13] *Ibid.*
[14] *Ibid.*, p. 506.
[15] *Ibid.*, Vol. XXXV, p. 355.
[16] *Ibid.*, Vol. XXXVI, p. 506.
[17] *Ibid.*, p. 507.

The Fourth Congress of the Third International (Comintern) met in Moscow and Petrograd from November 5 to December 5, 1922. Lenin received many of its delegations and individual delegates. During the second week of November he wrote out the usual detailed outline of an address he would deliver to the Congress, and on November 13 he delivered it in the Tsar's throne room in the Kremlin. I attended with other bourgeois journalists.

This time Lenin spoke German and I understood.

The Soviet Communist Party was the head and purse of the Comintern but it agreed to regard itself formally as under Comintern jurisdiction and obliged, therefore, to report to it, as other national parties did, at regular congresses. Lenin reported.

At Lenin's feet sat Karl Radek, his legs dangling over the sides of the platform, and whenever Lenin could not find the German word he needed he gave the Russian equivalent to Radek who raised his impish face and offered the translation. Once Lenin was not satisfied and threw the Russian word to the audience who made several attempts until they finally satisfied the speaker.

Lenin spoke with machine-gun rapidity in a rather high-pitched voice. The theme assigned to him, "Five Years of the Russian Revolution and the Prospects of the World Revolution," he said, was too broad for one speaker and one speech, and he would therefore limit himself to a single segment of the subject: "The New Economic Policy." It was an important question for all and important for him "because I am now working on it." He first discussed state capitalism, as he had on previous occasions, and recalled his earlier statement that "Though it is not a socialist form, state capitalism would be for us, and for Russia a more favorable form than the existing one": war communism. They were not prepared for this retreat, he confessed. He had talked about state capitalism, he reminded the delegates, in 1918, but "Those brief controversial lines were not by any means a plan of retreat. There was not a word in them about one very important point, for example, free trading, which is of fundamental significance for state capitalism." This confirmed the assumption that for Lenin, state capitalism was private capitalism permitted by the state, not state ownership and operation of enterprises.

The question of a retreat is one that all communist parties should study, Lenin continued, for "In view of the fundamental changes that have taken place all over the world, such as the overthrow of capitalism and the building of socialism, with all the difficulties accompanying it, this is a question to which we must unfailingly pay attention. . . . Moments always occur in times of revolution when the enemy loses his head, and if we make our onslaught on him at such a moment, we may achieve an easy victory. But this is not decisive; for if the enemy has sufficient endurance, he can rally his forces, etc. beforehand, he can easily provoke us to attack him, and then throw us back for many years." Therefore, "even from the practical point of view, all parties which are preparing to make a direct onslaught upon capitalism in the near future must think of ensuring the possibility of retreat for themselves."

After the end of the civil war, "we encountered a great—I think it was the greatest—internal crisis of Soviet Russia, which caused discontent among a considerable section, not only of the peasantry, but also of the workers. . . . Now, after eighteen months, at the end of 1922, we are able to make certain comparisons. . . . I think we can say with a clear conscience . . . that in the past eighteen months . . . we have passed our examination. . . .

"First of all I will deal with our celebrated rouble . . . celebrated if only for the reason that the number of these roubles now exceeds a quadrillion. That's something. . . . But we do not regard this figure to be very important even from the point of view of economic science, for the noughts can always be struck off." The need was to stabilize the rouble and "In that case, all these . . . trillions and quadrillions will not have mattered in the least." In 1921, the rouble was stable less than three months; in 1922, "more than five months . . . we have learned to make progress. Since we have learned this I as sure we shall achieve further successes on this road, if only we do not do anything particularly stupid. The most important thing, however, is trade, namely the circulation of commodities. . . . And since we have successfully grappled with this problem for two years, I think I can say that we can be pleased. After all, we are standing alone. . . .

"Now I come to our social aims. The most important thing, of course, is the peasantry." After the discontent early in 1921 came the famine "the monstrous result of the Civil War." (As though Russia had never had famines. As though the armed communist requisitions had nothing to do with the famine.) But since then the peasants had paid their food tax in hundreds of millions of poods to the state which had employed almost no measures of coercion. "Peasant uprisings, which previously, before 1921, shaped the general picture of Russia, so to speak, have almost completely disappeared. The peasants are contented with their present condition. We can honestly assert that. . . .

"Now I come to light industry"—the production of consumer goods. He noted "a general revival . . . and in connection with it a general improvement of the workers in Petrograd and in Moscow. In other districts this is observed to a smaller degree. . . .

"The third question is heavy industry"—steel, coal, machinery; capital goods. "We have not yet concluded a tolerable concession agreement." Nevertheless, the Soviet government had been able to save 20 million gold roubles—$10,000,000—to invest in heavy industry. "The salvation of Russia does not lie only in a good harvest on the peasant farms—that is not enough —and not only in the good condition of light industry . . . we also need *heavy* industry. . . . Heavy industry needs state subsidies. If we cannot provide them, then, as a civilized state, let alone as a socialist state, we are doomed." But the 20 million roubles were a beginning. "Hence we can say we have been successful."

However, "Undoubtedly, we have done, and will do in the future, an enormous number of absurd things. No one can judge or see this better than I can.

"Why do we do these absurd things? . . . firstly, because ours is a backward country; secondly, education in our country is at the lowest level; and thirdly, because we are receiving no assistance. . . . Very often the state apparatus works against us. . . . Actually, it often happens that at the top, as it were, where we have state power, the apparatus functions somehow; but down below . . . they function in such a way that very often they counteract our measures." But they had schools which were training new personnel. "If we do not work too hurriedly we shall within a few years have a large number of young people who will be capable of radically changing our apparatus."

He would be charged with giving food to the enemy by asserting that the Bolsheviks were doing stupid things. But "When the Bolsheviks do silly things, it is like saying, 'Twice two are five' "; when the capitalists and "the heroes of the Second International do silly things, it is like saying, 'Twice two are a tallow candle.' " As examples Lenin mentioned Western support of Kolchak, and the Versailles Peace Treaty.

Finally, he offered advice: "I think the most important thing for us all, Russian and foreign comrades, is to sit down and study things after five years of the Russian Revolution." The foreign delegates "must digest a good piece of Russian experience. How they will do this I do not know. . . . They, however, must study in the special sense that they may really understand the organization, structure, method, and content of revolutionary work. If they do that I am sure the prospects of the world revolution will not only be good, but excellent."[18]

The delegates and visitors gave Lenin a standing ovation. He hurried away.

After the recess, Trotsky spoke for an hour and a half in German, then for an hour and a half in French, and then for an hour and a half in Russian. Delegates who understood one language inspected the palace while Trotsky was speaking in the others. I watched the virtuoso performance for a time and then wandered into the private apartments of the Tsar and Tsarina. The furniture and the Tsarina's throne were protected by duckcloth. In a corner a French journalist banged out a story on his portable Corona. On a sofa sat Bela Kun, back from the revolutions in Hungary and Germany. The adjoining room was the royal bedroom, and on the immense bed, likewise covered with duckcloth, slept two delegates who had probably fought a committee battle through the night. All these private chambers were sumptuously decorated. Huge blue Sèvres vases stood on gold tables.

[18] Lenin, *Selected Works*, Vol. X, *The Communist International* (London, 1938), pp. 320-333. Russian text in Lenin, *Sochineniya*, Second ed., Vol. XXXVII, pp. 342-355.

The door handles were of gold, the knobs of green malachite. The doors themselves, some twelve feet high, were inlaid with imperial emblems and tiny round holy pictures studded with pearls. The bathroom had equipment imported from Glasgow, mirrors covering all walls, and parquet floors.[19]

When I returned to the throne room Trotsky was speaking in Russian. As I was about to leave to go home, Zinoviev, the chief of the Comintern, and another man preceded me. Zinoviev put his arm around the man's waist and said in German, "Well, when is the world revolution coming in Switzerland?"

Zinoviev was shot on Stalin's order in 1936. Switzerland still eludes the world revolution.

It taxes the imagination to believe that Zinoviev's remark to the Swiss was more than chitchat or that Lenin thought the prospects of world revolution "excellent." In 1922 a communist revolution anywhere might have exposed Russia to renewed military intervention or, at least, to intolerable foreign-policy and economic commitments. Propaganda for world revolution might have been good therapy for foreign communists and hope injections for Russian dreamers. But the reality of revolution would not have served Russia's national interests.

As Lenin spoke to the Comintern it was clear that his country could expect no aid from foreign capitalists, none from foreign communists. It was on its own, fated for decades to pay the high price of a farm policy the peasants disliked and of the inbuilt inefficiency of a bureaucracy unchecked by democracy, an expensive autocratic bureaucracy which, despite differences of form, dress, and verbiage, had a repelling resemblance to the bureaucracy of tsarist absolutism.

Earth hath no fury like a journalist scooped. Mr. Arthur Ransome of the *Manchester Guardian* had had many interesting talks with Lenin in the early years of the revolution and made friends with a number of leading Bolsheviks. Yet Michael Farbman of the London *Observer*, an occasional visitor to Soviet Russia, scooped him in an exclusive "first" interview with Lenin. Ransome, despite his great sense of humor, was vexed and asked Foreign Commissar Chicherin to arrange that he see Lenin. The appointment was made and put off and made again, in true Russian fashion, and finally Ransome was told that Lenin wished to see his written questions before receiving him.

A great British journalist, Ransome did not begin his write-up of the interview with what Lenin said but rather with a leisurely report on the story of how the interview came about. A slight dig at Farbman was natural in the circumstances: "I immediately drew up a series of questions, seven in all, of which only two were concerned with the immediate news of the day. It seemed to me that it would be of greater interest to get Lenin's views on the

---

[19] I remember some but not all of these details. I refreshed my memory from an article I wrote for the New York *Evening Post* of Dec. 16, 1922.

present phase of the Revolution, if he could be induced to state them, than to obtain conventional replies to questions on foreign policy, replies which, with the data at hand, one could perfectly give for oneself." This was Ransome's neat dismissal of Farbman's interview in October. He, on the other hand, intended to ask questions with a view to "provoking Lenin into personal expression. I do not think the result has been altogether satisfactory, because, in one or two cases, he refused to be provoked. . . . Still, the result has been the crystallization in a small space of Lenin's diagnosis of the present situation in Russia." Lenin had trouble with the questions, and, as shown in his *Collected Works*, he wrote two drafts of the replies.[20] "The immediate result" was the postponement of the interview. "It was postponed," Ransome stated in the *Manchester Guardian* of November 22, 1922, "from day to day, because the answers were not ready, and with each day I heard from different sources of the mild annoyance they had caused him." Not without enjoyment, Ransome elaborated: "From Radek I heard that he 'was swearing at me for putting such questions.' From Chicherin that he described them as having the character of snakes in the grass. There was indeed at one time a doubt whether he would answer them at all, and I said I was ready if necessary to withdraw them and submit others. Lenin, however, for the reasons he gave when I saw him, had made up his mind to answer them. In the meantime day after day went by and I was not allowed to see him. . . . Finally, I lost hope and prepared to leave Russia, and had already obtained my visa and place on the train when, on my going to say good-bye to him, Chicherin expressed great surprise that I had not already got my answers, said that he knew Lenin was actually writing them and that he wanted to see me before I left. Accordingly I gave up my place in the train and waited for the next, which was to leave on Monday.

"The next day (Friday) Mrs. Radek told me over the telephone that Lenin would receive me that night. I was to be at Radek's [in the Kremlin] about 8 o'clock. I was there, and had only waited a minute or two when Lenin telephoned to Radek and said he was very tired after a long committee meeting and could only be allowed to talk for a few minutes, whereas if I were to wait till the next morning he could manage a longer talk. I asked if the questions would be answered if I were to wait till morning. Radek repeated the question, and I could hear Lenin's chuckles at the other end of the wire. He said he could not get the questions done by morning, and that it was my own fault. 'Such questions!—such questions!' Then for the first time I believed that he really was answering the questions himself. I had had an unpleasant suspicion that other people were writing the answers for him. It was so unlike the old Lenin not to be ready and eager with jest and logic to deal with any question that might be put before him."

In the end, Ransome did get to Lenin. He reported: "I had not seen Lenin since his illness, and my first impression as we shook hands was that he had

[20] Lenin, *Sochineniya*, Second ed., Vol. XXVII, pp. 326-333.

not changed at all. My second, as we began to talk, was that he was extraordinarily tired. . . . His physical appearance, his charm of manner, these were the same. Something, however, was different. I had never before seen him tired. In the old days he used to keep up a machine-gun fire of questions, bombarding me to such an extent that it was difficult to squeeze in any particular subject on which I wanted to hear his opinion. He would be frightfully busy, but, getting interested, he would go on for half an hour, for an hour, for two hours, with inexhaustible vitality, chuckles of laughter, jokes, jeers, and cross-examination. He was the hardest phenomenon for a journalist to deal with, because he insisted on being the interviewer, not the interviewed. Now, instead of the excitement of old meetings, I felt rather wretched at seeing him make an effort who had seemed to do all he did without effort of any kind. . . .

"There was a little of the old Lenin when he flung back his head in laughter to think of the Fascists (Mussolini ruling in Rome—'A merry story!')—and a little in the interest he showed in the English election." But Lenin did not yet have the answers for Ransome. They were delivered "just in time to take them with me to the train."

"I find (in Moscow) immense economic activity, everybody buying and selling, and a new trading class obviously in existence," read Ransome's first question. How is it that these Nepmen did not wish to become a political force?

Lenin recalled street scenes in London Saturday evenings "about twenty years back." Crowds in London were buying and selling, but they too did not show signs of striving after political power.

Question No. 2: The Nepmen were making profits in trade, the Soviet state was engaged in unprofitable production. "Does this mean the steady economic strengthening of the Nepmen and the steady weakening of the State?"

Lenin replied in the negative. The peasants were paying their taxes "excellently," light industry was reviving, the rouble was being stabilized; only heavy industry was working at a loss. In reply to a third question, Lenin said taxes from Nepmen would help subsidize heavy industry.

Ransome then asked whether, since capitalism was prospering and the peasants were producing bigger crops while the state was losing money in heavy industry, Russia might not be slipping backwards toward a "feudal dictatorship"?

"Nothing of the kind is possible," Lenin affirmed, "for slowly, with intervals, from time to time, we are lifting ourselves along the line of State capitalism." Through state capitalism, by which Lenin meant NEP capitalism, Russia would move forward toward socialism and toward communism "as the highest grade of socialism," because "power in the State is in the hands of the working class."

The story about the interview was more interesting than the interview.

The man interviewed was more interesting than either. He ranks very high among the statesmen of the twentieth century, and made as much history as any of them. His face spoke of strength, shrewdness, will power, and premature age. When I saw him, and on many occasions, he wore buttoned-down shirt collars. I noted his hands, the hands of an aristocrat. His eyes had an X-ray quality; they also mocked. They flashed hate. He was the great hater, and the great doer, a modern proletarian Pugachev armed with an arsenal of stinging words and fabulous executive talent, the head of an intellectual leader mounted on the body of a Volga muzhik.

XLIX. ÖHE SECOND BELL

I WAS TRUDGING the streets of Moscow when word came to the hotel from the press section of the Foreign Commissariat that Lenin would address the Moscow Soviet in plenary session. This was the last speech of his life—November 20, 1922—and I missed it.

He gave the Moscow Soviet an optimistic report. In foreign affairs, all had been going well, and "we proceeded on our journey without having to change trains or horses," to use an old metaphor, he said.

Regarding the NEP, there were no differences in the communist party or the "vast mass of non-party workers and peasants." All agreed on its necessity. "We are now retreating . . . in order to get a better run for our longer leap forward." But they faced "the special difficulty" of being "unaided" by foreign countries. So we must "learn to trade, to make profit." Moreover, the government apparatus should be improved by distributing communists "properly" within it. But "These communists must become the masters of the apparatus which has been placed in their charge, and not, as is often the case now, the slaves of this apparatus." That had to be admitted frankly. "These are the difficulties that confront us just at the time when we have taken the business road, when we cannot approach socialism as if it were a solemnly painted icon . . . everything must be tested." Nothing on faith. "Shall we be able to organize efficiently? This question is by no means settled yet." A newspaper reports on a factory. The director is a communist. But "Does it produce a profit? Is it paying? . . . Socialism is no longer a matter of the distant future, or an abstract picture, or an icon. . . . Permit me to conclude by expressing the conviction that . . . NEP Russia will be transformed into Socialist Russia."[1]

[1] Lenin, *Selected Works*, Vol. IX, *New Economic Policy, Socialist Construction* (London, 1937), pp. 274-381. Russian text in Lenin, *Sochineniya*, Second ed., Vol. XXVII, pp. 360-366.

The peasants rarely read what Lenin said. But an epigram like "NEP Russia will be transformed into Socialist Russia" was sure to reach them through the two or three newspaper readers in a village or by word of mouth at markets and railway stations, and it undoubtedly spread uncertainty. When I traveled in the countryside in 1922 and 1923, muzhiks would ask whether Lenin might not rescind their right to trade. "Should I build myself a new house? Should I buy another cow?" they wondered, "because then the communists will put me in anathema and I'll be a kulak."

The question one cannot answer is whether Lenin was encouraging himself as well as others. He spoke to the Comintern and the Moscow Soviet in pink colors calculated to lift gloom. But he knew the truth. The coal-black facts were presented to the Congress of Soviets meeting in the Kremlin in December, 1922, when Lenin was absent. Chairman of the Supreme Economic Council Peter A. Bogdanov told that assembly: pig iron output equalled 4 percent of the prewar total; the Ukraine produced 2.5 percent of its 1914 iron and steel production; Turkestan and Azerbaijan were growing little cotton and two million tons would have to be imported for gold. Commissar of Finance Sokolnikov reported that in January, 1922, the Soviet government's revenue amounted to 1 percent of its budget and the rest came from the printing presses which turned out millions by the minute. Education Commissar Lunacharsky said: the number of pupils in elementary schools had fallen from 6,860,000 in 1921 to 5,300,000 in April, 1922, and 4,750,000 in October, 1922. Reason: insufficient funds.[2] Small wonder Lenin wrote two letters to Stalin, dated November 25, 1921, and November 29, 1921, urging sharp cuts in expenditures on the navy: "We don't need a fleet, but an increase in the expenditure on schools is desperately needed."[3] A small fleet is of no use to any country except as an easy target or for decoration, and Lenin was a realist. In response to Lenin's urging, two million gold roubles were transferred from the navy's budget to a fund for the feeding of school children and teachers.[4]

Would a better economy and less work have prolonged Lenin's life? When Lenin died his brain was lifted out of his skull and a special Institute of the Brain established which cut his gray matter into thousands of thin slices in the hope of plumbing the secret of his mental qualities. But after years of effort, the institute asked Krupskaya, Lenin's widow, and she answered its questionnaire: Lenin "was a militant person"; "colossal concentration"; "self-critical—very strict with himself. But he hated tortuous self-analysis of his soul"; "there was no quick change of moods"; "Impressionable. Reacted very strongly"; "grew pale when he was excited"; "wrote and spoke easily and freely"; "handwriting grew more distinct when he wrote something (in letters for instance) which especially interested and agitated him"; "always

---

[2] New York *Evening Post*, Jan. 27, 1923.
[3] *Leninskii Sbornik*, Vol. XXXVI, pp. 513-514.
[4] *Ibid.*, p. 516.

wrote a final draft of a manuscript immediately. Very few corrections";
"could not write and disliked writing when there was conversation, needed
absolute quiet"; "Just before making a speech he was very nervous"; "talked
quickly"; "preparing for a speech he would walk to and fro in the room and
whisper. . . . When he returned home after an argument, or discussion, he
was often gloomy, silent and upset. I never asked—later he would tell me,
without questions." She added that he became very tired when he heard
music; never played a musical instrument; never made drawings; could not
tolerate flowers in the room. "He was courageous and brave"; "Oh, how he
could laugh."[5]

The chemists of the brain institute had discovered none of these things in
their slices. But the autopsy did reveal the secret of his death. Dr. Rozanov
wrote: "Even for physicians the autopsy was a trial." Dissecting the brain of
a Lenin! They found "Colossal sclerosis of the blood vessels of the brain, and
only sclerosis. It is remarkable that he was able to think with a brain so
transformed by sclerosis and, too, that he could live so long with such a
brain."[6]

Was heredity decisive—Lenin's similarity to his father who died at the
same age? Or could rest and better political and economic conditions have
prolonged his life? The doctors tried to save him by urging that he withdraw
from active leadership and remain in ignorance of current events. But convincing Lenin was not easy, for as long as his brain functioned he insisted on
applying it to the purpose that had governed his adult life. Advancing sclerosis notwithstanding, Lenin's will remained a formidable force. He lacked inner peace. Adverse economic conditions worried him. But more tormenting
were unresolved problems: the monopoly of foreign trade; the nationalities
question; bureaucracy; and leadership. He wanted to work on these. Work
was his bread and butter, his tea and meat. He probably felt not that work
would kill him but that it would kill him not to work. How could he withdraw from leadership in the midst of chaos and when he differed so much
with Stalin?

The nationalities problem took a painful turn in Stalin's Georgia. The
Union of Soviet Socialist Republics to replace the R.S.F.S.R.—Lenin's
project—had not yet been approved. Meanwhile, trouble arose in one of the
constituent parts of the proposed Union: the Trans-Caucasus Federation,
itself a federation of Georgia, Armenia, and Azerbaijan, neighbors but different in history, temperament, and religion. The Azerbaijanis were Moslems;
the Armenians Monophysite Christians with their own pope at Echmiadzin;
the Georgians adherents of the Russian Orthodox Church yet hating everything Russian.

In 1924, following a Menshevik uprising in Georgia, I visited there with
Paul Scheffer of the *Berliner Tageblatt*. At Telav, deep in the mountains, we

[5] *Izvestia*, April 7, 1963.
[6] *Vospominaniya*, Vol. 2, p. 346.

took horses and rode with General Tchaikovsky, commander of a Russian cavalry brigade, to Tsinandali, site of the famous wine cellar once the property of the Tsar's relative, Grand Duke Nikolai Nikolaevich. At the inevitable Georgian banquet—wine served in ram's horns so they cannot be set down until emptied—a toast was pronounced in honor of the three foreigners. General Tchaikovsky looked around and said, "I see only two foreigners here." To which a Georgian replied, "A Russian is always a foreigner in Georgia."

Armenia and Azerbaijan, each eager for self-government however limited by Moscow, found the Trans-Caucasus Federation an additional hobble, and even Georgia, whose Sergo Orjonekidze, a national figure, dominated the Federation from the Georgian capital of Tiflis, was irked by the restraints placed on it as a member of the Federation. Georgia, once ruled by Turkey and Persia and far closer in blood and tradition to the Iranians than to the Russians, had enjoyed a quasi-independence under Menshevism from 1917 to 1921. The Menshevik leaders were democratic socialists, but it is probably fair to say that their popularity stemmed far more from anti-Moscovite sentiment than from the socialist ideology of a little country largely populated by small farmers, some of whom called themselves princes, and by mountain tribes, one of which, the Hevsurs, considered themselves descendants of the Crusaders and wore coats of mail while plowing their stony fields. Georgian nationalism was fed from the wells of the mountaineer's independent spirit.

Sergo Orjonekidze, Moscow's viceroy in Tiflis, known everywhere as "Sergo," was a giant of muscle and bone with a long face, huge beak of a nose, and a deep bass voice. As I sat in his office during several visits to the Caucasus in the 1920's, all I understood of his telephone conversations in Georgian was "ho" meaning yes and "ara" meaning no, and he intoned the words in a manner that made me think of Shaliapin turned politician. He was no misanthrope like Stalin; he was on the contrary a friendly man, sensitive and temperamental, and close at that time to Stalin who subsequently promoted him to the small leadership group in Moscow. In 1937, Sergo died of, the official announcement stated, a heart attack. In his secret speech of February 24-25, 1956, however, Chairman Khrushchev declared that Sergo, depressed by Stalin's cruel pressures on him and others, had committed suicide.

In 1922 the conflict in Georgia between the "independencers," who wanted Georgia to enjoy considerable self-government within a Soviet Union, and Orjonekidze, ruling by Stalin's Muscovite mandate, reached explosive fury. In an argument about autonomy versus independence, the big Sergo struck roly-poly "Boodoo" Mdivani, the communist champion of the "independencers." When Lenin heard of this he was incensed that a communist leader should use physical violence against a comrade. He was also perturbed by the nationalistic tensions which the incident revealed. On November 25, accordingly, the Politburo voted to send a commission led by Felix Djerzhinsky, ex-head of the Cheka, to investigate the "Georgian Question." At about the same time Lenin asked Rykov, resting in the North Caucasus from surgery in Germany, to join Djerzhinsky in making the study.[7] This action against Orjonekidze reflected Lenin's growing disfavor of Stalin. The situation shredded Lenin's nerves.

His condition became worse. On the morning of November 25 he was ill and came to his office for only five minutes; later he dictated three letters on the telephone from his apartment. Maria, Lenin's sister, told his secretaries not to disturb him. He returned to the office at 6 P.M. for an hour's talk with Deputy Chairman Tsurupa. After Tsurupa left, Lenin instructed his secretaries to forward to Tsurupa the two files on his desk on current matters and to submit to Chicherin an article he had written on the rejection of the Urquhart concession. During the seven days that followed, Lenin occasionally visited his office, used the telephone, looked at Politburo minutes, received Tsurupa, Molotov, and several others, but was relatively inactive. On the morning of December 2 the physician told Lenin he would have to take a vacation of several days once or even twice every two months.[8]

The statesman must attend to major issues without neglecting lesser matters. Lenin possessed this bifocal ability. He wrote Willy Muenzenberg, a young German communist, secretary of the International Workers Aid, stressing the importance of relief to the Russian famine victims and of working-class pressure in foreign countries on their governments to recognize Soviet Russia.[9] Two days later, December 4, Lenin drafted "Notes on the Question of the Tasks of Our Delegation to The Hague" whose cold precision and unsparing combativeness are reminiscent of the writings of his finest years. The Amsterdam Trade Union International had convoked a world conference in The Hague to discuss ways of preventing war, and Moscow was sending a strong delegation, including Karl Radek, Alexandra Kollontai, and Feodor Rothstein. "I think the greatest difficulty," Lenin began, "lies in overcoming the prejudice that this question is a simple, clear and comparatively easy one." The slogan of the reformists was, he said, "We shall retaliate to war with a strike or revolution." But, Lenin argued, "It must be explained to the people how great is the secrecy with which war arises, and how helpless the ordinary workers' organizations are in the face of war that is really impending, even if these organizations call themselves revolutionary." Moreover, when it comes to "the defense of the fatherland," Lenin admitted, "the overwhelming majority of the toilers will settle in favor of their bourgeoisie."

To combat war, Lenin said, requires "the preservation and formation of illegal organizations." Communists should not remain aloof from a war: "Boycott war—is a stupid phrase. Communists must take part even in the most reactionary war." And, clearly, spread propaganda and mutiny. Even

---

[7] Voprosi Istorii KPSS, Moscow, Vol. No. 2, February, 1963, p. 69.
[8] Ibid., pp. 71-73.
[9] Lenin, Sochineniya, Second ed., Vol. XXXVII, pp. 369-370.

communists did not understand their duty: "I recall that a number of declarations were made by our Communist deputies, in parliament as well as outside, which contained monstrously incorrect and monstrously frivolous statements about this subject."[10]

The same day, December 7, Lenin sent his autographed photograph with a long inscription to Karl Steinmetz, General Electric's wizard of Schenectady. Steinmetz had written Lenin on February 16, 1922, wishing him success and expressing confidence that he would complete the astonishing work of social and industrial construction which Russia had undertaken under difficult circumstances. Lenin replied in a letter written between April 2 and 10. He stated that "to my shame," he had heard the name of Steinmetz only several months ago from Comrade Krzhizhanovsky. "He told me of the prominent position you occupy among the electro-technicians of the entire world." Lenin declared that he observed in all countries of the world a growth in the number of representatives of science, technology, and art who are becoming convinced of the necessity of replacing capitalism with some other social-economic system. He thanked Steinmetz for his offer of help but suggested that the absence of diplomatic relations between the United States and Soviet Russia would impede its implementation. He was publishing the Steinmetz letter and his reply in the hope that this would advance the cause of trade and diplomatic relations between the two countries.[11] It was more than half a year after this exchange that Lenin sent Steinmetz his photograph. Below it, somebody had written, at Lenin's dictation, and in perfect penmanship without character, this message: "To the highly esteemed Charles Proteus Steinmetz, one of the few exceptions to the united front of representatives of science and culture opposed to the proletariat. I hope that a further deepening and widening of the breach in this front will not have to be awaited long. Let the example of the Russian workers and peasants holding their fate in their own hands serve as an encouragement to the American proletariat and farmers. In spite of the terrible consequence of the war destruction we are going ahead, though not possessing to the extent of one tenth the tremendous resources for the economic building of a new life that have been at the disposal of the American people for many years."

Lenin signed in a vigorous hand: "Moscow 7.XII.1922 Vladimir Oulianoff (Lenin)."[12]

Lenin disciplined others and disciplined himself, but he could not curb his

[10] Lenin, *Selected Works*, Vol. X, *The Communist International* (London, 1938), pp. 316-319. Russian text Lenin, *Sochineniya*, Second ed., Vol. XXVII, pp. 372-375, and editorial note p. 556.

[11] Lenin, *Sochineniya*, Second ed., Vol. XXVII, pp. 275-276 and 539. Also *Leninskii Sbornik*, Vol. XXXVI, p. 463. The Steinmetz letter and Lenin's reply were almost certainly written in English, but an assiduous search in the Schenectady Historical Society, where the Steinmetz archives are kept, failed to uncover them. I was compelled, therefore, to paraphrase the Russian translations.

[12] A copy of the photograph with inscription and signature was graciously sent to me by Mrs. Leslie S. Cormack, the curator of the Schenectady Historical Society.

appetite for work. From October 2, when he returned to Moscow after his first stroke in May, until December 16, he wrote 224 letters and memoranda, kept 125 appointments with 171 persons, and presided over 32 sessions of the Politburo, Sovnarkom, STO, and various commissions. This, his secretary, Lydia A. Fotieva, writes, is not a complete list. She also omitted his three public addresses. On December 7 Lenin arrived in his office at 10:55 A.M., participated in the session of the Politburo from 11 A.M. until 2:20 P.M., Kamenev presiding, and then retired before the conclusion of the discussions; he returned to his office at 5:30 P.M., talked on the telephone with Stalin, gave instructions to his secretary, and went home at 6:15, carrying some files with him. Later he drove to Gorky.[13]

From Gorky the same evening he telephoned a message to his secretary and the secretariat of the Sovnarkom: "All documents forwarded to me from the [party's] Central Committee should be recorded in a special book in briefest form in such a manner that the entry be in telegraphic style and in not more than three lines. If there is any unclarity or lack of precision in the document (on such questions as: what is wanted, how much is being requested, what is the complaint, what are they getting at), you will be responsible for such lack of precision."[14]

He intended to work at Gorky.

After Lenin withdrew from the Politburo session on December 7, it granted permission to Professor Nikolai A. Rozhkov, author of a classic twelve-volume history of Russia, to reside in Moscow. The next day, in Gorky, Lenin received the minutes of the Politburo meeting and read the Rozhkov decision. His obsessive hatred of the Mensheviks burst into a roaring fire and he dashed off a letter to Stalin.

Rozhkov had been a Bolshevik. Exiled to tsarist Siberia he broke with Lenin and in 1917 joined the Provisional (Kerensky) government and the Mensheviks. After the Kronstadt revolt, he abandoned the Mensheviks, devoted himself to scholarship, and privately expressed hope that Russia would evolve toward democratic socialism. Lenin did not trust him. ". . . essentially, I am very much afraid," he told Stalin. "He will tell any number of lies, *even in the press*. He will lie and we shall be circumvented. That is what I fear. Their"—the Mensheviks—"motto is, tell lies, quit the party, but stay in Russia."[15]

The day after he reached Gorky he telephoned an order to his Moscow office: The Politburo is to meet on Thursdays from 11 A.M. until not later than 2 P.M. Questions left over were to be taken up on Fridays or Mondays at the same hours. The agenda of the Politburo must be sent to members before noon on Wednesdays. Written data bearing on subjects to be discussed should accompany the agenda. New points could be added to the

[13] *Vospominaniya*, Vol. 3, p. 345.
[14] *Leninskii Sbornik*, Vol. XXXV, p. 359.
[15] *Vospominaniya*, Vol. 3, p. 346.

agenda on the day of meeting only in case of extreme urgency, "especially questions of foreign policy," only in writing, and only if all members agree.[16]

Such regulations might have been adopted years earlier. But the flag of Oblomov waved over the Kremlin too.

The next day, December 9, Lenin telephoned Lydia Fotieva and dictated to her a long letter for Tsurupa regarding the work of the Chairman (Lenin) and the three deputies (Tsurupa, Rykov, and Kamenev) of the Sovnarkom: he fixed the hours when the four would meet together and the duties of each deputy working separately. "Since," his last paragraph reads, "the work of improving and correcting the entire government apparatus is far more important than the presiding [over Cabinet meetings in Lenin's absence] and the chattering with assistant people's commissars and people's commissars which has hitherto entirely occupied the deputies, it is necessary that they adopt and strictly carry out the practice of 'descending to the depths' *no less than two hours* every week, and devote this time to the personal study of the most varied sections of the apparatus, the high and the low, and do it, moreover, in surprise. The record of such investigations, written down, confirmed, and disseminated (in certain cases) to *all* departments, should result in *a reduction* of staffs and tightening the discipline of everybody and everything in our government apparatus."[17]

As ever, Lenin saw the cause of bureaucracy in the conduct of individuals, which undoubtedly aggravated the evil, rather than in the character of the system. After Lenin's death, surprise "raids" by workers' squads became the vogue, and as the raids multiplied, so did the red tape.

On December 10 and 11, Lenin's office had no letters or instructions and only several brief telephone calls from him; he was writing the outline of his address to the Tenth All-Russian Congress of Soviets, scheduled for the end of the month, which would adopt the new constitution of the Union of Soviet Socialist Republics. This lent urgency to the "Georgian Question" and the controversy between Lenin and Stalin on the functions of the central Moscow government as compared with those of the constituent "independent" republics of the Union. Rykov and Djerzhinsky, who had gone to Georgia to investigate the incident in which Orjonekidze smacked Mdivani, were back in Moscow. Lenin wished to see them. He returned from Gorky to the Kremlin on December 12. Beginning at noon, he deliberated for two hours with his three deputy chairmen. At 6:45 P.M., he received Djerzhinsky, who remained an hour.

The day after Lenin talked with Djerzhinsky he had two cerebral thromboses.[18] These may not have been the result of Djerzhinsky's report on Georgia. Yet given Lenin's passionate involvement in the matter the connection is not precluded. For it developed that Djerzhinsky supported Stalin. The

[16] *Leninskii Sbornik*, Vol. XXXV, pp. 359-360.
[17] *Ibid.*, pp. 360-361.
[18] *Vospominaniya*, Vol. 3, p. 347.

Pole, like the Georgian, was aware of the strong nationalistic, secessionist tendencies among Russia's many ethnic strains and feared the divisive effect of granting real authority to the constituent republics of the Soviet Union.

M. S. Akhmedov, writing in the Moscow *Voprosi Istorii KPSS*, Volume No. 6 of 1962, and citing unpublished archive documents, states, "It is necessary to record that Stalin attempted to push his [autonomy] proposals through the [constitution-drafting] commission without regard to the opinions and the critical remarks of local party functionaries. In reality, he obstructed discussion in the party organizations of the Soviet republics of the question of establishing the Soviet Union. For instance, on September 24, when the commission examined Stalin's proposal of 'autonomy-ization,' Petrovsky [of the Ukraine] made a motion to permit debate on the commission's decisions 'in the bureaus of the provincial party committees of the republics.' " The four representatives in the commission of the national republics, an Ukrainian, a Byelorussian, a Georgian, and an Azerbaijani, voted for the motion. They were outvoted by the five Stalinmen: Molotov, Myasnikov, Orjonekidze, Sokolnikov, and Stalin. Petrovsky then asked that the minutes show that the Central Committee of the Ukranian Communist Party had not discussed the question of the Ukraine's relations with the R.S.F.S.R. "Those who opposed Stalin's plan were often indiscriminately called nationalists. Many honest members of the party, who in that period spoke against 'autonomy-ization,' were persecuted as 'counterrevolutionary' nationalists during Stalin's cult of personality." Their name is legion.

Stalin's future despotism was casting its black shadow before.

Lenin knew what Stalin was doing. Later in the month of December he blamed himself in writing for not opposing Stalin more resolutely on "autonomy-ization" and referred to the fears that came to him after conferring with Djerzhinsky on the evening of December 12.

The two cerebral thromboses of December 13, therefore, may have been due to purely physical or to emotional causes or both. In any case, Lenin's second bell had rung.

During the 1920's and 1930's I often crisscrossed the great expanses of Russia by train. Trains stopped frequently to allow their locomotives to drink and when that happened the passengers poured out of the railway cars like bees from a hive. Some made their way to the miserable "buffet" to grab a bun or a bottle of vodka, others rushed to the peasant women who uncertainly—for they never knew what the police might do—stood in the lee of the station selling hard-boiled eggs, pickles and bony chickens. Masses crowded around the battery of taps where anybody could fill his or her kettle (the women were usually jostled away) with free boiling water to make tea when they returned to the train. Shortly after the train halted, the station master himself rang the first bell. Depending on the state of the water hose, the weather, the relationship between the locomotive engineer and the stationmaster and how much gossip they had to exchange, the second bell sounded when the engine got up steam again. At that signal the passengers began scurrying back to their seats and bunks. Immediately the third bell sounded the train moved on.

The second bell was the final warning.

L. LENIN'S LAST WILL AND TESTAMENT

DECEMBER 12, 1922, was Lenin's last working day in his office. On December 13 the second bell rang, and he acceded to the physicians' demand that he retire from the active conduct of the affairs of state and go to Gorky for a prolonged rest. But he did not surrender the wheel. He still intended to address the Congress of Soviets at the end of the month. He still proposed to shape decisions on major issues like the role of the nationalities in the projected Soviet Union. For these reasons he rebuffed a suggestion by Deputy Chairman Rykov that the choice of his official visitors at home be made by his three deputies or by the secretariat of the party's Central Committee. He wanted "complete freedom" and "unlimited and even extension of visits," he told the three deputies in a letter dictated at noon on the 13th after the doctors' departure. As to other questions, he yielded to the deputies not, however, for three months as they had asked "but until my return to work if this occurs before the elapse of three months."[1]

He also dictated a letter to the Central Committee protesting the Polit-buro's vote to sanction Professor Rozhkov's residence in Moscow (Lenin never relinquished an issue until he won), and another to M. I. Frumkin on the foreign trade monopoly.

After thirty minutes of dictation, Stalin arrived in the apartment at 12:30 and stayed until 2:35 P.M.[2]

Nothing is known about this protracted conversation, but Lenin almost certainly dwelt on the nationalities question and certainly touched on the foreign trade monopoly, for after Stalin left Lenin dictated a letter to him on the monopoly. At 2:25 P.M. the next day he sent the letter to V. A. Avan-esov, former Deputy Commissar of Rabkrin (Workers and Peasants Inspec-tion), now Deputy Commissar of Foreign Trade, with a note: "I am sending you my letter. Return it by seven o'clock. Consider it very well, what to add, what to subtract. *How to prepare for battle.*"[3] The letter, as yet unpublished, was forwarded to Stalin on December 15.

On the 13th, after drafting the letter to Stalin, Lenin wrote a note to

---

[1] *Leninskii Sbornik*, Vol. XXXVI, p. 519.
[2] *Vospominaniya*, Vol. 3, p. 347.
[3] *Ibid.*, p. 350.

Trotsky: "I would earnestly urge you to take upon yourself at the coming plenum [of the party's Central Committee] the defense of our common view as to the unconditional necessity of preserving and enforcing the monopoly . . . the previous plenum took a decision in this matter wholly in conflict with the monopoly of foreign trade."[4]

Stalin and Trotsky held opposing views on the indispensability of a monopoly of foreign trade. At the plenary session of the Central Committee on October 6, Stalin had pushed through a resolution which Lenin regarded as a breach of the monopoly. On October 13, 1922, Lenin criticized Stalin's position in a letter addressed to Stalin but intended for the entire Central Committee. The resolution, he wrote, would have permitted imports and exports at certain points of entry. Lenin was concrete in his criticism: "Purchasing offices are opened for import and export. Then where is the control? Where are the means of control? The price of flax in Russia is four and a half roubles, in England fourteen roubles. . . . What force will restrain the peasants and merchants from profitable transactions? Cover Russia with a network of inspectors? Catch the neighbor of the purchasing office and prove that he sold his flax for secret export? . . . Without waiting to try out the monopoly regime which has only commenced to give us millions (and will give us tens of millions or more) we introduce complete chaos."

The monopoly, as Lenin showed, enabled the Soviet government to pay a low price for the peasant's produce and make a profit on it in the world market. "The question," he charged in his letter of October 13, "was decided in a hurry. Nothing like a serious discussion took place. . . . I am extremely sorry that illness prevented me from being at the session that day. . . . On such a matter, 'legality' in peasant Russia is absolutely impossible." The muzhik would find a way of selling to foreign exporters.

In a postscript Lenin added that he had talked to Stalin the day before and learned of a plan to make Petrograd and Novorossisk on the Black Sea temporary free ports. This, he argued, would swell the volume of contraband. "With the development of foreign trade we began to expect a flow of gold. I see no other income unless it be a state liquor monopoly" and he rejected that on moral grounds.[5] (It was introduced after his death.)

Now the December plenary session of the Central Committee drew near. Hence the long conversation with Stalin on December 13, and Lenin's letter to Trotsky on the same day urging him to defend the foreign trade monopoly. Lenin was concerned not only with the loss of revenue but equally with a possible alliance between the Russian muzhik and foreign business. Unlike Stalin, he wanted the monopoly strengthened.

[4] From the Trotsky Archives in the Houghton Library of Harvard University. Document T 766. Copy supplied.

[5] Lenin, *Sochineniya*, Fourth ed., Vol. 33, pp. 338-341. This volume, published in Moscow in 1950, contains an editorial note which puts the blame for the anti-monopoly resolution on Bukharin, Sokolnikov, Kamenev, and Zinoviev, but not on Stalin. p. 475.

Meanwhile, Lenin won the battle against Professor Rozhkov. Reversing itself, the Politburo, on December 14, granted Rozhkov permission to reside in Pskov (just as Lenin, after his Siberian exile, was allowed to settle in Pskov but not in the capital) and warned him that at the first anti-Soviet act he would be deported to the West. On the same day Lenin dictated a letter to Zinoviev in Petrograd to keep an eye on Rozhkov.[6]

Apparently, Lenin was in touch with Trotsky, for early on December 15 he wrote a letter to Trotsky: "I consider that we have reached full agreement. Please inform the plenum of our solidarity. I hope our solution passes, because some of those who voted against in October are now coming over to our side in part or altogether.

"If, contrary to expectation, our solution fails to pass, we will appeal to the [communist] fraction at the Congress of Soviets and declare that we shall raise the question at the Congress of the party.

"Let me know in that event and I will send my declaration."[7]

Several hours later Deputy Commissar of Foreign Trade Frumkin, who shared Lenin's views on the monopoly, informed him in writing that, according to rumor, the question of the monopoly might be removed from the plenum's agenda and transferred to the next plenum on the excuse that Lenin might attend it.[7]

Lenin immediately forwarded Frumkin's communication to Trotsky and dictated a note to go with it (the second letter to Trotsky that day): The question of the foreign trade monopoly had to be "finished with once and for all." Moreover, "If a fear exists that this question agitates me and might affect my health, then I think this is quite wrong, for I am ten thousand times more disturbed by a delay which makes our policy on a basic issue completely unstable." Lenin therefore pressed Trotsky to insist on an immediate discussion. He would, he wrote, accept no compromise except to have the plenum confirm the monopoly and raise the question again at the party congress.[7]

That night Lenin suffered a brain attack which lasted thirty minutes. The physicians were summoned, but before they arrived Lenin dictated a letter to Krupskaya on the distribution of his work among his three deputies. The same evening Krupskaya asked Lenin's staff to inform Stalin that Lenin would not address the imminent Congress of Soviets.[8] Lydia Fotieva, Lenin's chief secretary, states in her memoirs that "the inability to address the Tenth Congress of Soviets had a very serious effect on Vladimir Ilyich's health. His condition deteriorated gravely."[9] Lenin was trapped: every setback in his health reduced his ability to participate in politics, and every such constraint hurt his health.

[6] *Voprosi Istorii KPSS*, Vol. No. 2, 1963, p. 77.
[7] Trotsky Archives. Documents T 767; T 768; T 769.
[8] Pospelov and others, *Biografia*, Second ed., p. 620.
[9] *Vospominaniya*, Vol. 3, p. 352.

December 16, Lenin prepared to leave Moscow for the village of Gorky. He gave instructions on the disposition of his books and wrote a letter to the members of the Central Committee: "I have now completed the liquidation of my affairs and can go away in peace. I have also completed my agreement with Trotsky on the defense of my views regarding the monopoly of foreign trade. There remains only one circumstance which causes me extreme disquiet,—the impossibility of addressing the Congress of Soviets." But he still hoped. He suggested that another person be prepared to report for the government while leaving it open for him to speak if the doctors approved.[10]

Lenin's physicians insisted on his going away to Gorky. The roads, however, were blocked by snow; no automobile could make the trip. The family ruled out the use of an air sleigh because it involved danger and fatigue.

Every morning, P. P. Pakaln, the commander of the bodyguard, brought Aida, Lenin's dog, to the apartment. Lenin enjoyed playing with the beloved animal. His body and brain seemed to be fighting for survival. For several days he remained completely inactive.

Stalin watched suspiciously. He could, with reason, have concluded that Lenin and Trotsky were forming a united front to curb him, perhaps to oust him. He knew from Djerzhinsky how fiercely Lenin had reacted to Orjonekidze's temper and Stalin's "autonomy-ization" scheme; then there was Lenin's letter of December 16 to the Central Committee: "I have now completed my agreement with Trotsky on the defense of my views regarding the monopoly of foreign trade"—against Stalin's views. Indeed the plenum defeated Stalin and adopted the Lenin proposition as presented and seconded by Trotsky.

Lenin felt triumphant. On December 21 he dictated a letter for Trotsky which Krupskaya wrote out in longhand (Trotsky Archives, Document T 770): "Leon Davidovich," Krupskaya wrote on her own behalf, "today Professor Foerster permitted Vladimir Ilyich to dictate a letter and he dictated to me the following letter to you:

" 'Comrade Trotsky, It seems we succeeded in taking the position without a single shot by a simple maneuver. I propose that we do not stop and continue the attack. . . . N. Lenin.'

"V.I. also requests you to telephone your reply. N. K. Ulyanova."

The "simple maneuver" was the display of unity between Lenin and Trotsky.

Did someone "leak" this letter to Stalin? The conclusion is inescapable, for the next day, December 22, Stalin counterattacked; he attacked Krupskaya. Feigning solicitude for Lenin's health, he telephoned her, blamed her for disturbing her husband by giving him information on current party affairs,

[10] Pospelov and others, *op. cit.*, Second ed., p. 620. The first edition of this biography, published in Moscow in 1960, omits this letter. In Lydia Fotieva's contribution to *Vospominaniya*, Vol. 3, p. 351 (also published in 1960), the letter is reproduced without the sentence regarding his agreement with Trotsky and without any indication of a deletion.

showered her with curses, and threatened to bring her to trial before the party's disciplinary Central Control Commission.

It is not known whether Krupskaya told Lenin about Stalin's telephonic tirade. Exhausted by the long worrisome vigil over the man she had served and loved throughout her adult life, Stalin's assault tore at her exposed nerves, and since she was constantly in her husband's presence he could not have helped noticing her disquiet.

That night Lenin's right arm and right leg were paralyzed. The physicians arrived soon after daybreak. Lenin begged their permission to dictate for four minutes every day. They assented. Shortly after 9 A.M. on December 23, accordingly, he summoned Miss M. A. Volodicheva, one of his typists, and said, "I want to dictate to you a letter to the Congress" of the party. "Write this down." He then commenced to dictate his famous last will and testament.

A general impression prevails that this testament consisted of a demand to remove Stalin from the post of party General Secretary because he had amassed too much power. It was that and far more.

Lenin dictated: "A Letter to the Congress.

"I would very much advise this Congress to undertake a series of changes in our political system. I wish to share with you considerations which I regard as most important. I put ahead of everything else an increase in the number of members of the Central Committee to several tens or even to a hundred. [There were then twenty-seven members in the party's Central Committee.] It seems to me that unless we introduce such a reform our Central Committee would be threatened with great peril if the course of events were not wholly favorable to us. . . .

"Further, I think of directing the attention of the Congress to grant legislative force, under certain conditions, to the decisions of the Gosplan [Federal State Planning Commission], meeting the views of Comrade Trotsky in this regard to a certain extent and in certain conditions."

The expansion of the Central Committee would raise its authority and improve the work "of our apparatus" as well as "serve to prevent conflicts between small groups of the Central Committee from acquiring a quite exaggerated significance for the entire fate of the party."[11]

A copy of this letter was sent to Stalin the same day.[12] It would have reinforced his impression of an alliance between Lenin and Trotsky.

(The next, twelfth, Communist Party Congress met in April, 1923, when Lenin was mentally incapacitated. It followed his advice to the extent of electing a Central Committee of forty instead of twenty-seven. The Thirteenth Congress in May, 1924, expanded the Committee membership to sixty-three, and thereafter the size of the Committee continued to grow—

---

[11] Lenin, op. cit., Fourth ed., Vol. 36, p. 543.
[12] Vosprosi Istorii KPSS, Vol. No. 2, 1963. Note #102, p. 89.

with no beneficent effect from Lenin's magic of numbers. The larger the Committee the lighter the weight of each member and the easier Stalin's task of controlling the whole.)

Stalin's thrust at Krupskaya via the telephone breached her defenses. She felt she needed protection against him. The day Lenin dictated the above "Letter to the Congress," Krupskaya wrote an anguished note to Kamenev, one of Lenin's three deputies and, in Lenin's absence, chairman of the Politburo. She wrote: "Leo Borisovich!

"Because of a short letter which I had written in words dictated to me by Vladimir Ilyich by permission of the doctors, Stalin allowed himself yesterday an unusually rude outburst directed at me. This is not my first day in the party. During all these 30 years I have never heard from any comrade one word of rudeness. The business of the party and of Ilyich are not less dear to me than to Stalin. I need at present the maximum of self-control. What one can and what one cannot discuss with Ilyich I know better than any doctor, because I know what makes him nervous and what does not, in any case I know better than Stalin. I am turning to you and to Gregory [Zinoviev] as much closer comrades of V.I. and I beg you to protect me from rude interference with my private life and from vile invectives and threats. I have no doubt as to what will be the unanimous decision of the Control Commission, with which Stalin sees fit to threaten me; however, I have neither the strength nor the time to waste on this foolish quarrel. And I am a living person and my nerves are strained to the utmost. N. Krupskaya."[13]

On the basis of available information it is impossible to judge whether Lenin saw Krupskaya's letter before it was sent or whether her inner torment was communicated to him in some other way. But the day after she wrote it, Lenin dictated that part of his "Letter to the Congress" which is known throughout the world as his last testament. He cautioned Miss Volodicheva several times that this letter must remain "absolutely secret." On his instructions she typed five copies of everything he dictated that month and later; one for him, three for Krupskaya, and one to be placed in an envelope sealed

---

[13] Krupskaya's letter was first revealed in the secret speech of N. S. Khrushchev to the Twentieth Congress of the Soviet Communist Party on the night of Feb. 24 and in the early morning hours of Feb. 25, 1956. This "destalinization" address has never been published in the Soviet Union although the fact that it was delivered is mentioned in Khrushchev's biography in the *Large Soviet Encyclopedia*, Second ed., Vol. 46, p. 391. When I asked Anastas I. Mikoyan in the summer of 1956 why the speech had not been published in Russia, he replied, "It's too early." (Louis Fischer, *Russia Revisited* [New York, 1957], p. 70.) It is apparently still too early. The speech, however, was published in a State Department pamphlet, in the *New York Times* of June 5, 1956, and in a *New Leader* pamphlet, *The Crimes of the Stalin Era, Special Report to the 20th Congress of the Communist Party of the Soviet Union*, by Nikita S. Khrushchev, *annotated especially for this edition* by Boris I. Nicolaevsky.

with a wax seal and marked: Not to be opened except by Lenin or "after his death" by Krupskaya. The envelope was to be locked in a secret office file. Her original notes were burned.[14]

The December 24 installment of Lenin's last testament reads:

"Continuation of notes. December 24, 1922.

"By the stability of the Central Committee, of which I spoke above, I mean measures to prevent a split, so far as such measures can be undertaken at all. . . .

"Our party rests on the support of two classes and hence its instability and inescapably its fall if agreement cannot be reached between these two classes. In that event it would be useless to take any measures or in general to discuss the stability of our Central Committee. In such an event no measures would be able to prevent a split. But I hope that this future is too remote and the events too improbable to talk about them now.

"I am thinking of stability as a guarantee against a split in the very near future, and I intend to examine here a number of considerations of a purely personal character.

"I think that from this point of view the basic factor in the problem of stability is such members of the Central Committee as Stalin and Trotsky. In my view the relationship between them constitutes the large half of the danger of that split which could have been avoided and the avoidance of which, in my opinion, should be served, incidentally, by increasing the number of members of the Central Committee to fifty or one hundred persons.

"Having become General Secretary, Comrade Stalin has concentrated boundless power in his hands, and I am not certain he can always use this power with sufficient caution. On the other hand, Comrade Trotsky, as his struggle against the Central Committee in connection with the question of the Commissariat of Railways has already shown, is distinguished not only by his remarkable abilities. Personally he is, I think, the most able person in the present Central Committee, but he also has an exceptionally extensive self-confidence and an exceptional fascination for the purely administrative aspect of affairs.

"These two qualities of the two most prominent leaders of the present Central Committee might inadvertently lead to a split, and if our party does not take measures to prevent this, the split might arise unexpectedly.

"I shall not continue with the characteristics of the other members of the Central Committee according to their personal qualities. I will only mention that the October episode of Zinoviev and Kamenev [the opposition of these two leaders to the launching of the Bolshevik revolution in November, 1917] was not, of course, an accident, but that it can no more be counted against them personally than his non-Bolshevism against Trotsky.

"Of the younger members of the Central Committee I want to say a few

[14] *Voprosi Istorii KPSS*, Vol. No. 2, p. 90.

words about Bukharin and Pyatakov. They are, in my opinion, the ablest persons (of the very youngest persons) and the following must be borne in mind regarding them: Bukharin is not only the most valuable and the most distinguished theoretician of the party, he is also of right regarded as the darling of the entire party, but it is only with the greatest reserve that his theoretical views can be regarded as fully Marxist, for there is in him something scholastic (he has never studied and, I think, never fully understood dialectics)."

At this point Lenin apparently tired, or the time allocated him by the physicians had expired. But the next day he finished this note with the following two paragraphs: "December 25. Then as to Pyatakov—undoubtedly a person of exceptional willpower and abilities, but too attracted by authoritarian methods and the administrative aspect of affairs to be relied upon in a serious political matter.

"Of course, this and the other remarks are being made by me for the present situation on the assumption that these two very able and loyal party workers will find the opportunity to supplement their knowledge and alter their one-sidedness. Lenin. December 25, 1922. Noted by M.V."[15]

The physicians now permitted Lenin to read books. "Novels did not interest him," one of his secretaries noted in the diary they had been keeping of every large and small event in his life since November, 1922.[16] He began reading Volumes III and IV of Nikolai N. Himmer's (N. Sukhanov's) seven-volume *Zapiski o Revolustii* (*Notes on the Revolution*), published in Russian in Berlin and Moscow. Sukhanov, a Narodnik (populist), had once attempted to merge the Narodniks with the Marxists and, having failed, became a "non-fraction social democrat"—a one-man third force—and ultimately a Menshevik. Still later, and until 1930, he worked for the Soviet government and was a member of the Communist Academy. His memoirs are a detailed account, by an insider, of the first (Kerensky) and second (Bolshevik) revolutions.[17]

On December 26 Lenin dictated to Lydia Fotieva a further page of his last testament. It dealt, again, with the necessity for increasing the membership of the Central Committee to fifty or one hundred members in order to improve "our apparatus" which "in essence, was inherited from the old regime." In five years, he said, the communists could not have been expected to remake the government machinery. "It is enough that in the five years we established a new type of state in which the workers moved ahead of the peasants against the bourgeoisie, and this, in a hostile international environment, is a gigantic achievement." Nevertheless, "we must on no account close our eyes to the fact that we, in essence, took over the old ap-

[15] Lenin, *op. cit.*, Fourth ed., Vol. 36, pp. 544-545.

[16] *Voprosi Istorii KPSS*, Vol. No. 2, pp. 67-91.

[17] N. N. Sukhanov, *The Russian Revolution 1917, Eyewitness Account*, 2 vols., edited, abridged and translated by Joel Carmichael (New York, 1962).

paratus from the Tsar and the bourgeoisie." Now that peace had dawned it was time to improve it. He wanted several dozen workers elected to the Central Committee of the party; they would witness Politburo sessions and thereby add to the Central Committee's "stability."[18]

This was the old hammer-Lenin striking the same argument again and again, stressing organization as the key to success, stressing bureaucratic evils, and their cures by personnel, and ignoring the causes of virulent bureaucracy in an autocracy. Bolshevism had indeed inherited the tsarist apparatus, and by nationalizing much of the economy, expanded it to gigantic proportions. A hundred Central Committee members could no more alter this situation than a fly reverse an airplane propeller.

Lenin devoted his alloted dictation time during the next three days—December 27, 28, and 29—to notes on the granting of legislative functions to the Gosplan (Federal State Planning Commission). "This idea was first advanced by Comrade Trotsky, quite a long time ago it seems. I attacked it. . . . But after careful examination I find that, in essence, there is a healthy thought here." The Gosplan consisted of experts who supplied government departments with material that enabled them to make decisions on future plans and activities. But Lenin proposed that the Gosplan's prerogatives be increased so that it made decisions for the departments and that its decisions be law, subject only to the veto of the VTSIK—formally, Russia's legislative body.[19]

In all of these three installments of his last testament not the slightest diminution of Lenin's mental power is discernible. He displayed his usual intellectual vigor, grasp of organizational complexities, frankness, and clarity, cogency, and pungency of style.

On December 29, when Lenin dictated his last note on the Gosplan, he also dictated an additional page on the question of expanding the Central Committee, a measure which, he believed, would enable the Committee to inspect and improve "our apparatus which is good for nothing." He now saw the wisdom of combining the efforts of the Central Committee with those of the Rabkrin. The Rabkrin would be abolished as a separate commissariat and become an adjunct of the Central Committee.[20]

The next day, December 30, Lenin continued dictating the little "chapters" of his last testament. This time he grasped the sharpest nettle: the nationalities problem and the Georgian question and Stalin's "fatal" role in both. Lenin always complained to his secretaries who took down these notes that it was difficult for him to dictate, he liked to see before him what he had already said and then continue. The product, nevertheless, was tightly knit. He said:

"It seems I have greatly wronged the workers of Russia by not intervening

[18] Lenin, *op. cit.*, Fourth ed., Vol. 36, pp. 546-547.
[19] *Ibid.*, pp. 548-551.
[20] *Ibid.*, p. 552.

energetically enough and firmly enough in the infamous question of auton-omy-ization, officially known, I believe, as the question of the Union of the Soviet Socialist Republics.

"During the summer, when this question arose, I was ill, and then, in the autumn, I put too much faith in my recovery and expected that the October and December plenums would give me the possibility of intervening in this question. However, I was not able to be present at the October plenum (on this question) or at the December plenum, and so the question eluded me almost entirely.

"I was only able to talk with Comrade Djerzhinsky who arrived from the Caucasus and told me how this matter stood in Georgia. I was also able to exchange a few words with Comrade Zinoviev and to express to him my ap-prehensions on this question. What I heard from Comrade Djerzhinsky, who was chairman of the commission delegated by the Central Committee to 'investigate' the Georgian incident, only greatly increased my apprehen-sions. If things went so far that Orjonekidze could lose control of himself and resort to physical violence, and this is what Comrade Djerzhinsky told me, one can imagine the bog in which we have landed. It appears that this whole fuss of 'autonomy-ization' is basically wrong and inopportune.

"They say that we needed a unified apparatus. Where do these assertions come from? Is it not from that same Russian apparatus which, as I already indicated in one of the preceding entries of my diary, we borrowed from tsarism and only lightly smeared with Soviet ritual oil?

"Undoubtedly, we should have delayed this measure [the establishment of the Union of Soviet Socialist Republics] until we could say that we could vouch for this apparatus as our own. But now we must in all conscience say the opposite, that we call an apparatus our own which in fact is still thor-oughly alien to us and which represents the bourgeois and tsarist mechanism we had no possibility of eliminating in five years, what with the absence of aid from other countries and in view of the consuming 'preoccupation' with military affairs and the struggle against famine.

"In such circumstances it is very natural that 'the right of secession from the Union' with which we justified our policy, has proved to be an empty piece of paper incapable of defending the non-Russian minorities of Russia from the invasions of that true Russian, the Great Russian chauvinist who, in reality, is a scoundrel and tyrant—the typical Russian bureaucrat. There is no doubt that the negligible percentage of Soviet and sovietized workers will drown in this sea of chauvinistic Great-Russian riff-raff like a fly in milk. . . .

"I think that here Stalin's haste and disposition toward fiat administration played a fatal role and too his resentment against so-called 'social-national-ism.' In general resentment usually plays the worse possible role in politics.

"I also fear that Comrade Djerzhinsky who traveled to the Caucasus to investigate the affair of the 'crimes' of these 'social-nationalists,' also distinguished himself only by his purely Russian mood (it is known that a Russified non-Russian always puts too much salt into this purely Russian sentiment) and that the impartiality of his entire commission is adequately characterized by Orjonekidze's 'laying on of hands.' I think that this Russian use of physical force cannot be justified by any provocation or by any insult and that Comrade Djerzhinsky is irremediably guilty of a frivolous attitude toward this use of physical violence. . . . Orjonekidze had no right to the irritability to which he and Djerzhinsky refer. . . .

"Here the important question of principle arises: how is internationalism to be understood?" (Lenin then dictated a further sentence: "I believe that our comrades do not adequately understand this important question of principle." But he crossed it out.[21])

Lenin was saying that not only had the right of secession, granted by the Soviet constitution, become a worthless scrap of paper, even the craving of the national minorities for limited self-government, for freedom from total Muscovite dictation, was branded "social-nationalism," and Boodoo Mdivani, a veteran communist, colleague of Lenin's, won a smack in the face from Orjonekidze for championing the rights of small nationalities against Great Russian encroachments. To cap this anti-internationalism, Felix Djerzhinsky, the Pole, whitewashed Orjonekidze and charged Mdivani with irritating him by committing the political "crime" of social-nationalism. Lenin blamed Stalin for this distortion of internationalism within the Soviet Union. Stalin did indeed become the non-Russian who wreathed his personal despotism in Great Russian nationalism. After the Second World War, the same power madness, disguised as proletarian internationalism, engulfed small nations outside the Soviet Union as well.

Lenin could do nothing. He could have done nothing even if his second bell had not rung, for how can minority groups enjoy freedom where individuals have none? Lenin kept reiterating that the communists had borrowed the tsarist type of bureaucracy. But this was more than form. The form resulted from centralized government, more highly centralized in fact under Bolshevism than under tsarism. How, then, could the national minorities be independent?

Lenin ended his December 30 dictation with a question: "How is internationalism to be understood?" He did not answer it.

The argument between Lenin and Stalin revolved around the extent of self-government in the republics and regions inhabited by national minorities. Stalin's formula was: autonomy—the equivalent of no self-government. Lenin's was: "independence"—the equivalent of some self-government. In his testament entry of December 30 and in the two additional entries on the nationalities problem which he dictated on the last day of the year he wrestled with the question of: How? In the first of the two dictations on December 31 he stated that "nothing so retards the development and

[21] Ibid., pp. 553-555.

stability of proletarian class solidarity as nationalistic injustice." In the second he asked "What practical measures should be taken in the present situation?" And he replied, "First, the Union of Soviet Socialist Republics should be retained and reinforced." Secondly, the Union should be retained for foreign policy purposes. Third, Orjonekidze should be punished. He also mentioned that "Stalin and Djerzhinsky must of course be held politically responsible for this entire veritably Great-Russian-nationalistic campaign." He did not indicate what punishment might be meted out to the three transgressors. Fourth, the nationalities should be encouraged to use their own languages.

Lenin went much further: "There is no doubt that under the pretext of the unity of railway service, under the excuse of fiscal unity and so forth, and with our existing state apparatus, many abuses of a purely Russian character will make themselves felt in this country." They needed "a detailed code of laws" compiled by members of the national minorities. It might even be necessary, at the next Congress of Soviets, to restrict the activities of the Union of Soviet Socialist Republics to military and diplomatic affairs and "restore, in all other respects, the full independence of the separate people's commissariats" of the constituent republics of the Union.

It is nowhere recorded that they ever exercised full independence. But from the point of view of politics it was better to say "restore" than "introduce." Discounting the one propagandistic word, this was the first intimation —more came later—that Lenin was thinking in an unorthodox manner about the fundamental weaknesses of the Soviet system. For if, as he suggested, the activities of the government of the U.S.S.R. in Moscow were indeed restricted to defense and the conduct of foreign affairs while the national republics governed themselves in all other respects, the Kremlin would have been dismantled and its arms shortened. Decentralization would have replaced centralization. Such a measure involved a reversal of the philosophy of government Lenin had espoused since the beginning of the century, a philosophy fed from two sources: his own nervousness, which made him intolerant of dissent and favorable to a small, subservient political party, and, two, tsarist autocracy, administered by an oligarchy obedient to the monarchy and meeting the needs of a thin upper social crust. The Soviets turned tsarism inside out but retained its essential features: autocracy, oligarchy, bureaucracy, and proclaimed service to the needs of a thin social minority, the proletariat. In the ideas of the Russian Narodniks and of Friedrich Engels, as well as of some French revolutionists, Lenin found support for the seizure of power by a handful of aggressive willful men who, of necessity, would have to rule through centralized tyranny.

Now, late in December, 1922, when his Soviet state was five years old, Lenin suddenly discovered decentralization. It is easy to dismiss as mere words his proposal that the federal government in Moscow deal only with diplomacy and the armed forces. But Stalin's maneuvers and events in Georgia were as nerve-racking to Lenin as the worst forms of party indiscipline. Orjonekidze in Georgia had not only smacked Mdivani; the Georgian Cheka refused to become the GPU, and the peasants were being persecuted by the anti-NEP Stalinists. Moreover, Lenin had commenced to see the damage that could be inflicted on the revolution by the "typical Russian bureaucrat" who added Great Russian chauvinism to red tape and became "a scoundrel" as well as a "tyrant." Lenin had said to the Eighth Congress of the Communist Party on March 19, 1919, "Scratch some communists—and you will find a Great-Russian chauvinist." Then it was criticism. Now it was crisis. Great Russians and Stalin, who believed in Moscow autocracy, might wreck the revolution. These were reasons enough for a reassessment of the entire Soviet situation, and this, indeed, is what Lenin essayed in his last testament and, even more, in the articles he wrote in 1923.

To be sure, immediately after mentioning the possible necessity for reducing the central government's functions, Lenin took cognizance of the diffusion of power and lack of coordination with Moscow which might arise if his scheme were adopted, and therefore added that the divisiveness "can be adequately paralyzed by the authority of the communist party if it is applied with more or less adequate circumspection and impartiality." Knowing Lenin's attitude toward the party, this sentence could be regarded as the essence and the talk about decentralization as camouflage. But that was not the end of the sentence. Lenin went on to say, "the harm to our state which might be caused by the absence of unity between the government apparatuses of the nationalities and the Russian government apparatus would be immeasurably smaller, infinitely smaller than the harm that could come not only to us but to the entire International, and to the hundreds of millions of the peoples of Asia who, following after us, are about to appear on the stage of history in the very near future. . . . The necessity of cohesion against the Western imperialists who defend the capitalist world is one thing. Here there can be no doubt, and it is superfluous for me to say that I approve of these measures unconditionally. It is another thing when we slip, even in small matters, into an imperialistic relationship toward oppressed nationalities, thereby completely undermining all our sincerity of principle, all our defense of the principle of the struggle against imperialism. And the tomorrow of world history will be just such a day of the complete awakening of the peoples oppressed by imperialism when the decisive, long and difficult battle for their liberation will begin. Lenin."[22]

This was eloquent—and out of a brain that lost the power of thought and coherent speech seven weeks later. It has a ring of sincerity. Lenin did not pursue the idea far enough. Railway and airplane unity, fiscal unity, and planning unity, where much industry was state-owned, would conduce to centralization and reduce the prerogatives of the national republics. Nor did Lenin touch on the implications of decentralization for a dictatorship. No

[22] *Ibid.*, pp. 555-559.

large country in the world faces the dilemma of Russia, which is approximately half-Russian and half non-Russian. A racial problem often defies solution when the minority equals no more than 10 percent of the population. The solution is possible only if unabridged personal liberties and civil rights enable underprivileged groups to defend themselves and redress their grievances. State's rights that limit human rights are dross. Lenin was pleading for the rights of the national republics but not of their citizens. What would it benefit Georgians if they were free from Moscow but not free from the Orjonekidzes and Stalins? The corollary of regional, district, and local self-government is self-government: freedom without dictatorship. It was too difficult and too early for Lenin to draw all the logical conclusions from his plea for decentralization. He had, nevertheless, broached the subject. Perhaps he was having second thoughts about Sovietism. Perhaps too he was reacting against Stalin.

Although no one can say for certain whether Lenin was told, at the time, of Stalin's telephone attack on Krupskaya and of her letter to Kamenev, it is a safe surmise that he had learned about the incident by January 4, for on that day he asked to see the installment of the testament he had written on December 24, and added this postscript: "Stalin is too rude, and this fault, quite tolerable in the company of communists and among us, becomes intolerable for one who holds the office of General Secretary. Therefore I propose to the comrades to consider a means of removing Stalin from that post and appoint another person to this position who in all respects differs from Stalin only in superiority, namely, more patient, more loyal, more polite, and more attentive to comrades, less capricious, and so forth. This circumstance may seem to be an insignificant trifle. But I think that from the point of view of preventing a split and from the point of view of the relationship between Stalin and Trotsky which I discussed above, this is not a trifle, or it is a trifle that may acquire decisive significance."[23]

It acquired decisive significance far beyond Lenin's or anyone's imagination. It rocked Russia from 1924, when Lenin died, till 1940, when Trotsky was killed by an assassin in Mexico. The Moscow Trials of the 1930's, which cost the country its top leaders: Rykov, Bukharin, Zinoviev, Kamenev, Pyatakov, Rakovsky, Rudzutak, Sokolnikov, Radek, Tomsky (who committed suicide before he could be arrested and tried), Krestinsky, and scores of others of first rank, were in reality "trials" of Trotsky; he was the chief defendant in absentia; Stalin was attempting to prove Trotsky a demon of black deeds and himself the winged angel, Lenin's worthy "continuer," "the Lenin of today," as Stalin said of himself.[24] The blood purges of Russia's highest military leaders in 1937 and of thousands of her best industrial managers, authors, planners, and administrators—many have since been officially rehabilitated as innocent, and "rehabilitating" obituaries continue to appear in

[23] *Ibid.*, pp. 545-546.
[24] Krushchev's Secret Speech, *New Leader* pamphlet, p. 54.

Soviet newspapers and magazines to this day—were also, in part, an aspect of Stalin's vendetta against Trotsky. What this meant in World War II casualties and in industrial losses and agricultural setbacks no one can measure, for the Soviet Union has no social bookkeeping; the price of victory and progress in terms of human lives, limbs, and creativity is never reckoned. Nor is account taken of the effect of Stalin's psychotic hatred of Trotsky on policy: on the policy of the Comintern which brought death to many foreign communists; on premature and excessively speedy industrialization and on premature collectivization with its millions of victims and famine and reduced farm production—both timed as a response to Trotsky's criticism of Stalin. The entire history of the Soviet Union from 1924 to date could, in fact, be written, soberly, under the sign of the Stalin-Trotsky feud. To this day it stains all Soviet histories and biographies with lies.

Had Lenin lived and led Russia ten more years, say until the age of sixty-three, and a longer span is not above average, Stalin would either have had to shoot him, politically a formidable task, or have remained his subordinate without the power to punish Russia as he did. The Stalin-Trotsky feud might have burned slowly within the manageable limits where Lenin had kept it since its earliest manifestations in 1918. It was Lenin's illness that caused it to flare and his death that wrought the havoc.

Why, since Lenin wrote in his will on January 4 that the comrades should remove Stalin from the post of General Secretary of the communist party, did he not remove him? He still had the political influence and the intellectual thrust to do so. The puzzle remains. Did Lenin believe he would recover sufficiently to attend the next party congress in March or April, 1923, and lead the comrades in ousting Stalin? Writing a will is not the equivalent of being reconciled to imminent death. Or did Lenin underestimate Stalin's capacity for big intrigues while exaggerating the democracy within the party which he had built? Without Lenin the party was impotent in Stalin's steel hand.

Lenin, and Trotsky to his cost, underestimated Stalin. More than two thousand years ago Thucydides, the Athenian, writing *The History of the Peloponnesian War*, described the Stalin-Trotsky feud: "Inferior minds were as a rule more successful; aware of their defects and of the intelligence of their opponents, to whom they felt themselves inferior in debate . . . they struck boldly and at once. Their enemies despised them, were confident of detecting their plots and thought it needless to effect by violence what they could achieve by their brains, and so were taken off guard and destroyed."

Stalin read some—not all—of Lenin. But an aide might have opened the thick Volume XXV of Lenin's *Collected Works* (Second edition), turned to page 441, and moving his finger downward, stopped at a passage in which Lenin, after pouring vitriol and scorn on the Mensheviks and Kadets, explained what a dictatorship is: "The scientific concept of dictatorship means nothing other than unlimited government unrestrained by any laws or any absolute rules and supporting itself directly by force. *Nothing other than that* is the meaning of the concept 'dictatorship.' "

Stalin would have rubbed his hands and exclaimed in his Georgian-accented Russian: "Harasho [Good]."

Lenin wrote a letter to Commissar of Justice Dmitri I. Kursky, dated May 17, 1922: "To supplement our conversation I am sending you the draft of an additional paragraph of the Criminal Code. . . . The basic thought, I hope, is clear . . .: openly to proclaim the proposition, just in principle and just politically (and not only narrowly juridical), which motivates *the essence and the justification* of the terror, its necessity, its limits.

"The courts must not eliminate the terror; to promise that would be self-deceit or deceit."[25]

The question is whether Lenin, in the last three months of the life of his brain, had new thoughts on dictatorship and terror. Some time in November or December, 1922, Bukharin talked with Lenin and they discussed "leaderology." Lenin used the Russian word "leaderologiya." He was worried about the succession. He was more tolerant of criticism. Bukharin found Lenin reading Plekhanov's book *God na Rodine (A Year in the Homeland)*, on his impressions during the year he spent in revolutionary Russia just before his death. When Bukharin expressed surprise that he should be reading the views of an anti-Bolshevik, Lenin said, "There is much truth in it."[26]

Lenin's illness gave him something all statesmen need and few ever have: leisure for prolonged reflection. Some of the thoughts appeared in his writings in 1923.

LI. UNHAPPY LENIN

WITH HIS LAST TESTAMENT finished and locked away and his official duties transferred to his three deputies and to the party Secretariat, Lenin buoyantly resumed one of his prerevolutionary roles: that of political publicist.

Bukharin addressed a memorial meeting on the fifth anniversary of Lenin's death and, after reciting the titles of the five articles Lenin wrote between

[25] Lenin, *op. cit.*, Second ed., Vol. XXVII, p. 296.

[26] Bukharin visited Boris I. Nicolaevsky, the Menshevik, in Paris in 1936, on an official mission: to purchase some of Nicolaevsky's invaluable archives. The two had many heart-to-heart political talks. In one of these Bukharin told of this conversation with Lenin. Apropos of a remark by Bukharin, Nicolaevsky said, "It seems you have come to believe in the Ten Commandments." To which Bukharin replied, "They are not so bad."

January and March, 1923, called them "Lenin's Political Testament." "The principal thing that Lenin bequeathed to us," Bukharin said in his speech which covered almost a page of *Pravda* on January 24, 1929, "is contained in his five excellent articles most profound in their contents." These articles, Bukharin declared, were not "disparate pieces" but rather "organic parts of one large unity, of one *large plan* of Leninist strategy and tactics developed on the basis of a very definite *future*" which Lenin "foresaw."

The first of the five, dictated on January 2, 1923, and published in *Pravda* two days later over Lenin's name, was entitled "Pages from a Diary." It dealt with culture under communism. Citing statistics—he loved them to the last —on literacy in Russia, Lenin came to the conclusion "that we are still very backward in regard to general literacy and that even our progress compared with tsarist times (1897) has been too slow. This serves as a stern warning and reproach to those who are soaring in the empiric heights of 'proletarian culture.' It shows what imperative spadework still confronts us in order to reach the level of an ordinary West European civilized state."

Practical as ever, Lenin said, "We must not restrict ourselves, however, to this incontrovertible but too theoretical proposition." The budget of the People's Commissariat of Education should not be the first to suffer reduction. Instead, other departments should go hungry for money "in order that the sums thus released may be allocated to the needs of the People's Commissariat of Education. We must not be chary about increasing the bread ration for schoolteachers this year, as we are fairly well supplied." Old teachers should be enlisted and "interested in such problems as the problem of religion."

But the main thing was the village. ". . . if we are going to speak of any culture at all, whether proletarian or even bourgeois culture," the level of the village schoolteacher had to be raised. "We must bear in mind the semi-Asiatic state of lack of culture from which we have not yet emerged."

Not unexpectedly, he stressed the need for political organization: "We must systematically increase our work of organizing the village schoolteachers in order to transform them from the bulwark of the bourgeois system, which they still are in all capitalist countries without exception, into the bulwark of the Soviet system, in order, through them, to win the peasantry away from their alliance with the bourgeoisie and to bring them into an alliance with the proletariat."

Here he conservatively cautioned against excessive speed: "Under no circumstances must this be understood to mean that we must immediately propagate pure and strictly communist ideas in the rural districts. As long as our rural districts still lack the material basis for communism, that would be harmful, or one might say fatal, for communism."[1] These statements reflected Lenin's policy toward the peasantry which had been formulated as

[1] Lenin, *Selected Works*, Vol. IX (London, 1937), pp. 486-490; Russian original in *Sochineniya*, Fourth ed., Vol. 33, pp. 422-426.

"Keep in line with the peasants"; or, "We must move downhill, on brakes, to the muzhik." That is the core of the "Leninist strategy" based, as Bukharin put it, on Lenin's vision of the future. Plekhanov too predicted difficulties for a one-party dictatorship supported only or chiefly by the working class. In an article published three days after the November 7, 1917, revolution and included in the book *God na Rodine*, which Lenin read, Plekhanov, the father of Russian Marxism, once Lenin's mentor, affirmed that he, an old-time champion of the proletariat, was "saddened" by the overthrow of the Kerensky government because *"our working class is far from being capable of taking into its hands complete political power to the benefit of itself and the country."* For in Russia "the proletariat constitutes *a minority, not a majority.* . . . To be sure, the working class can count on the support of the peasants who, to this day, constitute the majority of the population of Russia. But the peasant needs land, he has no need of exchanging the capitalist system for a socialist system. . . . Consequently, the peasants are an altogether undependable ally of the worker in the construction of socialist methods of production." Moreover, Plekhanov denied Lenin's dictum that the German would finish what the Russian had commenced. Neither, he added, would the Frenchman, Englishman, or American complete the Bolshevik revolution by a revolution of his own. Therefore, "the Russian proletariat, having seized political power prematurely, will not carry out a social revolution but only provoke a civil war which, in the end, will force it to retreat far behind the positions conquered during March and April of this year"—1917.[2]

It is of these words that Lenin, if he read them, might have said to Bukharin that there is truth in them.

Events had unrolled as Plekhanov prophesied, and now, after the civil war, after moving downhill on brakes to the peasantry by legislating the NEP, Lenin, reviewing his handiwork, was saying that the peasant majority must be won over by the proletariat—slowly, and: No preaching communism in the villages.

A stand had been built for Lenin on which he could place books so that he did not have to hold them with his one functioning hand, the left hand. Thus aided, he continued reading Sukhanov's *Notes on the Revolution* and instructed his private librarian, Miss S. M. Manucharyants, to collect material for him on cooperatives. He listed especially: a book by Meshcheryakov, *Cooperation and Socialism*, in Russian; a book by Dr. Franz Staudinger of Darmstadt, Germany, *Marxism and Producers' Cooperatives*, in German, and by the same author, *From Schulze-Delitzsch to Kreuznach* which dealt with the dispute among German cooperators on whether to unite consumers' cooperatives with producers' cooperatives. The list also included works about

[2] G. V. Plekhanov, *God na Rodine (A Year in the Homeland). Complete Collection of Articles and Speeches of 1917-1918 in two volumes* (Paris, 1921), Vol. 2, pp. 244-248.

the theory of cooperatives and the history of the cooperative movement in tsarist Russia.[3]

Having digested this mass of printed data, Lenin devoted two dictation periods, approximately fifteen minutes in length, on January 4 and January 6, to an article entitled "On Cooperation," which was published in *Pravda* of May 26 and 27, 1923.[4]

Commenting on this article in his 1929 commemorative speech, Bukharin quoted one of its lines in thick capital letters: "WE ARE FORCED TO ADMIT A RADICAL CHANGE IN OUR ENTIRE VIEW OF SOCIALISM."

Lenin's words have often been employed inside and outside the Soviet Union as shields to ward off blows and as swords to stab opponents. In 1929, Bukharin, a key member of the Politburo, was fighting for his political life against Stalin's machinations. In June of that year his demotion began, and in the third great Moscow "Trial" in March, 1938, he was sentenced to death. In quoting Lenin in 1929, Bukharin showed what his own preferences were, but he could document Lenin's too, for Lenin went on to explain what this "radical change in our entire view of socialism" meant: "This radical change is that formerly we put and had to put the main emphasis on the political struggle, on revolution, the conquest of power, etc. But now the main emphasis is changing to such an extent that it is being shifted to organizational 'cultural' work."

This was Bukharin's policy in 1929; he opposed Stalin's forcible, fateful collectivization of the peasantry which had such disastrous effects on millions of human beings, and on the Soviet economy. Bukharin would have continued the NEP without trying to "socialize" the village. That was Lenin's thought in 1923 when he said in his article "On Cooperation" that if it were not for the international situation and "leaving that aside," and "limiting ourselves to domestic economic relations, then in fact the main emphasis of our work consists in cultural work."

This referred not so much to education as to consumers' cooperatives. "There is," Lenin dictated, "very little we still have to do from the point of view of the 'civilized' (first of all, literate) European in order to induce absolutely everyone to take not a passive, but an active part in cooperation. Properly speaking, there is 'only' one more thing that we have to do, and that is, to make our population so 'civilized' as to understand the advantages of the participation of the whole population in the work of the cooperatives, and to organize this participation. 'Only' this. We need no other devices to enable us to pass to Socialism."

Let not the Russian peasant who engages in private trade, Lenin cautioned, believe that he has become an efficient merchant. "He is trading, but

---

[3] *Voprosi Istorii KPSS*, Vol. No. 2, 1963, p. 90.

[4] Lenin, *Selected Works*, Vol. IX, pp. 402-409. Russian original in *Sochineniya*, Fourth ed., Vol. 33, pp. 427-435.

this is far from the ability to be a cultured merchant. He is now trading in an Asiatic manner; in order to be a merchant, one must be able to trade in a European manner. But he is a whole epoch removed from that position."

Here Lenin resumed his old discussion of state capitalism and stated that "concessions [granted to foreign capitalists] would have been a pure type of state capitalism. That is how I conceive the argument about state capitalism." Cooperatives, on the other hand, "coincide" with socialism.

"I think," he affirmed, "that inadequate attention is being paid to the cooperative movement." The early dreams of Robert Owen and other Europeans and of Russian cooperators in the tsarist period were sometimes "ridiculously fantastic," because they believed cooperatives could remake capitalism into socialism by gradual, peaceful means. But now that "state power is in the hands of the working class," and "since this state power owns all the means of production, the only task that really remains for us to perform is to organize the population in cooperative societies." When this will have been done, "socialism . . . automatically achieves its aims."

The NEP had made private trade legal, Lenin continued, but "it is precisely for this reason that cooperation acquires such enormous significance." He knew, however, that some people "think the very opposite." Soviet cooperatives "are looked down upon with contempt."

Lenin was considering consumers' cooperatives as a counterweight to private trade which he had once considered a "crime." He wrote: "We went too far in introducing the NEP, not in that we attached too much importance to the principle of free industry and trade; we went too far in introducing the NEP in that we forgot to think about the cooperatives."

He wanted this attitude reversed through concrete measures: loans to cooperatives from state banks at lower interest rates and in larger volume than to private businesses, "even those engaged in heavy industry, etc."

Further, the state should assist cooperatives so that *"real masses of the population really take part."* The peasant who participates in cooperative trade should be given a bonus. And the participation of the population should not be fictitious, on paper alone.

"And a system of civilized cooperators under the social ownership of the means of production, with the class victory of the proletariat over the bourgeoisie, is socialism." This Lenin statement has been condensed into the formula: "Cooperatives plus soviets equal socialism."

In the mid-1920's I visited Simferopol, a town in northern Crimea. Seeing a large sign marked "Cooperative Store," I walked in, sought out the manager, and asked what kind of cooperative this was, for I knew from a half-year's reading on cooperatives in the New York Public Library that there were various kinds of consumers' cooperatives: some paid dividends at the end of a year, some sold to members only at reduced prices. "This is a government cooperative," the manager told me. That was a contradiction in terms. A cooperative is a voluntary organization of members unconnected with a government. The "government cooperative" was in reality a government store and not a cooperative at all.

Since then the Soviets have dropped the fiction of consumers' cooperatives. There are none. The state is the great wholesale and retail trader, and the peasants conduct as much private trade as the government permits.

If soviets plus cooperatives equal socialism and there are no cooperatives (and no soviet except in name) there is no equation.

What was in Lenin's mind when he dictated these lines: "the participation of the whole population in the work of the cooperatives . . . real masses of the population really take part"? The whole population organized in cooperatives would have carried tremendous economic weight and hence political influence. In the trade-union debate Lenin specifically and vehemently opposed a concentration of economic power immune to communist party control. The people organized in cooperatives run by the people would have spelled democracy, democracy in competition with party dictatorship. Had a dying brain produced a new man?

Bukharin, analyzing Lenin's last five articles, said in January, 1929, "Anybody who knows Lenin's precision of expression, who knows how chaste Lenin was in his use of 'big' words, and who remembers this was his *political testament*, will not fail to read in these propositions the very deep uneasiness (the uneasiness of a serious thinker and wise strategist) for the fate of the entire socialist system, for the fate of the entire revolution."

Bukharin was fighting his own battles with Lenin's bullets. Yet he had talked with Lenin late in 1922 and had seen him reading Plekhanov's book with its grim prophecy of Bolshevik one-party rule over a recalcitrant peasantry which wanted capitalism and might be disloyal in the event of war. Lenin's cure was cooperatives which would show the peasant the disadvantages of semi-Asiatic private trade and convert him from an antisocialist to a decisive factor in the salvation of socialist Russia. Was Lenin then ready to countenance economic democracy and its political implications? In 1914, he quoted from Goethe's *Faust*:

> "Gray, dear friend, is all theory,
> And green is life's golden tree."

Lenin's first principle was party dictatorship. He identified it many times with the state and the revolution. But if all these were threatened by the muzhiks, who constituted the vast majority of the population, he might have thought that democratic cooperatives were preferable to runaway peasant-Nepman private trade which could drown the weak Soviet system.

Lenin's third article was a brief book review of Sukhanov's volumes on the two Russian revolutions of 1917. Dictated on January 16 and 17, it appeared in *Pravda* of May 30, 1923.[5] It was a masterpiece:

"These days I have been paging through Sukhanov's notes on revolution.

[5] Lenin, *Sochineniya*, Second ed., Vol. XXVII, pp. 398-401.

What stands out is the pedantry of all our petty-bourgeois democrats, as well as of all the heroes of the Second International. Not to mention the fact that they are extraordinarily cowardly, that even the best of them feeds himself with reservations when the slightest departure from the German model" of reform rather than revolution "is under discussion, not to speak of this characteristic of all petty-bourgeois democrats fully demonstrated by them throughout the revolution, what stands out is their slavish imitation of the past.

"They call themselves Marxists but their understanding of Marxism is impossibly pedantic. They have absolutely no understanding of the decisive aspect of Marxism: namely, its revolutionary dialectic. . . . All their conduct reveals them as cowardly reformists afraid to fall behind the bourgeoisie and even more to break with it, and at the same time they cover up their cowardice with the most reckless phrase-mongering and boasting. But what stands out is their complete inability to understand, even theoretically, the following view of Marxism: they have hitherto seen a certain pattern in the development of capitalism and bourgeois democracy in Western Europe. And so they cannot imagine that this pattern can be regarded, mutatis mutandis"—Lenin's Latin expression—"as other than a model with some changes (which are altogether negligible from the point of view of world history).

"*First*—the "—Bolshevik—" revolution was connected with the first imperialistic world war. In such a revolution new features or modifications arising out of that very war must manifest themselves, for no such war and no such situation had ever occurred. . . .

"*Second*— . . . It does not even enter their heads that Russia, standing on the borderline between civilized countries and the countries of the entire East, the non-European countries, which, for the first time, were finally drawn into civilization by this war, that Russia could and had to exhibit some peculiarities which, though they of course lay along the general line of world development, nevertheless distinguished her revolution from all previous revolutions in Western European countries and introduced some fractional innovations as it moved toward eastern countries.

"For instance, they uphold the endlessly banal proposition, which they learned by heart in the period of the development of European social democracy and which asserts that we are not grown up enough for socialism, that we, as a number of their 'academic' gentlemen put it, lack the objective economic prerequisites for socialism. And it does not enter anyone's head to ask himself: Could not a nation which encountered a revolutionary situation like that precipitated by the first imperialist war, could it not, under the pressure of the hopelessness of its position, throw itself into a struggle which would give it some chance of achieving for itself the not altogether usual conditions for the further growth of its civilization.

" 'Russia has not attained the level of development of its productive forces which make socialism possible.' This is the proposition the heroes of the Second International, and of course Sukhanov among them, fuss over like a child with a new toy. . . .

"If a definite level of culture is necessary for the establishment of socialism (although no one can say what that definite 'level of culture' is) then why should we not first begin, by means of revolution, to acquire the prerequisites for that definite level, and *after that*, on the foundation of a workers' and peasants' government and the Soviet system, advance to overtake other nations?

"You say: to establish socialism, civilization is necessary. Very good. Well, why could we not first create such prerequisites of civilization in our country as the eviction of the landowners and the eviction of the Russian capitalists and then begin the movement to socialism? In what books did you read that such a modification of the usual historic order of things is forbidden or impossible?

"I recall that Napoleon said: 'On s'engage et puis . . . on voit.' In free Russian translation this means: 'First it is necessary to engage in a serious battle, and then we'll see what happens.' " That is what the Bolsheviks did in November, 1917, "and there we discerned such details of development (details, of course, from the point of view of world history) as the Brest-Litovsk peace, the NEP, and so forth. And at present there is already no doubt that basically we have been victorious.

"It does not occur to our Sukhanovs, not to speak of the social democrats to the right of them, that a revolution cannot be made in any other way. It does not occur to our European middle-class people in their dreams that future revolutions in eastern countries with immeasurably larger populations and immeasurably more peculiarly varied social conditions will undoubtedly introduce greater originality than the Russian revolution.

"No doubt, the text book written in the spirit of Kautsky was very useful in its day. It is time, nevertheless, to renounce the thought that this textbook anticipated all forms of the further development of world history. Those who think so should now simply be called fools."

Two strokes had not dimmed Lenin's debating ardor or dulled his debating sword. The book review, moreover, contained creative thought. The dialectic to which Lenin referred is merely another way of saying, Circumstances change cases. Lenin was pleading that Russia's specific national circumstances—its location on the borderline between West and East and its resulting retarded civilization—made the case for revolution which, farther east, might assume still more startling shapes. (Was he thinking of China?) This represented a departure from the previous Leninist interpretation of Marxist universality according to which every country conforms to the same pattern. It follows that some countries lying to the west of Russia might make their revolutions by nonviolent reforms. Even Eastern countries with different civilizations could do so.

Lenin argued correctly that one enters the battle and then sees what can be done. He already saw what could not be done. But is it correct to affirm that these manifestations were the product only of Russia's lack of civilization? Lenin's own biography shows that tsarism treated its enemies with more humanity than Bolshevism. That there was culture in Russia as well as no culture is demonstrated by the eight months of the Provisional (Kerensky) government when, Lenin himself said, Russia was "the freest country in the world." Lenin's argument that Russia's geography shaped her history is partially right and partially wrong. Geography is not decisive without the aid of men. Men have some freedom of will. A Rykov or Kamenev in place of Lenin might have formed a workable coalition with the Mensheviks and Social Revolutionaries in November, 1917, and thereby limited the scope of the civil war and the terror. The monopoly-of-power streak in Lenin which prevented this unity also wrought the instruments that made Stalin and his quarter century of horrors possible. Lenin's review of Sukhanov's reminiscences reflected a fatalism which submits to a bad national past. But Russia had a Rasputin and a Tolstoy, an ugly secret police Okhrana and a freedom-loving intelligentsia, an autocratic Tsar and liberal zemstvo local authorities, the great mass of illiterate muzhiks and great mathematicians. Why did the European in Russia have to be dragged down by the Asiatic in Russia?

One cannot escape a faint suspicion, distinguishable from wishful thinking, that Lenin died at the wrong time, that had he lived even he might have changed. The illness which brought him death also brought him isolation from routine affairs and the time to meditate. In his last testament, and particularly in his statements on the nationalities question and Georgia, as well as in his articles on cooperatives and on Sukhanov, there is a thread that seems to lead to the conclusion that he knew something was wrong.

Lenin had no sooner finished dictating his review of Sukhanov's memoirs than he undertook the last literary effort of his life. On January 19 he dictated for thirty minutes about the Workers and Peasants Inspection (Rabkrin). Miss M. A. Volodicheva, who took the dictation, noted in the diary which Lenin's secretaries were keeping: "He said he wanted to write this quickly." The next day he read the typescript of the article, made alterations and additions. He asked Krupskaya and Lydia Fotieva, his secretary, to obtain some statistics he needed for the article. On January 21 Lenin summoned no one from his office. On the 22nd he continued to work on the article and asked that the final typescript be delivered to him in the evening. The following day he rapidly ran his eyes over the typescript, made a few minor corrections, ordered the corrections entered into his copy and the office copies, and instructed Miss Volodicheva to send one of the latter to his sister Maria who worked on *Pravda*. The article, entitled "How We Should Reorganize the Workers and Peasants Inspection. A Proposal to the Twelfth Party Congress," was published in *Pravda* on January 25.

"Undoubtedly," the first sentence reads, "the Workers and Peasants

Inspection presents an enormous difficulty for us, and this difficulty has not yet been solved." Those who believed that Rabkrin was useless and unnecessary were "wrong. At the same time I do not deny that the problem of our state apparatus and of improving it is a very difficult one, that it is not yet solved by far, and that it is an extremely urgent one."

With the exception of Chicherin's Commissariat of Foreign Affairs, "our state apparatus is very largely a survival of the old one. . . . It has only been slightly repainted on the surface, but in all other things it is a typical relic of our"—Russia's—"old state apparatus."

Lenin then propounded his plan for a reorganization not only of the Rabkrin, which was a government commissariat, but also of the top floor of the communist party apparatus. In Lenin's time the party Congress assembled once a year; a party conference, carrying less weight, convened every six months; the Central Committee met in plenary session every two months; between Central Committee plenums the Politburo conducted the current affairs of the party. In addition, a Central Control Commission served as the inspectorate of the party apparatus. Lenin urged in his article that the bi-monthly plenum of the Central Committee be converted into "a superior party conference which shall meet once in two months jointly with the Central Control Commission." He then unveiled a proposal for drastic reform: "The Central Control Commission should be amalgamated with the main body of the reorganized Workers and Peasants Inspection."

In past years it had been a basic tenet of Lenin and of his close co-workers that the party machine remain separate from the government apparatus. This had been debated at party congresses and elsewhere, and always the decision had been in favor of separation. Now Lenin proposed a radical departure, a merging of party and government machines. The article suggested that the party's Central Control Commission's membership be supplemented by seventy-five to one hundred "workers and peasants" elected by the party congress. Simultaneously, "the staff of the Workers and Peasants Inspection must be reduced to three or four hundred" and the Commission and the Inspection would become one. This organizational readjustment, Lenin contended, will give the Rabkrin "a high prestige."

Lenin foresaw objections. There would be, first, the no-change conservatives. Others would contend "that the change I propose will lead to chaos; that the members of the Central Control Commission will wander around all the offices, will not know to whom to apply on any particular question, will cause disorganization everywhere, distract employees from their daily work, etc., etc."

Lenin called this latter objection "malicious." To be sure, "the People's Commissar of the Workers and Peasants Inspection and his collegium (and also, in the proper cases, the Secretariat of our Central Committee), will need more than one year of persistent work in order properly to organize their Commissariat and its work in conjunction with the Central Control Commission."

That year would certainly be a year of chaos.

But Lenin put his hope in the reduction of Rabkrin's staff from several thousand to three or four hundred. The amalgamated Rabkrin-Central Control Commission, he believed, however, would be in a better position than theretofore to supply data for the deliberations of the Politburo whose sessions its superior officials would attend.

The party's Central Committee, Lenin wrote, "has grown into a strictly centralized and highly authoritative group, but the work of this group is not conducted in conditions that correspond to this authority. The reform that I propose should remove this defect." How? The Central Control Commission "will have to form a compact group which, 'without respect for persons,' should see to it that nobody's authority serves as an obstacle to their putting interpellations, seeing all documents, and in general to their keeping themselves informed of all things, and of seeing to it that affairs are properly conducted."

The Central Control Commission, merged with Rabkrin, would thus be assigned to watch the Central Committee which, between party congresses, had always been the supreme authority in communist Russia. Under Lenin's new plan, even it would submit to rigorous control.

Lenin's faith in the magic of organization and reorganization remained strong to the end.

In the final paragraph of the article Lenin gave a thumbnail sketch of the Soviet Republic's social system: it was based "on the collaboration of two classes: the workers and peasants, in which the 'Nepmen' that is, the bourgeoisie, are now permitted to participate on certain terms. If serious class disagreements arise between these classes, a split is inevitable." Everything depended on whether the Nepmen could "drive a wedge" between the peasants and the working class and thus "split them off from the working class." It was the principal task, he said, of the Central Committee and of the Central Control Commission to "forestall" this danger. ". . . the more clearly all workers and peasants understand it, the more chances are there that we shall avoid a split, which would be fatal for the Soviet Republic."[6]

When Lenin wrote in his article that the Central Control Commission should have access to all documents and see to it, "without respect for persons," that nobody in power could prevent subordinates from posing embarrassing questions, he was referring either to something he knew had happened during his illness or to something he thought might happen. To guard against such contingencies, he constructed a pyramid of blocks: the broad-based party congress; the narrower party conference; at the next higher level, two blocks of equal weight: the Central Committee and the Rabkrin-Control Commission; and to cap the structure: the Politburo. It did not occur to Lenin that this pyramid could be turned upside down so that all the power in the blocks drained out of them and flowed down to the

[6] Lenin, *Selected Works*, Vol. IX, pp. 382-386. Russian original in Lenin, *Sochineniya*, Second ed., Vol. XXVII, pp. 402-405.

apex on which it stood—the one-man dictator. That is exactly what Stalin did, and he held the pyramid in that precarious position for more than two decades by methods revealed by Nikita S. Khrushchev, methods which included the execution of the majority of the members of the Central Committee and of the Central Control Commission and of many members of the Politburo. Of what avail would Lenin's pyramid be against the power lust of men equipped with the weapons of dictatorship? Lenin's major contribution to communism was the idea of the one-party state exercising monopoly control. But he failed to make the party immune to one-man domination.

The second ingredient of communism—second only to party dictatorship —is nationalism. Hence Lenin's agitation over the problem of the formation of the U.S.S.R. and over the Georgian Question—an agitation which aggravated his illness. Late in December, 1922, he had dictated an article on the national question which he sent to Trotsky "whom Vladimir Ilyich instructed to defend his point of view on this question at the party Congress because of their agreement on this question." Lenin, however, did not authorize the publication of the article and it has not yet been published although Lenin attached "great significance to it." The nationalities "question utterly perturbed" Lenin "and he prepared himself to speak on it at the party Congress."[7] The Union of Soviet Socialist Republics had indeed been formally established by the First Congress of the U.S.S.R. on December 30, 1922. But the powers of the federal government and those of the constituent republics were not yet demarcated. And this was the aching problem that troubled Lenin. He therefore continued to study the subject. On January 24 he instructed Lydia Fotieva to ask Djerzhinsky or Stalin for the papers of the commission on the Georgian Question and to study them and report to him. He needed these, he said, "for the party Congress." Twenty-four hours later Lenin inquired whether she had received the material. She replied that Djerzhinsky was away from Moscow and would not return until Saturday, January 29. Saturday, Fotieva telephoned Djerzhinsky; he said Stalin had the files of the commission. She wrote a letter to Stalin. She was told he was not in Moscow. That same day, nevertheless, Stalin telephoned: "He could not give out the material without the permission of the Politburo. He asked," the secretaries' diary continues, "whether I hadn't said too much to Vladimir Ilyich, how was he so well informed on current business? For instance, his article on the Rabkrin"—in Pravda of January 25—"indicated that certain circumstances were known to him. I replied—I hadn't talked and had no reason to think that he was informed. Today," January 30, "Vladimir Ilyich summoned me to get the answer and he said he would fight to have the material laid before him."

A further entry in the diary for January 30 by Miss Fotieva reads: "Vladimir Ilyich said that yesterday, in answer to his question whether he

[7] Letter of Lydia Fotieva to Kamenev, copy to Trotsky, dated April 16, 1923, in Trotsky Archives, Document T 793.

could address the party Congress on March 30, the doctor replied in the negative, but said that by that time he could get out of bed, and a month later he would be allowed to read the newspapers." Reverting to the Georgian Question, Lenin remarked with a smile, "But that"—the commission's report—"isn't newspapers, which means that I can read it now. His mood, apparently, is not bad. There is no compress on his head."

This is the first indication that Lenin had been bedridden and had dictated his articles in bed.

On February 1 Lenin summoned Miss Fotieva at 6:30 P.M. She wrote in the diary: "I informed him that the Politburo had permitted him to receive the material" on the Georgian Question. He wanted his staff to study the report. "It was assumed that the study would require four weeks." Lenin then asked "about the reaction of Tsurupa," his deputy chairman, "and others to his article" in *Pravda* "on the Rabkrin and the reorganization of the party." She replied that Assistant Commissar of Rabkrin Svidersky "agreed entirely" whereas Tsurupa doubted whether three hundred or four hundred persons could perform the Rabkrin's work. Lenin also inquired whether the Central Committee had discussed the article. Miss Fotieva did not know.

The Georgian Question had become, for Lenin, the Stalin Question: his disagreement with Stalin on the division of power between the federal government and the national minorities. In case of war, the national minorities, organized in their republics or states on the periphery of the country, might defect; in years of peace, they might sabotage, revolt, drag their feet, and defeat Moscow's purpose. The issue was: how much "independence" would satisfy their national egos without cramping the Kremlin's monopoly. Lenin opposed the loss of Soviet territory just as adamantly as did Stalin. Independence equivalent to secession was precluded. But Lenin had seen through Stalin—late, and realized that he lacked the finesse to handle the subtle relationship between the center and the states, that if he could be rude to persons, including Krupskaya, he would be brutal toward the delicate sensibilities of ethnic minorities, and cause trouble. It tormented Lenin that he could not attend the party Congress and deal with this problem and simultaneously deal a blow at Stalin, remove him from the General Secretaryship as he had urged in his "Letter to the Congress," known to history as his last testament.

The "Letter" was secret. A public attack on Stalin by Lenin on personal grounds or on the explosive subject of the national minorities might release a whirlwind that would crack the party and split the country. Frustrated, imprisoned in his bed, Lenin found solace in reading and dictating. On February 2 he requested Krupskaya to obtain A. E. Hodorov's *World Imperialism and China. A Political-Economic Essay*, published in Shanghai in 1922, and M. P. Pavlovich's *Soviet Russia and Imperialist Japan*. They were procured by evening. Earlier, at 11:45 A.M. that day, Lenin had summoned

Miss Volodicheva and begun dictating another article, which, in reality, was the second part of his January 25 *Pravda* article on the Rabkrin. He dictated for forty-five minutes.

Volodicheva made this entry in the diary: "I hadn't seen him since January 23. His appearance has considerably improved: a fresh, cheerful look. He dictates extremely well, as always: without stopping, rarely encountering difficulty with a phrase, more correctly he doesn't dictate but talks and gesticulates. No compress on his head."

The following day Lenin summoned Lydia Fotieva for a few minutes. Had she looked over the material on the Georgian Question? She said she had glanced at it and found it more voluminous than expected. "He asked," she recorded, "whether the Politburo had considered the question. I replied that I had no right to speak about this."

Lenin: "You have been forbidden to speak specifically about this?"

Fotieva: "No, in general, I have no right to speak about current business."

Lenin: "This means it is current business."

"I realized that I had made an inadvertent mistake," Fotieva noted in the diary. She said again she had no right to speak about the matter.

Lenin said, "I know about this affair from Djerzhinsky, even before my illness. Did the [Djerzhinsky] commission report to the Politburo?"

"Yes," she said, "and the Politburo, as far as I remember, approved its conclusions." [The conclusions whitewashed Orjonekidze for smacking "independencer" Boodoo Mdivani.]

"Well," Lenin declared, "I think you will make your summary of the report in three weeks and then I'll descend on them with a letter."

She left when the physicians entered; they were Dr. Otfried Foerster, just arrived from Germany, and Dr. Kozhevnikov and Dr. Kramer. Lenin's appearance, Miss Fotieva wrote in the diary, "was gay and cheerful, perhaps somewhat animated before the visit of Foerster who had not seen him for a long time."

The next day, February 4, Lenin continued the dictation on the second part of the Rabkrin article which he was entitling "Better Fewer, But Better." Krupskaya told Miss Volodicheva, who took the dictation, that Professor Foerster had given Lenin permission to exercise and to extend the daily dictation period. "Vladimir Ilyich," Krupskaya said, "was very pleased." But when Volodicheva returned at eight in the evening with the typescript, his "speed of dictation was less than usual. Compress on his head. Face is pale. Seems tired."

On February 5 Lydia Fotieva was ill and absent; Lenin therefore talked for twenty minutes with another of his secretaries: Maria Ignatyevna Glyasser. This was the first time she saw him since his illness and she recorded her impressions in the office diary: "It seems to me he looks well and cheerful, only somewhat paler than before. He speaks slowly, gesticulating with his left hand while moving the fingers of the right. No compress on his head." The subject of their conversation was again the report of the Djerzhinsky commission on the Georgian Question. He thought he might have to send to the Caucasus for clarifying data.

The problem gave him no rest. It was obvious that he intended to challenge Stalin and Stalin's allies: "descend on them with a letter." He asked Miss Glyasser how many days remained until the Congress. "A month and twenty-five days," she said.

He still hoped to address that assembly.

Miss Volodicheva spent an hour and a half with Lenin on February 6. He read the typescript she brought of his new article and asked that, instead of making corrections on it in ink, as the secretaries had been doing, the typescripts be retyped in their entirety in the future. He dictated for fifteen-twenty minutes and stopped of his own accord. She found him in a joyful mood, only regretting that he could not write his article by hand, or, as he had once done, pacing up and down the room while dictating to Trotsky's stenographer in 1918. He found it trying to lie passive in bed when thoughts stirred him so deeply.

On February 7 Miss Fotieva answered his call. Lenin wanted the results of the recent census of government employees. She said she was forbidden to give them to him without Stalin's permission. All Lenin's secretaries were loyal to him, but they were party members and had to obey orders from the party's General Secretary. Further, he inquired how they were progressing with the reading of the commission's report on the Georgian Question. He also asked if the collegium of the Rabkrin intended to "take a step of significance to the state," in line with his *Pravda* article on the Rabkrin, or would it procrastinate until the Congress.

"Today," reads the diary entry, Dr. "Kozhevnikov said there had been a tremendous improvement in Vladimir Ilyich's health. He already moved his right hand and Lenin himself believed he would soon be able to use it." However, when Miss Volodicheva came to take dictation in the morning and in the evening she found him worse. Krupskaya told her he would not dictate the next day.

Lydia Fotieva went to Lenin's room on February 9. He told her firmly that he intended to raise the question of the Rabkrin at the coming party Congress. He also informed her that Professor Foerster was inclined to permit him to receive visitors but not to read newspapers. Miss Fotieva remarked that from the medical point of view this seemed to be the correct preference. Lenin thought a moment and disagreed. He said that in his opinion it was worse, because one read printed material and that was all, whereas personal visits provoked exchanges of opinion.

Lenin thus indicated that he knew he had opponents and if they came to see him they would discuss questions near to his heart and tear at his raw nerves.

That morning Miss Volodicheva took dictation on his "Better Fewer,

But Better" for about an hour. The article was now almost complete and met Lenin's approval. He instructed Miss Fotieva on February 10 to show it to Tsurupa on condition that he return it within forty-eight hours. After seeing Lenin, Miss Fotieva wrote in the diary: "Tired appearance, speaks with great difficulty, losing his thoughts and twisting words. Compress on his head." Nevertheless, Lenin gave her a list of books he wanted to read: one on new science and Marxism; another on Marxism as a study subject; a third on Soviet finances during the civil war and in the NEP period; a collection of articles on the theory of money; L. Axelrod, *Against Idealism. A Critique of Certain Idealistic Tendencies in Philosophic Thought*; A. Drevs, *The Christ Myth*; P. G. Kurlov, *The End of Russian Tsarism*; I. A. Modzalevsky, *Proletarian Myth-Making (Regarding Ideological Deviations in Contemporary Proletarian Poetry)*; and several other volumes.

Miss Fotieva's diary entry for February 12 records a sharp deterioration in Lenin's condition: "Vladimir Ilyich feels much worse. Bad headache. Summoned me for several minutes. According to Maria Ilyinichna [Lenin's younger sister] the physicians upset him so much that his lips shook. Last night Foerster categorically prohibited newspapers, visitors, and political information. In reply to a question what he meant by political information, Foerster replied: 'Well, now, for instance, you are interested in the census of Soviet employees.' Vladimir Ilyich was apparently upset by the fact that the physicians knew about this. Furthermore, Vladimir Ilyich has apparently gathered the impression that it was not the physicians who gave directions to the Central Committee, but the Central Committee who gave instructions to the physicians."

Lenin's reasoning was plausible and probably correct, for Foerster had permitted visits two days earlier. In any case, Lenin's mind was beset by suspicions of hostility to him in the highest ranks of the communist party. He could not be far wrong. It has even been suggested that Stalin, knowing Lenin's nervous tensions, aggravated them consciously and used the Soviet physicians, over whom he had control, to persuade Foerster to alter his instructions and thus irritate Lenin.

On February 14 Lenin called Miss Fotieva at 1 P.M. Her diary entry reads: "No headache. He said he was completely well. That his illness was a nervous one and such that he sometimes was well, that is, his head was perfectly clear, and at other times he felt worse. Therefore we must quickly perform the tasks he had given us, because he definitely wished to finish certain things before the Congress, and hoped that he could. But if we delay matters and thereby kill the thing he would be very and very displeased. The physicians arrived and we had to stop."

That evening Miss Fotieva answered his call again. He appeared tired and his speech was impeded. He talked about the matter "which disturbs him more than all others, that is, the Georgian Question. He urged us to work quickly." Miss Fotieva made a further note in the secretaries' diary: Somebody was to intimate to A. A. Solts, a member of the presidium of the Central Control Committee of the party, that Lenin "was on the side of the offended. Someone of the offended should be given to understand that he was on their side. Three points: 1. There should be no fight. 2. Concessions should be made. 3. It is impossible to compare a large state with a small one. Did Stalin know? Why did he not react? To call anybody a deviationist for a deviation towards chauvinism and Menshevism proves the great-power advocates guilty of that very deviation. Collect printed material for Vladimir Ilyich."

This rather cryptic notation seems to reflect Lenin's desire to let the representatives of the national minorities—"the offended"—know that he was their champion. A large state should make concessions to a small one and avoid a conflict. The great power advocates (Stalin, Djerzhinsky, and others) were charging Georgians like Mdivani with chauvinism and Menshevism when those were their own sins.

After February 14 and until March 5 there are no entries in the diary—at least, according to a footnote in Voprosi Istorii KPSS, Volume No. 2, for 1963. Whether this was due to Lenin's illness or to his work with Krupskaya on the article is not known. The article was finished on March 2, 1923, and appeared in Pravda on March 4. With it, Lenin's vast literary output came to an end. It was his last public utterance, written or oral.

The article "Better Fewer, But Better" directed attention to the Workers and Peasants Inspection (Rabkrin) but also ranged over a wider field. In the first paragraph Lenin stated that, "Up to now we have been able to devote so little attention to the quality of our state apparatus that it would be quite legitimate to display special concern for its organization and to concentrate in the Workers and Peasants Inspection human material of real modern quality, that is, quality not inferior to the best West European models. For a socialist republic this condition is too modest, of course; but the first five years have fairly crammed our heads with disbelief and skepticism. . . . For a start we would be satisfied with real bourgeois culture, for a start we would be satisfied to be able to dispense with the particularly crude types of pre-bourgeois culture, that is, bureaucratic or serf culture, etc. In matters of culture, haste and bustle are the worst possible things. Many of our young writers and communists should get this well into their heads.

"Thus, on the question of the state apparatus we should draw the conclusion from our past experience that it would be better to go more slowly.

"The situation in regard to our state apparatus is so deplorable, not to say outrageous, that we must first of all think very carefully how to eliminate its defects, bearing in mind that the roots of these defects lie in the past, which, although overturned, has not yet been overcome. . . .

"We must come to our senses in time. We must become highly skeptical of too rapid progress, of boastfulness, etc. We must think of testing the forward steps which we proclaim to the world every hour, which we take every minute, and which later prove to be flimsy, superficial and not understood every second. The worst thing of all would be haste. The worst thing of all would be to rely on the assumption that we know anything, or on the assumption that we possess any considerable quantity of the elements necessary for building a really new apparatus that would deserve the name of Socialist, Soviet, etc."

One can scarce forbear a comment here: This paragraph would make useful reading throughout the Soviet Union today.

"No," Lenin continued, "we have no such apparatus, and even the quantity of elements of it that we have is ridiculously small. . . .

"What elements have we for building this apparatus? Only two. First, the workers who are absorbed in the struggle for socialism. These elements are not sufficiently educated. They would like to build a better apparatus for us, but they do not know how to do it. They cannot do it. They have not yet developed the culture that is required for this; and it is precisely culture that is required for this. . . . Secondly, we have the element of knowledge, education and training, but to a degree that is ridiculously small compared with all other countries.

"Here, too, we must not forget that we are too prone to compensate (or imagine that we can compensate) our lack of knowledge by zeal, doing things in a rush, etc. . . .

"The conclusions to be drawn from the above are the following: we must make the Workers and Peasants Inspection, which is the instrument for improving our apparatus, a really exemplary institution.

"In order that it may achieve the necessary level we must follow the rule: 'It is better to get good human material in two years, or even in three years, than to work in haste without hope of getting any at all.'

". . . I know that the opposite rule will force its way through a thousand loopholes. . . . Nevertheless, I am convinced that only by such work shall we achieve our aim, and that only by achieving this aim shall we create a republic that is really worthy of the name of Soviet, Socialist, etc. . . .

"Let us say frankly that the People's Commissariat for Workers and Peasants Inspection does not enjoy a shadow of authority. Everybody knows that a more badly organized institution than our Workers and Peasants Inspection does not exist." Hence Lenin's proposal for a merger of the Rabkrin with the party's Central Control Commission. The personnel for both should be chosen with the greatest care from among communists with experience in administration and "knowledge of the principles of the theory of our state apparatus." Moreover, "several trained and conscientious persons" should be sent to Germany or England in case they could not visit America or Canada "to collect literature and to study this question."

But, Lenin asked, "Is there not something improper" in the suggestion to amalgamate a party institution with a government institution? His answer was a very simple one and very typical of Lenin's practicality which swept away considerations of theory, principle, precedence, and previous policy. He said, "but why, indeed, should we not amalgamate the two if it is in the interests of our work?" Did not the party's Politburo decide on government policy in foreign affairs and other domains? "I see no obstacle to this. More than that, I think that such amalgamation is the only guarantee of success in our work."

He knew how conservative bureaucrats, whether communist or noncommunist, could be. He wrote, "in all spheres of social, economic and political relationships we are 'frightfully' revolutionary. But in the sphere of precedence, in the observation of the forms and rites of office routine, our 'revolutionariness' very often yields to the mustiest routine. Here on more than one occasion we have witnessed the very interesting phenomenon of a great leap forward in social life being accompanied with monstrous hesitancy in the face of the smallest changes. . . . Among us, theoretical audacity in general constructions lived side by side with astonishing timidity in regard to some very minor reform in office routine."

Lenin now opened his literary lens to take in the entire Soviet scene: "The general feature of our present social life is the following: we have destroyed capitalist industry and have tried to raze to the ground the institution of medieval landlordism; in its place we have created a small and very small peasantry, which is following the lead of the proletariat because it believes in the results of its revolutionary work." Then surveying the world situation, he added glumly, "It is not easy, however, merely with the aid of this confidence, to hold on until the socialist revolution is victorious in the more developed countries, because, especially under the NEP, the small and very small peasantry is compelled by economic necessity to remain on an extremely low level of productivity of labor. Yes, and even the international situation threw Russia back and, taken as a whole, forced the productivity of the labor of the people considerably below the prewar level."

Beyond Russia's frontiers, Lenin saw "a number of countries—the East, India, China, etc." which have been "completely dislodged from their groove. . . . The general European ferment has begun to affect them, and it is now clear to the whole world that they have been drawn into a process of development that cannot but lead to a crisis in the whole of world capitalism."

Lenin then posed this question: "Shall we be able to hold on with our small and very small peasant production, and in our present state of ruin, until the West European capitalist countries accomplish their developments to socialism?" His reply was not weighted with optimism. The West European capitalist countries are not developing toward socialism, he wrote, "in the way we formerly expected. They are not accomplishing it by the normal 'ripening' of socialism, but by the exploitation of some countries by others." The "others" were the defeated countries in the First World War and the colonies. He was not altogether without hope, however. "On the other hand,"

Lenin said, "precisely as a result of the first imperialist war, the East has been completely drawn into the revolutionary movement . . . into the general maelstrom of the world revolutionary movement." (But neither here nor anywhere else in his voluminous writings, as far as I have been able to discover, did Lenin ever use the words so often attributed to him: "The road to Paris lies through Peking.")

What, in these circumstances, should the Soviet state do? Lenin asked. "Obviously the following: We must display extreme caution in order to preserve our workers' government and to retain our small and very small peasantry under its authority and leadership." On the one hand, "We have the advantage in that the whole world is now passing into a movement that must give rise to a world socialist revolution." On the other hand, "We are laboring under the disadvantage that the imperialists have succeeded in splitting the world into two camps; and this split is made more complicated by the fact that it is extremely difficult for Germany, which is really a land of advanced, cultured, capitalist development, to rise to her feet. All the capitalist powers of what is called the West are pecking at her and preventing her from rising to her feet." And in the East too, the hundreds of millions "of exploited toilers . . . have been reduced to the last degree of human endurance" and are much weaker physically, materially, and militarily than "any of the much smaller West European countries."

Lenin pondered the question: "Can we save ourselves from the impending conflict with these imperialist countries?" Would conflicts between these countries and within them "give us a second respite"?

Lenin was too wise to answer the question he raised: "I think the reply to this question should be that the answer depends upon too many circumstances, and that, taken as a whole, we can foretell the outcome of the struggle only inasmuch as, after all is said and done, capitalism itself is educating and training the enormous majority of the globe for that struggle."

The outcome of the struggle, Lenin affirmed, "will be determined by the fact that Russia, India, China, etc., constitute the overwhelming majority of the population" of the planet and this majority has been drawn into the battle for its emancipation with such "extraordinary rapidity" that "there cannot be the slightest shadow of a doubt" regarding the final outcome—"the final victory of socialism is fully and absolutely assured."

At this point, near the very end of the last article of his life, Lenin made a revealing statement: "But what interests us is not this final victory of socialism, but the tactics that we, the Russian Communist Party, we, the Russian Soviet Government, should pursue in order to prevent the West European counterrevolutionary states from crushing us." His consuming preoccupation was with the survival of his new Russian state. He formulated a broad strategy for the future: "In order to ensure our existence until the next military conflict between the counterrevolutionary imperialist West and the revolutionary and nationalist East, between the most civilized countries of the world and the orientally-backward countries which, however, are the majority, this majority must become civilized. We, too, lack sufficient civilization to pass directly to socialism, although we have the political requisites for this."

Lenin proposed these policies:

To retain the confidence of the peasants, the workers who lead them should exercise "the greatest economy" and avoid every trace of "excesses" or over-indulgence or intemperance "in our social relations."

Everything superfluous should be removed from the state apparatus.

Would this not, Lenin asked rhetorically, create "the kingdom of peasant narrowness"? He replied in the negative. Every kopek economized would be used to develop large-scale machine industry, to speed electrification, to construct the Volkhov hydroelectric power station begun in 1922 near Petrograd, and the modernization of methods of extracting peat. "In this and in this alone lies our hope," Lenin declared. "Only when we have done that shall we, figuratively speaking, be able to change . . . from the impoverished horse of the muzhik to the horse which the proletariat is seeking and cannot but seek—the horse of large-scale machine industry, electrification, . . . etc."

This is why, Lenin wrote, he wanted to purge the government apparatus. This is why he wanted to reorganize the Workers and Peasants Inspection. "If we do that we shall be able to hold on" and survive not in peasant narrowness but with a large-scale machine industry.

"These are the lofty tasks that I dream of for our Workers and Peasants Inspection. That is why I am planning for it, the merging of the most authoritative party body [The Central Control Commission] with an 'ordinary' people's commissariat."[8]

Those were Lenin's last words to appear in print.

The man who wrote the five articles was not a happy one. He was sinking into a morass of problems he could not solve; he felt helpless.

On March 5, Lenin dictated two letters, one to Stalin, one to Trotsky. The letter to Stalin demanded an apology to Krupskaya for insulting her on the telephone, otherwise he would break off relations with him. Krupskaya begged Miss Volodicheva, who took the dictation in shorthand, not to dispatch the letter, and it was held back during March 6. On March 7, however, the stenographer said she was obliged to carry out Lenin's orders. Krupskaya then consulted Kamenev, who advised sending the letter, with copies to himself and Zinoviev. Volodicheva handed the letter to Stalin personally. Stalin thereupon dictated his reply to her—an apology to Krupskaya. Lenin never saw it because he became ill.[9]

Lenin was apparently reconciled to being unable to attend the next party

[8] Lenin, *Selected Works*, Vol. IX, pp. 387-401. Russian original in Lenin, *Sochineniya*, Second ed., Vol. XXVII, pp. 406-418.

[9] *Voprosi Istorii KPSS*, Vol. No. 2, 1963, pp. 84-85 and 91. The text of neither Lenin's letter nor Stalin's has yet been published. This is the last entry in the secretaries' diary.

Congress, the biggest political event of any year. His March 5 letter to Trotsky, read to Trotsky over the telephone, therefore asked him to undertake the defense of the Georgian Question.[10] Trotsky gives the text: "Dear Comrade Trotsky: I wish very much to ask you to take upon yourself the defense of the Georgian case in the Central Committee of the Party. At present, the case is under the 'persecution' of Stalin and Djerzhinsky, and I cannot trust their impartiality. Quite the contrary. If you were to agree to undertake the defense, my mind would be at rest. If for some reason you cannot agree to do so, please return the entire dossier to me; I shall consider that a sign of refusal from you. With best comradely greetings, Lenin."[11]

The next day, March 6, 1923, Lenin dictated the last letter of which we have any knowledge. It was addressed to the Georgian opponents of Stalin: Mdivani, Philipp Y. Makharadze, President of Georgia, "and others"; "copies to Trotsky and Kamenev." It reads: "Respected Comrades, I am following your case with all my heart. I am shocked by crudeness of Orjonekidze and the conniving of Stalin and Djerzhinsky. I am preparing a memoranda and a speech for you. Respectfully, Lenin."[12]

Leon Trotsky had been ill during much of 1922. He therefore did not visit Gorky, as Stalin and Kamenev did, when Lenin was there from May to October. After Lenin returned to Moscow and to work, his relations with Trotsky were cordial. But, as Trotsky says in his autobiography, "Lenin needed practical, obedient assistants . . . I had my own views, my own ways of working." That was Trotsky's explanation for the appointment of Rykov, Kamenev, and Tsurupa, but not Trotsky, as Lenin's deputies.

Trotsky's illness lingered. Often the Politburo met in his apartment in the Kremlin so he could be present. Later he stayed at Arkhangelskoye, outside Moscow, for his health. The physicians told him to take a cure in the Caucasus, and he did. At the Tiflis railway station, en route to the Black Sea resort of Sukhum, he was handed a telegram: Lenin dead. It came from Stalin, who wired that the funeral would be on Saturday, too early for Trotsky to return to Moscow. The funeral actually took place on Sunday and Trotsky might have been there.

Much has been made of Trotsky's absence from Lenin's funeral. If he had been in Moscow, it is argued, he might have been the heir. This is superficial. Trotsky himself shows in his autobiography that Stalin, Zinoviev, and Kamenev had, by various stratagems and devices, already isolated him. Trotsky's illness helped them achieve their purpose. The timing of the funeral was not an essential factor. Why did Trotsky not return immediately from Tiflis to Moscow on hearing of Lenin's demise? He was chief of the armed services, a member of the Politburo. He could have flown in a military airplane. Prolonged ill-health had undermined his determination.

[10] *Ibid.*, p. 91 (footnote).
[11] *My Life*, p. 483.
[12] Trotsky Archives, T 788.

There were other ingredients in his defeat. In *My Life* Trotsky relates how he tried, and failed, to detach Kamenev, his brother-in-law, from the triumvirate (Stalin-Kamenev-Zinoviev) which worked assiduously, while Lenin lay partly paralyzed, to succeed him on his demise. Trotsky writes, "The renewal of the personnel in the war department had for some time been going on at full speed behind my back." The triumvirate controlled the party organization in Trotsky's own defense commissariat and were already grooming Michael Frunze to replace Trotsky.

For Trotsky to have condemned Orjonekidze and Stalin in these circumstances would have handed them a useful argument: he, the ex-Menshevik, who had written in defense of terror against Menshevik Georgia, now opposed Soviet terror against Mensheviks in Soviet Georgia. He could not do that because he believed in terror and was ever mindful of his compromising Menshevik past.

Trotsky, moreover, does not seem to have been of the stuff that makes a Number One leader. He was a great man, much abused by his comrades and fate, but great under Lenin. Without Lenin he was certainly no match for the aggressive triumvirate.

All these reasons played a part in Trotsky's response to Lenin's letter of March 5, asking him to defend the Georgian case against Stalin in the Central Committee.

Trotsky pondered and refused. This foreshadowed his defeat, demotion, deportation, and assassination.

On March 9 Lenin suffered a third stroke that spelled doom.

LII. ☉HE END

THE BRAIN of the political man was dead.

The third stroke on March 9 alarmed the few who knew about it. Dr. Vladimir N. Rozanov, called in on March 11, noted high temperature, paralysis of the right arm and leg, aphasia, and dimmed consciousness. Treatment was complicated, the doctor said, by the patient's inability to speak. Occasionally Lenin would pronounce "Lloyd George," "conferentsia" (conference), "nyevozmozhnost" (impossibility), and a few other words. He attempted to explain his condition to the physicians by gestures, and when they conveyed no meaning they became increasingly violent and, "especially in the first three or four months, sometimes brought on a fit of excitement. Vladimir Ilyich would then chase away the physicians, nurses, and orderlies."

A special edition of *Pravda* on March 12 informed the public of Lenin's grave illness. The government began issuing daily bulletins giving temperature, respiration, pulse, and other symptoms. Specialists were brought from abroad: from Sweden, Professor Hentschell and his son, both neurologists; from Leipzig, Professor Oswald Bumke, authority on circulatory disorders, and Professor Adolf von Strumpfell, a neurologist; from Hamburg, Professor Zonne, likewise a neurologist.

The official bulletin of March 22, signed "Hentschell, Strumpfell, Minkovsky, Foerster, Vittke, Kramer, Kozhevnikov, Semashko," stated that Lenin's illness "belongs to a category where complete restoration of health is possible."

Now and then intestinal trouble, in April catarrh in the left lung, raised Lenin's temperature and accelerated his pulse. Millions followed these ups and downs as though he were a relative. The physicians injected as much optimism into their bulletins as professional ethics—under political pressure —permitted. The leadership feared popular panic.

By May most of the snow was gone from Moscow's streets and the roads were passable. On May 12 attendants carried Lenin out of his Kremlin apartment on a stretcher and downstairs to a waiting ambulance. The secretaries in his office, hiding so he might not see them, peeped sadly as they saw him go. He was taken to the government rest house in the village of Gorky.

Here he improved startlingly. An orderly pushed him in a wheelchair through the leafy bowers while Krupskaya and Maria walked on either side. Soon he began to walk with assistance. In the beginning of August he commenced exercises for the restoration of speech. Lenin was so much better that Rozanov, as he writes in his memoirs, went on a month's vacation.

Lenin now objected to medicines, drove away the nurses, and refused to be examined by the physicians. Even Professor Foerster, whose company he had always enjoyed, was forced to diagnose and prescribe at a distance on the basis of the observations of members of the family.

In September the doctors, aided by shoemakers, fitted Lenin with orthopedic shoes and he started to walk in his room using a cane for support. The next month he showed further improvement. Krupskaya, with infinite patience, tried to teach him to utter a few simple words. He looked at the newspaper and indicated the items he wanted read to him.

The physicians apparently decided that politics would be therapy. In October, accordingly, Osip A. Pyatnitsky, a high official of the Third International, and Ivan I. Skvortsov-Stepanov, who was active in the Moscow Soviet, were brought out to Gorky. While Skvortsov-Stepanov told Lenin about the elections to the Moscow Soviet he paid little attention and looked at books lying on the table. But when the visitor mentioned the extension of streetcar service to the outlying proletarian wards of the city and the closing of beer saloons, Lenin "began to listen attentively" and uttered "the only word he had mastered well: 'Vot, vot,' "—That's it, that's it.

Pyatnitsky, in turn, reported to Lenin about developments in the Italian

Communist Party and communist participation in British elections. These matters failed to elicit Lenin's interest. On hearing of the progress of communist activities in Germany, however, Lenin nodded his head approvingly and said, "Vot, vot."

But now nothing could arrest the inexorable process that was taking place in his brain. Writing of the autopsy in the collected memoirs about Lenin, Health Commissar Semashko affirms that, while other organs showed negligible sclerosis, "the sclerosis of the blood vessels of Vladimir Ilyich's brain had gone so far that these blood vessels were calcified. When struck with a tweezer they sounded like stone. The walls of many blood vessels were so thickened and the blood vessels so overgrown that not even a hair could be inserted in the openings. Thus, whole segments of the brain were deprived of fresh blood."

That being the case, what Lenin did on October 19, 1923, is all the more remarkable. Deaf to all protestations from Krupskaya, Maria, and the physicians, he got into an automobile at Gorky and motioned the driver to proceed to Moscow. He went to his Kremlin apartment, looked around, walked into the adjoining Cabinet room, and came into his office and eyed everybody. Then, Lydia Fotieva writes, he descended to the car, drove to the permanent agricultural machinery exhibit in what is now the Park of Culture and Rest, and finally returned to Gorky.

The same month he began, with great difficulty, to write with his left hand. Lunacharsky recalls the hopes in government circles that Lenin would be restored to health and resume the leadership of the nation. Trotsky too says, "We all expected recovery." In December, 1923, the children at Gorky, including Victor, the only child of the Ulyanovs, decorated a Christmas tree. Lenin stayed all evening while the gifts were being distributed.

On January 19 Krupskaya writes in her *Memories of Lenin*, "I read to him in the evening a tale of Jack London's *Love of Life*—it is still lying on the table in his room. It is a very fine story. In a wilderness of ice, where no human being had set foot, a sick man, dying of hunger, is making for the harbor of a big river. His strength is giving out, he cannot walk but keeps slipping, and beside him there slides a wolf—also dying of hunger. There is a fight between them: the man wins. Half dead, half demented, he reaches his goal. That tale greatly pleased Ilyich." Perhaps Krupskaya was striving to strengthen Lenin's will to live.

"Next day," she continues, "he asked me to read him more Jack London. . . . The next tale happened to be of quite another type—saturated with bourgeois morals. Some captain promises the owner of a ship laden with corn to dispose of it at a good price; he sacrifices his life merely in order to keep his word. Ilyich smiled and dismissed it with a wave of the hand.

"That was the last time I read to him."

At 6 P.M. on the following day—January 21, 1924—Lenin's temperature rose sharply, he suffered a stormy attack which coincided with sharp muscular spasms throughout the body, and he lost consciousness. He never regained it. He died at 6:30. The doctors and nurses stood in a corner of the room, tears streaming down their faces. Krupskaya sat on the bed and caressed his hand.

Lenin's body was brought to Moscow on the 23rd. It lay in state in the Hall of Columns. For four days, while the northern city was in the deepest freeze it had known in years, hundreds of thousands of women, children, and men queued for hours night and day in the icy streets to get the split-second look allowed them as they passed the open coffin. Moscow mourned. Many millions elsewhere mourned. Meanwhile, a temporary wooden mausoleum was being built behind a fence in the Red Square near the Kremlin wall. Into it Lenin was borne on the 27th. Later, however, he was carried away to a laboratory, his organs and body fluids removed and preservative liquids substituted by a complex, never-disclosed chemical process to keep him life-like to this day. According to persistent word-of-mouth reports, Krupskaya, who survived her husband until 1939, opposed his mummification, and it is not difficult to understand the emotional reason. The political reason too is no secret, for she was an old-style Bolshevik who abhorred personal glorification, as he had, and must have been horrified at seeing the revolutionary regime imitating ancient Russian church practices. The Soviet government's anti-God campaign regularly featured public unsealing of the coffins of holy men believed to have been miraculously preserved and therefore possessing therapeutic qualities. Nothing was found inside, communist publications announced, except bones and hair. Unconsciously, or perhaps quite consciously and cynically, Moscow's Marxist materialists were paying tribute to religious Russian minds. The Kremlin needed Lenin. It needs him still, for the Soviet Union is a powerful country ruled by a pervasive, powerful government with weak popular support and unsure of its national minorities, peasantry, youth, and intelligentsia. Lenin is therefore mobilized for steady duty as the all-wise, all-good, all-time infallible oracle and binding cement. The atheistic Kremlin does not hesitate to employ reverse-anthropomorphism in this cause. "Lenin Lived, Lenin Lives, Lenin Shall Always Live," reads the inscription on a poster showing Lenin's head; before the poster, reproduced in *Pravda* of November 6, 1962, a group of boy and girl scouts are receiving instructions from a leader. "More Alive Than All The Living," is the two-column headline above a bibliographical note about Lenin in the *Literaturnaya Gazeta* of October 17, 1963. The second anniversary of the adoption of the new Soviet Communist Party program was celebrated on October 31, 1963. *Pravda* wrote on that day: "The radiant genius of the great teacher of the toilers of the world, V. I. Lenin, lights the path of mankind to communism. In the preparation of the Program, our party and its Central Committee constantly took counsel with Lenin and made their point of departure his brilliant ideas regarding the construction of socialism and communism. Therefore the Program of the Soviet Communist Party is, with complete justification, called Leninist."

"Lenin Lives." The Soviet leaders "took counsel with Lenin." The position is just on the edge of deification and resurrection. A leadership lacking confidence and new ideas leans on Lenin's words and deeds. It is symbolic that the massed multitudes see their leaders atop the Lenin Mausoleum on November 7 and May 1 and special occasions. They stand on him. Inside the pyramidal tomb made of red-black, gleaming granite brought from Vinnitsa in the Ukraine lies the lifelike dead man. The Kremlin is sensitive to aspersions on the chemical feat of his embalming. In the 1930's foreign newspapers stated that the pale mummy was a wax figure. Thereupon a group of foreigners, of which I was a member, were invited to descend into the depths of the shrine where Professor Boris I. Zbarsky, embalming chemist, alluded to the secret process by which the mummification was achieved and estimated that the body could last a century. Then he opened the hermetically sealed glass case containing the relic, tweaked Lenin's nose and turned his head to the right and left. It was not wax. It was Lenin. The iconoclast is now a modern Russian icon, and millions queue and gaze in wonder at the miracle of his preservation in the flesh.

APPENDIX. "DID STALIN POISON LENIN?"

"FINANCIAL DIFFICULTIES led him"—Trotsky—"to a strange quarrel with *Life* magazine," Isaac Deutscher writes in *The Prophet Outcast,* his third volume of a Trotsky biography. "At the end of September, 1939, on [James] Burnham's initiative, one of *Life's* editors came to Coyoacan and commissioned him to write a character sketch of Stalin and also an article on Lenin's death." The *Life* editor who journeyed to Mexico was Noel Busch, the magazine's text editor. Busch says he went there to see Trotsky's article and was highly pleased with it. Trotsky declared he too liked the article except that one thing had been omitted: he had not explained that Stalin poisoned Lenin. The gambit did not fail: Busch said he would be glad to consider a second article—for $2,000, the fee for the first.

However, when the article on Stalin's poisoning of Lenin arrived in New York, *Life* rejected it. This was unusual; Trotsky had a tremendous reputation and a brilliant style. Any literary contribution by him would grace a publication and increase sales. But *Life* refused to print Trotsky's tale of Lenin's death. The article was then submitted in turn to the *Saturday Evening Post,* which sent it back, and to *Collier's,* which also turned it down. Finally, *Liberty,* a Hearst periodical, published it on August 10, 1940, ten days before Trotsky's assassination.

The article in *Liberty* is entitled "Did Stalin Poison Lenin?" Nowhere in it does Trotsky answer this question in the affirmative. He never even attempts to introduce evidence that Stalin poisoned Lenin.

Trotsky merely states that "at the end of February, 1923" Lenin asked Stalin for poison so he could commit suicide if he felt the coming of a new stroke that would completely incapacitate him. Stalin reported this to a Politburo meeting attended by Trotsky, Kamenev, and Zinoviev.

Trotsky is not at all certain that Lenin made the request. "But did Lenin actually ask Stalin for poison?" Trotsky writes. At the same time, Trotsky believed that Lenin might have made the request: "it is possible that he wanted to test Stalin: just how eagerly would Stalin take advantage of this opportunity?"

Moreover, there is no record of an interview between Lenin and Stalin at the end of February, 1923. Trotsky offers no proof that such a meeting took place. Lenin had already angrily quarreled with Stalin and written his last testament and its January 4, 1923, postscript urging the removal of Stalin as the communist party's General Secretary. Lenin was incensed at Stalin's arrogant and insulting treatment of Krupskaya. Why should he have seen Stalin and asked him of all people for poison?

Did Stalin poison Lenin? Did Lenin's family or Lenin's physicians poison

Lenin at Stalin's behest? Trotsky does not say so. He simply states that at the Moscow trials in 1937 and 1938, the Soviet secret police was revealed as possessing a poison pharmacy. He also quotes Bukharin as saying that Stalin "is capable of anything."

No doubt he was, and yet Trotsky refrains from declaring that Stalin poisoned Lenin.

Trotsky tells in the article how Stalin had telegraphed him the news of Lenin's death and misinformed him about the date of the funeral. It took place on Sunday, not on Saturday as Stalin had wired. "It was safer in all respects to keep me away until the body had been embalmed and the viscera cremated." But if Trotsky had put any credence in the story of Lenin's request to Stalin for poison why did he not return from Tiflis to Moscow on Sunday and demand an investigation? The body was not embalmed until long after the death.

The real question is: Why did Trotsky keep this "secret" until 1939, when he wrote the article for *Life*? He was deported from the Soviet Union in 1929. In the following ten years he wrote several books and scores and scores of articles. Stalin was his political enemy. Many of the million words he penned in exile were directed at Stalin. The worst accusation he could have leveled against Stalin was that he had killed Lenin. Yet for an entire decade he made no mention of it and no allusion to it.

The detailed record of Lenin's illness before the end of February, 1923, and through March, 1923, to the end in January, 1924, offers no support for the sensational suspicion that Stalin poisoned Lenin.

ɳOTES TO THE READER

GANDHI AND LENIN. I began collecting material for a biography of Lenin in 1947. My wife, Markoosha, helped in the research. When Mahatma Gandhi was assassinated on January 30, 1948, John Fischer, chief editor of *Harper's*, and Simon Michael Bessie, a Harper editor, came to see me and said, "You have lived with Gandhi and written about him. Could you drop the Lenin book and do a biography of Gandhi?" I agreed. I was then equipped to write adequately about the Mahatma. If I had written the life of Lenin at that time it would have been a bad book. I lacked the long perspective and clear understanding. Since then, and especially in 1962 and 1963, moreover, a mass of revealing new material on Lenin has appeared in the Soviet Union and elsewhere.

FRIENDS, COLLEAGUES, SONS, AND CRITICS. While I was writing *The Life of Mahatma Gandhi* in New York, my friends would ask, "Where are you now?" I would reply, "I'm in South Africa in 1912." Fifteen months later they put the same question. "I'm in jail in India in 1943," I told them. Gandhi lived in the open twenty-four hours a day, and given his abhorrence of secrecy, one could live with him. It has not always been possible to do the same with Lenin, but I tried. He wrote so much, so much has been written about him, and so many of his notes and letters and his secretaries' diaries have been published that the man does emerge in all his stature and complexities; with him the course of the revolutionary movement before 1917 and the history of Soviet Russia till 1924 come into focus. I attempted not only to create the image of the person but also to picture the men and women with whom he worked, and to relate him and them to the people they ruled and to the Russia in which I resided for fourteen years.

I had many collaborators. When I encountered musicians and music lovers I told them about Lenin's attitude toward music and invited their comments. I consulted psychoanalysts and psychiatrists and gave them the germane facts about Lenin's conduct. Before I put down my own speculation on what would have happened to Marx if there had been no Lenin I posed the question to at least thirty philosophers, social scientists, and experts on the Soviet Union and on Afro-Asia and Latin America.

In describing the course of the bullets which struck Lenin in 1918 I was guided, as to both anatomy and terminology, by Dr. William B. Mather of the Princeton University Infirmary, by Ashley Montagu, well-known anthropologist and author, and by Dr. Harvey D. Rothberg of Princeton Hospital. Dr. Rothberg gracefully submitted to endless questioning while I was writing the final chapters about Lenin's illness. He also helped sustain my strength and health during the last year of my work on the biography.

I am impressed by the eager readiness of busy members of university faculties to assist an author in need. Dr. Merle Fainsod, Director of the Harvard University Russian Research Center, Professor Richard E. Pipes, Assistant Director, and Professor Marshall D. Shulman of the Center and of Tufts gave me access to the Trotsky Archives in Harvard's Houghton Library; the research and duplicating work there was done for me by Fritz Ermarth, a third-year graduate student in the Department of Government at Harvard, and by Daniel Mulholland, an advanced graduate student in history at the same university.

Professor James W. Morley, of Columbia University, sent me material on Japanese intervention in Siberia. At Princeton, Gregory Vlastos, Chairman of the Philosophy Department, Professor Robert C. Tucker, Director of Russian Studies, Professor Cyril E. Black, of the Department of History, and Professor of History Sidney Ratner of Rutgers University, as well as Professor Mirra Komarovsky, Chairman of the Sociology Department of Barnard College in New York, always lent me a friendly ear when I wanted to talk out a problem that arose in writing this book; I benefited from their knowledge and wisdom. Professor V. Lange, Princeton University's Chairman of the Department of Germanic Languages and Literatures, went to much trouble in establishing the full names of the German medical men summoned to treat Lenin in 1922 and 1923. Miss Helen Dukas, Dr. Albert Einstein's secretary, and the late Dr. Rudolf R. Ehrmann of Berkeley, California, also helped with these names.

A front-page *New York Times* report on February 7, 1962, recorded President John F. Kennedy's acceptance, for the Smithsonian Institution, of a gift from the late Rear Admiral Cary T. Grayson, President Woodrow Wilson's personal physician, of the old Hammond typewriter on which Wilson had typed many of his own state papers and letters. In the continuation of the story on an inside page, the *Times* reproduced the first line of a letter as a sample of Wilson's perfect typing. The line dealt with Soviet Russia. I thought I knew all of Wilson's published letters on Russia, but I did not know this one. Arthur S. Link, Professor of History at Princeton University, Director of the Woodrow Wilson Papers at that university, and author of a multi-volume biography of Wilson, said the letter had never been published; he gave me a copy. The text appears in this book. Subsequently he gave me copies of other Wilson documents which I quote.

From Miss Josephine L. Harper, Director of the State Historical Society of Wisconsin where the papers of Colonel Raymond Robins are deposited, I obtained photostats of correspondence between Lenin and Robins. Mrs. Leslie S. Cormack, of the Schenectady Historical Society, sent me a copy of the autographed photograph with inscription which Lenin mailed to Charles P. Steinmetz. Isaac Don Levine, American foreign correspondent and author, provided me with a photostat of Lenin's English-language handwritten letter to him dated October 5, 1919. Robert W. Hill, Keeper of Manuscripts of the New York Public Library, Xeroxed a 1913 handwritten letter of Lenin for me. I also had the benefit of two detailed letters from Mrs. Frank A. Vanderlip; an interview with Armand Hammer; a long talk with Italian novelist Ignazio Silone about the Italian Communist Party; interesting information from Madame William A. Bradley of Paris about *Les Exploits de Rocambole*; data from John M. McSweeney about Inessa Armand; an assist from John K. Jessup, chief editorial writer of *Life* magazine, in fixing a date; an elusive cutting from David Astor, editor of *The Observer* of London; a letter with clippings from Anna M. Bourgina; several helpful letters from Mrs. Olga Biryukova of Geneva, Switzerland; and from Dr. Lorenz Stucki of Zurich; and most valuable assistance from Michael Josselson, Director of the Congress for Cultural Freedom, in Geneva; as well as a sympathetic note from Professor Yves Collart of the Institut Universitaire de Haute Etudes Internationales in Geneva regarding the Swiss government's dossier on Lenin. Patrick Kelley, one of my finest students at the Woodrow Wilson School in Princeton, and Robert Eng, a Princeton undergraduate, did some research work for me in Firestone Library.

The person who helped me most was Boris Ivanovich Nicolaevsky. Born in the 1880's in a town near Ufa, now the capital of the Bashkir Republic, Boris Ivanovich was the son of an eighth-generation Russian Orthodox priest. But the tide of revolution ran so high that it caught the young student even in the remote province, and in 1903 he began organizing young people for the struggle against the tsarist regime. The next year he was expelled from the gymnasium and arrested. Between 1904 and 1917 his activity as a member of Russian Social Democratic Labor Party caused him to be arrested nine times and exiled to Siberia four times. He published his first major work in 1917 on the police archives of the tsarist government. From 1917 to 1919 he served as a member of the Central Committee of the Menshevik party. In 1919, working under David Ryazanov, he organized the Central Archive of the Soviet state and also concentrated on collecting the archives of the November 7, 1917, revolt. He was arrested by the Cheka in 1921 and banished in 1922 from Soviet territory for the rest of his life. From 1924 to 1931 he acted as representative in Western Europe for Ryazanov's Moscow Institute of Marx, Engels, and Lenin, and at the same time built his own private archive consisting of tons of invaluable material now at the Hoover Institute of War, Revolution, and Peace at Palo Alto, California. Early in the 1930's he published a biography of Karl Marx and in 1934, *Azef, The Spy*, the story of a tsarist double agent. Later he assembled and annotated an eight-volume collection on Marxism in Russia and Western Europe in the 1920's and 1930's.

Nicolaevsky is undoubtedly the greatest expert in the Western world on Soviet politics and Marx, so much so that Moscow overlooked his Menshevism to avail itself of his scholarship. I saw him innumerable times in his New York apartment where the floors, desks, tables, and floor-to-ceiling shelves were laden with books, documents, pamphlets, newspapers, etc. Like the true archivist, he has a photographic memory and could with ease summon up facts, dates, and reminiscences from the distant past. He gave me of his time and knowledge without stint, even writing me from his vacation place in Vermont and allowing me to telephone him there.

During my two years at the Institute for Advanced Study I enjoyed the intimate intellectual companionship of George F. Kennan. He read my chapters as I turned them out and I read his, and our criticisms were ever frank and friendly.

My sternest critic while writing this book was my senior son, George, Professor of Government at Cornell University. He wanted Papa's work to meet a high standard. His advice, bibliographical assistance, academic prods, and written detailed criticisms of the many chapters he read were enormously helpful.

READERS AND CRITICS. The entire book was read with endless care by Don M. Wolfe, Professor of English at Brooklyn College, and author of *Milton in the Puritan Revolution* and other books. He teaches creative writing and is a creative critic. He made typewritten comments on every chapter. His method is to laud the good to isolate the bad. The whole manuscript was proofread by Harry Sigmond and Deirdre Randall. Miss Randall also listened to numerous pages and paragraphs as they came out of my typewriter, and engaged in research in New York. One or more chapters were read in manuscript and criticized by Elias A. Lowe, Professor Emeritus of the Institute for Advanced Study, by Sir Llewellyn Woodward, British historian at the same Institute, Professor Cyril E. Black of Princeton University, Mrs. Corinne Manning Black, Mrs. Janet Gemmel, Nicolaevsky, Mrs. Jane Krieger Rosen, Professor Paul Massing of Rutgers University, Professor Milton R. Konvitz of Cornell University, Professor Herman S. Ermolaev of Princeton, and Peter M. Spackman, editor-in-chief of Columbia University's *Forum*. Mrs. Betty Allen, my hostess in the Bahamas and at Stone Ridge, New York, typed and read several chapters.

GRANTS. At the Institute for Advanced Study and at Princeton University I received generous financial assistance from the Rockefeller Foundation and from the University as well as a special research grant from President Robert F. Goheen.

LIBRARIES. In the summer of 1962, I travelled to London, Frankfurt, and Vienna to buy Soviet books not yet available in the United States, and from then to the time this biography was finished I received Soviet books by airmail from Les Livres Étrangèrs in Paris. But most of the volumes I needed were in the Firestone Library of Princeton University. The Library microfilmed for me eighteen volumes of the Russian-language *Collected Works* of Trotsky, a rarity which it did not have. At Firestone, readers have access to the stacks, a most useful arrangement, for sometimes, while reaching for a book one knows, one looks farther along on the shelf and discovers a book whose existence one had not suspected. Thus I found the official stenographic record in Russian of the one-day Constituent Assembly which the Bolsheviks suppressed in January, 1918, and was able to document the exact manner, often misrepresented by even the best scholars, of its dispersal. Dr. William S. Dix, Chief Librarian of Firestone, Frederick Lawrence Arnold, Assistant Librarian for Reference, Miss Rosemary V. Allen, Miss Eleanor V. Weld, Warren B. Kuhn, Assistant Librarian for Circulation, Mrs. Claralice Wolf, of the photoengraving and microfilm-reading division, and a score of their aides were always extremely helpful and patient.

During my two years at the Institute for Advanced Study, Miss Judith E. Sachs and her sensitive staff members were of great service.

Through Senator E. L. Bartlett, Miss Mary A. Nordale, his secretary, and my son Victor I obtained valuable information and photostats from the Library of Congress.

Whatever rare book or Russian magazine Firestone did not possess I usually obtained in the Slavonic Room of the New York Public Library where Mrs. Rissa Yachnin was exceptionally cooperative in research and photostating.

James T. Babb, Librarian of the Yale University Library, supplied me with a photostat of one of the twenty-five English-language handwritten letters Chicherin had written me; I had presented them to Yale years before I had any connection with Princeton.

In London I worked in the library of The Royal Institute of International Affairs at Chatham House and consulted Mrs. Jane Degras, author and editor of books on communist activities, who is a member of that Institute.

TYPING. Mrs. Jane McDowall and her ever-ready staff at the Center for International Studies of Princeton University and Miss Patricia La Rue and her corps of enthusiasts typed my bulky manuscript with the care that my careless two-finger typing requires. The secretaries at the Center and at the Woodrow Wilson School were always extremely accommodating. The typists at the Institute, and Miss Dorothy Hessman, as well as Miss Elizabeth I. Horton, secretary of the School of Historical Studies to which I was attached, and other Institute executives were equally helpful.

EDITORS. Mr. Cass Canfield, Jr., my editor at Harper & Row, read the manuscript as I wrote it and gave me every encouragement. Miss Julie Eidesheim, the copy editor, took infinite pains with the coordination of the style and accuracy of the manuscript.

To all these persons and institutions I express my profound gratitude. The willingness of people, out of the goodness of their hearts, to assist me has been a moving experience.

TRANSLATION. Except where otherwise indicated, all translations from the Russian and other languages were made by me. I endeavored to make them literary as well as literal. Sometimes, as in the case of the verb in a verse of Mayakovsky's poetry, when neither my Russian-English dictionary nor the four-volume, classic Russian-Russian dictionary of Vladimir Dal availed, I had to telephone, in turn, to Nicolaevsky, Vera Alexandrova, Sasha Schwartz, and Avrahm Yarmolinsky in New York, and to Russian-born John Turkevich, Professor of Chemistry at Princeton, to get a consensus.

EMPHASIS. I used no italics. The emphasis in the book is by Lenin, who loved to underline and capitalize words and phrases, or by others.

SPELLING. In transliterating from the Russian my purpose was to communicate the sound as nearly as possible. I could not write "Lenyin" phonetically for "Lenin" any more than one would write "Khrushchov" for "Khrushchev" although that would convey the correct pronunciation. In less-prominent names I aimed to be phonetic.

BIBLIOGRAPHY. The bibliography is in the footnotes. I read many books not mentioned in the footnotes; for instance: Isaiah Berlin, *Historical Inevitability*; *Documents on British Foreign Policy 1919-1939*, First Series, Vol. XII; Sidney Hook, *Marx and the Marxists*; Edmund Wilson, *To the Finland Station*; and I. G. Tsereteli, *Vospominaniya o Fevralskoi Revolyutsii* (*Memoirs of the February Revolution*), two vols., (The Hague, 1963). But since I did not quote them they are not included.

INDEX

sheviks urged, 86, 524, 657; Rozhkov and, 631; rupture with the Bolsheviks, 39, 49, 62, 64, 72, 82, 527; Stalin and, 440; at Third Congress of Soviets, 195; Trotsky and, 181, 671

Meshcheryakov, Nikolai L., 498, 651

Michaelis, Georg (Chancellor), 173

Mikhailov, V. M., 449, 596

Mikhailov regiment, 128

Mikhailovsky, Nikolai K., 27

Mikoyan, Anastas I., 546, 583, 639 n.

Mill, James, 102-03

Miller, General, 335

Milner, Lord, 165, 287 n., 331, 531

Milyukov, Paul N., 127, 129, 130, 147, 280

Milyutin, V., 158, 509

Minkovsky, 672

Minsk, 389

Minusinsk, 32

Mirbach, Count Wilhelm von, 226-28, 230, 232, 233, 235, 238, 240, 241, 242, 244, 268, 293

Modzalevsky, I. A., 664

Molotov, Vyacheslav M., 449, 509, 537, 546, 547, 581, 583, 596, 629, 633

Mongols, 5

Monopoly, growth of, 106

Montagu, Sir Edward, 531

Moon Sound Islands, 162, 200

Morality, communist, 416

Morozov, Pavel, 41, 70

Morozov Palace (Moscow), 242

Morris, Roland S., 290

Moscow, 31, 52, 127, 139, 141, 156, 157, 209, 216, 227, 262, 359, 611-12

Moscow Art Theater, 345, 498, 499

Moscow Consumers Association, 586

Moscow Regional Bureau, 214, 215

Moscow Soviet, 123, 346, 387, 467, 520, 625, 672

Moscow trials, 315, 380, 456, 601-02, 647, 652

Muenzenberg, Willy, 629

Munich, 22, 36, 37

Muraviov, General M. A., 242, 243, 255

Murmansk, 218, 235, 266-67, 268, 272-273, 289, 290, 291, 293, 298, 299, 302, 371

Murom, 293

Mussolini, Benito, 367, 411, 528

My Life (Trotsky), 188, 189, 671

Myasnikov, A. F., 609, 633

Naples, 63

Napoleon I, 30, 44, 91, 159, 656

Narimanov, Nariman, 455

Narishkin, Natalya, 270

Narodnaya Volya, see People's Freedom Party

Nationalism, 27, 86, 90, 93, 213, 235, 243, 660

Nationalization, 255, 259, 521

National minorities in Russia, 86, 90, 246, 248-51, 384, 607, 608, 610-11, 627, 660

Nechayev, Sergey G., 45

Nehru, B. K., 104

Nehru, Jawaharlal, 29

Nekrasov, N. A., 14, 489, 496, 497

Nepmen, 520, 565, 593, 605, 612, 614-615, 624, 659

Neue Rheinische Zeitung (newspaper), 308, 484

Neva River, 143, 414

New Data on the Laws of the Development of Capitalism in Agriculture (Lenin), 95

New Economic Policy (NEP), American reaction to, 557; application in Turkestan, 542-43; bureaucrats benefited by, 545; communist ideology corroded by, 518; economic surrender to survive, 472; Genoa conference and, 568, 570; introduced by Tenth Party Congress, 477; lasting nature of, 514; lease granted to capitalistic class, 116, 469, 487, 517, 522, 560, 586; Lenin and, 479, 480, 548, 553, 564, 569, 619, 625, 651, 653, 656, 667; Nepmen and, 520, 565, 605; peasants and, 564, 565, 584; Prolekult and, 494; state capitalism and, 593, 619; supported by the Congress, 478; trade union problems created by, 565; Trotsky and, 480, 591; unemployment increased by, 521; workers and, 586

"New Times, Old Errors in a New Form" (Lenin), 548

New York Evening Post, 615

New York Times, The, 126, 597

New York Tribune, 93

New York World, 412

Nicholas I, Tsar, 539

Nicholas II, Tsar, 10, 37, 52, 107, 126, 127, 129, 144, 149, 239, 294, 295

Nicolaevsky, Boris I., 328, 357, 367, 516, 547, 600, 601, 649 n.

Nigeria, 103

Nihilism, 62

Nikoforova, Anna N., 94

Nikolai, G. F., 461

Nikolai Mikhailovich, Grand Duke, 328

Nikolai Nikolaevich, 628

Nikolayevsky Bridge, 141, 142-43

Nikolayevsky railroad station (Petrograd), 142

Nikulina, N., 429

Nineteenth Party Congress (1952), 515

**PHOENIX
PRESS**

GENERAL EDITORS:
SIMON SCHAMA AND ANTONIA FRASER

Phoenix Press publishes and re-publishes hundreds of the very best new and out of print books about the past. For a free colour catalogue listing more than 400 titles please

telephone: +44 (0) 1903 828 503
fax: +44 (0) 1903 828 802
e-mail: mailorder@lbsltd.co.uk
or visit our website at www.phoenixpress.co.uk

The following books might be of particular interest to you:

The Fall of the Russian Monarchy

BERNARD PARES

The foremost expert on Russian history of his generation, Pares tells the story of the Russian Revolution from the point of view of the Romanovs, beginning with Nicholas II's accession in 1894 and ending with his and his family's murder at Ekaterinburg in 1918.

Paperback
UK: £12.99   528pp + Maps   1 84212 114 6
USA: $19.95
CAN: $29.95

Roots of Revolution

INTRODUCED BY ISAIAH BERLIN

FRANCO VENTURI

Venturi offers nothing less than a history of the populist and socialist movements in 19th-century Russia that spawned the events of 1917 that shook the world. Isaiah Berlin, who was himself uprooted by that Revolution, contributes an introduction, and a later essay by the author on Russian Populism is also included.

Paperback
UK: £18.99   960pp   1 84212 253 3
USA: $27.50
CAN: $39.95